INTERMEDIATE MICROECONOMICS

WALTER NICHOLSON
CHRISTOPHER SNYDER
PETER LUKE
MICHAEL WOOD

INTERMEDIATE MICROECONOMICS

SOUTH-WESTERN
CENGAGE Learning™

Australia • Brazil • Japan • Korea • Mexico • Singapore • Spain • United Kingdom • United States

SOUTH-WESTERN
CENGAGE Learning™

Intermediate Microeconomics
Walter Nicholson, Christopher Snyder, Peter Luke and Michael Wood

Publishing Director: John Yates

Publisher: Patrick Bond

Development Editor: James Clark

Content Project Editor: Leonora Dawson-Bowling

Manufacturing Manager: Helen Mason

Senior Production Controller: Maeve Healy

Marketing Manager: Anne-Marie Scoones

Typesetter: Integra, India

Cover design: Adam Renvoize

Text design: Design Deluxe, Bath, UK

Products and services that are referred to in this book may be either trademarks and/or registered trademarks of their respective owners. The publishers and author/s make no claim to these trademarks.

British Library Cataloguing-in-Publication Data
A catalogue record for this book is available from the British Library.

ISBN: 978-1-84480-629-4

Cengage Learning EMEA
High Holborn House, 50–51 Bedford Row
London WC1R 4LR

Cengage Learning products are represented in Canada by Nelson Education Ltd.

For your lifelong learning solutions, visit **www.cengage.co.uk**
Purchase e-books or e-chapters at: **http://estore.bized.co.uk**

Printed by G. Canale & C., Italy
1 2 3 4 5 6 7 8 9 10 – 10 09 08

BRIEF CONTENTS

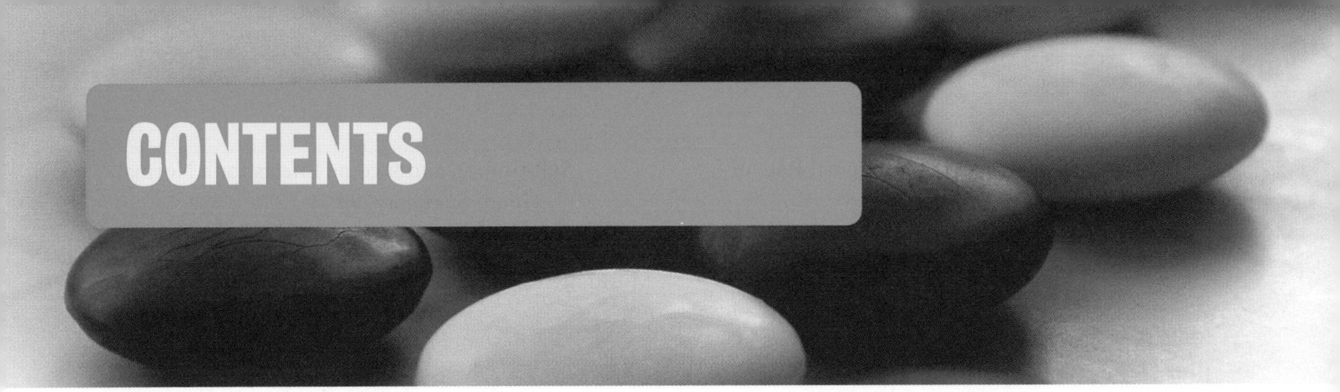

CONTENTS

PART FOUR PRODUCTION, COSTS, AND SUPPLY 203

LIST OF APPLICATIONS

PREFACE

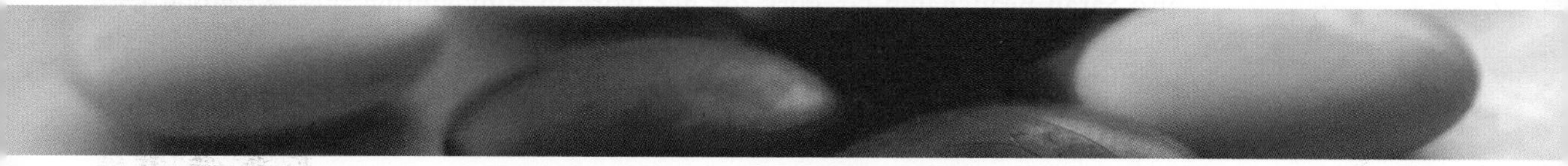

This is the first time that the excellent book by Professors Nicholson and Snyder has been adapted for the European market. In adapting this book the "British side" took a deliberate decision to leave the book substantially as it is; as the old saying goes, "If it isn't broke, then don't fix it." Indeed in canvassing views of those British and European academics who were currently using the American 10th Edition on their courses the general feeling was that the internal structure of the book is a core strength that should be kept intact in this adaptation.

So where then are the differences between this European edition and the American edition? Apart from the expected dollar signs to euros and pound weight to kilo, the main impact is to be found in the changing of many of the Applications that are peppered throughout the book. From an international perspective, while economic applications centered on America are legitimate, to have them exclusively American is to overlook the fact we live in an age of international student mobility. British and European universities in general are increasingly cosmopolitan in nature. Chinese students are ubiquitous and through the European Union Erasmus program it is not unusual to see and hear many a German, French and Scandinavian student (and many other nationalities!) attending courses within a UK university.

As such, many of the applications are now focused on examples taken from the "real world" of the UK and many other European Union countries. At the same time one could almost say that the adapted textbook is not just a European edition but an international edition with examples taken from China, India and South Africa. The reader will also notice that many applications remain based on experiences within America. This is first because many of these applications are simply good and should not be dropped; and second the US economy still *is* the biggest economy in the world! Any micro text book worth its name should surely have real world examples from the world's biggest economy.

In discussion within universities where the American textbook had been used, some calls did come for the book to be made more mathematical. While this may have been broadly appealing for those courses that are purely for students of economics we felt that to have gone too much down this path would have diluted the book's attractiveness to those lecturers who teach non-economic students on business degree courses, and in general social science courses where economics is not the main goal of the degree.

As with the previous American edition, online material is available to both lecturers who use the book and to students who use it. The information in the preface to the American 10th edition listing the supplements to the text is still valid and the reader – whether an instructor or student – is encouraged to make full use of them.

In closing may we thank Thomas Rennie and James Clark of Cengage Learning for the support they gave us and the patience they showed as we adapted this book while juggling all the other commitments we have had over the last year or so, and also Sarah Beauchamp-Gregory for her work in copy-editing the text along with Leonora Dawson-Bowling, the Content Project Editor, for her patience during the proof-reading stage.

Peter Luke and Michael Wood
London,
December 2007

Supplements to the Text

With this edition, a wide and helpful array of supplements is available to both students and instructors, on the companion website www.cengage.co.uk/nicholson including

- Instructor's Manual including full answers to question material in the book.
- PowerPoint® slides to accompany each chapter.
- Additional electronic-only Chapter 19 on Experimental Economics.
- Multiple-choice questions.
- Useful weblinks.

To the Instructor

Using this new edition should prove easy both for new adopters and for users of the previous editions. New adopters will find that the book proceeds in a very standard way through demand, supply, and market structure. It is possible to adopt a "bare bones" approach to the subject by covering only this material, or one may add extra topics from the final section of the book that covers factor markets, capital and time, asymmetric information, and externalities. Because principles of game theory provide the major focus for the chapters on imperfect competition and asymmetric information, it is important to cover the chapter introducing the topic (Chapter 6) before covering the extra topics.

For previous users of the text, there are few changes here that should affect class scheduling. The most important change are revisions to the Applications vignettes in the text. The general narrative structure and chapter order of the 10th edition of the American textbook has been maintained throughout this adaptation.

To the Student

This book really is intended to make it easier for you to learn microeconomics. Although the book pulls no punches in terms of insisting you learn "the real thing", it has been extensively reworked over the years to make that process as clear and streamlined as possible. In this edition, the core strengths of the original American textbook have been retained while many of the Application examples have been specifcally rewritten to be more relevant to non-American students and demonstrate how economic principles are applied in the real world.

Reviewer Acknowledgments

The publisher and authors would like to thank the following academics for reviewing material from this adaptation at proposal and draft chapter stage:

Paul Bishop	University of Plymouth
Susan Harkness	University of Bath
John Houston	Glasgow Caledonian University
Kim Kaivanto	Lancaster University Management School
Todd Kaplan	Univesity of Exeter
Thijs ten Raa	University of Tilburg
Marian Rizov	Middlesex University Business School
Jochen Runde	University of Cambridge
Emanuela Sciubba	Birkbeck, University of London
Indrajit Tay	University of Birmingham
Phil Tomlinson	University of Bath

ACKNOWLEDGMENTS

The following author acknowledgments from Walter Nicholson and Christopher Snyder have been reproduced from the most recent 10th edition of *Intermediate Microeconomics* which has formed the basis for this adaptation.

The key idea for this edition came from Peter Adams at Cengage South-Western. He had the foresight to see that Chris Snyder would be a great addition to the book at this time and convinced me to plunge ahead. Things have worked out even better than Peter anticipated – if he ever tires of publishing, he probably should consider a new career as a matchmaker. Susan Smart, despite being overworked in the extreme, helped us get organized at the start of this project and kept us in line and on target in getting to this final result. We joke with her about nagging us, but she really has a knack for getting things done with an insistent, though friendly, manner. Working with her is a pleasure, even when the pressure is on.

As to the specifics of this new edition, I drew especially on a series of very thoughtful reviews of the ninth edition that were kindly provided by Louis H. Amato, University of North Carolina, Charlotte; Gregory Besharov, Duke University; David M. Lang, California State University, Sacramento; Magnus Lofstrom, University of Texas, Dallas; Kathryn Nance, Fairfield University; Jeffrey O. Sundberg, Lake Forest College; Pete Tsournos, California State University, Chico; and Ben Young, University of Missouri, Kansas City. The suggestions of these reviewers about what should be covered in the book proved to be very good advice that I hope I have followed as faithfully as possible. These reviewers' thoughts on the suitability of various applications in the text were also most helpful.

Amherst students who assisted me with this and previous editions include: Mark Bruni, Stephanie Cogen, Morgan Delano, Adrian Dillon, Megan Kahn, David Macoy, Katie Merrell, Jeff Rodman, and Sujith Vijayan. To them and to all of their colleagues who used the text, I owe a debt of appreciation for keeping me "on message". I also appreciate all of the useful comments I have received from my Amherst colleague and longtime friend, Frank Westhoff. I am thankful that he uses the book voluntarily and seems none the worse for it.

I have been very impressed by the professional staff at Cengage South-Western who made this edition happen. In addition to Peter Adams and Susan Smart, I owe special gratitude to Emily Gross, who guided the production of the book. On more than one occasion, she caught my errors and made sure everything was here. Pamela Loos did a very fine job in copyediting the text; especially difficult was our decision to move to a more consistent and modern mathematical notation, which was (apparently) handled with ease. The very attractive and innovative design for this edition is the work of art director Michelle Kunkler. I believe users will appreciate the fine job she did in making the appearance of the book more lively and colorful. The production of pages for the book was directed by Jan Turner of Pre-Press Company. That this process went more smoothly than it ever has before is surely attributable to her talents.

Producing this edition was a somewhat more relaxed process than in the past, both because I have a lighter teaching schedule at Amherst College and because I had Chris Snyder to share the burden. Still, as the book entered its final phases, my mood deteriorated. With my children (Kate, David, Tory, and Paul) spread out across the country, the costs of this inevitably fell on my wife, Susan. As always, however, she was there for me, in every way making things easy. As Simon Schama would say, her presence provides an "embarrassment of riches" every day.

It is even harder to pretend to be young now that I have five grandchildren. My dedication of this edition to them is both a subtle attempt to lure them into pawing through the book and an announcement of how happy I am that they are here.

Walter Nicholson
Amherst, Massachusetts
October 2005

I was delighted to have been asked to collaborate with Walter Nicholson on the 10th edition of this text. I have used one or another of his books in my microeconomics classes since I began teaching 12 years ago. Walter's approach to the subject is similar to mine, so it has been easy to work together on it.

As did Walter, I encourage teachers and students to e-mail me if you have any comments on the text (Christopher.M.Snyder@dartmouth.edu).

I would like to add my thanks to those whom Walter acknowledged for contributing to the book. In addition, Karen Pelletier provided able administrative assistance. Conversations with my former colleagues at George Washington University and my present colleagues at Dartmouth College have helped me teach and write about microeconomics. I am grateful to Walter for his confidence in bringing me on the project, his continued patience while I apprenticed in the art of textbook writing, and his thorough comments and suggestions on my contributions to the book.

Committing to as extensive a project as this is in some sense a family decision. I thank my wife for accommodating the late nights that were sometimes required and for being willing to listen to the monotonous reports on the book's progress. Besides being well-behaved during the whole time I was writing the book, my children, Clare, Tess, and Meg, served as models for several of the end-of-chapter problems.

Christopher Snyder
Hanover, New Hampshire
October 2005

ABOUT THE AUTHORS

WALTER NICHOLSON is the Ward H. Patton Professor of Economics at Amherst College. He received a BA in mathematics from Williams College and a PhD in economics from the Massachusetts Institute of Technology (MIT). Professor Nicholson's primary research interests are in the econometric analyses of labor market problems, including welfare, unemployment, and the impact of international trade. For many years, he has been Senior Fellow at Mathematica, Inc. and has served as an advisor to the US and Canadian governments. He and his wife Susan live in Amherst, Massachusetts.

CHRISTOPHER SNYDER is Professor of Economics at Dartmouth College. He received his BA in economics and mathematics from Fordham University and his PhD in economics from MIT. Before his recent move to Dartmouth, he taught at George Washington University for more than a decade. His primary research interest is the strategic interaction among firms. He has studied markets for cable television, movies, and beer, among others, although as the father of three daughters he finds little time to participate in these markets as a consumer. Professor Snyder is President of the Industrial Organization Society and Associate Editor of the *International Journal of Industrial Organization* and *Review of Industrial Organization*. His wife Maura also teaches economics at Dartmouth.

PETER LUKE worked as a full-time fire-fighter with Lothian and Borders Fire Brigade in the early part of his career. Dr Luke then returned to full-time education as a mature student. After several years of undergraduate study Dr Luke graduated with a First in Economics from the University of Abertay in 1996 and then with an MSc Economics from Glasgow University in 1997 before graduating with his PhD in the same discipline from Heriot Watt University in 2004. From 2000 to 2002 Dr Luke worked as an economic consultant in Smolensk, Russia where, as the local Tacis[1] manager, he worked in close collaboration with the local employment service in establishing two apprenticeship units within their regional training centre. Following this he worked as a lecturer for four years at the University of Abertay where Dr Luke specialized in the teaching of micro and labor economics as well as econometrics. Moving on from there, and for two years until the end of 2007, Dr Luke was the long-term labor market expert on a EuropeAid[1] project in Kaliningrad, Russia where he worked in close collaboration with both the Immanuel Kant State University and the Planning and Strategy Department of the Regional Administration. Concurrent with this Dr Luke continues to work as a senior lecturer at London South Bank University.

[1] Tacis: Technical Assistance to the Commonwealth of Independent States which is now known simply as EuropeAid and is an ongoing project partnership agreement between the European Union and the Russian government.

MICHAEL WOOD graduated with a BA, and MA in Economics from Leicester University in 1976. He subsequently briefly taught at a number institutions before joining the economics team at London South Bank University, where he is a senior lecturer. He has worked on a number of overseas programs including a European Commission TEMPUS Programme in Poland, for a British Council International Link Programme in Bulgaria, as the UK author on a Trans European Policy Studies Association project into the Regulation of Public Services in Europe, and more recently as an external consultant on a EuropeAid project in Russia. His research and teaching interests are in area of microeconomics, privatization and regulation, and environmental economics. His work in labor economics has been supported by being a trade union official and by serving as an employment tribunal member for a number of years. He has also worked as a media expert on both television and radio.

WALKTHROUGH TOUR

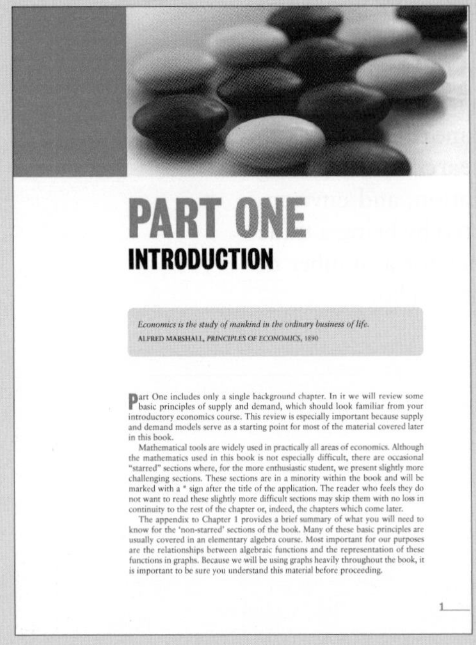

Part Openers divide the chapters into clearly defined groups; arranged to help your understanding of the subject.

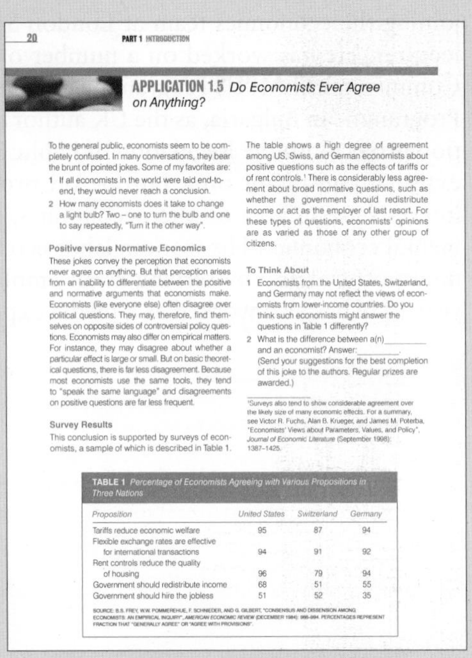

Applications explore core concepts from each chapter and demonstrate their direct relevance to the real world.

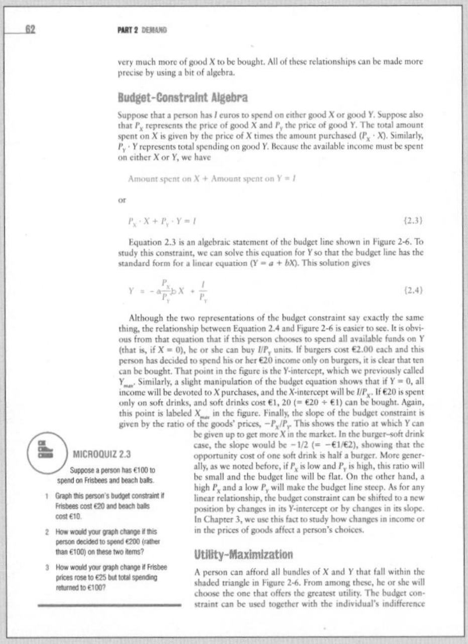

MicroQuizzes in every chapter directly test your comprehension of key chapter topics.

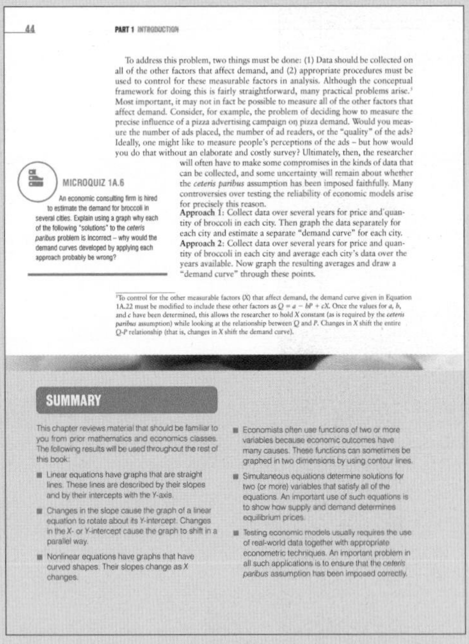

Summaries recap chapter content in helpful bite-size form.

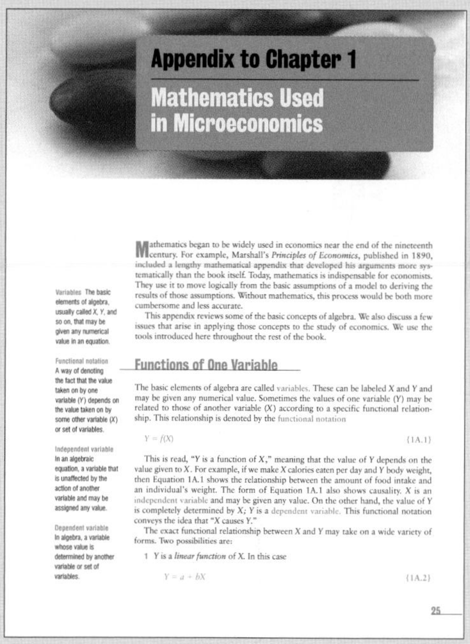

Appendix to Chapter 1

Mathematics Used in Microeconomics

Mathematics began to be widely used in economics near the end of the nineteenth century. For example, Marshall's *Principles of Economics*, published in 1890, included a lengthy mathematical appendix that developed his arguments more systematically than the book itself. Today, mathematics is indispensable for economists. They use it to move logically from the basic assumptions of a model to deriving the results of those assumptions. Without mathematics, this process would be both more cumbersome and less accurate.

This appendix reviews some of the basic concepts of algebra. We also discuss a few issues that arise in applying those concepts to the study of economics. We use the tools introduced here throughout the rest of the book.

Variables The basic elements of algebra, usually called X, Y, and so on, that may be given any numerical value in an equation.

Functional notation A way of denoting the fact that the value taken on by one variable (Y) depends on the value taken on by some other variable (X) or set of variables.

Independent variable In an algebraic equation, a variable that is unaffected by the action of another variable and may be assigned any value.

Dependent variable In algebra, a variable whose value is determined by another variable or set of variables.

Functions of One Variable

The basic elements of algebra are called variables. These can be labeled X and Y and may be given any numerical value. Sometimes the values of one variable (Y) may be related to those of another variable (X) according to a specific functional relationship. This relationship is denoted by the functional notation

$$Y = f(X) \tag{1A.1}$$

This is read, "Y is a function of X," meaning that the value of Y depends on the value given to X. For example, if we make X calories eaten per day and Y body weight, then Equation 1A.1 shows the relationship between the amount of food intake and an individual's weight. The form of Equation 1A.1 also shows causality. X is an independent variable and may be given any value. On the other hand, the value of Y is completely determined by X; Y is a dependent variable. This functional notation conveys the idea that "X causes Y."

The exact functional relationship between X and Y may take on a wide variety of forms. Two possibilities are:

1 Y is a *linear function* of X. In this case

$$Y = a + bX \tag{1A.2}$$

25

Chapter Appendices, included with several chapters, explore more advanced mathematical content related to chapter topics.

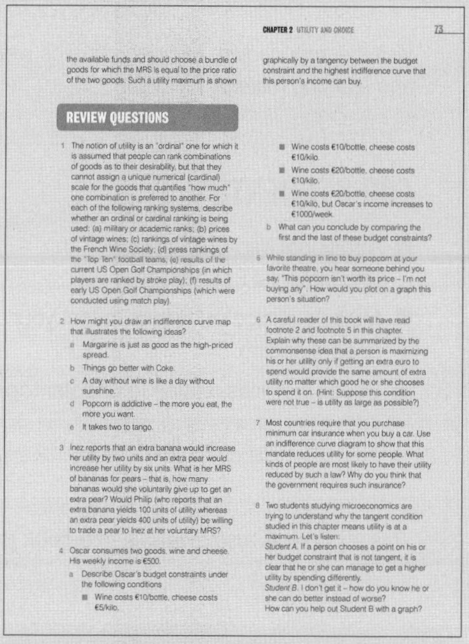

CHAPTER 2 UTILITY AND CHOICE 73

the available funds and should choose a bundle of goods for which the MRS is equal to the price ratio of the two goods. Such a utility maximum is shown graphically by a tangency between the budget constraint and the highest indifference curve that this person's income can buy.

REVIEW QUESTIONS

1 The notion of utility is an "ordinal" one for which it is assumed that people can rank combinations of goods as to their desirability, but that they cannot assign a unique numerical (cardinal) scale for the goods that quantifies "how much" one combination is preferred to another. For each of the following ranking systems, describe whether an ordinal or cardinal ranking is being used: (a) military or academic ranks; (b) prices of vintage wines; (c) rankings of vintage wines by the French Wine Society; (d) press rankings of the "Top Ten" football teams; (e) results of the current US Open Golf Championships (in which players are ranked by stroke play); (f) results of early US Open Golf Championships (which were conducted using match play).

2 How might you draw an indifference curve map that illustrates the following ideas?
- a Margarine is just as good as the high-priced spread.
- b Things go better with Coke.
- c A day without wine is like a day without sunshine.
- d Popcorn is addictive – the more you eat, the more you want.
- e It takes two to tango.

3 Inez reports that an extra banana would increase her utility by two units and an extra pear would increase her utility by six units. What is her MRS of bananas for pears – that is, how many bananas would she voluntarily give up to get an extra pear? Would Philip (who reports that an extra banana yields 100 units of utility whereas an extra pear yields 400 units of utility) be willing to trade a pear to Inez at her voluntary MRS?

4 Oscar consumes two goods, wine and cheese. His weekly income is €500.
- a Describe Oscar's budget constraints under the following conditions
  - Wine costs €10/bottle, cheese costs €5/kilo.
  - Wine costs €10/bottle, cheese costs €10/kilo.
  - Wine costs €20/bottle, cheese costs €10/kilo.
  - Wine costs €20/bottle, cheese costs €10/kilo, but Oscar's income increases to €1000/week.
- b What can you conclude by comparing the first and the last of these budget constraints?

5 While standing in line to buy popcorn at your favorite theatre, you hear someone behind you say, "This popcorn isn't worth its price – I'm not buying any". How would you plot on a graph this person's situation?

6 A careful reader of this book will have read footnote 2 and footnote 5 in this chapter. Explain why these can be summarized by the commonsense idea that a person is maximizing his or her utility only if getting an extra euro to spend would provide the same amount of extra utility no matter which good he or she chooses to spend it on. (Hint: Suppose this condition were not true – is utility as large as possible?)

7 Most countries require that you purchase minimum car insurance when you buy a car. Use an indifference curve diagram to show that this mandate reduces utility for some people. What kinds of people are most likely to have their utility reduced by such a law? Why do you think that the government requires such insurance?

8 Two students studying microeconomics are trying to understand why the tangent condition studied in this chapter means utility is at a maximum. Let's listen:
Student A. If a person chooses a point on his or her budget constraint that is not tangent, it is clear that he or she can manage to get a higher utility by spending differently.
Student B. I don't get it – how do you know he or she can do better instead of worse?
How can you help out Student B with a graph?

Review Questions at the end of each chapter, test your understanding, analysis and reasoning.

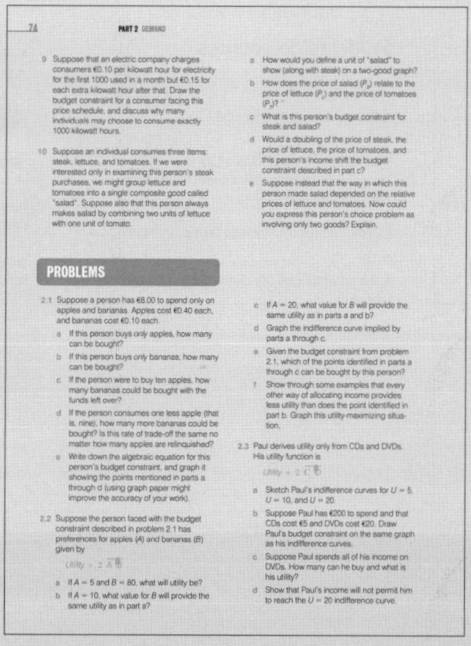

74 PART 2 DEMAND

9 Suppose that an electric company charges consumers €0.10 per kilowatt hour for electricity for the first 1000 used in a month but €0.15 for each extra kilowatt hour after that. Draw the budget constraint for a consumer facing this price schedule, and discuss why many individuals may choose to consume exactly 1000 kilowatt hours.

10 Suppose an individual consumes three items: steak, lettuce, and tomatoes. If we were interested only in examining this person's steak purchases, we might group lettuce and tomatoes into a single composite good called "salad". Suppose also that this person always makes salad by combining two units of lettuce with one unit of tomato.
- a How would you define a unit of "salad" to show (along with steak) on a two-good graph?
- b How does the price of salad (P_S) relate to the price of lettuce (P_L) and the price of tomatoes (P_T)?
- c What is this person's budget constraint for steak and salad?
- d Would a doubling of the price of steak, the price of lettuce, the price of tomatoes, and this person's income shift the budget constraint described in part c?
- e Suppose instead that the way in which this person made salad depended on the relative prices of lettuce and tomatoes. Now could you express this person's choice problem as involving only two goods? Explain.

PROBLEMS

2.1 Suppose a person has €8.00 to spend only on apples and bananas. Apples cost €0.40 each, and bananas cost €0.10 each.
- a If this person buys *only* apples, how many can be bought?
- b If this person buys *only* bananas, how many can be bought?
- c If the person were to buy ten apples, how many bananas could be bought with the funds left over?
- d If the person consumes one less apple (that is, nine), how many more bananas could be bought? Is this rate of trade-off the same no matter how many apples are relinquished?
- e Write down the algebraic equation for this person's budget constraint, and graph it showing the points mentioned in parts a through d (using graph paper might improve the accuracy of your work).

2.2 Suppose the person faced with the budget constraint described in problem 2.1 has preferences for apples (A) and bananas (B) given by

$$Utility = 2\sqrt{A \cdot B}$$

- a If $A = 5$ and $B = 80$, what will utility be?
- b If $A = 10$, what value for B will provide the same utility as in part a?
- c If $A = 20$, what value for B will provide the same utility as in parts a and b?
- d Graph the indifference curve implied by parts a through c.
- e Given the budget constraint from problem 2.1, which of the points identified in parts a through c can be bought by this person?
- f Show through some examples that every other way of allocating income provides less utility than does the point identified in part b. Graph this utility-maximizing situation.

2.3 Paul derives utility only from CDs and DVDs. His utility function is

$$Utility = 2\sqrt{C \cdot D}$$

- a Sketch Paul's indifference curves for $U = 5$, $U = 10$, and $U = 20$.
- b Suppose Paul has €200 to spend and that CDs cost €5 and DVDs cost €20. Draw Paul's budget constraint on the same graph as his indifference curves.
- c Suppose Paul spends all of his income on DVDs. How many can he buy and what is his utility?
- d Show that Paul's income will not permit him to reach the $U = 20$ indifference curve.

Problems, at the end of each chapter, test your understanding, knowledge and mathematical skills.

About the Website

Visit the Intermediate Microeconomics website at **www.cengage.co.uk/nicholson** *to find valuable teaching and learning material including:*

FOR STUDENTS

- Additional web-only chapter: Experimental Economics
- Multiple choice questions to test your understanding
- Useful weblinks related to chapter topics

FOR LECTURERS

- An Instructors Manual including teaching guidance, and answers to all questions
- PowerPoint® slides to accompany each chapter

This textbook is also available in e-book format, please visit the companion website for further details.

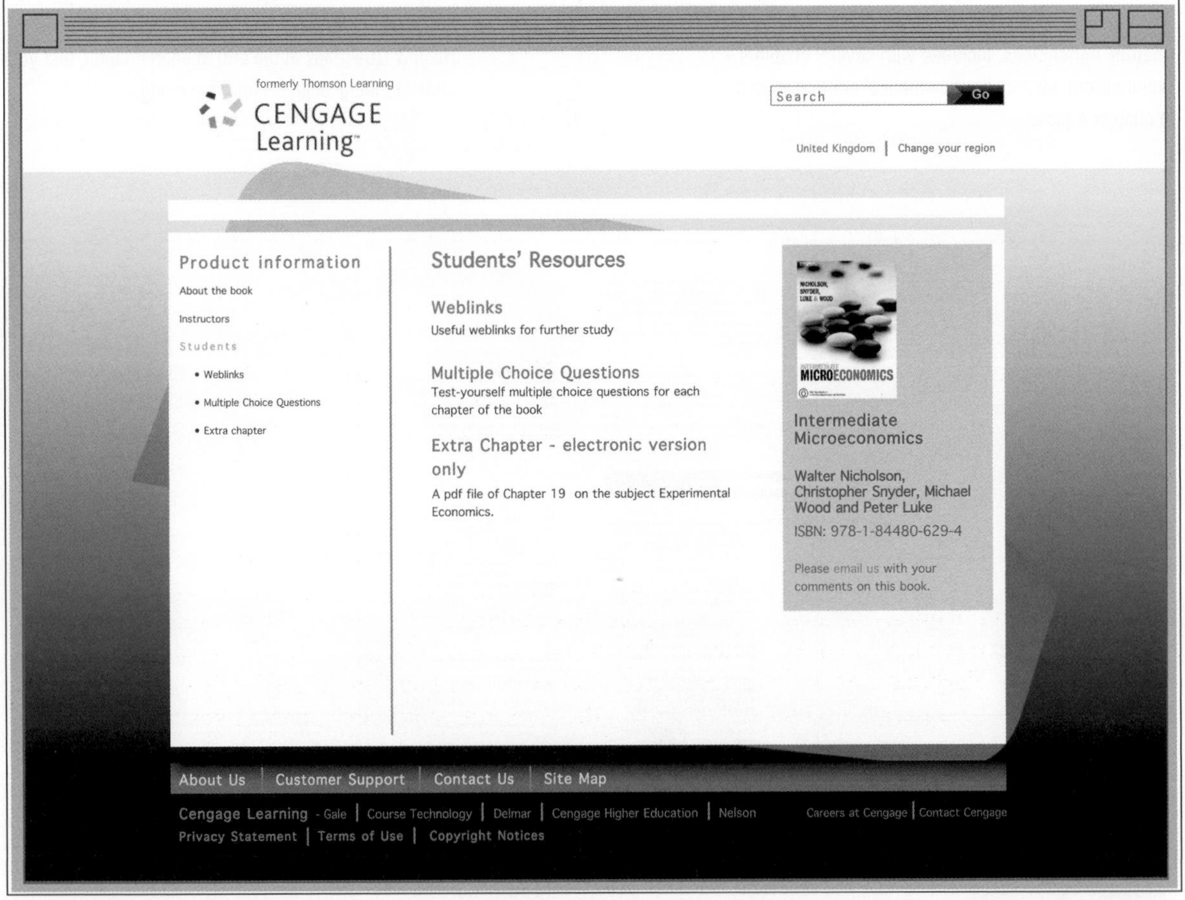

PART ONE
INTRODUCTION

Economics is the study of mankind in the ordinary business of life.
ALFRED MARSHALL, *PRINCIPLES OF ECONOMICS*, 1890

Part One includes only a single background chapter. In it we will review some basic principles of supply and demand, which should look familiar from your introductory economics course. This review is especially important because supply and demand models serve as a starting point for most of the material covered later in this book.

Mathematical tools are widely used in practically all areas of economics. The mathematics used in this book is not especially difficult and the appendix to Chapter 1 provides a brief summary of what you will need to know to follow the book and tackle the questions raised. Many of these basic principles are usually covered in an elementary algebra course. Most important for our purposes are the relationships between algebraic functions and the representation of these functions in graphs. Because we will be using graphs heavily throughout the book, it is important to be sure you understand this material before proceeding.

1

Economic Models

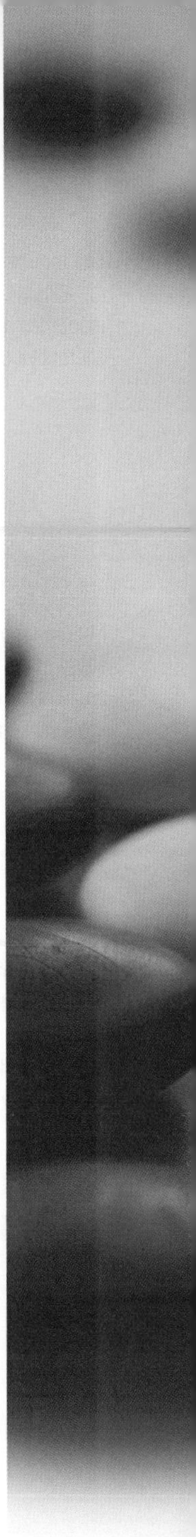

You have to deal with prices every day. When planning air travel, for example, you face a bewildering array of possible prices and travel-time restrictions. A quick look at any online travel agent will show you that for a flight between London and Paris ticket prices can vary significantly both within the fares on offer from an online agent and, indeed, between agents.[1] How can that be? Surely the cost is the same for an airline to carry each passenger; so why do passengers pay such different prices?

Or, consider buying beer or wine to go with your meal at a restaurant. You will probably have to pay at least €15 for a bottle of wine that would cost no more than €7 in a local retail store or off-license shop. How can that be? Why don't people balk at such extreme prices and why don't restaurants offer a better deal?

Finally, look at house prices. In recent times, these prices have been rising by 20 or even 50 per cent a year in many countries throughout the world. How can that be, when construction costs have risen no where near as quickly? It should be possible to build a new house relatively cheaply, so shouldn't that put a lid on the prices of existing houses? Won't these house price "bubbles" eventually collapse, just like the stock market did in 2000–2001?

If these are the kinds of questions that interest you, this is the right place to be. As the quotation in the introduction to this part states, economics (especially microeconomics) is the study of "the ordinary business of life". That is, economists take such things as airfares, house prices, or restaurants' menus as interesting topics, worthy of detailed study. Why? Because understanding these everyday features of our world goes a long way toward understanding the welfare of the actual people who live here. The study of economics cuts through the garble of television sound bites and the hot air of politicians that often obscure rather than enlighten these issues. By developing a thorough analysis of market forces, the goal here is to help you to understand better the many economic issues that affect all of our lives.

---

[1]One online agent for a flight from London, Heathrow to Paris, Charles De Gaul quoted £133.50 return from one airline while another airline wanted £242 return for traveling Saturday 31 March, 2006 and returning Tuesday 3 April, 2006. Another online agent quoted £108.30 to £225.30 for the same search criteria. All flights economy class and search conducted 12 March 2007.

What is Microeconomics?

Economics The study of the allocation of scarce resources among alternative uses.

As you probably learned in your introductory course, **economics** is formally defined as the "study of the allocation of scarce resources among alternative uses". This definition stresses that there simply are not enough basic resources (such as land, labor and capital equipment) in the world to produce everything that people want. Hence, every society must choose, either explicitly or implicitly, how its resources will be used. Of course, such "choices" are not made by an all-powerful dictator who specifies every citizen's life in minute detail. Instead, the way resources get allocated is determined by the actions of many people who engage in a bewildering variety of economic activities. Many of these activities involve participation in some sort of market transaction. Flying in aeroplanes, buying houses, or purchasing food are just three of the practically infinite number of things that people do that have market consequences for them and for society as a whole. **Microeconomics** is the study of all of these choices and of how well the resulting market outcomes meet basic human needs.

Microeconomics The study of the economic choices individuals and firms make and of how these choices create markets.

Of course, any real-world economic system is far too complicated to be described in detail. Just think about how many items are available in a typical corner shop (not to mention in the typical superstore, be it Tesco in Britain or Carrefour in France). Surely it would be impossible to study in detail how each tin of beans or DVD player was produced and how many were bought in each store. Not only would such a description take a very long time, but it seems likely no one would care to know such trivia, especially if the information gathered could not be used elsewhere. For this reason, all economists build simple **models** of various activities that they wish to study. These models may not be especially realistic, at least in terms of their ability to capture the details of how a hammer is sold; but, just as scientists use models of the atom or architects use models of what they want to build, economists use simplified models to describe the basic features of markets. Of course, these models are "unrealistic". But maps are unrealistic too – they do not show every house or parking lot. Despite this lack of "realism", maps help you see the overall picture and get you where you want to go. That is precisely what a good economic model should do. The economic models that you will encounter in this book have a wide variety of uses, even though, at first, you may think that they are unrealistic. The applications scattered throughout the book are intended to stress that point. But they only hint at the ways in which the study of microeconomics can help you understand the economic events that affect your life.

Models Simple theoretical descriptions that capture the essentials of how the economy works.

A Few Basic Principles

Much of microeconomics consists of simply applying a few basic principles to new situations. We can illustrate some of these by examining an economic model with which you already should be familiar – the **production possibility frontier**. This graph shows the various amounts of two goods that an economy can produce during some period (say, one year). Figure 1-1, for example, shows all the combinations of two goods (say, food and clothing) that can be produced with this economy's resources. For example, ten units of food and three units of clothing can be made, or four units of food and 12 units of clothing. Many other combinations of food and clothing can also be produced, and Figure 1-1 shows all of them. Any combination on or inside the frontier can be produced, but combinations of food and clothing outside the frontier cannot be made because not enough resources are available.

Production possibility frontier A graph showing all possible combinations of goods that can be produced with a fixed amount of resources.

This simple model of production illustrates five principles that are common to practically every situation studied in microeconomics:

- *Resources are scarce*. Some combinations of food and clothing (such as 10 units of food together with 12 units of clothing) are unattainable given the resources available. We simply cannot have all of everything we might want.
- *Scarcity involves* **opportunity costs**. That is, producing more of one good necessarily involves producing less of something else. For example, if this economy produces ten units of food and three units of clothing per year at point *A*, producing one more unit of clothing would "cost" $\frac{1}{2}$ unit of food. In other words, to increase the output of clothing by one unit means the production of food would have to decrease by $\frac{1}{2}$ unit.
- *Opportunity costs are increasing*. Expanding the output of one particular good will usually involve increasing opportunity costs as diminishing returns set in. Although the precise reasons for this will be explained later, Figure 1-1 shows this principle clearly. If clothing output were expanded to 12 units per year (point *B*), the opportunity cost of clothing would rise from $\frac{1}{2}$ a unit of food to two

Opportunity cost
The cost of a good as measured by the alternative uses that are foregone by producing it.

MICROQUIZ 1.1

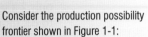

Consider the production possibility frontier shown in Figure 1-1:

1. Why is this curve called a "frontier"?
2. This curve has a "concave" shape. Would the opportunity cost of clothing production increase if the shape of the curve were convex instead?

FIGURE 1-1 Production Possibility Frontier *The production possibility frontier shows the different combinations of two goods that can be produced from a fixed amount of scarce resources. It also shows the opportunity cost of producing more of one good as the quantity of the other good that cannot then be produced. The opportunity cost at two different levels of production of a good can be seen by comparing points A and B. Inefficiency is shown by comparing points B and C.*

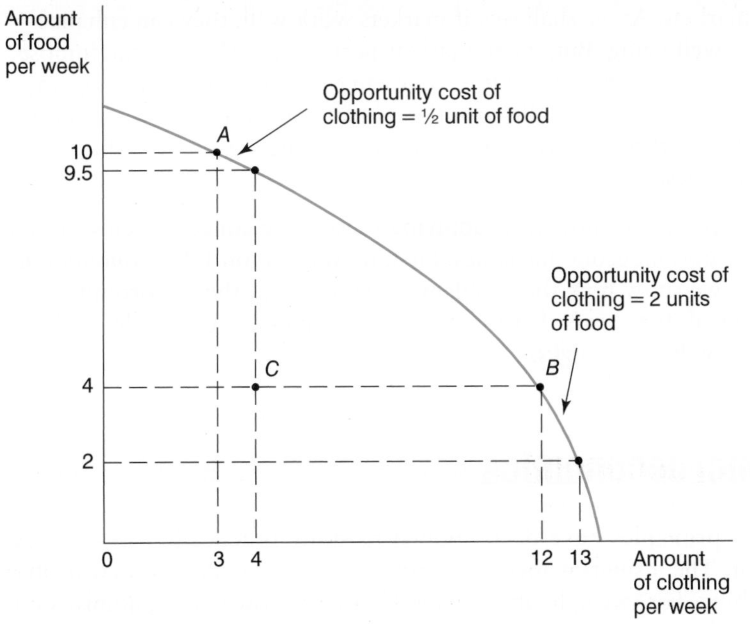

units of food. Hence, the opportunity cost of an economic action is not constant but varies with the circumstances.

- *Incentives matter.* When people make economic decisions, they will consider opportunity costs. Only when the extra (marginal) benefits from an action exceed the extra (marginal) opportunity costs will they take the action being considered. Suppose, for example, that the economy is operating at a place on its production possibility frontier where the opportunity cost of one unit of clothing is one unit of food. Then any person could judge whether he or she would prefer more clothing or more food and trade at this ratio. But if, say, there were a 100 per cent tax on clothing, it would seem as if you could get only $\frac{1}{2}$ a unit of clothing in exchange for giving up food – so you might choose to eat more and dress in last year's apparel. Or, suppose a rich uncle offers to pay $\frac{1}{2}$ your clothing costs. Now it appears that additional clothing only costs $\frac{1}{2}$ unit of food, so you might choose to dress much better, even though true opportunity costs (as shown on the production possibility frontier) are unchanged. Much of the material in this book looks at the problems that arise in situations like these, when people do not recognize the true opportunity costs of their actions and therefore take actions that are not the best from the perspective of the economy as a whole.
- *Inefficiency involves real costs.* An economy operating inside its production possibility frontier is said to be performing "inefficiently" – a term we will be making more precise later. Producing, say, four units of clothing and four units of food (at point C in Figure 1-1) would constitute an inefficient use of this economy's resources. Such production would involve the loss of, say, eight units of clothing that could have been produced along with the four units of food. When we study why markets might produce such inefficiencies, it will be important to keep in mind that such losses are not purely conceptual, being of interest only to economic researchers. These are real losses. They involve real opportunity costs. Avoiding such costs will make people better off.
- *Whether markets work well is important.* Most economic transactions occur through markets. As we shall see, if markets work well, they can enhance everyone's well-being. But, when markets perform poorly, they can impose real costs on any economy – that is, they can cause the economy to operate inside its production possibility frontier. Sorting out situations where markets work well from those where they don't is one of the key goals of the study of microeconomics.

In the next section, we show how applying these basic concepts helps in understanding some important economic issues. First, in Application 1.1: *Economics in the Natural World?*, we show how the problem of scarcity and the opportunity costs it entails are universal. It appears that these basic principles can even help explain the choices made by wolves or hawks.

Uses of Microeconomics

Microeconomic principles have been applied to study practically every aspect of human behavior. The insights gained by applying a few basic ideas to new problems can be far-reaching. For example, in Chapter 13, we see how one economist's initial fascination with the way prices were set for the rides at Disneyland opened the way

APPLICATION 1.1 *Economics in the Natural World?*

Scarcity is a dominant fact of nature. Indeed, the effect of scarcity is often easier to study in natural environments because they are less complex than modern human societies. In trying to understand the pressures that scarcity imposes on actions, economists and biologists have used models with many similarities. Charles Darwin, the founder of modern evolutionary biology, was well acquainted with the writings of the major eighteenth- and nineteenth-century economists. Their thinking helped to sharpen his insights in *The Origin of Species*. Here we look at the ways in which economic principles are illustrated in the natural world.

Foraging for Food

All animals must use time and energy in their daily search for food. In many ways, this poses an "economic" problem for them in deciding how to use these resources most effectively. Biologists have developed general theories of animal foraging behavior that draw largely on economic notions of weighing the (marginal) benefits and costs associated with various ways of finding food.[1]

Two examples illustrate this "economic" approach to foraging. First, in the study of birds of prey (eagles, hawks, and so forth), biologists have found that the length of time a bird will hunt in a particular area is determined both by the prevalence of food in that area and by the flight time to another location. These hunters recognize a clear trade-off between spending time and energy looking in one area and using those same resources to go somewhere else. Factors such as the types of food available and the mechanics of the bird's flight can explain observed hunting behavior.

A related observation about foraging behavior is the fact that no animal will stay in a given area until all of the food there is exhausted. For example, once a relatively large portion of the prey in a particular area has been caught, a hawk will go elsewhere. Similarly, studies of honeybees have found that they generally do not gather all of the nectar in a particular flower before moving on. To collect the last drop of nectar is not worth the time and energy the bee must expend to get it. Such weighing of marginal benefits and costs is precisely what an economist would predict.

[1]See, for example, David W. Stephens and John R. Krebs, *Foraging Theory* (Princeton, NJ: Princeton University Press, 1986).

Scarcity and Human Evolution

Charles Darwin's greatest discovery was the theory of evolution. Later research has tended to confirm his views that species evolve biologically over long periods of time in ways that adapt to their changing natural environments. In that process, scarcity plays a major role. For example, many of Darwin's conclusions were drawn from his study of finches on the Galapagos Islands. He discovered that these birds had evolved in ways that made it possible to thrive in this rather inhospitable locale. Specifically, they had developed strong jaws and beaks that made it possible for them to crack open nuts that are the only source of food during droughts.

It may even be the case that the evolution of economic-type activities led to the emergence of human beings. About 50 000 years ago *Homo sapiens* were engaged in active competition with *Neanderthals*. Although the fact that *Homo sapiens* eventually won out is usually attributed to their superior brainpower, some research suggests that this dominance may have derived instead from superior economic organization. Specifically, it appears that our forerunners were better at specialization in production and in trade than were *Neanderthals*. *Homo sapiens* made better use of the resources available than did *Neanderthals*.[2] Hence, Adam Smith's observation that humans have "the propensity to truck, barter, and trade one thing for another"[3] may indeed reflect an evolutionarily valuable aspect of human nature.

To Think About

1. Does it make sense to assume that animals consciously choose an optimal strategy for dealing with the scarcity of resources (see Friedman's pool player, p. 19)?
2. Why do some companies grow whereas others decline? Name one company for which the failure to adapt to a changing environment was catastrophic.

[2]See R.D. Horan, E.H. Bulte, and J.F. Shogren, "How Trade Saved Humanity from Biological Exclusion: An Economic Theory of Neanderthal Extinction", *Journal of Economic Behaviour and Organization*, Volume 58, Issue 1 (2005) pp. 1–29.

[3]Adam Smith, *The Wealth of Nations* (New York, Random House, 1937), 13. Citations are to the Modern Library edition.

for understanding pricing in such complex areas as air travel or the bundling and pricing of Internet connections; or, in Chapter 17, we look at another economist's attempt to understand the pricing of used cars. The resulting model of the pricing of "*lemons*" offers surprising insights about the markets for such important products as health care and legal services.[2] One must, therefore, be careful in trying to list the ways in which microeconomics is used because new uses are being discovered every day. Today's seemingly trivial discovery may aid in understanding complex transactions that may not occur until some distant future date.

One way to categorize the uses of microeconomics is to look at the types of people who use it. At the most basic level, microeconomics has a variety of uses for people in their own lives. An understanding of how markets work can help you make decisions about future jobs, about the wisdom of major purchases (such as houses), or about important financial decisions (such as retirement). Of course, economists are not much better than anyone else in predicting the future. There are legendary examples of economists who in fact made disastrous decisions. Topically, at the time of writing, many economists have been predicting a housing crash in Britain (and other countries) for some years now but with, as yet, no sign of any major correction on the scale of a crash. Time may prove them right but their timing may not go down in history as a having been close. Nevertheless, the study of microeconomics can help you to conceptualize the important economic decisions you must make in your life and that can often lead to better decision-making. For example, Application 1.2: *Is It Worth Your Time to Be Here?* illustrates how notions of opportunity cost can clarify whether university attendance is really a good investment.

Businesses, governments, and research institutes also use the tools of microeconomics. Any firm must try to understand the nature of the demand for its product. A firm that stubbornly continues to produce a good or service that no one wants will soon find itself in bankruptcy.

Firms must also be concerned with their costs; for this topic, too, microeconomics has found many applications. For example, in Chapter 8 we look at how the Renault car firm managed, through a reorganization of a section of their production, to cut costs substantially. Microeconomic tools can help to understand such efficiencies. They can also help to explore the implications of introducing these efficiencies into such notoriously high-cost markets as that for air travel within Europe.

Microeconomics is also often used to evaluate broad questions of government policy. At the deepest level, these investigations focus on whether certain laws and regulations contribute to or detract from overall welfare. As we see in later chapters, economists have devised a number of imaginative ways of measuring how various government actions affect consumers, workers, and firms. These measures often play crucial roles in the political debate surrounding the adoption or repeal of such policies. Later in this book, we look at many examples in such important areas as health care, antitrust policy, or minimum wages. Of course, there are two sides to most policy questions, and economists are no more immune than anyone else from the temptation to bend their arguments to fit a particular point of view. Knowledge of microeconomics does provide a basic framework – that is, a common language – in which many such discussions are conducted, and it should help you to sort out good arguments from self-serving ones.

[2] The word *lemon* is used in American English to denote a used car which is not as good as it is made out to be by the seller of the car.

APPLICATION 1.2 *Is It Worth Your Time to Be Here?*

As the student of this textbook plows their way through, hopefully finding enlightenment in the process, if you start to wonder whether being at university is worth all the effort then you are weighing up the benefits and costs of sitting where you are now instead of "out there" earning a salary in the world or work. In effect you are trying to calculate your *opportunity cost* of being here right now in a university or college.

There are two answers to this thought, which at some stage will inevitably cross the minds of every higher education student. The first is, be patient: the world of work will come soon enough and graduating in your early twenties some of you will have until your late sixties to exhaust your work desires. (Study *and* enjoy your student days while you can!)

The second reply is a bit more calculating: those who graduate with a higher level of education over those who do not tend to have greater lifetime earnings. In other words you are better off financially if you study for a higher level qualification.

Blundell *et al.* (2003) in a recent study found that the earnings premium associated with a higher educational qualification within the United Kingdom is roughly 23.5 per cent compared to those who have attained two or more British "A" levels.[1] This premium in monetary terms is the equivalent of £120 000 discounted lifetime earnings. (That is, the net present value figure.)

The study also took into account the personal circumstances and characteristics of the individuals. For example, an individual may come from a small, relatively well-off family which may help foster greater learning.

As one might expect the return to an education at a higher level will vary by subject area studied. In addition the returns seem to be much larger for females than for males regardless of the subject area as Figure 1 demonstrates. One should not conclude from this that females therefore earn more in wages than males; they do not – on average! It simply means that the earnings of females who do not go to university are so very low that relatively speaking the jump in earnings for females who do go to university is that much bigger compared to the situation for males.

To Think About

1 Why do you think that the return to a higher education is greater for females than it is for males?

2 Is innate ability the same thing as a good education? Justify your answer.

3 Do the higher lifetime earnings justify the introduction of tuition fees for those who receive higher lifetime earnings?

[1] R. Blundell, L. Dearden and B. Sianesi, *Estimating the Returns to Education: Models, Methods and Results* (2003), Institute for Fiscal Studies Working Paper No. WP03/20.

FIGURE 1 Earning Premia Associated with Different Degree Level Subjects

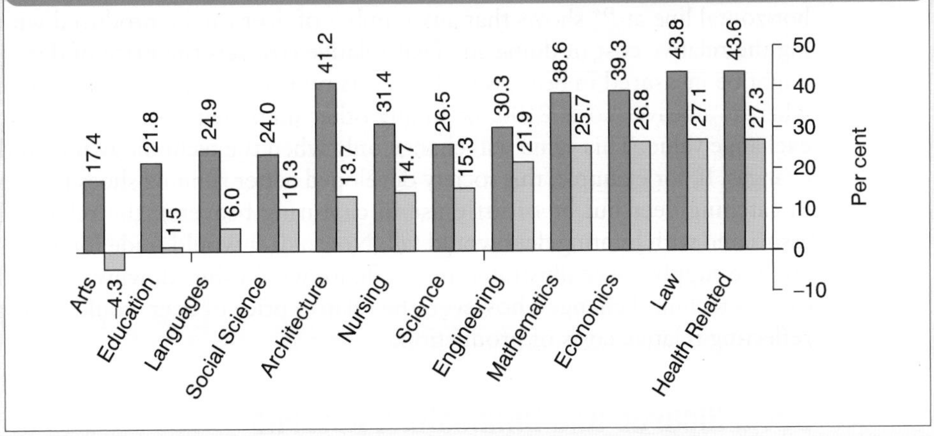

SOURCE: QUOTED IN *LONDON SOUTH BANK UNIVERSITY, DRAFT ECONOMIC IMPACT STUDY* (JUNE 2006) CONSULTANCY REPORT CARRIED OUT FOR SOUTH BANK UNIVERSITY BY PRICEWATERHOUSECOOPER. THE PREMIA ABOVE REFER TO THOSE GRADUATES FROM UK HIGHER EDUCATIONAL INSTITUTIONS.

The Basic Supply–Demand Model

Supply–demand model A model describing how a good's price is determined by the behavior of the individuals who buy the good and of the firms that sell it.

As the saying goes, "Even your pet parrot can learn economics – just teach it to say 'supply and demand' in answer to every question." Of course, there is often more to the story. But economists tend to insist that market behavior can usually be explained by the relationship between preferences for a good (demand) and the costs involved in producing that good (supply). The basic **supply–demand model** of price determination is a staple of all courses in introductory economics – in fact, this model may be the first thing you studied in your introductory course. Here we provide a quick review of the model, adding a bit of historical perspective.

Adam Smith and the Invisible Hand

The Scottish philosopher Adam Smith (1723–1790) is generally credited with being the first true economist. In *The Wealth of Nations* (published in 1776), Smith examined a large number of the pressing economic issues of his day and tried to develop economic tools for understanding them. Smith's most important insight was his recognition that the system of market-determined prices that he observed was not as chaotic and undisciplined as most other writers had assumed. Rather, Smith saw prices as providing a powerful "invisible hand" that directed resources into activities where they would be most valuable. Prices play the crucial role of telling both consumers and firms what resources are "worth" and thereby prompt these economic actors to make efficient choices about how to use them. To Smith, it was this ability to use resources efficiently that provided the ultimate explanation for a nation's "wealth".

Because Adam Smith placed great importance on the role of prices in directing how a nation's resources are used, he needed to develop some theories about how those prices are determined. He offered a very simple and only partly correct explanation. Because, in Smith's day (and, to some extent, even today), the primary costs of producing goods were costs associated with the labor that went into a good, it was only a short step for him to embrace a labor-based theory of prices. For example, to paraphrase an illustration from *The Wealth of Nations*, if it takes twice as long for a hunter to catch a deer as to catch a beaver, one deer should trade for two beavers. The relative price of a deer is high because of the extra labor costs involved in catching one.

Smith's explanation for the price of a good is illustrated in Figure 1-2(a). The horizontal line at P^* shows that any number of deer can be produced without affecting the relative cost of doing so. That relative cost sets the price of deer (P^*), which might be measured in beavers (a deer costs two beavers), in euros a deer costs €200, whereas a beaver costs €100, or in any other units that this society uses to indicate exchange value. This value will change only when the technology for producing deer changes. If, for example, this society developed better running shoes (which would aid in catching deer but be of little use in capturing beavers), the relative labor costs associated with hunting deer would fall. Now a deer would trade for, say, 1.5 beavers, and the supply curve illustrated in the figure would shift downward. In the absence of such technical changes, however, the relative price of deer would remain constant, reflecting relative costs of production.

David Ricardo and Diminishing Returns

The early nineteenth century was a period of considerable controversy in economics, especially in Britain. The two most pressing issues of the day were whether international trade was having a negative effect on the economy and whether industrial growth was harming farmland and other natural resources. It is testimony to the timelessness of economic questions that these are some of the same issues that dominate political discussions in throughout academic and political circles today. One of the most influential contributors to the earlier debates was the British financier and pamphleteer David Ricardo (1772–1823).

Ricardo believed that labor and other costs would tend to rise as the level of production of a particular good expanded. He drew this insight primarily from looking at the way in which farmland was expanding in England at the time. As new and less-fertile land was brought into use, it would naturally take more labor (say, to pick out the rocks in addition to planting crops) to produce an extra bushel of grain.[3] Hence, the relative price of grain would rise. Similarly, as deer hunters exhaust the stock of deer in a given area, they must spend more time locating their prey, so the relative price of deer would also rise. Ricardo believed that the phenomenon of increasing costs was quite general, and today we refer to his discovery as the law of **diminishing returns**. This generalization of Smith's notion of supply is reflected in Figure 1-2(b), in which the supply curve slopes upward as quantity produced expands.

Diminishing returns
Hypothesis that the cost associated with producing one more unit of a good rises as more of that good is produced.

The problem with Ricardo's explanation was that it really did not explain how prices are determined. Although the notion of diminishing returns made Smith's model more realistic, it did so by showing that relative price was not determined by production technology alone. Instead, according to Ricardo, the relative price of a good can be practically anything, depending on how much of it is produced.

To complete his explanation, Ricardo relied on a subsistence argument. If, for example, the current population of a country needs Q_1 units of output to survive, Figure 1-2(b) shows that the relative price would be P_1. With a growing population, these subsistence needs might expand to Q_2, and the relative price of this necessity would rise to P_2. Ricardo's suggestion that the relative prices of goods necessary for

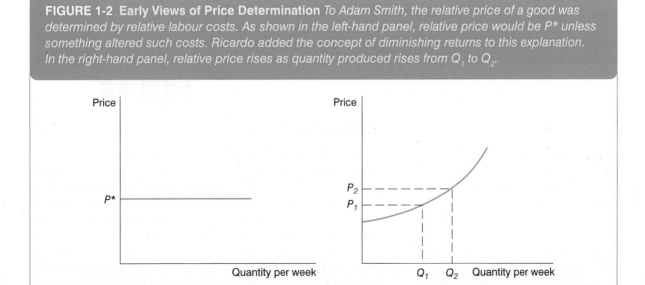

FIGURE 1-2 Early Views of Price Determination *To Adam Smith, the relative price of a good was determined by relative labour costs. As shown in the left-hand panel, relative price would be P* unless something altered such costs. Ricardo added the concept of diminishing returns to this explanation. In the right-hand panel, relative price rises as quantity produced rises from Q_1 to Q_2.*

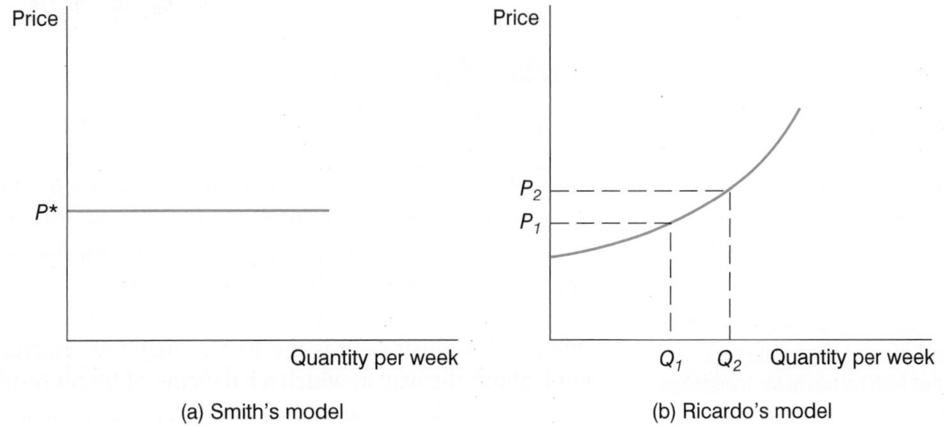

[3] A bushel is a measurement unit of dry volume equal to just over 35.24 liters in the American Customary System or just over 36.37 liters in the British Imperial System.

survival would rise in response to diminishing returns provided the basis for much of the concern about population growth in Britain during the 1830s and 1840s. It was largely responsible for the application of the term *dismal science* to the study of economics.

Marginalism and Marshall's Model of Supply and Demand

Contrary to the fears of many worriers, relative prices of food and other necessities did not rise significantly during the nineteenth century. Instead, as methods of production improved, prices tended to fall and levels of material well-being improved dramatically. As a result, subsistence became a less plausible explanation of the amounts of particular goods consumed, and economists found it necessary to develop a more general theory of demand. In the latter half of the nineteenth century, they adapted Ricardo's law of diminishing returns to this task. Just as diminishing returns mean that the cost of producing one more unit of a good rises as more is produced, so too, these economists argued, the willingness of people to pay for that last unit declines. Only if individuals are offered a lower price for a good will they be willing to consume more of it. By focusing on the value to buyers of the last, or *marginal*, unit purchased, these economists had at last developed a comprehensive theory of price determination.

The clearest statement of these ideas was first provided by the English economist Alfred Marshall (1842–1924) in his *Principles of Economics*, published in 1890. Marshall showed how the forces of demand and supply *simultaneously* determine price. Marshall's analysis is illustrated by the familiar cross diagram shown in Figure 1-3.

As before, the amount of a good purchased per period (say, each week) is shown on the horizontal axis and the price of the good appears on the vertical axis. The curve labeled "Demand" shows the amount of the good people want to buy at each price. The negative slope of this curve reflects the marginalist principle: Because people are willing to pay less and less for the last unit purchased, they will buy more only at a lower price. The curve labeled "Supply" shows the increasing cost of making one more unit of the good as the total amount produced increases. In other words, the upward slope of the supply curve reflects *increasing* marginal costs, just as the downward slope of the demand curve reflects *decreasing* marginal usefulness.

Equilibrium price
The price at which the quantity demanded by buyers of a good is equal to the quantity supplied by sellers of the good.

MICROQUIZ 1.2

Another way to describe the equilibrium in Figure 1-3 is to say that at P^*, Q^* neither the supplier nor the demander has any incentive to change behavior. Use this notion of equilibrium to explain:

1. Why the fact that P^*, Q^* occurs where the supply and demand curves intersect implies that both parties to the transaction are content with this result; and
2. Why no other P, Q point on the graph meets this definition of equilibrium.

Market Equilibrium

In Figure 1-3, the demand and supply curves intersect at the point P^*, Q^*. At that point, P^* is the **equilibrium price**. That is, at this price, the quantity that people want to purchase (Q^*) is precisely equal to the quantity that suppliers are willing to produce. Because both demanders and suppliers are content with this outcome, no one has an incentive to alter his or her behavior. The equilibrium P^*, Q^* will tend to persist unless something happens to change things. This illustration is the first of many we encounter in this book about the way in which a balancing of forces results in a sustainable equilibrium outcome. To conceptualize the nature of this balancing of forces, Marshall used the analogy of a pair of scissors: just as both blades of the scissors work together to do the cutting, so too the forces of demand and supply work together to establish equilibrium prices.

Non-equilibrium Outcomes

The smooth functioning of market forces envisioned by Marshall can, however, be thwarted in many ways. For example, a government decree that requires a price to be set in excess of P^* (perhaps because P^* was regarded as being the result of "unfair, ruinous competition") would prevent the establishment of equilibrium. With a price set above P^*, demanders would wish to buy less than Q^*, whereas suppliers would produce more than Q^*. This would lead to a surplus of production in the market – a situation that characterizes many agricultural markets. Similarly, a regulation that holds a price below P^* would result in a shortage. With such a price, demanders would want to buy more than Q^*, whereas supplies would produce less than Q^*. In Chapter 11, we look at several situations where this occurs.

Change in Market Equilibrium

The equilibrium pictured in Figure 1-3 can persist as long as nothing happens to alter demand or supply relationships. If one of the curves were to shift, however, the equilibrium would change. In Figure 1-4, people's demand for the good increases. In this case, the demand curve moves outward (from curve *D* to curve *D*'). At each price, people now want to buy more of the good. The equilibrium price increases (from P^* to P^{**}). This higher price both tells firms to supply more goods and restrains individuals' demand for the good. At the new equilibrium price of P^{**}, supply and demand again balance – at this higher price, the amount of goods demanded is exactly equal to the amount supplied.

MICROQUIZ 1.3

Supply and demand curves show the relationship between the price of a good and the quantity supplied or demanded when other factors are held constant. Explain:

1 What factors might shift the demand or supply curve for, say, personal computers.

2 Why a change in the price of PCs would shift neither curve. Indeed, would this price ever change if all of the factors identified previously did not change?

FIGURE 1-3 The Marshall Supply-Demand Cross *Marshall believed that demand and supply together determine the equilibrium price (P*) and quantity (Q*) of a good. The positive slope of the supply curve reflects diminishing returns (increasing marginal cost), whereas the negative slope of the demand curve reflects diminishing marginal usefulness. P* is an equilibrium price. Any other price results in either a surplus or a shortage.*

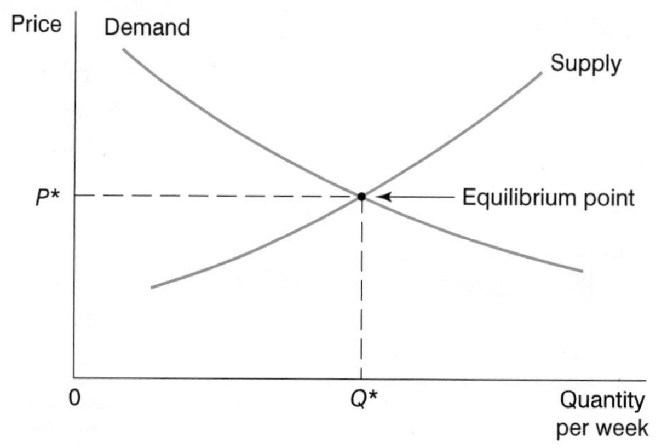

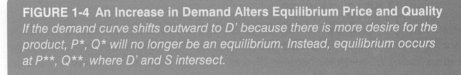

FIGURE 1-4 An Increase in Demand Alters Equilibrium Price and Quality *If the demand curve shifts outward to D' because there is more desire for the product, P*, Q* will no longer be an equilibrium. Instead, equilibrium occurs at P**, Q**, where D' and S intersect.*

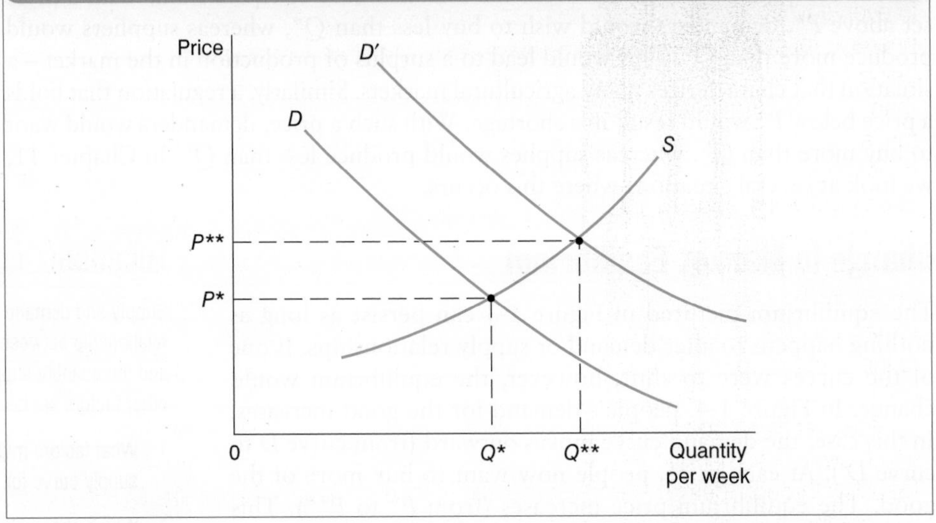

A shift in the supply curve also affects market equilibrium. In Figure 1-5, the effects of an increase in supplier costs (for example, an increase in wages paid to workers) are illustrated. For any level of output, marginal costs associated with the supply curve *S'* exceed those associated with *S*. This shift in supply causes the price of this product to rise (from *P** to *P***), and consumers respond to this price rise by reducing quantity demanded (from *Q** to *Q***) along the demand curve, *D*. As for the case of a shift in demand, the ultimate result of the shift in supply depicted in Figure 1-5 depends on the shape of both the demand curve and the supply curve.

FIGURE 1-5 A Shift in Supply Alters Equilibrium Price and Quality *A rise in costs would shift the supply curve upward to S'. This would cause an increase in equilibrium price from P* to P** and a decline in quantity from Q* to Q**.*

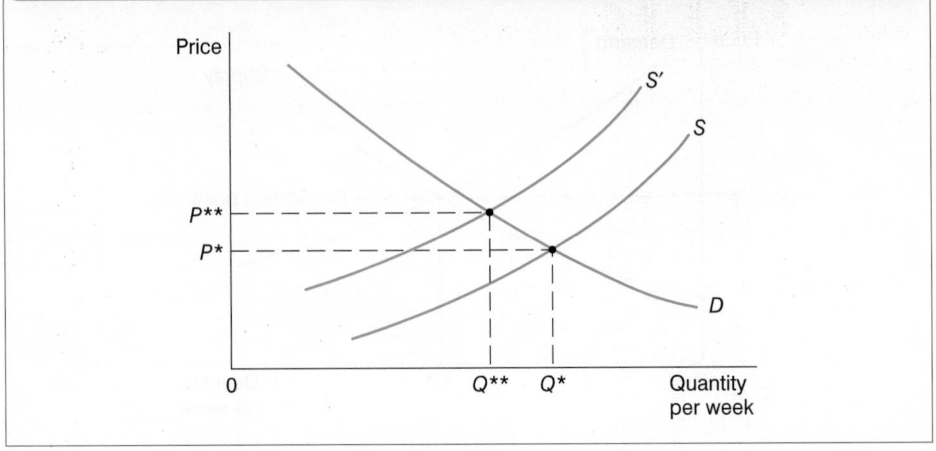

APPLICATION 1.3 *The Day They Paid You to Take Gas*

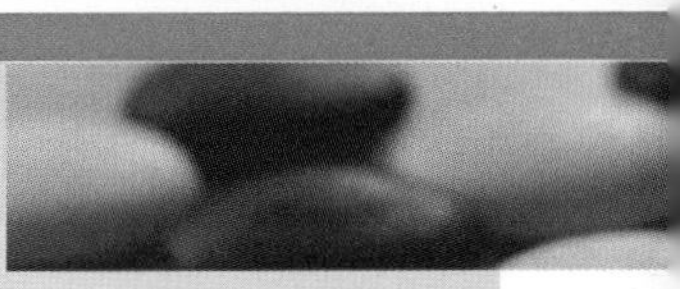

In everyday life most people will invariably think of prices – for television sets, cars, food, etc. – as being positive, i.e. the price of the good is greater than zero. Economists will occasionally point out that some goods which can be labeled as "bads" – household rubbish, nuclear waste for example – will often involve individuals or governments paying for other people to take these bads off the hands of those who currently possess them. These particular goods have, what economists call, a negative externality – they give negative satisfaction or utility to their current owners. We cover this in more detail in Chapter 18.

However, if we consider "run-of-the-mill" goods which give consumers positive satisfaction (or positive utility) through their consumption then it might be thought that it would be very unlikely, if not impossible, for a situation to arise when the owners of goods, which give positive satisfaction to consumers, would pay money *to* the consumer or buyer to take the good off their hands. In the example below we present the admittedly rare case of where such a situation occurred. This led to the situation where for the market to clear, i.e. where the quantity of the good demanded just equaled the quantity supplied – the price in the market was negative.[1]

Figure 1 represents the situation that developed in the market for gas imported into Britain on 3 October 2006.[2] A mild spell of weather had left stocks of gas high within Britain. This was exacerbated by the testing of a new gas pipeline from Norway, the Langeled pipeline, connecting the Norwegian gas fields with the East Yorkshire coast of England. Gas was piped, regardless of demand, to test the capacity of the pipe such that enough gas was being piped through to supply 12 gas-fired power stations each day. As such, this had the effect of shifting the supply of natural gas onto the British market from S_1 to S_2.

The result was that when shipments of gas arrived from abroad on 3 October 2006 the infrastructure did not exist on the part of traders to store the gas that could not be sold.

At the then existing market price (represented by £P in Figure 1) it was estimated by the National Grid, the UK gas network operator, that 344 m cubic meters were available compared with demand of 234 m cubic meters.

In the end some UK traders of gas sold the gas on at *negative* 5p per therm to eliminate the excess supply. This combined with producers cutting back supply from gas fields in the North Sea and even one coal-fired power station switching temporarily to gas brought supply and demand back into equilibrium at a positive price.

To Think About

Using the letters *A* through to *F* in Figure 1 along with any quantitative information given, show:

1. The equilibrium or market clearing position on 3 October 2006 *before* the importation of gas that could not be sold at a positive price both in terms of letters and in actual cubic meters of gas;
2. The excess supply of gas that could not be sold at a positive price in terms of letters and in actual cubic meters of gas;
3. In terms of letters, the equilibrium or market clearing position (where the supply curve equals the demand curve) *after* the importation of gas that could only be sold at a negative price;
4. The quantity of gas sold at a negative price in terms of letters.

[1] "*Gas given away as surge from Norway causes price plunge*", *Financial Times*, London, 4 October 2006.

[2] To the reader whose first language is not English and who may have learnt American English, it should be explained that in British English gas is not the material that you place in your car to make it run. Rather it is the material used in the kitchen via the cooker to cook your food; to heat your home through gas central heating; or to generate electricity in gas-fired power stations. In British English, the American word gas (short for gasoline) is translated as petrol.

(*Continued*)

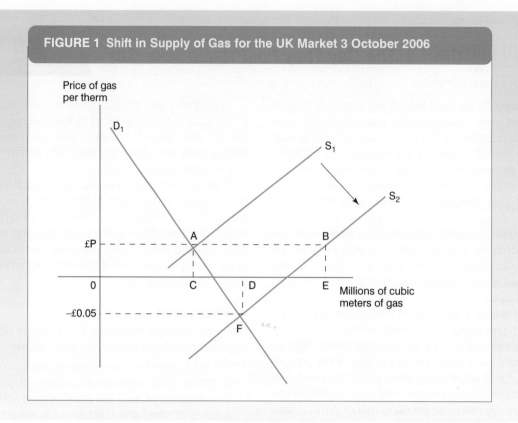

FIGURE 1 Shift in Supply of Gas for the UK Market 3 October 2006

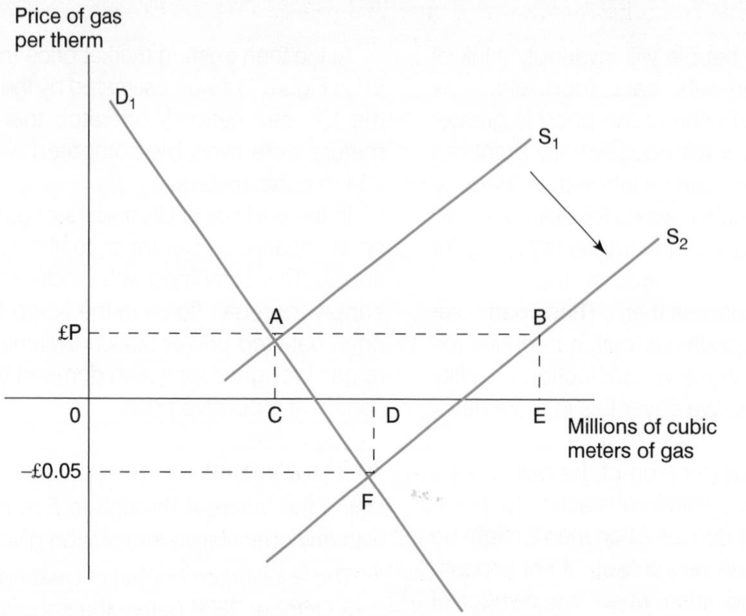

Marshall's model of supply and demand should be quite familiar to you, since it provides the principal focus of most courses in introductory economics. Indeed, the concepts of marginal cost, marginal value, and market equilibrium encountered in this model provide the starting place for most of the economic models you will learn about in this book. Application 1.3: *The Day They Paid You to Take Gas* examines the supply and demand situation from the unusual situation where, for a short period, the price of gas was negative.

How Economists Verify Theoretical Models

Not all models are as useful as Marshall's model of supply and demand. An important purpose of studying economics is to sort out bad models from good ones. Two methods are used to provide such a test of economic models. **Testing assumptions** looks at the assumptions upon which a model is based; **testing predictions**, on the other hand, uses the model to see if it can correctly predict real-world events. This book uses both approaches to try to illustrate the validity of the models that are presented. We now look briefly at the differences between the approaches.

Testing assumptions
Verifying economic models by examining the validity of the assumptions on which they are based.

Testing predictions
Verifying economic models by asking if they can accurately predict real-world events.

Testing Assumptions

One approach to testing the assumptions of an economic model might begin with intuition. Do the model's assumptions seem reasonable? Unfortunately, this question is fraught with problems, since what appears reasonable to one person may seem preposterous to someone else (try arguing with a non-economics student about whether people usually behave rationally, for example).

Assumptions can also be tested with empirical evidence. For example, economists usually assume that firms are in business to maximize profits – in fact, much of our discussion in this book is based on that assumption. Using the direct approach to test this assumption with real-world data, you might send questionnaires to managers asking them how they make decisions and whether they really do try to maximize profits. This approach has been used many times, but the results, like those from many opinion polls, are often difficult to interpret.

Testing Predictions

Some economists, such as the late Milton Friedman, did not believe that a theory can be tested by looking only at its assumptions. They argue that all theories are based on unrealistic assumptions; the very nature of theorizing demands that we make unrealistic assumptions.[4] Such economists believe that, in order to decide if a theory is valid, we must see if it is capable of explaining and predicting real-world events. The real test of any economic model is whether it is consistent with events from the economy itself.

Friedman gives a good example of this idea by asking what theory explains the shots an expert pool player will make. He argues that the laws of velocity, momentum, and angles from physics make a suitable theoretical model, because the pool player certainly shoots *as if* he or she followed these laws. If we asked the players whether they could state these physical principles, they would undoubtedly answer that they could not. That does not matter, Friedman argues, because the physical laws give very accurate predictions of the shots made and are therefore useful as theoretical models.

Going back to the question of whether firms try to maximize profits, the indirect approach would try to predict the firms' behavior by assuming that they do act *as if* they were maximizing profits. If we find that we can predict firms' behavior, then we can believe the profit-maximization hypothesis. Even if these firms said on questionnaires that they don't really try to maximize profits, the theory will still be valid, much as the pool players' disclaiming knowledge of the laws of physics does not make these laws untrue. The ultimate test in both cases is the theory's ability to predict real-world events. Application 1.4: *Forecasting Meat Production: Let Us Assume . . .* Looks at the output of meat during the BSE crisis of 1996 within the United Kingdom and asks whether it is a safe assumption to assume meat production declined at that period due to beef output going down. We use quantitative data to examine the "evidence".

The Positive–Normative Distinction

Related to the question of how the validity of economic models should be tested is the issue of how such models should be used. To some economists, the only proper analysis is "positive" in nature. As in the physical sciences, they argue, the correct role

[4]Milton Friedman, *Essays in Positive Economics* (Chicago: University of Chicago Press, 1953), Chapter 1. Another view stressing the importance of realistic assumptions can be found in H. A. Simon, "Rational Decision Making in Business Organizations", *American Economic Review* (September 1979): 493–513.

APPLICATION 1.4 *Forecasting Meat Production: Let Us Assume . . . (Or Lies, Damned Lies, and . . .)*

Imagine you are a new young agricultural economist specializing in the research of meat production within the United Kingdom. Over the last number of years you will have been aware of bovine spongiform encephalopathy (BSE) or as it became known "Mad Cow Disease". Due to the slaughter of infected cattle herds you suspect and therefore make what you think is the relatively safe assumption that the supply of meat onto the British consumer market slumped during the period when BSE was at its height.

From the point of view of empirically examining the impact of declining *beef* output on the overall output of *all types of meat* you start to uncover the data to ascertain if your assumption is correct.

You have made the assumption that due to declining beef output this must have led to meat output figures (which include beef, pork, venison, etc.) dropping quite significantly. Figure 1 displays monthly data of beef output. Such data are referred to as *non- or not-seasonally adjusted* (NSA). This means that, in this case, due to the breeding cycle of cattle, and the specifics of the farming industry beef production will be higher at some times of the year than at others. We could smooth out these variations by taking average output over three or four month periods and present seasonally adjusted data but we stick to the non-SA data.[1]

Sure enough, as displayed in Figure 1, there appears a distinct dip in *beef* output corresponding to the month and year of March, 1996. Your assumption of declining meat output must surely be confirmed since clearly beef production, which makes up a significant part of overall meat production, has fallen quite markedly.

However, when you download the relevant data and plot the data in a graph (see Figure 2), to your surprise, you find that meat production rose substantially one month after beef production plummeted.

It would appear that your initial assumption has been confounded. But why? It seemed a reasonable assumption but the testing of that assumption did not back up your original thoughts on overall meat output.

To Think About

1 Task for the student: Visit the website Biz/ed which is, as the sites' creators say themselves, "A website for students and educators in busi-

FIGURE 1 Monthly Beef Output within the United Kingdom

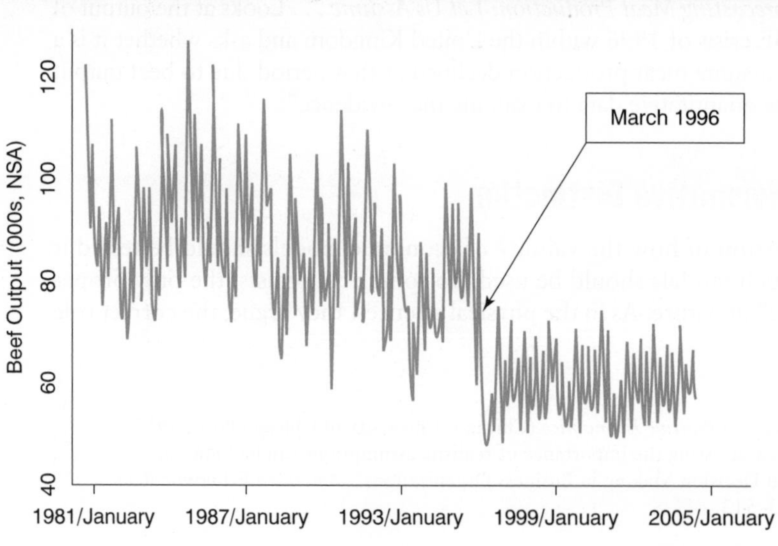

ness studies, economics, accounting, leisure, sport & recreation and travel & tourism". You can find this site at: http://www.bized.co.uk/dataserv/datahome.htm.

2 Through the section TimeWeb you should be able to access sample data for the output of various commodities including all types of meat. Download these and examine the output for all the different types of meat to try and figure out why all types of meat production went up when beef production went down. When you have answered the question to your satisfaction, ask yourself whether this implies that the young agricultural economist was wrong to assume what (s)he did?

[1]In general, whenever a variable of interest is linked to units of time during the year there can be seasonality in the figures reported. Unemployment among building workers, for example, can rise during the winter months in some countries because of deteriorations in the conditions of work on open air building sites. From a governmental perspective such a rise may not be seen as quite so serious (compared to unemployment brought about due to a general economic recession) since, it is assumed, once the weather improves so too will the job prospects of unemployed construction workers without the need for government intervention.

FIGURE 2 Monthly Output of All Types of Meat within the United Kingdom

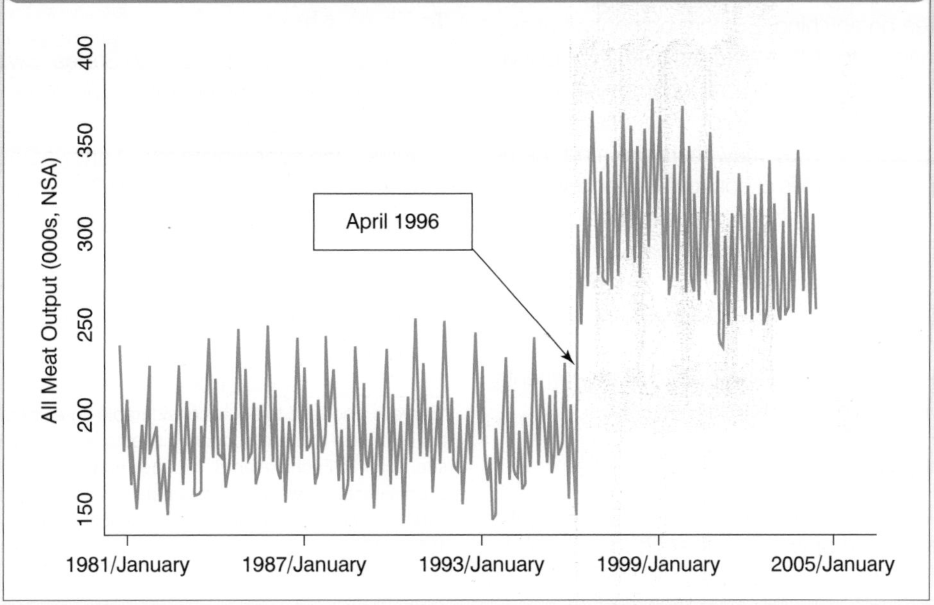

for theory is to explain the real world as it is. In this view, developing "normative" theories about how the world *should be* is an exercise for which economists have no more special skills than anyone else. For other economists, this **positive–normative distinction** is not so clear-cut. They argue that economic models invariably have normative consequences that should be recognized. Application 1.5: *Do Economists Ever Agree on Anything*? shows that, contrary to common perceptions, there is considerable agreement among economists about issues that are suitable for positive scientific analysis. There is far less agreement about normative questions related to what should be done. In this book, we take primarily a positive approach by using economic models to explain real-world events. The book's applications pursue these explanations in greater detail. You should feel free to adapt these models to whatever normative goals you believe are worth pursuing.

Positive–normative distinction Distinction between theories that seek to explain the world as it is and theories that postulate the way the world should be.

APPLICATION 1.5 *Do Economists Ever Agree on Anything?*

To the general public, economists seem to be completely confused. In many conversations, they bear the brunt of pointed jokes. Some of my favorites are:

1 If all economists in the world were laid end-to-end, they would never reach a conclusion.

2 How many economists does it take to change a light bulb? Two – one to turn the bulb and one to say repeatedly, "Turn it the other way".

Positive versus Normative Economics

These jokes convey the perception that economists never agree on anything. But that perception arises from an inability to differentiate between the positive and normative arguments that economists make. Economists (like everyone else) often disagree over political questions. They may, therefore, find themselves on opposite sides of controversial policy questions. Economists may also differ on empirical matters. For instance, they may disagree about whether a particular effect is large or small. But on basic theoretical questions, there is far less disagreement. Because most economists use the same tools, they tend to "speak the same language" and disagreements on positive questions are far less frequent.

Survey Results

This conclusion is supported by surveys of economists, a sample of which is described in Table 1. The table shows a high degree of agreement among US, Swiss, and German economists about positive questions such as the effects of tariffs or of rent controls.[1] There is considerably less agreement about broad normative questions, such as whether the government should redistribute income or act as the employer of last resort. For these types of questions, economists' opinions are as varied as those of any other group of citizens.

To Think About

1 Economists from the United States, Switzerland, and Germany may not reflect the views of economists from lower-income countries. Do you think such economists might answer the questions in Table 1 differently?

2 What is the difference between a(n)_________ and an economist? Answer:_________. (Send your suggestions for the best completion of this joke to the authors. Regular prizes are awarded.)

[1] Surveys also tend to show considerable agreement over the likely size of many economic effects. For a summary, see Victor R. Fuchs, Alan B. Krueger, and James M. Poterba, "Economists' Views about Parameters, Values, and Policy", *Journal of Economic Literature* (September 1998): 1387–1425.

TABLE 1 Percentage of Economists Agreeing with Various Propositions in Three Nations

Proposition	*United States*	*Switzerland*	*Germany*
Tariffs reduce economic welfare	95	87	94
Flexible exchange rates are effective for international transactions	94	91	92
Rent controls reduce the quality of housing	96	79	94
Government should redistribute income	68	51	55
Government should hire the jobless	51	52	35

SOURCE: B.S. FREY, W.W. POMMEREHUE, F. SCHNEIDER, AND G. GILBERT, "CONSENSUS AND DISSENSION AMONG ECONOMISTS: AN EMPIRICAL INQUIRY", *AMERICAN ECONOMIC REVIEW* (DECEMBER 1984): 986–994. PERCENTAGES REPRESENT FRACTION THAT "GENERALLY AGREE" OR "AGREE WITH PROVISIONS". USED WITH PERMISSION.

SUMMARY

This chapter provides you with some background to begin your study of microeconomics. Much of this material should be familiar to you from your introductory economics course, but that should come as no surprise. In many respects, the study of economics repeatedly investigates the same questions with an increasingly sophisticated set of tools. This course gives you some more of these tools. In establishing the basis for that investigation, this chapter reminds you of several important ideas:

- Economics is the study of allocating scarce resources among possible uses. Because resources are scarce, choices have to be made on how they will be used. Economists develop theoretical models to explain these choices.
- The production possibility frontier provides a simple illustration of the supply conditions in two markets. The curve clearly shows the limits imposed on any economy because resources are scarce. Producing more of one good means that less of something else must be produced. This reduction in output elsewhere measures the opportunity cost involved in such additional production.
- The most commonly used model of the allocation of resources is the model of supply and demand developed by Alfred Marshall in the latter part of the nineteenth century. The model shows how prices are determined by creating an equilibrium between the amount people want to buy and the amount firms are willing to produce. If supply and demand curves shift, new prices are established to restore equilibrium to the market.
- Proving the validity of economic models is difficult and sometimes controversial. Occasionally the validity of a model can be determined by whether it is based on reasonable assumptions. More often, however, models are judged by how well they explain actual economic events.

REVIEW QUESTIONS

1 "To an economist, a resource is 'scarce' only if it has a positive price. Resources with zero prices are, by definition, not scarce." Do you agree? Or does the term *scarce* convey some other meaning?

2 In many economic problems, time is treated as a resource. Describe how problems in using time meet our definition of "economics". Can you think of something that is different about using time than about using physical resources?

3 Develop a formal economic analysis of why honeybees find it in their interest to leave some nectar in each flower they visit. Can you think of any human activities that yield a similar result?

4 Classical economists struggled with the "Water–Diamond Paradox", which seeks an explanation for why water (which is very useful) has a low price, whereas diamonds (which are not particularly important to life) have a high price. How would Smith explain the relative prices of water and diamonds? Would Ricardo's concept of diminishing returns pose some problem for this explanation? Can you resolve matters by using Marshall's model of supply and demand? Is water "very useful" to the demanders in Marshall's model?

5 Marshall's model pictures price *and* quantity as being determined simultaneously by the interaction of supply and demand. Using this insight, explain the fallacies in the following paragraph:
A rise in the price of oranges reduces the number of people who want to buy. This reduction by itself reduces growers' costs by allowing them to use only their best trees. Price, therefore, declines along with costs, and the initial price rise cannot be sustained.

6 "Petrol sells for €1.50 per liter this year, and it sold for €1.30 per liter last year. But consumers

bought more petrol this year than they did last year. This is clear proof that the economic theory that people buy less when the price rises is incorrect." Do you agree? Explain.

7 "A shift outward in the demand curve always results in an increase in total spending (price times quantity) on a good. On the other hand, a shift outward in the supply curve may increase or decrease total spending." Explain.

8 Housing advocates often claim that "the demand for affordable housing vastly exceeds the supply". Use a supply–demand diagram to show whether you can make any sense out of this statement. In particular, show how a proper interpretation may depend on precisely how the word *affordable* is to be defined.

9 A key concept in the development of positive economic theories is the notion of "refutability" – a "theory" is not a "theory" unless there is some evidence that, if true, could prove it wrong. Use this notion to discuss whether one can conceive of evidence with which the following theories might be refuted:

- Friedman's claim that pool players play as if they were using the rules of physics.
- The theory that firms operate so as to maximize profits.
- The theory that demand curves slope downward.
- The theory that adoption of capitalism makes people who are poor more miserable.

10 The following conversation was heard among four economists discussing whether the minimum wage should be increased:

Economist A. "Increasing the minimum wage would reduce employment of minority teenagers."
Economist B. "Increasing the minimum wage would represent an unwarranted interference with private relations between workers and their employers."
Economist C. "Increasing the minimum wage would raise the incomes of some unskilled workers."
Economist D. "Increasing the minimum wage would benefit higher-wage workers and would probably be supported by the trade unions."

Which of these economists are using positive analysis and which are using normative analysis in arriving at their conclusions? Which of these predictions might be tested with empirical data? How might such tests be conducted?

PROBLEMS

Note: These problems focus on the mathematical material from the Appendix to Chapter 1. Hence they are primarily numerical.

1.1 The following data represent five points on the supply curve for red wine:

Price (€ per liter)	*Quantity (millions of liters)*
1	100
2	300
3	500
4	700
5	900

and these data represent five points on the demand curve for red wine:

Price (€ per liter)	*Quantity (millions of liters)*
1	700
2	600
3	500
4	400
5	300

a Graph the points of these supply and demand curves for red wine. Be sure to put price on the vertical axis and quantity on the horizontal axis.

b Do these points seem to lie along two straight lines? If so, figure out the precise algebraic equation of these lines. (Hint: If the points do lie on straight lines, you need only consider two points on each of them to calculate the lines.)

c Use your solutions from part b to calculate the "excess demand" for red wine if the market price is zero.

d Use your solutions from part b to calculate the "excess supply" of red wine if the red wine price is €6 per liter.

1.2 Marshall defined an equilibrium price as one at which the quantity demanded equals the quantity supplied.

a Using the data provided in problem 1.1, show that $P = 3$ is the equilibrium price in the red wine market.

b Using these data, explain why $P = 2$ and $P = 4$ are not equilibrium prices.

c Graph your results and show that the supply–demand equilibrium resembles that shown in Figure 1-3.

d Suppose the demand for red wine were to increase so that people want to buy 300 million more liters at every price. How would that change the data in problem 1.1? How would it shift the demand curve you drew in part c?

e What is the new equilibrium price in the red wine market, given this increase in demand? Show this new equilibrium in your supply–demand graph.

f Suppose now that a plague of aphids that eats the roots of grapevines reduces the supply by 300 million liters at every price listed in problem 1.1. How would this shift in supply affect the data in problem 1.1? How would it affect the algebraic supply curve calculated in that problem?

g Given this new supply relationship together with the demand relationship shown in problem 1.1, what is the equilibrium price in this market?

h Explain why $P = 3$ is no longer an equilibrium in the red wine market. How would the participants in this market know $P = 3$ is no longer an equilibrium?

i Graph your results for this supply shift.

1.3 Marshall used the analogy of scissors to explain how demand and supply work together in determining market outcomes.

a Use this observation to explain why a shift outward in the demand for diamonds (which have a nearly vertical supply curve) will have a greater impact on market price than will a similar-sized shift outward in the demand for pizzas (which have a flat supply curve).

b Explain your results from part a intuitively, by focusing on the post-shift positions of suppliers and demanders in these two markets.

c Devise an algebraic representation of these two markets that illustrates what was shown in part a.

1.4 "Economists must have failed Algebra I! They persist in putting the independent variable in supply–demand graphs on the vertical axis and the dependent variable on the horizontal axis. Everyone knows that dependent variables (like Y) belong on the vertical axis and independent variables (like X) belong on the horizontal axis." Do you agree? Why do you think economists made the axis choices that they did?

1.5 This problem involves solving demand and supply equations together to determine price and quantity.

a Consider a demand curve of the form

$$Q_D = -2P + 20$$

where Q_D is the quantity demanded of a good and P is the price of the good. Graph this demand curve. Also draw a graph of the supply curve

$$Q_S = 2P - 4$$

where Q_S is the quantity supplied. Be sure to put P on the vertical axis and Q on the horizontal axis. Assume that all the Qs and Ps are nonnegative for parts a, b, and c. At what values of P and Q do these curves intersect – that is, where does $Q_D = Q_S$?

b Now suppose at each price that individuals demand four more units of output – that the demand curve shifts to

$$Q_{D'} = -2P + 24$$

Graph this new demand curve. At what values of P and Q does the new demand curve intersect the old supply curve – that is, where does $Q_{D'} = Q_S$?

c Now, finally, suppose the supply curve shifts to

$$Q_{S'} = 2P - 8$$

Graph this new supply curve. At what values of P and Q does $Q_{D'} = Q_{S'}$? You may wish to refer to this simple problem when we discuss shifting supply and demand curves in later sections of this book.

1.6 Taxes in Oz are calculated according to the formula

$$T = 0.01I^2$$

where T represents thousand of euros of tax liability and I represents income measured in thousands of euros. Using this formula, answer the following questions:

a How much in taxes is paid by individuals with incomes of €10 000, €30 000, and €50 000? What are the average tax rates for these income levels? At what income level does tax liability equal total income?

b Graph the tax schedule for Oz. Use your graph to estimate marginal tax rates for the income levels specified in part a. Also show the average tax rates for these income levels on your graph.

c Marginal tax rates in Oz can be estimated more precisely by calculating tax owed if persons with the incomes in part a get one more euro. Make this computation for these three income levels. Compare your results to those obtained from the calculus-based result that, for the Oz tax function, its slope is given by $0.02I$.

1.7 The following data show the production possibilities for a hypothetical economy during one year:

Output of X	Output of Y
1000	0
800	100
600	200
400	300
200	400
0	500

a Plot these points on a graph. Do they appear to lie along a straight line? What is that straight line production possibility frontier?

b Explain why output levels of $X = 400$, $Y = 200$ or $X = 300$, $Y = 300$ are inefficient. Show these output levels on your graph.

c Explain why output levels of $X = 500$, $Y = 350$ are unattainable in this economy.

d What is the opportunity cost of an additional unit of X output in terms of Y output in this economy? Does this opportunity cost depend on the amounts being produced?

1.8 Suppose an economy has a production possibility frontier characterized by the equation

$$X^2 + 4Y^2 = 100$$

a In order to sketch this equation, first compute its intercept. What is the value of X if $Y = 0$? What is the value of Y if $X = 0$?

b Calculate three additional points along this production possibility frontier. Graph the frontier and show that it has a general elliptical shape.

c Is the opportunity cost of X in terms of Y constant in this economy or does it depend on the levels of output being produced? Explain.

d How would you calculate the opportunity cost of X in terms of Y in this economy? Give an example of this computation.

1.9 Suppose consumers in the economy described in problem 1.8 wished to consume X and Y in equal amounts.

a How much of each good should be produced to meet this goal? Show this production point on a graph of the production possibility frontier.

b Assume that this country enters into international trading relationships and decides to produce only good X. If it can trade one unit of X for one unit of Y in world markets, what possible combinations of X and Y might it consume?

c Given the consumption possibilities outlined in part b, what final choice will the consumers of this country make?

d How would you measure the costs imposed on this country by international economic sanctions that prevented all trade and required the country to return to the position described in part a?

1.10 Consider the function

$$Y = \sqrt{X \cdot Z}$$

where $X > 0$, $Z > 0$. Draw the contour lines (in the positive quadrant) for this function for $Y = 4$, $Y = 5$, and $Y = 10$. What do we call the shape of these contour lines? Where does the line $20X + 10Z = 200$ intersect the contour line $Y = \sqrt{50}$? (Hint: It may be easier to graph the contour lines for Y^2 here.)

Appendix to Chapter 1

Mathematics Used in Microeconomics

Mathematics began to be widely used in economics near the end of the nineteenth century. For example, Marshall's *Principles of Economics*, published in 1890, included a lengthy mathematical appendix that developed his arguments more systematically than the book itself. Today, mathematics is indispensable for economists. They use it to move logically from the basic assumptions of a model to deriving the results of those assumptions. Without mathematics, this process would be both more cumbersome and less accurate.

This appendix reviews some of the basic concepts of algebra. We also discuss a few issues that arise in applying those concepts to the study of economics. We use the tools introduced here throughout the rest of the book.

Variables The basic elements of algebra, usually called *X*, *Y*, and so on, that may be given any numerical value in an equation.

Functions of One Variable

The basic elements of algebra are called **variables**. These can be labeled *X* and *Y* and may be given any numerical value. Sometimes the values of one variable (*Y*) may be related to those of another variable (*X*) according to a specific functional relationship. This relationship is denoted by the **functional notation**

$$Y = f(X) \quad \{1A.1\}$$

This is read, "*Y* is a function of *X*", meaning that the value of *Y* depends on the value given to *X*. For example, if we make *X* calories eaten per day and *Y* body weight, then Equation 1A.1 shows the relationship between the amount of food intake and an individual's weight. The form of Equation 1A.1 also shows causality. *X* is an **independent variable** and may be given any value. On the other hand, the value of *Y* is completely determined by *X; Y* is a **dependent variable**. This functional notation conveys the idea that "*X* causes *Y*".

The exact functional relationship between *X* and *Y* may take on a wide variety of forms. Two possibilities are:

1 *Y* is a *linear function* of *X*. In this case

$$Y = a + bX \quad \{1A.2\}$$

Functional notation A way of denoting the fact that the value taken on by one variable (*Y*) depends on the value taken on by some other variable (*X*) or set of variables.

Independent variable In an algebraic equation, a variable that is unaffected by the action of another variable and may be assigned any value.

Dependent variable In algebra, a variable whose value is determined by another variable or set of variables.

where a and b are constants that may be given any numerical value. For example, if $a = 3$ and $b = 2$, this equation would be written as

$$Y = 3 + 2X \qquad \{1A.3\}$$

We could give Equation 1A.3 an economic interpretation. For example, if we make Y the labor costs of a firm and X the number of labor hours hired, then the equation could record the relationship between costs and workers hired. In this case, there is a fixed cost of €3 (when $X = 0$, $Y =$ €3), and the wage rate is €2 per hour. A firm that hired six labor hours, for example, would incur total labor costs of €15 [= 3 + 2(6) = 3 + 12]. Table 1A-1 illustrates some other values for this function for various values of X.

2 Y is a *nonlinear function* of X. This case covers a number of possibilities, including quadratic functions (containing X^2), higher-order polynomials (containing X^3, X^4, and so forth), and those based on special functions such as logarithms. All of these have the property that a given change in X can have different effects on Y depending on the value of X. This contrasts with linear functions for which a given change in X always changes Y by the same amount.

To see this, consider the quadratic equation

$$Y = -X^2 + 15X \qquad \{1A.4\}$$

Y values for this equation for values of X between −3 and +6 are shown in Table 1A-1. Notice that as X increases by one unit, the values of Y go up rapidly at first but then slow down. When X increases from 0 to 1, for example, Y increases from 0 to 14. But when X increases from 5 to 6, Y increases only from 50 to 54. This looks like Ricardo's notion of diminishing returns – as X increases, its ability to increase Y diminishes.[1]

TABLE 1A-1 Values of X and Y for Linear and Quadratic Functions

Linear Function Y = f(X)		*Quadratic Function Y = f(X)*	
X	$= 3 + 2X$	X	$= -X^2 + 15X$
−3	−3	−3	−54
−2	−1	−2	−34
−1	1	−1	−16
0	3	0	0
1	5	1	14
2	7	2	26
3	9	3	36
4	11	4	44
5	13	5	50
6	15	6	54

[1]Of course, for other nonlinear functions, increases in X may result in increasing amounts of Y (consider, for example, $X^2 + 15X$).

Graphing Functions of One Variable

When we write down the functional relationship between X and Y, we are summarizing all there is to know about that relationship. In principle, this book, or any book that uses mathematics, could be written using only these equations. Graphs of some of these functions, however, are very helpful. Graphs not only make it easier for us to understand certain arguments; they also can take the place of a lot of the mathematical notation that must be developed. For these reasons, this book relies heavily on graphs to develop its basic economic models. Here we look at a few simple graphic techniques.

A graph is simply one way to show the relationship between two variables. Usually, the values of the dependent variable (Y) are shown on the vertical axis and the values of the independent variable (X) are shown on the horizontal axis.[2] Figure 1A-1 uses this form to graph Equation 1A.3. Although we use heavy dots to show only the points of this function that are listed in Table 1A-1, the graph represents the function for every possible value of X. The graph of Equation 1A.3 is a straight line, which is why this is called a **linear function**. In Figure 1A-1, X and Y can take on both positive and negative values. The variables used in economics generally take on only positive values, and therefore we only have to use the upper-right-hand (positive) quadrant of the axes.

Linear function An equation that is represented by a straight-line graph.

Linear Functions: Intercepts and Slopes

Two important features of the graph in Figure 1A-1 are its slope and its **intercept** on the Y-axis. The Y-intercept is the value of Y when X is equal to 0. For example, as shown in Figure 1A-1, when $X = 0$, $Y = 3$; this means that 3 is the Y-intercept.[3] In the general linear form of Equation 1A.2,

Intercept The value of Y when X equals zero.

$$Y = a + bX$$

the Y-intercept will be $Y = a$, because this is the value of Y when $X = 0$.

We define the **slope** of any straight line to be the ratio of the change in Y to the change in X for a movement along the line. The slope can be defined mathematically as

Slope The direction of a line on a graph; shows the change in Y that results from a unit change in X.

$$Slope = \frac{Change\ in\ Y}{Change\ in\ X} = \frac{\Delta Y}{\Delta X} \tag{1A.5}$$

where the Δ ("delta") notation simply means "change in". For the particular function shown in Figure 1A-1, the slope is equal to 2. You can clearly see from the dashed lines, representing changes in X and Y, that a given change in X is met by a change of twice that amount in Y. Table 1A-1 shows the same result – as X increases from 0 to 1, Y increases from 3 to 5. Consequently

$$Slope = \frac{\Delta Y}{\Delta X} = \frac{5-3}{1-0} = 2 \tag{1A.6}$$

[2]In economics, this convention is not always followed. Sometimes a dependent variable is shown on the horizontal axis as, for example, in the case of demand and supply curves. In that case, the independent variable (price) is shown on the vertical axis and the dependent variable (quantity) on the horizontal axis.

[3]One can also speak of the X-intercept of a function, which is defined as that value of X for which $Y = 0$. For equation 1A.3, it is easy to see that $Y = 0$ when $X = -3/2$, which is then the X-intercept. The X-intercept for the general linear function in Equation 1A.2 is given by $-a/b$, as may be seen by substituting that value into the equation.

It should be obvious that this is true for all the other points in Table 1A-1. Everywhere along the straight line, the slope is the same. Generally, for any linear function, the slope is given by b in Equation 1A.2. The slope of a straight line may be positive (as it is in Figure 1A-1), or it may be negative, in which case the line would run from upper left to lower right.

A straight line may also have a slope of 0, which is a horizontal line. In this case, the value of Y is constant; changes in X will not affect Y. The function would be $Y = a + 0X$, or $Y = a$. This equation is represented by a horizontal line (parallel to the X-axis) through point a on the Y-axis.

MICROQUIZ 1A.1

Suppose that the quantity of cod caught each week in the North Sea is given by $Q = 100 + 5P$ (where Q is the quantity of cod measured in thousands of kilos and P is the price per kilo in euros). Explain:

1 What are the units of the intercept and the slope in this equation?

2 How would this equation change if the cod catch were measured in kilos and price measured in cents per kilo?

Slope and Units of Measurement

The slope of a function depends on the units in which X and Y are measured. For example, a study of a family's consumption of oranges might reveal that the number of oranges (Y) purchased in a week is equal to $3 + 2X$, where X is the family's income measured in hundreds of euros per week. Consequently, $\Delta Y/\Delta X = 2$; that is, a €100 increase in income one week causes 2 more oranges to be purchased. If income (X) is measured in single euros, the relationship is $Y = 3 + 0.02X$ and $\Delta Y/\Delta X = 0.02$. In this case, although the interpretation of this slope is the

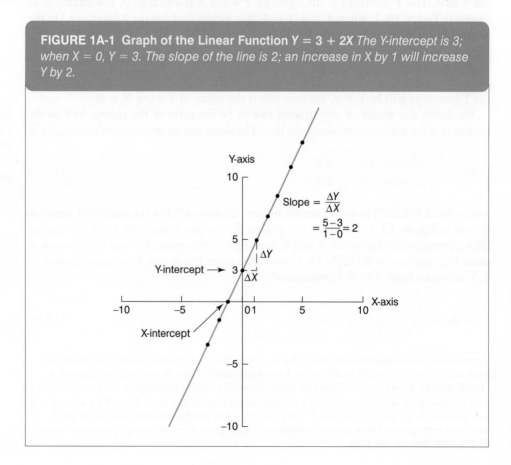

FIGURE 1A-1 Graph of the Linear Function Y = 3 + 2X *The Y-intercept is 3; when X = 0, Y = 3. The slope of the line is 2; an increase in X by 1 will increase Y by 2.*

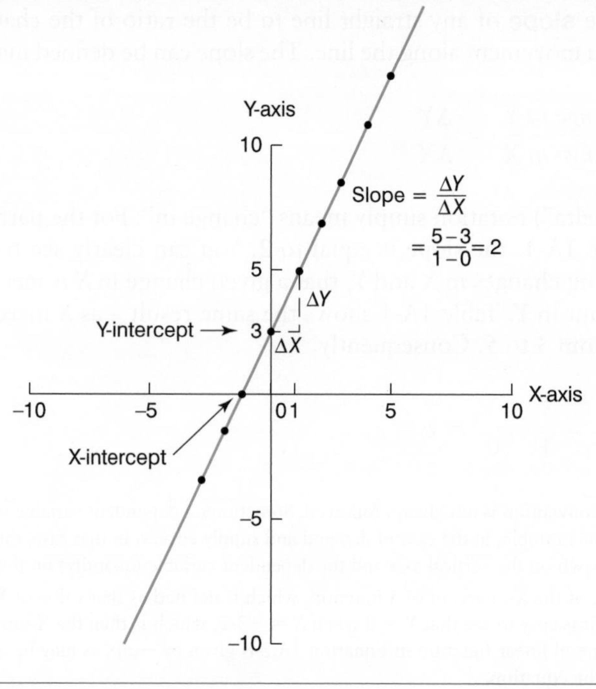

same (a €100 increase in income still increases orange purchases by 2 per week), the numerical value of the slope is very different. Similarly, if Y were measured in dozens of oranges per week and X in hundreds of euros, the relationship would be $Y = 1/4 + 1/6\ X$. An increase in family income of €100 still increases orange purchases by 2 (1/6 of a dozen), but now the slope is different again. Clearly, one must be very careful when discussing *the* slope of a function to know how the variables are measured. This is one reason economists have adopted the idea of "elasticity" (see Chapter 4), which is a unit-free measure of how one variable affects another.

Changes in Slope

Quite often in this text we are interested in changing the parameters (that is, a and b) of a linear function. We can do this in two ways: We can change the Y-intercept, or we can change the slope. Figure 1A-2 shows the graph of the function

$$Y = -X + 10 \qquad \{1A.7\}$$

This linear function has a slope of -1 and a Y-intercept of $Y = 10$. Figure 1A-2 also shows the function

$$Y = -2X + 10 \qquad \{1A.8\}$$

MICROQUIZ 1A.2

In Figure 1A-2, the X-intercept changes from 10 to 5 as the slope of the graph changes from -1 to -2. Explain:

1. What would happen to the X-intercept in Figure 1A-2 if the slope changed to $-5/6$?
2. What do you learn by comparing the graphs in Figure 1A-2 to those in Figure 1A-3?

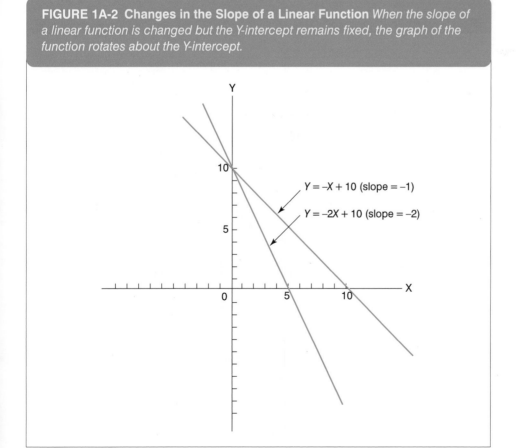

FIGURE 1A-2 Changes in the Slope of a Linear Function *When the slope of a linear function is changed but the Y-intercept remains fixed, the graph of the function rotates about the Y-intercept.*

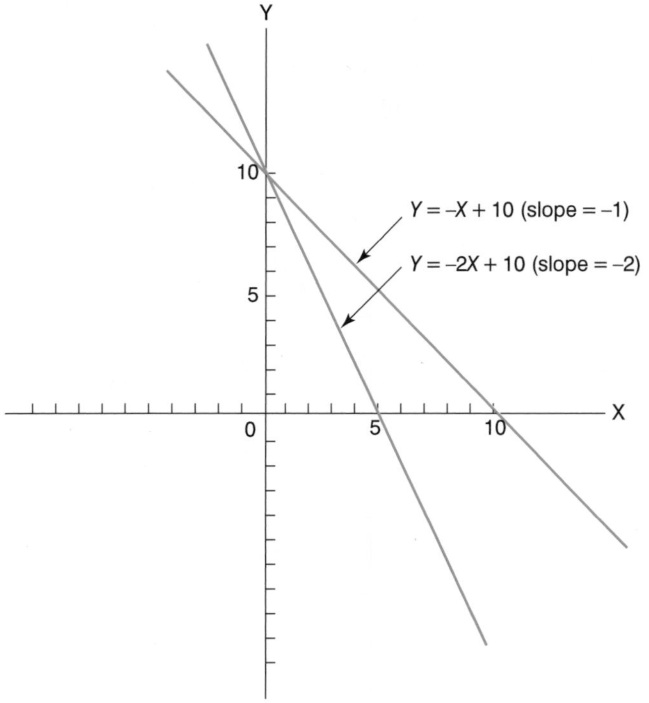

We have doubled the slope of Equation 1A.7 from −1 to −2 and kept the Y-intercept at Y = 10. This causes the graph of the function to become steeper and to rotate about the Y-intercept. In general, a change in the slope of a function will cause this kind of rotation without changing the value of its Y-intercept. Since a linear function takes on the value of its Y-intercept when X = 0, changing the slope will not change the value of the function at this point.

Changes in Intercept

Figure 1A-3 also shows a graph of the function Y = −X + 10. It shows the effect of changes in the constant term, that is, the Y-intercept only, while the slope stays at −1. Figure 1A-3 shows the graphs of

$$Y = -X + 12 \quad \{1A.9\}$$

and

$$Y = -X + 5 \quad \{1A.10\}$$

FIGURE 1A-3 Changes in the Y-Intercept of a Linear Function *When the Y-intercept of a function is changed, the graph of the function shifts up or down and is parallel to the other graphs.*

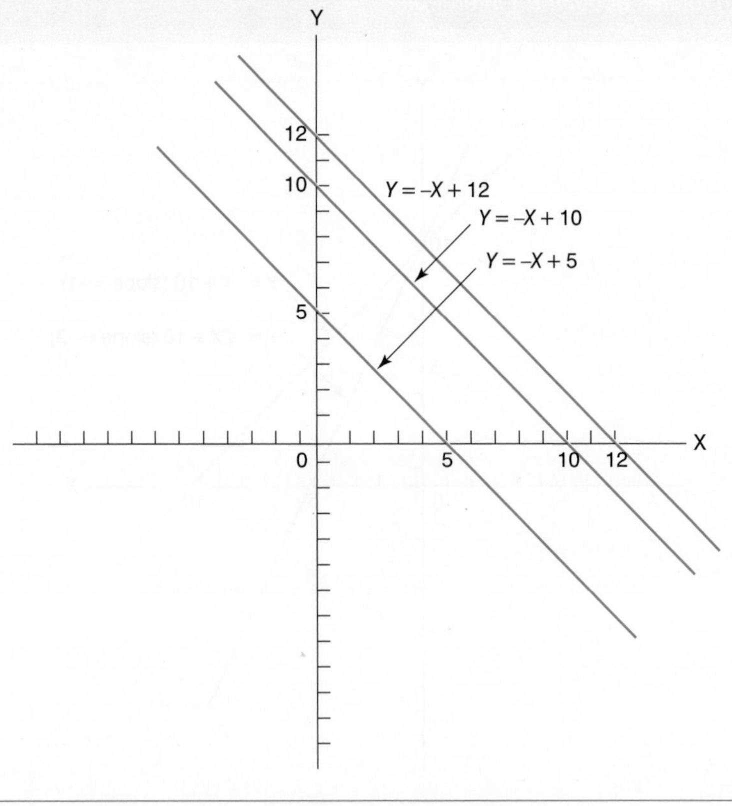

All three lines are parallel; they have the same slope. Changing the Y-intercept only makes the line shift up and down. Its slope does not change. Of course, changes in the Y-intercepts also cause the X-intercepts to change, and you can see these new intercepts.

In many places in this book, we show how economic changes can be represented by changes in slopes or in intercepts. Although the economic context varies, the mathematical form of these changes is of the general type shown in Figure 1A-2 and Figure 1A-3. Application 1A.1: *Property Tax Assessment* uses these concepts to illustrate one such use that may be depressingly familiar to home owners.

Nonlinear Functions

Graphing nonlinear functions is also straightforward. Figure 1A-4 shows a graph of

$$Y = -X^2 + 15X \tag{1A.11}$$

for relatively small, positive values of X. Heavy dots are used to indicate the specific values identified in Table 1A-1, though, again, the function is defined for all values of X. The general concave shape of the graph in Figure 1A-4 reflects the nonlinear nature of this function.

FIGURE 1A-4 Graph of the Quadratic Function $Y = -X^2 + 15X$ *The quadratic equation $Y = -X^2 + 15X$ has a concave graph—the slopes of the tangents to the curve diminish as X increases. This shape reflects the economic principle of diminishing marginal returns. The slope of a chord from the function to the origin shows the ratio y/x.*

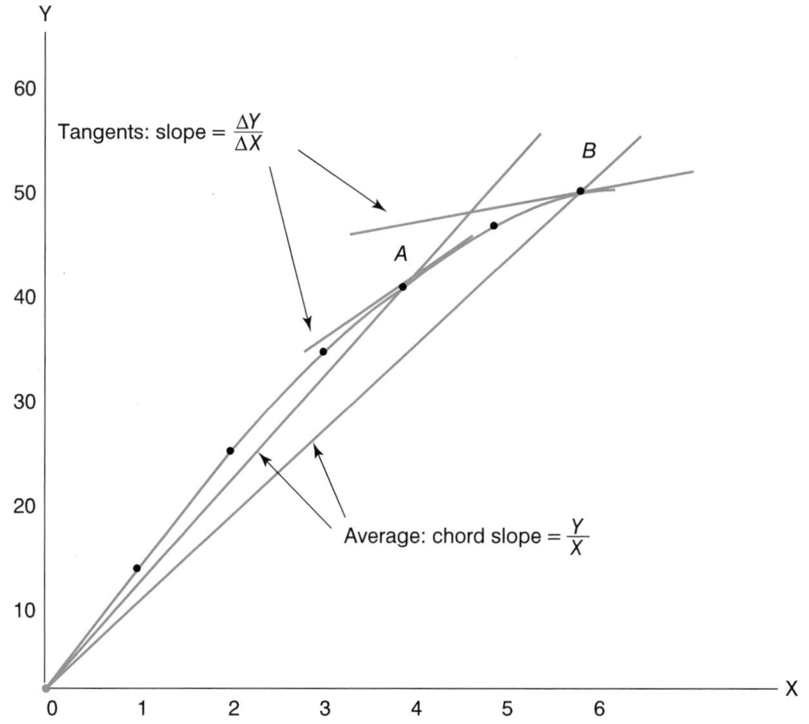

APPLICATION 1A.1 *Property Tax Assessment*

In most countries throughout the world, property taxes pay for schools, the local police force, the fire department, and so forth. Conceptually, figuring what a property owner owes in taxes is a simple matter – the town assessors multiply the tax rate by the market value of the property. A major problem with this procedure, however, is that current market values for most properties are not known because properties only rarely change hands. To come up with accurate market values, localities increasingly turn to sophisticated computer methods to assess properties.

A Simple Linear Method

Local property assessors begin by collecting information on all houses that were recently sold in the area. With these data, they can estimate a relationship between sale price (Y) and a relevant characteristic of the house, say, its square footage (X). Such a relationship might be stated as

$$Y = €50\,000 + €150X \tag{1}$$

This equation means that a house with zero square footage ($X = 0$) should sell for €50 000 (because of the value of its land) and each square meter of living space adds €150 to the value of the house. Using the square footage of a house, the assessor can predict its current value by using Equation 1. This procedure is shown in Figure 1. According to the figure, a house with 200 square meters would have a market value of €350 000 and one with 300 square meters would be worth €500 000.

Valuing Other Features of Homes

Of course, assessors must take into account more features of a house than just square footage. Suppose current sales suggest that a nice view is worth €100 000 in the current housing market. Assuming Equation 1 reflects the values of houses without views, the values of houses with views can be computed by

$$\begin{aligned} Y &= €100\,000 + €50\,000 + €150X \\ &= €150\,000 + €150X \end{aligned} \tag{2}$$

Equation 2 shows that the entire relationship between square footage and house value shifts upward by €100 000 if a house has a nice view. This relationship is also shown in Figure 1.

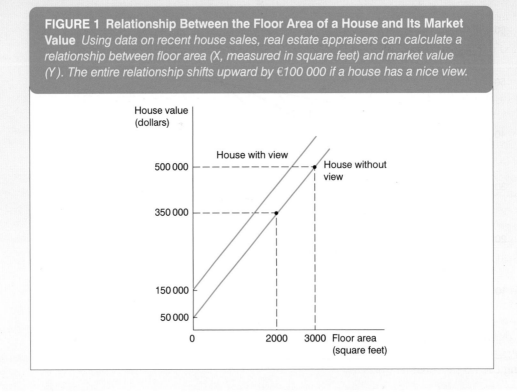

FIGURE 1 Relationship Between the Floor Area of a House and Its Market Value *Using data on recent house sales, real estate appraisers can calculate a relationship between floor area (X, measured in square feet) and market value (Y). The entire relationship shifts upward by €100 000 if a house has a nice view.*

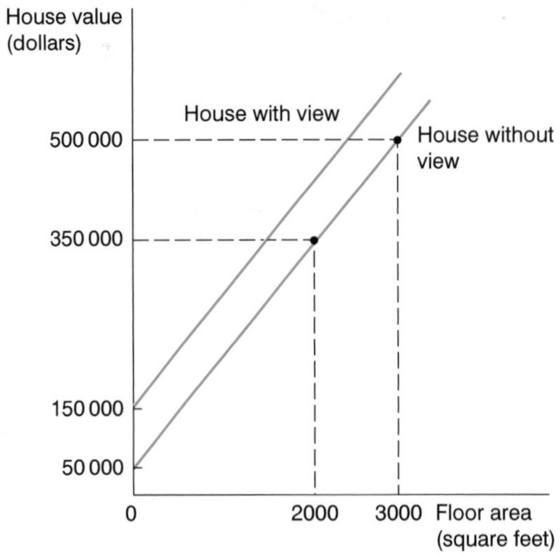

Hedonic Prices

Use of this procedure is not limited only to appraisers. Any analyst who wishes to examine how the features of a property affect its value can apply such "hedonic" procedures using information from sales prices. For example, one way to measure the costs of aircraft noise from airports is to compare prices for houses that lie under major flight paths to otherwise identical houses that do not. Similar calculations can be made for any other pollutant for which the impact is geographically localized.

To Think About

1. Suppose spectacular views are more valuable in large houses than in small ones. How would this effect be represented with algebra?
2. How would you measure the effect of traffic noise on housing values?

The Slope of a Nonlinear Function

Because the graph of a nonlinear function is, by definition, not a straight line, it does not have the same slope at every point. Instead, the slope of a nonlinear function *at a particular point* is defined to be the slope of the straight line that is tangent to the function at that point. For example, the slope of the function shown in Figure 1A-4 at point B is the slope of the tangent line illustrated at that point. As is clear from the figure, in this particular case, the slope of this function gets smaller as X increases. This graphical interpretation of "diminishing returns" to increasing X is simply a visual illustration of fact already pointed out in the discussion of Table 1A-1.

Marginal and Average Effects

Marginal effect The change in Y brought about by a one unit change in X at a particular value of X. (Also the slope of the function.)

Average effect The ratio of Y to X at a particular value of X. (Also the slope of the ray from the origin to the function.)

Economists are often interested in the size of the effect that X has on Y. There are two different ways of making this concept precise. The most usual is to look at the **marginal effect** – that is, how does a small change in X change Y? For this type of effect, the focus is on $\Delta Y/\Delta X$, the slope of the function. For the linear equations illustrated in Figure 1A-1 to Figure 1A-3, this effect is constant – in economic terms, the marginal effect of X on Y is constant for all values of X. For the nonlinear equation graphed in Figure 1A-4, this marginal effect diminishes as X gets larger. Diminishing returns and diminishing marginal effects amount to the same thing.

Sometimes economists speak of the **average effect** of X on Y. By this, they simply mean the ratio Y/X. For example, as shown in Chapter 7, the average productivity of labor in, say, automobile production is measured as the ratio of total car production (say, 10 million cars per year) to total labor employed (say, 250 000 workers). Hence, average productivity is 40 (= 10 000 000 ÷ 250 000) cars per year per worker.

Showing average values on a graph is more complex than showing marginal values (slopes). To do so, we take the point on the graph that is of interest (say, point A in Figure 1A-4 whose coordinates are $X = 4$, $Y = 44$) and draw the chord OA. The slope of OA is then $Y/X = 44/4 = 11$ – the average effect we seek to measure. By comparing the slope of OA to that of OB ($= 54/6 = 9$), it is hopefully easy to see that the average effect of X on Y also declines as X increases in Figure 1A-4. This is another reflection of the diminishing returns in this function. In later chapters, we show the relationship between marginal and average effects in many different contexts. Application 1A.2: *Can a "Flat" Tax Be Progressive?* shows how the concepts arise in disputes about revising the US personal income tax.

MICROQUIZ 1A.3

Suppose that the relationship between grapes harvested per hour (G, measured in kilos) and the number of workers hired (L, measured in worker hours) is given by $G = 100 + 20L$.

1. How many additional grapes are harvested by the 10th worker? The 20th worker? The 50th worker?
2. What is the average productivity when 10 workers are hired? When 20 workers are hired? When 50 workers are hired?

APPLICATION 1A.2 *Can a "Flat" Tax Be Progressive?*

Ever since the US federal income tax (FIT) was first enacted in 1913, there has been a running debate about its fairness, particularly about whether the rates of taxation fairly reflect a person's ability to pay. Historically, the FIT had steeply rising tax rates, though these were moderated during the 1970s and 1980s. Recently, a "flat tax" with a single tax rate has been proposed as a solution to some of the complexities and adverse economic incentives that arise with multiple rates. These ideas have been attacked as unfair in that they would eliminate the prevailing increasing rate structure.

Progressive Income Taxation

Advocates of tax fairness usually argue that income taxes should be "progressive" – that is, they argue that richer people should pay a *higher fraction* of their incomes in taxes because they are "more able to do so". Notice that the claim is that the rich should pay *proportionally* more, not just *more*, taxes. To achieve this goal, lawmakers in America have tended to specify tax schedules with increasing marginal rates. That is, an extra dollar of income is taxed at a higher rate the higher a person's income is. Figure 1 illustrates these increasing rates by the line *OT*.[1] The increasing slope of the various segments of *OT* reflects the increasing marginal tax rate structure.

Flat Taxes

Progressive rate structures are very hard to administer. For example, progressive rates make it difficult to withhold income tax from people because it is not often clear what rate to use. Also, a progressive rate structure usually requires some type of multiyear averaging to be fair to people whose incomes fluctuate a lot. One way to avoid problems like these and still have a "progressive" tax is to use a single rate system (a so-called "flat tax") together with an initial personal exemption. The line *OT′* in Figure 1 shows such a tax. In this case, the tax schedule provides an initial exemption of \$25 000 and then applies a flat rate of 25 per cent on remaining income. Although this structure does not have rising marginal tax rates, it still is a progressive tax structure. For example, people who make \$50 000 per year pay 12.5 per cent of their income in taxes (0.25(50 000 – 25 000)/50 000 = 0.125), whereas people who make \$150 000 pay

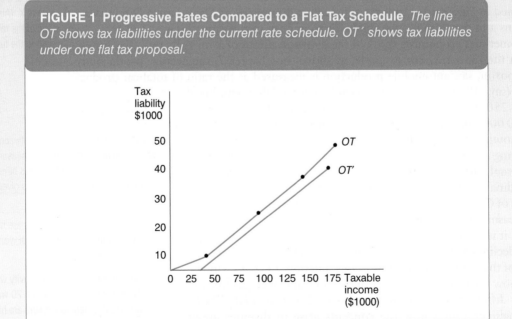

FIGURE 1 Progressive Rates Compared to a Flat Tax Schedule *The line OT shows tax liabilities under the current rate schedule. OT′ shows tax liabilities under one flat tax proposal.*

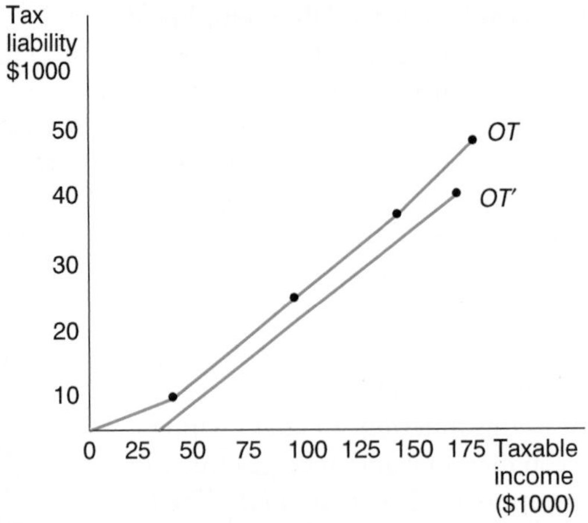

nearly 21 per cent of their income in taxes (0.25(150 000 − 25 000)/150 000 = 0.208).

Flat Tax Popularity

Many eastern European countries have recently introduced flat taxes. Estonia led the way in 1994 and was soon followed by Lithuania and Latvia. More recently many other countries have followed suit, including Russia, Georgia, Serbia, and Ukraine. What is unique about these countries is that they have all had recent major changes in their government structures, making it possible to do some fresh thinking about how income should be taxed.

Ironically a country which inspired some other countries to adopt a flat rate tax was Russia in 2001. Marginal tax rates on personal income of 12, 20, and 30 per cent were unified at 13 per cent. Russia also provides an example that a flat tax rate may not necessarily be suitable for all countries. While revenue in Russia from personal income tax (PIT) over the next year then rose by 46 per cent on the face of it suggesting that a flat rate tax increases revenue and does not decrease it. Ivanova *et al.* (2005) demonstrate that from an analysis of micro-level data (and macro), the strongest growth in personal taxation came from those who benefited little from the tax reform in Russia.[2] The increase in personal taxation revenue came largely, they conclude, from increases in real wages unrelated to the reform.

The authors conclude, ". . . the key lesson from the analysis here – whatever the reason for the PIT revenue boom, it lies in something other than behavioral responses to the PIT reform itself – serves as an important cautionary note for would-be emulators". Ivanova *et al.* (2005, page 41).

To Think About

1. Does the flat tax shown in Figure 1 collect as much revenue as the progressive tax in that figure? If not, how could the flat tax be changed so as to be "revenue neutral"?
2. How could the flat tax be made more progressive than the current actual tax structure in the US (line *OT*)?
3. In the quotation above from Ivanova *et al.*, what behavioral responses could possibly, in theory, stimulate higher tax revenues through the introduction of a flat rate tax?

[1]The tax does permit various deductions in calculating "taxable income". Hence, Figure 1 does not reflect the relationship between total income and taxes paid.

[2]A. Ivanova, M. Keen, and A. Klemm *The Russian Flat Tax Reform* (2005) IMF Working Paper WP/05/16.

Calculus and Marginalism

Although this course in microeconomics does not require that you know calculus, it should be clear that many of the concepts that we cover were originally discovered using that branch of mathematics. Specifically, many economic concepts are based on looking at the effect of a small (marginal) change in a variable X on some other variable Y. You should be familiar with some of these concepts (such as marginal cost, marginal revenue, or marginal productivity) from your introductory economics course. Calculus provides a way of making the definitions for these ideas more precise. For example, in calculus, mathematicians develop the idea of the *derivative* of a function, which is simply defined as the limit of the ratio $\Delta Y/\Delta X$ as ΔX gets very small. This limit is denoted as dY/dX and is termed the derivative of Y with respect to X. In graphical terms, the derivative of a function is identical to its slope. For linear functions, the derivative has a constant value that does not depend on the value of X being used. But for nonlinear functions, the value of the derivative varies, depending on which value of X is being considered. In economic terms, the derivative provides a convenient shorthand way of noting the *marginal* effect of X on Y.

Perhaps the most important use for calculus in microeconomics is to study the formal conclusions that can be derived from the assumption that an economic actor seeks to maximize something. All such problems reach the same general conclusion – that the dependent variable, Y, reaches its maximum value (assuming there is one) at that value of X for which $dY/dX = 0$. To see why, assume that this derivative (slope) is, say, greater than zero. Then Y can not be at its maximum value because an increase in X would, in fact, succeed in increasing Y. Alternatively, if the derivative (slope) of the function were negative, decreasing X would increase Y. Hence, only if the derivative is 0 can X be at its optimal value. Similar comments apply when one is seeking to find that value of X which yields a minimum value for Y.

Consider the most well-known application of this principle. Let X be the quantity of output a firm produces. The profits a firm receives from selling this output depend on how much is produced and are denoted by $\pi(X)$. But profits are defined as the difference between revenue and cost [that is $\pi(X) = R(X) - C(X)$]. Now applying the maximizing principle to profits yields:

$$\frac{d\pi(X)}{dX} = \frac{dR(X)}{dX} - \frac{dC(X)}{dX} = 0 \text{ or } \frac{dR(X)}{dX} = \frac{dC(X)}{dX} \qquad \{1A.12\}$$

In words, this says that for profits to be at a maximum, the firm should produce that level of output for which the derivative of revenue with respect to output (that is, *marginal revenue*) is equal to the derivative of costs with respect to output (that is, *marginal cost*). This calculus-based approach to profit-maximization was first employed by the French economist A. Cournot in the early nineteenth century. It represents both a simpler and more elegant approach to showing the "marginal revenue equals marginal cost" implication of profit maximization than the combination of graphs and intuition that you probably encountered in your introductory economics course. Although we will not use many calculus-based explanations in this book, such mathematical tools are the primary way in which modern-day economists construct most of their models.

Functions of Two or More Variables

Economists are usually concerned with functions of more than just one variable because there is almost always more than a single cause of an economic outcome. To see the effects of many causes, economists must work with functions of several variables. A two-variable function might be written in functional notation as

$$Y = f(X,Z) \qquad \{1A.13\}$$

This equation shows that Y's values depend on the values of two independent variables, X and Z. For example, an individual's weight (Y) depends not only on calories eaten (X) but also on how much the individual exercises (Z). Increases in X increase Y, but increases in Z decrease Y. The functional notation in Equation 1A.13 hints at the possibility that there might be trade-offs between eating and exercise. In Chapter 2, we start to explore such trade-offs because they are central to the choices that both individuals and firms make.

A Simple Example

In general, we could have Y depend on the values of more than two variables, but a simple two-variable function can be used to explain most of the relevant facts about how multiple variable functions work. Suppose the relationship between Y, X, and Z is given by

$$Y = X \cdot Z \tag{1A.14}$$

The form of this particular function is widely used in economics. Later chapters use a closely related form to show the utility (Y) that an individual receives from using two goods (X and Z) and also to show the production relationship between an output (Y) and two inputs (say, labor X and capital Z). Here, however, we are interested mainly in this function's mathematical properties.

Some values for the function in Equation 1A.14 are recorded in Table 1A-2. Two important facts are shown by this table. First, even if one of the variables is held constant (say, at $X = 2$), changes in the other independent variable (Z) will cause the value of the dependent variable (Y) to change. The value of Y increases from 4 to 6 as Z rises from 2 to 3, even though X is held constant. In economic terms, this illustrates the "marginal" influence of variable Z. Second, several different combinations of X and Z will result in the same value of Y. For example, $Y = 4$ if $X = 2$, $Z = 2$ or if $X = 1$, $Z = 4$ (or, indeed, for an infinite number of other X, Z combinations if fractions are used). Using this equality of values of Y for a number of X, Z combinations, functions of two variables can be graphed rather simply.

Graphing Functions of Two Variables

It would take three dimensions to graph a function of two variables completely: one axis for X, one for Z, and one for Y. Drawing three-dimensional graphs in a two-dimensional book is difficult. Not only must an artist be good enough to be able to show depth in only two dimensions, but the reader must have enough imagination to read the graph as a three-dimensional model. Since economists are not necessarily

TABLE 1A-2 Values of X, Z, and Y That Satisfy the Relationship $Y = X \cdot Z$

X	Z	Y
1	1	1
1	2	2
1	3	3
1	4	4
2	1	2
2	2	4
2	3	6
2	4	8
3	1	3
3	2	6
3	3	9
3	4	12
4	1	4
4	2	8
4	3	12
4	4	16

good artists (and some would argue because economists lack imagination), they graph these functions another way that is much like the techniques mapmakers use.

Contour lines Lines in two dimensions that show the sets of values of the independent variables that yield the same value for the dependent variable.

Mapmakers are also confined to working with two-dimensional drawings. They use **contour lines** to show the third dimension. These are lines of equal altitude that outline the physical features of the territory being mapped. For example, a contour line labeled "1000 meters" on a map shows all those points of land that are 1000 meters above sea level. By using a number of contour lines, mapmakers can show the heights and steepness of mountains and the depths of valleys and ocean trenches. In this way, they add the third dimension to a two-dimensional map.

Economists also use contour lines – that is, lines of equal "altitude". Equation 1A.14 can be graphed in two dimensions (one dimension for the values of *X* and another dimension for values of *Z*), with contour lines to show the values of *Y*, the third dimension. This equation is graphed in Figure 1A-5, with three contour lines: one each for $Y = 1$, $Y = 4$, and $Y = 9$.

Each of the contour lines in Figure 1A-5 is a rectangular hyperbola. The contour line labeled "Y = 1" is a graph of

$$Y = 1 = X \cdot Z \qquad \{1A.15\}$$

"Y = 4" is a graph of

$$Y = 4 = X \cdot Z \qquad \{1A.16\}$$

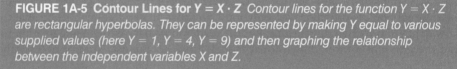

FIGURE 1A-5 Contour Lines for Y = X · Z *Contour lines for the function Y = X · Z are rectangular hyperbolas. They can be represented by making Y equal to various supplied values (here Y = 1, Y = 4, Y = 9) and then graphing the relationship between the independent variables X and Z.*

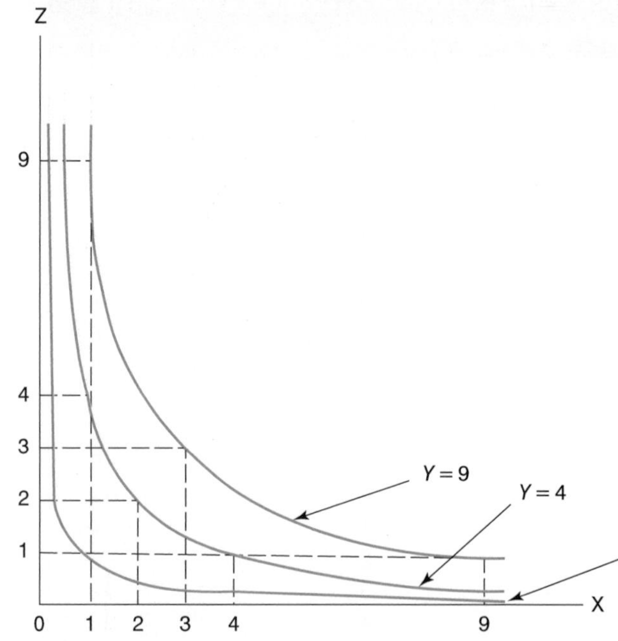

and the line labeled "$Y = 9$" is a graph of

$$Y = 9 = X \cdot Z \qquad \{1A.17\}$$

Some of the values along these contour lines are shown in Table 1A-2. It would be easy to compute other points on the curves. Other contour lines for the function could also be drawn by making Y equal to the desired level and graphing the resulting relationship between X and Z. Since we can give Y any value we want, an infinite number of contour lines can be drawn. In this way, we can show the original function as accurately as we want without resorting to three dimensions.

Simultaneous Equations

Another mathematical concept that is often used in economics is **simultaneous equations**. When two variables (say, X and Y) are related by two different equations, it is sometimes, though not always, possible to solve these equations together for a single set of values of X and Y that satisfies both of the equations. For example, it is easy to see that the two equations

Simultaneous equations A set of equations with more than one variable that must be solved together for a particular solution.

$$X + Y = 3$$
$$X - Y = 1 \qquad \{1A.18\}$$

have a unique solution of

$$X = 2$$
$$Y = 1 \qquad \{1A.19\}$$

These equations operate "simultaneously" to determine the solutions for X and Y. One of the equations alone cannot determine a specific value for either variable – the solution depends on both of the equations.

MICROQUIZ 1A.4

Figure 1A-5 shows three contour lines for the function $Y = X \cdot Z$. How do these lines compare to the following contour lines?

1 Contour lines for $Y = 3, 2,$ and 1 for the function $Y = \sqrt{X \cdot Z}$

2 Contour lines for $Y = 81, 16,$ and 1 for the function $Y = X^2 \cdot Z^2$.

Changing Solutions for Simultaneous Equations

It makes no sense in these equations to ask how a change in, say, X would affect the solution for Y. There is only one solution for X and Y from these two equations. As long as both equations must hold, the solution values for neither X nor Y can change. Of course, if the equations themselves are changed, then their solution will also change. For example, the equation system

$$X + Y = 5$$
$$X - Y = 1 \qquad \{1A.20\}$$

is solved as

$$X = 3$$
$$Y = 2 \qquad \{1A.21\}$$

MICROQUIZ 1A.5

Economists use the *ceteris paribus* assumption to hold "everything else" constant when looking at a particular effect. How is this assumption reflected in simultaneous equations? Specifically:

1 Explain how the changes illustrated in Figure 1A-6 represent a change in "something else"; and

2 Explain how the changes illustrated in Figure 1A-6 might occur in a supply–demand context in the real world.

Changing just one of the numbers in Equation Set 1A.18 yields an entirely different solution set.

Graphing Simultaneous Equations

These results are illustrated in Figure 1A-6. The two equations in Equation Set 1A.18 are straight lines that intersect at the point (2,1). This point is the solution to the two equations, since it is the only one that lies on both lines. Changing the constant in the first equation of this system provides a different intersection for Equation Set 1A.20. In that case, the lines intersect at point (3,2), and that is the new solution. Even though only one of the lines shifted, both *X* and *Y* take on new solutions.

The similarity between the algebraic graph in Figure 1A-6 and the supply and demand graphs in Figure 1-3 and Figure 1-4 is striking. The point of intersection of two curves is called a "solution" in algebra and an "equilibrium" in economics, but in both cases we are finding the point that satisfies both relationships. The shift of the demand curve in Figure 1-4 clearly resembles the change in the simultaneous equation set in Figure 1A-6. In both cases, the shift in one of the curves results in new solutions for both of the variables. If we could figure out the algebraic form for the supply and demand curves for a product, this example shows how we might make predictions about markets. Application 1A.3: *A Simple Model of World Oil Prices* provides a glimpse of this sort of analysis.

FIGURE 1A-6 Solving Simultaneous Equations *The linear equations X + Y = 3 (Y = 3 − X) and (X − Y = 1) can be solved simultaneously to find X = 2, Y = 1. This solution is shown by the point of intersection of the graphs of the two equations. If the first equation is changed (to Y = 5 − X), the solution will also change (to X = 3, Y = 2).*

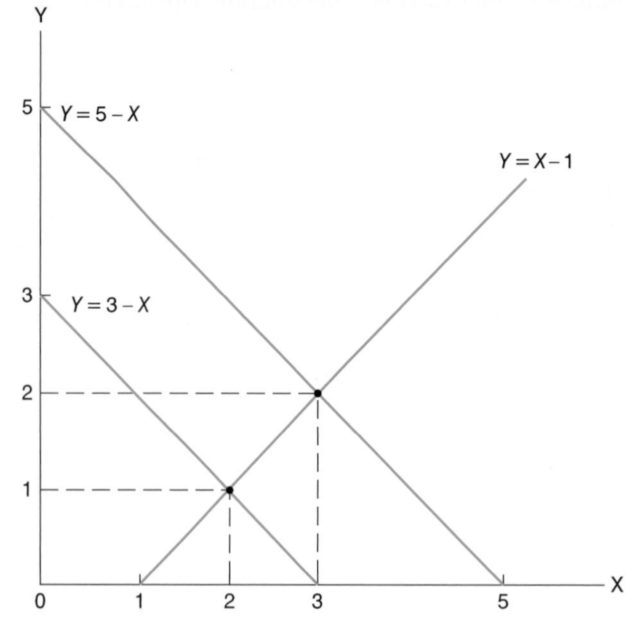

APPLICATION 1A.3 *A Simple Model of World Oil Prices*

To illustrate how a supply–demand model can help to understand economic events, consider the following representation of market equilibrium in the world market for crude oil. Suppose that the short-run demand for crude oil is given by

$$Q_D = 85 - 0.4P \qquad \{1\}$$

where Q_D is the quantity demanded of crude oil in millions of barrels per day and P is the price of crude oil in dollars per barrel. Suppose also that short-run supply is given by

$$Q_S = 55 + 0.6P \qquad \{2\}$$

Equilibrium in this market is given by equating demand and supply

$$Q_D = 85 - 0.4P = Q_S = 55 + 0.6P$$

$$\text{Or } P = 30 \; Q = 73 \qquad \{3\}$$

These are approximately the values that prevailed in the world oil market in 2002 – oil sold for about \$30 per barrel and about 73 million barrels per day were produced.[1] Now let's see how various factors might have changed this equilibrium in the years that followed.

The Iraq War

The US invasion of Iraq in early 2003 had the effect of completely disrupting oil production in that country. Prior to the war, Iraq produced about 2.5 million barrels per day of crude oil, so this disruption would shift the supply curve leftward by that amount, as shown in Figure 1. The new equilibrium can be found algebraically as:

$$Q_D = 85 - 0.4P = Q_S = (55 - 2.5) + 0.6P$$

$$\text{or } P = 32.5 \; Q = 72 \qquad \{4\}$$

[1]These data also reflect elasticities of demand and supply that are close to what economists estimate in empirical studies. Specifically, at the equilibrium values, the short-run price elasticity of demand for crude oil is −0.16 and the short-run price elasticity of supply is 0.25.

FIGURE 1 World Oil Market *Supply disruptions from the invasion of Iraq had the effect of increasing prices by about \$2.50 per barrel. Although Iraq's production was reduced by 2.5 million barrels per day, total supply was reduced by only 1 million barrels per day.*

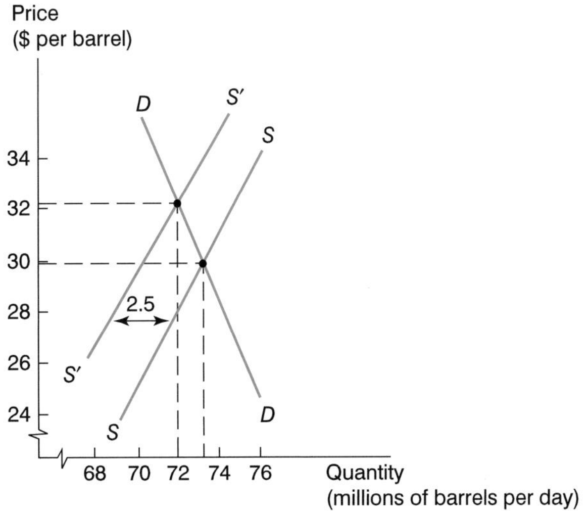

Hence, the cut-off of Iraq production would by itself have a relatively modest ($2.50) effect on increasing world oil prices. A major reason is the willingness of other producers to supply more as the price rises. Notice that our model predicts that production falls by only 1 million barrels per day after this reaction is taken into account.

The 2004 Price Increase

Despite this prediction, oil prices rose dramatically after the middle of 2004, sometimes reaching over $60 per barrel. Our model suggests that events in Iraq can explain only a small part of this increase. Probably a more important explanation is that demand for crude oil increased dramatically during 2004 as the US and other Western countries had fairly strong economic growth. Even more significant, the Chinese economy grew by a whopping 9 per cent in 2004, greatly increasing demand from that sector of the market as well.

To Think About

1. How would you model the increase in demand for crude oil in 2004? How big a shift in demand would be needed to explain a price of $50 per barrel? Does this seem likely?
2. In the short run the demand for oil may be less responsive to price than shown in Figure 1. How would a short-run disruption in supply (as in Hurricane Katrina in August 2005) affect price? Would this effect persist?

Empirical Microeconomics and Econometrics

As we discussed in Chapter 1, economists are not only concerned with devising models of how the economy works. They must also be concerned with establishing the validity of those models, usually by looking at data from the real world. The tools used for this purpose are studied in the field of *econometrics* (literally, "economic measuring"). Because many of the applications that appear in this book are taken from econometric studies, and because econometrics has come to play an increasingly important role in all of economics, here we briefly discuss a few aspects of this subject. Any extended treatment is, of course, better handled in a full course on econometrics; but discussion of a few key issues may be helpful in understanding how economists draw conclusions about their models. Specifically, we look at two topics that are relevant to all of econometrics: (1) random influences; and (2) the *ceteris paribus* assumption.

Random Influences

If real-world data fit economic models perfectly, econometrics would be a very simple subject. For example, suppose an economist hypothesizes that the demand for pizza (Q) is a linear function of the price of pizza (P) of the form

$$Q = a - bP \qquad \{1A.22\}$$

where the values for a and b were to be determined by the data. Because any straight line can be established by knowing only two points on it, all the researcher would have to do is: (1) find two places or time periods where "everything else" was the same (a topic we take up next); (2) record the values of Q and P for these observations; and (3) calculate the line passing through the two points. Assuming that the demand equation 1A.22 holds in other times or places, all other points on this curve could be determined with perfect accuracy.

In fact, however, no economic model exhibits such perfect accuracy. Instead, the actual data on Q and P will be scattered around the "true" demand curve because of the huge variety of random influences (such as whether people get a yearning for pizza on a given day) that affect demand. This situation is illustrated in Figure 1A-7. The true demand curve for pizza is shown by the line, *D*. Researchers do not know this line. They can "see" only the actual points shown. The problem the researcher faces then is how to infer what the true demand curve is from these scattered points.

Technically, this is a problem in **statistical inference**. The researcher uses various statistical techniques in an attempt to see through all of the random things that affect the demand for pizza and to *infer* what the relationship between *Q* and *P* actually is. A discussion of the techniques actually used for this purpose is beyond the scope of this book, but a glance at Figure 1A-7 makes clear that no technique will find a straight line that fits the points perfectly. Instead, some compromises will have to be made in order to find a demand curve that is "close" to most of the data points. Careful consideration of the kinds of random influences present in a problem can help in devising which technique to use.[4] A few of the applications in this text describe how researchers have adapted statistical techniques to their purposes.

Statistical inference Use of actual data and statistical techniques to determine quantitative economic relationships.

The *Ceteris Paribus* Assumption

All economic theories employ the assumption that "other things are held constant". In the real world, of course, many things do change. If the data points in Figure 1A-7 come from different weeks, for example, it is unlikely that conditions such as the weather or the prices of pizza substitutes (hamburgers?) have remained unchanged over these periods. Similarly, if the data points in the figure come from, say, different towns, it is unlikely that all factors that may affect pizza demand are exactly the same in every town. Hence, a researcher might reasonably be concerned that the data in Figure 1A-7 do not reflect a single demand curve. Rather, the points may lie on several different demand curves, and attempting to force them into a single curve would be a mistake.

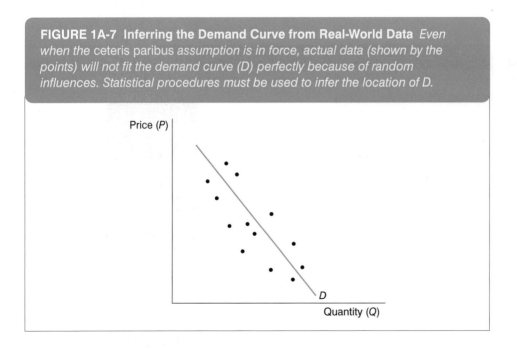

FIGURE 1A-7 Inferring the Demand Curve from Real-World Data *Even when the ceteris paribus assumption is in force, actual data (shown by the points) will not fit the demand curve (D) perfectly because of random influences. Statistical procedures must be used to infer the location of D.*

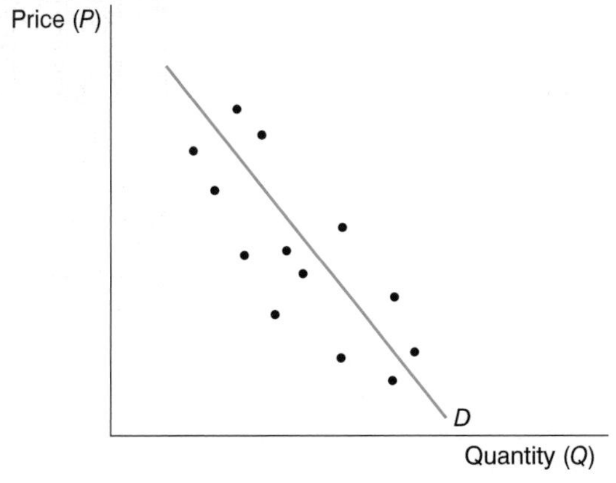

[4]In many problems, the statistical technique of "ordinary least squares" is the best available. This technique proceeds by choosing the line for which the sum of the squared deviations from the line for all of the data points is as small as possible. For a discussion, see R. Ramanathan, *Introductory Econometrics with Applications*, 5th ed. (Mason, OH: South-Western College Publishing, 2001).

MICROQUIZ 1A.6

An economic consulting firm is hired to estimate the demand for broccoli in several cities. Explain using a graph why each of the following "solutions" to the *ceteris paribus* problem is incorrect – why would the demand curves developed by applying each approach probably be wrong?

Approach 1: Collect data over several years for price and quantity of broccoli in each city. Then graph the data separately for each city and estimate a separate "demand curve" for each city.

Approach 2: Collect data over several years for price and quantity of broccoli in each city and average each city's data over the years available. Now graph the resulting averages and draw a "demand curve" through these points.

To address this problem, two things must be done: (1) Data should be collected on all of the other factors that affect demand, and (2) appropriate procedures must be used to control for these measurable factors in analysis. Although the conceptual framework for doing this is fairly straightforward, many practical problems arise.[5] Most important, it may not in fact be possible to measure all of the other factors that affect demand. Consider, for example, the problem of deciding how to measure the precise influence of a pizza advertising campaign on pizza demand. Would you measure the number of ads placed, the number of ad readers, or the "quality" of the ads? Ideally, one might like to measure people's perceptions of the ads – but how would you do that without an elaborate and costly survey? Ultimately, then, the researcher will often have to make some compromises in the kinds of data that can be collected, and some uncertainty will remain about whether the *ceteris paribus* assumption has been imposed faithfully. Many controversies over testing the reliability of economic models arise for precisely this reason.

[5]To control for the other measurable factors (X) that affect demand, the demand curve given in Equation 1A.22 must be modified to include these other factors as $Q = a - bP + cX$. Once the values for a, b, and c have been determined, this allows the researcher to hold X constant (as is required by the *ceteris paribus* assumption) while looking at the relationship between Q and P. Changes in X shift the entire Q-P relationship (that is, changes in X shift the demand curve).

SUMMARY

This chapter reviews material that should be familiar to you from prior mathematics and economics classes. The following results will be used throughout the rest of this book:

- Linear equations have graphs that are straight lines. These lines are described by their slopes and by their intercepts with the Y-axis.
- Changes in the slope cause the graph of a linear equation to rotate about its Y-intercept. Changes in the X- or Y-intercept cause the graph to shift in a parallel way.
- Nonlinear equations have graphs that have curved shapes. Their slopes change as X changes.
- Economists often use functions of two or more variables because economic outcomes have many causes. These functions can sometimes be graphed in two dimensions by using contour lines.
- Simultaneous equations determine solutions for two (or more) variables that satisfy all of the equations. An important use of such equations is to show how supply and demand determines equilibrium prices.
- Testing economic models usually requires the use of real-world data together with appropriate econometric techniques. An important problem in all such applications is to ensure that the *ceteris paribus* assumption has been imposed correctly.

PART TWO
DEMAND

There is one general law of demand . . . The amount demanded increases with a fall in price and diminishes with a rise in price.
ALFRED MARSHALL, *PRINCIPLES OF ECONOMICS*, 1890

Part Two examines how economists model people's economic decisions. Our main goal is to develop Marshall's demand curve for a product and to show why this demand curve is likely to be downward sloping. This "law of demand" (that price and quantity demanded move in opposite directions) is a central building block of microeconomics.

Chapter 2 describes how economists treat the consumer's decision problem. We first define the concept of utility, which represents a consumer's preferences. The second half of the chapter discusses how people decide to spend their limited incomes on different goods to get the greatest satisfaction possible – that is, to "maximize" their utility.

Chapter 3 investigates how people change their choices when their income changes or as prices change. This allows us to develop an individual's demand curve for a product. Chapter 3 also illustrates a few additional applications of the economic model of individual's choices.

Chapter 4, the final one in this part, shows how individual demand curves can be "added up" to make market demand curves. These curves provide a starting point for our study of the price determination process.

2

Utility and Choice

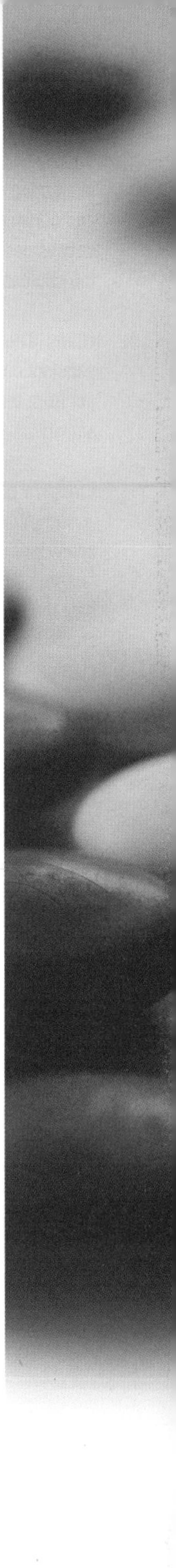

Every day you must make many choices: when to wake up; what to eat; how much time to spend working, studying, or relaxing; and whether to buy something or save your money. Economists investigate all these decisions because they all affect the way any economy operates. In this chapter, we look at the general model used for this purpose.

The economic **theory of choice** begins by describing people's preferences. This amounts to a complete cataloguing of how a person feels about all the things he or she might do. But people are not free to do anything they want – they are constrained by time, income and many other factors, in the choices open to them. Our model of choice must, therefore, describe how these constraints affect the ways in which individuals actually are able to make choices based on their preferences.

Utility

Economists model people's preferences using the concept of **utility**, which we define as the satisfaction that a person receives from his or her economic activities. This concept is very broad, and in the next few sections we define it more precisely. We use the simple case of a single consumer who receives utility from just two commodities. We will eventually analyze how that person chooses to allocate income between these two goods, but first we need to develop a better understanding of utility itself.

Ceteris Paribus Assumption

To identify all the factors affecting a person's feelings of satisfaction would be a lifelong task for an imaginative psychologist. To simplify matters, economists focus on basic, quantifiable economic factors and look at how people choose among them. Economists clearly recognize that all sorts of factors (aesthetics, love, security, envy, and so forth) affect behavior, but they develop models in which these kinds of factors are held constant and are not specifically analyzed.

Theory of choice The interaction of preferences and constraints that causes people to make the choices they do.

Utility The pleasure or satisfaction that people get from their economic activity.

***Ceteris paribus* assumption** In economic analysis, holding all other factors constant so that only the factor being studied is allowed to change.

Much economic analysis is based on this ***ceteris paribus*** (other things being equal) **assumption**. We can simplify the analysis of a person's consumption decisions by assuming that satisfaction is affected only by choices made among the options being considered. All other effects on satisfaction are assumed to remain constant. In this way, we can isolate the economic factors that affect consumption behavior. This narrow focus is not intended to imply that other things that affect utility are unimportant; we are conceptually holding these other factors constant so that we may study choices in a simplified setting.

Utility from Consuming Two Goods

This chapter concentrates on an individual's problem of choosing the quantities of two goods (which for most purposes we will call simply "X" and "Y") to consume. We assume that the person receives utility from these goods and that we can show this utility in functional notation by

$$\text{Utility} = U(X,Y; \text{other things}) \tag{2.1}$$

This notation indicates that the utility an individual receives from consuming X and Y over some period of time depends on the quantities of X and Y consumed and on "other things". These other things might include easily quantifiable items such as the amounts of other kinds of goods consumed, the number of hours worked, or the amount of time spent sleeping. They might also include such unquantifiable items as love, security and feeling of self-worth. These other things appear after the semicolon in Equation 2.1 because we assume that they do not change while we look at the individual's choice between X and Y. If one of the other things should change, the utility from some particular amounts of X and Y might be very different than it was before.

For example, several times in this chapter we consider the case of a person choosing how many burgers (Y) and soft drinks (X) to consume during one week. Although our example uses somewhat silly commodities, the analysis is quite general and will apply to any two goods. In analyzing the burger–soft drink choices, we assume that all other factors affecting utility are held constant. The weather, the person's basic preferences for burgers and soft drinks, the person's exercise pattern, and everything else are assumed not to change during the analysis. If the weather, for instance, were to become warmer, we might expect soft drinks to become relatively more desirable, and we wish to eliminate such effects from our analysis, at least for the moment. We usually write the utility function in Equation 2.1 as

$$\text{Utility} = U(X,Y) \tag{2.2}$$

with the understanding that many other things are being held constant. All economic analyses impose some form of this *ceteris paribus* assumption so that the relationship between a selected few variables can be studied.

Measuring Utility

You might think that economists would try to measure utility directly, but that goal has proven to be very elusive. The problems are of two general types. First, economists have found it very difficult to impose the *ceteris paribus* assumption. In the real world, things are constantly changing in people's lives, so it is hard to measure the utility of a few specific economic goods. Some progress has been made in this

APPLICATION 2.1 *Can Money Buy Happiness?*

A growth area of study in recent years is the Economics of Happiness, which mixes economics with a wider consideration involving sociology, psychology and more recently environmental issues. For over two hundred years, economics has been concerned with squeezing more output from society's scare resources. Increased utility has always been linked with an increase in the consumption of goods and services. Rising incomes mean more of these can be consumed, so individuals and societies should be happier. If not, a core tenet of economics is in trouble. Why are we working so hard to acquire more income and wealth if it appears to make us no more content?

The paradox is that although post-war capitalism has been extremely successful in raising incomes several fold throughout the world, and especially in the Western world, growing evidence suggests that happiness and contentment are not rising for many in society.[1] International surveys confirm the position elsewhere. The Japanese have experienced a six fold increase in GDP per head since 1950, but the proportion of the society that is "happy" has not changed at all. Many in Eastern Europe now claim they were actually happier under the older, poorer, communist regimes.

A large number of workers in the UK are now working longer, and more intense hours than their parents did in the 1970s; British workers work some of the longest hours in Europe. In the past, the great scourge of society and a major cause of unhappiness was unemployment. In the last decade Britain has seen unemployment fall dramatically to under a million, while 2.7 million workers are receiving incapacity benefit as long-term illness, stress or depression makes them unable to work.

Two factors seem to be important. First, consumers image that higher consumption and utility levels will make them happier. In the short-term it does, but this falls as the higher level of consumption soon becomes the norm. People easily get used to their bigger house or larger car, and it gives less and less satisfaction; it becomes a habit. The mobile phone industry very much plays on this belief that the next new mobile phone will always be much better than the old one, which needs to be replaced often. Second, people also adjust their requirements in response to what others have. This effect is shown in many studies of happiness, which suggest that if a person earns an extra 10 per cent and so does everyone else, he or she experiences only two-thirds of the extra happiness that would accrue if he or she alone had had the increase. Rivalry and status are important. In this sense, luxuries and the pleasure obtained from then appear to diminish once they become within the reach of others. Witness the exclusive holiday spot that loses its chic once mass tourism arrives, or how the celebrity three-star Michelin chief Gordon Ramsey is said to have decided to replace his Bentley Continental GT car when the model Jordan pulled up alongside him in one. It seems that consumers derive a large measure of the happiness from consuming goods and services, in the knowledge that others cannot. Social status and the pecking order really do seem to matter. This presents a dilemma for the "luxury goods" industry that are torn between keeping the product exclusive and limited, and appealing to the wider mass market with its higher profits.

Where does this leave governments who for decades have claimed that growth and higher incomes bring happiness? Richard Layard reflects that in comparing countries, once income rises above about £8000 even those in poor societies fail to see much of an increase in happiness. True, income is important, and richer people are happier than the poor, but other elements of life are very significant. The work experience, private life, community, health, freedom, and a philosophy of life are all crucial in the happiness equation.[2] Indeed, "work–life balance" courses are now taught, and are very popular in many universities.

In the eighteenth century Jeremy Bentham and others with their "utilitarian" approach proposed that the object of public policy should be to maximize the sum of happiness in society, and that economics should be concerned with utility or happiness. It may be that society has to have a major rethink.

(Continued)

To Think About

1 A higher income makes it possible for a person to consume bundles of goods that were previously unaffordable. He or she must necessarily be better off. Isn't that all we need to know?

2 Should governments follow policies to make people "happier", or is happiness something that only individuals can decide?

3 Sometimes people are said to be poor if they have to spend more than, say, 25 per cent of their income on food. Why would spending a large fraction of one's income on food tend to indicate some degree of economic deprivation? How would you want to adjust the 25 per cent figure for factors such as family size or the number of meals eaten in restaurants?

[1]H. Johns and P. Ormerod, 'Happiness, Economics and Public Policy', The Institute for Economic Affairs, Londons (2007).

[2]Richard Layard, Lord Robbins Memorial Lecture, ***Happiness: Has Social Science A Clue***? London School of Economics, 3–5 March 2003.

regard by using controlled experiments in laboratories (usually with students as subjects), but experimental economics remains in its infancy.

A second pervasive problem with measuring utility is in defining a unit of measurement. Economists have been rather unsuccessful in developing some sort of scale that might measure utility in, say, "happiness units" and allow comparisons of one person's units to those of someone else. One natural way for economists to think about this issue might be to treat income and utility synonymously. This would provide a direct measure of "happiness" and permit such statements as "a person with €50 000 per year is twice as happy as someone with €25 000". As Application 2.1: *Can Money Buy Happiness*? shows, however, this approach, though widely used, poses pitfalls of its own.

Fortunately, we do a fairly complete job of studying economic choices without actually measuring utility on any sort of a numerical scale. To do so, we only have to be willing to assume that people have well-defined preferences so that they can clearly state whether they prefer situation *A* to situation *B* or vice versa. That is, people can order the options available from most to least favorable, though they may not be able to give numerical values to the options. Together with a few more seemingly reasonable assumptions, this is all we need to get started.

Assumptions About Utility

What do we mean by saying that people's preferences are "consistent"? How can we describe the voluntary deals that people are willing to make? Can these preferences (utility) be shown graphically? We explore these questions as we begin our study of economists' model of choice.

Basic Properties of Preferences

Although we cannot measure utility, we might expect people to express their preferences in a reasonably consistent manner. Between two bundles of goods, A and B, we might expect a person to be able to state clearly either "I prefer *A* to *B*", or "I prefer *B* to *A*", or "*A* and *B* are equally attractive to me". We do not expect this person to be paralyzed by indecision but, rather, to be able to say precisely how he or she feels about potential consumption possibilities. This rules out such situations as the mythical donkey, who, finding himself midway between a pile of hay and a bag of oats, starved to death because he was unable to decide which way to go.

Complete preferences The assumption that an individual is able to state which of any two options is preferred.

Formally, we are assuming preferences are **complete preferences** – that people can always make a choice between any two options presented to them.

In addition to expecting people to be able to state preferences clearly and completely, we might also expect people's preferences not to be self-contradictory. We do not expect a person to make statements about his or her preferences that conflict with each other. One way of stating this idea precisely is to assume that preferences are **transitive**. If a person says, "I prefer *A* to *B*", and "I prefer *B* to *C*", then he or she can be expected to say, "I prefer *A* to *C*". A person who instead states the contrary (that is, "I prefer C to *A*") would appear to be hopelessly confused. We wish to rule out such inconsistency.

MICROQUIZ 2.1

How should the assumption of completeness and transitivity be reflected in Figure 2-1? Specifically:

1 What does the assumption of completeness imply about all of the points in the figure?

2 If it were known that a particular point in the "?" area in Figure 2-1 was preferred to point *X**, *Y**, how could transitivity be used to rank some other points in that area?

More Is Better: Defining an Economic "Good"

A third assumption we make about preferences is that a person prefers more of a good to less. In Figure 2-1, all points in the darkly shaded area are preferred to the amounts of X^* of good X and Y^* of good Y. Movement from point X^*, Y^* to any point in the shaded area is an unambiguous improvement, since in this area this person gets more of one good without taking less of another. This idea leads us to define an "economic good" as an item that yields positive benefits to people.[1] That is, more of a

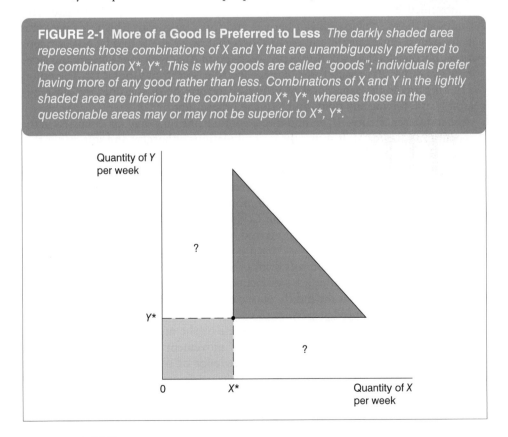

FIGURE 2-1 More of a Good Is Preferred to Less *The darkly shaded area represents those combinations of X and Y that are unambiguously preferred to the combination X*, Y*. This is why goods are called "goods"; individuals prefer having more of any good rather than less. Combinations of X and Y in the lightly shaded area are inferior to the combination X*, Y*, whereas those in the questionable areas may or may not be superior to X*, Y*.*

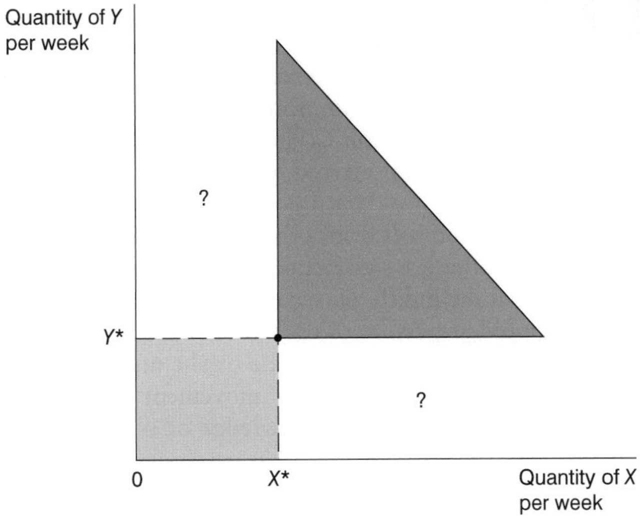

[1]Later in this chapter, we briefly describe a theory of "bads" – items for which less is preferred to more. Such items might include toxic wastes, mosquitoes, or, for your authors, butter beans.

Transitivity of preferences The property that if A is preferred to B, and B is preferred to C, then A must be preferred to C.

good is, by definition, better. Combinations of goods in the lightly shaded area of Figure 2-1 are definitely inferior to X^*, Y^* since they offer less of *both* goods.

Voluntary Trades and Indifference Curves

How people feel about getting more of some good when they must give up an amount of some other good is probably the most important reason for studying preferences. The areas identified with question marks in Figure 2-1 are difficult to compare to X^*, Y^* because they involve more of one good and less of the other. Whether a move from X^*, Y^* into these areas would increase utility is not clear. To be able to look into this situation, we need some additional tools. Because giving up units of one commodity (e.g., money) to get back additional units of some other commodity (say, bars of chocolate) is what gives rise to trade and organized markets, these new tools provide the foundation for the economic analysis of demand.

Indifference Curves

Indifference curve A curve that shows all the combinations of goods or services that provide the same level of utility.

To study voluntary trades, we use the concept of an **indifference curve**. Such a curve shows all those combinations of two goods that provide the same utility to an individual; that is, a person is *indifferent* about which particular combination of goods on the curve he or she actually has. Figure 2-2 records the quantity of soft drinks consumed by a person in one week on the horizontal axis and the quantity of burgers consumed in the same week on the vertical axis. The curve U_1 in Figure 2-2 includes all those combinations of burgers and soft drinks with which this person is equally happy. For example, the curve shows that he or she would be just as happy with six burgers and two soft drinks per week (point A) as with four burgers and three soft drinks (point B) or with three burgers and four soft drinks (point C). The points on U_1 all provide the same level of utility; therefore, he or she does not have any reason for preferring any point on U_1 to any other point.

The indifference curve U_1 is similar to a contour line on a map (as discussed in the Appendix to Chapter 1). It shows those combinations of burgers and soft drinks that provide an identical "altitude" (that is, amount) of utility. Points to the northeast of U_1 promise a higher level of satisfaction and are preferred to points on U_1. Point E (five soft drinks and four burgers) is preferred to point C because it provides more of both goods. As in Figure 2-1, our definition of economic goods assures that combination E is preferred to combination C. Similarly, the assumption of transitivity assures that combination E is also preferred to combinations A, B, and D and to all other combinations on U_1.

Combinations of burgers and soft drinks that lie below U_1, on the other hand, are less desirable because they offer less satisfaction. Point F offers less of both goods than does point C. The fact that the indifference curve U_1 has a negative slope (that is, the curve runs from the upper left-portion of the figure to the lower-right portion) indicates that if a person gives up some burgers, he or she must receive additional soft drinks to remain equally well-off. This type of movement along U_1 represents those trades that a person might freely make. Knowledge of U_1 therefore eliminates the ambiguity associated with the questionable areas we showed in Figure 2-1.

Indifference Curves and the Marginal Rate of Substitution

What happens when a person moves from point A (six burgers and two soft drinks) to point B (four burgers and three soft drinks)? This person remains equally well-off because the two commodity bundles lie on the same indifference curve. This person will voluntarily give up two of the burgers that were being consumed at point *A* in exchange for one additional soft drink. The slope of the curve U_1 between *A* and *B* is therefore approximately $-2/1 = -2$. That is, *Y* (burgers) declines two units in response to a one-unit increase in *X* (soft drinks). We call the absolute value of this slope the **marginal rate of substitution (MRS)**. Hence, we would say that the MRS (of soft drinks for burgers) between points *A* and *B* is 2: Given his or her current circumstances, this person is willing to give up two burgers in order to get one more soft drink. In making this trade, this person is substituting soft drinks *for* burgers in his or her consumption bundle. That is, by convention, we are looking at trades that involve more *X* and less *Y*.

Marginal rate of substitution (MRS) The rate at which an individual is willing to reduce consumption of one good when he or she gets one more unit of another good. The negative of the slope of an indifference curve.

Diminishing Marginal Rate of Substitution

The MRS varies along the curve U_1. For points like *A*, this person has quite a few burgers and is relatively willing to trade them away for soft drinks. On the other hand, for combinations such as those represented by point *D*, this person has a lot of soft drinks and is reluctant to give up any more burgers to get more soft drinks. The increasing reluctance to trade away burgers reflects the notion that the consumption of any one good (here, soft drinks) can be pushed too far. This characteristic can be seen by considering the trades that take place in moving from point *A* to *B*, from point *B* to *C*, and from point *C* to *D*. In the first trade, two burgers are given up to get one more soft drink – the MRS is 2 (as we have already shown). The second trade involves giving up one burger to get one additional soft drink. In this trade, the MRS has

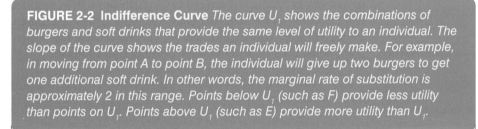

FIGURE 2-2 Indifference Curve *The curve U_1 shows the combinations of burgers and soft drinks that provide the same level of utility to an individual. The slope of the curve shows the trades an individual will freely make. For example, in moving from point A to point B, the individual will give up two burgers to get one additional soft drink. In other words, the marginal rate of substitution is approximately 2 in this range. Points below U_1 (such as F) provide less utility than points on U_1. Points above U_1 (such as E) provide more utility than U_1.*

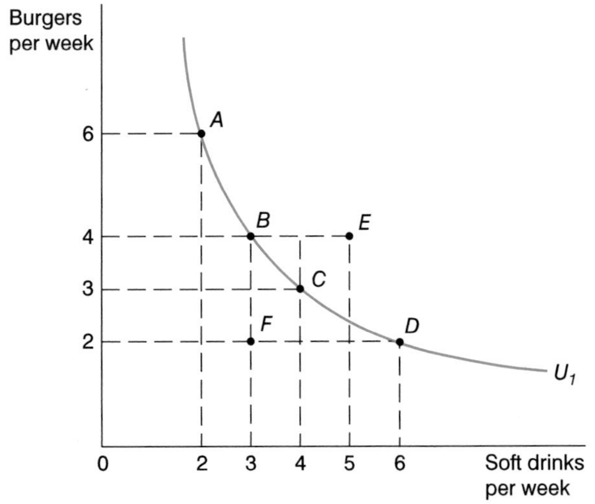

declined to 1, reflecting an increased reluctance to give up burgers to get more soft drinks. Finally, for the third trade, from point *C* to *D*, this person is willing to give up a burger only if two soft drinks are received in return. In this final trade, the MRS is 1/2 (the individual is willing to give up one-half of a burger to get one more soft drink), which is a further decline from the MRS of the previous trades. Hence, the MRS steadily declines as soft drinks (shown on the *X*-axis) increase.

Balance in Consumption

The conclusion of a diminishing MRS is based on the idea that people prefer balanced consumption bundles to unbalanced ones.[2] This assumption is illustrated precisely in Figure 2-3, where the indifference curve U_1 from Figure 2-2 is redrawn. Our discussion here concerns the two extreme consumption options *A* and *D*. In consuming *A*, this person gets six burgers and two soft drinks; the same satisfaction could be received by consuming *D* (two burgers and six soft drinks). Now consider a bundle of commodities (say, *G*) "between" these extremes. With *G* (four burgers and four soft drinks), this person obtains a higher level of satisfaction (point *G* is northeast of the indifference curve U_1) than with either of the extreme bundles *A* or *D*.

The reason for this increased satisfaction should be geometrically obvious. All of the points on the straight line joining *A* and *D* lie above U_1. Point *G* is one of these points (as the figure shows, there are many others). As long as the indifference curve obeys the assumption of a diminishing MRS, it will have the type of convex shape shown in Figure 2-3. Any consumption bundle that represents an "average" between two equally attractive extremes will be preferred to those extremes. The assumption of a diminishing MRS (or convex indifference curves) reflects the notion that people prefer variety in their consumption choices.

MICROQUIZ 2.2

The slope of an indifference curve is negative.

1. Explain why the slope of an indifference curve would not be expected to be positive for economic "goods".
2. Explain why the MRS (which is the negative of the slope of an indifference curve) cannot be calculated for points *E* and *F* in Figure 2-2 without additional information.

[2]If we assume utility is measurable, we can provide an alternative analysis of a diminishing MRS. To do so, we introduce the concept of the marginal utility of a good *X* (denoted by MU_X). Marginal utility is defined as the extra utility obtained by consuming one more unit of good X. The concept is meaningful only if utility can be measured and so is not as useful as the MRS. If the individual is asked to give up some *Y* (ΔY) to get some additional *X* (ΔX), the change in utility is given by

$$\text{Change in utility} = MU_Y \cdot \Delta Y + MU_X \cdot \Delta X \qquad \{i\}$$

It is equal to the utility gained from the additional *X* less the utility lost from the reduction in Y. Since utility does not change along an indifference curve, we can use Equation i to derive

$$\frac{-\Delta Y}{\Delta X} = \frac{MU_X}{MU_Y} \qquad \{ii\}$$

Along an indifference curve, the negative of its slope is given by MU_X/MU_Y. That is, by definition, the MRS. Hence we have

$$\text{MRS} = MU_X/MU_Y \qquad \{iii\}$$

As a numerical illustration, suppose an extra burger yields two utils (units of utility; $MU_Y = 2$) and an extra soft drink yields four utils ($MU_X = 4$). Now MRS = 2 because the individual will be willing to trade away two burgers to get an additional soft drink. If we can assume that MU_X falls and MU_Y increases as X is substituted for Y, Equation iii shows that MRS will fall as we move counter clockwise along U_1.

Indifference Curve Maps

Although Figure 2-2 and Figure 2-3 each show only one indifference curve, the positive quadrant contains many such curves, each one corresponding to a different level of utility. Because every combination of burgers and soft drinks must yield some level of utility, every point must have one (and only one[3]) indifference curve passing through it. These curves are, as we said earlier, similar to the contour lines that appear on topographical maps in that they each represent a different "altitude" of utility. In Figure 2-4, three of these curves have been drawn and are labeled U_1, U_2, and U_3. These are only three of the infinite number of curves that characterize an individual's entire **indifference curve map**. Just as a map may have many contour lines (say, one for each inch of altitude), so too the gradations in utility may be very fine, as would be shown by very closely spaced indifference curves. For graphic convenience, our analysis generally deals with only a few indifference curves that are relatively widely spaced.

Indifference curve map
A contour map that shows the utility an individual obtains from all possible consumption options.

The labeling of the indifference curves in Figure 2-4 has no special meaning except to indicate that utility increases as we move from combinations of good on U_1 to those on U_2 and then to those on U_3. As we have pointed out, there is no precise way to measure the level of utility associated with, say, U_2. Similarly, we have no way of measuring the amount of extra utility an individual receives from

FIGURE 2-3 Balance in Consumption Is Desirable *The consumption bundle G (four burgers, four soft drinks) is preferred to either of the extreme bundles A and D. This is a result of the assumption of a diminishing MRS. Because individuals become progressively less willing to give up burgers as they move in a south easterly direction along U_1, the curve U_1 will have a convex shape. Consequently, all points on a straight line joining two points such as A and D will lie above U_1. Points such as G will be preferred to any of those on U_1.*

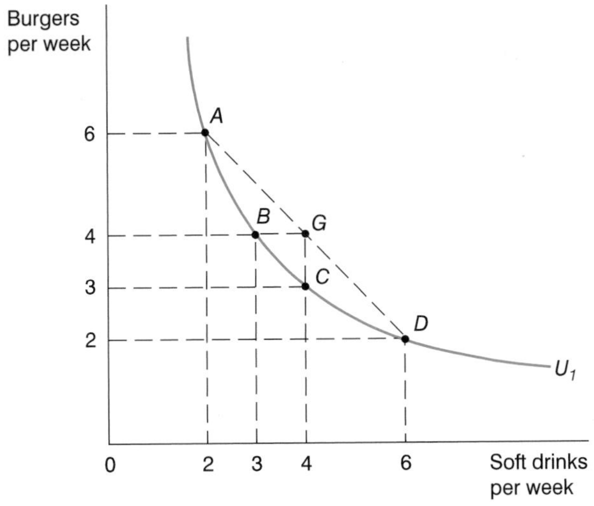

[3]One point cannot appear on two separate indifference curves because it cannot yield two different levels of utility. Each point in a map can have only a single altitude.

APPLICATION 2.2 *Product Positioning in Marketing*

A practical application of utility theory is in the field of marketing. Firms that wish to develop a new product that will appeal to consumers must provide the good with attributes that successfully differentiate it from its competitors. A careful positioning of the good that takes account of both consumers' desires and the costs associated with product attributes can make the difference between a profitable and an unprofitable product introduction.

Graphic Analysis

Consider, for example, the case of breakfast cereals. Suppose only two attributes matter to consumers – taste and crunchiness (shown on the axes of Figure 1). Utility increases for movements in the northeast direction on this graph. Suppose that a new breakfast cereal has two competitors – Brand *X* and Brand *Y*. The marketing expert's problem is to position the new brand in such a way that it provides more utility to the consumer than does Brand *X* or Brand *Y*, while keeping the new cereal's production costs competitive. If marketing surveys suggest that the typical consumer's indifference curve resembles U_1, this can be accomplished by positioning the new brand at, say, point *Z*.

Hotels

Hotel chains use essentially the same procedure in competing for business. For example, the Marriott Corporation gathers small focus groups of consumers.[1] It then asks them to rank various sets of hotel attributes such as check-in convenience, pools, and room service. Such information allows Marriott to construct (multidimensional) indifference curves for these various attributes. It then places its major competitors on these graphs and explores various ways of correctly positioning its own product.

Options Packages

Similar positioning strategies are followed by makers of complex products, such as cars or personal computers, supplied with various factory-installed options. These makers not only must position their basic product among many competitors but also they must decide when to incor-

FIGURE 1 Product Positioning *Market research indicates consumers are indifferent between the characteristics of cereals X and Y. Positioning a new brand at Z offers good market prospects.*

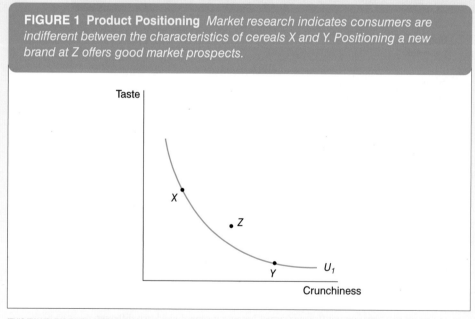

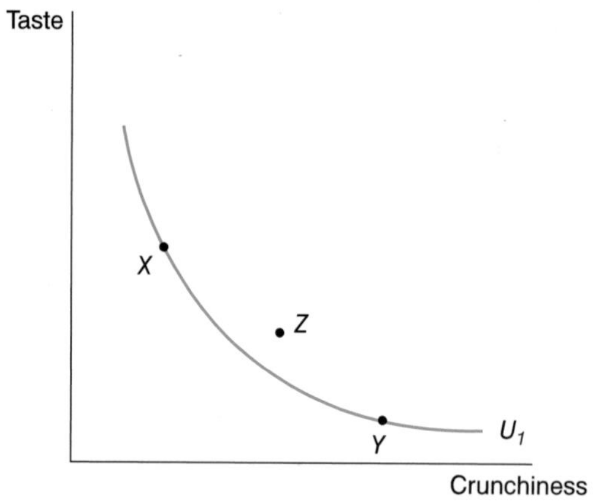

[1] THIS EXAMPLE IS TAKEN FROM ALEX HIAM, *THE VEST POCKET CEO* (ENGLEWOOD CLIFFS, NJ: PRENTICE HALL, 1990): 270–272.

porate options into their designs and how to price them. For example, throughout the 1980s, Japanese carmakers tended to incorporate such options as air-conditioning, electric windows, and sunroofs into their mid-range models, thereby giving them a "luxury feel" relative to their British competitors. The approach was so successful that most makers of such cars have adopted it. Similarly, in the personal computer market, producers such as Dell or Hewlett-Packard found they could gain market share by including carefully tailored packages of peripherals (larger hard drives, extra memory, and powerful modems) in their packages.

To Think About

1 How is the MRS concept relevant to the positioning analysis illustrated in Figure 1? How could firms take advantage of information about such a trade-off rate?

2 Doesn't the idea of a car "options package" seem inferior to a situation where each consumer chooses exactly what he or she wants? How do you explain the prevalence of such packages?

[1]This example is taken from M. Rehavi, "Policy Watch: Trade Adjustment Assistance", *Journal of Economic Perspectives*, Spring, 2004: 239–255.

consuming bundles on U_3 instead of U_2. All we can say is that utility increases as this person moves to higher indifference curves. That is, he or she would prefer to be on a higher curve rather than on a lower one. This map tells us all there is to know about this person's preferences for these two goods. Both economists and marketing experts have made use of these ideas, as Application 2.2: *Product Positioning in Marketing* illustrates.

FIGURE 2-4 Indifference Curve Map for Burgers and Soft Drinks *The positive quadrant is full of indifference curves, each of which reflects a different level of utility. Three such curves are illustrated. Combinations of goods on U_3 are preferred to those on U_2, which in turn are preferred to those on U_1. This is simply a reflection of the assumption that more of a good is preferred to less, as may be seen by comparing points C, G, and H.*

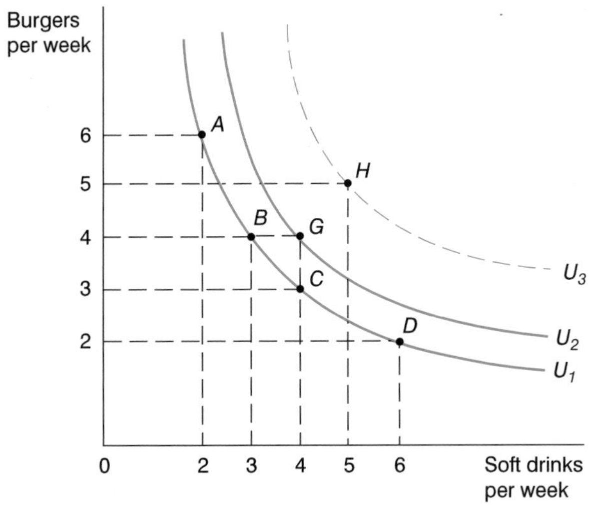

Illustrating Particular Preferences

To illustrate some of the ways in which indifference curve maps might be used to reflect particular kinds of preferences, Figure 2-5 shows four special cases.

A Useless Good

Figure 2-5(a) shows an individual's indifference curve map for food (on the horizontal axis) and waiting in a doctor's surgery (on the vertical axis). Because time spent waiting in a doctor's surgery is considered an utter waste of time, increasing the consumption of it does not increase utility. Only by getting more food does this person enjoy a higher level of utility. The vertical indifference curve U_2, for example, shows that utility will be U_2 as long as this person has 10 units of food no matter how much extra "waiting in the surgery" he or she has.

FIGURE 2-5 Illustrations of Specific Preferences *The four indifference curve maps in this figure geographically analyze different relationships between two goods.*

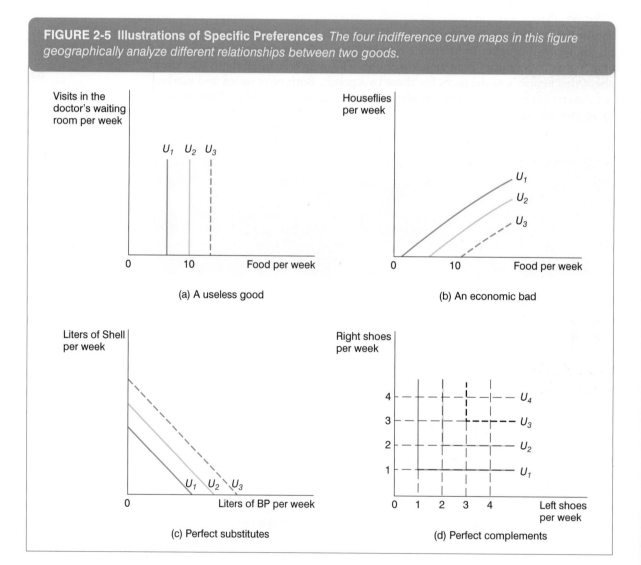

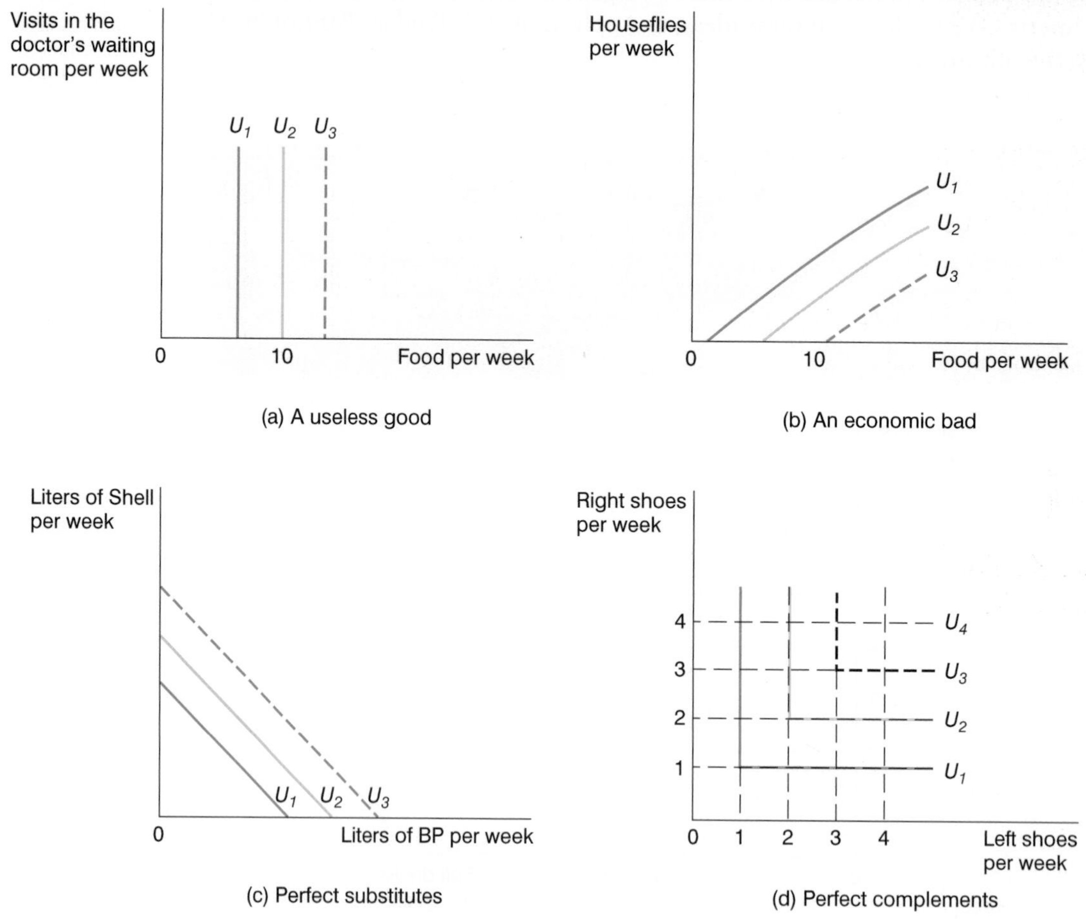

An Economic Bad

The situation illustrated in Figure 2-5(a) implicitly assumes that useless goods cause no harm – having more useless waits in the surgery causes no problem since there is nothing to throw away. In some cases, however, such free disposal is not possible, and additional units of a good can cause actual harm. For example, Figure 2-5(b) shows an indifference curve map for food and houseflies. Holding food consumption constant at 10, utility declines as the number of houseflies increases. Because additional houseflies reduce utility, an individual might even be willing to give up some food (and buy flypaper instead, for example) in exchange for fewer houseflies.

Perfect Substitutes

The illustrations of convex indifference curves in Figure 2-2 through Figure 2-4 reflected the assumption that diversity in consumption is desirable. If, however, the two goods we were examining were essentially the same (or at least served identical functions), we could not make this argument. In Figure 2-5(c), for example, we show an individual's indifference curve map for Shell and BP petrol. Because this buyer is unconvinced by television advertisements that stress various miracle ingredients, he or she has adopted the sensible proposition that all liters of petrol are pretty much the same. Hence, he or she is always willing to trade one liter of Shell for a liter of BP – the MRS along any indifference curve is 1.0. The straight-line indifference curve map in Figure 2-5(c) reflects the perfect substitutability between these two goods.

Perfect Complements

In Figure 2-5(d), on the other hand, we illustrate a situation in which two goods go together. This person (quite naturally) prefers to consume left shoes (on the horizontal axis) and right shoes (on the vertical axis) in pairs. If, for example, he or she currently has three pairs of shoes, additional right shoes provide no more utility (compare this to the situation in panel (a)). Similarly, additional left shoes alone provide no additional utility. An extra pair of shoes, on the other hand, does increase utility (from U_3 to U_4) because this person likes to consume these two goods together. Any situation in which two goods have such a strong complementary relationship to one another would be described by a similar map of L-shaped indifference curves.

Of course, these simple examples only hint at the variety in types of preferences that can be illustrated by indifference curve maps. Later in this chapter, we encounter other, more realistic, examples that help to explain observed economic behavior. Because indifference curve maps reflect people's basic preferences about the goods they might select, such maps provide an important first building block for studying demand.

Utility-Maximization: An Initial Survey

Economists assume that when a person is faced with a choice from among a number of possible options, he or she will choose the one that yields the highest utility – utility-maximization. As Adam Smith remarked more than two centuries ago, "We are not ready to suspect any person of being defective in selfishness".[4] In other words, economists

[4]Adam Smith, *The Theory of Moral Sentiments* (1759; reprint, New Rochelle, NY: Arlington House, 1969), 446.

assume that people know their own minds and make choices consistent with their preferences. This section surveys in general terms how such choices might be made.

Choices Are Constrained

The most important feature of the utility-maximization problem is that people are constrained in what they can buy by the size of their incomes. Of those combinations of goods that a person can afford, he or she will choose the one that is most preferred. This most preferred bundle of goods may not provide complete bliss; it may even leave this person in misery. It will, however, reflect the best (utility-maximizing) use of limited income. All other combinations of goods that can be bought with that limited income would leave him or her even worse off. It is the limitation of income that makes the consumer's choice an economic problem of allocating a scarce resource (the limited income) among alternative end uses.

A Simple Case

Consider the following problem: How should a person choose to allocate income among two goods (burgers and soft drinks) if he or she is to obtain the highest level of utility possible? Answering this question provides fundamental insights into all of microeconomics. The basic result can easily be stated at the outset. In order to maximize utility given a fixed amount of income to spend on two goods, this person should spend the entire amount and choose a combination of goods for which the marginal rate of substitution between the two goods is equal to the ratio of those goods' market prices.

The reasoning behind the first part of this proposition is straightforward. Because we assume that more is better, a person should obviously spend the entire amount budgeted for the two items. The alternative here is throwing the money away, which is obviously less desirable than buying something. If the alternative was saving the money, we would have to consider savings and the decision to consume goods in the future. We will take up this more complex problem in Chapter 16.

The reasoning behind the second part of the proposition is more complicated. Suppose that a person is currently consuming some combination of burgers and soft drinks for which the MRS is equal to 1; he or she is willing to do without one burger in order to get an additional soft drink. Assume, on the other hand, that the price of burgers is €2.00 and that of soft drinks is €1.00. The ratio of their prices is €1.00/€2.00 = 1/2. This person is able to afford an extra soft drink by doing without only one-half of a burger. In this situation, the individual's MRS is not equal to the ratio of the goods' market prices, and we can show that there is some other combination of goods that provides more utility.

Suppose this person consumes one less burger. This frees €2.00 in purchasing power. He or she can now buy one more soft drink (at a price of €1.00) and is now as well-off as before, because the MRS was assumed to be 1. However, another euro remains unspent that can now be spent on either soft drinks or burgers (or some combination of the two). This additional consumption clearly makes this person better off than in the initial situation.

Our numbers here were purely arbitrary. Whenever a person selects a combination of goods for which the MRS differs from the price ratio, a similar utility-improving change in spending patterns can be made. This reallocation will continue until the MRS is brought into line with the price ratio, at which time maximum utility is attained. We now present a more formal proof of this.

Showing Utility-Maximization on a Graph

To show the process of utility-maximization on a graph, we will begin by showing how to illustrate an individual's **budget constraint**. This constraint shows which combinations of goods are affordable. It is from among these combinations that a person can choose the bundle that provides the most utility.

Budget constraint The limit that income places on the combinations of goods that an individual can buy.

The Budget Constraint

Figure 2-6 shows the combinations of two goods (which we will call simply *X* and *Y*) that a person with a fixed amount of money to spend can afford. If all available income is spent on good *X*, the number of units that can be purchased is recorded as X_{max} in the figure. If all available income is spent on *Y*, Y_{max} is the amount that can be bought. The line joining X_{max} to Y_{max} represents the various mixed bundles of goods *X* and *Y* that can be purchased using all the available funds. Points in the shaded area below the budget line are also affordable, but these leave some portion of funds unspent, so these points would usually not be chosen.

The downward slope of the budget line shows that any person can afford more *X* only if *Y* purchases are cut back. The precise slope of this relationship depends on the prices of the two goods. If *Y* is expensive and *X* is cheap, the line will be relatively flat because choosing to consume one less *Y* will permit the purchasing of many units of *X* (an individual who decides not to purchase a new designer suit can instead choose to purchase many pairs of socks). Alternately, if *Y* is relatively cheap per unit and *X* is expensive, the budget line will be steep. Reducing *Y* consumption does not permit

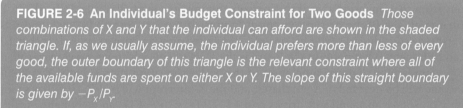

FIGURE 2-6 An Individual's Budget Constraint for Two Goods *Those combinations of X and Y that the individual can afford are shown in the shaded triangle. If, as we usually assume, the individual prefers more than less of every good, the outer boundary of this triangle is the relevant constraint where all of the available funds are spent on either X or Y. The slope of this straight boundary is given by* $-P_X/P_Y$.

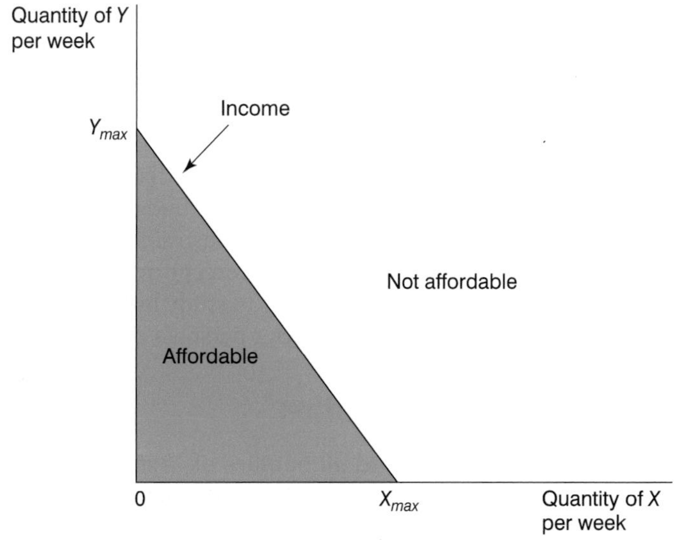

very much more of good X to be bought. All of these relationships can be made more precise by using a bit of algebra.

Budget-Constraint Algebra

Suppose that a person has I euros to spend on either good X or good Y. Suppose also that P_X represents the price of good X and P_Y the price of good Y. The total amount spent on X is given by the price of X times the amount purchased ($P_X \cdot X$). Similarly, $P_Y \cdot Y$ represents total spending on good Y. Because the available income must be spent on either X or Y, we have

$$\text{Amount spent on } X + \text{Amount spent on } Y = I$$

or

$$P_X \cdot X + P_Y \cdot Y = I \qquad \{2.3\}$$

Equation 2.3 is an algebraic statement of the budget line shown in Figure 2-6. To study this constraint, we can solve this equation for Y so that the budget line has the standard form for a linear equation ($Y = a + bX$). This solution gives

$$Y = -\left(\frac{P_X}{P_Y}\right) X + \frac{I}{P_Y} \qquad \{2.4\}$$

Although the two representations of the budget constraint say exactly the same thing, the relationship between Equation 2.4 and Figure 2-6 is easier to see. It is obvious from that equation that if this person chooses to spend all available funds on Y (that is, if $X = 0$), he or she can buy I/P_Y units. If burgers cost €2.00 each and this person has decided to spend his or her €20 income only on burgers, it is clear that 10 can be bought. That point in the figure is the Y-intercept, which we previously called Y_{max}. Similarly, a slight manipulation of the budget equation shows that if $Y = 0$, all income will be devoted to X purchases, and the X-intercept will be I/P_X. If €20 is spent only on soft drinks, and soft drinks cost €1, 20 (= €20 ÷ €1) can be bought. Again, this point is labeled X_{max} in the figure. Finally, the slope of the budget constraint is given by the ratio of the goods' prices, $-P_X/P_Y$. This shows the ratio at which Y can be given up to get more X in the market. In the burger–soft drink case, the slope would be $-1/2$ (= −€1/€2), showing that the opportunity cost of one soft drink is half a burger. More generally, as we noted before, if P_X is low and P_Y is high, this ratio will be small and the budget line will be flat. On the other hand, a high P_X and a low P_Y will make the budget line steep. As for any linear relationship, the budget constraint can be shifted to a new position by changes in its Y-intercept or by changes in its slope. In Chapter 3, we use this fact to study how changes in income or in the prices of goods affect a person's choices.

MICROQUIZ 2.3

Suppose a person has €100 to spend on Frisbees and beach balls.

1. Graph this person's budget constraint if Frisbees cost €20 and beach balls cost €10.
2. How would your graph change if this person decided to spend €200 (rather than €100) on these two items?
3. How would your graph change if Frisbee prices rose to €25 but total spending returned to €100?

Utility-Maximization

A person can afford all bundles of X and Y that fall within the shaded triangle in Figure 2-6. From among these, he or she will choose the one that offers the greatest utility. The budget constraint can be used together with the individual's indifference curve map to show this utility-maximization process. Figure 2-7 illustrates the procedure. This person would be irrational to choose a point such as *A*; he or she can get to a higher utility level (that is, higher than U_1) just by spending some of the unspent portion of his or her income. Similarly, by reallocating expenditures he or she can do better than point *B*. This is a case in which the MRS and the price ratio differ, and this person can move to a higher indifference curve (say, U_2) by choosing to consume less *Y* and more *X*. Point *D* is out of the question because income is not large enough to permit the purchase of that combination of goods. It is clear that the position of maximum utility will be at point C where the combination X^*, Y^* is chosen. This is the only point on indifference curve U_2 that can be bought with *I* dollars, and no higher utility level can be bought. C is the single point of tangency between the budget constraint and the indifference curve. Therefore all funds are spent and

$$\text{Slope of budget constraint} = \text{Slope of indifference curve} \quad \{2.5\}$$

or (neglecting the fact that both slopes are negative)

$$P_X/P_Y = \text{MRS} \quad \{2.6\}$$

The numerical example we started with is proved as a general result. For a utility maximum, the MRS should equal the ratio of the prices of the goods. The diagram shows that if this condition

MICROQUIZ 2.4

Simple utility-maximization requires MRS $= P_X/P_Y$.

1 Why does the price ratio P_X/P_Y show the rate at which any person can trade *Y* for *X* in "the market"? Illustrate this principle for the case of music CDs (which cost €10 each) and film DVDs (which cost €17 each).

2 If an individual's current stock of CDs and DVDs yields him or her an MRS of 2-to-1 (that is, he or she is willing to trade two CDs for one DVD), how should consumption patterns be changed to increase utility?

FIGURE 2-7 Graphic Demonstration of Utility-Maximization *Point C represents the highest utility that can be reached by this individual, given the budget constraint. The combination X*, Y* is therefore the rational way for this person to use the available purchasing power. Only for this combination of goods will two conditions hold: All available funds will be spent; and the individual's psychic rate of trade-off (marginal rate of substitution) will be equal to the rate at which the goods can be traded in the market (P_X/P_Y).*

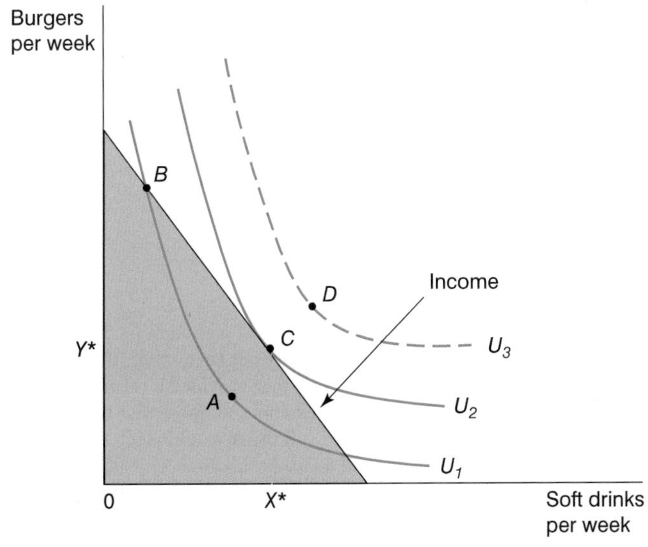

is not fulfilled, this person could be made better off by reallocating expenditures.[5] You may wish to try several other combinations of *X* and *Y* that this person can afford to show that all of them provide a lower utility level than does combination *C*. That is why *C* is a point of tangency – it is the only affordable combination that allows this person to reach U_2. For a point of nontangency (say *B*), a person can always get more utility because the budget constraint passes through the indifference curve (see U_1 in the figure). In Application 2.3: *Ticket Touting*, we examine a case in which people do not have such complete freedom in how they spend their incomes.

Using the Model of Choice

This model of utility-maximization can be used to explain a number of common observations. Figure 2-8, for example, provides an illustration of why people with the same income choose to spend this in different ways. In all three panels of Figure 2-8, the budget constraint facing each person is the same. However, Hungry Joe in panel (a) of the figure has a clear preference for burgers. He chooses to spend his €20 almost exclusively on burgers. Thirsty Teresa, on the other hand, chooses to spend most of her €20 on soft drinks. She does buy two burgers, however, because she feels some need for solid food. Extra-Thirsty Ed, whose situation is shown in panel (c), wants a totally liquid diet. He gets the most utility from spending his entire €20 on soft drinks. Even though he would, with more to spend, probably, buy burgers, in the current case he is so thirsty that the opportunity cost of giving up a soft drink to do so is just too high.

Figure 2-9 again shows the four specific indifference curve maps that were introduced earlier in this chapter. Now we have superimposed a budget constraint on each one and indicated the utility-maximizing choice by *E*. Some obvious implications can be drawn from these illustrations. Panel (a) makes clear that a utility-maximizing individual will never buy a useless good. Utility is as large as possible by consuming only food. There is no reason for this person to incur the opportunity cost involved in consuming any more "waiting in the doctor's surgery". A

MICROQUIZ 2.5

Figure 2-8 and Figure 2-9 show that the condition for utility-maximization should be amended sometimes to deal with special situations.

1. Explain how the condition should be changed for "boundary" issues such as those shown in Figure 2-8(c) and 2–9(c), where people buy zero amounts of some goods. Use this to explain why your author never buys any butter beans.
2. How do you interpret the condition in which goods are perfect complements, such as those shown in Figure 2-9(d)? If left and right shoes were sold separately, could any price ratio make you depart from buying pairs?

[5]If we use the results of note 2 on the assumption that utility is measurable, Equation 2.6 can be given an alternative interpretation. Because

$$P_X/P_Y = \text{MRS} = MU_X/MU_Y \qquad \{i\}$$

for a utility maximum, we have

$$\frac{MU_X}{P_X} = \frac{MU_Y}{P_Y} \qquad \{ii\}$$

The ratio of the extra utility from consuming one more unit of a good to its price should be the same for each good. Each good should provide the same extra utility per euro spent. If that were not true, total utility could be raised by reallocating funds from a good that provided a relatively low level of marginal utility per euro to one that provided a high level. For example, suppose that consuming an extra burger would yield 5 utils (units of utility), whereas an extra soft drink would yield 2 utils. Then each util costs €0.40 (= €2.00 ÷ 5) if hamburgers are bought and €0.50 (= €1.00 ÷ 2) if soft drinks are bought. Clearly burgers are a cheaper way to buy utility. So this person should buy more hamburgers and fewer soft drinks until each good becomes an equally costly way to get utility. Only when this happens will utility be as large as possible because it cannot be raised by further changes in spending.

APPLICATION 2.3 *Ticket Touting*

Tickets to major concerts or sporting events are not usually auctioned off to the highest bidder. Instead, promoters tend to sell most tickets at "reasonable" prices and then ration the resulting excess demand either on a first-come-first-served basis or by limiting the number of tickets each buyer can purchase. Such rationing mechanisms create the possibility for further selling of tickets at much higher prices in the secondary market – that is, ticket "touting".

A Graphical Interpretation

Figure 1 shows the motivation for ticket touting for, say, Cup Final tickets. With this consumer's income and the quoted price of tickets, he or she would prefer to purchase four tickets (point *A*). But the Football Association has decided to limit tickets to only one per customer. This limitation reduces the consumer's utility from U_2 (the utility he or she would enjoy with tickets freely available) to U_1. Notice that this choice of one ticket (point *B*) does not obey the tangency rule for a utility maximum – given the actual price of tickets, this person would prefer to buy more than one. In fact, this frustrated consumer would be willing to pay more than the prevailing price for additional Cup Final tickets. He or she would not only be more than willing to buy a second ticket at the official price (since point *C* is above U_1) but also would be willing to give up an additional amount of other goods (given by distance *CD*) to get this ticket. It appears that this person would be more than willing to pay quite a bit to a "tout" for the second ticket. For example, tickets for major events at the Olympic Games often sold for five times their face value, and resold tickets for the 2006 World Cup Final were on sale on eBay for upwards of €2000 to die-hard fans.

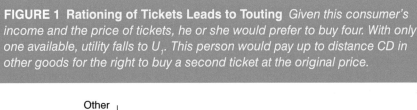

FIGURE 1 Rationing of Tickets Leads to Touting *Given this consumer's income and the price of tickets, he or she would prefer to buy four. With only one available, utility falls to U_1. This person would pay up to distance CD in other goods for the right to buy a second ticket at the original price.*

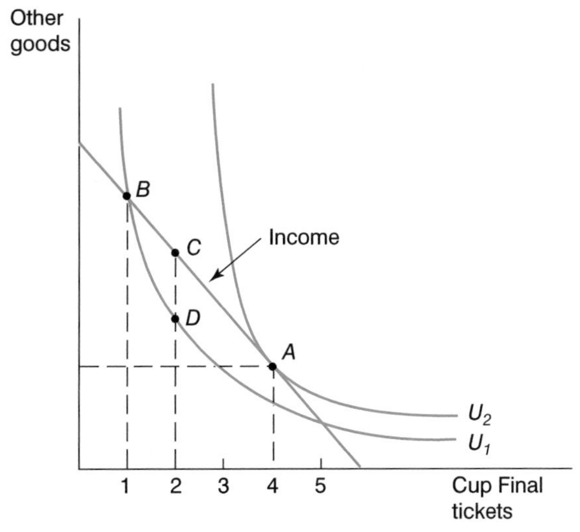

(Continued)

Anti-Touting Laws

Most economists hold a relatively benign view of ticket touting. They view the activity as being voluntary between a willing buyer and a willing seller. Central and local governments however, often seem to see things differently. Many have passed laws that seek either to regulate the prices of resold tickets or to outlaw ticket selling in locations near the events. The generally cited reason for such laws is that touting is "unfair" – perhaps because the "tout" makes profits that are "not deserved". This value judgment seems excessively harsh, however. Ticket touts do provide a valuable service by enabling transactions between those who place a low value on their tickets and those who would value them more highly. The ability to make such transactions can itself be valuable to people whose situations change. Forbidding these transactions may result in wasted resources if some seats remain unfilled. However, UK legislation such as section 166 of the Criminal Justice and Public Order Act 1994 was introduced to stop football fans who buy tickets from touts getting in to areas of the ground reserved for opposing fans. Fears over crowd violence and public order issues prompted the legislation. A side effect of this well-meaning policy is that the primary gainer from anti-touting laws may be ticket agencies who can gain a monopoly-like position as the sole source of sought-after tickets.

To Think About

1 Some promoters of sporting events favor anti-touting laws because they believe that such activity cuts into their profits. What do you make of this argument?
2 Touting is just one example of the "black markets" that arise when goods are rationed by means other than price. What are a few other examples? Are black market transactions undesirable?

similar result holds for panel (b) – there is no reason for this person to spend anything on houseflies (assuming there is a store that sells them).

In panel (c), the individual buys only Shell, even though Shell and BP are perfect substitutes. The relatively steep budget constraint in the figure indicates that Shell is the more expensive of the two brands, so this person opts to buy only Shell. Because the goods are all but identical, the utility-maximizing decision is to buy only the less expensive brand. People who buy only generic versions of prescription drugs or who buy all their brand-name household staples at a discount supermarket are exhibiting a similar type of behavior.

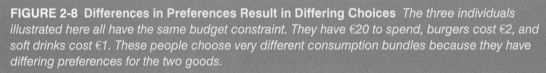

FIGURE 2-8 Differences in Preferences Result in Differing Choices *The three individuals illustrated here all have the same budget constraint. They have €20 to spend, burgers cost €2, and soft drinks cost €1. These people choose very different consumption bundles because they have differing preferences for the two goods.*

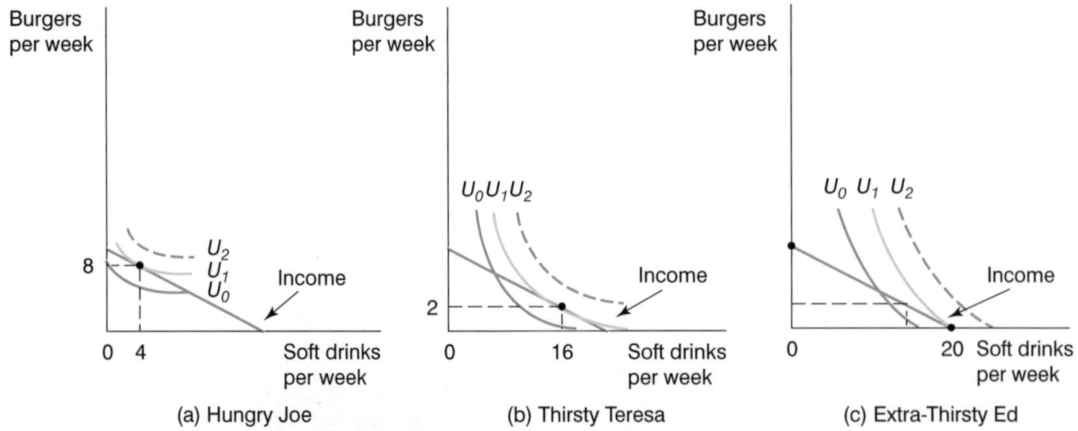

Finally, the utility-maximizing situation illustrated in Figure 2-9(d) shows that this person will buy shoes only in pairs. Any departure from this pattern would result in buying extra left or right shoes, which alone provide no utility. In similar circumstances involving complementary goods, people also tend to purchase those goods together. Other items of apparel (gloves, earrings, socks, and so forth) are also bought mainly in pairs. Most people have preferred ways of concocting the beverages they drink (coffee and cream, gin and tonic) or of making sandwiches (peanut butter and jam, cheese and tomato); and people seldom buy cars, stereos, or washing machines by the part. Rather, they consume these complex goods as fixed packages made up of their various components.

Overall then, the utility-maximizing model of choice provides a very flexible way of explaining why people make the choices that they do. Because people are faced with budget constraints, they must be careful to allocate their incomes so that they provide as much satisfaction as possible. Of course, they will not explicitly engage in the kinds of graphic analyses shown in the figures for this chapter. But this model seems to be a good way of making precise the notion that people "do the best with what they've got". We look at how this model can be used to illustrate a famous court case in Application 2.4: *What's a Rich Uncle's Promise Worth?*

FIGURE 2-9 Utility-Maximizing Choices for Special Types of Goods *The four panels in this figure repeat the special indifference curve maps from Figure 2-5. The resulting utility-maximizing positions (denoted by E in each panel) reflect the specific relationships among the goods pictured.*

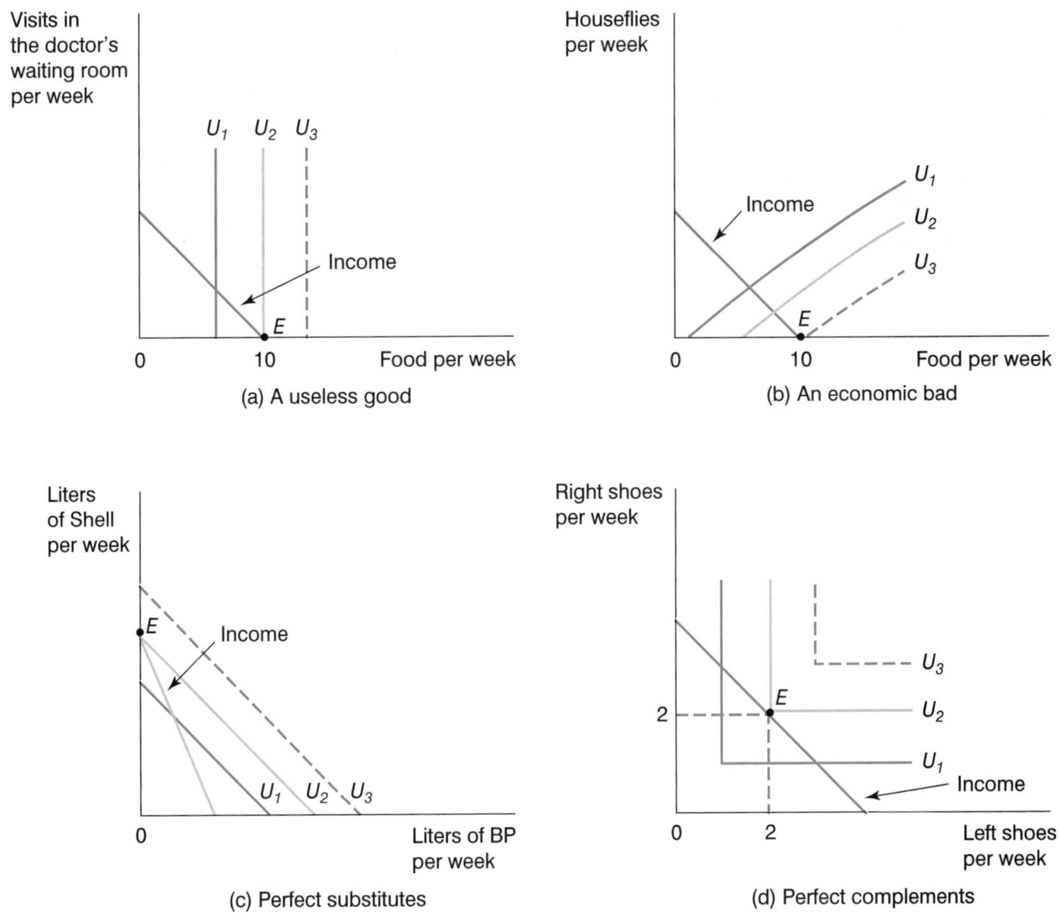

APPLICATION 2.4 *What's a Rich Uncle's Promise Worth?*

One of the strangest legal cases of the nineteenth century was the New York case of *Hamer v. Sidway*, in which nephew Willie sued his uncle for failing to carry through on the promise to pay him $5000 if he did not smoke, drink, or gamble until he reached the age of 21. No one in the case disagreed that the uncle had made this deal with Willie when he was about 15 years old. The legal issue was whether the uncle's promise was a clear "contract", enforceable in court. An examination of this peculiar case provides an instructive illustration of how economic principles can help to clarify legal issues.

Graphing the Uncle's Offer

Figure 1 shows Willie's choice between "sin" (that is, smoking, drinking, and gambling) on the *X*-axis and his spending on everything else on the *Y*-axis. Left to his own devices, Willie would prefer to consume point *A* – which involves some sin along with other things. This would provide him with utility of U_2. Willie's uncle is offering him point *B* – an extra $5000 worth of other things on the condition that sin = 0. In this graph, it is clear that the offer provides more utility (U_3) than point *A*, so Willie should take the offer and spend his teenage years sin-free.

When the Uncle Reneges

When Willie came to collect the $5000 for his abstinence, his uncle assured him that he would place the funds in a bank account that Willie would get once he was "capable of using it wisely". But the uncle died and left no provision for payment in his will. So Willie ended up with no money. The consequences of not being paid the $5000 can be shown in Figure 1 by point *C* – this is the utility Willie would get by spending all his income on non-sin items.

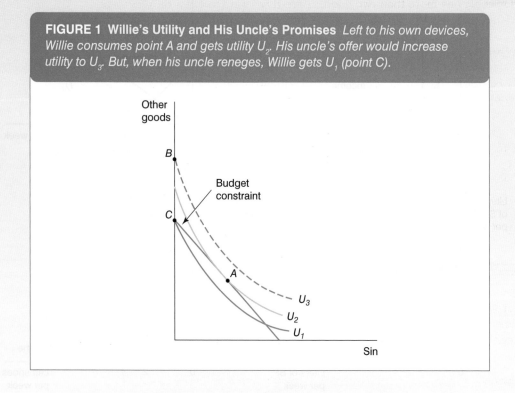

FIGURE 1 Willie's Utility and His Uncle's Promises *Left to his own devices, Willie consumes point A and gets utility U_2. His uncle's offer would increase utility to U_3. But, when his uncle reneges, Willie gets U_1 (point C).*

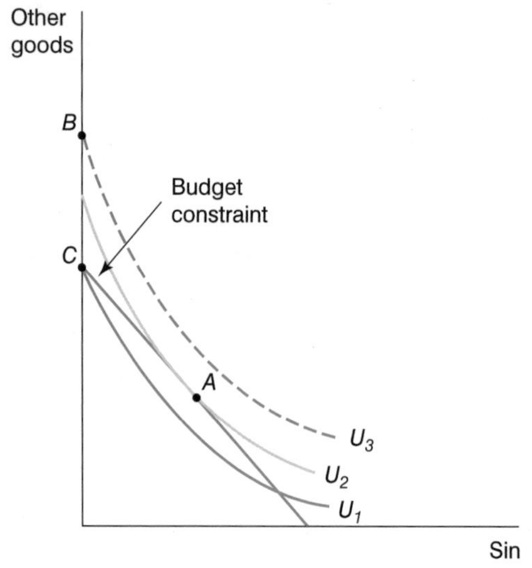

Willie Goes to Court

Not willing to take his misfortune lying down, Willie took his uncle's estate to court, claiming, in effect, that he had made a contract with his uncle and deserved to be paid. The primary legal question in the case concerned the issue of "consideration" in the purported contract between Willie and his uncle. In contract law the promise of party A to do something for party B is enforceable only if there is evidence that an actual bargain was reached. One sign that such an agreement has been reached is the payment of some form of consideration from B to A that seals the deal. Although there was no explicit payment from Willie to his uncle in this case, the court ultimately ruled that Willie's six years of abstinence itself played that role here. Apparently the uncle derived pleasure from seeing a "sin-free" Willie so this was regarded as sufficient consideration in this case. After much wrangling, Willie finally got paid.

To Think About

1 Suppose that the uncle's heirs had offered to settle by making Willie as well-off as he would have been by acting sinfully in his teenage years. In Figure 1, how could you show the amount they would have to pay?

2 Would the requirement that the uncle make Willie "whole" by paying the amount suggested in question 1 provide the right incentives for him to stick to the original deal?

Generalizations

The basic model of choice that we have been examining can be generalized in several ways. Here we look briefly at three of these.

Many Goods

Of course people buy more than two goods. Even if we were to focus on very large categories such as food, clothing, housing, or transport, it is clear that we would need a theory that includes more than two items. Once we looked deeper into the types of food that people might buy or how they might spend their housing euros, the situation would become very complex indeed. But the basic findings of this chapter would not really be changed in any major way. People who are seeking to make the best of their situations would still be expected to spend all of their incomes (because the only alternative is to throw it away – saving is addressed in Chapter 16). The logic of choosing combinations of goods for which the MRS is equal to the price ratio remains true, too. Our intuitive proof showed that any choice for which the slope of the indifference curve differs from the slope of the budget constraint offers the possibility for improvement. This proof would not be affected by situations in which there are more than two goods. Hence, although the formal analysis of the many-good case is indeed more complicated,[6] there is not much more to learn from what has already been covered in this chapter.

Complicated Budget Constraints

The budget constraints discussed in this chapter all had a very simple form – they could all be represented by straight lines. The reason for this is that we assumed that the price a person pays for a good is not affected by how much of that good he or she buys. We assumed there were no special deals for someone who purchased many burgers or

[6]For a mathematical treatment, see W. Nicholson, *Microeconomic Theory: Basic Principles and Extensions*, 9th ed. (Mason, OH: South-Western/Thomson Learning, 2005), Chapter 4.

who opted for "super" sizes of soft drinks. In many cases, people do not face such simple budget constraints. Instead, they face a variety of inducements to buy larger quantities or complex bundling arrangements that give special deals only if other items are also bought. For example, the pricing of telephone services has become extremely complex, involving cut rates for more extensive long-distance usage, special deals for services such as voice mail or caller ID, and tie-in sales that offer favorable rates to customers who also buy Internet or a mobile phone service from the same vendor. Describing precisely the budget constraint faced by a consumer in such situations can sometimes be quite difficult. But a careful analysis of the properties of such complicated budget constraints and how they relate to the utility-maximizing model can be revealing in showing why people behave in the ways they do. Application 2.5: *Frequent-Flier Programs* provides one such illustration.

Composite Goods

Composite good Combining expenditures on several different goods whose relative prices do not change into a single good for convenience in analysis.

Another important way in which the simple two-goods model in this chapter can be generalized is through the use of a **composite good**. Such a good is constructed by combining spending on many individual items into one aggregated whole. One way such a good is used is to study the way people allocate their spending among such major items as "food" and "housing". For example, in the next chapter, we show that spending on food tends to fall as people get richer, whereas spending on housing is, more or less, a constant fraction of income. Of course, these spending patterns are in reality made up of individual decisions about what kind of breakfast cereal to buy or whether to paint your house; but adding many things together can often help to illuminate important questions.

Probably the most common use of the composite good idea is in situations where we wish to study decisions to buy one specific item such as airline tickets or petrol. In this case, a common procedure is to show the specific item of interest on the horizontal (X) axis and spending on "everything else" on the vertical (Y) axis. This is the procedure we used in Application 2.3 and Application 2.4, and we use it many other times later in this book. Taking advantage of the composite good idea can greatly simplify many problems.

There are some technical issues that arise in using composite goods, though those do not detain us very long in this book. A first problem is how we are to measure a composite good. In our seemingly endless burger–soft drink example, the units of measurement were obvious. But the only way to add up all of the individual items that constitute "everything else" is to do so in euros (or some other currency). Looking at euros of spending on everything else will indeed prove to be a very useful graphical device. But one might have some lingering concerns that, because such adding up requires us to use the prices of individual items, we might get into some trouble when prices change. This then leads to a second problem with composite goods – what is the "price" of such a good. In most cases, there is no need to answer this question because we assume that the price of the composite good (good Y) does not change during our analysis. But, if we did wish to study changes in the price of a composite good, we would obviously have to define that price first.

In our treatment, therefore, we will not be much concerned with these technical problems associated with composite goods. If you are interested in the ways that some of the problems are solved, you may wish to do some reading on your own.[7]

[7]For an introduction, see W. Nicholson, *Microeconomic Theory: Basic Principles and Extensions*, 9th ed. (Mason, OH: South-Western/Thomson Learning, 2005), 167–169.

APPLICATION 2.5 *Frequent-Flier Programs*

The budget constraints we have studied in this chapter are plotted using straight lines because the prices of goods are unaffected by how much the consumer buys. In cases where consumers receive quantity discounts or may have to pay "excessive use" fees, this assumption is no longer valid and the budget constraint may not have such a simple shape.

Quantity Discounts and the Budget Constraint

The case of a quantity discount is illustrated in Figure 1. Here consumers who buy less than X_D pay full price and face the usual budget constraint. Purchases in excess of X_D entitle the buyer to a lower price (on the extra units), and this results in a flatter budget constraint beyond that point. The constraint, therefore, has a "kink" at X_D. Effects of this kink on consumer choices are suggested by the indifference curve U_1, which is tangent to the budget constraint at both point *A* and point *B*. This person is indifferent between consuming relatively little of *X* or a lot of it. A slightly larger quantity discount could tempt this consumer definitely to choose the larger amount. Notice that such a choice entails not only consuming low-price units of the good but also buying more of it at full price (up to X_D) in order to get the discount.[1]

Frequent-Flier Programs

All major airlines operate frequent-flier programs. These entitle customers to accumulate mileage with the airline at reduced fares. Because unused-seat revenues are lost forever, the airlines utilize these programs to tempt consumers to travel more on their airlines. Any additional full-fare travel that the programs may generate provides extra profits for the airline. One interesting side issue related to frequent-flier

FIGURE 1 Kinked Budget Constraint Resulting from a Quantity Discount
A quantity discount for purchases greater than X_D results in a kinked budget constraint. This consumer is indifferent between consuming relatively little X (point A) or a lot of X (point B).

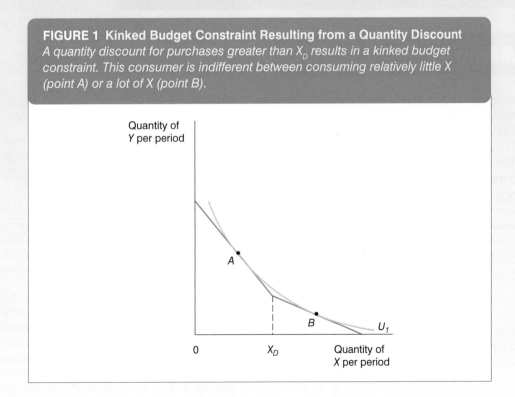

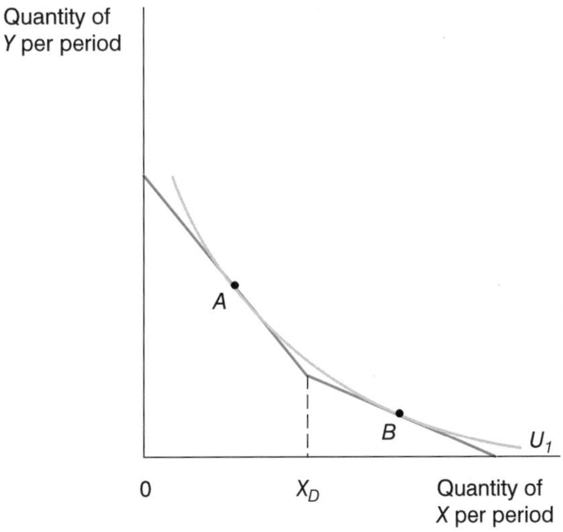

(Continued)

programs concerns business travel. When travelers have their fares reimbursed by their employers they may have extra incentives to accumulate frequent-flier miles. In such a case airlines may be especially eager to lure business travelers (who usually pay higher fares) with special offers such as "business class" service or airport-based lounges. Because a traveler pays the same zero-price no matter which airline is chosen, these extras may have a big influence on actual choices made. Of course travel departments of major companies recognize this and may adopt policies that seek to limit travelers' choices.

Some economists argue that frequent-flier plans reduce competition among airlines by tying a particular consumer to the airline with which he or she maintains such a plan. Of course, consumers are free to join a number of plans, and some airlines give credit for travel on other airlines. Hence, the overall effect of the plans may simply be to fill seats that would have gone empty, with little anticompetitive effect on full-fare prices.

To Think About

1. Most of the low cost airlines such as Ryanair and easyJet do not offer air miles, but most of the older legacy carriers such as British Airways or Lufthansa do. Explain what is the rational of these two different strategies.
2. Suppose frequent-flier points were transferable among people. How would this affect Figure 1 and, more generally, the overall viability of the program?

[1]For a more complete discussion of the kinds of pricing schemes that can be shown on a simple utility-maximization graph, see J. S. DeSalvo and M. Huq, "Introducing Nonlinear Pricing into Consumer Theory", *Journal of Economic Education* (Spring 2002):166–179.

SUMMARY

This chapter covers a lot of ground. In it we have seen how economists explain the kinds of choices people make and the ways in which those choices are constrained by economic circumstances. The chapter has been rather tough going in places. The theory of choice is one of the most difficult parts of any study of microeconomics, and it is unfortunate that it usually comes at the very start of the course. But that placement clearly shows why the topic is so important. Practically every model of economic behavior starts with the tools introduced in this chapter.

The principal conclusions in this chapter are

- Economists use the term *utility* to refer to the satisfaction that people derive from their economic activities. Usually only a few of the things that affect utility are examined in any particular analysis. All other factors are assumed to be held constant, so that a person's choices can be studied in a simplified setting.
- Utility can be shown by an indifference curve map. Each indifference curve identifies those bundles of goods that a person considers to be equally attractive. Higher levels of utility are represented by higher indifference curve "contour" lines.
- The slope of indifference curves shows how a person is willing to trade one good for another while remaining equally well-off. The negative of this slope is called the "marginal rate of substitution" (MRS), because it shows the degree to which an individual is willing to substitute one good for another in his or her consumption choices. The value of this trade-off depends on the amount of the two goods being consumed.
- People are limited in what they can buy by their "budget constraints". When a person is choosing between two goods, his or her budget constraint is usually a straight line because prices do not depend on how much is bought. The negative of the slope of this line represents the price ratio of the two goods – it shows what one of the goods is worth in terms of the other in the marketplace.
- If people are to obtain the maximum possible utility from their limited incomes, they should spend all

the available funds and should choose a bundle of goods for which the MRS is equal to the price ratio of the two goods. Such a utility maximum is shown graphically by a tangency between the budget constraint and the highest indifference curve that this person's income can buy.

REVIEW QUESTIONS

1 The notion of utility is an "ordinal" one for which it is assumed that people can rank combinations of goods as to their desirability, but that they cannot assign a unique numerical (cardinal) scale for the goods that quantifies "how much" one combination is preferred to another. For each of the following ranking systems, describe whether an ordinal or cardinal ranking is being used: (a) military or academic ranks; (b) prices of vintage wines; (c) rankings of vintage wines by the French Wine Society; (d) press rankings of the "Top Ten" football teams; (e) results of the current US Open Golf Championships (in which players are ranked by stroke play); (f) results of early US Open Golf Championships (which were conducted using match play).

2 How might you draw an indifference curve map that illustrates the following ideas?

- a Margarine is just as good as the high-priced spread.
- b Things go better with Coke.
- c A day without wine is like a day without sunshine.
- d Popcorn is addictive – the more you eat, the more you want.
- e It takes two to tango.

3 Inez reports that an extra banana would increase her utility by two units and an extra pear would increase her utility by six units. What is her MRS of bananas for pears – that is, how many bananas would she voluntarily give up to get an extra pear? Would Philip (who reports that an extra banana yields 100 units of utility whereas an extra pear yields 400 units of utility) be willing to trade a pear to Inez at her voluntary MRS?

4 Oscar consumes two goods, wine and cheese. His weekly income is €500.

- a Describe Oscar's budget constraints under the following conditions
  - Wine costs €10/bottle, cheese costs €5/kilo.
  - Wine costs €10/bottle, cheese costs €10/kilo.
  - Wine costs €20/bottle, cheese costs €10/kilo.
  - Wine costs €20/bottle, cheese costs €10/kilo, but Oscar's income increases to €1000/week.
- b What can you conclude by comparing the first and the last of these budget constraints?

5 While standing in line to buy popcorn at your favorite theatre, you hear someone behind you say, "This popcorn isn't worth its price – I'm not buying any". How would you plot on a graph this person's situation?

6 A careful reader of this book will have read footnote 2 and footnote 5 in this chapter. Explain why these can be summarized by the commonsense idea that a person is maximizing his or her utility only if getting an extra euro to spend would provide the same amount of extra utility no matter which good he or she chooses to spend it on. (Hint: Suppose this condition were not true – is utility as large as possible?)

7 Most countries require that you purchase minimum car insurance when you buy a car. Use an indifference curve diagram to show that this mandate reduces utility for some people. What kinds of people are most likely to have their utility reduced by such a law? Why do you think that the government requires such insurance?

8 Two students studying microeconomics are trying to understand why the tangent condition studied in this chapter means utility is at a maximum. Let's listen:
Student A. If a person chooses a point on his or her budget constraint that is not tangent, it is clear that he or she can manage to get a higher utility by spending differently.
Student B. I don't get it – how do you know he or she can do better instead of worse?
How can you help out Student B with a graph?

9 Suppose that an electric company charges consumers €0.10 per kilowatt hour for electricity for the first 1000 used in a month but €0.15 for each extra kilowatt hour after that. Draw the budget constraint for a consumer facing this price schedule, and discuss why many individuals may choose to consume exactly 1000 kilowatt hours.

10 Suppose an individual consumes three items: steak, lettuce, and tomatoes. If we were interested only in examining this person's steak purchases, we might group lettuce and tomatoes into a single composite good called "salad". Suppose also that this person always makes salad by combining two units of lettuce with one unit of tomato.

a How would you define a unit of "salad" to show (along with steak) on a two-goods graph?

b How does the price of salad (P_S) relate to the price of lettuce (P_L) and the price of tomatoes (P_T)?

c What is this person's budget constraint for steak and salad?

d Would a doubling of the price of steak, the price of lettuce, the price of tomatoes, and this person's income shift the budget constraint described in part c?

e Suppose instead that the way in which this person made salad depended on the relative prices of lettuce and tomatoes. Now could you express this person's choice problem as involving only two goods? Explain.

PROBLEMS

2.1 Suppose a person has €8.00 to spend only on apples and bananas. Apples cost €0.40 each, and bananas cost €0.10 each.

a If this person buys *only* apples, how many can be bought?

b If this person buys *only* bananas, how many can be bought?

c If the person were to buy ten apples, how many bananas could be bought with the funds left over?

d If the person consumes one less apple (that is, nine), how many more bananas could be bought? Is this rate of trade-off the same no matter how many apples are relinquished?

e Write down the algebraic equation for this person's budget constraint, and graph it showing the points mentioned in parts a through d (using graph paper might improve the accuracy of your work).

2.2 Suppose the person faced with the budget constraint described in problem 2.1 has preferences for apples (A) and bananas (B) given by

$$Utility = \sqrt{A \cdot B}$$

a If $A = 5$ and $B = 80$, what will utility be?

b If $A = 10$, what value for B will provide the same utility as in part a?

c If $A = 20$, what value for B will provide the same utility as in parts a and b?

d Graph the indifference curve implied by parts a through c.

e Given the budget constraint from problem 2.1, which of the points identified in parts a through c can be bought by this person?

f Show through some examples that every other way of allocating income provides less utility than does the point identified in part b. Graph this utility-maximizing situation.

2.3 Paul derives utility only from CDs and DVDs. His utility function is

$$Utility = \sqrt{C \cdot D}$$

a Sketch Paul's indifference curves for $U = 5$, $U = 10$, and $U = 20$.

b Suppose Paul has €200 to spend and that CDs cost €5 and DVDs cost €20. Draw Paul's budget constraint on the same graph as his indifference curves.

c Suppose Paul spends all of his income on DVDs. How many can he buy and what is his utility?

d Show that Paul's income will not permit him to reach the $U = 20$ indifference curve.

e If Paul buys five DVDs, how many CDs can he buy? What is his utility?

f Use a carefully drawn graph to show that the utility calculated in part e is the highest Paul can achieve with his €200.

2.4 Sometimes it is convenient to think about the consumer's problem in its "dual" form. This alternative approach asks how a person could achieve a given target level of utility at minimal cost.

a Develop a graphical argument to show that this approach will yield the same choices for this consumer as would the utility-maximization approach.

b Returning to problem 2.3, assume that Paul's target level of utility is $U = 10$. Calculate the costs of attaining this utility target for the following bundles of goods:

i $C = 100, D = 1$

ii $C = 50, D = 2$

iii $C = 25, D = 4$

iv $C = 20, D = 5$

v $C = 10, D = 10$

vi $C = 5, D = 20$

c Which of the bundles in part b provides the least costly way of reaching the $U = 10$ target? How does this compare to the utility-maximizing solution found in problem 2.3?

2.5 Ms Caffeine enjoys coffee (C) and tea (T) according to the function $U(C, T) = 3C + 4T$. What does her utility function say about her MRS of coffee for tea? What do her indifference curves look like? If coffee and tea cost €3 each and Ms Caffeine has €12 to spend on these products, how much coffee and tea should she buy to maximize her utility? Draw the graph of her indifference curve map and her budget constraint, and show that the utility-maximizing point occurs only on the T-axis where no coffee is bought. Would she buy any coffee if she had more money to spend? How would her consumption change if the price of coffee fell to €2?

2.6 Vera is an impoverished graduate student who has only €100 a month to spend on food. She has read in a government publication that she can assure an adequate diet by eating only peanut butter and carrots in the fixed ratio of 2 kilos of peanut butter to 1 kilo of carrots, so she decides to limit her diet to that regime.

a If peanut butter costs €4 per kilo and carrots cost €2 per kilo, how much can she eat during the month?

b Suppose peanut butter costs rise to €5 because of peanut subsidies introduced by a politically sensitive government. By how much will Vera have to reduce her food purchases?

c How much in social security aid would the government have to give Vera to compensate for the effects of the peanut subsidy?

d Explain why Vera's preferences are of a very special type here. How would you graph them?

2.7 Assume consumers are choosing between housing services (H) measured in square meters and consumption of all other goods (C) measured in euros.

a Show the equilibrium position in a diagram.

b Now suppose the government agrees to subsidize consumers by paying 50 per cent of their housing cost. How will their budget line change? Show the new equilibrium.

c Show in a diagram the minimum amount of income supplement the government would have to give individuals instead of a housing subsidy to make them as well-off as they were in part b.

d Describe why the amount shown in part c is smaller than the amount paid in subsidy in part b.

2.8 Suppose low-income people have preferences for non-food consumption (NF) and for food consumption (F). In the absence of any income transfer programs, a person's budget constraint is given by

$$NF + P_F F = I$$

where P_F is the price of food relative to non-food items and NF and I are measured in terms of non-food prices (that is, euros).

a Plot on a graph the initial utility-maximizing situation for this low-income person.

b Suppose now that a social security program is introduced that requires low-income people to pay C (measured in terms of non-food prices) in order to receive benefits sufficient to buy F^* units of food (presumably $P_F F^* > C$). Show this person's budget constraint if he or she participates in the program.

c Show graphically the factors that will determine whether the person chooses to participate in the program.

d Show graphically what it will cost the government to finance benefits for the typical welfare recipient. Show also that some people might reach a higher utility level if this amount were simply given with no strings attached.

2.9 Suppose that people derive utility from two goods – housing (H) and all other consumption goods (C).

a Show a typical consumer's allocation of his or her income between H and C.

b Suppose that the government decides that the level of housing shown in part a (say, H^*) is "substandard" and requires that all people buy $H^{**} > H^*$ instead. Show that this law would reduce this person's utility.

c One way to return this person to the initial level of utility would be to give him or her extra income. On your graph, show how much extra income this would require.

d Another way to return this person to his or her initial level of utility would be to provide a housing subsidy that reduces the price of housing. On your graph, show this solution as well.

2.10 A common utility function used to illustrate economic examples is the Cobb–Douglas function where $U(X,Y) = X^{\alpha}Y^{\beta}$ where α and β are decimal exponents that sum to 1.0 (that is, for example, 0.3 and 0.7).

a Explain why the utility function used in problem 2.2 and problem 2.3 is a special case of this function.

b It can be shown that a person with this utility function will spend a fraction α of his or her income on good X and a fraction β on good Y. Use this result to solve part e and part f of problem 2.3. Use the result also to solve parts c to e of this problem.

c Show that with this utility function, a person's total spending on good X will not change if the price of X changes, so long as his or her income stays constant.

d Show that with this utility function a change in the price of Y will not affect the amount of X purchased.

e Show that with this utility function, a 50 per cent increase in income accompanied by no changes in the price of X or Y will cause purchases of both X and Y to rise by 50 per cent.

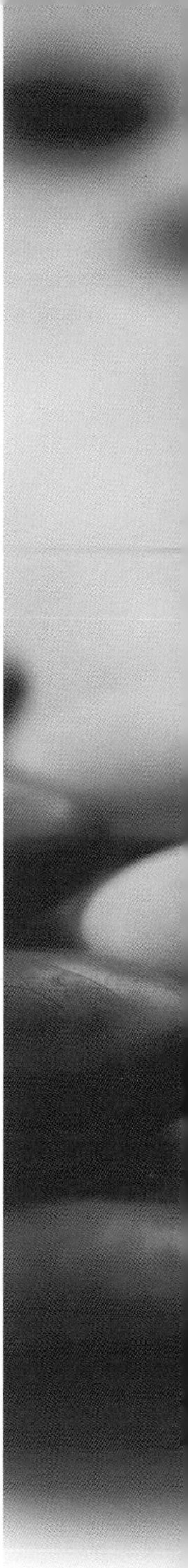

3

Individual Demand Curves

This chapter shows how people change their consumption choices when conditions change. In particular, we study how changes in income or changes in the price of a good affect the amount that people choose to consume. We compare the new choices with those that were made before conditions changed. The main result of this approach is to construct an individual's demand curve for a good. This curve shows the amounts of a good that a person chooses to buy at different prices.

Demand Functions

Chapter 2 concluded that the quantities of X and Y that a person chooses depend on that person's preferences and on the shape of his or her budget constraint. If we knew a person's preferences and all the economic forces that affect his or her choices, we could predict how much of each good would be chosen. We can summarize this conclusion using the **demand function** for some particular good, say, X

$$\text{Quantity of } X \text{ demanded} = d_X(P_X, P_Y, I; \text{preferences}) \quad \{3.1\}$$

This function contains the three elements that determine what the person can buy – the prices of X and Y and the person's income (I) – as well as a reminder that choices are also affected by preferences for the goods. These preferences appear to the right of the semicolon in Equation 3.1 because for most of our discussion we assume that preferences do not change. People's basic likes and dislikes are developed through a lifetime of experience. They are unlikely to change as we examine their reactions to relatively short-term changes in their economic circumstances caused by changes in commodity prices or incomes.

The quantity demanded of good Y depends on these same general influences and can be summarized by

$$\text{Quantity of } Y \text{ demanded} = d_Y(P_X, P_Y, I; \text{preferences}) \quad \{3.2\}$$

Demand function A representation of how quantity demanded depends on prices, income, and preferences.

Preferences again appear to the right of the semicolon in Equation 3.2 because we assume that the person's taste for good *Y* will not change during our analysis.

Homogeneity

One important result that follows directly from Chapter 2 is that if the prices of *X* and *Y* and income (*I*) were all to double (or to change by any identical percentage), the amounts of *X* and *Y* demanded would not change. The budget constraint

$$P_X X + P_Y Y = I \quad \{3.3\}$$

is the same as the budget constraint

$$2P_X X + 2P_Y Y = 2I \quad \{3.4\}$$

Graphically, these are exactly the same lines. Consequently, both budget constraints are tangent to a person's indifference curve map at precisely the same point. The quantities of *X* and *Y* the individual chooses when faced by the constraint in Equation 3.3 are exactly the same as when the individual is faced by the constraint in Equation 3.4.

This is an important result: The amounts a person demands depend only on the relative prices of goods *X* and *Y* and on the "real" value of income. Proportional changes in both the prices of *X* and *Y* and in income change only the units we count in (such as euros instead of cents). They do not affect the quantities demanded. Individual demand is said to be **homogeneous** (of degree zero) for proportional changes in all prices and income. People are not hurt by general inflation of prices if their incomes increase in the same proportion. They will be on exactly the same indifference curve both before and after the inflation. Only if inflation increases some incomes faster or slower than prices change does it then have an effect on budget constraints, on the quantities of goods demanded, and on people's well-being.

Homogeneous demand function Quantity demanded does not change when prices and income increase in the same proportion.

Changes in Income

As a person's total income rises, assuming prices do not change, we might expect the quantity purchased of each good also to increase. This situation is illustrated in Figure 3-1. As income increases from I_1 to I_2 to I_3, the quantity of *X* demanded increases from X_1 to X_2 to X_3 and the quantity of *Y* demanded increases from Y_1 to Y_2 to Y_3. Budget lines I_1, I_2, and I_3 are all parallel because we are changing only income, not the relative prices of *X* and *Y*. Remember, the slope of the budget constraint is given by the ratio of the two goods' prices, and these prices are not changing in this figure. Increases in income do, however, make it possible for this person to consume more; this increased purchasing power is reflected by the outward shift in the budget constraint and an increase in overall utility.

Normal good A good that is bought in greater quantities as income increases.

Inferior good A good that is bought in smaller quantities as income increases.

Normal Goods

In Figure 3-1, both good *X* and good *Y* increase as income increases. Goods that follow this tendency are called **normal goods**. Most goods seem to be normal goods – as their incomes increase, people tend to buy more of practically everything. Of course, as Figure 3-1 shows, the demand for some "luxury" goods (such as *Y*) may increase rapidly when income rises, but the demand for "necessities" (such as X) may grow less rapidly. The relationship between income and the amounts of various goods purchased has been extensively examined by economists, as Application 3.1: *Engel's Law* shows.

Inferior Goods

The demand for a few unusual goods may decrease as a person's income increases. Some proposed examples of such goods are "home-distilled" whiskey, potatoes, and second-hand clothing. This kind of good is called an **inferior good**. How the demand for an inferior good responds to rising income is shown in Figure 3-2. The good Z is inferior because the individual chooses less of it as his or her income increases. Although the curves in Figure 3-2 continue to obey the assumption of a diminishing MRS, they exhibit inferiority. Good Z is inferior only because of the way it relates to the other goods available (good Y here), not because of its own qualities. Purchases of home-distilled whiskey decline as income increases, for example, because an individual is able to afford more expensive beverages (such as French champagne). Although, as our examples suggest, inferior goods are relatively rare, the study of them does help to illustrate a few important aspects of demand theory.

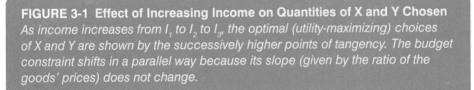

MICROQUIZ 3.1

The theory of utility-maximization implies that the relationship between a person's income and the amounts of goods he or she buys will be determined solely by his or her preferences. How would the relationship between income and house purchases look in the following circumstances?

1. The person's MRS of housing for other goods is the same along any ray through the origin of the indifference curve map (that is, along a line where the ratio of other goods to housing is fixed).
2. The person's MRS of housing for other goods follows the pattern in question 1 until housing reaches a certain "adequate" level and then the MRS becomes zero.

FIGURE 3-1 Effect of Increasing Income on Quantities of X and Y Chosen

As income increases from I_1 to I_2 to I_3, the optimal (utility-maximizing) choices of X and Y are shown by the successively higher points of tangency. The budget constraint shifts in a parallel way because its slope (given by the ratio of the goods' prices) does not change.

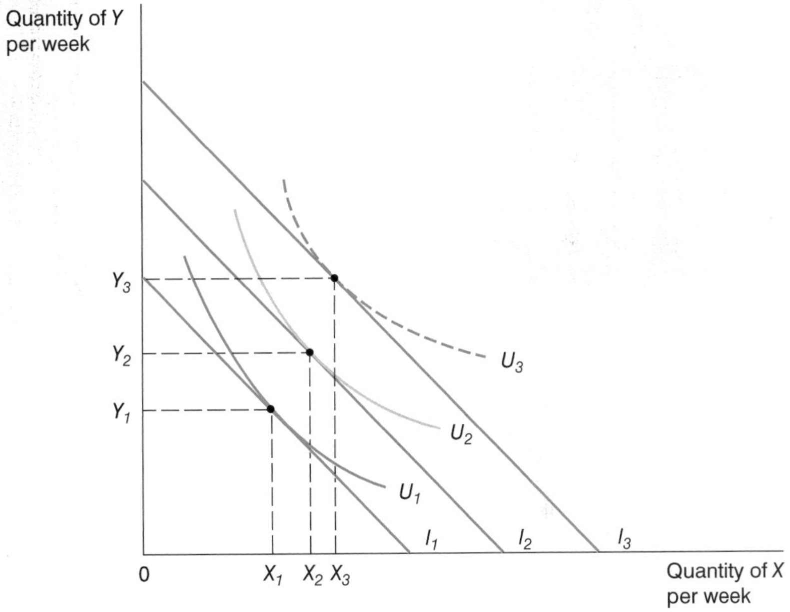

APPLICATION 3.1 *Engel's Law*

One of the most important generalizations about consumer behavior is that the fraction of income spent on food tends to decline as income increases. This finding was first discovered by the Prussian economist, Ernst Engel (1821–1896) in the nineteenth century and has come to be known as Engel's Law. Table 1 illustrates the data that Engel used. They clearly show that richer families spent a smaller fraction of their income on food.

Recent Data

Recent data for US consumers (see Table 2) tend to confirm Engel's observations. Affluent families devote a smaller proportion of their purchasing power to food than do poor families. Comparisons of the data from Table 1 and Table 2 also confirm Engel's Law – even current low income US consumers are much more affluent than nineteenth-century Belgians and, as might be expected, spend a much smaller fraction of their income on food.

Are There Other Laws?

Whether other Engel-like laws apply to the relationship between income and consumption of particular categories of goods is open to question. For example, Table 2 shows little tendency for the fraction of income spent on housing to decline with income. One must therefore be careful in thinking about what "necessities" really are for US consumers.

To Think About

1. The data in Table 2 include food both eaten at home and in restaurants. Do you think eating at restaurants follows Engel's law?
2. Property taxes are based on housing values. Are these taxes regressive?

TABLE 1 Percentage of Total Expenditures on Various Items in Belgian Families in 1853

	Annual Income		
Expenditure Item	*€225–€300*	*€450–€600*	*€750–€1000*
Food	62.0%	55.0%	50.0%
Clothing	16.0	18.0	18.0
Lodging, light, and fuel	17.0	17.0	17.0
Services (education, legal, health)	4.0	7.5	11.5
Comfort and recreation	1.0	2.5	3.5
Total	*100.0*	*100.0*	*100.0*

SOURCE: BASED ON A. MARSHALL, *PRINCIPLES OF ECONOMICS*, 8TH ED. (LONDON: MACMILLAN, 1920), 97. SOME ITEMS HAVE BEEN AGGREGATED.

TABLE 2 Percentage of Total Expenditures by US Consumers on Various Items, 2002

	Annual Income (000)		
Item	*$20–25*	*$50–70*	*$100+*
Food	15.2%	13.0%	12.4%
Clothing	4.3	4.1	4.6
Housing	33.6	30.4	31.0
Other items	46.9	52.5	52.0
Total	*100.0*	*100.0*	*100.0*

SOURCE: US BUREAU OF LABOR STATISTICS WEBSITE: *HTTP://STATS.BLS.GOV/CEX/CSXANN02.PDF*

Changes in a Good's Price

Examining how a price change affects the quantity demanded of a good is more complex than looking at the effect of a change in income. Changing the price geometrically involves not only changing the intercept of the budget constraint but also changing its slope. Moving to the new utility-maximizing choice means moving to indifference curve and to a point on that curve with a different MRS.

When a price changes, it has two different effects on people's choices. There is a **substitution effect** that occurs even if the individual stays on the same indifference curve because consumption has to be changed to equate the MRS to the new price ratio of the two goods. There is also an **income effect** because the price change also changes "real" purchasing power. People will have to move to a new indifference curve that is consistent with their new purchasing power. We now look at these two effects in several different situations.

Substitution effect The part of the change in quantity demanded that is caused by substitution of one good for another. A movement along an indifference curve.

Income effect The part of the change in quantity demanded that is caused by a change in real income. A movement to a new indifference curve.

Substitution and Income Effects from a Fall in Price

Let's look first at how the quantity consumed of good X changes in response to a fall in its price. This situation is illustrated in Figure 3-3. Initially, the person maximizes utility by choosing the combination X^*, Y^* at point *A*. When the price of X falls, the budget line shifts outward to the new budget constraint as shown in the figure. Remember that the budget constraint meets the Y-axis at the point where all available income is spent on good Y. Because neither the person's income nor the price of good Y has changed here, this Y-intercept is the same for both constraints. The new X-intercept is to the right of the old one because the lower price of X means that, with

FIGURE 3-2 Indifference Curve Map Showing Inferiority *Good Z is inferior because the quantity purchased declines as income increases. Y is a normal good (as it must be if only two goods are available), and purchases of it increase as total expenditures increase.*

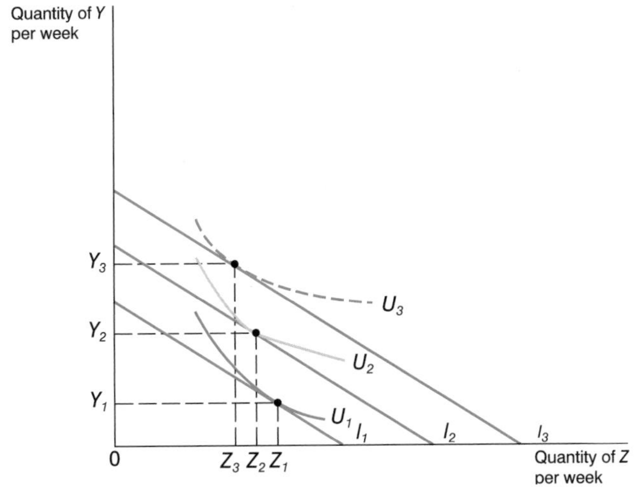

the lower price, this person could buy more X if he or she devoted all income to that purpose. The flatter slope of the budget constraint shows us that the relative price of X to Y (that is, P_X/P_Y) has fallen.

Substitution Effect

With this change in the budget constraint, the new position of maximum utility is at X^{**}, Y^{**} (point C). There, the new budget line is tangent to the indifference curve U_2. The movement to this new set of choices is the result of two different effects. First, the change in the slope of the budget constraint would have motivated this person to move to point B even if the person had stayed on the original indifference curve U_1. The dashed line in Figure 3-3 has the same slope as the new budget constraint, but it is tangent to U_1 because we are holding "real" income (that is, utility) constant. A relatively lower price for X causes a move from A to B if this person does not become better off as a result of the lower price. This movement is a graphic demonstration of the substitution effect. Even though the individual is no better off, the change in price still causes a change in consumption choices.

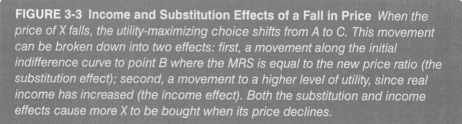

FIGURE 3-3 Income and Substitution Effects of a Fall in Price *When the price of X falls, the utility-maximizing choice shifts from A to C. This movement can be broken down into two effects: first, a movement along the initial indifference curve to point B where the MRS is equal to the new price ratio (the substitution effect); second, a movement to a higher level of utility, since real income has increased (the income effect). Both the substitution and income effects cause more X to be bought when its price declines.*

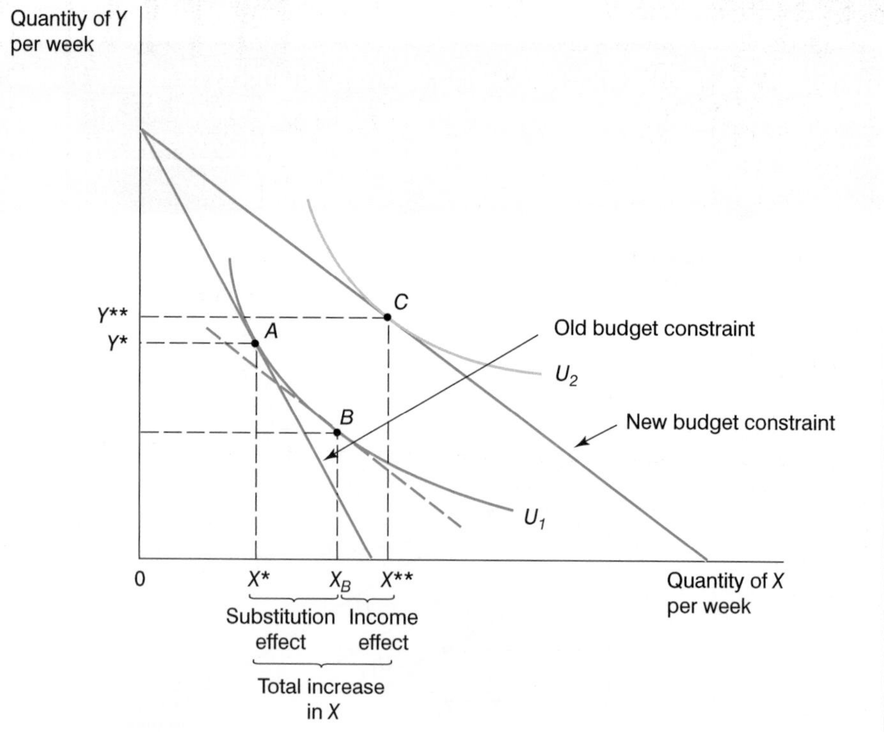

Another way to think about the substitution effect involved in the movement from point *A* to point *B* is to ask how this person can get to the indifference curve U_1 with the least possible expenditures. With the initial budget constraint, point *A* does indeed represent the least costly way to reach U_1 – with these prices every other point on U_1 costs more than does point *A*. When the price of *X* falls, however, commodity bundle *A* is no longer the cheapest way to obtain the level of satisfaction represented by U_1. Now this person should take advantage of the changed prices by substituting *X* for *Y* in his or her consumption choices if U_1 is to be obtained at minimal cost. Point *B* is now the least costly way to reach U_1. With the new prices, every point on U_1 costs more than point *B*.

Income Effect

The further move from *B* to the final consumption choice, *C*, is identical to the kind of movement we described in Figure 3-1 for changes in income. Because the price of *X* has fallen but nominal income (I) has stayed the same, this person has a greater "real" income and can afford a higher utility level (U_2). If *X* is a normal good, he or she will now demand more of it. This is the income effect. Notice that for normal goods this effect also causes price and quantity to move in opposite directions. When the price of *X* falls, this person's real income is increased and he or she buys more *X* because *X* is a normal good. A similar statement applies when the price of *X* rises. Such a price rise reduces real income and, because *X* is a normal good, less of it is demanded. Of course, as we shall see, the situation is more complicated when *X* is an inferior good. But that is a rare case, and ultimately it will not detain us very long.

The Effects Combined

People do not actually move from *A* to *B* to *C* when the price of good *X* falls. We never observe the point *B*; only the two actual choices of *A* and *C* are reflected in this person's behavior. But the analysis of income and substitution effects is still valuable because it shows that a price change affects the quantity demanded of a good in two conceptually different ways.

We can use the burger–soft drink example from Chapter 2 to show these effects at work. Suppose that the price of soft drinks falls to €0.50 from the earlier price of €1.00. This price change will increase this person's purchasing power. Whereas earlier 20 soft drinks could be bought with an income of €20.00, now 40 of them can be bought. The price decrease shifts the budget constraint outward and increases utility. This person now will choose some different combination of burgers and soft drinks than before, if only because the previous choice of five burgers and ten soft drinks (under the old budget constraint) now costs only €15 – there is €5 left unspent, and this person will choose to do something with it.

In making the new choices, this person is influenced by two different effects. First, even if we hold utility constant by somehow compensating for the beneficial effect that the fall in price has, this person will still act so that the MRS is brought into line with the new price ratio (now one burger to four soft drinks). This compensated response is the substitution effect. Even with a constant real income, this person will still choose more soft drinks and fewer burgers because the opportunity cost of eating a burger in terms of soft drinks forgone is now higher than before.

In actuality, real income has also increased; in order to assess the total effect of the price change on the demand for soft drinks, we must also investigate the effect of the change in purchasing power. The increase in real income would (assuming soft drinks are normal goods) be another reason to expect soft drink purchases to increase.

The Importance of Substitution Effects

Any price change induces both substitution and income effects. In general, however, economists believe that substitution effects are more important in determining why people respond more to changes in the prices of some kinds of goods than they do to changes in the prices of other kinds of goods. It is the availability of substitute goods that primarily determines how people react to price changes. One reason for the relative importance of substitution effects is that in most cases income effects will be small because we are looking at goods that constitute only a small portion of people's spending. Changes in the price of chewing gum or bananas have little impact on real income because these goods make up much less than 1 per cent of total spending for most people. Of course, in some cases income effects may be large – changes in the price of energy, for example, can have important effects on real incomes. But in most situations that will not be the case.

A second reason the economists tend to focus mainly on the substitution effects of price changes is that the sizes of these effects can be quite varied, depending on which specific goods are being considered. Figure 3-4 illustrates this observation by returning to some of the cases we looked at in the previous chapter. Panel (a) of Figure 3-4 illustrates the left shoe–right shoe example. When the price of left shoes falls, the slope of the budget constraint becomes flatter, moving from I to I'. But, because of the shape of the U_1 indifference curve in the figure, this causes no substitution effect at all – the initial bundle of goods (A) and the bundle illustrating the substitution effect (B) are the same point. As long as this person stays on the U_1 indifference curve, he or she will continue to buy the same number of pairs of shoes, no matter how the relative price of left shoes changes.

This situation is substantially different when two goods are very close substitutes. Panel (b) of Figure 3-4 returns to the Shell–BP example from the previous chapter. Suppose initially that the price of Shell petrol is lower than that of BP. Then the budget constraint (I) will be steeper than the indifference curve U_1 (which has a slope of -1 because the two brands are perfect substitutes) and this person will buy only Shell (point A). When the price of BP falls below that of Shell, the budget constraint will become flatter (I') and this person can achieve U_1 most cheaply by purchasing only BP

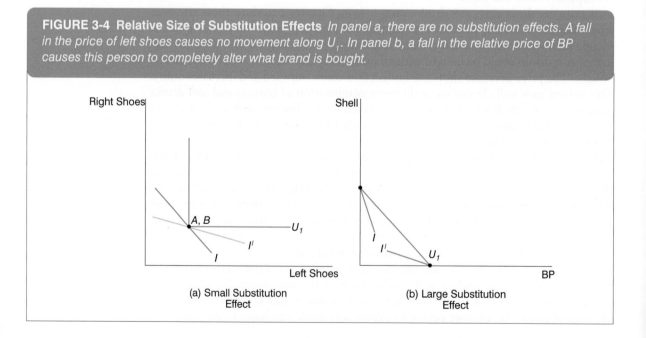

FIGURE 3-4 Relative Size of Substitution Effects *In panel a, there are no substitution effects. A fall in the price of left shoes causes no movement along U_1. In panel b, a fall in the relative price of BP causes this person to completely alter what brand is bought.*

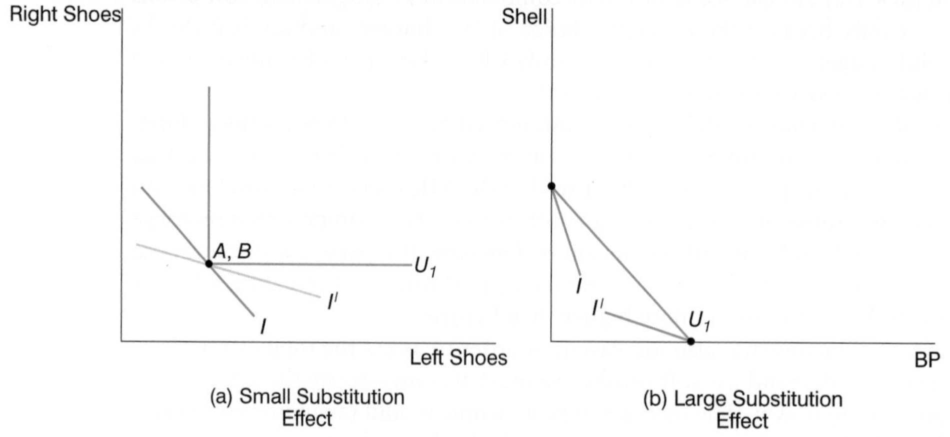

(point *B*). The substitution effect in this case is therefore huge, causing this person to completely alter the preferred petrol choice.

Of course, the examples illustrated in Figure 3-4 are extreme cases. But they do illustrate the wide range of possible substitution responses to a price change. The size of such responses in the real world will ultimately depend on whether the good being considered has many close substitutes or not.

MICROQUIZ 3.2

Use the discussion of substitution effects to explain

1. Why most petrol stations along a particular stretch of road charge about the same price.
2. Why the entry of large supermarket retailers like Tesco or Sainsbury's into a market causes prices at small local retailers to fall.

Substitution and Income Effects from an Increase in Price

We can use a similar analysis to see what happens if the price of good *X* increases. Now the budget line in Figure 3-5 shifts

FIGURE 3-5 Income and Substitution Effects of an Increase in Price *When the price of good X increases, the budget constraint shifts inward. The movement from the initial utility-maximizing point (A) to the new point (C) can again be analyzed as two separate effects. The substitution effect causes a movement to point B on the initial indifference curve (U_2). The price increase also creates a loss of purchasing power. This income effect causes a consequent movement to a lower indifference curve. The income and substitution effects together cause the quantity demanded of X to fall as a result of the increase in its price.*

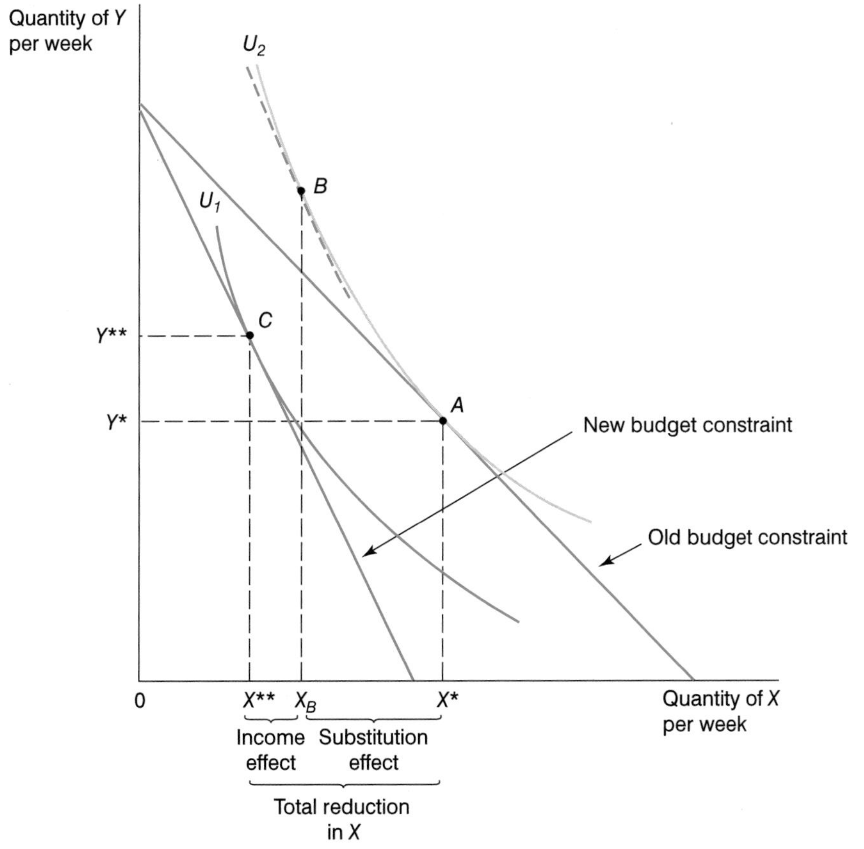

inward because of an increase in the price of X. The Y-intercept for the budget constraint again does not change since neither income nor P_Y has changed. The slope of the budget constraint is now steeper, however, because X costs more than it did before.

The movement from the initial point of utility-maximization (A) to the new point C is again caused by two forces. First, even if this person stayed on the initial indifference curve (U_2), he or she would substitute Y for X and move along U_2 to point B. At this point, the dashed line (with the same slope as the new budget constraint) is just tangent to the indifference curve U_2. The movement from A to B along U_2 is the substitution effect. However, because purchasing power is reduced by the increase in the price of X (the amount of income remains constant, but now X costs more), the person must move to a lower level of utility. This is the income effect that results from the higher price of X. In Figure 3-5, both the income and substitution effects work in the same direction and cause the quantity demanded of X to fall in response to an increase in its price.

Substitution and Income Effects for a Normal Good: Summary

Figure 3-3 and Figure 3-5 show that, for a normal good, substitution and income effects work in the same direction to yield the expected result: People choose to consume more of a good whose price has fallen and less of a good whose price has risen. As we illustrate later, this provides the rationale for drawing downward-sloping demand curves. If other things do not change, price and quantity move in opposite directions along such a curve. Recognizing that price changes lead to both substitution and income effects also helps to analyze whether such moves will be large or small. In general, price changes that induce big substitution effects or that have big effects on purchasing power (because the good is an important component of people's budgets) will have large effects on quantity demanded. Price changes that cause only modest substitutions among goods or that have trivial effects on purchasing power will have correspondingly small effects on quantity demanded. This kind of analysis also offers a number of insights about some commonly used economic statistics, as Application 3.2: *The Consumer Prices Index and Its Biases* illustrates.

Substitution and Income Effects for Inferior Goods

For the rare case of inferior goods, we cannot make such blanket statements about the effects of price changes. In this case, substitution and income effects work in opposite directions. The net effect of a price change on quantity demanded will be ambiguous. Here we show that ambiguity for the case of an increase in price, leaving it to you to explain the case of a fall in price.

Figure 3-6 shows the income and substitution effects from an increase in price when X is an inferior good. As the price of X rises, the substitution effect causes this person to choose less X. This substitution effect is represented by a movement from A to B in the initial indifference curve, U_2. This movement is exactly the same as in Figure 3-5 for a normal good. Because price has increased, however, this person now has a lower real income and must move to a lower indifference curve, U_1. The individual will choose combination C. At C, more X is chosen than at point B. This happens because good X is an inferior good: As real income falls, the quantity demanded of X increases rather than declines as it would for a normal good. In Figure 3-5, however, X^{**} is less than X^{*}; less X is ultimately demanded in response to the rise in its price. In our example here, the substitution effect is strong enough to outweigh the "perverse" income effect from the price change of this inferior good.

Giffen's Paradox

If the income effect of a price change for an inferior good is strong enough, the change in price and the resulting change in the quantity demanded could move in the same direction. Legend has it that the English economist Robert Giffen observed this paradox in nineteenth-century Ireland – when the price of potatoes rose, people consumed more of them. This peculiar result can be explained by looking at the size of the income effect of a change in the price of potatoes. Potatoes were not only inferior goods but also used up a large portion of the Irish people's income. An increase in the price of potatoes therefore reduced real income substantially. The Irish were forced to cut back on other food consumption in order to buy more potatoes. Even though this rendering of events is economically implausible, the possibility of an increase in the quantity demanded in response to the price increase of a good has come to be known as **Giffen's paradox.**[1]

Giffen's paradox A situation in which an increase in a good's price leads people to consume more of the good.

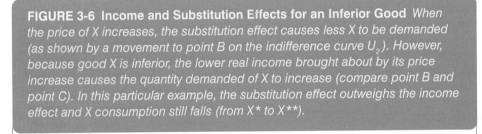

FIGURE 3-6 Income and Substitution Effects for an Inferior Good *When the price of X increases, the substitution effect causes less X to be demanded (as shown by a movement to point B on the indifference curve U_2). However, because good X is inferior, the lower real income brought about by its price increase causes the quantity demanded of X to increase (compare point B and point C). In this particular example, the substitution effect outweighs the income effect and X consumption still falls (from X* to X**).*

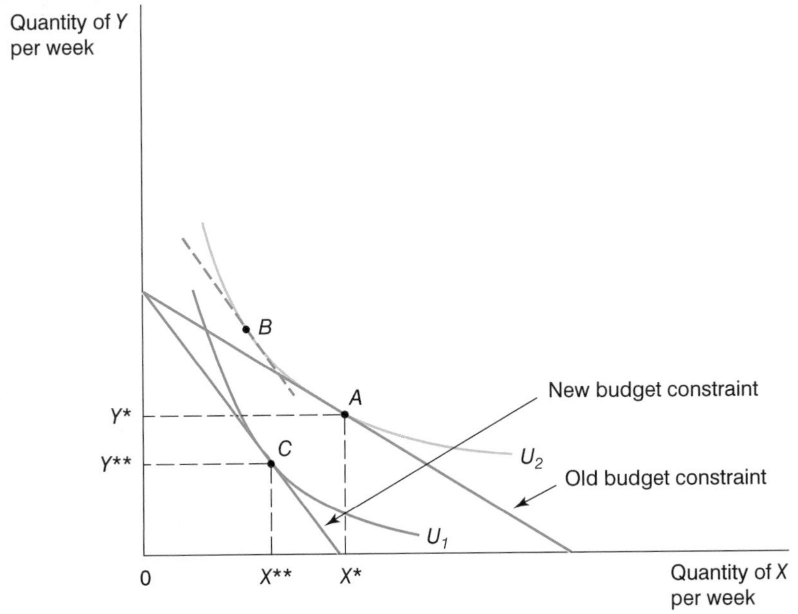

[1]A major problem with this explanation is that it disregards Marshall's observations that both supply and demand factors must be taken into account when analyzing price changes. If potato prices increased because of a decline in supply due to the potato blight, how could *more* potatoes possibly have been consumed? Also, since many Irish people were potato farmers, the potato price increase should have increased real income for them. For a detailed discussion of these and other fascinating bits of potato lore, see G. P. Dwyer and C. M. Lindsey, "Robert Giffen and the Irish Potato", *American Economic Review* (March 1984): 188–192.

APPLICATION 3.2 *The Consumer Price Index and Its Biases*

One of the principal measures of inflation in the United Kingdom is provided by the Consumer Prices Index (CPI), which is published monthly by the Office of National Statistics, and is comparable to the Harmonized Index of Consumer Prices (HCIP) used by the Member States of the European Union. To construct the CPI, the Office of National Statistics first defines a typical market basket of goods and services purchased by consumers in a base year (2005 is the year currently used). This is based on the cost of 650 everyday goods and services. Then data are collected every month (over 120 000 prices) about how much this market basket of commodities currently costs the consumer. The ratio of the current cost to the bundle's original cost (in 2005) is then published as the current value of the CPI. The rate of change in this index between two periods is reported to be the rate of inflation.

An Algebraic Example

This construction can be clarified with a simple two-goods example. Suppose that in 2005 the typical market basket contained X_{05} of good X and Y_{05} of good Y. The prices of these goods are given by

$$P^X_{05} \text{ and } P^Y_{05}$$

The cost of this bundle in the 2005 base year would be written as

$$\text{Cost in 2005} = B_{05} = P^X_{05}X_{05} + P^X_{05}Y_{05} \quad \{1\}$$

To compute the cost of the same bundle of goods in, say, 2007, we must first collect information on the goods' prices in that year

$$P^X_{07}, P^Y_{07}$$

and then compute

$$\text{Cost in 2007} = B_{07} = P^X_{07}X_{05} + P^Y_{07}Y_{05} \quad \{2\}$$

Notice that the quantities purchased in 2005 are being valued at 2007 prices. The CPI is defined as the ratio of the costs of these two market baskets multiplied by 100:

$$CPI_{07} = \frac{B_{07}}{B_{05}} \cdot 100 \quad \{3\}$$

The rate of inflation can be computed from this index. For example, if the same market basket of items that cost €100 in 2005 costs €110 in 2007, the value of the CPI would be 10 and we would say there had been a 100 per cent increase in prices over this two-year period. It might (probably incorrectly) be said that people would need a 10 per cent increase in nominal 2005 income to enjoy the same standard of living in 2007 that they had in 2007. Cost-of-living adjustments (COLAs) in Social Security benefits and in many job agreements are calculated in precisely this way. Unfortunately, this approach poses a number of problems.

Substitution Bias in the CPI

One conceptual problem with the preceding calculation is that it assumes that people who are faced with year 2007 prices will continue to demand the same basket of commodities that they consumed in 2005. This treatment makes no allowance for substitutions among commodities in response to changing prices. The calculation may overstate the decline in purchasing power that inflation has caused because it takes no account of how people will seek to get the most utility for their incomes when prices change.

In Figure 1, for example, a typical individual initially is consuming X_{05}, Y_{05}. Presumably this choice provides maximum utility (U_1), given his or her budget constraint in 2005 (which we call I). Suppose that by 2007 relative prices have changed in such a way that good Y becomes relatively more expensive. This would make the budget constraint flatter than it was in 2005. Using these new prices, the CPI calculates what X_{05}, Y_{05} would cost. This cost would be reflected by the budget constraint I', which is flatter than I (to reflect the changed prices) and passes through the 2005 consumption point.

As the figure makes clear, the erosion in purchasing power that has occurred is overstated. With I', this typical person could now reach a higher utility level than could have been attained in 2005. The CPI overstates the decline in purchasing power that has occurred.

A true measure of inflation would be provided by evaluating an income level, say, I'', which reflects the new prices but just permits the individual to remain on U_1. This would take account of the substitution in consumption that people might make in response to changing relative prices (they consume more X and less Y in moving along U_1). Unfortunately, adjusting the CPI to take such substitutions into account is a difficult task – primarily because the typical consumer's utility function cannot be measured accurately.

New Product and Quality Bias

The introduction of new or improved products produces a similar bias in the CPI. New products usually experience sharp declines in prices and rapidly growing rates of acceptance by consumers (consider mobile phones or DVDs, for example). If these goods are not included in the CPI market basket, a major source of welfare gain for consumers will have been omitted. Of course, the CPI market basket is updated every few years to permit new goods to be included. But that rate of revision is often insufficient for rapidly changing consumer markets. These changes can be very significant as markets are inundated with new products.

In March 2007, the UK Office of National Statistics announced significant changes in its annual update of the index. Brussels sprouts which had been in the survey since 1947 were replaced by broccoli, which was thought to be a better indicator of people's shopping lists. New items were added, but were mainly dominated by hi-tech gadgets, reflecting a big technological shift in Britain. As households switch to DVD recorders and recordable DVDs, video cassette players have finally been dropped, as well as VHS tapes, which since 1991 had been a feature of the basket. Ten years before, subscription rates to cable television and Internet servers were new additions. Today, mobile phone

FIGURE 1 Substitution Bias of the Consumer Price Index *In 2005 with income I the typical consumer chose X_{05}, Y_{05}. If this market basket is with different relative prices, the basket's cost will be given by I'. This cost exceeds what is actually required to permit the consumer to reach the original level of utility, I^*.*

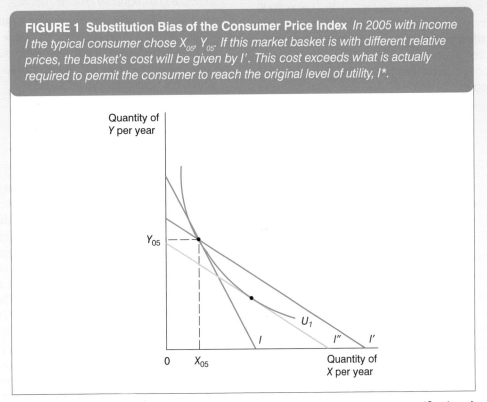

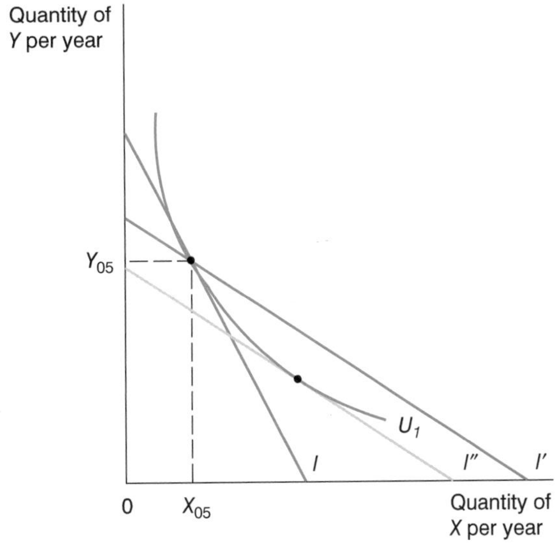

(Continued)

downloads, which include ring tones, games and music, have been included for the first time. The new "digital age" was also shown by the inclusion of digital photo processing, now readily available in many shops and supermarkets and driven by a rise in spending on digital cameras, which were first included in 2004. This replaced mail order film developing and the 35mm compact camera. Globalization also reflects changes, as goods become more available throughout the year, due to the rise of the internet, globalization and supermarket shopping. The prices of strawberries, for instance, are now collected every month.

Adjusting the CPI for the improving quality poses similar difficulties. In many cases the price of a specific consumer good will stay relatively constant from year to year, but more recent models of the product will be much better. For example, a good quality laptop computer has had a price in the €1500 to €2500 price range for many years. But this year's version is much more powerful than the models available, say, five years ago. In effect, the price of a fixed-quality laptop has fallen dramatically, but this will not be apparent when the CPI shoppers are told to purchase a "new laptop". In the UK in 2006, measuring the quality of a vacuum cleaner became more difficult when Dyson started to offer a five-year guarantee in contrast to LG's three years. Bosch, Numatic and Sebo offer two years, while Panasonic and Hoover just one.

Statisticians who compute the CPI have grappled with this problem for many years and have come up with a variety of ingenious solutions (including the use of "hedonic price" models – see Application 1A.1). Still, many economists believe that the CPI continues to miss many improvements in goods' quality.

Outlet Bias

Finally, the fact that the Office of National Statistics sends buyers to the same retail outlets each month may overstate inflation. Actual consumers tend to seek out temporary sales or other bargains. They shop where they can make their money go the farthest. In recent years this has meant shopping at giant discount stores and clubs such as Costco rather than at traditional outlets. The CPI as currently constructed does not take such price-reducing strategies into account.

To Think About

1. Would more frequent revisions of the market basket used for the CPI ameliorate the various biases outlined here? What problems would arise from using a frequently changing market basket?
2. How should quality improvements be reflected in the CPI? Is a 2008 television the same good as a 1976 television? If not, how will inclusion of "one television" in the CPI market basket affect whether it measures true inflation?

The Lump-Sum Principle

Economists have had a long-standing interest in studying taxes. We look at such analyses at many places in this book. Here we use our model of individual choice to show how taxes affect utility. Of course, it seems obvious (if we don't consider the government services that taxes provide) that paying taxes must reduce a person's utility because purchasing power is reduced. But, through the use of income and substitution effects, we can show that the size of this welfare loss will depend on how a tax is structured. Specifically, taxes that are imposed on general purchasing power will have smaller welfare costs than will taxes imposed on a narrow selection of commodities. This "lump-sum principle" lies at the heart of the study of the economics of optimal taxation.

A Graphical Approach

A graphical proof of the lump-sum principle is presented in Figure 3-7. Initially, this person has I euros to spend and chooses to consume X^* and Y^*. This combination yields utility level U_3. A tax on good X alone would raise its price, and the budget constraint would become steeper. With that budget constraint (shown as line I' in the figure), a person would be forced to accept a lower utility level (U_1) and would choose to consume the combination X_1, Y_1.

Suppose now that the government decided to institute a general income tax that raised the same revenue as this single-good excise tax. This would shift the individual's budget constraint to I''. The fact that I'' passes through X_1, Y_1 shows that both taxes raise the same amount of revenue.[2] However, with the income tax budget constraint I'', this person will choose to consume X_2, Y_2 (rather than X_1, Y_1). Even though this person pays the same tax bill in both instances, the combination chosen under the income tax yields a higher utility (U_2) than does the tax on a single commodity.

FIGURE 3-7 The Lump-Sum Principle *An excise tax on good X shifts the budget constraints to I'. The individual chooses X_1, Y_1 and receives utility of U_1. A lump-sum tax that collects the same amount shifts the budget constraint to I''. The individual chooses X_2, Y_2 and receives more utility (U_2).*

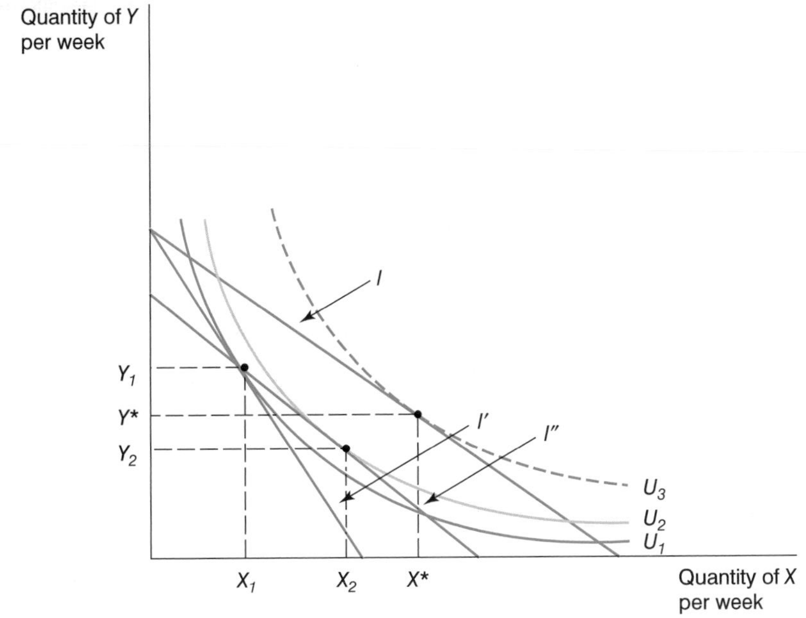

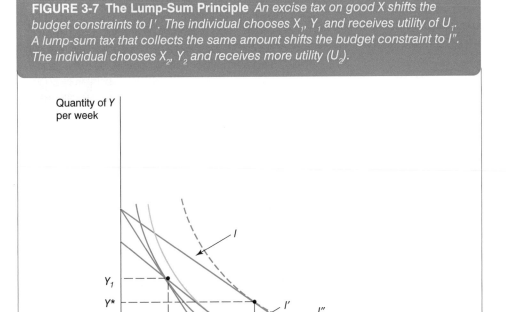

[2]Algebra shows why this is true. With the sales tax (where the per-unit tax rate is given by t) the individual's budget constraint is

$$I = I' = (P_X + t)\,X_1 + P_Y Y_1$$

Total tax revenues are given by

$$T = tX_1$$

With an income tax that collected the same revenue, after-tax income is

$$I'' = I - T = P_X X_1 + P_Y Y_1$$

which shows that I^* passes through the point X_1, Y_1 also. That is, the bundle X_1, Y_1 is affordable with either tax, but it provides less utility than another bundle (X_2, Y_2) affordable with the income tax.

APPLICATION 3.3 *Why Not Just Give the Poor Cash?*

Most countries provide a wide variety of programs to help poor people. In the United Kingdom and much of continental Europe, there are programs for cash assistance to low-income families, but much anti-poverty spending is done through a variety of "in-kind" programs such as free medical prescriptions, optical and dental services, subsidized travel, and low-income housing assistance. Such programs have expanded quite rapidly during the past 30 years, whereas cash programs have not.

Inefficiency of In-Kind Programs

The lump-sum principle suggests that these trends may be unfortunate because the in-kind programs do not generate as much welfare for poor people as would the spending of the same funds on a cash program. The argument is illustrated in Figure 1. The typical low-income person's budget constraint is given by the line I prior to any assistance. This yields a utility of U_1. An anti-poverty program that provided, say, good X at a highly subsidized price would shift this budget constraint to I' and raise this person's utility to U_2. If the government were instead to spend the same funds on a pure income grant to this person,[1] his or her budget constraint would be I'', and this would permit a higher utility to be reached (U_3). Hence, the in-kind program is not cost-effective in terms of raising the utility of this low-income person.

There is empirical evidence supporting this conclusion. Careful studies of spending patterns of poor people suggest that a euro spent on welfare subsidy programs is "worth" only about €0.90 to the recipients. A euro in medical or dental subsidies may be worth only about €0.70, and housing assistance may be worth less than €0.60. Spending on these kinds of in-kind programs therefore may not be an especially effective way of raising the utility of poor people.

Paternalism and Donor Preferences

Why have most countries favored in-kind programs over cash assistance? Undoubtedly, some of this

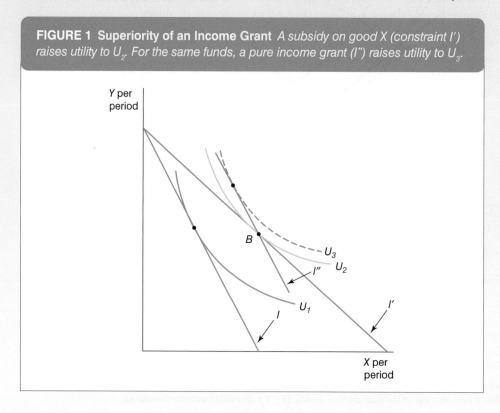

FIGURE 1 Superiority of an Income Grant *A subsidy on good X (constraint I') raises utility to U_2. For the same funds, a pure income grant (I") raises utility to U_3.*

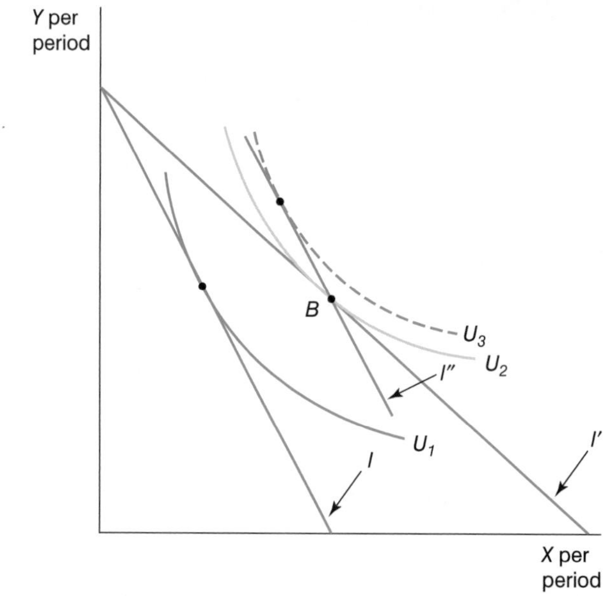

focus stems from paternalism – policymakers in the government may feel that they have a better idea of how poor people should spend their incomes than do poor people themselves. In Figure 1, for example, X purchases are indeed greater under the in-kind program than under the cash grant, though utility is lower. A related possibility is that "donors" (usually taxpayers) have strong preferences for how aid to poor people should be provided. Donors may care more about providing housing or dental care to poor people than about increasing their welfare overall. Political support for (seemingly less effective) cash payments is not generally popular.

To Think About

1 How should the welfare of children be factored into Figure 1 (which may only reflect the decision-making of the head-of-household)?

2 Some people fear that cash payments may affect the work incentives of poor people. Would similar concerns apply to in-kind programs?

[1]Budget constraints I' and I'' represent the same government spending because both permit this person to consume point *B*.

An intuitive explanation of this result is that a single-commodity tax affects people's well-being in two ways: It reduces general purchasing power (an income effect), and it directs consumption away from the taxed commodity (a substitution effect). An income tax incorporates only the first effect, and, with equal tax revenues raised, individuals are better off under it than under a tax that also distorts consumption choices.

Generalizations

More generally, the demonstration of the lump-sum principle in Figure 3-7 suggests that the utility loss associated with the need to collect a certain amount of tax revenue can be kept to a minimum by taxing goods for which substitution effects are small. By doing so, taxes will have relatively little welfare effect beyond their direct effect on purchasing power. On the other hand, taxes on goods for which there are many substitutes will cause people to alter their consumption plans in major ways. This additional distortionary effect raises the overall utility cost of such taxes to consumers. In Application 3.3: *Why Not Just Give the Poor Cash*? we look at a few implications of these observations for welfare policy.

Changes in The Price of Another Good

An examination of our work so far would reveal that a change in the price of X will also affect the quantity demanded of the other good (Y). In Figure 3-3, for example, a decrease in the price of X causes not only the quantity demanded of X to increase but the quantity demanded of Y to increase as well. We can explain this result by looking at the substitution and income effects on the demand for Y associated with the decrease in the price of X.

First, as Figure 3-3 shows, the substitution effect of the lower X price caused less Y to be demanded. In moving along the indifference curve U_1 from *A* to *B*, X is substituted for Y because the lower ratio of P_X/P_Y required an adjustment in the MRS. In this figure, the income effect of the decline in the price of good X is strong enough to reverse this result. Because Y is a normal good and real income has increased, more Y is demanded: The individual moves from *B* to *C*. Here Y^{**} exceeds Y^{*}, and the total effect of the price change is to increase the demand for Y.

A slightly different set of indifference curves (that is, different preferences) could have shown different results. Figure 3-8 shows a relatively flat set of indifference curves where the substitution effect from a decline in the price of X is very large. In moving from A to B, a large amount of X is substituted for Y. The income effect on Y is not strong enough to reverse this large substitution effect. In this case, the quantity of Y finally chosen (Y^{**}) is smaller than the original amount. The effect of a decline in the price of one good on the quantity demanded of some other good is ambiguous; it all depends on what the person's preferences, as reflected by his or her indifference curve map, look like. We have to examine carefully income and substitution effects that (at least in the case of only two goods) work in opposite directions.

Substitutes and Complements

Economists use the terms *substitutes* and *complements* to describe the way people look at the relationships between goods. Complements are goods that go together in the sense that people will increase their use of both goods simultaneously. Examples of complements might be coffee and cream, fish and chips, peanut butter and jam, or petrol and cars. Substitutes, on the other hand, are goods that can replace one another. Tea and coffee, Hondas and Toyotas, or owned versus rented housing are some goods that are substitutes for each other.

Whether two goods are substitutes or complements of each other is primarily a question of the shape of people's indifference curves. The market behavior of individuals in their purchases of goods can help economists to discover these relationships. Two goods

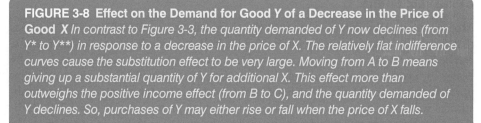

FIGURE 3-8 Effect on the Demand for Good Y of a Decrease in the Price of Good X *In contrast to Figure 3-3, the quantity demanded of Y now declines (from Y* to Y**) in response to a decrease in the price of X. The relatively flat indifference curves cause the substitution effect to be very large. Moving from A to B means giving up a substantial quantity of Y for additional X. This effect more than outweighs the positive income effect (from B to C), and the quantity demanded of Y declines. So, purchases of Y may either rise or fall when the price of X falls.*

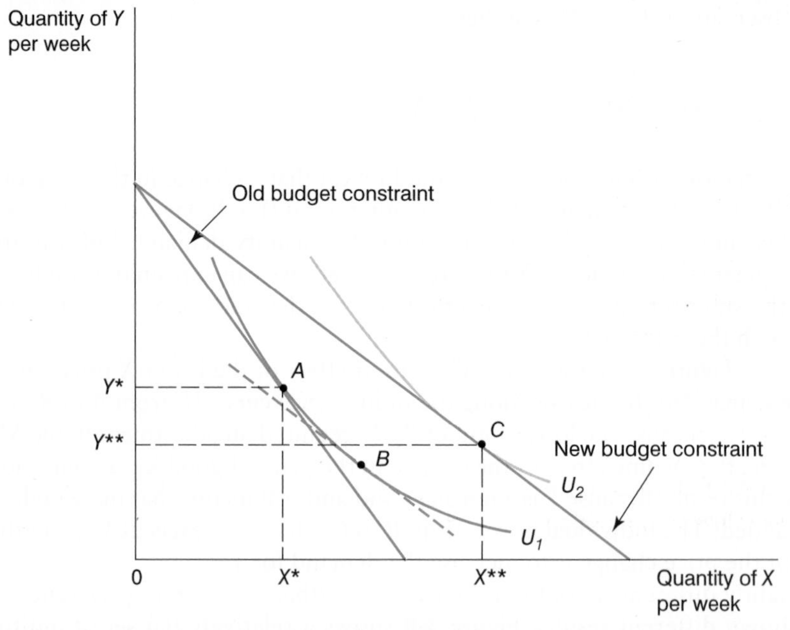

APPLICATION 3.4 *SUVs and Petrol Prices*

Motor vehicle registrations in the United States showed a remarkable change during the 1990s. In 1990, fewer than 30 per cent of the vehicles on US roads were "trucks", whereas by 2000 that figure had increased to over 40 per cent. Virtually all of the net new vehicle registrations during the 1990s were "trucks". Of course, the huge gain in truck registrations does not mean that most people in the United States are driving 18-wheelers. Rather, the issue is one of definition. The US Department of Transportation regards a wide variety of car-like vehicles as "trucks" for purposes of data collection. These include vans, minivans, mobile homes, and (most important) sport-utility vehicles (SUVs). The data reflect a huge increase in the popularity of these car-like vehicles during the 1990s. People in the United States have proven more than willing to make substitutions in the types of vehicles they buy. Of course, the factors propelling SUV ownership can also turn around, and that appears to have happened after 2000.

Earlier Effects of Petrol Prices

One of the most important reasons for the trend toward SUVs in the 1990s was a sharp decline in real petrol prices. In the late 1980s, petrol sold for about \$1.50 per gallon, with that price falling to about \$1.10 by 1999. In inflation-adjusted terms, the real price of petrol declined by over 40 per cent. This had the effect of significantly reducing the relative costs of operating truck-like vehicles. Suppose that the typical SUV averages about 15 miles per gallon of petrol and is driven 15 000 miles per year. The savings from lower fuel prices on the 1000 gallons of petrol used during the year would amount to perhaps \$800. This might be as much as 15 to 20 per cent of the overall operating cost of an SUV during the year. For a similarly priced but higher-mileage car, the percentage reduction might only be in the 5 to 10 per cent range. Hence, the relative price (remember, relative prices are what matter in consumers' choices) of operating SUV-size vehicles fell rather significantly during this ten-year period.

The Unintended Effects of Regulations

Part of the increased buying of SUVs during the 1990s can also be explained as unintended side effects of various governmental regulations that were (perhaps paradoxically) intended to reduce petrol usage. One set of regulations was the Corporate Average Fuel Economy (CAFE) standards that required carmakers to achieve certain average miles-per-gallon goals on their annual car sales. SUVs (which were defined as "trucks") were generally exempt from the CAFE standards, so firms could freely market all types of SUVs, but had to be more careful about the numbers of large cars they sold. A 1991 tax on "gas guzzlers" put large automobiles at a further disadvantage relative to SUVs, by imposing taxes of as much as \$5000 on cars with especially low mileage ratings.

The End of the Large SUV Era

Several factors suggest that US consumers' infatuation with SUVs is coming to an end. Most importantly, after 2000, petrol prices moved sharply upward, reaching over \$3.00 in September 2005. As might have been expected, sales of large SUVs slumped badly in 2004–05. This had negative consequences for many carmakers because SUVs were among their most profitable vehicles. As a further sign of reactions to petrol prices, several carmakers introduced smaller, more fuel-efficient SUVs that are built on car bodies (the Honda CRV, for example, is built on the Civic frame). These are much lighter and more fuel-efficient than large SUVs (which are built mainly on truck bodies). For many buyers, these may provide a better match to the characteristics they are seeking at much lower operating costs. Finally, in 2005 the Federal government moved to fill the "SUV loophole" by starting to include these vehicles under the CAFE standards. To economists the necessity of this further regulation is not obvious – presumably consumers will demand more fuel-efficient SUVs in response to higher petrol prices and competition among carmakers will ensure that such vehicles will

(Continued)

be produced. It is doubtful that government prodding will be more effective than such market forces.

To Think About

1 In real, inflation-adjusted terms petrol prices in 2005 were still lower than they were in 1980. Why is it important to make such an adjustment for inflation when comparing consumption behavior over time?

2 Both pedestrians and drivers of smaller cars are more likely to be injured when they are struck by an SUV than when struck by a standard-sized car. Is this an additional area where the government should seek to limit consumer choices by prescribing upper size limits for cars? Or should people be able to buy as much "safety" as they like?

Complements Two goods such that when the price of one increases, the quantity demanded of the other falls.

Substitutes Two goods such that if the price of one increases, the quantity demanded of the other rises.

are **complements** if an increase in the price of one causes a decrease in the quantity consumed of the other. For example, an increase in the price of coffee might cause not only the quantity demanded of coffee to decline but also the demand for cream to decrease because of the complementary relationship between cream and coffee. Similarly, coffee and tea are **substitutes** because an increase in the price of coffee might cause the quantity demanded of tea to increase as tea replaces coffee in use.

How the demand for one good relates to the price increase of another good is determined by both income and substitution effects. It is only the combined gross result of these two effects that we can observe. Including both income and substitution effects of price changes in our definitions of substitutes and complements can sometimes lead to problems. For example, it is theoretically possible for X to be a complement for Y and at the same time for Y to be a substitute for X. This perplexing state of affairs has led some economists to favor a definition of substitutes and complements that looks only at the direction of substitution effects.[3] We do not make that distinction in this book. In Application 3.4: *SUVs and Petrol Prices*, we take a brief look at some of the complex relationships between petrol prices and what people drive.

MICROQUIZ 3.3

Changes in the price of another good create both income and substitution effects in a person's demand for, say, coffee. Describe those effects in the following cases and state whether they work in the same direction or in opposite directions in their total impact on coffee purchases.

1 A decrease in the price of tea.

2 A decrease in the price of cream.

Construction of Individual Demand Curves

We have now completed our discussion of how the individual's demand for good X is affected by various changes in economic circumstances. We started by writing the demand function for good X as

$$\text{Quantity of } X \text{ demanded} = d_X\,(P_X, P_Y, I; \text{preferences})$$

Then we examined how changes in each of the economic factors P_X, P_Y, and I might affect an individual's decision to purchase good X. The principle purpose of this examination has been to permit us to derive individual demand curves and to be precise

[3]For a slightly more extended treatment for this subject, see Walter Nicholson, *Microeconomic Theory: Basic Principles and Extensions*, 9th ed. (Mason, OH: South-Western/Thomson Learning, 2005), 164–167. For a complete treatment, see J. R. Hicks, *Value and Capital* (London: Cambridge University Press, 1939), Chapter 3 and the mathematical appendix.

about those factors that might cause a demand curve to change its position. This section shows how a demand curve can be constructed. The next section looks at why this curve might shift.

An **individual demand curve** shows the *ceteris paribus* relationship between the quantity demanded of a good (say, X) and its price (P_X). Not only are preferences held constant under the *ceteris paribus* assumption (as they have been throughout our discussion in this chapter), but the other factors in the demand function (that is, the price of good Y and income) are also held constant. In demand curves, we are limiting our study to only the relationship between the quantity of a good chosen and changes in its price.

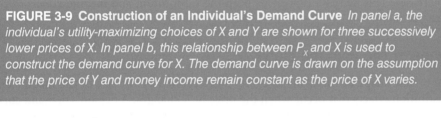

Individual demand curve A graphic representation of the relationship between the price of a good and the quantity of it demanded by a person, holding all other factors constant.

Figure 3-9 shows how to construct a person's demand curve for good X. In panel (a), a person's indifference curve map is drawn using three different budget constraints in

FIGURE 3-9 Construction of an Individual's Demand Curve *In panel a, the individual's utility-maximizing choices of X and Y are shown for three successively lower prices of X. In panel b, this relationship between P_X and X is used to construct the demand curve for X. The demand curve is drawn on the assumption that the price of Y and money income remain constant as the price of X varies.*

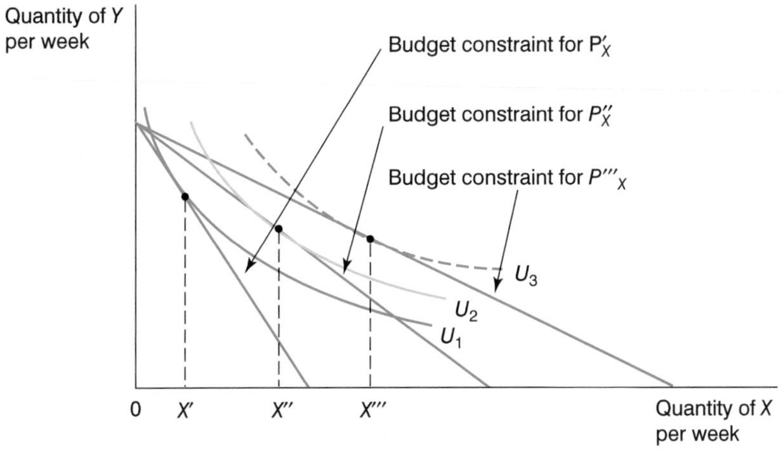

(a) Individual's indifference curve map

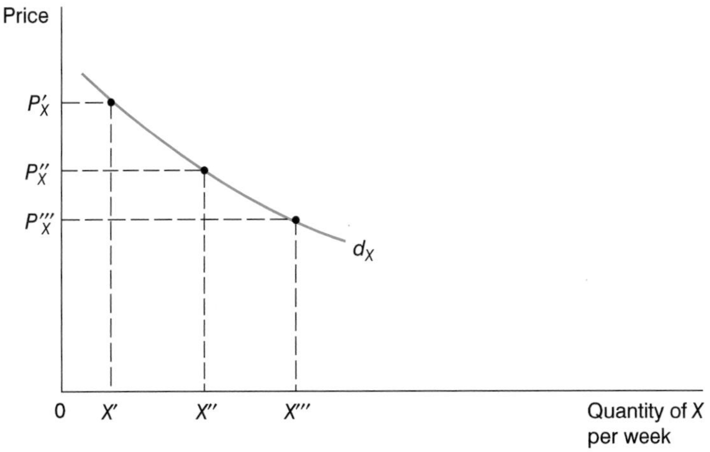

(b) Demand curve

which the price of X decreases. These decreasing prices are P'_X, P''_X, and P'''_X. The other economic factors that affect the position of the budget constraint (the price of good Y and income) do not change. In graphic terms, all three constraints have the same Y-intercept. The successively lower prices of X rotate this constraint outward. Given the three separate budget constraints, this person's utility-maximizing choices of X are given by X', X'', and X'''. These three choices show that the quantity demanded of X increases as the price of X falls on the presumption that substitution and income effects operate in the same direction.

The information in panel (a) in Figure 3-9 can be used to construct the demand curve shown in panel (b). The price of X is shown on the vertical axis, and the quantity chosen continues to be shown on the horizontal axis. The demand curve (d_X) is downward sloping, showing that when the price of X falls, the quantity demanded of X increases. This increase represents both the substitution and income effects of the price decline.

Shape of the Demand Curve

The precise shape of the demand curve is determined by the size of the income and substitution effects that occur when the price of X changes. A person's demand curve may be either rather flat or quite steeply sloped, depending on the nature of his or her indifference curve map. If X has many close substitutes, the indifference curves will be nearly straight lines (such as those shown in panel (b) of Figure 3-4), and the substitution effect from a price change will be very large. The quantity of X chosen may fall substantially in response to a rise in its price; consequently, the demand curve will be relatively flat. For example, consider a person's demand for one particular brand of cereal (say, the famous Brand X). Because any one brand has many close substitutes, the demand curve for Brand X will be relatively flat. A rise in the price of Brand X will cause people to shift easily to other kinds of cereal, and the quantity demanded of Brand X will be reduced significantly.

On the other hand, a person's demand curve for some goods may be steeply sloped. That is, price changes will not affect consumption very much. This might be the case if the good has no close substitutes. For example, consider a person's demand for water. Because water satisfies many unique needs, it is unlikely that it would have any substitutes when the price of water rose, and the substitution effect would be very small. However, since water does not use up a large portion of a person's total income, the income effect of the increase in the price of water would also not be large. The quantity demanded of water probably would not respond greatly to changes in its price; that is, the demand curve would be nearly vertical.

As a third possibility, consider the case of food. Because food as a whole has no substitutes (although individual food items obviously do), an increase in the price of food will not induce important substitution effects. In this sense, food is similar to our water example. However, food is a major item in a person's total expenditures, and an increase in its price will have a significant effect on purchasing power. It is possible, therefore, that the quantity demanded of food may be reduced substantially in response to a rise in food prices because of this income effect. The demand curve for food might be flatter (that is, quantity demanded reacts more to price) than we might expect if we thought of food only as a "necessity" with few, if any, substitutes.[4]

[4]For this and other reasons, sometimes it is convenient to talk about demand curves that reflect only substitution effects. We do not study such "compensated" demand curves in this book, however.

Shifts in an Individual's Demand Curve

An individual's demand curve summarizes the relationship between the price of X and the quantity demanded of X when all the other things that might affect demand are held constant. The income and substitution effects of changes in that price cause the person to move along his or her demand curve. If one of the factors (the price of Y, income, or preferences) that we have so far been holding constant were to change, the entire curve would shift to a new position. The demand curve remains fixed only while the *ceteris paribus* assumption is in effect. Figure 3-10 shows the kinds of shifts that might take place. In panel (a), the effect on good X of an increase in income is shown. Assuming that good X is a normal good, an increase in income causes more X to be demanded at each price. At P_1, for example, the quantity of X demanded rises from X_1 to X_2. This is the kind of effect we described early in this chapter (Figure 3-1). When income increases, people buy more X even if its price has not changed, and the demand curve shifts outward. Panels (b) and (c) in Figure 3-9 record two possible effects that an increase in the price of Y might have on the demand curve for good X. In panel (b), X and Y are assumed to be substitutes – for example, coffee (X) and tea (Y). An increase in the price of tea causes the individual to substitute coffee for tea. More coffee (that is, good X) is demanded at each price than was previously the case. At P_1, for example, the quantity of coffee demanded increases from X_1 to X_2.

On the other hand, suppose X and Y are complements – for example, coffee (X) and cream (Y). An increase in the price of cream causes the demand curve for coffee to shift inward. Because coffee and cream go together, less coffee (that is, good X) will

MICROQUIZ 3.4

The following statements were made by two reporters describing the same event. Which reporter (if either) gets the distinction between shifting a demand curve and moving along it correct?

Reporter 1. The freezing weather in Kent will raise the price of apples, and people will reduce their demand for apples. Because of this reduced demand, producers will now get lower prices for their apples than they might have and these lower prices will help restore apple purchases to their original level.

Reporter 2. The freezing weather in Kent raises apple prices and reduces the demand for apples. Apple growers should therefore accustom themselves to lower sales even when the weather returns to normal.

FIGURE 3-10 Shifts in an Individual's Demand Curve *In panel (a), the demand curve shifts outward because the individual's income has increased. More X is now demanded at each price. In panel (b), the demand curve shifts outward because the price of Y has increased, and X and Y are substitutes for the individual. In panel (c), the demand curve shifts inward because of the increase in the price Y; that is, X and Y are complements.*

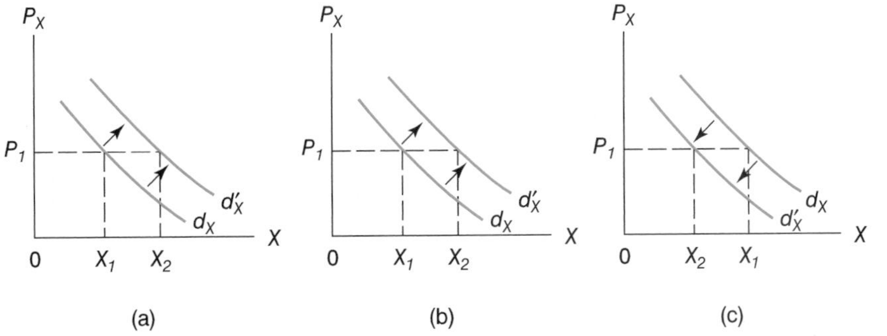

APPLICATION 3.5 *Fads, Seasons, and Health Scares*

The notion that changes in "preferences" can influence the demand for a product is a very broad concept that can include a wide variety of cultural and psychological influences. Let's look at a few.

Fads

Products such as Hula Hoops, Tamagotchis, Super Nintendo, and Rubik's Cube all experienced extremely rapid growth in demand when they were initially introduced, followed by an equally rapid loss of consumer interest. The widespread use of a product among consumers actually generates additional demand until a saturation point is reached. Then, demand falls precipitously. Such temporary bursts of demand (sometimes termed "bandwagon effects") arise because of the interdependence among people's preferences – everyone wants to be part of the latest craze. This recurring pattern in a fad's purchases lends some predictability to fads once they start. But predicting which products will catch on is a mystery.

Seasonality

Season-sensitive goods are the polar opposites of fad products when it comes to predictability. Everyone knows that the demand for wedding cakes increases in June, that Easter eggs are mostly consumed in March or April, and that Christmas trees are bought in December. Seasonality also affects the demand for less-familiar items. A famous early study of New England fishing, for example, found that the demand for scrod (New England speak for small cod) regularly increased by about 13 per cent during Lent because of the dietary restrictions imposed during this period by the Catholic Church upon its members.[1] All these seasonal patterns show that preferences are formed through a variety of long-term historical and cultural influences. This is one reason why economists tend to treat them as being stable over short periods.

Health Scares

Some of the more rapid shifts in demand in recent years have been associated with changing perceptions by consumers about the health risks associated with various products. Concern about the risks of smoking, for example, has resulted in a long-term reduction in the number of smokers in the United Kingdom since early research of a link with lung cancer by Professor (now Sir) Richard Doll and Austin Bradford Hill in 1950. Concern about cholesterol has led to similar long-term declines in individuals' demands for beef and dairy products.

Health concerns have also had dramatic effects on demand in both the short- and long-term. A striking example concerns the fall in demand for British beef following the discovery of bovine spongiform encephalopathy (BSE) in some cattle. By 1993 more than 1000 cases per week were being reported, involving more than 50 per cent of the dairy herds in the UK. Domestic demand for beef was down by 37 per cent from 1987 to 1995. In addition, the European Commission imposed a ten-year ban from 1996 to 2006 on British beef exports to the EU. Many other countries followed, and what were once lucrative export markets, with strong demand, dried up for British producers, many of whom were financially ruined. Many restaurants, worried about their dependence on British beef and the subsequent consumer reaction, switched suppliers. In March 1996 Macdonald's announced that it was suspending the use of British beef in its restaurants because of consumer expectations. They had been the biggest purchaser in Britain, accounting for £50 m per annum, or nearly 10 per cent of British beef production.

In June 2006, Cadburys removed millions of bars of chocolate from shelves after a salmonella scare. Within a month, supermarkets reported a slump in the sales of Cadburys' chocolate products of over 25 per cent. Similarly, in February 2007, a case of bird flu at the turkey producer Bernard Mathews saw UK sales of turkey fall by over 30 per cent in the following week. YouGov's Brand Index, which monitors consumer attitudes to 1100 brands every day, revealed that Bernard Matthews had fallen to the second least liked brand in Britain. Only McDonald's had a worse public image problem.

Many times the demand for food items may react strongly to the release of "scientific" studies. European demand for American beef dropped sharply in 1997 following some suggestions (subsequently disproved) that growth hormones fed to cattle are unsafe. Studies purporting to show health benefits from eating tomatoes had an important effect on demand in 1998, though many were skeptical of the study's methods. Similar purported health benefits have had the effect of increasing the demand for oat-based products, broccoli, and (even) red wine.

To Think About

1. Does the unpredictability of demand affect the profits firms might earn on a product? Why might turkeys or Christmas trees yield relatively small profits, whereas fad products often are quite profitable?
2. Do you think people often overreact to "scientific" studies of the health effects of consuming certain foods? How should a consumer choose among food items when the science is unclear?

[1]F. W. Bell, "The Pope and the Price of Fish", *American Economic Review* (December 1968): 346–350.

now be demanded at each price. This shift in the demand curve is shown in panel (c) – at P_1, the quantity of coffee demanded falls from X_1 to X_2.

Changes in preferences might also cause the demand curve to shift. For example, a sudden warm spell would shift the entire demand curve for cold drinks outward. More drinks would be demanded at each price because now each person's desire for them has increased. Similarly, increased environmental consciousness during the 1980s and 1990s vastly increased the demand for such items as recycling containers and organically grown food. Application 3.5: *Fads, Seasons, and Health Scares* explores a few other reasons why demand curves might shift.

Be Careful in Using Terminology

It is important to be careful in making the distinction between the shift in a demand curve and movement along a stationary demand curve. Changes in the price of X lead to movements along the demand curve for good X. Changes in other economic factors (such as a change in income, a change in another good's price, or a change in preferences) cause the entire demand curve for X to shift. If we wished to see how a change in the price of steak would affect a person's steak purchases, we would use a single demand curve and study movements along it. On the other hand, if we wanted to know how a change in income would affect the quantity of steak purchased, we would study the shift in the position of the entire demand curve.

To reiterate, economists must speak carefully. The movement downward along a stationary demand curve in response to a fall in price is called an **increase in quantity demanded**. A shift outward in the entire curve is an **increase in demand**. A rise in the price of a good causes a **decrease in quantity demanded** (a move along the demand curve), whereas a change in some other factor may cause a **decrease in demand** (a shift of the entire curve to the left). It is important to be precise in using those terms; they are not interchangeable.

Increase or decrease in quantity demanded The increase or decrease in quantity demanded caused by a change in the good's price. Graphically represented by the movement along a demand curve.

Increase or decrease in demand The change in demand for a good caused by changes in the price of another good, in income, or in preferences. Graphically represented by a shift of the entire demand curve.

Consumer Surplus

Demand curves provide a considerable amount of information about the willingness of people to make voluntary transactions. Because demand curves are in principle measurable, they are much more useful for studying economic behavior in the real world than are utility functions. One important application uses demand curves to study the consequences of price changes for people's overall welfare. This technique relies on the concept of *consumer surplus* – a concept we examine in this section. The tools developed here are widely used by economists to study the effects of public policies on the welfare of citizens.

Demand Curves and Consumer Surplus

In order to understand the consumer surplus idea, we begin by thinking about an individual's demand curve for a good in a slightly different way. Specifically, each point on the demand curve can be regarded as showing what a person would be willing to pay for *one more unit* of the good. Demand curves slope downward because this "marginal willingness to pay" declines as a person consumes more of a given good. On the demand curve for T-shirts in Figure 3-11, for example, this person chooses to consume ten T-shirts when the price is €11. In other words, this person is willing to pay €11 for the tenth T-shirt he or she buys. With a price of €9, on the other hand, this person chooses 15 T-shirts, so, implicitly, he or she values the 15th shirt at only €9. Viewed from this perspective then, a person's demand curve tells us quite a bit about his or her willingness to pay for different quantities of a good.

Because a good is usually sold at a single market price, people choose to buy additional units of the good up to the point at which their marginal valuation is equal to that price. In Figure 3-11, for example, if T-shirts sell for €7, this person will buy 20 T-shirts because the 20th T-shirt is worth precisely €7. He or she will not buy the 21st T-shirt because it is worth less than €7 (once this person already has 20 T-shirts). Because this person would be willing to pay more than €7 for the tenth or the 15th T-shirt, it is clear that this person gets a "surplus" on those shirts because he or she is actually paying less than the maximal amount that would willingly be paid. Hence, we have a formal

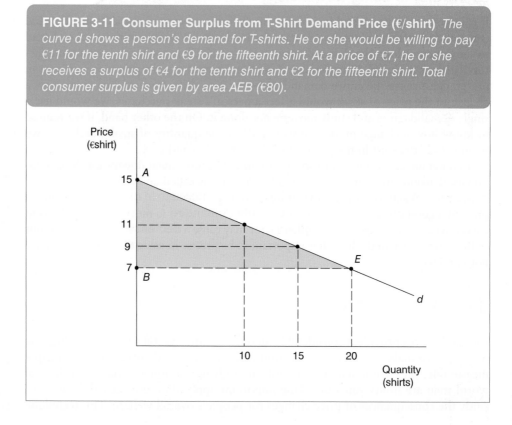

FIGURE 3-11 Consumer Surplus from T-Shirt Demand Price (€/shirt) *The curve d shows a person's demand for T-shirts. He or she would be willing to pay €11 for the tenth shirt and €9 for the fifteenth shirt. At a price of €7, he or she receives a surplus of €4 for the tenth shirt and €2 for the fifteenth shirt. Total consumer surplus is given by area AEB (€80).*

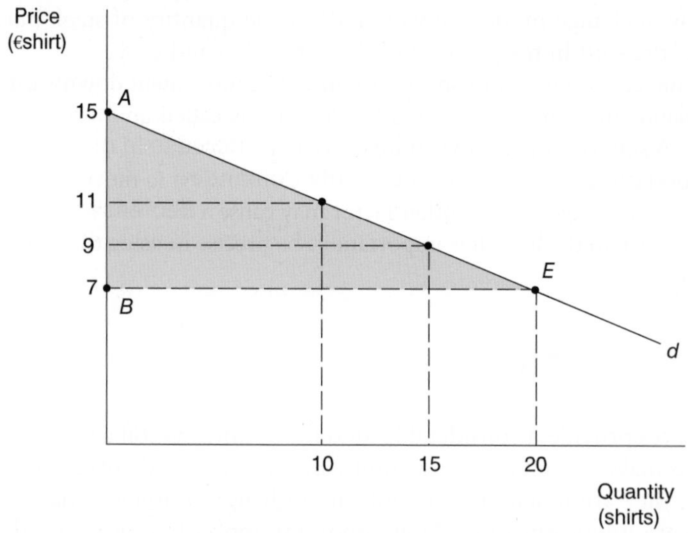

definition of **consumer surplus** as the difference between the maximal amounts a person would pay for a good and what he or she actually pays. In graphical terms, consumer surplus is given by the area below the demand curve and above the market price. The concept is measured in monetary values (dollars, euros, yen, etc.).

Consumer surplus The extra value individuals receive from consuming a good over what they pay for it. What people would be willing to pay for the right to consume a good at its current price.

Because the demand curve in Figure 3-11 is a straight line, the computation of consumer surplus is especially simple. It is just the area of triangle *AEB*. When the price of T-shirts is €7, the size of this area is 0.5 · 20 · (€15 − €7) = €80. When this person buys 20 T-shirts at €7, he or she actually spends €140 but also receives a consumer surplus of €80. If we were to value each T-shirt at the maximal amount this person would pay for that shirt, we would conclude that the total value of the 20 T-shirts he or she consumes is €220, but they are bought for only €140.

A rise in price would reduce this person's consumer surplus from T-shirt purchases. At a price of €11, for example, he or she buys ten T-shirts and consumer surplus would be computed as 0.5 · 10 · (€15 − €11) = €20. Hence, €60 of consumer surplus has been lost because of the rise in the price of T-shirts from €7 to €11. Some of this loss in consumer surplus went to shirt-makers because this person must pay €40 more for the ten T-shirts he or she does buy than was the case when the price was €7. The other €20 in consumer surplus just disappears. In later chapters, we see how computations of this type can be used to judge the consequences of a wide variety of economic situations in which prices change.

Consumer Surplus and Utility

The concept of consumer surplus can be tied directly to the theory of utility-maximization we have been studying. Specifically, consumer surplus provides a way of putting a monetary value on the effects that changes in the marketplace have on people's utility. Consumer surplus is not really a new concept but just an alternative way of getting at the utility concepts with which we started the study of demand.

Figure 3-12 illustrates the connection between consumer surplus and utility. The figure shows a person's choices between a particular good (here again we use the T-shirt example) and "all other" goods he or she might buy. The budget constraint shows that with a €7 price and a budget constraint given by line *I*, this person would choose to consume 20 T-shirts along with €500 worth of other items. Including the €140 spent on T-shirts, total spending on all items would be €640. This consumption plan yields a utility level of U_1 to this person.

Now consider a situation in which T-shirts were not available – perhaps they are banned by a paternalistic government that objects to slogans written on the shirts. In this situation, this person requires some compensation if he or she is to continue to remain on the U_1 indifference curve. Specifically, an extra income given by distance *AB* would just permit this person to reach U_1 when there are no T-shirts available. It is possible to show that this euro value is approximately equal to the consumer surplus figure computed in the previous section – that is, distance *AB* is approximately €80. Hence, consumer surplus can also be interpreted as measuring the amount one would have to compensate a person for withdrawing a product from the marketplace.

A somewhat different way to measure consumer surplus would be to ask how much income this person would be willing to pay for the right to consume T-shirts at €7 each. This amount would be given by distance *BC* in Figure 3-12. With a budget constraint given by I', this person can achieve that same utility level (U_0) that he or she could

MICROQUIZ 3.5

Throughout this book, we see that consumer surplus areas are often triangular.

1. Explain why this area is measured in monetary values. (Hint: What are the units of the height and width of the consumer surplus triangle?)
2. Suppose that the price of a product rose by 10 per cent. Would you expect the size of the consumer surplus triangle to fall by more or less than 10 per cent?

APPLICATION 3.6 *Valuing New Goods*

Estimating how consumers value a new good poses problems both for the firms that might wish to sell the good and for government agencies that have to assess the impact of such goods on overall welfare. One way that has been used for this purpose is illustrated in Figure 1. In the figure, the typical person's demand curve for a newly introduced good is given by *d*. After introduction of the product, this typical person consumes X^* at a price of P^*_X. This is the only point observed on the demand curve for this product because the good did not exist previously. However, some authors have proposed using the information in Figure 1 to draw a tangent to *d* at this initial point and thereby calculate the "virtual price" at which demand for this good would have been zero (P^{**}_X)[1]. This price is then taken to be the price before the new good was marketed. The welfare gain from introducing the new good is given by the consumer surplus triangle $P^{**}_X E P^*_X$. This is an approximation to the gain that consumers experience by being able to consume the new good at its current market price relative to a situation where the good did not exist. In some cases, the size of this gain can be quite large.

The Value of Mobile Phones

Jerry Hausman used this approach in an influential series of papers to estimate the value of mobile phones to consumers. He found very large gains indeed, amounting to perhaps as much as $50 billion. Apparently people really value the freedom of communication that mobile phones provide. A major advantage of Hausman's work was to reiterate the notion that the standard methods used to calculate the Consumer Price Index (CPI – see Application 3.2) significantly understate the welfare gains consumers experience from new products. In the case of mobile phones, for example, these goods did not enter the CPI until 15 years after they were introduced in the United States. Once mobile phones were considered part of the CPI "market basket", no explicit account was taken of the benefits they provided to consumers relative to prior versions of mobile phones.

Mobile Phones in the Developing World

This effect is even more pronounced in the developing world where tens of millions of people are using mobile phones even though they are struggling to meet their basic needs. This rush to mobiles raises fascinating questions about the value of mobiles on people's lives. Of the one million people who become new mobile phone subscribers everyday, about 85 per cent live in emerging markets, according to the mobile phone industry body, the GSMA. By bypassing antiquated fixed line systems, the mobile phone boom has transformed many ordinary people into micro-entrepreneurs.

An increase of ten mobile phones per 100 people in African developing countries can boost GDP growth by 0.6 per cent.[2] A recent Deloitte study suggested the increase in GDP could be as much as 1.2 per cent. McKinsey surveyed more than 600 workers in China who travel for their jobs: taxi drivers, plumbers, and salesmen, for example. Mobile phones offered these workers time savings of nearly 6 per cent – a productivity gain worth some €33 billion in 2005.

The value placed on a mobile is shown in Namibia, Ethiopia, and Zambia, where households spend more than 10 per cent of their monthly household income on the phone. This is equally true in rural areas where low-income households are prepared to spend relatively large amounts of their revenue on telecommunications because it helps them save money in other areas. Even if phone ownership is impossible, other options exist. One of the most famous examples of mobile phone entrepreneurship is the Village Phone Program in Bangladesh. Run by a sister firm of the 2006 Nobel Peace Prize-winning Grameen Bank, it enables local women to earn an income from renting mobile phones to fellow villagers who could not afford to purchase and operate a phone themselves.

Farmers in Kenya check crop prices on a service offered by local provider Safaricom, and in India, fishermen can now call ahead to ports to see where they will get the best deal on their catch. In South

Africa, mobile phones serve as a virtual office for carpenters, painters and other laborers who post their numbers on handwritten signs advertising their skills. Throughout the developing world millions of consumers who might never operate a bank account are now 'banking on-mobile'. In the Philippines since 2000, Smart Communications Inc., the country's largest carrier, has allowed subscribers in its Smart Money program to hold limited amounts of cash in electronic wallets linked to their mobile accounts. Using their mobile phones, members can withdraw cash from their bank accounts, pay for goods and services and transfer money and airtime credit. The phone records all transactions. Overseas Filipinos are even using this service to send money home. The multiplier effect continues as an expanded mobile system lures more foreign investment, gives families better access to health and educational information and provides governments with more revenue from licenses and taxes. Even Afghanistan now has two million cell phone subscribers but only 20 000 fixed-line phones. Mobile phones are, in short, a classic example of technology that helps people to help themselves.

To Think About

1. The size of the welfare gains from introducing a new product seems to depend on the slope of the demand curve (see Figure 1). Can you give an intuitive reason for this?
2. Figure 1 may give the misleading impression that *any* new good will increase welfare, even if firms can't sell it at a profit. How might the cost of producing a new good affect the evaluation of its welfare benefits?

---

[1]See J. Hausman, "Cellular Telephone, New Products, and the CPI", *Journal of Business and Economic Statistics* (April, 1999):188–194. Hausman shows how information from micro sales data on the new product can be used to estimate the slope of *d* at the initial market equilibrium.

[2]L. Waverman, M. Meschi and M. Fuss, "The Impact of Telecoms on Economic Growth in Developing Countries", *Africa: The Impact of Mobile Phones* (2005), The Vodafone Policy Paper Series, Number 2.

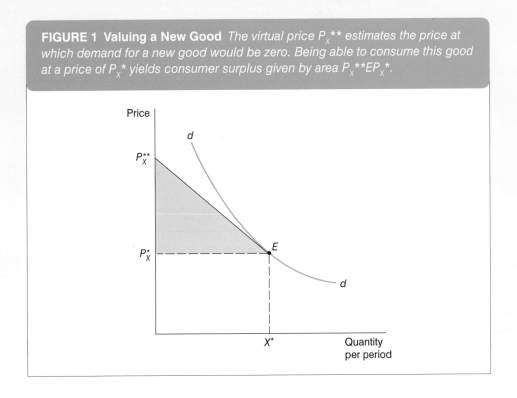

FIGURE 1 Valuing a New Good *The virtual price P_X^{**} estimates the price at which demand for a new good would be zero. Being able to consume this good at a price of P_X^{*} yields consumer surplus given by area $P_X^{**}EP_X^{*}$.*

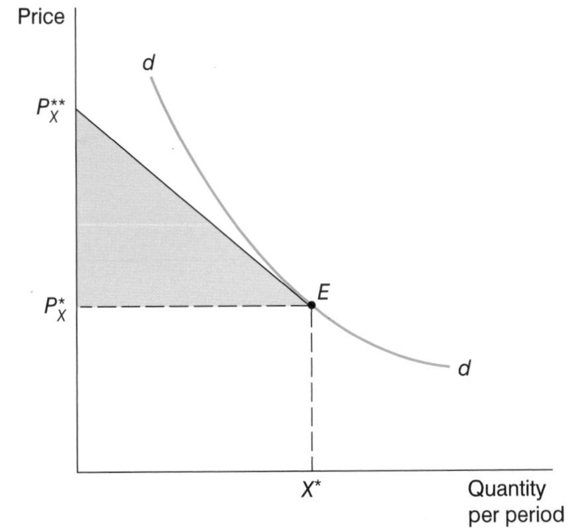

obtain with budget constraint *I* if no T-shirts were available. Again, it is possible to show[5] that this amount also is approximately equal to the consumer surplus figure calculated in the previous section (€80). In this case, the figure represents the amount that a person would voluntarily give up in exchange for dropping a no-T-shirt law. Hence, both approaches reach the same conclusion – that consumer surplus provides a way of putting an euro value on the utility people gain from being able to make market transactions.

Increases in the market price of T-shirts would again reduce these consumer surplus/utility measures. The correspondence between Figure 3-11 and Figure 3-12 would permit us to continue to study the welfare consequences of price changes using either graph. Because it is usually much easier to study these matters using a demand curve, however, that is the approach we take in later chapters. Application 3.6: *Valuing New Goods* shows how using a demand curve can solve a major problem in devising cost-of-living statistics.

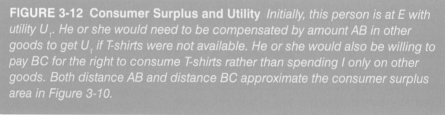

FIGURE 3-12 Consumer Surplus and Utility *Initially, this person is at E with utility U_1. He or she would need to be compensated by amount AB in other goods to get U_1 if T-shirts were not available. He or she would also be willing to pay BC for the right to consume T-shirts rather than spending I only on other goods. Both distance AB and distance BC approximate the consumer surplus area in Figure 3-10.*

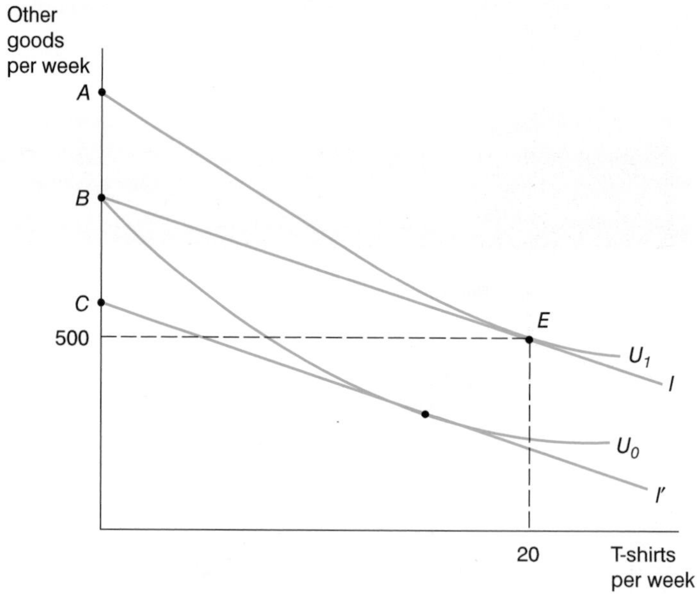

[5]For a theoretical treatment of these issues, see R. D. Willig, "Consumer's Surplus without Apology", *American Economic Review* (September 1976): 589–597. Willig shows that distance *AB* in Figure 3-12 (which is termed the "compensating income variation") exceeds total consumer surplus, whereas distance *BC* (termed the "equivalent income variation") is smaller than consumer surplus. All three measures approach the same value if income effects in the demand for the good in question are small.

SUMMARY

This chapter uses the model of individual choice to examine how people react to changes in income or prices. We have come to several important conclusions about the demand for a good:

- Proportionate changes in all prices and income will not affect choices because such changes do not shift the budget constraint.
- When income alone increases, the demand for a good will increase, except in the rare case when a good is inferior.
- A change in the price of a good has substitution and income effects that together cause changes in consumption choices. Except in the unlikely case of Giffen's paradox, a reduction in a good's price will cause more of it to be demanded. An increase in price will cause less of the good to be demanded.
- A change in the price of one good will usually affect the demand for other goods. If two goods are complements, an increase in the price of one will reduce the demand for the other. If the goods are substitutes, an increase in the price of one will increase the demand for the other.
- The demand for a good is also affected by preferences. Preferences are usually held constant under the *ceteris paribus* assumption in theoretical analysis, but changes in preferences can cause important shifts in real-world demand functions.
- Consumer surplus is the area below the demand curve and above the market price for a good. The area measures what people would pay for the right to consume the good at its current market price. Increases in the market price reduce the amount of consumer surplus that a person gets.

REVIEW QUESTIONS

1 Monica always buys one unit of food together with three units of housing, no matter what the prices of these two goods. If food and housing start with equal prices, decide whether the following events would make her better off or worse off or leave her welfare unchanged.

- a The prices of food and housing increase by 50 per cent, with Monica's income unchanged.
- b The prices of food and housing increase by 50 per cent, and Monica's income increases by 50 per cent.
- c The price of food increases by 50 per cent, the price of housing remains unchanged, and Monica's income increases by 25 per cent.
- d The price of food remains unchanged, the price of housing increases by 50 per cent, and Monica's income increases by 25 per cent.
- e How might your answers to part c and part d change if Monica were willing to alter her mix of food and housing in response to price changes?

2 Suppose a person consumes only two goods, *X* and *Y*, and that the prices of these goods are fixed. How would the set of utility-maximizing points traced out by successively higher incomes look if

- a this person always split his or her income equally between *X* and *Y*?
- b *X* were a luxury, *Y* a necessity?
- c *Y* were a luxury, *X* a necessity?
- d an unchanging amount of *X* were bought as income expanded above some minimal amount?
- e *X* were an inferior good? (Can *Y* be inferior here too?)

3 Suppose Jennifer always spends half her income on food. How will changes in the price of food affect the quantity of food consumed? How will changes in the price of food affect total spending on food? How large an increase in income would be needed to offset the effect of a 10 per cent increase in the price of food?

4 When there are only two goods, the assumption of a diminishing MRS requires that substitution effects have price and quantity move in opposite directions for any good. Explain why this is so. Do you think the result holds when there are more than two goods?

5 George has rather special preferences for DVD rentals. As his income rises, he will increase his rentals until he reaches a total of seven per week. Once he is regularly renting seven DVDs per week, however, further increases in his income do not cause him to buy any more DVDs.

a Provide a simple sketch of George's indifference curve map.

b Explain how George will respond to a fall in the price of DVD rentals.

6 Is the following statement true or false? Explain. "Every Giffen good must be inferior, but not every inferior good exhibits the Giffen paradox."

7 Suppose that Sarah never changes the quantity of water she consumes when the price of water changes. How do income and substitution effects work in this case?

8 When coffee prices rise, John buys more tea but fewer coffee mugs. Explain the substitution and income effects of the coffee price change on these two goods.

9 Does the theory of consumer choice require that an individual's demand curve for a good be downward sloping? In what case would a demand curve be vertical? When might it be positively sloped?

10 Explain whether the following events would result in a move along an individual's demand curve for popcorn or in a shift of the curve. If the curve would shift, in what direction?

a An increase in the individual's income.

b A decline in popcorn prices.

c An increase in prices for pretzels.

d A reduction in the amount of butter included in a box of popcorn.

e The presence of long waiting lines to buy popcorn.

f A sales tax on all popcorn purchases.

PROBLEMS

3.1 Elizabeth M. Suburbs makes €200 a week at her summer job and spends her entire weekly income on new running shoes and designer jeans, since these are the only two items that provide utility to her. Furthermore, Elizabeth insists that for every pair of jeans she buys, she must also buy a pair of shoes (without the shoes, the new jeans are worthless). Therefore, she buys the same number of pairs of shoes and jeans in any given week.

a If jeans cost €20 and shoes cost €20, how many will Elizabeth buy of each?

b Suppose that the price of jeans rises to €30 a pair. How many shoes and jeans will she buy?

c Show your results by graphing the budget constraints from part a and part b. Also draw Elizabeth's indifference curves.

d To what effect (income or substitution) do you attribute the change in utility levels between part a and part b?

e Now we look at Elizabeth's demand curve for jeans. First, calculate how many pairs of jeans she will choose to buy if jeans prices are €30, €20, €10, or €5.

f Use the information from part e to graph Ms Suburbs' demand curve for jeans.

g Suppose that her income rises to €300. Plot on a graph her demand curve for jeans in this new situation.

h Suppose that the price of running shoes rises to €30 per pair. How will this affect the demand curves drawn in part b and part c?

3.2 Mr Wright, a clothing salesman, is forced by his employer to spend at least €100 of his weekly income of €500 on clothing. Show that his utility level is lower than if he could freely allocate his income between clothing and other goods.

3.3 The Jones family spends all its income on food and shelter. It derives maximum utility when it spends two-thirds of its income on shelter and one-third on food.

a Use this information to calculate the demand functions for shelter and food. Show that demand is homogeneous with respect to changes in all prices and income.

b Graph the demand curves for shelter and food for the Jones family if family income is €20 000.

c Show how the demand curves for shelter and food would shift if income rose to €50 000.

d Explain why a change in food prices does not affect shelter purchases in this problem.

3.4 Currently Paula is maximizing utility by purchasing five TV dinners (T) and four Lean Cuisine meals (L) each week.

a Graph Paula's initial utility-maximizing choice.

b Suppose that the price of T rises by €1 and the price of L falls by €1.25. Can Paula still afford to buy her initial consumption choices? What do you know about her new budget constraint?

c Use your graph to show why Paula will choose to consume more L and less T given her new budget constraint. How do you know that her utility will increase?

d Some economists define the "substitution effect" of a price change to be the kind of change shown in part c. That is, the effect represents the change in consumption when the budget constraint rotates about *the initial consumption bundle*. Precisely how does this notion of a substitution effect differ from the one defined in the text?

e If the substitution effect were defined as in part d, how would you define "the income effect" in order to get a complete analysis of how a person responds to a price change?

3.5 The Lump-Sum Principle applies only in situations where there are substitution effects. If there are no substitution effects (say, because the person consumes two goods in fixed proportions), the principle no longer holds. That is, in this case, there is no utility difference between a tax on one good and a tax on income.

a Explain this result intuitively.

b Show this result formally with a graph.

c Describe how your conclusions would affect the conclusions about programs to aid the poor discussed in Application 3.3.

3.6 David gets €3 per month as an allowance to spend any way he pleases. Since he likes only peanut butter and jam sandwiches, he spends the entire amount on peanut butter (at €0.05 per gram) and jam (at €0.10 per gram). Bread is provided free of charge by a concerned neighbor. David is a picky eater and makes his sandwiches with exactly 1 gram of jam and 2 grams of peanut butter. He is set in his ways and will never change these proportions.

a How much peanut butter and jam will David buy with his €3 allowance in a week?

b Suppose the price of jam were to rise to €0.15 per gram. How much of each commodity would be bought?

c By how much should David's allowance be increased to compensate for the rise in the price of jam in part b?

d Graph your results of part a through part c.

e In what sense does this problem involve only a single commodity – peanut butter and jam sandwiches? Graph the demand curve for this single commodity.

f Discuss the results of this problem in terms of the income and substitution effects involved in the demand for jam.

3.7 For most of the situations we studied in Chapter 3 the consumer's (nominal) income was held fixed as prices changed. This would be an appropriate type of analysis for instances where the person's income was unaffected by the changing prices we were studying. But suppose that changing prices also affected a person's purchasing power. This problem looks at one simple case. To do so, suppose that an individual has in his or her possession certain amounts of X (say X^*) and Y (say Y^*) – we call these amounts this person's "initial endowments". This person can, of course, consume these amounts directly without making any market transactions. But he or she can also sell units of one good in order to buy more of the other goods.

a Graph this person's initial endowments on his or her indifference curve map. What utility will be received if no market transactions are made?

b Describe this person's "budget constraint" when he or she can freely sell one good to buy another.

c What will determine whether this person is a net seller or buyer of good X? What will determine whether he or she is a net seller or buyer of good Y?

d Explain how the assumption of a diminishing MRS can help you answer part c.

e Would a rise in the price of X make this person better off or worse off? Or does it all depend?

3.8 Irene's demand for pizza is given by

$$Q = \frac{0.3I}{P}$$

where Q is the weekly quantity of pizza bought (in slices), I is weekly income, and P is the price of pizza. Using this demand function, answer the following

a Is this function homogeneous in I and P?

b Graph this function for the case $I = 200$.

c One problem in using this function to study consumer surplus is that Q never reaches zero, no matter how high P is. Hence, suppose that the function holds only for $P \leq 10$ and that $Q = 0$ for $P > 10$. How should your graph in part b be adjusted to fit this assumption?

d With this demand function (and $I = 200$), it can be shown that the area of consumer surplus is approximately $CS = 198 - 6P - 60\ \ln(P)$, where "ln($P$)" refers to the natural logarithm of P. Show that if $P = 10$, $CS = 0$.

e Suppose $P = 3$. How much pizza is demanded, and how much consumer surplus does Irene receive? Give an economic interpretation to this magnitude.

f If P were to increase to 4, how much would Irene demand and what would her consumer surplus be? Give an economic interpretation to why the value of CS has fallen.

3.9 The demand curves we studied in this chapter were constructed holding a person's nominal income constant – hence, changes in prices introduced changes in real income (that is, utility). Another way to draw a demand curve is to hold utility constant as prices change. That is, the person is "compensated" for any effects that the prices have on his or her utility. Such *compensated demand curves* illustrate only substitution effects, not income effects. Using this idea, show that

a For any initial utility-maximizing position, the regular demand curve and the compensated demand curve pass through the same price/quantity point.

b The compensated demand curve is generally steeper than the regular demand curve.

c Any regular demand curve intersects many different compensated demand curves.

d If Irving consumes only pizza and Chianti in fixed proportions of one slice of pizza to one glass of Chianti, his regular demand curve for pizza will be downward-sloping but his compensated demand curve(s) will be vertical.

3.10 The residents of Uurp consume only pork chops (X) and Coca-Cola (Y). The utility function for the typical resident of Uurp is given by

$$Utility = U(X,Y) = \sqrt{X \cdot Y}$$

In 2005, the price of pork chops in Uurp was €1 each; Cokes were also €1 each. The typical resident consumed 40 pork chops and 40 Cokes (saving is impossible in Uurp). In 2006, swine fever hit Uurp and pork chop prices rose to €4; the Coke price remained unchanged. At these new prices, the typical Uurp resident consumed 20 pork chops and 80 Cokes.

a Show that utility for the typical Uurp resident was unchanged between the two years.

b Show that using 2005 prices would show an increase in real income between the two years.

c Show that using 2006 prices would show a decrease in real income between the years.

d What do you conclude about the ability of these indexes to measure changes in real income?

4

Market Demand and Elasticity

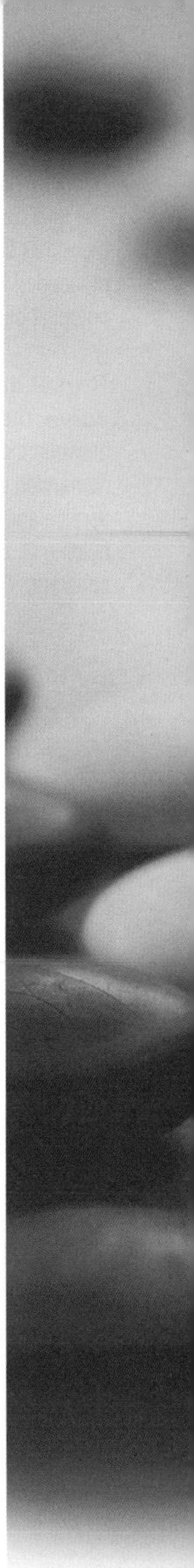

In this chapter, we show how individual demand curves are "added up" to create the market demand curve for a good. Market demand curves reflect the actions of many people and show how these actions are affected by market prices.

This chapter also describes a few ways of measuring market demand. We introduce the concept of elasticity and show how we can use it to summarize how the quantity demanded of a good changes in response to changes in income and prices.

Market Demand Curves

The **market demand** for a good is the total quantity of the good demanded by all potential buyers. The **market demand curve** shows the relationship between this total quantity demanded and the market price of the good, when all other things that affect demand are held constant. The market demand curve's shape and position are determined by the shape of individuals' demand curves for the product in question. Market demand is nothing more than the combined effect of economic choices by many consumers.

Construction of the Market Demand Curve

Figure 4-1 shows the construction of the market demand curve for good X when there are only two buyers. For each price, the point on the market demand curve is found by summing the quantities demanded by each person. For example, at a price of P^*_X, individual 1 demands X^*_1, and individual 2 demands X^*_2. The total quantity demanded at the market at P^*_X is therefore the sum of these two amounts: $X^* = X^*_1 + X^*_2$. Consequently the point X^*, P^*_X is one point on the market demand curve D. The other points on the curve are plotted in the same way. The market curve is simply the horizontal sum of each person's demand curve. At every possible price, we ask

Market demand The total quantity of a good or service demanded by all potential buyers.

Market demand curve The relationship between the total quantity demanded of a good or service and its price, holding all other factors constant.

how much is demanded by each person, and then we add up these amounts to arrive at the quantity demanded by the whole market. The demand curve summarizes the *ceteris paribus* relationship between the quantity demanded of X and its price. If other things that influence demand do not change, the position of the curve will remain fixed and will reflect how people as a group respond to price changes.

Shifts in the Market Demand Curve

Why would a market demand curve shift? We already know why individual demand curves shift. To discover how some event might shift a market demand curve, we must, obviously, find out how this event causes individual demand curves to shift. In some cases, the direction of a shift in the market demand curve is reasonably predictable. For example, using our two-buyer case, if both of the buyers' incomes increase and both regard X as a normal good, then each person's demand curve would shift outward. Hence, the market demand curve would also shift outward. At each price, more would be demanded in the market because each person could afford to buy more. This situation, in which a general rise in income increases market demand, is illustrated in Figure 4-2. Application 4.1: *The 2001 US Tax Cut* shows how this notion can be used to study the effects of tax cuts, although, as is often the case in economics, the story is not quite as simple as it appears to be.

In some cases, the direction that a market demand curve shifts may be ambiguous. For example, suppose that one person's income increases but a second person's income decreases. The location of the new market demand curve now depends on the relative sizes of the shifts in the individual demand curves that these income changes cause. The market demand curve could either shift inward or shift outward.

What holds true for our simple two-person example also applies to much larger groups of demanders – perhaps even to the entire economy. In this case, the market demand summarizes the behavior of all possible consumers. If personal income in the United Kingdom as a whole were to rise, the effect on the market demand curve for pizza would depend on whether the income gains went to people who love pizza or

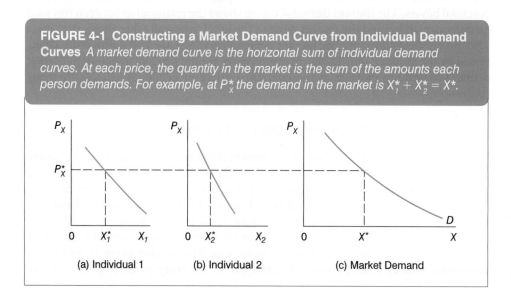

FIGURE 4-1 Constructing a Market Demand Curve from Individual Demand Curves *A market demand curve is the horizontal sum of individual demand curves. At each price, the quantity in the market is the sum of the amounts each person demands. For example, at P_X^* the demand in the market is $X_1^* + X_2^* = X^*$.*

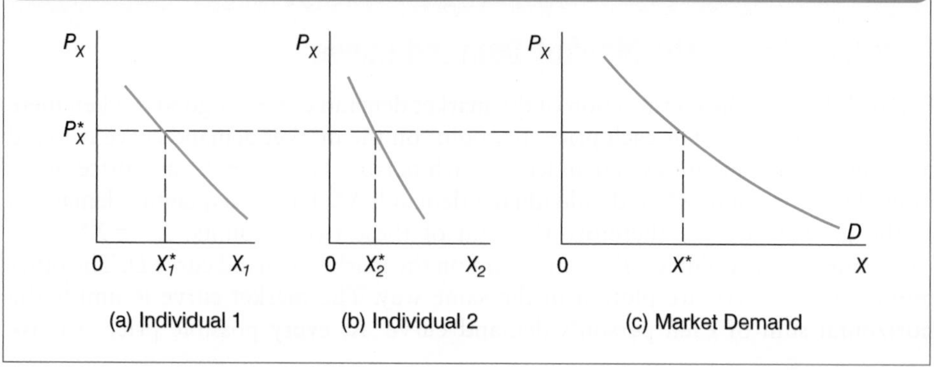

to people who never touch it. If the gains went to pizza lovers, the United Kingdom market demand for pizza would shift outward significantly. It would not shift at all if the income gains went only to pizza haters.

A change in the price of some other good (*Y*) will also affect the market demand for *X*. If the price of *Y* rises, for example, the market demand curve for *X* will shift outward if most buyers regard *X* and *Y* as substitutes. On the other hand, an increase in the price of *Y* will cause the market demand curve for *X* to shift inward if most people regard the two goods as complements. For example, an increase in the price of Corn Flakes would shift the demand curve for Wheat Flakes outward because these two cereals are close substitutes for each other. At every price, people would now demand more boxes of Wheat Flakes than they did before Corn Flakes became more expensive. On the other hand, an increase in the price of strawberries might shift the demand curve for Wheat Flakes inward because some people only like the taste of Wheat Flakes if they have strawberries on top. Higher-priced strawberries result in people demanding fewer boxes of Wheat Flakes at every price.

A Simplified Notation

Often in this book we look at only one market. In order to simplify the notation, we use the letter *Q* for the quantity of a good demanded (per week) in this market, and we use *P* for its price. When we draw a demand curve in the *Q*, *P* plane, we assume that all other factors affecting demand are held constant. That is, income, the price of other goods, and preferences are assumed not to change. If one of these factors happened to change, the demand curve would shift to a new location. As was the case for individual demand curves, the term "change in quantity demanded" is used

MICROQUIZ 4.1

A shift outward in a demand curve can be described either by the extent of its shift in the horizontal direction or by its shift in the vertical direction. How would the following shifts be shown graphically?

1. News that nutmeg cures the common cold causes people to demand two million kilos more nutmeg *at each price*.
2. News that nutmeg cures the common cold causes people to be willing to pay $1 more per kilo of nutmeg *for each possible quantity*.

FIGURE 4-2 Increases in Each Individual's Income Cause the Market Demand Curve to Shift Outward *An increase in income for each individual causes the individual demand curve for X to shift out (assuming X is a normal good). For example, at P^*_X, individual 1 now demands X^{**}_1 instead of X^*_1. The market demand curve shifts out to D9. X* was demanded at P^*_X before the income increase. Now X** (= $X^{**}_1 + X^{**}_2$) is demanded.*

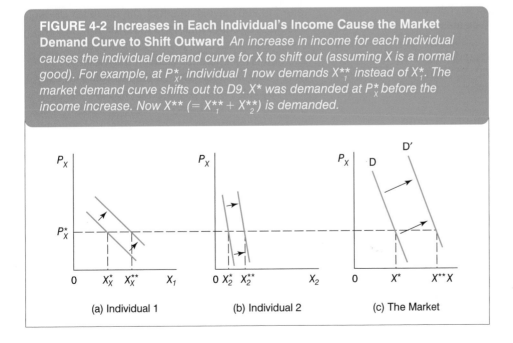

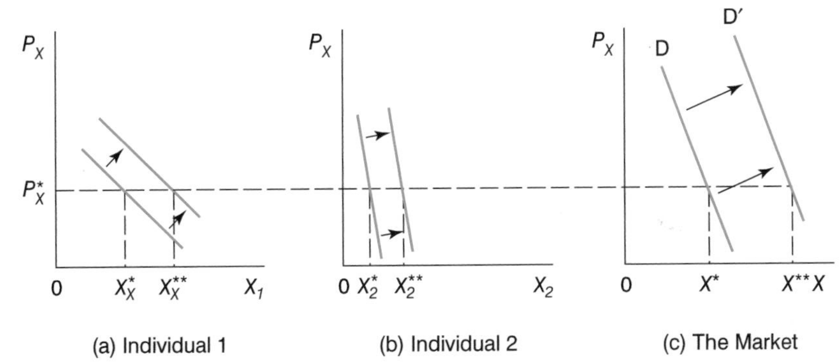

APPLICATION 4.1 *The 2001 US Tax Cut*

In May 2001, the US Congress passed one of the largest cuts in personal income taxes in history. The cuts are to be implemented over a ten-year period and will (over that period) amount to more than $1.6 trillion. As a "down payment" on this sum, the law provided that most US taxpayers receive an immediate check for $300 (or $600 for a married couple), and these checks rolled out of the Treasury at the rate of nine million per week during the summer of 2001. Many politicians argued that such a large tax reduction would have an important effect on fighting the recession that was then beginning, by boosting the demand for virtually every good. But such a prediction ignored both economic theory and the realities of the bizarre US tax system. Ultimately, the tax cut seems to have had virtually no immediate impact on consumer spending.

The Permanent Income Hypothesis

Our discussion of demand theory showed that changes in people's incomes do indeed shift demand curves outward. But we have been a bit careless in defining exactly what income is. Milton Friedman made one of the most important discoveries that clarify this question in the 1950s. He argued that spending decisions are based on a person's long-term view of his or her economic circumstances.[1] Short-term increases or decreases in income have little effect on spending patterns. Friedman's view that spending decisions are based on a person's "permanent" income is now widely accepted by economists.

Tax Cuts and Permanent Income

According to Friedman's theory, a tax reduction will affect a person's spending only to the extent that it affects his or her permanent income. This insight suggests that the 2001 tax act had little impact for two reasons. First, consider the $300 checks. These came to people "out of the blue", and everyone knew that such largess would not continue. The checks were too small to stimulate spending on any major goods, so they were largely saved. In this, they were exhibiting exactly the same sort of non-response that they had shown in many previous episodes, including temporary tax increases in the late 1960s and temporary reductions in the 1970s.

Now consider the effect of the overall tax act, a plan that was intended to be implemented over a ten-year period. Because of wrangling in Congress, the actual schedule of tax cuts is "back-loaded". That is, most of the cuts would not begin until 2006, and the largest cuts are reserved until 2009–2010. Such distant tax cuts probably have little immediate impact on people's perceptions of their economic situations. In purely dollar terms, the present value of such distant tax savings is much smaller than their actual stated amounts.[2] Perhaps more important, taxpayers may have had little faith that tax cuts projected for many years in the future will actually occur. That is, many of the tax reductions promised under the 2001 act were simply not "credible".

Complexities in the Income Tax

Another set of reasons that led to the sluggish response to the 2001 tax cuts relates to the complexities in the US income tax itself. First, all of the rate changes in the bill were subject to "sunset" provisions – in 2011, tax rates are supposed to return to 2001 levels. In effect, the entire tax bill is a temporary one. What happens after 2011 is anyone's guess. Second, the bill did not deal with the alternative minimum tax (AMT) – a provision of the US income tax originally intended to catch fat cats who pay little taxes, but one that has increasingly affected middle-income taxpayers. Under this arcane provision, much of the effect of the tax reductions promised under the 2001 act will be neutralized by increased taxes collected under the AMT. Finally, many of the tax reductions in the 2001 bill came about through special credits for all sorts of items such as college tuitions and energy conservation. How these actually affect the purchasing power of the average citizen obviously depends on whether they wish to spend their incomes on the especially favored items. Certainly not everyone's budget was positively affected.

To Think About

1 If a person makes economic decisions based on his or her permanent income, how much might be spent currently out of an unexpected $300 check from the government?

2 How might various people differ in the ways in which they respond to getting a tax rebate check from the government?

[1]Milton Friedman, *A Theory of the Consumption Function* (Princeton, NJ: Princeton University Press, 1957). Recent amendments to Friedman's theory stress the "life-cycle" nature of income and spending decisions – that is, people are assumed to plan their spending over their entire lives.

[2]The present value of a sum payable in the future is less than the actual amount because of forgone interest. For a discussion of this concept, see Chapter 16 and its Appendix.

for a movement along a given market demand curve (in response to a price change), and the term "change in demand" is used for a shift in the entire curve.

Elasticity

Economists frequently need to show how changes in one variable affect some other variable. They ask, for example, how much does a change in the price of electricity affect the quantity of it demanded, or how does a change in income affect total spending on automobiles? One problem in summarizing these kinds of effects is that goods are measured in different ways. For example, steak is typically sold per kilo, whereas oranges are generally sold per dozen. A €0.10 per pound rise in the price of steak might cause national consumption of steak to fall by 100 000 kilos per week, and a €0.10 per dozen rise in the price of oranges might cause national orange purchases to fall by 50 000 dozen per week. But there is no good way to compare the change in steak sales to the change in orange sales. When two goods are measured in different units, we cannot make a simple comparison between the demand for them to determine which demand is more responsive to changes in its price.

Economists solve this measurement problem in a two-step process. First, they practically always talk about changes in percentage terms. Rather than saying that the price of oranges, say, rose by €0.10 per dozen, from €2.00 to €2.10, they would instead report that orange prices rose by 5 per cent. Similarly, a fall in orange prices of €0.10 per dozen would be regarded as a change of minus 5 per cent.

Percentage changes can, of course, also be calculated for quantities. If national orange purchases fell from 500 000 dozen per week to 450 000, we would say that such purchases fell by 10 per cent (that is, they changed by minus 10 per cent). An increase in steak sales from 2 million kilos per week to 2.1 million kilos per week would be regarded as a 5 per cent increase.

The advantage of always talking in terms of percentage changes is that we don't have to worry very much about the actual units of measurement being used. If orange prices fall by 5 per cent, this has the same meaning regardless of whether we are paying for them in euros, dollars, yen, or pesos. Similarly, an increase in the quantity of oranges sold of 10 per cent means the same thing regardless of whether we measure orange sales in dozens, crates, or lorry loads.

The second step in solving the measurement problem is to link percentage changes when they have a cause/effect relationship. For example, if a 5 per cent fall in the price of oranges typically results in a 10 per cent increase in quantity bought (when everything else is held constant), we could link these two facts and say that each percent fall in the price of oranges leads to an increase in sales of about 2 per cent. That is, we would say that the "elasticity" of orange sales with respect to price changes is about 2 (actually, as we discuss in the next section, *minus* 2 because price and quantity move in opposite directions). This approach is quite general and is used throughout economics. Specifically, if economists believe that variable *A* affects variable *B*, they define the **elasticity** of *B* with respect to *A* as the percent change in *B* for each percentage point change in *A*. The number that results from this calculation is unit-free. It can readily be compared across different goods, between different countries, or over time.

Elasticity The measure of the percentage change in one variable brought about by a 1 percent change in some other variable.

Price Elasticity of Demand

Price elasticity of demand The percentage change in the quantity demanded of a good in response to a 1 percent change in its price.

Although economists use many different applications of elasticity, the most important is the **price elasticity of demand**. Changes in *P* (the price of a good) will lead to changes in *Q* (the quantity of it purchased), and the price elasticity of demand measures this relationship. Specifically, the price elasticity of demand ($e_{Q,P}$) is defined as the percentage change in quantity in response to a 1 per cent change in price. In mathematical terms,

$$\text{Price in elasticity of demand} = e_{Q,P} = \frac{\text{Percentage change in } Q}{\text{Percentage change in } P} \qquad \{4.1\}$$

This elasticity records how *Q* changes in percentage terms in response to a percentage change in *P*. Because *P* and *Q* move in opposite directions (except in the rare case of Giffen's paradox), $e_{Q,P}$ will be negative.[1] For example, a value of $e_{Q,P}$ of -1 means that a 1 per cent rise in price leads to a 1 per cent decline in quantity, whereas a value of $e_{Q,P}$ of -2 means that a 1 per cent rise in price causes quantity to decline by 2 per cent.

It takes a bit of practice to get used to speaking in elasticity terms. Probably the most important thing to remember is that the price elasticity of demand looks at movements along a given demand curve and tells you how much (in percentage terms) quantity changes for *each* per cent change in price. You should also keep in mind that price and quantity move in opposite directions, which is why the price elasticity of demand is negative. For example, suppose that studies have shown that the price elasticity of demand for petrol is -2. That means that every per cent rise in price will cause a movement along the petrol demand curve reducing quantity demanded by 2 per cent. So, if petrol prices rise by, say, 6 per cent, we know that (if nothing else changes) quantity will fall by 12 per cent ($= 6 \times [-2]$). Similarly, if the petrol price were to fall by 4 per cent, this price elasticity could be used to predict that petrol purchases would rise by 8 per cent ($= [-4] \times [-2]$). Sometimes price elasticities take on decimal values, but this should pose no problem. If, for example, the price elasticity of demand for aspirin were found to be -0.3, this would mean that each percentage point rise in aspirin prices would cause quantity demanded to fall by 0.3 per cent (that is, by three-tenths of 1 per cent). So, if aspirin prices rose by 15 per cent (and everything else that affects aspirin demand stayed fixed), we could predict that the quantity of aspirin demanded would fall by 4.5 per cent ($= 15 \times [-0.3]$).

[1]Sometimes the price elasticity of demand is defined as the absolute value of the definition in Equation 4.1. Using this definition, elasticity is never negative; demand is classified as elastic, unit elastic, or inelastic, depending on whether $e_{Q,P}$ is greater than, equal to, or less than 1. You need to recognize this distinction as there is no consistent use in economic literature.

Values of the Price Elasticity of Demand

A distinction is usually made among values of $e_{Q,P}$ that are less than, equal to, or greater than -1. Table 4-1 lists the terms used for each value. For an elastic curve ($e_{Q,P}$ is less than -1),[2] a price increase causes a more than proportional quantity decrease. If $e_{Q,P} = -3$, for example, each 1 per cent rise in price causes quantity to fall by 3 per cent. For a unit elastic curve ($e_{Q,P}$ is equal to -1), a price increase causes a decrease in quantity of the same proportion. For an inelastic curve ($e_{Q,P}$ is greater than -1), price increases proportionally more than quantity decreases. If $e_{Q,P} = -1/2$, a 1 per cent rise in price causes quantity to fall by only 1/2 of 1 per cent. In general then, if a demand curve is elastic, changes in price along the curve affect quantity significantly; if the curve is inelastic, price has little effect on quantity demanded.

Price Elasticity and the Substitution Effect

The discussion of income and substitution effects in Chapter 3 provides a basis for judging what the size of the price elasticity for particular goods might be. Goods with many close substitutes (brands of breakfast cereal, small cars, brands of electronic calculators, and so on) are subject to large substitution effects from a price change. For these kinds of goods, we can presume that demand will be elastic ($e_{Q,P} < -1$). On the other hand, goods with few close substitutes (water, insulin, and salt, for example) have small substitution effects when their prices change. Demand for such goods will probably be inelastic with respect to price changes ($e_{Q,P} > -1$; that is, $e_{Q,P}$ is between 0 and -1). Of course, as we mentioned previously, price changes also create income effects on the quantity demanded of a good, which we must consider to completely assess the likely size of overall price elasticities. Still, because the price changes for most goods have only a small effect on people's real incomes, the existence (or non-existence) of substitutes is probably the principal determinant of price elasticity.

Price Elasticity and Time

Making substitutions in consumption choices may take time. To change from one brand of cereal to another may only take a week (to finish eating the first box), but to change from heating your house with oil to heating it with electricity may take years because

TABLE 4-1 Terminology for the Ranges of $E_{Q,P}$

Value of $e_{Q,P}$ at a Point on Demand Curve	*Terminology for Curve at This Point*
$e_{Q,P} < -1$	Elastic
$e_{Q,P} = -1$	Unit elastic
$e_{Q,P} > -1$	Inelastic

[2]Remember, numbers like -3 are *less than* -1, whereas $-1/2$ is *greater than* -1. Because we are accustomed to thinking only of positive numbers, statements about the size of price elasticities can sometimes be confusing.

APPLICATION 4.2 *Brand Loyalty*

One reason that substitution effects are larger over longer periods than over shorter ones is that people develop spending habits that do not change easily. For example, when faced with a variety of brands consisting of the same basic product, you may develop loyalty to a particular brand, purchasing it on a regular basis. This behavior makes sense because you don't need to revaluate products continually. Thus, your decision-making costs are reduced. Brand loyalty also reduces the likelihood of brand substitutions, even when there are short-term price differentials. Over the long-term, however, price differences can tempt buyers into trying new brands and thereby switch their loyalties.

Cars

The competition between British and Japanese car manufacturers provides a good example of changing loyalties. Prior to the 1980s, many British consumers exhibited considerable loyalty to British cars. Repeat purchases of the same brand were a common pattern. In the early 1970s, Japanese car producers began making inroads into the UK market, often with cars specified to a much higher level than British vehicles. These "extras" often seduced buyers into making their first Japanese purchase. Satisfied with their experiences, by the 1980s many consumers developed a loyalty to Japanese brands. This loyalty was encouraged, in part, by large differences in quality between Japanese and British cars, which became noticeably significant in the mid-1980s. Survey after survey suggested that reliability had become a crucial factor in the eyes of consumers. This brand loyalty became even stronger as Japanese firms started to produce cars in the UK. Firstly, Nissan in Sunderland in 1986, then Toyota in Derbyshire, and Honda in Swindon both in 1992, mean British motorists could now feel good by buying a "British Toyota".

Licensing of Brand Names

The advantages of brand loyalty have not been lost on innovative marketers. Famous trademarks such as Coca-Cola, Harley-Davidson, or Disney's Mickey Mouse have been applied to products rather different from the originals. For example, Mickey Mouse is one of the most popular trademarks in Japan, appearing on products both conventional (watches and lunchboxes) and unconventional (fashionable handbags and neckties). The Harry Potter films have spawned five video games and have in conjunction with them led to the licensing of over 400 additional Harry Potter products (including an iPod). The Harry Potter brand is worth an estimated four billion euros and J.K. Rowling is by some reports richer than Queen Elizabeth II.

The economics behind these moves are straightforward. Prior to licensing, products are virtually perfect substitutes and consumers shift readily among various makers. Licensing creates somewhat lower price responsiveness for the branded product, so producers can charge more for it without losing all their sales. The large fees paid to companies, or individuals such as football star David Beckham provide strong evidence of the strategy's profitability.

Overcoming Brand Loyalty

A useful way to think about brand loyalty is that people incur "switching costs" when they decide to depart from a familiar brand. Producers of a new product must overcome those costs if they are to be successful. Temporary price reductions are one way in which switching costs might be overcome. Heavy advertising of a new product offers another route to this end. In general firms would be expected to choose the most cost-effective approach. For example, in a study of brand loyalty to breakfast cereals M. Shum[1] used scanner data to look at repeat purchases of a number of national brands such as Cheerios or Rice Krispies. He found that an increase in a new brand's advertising budget of 25 per cent reduced the costs associated with switching from a major brand by about €0.68 – a figure that represents about a 15 per cent reduction. The author showed that obtaining a similar reduction in switching costs through temporary price reductions would be considerably more costly to the producers of a new brand.

To Think About

1 Does the speed with which price differences erode brand loyalties depend on the frequency

with which products are bought? Why might differences between short-term and long-term price elasticities be much greater for brands of cars than for brands of toothpaste?

2 Why do people buy licensed products when they could probably buy generic brands at much lower prices? Does the observation that people pay 50 per cent more for Nike golf shoes endorsed by Tiger Woods than for identical no-name competitors violate the assumptions of utility-maximization?

[1]M. Shum, "Does Advertising Overcome Brand Loyalty? Evidence from the Breakfast Cereals Market", *Journal of Economics and Management Strategy*, Summer, 2004: 241–272.

a new heating system must be installed. We already have seen in Application 3.4: *SUVs and Petrol Prices* that trends in petrol prices may have little short-term impact because people already own their cars and have relatively fixed travel needs. Over a longer term, however, there is clear evidence that people will change the kinds of cars they drive in response to changing real petrol prices. In general then, it might be expected that substitution effects and the related price elasticities would be larger the longer the time period that people have to change their behavior. In some situations it is important to make a distinction between short-term and long-term price elasticities of demand, because the long-term concept may show much greater responses to price change. In Application 4.2: *Brand Loyalty*, we look at a few cases where this distinction can be important.

Price Elasticity and Total Expenditures

The price elasticity of demand is useful for studying how total expenditures on a good change in response to a price change. Total expenditures on a good are found by multiplying the good's price (P) times the quantity purchased (Q). If demand is elastic, a price increase will cause total expenditures to fall. When demand is elastic, a given percentage increase in price is more than counterbalanced in its effect on total spending by the resulting large decrease in quantity demanded. For example, suppose people are currently buying 1 million cars at €10 000 each. Total expenditures on cars amount to €10 billion. Suppose also that the price elasticity of demand for cars is −2. Now, if the price increases to €11 000 (a 10 per cent increase), the quantity purchased would fall to 800 000 cars (a 20 per cent fall). Total expenditures on cars are now €8.8 billion (€11 000 times 800 000). Because demand is elastic, the price increase causes total spending to fall. This example can be easily reversed to show that, if demand is elastic, a fall in price will cause total spending to increase. The extra sales generated by a fall in price more than compensate for the reduced price in this case. For example, a number of computer software producers have discovered that they can increase their total revenues by selling software at low, cut-rate prices. The extra users attracted by low prices more than compensate for those low prices.[3]

If demand is unit elastic ($e_{Q,P} = -1$), total expenditures stay the same when prices change. A movement of P in one direction causes an exactly opposite proportional movement in Q, and the total price-times-quantity stays fixed. Even if prices fluctuate substantially, total spending on a good with unit elastic demand never changes.

[3]Of course, costs are also important to software producers, but the extra cost of producing more copies of a software program is very low.

Finally, when demand is inelastic, a price rise will cause total expenditures to rise. A price rise in an inelastic situation does not cause a very large reduction in quantity demanded, and total expenditures will increase. For example, suppose people buy 100 million kilos of coffee per year at a price of €3 per kilo. Total expenditures on coffee are €300 million. Suppose also that the price elasticity of demand for coffee is −0.5 (demand is inelastic). If the price of coffee rises to €3.60 per kilo (a 20 per cent increase), quantity demanded will fall by 10 per cent (to 90 million kilos). The net result of these actions is to increase total expenditures on coffee from €300 million to €324 million. Because the quantity of coffee demanded is not very responsive to changes in price, total revenues are increased by a price rise. This same example could also be reversed to show that, in the inelastic case, total revenues are reduced by a fall in price. Application 4.3: *Volatile Farm Prices* illustrates how inelastic demand can result in highly unstable prices when supply conditions change.

The relationship between price elasticity and total expenditures is summarized in Table 4-2. To help you keep the logic of this table in mind, consider the rather extremely shaped demand curves shown in Figure 4-3. Total spending at any point on these demand curves is given by the price shown on the demand curve times the quantity associated with that price. In graphical terms, total spending is shown by the rectangular area bounded by the specific price–quantity combination chosen on the curve. In each case shown in Figure 4-3, the initial position on the demand curve is given by P_0, Q_0. Total spending is shown by the area of the hatched rectangle. If price rises to P_1, quantity demanded falls to Q_1. Now total spending is given by the brown rectangle. Comparing the hatched and brown rectangles gives very different results in the two cases in Figure 4-3. In panel (a) of the figure, demand is very inelastic – the demand curve is nearly vertical. In this case, the red rectangle is much larger than the hatched one. Because quantity changes very little in response to the higher price, total spending rises. In panel (b), however, demand is very elastic – the demand curve is nearly horizontal. In this case, the brown rectangle is much smaller than the hatched one. When price rises, quantity falls so much that total spending falls. Keeping a mental picture of these extreme demand curves can be a good way to remember the relationship between price elasticity and total spending.

Demand Curves and Price Elasticity

The relationship between a particular demand curve and the price elasticity it exhibits is relatively complicated. Although it is common to talk about *the* price elasticity of demand for a good, this usage conveys the false impression that price

TABLE 4-2 Relationship Between Price Changes and Changes in Total Expenditure

If Demand Is	*In Response to an Increase in Price, Expenditures Will*	*In Response to a Decrease in Price, Expenditures Will*
Elastic	Fall	Rise
Unit elastic	Not change	Not change
Inelastic	Rise	Fall

elasticity necessarily has the same value at every point on a market demand curve. A more accurate way of speaking is to say that "at current prices, the price elasticity of demand is . . ." and, thereby, leave open the possibility that the elasticity may take on some other value at a different point on the demand curve. In some cases, this distinction may be unimportant because the price elasticity of demand has the same value over a relatively broad range of a demand curve. In other cases, the distinction may be important, especially when large movements along a demand curve are being considered.

Linear Demand Curves and Price Elasticity

Probably the most important illustration of this warning about elasticities occurs in the case of a linear (straight-line) demand curve. As one moves along such a demand curve, the price elasticity of demand is always changing value. At high price levels, demand is elastic; that is, a fall in price increases quantity purchased more than proportionally. At low prices, on the other hand, demand is inelastic; a further decline in price has relatively little proportional effect on quantity.

This result can be most easily shown with a numerical example. Figure 4-4 illustrates a straight-line (linear) demand curve for, say, portable CD players. In looking at the changing elasticity of demand along this curve, we will assume it has the specific algebraic form

$$Q = 100 - 2P \qquad \{4.2\}$$

where Q is the quantity of CD players demanded per week and P is their price in euros. The demonstration would be the same

MICROQUIZ 4.2

The relationship between the price elasticity of demand and total spending can also be used "in reverse" – elasticities can be inferred from changes in spending.

1. Use the two panels of Figure 4-3 to show how the response of total spending to a *fall* in price can indicate what the price elasticity of demand is.
2. Suppose a researcher could measure the per cent change in total spending for each per cent change in market price. How could he or she use this information to infer the precise value of the price elasticity of demand?

FIGURE 4-3 Relationship between Price Elasticity and Total Revenue *In both panels, price rises from P_0 to P_1. In panel (a), total spending increases because demand is inelastic. In panel (b), total spending decreases because demand is elastic.*

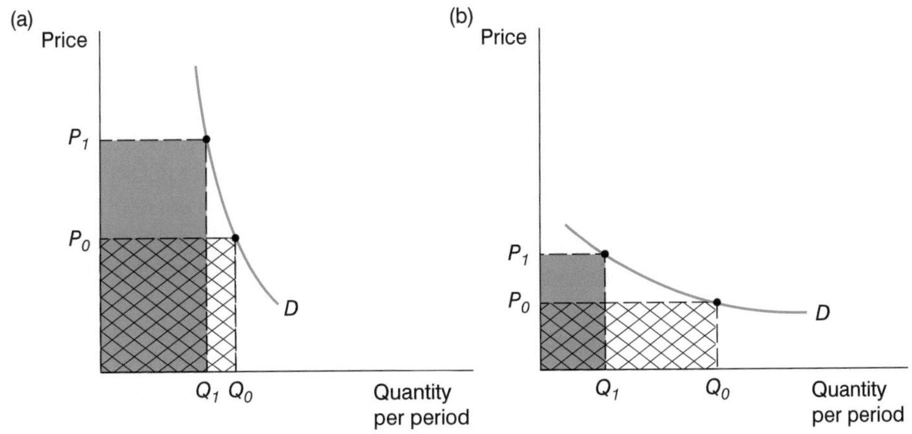

APPLICATION 4.3 *Volatile Farm Prices*

The demand for agricultural products is relatively price-inelastic. That is especially true for basic crops such as wheat, corn, or soybeans. An important implication of this inelasticity is that even modest changes in supply, often brought about by weather patterns, can have large effects on the prices of these crops. This volatility in crop prices has been a feature of farming throughout all of history.

The Paradox of Agriculture

Recognition of the fundamental economics of farm crops yields paradoxical insights about the influence of the weather on farmers' well-being. "Good" weather can produce bountiful crops and abysmally low prices, whereas "bad" weather (in moderation) can result in attractively high prices. For example, relatively modest supply disruptions in the US grain belt during the early 1970s caused an explosion in farm prices. Farmers' incomes increased more than 40 per cent over a short, two-year period. These incomes quickly fell back again when more normal weather patterns returned.

This paradoxical situation also results in misleading news coverage of localized droughts. Television news reporters will usually cover droughts by showing the viewer a shriveled ear of corn, leaving the impression that all farmers are being devastated. That is undoubtedly true for the farmer whose parched field is being shown (though he or she may also have irrigated fields next door). But the larger story of local droughts is that the price increases they bring benefit most farmers outside the immediate area – a story that is seldom told.

Volatile Prices and EU Programs

After the experiences of the Great Depression, and Second World War the European Union was determined to reduce the volatility of farm prices and the associated rural and national difficulties that are connected with it. The Common Agricultural Policy has been a core element of the EU from its inception. First, import tariffs are applied to specified goods imported into the EU. These are set at a level to raise the world market price up to the EU target price. The target price is chosen as the maximum desirable price for those goods within the EU. An internal intervention price is set. If the internal market price falls below the intervention level then the EU will buy up goods to raise the price to the intervention level. The intervention price is set lower than the target price. The internal market price can only vary in the range between the intervention price and target price. Should prices rise above the intervention price the EU could sell produce back onto the market to lower prices.

This system has not, however, been without problems. Knowing that the EU would always buy up any surpluses, farmers, and especially the large efficient producers, have had little incentive to reduce production. It is as if Jaguar Cars had a man at the end of the day buying up any car they could not sell through their garage network. The policy was a victim of its own success. The use of interventionist measures such as price support, import tariffs, export subsidies, and production quotas to promote domestic food production, led to the "food mountains and wine lakes" of the 1980s as well as environmental problems and trade distortion which damaged industries in developing countries. The program also accounts for over 40 per cent of all EU funds, and has been under pressure as newer members have joined the union. Reforms have started, but it has been painfully slow, as deep agricultural, political, and national interests prevail. The farming lobby which represents only a few per cent of workers still wields influence disproportionate to its importance to the economy.

A radical approach has been tried in New Zealand where most agricultural subsidies have been abolished and farming has had to stand on its own feet. Since subsidy removal the agricultural sector has grown faster than the rest of the economy. Agriculture's contribution to the New Zealand's gross domestic product (GDP) rose from 14.2 per cent in 1986–87 to 16.6 per cent in 1999–2000. Agriculture accounts for 11.4 per cent of the total workforce.[1] New Zealand agriculture is thriving without subsidy.

However, the basic price inelasticity of demand for most farm products ensures that even modest variations in supply will continue to have major consequences for price. The 2006 droughts in Southern

England, and the 2007 floods in the Midlands caused sharp rises in some grain and vegetable prices.

To Think About

1 The volatility of farm prices is both good and bad news for farmers. Since periods of low prices are often followed by periods of high prices, the long-term welfare of farmers is hard to determine. Would farmers be better off if their prices had smaller fluctuations around the same trend levels?

2 Should governments intervene to reduce the volatility of farm prices? What might be the side-effects of such intervention?

[1] Federated Farmers of New Zealand, *'Life After Subsidies: The New Zealand Farming Experience 15 Years Later'* (2002).

for any other linear demand curve we might choose. Table 4-3 shows a few price-quantity combinations that lie on the demand curve, and these points are also reflected in Figure 4-4. Notice, in particular, that the quantity demanded is zero for prices of €50 or greater.

Table 4-3 also records total spending on CD players ($P \cdot Q$) represented by each of the points on the demand curve. For prices of €50 or above, total expenditures are €0. No matter how high the price, if nothing is bought, expenditures are €0. As price falls below €50, total spending increases. At $P =$ €40, total spending is €800 (€40 · 20), and for $P =$ €30, the figure rises to €1200 (€30 · 40).

For high prices, the demand curve in Figure 4-4 is elastic; a fall in price causes enough additional sales to increase total spending. This increase in total expenditures begins to slow as price drops still further. In fact, total spending reaches a maximum at a price of €25. When $P =$ €25, $Q = 50$ and total spending on CD players are

FIGURE 4-4 Elasticity Varies along a Linear *Demand Curve* *A straight-line demand curve is elastic in its upper portion, inelastic in its lower portion. This relationship is illustrated by considering how total expenditures change for different points on the demand curve.*

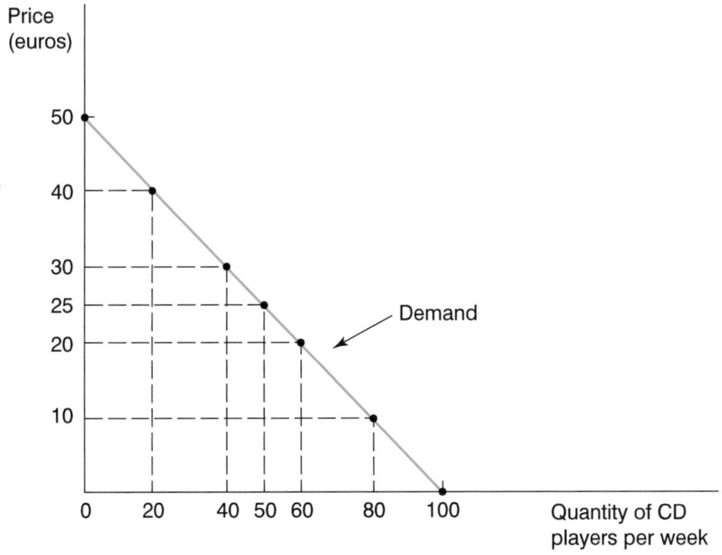

€1250. For prices below €25, reductions in price cause total expenditures to fall. At P = €20, expenditures are €1200 (€20 · 60), whereas at P = €10, they are only €800 (€10 · 80). At these lower prices, the increase in quantity demanded brought about by a further fall in price is simply not large enough to compensate for the price decline itself, and total spending falls.

This relationship is quite general. At high prices on a linear demand curve, demand is elastic ($e_{Q,P} < -1$). Demand is unit elastic ($e_{Q,P} = -1$) at a price halfway between €0 and the price at which demand drops to nothing (given by P = €50 in the prior example). Hence, demand is unit elastic at a price of P = €25. Below that price, demand is inelastic. Further reductions in price actually reduce total revenues.

Because of this property of linear demand curves, it is particularly important when using them to note clearly the point at which price elasticity is to be measured.[4] When looking at economic data from such a demand curve, if the price being examined has not changed very much over the period being analyzed, the distinction may be unimportant. But, if the analysis is being conducted over a period of substantial price change, the possibility that elasticity may have changed should be considered.

TABLE 4-3 Price, Quantity, and Total Expenditures of CD Players for the Demand Function

Price (P)	Quantity (Q)	Total Expenditures (P × Q)
$50	0	$0
40	20	800
30	40	1200
25	50	1250
20	60	1200
10	80	800
0	100	0

[4]The changing price elasticity along a linear demand curve can be shown algebraically as follows: Assume a demand curve of the form

$$Q = a - bP \qquad \{i\}$$

Because

$$e_{Q,P} = \frac{\frac{\Delta Q}{Q}}{\frac{\Delta P}{P}} = \frac{\Delta Q}{\Delta P} \times \frac{P}{Q}$$

for the case of the demand curve in equation i,

$$e_Q = -b \cdot \frac{P}{Q} \qquad \{ii\}$$

For large P, P/Q is large and $e_{Q,P}$ is a large negative number. For small P, P/Q is small and $e_{Q,P}$ is a small negative number. Equation ii provides a convenient way to compute $e_{Q,P}$: use two points on the demand curve to derive the curve's slope, b, then multiply by P/Q for the point being examined. Alternatively, equation ii can be used to derive $-b$ (the slope of the demand curve) if $e_{Q,P}$, P, and Q are known.

A Unitary Elastic Curve

Suppose that instead of being characterized by Equation 4.2, the demand for CD players took the form

$$Q = \frac{1200}{P} \tag{4.3}$$

As shown in Figure 4-5, the graph of this equation is a hyperbola – it is not a straight line. In this case, $P \cdot Q = 1200$ regardless of the price. This can be verified by examining any of the points identified in Figure 4-5. Because total expenditures are constant everywhere along this hyperbolic demand curve, the price elasticity of demand is always -1. Therefore, this is one simple example of a demand curve that has the same price elasticity along its entire length.[5] Unlike the linear case, for this curve, there is no need to worry about being specific about the point at which elasticity is to be measured. Application 4.4: *An Experiment in Health Insurance* illustrates how you might calculate elasticity from actual data and why your results could be very useful indeed.

FIGURE 4-5 A Unitary Elastic Demand Curve *This hyperbolic demand curve has a price elasticity of demand of −1 along its entire length. This is shown by the fact that total spending on CD players is the same (€1200) everywhere on the curve.*

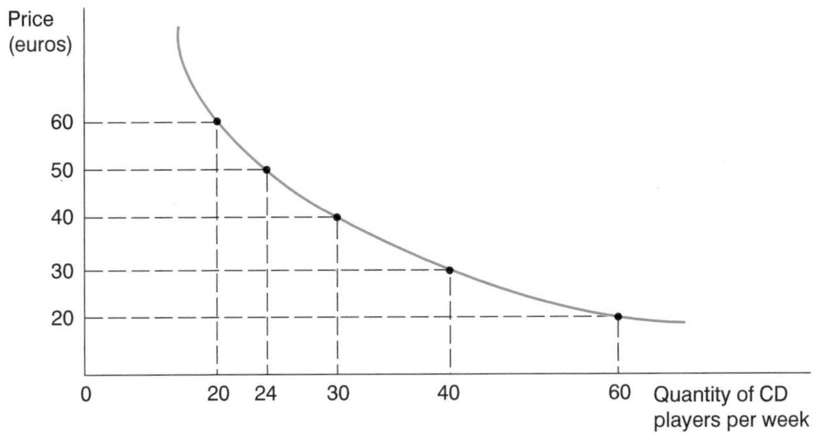

[5]More generally, if demand takes the form

$$Q = aP^b \ (b < 0) \tag{i}$$

the price elasticity of demand is given by b. This elasticity is the same everywhere along such a demand curve. Equation 4.3 is a special case of equation i for which

$$e_{Q,P} = b = -1 \text{ and } a = 1200 \tag{ii}$$

Taking logarithms of equations i yields

$$\ln Q = \ln a + b \ln P \tag{iii}$$

which shows that the price elasticity of demand can be found by studying the relationship between the logarithms of Q and P.

APPLICATION 4.4 *An Experiment in Health Insurance*

The provision of health insurance is one of the most universal and expensive social policies throughout the world. Although many nations have comprehensive insurance schemes that cover most of their populations, policymakers in the United States have resisted such an all-inclusive approach. Instead, US policies have evolved as a patchwork, stressing employer-provided insurance for workers together with special programs for the aged (Medicare) and the poor (Medicaid). Regardless of how health insurance plans are designed, however, all face a similar set of problems.

Moral Hazard

One of the most important such problems is that insurance coverage of health care needs tends to increase the demand for services. Because insured patients pay only a small fraction of the costs of the services they receive, they will demand more than they would have if they had to pay market prices. This tendency of insurance coverage to increase demand is (perhaps unfortunately) called "moral hazard", though there is nothing especially immoral about such behavior.

The Rand Experiment

The Medicare program was introduced in the United States in 1965, and the increase in demand for medical services by the elderly was immediately apparent. In order to understand better the factors that were leading to this increase in demand, the government funded a large-scale experiment in four cities. In that experiment, which was conducted by the Rand Corporation, people were assigned to different insurance plans that varied in the fraction of medical costs that people would have to pay out of their own pockets for medical care.[1] In insurance terms, the experiment varied the "coinsurance" rate from zero (free care) to nearly 100 per cent (patients pay everything).

Results of the Experiment

Table 1 shows the results from the experiment. People who faced lower out-of-pocket costs for medical care tended to demand more of it. A rough estimate of the elasticity of demand can be obtained by averaging the percentage changes across the various plans in the table. That is,

$$e_{Q,P} = \frac{\textit{percent change in Q}}{\textit{percent change in P}} = \frac{+12}{-66} = -0.18$$

So, as might have been expected, the demand for medical care is inelastic, but it clearly is not zero. In fact, the Rand study found much larger price effects for some specific medical services such as mental health care and dental care. It is these kinds of services for which new insurance coverage would be expected to have the greatest impact on market demand.

To Think About

1 The data in Table 1 show average spending for families who faced differing out-of-pocket

TABLE 1 Results of the Rand Health Insurance Experiment

Coinsurance Rate	*Per cent Change in Price*	*Average Total Spending in $*	*Per cent Change in Quantity*
0.95		540	
0.50	−47	573	+6.1
0.25	−50	617	+7.7
0.00	−100	750	+21.6
Average	−66		+12.0

SOURCE: MANNING ET AL., "HEALTH INSURANCE AND THE DEMAND FOR MEDICAL CARE: EVIDENCE FROM A RANDOMIZED EXPERIMENT", *AMERICAN ECONOMIC REVIEW* (JUNE 1987): 251–277. USED WITH PERMISSION.

prices for medical care. Why do these data accurately reflect the changes in *quantity* (rather than spending) that are required in the elasticity formula?

2 In recent years, prepaid health plans (i.e., HMOs) have come to be the dominant form of employer-provided health plans. How do prepaid plans seek to control the moral hazard problem?

[1]Details of the experiment are reported in W. G. Manning, J. P Newhouse, E. B. Keeler, A. Liebowitz, and M. S. Marquis, "Health Insurance and the Demand for Medical Care: Evidence from a Randomized Experiment", *American Economic Review* (June 1987): 251–277.

Income Elasticity of Demand

Another type of elasticity is the **income elasticity of demand** ($e_{Q,I}$). This concept records the relationship between changes in income and changes in quantity demanded:

Income elasticity of demand The percentage change in the quantity demanded of a good in response to a 1 percent change in income.

$$\textit{Income elasticity of demand} = e_{Q,I} = \frac{\textit{Percentage change in } Q}{\textit{Percentage change in } I} \quad \{4.4\}$$

For a normal good, $e_{Q,I}$ is positive because increases in income lead to increases in purchases of the good. For the unlikely case of an inferior good, on the other hand, $e_{Q,I}$ would be negative, implying that increases in income lead to decreases in quantity purchased. Such negative income elasticities are rarely encountered, however.

Among normal goods, whether $e_{Q,I}$ is greater than or less than 1 is a matter of some interest. Goods for which $e_{Q,I} > 1$ might be called luxury goods, in that purchases of these goods increase more rapidly than income. For example, if the income elasticity of demand for cars is 2, then a 10 per cent increase in income will lead to a 20 per cent increase in car purchases. Car sales would therefore be very responsive to business cycles that produce changes in people's incomes. On the other hand Engel's Law suggests that food has an income elasticity of much less than 1. If the income elasticity of demand for food were 0.5, for example, then a 10 per cent rise in income would result in only a 5 per cent increase in food purchases. Considerable research has been done to determine the actual values of income elasticities for various items, and we discuss the results of some of these studies in the final section of this chapter.

MICROQUIZ 4.3

Possible values for the income elasticity of demand are restricted by the fact that consumers are bound by budget constraints. Use this fact to explain

1 Why is it that not every good can have an income elasticity of demand greater than 1? Can every good have an income elasticity of demand less than 1?

2 If a set of consumers spend 95 per cent of their incomes on housing, why can't the income elasticity of demand for housing be much greater than 1?

Cross-Price Elasticity of Demand

In Chapter 3 we showed that a change in the price of one good will affect the quantity demanded of many other goods. To measure such effects, economists use the **cross-price elasticity of demand**. This concept records the percentage change in quantity demanded (Q) that results from a 1 percentage point change in the price of some other good (call this other price P'). That is,

$$\text{Cross-price elasticity of demand} = e_{Q,P'} = \frac{\text{Percentage change in } Q}{\text{Percentage change in } P'} \qquad \{4.5\}$$

Cross-price elasticity of demand
The percentage change in the quantity demanded of a good in response to a 1 percent change in the price of another good.

If the two goods in question are substitutes, the cross-price elasticity of demand will be positive because the price of one good and the quantity demanded of the other good will move in the same direction. For example, the cross-price elasticity for changes in the price of tea on coffee demand might be 0.2. Each 1 percentage point increase in the price of tea results in a 0.2 percentage point increase in the demand for coffee because coffee and tea are substitutes in people's consumption choices. A fall in the price of tea would cause the demand for coffee to fall also, since people would choose to drink tea rather than coffee.

If two goods in question are complements, the cross-price elasticity will be negative, showing that the price of one good and the quantity of the other good move in opposite directions. The cross-price elasticity of doughnut prices on coffee demand might be, say, −1.5. This would imply that each 1 per cent increase in the price of doughnuts would cause the demand for coffee to fall by 1.5 per cent. When doughnuts are more expensive, it becomes less attractive to drink coffee because many people like to have a doughnut with their morning coffee. A fall in the price of doughnuts would increase coffee demand because, in that case, people will choose to consume more of both complementary products. As for the other elasticities we have examined, considerable empirical research has been conducted to try to measure actual cross-price elasticities of demand.

Empirical Studies of Demand

Economists have for many years studied the demand for all sorts of goods. Some of the earliest studies generalized from the expenditure patterns of a small sample of families. More recent studies have examined a wide variety of goods to estimate both income and price elasticities. Although it is not possible for us to discuss in detail here the statistical techniques used in these studies, we can show in a general way how these economists have gone about getting their estimates.

MICROQUIZ 4.4

Suppose that a set of consumers spend their incomes only on beer and pizza.

1 Explain why a fall in the price of beer will have an ambiguous effect on pizza purchases.

2 What can you say about the relationship between the price elasticity of demand for pizza, the income elasticity of demand for pizza, and the cross-price elasticity of the demand for pizza with respect to beer prices? (Hint: Remember the demand for pizza must be homogeneous.)

Estimating Demand Curves

Estimating the demand curve for a product is one of the more difficult and important problems in econometrics. The importance of the question is obvious. Without some idea of what the demand curve for a product looks like, economists could not describe with any precision how the market for a good might be affected by various events. Usually the notion that a rise in price will cause quantity demanded to fall will not be precise enough – we need some way to estimate the size of the effect.

Problems in deriving such an estimate are of two general types. First are those related to the need to implement the *ceteris paribus* assumption. One must find some way to hold constant all of the other factors that affect quantity demanded so that the direct relationship between price and quantity can be observed. Otherwise, we will be looking at points on several demand curves rather than on only one. We have already discussed this problem in the Appendix to Chapter 1, which shows how it can often be solved through the use of relatively simple statistical procedures.[6]

A second problem in estimating a demand curve goes to the heart of microeconomic theory. From the early days in your introductory economics course, you have (hopefully) learned that quantity and price are determined by the simultaneous operation of demand and supply. A simple plot of quantity versus price will be neither a demand curve nor a supply curve, but only points at which the two curves intersect. The econometric problem then is to penetrate behind this confusion and "identify" the true demand curve. There are indeed methods for doing this, though we will not pursue them here.[7] All studies of demand, including those we look at in the next section, must address this issue, however.

Some Elasticity Estimates

Table 4-4 gathers a number of estimated income and price elasticities of demand. As we shall see, these estimates often provide the starting place for analyzing how activities such as changes in taxes or import policy might affect various markets. In several later chapters, we use these numbers to illustrate such applications.

Although interested readers are urged to explore the original sources of these estimates to understand more details about them, in our discussion we just take note of a few regularities they exhibit. With regard to the price elasticity figures, most estimates suggest that product demands are relatively inelastic (between 0 and -1). For the groupings of commodities listed, substitution effects are not especially large, although they may be large within these categories. For example, substitutions between beer and other commodities may be relatively small, though substitutions among brands of beer may be substantial in response to price differences. Still, all the estimates are less than 0, so there is clear evidence that people do respond to price changes for most goods.[8] Application 4.5: *Alcohol Taxes, Price and Public Health* shows how price elasticity estimates can inform an important policy debate.

As expected, the income elasticities in Table 4-4 are positive and are roughly centered about 1.0. Luxury goods, such as cars or transatlantic travel ($e_{Q,I} > 1$), tend to be balanced by necessities, such as food or medical care ($e_{Q,I} < 1$). Because none of the income elasticities are negative, it is clear that Giffen's paradox must be very rare.

[6]The most common technique, multiple regression analysis, estimates a relationship between quantity demanded (Q), price (P), and other factors that affect quantity demanded (X) of the form $Q = a + bP + cX$. Given this relationship, X can be held constant while looking at the relationship between Q and P. Following footnote 5, it is common practice to use logarithms to provide estimates of elasticities.

[7]For a good discussion, see R. Ramanathan, *Introductory Econometrics with Applications*, 5th ed. (Mason, OH: South-Western, 2002), Chapter 13.

[8]Although the estimated price elasticities in Table 4-4 incorporate both substitution and income effects, they predominantly represent substitution effects. To see this, note that the price elasticity of demand ($e_{Q,P}$) can be disaggregated into substitution and income effects by

$$e_{Q,P} = e_S - s_i e_i$$

where e_S is the "substitution" price elasticity of demand representing the effect of a price change holding utility constant, s_i is the share of income spent on the good in question, and e_i is the good's income elasticity of demand. Because s_i is small for most of the goods in Table 4-4, $e_{Q,P}$ and e_S have values that are reasonably close.

Some Cross-Price Elasticity Estimates

Table 4-5 shows a few cross-price elasticity estimates that economists have derived. All of the pairs of goods illustrated are probably substitutes, and the positive values for the elasticities confirm that view. The figure for the relationship between butter and margarine is the largest in Table 4-5. Even in the absence of health issues, the competition between these two spreads on the basis of price is clearly very intense. Similarly, natural gas prices have an important effect on electricity sales because they help determine how people heat their homes.

TABLE 4-4 Representative Price and Income Elasticities of Demand

	Price Elasticity	*Income Elasticity*
Food	−0.21	+0.28
Medical services	−0.18	+0.22
Housing		
Rental	−0.18	+1.00
Owner-occupied	−1.20	+1.20
Electricity	−1.14	+0.61
Automobiles	−1.20	+3.00
Beer	−0.26	+0.38
Wine	−0.88	+0.97
Marijuana	−1.50	0.00
Cigarettes	−0.35	+0.50
Abortions	−0.81	+0.79
Transatlantic air travel	−1.30	+1.40
Imports	−0.58	+2.73
Money	−0.40	+1.00

Sources: Food: H. Wold and L. Jureen, *Demand Analysis* (New York: John Wiley & Sons, Inc., 1953): 203. Medical Services: income elasticity from R. Andersen and L. Benham, "Factors Affecting the Relationship between Family Income and Medical Care Consumption" in *Empirical Studies in Health Economics*, ed. Herbert Klarman (Baltimore: Johns Hopkins Press, 1970). Price elasticity from Manning *et al.*, "Health Insurance and the Demand for Medical Care: Evidence from a Randomized Experiment", *American Economic Review* (June 1987): 251–277. Housing: income elasticities from F. de Leeuw, "The Demand for Housing", *Review of Economics and Statistics* (February 1971); price elasticities from H. S. Houthakker and L. D. Taylor, *Consumer Demand in the United States* (Cambridge, Mass.: Harvard University Press, 1970), 166–167. Electricity: R. F. Halvorsen, "Residential Demand for Electricity", unpublished Ph.D. dissertation, Harvard University, December 1972. Automobiles: Gregory C. Chow, *Demand for Automobiles in the United States* (Amsterdam: North Holland Publishing Company, 1957). Beer and Wine: J. A. Johnson, E. H. Oksanen, M. R. Veall, and D. Fritz, "Short-Run and Long-Run Elasticities for Canadian Consumption of Alcoholic Beverages", *Review of Economics and Statistics* (February 1992): 64–74. Marijuana: T. C. Misket and F. Vakil, "Some Estimates of Price and Expenditure Elasticities among UCLA Students", *Review of Economics and Statistics* (November 1972): 474–475. Cigarettes: F. Chalemaker, "Rational Addictive Behavior and Cigarette Smoking", *Journal of Political Economy* (August 1991): 722–742. Abortions: M. J. Medoff, "An Economic Analysis of the Demand for Abortions", *Economic Inquiry* (April 1988): 253–259. Transatlantic air travel: J. M. Cigliano, "Price and Income Elasticities for Airline Travel", *Business Economics* (September 1980): 17–21. Imports: M. D. Chinn, "Beware of Econometricians Bearing Estimates", *Journal of Policy Analysis and Management* (Fall 1991): 546–567. Money: "Long-Run Income and Interest Elasticities of Money Demand in the United States", *Review of Economics and Statistics* (November 1991): 665–674. Price elasticity refers to interest rate elasticity.

TABLE 4-5 Representative Cross-Price Elasticities of Demand

Demand for	*Effect of Price of*	*Elasticity Estimate*
Butter	Margarine	1.53
Electricity	Natural gas	0.50
Coffee	Tea	0.15

Sources: Butter: Dale M. Heien, "The Structure of Food Demand: Interrelatedness and Duality", *American Journal of Agricultural Economics* (May 1982): 213–221. Electricity: G. R. Lakshmanan and W. Anderson, "Residential Energy Demand in the United States", *Regional Science and Urban Economics* (August 1980): 371–386. Coffee: J. Huang, J. J. Siegfried, and F. Zardoshty, "The Demand for Coffee in the United States, 1963–77", *Quarterly Journal of Business and Economics* (Summer 1980): 36–50.

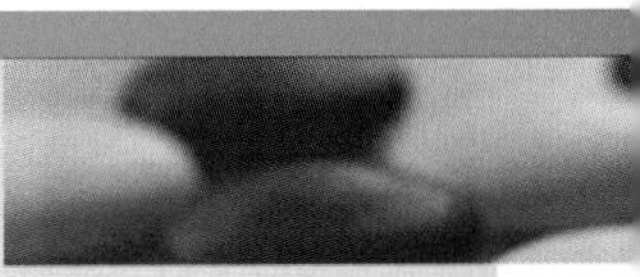

APPLICATION 4.5 *Alcohol Taxes, Price and Public Health*

A number of European countries, especially the United Kingdom, have had a growing problem with alcohol related accidents, drink driving, violence, and public health issues. Over many years, research has suggested that alcohol consumption could be reduced if alcohol taxes were increased. A recent illustration of the link between tax, price and health is provided by Finland, where in 2004 the Government reduced alcohol excise duty by an average of 33 per cent. The result was an immediate 17 per cent increase in alcohol-related mortality, equivalent to approximately eight additional alcohol-related deaths per week.[1]

Throughout Europe different countries have very different ideas about how sensitive alcohol consumption is to the level of taxes. Generally speaking wine producing nations have lower tax levels, and northern countries tax higher than southern ones.

Price Elasticity Estimates – The Importance of Beer

Most empirical studies of alcohol consumption show that it is sensitive to price. While all alcohol consumption appears to be relatively price sensitive, price elasticities for beer are usually found to be less than those for wine (and other spirits). Unfortunately, most teenage alcohol consumption is beer or lager. The lower price elasticity of demand for this product therefore poses a problem for those who would use alcohol taxes as a deterrent to binge drinking.

Why beer should have a lower price elasticity of demand than other alcoholic beverages is a puzzle. Two factors may provide a partial explanation. First, a significant portion of beer consumption is done in a group setting (while "clubbing" for example). In this case, many establishments have "happy hours" or price reductions, for the price of alcohol is an important competitive aspect of the club trade. A second possible reason for the lower price elasticity of beer consumption relates to differences among beer consumers. Most beer is consumed by people who drink quite a bit of it at a session. Unlike wine, which is often drunk with food. This is a group of consumers for whom demand has been found to be less responsive to price than is the case for most other consumers. Indeed elasticity is very low among heavy, dependent drinkers.

Alcohol Consumption and the Tax Dilemma

Even if increased prices might reduce consumption, rising incomes can mitigate against this. In the UK, between 1980 and 2003 the price of alcohol increased by 24 per cent more than prices generally, but household incomes increased by 91 per cent in real terms making alcohol 54 per cent more affordable. As a percentage of final household expenditure, it is also falling.

Moreover, other government policies may have precedent. In an attempt to revitalize decaying urban centers, the UK government encouraged more clubs, pubs and restaurants. Manchester saw a 242 per cent increase in licensed premises between 1966 and 1999. The drinks industry is also a powerful lobby group. The UK spirits duty has been largely static for many years, reflecting the concerns of the Scottish whisky industry. The large personal imports of alcohol from low to high tax countries, (now allowed under the EU Single European Market), have made many governments fearful of raising taxes by too much, as consumers by-pass traditional retail outlets, and smuggling increases. It must also be remembered that alcohol taxes raise over £14 billion, or more than 7 per cent of all UK government revenue.

To Think About

1. Reducing alcohol consumption by raising taxes would have a number of other additional effects apart from reduced consumption. What are some of these effects? Do these also provide a rationale for higher alcohol taxes?
2. One principle of efficient taxation is that taxes should be imposed directly on the "problem". Alcohol taxes do not do that because they tax alcohol consumers who do not drive, engage in violence, or need medical care because of alcohol related accidents. Is raising alcohol taxes still a desirable solution?

[1] T. Babor *et al.*, *"Alcohol: No Ordinary Commodity"*. Research and Public Policy (Oxford, Oxford University Press, 2003).

SUMMARY

In this chapter, we constructed a market demand curve by adding up the demands of all potential consumers. This curve shows the relationship between the market price of a good and the amount that people choose to purchase of that good, assuming all the other factors that affect demand do not change. The market demand curve is a basic building block for the theory of price determination. We use the concept frequently throughout the remainder of this book. You should therefore keep in mind the following points about this concept:

- The market demand curve represents the summation of the demands of a given number of potential consumers of a particular good. The curve shows the *ceteris paribus* relationship between the market price of the good and the amount demanded by all consumers.
- Factors that shift individual demand curves also shift the market demand curve to a new position. Such factors include changes in incomes, changes in the prices of other goods, and changes in people's preferences.
- The price elasticity of demand provides a convenient way of measuring the extent to which market demand responds to price changes for movement along a given demand curve. Specifically, the price elasticity of demand shows the percentage change in quantity demanded in response to a 1 per cent change in market price. Demand is said to be elastic if a 1 per cent change in price leads to a greater than 1 per cent change in quantity demanded. Demand is inelastic if a 1 per cent change in price leads to a smaller than 1 per cent change in quantity.
- There is a close relationship between the price elasticity of demand and total spending on a good. If demand is elastic, a rise in price will reduce total expenditures. If demand is inelastic, a rise in price will increase total spending.
- Other elasticities of demand are defined in a way similar to that used for the price elasticity. For example, the income elasticity of demand measures the percentage change in quantity demanded in response to a 1 per cent change in income.
- The price elasticity of demand is not necessarily the same at every point on a demand curve. For a linear demand curve, demand is elastic for high prices and inelastic for low prices.
- Economists have estimated elasticities of demand for many different goods using real-world data. A major problem in making such estimates is to devise ways of holding constant all other factors that affect demand so that the price–quantity points being used lie on a single demand curve.

REVIEW QUESTIONS

1 In the construction of the market demand curve shown in Figure 4-1, why is a horizontal line drawn at the prevailing price, P^*_x? What does this assume about the price facing each person? How are people assumed to react to this price?

2 Explain how the following events might affect the market demand curve for prime filet steak.

   a A fall in the price of filet steak because of a decline in cattle prices.

   b A general rise in consumers' incomes.

   c A rise in the price of lobster.

   d Increased health concerns about cholesterol.

   e An income tax increase for high-income people, used to increase welfare benefits.

   f A cut in income taxes and welfare benefits.

3 Why is the price elasticity of demand usually negative? If the price elasticity of demand for cars is less than the price elasticity of demand for medical care, which demand is more elastic? Give a numerical example.

4 "Gaining extra revenue is easy for any producer – all it has to do is raise the price of its product". Do you agree? Explain when this would be true and when it would not be true.

5 Suppose that the market demand curve for pasta is a straight line of the form $Q = 300 - 50P$ where Q is the quantity of pasta bought in thousands of boxes per week and P is the price per box (in euros).

  a At what price does the demand for pasta go to 0? Develop a numerical example to show that the demand for pasta is elastic at this point.

  b How much pasta is demanded at a price of €0? Develop a numerical example to show that demand is inelastic at this point.

  c How much pasta is demanded at a price of €3? Develop a numerical example that suggests that total spending on pasta is as large as possible at this price.

6 Marvin currently spends 35 per cent of his €100 000 income on housing. If his income elasticity of demand for housing is 0.8, will this fraction rise or fall when he gets a raise to €120 000? What is the new fraction of income spent on housing? Would you give different answers to the questions if Marvin's income elasticity of demand for housing were 1.3?

7 John Bull always spends one-third of his income on Union Jack flags. What is the income elasticity of his demand for such flags? What is the price elasticity of his demand for flags?

8 Table 4-4 reports an estimated price elasticity of demand for electricity of −1.14. Explain what this means with a numerical example. Does this number seem large? Do you think this is a short- or long-term elasticity estimate? How might this estimate be important for owners of electric utilities or for bodies that regulate them?

9 Table 4-5 reports that the cross-price elasticity of demand for electricity with respect to the price of natural gas is 0.50. Explain what this means with a numerical example. What does the fact that the number is positive imply about the relationship between electricity and natural gas use?

10 An economist hired by a home building firm has been asked to estimate a demand curve for homes. He gathers data on the price of new houses and on the number sold from the top 100 metropolitan areas in the United Kingdom. He plots these data, draws a line that seems to pass near the points, and labels that line "demand". How many problems can you identify in this approach to estimating the demand for houses?

PROBLEMS

4.1 Suppose the demand curve for flyswatters is given by

$$Q = 500 - 50P$$

where Q is the number of flyswatters demanded per week and P is the price in euros.

  a How many flyswatters are demanded at a price of €2? How about a price of €3? €4? Suppose flyswatters were free; how many would be bought?

  b On a graph, plot the flyswatter demand curve. Remember to put P on the vertical axis and Q on the horizontal axis. To do so, you may wish to solve for P as a function of Q.

  c Suppose during July the flyswatter demand curve shifts to

$$Q = 1000 - 50P$$

  Answer part a and part b for this new demand curve.

4.2 Suppose that the demand curve for kidney beans is given by

$$Q = 20 - P$$

where Q is thousands of kilos of beans bought per week and P is the price in euros per kilo.

  a How many beans will be bought at $P = 0$?

  b At what price does the quantity demanded of beans become 0?

c Calculate total expenditures ($P \cdot Q$) for beans of each whole euro price between the prices identified in part a and part b.

d What price for beans yields the highest total expenditures?

e Suppose the demand for beans shifted to $Q = 40 - 2P$. How would your answers to part a through part d change? Explain the differences intuitively and with a graph.

4.3 Consider the three demand curves

$$Q = \frac{100}{P} \quad \{i\}$$

$$Q = \frac{100}{\sqrt{P}} \quad \{ii\}$$

$$Q = \frac{100}{P^{3/2}} \quad \{iii\}$$

a Use a calculator to compute the value of Q for each demand curve for $P = 1$ and for $P = 1.1$.

b What do your calculations show about the price elasticity of demand at $P = 1$ for each of the three demand curves?

c Now perform a similar set of calculations for the three demand curves at $P = 4$ and $P = 4.4$. How do the elasticities computed here compare to those from part b? Explain your results using footnote 5 of this chapter.

4.4 The market demand for potatoes is given by

$$Q = 1000 + 0.3I - 300P + 299P'$$

where

Q = Annual demand in kilos

I = Average income in euros per year

P = Price of potatoes in cents per kilo

P' = Price of rice in cents per kilo.

a Suppose I = €10 000 and P' = €0.25; what would be the market demand for potatoes? At what price would $Q = 0$? Graph this demand curve.

b Suppose I rose to €20 000 with P' staying at €0.25. Now what would the demand for potatoes be? At what price would $Q = 0$? Plot this demand curve. Explain why more potatoes are demanded at every price in this case than in part a.

c If I returns to €10 000 but P' falls to €0.10, what would the demand for potatoes be? At what price would $Q = 0$? Graph this demand curve. Explain why fewer potatoes are demanded at every price in this case than in part a.

4.5 Tom, Dick, and Harry constitute the entire market for the fresh fish catch of the day. Tom's demand curve is given by

$$Q_1 = 100 - 2P$$

for $P \leq 50$. For $P > 50$, $Q_1 = 0$. Dick's demand curve is given by

$$Q_2 = 160 - 4P$$

for $P \leq 40$. For $P > 40$, $Q_2 = 0$. Harry's demand curve is given by

$$Q_3 = 150 - 5P$$

for $P \leq 30$. For $P > 30$, $Q_3 = 0$. Using this information, answer the following:

a How much fish is demanded by each person at $P = 50$? At $P = 35$? At $P = 25$? At $P = 10$? And at $P = 0$?

b What is the total market demand for fish at each of the prices specified in part a?

c Plot each individual's demand curve.

d Use the individual demand curves and the results of part b to construct the total market demand for fish.

4.6 Suppose the quantity of good X demanded by individual 1 is given by

$$X_1 = 10 - 2P_X + 0.01I_1 + 0.4P_Y$$

and the quantity of X demanded by individual 2 is

$$X_2 = 5 - P_X + 0.02I_2 + 0.2P_Y$$

a What is the market demand function for total X ($= X_1 + X_2$) as a function of P_X, I_1, I_2, and P_Y?

b Plot the two individual demand curves (with X on the horizontal axis, P_X on the vertical axis) for the case $I_1 = 1000$, $I_2 = 1000$, and $P_Y = 10$.

c Using these individual demand curves, construct the market demand curve for total X. What is the algebraic equation for this curve?

d Now suppose I_1 increases to 1100 and I_2 decreases to 900. How would the market demand curve shift? How would the individual demand curves shift? Plot these new curves.

e Finally, suppose P_Y rises to 15. Plot the new individual and market demand curves that would result.

4.7 Suppose that the current market price of VCRs is €300, that average consumer disposable income is €30 000, and that the price of DVD players (a substitute for VCRs) is €500. Under these conditions, the annual UK demand for VCRs is 5 million per year. Statistical studies have shown that for this product $e_{Q,P} = -1.3$, $e_{Q,I} = 1.7$, and $e_{Q,P}{}' = 0.8$ where P' is the price of DVD players.
Use this information to predict the annual number of VCRs sold under the following conditions:

a Increasing competition from China causes VCR prices to fall to €270 with I and P' unchanged.

b Income tax reductions raise average disposable income to €31 500 with P and P' unchanged.

c Technical improvements in DVD players cause their price to fall to €400 with P and I unchanged.

d All of the events described in part a through part c occur simultaneously.

4.8 In Chapter 3 we introduced the concept of consumer surplus as measured by the area above market price and below an individual's demand for a good. This problem asks you to think about that concept for the market as a whole.

a Consumer surplus in the market as a whole is simply the sum of the consumer surplus received by each individual consumer. Use Figure 4-1 to explain why this total consumer surplus is also given by the area under the *market* demand curve and above the current price.

b Use a graph to show that the loss of consumer surplus resulting from a given price rise is greater with an inelastic demand curve than with an elastic one. Explain your result intuitively. (Hint: What is the primary reason a demand curve is elastic?)

c How would you evaluate the following assertion: "The welfare loss from any price increase can be readily measured by the increased spending on a good made necessary by that price increase."

4.9 In Problem 3.9, we introduced compensated demand curves along which utility is held constant and only the substitution effect of price changes is considered. This problem shows how the price elasticity of demand along such a curve is related to the customary measure of price elasticity.

a Suppose consumers buy only two goods, food and shelter, and that they buy these in fixed proportions – one unit of food for each unit of shelter. In this case, what does the compensated demand curve for food look like? What is the price elasticity of demand along this curve (call this elasticity e_s – the substitution elasticity)? Are there any substitution effects in this demand?

b Under the conditions of part a, what is the income elasticity of demand for food ($e_{F,I}$)?

c Continuing as in part a, suppose one unit of food costs half what one unit of housing costs. What fraction of income will be spent on food (call this s_F)?

d Using the information in part c, what is the overall price elasticity of demand (including both substitution and income effects) for food ($e_{F,P}$)? (Hint: A numerical example may help here.)

e Use your answers to part a through part d to show that the numbers calculated in this problem obey the formula in footnote 8 of this chapter:

$$e_{F,P} = e_s - s_F e_{F,I}$$

This formula is quite general. It is sometimes called the "Slutsky Equation" after its discoverer.

f Let us change this problem a bit now to assume that people *always* spend one-third of their income on food, no matter what their income or what the price of food is. What is the demand function for food in this case?

g Under the conditions of part f, what are the values of $e_{F,P}$, s_F, $e_{F,I}$, and (using the formula in part e) e_s for this case? Explain why the value for e_s differs between this case and the value calculated in part a.

h How would your answers to part a through part g change if we focused on shelter instead of food?

4.10 Consider the linear demand curve shown in the following figure.

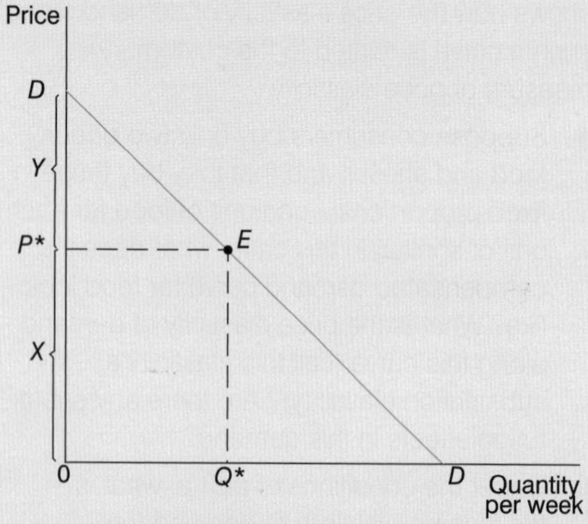

There is a geometric way of calculating the price elasticity of demand for this curve at any arbitrary point (say point E). To do so, first write the algebraic form of this demand curve as $Q = a + bP$.

a With this demand function, what is the value of P for which $Q = 0$?

b Use your results from part a together with the fact that distance X in the figure is given by the current price, P^*, to show that distance Y is given by

$$-\frac{Q^*}{b}$$

(remember, b is negative here, so this really is a positive distance).

c Footnote 4 of this chapter shows that the price elasticity of demand at point E can be defined as

$$e_{Q,P} = \frac{\Delta Q}{\Delta P} \cdot \frac{P^*}{Q^*} = b \cdot \frac{P^*}{Q^*}$$

where the final equation follows because of the algebraic form of this demand curve. Use this result to show that

$$|e_{Q,P}| = \frac{X}{Y}$$

(we use absolute values here because the price elasticity of demand is actually negative).

d Explain how the result of part c can be used to demonstrate how the price of elasticity of demand changes as one moves along a linear demand curve.

e Explain how the results of part c might be used to approximate the price elasticity of demand at any point on a nonlinear demand curve.

PART THREE
UNCERTAINTY AND STRATEGY

It is a world of change in which we live . . . the problems of life arise from the fact that we know so little.

FRANK H. KNIGHT, *RISK, UNCERTAINTY AND PROFIT,* 1921

In the previous part of this book, we looked at the choices people make when they know exactly what will happen. This study left us with a quite complete theory of demand and of how prices affect decisions. In this part, we expand our scope a bit by looking at how people make decisions when they are not certain what will happen. As for the simple theory of demand, the tools developed here to deal with such uncertainty are used in all of economics.

Part Three has only two chapters. The first (Chapter 5) focuses on defining the notion of "risk" and showing why people generally do not like it. Most of the chapter is concerned with methods that people may use to reduce the risks to which they are exposed. Use of insurance, diversification, and options are highlighted as ways in which various risks can be reduced.

Chapter 6 then looks at a somewhat different kind of uncertainty – the uncertainty that can arise in strategic relationships with others. The chapter introduces the formal topic of game theory and shows, through increasingly complex formulations, how games can capture the essence of many strategic situations. Probably the most important conclusion of Chapter 6 is that many games contain a set of strategic choices that constitute an "equilibrium" among the game's players. In such an equilibrium, once it is established, no player has an incentive to change what he or she is doing.

5

Uncertainty

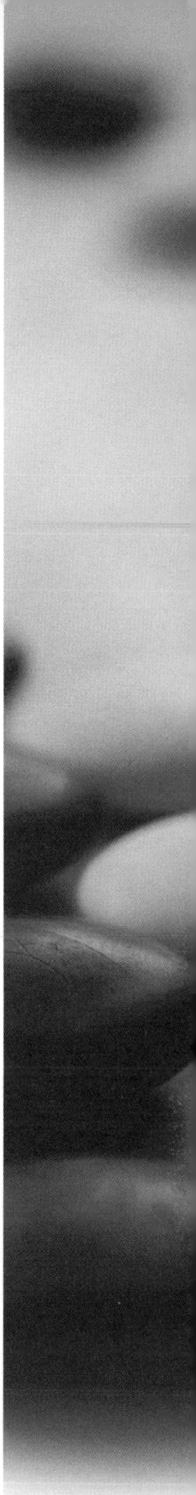

So far, we have assumed that people's choices do not involve any degree of uncertainty; once they decide what to do, they get what they have chosen. That is not always the way things work in many real-world situations. When you buy a lottery ticket, invest in shares of common stock, or play poker, what you get back is subject to chance. Many choices involve incomplete information (such as deciding which second-hand car is a lemon and which isn't), and these choices must be made somewhat "in the dark". In this chapter, we look at three questions raised by economic problems involving uncertainty: (1) Why do people generally dislike risky situations? (2) What can people do to avoid or reduce risks? and (3) How can the problem of uncertainty be treated more generally as one of incomplete information?

Probability and Expected Value

The study of individual behavior under uncertainty and the mathematical study of probability and statistics have a common historical origin in games of chance. Gamblers who try to devise ways of winning at blackjack and casinos trying to keep the game profitable are modern examples of this concern. Two statistical concepts that originated from studying games of chance, *probability* and *expected value*, are very important to our study of economic choices in uncertain situations.

The **probability** of an event happening is, roughly speaking, the relative frequency with which it occurs. For example, to say that the probability of heads coming up on the toss of a fair coin is 1/2 means that if a coin is tossed a large number of times, we can expect heads to come up in approximately one-half of the tosses. Similarly, the probability of rolling a "2" on a single die is 1/6. In approximately one out of every six rolls, a "2" should come up. Of course, before a coin is tossed or a die is rolled, we have no idea what will happen, so each toss or roll has an uncertain outcome.

The **expected value** of a game with a number of uncertain outcomes (or prizes) is the size of the prize that the player will win on average. Suppose Jones and Smith agree to toss a coin once. If heads comes up, Jones will pay Smith €1; if tails comes up, Smith will pay Jones €1. From Smith's point of view, there are two prizes or outcomes (X_1 and X_2) in this game: If the coin is a head, $X_1 = +€1$; if a tail comes up, $X_2 = -€1$ (the minus sign indicates that Smith must pay). From Jones's point of view, the game is exactly the same except that the signs of the outcomes are reversed. The expected value of the game is then

$$\frac{1}{2}X_1 + \frac{1}{2}X_2 = \frac{1}{2}€ + \frac{1}{2}(-€1) = 0 \qquad \{5.1\}$$

The expected value of this game is zero. If the game were played a large number of times, it is not likely that either player would come out very far ahead.

Now suppose the prizes of the game were changed so that, from Smith's point of view, $X_1 = €10$, and $X_2 = -€1$. Smith will win €10 if a head comes up but will lose only €1 if a tail comes up. The expected value of this game is €4.50:

Probability The relative frequency with which an event occurs.

$$\frac{1}{2}X_1 + \frac{1}{2}X_2 = \frac{1}{2}(€10) + \frac{1}{2}(-€1) = €5 - €0.50 = €4.50 \qquad \{5.2\}$$

Expected value The average outcome from an uncertain gamble.

Fair games Games that cost their expected value.

Risk aversion The tendency of people to refuse to accept fair games.

If this game is played many times, Smith will certainly end up the big winner, averaging €4.50 each time the coin is tossed. The game is so attractive that Smith might be willing to pay Jones something for the privilege of playing. She might even be willing to pay as much as €4.50, the expected value, for a chance to play. Games with an expected value of zero and games that cost their expected values for the right to play (here, €4.50) are called **fair games**. If fair games are played many times, the monetary losses or gains are expected to be rather small. Application 5.1: *Blackjack Systems* looks at the importance of the expected value idea to gamblers and casinos alike.

Risk Aversion

Economists have found that, when people are faced with a risky but fair situation, they usually choose not to participate.[1] A major reason for this **risk aversion** was first identified by the Swiss mathematician Daniel Bernoulli in the eighteenth century. In his early study of behavior under uncertainty, Bernoulli theorized that it is not the monetary payoff of a game that matters to people. Rather, it is the expected utility (what Bernoulli called the *moral value*) associated with the game's prizes that is important for people's decisions. If differences in a game's money prizes do not completely reflect utility, people may find that games that are fair in euro terms are in fact unfair in terms of utility. Specifically, Bernoulli (and most later economists) assumed that the utility associated with the payoffs in a risky situation

MICROQUIZ 5.1

What is the actuarially fair price for each of the following games?

1. Winning €1000 with probability 0.5 and losing €1000 with probability 0.5.
2. Winning €1000 with probability 0.6 and losing €1000 with probability 0.4.
3. Winning €1000 with probability 0.7, winning €2000 with probability 0.2, and losing €10 000 with probability 0.1.

[1]The games we discuss here are assumed to yield no utility in their play other than the prizes. Because economists wish to focus on the purely risk-related aspects of a situation, they must abstract from any pure consumption benefit that people get from gambling. Clearly, if gambling is fun to someone, he or she will be willing to pay something to play.

APPLICATION 5.1 *Blackjack Systems*

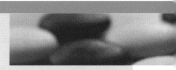

The game of blackjack (or twenty-one) provides an illustration of the expected-value notion and its relevance to people's behavior in uncertain situations. Blackjack is a very simple game. Each player is dealt two cards (with the dealer playing last). The dealer asks each player if he or she wishes another card. The player getting a hand that totals closest to 21, without going over 21, is the winner. If the receipt of a card puts a player over 21, that player automatically loses.

Played in this way, blackjack offers a number of advantages to the dealer. Most important, the dealer, who plays last, is in a favorable position because other players can go over 21 (and therefore lose) before the dealer plays. Under the usual rules, the dealer has the additional advantage of winning hands that are ties. These two advantages give the dealer a margin of winning of about 6 per cent on average. Players can expect to win 47 per cent of all hands played, whereas the dealer will win 53 per cent of the time.

Card Counting

Because the rules of blackjack make the game unfair to players, casinos have gradually eased the rules in order to entice more people to play. At many Las Vegas casinos, for example, dealers must play under fixed rules that allow no discretion depending on the individual game situation; and, in the case of ties, rather than winning them, dealers must return bets to the players. These rules alter fairness of the game quite a bit. By some estimates, Las Vegas casino dealers enjoy a blackjack advantage of as little as 0.1 per cent, if that. In fact, in recent years a number of systems have been developed by players that they claim can even result in a net advantage for the player. The systems involve counting face cards, systematic varying of bets, and numerous other strategies for special situations that arise in the game.[1] Computer simulations of literally billions of potential blackjack hands have shown that careful adherence to a correct strategy can result in an advantage to the player of as much as 1 or 2 per cent. Actor Dustin Hoffman illustrated these potential advantages in his character's remarkable ability to count cards in the 1989 film *Rain Man*.

Casino vs. Card Counter

It should come as no surprise that players' use of these blackjack systems is not particularly welcomed by those who operate Las Vegas casinos. The casinos made several rule changes (such as using multiple card decks to make card counting more difficult) in order to reduce system players' advantages. They have also started to refuse admission to known system players. Such care has not been foolproof, however. For example, in the late 1990s a small band of MIT students used a variety of sophisticated card counting techniques to take Las Vegas casinos for more than $2 million.[2] Their clever efforts did not amuse casino personnel, however, and the students had a number of unpleasant encounters with security personnel.

All of this turmoil illustrates the importance of small changes in expected values for a game such as blackjack that involves many repetitions. Card counters pay little attention to the outcome on a single hand in blackjack. Instead, they focus on improving the average outcome after many hours at the card table. Even small changes in the probability of winning can result in large expected payoffs.

Expected Values of Other Games

The expected value concept plays an important role in all of the games of chance offered at casinos. For example, slot machines can be set to yield a precise expected return to players. When a casino operates hundreds of slot machines in a single location it can be virtually certain of the return it can earn each day even though the payouts from any particular machine can be quite variable. Similarly, the game of roulette includes 36 numbered squares together with squares labeled "0" and "00". By paying out 36-to-1 on the numbered squares the casino can expect to earn about 5.3 cents (= 2 ÷ 38) on each dollar bet. Bets on Red or Black or on Even or Odd are equally

(*Continued*)

profitable. According to some experts the game of baccarat has the lowest expected return for casinos, though in this case the game's high stakes may still make the game quite profitable.

To Think About

1 If blackjack systems increase people's expected winnings, why doesn't everyone use them? Who do you expect would be most likely to learn how to use the systems?

2 How does the fact that casinos operate many blackjack tables, slot machines, and roulette tables simultaneously reduce the risk that they will lose money? Is it more risky to operate a small casino than a large one?

[1]The classic introduction to card-counting strategies is in Edward O. Thorp, *Beat the Dealer* (New York: Random House, 1962).

[2]See Ben Merzrich, *Bringing Down the House* (New York: Free Press, 2002).

increases less rapidly than the euro value of these payoffs. That is, the extra (or marginal) utility that winning an extra euro in prize money provides is assumed to decline as more euros are won.

Diminishing Marginal Utility

This assumption is illustrated in Figure 5-1, which shows the utility associated with possible prizes (or incomes) from €0 to €50 000. The concave shape of the curve reflects the assumed diminishing marginal utility of these prizes. Although additional income always raises utility, the increase in utility resulting from an increase in income from €1000 to €2000 is much greater than the increase in utility that results from an increase in income from €49 000 to €50 000. It is this assumed

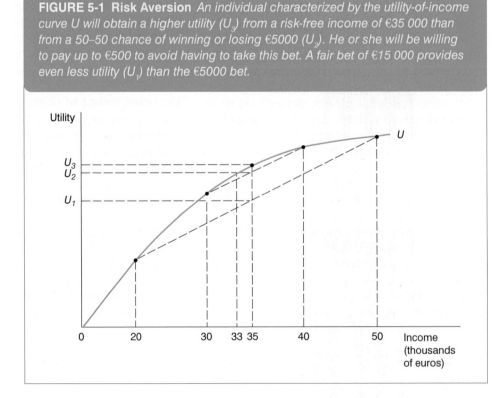

FIGURE 5-1 Risk Aversion *An individual characterized by the utility-of-income curve U will obtain a higher utility (U_3) from a risk-free income of €35 000 than from a 50–50 chance of winning or losing €5000 (U_2). He or she will be willing to pay up to €500 to avoid having to take this bet. A fair bet of €15 000 provides even less utility (U_1) than the €5000 bet.*

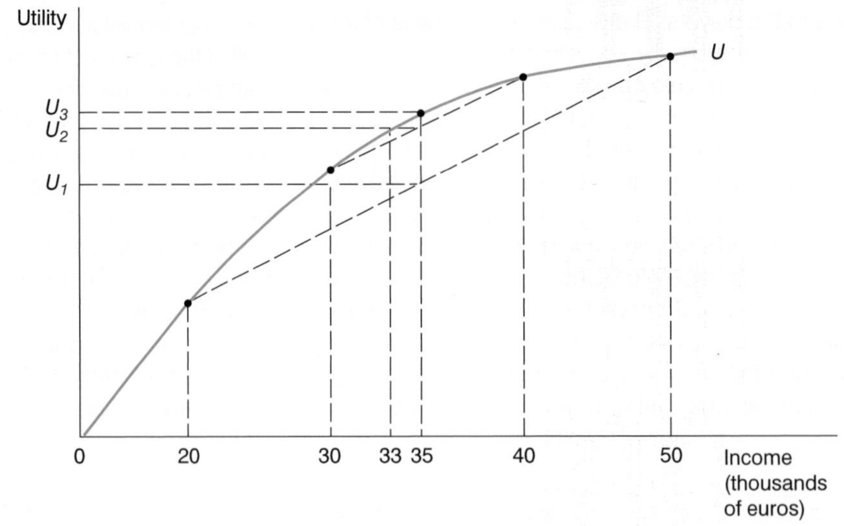

diminishing marginal utility of income (which is in some ways similar to the assumption of a diminishing MRS introduced in Chapter 2) that gives rise to risk aversion.

A Graphical Analysis of Risk Aversion

Figure 5-1 illustrates risk aversion. The figure assumes that three options are open to this person. He or she may (1) retain the current level of income (€35 000) without taking any risk; (2) take a fair bet with a 50–50 chance of winning or losing €5000; or (3) take a fair bet with a 50–50 chance of winning or losing €15 000. To examine the person's preferences among these options, we must compute the expected utility available from each.

The utility received by staying at the current €35 000 income is given by U_3. The *U* curve shows directly how the individual feels about this current income. The utility level obtained from the €5000 bet is simply the average of the utility of €40 000 (which the individual will end up with by winning the game) and the utility of €30 000 (which he or she will end up with when the game is lost). This average utility is given by U_2.[2] Because it falls short of U_3, we can assume that the person will refuse to make the €5000 bet. Finally, the utility of the €15 000 bet is the average of the utility from €50 000 and the utility from €20 000. This is given by U_1, which falls below U_2. In other words, the person likes the risky €15 000 bet even less than the €5000 bet.

Willingness to Pay to Avoid Risk

Diminished marginal utility of income, as shown in Figure 5-1, means that people will be averse to risk. Among options with the same expected euro values (€35 000 in all of our examples), people will prefer risk-free incomes to risky options because the gains such risky options offer are worth less in utility terms than the losses. In fact, a person would be willing to give up some amount of income to avoid taking a risk. In Figure 5-1, for example, a risk-free income of €33 000 provides the same utility as the €5000 gamble (U_2). The individual is willing to pay up to €2000 to avoid taking that risk. There are a number of ways this person might spend these funds to reduce the risk or avoid it completely.

Methods for Reducing Risk

In many situations, taking risks is unavoidable. Even though driving your car or eating a meal at a restaurant subjects you to some uncertainty about what will actually happen, short of becoming a hermit, there is no way you can avoid every risk in your life. Our analysis in the previous section suggests, however, that people are generally willing to pay something to reduce these risks. In this section, we examine three methods for doing so – insurance, diversification, and using options.

MICROQUIZ 5.2

Under what conditions would an individual be neutral to risk (that is, receive the same utility from taking a fair bet as from refusing the bet)? What kind of preferences would give rise to a preference for risky situations?

Insurance

Each year, people in the United Kingdom spend millions of pounds on insurance of all types. Most commonly, they buy coverage for their own life, for their home and cars, and for any private health

[2]This average utility can be found by drawing the chord joining *U*(€40 000) and *U*(€30 000) and finding the midpoint of that chord. Because the vertical line at €35 000 is midway between €40 000 and €30 000, it will also bisect the chord.

care costs. But, insurance can be bought (perhaps at a very high price) for practically any risk imaginable. For example, many people in California buy earthquake insurance, outdoor swimming pool owners can buy special coverage for injuries to falling parachutists, and surgeons or piano players can insure their hands. In all of these cases, people are willing to pay a premium to an insurance company in order to be assured of compensation if something goes wrong.

The underlying motive for insurance purchases is illustrated in Figure 5-2. Here, we have repeated the utility-of-income curve from Figure 5-1, but now we assume that during the next year this person with a €35 000 current income (and consumption) faces a 50 per cent chance of having €15 000 in unexpected medical bills, which would reduce his or her consumption to €20 000. Without insurance, this person's utility would be U_1 – the average of the utility from €35 000 and the utility from €20 000.

Fair insurance Insurance for which the premium is equal to the expected value of the loss.

Fair Insurance This person would clearly be better off with an actuarially **fair insurance** policy for his or her private health care needs. This policy would cost €7500 – the expected value of what insurance companies would have to pay each year in health claims. A person who bought the policy would be assured of €27 500 in consumption. If he or she bought the policy and stayed well, income would be reduced by the €7500 premium. If this person suffered the illness, the insurance

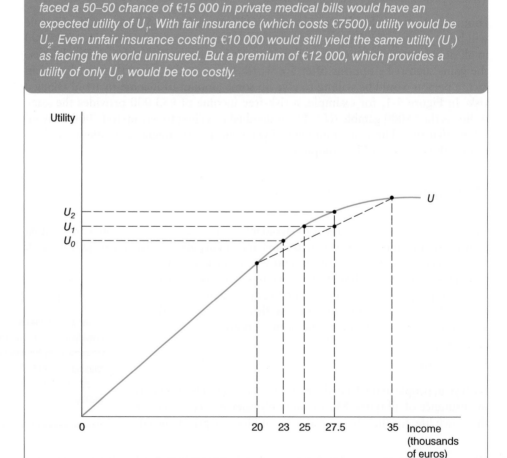

FIGURE 5-2 Insurance Reduces Risk *A person with €35 000 in income who faced a 50–50 chance of €15 000 in private medical bills would have an expected utility of U_1. With fair insurance (which costs €7500), utility would be U_2. Even unfair insurance costing €10 000 would still yield the same utility (U_1) as facing the world uninsured. But a premium of €12 000, which provides a utility of only U_0, would be too costly.*

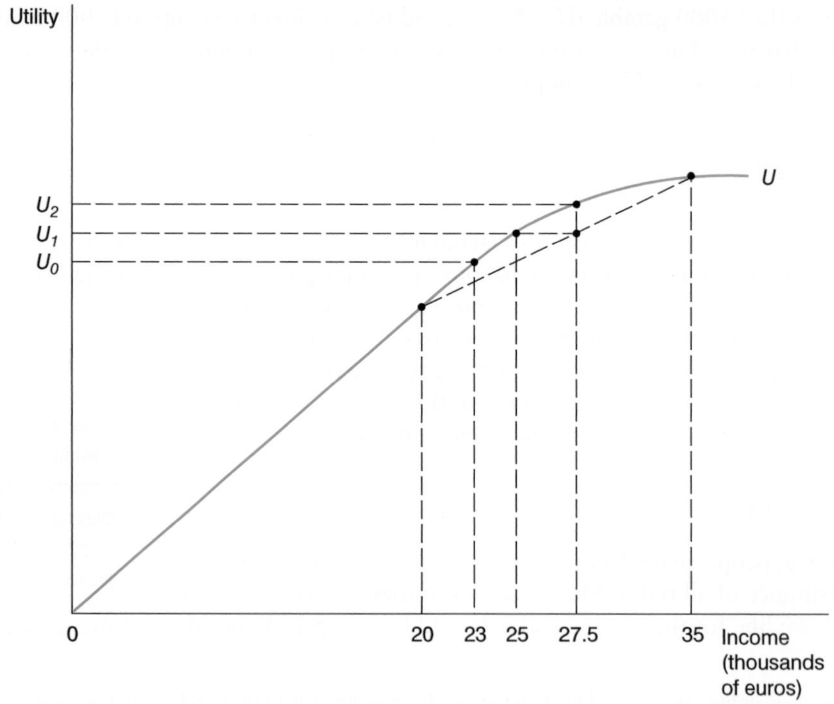

company would pay the €15 000 in medical bills but this person would have paid the €7500 premium so consumption would still be €27 500. As Figure 5-2 shows, the utility from a certain income of €27 500 (U_2) exceeds that attainable from facing the world uninsured, so the policy represents a utility-enhancing use for funds.

Unfair Insurance No insurance company can afford to sell insurance at actuarially fair premiums. Not only do insurance companies have to pay benefits, but they must also maintain records, collect premiums, and investigate claims to ensure they are not fraudulent. Hence, a would-be insurance purchaser can always expect to pay more than an actuarially fair premium. Still, a buyer may decide that the risk reduction that insurance provides is worth the extra charges. In the health care illustration in Figure 5-2, for example, this person would be willing to pay up to €10 000 for health insurance since the risk-free consumption stream of €25 000 that buying such "unfair" insurance would yield provides as much utility (U_1) as does facing the world uninsured. Of course, even a desirable product such as insurance can become too expensive. At a price of €12 000, the utility provided with full insurance (U_0) falls short of what would be obtained from facing the world uninsured. In this case, this person is better off taking the risk of paying his or her own medical bills than accepting such an unfair insurance premium. In Application 5.2: *Excesses in Insurance*, we look at one way to avoid unfair insurance associated with small risks.

Uninsurable Risks The preceding discussion shows that risk-averse individuals will always buy insurance against risky outcomes unless insurance premiums exceed the expected value of a loss by too much. Three types of factors may result in such high premiums and thereby cause some risks to become uninsurable. First, some risks may be so unique or difficult to evaluate that an insurer may have no idea how to set the premium level. Determining an actuarially fair premium requires that a given risky situation must occur frequently enough so that the insurer can both estimate the expected value of the loss and rely on being able to cover expected payouts with premiums from individuals who do not suffer losses. For rare or very unpredictable events such as wars, nuclear power station mishaps, or invasions from Mars, would-be insurers may have no basis for establishing insurance premiums and therefore refrain from offering any coverage.

Two other reasons for absence of insurance coverage relate to the behavior of the individuals who want to buy insurance. In some cases, these individuals may know more about the likelihood that they will suffer a loss than does an insurer. Those who expect large losses will buy insurance, whereas those who expect small ones will not. This *adverse selection* results in the insurer paying out more in losses than expected unless the insurer finds a way to control who buys the policies offered. As we will see later, in the absence of such controls, no insurance would be provided even though people would willingly buy it.

The behavior of individuals once they are insured may also affect the possibility for insurance coverage. If having insurance makes people more likely to incur losses, insurers' premium calculations will be incorrect and again, they may be forced to charge premiums that are too unfair in an actuarial sense. For example, if people who have insurance on the cash they carry in their pockets are far more likely to lose it through carelessness than those who do not have insurance, insurance premiums to cover such losses may have to be very high. This *moral hazard* in people's behavior means that insurance against accidental losses of cash will not be available on any reasonable terms. In Chapter 17, we explore both adverse selection and moral hazard in much more detail.

APPLICATION 5.2 *Excesses in Insurance*

An "excess" provision in an insurance policy is the requirement that the insured pay the first *X* euros in the event of a claim; after that, insurance pays the rest. With car insurance policies, for example, a €200 excess provision is quite standard. If you have a collision, you must pay the first €200 in damages, then the insurance company will pay the rest. Most other accident insurance policies have similar provisions.

Excesses and Administrative Costs

The primary reason for excess provisions in insurance contracts is to deter small claims. Because administrative costs to the insurance company of handling a claim are about the same regardless of a claim's size, such costs will tend to be a very high fraction of the value of a small claim. Hence, insurance against small losses will tend to be actuarially "unfair". Most people will find that they would rather incur the risks of such losses (such as scratches to the paintwork of their cars) themselves rather than paying such unfair premiums. Similarly, increasing the excess in a policy may sometimes be a financially attractive option.

These features of excesses in insurance policies are illustrated by the choices made by two of your authors. For example, both of their car policies offer either a €500 or a €1000 excess associated with collision coverage. The lower €500 excess policy costs about €100 more each year. Both authors have opted for the €1000 policy on the principle that paying €100 for an extra €500 coverage each year seems like a bad deal.

Homeowners' policies offer a similar set of choices. In this case, excesses can be applied to both accident and theft losses of property. Excesses per claim of €500 are fairly standard in these policies and the benefits of increasing to a €1000 excess or more are very modest. Insurance companies do offer lower premiums (in the form of "no claims bonuses") for "claims free" experience, however. This, in combination with the paperwork costs that filing a claim entails, may be sufficient to deter most claims under €1000 anyway.

Excesses in Private Health Insurance

Although the logic of excesses applies to health insurance too, the presence of such features has proven to be quite controversial.[1] For example, in the United States in 1988, Congress passed the Medicare Catastrophic Coverage Act. This act provided extra coverage for Medicare recipients, with a large annual excess being required before coverage began. This policy proved unpopular for two reasons: (1) People argued that it was unfair to ask elderly people suffering "catastrophic" illnesses to pay the initial portion of their costs; and (2) the premium for the policy was to be paid by the elderly themselves rather than by the working population (as is the case for a major portion of the rest of the Medicare program). The uproar over the program was so large that it was repealed after only one year.

More recently, arguments over excesses surrounded the adoption of a Medicare drug benefit in 2003. Under the provisions of this plan (which came fully into effect in 2006), elderly consumers of prescription drugs would face a complex excess scheme: (1) The first $250 spent annually on drugs is not covered by the drug benefit, (2) 75 per cent of annual spending on drugs between $250 and $2100 is covered by Medicare, (3) No spending between $2100 and $5100 annually is covered by Medicare, and (4) 95 per cent of annual spending over $5100 is reimbursed by Medicare. Observers have had a difficult time trying to find a rationale for such a complex scheme – especially for the odd "doughnut hole" of coverage between $2100 and $5100 in annual spending. Clearly the provision cannot have much to do with the administrative cost issue. The $250 excess at the bottom of the schedule prevents the filing of claims for every aspirin bought. It may be that the hole is intended mainly to save money so that available funds can be focused on the most needy elderly (those with drug expenses over $5100), but whether it has a rationale in the theory of insurance is anyone's guess.

To Think About

1 In some cases, you can buy another insurance policy to cover an excess in your underlying insurance. That is the case, for example, when you rent a car, and for "Medigap" policies that

cover Medicare deductibles. Does buying such a policy make sense?

2 Why are excesses usually stated on an annual basis? If losses occur randomly, wouldn't a "lifetime" deductible be better?

[1]Many private health insurance policies also have "co-payment" provisions that require people to pay, say, 25 per cent of their claim's cost. Co-payments increase the price people pay for health care *at the margin*. Excesses reduce the average price paid, but, after the excess is met, the marginal price of added care is zero. For a discussion of co-payments in health (and other) insurance, see Chapter 17.

Diversification

A second way for risk-averse individuals to reduce risk is by diversifying. This is the economic principle underlying the adage, "Don't put all your eggs in one basket". By suitably spreading risk around, it may be possible to raise utility above that provided by following a single course of action. This possibility is illustrated in Figure 5-3, which shows the utility of income for an individual with a current income of €35 000 who must invest €15 000 of that income in risky assets.

For simplicity, assume there are only two such assets, shares of stock in company A or company B. One share of stock in either company costs €1, and the investor believes that the stock will rise to €2 if the company does well during the next year; if the company does poorly, however, the stock will be worthless. Each company has a 50–50 chance of doing well. How should this individual invest his or her funds? At

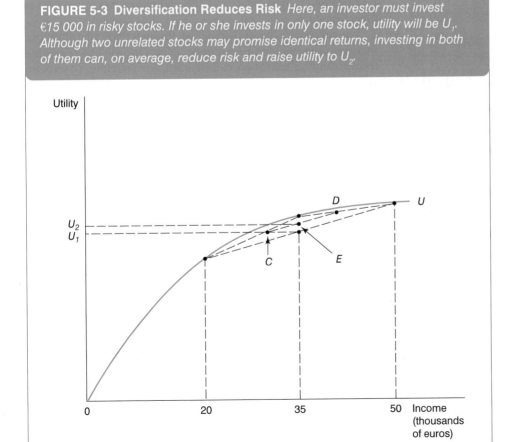

FIGURE 5-3 Diversification Reduces Risk *Here, an investor must invest €15 000 in risky stocks. If he or she invests in only one stock, utility will be U_1. Although two unrelated stocks may promise identical returns, investing in both of them can, on average, reduce risk and raise utility to U_2.*

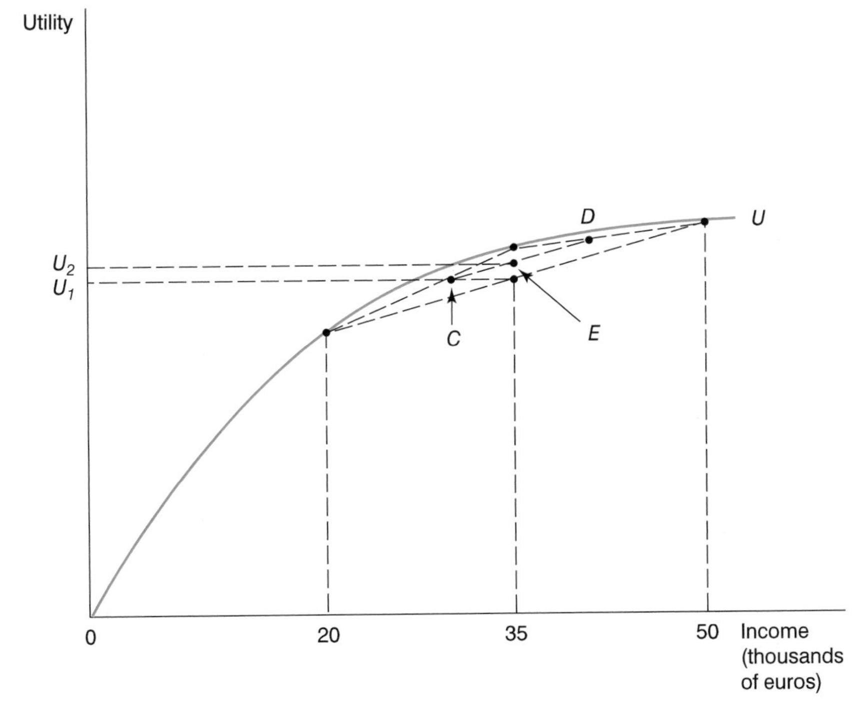

first, it would seem that it does not matter since the two companies' prospects are identical. But, if we assume the company's prospects are unrelated to one another, we can show that holding both stocks will reduce this person's risks.

Suppose this person decides to plunge into the market by investing only in 15 000 shares of company A. Then he or she has a 50 per cent chance of having €50 000 at the end of the year and a 50 per cent chance of having €20 000. This undiversified investment strategy will therefore yield a utility of U_1.

Let's consider a diversified strategy in which the investor buys 7500 shares of each stock. There are now four possible outcomes, depending on how each company does. These are illustrated in Table 5-1 together with the individual's income in each of these eventualities. Each of these outcomes is equally likely. Notice that the diversified strategy only achieves very good or very bad results when both companies do well or poorly, respectively. In half the cases, the gains in one company's shares balance the losses in the others, and the individual ends up with the original $35 000. The diversified strategy, although it has the same expected value (€35 000 $= 0.25 \cdot$ €20 000 $+ 0.50 \cdot$ €35 000 $+ 0.25 \cdot$ €50 000) as the single stock strategy, is less risky.

Diversification The spreading of risk among several alternatives rather than choosing only one.

Illustrating the utility gain from this reduction in risk requires a bit of ingenuity because we must average the utilities from the four outcomes shown in Table 5-1. We do so in a two-step process. Point *C* in Figure 5-3 represents the average utility for the case where company B does poorly (the average of the utility from €20 000 and €35 000), whereas point *D* represents the average utility when company B does well (€35 000 and €50 000). The final average of points C and D is found at point *E*, which represents a utility level of U_2. Because U_2 exceeds U_1, it is clear that this individual has gained from diversification.

The conclusion that spreading risk through **diversification** can increase utility applies to a number of situations. The reasoning in our simple illustration can be used, for example, to explain why individuals opt to buy mutual funds that invest in many stocks rather than choosing only a few stocks on their own (see Application 5.3: *Mutual (or Unit Trust) Funds*. It also explains why people invest in many kinds of assets (stocks, bonds, cash, precious metals, real estate, and durable goods such as classic cars) rather than in only one. Individuals may also choose to diversify their earnings stream by obtaining skills that can be used in many kinds of jobs or by choosing jobs whose success does not depend on the fortunes of a single product. In all of these cases, our analysis shows that individuals will not only obtain higher utility levels because of the risk reduction from diversification but that they might even be willing to pay something (say, mutual fund fees or educational costs) to obtain these gains.

MICROQUIZ 5.3

Explain why the following are examples of diversification – that is, explain why each choice specified offers the same expected value, though the preferred choice is lower in risk.

1. Preferring to bet €100 on each of 10 coin tosses over €1000 on a single toss.
2. Preferring single feed lines at banks to lines for each teller.
3. Preferring basketball to football if a single game is to determine the best team (this example may reflect a peculiarity of your authors).

TABLE 5-1 Possible Outcomes from Investing in Two Companies

		Company B's Performance	
		Poor	Good
Company A's Performance	Poor	€20 000	€35 000
	Good	35 000	50 000

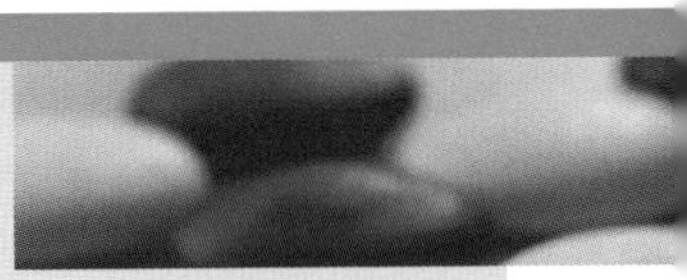

APPLICATION 5.3 *Mutual (or Unit Trust) Funds*

One of the most convenient ways for individuals to invest in common stocks is by purchasing mutual fund (or unit trust) shares. Mutual funds pool money from many investors to buy shares in several different companies. For this service, individuals pay an annual management fee of about 0.5 to 1.5 per cent of the value of the money they have invested.

Diversification and Risk Characteristics of Funds

Although mutual fund managers often sell their services on the basis of their supposed superiority in picking shares, the diversification that funds offer probably provides a better explanation of why individuals choose them. Any single investor who tried to purchase shares in, say, 100 different companies would find that most of his or her funds would be used for brokerage commissions, with little money left over to buy the shares themselves. Because mutual funds deal in large volume, brokerage commissions are lower. It then becomes feasible for an individual to own a proportionate share in the stocks of many companies. For the reasons illustrated in Figure 5-3, this diversification reduces risk.

Still, investing in shares generally is a risky enterprise, so mutual fund managers offer products that allow investors to choose the amount of risk they are willing to tolerate. Money market and short-term bond funds tend to offer little risk; balanced funds (which consist of both common shares and bonds) are a bit riskier; growth funds offer the greatest risk. On average, the riskier funds have tended to yield a somewhat higher return for investors. For example, one well-known study of mutual fund performance during the 1960s found that each 10 per cent increase in risk resulted in an increase in average total yield from the funds of about one percentage point.[1]

Portfolio Management

Managers of mutual funds can reduce risk further by the choices they make when purchasing specific shares. Our numerical illustration of the benefits of diversification assumed that the returns on the shares of the two companies were independent of each other; it was that fact that resulted in the benefits from diversification. Further benefits in terms of risk reduction can be achieved if mutual fund managers find investments whose returns tend to move in opposite directions (that is, when one does well, the other does not, and vice versa). For example, some fund managers may choose to hold some of their funds in mining companies because precious metal prices tend to rise when share prices fall. Another way to achieve this balancing of risk is to purchase shares from companies in many countries. Such global mutual funds and international funds (which specialize in securities from individual countries) have grown rapidly in recent years. More generally, fund managers may even be able to develop complex strategies involving short sales or share options that allow them to hedge their returns from a given investment even further. Recent financial innovations such as standardized put and call options, stock index options, interest rate futures, and a bewildering variety of computer-program trading schemes illustrate the increasing demand for such risk-reduction vehicles.

Index Funds (or Index Tracking Funds)

Index funds represent a more systematic approach to diversification. These funds, which were first introduced in the 1970s, seek to mimic (or track), the performance of an overall market average. Some of the most popular funds track the Financial Times Index. There are also index funds that mimic foreign stock market indices such as the Nikkei Stock Average (Japan) or track Standard and Poor's 500 Stock Market index, the Dow Jones Industrial Average, or the Wiltshire 5000 Stock Average (the United States). Managers of these index funds use complex computer algorithms to ensure that they closely track their underlying index. The primary advantage of these funds is their very low management cost. Most large index funds have annual expenses of less than 0.25 per cent of their assets whereas actively managed funds have expenses that average about 1.3 per cent of assets. Historically few managed funds have been able to overcome this cost disadvantage.

(*Continued*)

To Think About

1 Most studies of mutual fund performance conclude that managers cannot consistently exceed the average return in the stock market as a whole. Why might you expect this result? What does it imply about investors' motives for buying managed mutual funds?

2 Mutual funds compute the net asset value of each share daily. Should the fund's shares sell for this value in the open market?

[1] M. Jensen, "Risk, the Pricing of Capital Assets, and the Evaluation of Investment Performance", *Journal of Business* (April 1969).

Options

Option A contract offering the right, but not the obligation, to complete an economic transaction over a specified period.

A third way to reduce risk is through the use of options. As the name implies, "options" are various kinds of contracts you can purchase that increase your flexibility in coping with uncertain situations. Technically an **option** is defined as a contract that gives a person the right, but not the obligation, to complete an economic transaction over some specified time period into the future. Because options only bestow rights, not obligations, they increase the flexibility people have in facing the future and can thereby reduce risks. In general, we would expect people to be willing to pay something for such valuable rights.

Although the term "options" is most often encountered in financial literature (for example in the term "stock options"), the concept is much broader than that. Consider a simple example. You are buying a used car and have located two sellers, each of whom seems to be offering the identical vehicle. The first seller is providing the car on an "as-seen" basis. Once you buy it, it's yours, potential problems and all. The second seller is offering a money-back guarantee – if for any reason you wish to return the car over the next month, he or she will give you your money back, no questions asked. Such a guarantee is an option – it gives you the right, but not the obligation, to resell the car to its original owner at any time over the next month for your original purchase price. Buying the car with this option reduces the problems of uncertainty that you face in buying a used car. If during the first month you discover the car is a lemon, you can readily sell it back. With the as-seen car, that is not possible and you will be stuck. Because of the value of this option, you will be willing to pay more for the second used car than for the first – you are willing to pay something to reduce your risks. Hence, the market for options gives you a way to reduce risks.

Attributes of Options Although there are many different and sometimes quite complex options, all share three fundamental attributes:

1 **Specification of the underlying transaction.** Options must include details of the transaction being considered. This includes what is being bought or sold, at what price the transaction will take place, and any other details that are relevant (such as where the transaction will occur). In the used car example, the option specifies that the transaction being optioned is for the resale of the car at the original purchase price. If the parties wished, this intended transaction could be made more precise by specifying where it will occur, whether wear and tear on the car during the month will be considered, or even whether the petrol tank should be full.

2 **Definition of the period during which the option may be exercised.** In the car example, the period specified was one month. But the parties to an option

could agree on any exercise period ranging from the very specific (the option may only be exercised on 5 June at 10am) to the very general (the option may be exercised anytime).

3. **The price of the option.** In some cases, the price of an option is explicit. You can, for example, buy a wide variety of options on stocks, and the prices for those are quoted in the newspapers. At other times, the price of an option may only be implicit because it is part of a larger transaction. That is the situation in the car example – the price of the resale option is implicit in the higher asking price for the car.

In order to understand any option, you need to be able to identify these three components. Whether the option is worth its price will depend on the details of the underlying transaction and on the nature of the option's exercise period. Let's look at how these details might affect an option's value to a would-be buyer.

How the Value of the Underlying Transaction Affects Option Value

Because the transaction that underlies an option will occur in the future, its value is subject to many uncertainties. The value of selling your recently purchased car back to the original owner depends on what ultimately happens to the car. If the car performs as you thought it would, the transaction may have little value. You paid what the car was worth and in a month that price may be still what you think the car is worth. The option to resell at the original price has no value. But it is also possible that you will have trouble with the car – the gearbox may fail, the doors may fall off, or the engine may explode. Each of these negative outcomes implies a different value for the transaction of selling the car back at its original purchase price. The worse the problem that turns up, the greater is the value, to you, of the option of selling it at this pre-arranged price. Of course, it is also possible that you will discover the car is better than you thought, making it unlikely you will sell it back.

As for any uncertain outcome, it is useful to think of the value of the underlying transaction in an option as having two general dimensions: (1) the expected value of the transaction and (2) the variability of the value of the transaction. Clearly, the greater the expected value of the transaction, the greater will be the value of an option to undertake that transaction. If you expect that you will have a lot of trouble with the car you buy, the option of a resale will be quite valuable. If you expect little or no trouble, the value of a resale option isn't very great. Suppose, for instance, that you believe there is a 50 per cent chance that the car will need a €500 repair during the next month and a 50 per cent chance it will not. In this case, the expected value of the resale option is €250. By reselling the car when it needs the repair, you make €500, but reselling it when it doesn't need the repair yields nothing. Hence the expected value is given by $0.5 \cdot 500 + 0.5 \cdot 0 = 250$. If instead you thought there was a 50–50 chance of the car needing a €1000 repair, the expected value of the transaction would be €500 and you would be willing to pay more for the resale option.

The effect of the variability of a transaction's potential value on the price of an option requires a more complicated logic, but this is where the notion of an *option* to resell becomes especially important. Basically, the more variable the potential value of a transaction, the more valuable will be the option to undertake it or not. To see this, it is easiest to deal with some numbers. Consider first the situation where you believe there is a 50–50 chance that the car you are thinking of buying will need €500 worth of repairs during the next month. In this case, as we saw, the expected value of the transaction is €250. Now consider a situation where you instead believe there is a 50–50 chance that the car will need either a €1000 repair over the next month or that you will discover that the car is great and worth €500 more than you paid for it. In this case, half the time the transaction yields you €1000 because you can resell the car needing the repair. But also, half the time the transaction would have a negative value – you would be reselling the car for €500 less than you had discovered it was worth. Hence the expected value of the transaction is $0.5 \cdot 1000 + 0.5 \cdot (-500) = 250$. Both situations therefore yield the same expected value for the transaction.

Ultimately, however, the option for resale is more valuable in our second case. The key reason is that the option for resale need not be exercised – you can decide whether or not to exercise it after you see how the car works out. In the first case, 50 per cent of the time the transaction is worth €500 because you get to resell the car for €500 more than it has been shown to be worth. And 50 per cent of the time you will discover that the transaction is worthless because you can just sell the car for what it's worth. So you probably won't opt for the resale anyway. Hence, the expected value of the transaction *after the uncertainty is resolved* is still €250. In the second case, however, the calculation yields a different result. Now, 50 per cent of the time the transaction is worth €1000 once the uncertainty is resolved because you can resell the car for €1000 more than it is worth. The other 50 per cent of the time the transaction is worthless because you would never sell a car worth €500 more than was being offered. Hence, the expected value of the transaction now is €500 ($= 0.5 \cdot 1000 + 0.5 \cdot 0$) – considerably more than in the less variable case.

It is worth repeating the mathematical reason why the more variable transaction is more valuable. The desirable outcome of having a better car enters into calculating the expected value of the transaction *before* the uncertainty is resolved. But the added value of the car is not relevant to assessing the value of the resale transaction once the uncertainty is resolved because you would not sell the car at the specified price anyway. It is this difference in expected values before and after uncertainty is resolved that causes variability to add value to an option.[3] Intuitively, the more variable the value of the transaction specified in the option, the more valuable will be the ability to choose to exercise the option or not.

MICROQUIZ 5.4

George Lucas has offered to sell you the option to buy his seventh *Star Wars* feature for €100 million should that film ever be made.

1. Identify the underlying transaction involved in this option. How would you decide on the expected value of this transaction? How would you assess the variability attached to the value of the transaction? What is the duration of this option?
2. How would you decide how much to pay Mr Lucas for this option?

How the Duration of an Option Affects Its Value The effect of the duration of an option on its value is much easier to understand. Simply put, the longer an option lasts, the more valuable it is. Intuitively, the more time you have to take advantage of the flexibility an option offers, the more likely it is that you will want to do so. An option that lets you buy a liter of petrol tomorrow at today's price isn't worth very much because the price is unlikely to change by very much over the next 24 hours. An option that lets you buy a liter of petrol at today's price over the next year is valuable because prices could explode over such a long period.

The level of interest rates can also affect the value of an option, but this is usually a relatively minor concern. Because buying an option gives you the right to make a transaction in the future, a correct accounting must consider the "present value" of that transaction (see Chapter 16). In that way, the return to being able to invest your other funds (say, in a bank) between the time

[3]In fact, some authors define the "option value" of a contract to be the difference in the expected value of the underlying transaction before and after the uncertainty is resolved and the option exercised (or not).

you buy the option and when it is exercised can be taken into account. With normal levels of interest rates, however, only for options that are very long-lasting will this be a major element in the value of an option.

Buying Options to Reduce Risk There are many ways in which individuals can take advantage of the risk-reducing features of options. One way that has been extensively studied is to use options to buy or sell stock as a way of limiting the risks involved in owning shares. In Application 5.4: *Puts, Calls, and Black-Scholes*, we describe some of these financial options and show how information on their pricing has been used to study a number of risk-related topics.

But financial options are only a small segment of the options universe. Many things people do in their everyday lives involve the purchasing of options. We have already seen how money-back guarantees are a type of option. Other features of purchasing contracts such as allowances for upgrades or service agreements also have option-like features. More broadly, getting an education that allows for flexibility in your future choice of profession or tending to some long-term healthcare needs may also share characteristics of options. That is, you may pay something up front (by taking a course in accounting or by getting braces on your teeth) in order to have the option of making transactions (becoming a chartered accountant or eating a crisp apple) in the future. Sometimes the issues underlying such choices can be clarified by thinking about basic questions such as: (1) What kinds of transactions are you buying options on? (2) How will options help you address the uncertainty involved in this transaction? and (3) How much does the option cost? The fact that people do many things to add flexibility to their future lives shows that "buying options" is not just an arcane financial manoeuvre.[4]

Pricing of Risk in Financial Assets

Because people are willing to pay something to avoid risks, it seems as if one should be able to study this process directly. That is, we could treat "risk" like any other commodity and study the factors that influence its demand and supply. One result of such a study would be to be able to say how much risk there is in the economy and how much people would be willing to pay to have less of it. Although, as we shall see, there are several problems with this approach, financial markets do indeed provide a good place to get useful information about the pricing of risk.

With financial assets, the risks people face are purely monetary and relatively easy to measure. One can, for example, study the history of the price of a particular financial asset and determine whether this price has been stable or volatile. Presumably, less-volatile assets are more desirable to risk-averse people, so they should be willing to pay something for them. Economists are able to get some general idea of people's attitudes toward risk by looking at differences in financial returns on risky versus non-risky assets.

Investors' Market Options

Figure 5-4 shows a simplified illustration of the market options open to a would-be investor in financial assets. The vertical axis of the figure shows the expected annual return that the investor might earn from an asset, whereas the horizontal axis shows the level of risk associated with each asset. The points in the figure represent the

[4]In the theory of investment, some authors talk about "real options" as a way of incorporating options-like flexibility into the way in which firms buy new plants and equipment.

APPLICATION 5.4 *Puts, Calls, and Black–Scholes*

Options on financial assets are widely traded in organized markets. Not only are there options available on most company's stocks, but there are also a bewildering variety of options on such assets as bonds, foreign exchange, commodities, or even on indexes based on groups of these assets. Probably the most common options are those related to the stock of a single company. The potential transactions underlying these options are simply promises to buy or sell the stock at a specific ("strike") price over some period in the future. Options to buy a stock at a certain strike price are termed "call" options because the buyer has the right to "call" the stock from someone else if he or she wishes to exercise the option. Options to sell a stock at a certain price are called "put" options (perhaps because you have the option to put the stock into someone else's hands).

As an example, suppose that Microsoft stock is currently selling at $25 per share. A call option might give you the right (but, again, not the obligation) to buy Microsoft in one month at, say, $27 per share.[1] Suppose you also believe there is a 50–50 chance that Microsoft will sell for either $30 or $20 in one month's time. Clearly the option to buy at $27 is valuable – the stock might end up at $30. But how much is this option worth?

An Equivalent Portfolio

One way that financial economists evaluate options is by asking whether there is another set of assets that would yield the same outcomes as would the option. If such a set exists, one can then argue that it should have the same price as the option because markets will ensure that the same good always has the same price. So, let's consider the outcomes of the Microsoft option. If Microsoft sells for $20 in a month's time, the option is worthless – why pay $27 when the stock can readily be bought for $20. If Microsoft sells for $30, however, the option will be worth $3. Could we duplicate these two payouts with some other set of assets? Suppose, for example, we borrow some funds (L) from a bank (with no interest, to make things simple) and buy a fraction (k) of a Microsoft share. After a month, we will sell the fractional share of Microsoft and pay off the loan. In this example, L and k must be chosen to yield the same outcomes as the option. That is

$$k(\$20) - L = 0 \text{ and } k(\$30) - L = 3 \qquad \{1\}$$

These two equations can easily be solved as $k = 0.3, L = 6$. That is, buying 0.3 of a Microsoft share and taking a loan of $6 will yield the same outcomes as buying the option. The net cost of this strategy is $1.50 – $7.50 to buy 0.3 of a Microsoft share at $25 less the loan of $6 (which in our simple case carries no interest). Hence, this also is the value of the option.

The Black–Scholes Theorem

Of course, valuing options in the real world is much more complicated than this simple example suggests. Three specific complications that need to be addressed in developing a more general theory of valuation are (1) There are far more possibilities for Microsoft stock's price in one month than just the two we assumed; (2) Most popular options can be exercised at any time during a specified period, not just on a specific date; and (3) Interest rates matter for any economic transaction that occurs over time. Taking account of these factors proved to be very difficult, and it was not until 1973 that Fisher Black and Myron Scholes developed an acceptable valuation model.[2] Since that time, the Black–Scholes model has been widely applied to options and other markets. In one of its more innovative applications, the model is now used in reverse to calculate an "implied volatility" expected for stocks in the future. The Chicago Board Options Exchange Volatility Index (VIX) is widely followed in the financial press, where it is taken as a good measure of the current uncertainties involved in stock market investing.

To Think About

1 For every buyer of, say, a call option, there must of course also be a seller. Why would someone sell a call option on some shares

he or she already owned? How would this be different than buying a put option on this stock?

2 The Black–Scholes model assumes that share returns are random and that they follow a bell-shaped (normal) distribution. Does this seem a reasonable assumption?

[1]Options with a specific exercise date are called "European" options. "American" options can be exercised at any time during a specified time interval.

[2]F. Black and M. Scholes, "The Pricing of Options and Corporate Liabilities", *Journal of Political Economy* (May–June 1973): 637–654. This is a very difficult paper. Less difficult treatments (together with some criticisms of Black–Scholes) can be found in most corporate finance texts.

various kinds of financial assets available. For example, point *A* represents a risk-free asset such as money in a current account. Although this asset has (practically) no risks associated with its ownership, it promises a very low annual rate of return. Asset *B*, on the other hand, represents a relatively risky stock – this asset promises a high expected annual rate of return, but any investor must accept a high risk to get that return. All of the other points in Figure 5-4 represent the risks and returns associated with assets that an investor might buy.

Because investors like high annual returns but dislike risk, they will choose to hold combinations of these available assets that lie on their "northwest" periphery. By mixing various risky assets with the risk-free asset (*A*), they can choose any point along the line *AC*. This line is labeled the **market line** because it shows the possible combinations of annual returns and risk that an investor can achieve by taking advantage of what the market offers.[5] The slope of this line shows the trade-off between annual

Market line A line showing the relationship between risk and annual returns that an investor can achieve by mixing financial assets.

FIGURE 5-4 Market Options for Investors *The points in the figure represent the risk/return features of various assets. The market line shows the best options a risk-averse investor can obtain by mixing risk assets with the risk-free asset A.*

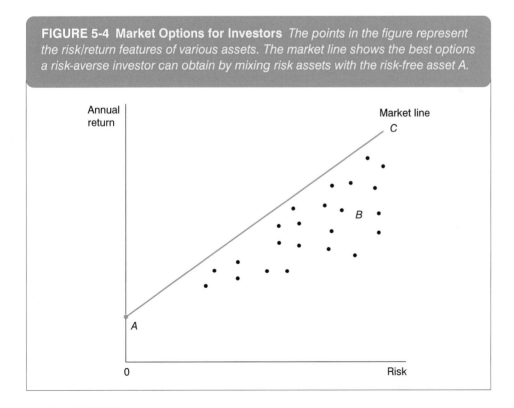

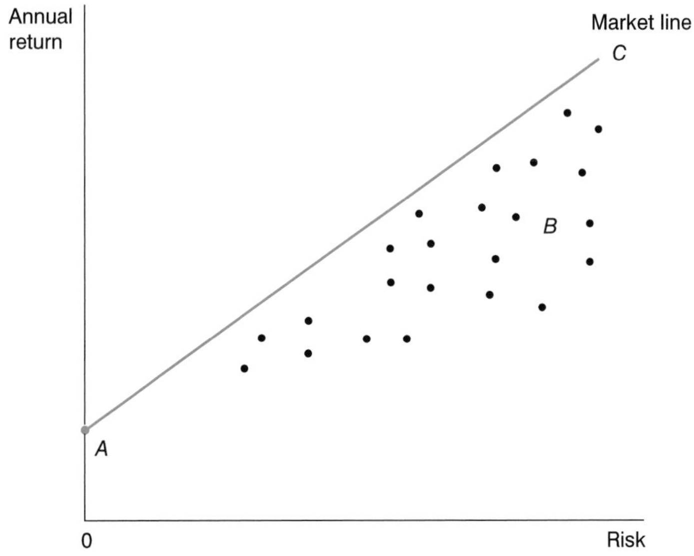

[5]The actual construction of the market line is relatively complicated. For a discussion, see W. Nicholson, *Microeconomic Theory: Basic Principles and Extensions*, 9th ed. (Mason, OH: Thomson Learning, 2005): 556–558.

APPLICATION 5.5 *The Equity Premium Puzzle*

As shown in Figure 5-4, differences in the rates of return of financial assets reflect, in part, the differing risks associated with those assets. The historical data show that shares have indeed had higher returns than bonds to compensate for that risk. In fact, returns on common shares have been so favorable that they pose a puzzle to economists.

Historical Rates of Return

Table 1 illustrates the most commonly used rate of return data for US financial markets, published by the Ibbotson firm in Chicago. These data show that over the period 1926–1994,[1] shares provided average annual rates of return that exceeded those on long-term government bonds by 7 per cent per year. Average returns on short-term government bonds fell short of those on stocks by a massive 8.5 per cent. Indeed, given the rate of inflation during this period (averaging 3.2 per cent per year), the very low real return on short-term government bonds – about 0.5 per cent per year – is a bit of a puzzle.

One way to measure the risk associated with various assets uses the "standard deviation" of their annual returns. This measure shows the range in which roughly two-thirds of the returns fall. For the case of, say, common shares, the average annual return was 12.2 per cent, and the standard deviation shows that in two-thirds of the years the average was within ± 20.2 per cent of this figure. In other words, in two-thirds of the years, common stocks returned more than −8 per cent and less than +32.4 per cent. Rates of return on shares were much more variable than those on bonds.

The Excess Return on Common Shares

Although the qualitative findings from data such as those in Table 1 are consistent with risk aversion, the quantitative nature of the extra returns to common stock holding are inconsistent with many other studies of risk. These other studies suggest that individuals would accept the extra risk that shares carry for an extra return of between 1 and 2 per cent per year – significantly less than the 7 per cent extra actually provided.

One set of explanations focuses on the possibility that the figures in Table 1 understate the risk of shares. The risk individuals really care about is changes in their consumption plans. If returns on shares were highly correlated with the business cycle, then they might pose extra risks because individuals would face a double risk from economic downturns – a fall in income and a fall in returns from investments. Other suggested explanations for the high return on common shares include the possibility that there are much higher transaction costs on shares (hence, the returns are necessary to compensate) and that only people whose incomes are excessively affected by the business cycle buy shares. However, none of these explanations has survived close scrutiny.[2]

To Think About

1 Holding shares in individual companies probably involves greater risks than are reflected in the data for all stocks in Table 1. Do you think these extra risks are relevant to apprais-

TABLE 1 Total Annual Returns, 1926–1994

Financial asset	*Average annual rate of return*	*Standard deviation of rate of return*
Common stocks	12.2%	20.2%
Long-term government bonds	5.2	8.8
Short-term government bonds	3.7	3.3

SOURCE: STOCKS, BONDS, BILLS, AND INFLATION: 1995 YEARBOOK (Chicago: Ibbotson Associates, 1995).

ing the extra rate of return that shares provide?

2 The real return on short-term government bonds implied by Table 1 is less than 1 per cent per year. Why do people save at all if this relatively risk-free return is so low?

[1]Years after 1994 were eliminated here so as not to bias the results by the very strong performance of shares in the period 1996–2000.

[2]For an extensive discussion, see N. R. Kocherlakota, "The Equity Premium: It's Still a Puzzle", *Journal of Economic Literature* (March 1996): 42–71.

returns and risk that is available from financial markets. By studying the terms on which such trade-offs can be made in actual financial markets, economists can learn something about how those markets price risks. Application 5.5: *The Equity Premium Puzzle* illustrates these calculations but also highlights some of the uncertainties that arise in making them.

Choices by Individual Investors

The market line shown in Figure 5-4 provides a constraint on the alternatives that financial markets provide to individual investors. These investors then choose among the available assets on the basis of their own attitudes toward risk. This process is illustrated in Figure 5-5. The figure shows a typical indifference curve for three different types of investors. Each of these indifference curves has a positive slope because of the assumption that investors are risk averse – they can be induced to take on more

FIGURE 5-5 Choices by Individual Investors *Points L, M, and N show the investment choices made by three different investors. Investor I is very risk-averse and has a high proportion of the risk-free asset. Investor II has modest toleration for risk and chooses the "market" portfolio. Investor III has a great toleration for risk and leverages his/her position.*

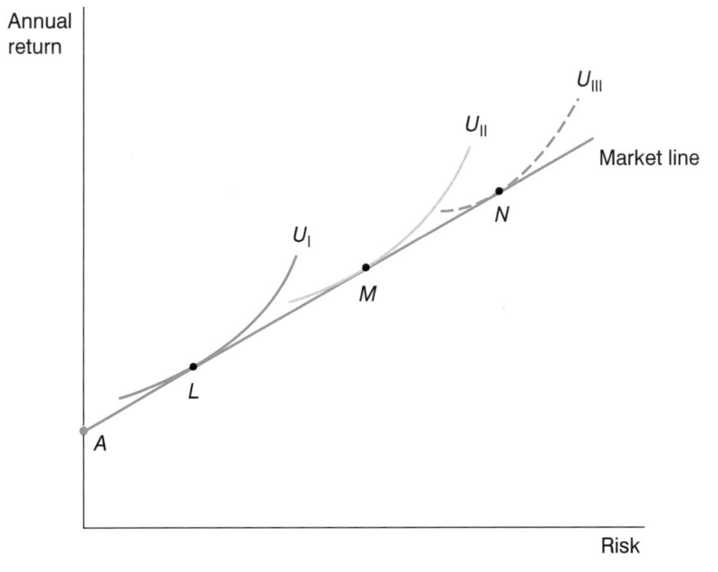

risk only by the promise of a higher return. The curves also have a convex curvature on the presumption that investors will become increasingly less willing to take on more risk as the overall riskiness of their positions increases.

The three investors illustrated in Figure 5-5 have different attitudes toward risk. Investor I has a very low tolerance for risk. He or she will opt for a mix of investments that includes a lot of the risk-free option (point L). Investor II has a modest toleration for risk, and he or she will opt for a combination of assets that is reasonably representative of the overall market (M). Finally, investor III is a real speculator. He or she will accept a very risky combination of assets (N) – more risky than the overall market. One way for this investor to do that is to borrow to invest in stocks. The impact of any fluctuations in stock prices will then be magnified in its impact on this investor's wealth. Actual financial markets therefore accommodate a wide variety of risk preferences by providing the opportunity to choose various mixes of asset types.

The Economics of Information

In a sense, all individual behavior in uncertain situations can be regarded as a response to a lack of information. If people knew that a coin was going to come up heads, or knew how their investments would fare next year, they would be better off. They may even be willing to pay for additional information to reduce uncertainty, and probably will do so as long as the expected gains from this information exceed its cost. For example, someone trying to decide whether to buy a used car may pay an impartial mechanic to evaluate the car's condition before buying it; someone wishing to buy a color television may check around to find the best price. He or she may also consult *Which* magazine, which gives its subscribers detailed information on various consumer goods. Similarly, farmers may use information about the weather to make decisions about what to grow and when to harvest their crops. In this section, we look briefly at a model that can be used to study such activities.

A Utility-Maximizing Model

Many of the issues that arise in studying the economics of information can be examined by using a utility-maximizing model similar to the one we presented in Chapters 2 and 3. The basic outline of the model is presented in Figure 5-6. For this model, an individual is assumed to face two possible outcomes (sometimes called *states of the world*), but he or she does not know which outcome will occur. The individual's consumption in the two states is denoted by C_1 and C_2, and possible values for these are recorded on the axes in Figure 5-6. A particular risk such as point A in the figure promises C^A_1 if state 1 occurs and C^A_2 if state 2 occurs.

In the situation illustrated at point A, this person has considerably more consumption in state 1 than in state 2. If there were ways to give up some consumption from state 1 to increase consumption in state 2, this person might jump at the chance. He or she could then avoid the possibility of ending up impoverished should state 2 occur. Insurance, as we learned previously, is one mechanism that might be used for this purpose. By paying an insurance premium, this person reduces C_1 (consumption during a good time when things don't go wrong) in order to increase C_2 (consumption when things do go wrong). For example, if the terms at which insurance can be bought are reflected by the slope of the line AE, this person can increase utility from U_1 to U_2 by purchasing complete insurance and moving to point E where $C_1 = C_2$. This outcome is similar to the complete insurance solution examined in Figure 5-2. In other words, by paying a premium of $C_1^A - C_1^E$, this person has assured enough additional consumption when things go wrong ($C_2^E - C_2^A$) that consumption is the same no matter what happens. Buying complete insurance has allowed this person to obtain C_1^E (which equals C_2^E) with certainty.

There are many other ways in which the person in Figure 5-6 might improve his or her situation. For example, if insurance were more costly than indicated by the slope of the line *AE*, some utility improvement might still be possible. In this case, the budget line would be flatter than *AE* (because more expensive insurance means that obtaining additional C_2 requires a greater sacrifice of C_1) and this person could not attain utility level U_2. He or she might not opt for complete insurance, selecting instead a point where C_1 still exceeded C_2. But achieving a utility level greater than U_1 might still be possible.

MICROQUIZ 5.5

Let's examine Figure 5-6 more closely.

1. Why do choices along the "certainty line" imply that there is no risk?
2. If the probability of state 1 is 0.6 and the probability of state 2 is 0.4, what is the actuarially fair slope for the line *AE*?
3. In general, what determines the slope of the indifference curve U_2?
4. Given your answer to part 2, can you explain why *AE* and U_2 have the same slope at point *E*? (This question is relatively hard.)

Balancing the Gains and Costs of Information

Another way that this person might better his or her situation would be to gather additional information. The key question, of course, is whether such actions are worth the cost and effort they may entail. Consulting *Which* when buying a new car might make sense because the cost is low and the potential gains (in terms of getting a better car for one's money) may be

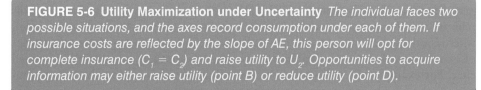

FIGURE 5-6 Utility Maximization under Uncertainty *The individual faces two possible situations, and the axes record consumption under each of them. If insurance costs are reflected by the slope of AE, this person will opt for complete insurance ($C_1 = C_2$) and raise utility to U_2. Opportunities to acquire information may either raise utility (point B) or reduce utility (point D).*

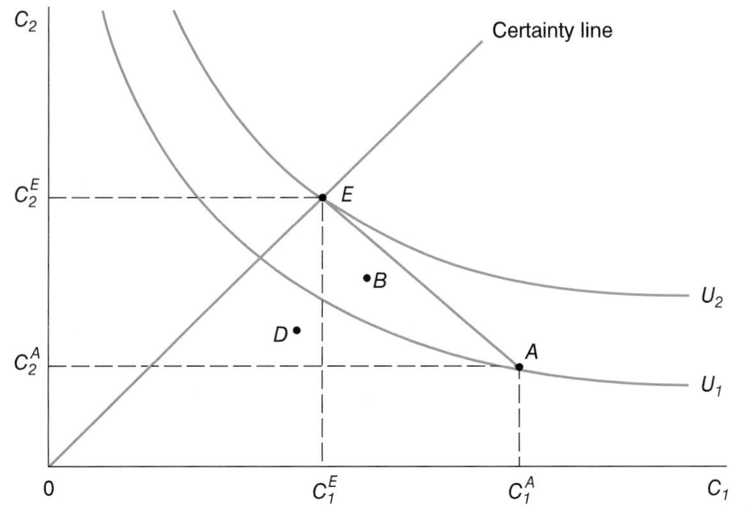

significant. Similarly, investing in a few phone calls to discount stores may be worth the time before buying a new television. On the other hand, visiting every store in town to find a lower-priced chocolate bar clearly carries the information search too far.

These ideas can also be illustrated with the model in Figure 5-6. For an individual initially facing the prospects represented by point A, the issue is whether acquiring information will raise utility above U_1. Because most information is costly to obtain, gathering it will usually result in lower consumption in favorable situations. Reading *Which* or checking around for low prices won't improve your consumption prospects if you would have chosen correctly in any case; moreover, the magazine or phone calls cost both time and money. But, gathering the information will probably raise C_2 because the information makes it possible to be a wiser consumer when things go wrong. Point B, for example, represents a utility-improving investment in information acquisition. For that point, the sacrifice of C_1 is more than compensated for by the rise in C_2 and utility rises above U_1. An investment in information that yielded point D would be a poor one, however. Even though the information does have value (C_2 rises), its cost in terms of C_1 is too great and utility would fall below U_1. Again, visiting every store in town in search of a cheaper chocolate bar is a poor use of time.

Information Differences among Economic Actors

This discussion suggests two observations about acquiring information. First, the level of information that an individual acquires will depend on how much the information costs. Unlike market prices for most goods (which are usually assumed to be the same for everyone), there are many reasons to believe that information costs may differ significantly among individuals. Some people may possess specific skills relevant to information acquisition (they may be trained mechanics, for example), whereas others may not possess such skills. Some individuals may have other types of experiences that yield valuable information while others may lack that experience. For example, the seller of a product will usually know more about its limitations than will a buyer because the seller knows precisely how the good was made and what possible problems might arise. Similarly, large-scale repeat buyers of a good may have greater access to information about it than do first-time buyers. Finally, some individuals may have invested in some types of information services (for example, by having a computer link to a brokerage firm or by subscribing to *Which*) that make the cost of obtaining additional information lower than for someone without such an investment.

Differing preferences provide a second reason why information levels may differ among buyers of the same good. Some people may care a great deal about getting the best buy. Others may have a strong aversion to seeking bargains and will take the first model available. As for any good, the trade-offs that individuals are willing to make are determined by the nature of their preferences.

The possibility that information levels will differ among people raises a number of difficult problems about how markets operate. Although it is customary to assume that all buyers and sellers are fully informed, in a number of situations this assumption is untenable. In Chapter 17, we will look at some of the issues that arise in such situations.

SUMMARY

In this chapter, we have briefly surveyed the economic theory of uncertainty and information. From that survey, we reached several conclusions that have relevance throughout the study of microeconomics.

- In uncertain situations, individuals are concerned with the expected utility associated with various outcomes. If individuals have a diminishing marginal utility for income, they will be risk averse. That is, they will generally refuse bets that are actuarially fair in monetary terms but result in an expected loss of utility.
- Risk-averse individuals may purchase insurance that allows them to avoid participating in fair bets. Even if the premium is somewhat unfair (in an actuarial sense), they may still buy insurance in order to increase utility.
- Diversification among several uncertain options may reduce risk. Such risk spreading may sometimes be costly, however.
- Buying options is another way to reduce risk. Because the buyer has the right, but not the obligation, to complete a market transaction on specified terms, such options can add flexibility to the ways people plan in uncertain situations. Options are more valuable when the expected value of the underlying market transaction is more valuable, the value of that transaction is more variable, and the duration of the option is longer.
- Financial markets allow people to choose the risk-return combination that maximizes their utility. These markets therefore provide evidence on how risk is priced.
- New information is valuable because it may permit individuals to make new choices that increase expected utility. However, individuals may face differing costs of obtaining information and may therefore acquire different amounts of it.

REVIEW QUESTIONS

1. What does it mean to say we expect a fair coin to come up heads about half the time? Would you expect the fraction of heads to get closer to exactly 0.5 as more coins are tossed? Explain how this law of large numbers applies to the risks faced by casinos or insurance companies.

2. Why does the assumption of diminishing marginal utility of income imply risk aversion? Can you think of other assumptions that would result in risk-averse behavior (such as the purchase of insurance) but would not require the difficult-to-verify notion of diminishing marginal utility?

3. "The purchase of actuarially fair insurance turns an uncertain situation into a situation where you receive the expected value of income with certainty." Explain why this is true. Can you think of circumstances where it might not be true?

4. The diversification example illustrated in Table 5-1 and Figure 5-3 requires that returns on the two stocks be independent. Explain what "independent" means in this context and why independence of returns provides opportunities for diversification. Why would such opportunities be limited if the returns on the stocks in the example moved together?

5. Suppose that historical data showed that returns of Japanese stocks and returns on US stocks tended to move in opposite directions. Would it be better to own only one country's stocks or to hold a mixture of the two? How would your

answer change if the Japanese stock market always precisely mirrored the US stock market?

6 As discussed in Application 5.4, a call option provides you with the option to buy a share of, say, Microsoft stock at a specified price of €60. Suppose that this option can only be exercised at exactly 10am on 1 June 2006. What will determine the expected value of the transaction underlying this option? What will determine the variability around this expected value? Explain why the greater this expected variability, the greater is the value of this option.

7 In order to understand the market line shown in Figure 5-4, it is easiest to assume there are only two assets: a risk-free asset (*A*) and a risky asset (*M*). Explain why an individual who mixes these assets in various proportions will be located along the market line. What will determine where on the line he or she actually is?

8 Explain why the slope of the market line in Figure 5-4 and Figure 5-5 shows how risk is "priced" in this market. How might the data in Application 5.4 be plotted to determine this slope?

9 "The model in Figure 5-6 differs from other models because the individual does not ultimately consume both C_1 and C_2; rather, these are the two possible outcomes from one random event." Explain exactly how this model does differ from the one in Chapters 2 and 3 and provide a simple example of how Figure 5-6 might apply to an actual situation.

10 Our analysis in this chapter suggests that individuals have a utility-maximizing amount of information. Explain why some degree of ignorance is optimal.

PROBLEMS

5.1 Suppose a person must accept one of three bets:

Bet 1: Win €100 with probability 1/2; lose €100 with probability 1/2.

Bet 2: Win €100 with probability 3/4; lose €300 with probability 1/4.

Bet 3: Win €100 with probability 9/10; lose €900 with probability 1/10.

- a Show that all of these are fair bets.
- b Plot on a graph each bet on a utility of income curve similar to Figure 5-1.
- c Explain carefully which bet will be preferred and why.

5.2 Two fast-food restaurants are located next to each other and offer different procedures for ordering food. The first offers five lines leading to a server, whereas the second has a single line leading to five servers, with the next person in the line going to the first available server. Use the assumption that most individuals are risk averse to discuss which restaurant will be preferred.

5.3 A person purchases a dozen eggs and must take them home. Although making trips home is costless, there is a 50 per cent chance that all of the eggs carried on one trip will be broken during the trip. This person considers two strategies:

Strategy 1: Take the dozen eggs in one trip.

Strategy 2: Make two trips, taking six eggs in each trip.

- a List the possible outcomes of each strategy and the probabilities of these outcomes. Show that, on average, six eggs make it home under either strategy.
- b Develop a graph to show the utility obtainable under each strategy.
- c Could utility be improved further by taking more than two trips? How would the desirability of this possibility be affected if additional trips were costly?

5.4 Suppose there is a 50–50 chance that a risk-averse individual with a current wealth of €20 000 will contract a debilitating disease and suffer a loss of €10 000.

a Calculate the cost of actuarially fair insurance in this situation and use a utility-of-income graph (Figure 5-2) to show that the individual will prefer fair insurance against this loss to accepting the gamble uninsured.

b Suppose two types of insurance policies were available

1 A fair policy covering the compete loss.

2 A fair policy covering only half of any loss incurred.

Calculate the cost of the second type of policy and show that the individual will generally regard it as inferior to the first.

c Suppose individuals who purchase cost-sharing policies of the second type take better care of their health, thereby reducing the loss suffered when ill to only €7000. In this situation, what will be the cost of a cost-sharing policy? Show that some individuals may now prefer this type of policy. (This is an example of the moral hazard problem in insurance theory.)

5.5 Ms Fogg is planning an around-the-world trip. The utility from the trip is a function of how much she spends on it (*Y*) given by

$$U(Y) = \log Y$$

Ms Fogg has €10 000 to spend on the trip. If she spends all of it, her utility will be

$$U(10\,000) = \log 10\,000 = 4$$

(In this problem, we are using logarithms to the base 10 for ease of computation.)

a If there is a 25 per cent probability that Ms Fogg will lose €1000 of her cash on the trip, what is the trip's expected utility?

b Suppose that Ms Fogg can buy insurance against losing the €1000 (say, by purchasing travelers checks) at an actuarially fair premium of €250. Show that her utility is higher if she purchases this insurance than if she faces the chance of losing the €1000 without insurance.

c What is the maximum amount that Ms Fogg would be willing to pay to insure her €1000?

d Suppose that people who buy insurance tend to become more careless with their cash than those who don't, and assume that the probability of their losing €1000 is 30 per cent. What will be the actuarially fair insurance premium? Will Ms Fogg buy insurance in this situation?

5.6 Sometimes economists speak of the *certainty equivalent* of a risky stream of income. This problem asks you to compute the certainty equivalent of a risky bet that promises a 50–50 chance of winning or losing €5000 for someone with a starting income of €50 000. We know that a certain income of somewhat less than €50 000 will provide the same expected utility as will taking this bet. You are asked to calculate precisely the certain income (that is, the certainty equivalent income) that provides the same utility as does this bet for three simple utility functions:

a. $U(I) = \sqrt{I}$.

b. $U(I) = ln(I)$ (where *ln* means "natural logarithm"

c. $U(I) = \frac{-1}{I}$.

What do you conclude about these utility functions by comparing these three cases?

5.7 Suppose Molly Jock wishes to purchase a high-definition television to watch the Olympic Greco-Roman wrestling competition in Beijing. Her current income is €20 000, and she knows where she can buy the television she wants for €2000. She had heard the rumor that the same set can be bought at Crazy Eddie's (recently out of bankruptcy) for €1700 but is unsure if the rumor is true. Suppose this individual's utility is given by

$$\text{Utility} = ln(Y)$$

where *Y* is her income after buying the television.

a What is Molly's utility if she buys from the location she knows?

b What is Molly's utility if Crazy Eddie's really does offer a lower price?

c Suppose Molly believes there is a 50–50 chance that Crazy Eddie does offer the lower-priced television, but it will cost her €100 to drive to the discount store to find out for sure (the store is far away and has had its phone disconnected). Is it worth it to her to invest the money in the trip? (Hint: To calculate the utility associated with part c, simply average Molly's utility from the two states: [1] Eddie offers the television; [2] Eddie doesn't offer the television.)

5.8 Sophia is a contestant on a game show and has selected the prize that lies behind door number 3. The show's host tells her that there is a 50 per cent chance that there is a €15 000 diamond ring behind the door and a 50 per cent chance that there is a goat behind the door (which is worth nothing to Sophia, who is allergic to goats). Before the door is opened, someone in the audience shouts "I will give you the option of selling me what is behind the door for €8000 if you will pay me €4500 for this option."

- a If Sophia cares only about the expected euro values of various outcomes, will she buy this option?
- b Explain why Sophia's degree of risk aversion might affect her willingness to buy this option.

5.9 The option on Microsoft stock described in Application 5.4 gave the owner the right to buy one share at $27 one month from now. Microsoft currently sells for $25 per share, and investors believe there is a 50–50 chance that it could become either $30 or $20 in one month. Now let's see how various features of this option affect its value:

- a How would an increase in the strike price of the option, from $27 to $28, affect the value of the option?
- b How would an increase in the current price of Microsoft stock, from $25 to $27 per share, affect the value of the original option?
- c How would an increase in the volatility of Microsoft stock, so that there was a 50–50 chance that it could sell for either $32 or $18, affect the value of the original option?
- d How would a change in the interest rate affect the value of the original option? Is this an unrealistic feature of this example? How would you make it more realistic?

5.10 In this problem, you will see why the "Equity Premium Puzzle" described in Application 5.5 really is a puzzle. Suppose that a person with €100 000 to invest believes that stocks will have a real return over the next year of 7 per cent. He or she also believes that bonds will have a real return of 2 per cent over the next year. This person believes (probably contrary to fact) that the real return on bonds is certain – an investment in bonds will definitely yield 2 per cent. For stocks, however, he or she believes that there is a 50 per cent chance that stocks will yield 16 per cent, but also a 50 per cent chance they will yield −2 per cent. Hence stocks are viewed as being much riskier than bonds.

- a Calculate the certainty equivalent yield for stocks using the three utility functions in Problem 5.6. What do you conclude about whether this person will invest the €100 000 in stocks or bonds?
- b The most risk-averse utility function economists usually ever encounter is $U(I) = -I^{-10}$. If your scientific calculator is up to the task, calculate the certainty equivalent yield for stocks with this utility function. What do you conclude?

(Hint: The calculations in this problem are most easily accomplished by using outcomes in euros – that is, for example, those that have a 50–50 chance of producing a final wealth of €116 000 or €98 000. If this were to yield a certainty equivalent wealth of, say, €105 000, the certainty equivalent yield would be 5 per cent.)

6

Game Theory

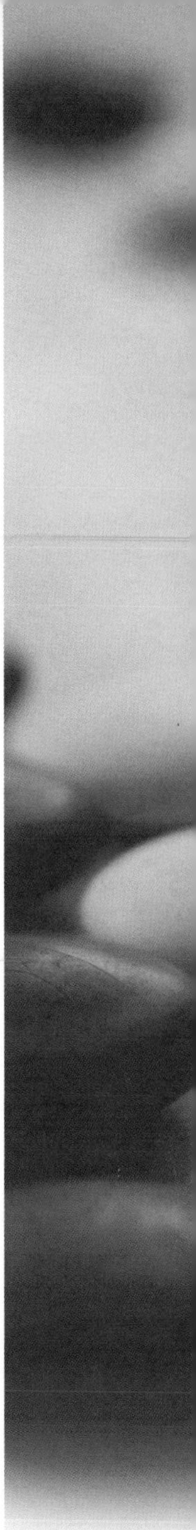

The central assumption behind the analysis in this text is that people make the best choices they can given their objectives. For example, in the theory of choice in Chapter 2, a consumer chooses the affordable bundle maximizing his or her utility. The setting was made fairly simple by considering a single consumer in isolation, justified by the assumption that consumers are price takers, small enough relative to the market that their actions do not measurably impact others. Many situations are more complicated in that they involve strategic interaction. The best one person can do may often depend on what another does. For example, how loud a student plays his or her music may depend on how loud the student in the next room plays his or hers, and vice versa. A petrol station's profit-maximizing price may depend on what the competitor across the street charges. In this chapter, we will learn the tools economists use to deal with these strategic situations. The tools are quite general, applying to problems anywhere from the interaction between students in a hall of residence or players in a card game, all the way up to wars between countries. The tools are also particularly useful for analyzing the interaction among oligopoly firms, and we will draw on them extensively for this purpose later in the book.

Background

Game theory was originally developed during the 1920s and grew rapidly during World War II in response to the need to develop formal ways of thinking about military strategy.[1] One branch of game theory, called cooperative game theory, assumes the group of players reaches an outcome that is best for the group as a whole, producing the largest "pie" to be shared among them; the theory focuses on rules for how the "pie" should be divided. We will focus mostly on the second branch, called non-cooperative game theory, in which players are guided instead by self-interest. We focus

[1]Much of the pioneering work in game theory was done by the mathematician John von Neumann. The main reference is J. von Neumann and O. Morgenstern, *The Theory of Games and Economic Behavior* (Princeton, NJ: Princeton University Press, 1944).

on non-cooperative game theory for several reasons. Self-interested behavior does not always lead to an outcome that is best for the players as a group, and such outcomes are interesting (as we will see from the Prisoners' Dilemma to follow) and practically relevant. Second, the assumption of self-interested behavior is the natural extension of our analysis of single-player decision problems in earlier chapters to a strategic setting. Third, one can analyze attempts to cooperate using non-cooperative game theory. Perhaps most importantly, non-cooperative game theory is more widely used by economists. Still, cooperative game theory has proved useful to model bargaining games and political processes.

Basic Concepts

Game theory models seek to portray complex strategic situations in a simplified setting. Much like the previous models in this book, a game theory model abstracts the details of a problem to arrive at its mathematical representation. The greatest strength of this type of modeling is that it enables us to get to the heart of the problem.

Any situation in which individuals must make strategic choices and in which the final outcome depends on what each person chooses to do can be viewed as a game. All games have three basic elements: (1) players, (2) strategies, and (3) payoffs.

Players

Each decision-maker in a game is called a *player*. The players may be individuals (as in card games), firms (as in an oligopoly), or entire nations (as in military conflicts). Players are characterized as having the ability to choose among a set of possible actions. The number of players, usually fixed throughout the "play" of the game, varies from game to game, with two-player, three-player, or n-player games being possible. In this chapter, we primarily study two-player games since many of the important concepts can be illustrated in this simple setting. We usually denote these players by A and B.

Strategies

A player's choice in a game is called a *strategy*. A strategy may simply be one of the set of possible actions available to the player, leading to the use of the terms *strategy* and *action* interchangeably in informal discourse. But a strategy can be more complicated than an action. A strategy can be a contingent plan of action based on what another player does first (as will be important when we get to sequential games). A strategy can involve probabilities of playing several actions (as will be important when we get to mixed strategies). The actions underlying the strategies can range from the very simple (taking another card in blackjack) to the very complex (building an anti-missile defense system). Although some games offer the players a choice among many different actions, most of the important concepts in this chapter can be illustrated for situations in which each player has only two actions available. Even when the player has only two actions available, the set of strategies may be much larger once we allow for contingent plans or for a range of probabilities of playing the actions.

Payoffs

The final returns to the players of a game at its conclusion are called *payoffs*. Payoffs include the utilities players obtain from explicit monetary payments plus any implicit feelings they have about the outcome, such as whether they are embarrassed or gain self-esteem. It is sometimes convenient to ignore these complications and take payoffs simply to be the explicit monetary payments involved in the game. This is sometimes a reasonable assumption (for example, in the case of profit for a profit-maximizing firm), but it should be recognized as a simplification. Players prefer to earn the highest payoffs possible.

Equilibrium

Students who have taken a basic microeconomics course are familiar with the concept of market equilibrium (we will study this in detail in Chapter 10), defined as the point where supply equals demand. Both suppliers and demanders are content with the market equilibrium: given the equilibrium price and quantity, no market participant has an incentive to change his or her behavior. The question arises whether there are similar concepts in game theory models. Are there strategic choices that, once made, provide no incentives for the players to alter their behavior given what others are doing?

The most widely used approach to defining equilibrium in games is that proposed by Cournot (see Chapter 14) and generalized in the 1950s by John Nash (see Application 6.1: *A Beautiful Mind* for a discussion of the movie that increased his fame). An integral part of this definition of equilibrium is the notion of a best response. Player *A*'s strategy *a* is a **best response** against player *B*'s strategy *b* if *A* cannot earn more from any other possible strategy given that *B* is playing *b*. A **Nash equilibrium** is a set of strategies, one for each player, that are each best responses against one another. In a two-player game, a set of strategies (a^*,b^*) is a Nash equilibrium if a^* is a best response for *A* against b^* and b^* is a best response for *B* against a^*. A Nash equilibrium is stable in the sense that no single player has an incentive to deviate unilaterally to some other strategy. Put another way, outcomes that are not Nash equilibria are unstable because at least one player can switch to a strategy that would increase his or her payoffs given what the other players are doing.

Best response A strategy that produces the highest payoff among all possible strategies for a player given what the other player is doing.

Nash equilibrium A set of strategies, one for each player, that are each best responses against one another.

Nash equilibrium is so widely used by economists as an equilibrium definition because, in addition to selecting an outcome that is stable, a Nash equilibrium exists for all games. (As we will see, some games that at first appear not to have a Nash equilibrium will end up having one in mixed strategies.) The Nash equilibrium concept does have some problems. Some games have several Nash equilibria, some of which may be more plausible than others. In some applications, other equilibrium concepts may be more plausible than Nash equilibrium. The definition of Nash equilibrium leaves out the process by which players arrive at strategies they are prescribed to play. Economists have devoted a great deal of recent research to these issues, and the picture is far from settled. Still, Nash's concept provides an initial working definition of equilibrium that we can use to start our study of game theory.

Illustrating Basic Concepts

We can illustrate the basic components of a game and the concept of Nash equilibrium in perhaps the most famous of all non-cooperative games, the Prisoners' Dilemma.

The Prisoners' Dilemma

First introduced by A. Tucker in the 1940s, its name stems from the following situation. Two suspects, *A* and *B*, are arrested for a crime. The local prosecutor has

APPLICATION 6.1 *A Beautiful Mind*

In 1994, John Nash received the Nobel Prize in economics for the development of the equilibrium concept now known as Nash equilibrium. The publication of the best-selling biography *A Beautiful Mind* and the Oscar-award-winning film of the same title has made Nash world famous.[1]

A Beautiful Blond

The movie dramatizes the development of Nash equilibrium in a single scene in which Nash is in a bar talking with his male classmates. They notice several women at the bar, one blond and the rest brunette, and it is posited that the blond is more desirable than the brunettes. Nash conceives of the situation as a game among the male classmates. If they all go for the blond, they will block each other and fail to get her, and indeed fail to get the brunettes because the brunettes will be annoyed at being second choice. He proposes that they all go for the brunettes. (The assumption is that there are enough brunettes that they do not have to compete for them, so the males will be successful in getting dates with them.) While they will not get the more desirable blond, each will at least end up with a date.

Confusion About Nash Equilibrium?

If it is thought that the Nash character was trying to solve for the Nash equilibrium of the game, he is guilty of making an elementary mistake! The outcome in which all male graduate students go for brunettes is not a Nash equilibrium. In a Nash equilibrium, no player can have a strictly profitable deviation given what the others are doing. But if all the other male graduate students went for brunettes, it would be strictly profitable for one of them to deviate and go for the blond because the deviator would have no competition for the blond, and she is assumed to provide a higher payoff. There are many Nash equilibria of this game, involving various subsets of males competing for the blond, but the outcome in which all males avoid the blond is not one of them.[2]

Nash Versus the Invisible Hand

Some sense can be made of the scene if we view the Nash character's suggested outcome not as what he thought was the Nash equilibrium of the game but as a suggestion for how they might cooperate to move to a different outcome and increase their payoffs. One of the central lessons of game theory is that equilibrium does not necessarily lead to an outcome that is best for all. In this chapter, we study the Prisoners' Dilemma, in which the Nash equilibrium is for both players to confess when they could both benefit if they could agree to be silent. In this chapter we also study the Battle of the Sexes, in which there is a Nash equilibrium where the players sometimes show up at different events, and this failure to coordinate ends up harming them both. The payoffs in the Beautiful Blond game can be specified in such a way that players do better if they all agree to ignore the blond than in the equilibrium in which all compete for the blond with some probability.[3] Adam Smith's famous "invisible hand", which directs the economy toward an efficient outcome under perfect competition, does not necessarily operate when players interact strategically in a game. Game theory opens up the possibility of conflict, miscoordination, and waste, just as observed in the real world.

To Think About

1. How would you write down the game corresponding to the bar scene from *A Beautiful Mind*? What are the Nash equilibria of your game? Should the females be included as players in the setup along with the males?
2. One of Nash's classmates suggested that Nash was trying to convince the others to go after the brunettes so that Nash could have the blond for himself. Is this a Nash equilibrium? Are there others like it? How can one decide how a game will be played if there are multiple Nash equilibria?

[1]The book is S. Nasar, *A Beautiful Mind* (New York: Simon and Schuster, 1997) and the movie is *A Beautiful Mind* (Universal Pictures, 2001).

[2]S. P. Anderson and M. Engers, "A Beautiful Blond: A Nash Coordination Game", University of Virginia working paper (February 2004).

[3]For example, the payoff to getting the blond can be set to 3, getting no date to 0, getting a brunette when no-one else has got the blond to 2, and getting a brunette when someone else has got the blond to 1. Thus there is a loss due to envy if one gets the brunette when another has got the blond.

little evidence in the case and is anxious to extract a confession. She separates the suspects and privately tells each, "If you confess and your partner doesn't, I can promise you a reduced (one-year) sentence, and on the basis of your confession, your partner will get ten years. If you both confess, you will each get a three-year sentence." Each suspect also knows that if neither of them confesses, the lack of evidence will cause them to be tried for a lesser crime for which they will receive two-year sentences.

The Game in Normal Form

The players in the game are the two suspects, *A* and *B*. (Though a third person, the prosecutor, plays a role in the story, once she sets up the payoffs from confessing she does not make strategic decisions, so she does not need to be included in the game.) The players can choose one of two possible actions, Confess or Silent. The payoffs, as well as the players and actions, can be conveniently summarized, as shown in the matrix in Table 6-1. The representation of a game in a matrix like this is called the **normal form**. In the table, player *A*'s strategies, Confess or Silent, head the rows and *B*'s strategies head the columns. Payoffs corresponding to the various combinations of strategies are shown in the body of the table. Since more prison time causes disutility, the prison terms for various outcomes enter with negative signs. We will adopt the convention that the first payoff in each box corresponds to the row player (player *A*) and the second corresponds to the column player (player *B*). To make this convention even clearer, we will make all of player *A*'s strategies and payoffs brown and all of player *B*'s black. For an example of how to read the table, if *A* confesses and *B* is silent, *A* earns −1 (for one year of prison) and *B* earns −10 (for 10 years of prison). The fact that the prosecutor approaches each separately indicates that the game is simultaneous: a player cannot observe the other's action before choosing his or her own action.

Normal form
Representation of a game using a payoff matrix.

TABLE 6-1 Prisoners' Dilemma in Normal Form

		B	
		Confess	*Silent*
A	*Confess*	−3, −3	−1, −10
	Silent	−10, −1	−2, −2

The Game in Extensive Form

Extensive form Representation of a game as a tree.

The Prisoners' Dilemma game can also be represented as a game tree as in Figure 6-1, called the **extensive form**. Action proceeds from top to bottom. Each point or node is a decision point for the player indicated there. The first move belongs to *A*, who can choose to confess or be silent. The next move belongs to *B*, who can also choose to confess or be silent. Payoffs are given at the bottom of the tree.

To reflect the fact that the Prisoners' Dilemma is a simultaneous game, we would like to put the two players' moves at the same level in the tree, but the structure of a tree prevents us from doing that. To avoid this problem, we can arbitrarily choose one player (here *A*) to be at the top of the tree as the first mover and the other to be lower as the second mover, but then we draw an oval around *B*'s decision points to reflect the fact that *B* does not observe which action *A* has chosen and so does not observe which decision point has been reached when he or she makes his or her decision.

The choice to put *A* above *B* in the extensive form was arbitrary: we would have obtained the same representation if we put *B* above *A* and then had drawn an oval around *A*'s decision points. As we will see when we discuss sequential games, having an order to the moves only matters if the second mover can observe the first mover's action. It usually is easier to use the extensive form to analyze sequential games and the normal form to analyze simultaneous games. Therefore, we will return to the normal-form representation of the Prisoners' Dilemma to solve for its Nash equilibrium.

Solving for the Nash Equilibrium

Return to the normal form of the Prisoners' Dilemma in Table 6-1. Consider each box in turn to see if any of the corresponding pairs of strategies constitute a Nash

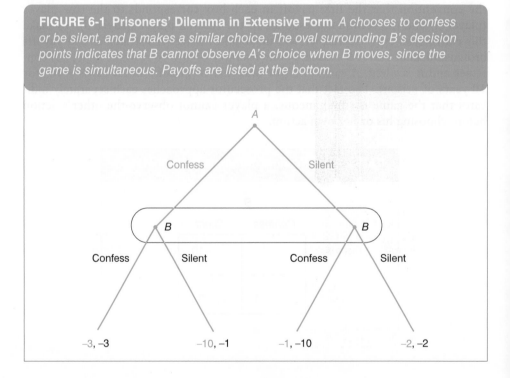

FIGURE 6-1 Prisoners' Dilemma in Extensive Form *A chooses to confess or be silent, and B makes a similar choice. The oval surrounding B's decision points indicates that B cannot observe A's choice when B moves, since the game is simultaneous. Payoffs are listed at the bottom.*

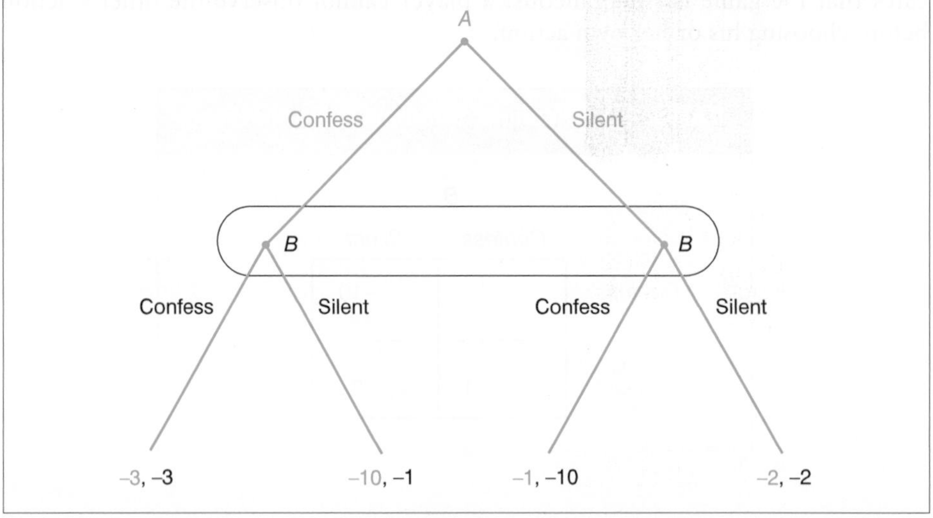

equilibrium. First consider the lower right box, corresponding to both players choosing Silent. There is reason to think this is the equilibrium of the game since the sum of the payoffs, −4, is greater than the sum of the payoffs in any of the other three outcomes (since all sums are negative, by "the greatest sum" we mean the one closest to 0). However, both playing Silent is in fact not a Nash equilibrium. To be a Nash equilibrium, both players' strategies must be best responses to each other. But given that *B* plays Silent, *A* can increase his or her payoff from −2 in the proposed equilibrium to −1 by deviating from Silent to Confess. Therefore, Silent is not *A*'s best response to *B*'s playing Silent. It is also true that *B*'s playing Silent is not a best response to *A*'s playing Silent (although demonstrating that at least one of the two players was not playing his or her best response was enough to rule out an outcome as being a Nash equilibrium). Next consider the top right box, where *A* plays Confess and *B* plays Silent. This is not a Nash equilibrium either. Given that *A* plays Confess, *B* can increase his or her payoff from −10 in the proposed equilibrium to −3 by deviating from Silent to Confess. Similarly, the bottom left box, in which *A* plays Silent and *B* plays Confess, can be shown not to be a Nash equilibrium since *A* is not playing a best response.

The remaining upper left box corresponds to both playing Confess. This is a Nash equilibrium. Given *B* plays Confess, *A*'s best response is Confess since this leads *A* to earn −3 rather than −10. By the same logic, Confess is *B*'s best response to *A*'s playing Confess.

Rather than going through each outcome one by one, there is a shortcut to finding the Nash equilibrium directly by underlining payoffs corresponding to best responses. This method is useful in games having only two actions having small payoff matrices, but it becomes extremely useful when the number of actions increases and the payoff matrix grows. The method is outlined in Table 6-2. The first step is to compute *A*'s best response to *B*'s playing Confess. *A* compares his or her payoff in the first column from playing Confess, −3, to playing Silent, −10. The payoff −3 is higher than −10, so Confess is *A*'s best response, and we underline −3. In step 2, we underline −1, corresponding to *A*'s best response, Confess, to *B*'s playing Silent. In step 3, we underline −3, corresponding to *B*'s best response to *A*'s playing Confess. In step 4, we underline −1, corresponding to *B*'s best response to *A*'s playing Silent.

For an outcome to be a Nash equilibrium, both players must be playing a best response to each other. Therefore, both payoffs in the box must be underlined. As seen in step 5, the only box in which both payoffs are underlined is the upper left, with both players choosing Confess. In the other boxes, either one or no payoffs are underlined, meaning that one or both of the players are not playing a best response in these boxes, so they cannot be Nash equilibria.

The temptation is to say that the Nash equilibrium is −3,−3. This is not technically correct. Recall that the definition of Nash equilibrium involves a set of strategies, so it is proper to refer to the Nash equilibrium in the Prisoners' Dilemma as "both players choose Confess". True, each outcome corresponds to unique payoffs in this game, so there is little confusion in referring to an equilibrium by the associated payoffs rather than strategies. However, we will come across games later in the chapter in which different outcomes have the same payoffs, so referring to equilibria by payoffs leads to ambiguity.

Dominant Strategies

Referring to step 5 in Table 6-2, not only is Confess a best response to the other players' equilibrium strategy (all that is required for Nash equilibrium), Confess is a best

TABLE 6-2 Solving for Nash Equilibrium in Prisoners' Dilemma Using the Underlining Method

Step 1: Underline payoff for *A*'s best response to *B*'s playing Confess (indicated by box shading).

A \ *B*	*Confess*	*Silent*
Confess	−3, −3	−1, −10
Silent	−10, −1	−2, −2

Step 2: Underline payoff for *A*'s best response to *B*'s playing Silent.

A \ *B*	*Confess*	*Silent*
Confess	−3, −3	−1, −10
Silent	−10, −1	−2, −2

Step 3: Underline payoff for *B*'s best response to *A*'s playing Confess.

A \ *B*	*Confess*	*Silent*
Confess	−3, −3	−1, −10
Silent	−10, −1	−2, −2

Step 4: Underline payoff for *B*'s best response to *A*'s playing Silent.

A \ *B*	*Confess*	*Silent*
Confess	−3, −3	−1, −10
Silent	−10, −1	−2, −2

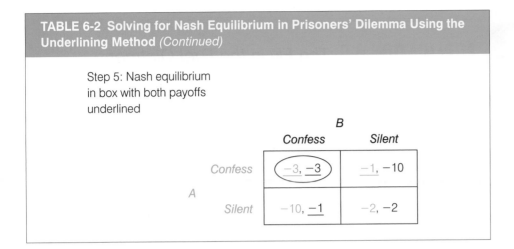

TABLE 6-2 Solving for Nash Equilibrium in Prisoners' Dilemma Using the Underlining Method *(Continued)*

Step 5: Nash equilibrium in box with both payoffs underlined

		B: *Confess*	B: *Silent*
A	*Confess*	(−3, −3)	−1, −10
	Silent	−10, −1	−2, −2

response to all strategies the other player might choose, called a **dominant strategy**. When a player has a dominant strategy in a game, there is good reason to predict that this is how the player will play the game. The player does not need to make a strategic calculation, imagining what the other might do in equilibrium. The player has one strategy that is best, regardless of what the other does. In most games, players do not have dominant strategies, so dominant strategies would not be a generally useful equilibrium definition (while Nash equilibrium is, since it exists for all games).

Dominant strategy Best response to all of the other player's strategies.

The Dilemma

The game is called the Prisoners' "Dilemma" because there is a better outcome for both players than the equilibrium. If both were Silent, they would each only get two years rather than three. But both being Silent is not stable; each would prefer to deviate to Confess. If the suspects could sign binding contracts, they would sign a contract that would have them both choose Silent. But such contracts would be difficult to write in the game because the local prosecutor approaches each suspect privately, so they cannot communicate; and even if they could sign a contract, the court would refuse to enforce it.

Situations resembling the Prisoners' Dilemma arise in many real world settings. (See Application 6.2 *The Fly in the Fuel Ointment*.) The best outcome for students working on a group project together might be for all to work hard and earn a high grade on the project, but the individual incentive to shirk, each relying on the efforts of others, may prevent them from attaining such an outcome. A cartel agreement among dairy farmers to restrict output would lead to higher prices and profits if it could be sustained, but may be unstable because it may be too tempting for an individual farmer to try to sell more milk at the high price. We will study the stability of business cartels more formally in Chapter 14.

Mixed Strategies

To analyze some games, we need to allow for more complicated strategies than simply choosing an action. We will consider **mixed strategies**, which have the player randomly select one of several possible actions. In contrast, the strategies we have considered so far that have each player choose one action or another with certainty, are called **pure strategies**. We will illustrate mixed strategies in another classic game, Matching Pennies.

Mixed strategy Randomly selecting from several possible actions.

Pure strategy A single action played with certainty.

APPLICATION 6.2 *The Fly in the Fuel Ointment . . .*

A form of the Prisoners Dilemma was provided in the case of British Airways (BA) and Virgin Atlantic Airlines (VAA) – two large airline companies. Both companies – or more accurately certain individuals within both companies – had decided to cooperate in setting fuel surcharges on airline tickets on their trans-Atlantic routes in response to the rising cost of aviation fuel. (This sort of thing, being illegal in both the United Kingdom and the United States, is not discussed and minuted at company board meetings.) In July and August of 2007 the British Government's Office of Fair Trading (OFT) fined BA £121.5 million after the airline admitted that it had colluded with VAA between August 2004 and January 2006 in imposing the surcharges. Both firms had on at least six separate occasions contacted each other about proposed changes to surcharges, rather than setting levels independently as they should have done under competition law.

Under the rules laid out by the OFT, the first firm (and only the first firm) which is involved in any anti-competitive practice that comes forward and admits its "guilt" will walk away completely unscathed, i.e. it will not be fined one British penny. The full force of the law will then come down on the remaining firms in the cartel. In this particular case the cartel only consisted of two firms. BA set aside a total of £350 million for fines that it anticipated from the OFT, the United States Department of Justice and the European Union. This should be compared with the £519 million that BA made in fuel surcharges in 2006 alone.

Figure 1 shows an indicative pay-off matrix for both firms where it is assumed that VAA, being a smaller firm, made less in fuel surcharges and would have been fined less than BA if BA had been the first to confess. As it was VAA confessed first. One interesting difference with our original prisoner's dilemma is that the party which confesses not only walks free but takes its "ill-gotten gains" with it! However, precisely because of this the OFT strategy has over the years been remarkably successful in causing a "breaking of ranks". Each member of a cartel must at some stage reason that not only could they confess and then keep the benefit of the collusion but in the process they could, temporarily at least, inflict a substantial cost penalty on a market rival.

The "game" is also interesting because there would appear to be a pay-off matrix within a pay-off matrix (not shown in the figure). An individual, Mr Martin George, who had responsibility for the department within BA which initially contacted VAA and resigned because of the price-fixing scandal left with £467 000 which included his salary, benefits and a termination fee of £263 000. He also got £356 000 towards his legal fees and a £555 397 pay-out from a BA long-term incentive plan. All the above was part of Mr George's contractual arrangements with BA.

To think About

1 In chapter 17 we discuss in detail the "principal–agent problem" where (briefly here) because an individual (the agent) acting on behalf of someone else (the principal) is not observed all of the time, this can lead to opportunistic behavior on the part of the agent which lowers the overall well-being of the principle. From the application Mr George was the agent acting on behalf of BA. Do Mr George's payouts on leaving BA prove that such contracts do not work in terms of making, in this case Mr George, more productive for BA? Was the long-term incentive plan part of the problem or solution to behavior which put BA at risk? [These are open-ended questions which cannot be proved one way or another from the text alone and are meant to make you think and express an opinion!]

2 Is it right that one party who breaks the law should walk away unscathed or is it a "necessary evil" to ensure the greater problem of cartels and anti-competitive behavior is tackled? [Again, like question one, there is no right or wrong answer.]

3 Is any other airline likely to approach VAA to fix prices of any form in the future? Explain your reasoning. Recall as well that it was individuals who colluded and not *per se* the firms themselves. Does that make a difference to your reasoning? If not, why not?

TABLE 1 Collusion on Fuel Surcharges between British Airways and Virgin Atlantic Airlines

		Virgin Atlantic Airlines	
		Confess	Silent/found out
British Airways	Confess	−350, −150	500, −150
	Silent/found out	−350, 250	500, 250

Matching Pennies

Matching Pennies is based on a children's game in which two players, *A* and *B*, each secretly choose whether to leave a penny with its head or tail facing up. The players then reveal their choices simultaneously. *A* wins *B*'s penny if the coins match (both Heads or both Tails), and *B* wins *A*'s penny if they do not. The normal form for the game is given in Table 6-3 and the extensive form in Figure 6-2. The game has the special property that the two players' payoffs in each box add to zero, called a zero-sum game. By contrast, the reader can check that the Prisoner's Dilemma is not a zero-sum game because the sum of players' payoffs varies across the different boxes.

To solve for the Nash equilibrium, we will use the method of underlining payoffs for best responses introduced previously for the Prisoners' Dilemma. Table 6-4 presents the results from this method. *A* always prefers to play the same action as *B*. *B* prefers to play a different action from *A*. There is no box with both payoffs underlined, so we have not managed to find a Nash equilibrium. One might be tempted to say that no Nash equilibrium exists for this game. But this contradicts our earlier claim that all games have Nash equilibria. The contradiction can be resolved by noting that the Matching Pennies game does have a Nash equilibrium, not in pure strategies, as would be found by our underlining method, but in mixed strategies.

TABLE 6-3 Matching Pennies Game in Normal Form

		B	
		Heads	Tails
A	Heads	1, −1	−1, 1
	Tails	−1, 1	1, −1

FIGURE 6-2 Matching Pennies Game in Extensive Form

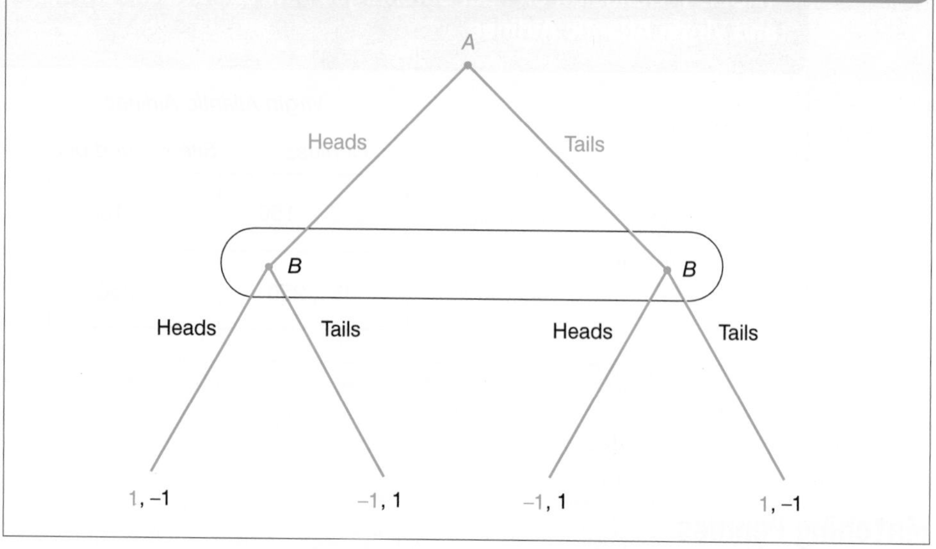

Solving for a Mixed-Strategy Nash Equilibrium

Rather than choosing Heads or Tails, suppose players secretly flip the penny and play whatever side turns up. The result of this strategy is a random choice of Heads with probability 1/2 and Tails with probability 1/2. This set of strategies, with both playing Heads or Tails with equal chance, is the mixed-strategy Nash equilibrium of the game. To verify this, we need to show that both players' strategies are best responses to each other.

In the proposed equilibrium, all four outcomes corresponding to the four boxes in the normal form in Table 6-3 are equally likely to occur, each occurring with probability 1/4. Using the formula for expected payoffs from the previous chapter, *A*'s expected payoff equals the probability-weighted sum of the payoffs in each outcome:

$$(1/4)(1) + (1/4)(-1) + (1/4)(-1) + (1/4)(1) = 0.$$

Similarly, *B*'s expected payoff is also 0. The mixed strategies in the proposed equilibrium are best responses to each other if neither player can deviate to a strategy

TABLE 6-4 Solving for Pure-Strategy Nash Equilibrium in Matching Pennies Game

		B	
		Heads	*Tails*
A	*Heads*	1, −1	−1, 1
	Tails	−1, 1	1, −1

that produces a strictly higher payoff than 0. But there is no such profitable deviation. Given that *B* plays Heads and Tails with equal probabilities, the players' coins will match exactly half the time, whether *A* chooses Heads or Tails (or indeed even some random combination of the two actions); so *A*'s payoff is 0 no matter what strategy it chooses. *A* cannot earn more than the 0 it earns in equilibrium. Similarly, given *A* is playing Heads and Tails with equal probabilities, *B*'s expected payoff is 0 no matter what strategy it uses. So neither player has a strictly profitable deviation. (It should be emphasized here that if a deviation produces a tie with the player's equilibrium payoff, this is not sufficient to rule out the equilibrium; to rule out an equilibrium, one must demonstrate a deviation produces a strictly higher payoff than in equilibrium.)

Both players playing Heads and Tails with equal probabilities is the only mixed-strategy Nash equilibrium in this game. No other probabilities would work. For example, suppose *B* were to play Heads with probability 1/3 and Tails with probability 2/3. Then *A* would earn an expected payoff of $(1/3)(1) + (2/3)(-1) = -1/3$ from playing Heads and $(1/3)(-1) + (2/3)(1) = 1/3$ from playing Tails. Therefore, *A* would strictly prefer to play Tails as a pure strategy rather than playing a mixed strategy involving both Heads and Tails, and so *B*'s playing Heads with probability 1/3 and Tails with probability 2/3 cannot be a mixed-strategy Nash equilibrium.

It should be emphasized that in mixed-strategy Nash equilibrium of Matching Pennies or indeed any game, players must be indifferent between the actions that are played with positive probability. If a player strictly preferred one action over another, the player would want to put all of the probability on the preferred action and none on the other action.

The Nash equilibrium in Matching Pennies involved equal probabilities of the two actions. In other games, the mixed-strategy Nash equilibrium can involve different probabilities of playing the two actions. We will see such a case in the Battle of the Sexes game below. In games with more than two actions, the mixed-strategy Nash equilibrium can sometimes involve playing more than two actions with positive probability.

Interpretation of Random Strategies

While at first glance it may seem bizarre to have players flipping coins or rolling dice in secret to determine their strategies, it may not be so unnatural in children's games such as Matching Pennies. Mixed strategies are also natural and common in sports, as discussed in Application 6.3: *Mixed Strategies in Sports*. Mixed strategies are important in law enforcement. Consider the enforcement of traffic laws such as speeding. Having police stationed continuously on every street may be prohibitively expensive. But having police stationed on only some of the streets only some of the time may deter speeding everywhere, especially if the punishment for speeding is high enough. Of course, if drivers knew which streets the police patrolled, they would drive within the limit on those and speed on the others. So, in practice, police are stationed at random places and times. Perhaps most familiar to students is the role of mixed strategies in class exams. Class time is usually too limited for the professor to examine students on every topic taught in class. But it may be sufficient to test students on a subset of topics to get them to study all of the material. If students knew which topics are on the test, they may be inclined to study only those and not the others, so the professor must choose which topics to include at random to get the students to study everything.

MICROQUIZ 6.1

In Matching Pennies, suppose *B* plays the equilibrium mixed strategy of Heads with probability 1/2 and Tails with probability 1/2. Use the formula for expected values to verify that *A*'s expected payoff equals 0 from using any of the following strategies.

1. The pure strategy of Heads.
2. The pure strategy of Tails.
3. The mixed strategy of Heads with probabilit[y] 1/2 and Tails with probability 1/2.
4. The mixed strategy of Heads with probabili[ty] 1/3 and Tails with probability 2/3.

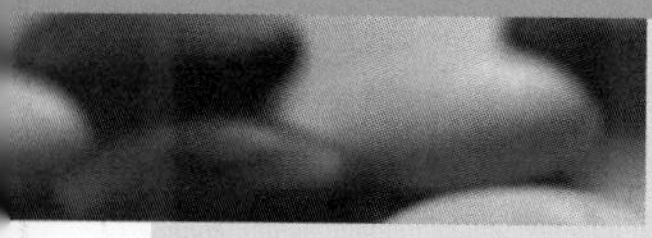

APPLICATION 6.3 *Mixed Strategies in Sports*

Sports provide a setting in which mixed strategies arise quite naturally, and in a simple enough setting that we can see game theory in operation.

Football Penalty Kicks

In football, if a team commits certain offences near its own goal, the other team is awarded a penalty kick, effectively setting up a game between the taker of the penalty shot and the goal keeper (or simply keeper). Table 1 is based on a study of penalty kicks in elite European soccer leagues.[1] The first entry in each box is the frequency the penalty kick scores (taken to be the penalty taker's payoff), and the second entry is the frequency it does not score (taken to be the keeper's payoff). Penalty takers are assumed to have two actions: aim toward the "natural" side of the goal (left for right-footed kickers and right for left-footed players) or aim toward the other side. Penalty takers can typically kick harder and more accurately to their natural side. Keepers can try to jump one way or the other to try to block the kick. The ball travels too fast for the goalie to react to its direction, so the game is effectively simultaneous. Keepers know from scouting reports what side is natural for each penalty taker, so they can condition their actions on this information.

Do Mixed Strategies Predict Actual Outcomes?

Using the method of underlining payoffs corresponding to best responses, as shown in Table 1, we see that no box has both payoffs underlined, so there is no pure-strategy Nash equilibrium.

Using the same steps we will use to compute the mixed-strategy Nash equilibrium in the Battle of the Sexes below, one can show that the kicker kicks to his natural side 3/5 of the time and 2/5 of the time to his other side; the keeper jumps to the side that is natural for the kicker 2/3 of the time and the other side 1/3 of the time. Several important implications emerge from the theoretical analysis of the mixed-strategy Nash equilibrium that can be checked in the data. First, both actions have at least some chance of being played. This is borne out in the Chiappori *et al.* data: almost all of the penalty takers and keepers who are involved in three or more penalty kicks in the data choose each action at least once. Second, players obtain the same expected payoff in equilibrium regardless of the action taken. This is again borne out in the data, with penalty takers scoring about 75 per cent of the time, whether they kick to their natural side or the opposite, and keepers being scored on about 75 per cent of the time, whether they jump to the kicker's natural side or the opposite. Third, the keeper should jump to the side that is natural for the taker of the penalty more often. Otherwise, the higher speed and accuracy going to his natural side would lead the penalty taker to play the pure strategy of always kicking that way. Again, this conclusion is borne out in the data, with the keeper jumping to the penalty taker's natural side 60 per cent of the time (note how close this is to the prediction of 2/3 we made above).

To Think About

1 Verify the mixed-strategy Nash equilibrium computed above for the penalty-kick game using the methods we will use for the Battle of the Sexes game.

2 Economists have studied mixed strategies in other sports, for example whether a tennis serve is aimed to the returner's backhand or forehand.[2] Can you think of other sports settings in which mixed strategies may be involved? Can you think of settings involving mixed strategies outside of sports and games and besides the ones noted in the text?

TABLE 1 Football Penalty Kick Game

	Goalie	
Kicker	*Natural Side for the Kicker*	*Other Side*
Natural Side for the Kicker	.64, .36	.94, .06
Other Side	.89, .11	.44, .56

[1] P.-A. Chiappori, S. Levitt, and T. Groseclose, "Testing Mixed-Strategy Equilibria When Players Are Heterogeneous: The Case of Penalty Kicks in Soccer", *American Economic Review* (September 2002): 1138–1151.

[2] M. Walker and J. Wooders, "Minimax Play at Wimbledon", *American Economic Review* (December 2001), 1521–1538.

Multiple Equilibria

Nash equilibrium is a useful solution concept because it exists for all games. A drawback is that some games have several or even many Nash equilibria. The possibility of multiple equilibria causes a problem for economists who would like to use game theory to make predictions, since it is unclear which of the Nash equilibria one should predict will happen. The possibility of multiple equilibria is illustrated in yet another classic game, the Battle of the Sexes.

Battle of the Sexes

The game involves two players, a wife (*A*) and a husband (*B*) who are planning an evening out. Both prefer to be together rather than apart. Conditional on being together, the wife would prefer to go to a ballet performance and the husband to a boxing match. The normal form for the game is given in Table 6-5 and the extensive form in Figure 6-3.

To solve for the Nash equilibria, we will use the method of underlining payoffs for best responses introduced previously. Table 6-6 presents the results from this method. A player's best response is to play the same action as the other. Both payoffs are underlined in two boxes: the box in which both play Ballet and also in the box in which both

TABLE 6-5 Battle of the Sexes in Normal Form

		B (Husband)	
		Ballet	*Boxing*
A (Wife)	*Ballet*	2, 1	0, 0
	Boxing	0, 0	1, 2

FIGURE 6-3 Battle of the Sexes in Extensive Form

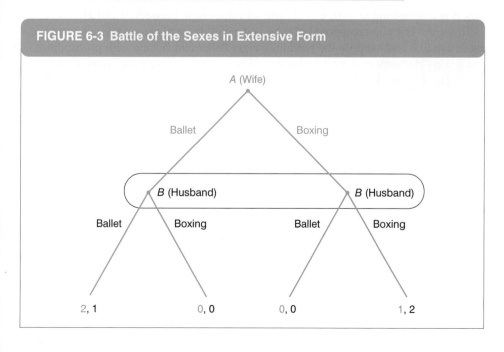

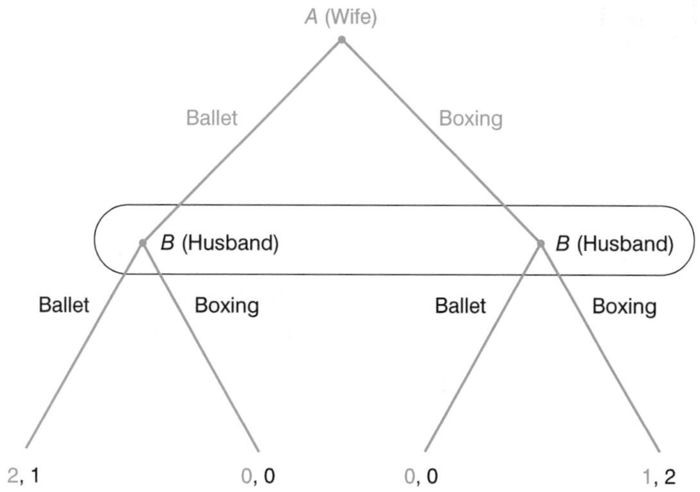

play Boxing. Therefore, there are two pure-strategy Nash equilibria: (1) both play Ballet and (2) both play Boxing.

The problem of multiple equilibria is even worse than at first appears. Besides the two pure-strategy Nash equilibria, there is a mixed-strategy one. How does one know this? It is impossible to know exactly unless one performs all the calculations necessary to find a mixed-strategy Nash equilibrium. However, one could guess that there would be a mixed-strategy Nash equilibrium based on a famous but peculiar result that Nash equilibria tend to come in odd numbers. Therefore, finding an even number of pure-strategy Nash equilibria (two in this game, zero in Matching Pennies) should lead one to suspect that the game also has another Nash equilibrium, in mixed strategies.

Computing Mixed Strategies in the Battle of the Sexes

It is instructive to go through the calculation of the mixed-strategy Nash equilibrium in the Battle of the Sexes since, unlike in Matching Pennies, the equilibrium probabilities do not end up being equal (1/2) for each action. Let w be the probability the wife plays Ballet and h the probability the husband plays Ballet. Remembering that the probabilities of exclusive and exhaustive events must add to one, the probability of playing Boxing is $1 - w$ for the wife and $1 - h$ for the husband; so once we know the probability each plays Ballet, we automatically know the probability each plays Boxing. Our task then is to compute the equilibrium values of w and h. The difficulty now is that w and h may potentially be any one of a continuum of values between 0 and 1, so we cannot set up a payoff matrix and use our underlining method to find best responses. Instead, we will graph players' **best-response functions.**

Best-response function Function giving the payoff-maximizing choice for one player for each of a continuum of actions of the other player.

Let us start by computing the wife's best-response function. The wife's best-response function gives the w that maximizes her payoff for each of the husband's possible strategies, h. For a given h, there are three possibilities: she may strictly prefer to play Ballet; she may strictly prefer to play Boxing; or she may be indifferent between Ballet and Boxing. In terms of w, if she strictly prefers to play Ballet, her best response is $w = 1$. If she strictly prefers to play Boxing, her best response is $w = 0$. If she is indifferent about Ballet and Boxing, her best response is a tie between $w = 1$ and $w = 0$; in fact, it is a tie among $w = 0$, $w = 1$, and all values of w between 0 and 1!

To see this last point, suppose her expected payoff from playing both Ballet and Boxing is, say, 2/3, and suppose she randomly plays Ballet and Boxing with probabilities w and $1 - w$. Her expected payoff (this should be reviewed, if necessary, from Chapter 5) would equal the probability she plays Ballet times her expected payoff if she plays Ballet plus the probability she plays Boxing times her expected payoff if she plays Boxing:

$$(w)(2/3) + (1 - w)(2/3) = 2/3.$$

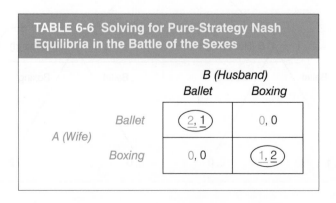

TABLE 6-6 Solving for Pure-Strategy Nash Equilibria in the Battle of the Sexes

		B (Husband)	
		Ballet	Boxing
A (Wife)	Ballet	(2, 1)	0, 0
	Boxing	0, 0	(1, 2)

This shows that she gets the same payoff, 2/3, whether she plays Ballet for sure, Boxing for sure, or a mixed strategy involving any probabilities w, $1 - w$ of playing Ballet and Boxing. So her best response would be a tie among $w = 0$, $w = 1$, and all values in between.

Returning to the computation of the wife's best-response function, suppose the husband plays a mixed strategy of Ballet probability h and Boxing with probability $1 - h$. Referring to Table 6-7, her expected payoff from playing Ballet equals h (the probability the husband plays Ballet, and so they end up in Box 1) times 2 (her payoff in Box 1) plus $1 - h$ (the probability he plays Boxing, and so they end up in Box 2) times 0 (her payoff in Box 2), for a total expected payoff, after simplifying, of $2h$. Her expected payoff from playing Boxing equals h (the probability the husband plays Ballet, and so they end up in Box 3) times 0 (her payoff in Box 3) plus $1 - h$ (the probability he plays Boxing, and so they end up in Box 4) times 1 (her payoff in Box 4) for a total expected payoff, after simplifying, of $1 - h$.

Based on the calculations from the previous paragraph, we can see that she prefers Ballet if $2h > 1 - h$ or, rearranging, $h > 1/3$. Therefore, in other words, her best response to any h greater than 1/3 is $w = 1$. She prefers Boxing if $2h < 1 - h$ or, rearranging, $h < 1/3$. Therefore, her best response to any h less than 1/3 is $w = 0$. She is indifferent between Ballet and Boxing if $h = 1/3$. Therefore, her best response to $h = 1/3$ includes $w = 0$, $w = 1$, and all values in between.

Figure 6-4 graphs her best-response function as the thick brown line. Similar calculations can be used to derive the husband's best-response function, the thick black line. The best-response functions intersect in three places, the three Nash equilibria. The figure allows us to recover the two pure-strategy Nash equilibria found before: the one in which $w = h = 1$ (that is, both play Ballet for sure) and the one in which $w = h = 0$ (that is, both play Boxing for sure). We also obtain the mixed-strategy Nash equilibrium $w = 2/3$ and $h = 1/3$. In words, the mixed-strategy Nash equilibrium involves the wife's playing Ballet with probability 2/3 and Boxing with probability 1/3 and the husband's playing Ballet with probability 1/3 and Boxing with probability 2/3.

At first glance, it seems that the wife puts more probability on Ballet because she prefers Ballet conditional on coordinating and the husband puts more probability on Boxing because he prefers Boxing conditional on coordinating. This intuition is misleading. The wife, for example, is indifferent between Ballet and Boxing in the mixed-strategy Nash equilibrium given her husband's strategy. She does not care what probabilities she plays Ballet and Boxing. What pins down her equilibrium probabilities is not her

MICROQUIZ 6.2

1. In the Battle of the Sexes, does either player have a dominant strategy?
2. In general, can a game have a mixed-strategy Nash equilibrium if a player has a dominant strategy? Why or why not?

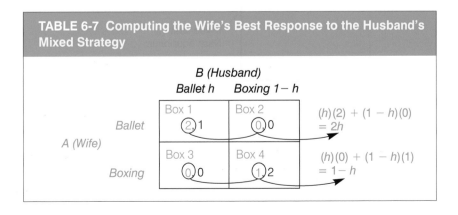

TABLE 6-7 Computing the Wife's Best Response to the Husband's Mixed Strategy

		B (Husband) Ballet h	B (Husband) Boxing $1 - h$	
A (Wife)	Ballet	Box 1: (2), 1	Box 2: (0), 0	$(h)(2) + (1 - h)(0) = 2h$
A (Wife)	Boxing	Box 3: (0), 0	Box 4: (1), 2	$(h)(0) + (1 - h)(1) = 1 - h$

payoffs but her husband's. She has to put less probability on the action he prefers conditional on coordinating (Boxing) than on the other action (Ballet) or else he would not be indifferent between Ballet and Boxing and the probabilities would not form a Nash equilibrium.

The Problem of Multiple Equilibria

Given that there are multiple equilibria, it is difficult to make a unique prediction about the outcome of the game. To solve this problem, game theorists have devoted a considerable amount of research to refining the Nash equilibrium concept, that is, coming up with good reasons for picking out one Nash equilibrium as being more "reasonable" than others. One suggestion would be to select the outcome with the highest total payoffs for the two players. This rule would eliminate the mixed-strategy Nash equilibrium in favor of one of the two pure-strategy equilibria. In the mixed-strategy equilibrium, we showed that each player's expected payoff is 2/3 no matter which action is chosen, implying that the total expected payoff for the two players is $2/3 + 2/3 = 4/3$. In the two pure-strategy equilibria, total payoffs, equal to 3, exceed the total expected payoff in the mixed-strategy equilibrium.

Focal point Logical outcome on which to coordinate, based on information outside of the game.

A rule that selects the highest total payoff would not distinguish between the two pure-strategy equilibria. To select between these, one might follow T. Schelling's suggestion and look for a **focal point**.[2] For example, the equilibrium in which both play Ballet might be a logical focal point if the couple had a history of deferring to the wife's wishes on previous occasions. Without access to this external information on

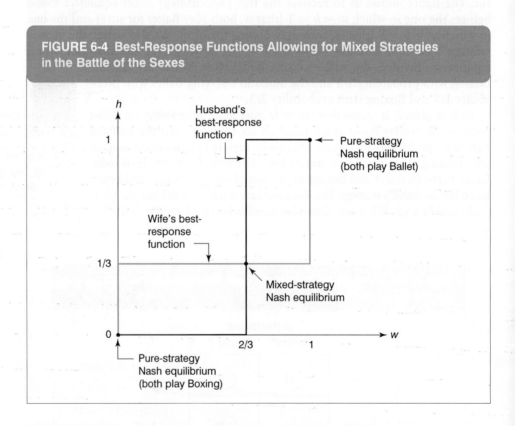

FIGURE 6-4 Best-Response Functions Allowing for Mixed Strategies in the Battle of the Sexes

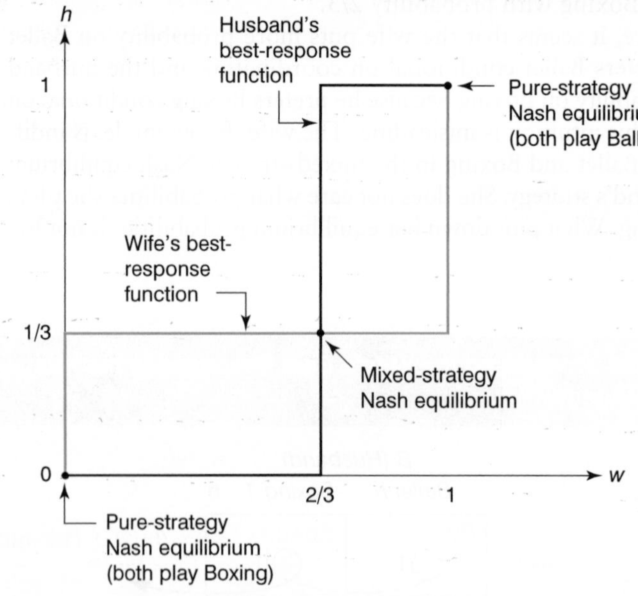

[2]T. Schelling, *The Strategy of Conflict* (Cambridge, MA: Harvard University Press, 1960).

previous interactions, it would be difficult for a game theorist to make predictions about focal points, however. Another suggestion would be that, since we have no reason to think one player is favored over another, to select the symmetric equilibrium. This rule might select the mixed-strategy Nash equilibrium because it is the only one that has equal payoffs (the wife's and husband's expected payoffs are both 2/3). In sum, the basis for any of these selection rules is fairly weak. The Battle of the Sexes is one of those games for which there is simply no good way to solve the problem of multiple equilibria.

Coming up with a suitable refinement of Nash equilibrium allowing the selection of one from a set of multiple Nash equilibria is an issue at the forefront of current research in game theory. Perhaps an even more basic question, also at the forefront of current research, is why players are led to play Nash equilibria to begin with. One approach, described in Application 6.4: *Evolutionary Game Theory* is to suppose that players are guided more by instinct than reason, instinct that has been honed by generations of evolution.

Sequential Games

In some games, the order of moves matters. For example, in a bicycle race with a staggered start, the last racer has the advantage of knowing the time to beat. With new consumer technologies, for example HDTV sets, it may help to wait to buy until a critical mass of others have and so there are a sufficiently large number of program channels available.

Sequential games differ from the simultaneous games we have considered so far in that a player that moves after another can learn information about the play of the game up to that point, including what actions other players have chosen. The player can use this information to form more sophisticated strategies than simply choosing an action; the player's strategy can be a contingent plan, with the action played depending on what the other players do.

To illustrate the new concepts raised by sequential games, and in particular to make a stark contrast between sequential and simultaneous games, we will take a simultaneous game we have discussed already, the Battle of the Sexes, and turn it into a sequential game.

The Sequential Battle of the Sexes

Consider the Battle of the Sexes game analyzed previously with all the same actions and payoffs, but change the order of moves. Rather than the wife and husband making a simultaneous choice, the wife moves first, choosing Ballet or Boxing, the husband observes this choice (say the wife calls him from her chosen location), and then the husband makes his choice. The wife's possible strategies have not changed: she can choose the simple actions Ballet or Boxing (or perhaps a mixed strategy involving both actions, although this will not be a relevant consideration in the sequential game). The husband's set of possible strategies has expanded. For each of the wife's two actions, he can choose one of two actions, so he has four possible strategies, which are listed in Table 6-8. The vertical bar in the second equivalent way of writing the strategies means "conditional on", so, for example, "Boxing | Ballet" should be read "the husband goes to Boxing conditional on the wife's going to Ballet". The husband still can choose a simple action, with "Ballet" now interpreted as "always go to Ballet" and "Boxing" as "always go to Boxing", but he can also follow her or do the opposite.

APPLICATION 6.4 *Evolutionary Game Theory*

The development of the theory of evolution had been so successful in describing how living things' physical structure came to be that biologists began wondering if the theory could also explain animal behavior. Could the theory of evolution explain how hard two dogs were willing to fight over a bone? Could it explain why a bee might sacrifice itself to defend the hive?

A Biologist's Conception

John Maynard Smith pioneered the use of evolutionary game theory to understand animal behavior.[1] The theory assumes that animals behave according to instinctual strategies passed down from generation to generation through one's genes, just as physical characteristics are passed down. The more successful a particular strategy, the more "fit" is an animal in terms of the ability to survive and pass down its genes to subsequent generations. New strategies arise through mutations. Mutations quickly disappear in the population if they are not successful against the strategies that are predominant in the population. But if the mutations are successful, they can come to dominate in the population.

The Hawk–Dove Game

To see these ideas more concretely, consider the famous Hawk–Dove game shown in Table 1. Animals *A* and *B* play one of two possible actions when confronting each other over a piece of food. An animal may fight aggressively for the food (the Hawk strategy), or it may be more passive (the Dove strategy). If an animal playing Dove meets one playing Hawk, the Hawk gets the food without a fight. If two Hawks meet, they divide the benefit from the food, v, less the cost of fighting, c, in half. If two Doves meet, they divide v in half and do not fight. Animals from a large population are matched at random to play the game. The animal that gets the higher payoff in their meeting passes the genes for its strategy on to the next generation.

A strategy is said to be evolutionarily stable if, given it is pervasive in the population, any other strategy is introduced as a small mutation, this mutation will not spread in the population. Dove is not an evolutionarily stable strategy. If the whole population is playing Dove and a few Hawks are introduced, random matching will lead the Hawks nearly always to be matched against Doves, and Hawks will get a higher payoff in these matches (v compared to 0). On the other hand, Hawk is evolutionarily stable as long as the cost of fighting c does not exceed the benefit v.

Evolutionary Game Theory in Economics

Evolutionary game theory has received considerable recent attention in economics. First, it provides a way of selecting among multiple Nash equilibria. It can be shown that evolutionarily stable strategies are Nash equilibria, but not all Nash equilibria are evolutionarily stable.

Second, and more importantly, evolutionary game theory provides an equilibrium concept that does not depend on players being hyper rational as does Nash equilibrium. In a two-player game, for example, Nash equilibrium requires player *A* to be rational in the sense that *A* plays a best response to *B*'s equilibrium action, but *A* must also know that *B* is rational, since *A* expects *B* to play a best response, and *A* must know that *B* knows that *A* is rational, and so on, a mind-boggling chain of reasoning. There is thus appeal in a concept such as evolutionarily stable strategies, which require no rationality and can explain regularities in even animal behavior.

To Think About

1. Researchers have applied evolutionary arguments to explain norms regarding sexual behavior (monogamy, polygamy, adultery).[2] How might one construct such arguments?
2. Are humans evolving faster than other animals? What factors might affect human evolution, given that nature plays less of a role in preventing survival to maturity as civilization advances?

TABLE 1 Hawk–Dove Game

		B: Hawk	B: Dove
A	Hawk	$(v-c)/2, (v-c)/2$	$v, 0$
A	Dove	$0, v$	$v/2, v/2$

[1] J. Maynard Smith, *Evolution and the Theory of Games* (Cambridge: Cambridge University Press, 1982).

[2] T. Burnham and J. Phelan, *Mean Genes: From Sex to Money to Food: Taming Our Primal Instincts* (New York: Penguin Books, 2000).

Given that the husband has four pure strategies rather than just two, the normal form, given in Table 6-9, must now be expanded to have eight boxes. Roughly speaking, the normal form is twice as complicated as that for the simultaneous version of the game in Table 6-5. By contrast, the extensive form, given in Figure 6-5, is no more complicated than the extensive form for the simultaneous version of the game in Figure 6-3. The only difference between the extensive forms is that the oval around the husband's decision points has been removed. In the sequential version of the game, the husband's decision points are not gathered together in an oval because the husband observes his wife's action and so knows which one he is on before moving. We can begin to see why the extensive form becomes more useful than the normal form for sequential games, especially in games with many rounds of moves.

To solve for the Nash equilibria, we will return to the normal form and use the method of underlining payoffs for best responses introduced previously. Table 6-10 presents the results from this method. One complication that arises in the method of underlining payoffs is that there are ties for best responses in this game. For example, if the husband plays the strategy "Boxing | Ballet, Ballet | Boxing", that is, if he does the opposite of his wife, then she earns zero no matter what action she chooses. To apply the underlining method properly, we need to underline both zeroes in the third column. There are also ties between the husband's best responses to his wife's playing Ballet (his payoff is 1 if he plays either "Ballet | Ballet, Ballet | Boxing" or "Ballet | Ballet, Boxing | Boxing") and to his wife's playing Boxing (his payoff is 2 if he plays either "Ballet | Ballet, Boxing | Boxing" or "Boxing | Ballet, Boxing | Boxing"). Again, as shown in the table, we need to underline the payoffs for all the strategies that tie for the best response. There are three pure-strategy Nash equilibria:

1 Wife plays Ballet, husband plays "Ballet | Ballet, Ballet | Boxing".
2 Wife plays Ballet, husband plays "Ballet | Ballet, Boxing | Boxing".
3 Wife plays Boxing, husband plays "Boxing | Ballet, Boxing | Boxing".

As we saw with the simultaneous version of the Battle of the Sexes, here again with the sequential version we have multiple equilibria. Here, however, game theory offers a good way to select among the equilibria. Consider the third Nash equilibrium. The husband's strategy, "Boxing | Ballet, Boxing | Boxing", involves an implicit threat that he will choose Boxing even if his wife chooses Ballet. This threat

TABLE 6-8 Husband's Contingent Strategies

Contingent strategy	*Strategy written equivalently in conditional format*
Always go to Ballet	Ballet | Ballet, Ballet | Boxing
Follow his wife	Ballet | Ballet, Boxing | Boxing
Do the opposite	Boxing | Ballet, Ballet | Boxing
Always go to boxing	Boxing | Ballet, Boxing | Boxing

> **MICROQUIZ 6.3**
>
> Refer to the normal form of the sequential Battle of the Sexes.
>
> 1 Provide examples in which referring to equilibria using payoffs is ambiguous but with strategies is unambiguous.
>
> 2 Explain why "Boxing" or "Ballet" is not a complete description of the second-mover's strategy.

is sufficient to deter her from choosing Ballet. Given she chooses Boxing in equilibrium, his strategy earns him 2, which is the best he can do in any outcome. So the outcome is a Nash equilibrium. But the husband's threat is not credible, that is, it is an empty threat. If the wife really were to choose Ballet first, he would be giving up a payoff of 1 by choosing Boxing rather than Ballet. It is clear why he would want to threaten to choose Boxing, but it is not clear that such a threat should be believed. Similarly, the husband's strategy, "Ballet | Ballet, Ballet | Boxing", in the first Nash equilibrium also involves an empty threat, the threat that he will choose Ballet if his wife chooses Boxing. (This is an odd threat to make since he does not gain from making it, but it is an empty threat nonetheless.)

TABLE 6-9 Sequential Version of the Battle of the Sexes in Normal Form

		B (Husband)			
		Ballet | Ballet Ballet | Boxing	Ballet | Ballet Boxing | Boxing	Boxing | Ballet Ballet | Boxing	Boxing | Ballet Boxing | Boxing
A (Wife)	Ballet	2, 1	2, 1	0, 0	0, 0
	Boxing	0, 0	1, 2	0, 0	1, 2

FIGURE 6-5 Sequential Version of the Battle of the Sexes in Extensive Form

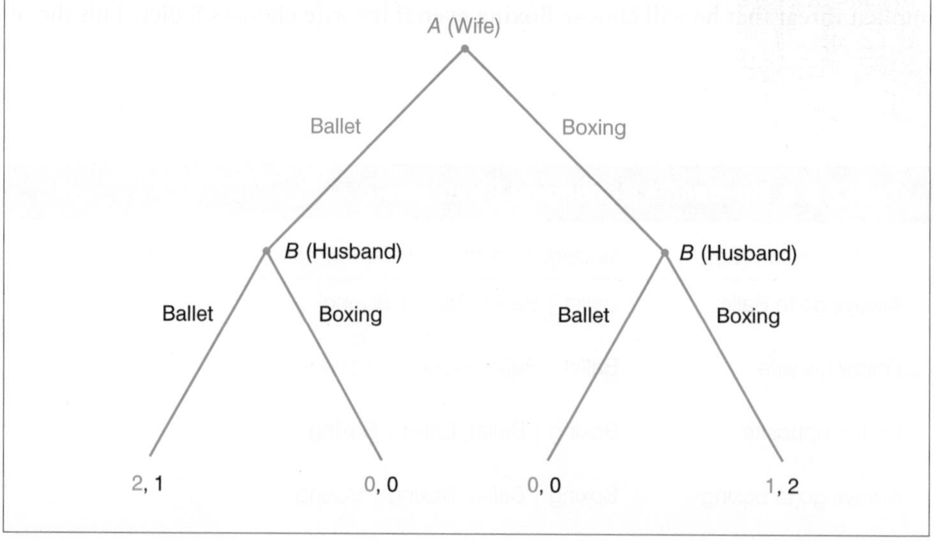

Subgame-Perfect Equilibrium

Game theory offers a formal way of selecting the reasonable Nash equilibria in sequential games using the concept of subgame-perfect equilibrium. Subgame-perfect equilibrium is a refinement that rules out empty threats by requiring strategies to be rational even for contingencies that do not arise in equilibrium.

Before defining subgame-perfect equilibrium formally, we need to say what a proper subgame is. A subgame is a part of the extensive form beginning with a decision point and including everything that branches out below it. The decision point at the top of a **proper subgame** is not connected to another in the same oval. Conceptually, this means that the player who moves first in a proper subgame knows the actions played by others that have led up to that point. It is easier to see what a proper subgame is than to define it in words. Figure 6-6 shows the extensive forms from the simultaneous and sequential versions of the Battle of the Sexes, with dotted lines drawn around the proper subgames in each. In the simultaneous Battle of the Sexes, there is only one decision point that is not connected to another in an oval, the topmost one. Therefore, there is only one proper subgame, the game itself. In the sequential Battle of the Sexes, there are three proper subgames: the game itself, and two lower subgames starting with decision points where the husband gets to move.

Proper subgame Part of the game tree including an initial decision not connected to another in an oval and everything branching out below it.

A **subgame-perfect equilibrium** is a set of strategies, one for each player, that form a Nash equilibrium on every proper subgame. A subgame-perfect equilibrium is always a Nash equilibrium. This is true since the whole game is a proper subgame of itself, so a subgame-perfect equilibrium must be a Nash equilibrium on the whole game. In the simultaneous version of the Battle of the Sexes, there is nothing more to say since there are no other subgames besides the whole game itself.

Subgame-perfect equilibrium Strategies that form a Nash equilibrium on every proper subgame.

In the sequential version of the Battle of the Sexes, the concept of subgame-perfect equilibrium has more bite. In addition to strategies having to form a Nash equilibrium on the whole game itself, they must form Nash equilibria on the two other proper subgames, starting with the decision points at which the husband moves. These subgames are simple decision problems, and so it is easy to compute the corresponding Nash equilibria. For the left-hand subgame, beginning with the husband's decision point following his wife's choosing Ballet, he has a simple decision between Ballet, which earns him a payoff of 1, and Boxing, which earns him a

TABLE 6-10 Solving for Nash Equilibria in the Sequential Version of the Battle of the Sexes

		B (Husband)			
		Ballet | Ballet *Ballet | Boxing*	*Ballet | Ballet* *Boxing | Boxing*	*Boxing | Ballet* *Ballet | Boxing*	*Boxing | Ballet* *Boxing | Boxing*
A (Wife)	*Ballet*	Nash equilibrium 1 2, 1	Nash equilibrium 2 2, 1	0, 0	0, 0
	Boxing	0, 0	1, 2	0, 0	Nash equilibrium 3 1, 2

payoff of 0. The Nash equilibrium in this simple decision subgame is for the husband to choose Ballet. For the right-hand subgame, beginning with the husband's decision point following from his wife's choosing Boxing, he has a simple decision between Ballet, which earns him 0, and Boxing, which earns him 2. The Nash equilibrium in this simple decision subgame is for him to choose Boxing. Thus we see that the husband has only one strategy that can be part of a subgame-perfect equilibrium: "Ballet | Ballet, Boxing | Boxing". Any other strategy has him playing something that is not a Nash equilibrium on some proper subgame. Returning to the three

FIGURE 6-6 Proper Subgames in the Battle of the Sexes

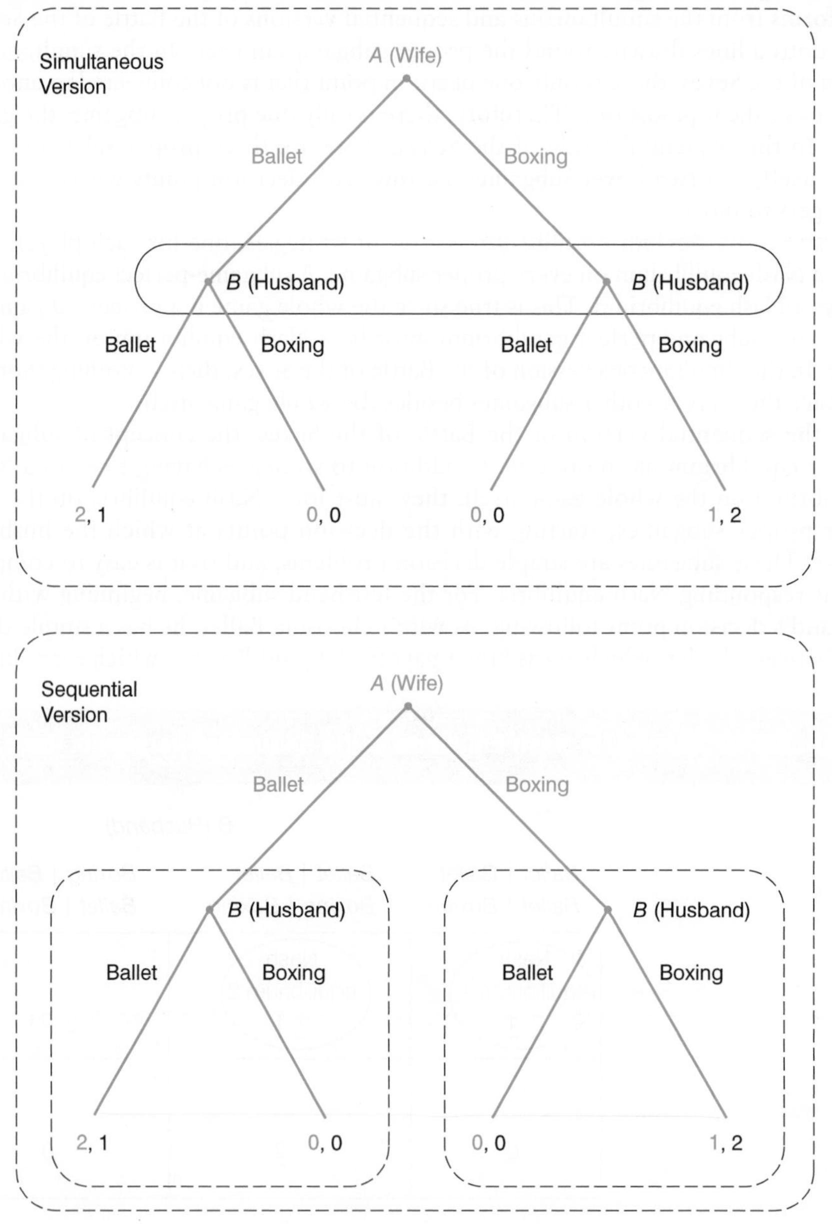

enumerated Nash equilibria, only the second one is subgame-perfect. The first and the third are not. For example, the third equilibrium, in which the husband always goes to Boxing, is ruled out as a subgame-perfect equilibrium because the husband would not go to Boxing if the wife indeed went to Ballet; he would go to Ballet as well. Subgame-perfect equilibrium thus rules out the empty threat of always going to Boxing that we were uncomfortable with in the previous section.

More generally, subgame-perfect equilibrium rules out any sort of empty threat in any sequential game. In effect, Nash equilibrium only requires behavior to be rational on the part of the game tree that is reached in equilibrium. Players can choose potentially irrational actions on other parts of the game tree. In particular, a player can threaten to damage both of them in order to "scare" the other from choosing certain actions. Subgame-perfect equilibrium requires rational behavior on all parts of the game tree. Threats to play irrationally, that is, threats to choose something other than one's best response, are ruled out as being empty.

Subgame-perfect equilibrium is not a useful refinement in a simultaneous game because a simultaneous game has no proper subgames besides the game itself, and so subgame-perfect equilibrium would not reduce the set of Nash equilibria.

Backward Induction

Our approach to solving for the equilibrium in the sequential Battle of the Sexes was to find all the Nash equilibria using the normal form, and then to sort through them for the subgame-perfect equilibrium. A shortcut to find the subgame-perfect equilibrium directly is to use **backward induction**. Backward induction works as follows: identify all of the subgames at the bottom of the extensive form; find the Nash equilibria on these subgames; replace the (potentially complicated) subgames with the actions and payoffs resulting from Nash equilibrium play on these subgames; then move up to the next level of subgames and repeat the procedure.

Backward induction
Solving for equilibrium by working backwards from the end of the game to the beginning.

Figure 6-7 illustrates the use of backward induction to solve for the subgame-perfect equilibrium of the sequential Battle of the Sexes. First compute the Nash equilibria of the bottom-most subgames, in this case the subgames corresponding to the husband's decision problems. In the subgame following his wife's choosing Ballet, he would choose Ballet, giving payoffs 2 for her and 1 for him. In the subgame following his wife's choosing Boxing, he would choose Boxing, giving payoffs 1 for her and 2 for him. Next, substitute the husband's equilibrium strategies for the subgames themselves. The resulting game is a simple decision problem for the wife, drawn in the lower panel of the figure, a choice between Ballet, which would give her a payoff of 2 and Boxing, which would give her a payoff of 1. The Nash equilibrium of this game is for her to choose the action with the higher payoff, Ballet. In sum, backward induction allows us to jump straight to the subgame-perfect equilibrium, in which the wife chooses Ballet and the husband chooses "Ballet | Ballet, Boxing | Boxing", and bypass the other Nash equilibria.

Backward induction is particularly useful in games in which there are multiple rounds of sequential play. As rounds are added, it quickly becomes too hard to solve for all the Nash equilibria and then to sort through which are subgame-perfect. With backward induction, an additional round is simply accommodated by adding another iteration of the procedure.

Application 6.5: *Laboratory Experiments* discusses whether human subjects play games the way theory predicts in experimental settings, including whether subjects play the subgame-perfect equilibrium in sequential games.

APPLICATION 6.5 *Laboratory Experiments*

Experimental economics tests how well economic theory matches the behavior of experimental subjects in laboratory settings. The methods are similar to those used in experimental psychology – often conducted on campus using undergraduates as subjects – the main difference being that experiments in economics tend to involve incentives in the form of explicit monetary payments paid to subjects. The importance of experimental economics was highlighted in 2002, when Vernon Smith received the Nobel prize in economics for his pioneering work in the field.

Experiments with the Prisoners' Dilemma

There have been hundreds of tests of whether players Confess in the Prisoners' Dilemma, as predicted by Nash equilibrium, or whether they play the cooperative outcome of Silent. In the experiments of Cooper *et al.*,[1] subjects played the game 20 times, against different, anonymous opponents. Play converged to the Nash equilibrium as subjects gained experience with the game. Players played the cooperative action 43 per cent of the time in the first five rounds, falling to only 20 per cent of the time in the last five rounds.

Experiments with the Ultimatum Game

Experimental economics has also tested to see whether subgame-perfect equilibrium is a good predictor of behavior in sequential games. In one widely studied sequential game, the Ultimatum Game, the experimenter provides a pot of money to two players. The first mover (Proposer) proposes a split of this pot to the second mover. The second mover (Responder) then decides whether to accept the offer, in which case players are given the amount of money indicated, or reject the offer, in which case both players get nothing. As one can see by using backward induction, in the subgame-perfect equilibrium, the Proposer should offer a minimal share of the pot and this should be accepted by the Responder.

In experiments, the division tends to be much more even than in the subgame-perfect equilibrium.[2] The most common offer is a 50–50 split. Responders tend to reject offers giving them less than 30 per cent of the pot. This result is observed even when the pot is as high as €100, so that rejecting a 30 per cent offer means turning down €30. Some economists have suggested that money may not be a true measure of players' payoffs, which may include other factors such as how fairly the pot is divided.[3] Even if a Proposer does not care directly about fairness, the fear that the Responder may care about fairness and thus might reject an uneven offer out of spite may lead the Proposer to propose an even split.

Experiments with the Dictator Game

To test whether players care directly about fairness or act out of fear of the other player's spite, researchers experimented with a related game, the Dictator Game. In the Dictator Game, the Proposer chooses a split of the pot, and this split is implemented without input from the Responder. Proposers tend to offer a less-even split than in the Ultimatum Game, but still offer the Responder some of the pot, suggesting Responders had some residual concern for fairness. The details of the experimental design are crucial, however, as one ingenious experiment showed.[4] The experiment was designed so that the experimenter would never learn which Proposers had made which offers. With this element of anonymity, Proposers almost never gave an equal split to Responders and, indeed, took the whole pot for themselves two-thirds of the time. The results suggest that Proposers care more about being thought of as fair rather than truly being fair.

To Think About

1 As an experimenter, how would you choose the following aspects of experimental design? Are there any tradeoffs involved?
   a Size of the payoffs.
   b Ability of subjects to see opponents.
   c Playing the same game against the same opponent repeatedly.
   d Informing subjects fully about the experimental design.

2 How would you construct an experiment involving the Battle of the Sexes? What theoretical issues might it be interesting to test with your experiment?

[1]R. Cooper, D. V. DeJong, R. Forsythe, and T. W. Ross, "Cooperation Without Reputation: Experimental Evidence from Prisoner's Dilemma Games", *Games and Economic Behavior* (February 1996): 187–218.

[2]For a review of Ultimatum Game experiments and a textbook treatment of experimental economics more generally, see D. D. Davis and C. A. Holt, *Experimental Economics* (Princeton: Princeton University Press, 1993).

[3]See, for example, M. Rabin, "Incorporating Fairness into Game Theory and Economics", *American Economic Review* (December 1993): 1281–1302.

[4]E. Hoffman, K. McCabe, K. Shachat, and V. Smith, "Preferences, Property Rights, and Anonymity in Bargaining Games", *Games and Economic Behavior* (November 1994): 346–380.

FIGURE 6-7 Backward Induction in the Sequential Battle of the Sexes

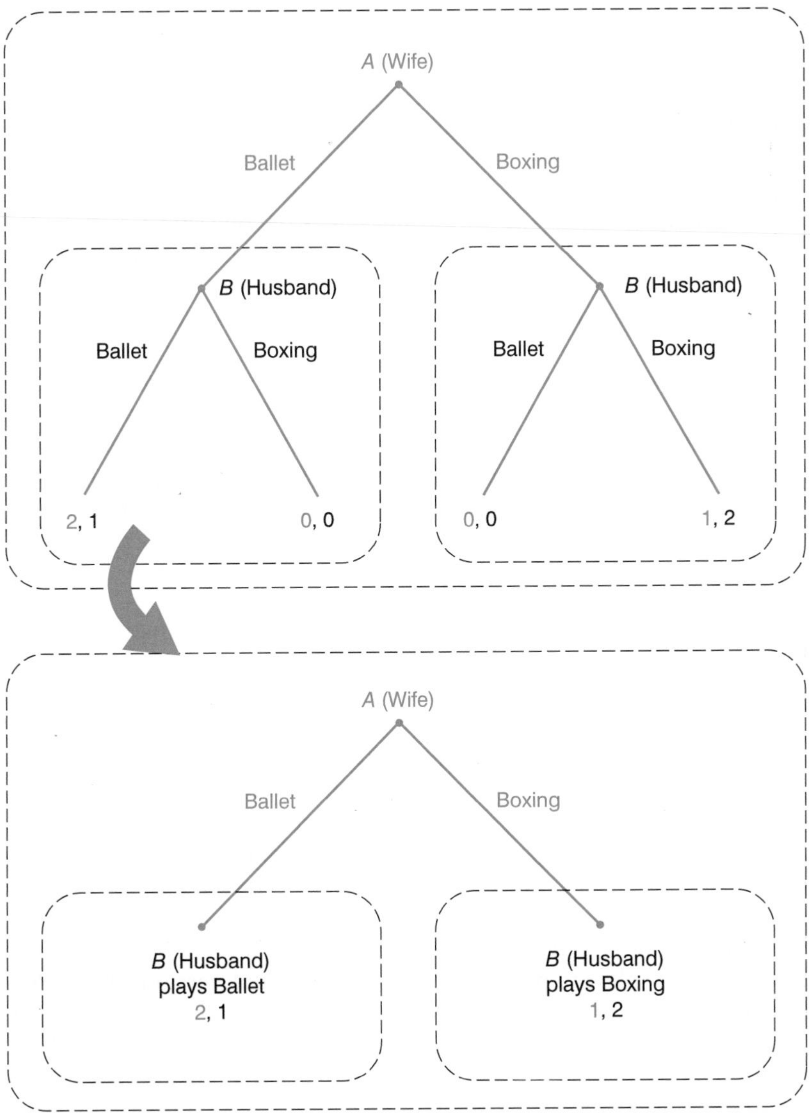

Repeated Games

Stage game Simple game that is played repeatedly.

Trigger strategy Strategy in a repeated game where the player stops cooperating in order to punish another player's break with cooperation.

So far, we have examined one-shot games in which each player is given one choice and the game ends. In many real-world settings, the same players play the same **stage game** several or even many times. For example, the players in the Prisoners' Dilemma may anticipate committing future crimes together and thus playing future Prisoners' Dilemmas together. Petrol stations located across the street from each other, when they set their prices each morning, effectively play a new pricing game every day. As we saw with the Prisoners' Dilemma, when such games are played once, the equilibrium outcome may be worse for all players than some other, more cooperative, outcome. Repetition opens up the possibility of the cooperative outcome being played in equilibrium. Players can adopt **trigger strategies**, whereby they play the cooperative outcome as long as all have cooperated up to that point, but revert to playing the Nash equilibrium if anyone breaks with cooperation. We will investigate the conditions under which trigger strategies work to increase players' payoffs. We will focus on subgame-perfect equilibria of the repeated games.

Definite Time Horizon

For many stage games, repeating them a known, finite number of times does not increase the possibility for cooperation. To see this point concretely, suppose the Prisoners' Dilemma were repeated for ten periods. Use backward induction to solve for the subgame-perfect equilibrium. The lowest subgame is the one-shot Prisoners' Dilemma played in the tenth period. Regardless of what happened before, the Nash equilibrium on this subgame is for both to play Confess. Folding the game back to the ninth period, trigger strategies that condition play in the tenth period on what happens in the ninth are ruled out. Nothing that happens in the ninth period affects what happens subsequently because, as we just argued, the players both Confess in the tenth period no matter what. It is as if the ninth period is the last, and the Nash equilibrium on this subgame is again for both to play Confess. Working backward in this way, we see that players will Confess each period; that is, players will simply repeat the Nash equilibrium of the stage game ten times. The same argument would apply for any definite number of repetitions.

Indefinite Time Horizon

If the number of times the stage game is repeated is indefinite, matters change significantly. The number of repetitions is indefinite if players know the stage game will be repeated but are uncertain of exactly how many times. For example, the partners in crime in the Prisoners' Dilemma may know that they will participate in many future crimes together, sometimes be caught, and thus have to play the Prisoners' Dilemma game against each other, but may not know exactly how many opportunities for crime they will have or how often they will be caught, and so will not know exactly how many times they will play the stage game. With an indefinite number of repetitions, there is no final period from which to start applying backward induction, and thus no final period for trigger strategies to begin unraveling. Under certain conditions, more cooperation can be sustained than in the stage game.

Suppose the two players play the following repeated version of the Prisoners' Dilemma. The game is played in the first period for certain, but for how many more periods after that the game is played is uncertain. Let r be the probability the game is repeated for another period and $1 - r$ the probability the repetitions stop for good. Thus, the probability the game lasts at least one period is 1, at least two periods is r, at least three periods is r^2, and so forth.

Suppose players use the trigger strategies of playing the cooperative action, Silent, as long as no one cheats by playing Confess, but that players both play Confess forever afterward if either of them had ever cheated. To show that such strategies form a subgame-perfect equilibrium, we need to check that a player cannot gain by cheating. In equilibrium, both players play Silent and each earns −2 each period the game is played, implying a player's expected payoff over the course of the entire game is

$$(-2)\,(1 + r + r^2 + r^3 + \ldots) \qquad \{6.1\}$$

If a player cheats and plays Confess, given the other is playing Silent, the cheater earns −1 in that period, but then both play Confess every period, from then on, each earning −3 each period, for a total expected payoff of

$$-1 + (-3)\,(r + r^2 + r^3 + \ldots) \qquad \{6.2\}$$

For cooperation to be a subgame-perfect equilibrium, (6.1) must exceed (6.2). Adding 2 to both expressions, and then adding $3(r + r^2 + r^3 + \ldots)$ to both expressions, (6.1) exceeds (6.2) if

$$r + r^2 + r^3 + \ldots > 1 \qquad \{6.3\}$$

To proceed further, we need to find a simple expression for the series $r + r^2 + r^3 + \ldots$. A standard mathematical result is that the series $r + r^2 + r^3 + \ldots$ equals $r/(1 - r)$.[3] Substituting this result in (6.3), we see that (6.3) holds, and so cooperation on Silent can be sustained, if r is greater than 1/2.[4]

This result means that players can cooperate in the repeated Prisoners' Dilemma only if the probability of repetition r is high enough. Players are deterred from getting the short-run gain that cheating and playing Confess provides (a payoff of −1 rather than −2) with the threat of the loss of future payoffs as cheating leads them to revert to both playing Confess thereafter. This threat only works if the probability the game is repeated, and so future payoffs are actually realized, is high enough.

Other strategies can be used to try to elicit cooperation in the repeated game. We considered strategies that had players revert to the Nash equilibrium of Confess each period forever. This strategy, which involves the harshest possible punishment for deviation, is called the grim strategy. Less harsh punishments include the so-called tit-for-tat strategy, which involves only one round of punishment for cheating. Since it involves the harshest punishment possible, the grim strategy elicits cooperation for the largest range of cases (the lowest value of r) of any strategy. Harsh punishments work well because, if players succeed in cooperating, they never experience the losses from the punishment in equilibrium. If there were uncertainty about the economic environment, or about the rationality of the other player, the grim strategy may not lead to as high payoffs as less-harsh strategies.

One might ask whether the threat to punish the other player (whether forever as in the grim strategy or for one round with tit-for-tat) is an empty threat since punishment harms

[3]Let $S = r + r^2 + r^3 + \ldots$. Multiplying both sides by r, $rS = r^2 + r^3 + r^4 + \ldots$. Subtracting rS from S, we have $S - rS = (r + r^2 + r^3 + \ldots) - (r^2 + r^3 + r^4 + \ldots) = r$ since all of the terms on the right-hand side cancel except for the leading r. Thus $(1 - r)S = r$, or, rearranging, $S = r/(1 - r)$.

[4]The mathematics are the same in an alternative version of the game in which the stage game is repeated with certainty each period for an infinite number of periods, but in which future payoffs are discounted according to a per-period interest rate. One can show that cooperation is possible if the per-period interest rate is less than 100 per cent.

both players. The answer is no. The punishment involves reverting to the Nash equilibrium, in which both players choose best responses, and so it is a credible threat and is consistent with subgame-perfect equilibrium.

Continuous Actions

Most of the insight from economic situations can often be gained by distilling the situation down to a game with two actions, as with all the games studied so far. Other times, additional insight can be gained by allowing more actions, sometimes even a continuum. Firms' pricing, output or investment decisions, bids in auctions, and so forth are often modeled by allowing players a continuum of actions. Such games can no longer be represented in the normal form we are used to seeing in this chapter, and the underlining method cannot be used to solve for Nash equilibrium. Still, the new techniques for solving for Nash equilibria will have the same logic as those seen so far. We will illustrate the new techniques in a game called the Tragedy of the Commons.

Tragedy of the Commons

The game involves two shepherds, A and B, who graze their sheep on a common (land that can be freely used by community members). Let s_A and s_B be the number of sheep each grazes, chosen simultaneously. Because the common only has a limited amount of space, if more sheep graze, there is less grass for each one, and they grow less quickly. To be concrete, suppose the benefit A gets from each sheep (in terms of mutton and wool) equals

$$120 - s_A - s_B \tag{6.4}$$

The total benefit A gets from a flock of s_A sheep is therefore

$$s_A(120 - s_A - s_B) \tag{6.5}$$

While we cannot use the method of underlining payoffs for best responses, we can compute A's best-response function. Recall the use of best-response functions in computing the mixed-strategy Nash equilibrium in the Battle of the Sexes game. We resorted to best-response functions because, although the Battle of the Sexes game has only two actions, there is a continuum of possible mixed strategies over those two actions. In the Tragedy of the Commons here, we need to resort to best-response functions because we start off with a continuum of actions.

A's best-response function gives the s_A that maximizes A's payoff for any s_B. A's best response will be the number of sheep such that the marginal benefit of an additional sheep equals the marginal cost. His marginal benefit of an additional sheep is[5]

$$120 - 2s_A - s_B \tag{6.6}$$

MICROQUIZ 6.4

Consider the indefinitely repeated Prisoners' Dilemma.

1. For what value of r does the repeated game become simply the stage game?
2. Suppose at some point while playing the grim strategy, players relent and go back to the cooperative outcome (Silent). If this relenting were anticipated, how would it affect the ability to sustain the cooperative outcome using trigger strategies to begin with?

[5]One can take the formula for the marginal benefit in (6.6) as given or can use calculus to verify it. Differentiating the benefit function (6.5), which can be rewritten $120s_A - s_A^2 - s_As_B$, term by term with respect to s_A (treating s_B as a constant) yields the marginal benefit (6.6).

The total cost of grazing sheep is 0 since they graze freely on the common, and so the marginal cost of an additional sheep is also 0. Equating the marginal benefit in (6.6) with the marginal cost of 0 and solving for s_A, A's best-response function equals

$$s_A = 60 - \frac{s_B}{2} \qquad \{6.7\}$$

By symmetry, B's best-response function is

$$s_B = 60 - \frac{s_A}{2} \qquad \{6.8\}$$

For actions to form a Nash equilibrium, they must be best responses to each other; in other words, they must be the simultaneous solution to (6.7) and (6.8). The simultaneous solution is shown graphically in Figure 6-8. The best-response functions are graphed with s_A on the horizontal axis and s_B on the vertical (the inverse of A's best-response function is actually what is graphed). The Nash equilibrium, which lies at the intersection of the two functions, involves each grazing 40 sheep.

The game is called a tragedy because the shepherds end up overgrazing in equilibrium. They overgraze because they do not take into account the reduction in the value of other's sheep when they choose the size of their flocks. If each grazed 30 rather than 40 sheep, one can show that each would earn a total payoff of 1800 rather than the 1600 they each earn in equilibrium. Over-consumption is a typical finding in settings where multiple parties have free access to a common resource, such as multiple wells pumping oil from a common underground pool or multiple fishing boats fishing in the same ocean area, and is often a reason given for restricting access to such common resources through licensing and other government interventions.

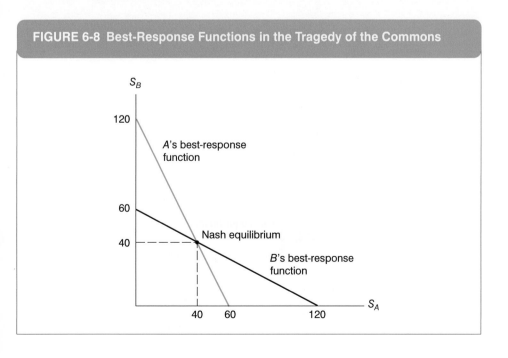

FIGURE 6-8 Best-Response Functions in the Tragedy of the Commons

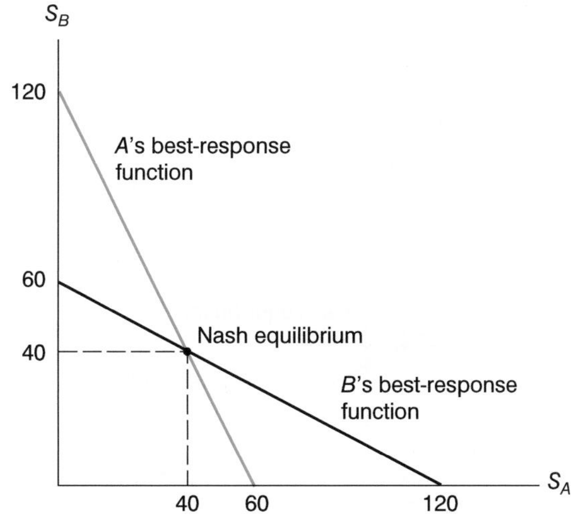

Shifting Equilibria

One reason it is useful to allow players to have continuous actions is that it is easier in this setting to analyze how a small change in one of the game's parameters shifts the equilibrium. For example, suppose *A*'s benefit per sheep rises from (6.4) to

$$132 - s_A - s_B \tag{6.9}$$

A's best-response function becomes

$$s_A = 66 - \frac{s_B}{2} \tag{6.10}$$

B's stays the same as in (6.8). As shown in Figure 6-9, in the new Nash equilibrium, *A* increases his flock to 48 sheep and *B* decreases his to 36. It is clear why the size of *A*'s flock increases: the increase in *A*'s benefit shifts his best-response function out. The interesting strategic effect is that – while nothing about *B*'s benefit has changed, and so *B*'s best-response function remains the same as before – having observed *A*'s benefit increasing from (6.4) to (6.9), *B* anticipates that it must choose a best response to a higher quantity by *A*, and so ends up reducing the size of his flock.

Games with continuous actions offer additional insights in other contexts, as shown in Application 6.6: *Terrorism*.

N-Player Games

Just as we can often capture the essence of a situation using a game with two actions, as we have seen with all the games studied so far, we can often distil the number of players down to two as well. However in some cases, it is useful to study

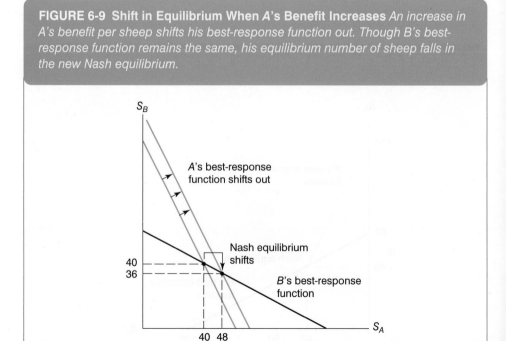

FIGURE 6-9 Shift in Equilibrium When *A*'s Benefit Increases *An increase in A's benefit per sheep shifts his best-response function out. Though B's best-response function remains the same, his equilibrium number of sheep falls in the new Nash equilibrium.*

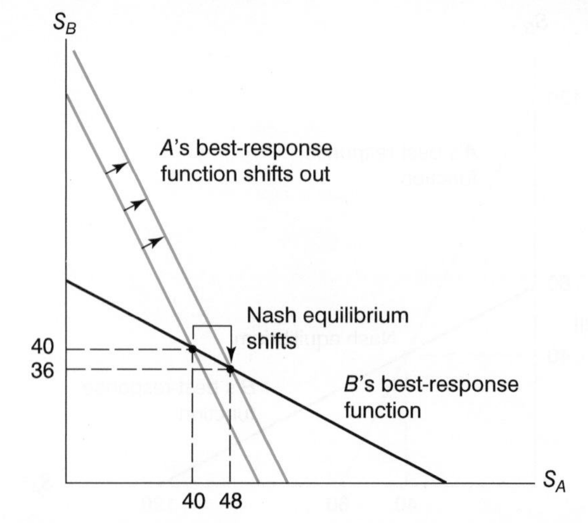

APPLICATION 6.6 *Terrorism*

Few issues raise as much public-policy concern as terrorism, given the continued attacks in the Middle East and Europe and the devastating attack on the World Trade Center and Pentagon in the United States on September 11, 2001. In this application, we will see that game theory can be usefully applied to analyze terrorism and the best defensive measures against it.

Defending Targets against Terrorism

Consider a sequential game between a government and a terrorist. The players have the opposite objectives: the government wants to minimize the expected damage from terrorism, and the terrorist wants to maximize expected damage. For simplicity, assume the terrorist can attack one of two targets: target 1 (say a nuclear power plant) leads to considerable damage if successfully attacked; target 2 (say a restaurant) leads to less damage. The government moves first, choosing s_1, the proportion of its security force guarding target 1. The remainder of the security force, $1 - s_1$, guards target 2. (Note that the government's action is a continuous variable between 0 and 1, so this is an application of our general discussion of games with continuous actions in the text.) The terrorist moves second, choosing which target to attack. Assume the probability of successful attack on target 1 is $1 - s_1$ and on target 2 is s_1, implying that the larger the security force guarding a particular target, the lower the probability of a successful attack.

To solve for the subgame-perfect equilibrium, we will apply backward induction, meaning in this context that we will consider the terrorist's (the second-mover's) decision first. The terrorist will compute the expected damage from attacking each target, equal to the probability of a successful attack multiplied by the damage caused if the attack is successful. The terrorist will attack the target with the highest expected damage. Moving backward to the first mover's (the government's) decision, the way for the government to minimize the expected damage from terrorism is to divide the security force between the two targets so that the expected damage is equalized. (Suppose the expected damage from attacking target 1 were strictly higher than target 2. Then the terrorist would definitely attack target 1, and the government could reduce expected damage from this attack by shifting some of the security force from target 2 to target 1.) Using some numbers, if the damage from a successful attack on target 1 is ten times that on target 2, the government should put ten times the security force on target 1. The terrorist ends up playing a mixed strategy in equilibrium, with each target having a positive probability of being attacked.

Bargaining with Terrorists

Terrorism raises many more issues than those analyzed above. Suppose terrorists have taken hostages and demand the release of prisoners in return for the hostages' freedom. Should a country bargain with the terrorists?[1] The official policy of countries, including the United States, the United Kingdom and Israel, is no. Using backward induction, it is easy to see why countries would like to commit to not bargaining, since this would preclude any benefit from taking hostages and deter the terrorists from taking hostages in the first place. But a country's commitment to not bargain may not be credible, especially if the hostages are "important" enough, as was the case when the Israeli parliament voted to bargain for the release of 21 students taken hostage in a high school in Maalot, Israel, in 1974. (The vote came after the deadline set by the terrorists, and the students ended up being killed.) The country's commitment may still be credible in some scenarios. If hostage incidents are expected to arise over time repeatedly, the country may refuse to bargain as part of a long-term strategy to establish a reputation for not bargaining. Another possibility is that the country may not trust the terrorists to free the hostages after the prisoners are released, in

(Continued)

which case there would be little benefit from bargaining with them.

To Think About

1 The US government has considered analyzing banking transactions to look for large, suspicious movements of cash as a screen for terrorists. What are the pros and cons of such a screen? How would the terrorists respond in equilibrium if they learned of this screen? Would it still be a useful tool?

2 Is it sensible to model the terrorist as wanting to maximize expected damage? Instead, the terrorist may prefer to attack "high-visibility" targets, even if this means lower expected damage, or may prefer to maximize the sum of damage plus defense/deterrence expenditures. Which alternative is most plausible? How would these alternatives affect the game?

[1]See H. E. Lapan and T. Sandler, "To Bargain or not to Bargain: That Is the Question", *American Economic Review* (May 1988): 16–20.

games with more than two players. This is particularly useful to answer the question of how a change in the number of players would affect the equilibrium (see, for example, MicroQuiz 6.5). The problems at the end of the chapter will provide some examples of how to draw the normal form in games with more than two players.

Incomplete information Some players have information about the game that others do not.

Incomplete Information

In all the games studied so far, there was no private information. All players knew everything there was to know about each others' payoffs, available actions, and so forth. Matters become more complicated, and potentially more interesting, if players know something about themselves that others do not know. For example, one's bidding strategy in a sealed-bid auction for a painting would be quite different if one knew the valuation of everyone else at the auction compared to the (more realistic) case in which one did not. Card games would be quite different, certainly not as fun, if all hands were played face up. Games in which players do not share all relevant information in common are called games of **incomplete information**.

MICROQUIZ 6.5

Suppose the Tragedy of the Commons involved three shepherds (A, B, and C). Suppose the benefit per sheep is $120 - s_A - s_B - s_C$, implying that, for example, A's total benefit is $s_A(120 - s_A - s_B - s_C)$ and marginal benefit is $120 - 2s_A - s_B - s_C$.

1 Solve the three equations that come from equating each of the three shepherds' marginal benefit of a sheep to the marginal cost (zero) to find the Nash equilibrium.

2 Compare the total number of sheep on the common with three shepherds to that with two.

We will devote most of Chapter 17 to studying games of incomplete information. We will study signaling games, which include students choosing how much education to obtain in order to signal their underlying aptitude, which might be difficult to observe directly, to prospective employers. We will study screening games, which include the design of deductible policies by insurance companies in order to deter high-risk consumers from purchasing. As mentioned, auctions and card games also fall in the realm of games of incomplete information. Such games are at the forefront of current research in game theory.

SUMMARY

This chapter provided a brief overview of game theory. Game theory provides an organized way of understanding decision making in strategic environments. We introduced the following broad ideas:

- The basic building blocks of all games are players, actions, and payoffs.
- Nash equilibrium is the most widely used equilibrium concept. Strategies form a Nash equilibrium if all players' strategies are best responses to each other. All games have at least one Nash equilibrium. Sometimes the Nash equilibrium is in mixed strategies, which we learned how to compute. Some games have multiple Nash equilibria, and it may be difficult in these cases to make predictions about which one will end up being played.
- We studied several classic games, including the Prisoners' Dilemma, Matching Pennies, and Battle of the Sexes. These games each demonstrated important principles. Many strategic situations can be distilled down to one of these games.
- Sequential games introduce the possibility of contingent strategies for the second mover and often expand the set of Nash equilibria. Subgame-perfect equilibrium rules out outcomes involving non-credible threats. One can easily solve for subgame-perfect equilibrium using backward induction.
- In some games such as the Prisoners' Dilemma, all players are worse off in the Nash equilibrium than in some other outcome. If the game is repeated an indefinite number of times, players can use trigger strategies to try to enforce the better outcome.

REVIEW QUESTIONS

1 In game theory, players maximize payoffs. Is this assumption different from the one we used in Chapter 2 through Chapter 4?

2 What is the difference between an action and a strategy?

3 Why are Nash equilibria identified by the strategies rather than the payoffs involved?

4 Which of the following activities might be represented as a zero-sum game? Which are clearly not zero-sum?

a Flipping a coin for €1.

b Playing blackjack.

c Choosing which chocolate bar to buy from a shop.

d Reducing taxes through various "creative accounting" methods and seeking to avoid detection by the tax authorities.

e Deciding when to rob a particular house, knowing that the residents may adopt various countertheft strategies.

5 Why is the Prisoners' Dilemma a "dilemma" for the players involved? How might they solve this dilemma through pregame discussions or postgame threats? If you were arrested and the prosecutor tried this ploy, what would you do? Would it matter whether you were very close friends with your criminal accomplice?

6 The Battle of the Sexes is a coordination game. What coordination games arise in your experience? How do you go about solving coordination problems?

7 In the sequential games such as the sequential Battle of the Sexes, why does Nash equilibrium allow for outcomes with non-credible threats? Why does subgame-perfect equilibrium rule them out?

8 Which of these relationships would be better modeled as involving repetitions and which not, or does it depend? For those that are repeated, which are more realistically seen as involving a definite number of repetitions and which an indefinite number?

a Two nearby petrol stations posting their prices each morning.

b A professor testing students in a course.

c Students entering a lottery syndicate together.

d Accomplices committing a crime.

e Two lions fighting for a mate.

9 In the Tragedy of the Commons, we saw how a small change in *A*'s benefit resulted in a shift in *A*'s best response function and a movement along *B*'s best-response function. Can you think of other factors that might shift *A*'s best-response function? Relate this discussion to shifts in an individual's demand curve versus movements along it.

10 Choose a setting from student life. Try to model it as a game, with a set number of players, payoffs, and actions. Is it like any of the classic games studied in this chapter?

PROBLEMS

6.1 Consider a simultaneous game in which player *A* chooses one of two actions (Up or Down), and *B* chooses one of two actions (Left or Right). The game has the following payoff matrix, where the first payoff in each entry is for *A* and the second for *B*.

		B	
		Left	**Right**
A	**Up**	3, 3	5, 1
	Down	2, 2	4, 4

a Find the Nash equilibrium or equilibria.

b Which player, if any, has a dominant strategy?

6.2 Suppose *A* can somehow change the game in problem 6.1 to a new one in which his payoff from Up is reduced by 2, producing the following payoff matrix.

		B	
		Left	**Right**
A	**Up**	1, 3	3, 1
	Down	2, 2	4, 4

a Find the Nash equilibrium or equilibria.

b Which player, if any, has a dominant strategy?

c Does *A* benefit from changing the game by reducing his or her payoff in this way?

6.3 Return to the game given by the payoff matrix in Problem 6.1.

a Write down the extensive form for the simultaneous-move game.

b Suppose the game is now sequential move, with *A* moving first and then *B*. Write down the extensive form for this sequential-move game.

c Write down the normal form for the sequential-move game. Find all the Nash equilibria. Which Nash equilibrium is subgame-perfect?

6.4 The Chicken Game is played by two macho teens who speed toward each other on a single-lane road. The first to veer off is branded a coward or "chicken", whereas the one who doesn't turn gains peer group esteem. Of course, if neither veers, both die in the resulting crash. Payoffs to the Chicken Game are provided in the following table.

		Teen B	
		Chicken	**Not Chicken**
Teen A	**Chicken**	2, 2	1, 3
	Not Chicken	1, 3	0, 0

a Find the pure-strategy Nash equilibrium or equilibria.

b Compute the mixed-strategy Nash equilibrium. As part of your answer, draw the best-response function diagram for the mixed strategies.

c Suppose the game is played sequentially, with teen *A* moving first and committing to this action by throwing away the steering wheel. What are teen *B*'s contingent strategies? Write down the normal and extensive forms for the sequential version of the game.

d Using the normal form for the sequential version of the game, solve for the Nash equilibria.

e Identify the proper subgames in the extensive form for the sequential version of the game. Use backward induction to solve for the subgame-perfect equilibrium. Explain why the other Nash equilibria of the sequential game are "unreasonable".

6.5 Two classmates *A* and *B* are assigned a group exercise project. Each student can choose to Shirk or Work. If one or more players choose Work, the project is completed and provides each with extra credit valued at 4 payoff units each. The cost of completing the project is that 6 total units of effort (measured in payoff units) is divided equally among all players who choose to Work and this is subtracted from their payoff. If both Shirk, they do not have to expend any effort but the project is not completed, giving each a payoff of 0. The teacher can only tell whether the project is completed and not which students contributed to it.

a Write down the normal form for this game, assuming students choose to Shirk or Work simultaneously.

b Find the Nash equilibrium or equilibria.

c Does either player have a dominant strategy? What game from the chapter does this resemble?

6.6 Return to the Battle of the Sexes in Table 6-5. Compute the mixed-strategy Nash equilibrium under the following modifications and compare it to the one computed in the text. Draw the corresponding best-response-function diagram for the mixed strategies.

a Double all of the payoffs.

b Double the payoff from coordinating on one's preferred activity from 2 to 4 but leave all other payoffs the same.

c Change the payoff from choosing one's preferred activity alone (that is, not coordinating with one's spouse) from 0 to 1/2 for each but leave all the other payoffs the same.

6.7 The following game is a version of the Prisoners' Dilemma, but the payoffs are slightly different than in Table 6-1.

		B	
		Confess	***Silent***
A	***Confess***	0, 0	3, −1
	Silent	−1, 3	1, 1

a Verify that the Nash equilibrium is the usual one for the Prisoners' Dilemma and that both players have dominant strategies.

b Suppose the stage game is played infinitely often with a probability *r* the game is continued to the next stage and $1 - r$ that the game ends for good. Compute the level of *r* that is required for a subgame-perfect equilibrium in which both players play a trigger strategy where both are Silent if no one deviates but resort to a grim strategy (that is, both play Confess forever after) if anyone deviates to Confess.

c Continue to suppose the stage game is played infinitely often, as in b. Is there a value of *r* for which there exists a subgame-perfect equilibrium in which both players play a trigger strategy where both are Silent if no one deviates but resort to tit-for-tat (that is, both play Confess for one period and go back to Silent forever after that) if anyone deviates to Confess. Remember that *r* is a probability so it must be between 0 and 1.

6.8 Find the pure-strategy Nash equilibrium or equilibria of the following game with three actions for each player.

		B		
		Left	***Center***	***Right***
A	***Up***	4, 3	5, −1	6, 2
	Middle	2, 1	7, 4	3, 6
	Down	3, 0	9, 6	0, 8

6.9 Three department stores, *A*, *B*, and *C*, simultaneously decide whether or not to locate in a shopping center that is being constructed in town. A store likes to have another with it in the shopping center since then there is a critical mass of stores to induce shoppers to come out. However, with three stores in the shopping center, there begins to be too much competition among them and store profits fall drastically. Read the payoff matrix as follows: the first payoff in each entry is for *A*, the second for *B*, and the third for *C*; *C*'s choice determines which of the bold boxes the other players find themselves in.

a Find the pure-strategy Nash equilibrium or equilibria of the game. You can apply the underlying method from the text as follows. First, find the best responses for *A* and *B*, treating each bold box corresponding to *C*'s choice as a separate game. Then find *C*'s best responses by comparing corresponding entries in the two boxes (the two entries in the upper-left corners of both, the upper-right corners of both, etc.) and underlining the higher of the two payoffs.

b What do you think the outcome would be if players chose cooperatively rather than non-cooperatively?

		C chooses Shopping Center		*C* chooses Not Shopping Center	
		B: Shopping Center	*B*: Not Shopping Center	*B*: Shopping Center	*B*: Not Shopping Center
A	Shopping Center	−2, −2, −2	2, 0, 2	2, 1, 0	−1, 0, 0
	Not Shopping Center	0, 1, 2	0, 0, −1	0, −1, 0	0, 0, 0

6.10 Consider the Tragedy of the Commons game from the chapter with two shepherds, *A* and *B*, where s_A and s_B denote the number of sheep each grazes on the common pasture. Assume that the benefit per sheep (in terms of mutton and wool) equals

$$300 - s_A - s_B$$

implying that the total benefit from a flock of s_A sheep is

$$s_A(300 - s_A - s_B)$$

and that the marginal benefit of an additional sheep (as one can use calculus to show or can take for granted) is

$$300 - 2s_A - s_B$$

Assume the (total and marginal) cost of grazing sheep is zero since the common can be freely used.

a Compute the flock sizes and shepherds' total benefits in the Nash equilibrium.

b Draw the best-response-function diagram corresponding to your solution.

c Suppose *A*'s benefit per sheep rises to $330 - s_A - s_B$. Compute the new Nash equilibrium flock sizes. Show the change from the original to the new Nash equilibrium in your best-response-function diagram.

PART FOUR
PRODUCTION, COSTS, AND SUPPLY

The laws and conditions of production partake of the character of physical truths. There is nothing arbitrary about them.
J. S. MILL, *PRINCIPLES OF POLITICAL ECONOMY,* 1848

Part Four describes the production and supply of economic goods. The organizations that supply goods are called *firms*. They may be large, complex organizations, such as Tata Steel or the United Nations, or they may be quite small, such as the local corner shop or self-employed consultant. All firms must make choices about what inputs they will use and the level of output they will supply. Part Four looks at these choices.

To be able to produce any output, firms must hire many inputs (labor, capital, natural resources, and so forth). Because these inputs are scarce, they have costs associated with their use. Our goal in Chapter 7 and Chapter 8 is to show clearly the relationship between input costs and the level of the firm's output. In Chapter 7, we introduce the firm's production function, which shows the relationship between inputs used and the level of output that results. Once this physical relationship between inputs and outputs is known, the costs of needed inputs can be determined for various levels of output. This we show in Chapter 8.

Chapter 9 uses the cost concepts developed in Chapter 8 to discuss firms' supply decisions. It provides a detailed analysis of the supply decisions of profit-maximizing firms. Later, in Chapter 17, we will look at problems in modeling the internal organization of firms, especially in connection with the incentives faced by the firms' managers and workers.

7

Production

In this chapter, we show how economists illustrate the relationship between inputs and outputs using production functions. This is the first step in showing how input costs affect firms' supply decisions.

Production Functions

The purpose of any **firm** is to turn inputs into outputs: Daimler combines steel, glass, workers' time, and hours of assembly line operation to produce cars; farmers combine their labor with seed, soil, rain, fertilizer, and machinery to produce crops; and universities combine professors' time with books and (hopefully) hours of student study to produce educated students. Because economists are interested in the choices that firms make to accomplish their goals, they have developed a rather abstract model of production. In this model, the relationship between inputs and outputs is formalized by a **production function** of the form

$$q = f(K,L,M\ldots) \tag{7.1}$$

where q represents the output of a particular good during a period,[1] K represents the machine hours (that is, capital) used during the period, L represents hours of labor input, and M represents raw materials used. The form of the notation indicates the possibility of other variables affecting the production process. The production function summarizes what the firm knows about mixing various inputs to yield output.

For example, this production function might represent a farmer's output of wheat during one year as being dependent on the quantity of machinery employed, the amount of labor used on the farm, the amount of land under cultivation, the amount of fertilizer

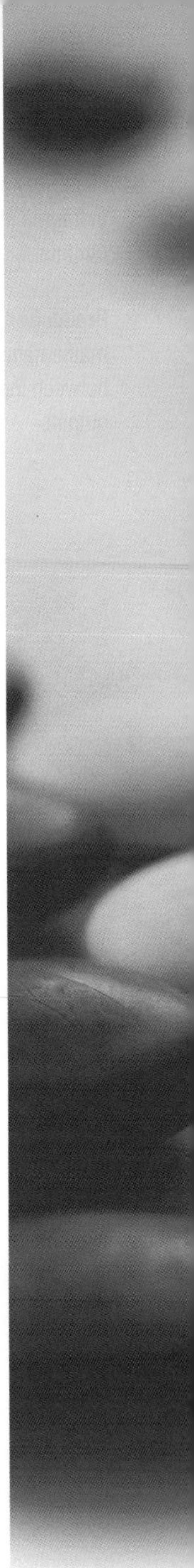

[1] Sometimes the output for a firm is defined to include only its "value added"; that is, the value of raw materials used by the firm is subtracted to arrive at a net value of output for the firm. This procedure is also used in adding up gross domestic product to avoid double-counting of inputs. Throughout our discussion, a single firm's output is denoted by q.

Firm Any organization that turns inputs into outputs.

Production function The mathematical relationship between inputs and outputs.

and seeds used, and so forth. The function shows that, say, 100 kilograms of wheat can be produced in many different ways. The farmer could use a very labor-intensive technique that would require only a small amount of mechanical equipment (as tends to be the case in China). The 100 kilograms could also be produced using large amounts of equipment and fertilizer with very little labor (as in the United States). A great deal of land might be used to produce the 100 kilograms of wheat with less of the other inputs (as in Brazil or Australia); or relatively little land could be used with great amounts of labor, equipment, and fertilizer (as in British or Japanese agriculture). All of these combinations are represented by the general production function in Equation 7.1. The important question about this production function from an economic point of view is how the firm chooses its levels of q, K, L, and M. We take this question up in detail in the next three chapters.

Two-Input Production Function

We simplify the production function here by assuming that the firm's production depends on only two inputs: capital (K) and labor (L). Hence, our simplified production function is now

$$q = f(K,L) \tag{7.2}$$

The decision to focus on capital and labor is arbitrary. Most of our analysis here holds true for any two inputs that might be investigated. For example, if we wish to examine the effects of rainfall and fertilizer on crop production, we can use those two inputs in the production function while holding other inputs (quantity of land, hours of labor input, and so on) constant. In the production function that characterizes a school system, we can examine the relationship between the "output" of the system (say, academic achievement) and the inputs used to produce this output (such as teachers, buildings, and learning aids). The two general inputs of capital and labor are used here for convenience, and we frequently show these inputs on a two-dimensional graph. Application 7.1: *Everyone Is a Firm* shows how the production function idea can yield surprising insights about quite ordinary behavior.

Marginal Product

Marginal product The additional output that can be produced by adding one more unit of a particular input while holding all other inputs constant.

The first question we might ask about the relationship between inputs and outputs is how much extra output can be produced by adding one more unit of an input to the production process. The marginal physical productivity, or more simply, **marginal product** of an input is defined as the quantity of extra output provided by employing one additional unit of that input while holding all other inputs constant. For our two principal inputs of capital and labor, the marginal product of labor (MP_L) is the extra output obtained by employing one more worker while holding the level of capital equipment constant. Similarly, the marginal product of capital (MP_K) is the extra output obtained by using one more machine while holding the number of workers constant.

As an illustration of these definitions, consider the case of a farmer hiring one more person to harvest a crop while holding all other inputs constant. The extra output produced when this person is added to the production team is the marginal product of labor input. The concept is measured in physical quantities such as kilograms of wheat, crates of oranges, or heads of lettuce. We might, for example, observe that 25 workers in an orange grove are able to produce 10 000 crates of oranges per week, whereas 26 workers (with the same trees and equipment) can produce 10 200 crates. The marginal product of the 26th worker is 200 crates per week.

APPLICATION 7.1 *Everyone Is a Firm*

Turning inputs into outputs is something we all do every day without thinking about it. When you drive somewhere, you are combining labor (your time) with capital (the car) to produce economic output (a trip). Of course, the output from this activity is not traded in organized markets; but there is not very much difference between providing "taxi services" to yourself or selling them to someone else. In both cases, you are performing the economic role that economists assign to firms. In fact, "home production" constitutes a surprisingly large segment of the overall economy.

Looking at people as "firms" can yield some interesting insights. In measuring household production we can adopt, in principle, one of two methods: we can measure the value of inputs or measure the value of outputs. Measuring inputs relies, in the main, on time surveys where individuals as part of a survey will keep detailed diaries of exactly they have done over each 10 or 15 minute period of the day.

In Table 1 we present the findings of Eurostat, the European Union statistical agency, who provide a very interesting breakdown of how individuals spend their time across a range of European countries broken down by gender (Aliaga, 2006).[1] The average time spent on various activities is calculated for all persons in the survey aged between 20 and 74 from a representative sample of people who complete a diary during one weekday and one weekend day distributed throughout the year. Since people record their time activities for holiday periods, weekends as well as work days this explains why the amount of time spent on gainful work is considerably lower than one might expect but this is simply due to this representing an average across all types of days.

In more detailed tables (not shown) Eurostat reveal that in the countries surveyed, at least 80 per cent of women perform food preparation every day, while in some countries less than a third of men do. Food preparation is most equitably distributed in Sweden, Norway and the United Kingdom. Even in these countries, the time spent by women on preparing meals is double that spent by men. Dish washing is also a typically female task along with laundry, ironing and handicraft which are almost entirely performed by women.

Turning to the value of total household production, in the UK for the year 2000 this came to £641 533 million. This should be compared with the gross domestic product of the UK for the same year of £892 182 million. That is, the value of household production in the UK stood at 72 per cent of official GDP.

Finally we note from Table 2 as regards domestic work, where much of the value added in household production is created, that in every European country listed women work

TABLE 1 Hours Spent by Women on Domestic Work for Every One Hour Spent by Men on Domestic Work

Country	*Female Hours to 1 Male Hour*	*Country*	*Female Hours to 1 Male Hour*
BE	1.82	HU	1.91
DE	1.86	PL	2.00
EE	2.02	SI	1.91
ES	3.33	FI	1.65
FR	1.94	SE	1.49
IT	3.85	UK	1.90
LV	2.37	NO	1.56
LT	2.05		

SOURCE: AUTHOR'S OWN CALCULATION BASED ON TABLE 3 CONTAINED WITHIN CHRISTEL ALIAGA (2006) *HOW IS THE TIME OF MEN AND WOMEN DISTRIBUTED?* STATISTICS IN FOCUS, POPULATION AND SOCIAL CONDITIONS. PUBLISHER, EUROSTAT. DOMESTIC WORK INCLUDES: FOOD PREPARATION, DISH WASHING, CLEANING AND OTHER UPKEEP, LAUNDRY IRONING AND HANDICRAFTS, GARDENING, CONSTRUCTION AND REPAIRS, SHOPPING AND SERVICES, CHILDCARE, AND OTHER DOMESTIC WORK. BELGIUM (BE), DENMARK (DK), GERMANY (DE), ESTONIA (EE), SPAIN (ES), FRANCE (FR), ITALY (IT), LATVIA (LV), LITHUANIA (LT), HUNGARIAN (HU), NETHERLANDS (NL), POLAND (PL), SLOVENIA (SI), FINLAND (FI), SWEDEN (SE), UNITED KINGDOM (UK), NORWAY (NO), ROMANIA (RO).

(Continued)

more hours than men. Scandinavian men would seem to be able to hold their heads up the highest in terms of their contribution to household chores whilst Italian men . . ., well . . . Italian men clearly have some way to go. Regardless of the socio-economic reasons that lie behind these figures there would appear to be an explicit subsidy in terms of time and an implicit subsidy in terms of unpaid work from women to men that is not often spelt out.

To Think About

1 If people produce goods such as housing services and transport for their own consumption, how should we define the "prices" of these goods in the model of utility maximization used in prior chapters?

2 How does a family with more than one adult decide how to allocate each person's work time between home production and work in the market?

[1]Christel Aliaga (2006) *How is the Time of Men and Women Distributed?* Statistics in Focus, Population and Social Conditions. Publisher, Eurostat.

TABLE 2 Time Use Structure of Women and Men Aged 20 to 72

Women	*BE*	*DE*	*EE*	*ES*	*FR*	*IT*	*LV*	*LT*	*HU*	*PL*	*SI*	*FI*	*SE*	*UK*	*NO*
Gainful work, study	2:07	2:05	2:33	2:26	2:31	2:06	3:41	3:41	2:32	2:29	2:59	2:49	3:12	2:33	2:53
Domestic work	4:32	4:11	5:02	4:55	4:30	5:20	3:56	4:29	4:58	4:45	4:58	3:56	3:42	4:15	3:47
Travel	1:19	1:18	1:06	1:05	0:54	1:14	1:20	1:04	0:51	1:06	1:02	1:07	1:23	1:25	1:11
Sleep	8:29	8:19	8:35	8:32	8:55	8:19	8:44	8:35	8:42	8:35	8:24	8:32	8:11	8:27	8:10
Meals, personal care	2:43	2:43	2:08	2:33	3:02	2:53	2:10	2:22	2:19	2:29	2:08	2:06	2:28	2:16	2:08
Free time	4:50	5:24	4:36	4:29	4:08	4:08	4:09	3:49	4:38	4:36	4:29	5:30	5:04	5:04	5:51
Total	24	24	24	24	24	24	24	24	24	24	24	24	24	24	24

Men	*BE*	*DE*	*EE*	*ES*	*FR*	*IT*	*LV*	*LT*	*HU*	*PL*	*SI*	*FI*	*SE*	*UK*	*NO*
Gainful work, study	3:30	3:35	3:40	4:39	4:03	4:26	5:09	4:55	3:46	4:15	4:07	4:01	4:25	4:18	4:16
Domestic work	2:38	2:21	2:48	1:37	2:22	1:35	1:50	2:09	2:40	2:22	2:40	2:16	2:29	2:18	2:22
Travel	1:35	1:27	1:17	1:16	1:03	1:35	1:28	1:13	1:03	1:13	1:09	1:12	1:30	1:30	1:20
Sleep	8:15	8:12	8:32	8:36	8:45	8:17	8:35	8:28	8:31	8:21	8:17	8:22	8:01	8:18	7:57
Meals, personal care	2:40	2:33	2:15	2:35	3:01	2:59	2:10	2:25	2:31	2:23	2:13	2:01	2:11	2:04	2:02
Free time	5:22	5:52	5:28	5:17	4:46	5:08	4:48	4:50	5:29	5:25	5:34	6:08	5:24	5:32	6:03
Total	24	24	24	24	24	24	24	24	24	24	24	24	24	24	24

SOURCE: CHRISTEL ALIAGA (2006) *HOW IS THE TIME OF MEN AND WOMEN DISTRIBUTED*? STATISTICS IN FOCUS, POPULATION AND SOCIAL CONDITIONS. PUBLISHER, EUROSTAT. INFORMATION GATHERED FROM NATIONAL TIME USE SURVEYS BETWEEN 1998 AND 2004 FOR THE VARIOUS COUNTRIES LISTED. BELGIUM (BE), DENMARK (DK), GERMANY (DE), ESTONIA (EE), SPAIN (ES), FRANCE (FR), ITALY (IT), LATVIA (LV), LITHUANIA (LT), HUNGARIAN (HU), NETHERLANDS (NL), POLAND (PL), SLOVENIA (SI), FINLAND (FI), SWEDEN (SE), UNITED KINGDOM (UK), NORWAY (NO), ROMANIA (RO). EUROSTAT © EUROPEAN COMMUNITIES, 2006.

Diminishing Marginal Product

We might expect the marginal product of an input to depend on how much of that input is used. For example, workers cannot be added indefinitely to the harvesting of oranges (while keeping the number of trees, amount of equipment, fertilizer, and so forth fixed) without the marginal product eventually deteriorating. This possibility is illustrated in Figure 7-1. The top panel of the figure shows the relationship between output per week and labor input during the week when the level of capital input is held fixed. At first, adding new workers also increases output significantly, but these gains diminish as even more labor is added and the fixed amount of capital becomes over utilized. The concave shape of the total output curve in panel a therefore reflects the economic principle of diminishing marginal product.

Marginal Product Curve

A geometric interpretation of the marginal product concept is straightforward – it is the slope of the total product curve,[2] shown in panel a of Figure 7-1. The decreasing slope of the curve shows diminishing marginal product. For higher values of labor input,

FIGURE 7-1 Relationship between Output and Labour Input, Holding Other Inputs Constant *Panel (a) shows the relationship between output and labour input, holding other inputs constant. Panel (b) shows the marginal product of labour input, which is also the slope of the curve in panel (a). Here, MP_L diminishes as labour input increases. MP_L reaches zero at L^*.*

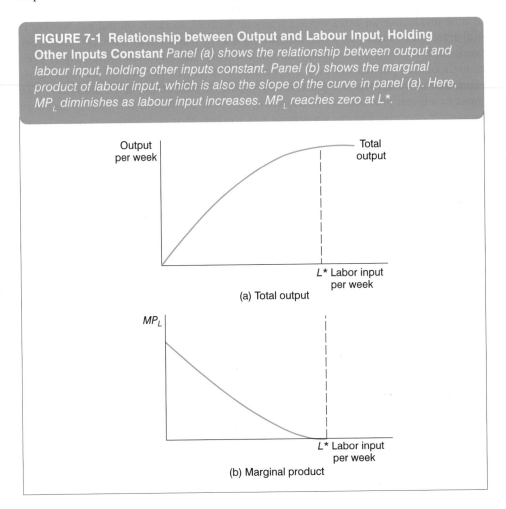

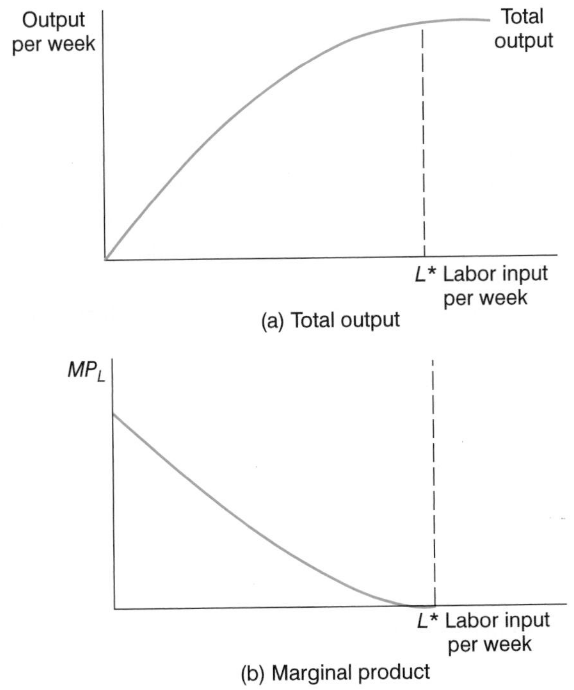

[2]In mathematical terms, the MP_L is the derivative of the production function with respect to L. Because K is held constant in defining the MP_L, this derivative should be a "partial" derivative.

the total curve is nearly flat – adding more labor raises output only slightly. The bottom panel of Figure 7-1 illustrates this slope directly by the marginal product of labor curve (MP_L). Initially, MP_L is high because adding extra labor results in a significant increase in output. As labor input expands, however, MP_L falls. Indeed, at L^*, additional labor input does not raise total output at all. It might be the case that 50 workers can produce 12 000 crates of oranges per week, but adding a 51st worker (with the same number of trees and equipment) fails to raise this output at all. This may happen because he or she just gets in the way in an already crowded orange grove. The marginal product of this new worker is therefore zero.

Average Product

When people talk about the productivity of workers, they usually do not have in mind the economist's notion of marginal product. Rather, they tend to think in terms of "output per worker". In our orange grove example, with 25 workers, output per worker is 400 (=10 000 ÷ 25) crates of oranges per week. With 50 workers, however, output per worker falls to 240 (=12 000 ÷ 50) crates per week. Because the marginal productivity of each new worker is falling, output per worker is also falling. Notice, however, that the output-per-worker figures give a misleading impression of how productive an extra worker really is. With 25 workers, output-per-worker is 400 crates of oranges per week, but adding a 26th worker only adds 200 crates per week. Indeed, with 50 workers, an extra worker adds no additional output even though output-per-worker is a respectable 240 crates per week.[3] Because most economic analysis involves questions of adding or subtracting small amounts of an input in a given production situation, the marginal product idea is clearly the more important concept. Figures on output per worker (that is, "average product") can be quite misleading if they do not accurately reflect these marginal ideas.

Appraising the Marginal Product Concept

The concept of marginal product itself may sometimes be difficult to apply because of the *ceteris paribus* assumption used in its definition. Both the levels of other inputs and the firm's technical knowledge are assumed to be held constant when we perform the conceptual experiment of, say, adding one more worker to an orange grove. But, in the real world, that is not how such hiring would likely occur. Rather, additional hiring would probably also necessitate adding additional equipment (ladders, crates, tractors, and so forth). From a broader perspective, additional hiring might be accompanied by the opening up of entirely new orange groves and the adoption of improved methods of production. In such cases, the *ceteris paribus* assumptions incorporated in the definition of marginal productivity would be violated and the combinations of q and L observed would lie on many different marginal product curves. For this reason, it is more common to study the entire production function for a good, using the marginal product concept to help understand the overall function.

MICROQUIZ 7.1

Average and marginal productivities can be derived directly from the firm's production function. For each of the following cases, discuss how the values of these measures change as labor input expands. Explain why the cases differ.

Case 1. Apples harvested (q) depend on hours of labor employed (L) as: $q = 10 + 50L$.

Case 2. Books dusted (q) depend on minutes spent dusting (L) as: $q = -10 + 5L$.

[3] Output per worker can be shown geometrically in the top panel of Figure 7-1 as the slope of a chord from the origin to the relevant point in the total product curve. Because of the concave shape of the total product curve, this slope too decreases as labor input is increased. Unlike the marginal product of labor, however, average productivity will never reach zero unless extra workers actually reduce output.

APPLICATION 7.2 *High Value-Added Production: What it is and how to achieve it*

While we have yet to cover the market as a whole in terms of supply and demand with the ultimate aim of determining under what conditions a firm will make and maximize profit, it should be intuitively clear that activities inside the firm as well as market conditions outside the firm will interact to determine the overall profit.

A significant issue in market economies contributing to the profit level is the value added within the firm. Firms take inputs – raw materials, land, labor (including management input), and capital – and combine them in such a way that the good or service produced has a value greater than the sum of the value of the parts used to make the good or service. If this was not the case there would not be much point in the production process taking place.

Formally we can define value added as the difference between "the cost of materials, components and services purchased by a firm and the market price for which it sells the goods and services produced using those inputs" (Mason, 2005, p. 8).[1]

The report by Mason looks at sections of the Plastics Processing, Printing, Logistics and Insurance Industries in the United Kingdom. He compares firms with medium value added (MVA) with high value added (HVA) firms to see what is peculiar and what is common between these industries as regards the reasons for some firms engaging in HVA activities while others do not.

He defines HVA firms as those in the upper quartile for average value added per employee between 2000–02 and MVA firms as those in the inter-quartile range for average value added per employee over the same period. Figures on average value added per employee were obtained from the FAME data set available, indeed, to many undergraduate students in their university libraries. Table 1 presents information on several industries in terms of average value added per employee.

The study by Mason included visits to firms represented both in the HVA and LVA sectors of the economy. In short, HVA production takes different forms in different industries; for plastics, for example, the more complex the product and the more flexible the company can be in responding to customer demands then the higher the value added. Much of this depended on previous research and development (R & D). For commercial printing HVA firms tended to have won long-term contracts and thus to be able to have long production runs or they were able to cater to specialized markets segments.

Interestingly the intensity of competition in low value added product areas had a tendency to "drive" firms up-market into high value products. However, a firm's ability to do this was often limited by previous management decisions; the quantity and quality of physical capital; the human resources available to the firm and the organizational culture of the firm. Some of these reasons tended to be stronger in some industries than others. So in plastics and printing capital requirements were more important than in other sectors.

While skill deficiencies were cited by managers only in Logistics was it a major issue with managers reporting a lack of "high-quality graduates, experienced freight forwarders, qualified drivers and warehouse employees with adequate basic skills (literacy and numeracy)". In plastics processing firms also had difficulties in recruiting qualified "engineers of adequate quality along with gaps in production, maintenance, management and supervisory skills among existing employees". (Mason, *opt cit.*, p. 4 both quotations.)

In conclusion, and being slightly selective, Mason concludes that, "these findings clearly support a hypothesis that workforce skill levels are positively related to value added per employee at the enterprise level". (Mason, *opt cit.*, p. 130.)

(*Continued*)

To Think About

1. If skill levels are positively related to value added per employee does this mean that high skills cause the creation of high value added production or is it high value added production that creates the need for high skills?
2. Explain to a colleague what you understand by profit and value-added. What are the differences and similarities?

[1]Geoff Mason, *In Search of High Value Added Production: How Important are Skills? Investigations in the Plastics Processing, Printing, Logistics and Insurance Industries in the UK* (National Institute of Economic and Social Research, London, 2005). Report prepared for the Department for Education and Skills, Research Report RR663. In reality there are several ways to approach this issue. In the study quoted here Mason follows the practice of calculating value added by summing operating profits, employee costs, depreciation and amortization. This is defined as Gross Value Added (GVA). Once the latter three items of employee costs, depreciation and amortization are removed from GVA we have, in effect, (net) value added.

TABLE 1 Gross value added per employee in printing, plastics processing, logistics, general (non-life) insurance services, all manufacturing and all market services, 2000–02, derived from FAME company accounts dataset

Description	*Manu-facturing*	*Printing and related services*	*Manu-facture of plastic products*	*Market services*	*Logistics*	*General insurance services*
Year	*2000–02*	*2000–02*	*2000–02*	*2000–02*	*2000–02*	*2000–02*
Number of enterprises	12871	806	575	13706	1039	336
Average GVA per employee (£)	30519	35761	29354	35976	30259	50465
Number of enterprises reporting consolidated accounts data	2501	122	87	3825	178	100
Average GVA per employee, consolidated accounts only (£), Index numbers (Median = 100)	32470	35421	30381	38870	32602	44352
10th percentile	57	69	67	23	71	57
25th percentile	76	81	80	62	85	69
50th percentile	100	100	100	100	100	100
75th percentile	133	123	130	155	120	170
90th percentile	179	146	171	247	165	217

ORIGINAL SOURCE: FAME COMPANY ACCOUNTS DATASET. CITED IN MASON (2005). VALUE ADDED IS HERE DEFINED AS IN FOOTNOTE 1.

Isoquant Maps

One way to picture an entire production function in two dimensions is to look at its **isoquant map**. We can again use a production function of the form $q = f(K,L)$, using capital and labor as convenient examples of any two inputs that might happen to be of interest. To show the various combinations of capital and labor that can be employed to produce a particular output level, we use an **isoquant** (from the Greek *iso*, meaning "equal"). For example, all the combinations of K and L that fall on the curve labeled $q = 10$ in Figure 7-2 are capable of producing ten units of output per period. This single isoquant records the many alternative ways of producing ten units of output. One combination is represented by point A. A firm could use L_A and K_A to produce ten units of output. Alternatively, the firm might prefer to use relatively less capital and more labor and would therefore choose a point such as B. The isoquant demonstrates that a firm can produce ten units of output in many different ways, just as the indifference curves in Part 2 showed that many different bundles of goods yield the same utility.

Isoquant map A contour map of a firm's production function.

Isoquant A curve that shows the various combinations of inputs that will produce the same amount of output.

There are infinitely many isoquants in the K–L plane. Each isoquant represents a different level of output. The isoquants record successively higher levels of output as we move in a north-easterly direction because using more of each of the inputs will permit output to increase. Two other isoquants (for $q = 20$ and $q = 30$) are also shown in Figure 7-2. They record those combinations of inputs that can produce the specified level of output. You should notice the similarity between an isoquant map and the individual's indifference curve map discussed in Part Two. Both are "contour" maps that show the "altitude" (that is, of utility or output) associated with various input combinations. For isoquants, however, the labeling of the curves is measurable (an output of ten units per week has a precise meaning), and we are more interested in the characteristics of these curves than we were in determining the exact shape of indifference curves.

FIGURE 7-2 Isoquant Map *Isoquants record the alternative combinations of inputs that can be used to produce a given level of output. The slope of these curves shows the rate at which L can be substituted for K while keeping output constant. The negative of this slope is called the (marginal) rate of technical substitution (RTS). In the figure, the RTS is positive, and it is diminishing for increasing inputs of labour.*

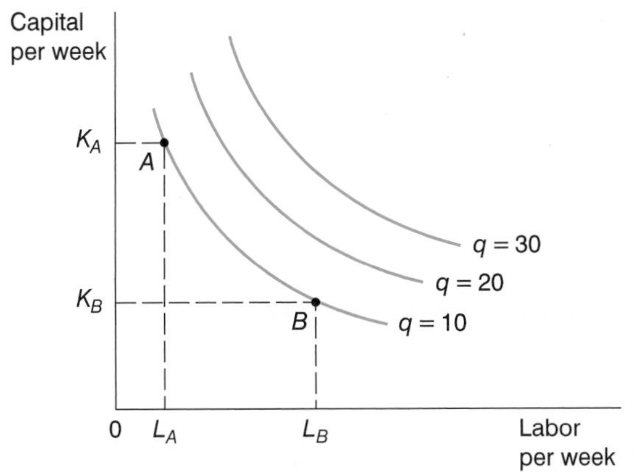

Rate of Technical Substitution

Marginal rate of technical substitution (RTS) The amount by which one input can be reduced when one more unit of another input is added while holding output constant. The negative of the slope of an isoquant.

The slope of an isoquant shows how one input can be traded for another while holding output constant. Examining this slope gives some information about the technical possibilities for substituting labor for capital – an issue that can be quite important to firms. The slope of an isoquant (or, more properly, its negative) is called the **marginal rate of technical substitution (RTS)** of labor for capital. Specifically, the RTS is defined as the amount by which capital input can be reduced while holding quantity produced constant when one more unit of labor input is used. Mathematically,

$$\begin{aligned}\textit{Rate} \text{ of technical substitution} \\ \text{(of labor for capital)} &= RTS \text{ (of } L \text{ for } K) \\ &= -(\text{Slope of isoquant}) \\ &= -\frac{\text{Change in capital input}}{\text{Change in labor input}}\end{aligned} \quad \{7.3\}$$

where all of these changes refer to a situation in which output (q) is held constant. The particular value of this trade-off rate will depend not only on the level of output but also on the quantities of capital and labor being used. Its value depends on the point on the isoquant map at which the slope is to be measured. At a point such as A in Figure 7-2, relatively large amounts of capital can be given up if one more unit of labor is employed – at point A, the RTS is a high positive number. On the other hand, at point B, the availability of an additional unit of labor does not permit much of a reduction in capital input, and the RTS is relatively small.

The RTS and Marginal Products

We can use the RTS concept to discuss the likely shape of a firm's isoquant map. Most obviously, it seems clear that the RTS should be positive; that is, each isoquant should have a negative slope. If the quantity of labor employed by the firm increases, the firm should be able to reduce capital input and still keep output constant. Because labor presumably has a positive marginal product, the firm should be able to get by with less capital input when more labor is used. If increasing labor actually required the firm to use more capital, it would imply that the marginal product of labor is negative, and no firm would be willing to pay for an input that had a negative effect on output.

We can show this result more formally by noting that the RTS is precisely equal to the ratio of the marginal product of labor to the marginal product of capital. That is

$$RTS \text{ (of } L \text{ for } K) = \frac{MP_L}{MP_K} \quad \{7.4\}$$

Suppose, for example, that $MP_L = 2$ and $MP_K = 1$. Then, if the firm employs one more worker, this will generate two extra units of output if capital input remains constant. Put another way, the firm can reduce capital input by two when there is another worker and output will not change – the extra labor adds two units of output, whereas the reduced capital reduces output by two. Hence, by definition, the RTS is 2 – the ratio of the marginal products.

Now, applying Equation 7.4, it is clear that if the RTS is negative, one of the marginal products must also be negative. But no firm would pay anything for an input that reduced output. Hence, at least for those portions of isoquants where firms actually operate, the RTS must be positive (and the slope of the isoquant negative).

Diminishing RTS

The isoquants in Figure 7-2 are drawn not only with negative slopes (as they should be) but also as convex curves. Along any one of the curves, the RTS is *diminishing*. For a high ratio of K to L, the RTS is a large positive number, indicating that a great deal of capital can be given up if one more unit of labor is employed. On the other hand, when a lot of labor is already being used, the RTS is low, signifying that only a small amount of capital can be traded for an additional unit of labor if output is to be held constant. This shape seems intuitively reasonable: The more labor (relative to capital) that is used, the less able labor is to replace capital in production. A diminishing RTS shows that use of a particular input can be pushed too far. Firms will not want to use "only labor" or "only machines" to produce a given level of output.[4] They will choose a more balanced input mix that uses at least some of each input. In Chapter 8, we see exactly how an optimal (that is, minimum cost) mix of inputs might be chosen. Application 7.3: *Moving Along and Between Production Isoquants: The example of Renault (I)* gives a real-life example of how the same amount of output can be produced with different combinations of labor and capital.

Returns to Scale

Because production functions represent actual methods of production, economists pay considerable attention to the form of these functions. The shape and properties of a firm's production function are important for a variety of reasons. Using such information, a firm may decide how its research funds might best be spent on developing technical improvements. Or, public policymakers might study the form of production functions to argue that laws prohibiting very large-scale firms would harm economic efficiency. In this section, we develop some terminology to aid in examining such issues.

Returns to scale The rate at which output increases in response to proportional increases in all inputs.

Adam Smith on Returns to Scale

The first important issue we might address about production functions is how the quantity of output responds to increases in all inputs together. For example, suppose all inputs were doubled. Would output also double, or is the relationship not quite so simple? Here we are asking about the **returns to scale** exhibited by a production function, a concept that has been of interest to economists ever since Adam Smith intensively studied (of all things) the production of pins in the eighteenth century. Smith identified two forces that come into play when all inputs are doubled (for a doubling of scale). First, a doubling of scale permits a greater "division of labor". Smith was intrigued by the skill of people who made only pin heads, or who sharpened pin shafts, or who stuck

MICROQUIZ 7.2

A hole can be dug in one hour with a small shovel and in half an hour with a large shovel.

1. What is the RTS of labor time for shovel size?
2. What does the "one-hole" isoquant look like? How much time would it take a worker to dig a hole if he or she used a small shovel for half the hole, then switched to the large shovel?

[4]An incorrect, but possibly instructive, argument based on Equation 7.4 might proceed as follows. In moving along an isoquant, more labor and less capital are being used. Assuming that each factor exhibits a diminishing marginal product, we might say that MP_L would decrease (because the quantity of labor has increased) and that MP_K would increase (because the quantity of capital has decreased). Consequently, the RTS ($= MP_L/MP_K$) should decrease. The problem with this argument is that *both* inputs are changing together. It is not possible to make such simple statements about changes in marginal productivities when two inputs are changing, because the definition of the marginal product of any one input requires that the level of all other inputs be held constant.

APPLICATION 7.3 *Moving Along and Between Production Isoquants: The example of Renault (I)*

We have looked at isoquant curves; curves which demonstrated how the same amount of output can be produced with different combinations of capital and labor. Just as students sometimes prefer numbers in formula rather than letters to gain an intuitive grasp, here we present a concrete example of how a change in the production function (the way in which output and inputs are related) led to one car manufacturer, Renault, changing the production process of making car exhausts. In so doing the combination of labor and capital needed to make a given quantity of car exhausts for its various models of cars changed[1].

In addition, Renault *simultaneously* cut back on the quantity of factor inputs needed to produce a fixed amount of output with a concomitant knock-on effect on costs of production (see Application 8-5: "*Moving Down the Short-Run Average Cost Curve – but which one?: The example at Renault (II)*" in Chapter 8).

In the 1990s Renault built exhaust systems using specialized production lines with each production line corresponding to each category of engine. With ten production lines the production of the exhaust systems were organized in batches. The upshot of this was that too many or too little exhausts were produced depending on market demand for any particular model of car at a given time. Forecasting models to predict demand were just too inaccurate to prevent inventory stocks form either building up or running down too quickly.

The choice facing senior management was to outsource the production of exhausts or find a cheaper way of doing it in-house. The original, or classical, approach in the 1990s involved 500 people in exhaust production at sites in Flins and Douai in France and Valladolid in Spain. The traditional approach to exhaust production is illustrated in Figure 1.

FIGURE 1 The Traditional Production Cycle at Renault in Making Car Exhausts

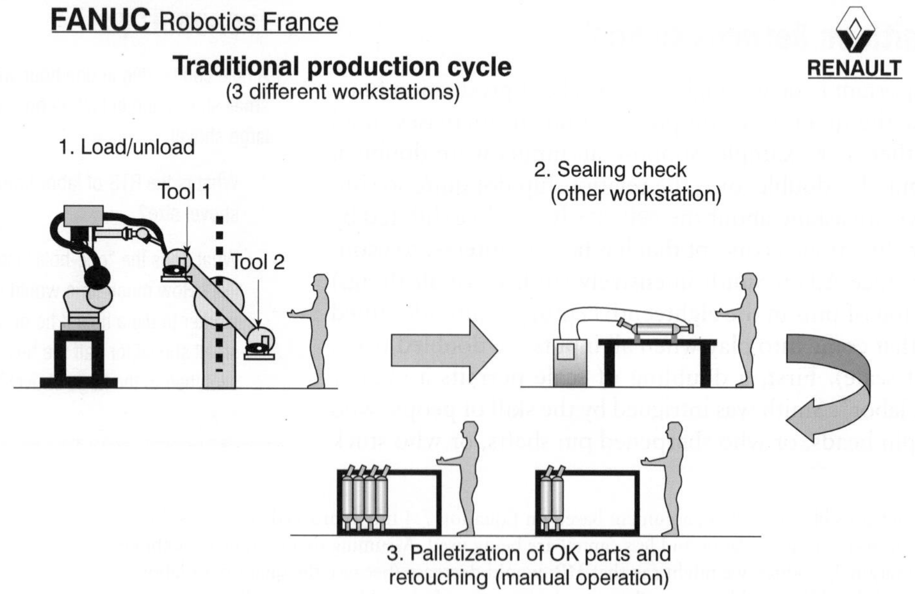

SOURCE: M. DEFAUX "RENAULT DEVELOPS INNOVATIVE ARC WELDING SOLUTIONS FOR EXHAUST SYSTEMS THAT CUT PRODUCTION COSTS BY 30 PER CENT", *INDUSTRIAL ROBOT: AN INTERNATIONAL JOURNAL*, VOL. 29, ISSUE 4 (2002): 318–321. PUBLISHED WITH PERMISSION FROM EMERALD GROUP PUBLISHING LTD.

The gentleman in charge of solving the problem of over or under-stocking of exhausts, M. Lionel Ollivon, commented that

Our idea was to define a flexible process and to be able to use the same welding installation for the complete family of a product. In that way, we would be able to produce the exhaust components as needed, in fact in the same order as we assemble the vehicles in the assembly plant. And that would avoid all stocks.

The resolution to the problem lay in having two industrial robots work in synchronization. It turned out that very few robotic manufacturers (who supplied Renault) were able to offer such industrial robots. One firm that could assist was Fanuc Robotics based in Luxembourg. Without getting too technical the solution lay in the "dual-arc concept" whereby during the production process the two robots move at the same speed being controlled through a single "control cabinet". In the past two such control points were needed with a slowing down in the process due to information exchange which, with the new process, was no longer needed. "Using a single controller we gain time on the data exchange process" (Lionel Ollivon).

The new system, initialy trialled in real production at Renault's Valladolid plant in Spain used the new arc welding system as follows.

- First, the operator places the component parts of the exhaust to be assembled on a turntable.
- Then he rotates the turntable and pushes the button which sets the next stage in motion.
- The robot picks up the components in the correct manner for assembly and loads the components into their positions. This results in a saving of time since formerly it was the employee's role to place the components in the correct position.
- Once the parts are loaded, the robot moves them in front of two cameras (known as the vision system) to check the exact positions of the surfaces to be welded. Using this new vision system reduces inaccuracies in

FIGURE 2 The Production Cycle with the New Production Techniques

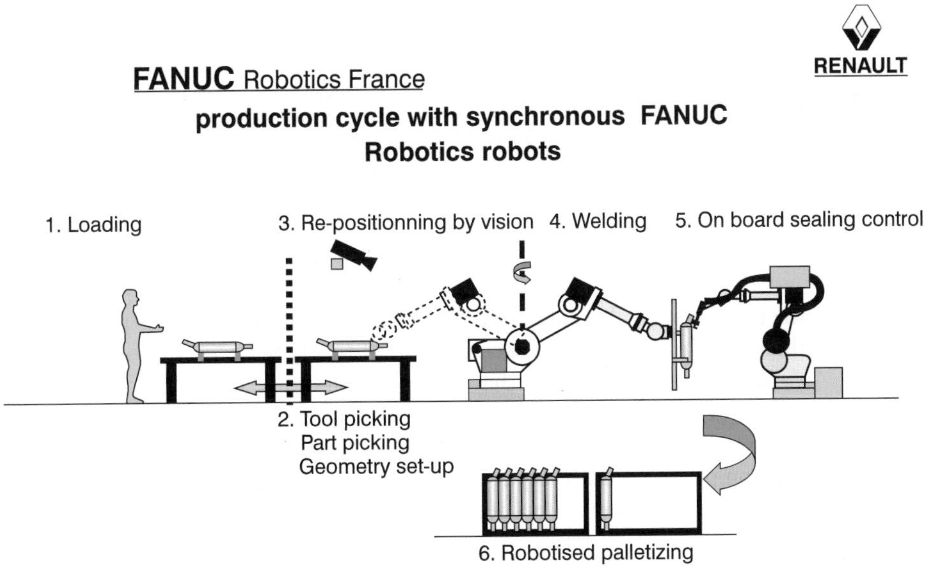

Note: Three workstations from the traditional set are replaced by a single workstation

SOURCE: M. DEFAUX "RENAULT DEVELOPS INNOVATIVE ARC WELDING SOLUTIONS FOR EXHAUST SYSTEMS THAT CUT PRODUCTION COSTS BY 30 PER CENT", *INDUSTRIAL ROBOT: AN INTERNATIONAL JOURNAL*, VOL. 29, ISSUE 4 (2002): 318–321. PUBLISHED WITH PERMISSION FROM EMERALD GROUP PUBLISHING LTD.

(*Continued*)

alignment from 3 mm down to 0.1 mm. "We used to have to cope with three sources of deviation: the parts tolerance was 0.7 mm, and the position of the parts in the tool could incur inaccuracies as could the location of the arc welding torch", comments M. Ollivon.

- An additional efficiency measure occurred when the seam to be welded was laid in a horizontal position first. During welding, gravity then helped to fully fill the weld gap in a quicker manner.

The end result, as M Ollivon comments, is that, "We are working today at a linear speed of 1.5 m/min using exactly the same gas and welding materials we previously used to achieve a working speed of 0.7 m/min".

Yet a further improvement was to take the so-called leak test, which tests the quality of the weld and was previously carried out separately, and integrate it with the welding process. "The result is a tremendous saving in cycle time. The complete cycle is performed in 44 seconds."

- The last piece of this new process is for the robot to place the welded and tested exhaust onto the right conveyer – one for those that pass the test and the other for those that do not and require rewelding.

After three weeks at the Valladolid plant re-working fell off. The end result of the new production process was a greater flexibility; tighter tolerances and a doubling of welding speed; fewer personnel required; lower investment and a smaller floor space. In February 2002, having patented the synchronous robot technique, Renault took the decision to introduce it throughout the Renault group. Indeed the manufacturer soon found the technique could be applied to other jobs including the "welding of engine cradles, the assembly of body sides, gear box assembly, plasma cutting, laser cutting and so on".

To Think About

1. Learning-by-doing is the process whereby the efficiency and productivity of an employee or group of employees can improve over time as they become more familiar with how the specific job they are doing is done. Is there any evidence of learning-by-doing in the above case study?
2. List and describe the various ways in which the new production process has become more efficient?
3. Based on the above summary of the article by Defaux (2002) draw an isoquant to represent the classical production method of exhausts and underneath the diagram show a different isoquant representing the new process of exhaust production.

[1]The material presented here draws heavily from "Renault develops innovative arc welding solutions for exhaust systems that cut production costs by 30 per cent" by Michel Defaux, *Industrial Robot* (2002) Volume 29 Number 4. All quotations are from the above article.

the two together. He suggested that efficiency might increase – production might more than double – as greater specialization of this type becomes possible.

Smith did not envision that these benefits to large-scale operations would extend indefinitely, however. He recognized that large firms may encounter inefficiencies in managerial direction and control if scale is dramatically increased. Coordination of production plans for more inputs may become more difficult when there are many layers of management and many specialized workers involved in the production process.

A Precise Definition

Which of these two effects of scale is more important is an empirical question. To investigate this question, economists need a precise definition of returns to scale. A production function is said to exhibit *constant returns to scale* if a doubling of all inputs results in a precise doubling of output. If a doubling of all inputs yields less than a doubling of output, the production function is said to exhibit *decreasing returns to scale*. If a doubling of all inputs results in more than a doubling of output, the production function exhibits *increasing returns to scale*.

Graphic Illustrations

These possibilities are illustrated in the three graphs of Figure 7-3. In each case, production isoquants for $q = 10, 20, 30$, and 40 are shown, together with a ray (labeled *A*) showing a uniform expansion of both capital and labor inputs. Panel (a) illustrates constant returns to scale. There, as both capital and labor inputs are successively increased from 1 to 2, and 2 to 3, and then 3 to 4, output expands proportionally. That is, output and inputs move in unison. In panel (b), by comparison, the isoquants get farther apart as output expands. This is a case of decreasing returns to scale – an expansion in inputs does not result in a proportionate rise in output. For example, the doubling of both capital and labor inputs from 1 to 2 units is not sufficient to increase output from 10 to 20. That increase in output would require more than a doubling of inputs. Finally, panel (c) illustrates increasing returns to scale. In this case, the isoquants get closer together as input expands – a doubling of inputs is more than sufficient to double output. Large-scale operation would in this case appear to be quite efficient.

FIGURE 7-3 Isoquant Maps Showing Constant, Decreasing, and Increasing Returns to Scale *In panel (a), an expansion in both inputs leads to a similar, proportionate expansion in output. This shows constant returns to scale. In panel (b), an expansion in inputs yields a less-than-proportionate expansion in output, illustrating decreasing returns to scale. Panel (c) shows increasing returns to scale–output expands proportionately faster than inputs.*

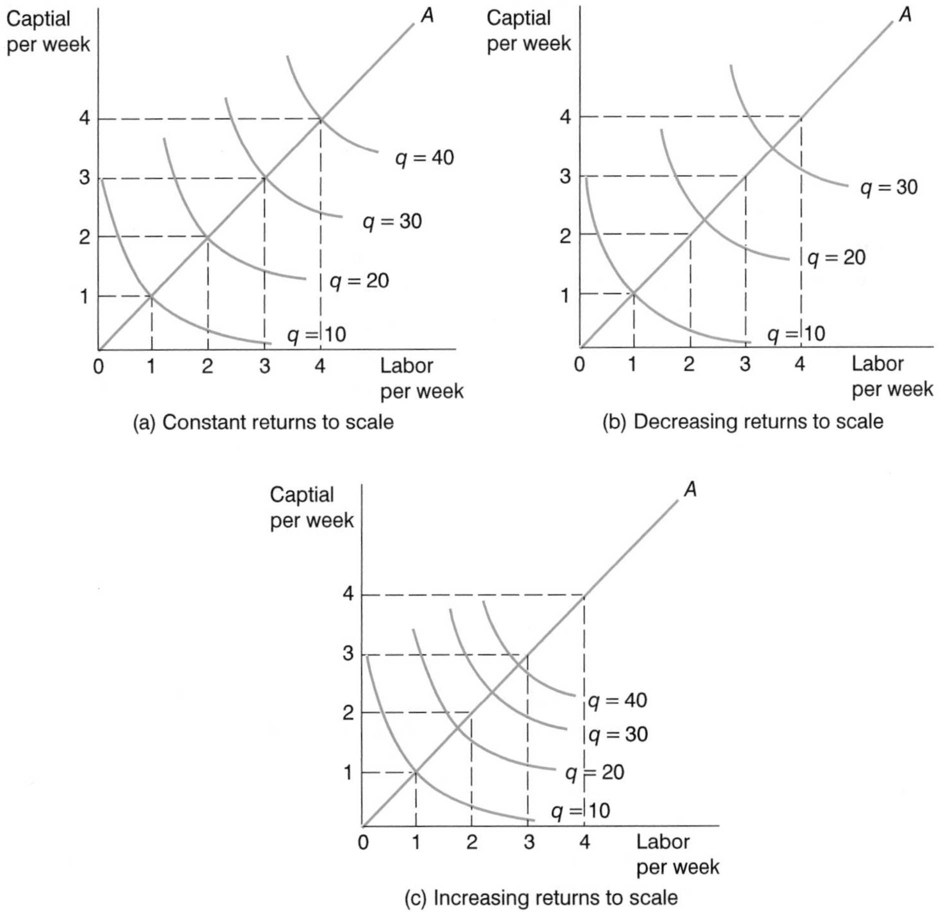

APPLICATION 7.4 *Economies of Scale in the South African Car Industry*

The classic example for economies of scale is the oft cited car industry. It remains a good example today.

Developments in the automotive industry in South Africa present an interesting picture of how smaller developing countries can try to foster important sectors of their economy.[1]

Developed initially in the 1920s when Ford and General Motors established subsidiary plants, the South African motor industry moved from an assembly operation to a more capital-intensive industry in the 1960s. Due in part to business related reasons and in part due to the growing international demands for trade sanctions during the apartheid era, there was a growing move towards indigenous ownership of the industry.[2]

This trend speeded up in the second half of the 1980s whereby the end of 1987 there were seven motor vehicle assemblers remaining in South Africa – four locally owned companies and three foreign owned. Come the 1980s demand was muted with vehicle sales in 1995, for example reaching 376 784. (Compare equivalent figures for Brazil with 1.6 million units, Mexico at 936 437 and India at 634 021 to give but three comparison cases.) Clearly something needed to be done.

A major departure from this policy took place from 1995 when the South African government, determined to make the industry more competitive, launched the Motor Industry Development Program. This was an attempt, through a series of incentives, to integrate the industry into the global value chain of major car manufacturers and at the same time make the industry more competitive. This was made all the more urgent given the large trade deficit that existed on vehicles and parts of roughly 4 bn Rand.

As such, any policy which might ameliorate these issues was to be welcome. Economies of scale through consolidation within the industry and linking the small car industry into the international division of multinational manufacturing were seen as the way forward.

That economies of scale could indeed be one way forward was in part demonstrated by other studies which showed that such economies of scale were feasible with relatively low levels of production. The Australian Industry Commission (1990, p. 19) note that, "assembly volumes of 200 000 per plant are generally regarded as necessary for efficient production". A study by Booz, Allen and Hamilton and INFOTECC (1987, p. 28) of the Mexican car sector concluded that production of 150 000 units per car model are required to achieve internationally competitive cost levels.[3]

Truett and Truett (2006) estimated whether economies of scale had the potential to operate within the car sector of the South African economy. In the process own price elasticities of demand and cross-price elasticities of demand for the various factor inputs are estimated also. They estimate economies of scale (depending on the model estimated) of 2.02 and 2.91.

To Think About

1. How might a government go about influencing firms to merge? Is it the role of a government to do such a thing? Or do the ends of greater efficiency justify the means of governments intervening into an economy?
2. If economies of scale are estimated at 2.02 and 2.91 what exactly does that mean in terms of a doubling of all inputs into the production of cars in the South African economy?
3. Switching from South Africa to Europe, did the creation of the European Union foster or hinder the development of economies of scale in industry in general? (You will probably not have actual data to hand but from a theoretical perspective what do you think was more likely to happen?)

[1]The following draws on Lila J. Truett and Dale B. Truett, "Production and costs in the South African motor vehicle industry", *Applied Economics*, Vol. 38 (2006): 2381–2392; and John Humphrey and Olga Memedovic, "The Global Automotive Industry Value Chain: What Prospects for Upgrading by Developing Countries" (Vienna: United Nations Industrial Organization (UNIDO), 2003), http://www.unido.org/en/doc/.

[2]For the younger generation that has not dwelled too much on international politics, apartheid was a system of keeping non-white and white elements of the population separated in virtually all aspects of social, economic and political life. Through this system the white minority ruled the country and enjoyed the overwhelming wealth created in the country by the majority non-white population.

[3]Both studies cited in Truett and Truett (2006).

The types of scale economies experienced in the real world may, of course, be rather complex combinations of these simple examples. A production function may exhibit increasing returns to scale over some output ranges and decreasing returns to scale over other ranges. Or, some aspects of a good's production may illustrate scale economies, whereas other aspects may not. For example, the production of computer chips can be highly automated; but the assembly of chips into electronic components is more difficult to automate and may exhibit few such scale economies. Application 7.4: *Economies of Scale in the South African Car Industry* illustrates the classic example of the car industry in exploiting economies of scale. Problem 7.7 and problem 7.8 at the end of this chapter show how the returns to scale concept can be captured with a simple mathematical equation called the Cobb-Douglas production function. This form of the production function (or a simple generalization of it) has been used to study production in a wide variety of industries.

Input Substitution

Another important characteristic of a production function is how "easily" capital can be substituted for labor, or, more generally, how any one input can be substituted for another. This characteristic depends primarily on the shape of a single isoquant. So far we have assumed that a given output level can be produced with a variety of different input mixes – that is, we assumed firms could substitute labor for capital while keeping output constant. How easily that substitution can be accomplished may, of course, vary. In some cases, the substitution can be made easily and quickly in response to changing economic circumstances. Mine owners found it relatively easy to automate in response to rising wages for miners, for example. In other cases, firms may have little choice about the input combination they must use. Producers of operas have little chance to substitute capital (scenery) for labor (singers). Economists can measure this degree of substitution very technically, but for us to do so here would take us too far afield.[5] We can look at one special case in which input substitution is impossible. This example illustrates some of the difficulties in input substitution that economists have explored.

Fixed-Proportions Production Function

Figure 7-4 demonstrates a case where no substitution is possible. This case is rather different from the ones we have looked at so far. Here, the isoquants are L-shaped, indicating that machines and labor must be used in absolutely fixed proportions. Every machine has a fixed complement of workers that cannot be varied. For example, if K_1 machines are in use, L_1 workers are required to produce output level q_1. Employing more workers than L_1 will not increase output with K_1 machines. This is shown by the fact that the q_1 isoquant is horizontal beyond the point K_1, L_1. In other words, the marginal productivity of labor is zero beyond L_1. On the other hand, using fewer workers would result in excess machines. If only L_0 workers were hired, for instance, only q_0 units could be produced, but these units could be produced with only K_0 machines. When L_0 workers are hired, there is an excess of machines of an amount given by $K_1 - K_0$.

The production function whose isoquant map is shown in Figure 7-4 is called a **fixed-proportions production function**. Both inputs are fully employed only if a combination of K and L that lies along the ray A, which passes through the vertices of the isoquants, is chosen. Otherwise, one input will be excessive in the sense that it could be cut back

Fixed-proportions production function
A production function in which the inputs must be used in a fixed ratio to one another.

[5]Formally, the case of input substitution is measured by the *elasticity of substitution*, which is defined as the ratio of the percentage change in K/L to the percentage change in the RTS along an isoquant. For the fixed-proportions case, this elasticity is zero because K/L does not change at the isoquant's vertex.

without reducing output. If a firm with such a production function wishes to expand, it must increase all inputs simultaneously so that none of the inputs is redundant.

The fixed-proportions production function has a wide variety of applications to the study of real-world production techniques. Many machines do require a fixed complement of workers; more than these would be redundant. For example, consider the combination of capital and labor required to mow a lawn. The lawn mower needs one person for its operation, and a worker needs one lawn mower in order to produce any output. Output can be expanded (that is, more grass can be mowed at the same time) only by adding capital and labor to the productive process in fixed proportions. Many production functions may be of this type, and the fixed-proportions model is in many ways appropriate for production planning.[6]

The Relevance of Input Substitutability

The ease with which one input can be substituted for another is of considerable interest to economists. They can use the shape of an isoquant map to see the relative ease with which different industries can adapt to the changing availability of productive inputs. For example, rapidly rising energy prices during the late 1970s caused many industries to adopt energy-saving capital equipment. For these firms, their costs did not rise very rapidly because they were able to adapt to new circumstances. Firms that could not make such substitutions had large increases in costs and may have become non-competitive. Another example of input substitutability is found in the

FIGURE 7-4 Isoquant Map with Fixed Proportions *The isoquant map shown here has no substitution possibilities. Capital and labour must be used in fixed proportions if neither is to be redundant. For example, if K_1 machines are available, L_1 units of labour should be used. If L_2 units of labour are used, there will be excess labour since no more than q_1 can be produced from the given machines. Alternatively, if L_0 labourers were hired, machines would be in excess to the extent $K_1 - K_0$.*

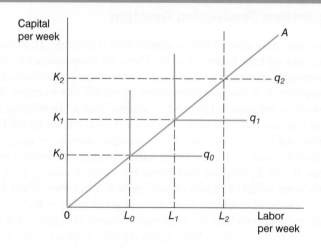

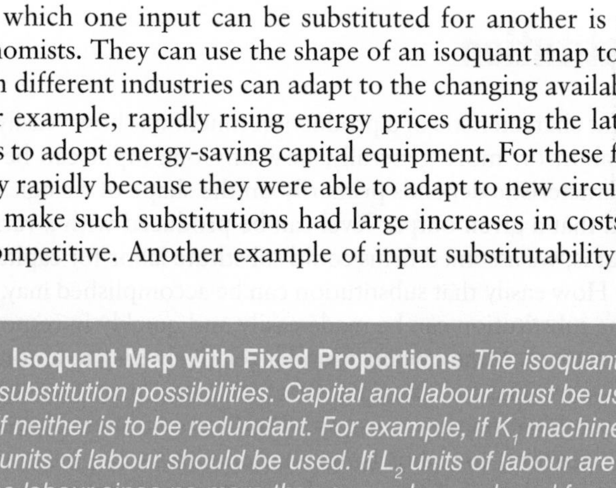

[6]The lawn mower example points up another important possibility. Presumably there is some leeway in choosing what size and type of lawn mower to buy. Any device, from a pair of clippers to a gang mower, might be chosen. Prior to the actual purchase, the capital–labor ratio in lawn mowing can be considered variable. Once the mower is purchased, however, the capital–labor ratio becomes fixed.

huge changes in agricultural production that have occurred during the past 100 years. As farmers gained access to better farm equipment, they discovered it was very possible to substitute capital for labor while continuing to harvest about the same number of acres. Employment in agriculture declined from about half the labor force to fewer than 3 per cent of workers today. The fact that the workers who left farms found employment in other industries also shows that these other industries were able to make substitutions in how they produce their goods.

Changes in Technology

A production function reflects firms' technical knowledge about how to use inputs to produce outputs. When firms learn new ways to operate, the production function changes. This kind of technical advancement occurs constantly as older, outmoded machines are replaced by more efficient ones that embody state-of-the-art techniques. Workers too are part of this technical progress as they become better educated and learn special skills for doing their jobs. Today, for example, steel is made far more efficiently than in the nineteenth century both because blast furnaces and rolling mills are better and because workers are better trained to use these facilities.

The production function concept and its related isoquant map are important tools for understanding the effect of technical change. Formally, technical progress represents a shift in the production function, such as that illustrated in Figure 7-5 (on p. 226). In this figure, the isoquant q_0 summarizes the initial state of technical knowledge. That level of output can be produced using K_0, L_0, or any of a number of input combinations. With the discovery of new production techniques, the q_0 isoquant shifts toward the origin – the same output level can now be produced using smaller quantities of inputs. If, for example, the q_0 isoquant shifts inward to q'_0, it is now possible to produce q_0 with the same amount of capital as before (K_0) but with much less labor (L_1). It is even possible to produce q_0 using both less capital and less labor than previously by choosing a point such as *A*. **Technical progress** represents a real saving on inputs and (as we see in the next chapter) a reduction in the costs of production.

Technical progress
A shift in the production function that allows a given output level to be produced using fewer inputs.

MICROQUIZ 7.3

Suppose that artichokes are produced according to the production function $q = 100K + 50L$, where q represents kilos of artichokes produced per hour, K is the number of hectares of land devoted to artichoke production, and L represents the number of workers hired each hour to pick artichokes.

1. Does this production function exhibit increasing, constant, or decreasing returns to scale?
2. What does the form of this production function assume about the substitutability of L for K?
3. Give one reason why this production function is probably not a very reasonable one.

Technical Progress versus Input Substitution

We can use Figure 7-5 to show an important distinction between true technical advancement and simple capital–labor substitution. With technical progress, the firm can continue to use K_0, but it produces q_0 with less labor (L_1). The output per unit of labor input rises from q_0/L_0 to q_0/L_1. Even in the absence of technical improvements, the firm could have achieved such an increase by choosing to use K_1 units of capital. This substitution of capital for labor would also have caused the average productivity of labor to rise from q_0/L_0 to q_0/L_1. This rise would not mean any real improvement in the way goods are made, however. In studying productivity data, especially data on output per worker, we must be careful that the changes being observed represent true technical improvements rather than capital-for-labor substitution. Application 7.5: *Measuring Multifactor Productivity* illustrates this distinction. Problems 7.9 and 7.10 look at some of the mathematics of measuring technical change.

APPLICATION 7.5 *Measuring Multifactor Productivity*

Differences in the way productivity is measured can have an important effect on the economic insights that the data provide. Sometimes total output is simply divided by the total number of employees in a firm. This is then repeated at some point in time later and the percentage increase or growth rate is worked out. But these figures can be rather misleading because they may reflect simple capital-for-labor substitution rather than real technical gains.[1] To explore this further, in what follows, we closely follow Harris (2004).[2] We start by looking at the Cobb-Douglas production function. Normally, this is presented as output being a function of capital and labor and is written as

$$Y = f(K, L) = A_0 K^{\alpha_K} L^{\alpha_L} \qquad \{1\}$$

Where A_0, α_K, and α_L in equation {1} are positive constants less than one; and K and L represents the capital stock and employment respectively. There is nothing to say, however, that only two variables need enter into this specific function. If we add in real intermediate inputs (i.e. raw materials, semi-finished products etc.) represented by M, and also add in time, T, we arrive at equation {2} below.

$$Y = f(K, L) = A_0 K^{\alpha_K} L^{\alpha_L} M^{\alpha_M} T^{\alpha_T} \qquad \{2\}$$

The next step is to take the natural logarithms of both sides of equation {2} to give equation {3} below.

$$y = \alpha_0 + \alpha_K k + \alpha_L l + \alpha_M m + \alpha_T t \qquad \{3\}$$

The coefficients on the various inputs on the right hand side of {3}, including the "input" of time, measure the elasticity of output with respect to that particular input. So, if α_L, say, equaled 0.23 then this would imply that for a 1 per cent increase in employment output would rise by 0.23 per cent.

We now totally differentiate this equation with respect to time to derive an expression that gives us the rate of change of the various variables with respect to time itself. We have equation {4}, where terms such as dY/dT are expressed as $\dot{y}$,

$$\dot{y} = \alpha_K \dot{k} + \alpha_L \dot{l} + \alpha_M \dot{m} + \alpha_T \qquad \{4\}$$

Rearranging {4} above gives us:

$$\alpha_T = \dot{y} - \alpha_K \dot{k} - \alpha_L \dot{l} - \alpha_M \dot{m} \qquad \{5\}$$

The term α_T represents what is leftover or the residual after capital, intermediate inputs and labor have all contributed towards final output. It measures the contribution to growth by all other factors such as technological progress and increases (or decreases) in efficiency.[3] α_T can also be called the change in Total Factor Productivity Growth or $\dot{TFP}$

To see how this helps us to measure properly, and so understand better, productivity changes we rearrange {5} above to give us {6} below.

$$\dot{y} - \dot{l} = (\alpha_L - 1)\dot{l} + \alpha_K \dot{k} + \alpha_M \dot{m} + \alpha_T \qquad \{6\}$$

The left hand side of {6} represents labor productivity. To see this recall that the LHS can be written as

$$ln\left(\frac{dY}{dT}\right) - ln\left(\frac{dL}{dT}\right) = ln\left(\frac{dY/dT}{dl/dT}\right)$$

$$= ln\left(\frac{dY}{dL}\right) \approx \frac{\Delta Y/Y}{\Delta L} \qquad \{7\}$$

So for a one unit change in employment we get the proportionate change in output.

Referring to equation {6}, since α_L is a positive constant less than one then $(\alpha_L - 1)$ is negative; which simply implies that as you employ more labor (represented by $\dot{l}$) then labor productivity falls. Equation {6} also shows that labor productivity is increasing in the growth of capital and intermediate inputs. If capital is substituted for labor, due to automation, then this would imply an increase in the capital/labor ratio (K/L, what is called capital deepening). This could be combined with outsourcing where more of the intermediate products are made outside the firm (M/L would increase) and then purchased from suppliers. Finally, improvements in technology or efficiency represented by α_T also contribute to labor productivity.

Figure 1 shows the situation in UK manufacturing between 1973 to 1998 in terms of output per employee, capital per employee, and intermediate inputs per employee. Given how steeply K/L and M/L rose throughout the 1970s and 1980s then much of any gross output measurement of labor productivity cannot be put down to genuine labor productivity improvements. It is now, hopefully, clear why TFP is seen as a better way to measure efficiency changes and technological progress.

To Think About

1 Is TFP influenced by changes in the quantity of labor, capital or intermediate inputs? What is TFP influenced by?

2 Thinking of the production possibility frontier what will happen to this curve, all other things being equal, when TFP increases due to technical improvements in the production process or improvements due to efficiency?

3 In a general sense, why do you think that the ratio M/E increased so significantly throughout the middle to late 1980s and beyond?

[1]Productivity can also be measured as "output per hour" but this suffers from the same problems as output per employee.

[2]Richard Harris (March, 2004) *DTI Industrial Support Policies: Key Findings from New Micro-data Analysis.* Contained within DTI Economics Paper *Raising UK Productivity – Developing the Evidence Base for Policy.* Papers and Proceedings from a DTI Seminar. This paper can be downloaded free of charge from the UK Government's Department of Trade and Industry website at http://www.dti.gov.uk/files/file14765.pdf.

[3]While it is common to see written that α_T represents technological progress it can conceivably be due to what is called "learning-by-doing" which also goes by the name of the Horndal Effect. This can occur with no technological progress at all but simply that the employees in the production of service process become better, overtime, at what they are doing.

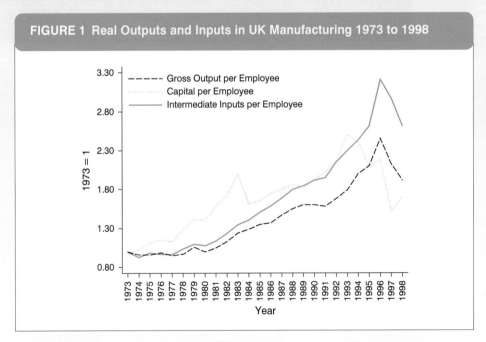

FIGURE 1 Real Outputs and Inputs in UK Manufacturing 1973 to 1998

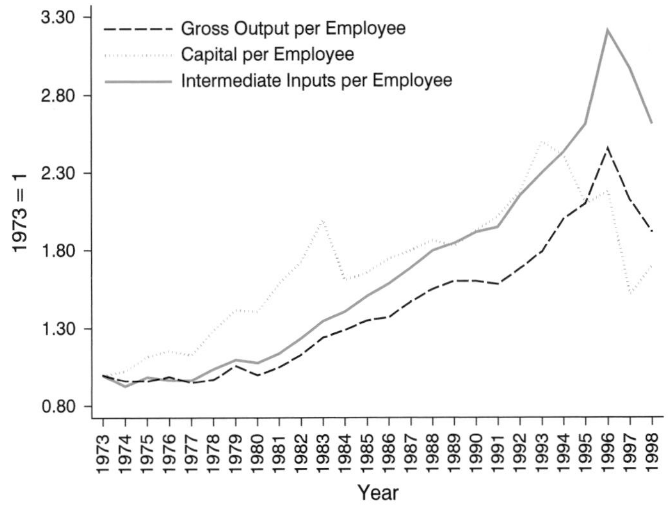

SOURCE: HARRIS (MARCH, 2004). CROWN COPYRIGHT

A Numerical Example

Additional insights about the nature of production functions can be obtained by looking at a numerical example. Although this example is obviously unrealistic (and, we hope, a bit amusing), it does reflect the way production is studied in the real world.

The Production Function

Suppose we looked in detail at the production process used by the fast-food chain Hamburger Heaven (HH). The production function for each outlet in the chain is

$$\textit{Hamburgers per hour} = q = 10\sqrt{KL} \qquad \{7.5\}$$

where K represents the number of grills used and L represents the number of workers employed during an hour of production. One aspect of this function is that it exhibits constant returns to scale.[7] Table 7-1 shows this fact by looking at input levels for K and L ranging from 1 to 10. As both workers and grills are increased together, hourly hamburger output rises proportionally. To increase the number of hamburgers it serves, HH must simply duplicate its kitchen technology over and over again.

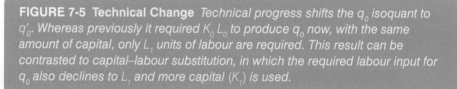

FIGURE 7-5 Technical Change *Technical progress shifts the q_0 isoquant to q'_0. Whereas previously it required K_0 L_0 to produce q_0 now, with the same amount of capital, only L_1 units of labour are required. This result can be contrasted to capital–labour substitution, in which the required labour input for q_0 also declines to L_1 and more capital (K_1) is used.*

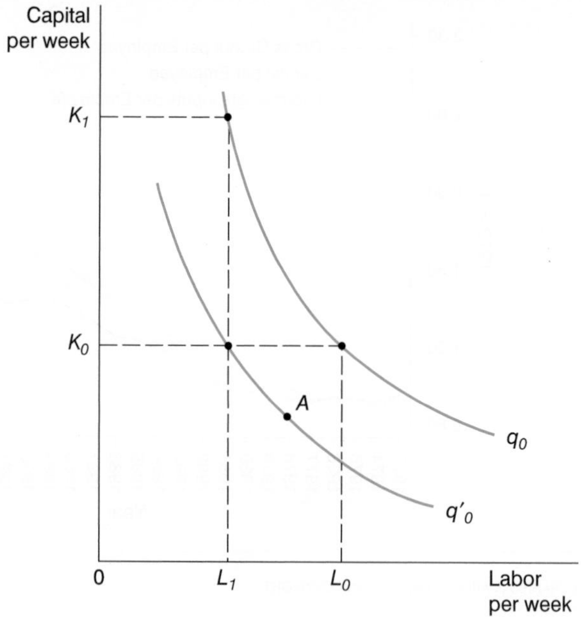

[7]Because this production function can be written $q = 10K^{1/2}L^{1/2}$, it is a Cobb-Douglas function with constant returns to scale (since the exponents sum to 1.0). See problem 7.7.

Average and Marginal Productivities

To show labor productivity for HH, we must hold capital constant and vary only labor. Suppose that HH has four grills ($K = 4$, a particularly easy number of which to take a square root). In this case

$$q = 10\sqrt{4 \cdot L} = 20\sqrt{L} \quad \{7.6\}$$

and this provides a simple relationship between output and labor input. Table 7-2 shows this relationship. Notice two things about the table. First, output per worker declines as more hamburger flippers are employed. Because K is fixed, this occurs because the flippers get in each other's way as they become increasingly crowded around the four grills. Second, notice that the productivity of each additional worker hired also declines. Hiring more workers drags down output per worker because of the diminishing marginal productivity arising from the fixed number of grills. Even though HH's production

TABLE 7-1 Hamburger Production Exhibits Constant Returns to Scale

Grills (K)	Workers (L)	Hamburgers per hour
1	1	10
2	2	20
3	3	30
4	4	40
5	5	50
6	6	60
7	7	70
8	8	80
9	9	90
10	10	100

SOURCE: Equation 7.5.

TABLE 7-2 Total Output, Average Productivity, and Marginal Productivity with Four Grills

Grills (K)	Workers (L)	Hamburgers per hour (q)	q/L	MP_L
4	1	20.0	20.0	—
4	2	28.3	14.1	8.3
4	3	34.6	11.5	6.3
4	4	40.0	10.0	5.4
4	5	44.7	8.9	4.7
4	6	49.0	8.2	4.3
4	7	52.9	7.6	3.9
4	8	56.6	7.1	3.7
4	9	60.0	6.7	3.4
4	10	63.2	6.3	3.2

SOURCE: Equation 7.5.

exhibits constant returns to scale when both K and L can change, holding one input constant yields the expected declining average and marginal productivities.

The Isoquant Map

The overall production technology for HH is best illustrated by its isoquant map. Here, we show how to get one isoquant, but any others desired could be computed in exactly the same way. Suppose HH wants to produce 40 hamburgers per hour. Then its production function becomes

$$q = 40 \text{ hamburgers per hour} = 10\sqrt{KL} \tag{7.7}$$

or

$$4 = \sqrt{KL} \tag{7.8}$$

or

$$16 = K \cdot L \tag{7.9}$$

Table 7-3 shows a few of the K, L combinations that satisfy this equation. Clearly, there are many ways to produce 40 hamburgers, ranging from using a lot of grills with workers dashing among them to using many workers gathered around a few grills. All possible combinations are reflected in the "$q = 40$" isoquant in Figure 7-6. Other isoquants would have exactly the same shape, showing that HH has many substitution possibilities in the ways it actually chooses to produce its heavenly burgers.

Technical Progress

The possibility for scientific advancement in the art of hamburger production can also be shown in this simple case. Suppose that genetic engineering leads to the invention of self-flipping burgers so that the production function becomes

$$q = 20\sqrt{K \cdot L} \tag{7.10}$$

TABLE 7-3 Construction of the $q = 40$ Isoquant

Hamburgers per hour (q)	Grills (K)	Workers (L)
40	16.0	1
40	8.0	2
40	5.3	3
40	4.0	4
40	3.2	5
40	2.7	6
40	2.3	7
40	2.0	8
40	1.8	9
40	1.6	10

SOURCE: Equation 7.9.

We can compare this new technology to that which prevailed previously by recalculating the $q = 40$ isoquant:

$$q = 40 = 20\sqrt{KL} \tag{7.11}$$

or

$$20\sqrt{KL} \tag{7.12}$$

or

$$4 = KL \tag{7.13}$$

The combinations of K and L that satisfy this equation are shown by the "$q = 40$ after invention" isoquant in Figure 7-6. One way to see the overall effect of the invention is to calculate output per worker-hour in these two cases. With four grills, Figure 7-6 shows that it took four workers using the old technology to produce 40 hamburgers per hour. Average productivity was 10 hamburgers per hour per worker. Now a single worker can produce 40 hamburgers per hour because each burger flips itself. Average productivity is 40 hamburgers per hour per worker. This level of output per worker hour could have been attained using the old technology, but that would have required 16 grills and would have been considerably more costly.

MICROQUIZ 7.4

Consider the following historical changes in labor productivity. Which of these were "technical progress"? Which were primarily substitution of capital for labor? If the case seems ambiguous, explain why.

1. The increase in coal output per worker when open-pit mining began.
2. The increase in car output per worker with the introduction of the assembly line.
3. The increase in electricity output per worker with larger power stations.
4. The increase in computer-power output per worker with the availability of better microchips.

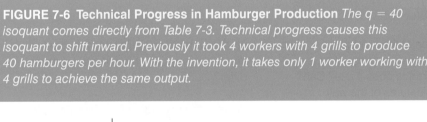

FIGURE 7-6 Technical Progress in Hamburger Production *The $q = 40$ isoquant comes directly from Table 7-3. Technical progress causes this isoquant to shift inward. Previously it took 4 workers with 4 grills to produce 40 hamburgers per hour. With the invention, it takes only 1 worker working with 4 grills to achieve the same output.*

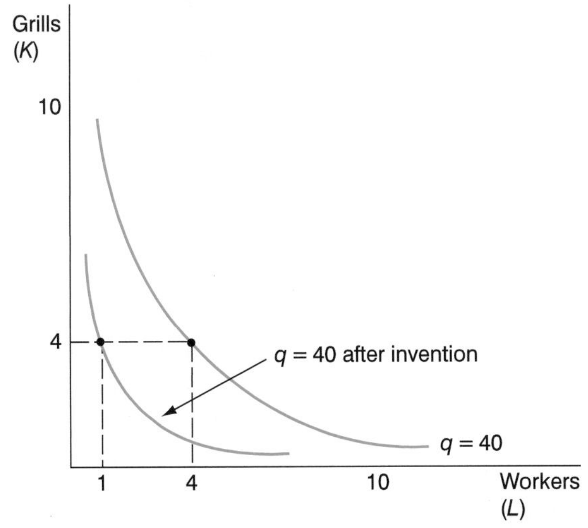

SUMMARY

Chapter 7 shows how economists conceptualize the process of production. We introduce the notion of a production function, which records the relationship between input use and output, and we show how this function can be illustrated with an isoquant map. Several features of the production function are analyzed in the chapter.

- The marginal product of any input is the extra output that can be produced by adding one more unit of that input while holding all other inputs constant. The marginal product of an input declines as more of that input is used.
- The possible input combinations that a firm might use to produce a given level of output are shown on an isoquant. The (negative of the) slope of the isoquant is called the rate of technical substitution (RTS) – it shows how one input can be substituted for another while holding output constant.
- "Returns to scale" refers to the way in which a firm's output responds to proportionate increases in all inputs. If a doubling of all inputs causes output to more than double, there are increasing returns to scale. If such a doubling of inputs causes output to less than double, returns to scale are decreasing. The middle case, when output exactly doubles, reflects constant returns to scale.
- In some cases, it may not be possible for the firm to substitute one input for another. In these cases, the inputs must be used in fixed proportions. Such production functions have L-shaped isoquants.
- Technical progress shifts the firm's entire isoquant map. A given output level can be produced with fewer inputs.

REVIEW QUESTIONS

1 Provide a brief description of the production function for each of the following firms. What is the firm's output? What inputs does it use? Can you think of any special features of the way production takes place in the firm?

   a A wheat farm
   b A vegetable farm
   c Tata Steel Corporation
   d A local arc welding firm
   e Sears
   f Joe's Coffee Stand
   g The Metropolitan Opera
   h The British Museum
   i The National Health Service
   j Dr Smith's private practice
   k Paul's lemonade stand

2 In what ways are firms' isoquant maps and individuals' indifference curve maps based on the same idea? What are the most important ways in which these concepts differ?

3 Pierre is the manager of a croissant outlet that uses only labor and capital to produce the coffee and croissants. The firm usually produces 1000 croissants a day with five workers and four ovens. One day a worker is absent but the stand still produces 1000 croissants. What does this imply about the 1000 croissants isoquant? What does this tell us about Pierre's management skills?

4 A recent news headline read: "Productivity rises by record amount as economy roars out of recession". Assuming that the "productivity" referred to in this headline is the customary "Average Output per Worker Hour" that is usually reported, how would you evaluate whether this increase really is an increase in workers' marginal products?

5 Marjorie Cplus wrote the following answer on her micro examination: "Virtually every production function exhibits diminishing returns to scale because my professor said that all inputs have diminishing marginal productivities. So when all inputs are doubled, output must be less than double". How would you grade Marjorie's answer?

6 Answer question 5 using two specific production functions as examples:

a A fixed-proportions production function

b A Cobb-Douglas production function of the form

$$q = \sqrt{K \cdot L}$$

(See problems 7.4, 7.7, and 7.8 for a discussion of this case.)

7 Universal Gizmo operates a large number of plants that produce gizmos using a special technology. Each plant produces exactly 100 gizmos per day using 5 gizmo presses and 15 workers. Explain why the production function for the entire UG firm exhibits constant returns to scale.

8 Continuing the prior question, suppose that Universal Gizmo devises a new plant design that uses 15 gizmo presses and 5 workers also to produce 100 gizmos per day. How would you construct an isoquant for the firm for 100 000 gizmos per day based on the following assumptions:

a The firm uses plants only of the type specified in question 7.

b The firm uses plants only of its new type.

c The firm uses 500 plants of the type in question 7 and 500 plants of the new type.

What do you conclude about the ability of UG to substitute workers for gizmo presses in its production?.

9 Can a fixed-proportions production function exhibit increasing or decreasing returns to scale? What would its isoquant map look like in each case?

10 Capital and labor are used in fixed proportions to produce an airline flight. It takes two workers (pilots) and one plane to produce a trip. Safety concerns require that every plane has two pilots.

a Describe the isoquant map for the production of air trips.

b Suppose an airline rented 10 planes and hired 30 pilots. Explain both graphically and in words why this would be a foolish thing to do.

c Suppose technical progress in avionic equipment made it possible for a single pilot to handle a plane safely. How would this shift the isoquant map described in part a? How would this affect the average productivity of labor in this industry? How would this affect the average productivity of capital (planes) in this industry?

PROBLEMS

7.1 Imagine that the production function for tuna cans is given by

$$q = 6K + 4L$$

where

q = Output of tuna cans per hour

K = Capital input per hour

L = Labor input per hour

a Assuming capital is fixed at $K = 6$, how much L is required to produce 60 tuna cans per hour? To produce 100 per hour?

b Now assume that capital input is fixed at $K = 8$; what L is required to produce 60 tuna cans per hour? To produce 100 per hour?

c Graph the $q = 60$ and $q = 100$ isoquants. Indicate the points found in part a and part b. What is the RTS along the isoquants?

7.2 Frisbees are produced according to the production function

$$q = 2K + L$$

where

q = Output of Frisbees per hour

K = Capital input per hour

L = Labor input per hour

a If $K = 10$, how much L is needed to produce 100 Frisbees per hour?

b If $K = 25$, how much L is needed to produce 100 Frisbees per hour?

c Graph the $q = 100$ isoquant. Indicate the points on that isoquant defined in part a and part b. What is the RTS along this isoquant? Explain why the RTS is the same at every point on the isoquant.

d Graph the $q = 50$ and $q = 200$ isoquants for this production function also. Describe the shape of the entire isoquant map.

e Suppose technical progress resulted in the production function for Frisbees becoming

$$q = 3K + 1.5L$$

Answer part a through part d for this new production function and discuss how it compares to the previous case.

7.3 Digging clams by hand in Sunset Bay requires only labor input. The total number of clams obtained per hour (q) is given by

$$q = 100\sqrt{L}$$

where L is labor input per hour.

a Graph the relationship between q and L.

b What is the average productivity of labor (output per unit of labor input) in Sunset Bay? Graph this relationship and show that output per unit of labor input diminishes for increases in labor input.

c The marginal productivity of labor in Sunset Bay is given by

$$MP_L = 50/\sqrt{L}$$

Graph this relationship and show that labor's marginal productivity is less than average productivity for all values of L. Explain why this is so.

7.4 Suppose that the hourly output of chili at a barbecue (q, measured in kilos) is characterized by

$$q = 20\sqrt{KL}$$

where K is the number of large pots used each hour and L is the number of worker hours employed.

a Graph the $q = 2000$ kilos per hour isoquant.

b The point $K = 100$, $L = 100$ is one point on the $q = 2000$ isoquant. What value of K corresponds to $L = 101$ on that isoquant? What is the approximate value for the RTS at $K = 100$, $L = 100$?

c The point $K = 25$, $L = 400$ also lies on the $q = 2000$ isoquant. If $L = 401$, what must K be for this input combination to lie on the $q = 2000$ isoquant? What is the approximate value of the RTS at $K = 25$, $L = 400$?

d For this production function, the RTS is

$$RTS = K/L$$

Compare the results from applying this formula to those you calculated in part b and part c. To convince yourself further, perform a similar calculation for the point $K = 200$, $L = 50$.

e If technical progress shifted the production function to

$$q = 20\sqrt{KL}$$

all of the input combinations identified earlier can now produce $q = 4000$ kilos per hour. Would the various values calculated for the RTS be changed as a result of this technical progress, assuming now that the RTS is measured along the $q = 4000$ isoquant?

7.5 Grapes must be harvested by hand. This production function is characterized by fixed proportions – each worker must have one pair of stem clippers to produce any output. A skilled worker with clippers can harvest 50 kilos of grapes per hour.

a Sketch the grape production isoquants for $q = 500$, $q = 1000$, and $q = 1500$ and indicate where on these isoquants firms are likely to operate.

b Suppose a vineyard owner currently has 20 clippers. If the owner wishes to utilize fully these clippers, how many workers should be hired? What should grape output be?

c Do you think the choices described in part b are necessarily profit-maximizing? Why might the owner hire fewer workers than indicated in this part?

d Ambidextrous harvesters can use two clippers – one in each hand – to produce 75 kilos of grapes per hour. Draw an isoquant map (for $q = 500$, 1000, and

1500) for ambidextrous harvesters. Describe in general terms the considerations that would enter into an owner's decision to hire such harvesters.

7.6 Power Goat Lawn Company uses two sizes of mowers to cut lawns. The smaller mowers have a 50 cm blade and are used on lawns with many trees and obstacles. The larger mowers are exactly twice as big as the smaller mowers and are used on open lawns where maneuverability is not so difficult. The two production functions available to Power Goat are:

	Output per hour (square meters)	Capital input (no. of 50 cm mowers)	Labor input
Large mowers	8000	2	1
Small mowers	5000	1	1

a Graph the $q = 40\,000$ square meters isoquant for the first production function. How much K and L would be used if these factors were combined without waste?

b Answer part a for the second function.

c How much K and L would be used without waste if half of the 40 000-square-meter lawn were cut by the method of the first production function and half by the method of the second? How much K and L would be used if three-fourths of the lawn were cut by the first method and one-fourth by the second? What does it mean to speak of fractions of K and L?

d On the basis of your observations in part c, draw a $q = 40\,000$ isoquant for the combined production functions.

7.7 The production function

$$q = K^a L^b$$

where $0 \leq a, b \leq 1$, is called a Cobb-Douglas production function. This function is widely used in economic research. Using the function, show that

a The chili production function in problem 7.4 is a special case of the Cobb-Douglas.

b If $a + b = 1$, a doubling of K and L will double q.

c If $a + b < 1$, a doubling of K and L will less than double q.

d If $a + b > 1$, a doubling of K and L will more than double q.

e Using the results from part b through part d, what can you say about the returns to scale exhibited by the Cobb-Douglas function?

7.8 For the Cobb-Douglas production function in problem 7.7, it can be shown (using calculus) that

$$MP_K = aK^{a-1}L^b$$
$$MP_L = bK^aL^{b-1}$$

If the Cobb-Douglas exhibits constant returns to scale ($a + b = 1$), show that

a Both marginal productivities are diminishing.

b The RTS for this function is given by

$$RTS = \frac{bK}{aL}$$

c The function exhibits a diminishing RTS.

7.9 The production function for puffed rice is given by

$$q = 100\sqrt{KL}$$

where q is the number of boxes produced per hour, K is the number of puffing guns used each hour, and L is the number of workers hired each hour.

a Calculate the $q = 1000$ isoquant for this production function and show it on a graph.

b If $K = 10$, how many workers are required to produce $q = 1000$? What is the average productivity of puffed-rice workers?

c Suppose technical progress shifts the production function to

$$q = 200\sqrt{KL}$$

Answer parts a and b for this new situation.

d Suppose technical progress proceeds continuously at a rate of 5 per cent per year. Now the production function is given by

$$q = (1.05)^t\, 100\sqrt{KL}$$

where t is the number of years that have elapsed into the future. Now answer parts a and b for this production function. (Note: Your answers should include terms in $(1.05)^t$. Explain the meaning of these terms.)

7.10 You will need to read Application 7.5 before attempting this question. One way economists measure total factor productivity is to use a Cobb-Douglas production function of the form,

$$q = A(t)K^{a}L^{1-a}$$

where $A(t)$ is a term representing technical change and a is a positive fraction representing the relative importance of capital input.

a Describe why this production function exhibits constant returns to scale (see problem 7.7)

b Taking logarithms of this production function yields

$$\ln q = \ln A(t) + a \ln K + (1 - a) \ln L$$

One useful property of logarithms is that the change in the log of X is approximately equal to the percentage change in X itself. Explain how this would allow you to calculate annual changes in the technical change factor from knowledge of changes in q, K, and L and of the parameter a.

c Use the results from part b to calculate an expression for the annual change in labor productivity (q/L) as a function of changes in $A(t)$ and in the capital–labor ratio (K/L). Under what conditions would changes in labor productivity be a good measure of changes in total factor productivity? When would the measures differ greatly?

8

Costs

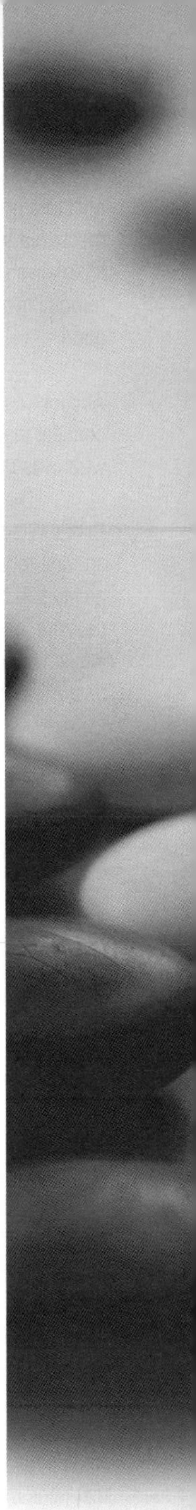

Production costs are a crucial determinant of firms' supply decisions. If the producers of mechanical adding machines discover that no one is willing to pay as much for these obsolete devices as it costs to make them, they will go out of business. On the other hand, if someone invents a better mousetrap that can be made more cheaply than existing ones, he or she will have to build them frantically to keep up with demand. In this chapter, we will develop some ways of thinking about costs that will help in explaining such decisions. We begin by showing how any firm will choose the inputs it uses to produce a given level of output as cheaply as possible. We then proceed to use this information on input choices to derive the complete relationship between how much a firm produces and what that output costs. Possible reasons why this relationship might change are also examined. By the end of this chapter, you should have a good understanding of all the factors that go into determining the cost structure of any firm. These concepts are central to the study of supply and will be useful throughout the remainder of this book.

Basic Concepts of Costs

There are at least three different concepts of costs encountered in economics: opportunity cost, accounting cost, and economic cost. For economists, the most general of these is **opportunity cost** (sometimes called *social cost*). Because resources are limited, any decision to produce more of one good means doing without some other good. When an automobile is produced, for example, an implicit decision has been made to do without 15 bicycles, say, that could have been produced using the labor, steel, and glass that goes into the automobile. The opportunity cost of one automobile is 15 bicycles.

Because it is inconvenient to express opportunity costs in terms of physical goods, we usually use monetary units instead. The price of a car may often be a good reflection of the costs of the goods that were given up to produce it. We could then say the opportunity cost of an automobile is €20 000 worth of other goods. This may not always be the case, however. If something were produced with resources that could not be usefully employed elsewhere, the opportunity cost of this good's production may be close to zero.

Opportunity cost The cost of a good as measured by the alternative uses that are forgone by producing the good.

Accounting cost The concept that inputs cost what was paid for them.

Economic cost The amount required to keep an input in its present use; the amount that it would be worth in its next best alternative use.

Wage rate (w) The cost of hiring one worker for one hour.

Although the concept of opportunity cost is fundamental for all economic thinking, it is too abstract to be of practical use to firms in looking at the costs of their inputs. The two other concepts of cost are directly related to the firm's input choices. **Accounting cost** stresses what was actually paid for inputs, even if those amounts were paid long ago. **Economic cost** (which draws, in obvious ways, on the idea of opportunity cost), on the other hand, is defined as the payment required to keep an input in its present employment, or (what amounts to the same thing) the remuneration that the resource would receive in its next best alternative use.

To see how the economic definition of cost might be applied in practice and how it differs from accounting ideas, let's look at the economic costs of three inputs: labor, capital, and the services of entrepreneurs (owners).

Labor Costs

Economists and accountants view labor costs in much the same way. To the accountant, firms' spending on wages and salaries is a current expense and therefore is a cost of production. Economists regard wage payments as an *explicit cost*: labor services (worker-hours) are purchased at some hourly **wage rate** (which we denote by w), and we presume that this rate is the amount that workers would earn in their next best alternative employment. If a firm hires a worker at, say, €20 per hour, this figure probably represents about what the worker would earn elsewhere. There is no reason for the firm to offer more than this amount, and no worker would willingly accept less. Of course, there are cases in the real world where a worker's wage does not fairly reflect economic cost. The wages of the dunderhead son of the boss exceed his economic cost because no one else would be willing to pay him very much; or, prisoners who are paid €0.50/hour to make license plates probably could earn much more were they out of jail. Noticing such differences between wages paid and workers' opportunity costs can provide an interesting start to an economic investigation; but, for now, it seems most useful to start with the presumption that wages paid are about equal to true economic costs.

Capital Costs

Sunk cost Expenditure that once made cannot be recovered.

Rental rate (v) The cost of hiring one machine for one hour.

In the case of capital services (machine-hours), accounting and economic definitions of costs differ greatly. Accountants, in calculating capital costs, use the historical price of a particular machine and apply some (more or less) arbitrary depreciation rule to determine how much of that machine's original price to charge to current costs. For example, a machine purchased for €1000 and expected to last ten years might be said to "cost" €100 per year, in the accountant's view. Economists, on the other hand, regard the amount paid for a machine as a **sunk cost**. Once such a cost has been incurred, there is no way to get it back. Because sunk costs do not reflect forgone opportunities, economists instead focus on the *implicit cost* of a machine as being what someone else would be willing to pay to use it. Thus, the cost of one machine-hour is the **rental rate** for that machine in the best alternative use. By continuing to employ the machine, the firm is implicitly forgoing the rent someone else would be willing to pay for its use. We use v to denote this rental rate for one machine-hour. This is the rate that the firm must pay for the use of the machine for one hour, regardless of whether the firm owns the machine and implicitly rents it from itself or if it rents the machine from someone else such as Hertz Rent-a-Car. In Chapter 16, we examine the determinants of capital rental rates in more detail. For now, Application 8.1: *Stranded Costs and Deregulation in America* looks at a controversy over costs that has important implications for people's electric and phone bills in America but also other countries where these issues arise.

APPLICATION 8.1 *Stranded Costs and Deregulation in America*

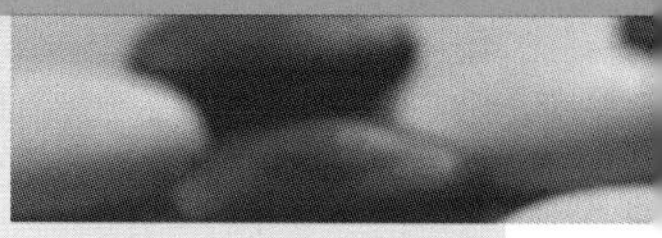

For many years, the electric power, natural gas, and telecommunications industries in the United States were heavily regulated. The prices for electricity or phone service were set by public regulatory commissions in such a way as to allow each firm a "fair" return on its investment. This regulatory structure began to crumble after 1980 as government at both the state and the federal level began to introduce competition into the pricing of electricity, natural gas, and long-distance telephone service. Declining prices for all of these goods raised panic among many tradition-bound utilities. The resulting debate over "stranded costs" will continue to plague consumers of all of these goods for many years to come.

The Nature of Stranded Costs

The fundamental problem for the regulated firms is that some of their production facilities became "uneconomic" with deregulation because their average costs exceeded the lower prices for their outputs in newly deregulated markets. In electricity production, that was especially true for nuclear power plants and for generating facilities that use alternative energy sources such as solar or wind power. For long-distance telephone calls, introduction of high-capacity fiber optics cables meant that older cables and some satellite systems were no longer viable. The historical costs of these facilities had therefore been "stranded" by deregulation, and the utilities believed that their "regulatory contracts" had promised them the ability to recover these costs, primarily through surcharges on consumers.

From an economist's perspective, of course, this plea rings a bit hollow. The historical costs of electricity-generating plants, natural gas transmission pipelines, or telephone cables are sunk costs. The fact that these facilities are currently uneconomic to operate implies that their market values are zero because no buyer would pay anything for them. Such a decline in the value of productive equipment is common in many industries – machinery for making slide rules, 78 rpm recordings, or high-button shoes are also worthless now (though sometimes collected as an antique). But no one suggests that the owners of this equipment should be compensated for these losses. Indeed, the economic historian Joseph Schumpeter coined the term "creative destruction" to refer to this dynamic hallmark of the capitalist system. Why should regulated firms be any different?

Socking It to the Consumer

The utility industry argues that its regulated status does indeed make it different. Because regulators promised them a "fair" return on their investments, they argue, the firms have the right to some sort of compensation for the impact of deregulation. This argument has had a major impact in some instances. In the American state of California, for example, electric utilities were awarded more than $28 billion in compensation for their stranded costs – a figure that will eventually show up on every electricity customer's bill. Natural gas customers have had to pay similar charges as they attempt to bypass local delivery systems to buy lower-priced gas. And everyone has become familiar with the bewildering array of special charges and taxes on their telephone bills, all with the intention of cross-subsidizing formerly regulated firms.

The Future of Deregulation

Allowing firms to charge customers for their stranded costs has reduced the incentives for deregulation in many markets because paying such costs reduces the incentives that consumers have to use alternative suppliers. Moves toward deregulation (especially in electricity production) were further stalled by the Enron debacle that broke in late 2001. As one aspect of that case, the firm was accused of conspiring to manipulate wholesale electricity prices, especially in California during the summer of 2000. Indeed in June 2007 the US Federal Energy Regulatory Commission ordered Enron to repay $1.6 billion of unjust profits.

To Think About

1. Many regulated firms believe that they had an "implicit contract" with state regulators to ensure a fair return on their investments. What kind of incentives would such a contract provide to the firms in their decisions about what types of equipment to buy?
2. How would the possibility that equipment may become obsolete be handled in unregulated markets? That is, how could this possibility be reflected in an unregulated firm's economic costs?

Entrepreneurial Costs

The owner of a firm is entitled to whatever is left from the firm's revenues after all costs have been paid. To an accountant, all of this excess would be called "profits" (or "losses" if costs exceed revenues). Economists, however, ask whether owners (or entrepreneurs) also encounter opportunity costs by being engaged in a particular business. If so, their entrepreneurial services should be considered an input to the firm, and economic costs should be imputed to that input. For example, suppose a highly skilled computer programmer starts a software firm with the idea of keeping any (accounting) profits that might be generated. The programmer's time is clearly an input to the firm, and a cost should be imputed to it. Perhaps the wage that the programmer might command if he or she worked for someone else could be used for that purpose. Hence, some part of the accounting profits generated by the firm would be categorized as entrepreneurial costs by economists. Residual economic profits would be smaller than accounting profits. They might even be negative if the programmer's opportunity costs exceeded the accounting profits being earned by the business.

The Two-Input Case

We will make two simplifying assumptions about the costs of inputs a firm uses. First, we can assume, as before, that there are only two inputs: labor (L, measured in labor-hours) and capital (K, measured in machine-hours). Entrepreneurial services are assumed to be included in capital input. That is, we assume that the primary opportunity costs faced by a firm's owner are those associated with the capital the owner provides.

A second assumption we make is that inputs are hired in perfectly competitive markets. Firms can buy (or sell) all the labor or capital services they want at the prevailing rental rates (w and v). In graphic terms, the supply curve for these resources that the firm faces is horizontal at the prevailing input prices.

Economic profits (π)
The difference between a firm's total revenues and its total economic costs.

Economic Profits and Cost Minimization

Given these simplifying assumptions, total costs for the firm during a period are

$$\text{Total costs} = TC = wL + vK \qquad \{8.1\}$$

where, as before, L and K represent input usage during the period. If the firm produces only one output, its total revenues are given by the price of its product (P) times its total output [$q = f(K,L)$, where $f(K,L)$ is the firm's production function]. **Economic profits** (π) are then the difference between total revenues and total economic costs:

$$\begin{aligned}\pi &= \text{Total revenues} - \text{Total costs}\\ &= Pq - wL - vK = Pf(K,L) - wL - vK \qquad \{8.2\}\end{aligned}$$

Equation 8.2 makes the important point that the economic profits obtained by a firm depend only on the amount of capital and labor it hires. If, as we assume in many places in this book, the firm seeks maximum profits, we might study its behavior by examining how it chooses K and L. This would, in turn, lead to a theory of the "derived demand" for capital and labor inputs – a topic we explore in detail in Chapter 15.

MICROQUIZ 8.1

Young homeowners often get bad advice that confuses accounting and economic costs. What is the fallacy in each of the following pieces of advice? Can you alter the advice so that it makes sense?

1. Owning is always better than renting. Rent payments are just money down a "rat hole" – making house payments as an owner means that you are accumulating a real asset.
2. One should pay off a mortgage as soon as possible. Being able to close out your mortgage and burn the papers is one of the great economic joys of your life!

Here, however, we wish to develop a theory of costs that is somewhat more general and might apply to firms that pursue goals other than profits. To do that, we begin our study of costs by finessing a discussion of output choice for the moment. That is, we assume that for some reason the firm has decided to produce a particular output level (say, q_1). The firm's revenues are therefore fixed at $P \cdot q_1$. Now we want to show how the firm might choose to produce q_1 at minimal costs. Because revenues are fixed, minimizing costs will make profits as large as possible for this particular level of output. The details of how a firm chooses the actual level of output it will produce are taken up in the next chapter.

Cost-Minimizing Input Choice

In order to minimize the cost of producing q_1, a firm should choose that point on the q_1 isoquant that has the lowest cost. That is, it should explore all feasible input combinations to find the cheapest one. This will require the firm to choose that input combination for which the marginal rate of technical substitution (RTS) of L for K is equal to the ratio of the inputs' costs, w/v. To see why this is so intuitively, let's ask what would happen if a firm chose an input combination for which this were not true. Suppose the firm is producing output level q_1 using $K = 10, L = 10$, and the RTS is 2 at this point. Assume also that $w =$ €1, $v =$ €1, and hence that $w/v = 1$, which is unequal to the RTS of 2. At this input combination, the cost of producing q_1 is €20, which is not the minimal input cost. Output q_1 can also be produced using $K = 8$ and $L = 11$; the firm can give up 2 units of K and keep output constant at q_1 by adding 1 unit of L. At this input combination, the cost of producing q_1 is only €19. So, the original input combination of $K = 10, L = 10$ was not the cheapest way to make q_1. A similar result would hold any time the RTS and the ratio of the input costs differ. Therefore, we have shown that to minimize total cost, the firm should produce where the RTS is equal to the ratio of the prices of the 2 inputs. Now let's look at the proof in more detail.

Graphic Presentation

This cost-minimization principle is demonstrated graphically in Figure 8-1. The isoquant q_1 shows all the combinations of K and L that are required to produce q_1. We wish to find the least costly point on this isoquant. Equation 8.1 shows that those combinations of K and L that keep total costs constant lie along a straight line with slope $-w/v$.[1] Consequently, all lines of equal total cost can be shown in Figure 8-1 as a series of parallel straight lines with slopes $-w/v$. Three lines of equal total cost are shown in Figure 8-1: $TC_1 < TC_2 < TC_3$. It is clear from the figure that the minimum total cost for producing q_1 is given by TC_1 where the total cost curve is just tangent to the isoquant. The cost-minimizing input combination is L^*, K^*.

You should notice the similarity between this result and the conditions for utility maximization that we developed in Part 2. In both cases, the conditions for an optimum require that decision-makers focus on relative prices from the market. These prices provide a precise measure of how one good or productive input can be traded for another through market transactions. In order to maximize utility or minimize costs, decision makers must adjust their choices until their own tradeoff rates are

[1]For example, if $TC =$ €100, Equation 8.1 would read $100 = wL + vK$. Solving for K gives $K = -w/vL + 100/v$. Hence the slope of this total costline is $-w/v$, and the intercept is $100/v$ (which is the amount of capital that can be purchased with €100).

brought into line with those being objectively quoted by the market. In this way, the market conveys information to all participants about the relative scarcity of goods or productive inputs and encourages them to use them appropriately. In later chapters (especially Chapter 12), we will see how this informational property of prices provides a powerful force in directing the overall allocation of resources.

An Alternative Interpretation

Another way of looking at the result pictured in Figure 8-1 may provide more intuition about the cost-minimization process. In Chapter 7, we showed that the absolute value of the slope of an isoquant (the RTS) is equal to the ratio of the two inputs' marginal productivities

$$RTS\,(L\ for\ K) = \frac{MP_L}{MP_K} \qquad \{8.3\}$$

The cost-minimization procedure shown in Figure 8-1 requires that this ratio also equal the ratio of the inputs' prices

$$RTS\,(L\ for\ K) = \frac{MP_L}{MP_K} = \frac{w}{v} \qquad \{8.4\}$$

FIGURE 8-1 Minimizing the Costs of Producing q_1 *A firm is assumed to choose capital (K) and labour (L) to minimize total costs. The condition for this minimization is that the rate at which L can be substituted for K (while keeping $q = q_1$) should be equal to the rate at which these inputs can be traded in the market. In other words, the RTS (of L for K) should be set equal to the price ratio w/v. This tangency is shown here in that costs are minimized at TC_1 by choosing inputs K* and L*.*

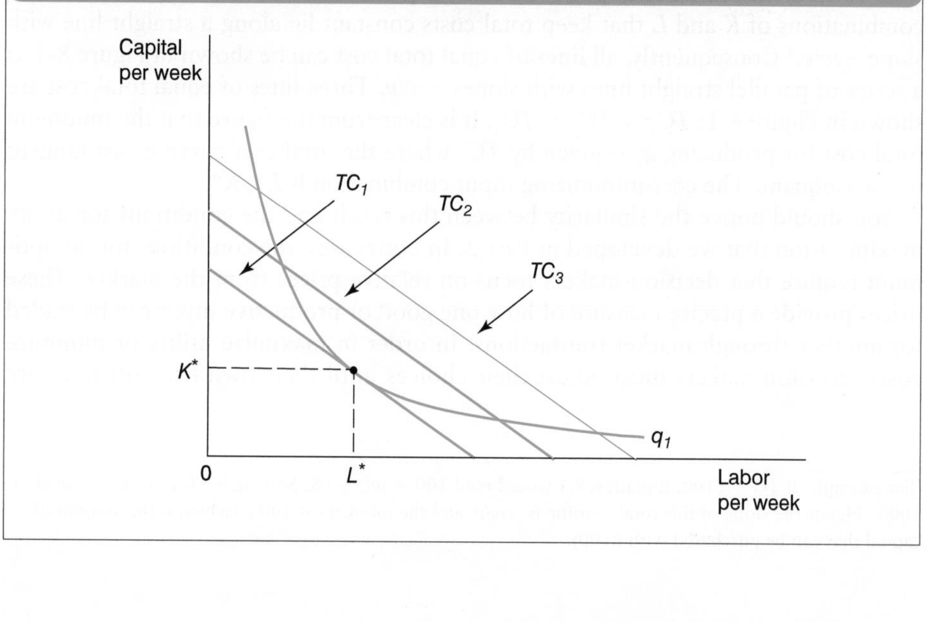

Some minor manipulation of this equation yields

$$\frac{MP_L}{w} = \frac{MP_K}{v} \quad \{8.5\}$$

This condition for cost minimization says that the firm should employ its inputs so that, at the margin, it gets the same "bang for the buck" from each kind of input hired. For example, consider the owner of an orange grove. If MP_L is 20 crates of oranges per hour and the wage is €10 per hour, the owner is getting two crates of oranges for each euro he or she spends on labor input. If tree-shaking machinery would provide a better return on euros spent, the firm would not be minimizing costs. Suppose that MP_K is 300 crates per hour from hiring another tree-shaker and that these wondrous machines rent for €100 per hour. Then each euro spent on machinery yields three crates of oranges and the firm could reduce its costs by using fewer workers and more machinery. Only if Equation 8.5 holds will each input provide the same marginal output per euro spent, and only then will costs be truly minimized.

The Firm's Expansion Path

Any firm can perform an analysis such as the one we just performed for every level of output. For each possible output level (q), it would find that input combination that minimizes the cost of producing it. If input costs (w and v) remain constant for all amounts the firm chooses to use, we can easily trace out this set of cost-minimizing choices, as shown in Figure 8-2. This ray

MICROQUIZ 8.2

Suppose a firm faces a wage rate of 10 and a capital rental rate of 4. In the following two situations, how much of each input should this firm hire in order to minimize the cost of producing an output of 100 units? What are the firm's total costs? How would the firm's total costs change if capital rental rates rose to 10?

1. The firm produces with a fixed-proportions production function that requires 0.1 labor hours and 0.2 machine hours for each unit of output.
2. The firm's production function is given by $Q = 10L + 5K$.

FIGURE 8-2 Firm's Expansion Path *The firm's expansion path is the locus of cost-minimizing tangencies. On the assumption of fixed input prices, the curve shows how input use increases as output increases.*

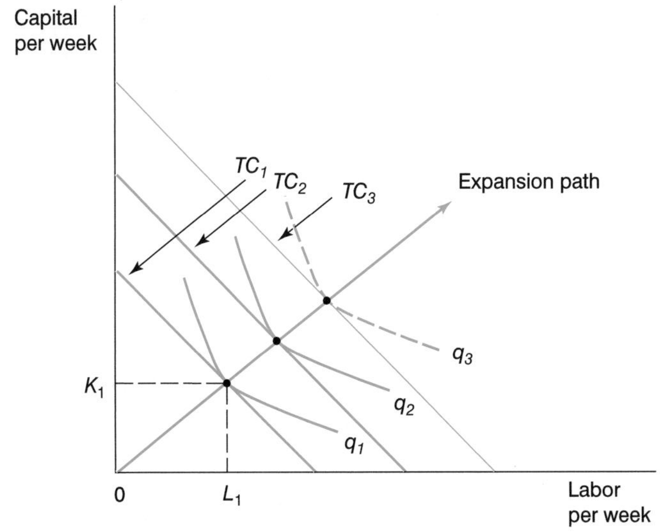

records the cost-minimizing tangencies for successively higher levels of output. For example, the minimum cost for producing output level q_1 is given by TC_1, and inputs K_1 and L_1 are used. Other tangencies in the figure can be interpreted in a similar way. The set of all of these tangencies is called the firm's **expansion path** because it records how input use expands as output expands while holding the per-unit prices of the inputs constant. The expansion path need not necessarily be a straight line. The use of some inputs may increase faster than others as output expands. Which inputs expand more rapidly will depend on the precise nature of production.

Expansion path The set of cost-minimizing input combinations a firm will choose to produce various levels of output (when the prices of inputs are held constant).

Cost Curves

The firm's expansion path shows how minimum-cost input use increases when the level of output expands. The path allows us to develop the relationship between output levels and total input costs. Cost curves that reflect this relationship are fundamental to the

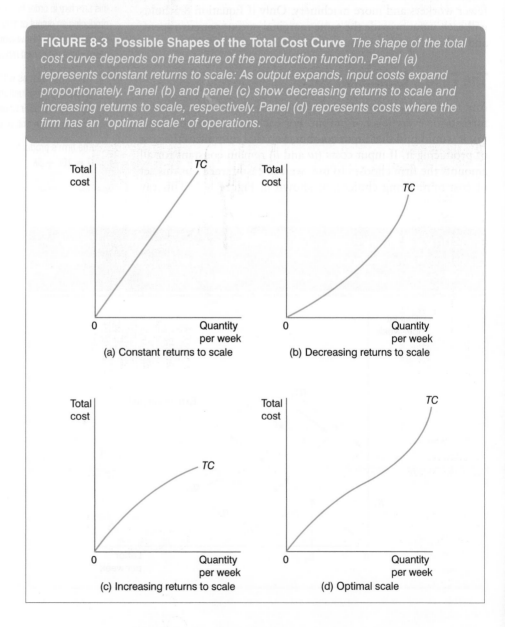

FIGURE 8-3 Possible Shapes of the Total Cost Curve *The shape of the total cost curve depends on the nature of the production function. Panel (a) represents constant returns to scale: As output expands, input costs expand proportionately. Panel (b) and panel (c) show decreasing returns to scale and increasing returns to scale, respectively. Panel (d) represents costs where the firm has an "optimal scale" of operations.*

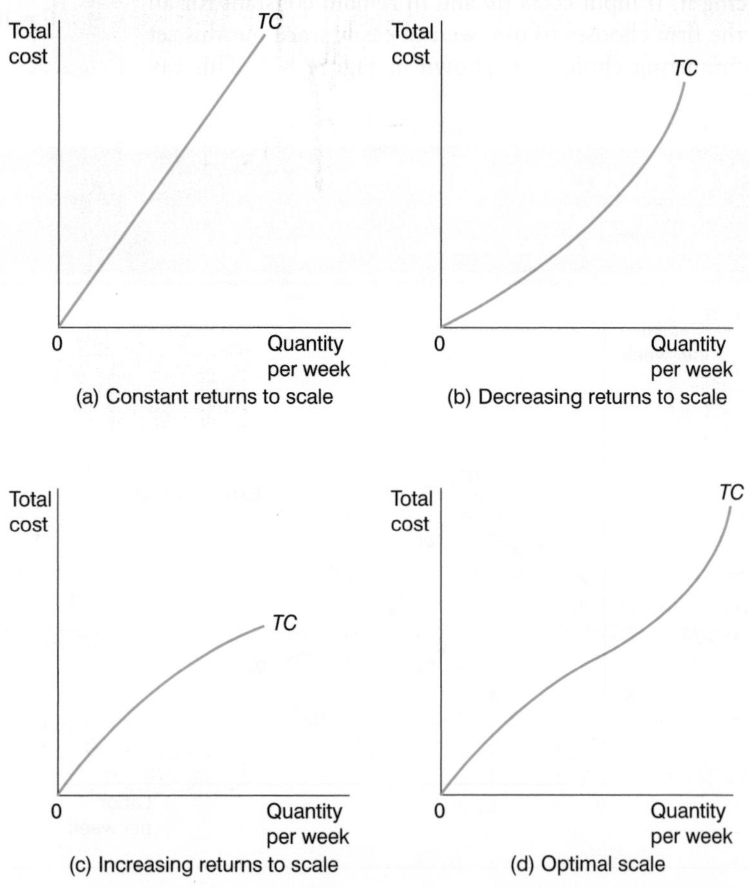

theory of supply. Figure 8-3 illustrates four possible shapes for this cost relationship. Panel a reflects a situation of constant returns to scale. In this case, as Figure 7-3 showed, output and required input use are proportional to one another. A doubling of output requires a doubling of inputs. Because input prices do not change, the relationship between output and total input costs is also directly proportional – the total cost curve is simply a straight line that passes through the origin (since no inputs are required if $q = 0$).[2]

Panel (b) and panel (c) in Figure 8-3 reflect the cases of decreasing returns to scale and increasing returns to scale, respectively. With decreasing returns to scale, successively larger quantities of inputs are required to increase output and input costs rise rapidly as output expands. This possibility is shown by the convex total cost curve in panel (b).[3] In this case, costs expand more rapidly than output. With increasing returns to scale, on the other hand, successive input requirements decline as output expands. In that case, the total cost curve is concave, as shown in panel (c). In this case, considerable cost advantages result from large-scale operations.

Finally, panel (d) in Figure 8-3 demonstrates a situation in which the firm experiences ranges of both increasing and decreasing returns to scale. This situation might arise if the firm's production process required a certain "optimal" level of internal coordination and control by its managers. For low levels of output, this control structure is underutilized and expansion in output is easily accomplished. At these levels, the firm would experience increasing returns to scale – the total cost curve is concave in its initial section. As output expands, however, the firm must add additional workers and capital equipment, which perhaps need entirely separate buildings or other production facilities. The coordination and control of this larger-scale organization may be successively more difficult, and diminishing returns to scale may set in. The convex section of the total cost curve in panel (d) reflects that possibility.

The four possibilities in Figure 8-3 illustrate the most common types of relationships between a firm's output and its input costs. This cost information can also be depicted on a per-unit-of-output basis. Although this depiction adds no new details to the information already in the total cost curves, per-unit curves will be quite useful when we analyze the supply decision in the next chapter.

Average and Marginal Costs

Two per-unit-of-output cost concepts are average and marginal costs. **Average cost** (*AC*) measures total costs per unit. Mathematically,

Average cost Total cost divided by output; a common measure of cost per unit.

$$Average\ Cost = AC = \frac{TC}{q} \qquad \{8.6\}$$

This is the per-unit-of-cost concept with which people are most familiar. If a firm has total costs of €100 in producing 25 units of output, it is natural to consider the cost per unit to be €4. Equation 8.6 reflects this common averaging process.

For economists, however, average cost is not the most meaningful cost-per-unit figure. In Chapter 1, we introduced Marshall's analysis of demand and supply. In his model of price determination, Marshall focused on the cost of the last unit produced because

[2]A technical property of constant returns to scale production functions is that the RTS depends only on the ratio of *K* to *L*, not on the scale of production. For given input prices, the expansion path is a straight line, and cost-minimizing inputs expand proportionally along with output. For an illustration, see the numerical example at the end of this chapter.

[3]One way to remember how to use the terms "convex" and "concave" is to note that the curve in Figure 8-3(c) resembles (part of) a cave entrance and is therefore "concave".

Marginal cost The additional cost of producing one more unit of output.

it is that cost that influences the supply decision for that unit. To reflect this notion of incremental cost, economists use the concept of **marginal cost** (*MC*). By definition then

$$Marginal\ Cost = MC = \frac{Change\ in\ TC}{Change\ in\ q} \qquad \{8.7\}$$

That is, as output expands, total costs increase, and the marginal cost concept measures this increase only *at the margin*. For example, if producing 24 units costs the firm €98 but producing 25 units costs it €100, the marginal cost of the 25th unit is €2: To produce that unit, the firm incurs an increase in cost of only €2. This example shows that the average cost of a good (€4) and its marginal cost (€2) may be quite different. This possibility has a number of important implications for pricing and overall resource allocation.

Marginal Cost Curves

Figure 8-4 compares average and marginal costs for the four total cost relationships shown in Figure 8-3. As our definition makes clear, marginal costs are reflected by the

FIGURE 8-4 Average and Marginal Cost Curves *The average and marginal cost curves shown here are derived from the total cost curves in Figure 8-3. The shapes of these curves depend on the nature of the production function.*

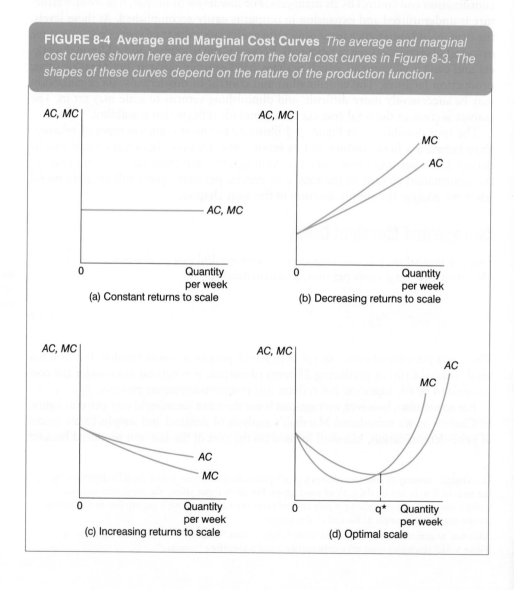

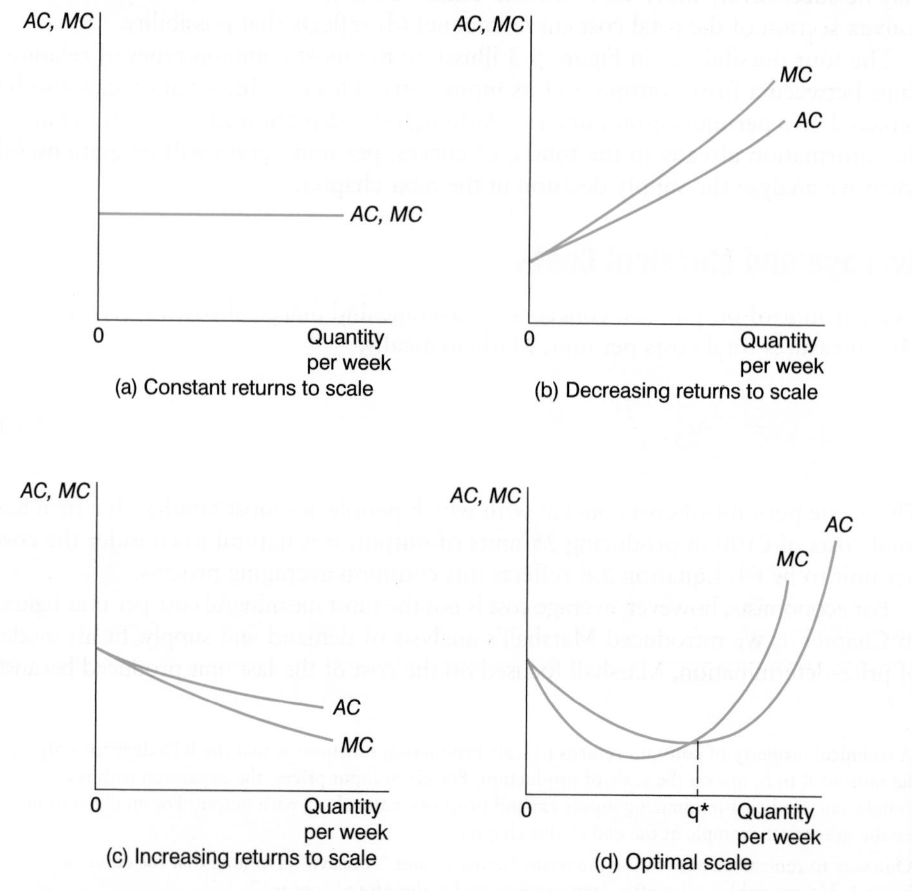

slope of the total cost curve since (as discussed in Appendix to Chapter 1) the slope of any curve shows how the variable on the vertical axis (here, total cost) changes for a unit change in the variable on the horizontal axis (here, quantity).[4] In panel (a) of Figure 8-3, the total cost curve is a straight line – it has the same slope throughout. In this case, marginal cost (*MC*) is constant. No matter how much is produced, it will always cost the same to produce *one more unit*. The horizontal *MC* curve in panel a of Figure 8-4 reflects this fact.

In the case of decreasing returns to scale (panel (b) in Figure 8-3), marginal costs are increasing. The total cost curve becomes steeper as output expands, so, at the margin, the cost of one more unit is becoming greater. The *MC* curve in panel (b) in Figure 8-4 is positively sloped, reflecting these increasing marginal costs.

For the case of increasing returns to scale (panel (c) in Figure 8-3), this situation is reversed. Because the total cost curve becomes flatter as output expands, marginal costs fall. The marginal cost curve in panel (c) in Figure 8-4 has a negative slope.

Finally, the case of first concave, then convex, total costs (panel (d) in Figure 8-3) yields a U-shaped marginal cost curve in panel (d) in Figure 8-4. Initially, marginal costs fall because the coordination and control mechanism of the firm is being utilized more efficiently. Diminishing returns eventually appear, however, and the marginal cost curve turns upward. The *MC* curve in panel (d) in Figure 8-4 reflects the general idea that there is some optimal level of operation for the firm – if production is pushed too far, very high marginal costs will be the result. We can make this idea of optimal scale more precise by looking at average costs.

Average Cost Curves

Developing average cost (*AC*) curves for each of the cases in Figure 8-4 is also relatively simple. The average and marginal cost concepts are identical for the very first unit produced. If the firm produced only one unit, both average and marginal cost would be the cost of that one unit. Graphing the *AC* relationship begins at the point where the marginal cost curve intersects the vertical axis. For panel (a) in Figure 8-4, marginal cost never varies from its initial level. It always costs the same amount to produce one more unit, and *AC* must also reflect this amount. If it always costs a firm €4 to produce one more unit, both average and marginal costs are €4. Both the *AC* and the *MC* curves are the same horizontal line in panel (a) in Figure 8-4.

In the case of decreasing returns to scale, rising marginal costs also result in rising average costs. Because the last unit produced is becoming more and more costly as output expands, the overall average of such costs must be rising. Because the first few units are produced at low marginal costs, however, the overall average will always lag behind the high marginal cost of the last unit produced. In panel (b) in Figure 8-4, the *AC* curve is upward sloping, but it is always below the *MC* curve.

In the case of increasing returns to scale, the opposite situation prevails. Falling marginal costs cause average costs to fall as output expands, but the overall average also reflects the high marginal costs involved in producing the first few units. As a consequence, the *AC* curve in panel (c) in Figure 8-4 is negatively sloped and always lies above the *MC* curve. Falling average cost in this case is, as we shall see in Chapter 13, a principal force leading to the creation of monopoly power for firms with such increasing-returns-to-scale technologies.

[4] If total costs are given by $TC(q)$, then mathematically marginal cost is given by the derivative function $MC(q) = dTC/dq$.

The case of a U-shaped marginal cost curve represents a combination of the two preceding situations. Initially, falling marginal costs cause average costs to decline also. For low levels of output, the configuration of average and marginal cost curves in panel (d) in Figure 8-4 resembles that in panel (c). Once the marginal costs turn up, however, the situation begins to change. As long as marginal cost is below average cost, average cost will continue to decline because the last unit produced is still less expensive than the prior average. When $MC < AC$, producing one more unit pulls AC down. Once the rising segment of the marginal cost curve cuts the average cost curve from below, however, average costs begin to rise. Beyond point q^* in panel (d) in Figure 8-4, MC exceeds AC. The situation now resembles that in panel (b), and AC must rise. Average costs are being pulled up by the high cost of producing one more unit. Because AC is falling to the left of q^* and rising to the right of q^*, average costs of production are lowest at q^*. In this sense, q^* represents an "optimal scale" for a firm whose costs are represented in panel (d) in Figure 8-4. Later chapters show that this output level plays an important role in the theory of price determination. Application 8.2: *The Cost Structure of Small and Medium-Sized Enterprises (SMEs) and Large Enterprises (LEs) within Europe* looks at real life cost structures for various economic sectors in Europe.

Distinction Between the Short Run and the Long Run

Short run The period of time in which a firm must consider some inputs to be fixed in making its decisions.

Long run The period of time in which a firm may consider all of its inputs to be variable in making its decisions.

Economists sometimes wish to distinguish between the **short run** and the **long run** for firms. These terms denote the length of time over which a firm may make decisions. This distinction is useful for studying market responses to changed conditions. For example, if only the short run is considered, a firm may need to treat some of its inputs as fixed because it may be technically impossible to change those inputs on short notice. If a time interval of only one week is involved, the size of a Honda assembly plant would have to be treated as fixed. Similarly, an entrepreneur who is committed to an Internet start-up firm would find it impossible (or extremely costly) to change jobs quickly – in the short run, the entrepreneur's input to his or her firm is essentially fixed. Over the long run, however, neither of those inputs needs to be considered fixed, since Honda's factory size can be altered and the entrepreneur can indeed quit the business.

MICROQUIZ 8.3

Suppose that there are to be ten quizzes in your economics course. You have scored 80 on every one of the first five quizzes.

1. What will happen to your average for the course if your grade falls to 60 on each of the next two quizzes?
2. What will you have to score on the final three quizzes in the course to get your average back to 80?
3. Explain how this example illustrates the relationship between average and marginal costs studied in this section.

Holding Capital Input Constant

Probably the easiest way to introduce the distinction between the short run and the long run into the analysis of a firm's costs is to assume that one of the inputs is held constant in the short run. Specifically, we assume that capital input is held constant at a level of K_1 and that (in the short run) the firm is free to vary only its labor input. For example, a haulage firm with a fixed number of articulated vehicles and loading facilities can still hire and fire workers to change its output. We already studied this possibility in Chapter 7, when we examined the marginal productivity of labor. Here, we are interested in analyzing how changes in a firm's output level in the short run are related to changes in total costs. We can then contrast this relationship to the cost relationships studied earlier, in which both inputs could be changed.

APPLICATION 8.2 *The Cost Structure of Small and Medium-Sized Enterprises (SMEs) and Large Enterprises (LEs) within Europe*

There are many differences in Europe between small and medium-sized enterprises (SMEs) and large enterprises (LEs). We look at the differences in cost structure of these two segments of the economies of Europe to allow you to get a feel how different sectors "experience" costs differently. We also touch on the evolving relationship between LEs and SMEs and how this has affected costs.[1]

SMEs make up 99.8 per cent of all firms, 66 per cent of all employment, and 54 per cent of turnover. As might be expected they differ somewhat in their cost structure from LEs. In Table 1 we present the cost structure for different economic sectors over the 1990s.

Table 1 shows that many costs that firms incur correspond to the economic sector and hence the specific type of economic activities they are involved with. Trade specific firms have very high expenditures on the purchase of goods and services (81.4 per cent). This reflects that they primarily act as intermediaries between the producer of the good or service and the consumer. Value added, and hence profit, is derived from marketing and distribution rather than in the production itself. On the other hand, the other sectors in the table have costs of intermediate purchases similar to each other of 53 per cent or 64 per cent depending on the sector.

Looking at staff costs, however, shows that the trade sector has the smallest costs of all the sectors again reflecting on the nature of the economic activities that sector engages in; selling in shops and other retail outlets require individual staff employees with good social skills in dealing with the public but, in general, these skills are not well paid. Nevertheless, staff costs fell over time in all sectors apart from other services.

Although not clear from Table 1 the intermediate consumption of goods by a firm (and hence part of its variable costs) was significantly higher in LEs than SMEs. However, when we come to look at staff costs the opposite situation holds. This can be put down to the change in strategy adopted by many LEs in the 1990s who increasingly subcontracted out work to SMEs who became part of a new hierarchical structure often tied into a dependency relationship with the LEs.

Another significant cost of enterprises can be interest payments which they have to make to service debts used to help finance their operations. Financial charges that firms had to pay declined

TABLE 1 Cost Structures as a Percentage 1990–1999

EUR-8	*Manufacturing*		*Construction and Civil Engineering*		*Trade*		*Transport and Communications*		*Other Services*	
	90–95	*95–99*	*90–95*	*90–99*	*90–95*	*95–99*	*90–95*	*90–99*	*90–95*	*95–99*
Purchases of Goods and Services	62.4	64.3	61.6	64.0	81.4	81.7	50.8	53.2	55.4	53.9
Staff Costs	21.1	18.5	27.2	24.9	8.2	7.7	34.7	31.6	35.8	35.9
Financial Charges	2.4	1.5	2.6	2.0	1.4	0.9	8.5	6.5	6.2	3.8
Other Costs	12.9	13.0	8.1	8.6	8.2	8.5	6.1	7.5	0.9	1.5
Net Profit Margin	1.3	2.7	0.4	0.5	0.9	1.1	−0.1	1.2	1.7	5.0
Turnover	100.0	100.0	100.0	100.0	100.0	100.0	100.0	100.0	100.0	100.0

(Continued)

throughout the 1990s. This reflected both falling debt across sectors and also the lower cost of servicing debt as both short- and long-term interest rates fell.

The Table, however, hides significant differences between countries. In Sweden, Portugal, Germany, Italy, Denmark, Spain, and Austria the relative share of financial charges was higher for SMEs than LEs. Perhaps SMEs needed a much higher proportion of working capital to be financed through short-term loans. That said, one or two countries such as Germany and Austria, have traditionally a much closer relationship between SMEs and banks resulting in higher levels of debt and hence interest charges.

France, the Netherlands, Finland and Belgium have the opposite characteristics, explained by the fact that LEs have a higher proportion of their debt in the form of bond issues which carry higher interest rate charges than on short-term loans.

All in all, as LEs sub-contracted throughout the 1990s this led to a lower level of working capital which allowed them to direct their energies into activities that created value such as advertising, after-sales service, and R & D. In general after 1993, outsourcing led to a higher spend on intermediate products that had formally been done in-house. With less raw materials transformed inside LEs this implies lees staff needed to work in LEs hence the reduction in staff costs.

Staff costs did fall in SMEs but not to the same extent. Faced with pressure from their "principals", the LEs (see Chapter 17 for an explanation of this term) SMEs relocated, redesigned production techniques and kept wage growth down.

To Think About

1 Do financial charges represent fixed or variable costs? Or can they at one time be fixed and at others variable?

2 To what extent, do you think, does the relationship between LEs and SMEs reflect market structure?

[1]The material presented here follows *European Economy, Financial situation of European enterprises*, Supplement A Economic Trends No. 8/9 August/September 2001, European Commission Directorate-General for Economic and Financial Affairs.

We will see that the diminishing marginal productivity that results from the fixed nature of capital input causes costs to rise rapidly as output expands.

Of course, any firm obviously uses far more than two inputs in its production process. The level of some of these inputs may be changed on rather short notice. Firms may ask workers to work overtime, hire part-time replacements from an employment agency, or rent equipment (such as power tools or automobiles) from some other firm. Other types of inputs may take somewhat longer to be adjusted; for example, to hire new, full-time workers is a relatively time-consuming (and costly) process, and ordering new machines designed to unique specifications may involve a considerable time lag. Still, most of the important insights from making the short-run/long-run distinction can be obtained from the simple two-input model by holding capital input constant.

Types of Short-Run Costs

Because capital input is held fixed in the short run, the costs associated with that input are also fixed. That is, the amount of capital costs that the firm incurs is the same no matter how much the firm produces – it must pay the rent on its fixed number of machines even if it chooses to produce nothing. Such **fixed costs** play an important role in determining the firm's profitability in the short run, but (as we shall see) they play no role in determining how firms will react to changing prices because they must pay the same amount in capital costs no matter what they do.

Fixed costs Costs associated with inputs that are fixed in the short run.

Short-run costs associated with inputs that can be changed (labor in our simple case) are called **variable costs**. The amount of these costs obviously will change as the firm changes its labor input so as to bring about changes in output. For example, although a Honda assembly plant may be of fixed size in the short run (and

Variable costs Costs associated with inputs that can be varied in the short run.

the rental costs of the plant are the same no matter how many cars are made), the firm can still vary the number of cars produced by varying the number of workers employed. By adding a third shift, for example, the firm may be able to expand output significantly. Costs involved in paying these extra workers would be variable costs.

Input Inflexibility and Cost Minimization

The total costs that firms experience in the short run may not be the lowest possible for some output levels. Because we are holding capital fixed in the short run, the firm does not have the flexibility in input choice that was assumed when we discussed cost minimization and the related (long-run) cost curves earlier in this chapter. Rather, to vary its output level in the short run, the firm will be forced to use "non-optimal" input combinations.

This is shown in Figure 8-5. In the short run, the firm can use only K_1 units of capital. To produce output level q_0, it must use L_0 units of labor, L_1 units of labor to produce q_1, and L_2 units to produce q_2. The total costs of these input combinations are given by STC_0, STC_1, and STC_2, respectively. Only for the input combination K_1, L_1 is output being produced at minimal cost. Only at that point is the RTS equal to the ratio of the input prices. From Figure 8-5, it is clear that q_0 is being produced with "too much" capital in this short-run situation. Cost minimization should suggest a south-easterly movement along the q_0 isoquant, indicating a substitution of labor for capital in production. On the other hand, q_2 is being produced with "too little" capital, and costs could be reduced by substituting capital for labor. Neither of these substitutions is possible in

FIGURE 8-5 "Non-optimal" Input Choices Must Be Made in the Short Run
Because capital input is fixed at K_1 in the short run, the firm cannot bring its RTS into equality with the ratio of input prices. Given the input prices, q_0 should be produced with more labour and less capital than it will be in the short run, whereas q_2 should be produced with more capital and less labour than it will be.

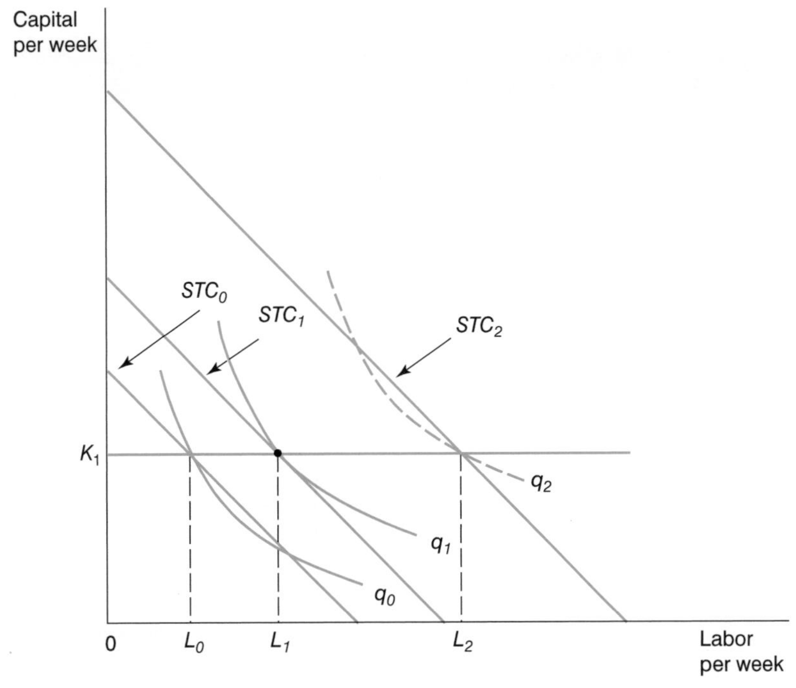

the short run. However, over the long run, the firm will be able to change its level of capital input and will adjust its input usage to the cost-minimizing combinations.

Per-Unit Short-Run Cost Curves

The relationship between output and short-run total costs shown in Figure 8-5 can be used in a way similar to what we did earlier in this chapter to define a number of per-unit notions of short-run costs. Specifically, short-run average cost can be defined as the ratio of short-run total cost to output. Similarly, short-run marginal cost is the change in short-run total cost for a one-unit increase in output. Because we do not use the short-run/long-run distinction extensively in this book, it is unnecessary to pursue the construction of all of these cost curves in detail. Rather, our earlier discussion of the relationship between the shapes of total cost curves and their related per-unit curves will usually suffice.

One particular set of short-run cost curves is especially instructive, however. Figure 8-6 shows the case of a firm with a U-shaped (long-run) average cost curve.

For this firm, long-run average costs reach a minimum at output level q^*, and, as we have noted in several places, at this output level, $MC = AC$. Also associated with q^* is a certain level of capital usage, K^*. What we wish to do now is to examine the short-run average and marginal cost curves (denoted by *SAC* and *SMC*, respectively) based on this level of capital input. We now look at the costs of a firm whose level of capital input is fixed at K^* to see how costs vary in the short run as output departs from its optimal level of q^*.

Our discussion about the total cost curves in Figure 8-5 shows that when the firm's short-run decision causes it to use the cost-minimizing amount of capital input, short-run and long-run total costs are equal. Average costs then are equal also. At q^*, *AC* is equal to *SAC*. This means that at q^*, *MC* and *SMC* are also equal, since both of the average cost curves are at their lowest points. At q^* in Figure 8-6, the following equality holds:

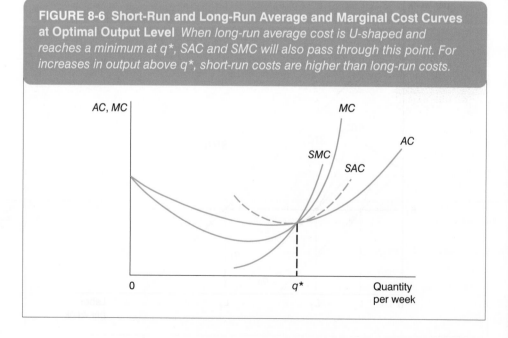

FIGURE 8-6 Short-Run and Long-Run Average and Marginal Cost Curves at Optimal Output Level *When long-run average cost is U-shaped and reaches a minimum at q*, SAC and SMC will also pass through this point. For increases in output above q*, short-run costs are higher than long-run costs.*

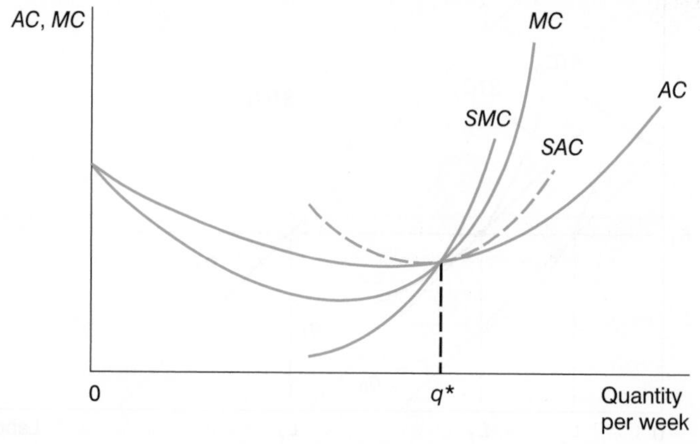

$$AC = MC = SAC(K^*) = SMC(K^*) \quad \{8.8\}$$

For increases in q above q^*, short-run costs are greater than long-run costs. These higher per-unit costs reflect the firm's inflexibility in the short run because some inputs are fixed. This inflexibility has important consequences for firms' short-run supply responses and for price changes in the short run. In Application 8.3: *Congestion on the Roads*, we look at some cases where short-run costs rise rapidly as the output increases.

Shifts in Cost Curves

We have shown how any firm's cost curves are derived from its cost-minimizing expansion path. Any change in economic conditions that affects this expansion path will also affect the shape and position of the firm's cost curves. Three kinds of economic changes are likely to have such effects: changes in input prices, technological innovations, and economies of scope.

Changes in Input Prices

A change in the price of an input tilts the firm's total cost lines and alters its expansion path. A rise in wage rates, for example, causes firms to produce any output level using relatively more capital and relatively less labor. To the extent that a substitution of capital for labor is possible (remember that substitution possibilities depend on the shape of the isoquant map), the entire expansion path of the firm rotates toward the capital axis. This movement in turn implies a new set of cost curves for the firm. A rise in the price of labor input causes the entire relationship between output levels and costs to change. Presumably, all cost curves are shifted upward, and the extent of the shift depends both on how "important" labor is in production and on how successful the firm is in substituting other inputs for labor. If labor is relatively unimportant or if the firm can readily shift to more mechanized methods of production, increases in costs resulting from a rise in wages may be rather small. Wage costs have relatively little impact on the costs of oil refineries because labor constitutes a small fraction of total cost. On the other hand, if labor is a very important part of a firm's costs and input substitution is difficult (remember the case of lawn mowers), production costs may rise significantly. A rise in carpenters' wages raises homebuilding costs significantly.

> **MICROQUIZ 8.4**
>
> Give an intuitive explanation for the following questions about Figure 8-6:
>
> 1 Why does *SAC* exceed *AC* for every level of output except q^*?
>
> 2 Why does *SMC* exceed *MC* for output levels greater than q^*?
>
> 3 What would happen to this figure if the firm increased its short-run level of capital beyond K^*?

Technological Innovation

In a dynamic economy, technology is constantly changing. Firms discover better production methods, workers learn how to do their jobs better, and the tools of managerial control may improve. Because such technical advances alter a firm's production function, isoquant maps – as well as the firm's expansion path – shift when technology changes. For example, an advance in knowledge may simply shift all isoquants toward the origin, with the result that any output level can then be produced with a lower level of input use and a lower cost. Alternatively, technical change may be "biased" in that it may save only on the use of one input – if workers become more skilled, for instance, this saves only on labor

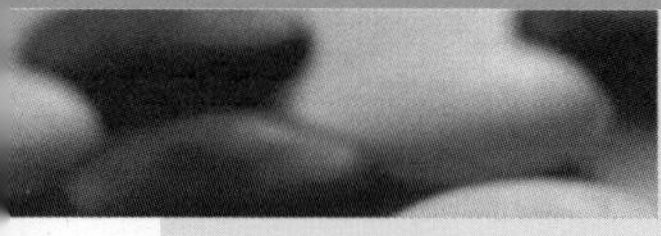

APPLICATION 8.3 *Congestion on the Roads*

Road congestion can also be looked at from the point of view of "externalities" as we do in chapter 18. Here we present a brief introduction as to how the action of individuals can have unintended costs on other individuals and businesses and in doing so examples of rapidly increasing short-run marginal costs. For many facilities such as roads, airports, or tourist attractions, "output" is measured by the number of people that are served during a specified period of time (say, per hour). Because capital (that is roads, terminals, or buildings) is fixed in the short run, the variable costs associated with serving more people primarily consist of the time costs these people incur. In many cases, the increase in these time costs with increasing output can be quite large.

In countries such as the United Kingdom, where car ownership is widespread and it may have been thought that saturation levels of car ownership would have been reached, expansion continues. In 1996 there were 26 million registered vehicles; in 2005 this had jumped to 33 million with the number of kilometers traveled rising from 440 *billion* in 1996 to 500 *billion* in 2006.[1] Much of this is also due to just under a third of households owning a second car.[2]

One (partial) solution that is being put forward by the United Kingdom government is road pricing. In short, the more you drive, the more you pay. This provoked an unprecedented wave of online opposition with over 1.3 million people visiting a UK Government Internet website to sign a 'virtual petition' opposing the idea.

The Feasibility Study of Road Pricing in the UK (2004) looked at a range of scenarios and reported that a significant reduction in congestion could be achieved through a small reduction in peak time traffic.[3] The independent report by Sir Rod Eddington estimated that by 2025, congestion could cost all road users between £22–24 billion more than today, including £10–12 billion to business. The Eddington report said that a distance based marginal social cost national road pricing scheme has potential benefits of around £28 billion per annum by 2025, and could reduce road-building requirement by up to 80 per cent.[4]

While a national UK road pricing scheme is still at the proposal stage one area of the United Kingdom where a road pricing policy has been introduced and tested is in the capital, namely London. In London on February 17, 2003 a £5 per day charge was levied on any vehicle entering a centrally designated area between the hours of 7 am and 6.30 pm Monday to Friday.

Following Blow *et al.* (2003) we present the economics of congestion charging below.[5]

If traffic is light (11 pm to 5 am) then no additional unanticipated costs are imposed by the driver on other drivers (or pedestrians) and this is reflected up to point A in Figure 1 where trips per hour are measured on the horizontal axis and total costs of making these trips is measured on the vertical axis. After point A each extra road user slows down other drivers but does not see this as a cost as it is not included in his or her own personal journey costs. This will lead to too many road users compared to the situation if they had faced such a cost. These costs include petrol costs, individual time costs, increased fumes to pedestrians and those living near to congested roads with associated health expenses (asthma, bronchitis, etc.), increased wear and tear on the road surface through excessive road use, delays to businesses expediting their daily activities, etc.

The results of the charge were quite dramatic at least in the initial stage as Table 1 below demonstrates.

See Leape (2006) for details; however, it is estimated that in the early years of the scheme annual benefits ran to roughly £70 million in 2005 prices and would have been more but for running costs higher than expected.

To Think About

1. In Athens, Greece cars with odd or even number plates are banned on alternate days. Are there any possible weaknesses in such a scheme?
2. Raising the tax on the petrol motorists buy has been put forward as one way to reduce traffic on the roads especially for cars which consume larger amounts of petrol. Do you think this is the most efficient way to go about reducing costs in this case?
3. Given that costs vary throughout the day, should the congestion charge vary throughout the day? What problems might arise in making pricing variable throughout the day?

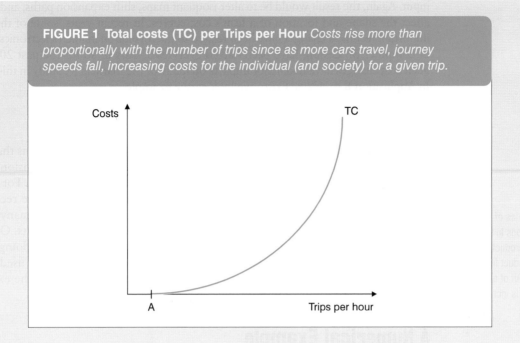

FIGURE 1 Total costs (TC) per Trips per Hour *Costs rise more than proportionally with the number of trips since as more cars travel, journey speeds fall, increasing costs for the individual (and society) for a given trip.*

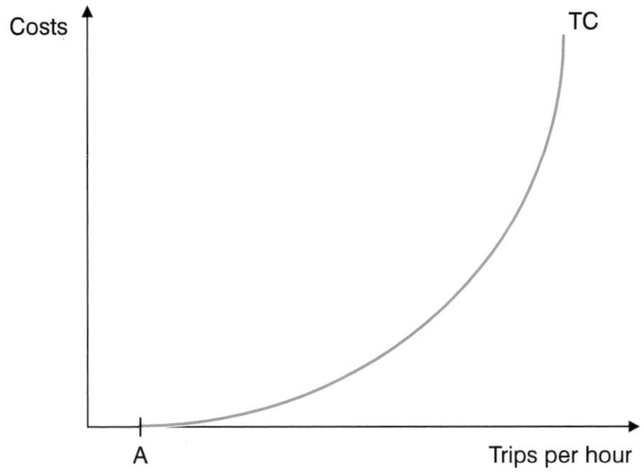

TABLE 1 Impact of the Congestion Charge on Traffic in the Congestion Charging Zone

(in thousands of vehicle-kilometers and per cent)

	2002	2003	Percentage change
Cars	771 (47%)	507 (35%)	−34.0%
Vans	287 (18%)	273 (19%)	−5.0%
Trucks	73 (4%)	68 (5%)	−7.0%
Taxis	256 (16%)	312 (21%)	22.0%
Busses	54 (3%)	65 (5%)	21.0%
Motorcycles	129 (8%)	137 (9%)	6.0%
Bicycles	69 (4%)	89 (6%)	28.0%
All vehicles	1640 (100%)	1451 (100%)	−12.0%

SOURCE: Transport for London. Cited in Leape (2006)[6]

[1]Vehicle Licensing Statistics: http://www.dft.gov.uk/pgr/statistics/datatablespublications/vehicles/licensing/ and Transport Statistics for Great Britain: http:// www.dft.gov.uk/pgr/statistics/datatablespublications/tsgb/.

[2]Transport's role in sustaining the UK's productivity and competitiveness – Sir Rod Eddington, 2006, http://www.hm-treasury.gov.uk/independent_reviews/eddington_transport_study/eddington_index.cfm

[3]See http://www.dft.gov.uk/pgr/roads/roadpricing/feasibilitystudy/.

[4]See http://www.hm-treasury.gov.uk/independent_reviews/eddington_transport_study/eddington_index.cfm.

[5]Laura Blow, Andrew Leicester, and Zoë Smith, "London's Congestion Charge", The Institute for Fiscal Studies, Briefing Note Number 31 (2003).

[6]Jonathan Leape *Journal of Economic Perspectives*, Volume 20, Number 4, Fall 2006: 157–176.

input. Again, the result would be to alter isoquant maps, shift expansion paths, and finally affect the shape and location of a firm's cost curves. In recent years, some of the most important technical changes have been related to the revolution in microelectronics. Costs of computer processing have been halved every two years or so for the past 20 years. Such cost changes have had major impacts on many of the markets we study in this book. In Application 8.4: *Airline Costs*, we look at one example.

Economies of Scope

Economies of scope
Reductions in the costs of one product of a multiproduct firm when the output of another product is increased.

A third factor that may cause cost curves to shift arises in the case of firms that produce several different kinds of output. In such multiproduct firms, expansion in the output of one good may improve the ability to produce some other good. For example, the experience of the Sony Corporation in producing videocassette recorders undoubtedly gave it a cost advantage in producing DVD players because many of the underlying electronic circuits were quite similar between the two products. Or, hospitals that do many surgeries of one type may have a cost advantage in doing other types because of the similarities in equipment and operating personnel used. Such cost effects are called **economies of scope** because they arise out of the expanding scope of operations of multiproduct firms.

A Numerical Example

If you have the stomach for it, we can continue the numerical example we began in Chapter 7 to derive cost curves for Hamburger Heaven (HH). To do so, let's assume HH can hire workers at €5 per hour and that it rents all of its grills from the Hertz Grill Rental Company for €5 per hour. Hence, total costs for HH during one hour are

$$TC = 5K + 5L \qquad \{8.9\}$$

where K and L are the number of grills and the number of workers hired during that hour, respectively. To begin our study of HH's cost-minimization process, suppose the firm wishes to produce 40 hamburgers per hour. Table 8-1 repeats the various ways HH can produce 40 hamburgers per hour and uses Equation 8.9 to compute the total cost of each method. It is clear in Table 8-1 that total costs are minimized when K and L are each 4. With this employment of inputs, total cost is €40, with half being spent on grills (€20 = €5 × 4 grills) and the other half being spent on workers. Figure 8-7 shows this cost-minimizing tangency.

MICROQUIZ 8.5

An increase in the wages of fast-food workers will increase McDonald's costs.

1 How will the extent of the increase in McDonald's costs depend on whether labor costs account for a large or a small fraction of the firm's total costs?

2 How will the extent of the increase in McDonald's costs depend on whether the firm is able to substitute capital for labor?

Long-Run Cost Curves

Because HH's production function has constant returns to scale, computing its expansion path is a simple matter; all of the cost-minimizing tangencies will resemble the one shown in Figure 8-7. As long as $w = v =$ €5, long-run cost minimization will require $K = L$ and each hamburger will cost exactly €1. This result is shown graphically in Figure 8-8. HH's long-run total cost curve is a straight line through the origin, and its long-run average and marginal costs are constant at €1

APPLICATION 8.4 *Airline Costs*

Economists have extensively studied costs for airlines. The interest was sparked by the many changes that have taken place in this industry in recent years, such as deregulation, bankruptcy, and mergers. The analysis of costs provides a first step to understanding the economic forces that have motivated these changes.

Two general findings characterize airlines' costs in the United States. First, notwithstanding rising aviation fuel costs in recent years, costs seem to have fallen rather significantly over the past 30 years, primarily in response to technical improvements in the ways that airlines operate. Second, the level of costs seems to differ substantially among US firms. When average costs are measured on a per-passenger-mile basis, those at high-cost airlines (such as US Air) exceed those at low-cost airlines (Southwest) by more than 50 per cent. Here we look at some underlying reasons for both of these facts.

Technical Improvement in Air Travel

Productivity growth in the air transportation industry over the past 30 years was nearly three times as rapid as in the economy as a whole.[1] During the 1970s and 1980s, a large part of these gains came from the introduction of more efficient aircraft and jet engines. In recent years, however, productivity gains have been derived largely from gains in the ways in which air traffic is handled. Introduction of satellite-oriented global positioning technology gave airlines a much more accurate way to plan routes and airport approaches. Better weather detection together with the adoption of new air traffic control technology allowed planes to make more efficient routings between airports. The advent of on-line reservation systems further reduced costs associated with airlines' operations. Deregulation of airline fares in 1978 (see Application 9.2) also had a major effect on operating efficiency by permitting airlines to adopt pricing schemes that resulted in higher passenger loads per plane.[2]

Differences in Costs among Airlines

Economists have explored a wide variety of reasons that might explain the large variation in airlines' costs. Some of the differences may be explained by the nature of airlines' routes. Airlines that fly longer average distances or operate a greater number of flights over a given network tend to have lower costs. In such cases, the firms can spread the fixed costs associated with terminals, maintenance facilities, and reservation systems over a larger output volume. Characteristics of the fleet of planes operated by various airlines can also affect costs. Firms that operate older fleets or that operate fleets with many different types of planes tend to have higher maintenance and fuel costs. One secret of Southwest Airlines' low costs, for example, is that their fleet is composed almost exclusively of relatively fuel-efficient newer Boeing 737s. Wage costs, especially for pilots, also differ significantly among the airlines. Friction over non-competitive wage contracts has been a repeated cause of labor strife in the airline industry and was one of the primary factors that led to the purchase of United Airlines by its employees in 1991. In exchange for about 55 per cent of the company, United employees agreed to wage concessions that may have reduced costs per passenger mile by as much as 25 cents. A 1999 strike at American Airlines focused on wages to be paid to pilots of new, smaller jet aircraft intended to serve regional airports. During the 2003–2005 period, several major airlines (for example United, US Air, and Northwest) declared bankruptcy, in part motivated by the need to get control over their costs. Bankruptcy proceedings would allow them to do so by permitting the breaking of prior labor contracts that have become non-competitive.

To Think About

1 Some of the improvements in airline productivity resulted from government investments in airports or air-traffic-control systems. Who should pay for such investments – airline travelers or general taxpayers?

(Continued)

2 Airline costs in Europe exceed those in the United States by a substantial margin. Can such differences be the result of differences in technology? What other features of air travel in Europe might explain the differences?

[1]See J. Duke and V. Torres, "Multifactor Productivity Change in the Air Transportation Industry", *Monthly Labor Review* (March 2005): 32–45.

[2]See C. K. Ng and P. Seabright, "Competition, Privatization, and Productive Efficiency: Evidence from the Airline Industry", *Economic Journal* (July 2001): 591–619.

per burger. The very simple shapes shown in Figure 8-8 are a direct result of the constant-returns-to-scale production function HH has.

Short-Run Costs

If we hold one of HH's inputs constant, its cost curves have a more interesting shape. For example, with the number of grills fixed at 4, Table 8-2 repeats the labor input required to produce various output levels (see Table 7-3). Total costs of these input combinations are also shown in the table. Notice how the diminishing marginal productivity of labor for HH causes its costs to rise rapidly as output expands. This is shown even more clearly by computing the short-run average and marginal costs implied by those total cost figures. The marginal cost of the 100th hamburger amounts to a whopping €2.50 because of the 4-grill limitation in the production process.

Finally, Figure 8-9 shows the short-run average and marginal cost curves for HH. Notice that *SAC* reaches its minimum value of €1 per hamburger at an output of 40 burgers per hour because that is the optimal output level for 4 grills. For increases in output above 40 hamburgers per hour, both *SAC* and *SMC* increase rapidly.[5]

TABLE 8-1 Total Costs of Producing 40 Hamburgers per Hour

Output (q)	*Workers (L)*	*Grills (K)*	*Total cost (TC)*
40	1	16.0	€85.00
40	2	8.0	50.00
40	3	5.3	41.50
40	4	4.0	40.00
40	5	3.2	41.00
40	6	2.7	43.50
40	7	2.3	46.50
40	8	2.0	50.00
40	9	1.8	54.00
40	10	1.6	58.00

SOURCE: Table 7-2 and Equation 8.9.

[5]For some examples of how the cost curves for HH might shift, see problem 8.9 and problem 8.10.

FIGURE 8-7 Cost-Minimizing Input Choice for 40 Hamburgers per Hour *Using 4 grills and 4 workers is the minimal cost combination of inputs that can be used to produce 40 hamburgers per hour. Total costs are €40.*

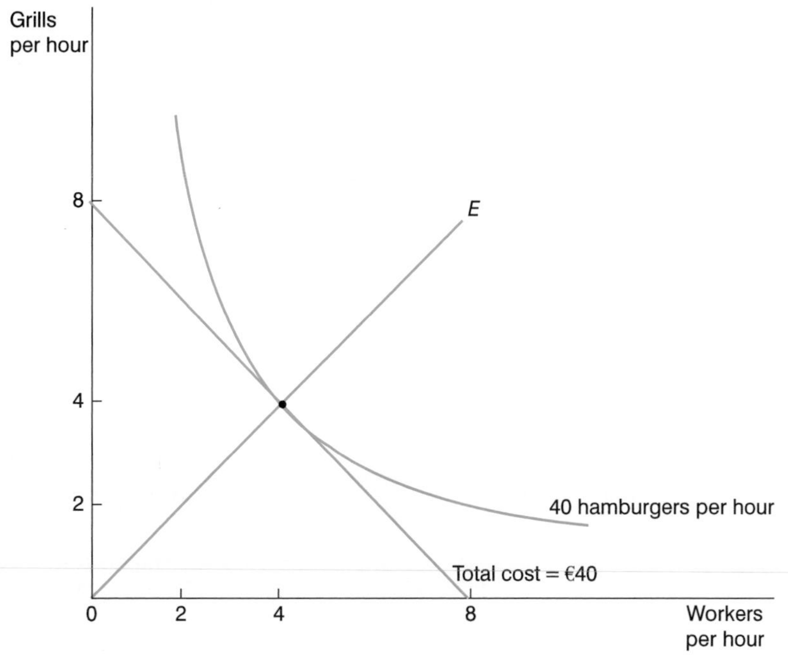

FIGURE 8-8 Total, Average, and Marginal Cost Curves *The total cost curve is simply a straight line through the origin reflecting constant returns to scale. Long-run average and marginal costs are constant at €1 per hamburger.*

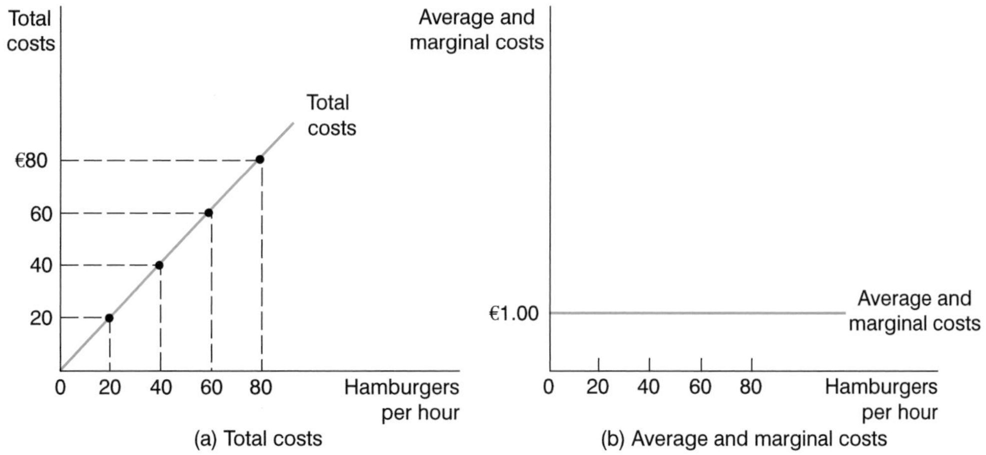

TABLE 8-2 Short-Run Costs of Hamburger Production

Output (q)	*Workers (L)*	*Grills (K)*	*Total cost (STC)*	*Average cost (SAC)*	*Marginal cost (SMC)*
10	0.25	4	€21.25	€2.125	—
20	1.00	4	25.00	1.250	€0.50
30	2.25	4	31.25	1.040	0.75
40	4.00	4	40.00	1.000	1.00
50	6.25	4	51.25	1.025	1.25
60	9.00	4	65.00	1.085	1.50
70	12.25	4	81.25	1.160	1.75
80	16.00	4	100.00	1.250	2.00
90	20.25	4	121.25	1.345	2.25
100	25.00	4	145.00	1.450	2.50

SOURCE: Table 7-3 and Equation 8.9. Marginal costs have been computed using calculus.

FIGURE 8-9 Short-Run and Long-Run Average and Marginal Cost Curves for Hamburger Heaven *For this constant returns-to-scale production function, AC and MC are constant over all ranges of output. This constant average cost is €1 per unit. The short-run average cost curve does, however, have a general U-shape since the number of grills is held constant. The SAC curve is tangent to the AC curve at an output of 40 hamburgers per hour.*

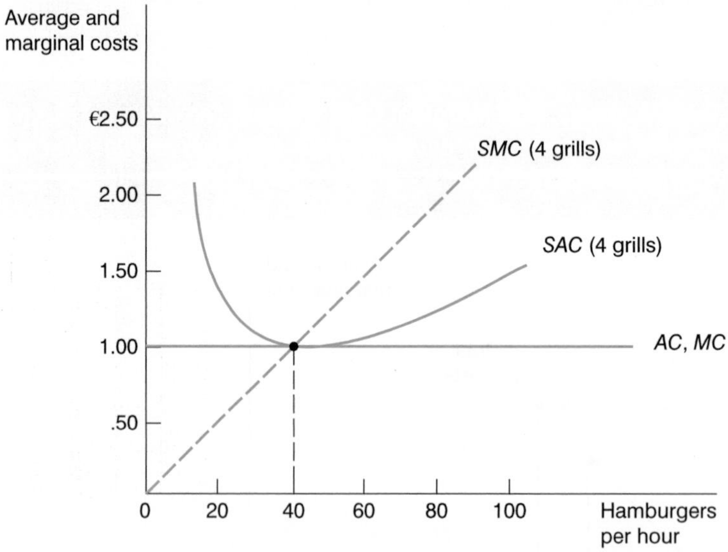

APPLICATION 8.5 *Moving Down the Average Cost Curve – but which one? The example at Renault (II)*

In Chapter 7 we looked at how Renault with the introduction of new production techniques increased productivity at their car plants. This led to a change in the optimal combination of labor and capital and hence the point on the isoquant for any given level of output. Here we present the cost savings that resulted from the introduction of the new production techniques over the classical solution.

To Think About

1 Given the information in Table 1, how will this affect the isocost lines for the Renault car plants where this new technique has been introduced?

2 In introducing this new production technique has the car company moving down its short-run average cost curve or has it moved down its long-run average cost curve? Explain your answer.

TABLE 1 Cost Efficiencies Over the Classic Solution

Percentage gain on previous classic solution	*Description of gain over classic solution*
Gains on Investments: 14%	• A single tool is needed (2 tools for the classical solution)
Gains on direct labor: 40%	• Reduction of handling/ checking by operator: one operator can tend two sites in parallel;
	• Improved productivity (cycle time = 44 seconds compared to 60 seconds for classical solution);
	• Improved quality: retouching ratio is less than 2%.
Gains on material consumption: 25%	• The visions systems deposit the welding wire directly onto the welding plan (suppression of weaving)
Gains on working expenses: (no figure given)	• Suppression of stocks;
	• Suppression of inter-shop handling.

SUMMARY

This chapter shows how to construct the firm's cost curves. These curves show the relationship between the amount that a firm produces and the costs of the inputs required for that production. In later chapters, we see how these curves are important building blocks for the theory of supply. The primary results of this chapter are

- To minimize the cost of producing any particular level of output, the firm should choose a point on the isoquant for which the rate of technical substitution (RTS) is equal to the ratio of the inputs' market prices. Alternatively, the firm should choose its inputs so that the ratio of an input's marginal productivity to its price is the same for every input.

- By repeating this cost-minimization process for every possible level of output, the firm's expansion path can be constructed. This shows the minimum-cost way of producing any level of output. The firm's total cost curve can be calculated directly from the expansion path.
- The two most important unit-cost concepts are average cost (that is, cost per unit of output) and marginal cost (that is, the incremental cost of the last unit produced). Average and marginal cost curves can be constructed directly from the total cost curve. The shape of these curves depends on the shape of the total cost curve.
- Short-run cost curves are constructed by holding one (or more) of the firm's inputs constant in the short run. These short-run costs will not generally be the lowest cost the firm could achieve if all inputs could be adjusted. Short-run costs increase rapidly as output expands because the inputs that can be increased experience diminishing marginal productivities.
- Cost curves shift to a new position whenever the prices of inputs change. Improvements in production techniques also shift cost curves because the same level of output can then be produced with fewer inputs. Expanding one output in a multiproduct firm may reduce costs of some other output when there are economies of scope.

REVIEW QUESTIONS

1 Trump Airlines is thinking of buying a new plane for its shuttle service. Why does the economist's notion of cost suggest that Trump should consider the plane's price in deciding whether it is a profitable investment but that, once bought, the plane's price is not directly relevant to Trump's profit-maximizing decisions? In such a case of "sunk costs", which cost should be used for deciding where to use the plane?

2 Farmer McDonald was heard to complain, "Although my farm is still profitable, I just can't afford to stay in this business any longer. I'm going to sell out and start a fast-food business." In what sense is McDonald using the word *profitable* here? Explain why his statement might be correct if he means profits in the accountant's sense but would be dubious if he is referring to economic profits.

3 Explain why the assumption of cost minimization implies that the total cost curve must have a positive slope: An increase in output must always increase total cost.

4 Suppose a firm had a production function with linear isoquants, implying that its two inputs were perfect substitutes for each other. What would determine the firm's expansion path in this case? For the opposite case of a fixed-portions production function, what would the firm's expansion path be?

5 Consider two possible definitions of marginal cost

a The extra cost involved in producing one more unit of output.

b The cost of the last unit produced.

Are these definitions identical? If not, which is more correct? Why might the other be misleading?

6 Leonardo is a mechanically minded person who always builds things to help him understand his courses. To help in his understanding of average and marginal cost curves, he draws a *TC-q* axis pair on a board and attaches a thin wood pointer by a single nail through the origin. He now claims that he can find the level of output for which average cost is a minimum for any cost curve by the following mechanical process: (1) Draw the total cost curve on his graph; (2) Rotate his pointer until it is precisely tangent to the total cost curve he has drawn; and (3) Find the quantity that corresponds to this tangency. Leonardo claims that this is the

quantity where average cost is minimized. Is he right? For which of the total cost curves in Figure 8-3 would this procedure work? When would it not work?

7 Late Bloomer is taking a course in microeconomics. Grading in the course is based on ten weekly quizzes, each with a 100-point maximum. On the first quiz, Late Bloomer receives a 10. In each succeeding week, he raises his score by ten points, scoring a 100 on the final quiz of the year.

a Calculate Late Bloomer's quiz average for each week of the semester. Why, after the first week, is his average always lower than his current week's quiz?

b To help Late Bloomer, his kindly professor has decided to add 40 points to the total of his quiz scores before computing the average. Recalculate Late Bloomer's weekly averages given this professorial gift.

c Explain why Late Bloomer's weekly quiz averages now have a U shape. What is his lowest average during the term?

d Explain the relevance of this problem to the construction of cost curves. Why does the presence of a "fixed cost" of 40 points result in a U-shaped curve? Are Late Bloomer's average and marginal test scores equal at his minimum average?

8 Beth is a mathematical whiz. She has been reading this chapter and remarks, "All this short-run/long-run stuff is a trivial result of the mathematical fact that the minimum value for any function must be as small as or smaller than the minimum value for the same function when some additional constraints are attached." Use Beth's insight to explain the following:

a Why short-run total costs must be equal to or greater than long-run total costs for any given output level?

b Why short-run average cost must be equal to or greater than long-run average cost for any given output level?

c Whether you can make a definite statement about the relationship between short-run and long-run marginal cost.

9 Taxes can obviously affect firms' costs. Explain how each of the following taxes would affect total, average, and marginal cost. Be sure to consider whether the tax would have a different effect depending on whether one discusses short-run or long-run costs.

a A franchise tax of €10 000 that the firm must pay in order to operate.

b An output tax of €2 on each unit of output.

c An employment tax on each worker's wages.

d A capital use tax on each machine the firm uses.

10 Use Figure 8-1 to explain why a rise in the price of an input must increase the total cost of producing any given output level. What does this result suggest about how such a price increase shifts the *AC* curve? Do you think it is possible to draw any definite conclusion about how the *MC* curve would be affected?

PROBLEMS

8.1 A widget manufacturer has an infinitely substitutable production function of the form

$$q = 2K + L$$

a Graph the isoquant maps for $q = 20$, $q = 40$, and $q = 60$. What is the RTS along these isoquants?

b If the wage rate (w) is €1 and the rental rate on capital (v) is €1, what cost-minimizing combination of K and L will the manufacturer employ for the three different production levels in part a? What is the manufacturer's expansion path?

c How would your answer to part b change if v rose to €3 with w remaining at €1?

8.2 A stuffed-wombat manufacturer determined that the lowest average production costs were achieved when eight wombats were produced at an average cost of €1000 each. If the marginal cost curve is a straight line intersecting the origin, what is the marginal cost of producing the ninth wombat?

8.3 The long-run total cost function for a firm producing skateboards is

$$TC = q^3 - 40q^2 + 430q$$

where q is the number of skateboards per week.

a What is the general shape of this total cost function?

b Calculate the average cost function for skateboards. What shape does the graph of this function have? At what level of skateboard output does average cost reach a minimum? What is the average cost at this level of output?

c The marginal cost function for skateboards is given by

$$MC = 3q^2 - 80q + 430$$

Show that this marginal cost curve intersects average cost at its minimum value.

d Graph the average and marginal cost curves for skateboard production.

8.4 Trapper Joe, the fur trader, has found that his production function in acquiring pelts is given by

$$q = 2\sqrt{H}$$

where q = the number of pelts acquired in a day, and H = the number of hours Joe's employees spend hunting and trapping in one day. Joe pays his employees €8 an hour.

a Calculate Joe's total and average cost curves (as a function of q).

b What is Joe's total cost for the day if he acquires four pelts? Six pelts? Eight pelts? What is Joe's average cost per pelt for the day if he acquires four pelts? Six pelts? Eight pelts?

c Graph the cost curves from part a and indicate the points from part b.

8.5 A firm producing hockey sticks has a production function given by

$$q = 2\sqrt{K \cdot L}$$

In the short run, the firm's amount of capital equipment is fixed at $K = 100$. The rental rate for K is v = €1, and the wage rate for L is w = €4.

a Calculate the firm's short-run total cost function. Calculate the short-run average cost function.

b The firm's short-run marginal cost function is given by $SMC = q/50$. What are the STC, SAC, and SMC for the firm if it produces 25 hockey sticks? 50 hockey sticks? 100 hockey sticks? 200 hockey sticks?

c Graph the SAC and the SMC curves for the firm. Indicate the points found in part b.

d Where does the SMC curve intersect the SAC curve? Explain why the SMC curve will always intersect the SAC at its lowest point.

8.6 Professor Smith and Professor Jones are going to produce a new economics textbook. As true economists, they have laid out the production function for the book as

$$q = \sqrt{SJ}$$

where

q = the number of pages in the finished books

S = the number of working hours spent by Smith

J = the number of working hours spent by Jones

Smith, the less experienced of the two, values her labor at €40 per working hour. She has spent 900 hours preparing the first draft. Jones, whose labor is valued at €80 per working hour, will revise Smith's draft to complete the book.

a How many hours will Jones have to spend to produce a finished book of 150 pages? Of 300 pages? Of 450 pages?

b What is the marginal cost of the 150th page of the finished book? Of the 300th page? Of the 450th page?

8.7 Venture capitalist Sarah purchases two firms to produce widgets. Each firm produces identical products and each has a production function given by

$$q_1 = \sqrt{K_1 \cdot L_1}$$

where

$$i = 1, 2$$

The firms differ, however, in the amount of capital equipment each has. In particular, firm 1 has $K_1 = 25$, whereas firm 2 has $K_2 = 100$. The marginal product of labor is

$$MP_L = 5/(2\sqrt{L})$$

for firm 1, and

$$MP_L = 5/\sqrt{L}$$

for firm 2. Rental rates for K and L are given by $w = v = €1$.

a If Sarah wishes to minimize short-run total costs of widget production, how would output be allocated between the two firms?

b Given that output is optimally allocated between the two firms, calculate the short-run total and average cost curves. What is the marginal cost of the 100th widget? The 125th widget? The 200th widget?

c How should Sarah allocate widget production between the two firms in the long run? Calculate the long-run total and average cost curves for widget production.

d How would your answer to part c change if both firms exhibited diminishing returns to scale?

8.8 Suppose a firm's constant-returns-to-scale production function requires it to use capital and labor in a fixed ratio of two workers per machine to produce ten units and that the rental rates for capital and labor are given by $v = 1$, $w = 3$.

a Calculate the firm's long-run total and average cost curves.

b Suppose K is fixed at 10 in the short-run. Calculate the firm's short-run total and average cost curves. What is the marginal cost of the 10th unit? The 25th unit? The 50th unit? The 100th unit?

8.9 In the numerical example of Hamburger Heaven's production function in Chapter 7, we examined the consequences of the invention of a self-flipping burger that changed the production function to

$$q = 20\sqrt{KL}$$

a Assuming this shift does not change the cost-minimizing expansion path (which requires $K = L$), how are long-run total, average, and marginal costs affected? (See the numerical example at the end of Chapter 8.)

b More generally, technical progress in hamburger production might be reflected by

$$q = (1 + r)\sqrt{KL}$$

where r is the annual rate of technical progress (that is, a rate of increase of 3 per cent would have $r = 0.03$). How will the year-to-year change in the average cost of a hamburger be related to the value of r?

8.10 In our numerical example, Hamburger Heaven's expansion path requires $K = L$ because w (the wage) and v (the rental rate of grills) are equal. More generally, for this type of production function, it can be shown that

$$K/L = w/v$$

for cost minimization. Hence, relative input usage is determined by relative input prices.

a Suppose both wages and grill rents rise to €10 per hour. How would this affect the firm's expansion path? How would long-run average and marginal cost be affected? What can you conclude about the effect of uniform inflation of input costs on the costs of hamburger production?

b Suppose wages rise to €20 but grill rents stay fixed at €5. How would this affect the firm's expansion path? How would this affect the long-run average and marginal cost of hamburger production? Why does a multiplication of the wage by four result in a much smaller increase in average costs?

9

Profit Maximization and Supply

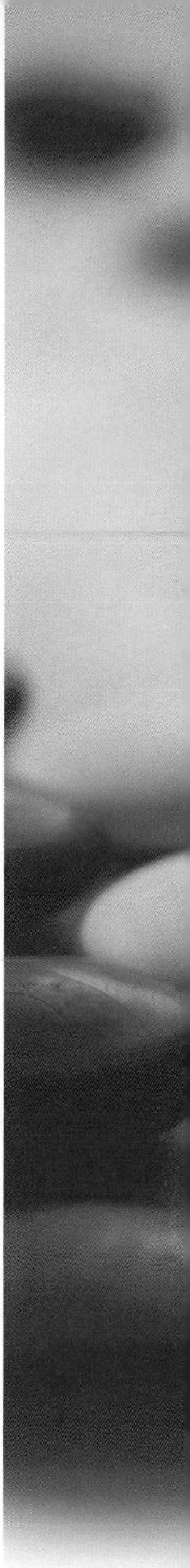

In this chapter, we use the cost curves developed in Chapter 8 to study firms' output decisions. This results in a detailed model of supply. First, however, we briefly look at some conceptual issues about firms.

The Nature of Firms

Our definition of a firm as any organization that turns inputs into outputs suggests a number of questions about the nature of such organizations. These include: (1) Why do we need such organizations? (2) How are the relationships among the people in a firm structured? and (3) How can the owners of a firm ensure that their employees perform in ways that are best from an overall perspective? Because firms may involve thousands of owners, employees, and other input providers, these are complicated questions, many of which are at the forefront of current economic research. In this section, we provide a very brief introduction to the current thinking on each of them.

Why Firms Exist

In order to understand why large and complex firms are needed, it is useful to ask first what the alternative might be. If cars were not produced by big enterprises like Toyota, how would peoples' demands for them be met? One conceptual possibility would be for individual workers to specialize in making each car part and in putting various collections of parts together. Coordination of this process could, at least in principle, be accomplished through markets. That is, each person could contract with the suppliers he or she needed and with people who use the parts being produced. Of course, making all of these contracts and moving partly assembled cars from one place to the next would be very costly. Getting the details of each transaction right and establishing procedures on what to do when something goes wrong would involve endless negotiations. Organizing people into firms helps to economize on these costs.

The British-born economist Ronald Coase is usually credited with the idea that firms arise to minimize transactions costs.[1] In the case of the car industry, for example, the scope of car firms will expand to include parts production and assembly so long as there are gains from handling such operations internally. These gains consist mainly of the ability to invest in machinery uniquely suited to the firm's specific production tasks and to avoid the need to contract with outside suppliers. The fact that such gains exist does not mean that they occur in all cases, however. In some instances, car firms may find it attractive to contract with outside suppliers for certain parts (such as tires, for example), perhaps because such outsiders are very good at making them. In Coase's view, then, a generalized process of seeking the minimum-cost way of making the final output determines the scope of any firm. This insight about transactions provides the starting point for much of the modern theory on how complex organizations arise.

Contracts within Firms

The organization of production within firms arises out of an understanding by each supplier of inputs to the firm about what his or her role will be. In some cases, these understandings are explicitly written out in formal contracts. Workers, especially workers who enjoy the negotiating benefits of trade unions, often arrive at contracts that specify in considerable detail what hours are to be worked, what work rules are to be followed, and what rate of pay can be expected. Similarly, the owners of a firm invest their capital in the enterprise under an explicit set of legal principles about how the capital will be used and how the resulting returns will be shared. In many cases, however, the understandings among the input suppliers in a firm may be less formal. For example, managers and workers may follow largely implicit beliefs about who has the authority to do what in the production process. Or capital owners may delegate most of their authority to a hired manager or to workers themselves. Shareholders in large firms like Microsoft or Rolls Royce do not want to be involved in every detail about how these firms' equipment is used, even though technically they own it. All of these understandings among input suppliers may change over time in response to experiences and to events external to the firm. Much as a basketball or football team tries out new attacking or defensive strategies in response to the competition they encounter, firms also alter the details of their internal structures in order to obtain better long-term results.

Contract Incentives

Some of the most important questions about a firm's contracts with input suppliers concern the kinds of incentives these contracts provide. Only if these incentives are compatible with the general goals of the firm will operations proceed efficiently. The primary reason that such incentives matter is that information about the actual performance of a firm's managers or its employees may be difficult to observe. No boss wants to be constantly looking over the shoulders of all his or her workers to make sure they work effectively. And no shareholder wants to scrutinize managers constantly to make sure they do not waste money. Rather, it may be much less costly to establish the proper incentives in a contract and then leave the individuals involved more or less on their own. For example, a manager who hires a worker to build a brick wall could watch him or her laying each brick to make sure it was placed

[1]R. Coase, "The Nature of the Firm", *Economica* (November 1937): 386–405.

correctly. A much less costly solution, however, would be to pay the worker on the basis of how well the wall was built and how long it took to do the job. In other cases, measuring a worker's output may not be so easy (How would you assess the productivity of, say, a receptionist in a doctor's office?) and some less direct incentive scheme may be needed. Similarly, a firm's owners will need some way to assess how well their hired manager is doing, even though outside influences may also affect the firm's bottom line. Studying the economics behind such incentive contracts at this stage would take us away from our primary focus on supply, but in Chapter 17 we look in detail at how certain information problems in the management of firms (and in other applications) can be solved through the appropriate specification of contract incentives.

Firms' Goals and Profit Maximization

All of these complexities in how firms are actually organized can pose some problems for economists who wish to make some simple statements about how firms supply economic goods. In demand theory, it made sense to talk about the choices made by a utility-maximizing consumer because we were looking only at the decisions of a single person. But, in the case of firms, many people may be involved in supply decisions, and any detailed study of the process may quickly become too complex for easy generalizations. To avoid this difficulty, economists usually treat the firm as a single decision-making unit. That is, the firm is assumed to have a single owner-manager who makes all decisions in a rather dictatorial way. Usually we will also assume that this person seeks to maximize the profits that are obtained from the firm's productive activities. Of course, we could assume that the manager seeks some other goal, and in some cases that might make more sense than to assume profit maximization. For example, the manager of a public junior school would probably not pursue profitability but instead would have some educational goal in mind. Or the manager of the transport and roads department might seek safe roads (or, more cynically, nice contracts for his or her friends). But for most firms, the profit maximization assumption seems reasonable because it is consistent with the owner doing the best with his or her investment in the firm. In addition, profit maximization may be forced on firms by external market forces – if a manager doesn't make the most profitable use of a firm's assets, someone else may come along who will do better and buy them out. This is a situation we explore briefly in Application 9.1: *Corporate Profits Taxes and Private Equity*. Hence, assuming profit maximization seems to be a reasonable way to start our study of supply behavior.

Profit-Maximization

If the manager of a firm is to pursue the simple goal of profit-maximization, he or she must, by definition, make the difference between the firm's revenue and its total costs as large as possible. In making such calculations, it is important that the manager use the economist's notion of costs – that is, the cost figure should include allowances for all opportunity costs. With such a definition, economic profits are indeed a residual over and above all costs. For the owner of the firm, profits constitute an above-competitive return of his or her investment because allowance for a "normal" rate of return is already considered as a cost. Hence, the prospect for economic profits represents a powerful inducement to enter a business. Of course, economic profits may also be negative, in which case the owner's return on investment is lower than he or she could get elsewhere – this would provide an inducement to exit the business.

APPLICATION 9.1 *Corporate Profits Taxes and Private Equity*

Corporate income taxes were first levied in the United States in 1909, about four years before the personal income tax was put into effect. In 2004, corporate income tax revenues amounted to more than $200 billion, more than 10 per cent of total federal tax collections. Many people view the tax as a natural complement to the personal income tax. Under US law, corporations share many of the same rights as do people, so it may seem only reasonable that corporations should be taxed in a similar way. Some economists, however, believe that the corporate profits tax seriously distorts the allocation of resources, both because of its failure to use an economic profit concept under the tax law and because a substantial portion of corporate income is taxed twice.

Definition of Profits

A large portion of what are defined as corporate profits under the tax laws is in fact a normal return to shareholders for the equity they have invested in corporations. Shareholders expect a similar return from other investments they might make: If they had deposited their funds in a bank, for instance, they would expect to be paid interest. Hence, some portion of corporate profits should be considered an economic cost of doing business because it reflects what owners have forgone by making an equity investment. Because such costs are not allowable under tax accounting regulations, equity capital is a relatively expensive way to finance a business.

Effects of the Double Tax

The corporate profits tax is not so much a tax on profits as it is a tax on the equity returns of corporate shareholders. Such taxation may have two consequences. First, corporations will find it more attractive to finance new capital investments through loans and bond offerings (whose interest payments are an allowable cost) than through new stock issues (whose implicit costs are not an allowable cost under the tax law). A second effect occurs because a part of corporate income is double taxed – first when it is earned by the corporation and then later when it is paid out to shareholders in the form of dividends. Hence, the total rate of tax applied to corporate equity capital is higher than that applied to other sources of capital.

Are Private Equity Firms a Problem?

These peculiarities of the corporate income tax are at least partly responsible for the wave of private equity buyouts that have swept financial markets in recent years. Many familiar UK household names such as the AA, Birds Eye, Boots, Pizza Express, and even the makers of Jaffa Cakes, (United Biscuits), have seen their position dramatically change due to private equity firms. These firms acting on behalf of investors, such as pension funds, banks, financial institutions and wealthy individuals, use borrowed funds to acquire most of the outstanding publicly traded shares, and then takeover and manage the firm as a private activity. The larger private equity firms such as KKR, Blackstone and Vestar Capital Partners have borrowed billions of euros in this way and caused great controversy in the UK and elsewhere. Those involved in such buyouts are substituting a less highly taxed source of capital (debt) for a more highly taxed form (equity). Private equity owners reduce the corporation tax payable by the businesses they buy by injecting huge debt into their companies, and the interest paid on these borrowings wipes out any significant taxable profits – thereby minimizing their liability to tax. In 2006, the AA made an operating profit of £252 m, which was 29 per cent higher than in the previous year, but almost all this profit was wiped out by £222.3 m "finance costs" on its £1.7 bn of debts. The AA's accounts show that it ended 2006 with the taxman actually owing it money – £11.9 m.

Often making vast fortunes, those involved in buyouts have had to defend themselves before a wide body of critics, and even Parliament. TUC General Secretary Brendan Barber has challenged the private equity industry on three fronts.[1] The responsibility to the workforce and wider community, particularly after any rationalization; whether private equity can establish long-term sustainability and not just fuel a short-term, debt-based high risk bubble that is waiting to burst; and the transparency that these private firms operate under, particularly with respect to company and executive rewards and tax. He has also warned pension trustees, looking for high returns, to be "very careful" of investing in such ventures.

The industry has countered by arguing that in today's globalized capital and product markets, and particularly in Britain's very open economy, private equity ventures give investors (many of which are pension holders) a good return on their assets that comes from turning sleepy or problematic firms around. This is possible with a dynamic management that can operate away from the constant demands and scrutiny of a public traded firm. However, the tax question is now a growing political issue.[2] Some of private equity's most noted figures Sir Ronald Cohen, Nicholas Ferguson, and Jon Moulton, have said in recent statements that partners in buyout firms ought to pay more tax. Indeed, while Parliament's Treasury Committee fiercely questioned executives from Permira, Kohlberg Kravis Roberts (KKR), 3i, and the Carlyle Group, four of the world's biggest buyout firms, Nicholas Ferguson, the chairman of SVG Capital, added that private-equity executives were "paying less tax than a cleaning lady", and that this was wrong.

To Think About

1 How does the taxation of capital gains to stockholders affect the cost of capital? Can you think of any reasons why it might be a good idea to tax dividends and capital gains at the same rate?

2 A popular slogan of some tax reformers is: "Corporations don't pay taxes, people do". Do you agree? If so, why do we have a separate tax for corporations? Which "people" pay that tax?

[1] A fuller explanation of the TUC's concerns can be found in "*Private Equity – a TUC Perspective*" (2007), TUC Evidence to the Treasury Committee Inquiry, 23 May.

[2] Much of the concern over tax has centered on the fact that most executives make their money in the form of "carried interest" or their share (usually around 20 per cent) of a private-equity fund's profits. This is treated as a capital gain on investment rather than as income from employment, and so attracts a much more lenient tax treatment.

Marginalism

If managers are profit-maximizers, they will make decisions in a marginal way. They will adjust the things that can be controlled until it is impossible to increase profits further. The manager looks, for example, at the incremental (or marginal) profit from producing one more unit of output or the additional profit from hiring one more employee. As long as this incremental profit is positive, the manager decides to produce the extra output or hire the extra worker. When the incremental profit of an activity becomes zero, the manager has pushed the activity far enough – it would not be profitable to go further.

The Output Decision

We can show this relationship between profit-maximization and marginalism most directly by looking at the output level that a firm chooses to produce. A firm sells some level of output, q, and from these sales the firm receives its revenues, $R(q)$. The amount of revenues received obviously depends on how much output is sold and on what price it is sold for. Similarly, in producing q, certain economic costs are incurred, $TC(q)$, and these also depend on how much is produced. Economic profits (π) are defined as

$$\pi q = R(q) - TC(q) \qquad \{9.1\}$$

Notice that the level of profits depends on how much is produced. In deciding what output should be, the manager chooses that level for which economic profits are as large as possible. This process is illustrated in Figure 9-1. The top panel of this figure shows rather general revenue and total cost curves. As might be expected, both have positive slopes – producing more causes both the firm's revenues and its costs to increase. For any level of output, the firm's profits are shown by the vertical distance between these two curves. These are shown separately in the lower panel of Figure 9-1. Notice that profits are initially negative. At an output of $q = 0$ the firm obtains no revenue but must pay fixed costs (if there are any). Profits then increase as some output is produced and sold. Profits reach zero at q_1 – at that output level revenues and costs are equal. Beyond q_1, profits increase, reaching their highest level at q^*. At this level of output, the revenue and cost curves are furthest apart. Increasing output even beyond q^* would reduce total profits – in fact, in this case, increasing output enough (to more than q_2) would eventually result in profits becoming negative. Hence, the graph suggests that a manager who pursues the goal of profit-maximization would opt to produce output level q^*. Examining the characteristics of both the revenue and cost curves at this output level provides one of the most familiar and important results in all of microeconomics.

FIGURE 9-1 Marginal Revenue Must Equal Marginal Cost for Profit Maximization *Economic profits are defined as total revenues minus total economic costs and can be measured by the vertical distance between the revenue and cost curves. Profits reach a maximum when the slope of the revenue function (marginal revenue) is equal to the slope of the cost function (marginal cost). In the figure, this occurs at q^*. Profits are zero at both q_1 and q_2.*

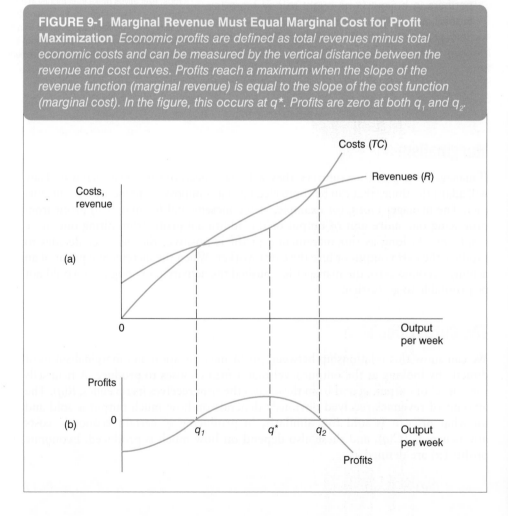

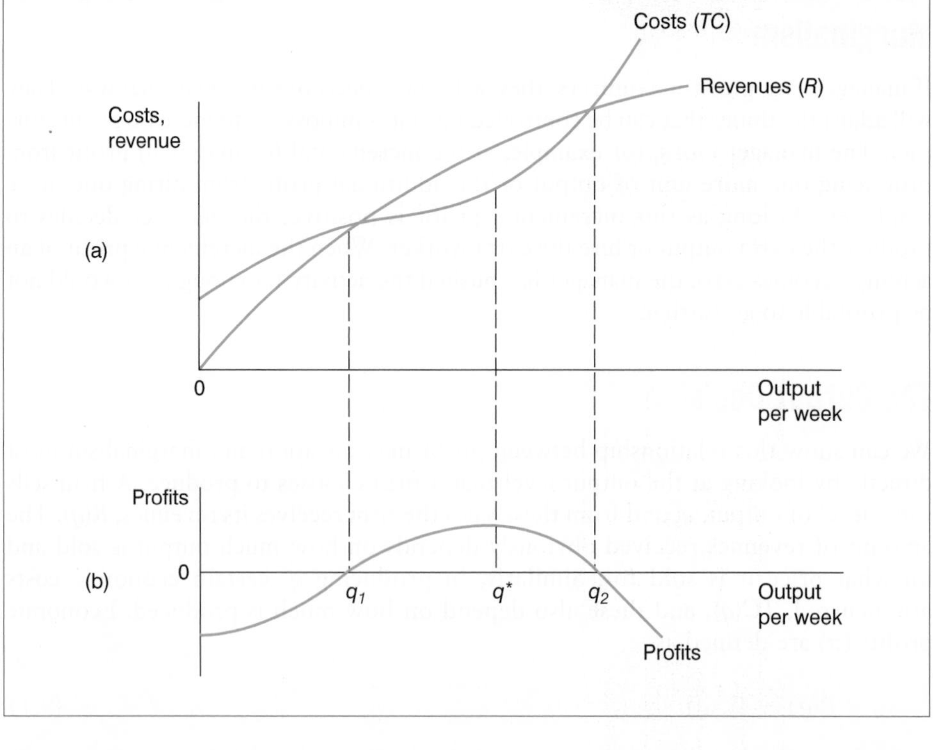

The Marginal Revenue/Marginal Cost Rule

In order to examine the conditions that must hold at q^*, consider a firm that produces slightly less than this amount. It would find that, if it were to increase its output by one unit, additional revenues would rise faster than would additional costs – so, profits would grow. In economic jargon, a firm that opted to produce less than q^* would find that its **marginal revenue** would be greater than its marginal cost – a sure sign that increasing output will raise profits. Increasing output beyond q^* would, however, cause profits to fall. Beyond q^*, the extra revenue from selling one more unit is not as great as the cost of producing that extra unit, so producing it would cause a drop in profits. Hence, the characteristics of output level q^* are clear – at that output, marginal revenue is precisely equal to marginal cost. More succinctly, at q^*

Marginal revenue The extra revenue a firm receives when it sells one more unit of output.

$$\text{Marginal revenue} = \text{Marginal cost} \tag{9.2}$$

or

$$MR = MC \tag{9.3}$$

Because both marginal revenue and marginal cost are functions of q, Equation 9.3 can usually be solved for q^*. For output levels less than q^*, $MR > MC$, whereas, for output levels greater than q^*, $MR < MC$.

A geometric proof of this key proposition can be developed from Figure 9-1. We are interested in the conditions that must hold if the vertical distance between the revenue and cost curves is to be as large as possible. Clearly this requires that the slopes of the two curves be equal. If the curves had differing slopes, profits could be increased by adjusting output in the direction in which the curves diverged. Only when the two curves are parallel would such a move not raise profits. But the slope of the total cost curve is in fact marginal cost and (as we shall see) the slope of the total revenue curve represents marginal revenue. Hence, the geometric argument also proves the $MR = MC$ output rule for profit maximization.[2]

Marginalism in Input Choices

Similar marginal decision rules apply to firms' input choices as well. Hiring another worker, for example, entails some increase in costs, and a profit-maximizing firm should balance the additional costs against the extra revenue brought in by selling the output produced by this new worker. A similar analysis holds for the firm's decision on the number of machines to rent. Additional machines should be hired only as long as their marginal contributions to profits are positive. As the marginal productivity of machines begins to decline, the ability of machines to yield additional revenue also declines. The firm eventually reaches a point at which the marginal contribution of an additional machine to profits is exactly zero – the extra sales generated precisely match

[2]The result can also be derived from calculus. We wish to find the value of q for which $\pi(q) = R(q) - TC(q)$ is as large as possible. The first order condition for a maximum is

$$\frac{d\pi(q)}{dq} = \frac{dR(q)}{dq} - \frac{dTC(q)}{dq} = MR(q) - MC(q) = 0$$

Hence the profit-maximizing level for q solves the equation $MR(q) = MC(q)$. To be a true maximum, the second order conditions require that at the optimal value of q, profits be diminishing for increases in q.

the costs of the extra machines. The firm should not expand the rental of machines beyond this point. In Chapter 15, we look at such hiring decisions in more detail.

Marginal Revenue

Price taker A firm or individual whose decisions regarding buying or selling have no effect on the prevailing market price of a good.

It is the revenue from selling one more unit of output that is relevant to a profit-maximizing firm. If a firm can sell all it wishes without affecting market price – that is, if the firm is a **price taker** – the market price will indeed be the extra revenue obtained from selling one more unit. In other words, if a firm's output decisions do not affect market price, marginal revenue is equal to price. Suppose a firm was selling 50 widgets at €1 each. Then total revenues would be €50. If selling one more widget does not affect price, that additional widget will also bring in €1 and total revenue will rise to €51. Marginal revenue from the 51st widget will be €1 (= €51 − €50). For a firm whose output decisions do not affect market price, we therefore have

$$MR = P \tag{9.4}$$

Marginal Revenue for a Downward-Sloping Demand Curve

A firm may not always be able to sell all it wants at the prevailing market price. If it faces a downward-sloping demand curve for its product, it can sell more only by reducing its selling price. In this case, marginal revenue will be less than market price. To see why, assume in our prior example that to sell the 51st widget the firm must reduce the price of all its widgets to €.99. Total revenues are now €50.49 (= €0.99 × 51), and the marginal revenue from the 51st widget is only €0.49 (= €50.49 − €50.00). Even though the 51st widget sells for €0.99, the extra revenue obtained from selling the widget is a net gain of only €0.49 (a €0.99 gain on the 51st widget less a €0.50 reduction in revenue from charging one penny less for each of the first 50). When selling one more unit causes market price to decline, marginal revenue is less than market price:

$$MR < P \tag{9.5}$$

Firms that must reduce their prices to sell more of their products (that is, firms facing a downward-sloping demand curve) must take this fact into account in deciding how to obtain maximum profits.

MICROQUIZ 9.1

Use the marginal revenue/marginal cost rule to explain why each of the following purported rules for obtaining maximum profits is *incorrect*.

1. Maximum profits can be found by looking for that output for which profit per unit (that is, price minus average cost) is as large as possible.
2. Because the firm is a price taker, the scheme outlined in point 1 can be made even more precise – maximum profits may be found by choosing that output level for which average cost is as small as possible. That is, the firm should produce at the low point of its average-cost curve.

A Numerical Example

The result that marginal revenue is less than price for a downward-sloping demand curve is illustrated with a numerical example in Table 9-1. There, we have recorded the quantity of, say, CDs demanded from a particular shop per week (q), their price (P), total revenues from CD sales ($P \cdot q$), and marginal revenue (MR) for a simple linear demand curve of the form

$$q = 10 - P \tag{9.6}$$

Total revenue from CD sales reaches a maximum at $q = 5$, $P = 5$. For $q > 5$, total revenues decline. Increasing sales beyond five per week actually causes marginal revenue to be negative.

In Figure 9-2, we have drawn this hypothetical demand curve and can use the figure to illustrate the marginal revenue concept. Consider, for example, the extra revenue obtained if the firm sells four CDs instead of three. When output is three, the market price per CD is €7 and total revenues ($P \cdot q$) are €21. These revenues are shown by the area of the rectangle P^*Aq^*0. If the firm produces four CDs per week instead, price must be reduced to €6 to sell this increased output level. Now total revenue is €24, illustrated by the area of the rectangle $P^{**}Bq^{**}0$. A comparison of the two revenue rectangles shows why the marginal revenue obtained by producing the fourth CD is less than its price. The sale of this CD does indeed increase revenue by the price at which it sells (€6). Revenue increases by the area of the darkly shaded rectangle in Figure 9-2. But, to sell the fourth CD, the firm must reduce its selling price from €7 to €6 on the first three CDs sold per week. That price reduction causes a fall in revenue of €3, shown as the area of the lightly shaded rectangle in Figure 9-2.

The net result is an increase in revenue of only €3 (€6 − €3), rather than the gain of €6 that would be calculated if only the sale of the fourth CD is considered in isolation. The marginal revenue for other points in this hypothetical demand curve could also be illustrated. In particular, if you draw the case of a firm producing six CDs instead of five, you will see that marginal revenue from the sixth CD is negative. Although the sixth CD itself sells for €4, selling it requires the firm to reduce price by €1 on the other five CDs it sells. Hence, marginal revenue is – €1 (= €4 − €5).

Marginal Revenue and Price Elasticity

In Chapter 4, we introduced the concept of the price elasticity of demand ($e_{Q,P}$), which we defined as

$$e_{Q,P} = \frac{\text{Percentage change in } Q}{\text{Percentage change in } P} \qquad \{9.7\}$$

TABLE 9-1 Total and Marginal Revenue for CDs ($q = 10 - P$)

Price (P)	Quantity (q)	Total revenue ($P \cdot q$)	Marginal revenue (MR)
€10	0	€ 0	
9	1	9	€ 9
8	2	16	7
7	3	21	5
6	4	24	3
5	5	25	1
4	6	24	−1
3	7	21	−3
2	8	16	−5
1	9	9	−7
0	10	0	−9

Although we developed this concept as it relates to the entire market demand for a product (Q), the definition can be readily adapted to the case of the demand curve that faces an individual firm. We define the price elasticity of demand for a single firm's output (q) as

$$e_{q,P} = \frac{\text{Percentage change in } q}{\text{Percentage change in } P} \qquad \{9.8\}$$

where P now refers to the price at which the firm's output sells.[3]

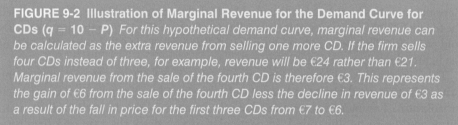

FIGURE 9-2 Illustration of Marginal Revenue for the Demand Curve for CDs ($q = 10 - P$) *For this hypothetical demand curve, marginal revenue can be calculated as the extra revenue from selling one more CD. If the firm sells four CDs instead of three, for example, revenue will be €24 rather than €21. Marginal revenue from the sale of the fourth CD is therefore €3. This represents the gain of €6 from the sale of the fourth CD less the decline in revenue of €3 as a result of the fall in price for the first three CDs from €7 to €6.*

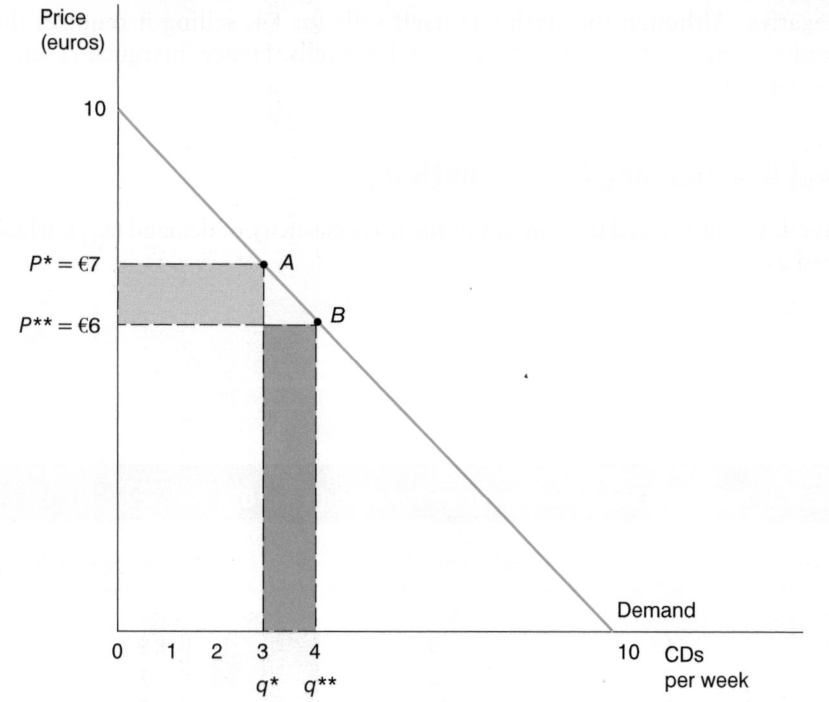

[3]This definition assumes that competitors' prices do not change when the firm varies its own price. Under such a definition, the demand curve facing a single firm may be quite elastic, even if the demand curve for the market as a whole is not. Indeed, if other firms are willing to supply all that consumers want to buy at a particular price, the firm cannot raise its price above that level without losing all its sales. Such behavior by rivals would therefore force price-taking behavior on the firm (see the discussion in the next section). For a more complete discussion of interfirm price competition, see Chapter 14.

Our discussion in Chapter 4 about the relationship between elasticity and total expenditures also carries over to the case of a single firm. Total spending on the good ($P \cdot q$) is now the same as total revenue for the firm. If demand facing the firm is inelastic ($0 \geq e_{q,P} > -1$), a rise in price will cause total revenues to rise. But, if this demand is elastic ($e_{q,P} < -1$), a rise in price will result in smaller total revenues. Clearly, therefore, there is a connection between the price elasticity and marginal revenue concepts. However, because price elasticity concerns reactions to changing prices whereas marginal revenue concerns the effect of changes in quantity sold, we must be careful to clarify exactly what this connection is.

Table 9-2 summarizes the connection between the price elasticity of the demand curve facing a firm and marginal revenue. Let's work through the entries in the table. When demand is elastic ($e_{q,P} < -1$), a fall in price raises quantity sold to such an extent that total revenues rise. Hence, in this case, an increase in quantity sold lowers price and thereby raises total revenue – marginal revenue is positive ($MR > 0$). When demand is inelastic ($0 \geq e_{q,P} > -1$), a fall in price, although it allows a greater quantity to be sold, reduces total revenue. Since an increase in output causes price and total revenue to decline, *MR* is negative. Finally, if demand is unit elastic ($e_{q,P} = -1$), total revenue remains constant for movements along the demand curve, so *MR* is zero. More generally, the precise relation between *MR* and price elasticity is given by:

$$MR = P\left(1 + \frac{1}{e_{q,P}}\right) \quad \{9.9\}$$

and all of the relationships in Table 9-2 can be derived from this basic equation. For example, if demand is elastic ($e_{q,P} < -1$), Equation 9-9 shows that *MR* is positive. Indeed, if demand is infinitely elastic ($e_{q,P} = -\infty$), *MR* will equal price since, as we showed before, the firm is a price taker and cannot affect the price it receives.

To see how Equation 9.9 might be used in practice, suppose that a firm knows that the elasticity of demand for its product is –2. It may derive this figure from historical data that show that each 10 per cent decline in its price has usually led to an increase in sales of about 20 per cent. Now assume that the price of the firm's output is €10 per unit and the firm wishes to know how much additional revenue the sale of one more unit of output will yield. The additional unit of output will not yield €10 because the firm faces a downward-sloping demand curve: To sell the unit requires a reduction in its overall selling price. The firm can, however, use Equation 9.9 to calculate that the additional revenue

MICROQUIZ 9.2

How does the relationship between marginal revenue and price elasticity explain the following economic observations?

1 There are five major toll routes for cars from New Jersey into New York City. Raising the toll on one of them will cause total revenue collected on that route to fall. Raising the tolls on all of the routes will cause total revenue collected on any one route to rise.

2 A doubling of the restaurant tax from 3 per cent to 6 per cent only in Amherst, Massachusetts, causes meal tax revenues to fall in that town, but a state-wide increase of a similar amount causes tax revenues to rise.

TABLE 9-2 Relationship Between Marginal Revenue and Elasticity

Demand curve	Marginal revenue
Elastic ($e_{q,P} < -1$)	$MR > 0$
Unit elastic ($e_{q,P} = -1$)	$MR = 0$
Inelastic ($e_{q,P} > -1$)	$MR < 0$

yielded by the sale will be €5 [= €10 · (1 + 1/−2) = €10 · 1/2]. The firm will produce this extra unit if marginal costs are less than €5; that is, if $MC <$ €5, profits will be increased by the sale of one more unit of output. Although firms in the real world use more complex means to decide on the profitability of increasing sales (or of lowering prices), our discussion here illustrates the logic these firms must use. They must recognize how changes in quantity sold affect price (or vice versa) and how these price changes affect total revenues.

Marginal Revenue Curve

Marginal revenue curve
A curve showing the relation between the quantity a firm sells and the revenue yielded by the last unit sold. Derived from the demand curve.

Any demand curve has a **marginal revenue curve** associated with it. It is sometimes convenient to think of a demand curve as an *average revenue curve* because it shows the revenue per unit (in other words, the price) at various output choices the firm might make. The marginal revenue curve, on the other hand, shows the extra revenue provided by the last unit sold. In the usual case of a downward-sloping curve, the marginal revenue curve will lie below the demand curve because, at any level of output, marginal revenue is less than price.[4] In Figure 9-3, we have drawn a marginal revenue curve together with the demand curve from which it was derived. For output levels greater than q_1, marginal revenue is negative. As q increases from 0 to

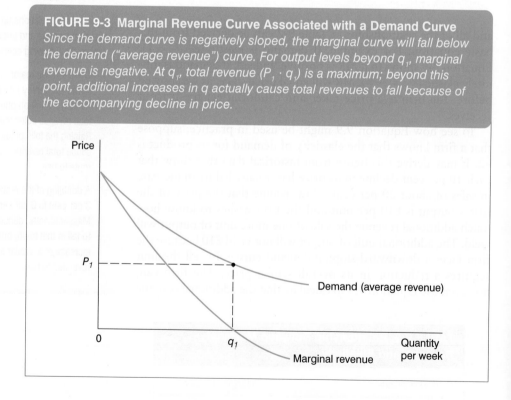

FIGURE 9-3 Marginal Revenue Curve Associated with a Demand Curve
Since the demand curve is negatively sloped, the marginal curve will fall below the demand ("average revenue") curve. For output levels beyond q_1, marginal revenue is negative. At q_1, total revenue ($P_1 \cdot q_1$) is a maximum; beyond this point, additional increases in q actually cause total revenues to fall because of the accompanying decline in price.

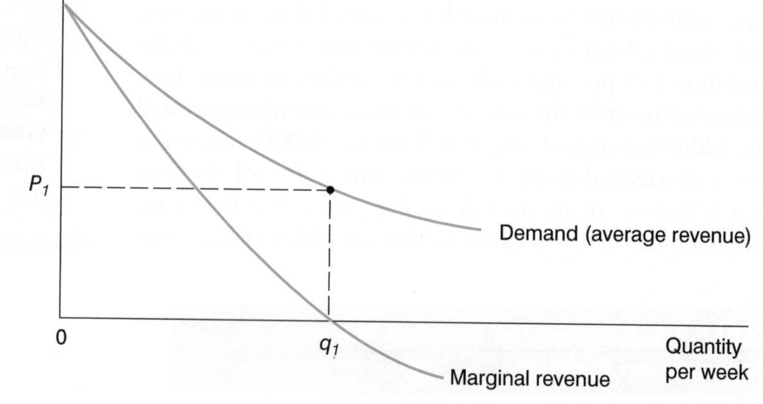

[4]If the firm is a price-taker and can sell all its owners want at the prevailing market price, the demand curve facing the firm is infinitely elastic (that is, if the demand curve is a horizontal line at the market price) and the average and marginal revenue curves coincide. Selling one more unit has no effect on price; therefore, marginal and average revenue are equal.

q_1, total revenues ($P \cdot q$) increase. However, at q_1, total revenues ($P_1 \cdot q_1$) are as large as possible; beyond this output level, price falls proportionately faster than output rises, so total revenues fall.

Shifts in Demand and Marginal Revenue Curves

In Chapter 4, we talked in detail about the possibility of a demand curve's shifting because of changes in such factors as income, other prices, or preferences. Whenever a demand curve shifts, its associated marginal revenue curve shifts with it. This should be obvious. The marginal revenue curve is always calculated by referring to a specific demand curve. In later analysis, we will have to keep in mind the kinds of shifts that marginal revenue curves might make when we talk about changes in demand. Application 9.2: *How Did Airlines Respond to Deregulation?* shows the importance of marginal decisions to the behavior of the airline industry following deregulation.

Supply Decisions of a Price-Taking Firm

In this section, we look in detail at the supply decisions of a single price-taking firm. This analysis leads directly to the study of market supply curves and price determination – a topic that we take up in the next part. Here, however, we are concerned only with the decisions of the owner-manager of a single firm.

Price-Taking Behavior

Before looking at supply decisions, let's briefly explore the price-taker assumption. In the theory of demand, the assumption of price-taking behavior seemed to make sense because we all have had the experience of buying something at a fixed price from a vending machine or from a supermarket. Of course there are situations where you might bargain over price (buying a car or a house), but usually you treat prices as given. The primary reason is that for most of your transactions there are many other buyers doing the same thing. Whether you buy a Coke from a given vending machine or not will make little difference to the owner of the machine, especially since he or she probably owns many others. On the other hand, buying a car or a house is a unique transaction, and you may be able to influence what the seller gets.

The same logic applies to firms. If a firm is producing a good that is just like that produced by many others, it will make little difference how much of it is brought to market because buyers can always buy from another firm. In this case, the firm's only option is to adapt its behavior to the prevailing market price because its decisions won't affect it. On the other hand, if a firm has few competitors, its decisions may affect market price, and it would have to take those effects into account by using the marginal revenue concept. In Part Six we will look at this situation in detail. But before we get there, we will retain the price-taking assumption.

MICROQUIZ 9.3

Use Equation 9.9 and Figure 9-3 to answer the following questions about the relationship between a demand curve and its associated marginal revenue curve.

1. How does the vertical distance between the demand curve and its marginal revenue curve at a given level of output depend on the price elasticity of demand at that output level?
2. Suppose that an increase in demand leads consumers to be willing to pay 10 per cent more for a particular level of output. Will the marginal revenue associated with this level of output increase by more or less than 10 per cent? Does your answer depend on whether the elasticity of demand changes as a result of the shift?

APPLICATION 9.2 *How Did Airlines Respond to Deregulation?*

Under the Airline Deregulation Act of 1978, a number of laws restricting US airline operations were gradually phased out. In Europe too, the liberalization packages implemented by the EU from 1987 to 1997 finally deregulated the previously heavily controlled industry. Regulation of airline fares was reduced or eliminated entirely, and rules governing the assignment of airline routes were relaxed significantly so that airlines had much more choice about which routes to fly. These dramatic changes in the legal environment in which airlines operated provided economists with an ideal opportunity to observe how firms respond to altered circumstances. In general, the responses were quite consistent with the profit-maximization hypothesis.

Marginal Revenue

A clear example of airlines' attention to marginal revenue was the development of new fare structures following deregulation. Prices for unrestricted business class fares dropped little because business people, whose demands are relatively inelastic, usually pay these fares. Consequently, little if any extra revenue would have been earned by the airlines' attempting to lure additional full-fare passengers into flying. For special discount fares, however, it was an entirely different story. Discount fares were generally targeted toward people with highly elastic travel demands (tourists, families traveling together, students, and so forth). In these cases, large price reductions increased passenger demand significantly, thereby improving the passenger loads on many flights. Overall, the increased use of discount fares resulted in a 33 per cent decline in the average price per passenger mile flown.[1] The structure of the price declines ensured that these discount fares generated far more additional revenue for the airlines than an across-the-board fare cut of a similar magnitude would have. It also resulted in a much wider price dispersion among airlines on the same route (averaging 36 per cent of price) than had existed prior to deregulation.[2] This price dispersion provided even further room to focus their pricing efforts on filling planes. The research departments of the major airlines developed computer programs to collect data on what their rivals were charging for a specific trip on a minute-by-minute basis. If an airline found that its rivals were offering prices close to their fares, the demand for their travel would be quite elastic. Modest fare reductions might garner many additional travelers. On the other hand, if an airline discovered that its current fare was the lowest in a given market by a wide margin, it could increase the fare without losing many travelers (demand would be inelastic).

Marginal Cost

Airlines' attention to marginal costs in response to deregulation is also what might have been expected based on the profit-maximization hypothesis. The firms' fleets of aircraft could not be changed significantly in the short run, so airlines altered their route structures to coincide with those aircraft they already had. As Alfred Kahn has observed, from an economic point of view, their planes represented "marginal costs with wings", which could easily be moved around among cities once deregulation came.

Effects of such reallocations by airlines were readily apparent. Service to many small communities (previously required under Civil Aeronautics Board regulation) was curtailed. Flight lengths were generally brought into greater correspondence with the optimal operating characteristics of the aircraft. Many airlines adopted a hub-and-spoke procedure for connecting flights, which also had the effect of allowing them to use different types of aircraft for different routes.

One particularly interesting innovation in airline practices is the creative use of overbooking. The airlines have tried very hard to reduce the losses they suffer from "no shows" by selling more space than is available. Waiting for a flight to leave has come to resemble a frantic auction as airline personnel make increasingly attractive offers to get some passengers to give up their seats voluntarily. The value of these giveaways (free fares to anywhere) shows that airlines gain substantially by filling their planes.

To Think About

1. Airline pricing has led to much grumbling from passengers; a passenger will complain that he "paid twice what the fellow sitting next to me did". Should the government seek to stamp out such price differences?
2. Some critics of airline deregulation charge that it has caused airlines to skimp on safety. Does this claim seem plausible?

[1]See C. Winston, "US Industry Adjustment to Economic Deregulation", *Journal of Economic Perspectives* (Summer 1998): 89–110.

[2]S. Borenstein and N. L. Rose, "Competition and Price Dispersion in the US Airline Industry", *Journal of Political Economy* (August 1994): 653–682.

A numerical example can help illustrate why it may be reasonable for a firm to be a price-taker. Suppose that the demand for, say, corn is given by

$$Q = 16\,000\,000\,000 - 2\,000\,000\,000\,P \tag{9.10}$$

where Q is quantity demanded in bushels per year and P is the price per bushel in euros. Suppose also that there are one million corn growers and that each produces 10 000 bushels a year. In order to see the consequences for price of any one grower's decision, we first solve Equation 9.10 for price:

$$P = 8 - \frac{Q}{2\,000\,000\,000} \tag{9.11}$$

If $Q = 10\,000 \times 1\,000\,000 = 10\,000\,000\,000$, price will be $P =$ €3.00. These are the approximate values for all US corn production – output is about 10 billion bushels per year, and price is about €3 per bushel. Now suppose one grower tries to decide whether his or her actions might affect price. If he or she produces $q = 0$, total output will be $Q = 10\,000 \times 999\,999 = 9\,999\,990\,000$, and the market price will rise to:

$$P = 8 - \frac{9\,999\,990\,000}{2\,000\,000\,000} = 3.00005 \tag{9.12}$$

So, for all practical purposes, price is still €3. In fact, this calculation probably exaggerates the price increase that would be felt if one grower produced nothing because others would surely provide some of the lost production.

A similar argument applies if a single grower thought about expanding production. If, for example, one very hard-working farmer decided to produce 20 000 bushels in a year, a computation similar to the one we just did would show that price would fall to about $P =$ €2.999995. Again, price would hardly budge. Hence, in situations where there are many suppliers, it appears that it is quite reasonable for any one firm to adopt the position that its decisions cannot affect price. In Application 9.3: *Price-Taking Behavior*, we look at a few examples where such behavior seems reasonable but some complications may arise.

Short-Run Profit Maximization

In Figure 9-4, we look at the supply decision of a single price-taking firm. The figure shows the short-run average and marginal cost curves for a typical firm (see Figure 8-6). We also have drawn a horizontal line at the prevailing price for this

APPLICATION 9.3 *Price-Taking Behavior*

Finding examples of price-taking behavior by firms in the real world is not easy. Of course, we are all familiar with our roles as price-taking consumers – you either pay the price that the supermarket wants for bread or do without. But for firms, it is sometimes difficult to know how they are actually making production decisions. One approach is to ask where firms get price information. When such information comes from sources that could not reasonably be affected by the firm's output decisions, price-taking behavior seems plausible. Here we look at two examples.

Futures Markets

Futures contracts are agreements to buy or sell a good at a specified date in the future. Such contracts are actively traded for all major crops, for livestock, for energy resources, for precious and industrial metals, and for a variety of financial assets. The prices specified in these contracts are set by the forces of supply and demand on major commodity exchanges and are reported daily in newspapers. This source of price information is widely used both by speculators and by firms for whom the act of production may take some time. For example, consumers may heat their homes with oil. Each winter, dealers offers to sell a predetermined amount of heating oil at a price determined by the futures price that the dealer must pay. Hence, the price the consumer pays and the price the dealer receives, is primarily determined in a market that is worldwide.

Similar examples of the importance of futures prices are easy to find. One study of broiler chickens,[1] for example, found that firms based their sales decisions primarily on an index of prices from the broiler futures market. Other researchers have found similar results for such diverse markets as the market for electricity, the market for frozen orange juice, and the market for fresh shrimp. In all of these cases, the firms' primary sources of price information are large, organized markets, results from which can be readily obtained from the media or over the Internet. It seems reasonable that any one firm would assume that its decisions cannot affect the price received.

Market Orders

One reason that price-taking behavior may occur is simply because other ways of proceeding may be too costly. For example, when you wish to buy shares of stock from a broker, there are several ways you can specify what price you are willing to pay. The most common procedure is to place a "market order", which states that you are willing to pay the price that prevails when the order arrives. But you can also place other types of orders featuring various limits on what you are willing to pay. Economists who have looked in detail at these various ways of buying stock generally conclude that it makes little difference what a buyer does.[2] Any gains from using complicated buying strategies are counterbalanced by the extra costs involved in using those strategies.

For some firms, a similar logic may prevail. A soybean farmer, for example, may have two options in selling the crop. He or she may take it to the local dealer and accept the price being offered (which, in turn, is based on what the dealer can sell soybeans for in major markets), or the farmer may set conditions on the sale or try to search out other dealers with better offers. But often it may be the case that the gains of more sophisticated sales methods are simply outweighed by the costs of undertaking them. Costs may be minimized by simply taking the price being offered by the local dealer. The dealer, in turn, is probably determining what to pay based on national information about prices.

To Think About

1 When a firm's production takes some time to accomplish, it may prefer to sell its output in the futures market rather than waiting to see what price prevails when the goods are finally ready for market. Would the same logic apply if the quantity produced could be easily adapted to prevailing market conditions?

2 Under what conditions would a firm spend resources searching for a better price for its output? When would it be content with a readily available offer, even though it is possible there is a better price elsewhere?

[1] L.J. Maynard, C.R. Dillon, and J. Carter "Go Ahead, Count Your Chickens: Cross-Hedging Strategies in the Broiler Industry", *Journal of Agricultural and Applied Economics* (April 2001): 79–90.

[2] See D.P. Brown and Z.M. Zhang, "Market Orders and Market Efficiency", *Journal of Finance* (March 1997): 277–308.

firm's product, P^*. This line is also labeled MR to show that this is the marginal revenue for this firm – it can sell all it wants and receive this additional revenue from each additional unit sold. Clearly, output level q^* provides maximum profits here – at this output level, price (marginal revenue) is indeed equal to marginal cost. You can tell that profits are as large as possible at q^* by simply asking what would happen if the firm produced either slightly more or slightly less. For any q less than q^*, price (P^*) exceeds marginal cost. Hence, an expansion in output would yield more in extra revenues than in extra costs – profits would rise by moving toward q^*. Similarly, if the firm opted for $q > q^*$, now marginal cost would exceed P^*. Cutting back on output would save more in costs than would be lost in sales revenue. Again, profits would rise by moving toward q^*.

Showing Profits

The actual amount of profits being earned by this firm when it decides to produce q^* is easiest to show by using the short-run, average-cost curve. Because profits are given by

$$\text{Profits} = \pi = \text{Total revenue} - \text{Total cost} = P^*q^* - STC\,(q^*) \qquad \{9.13\}$$

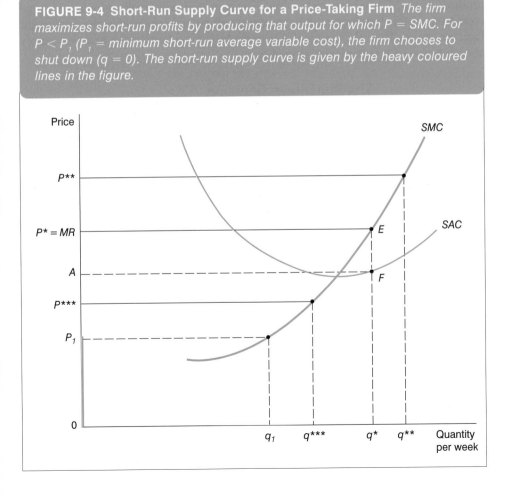

FIGURE 9-4 Short-Run Supply Curve for a Price-Taking Firm *The firm maximizes short-run profits by producing that output for which P = SMC. For P < P_1 (P_1 = minimum short-run average variable cost), the firm chooses to shut down (q = 0). The short-run supply curve is given by the heavy coloured lines in the figure.*

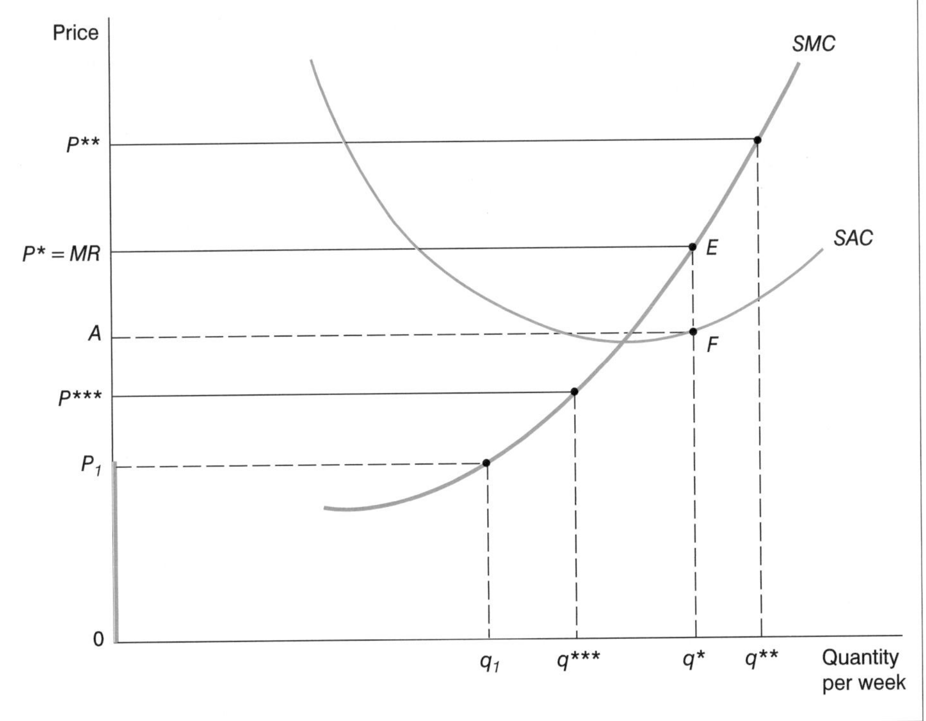

We can factor q^* out of this expression to get

$$\text{Profits} = \pi = q^*\left(P^* - \frac{STC}{q^*}\right) = q^*\,[P^* - SAC(q^*)] \qquad \{9.14\}$$

So, total profits are given by profits-per-unit (price minus average cost) times the number of units sold. Geometrically, profits per unit are shown in Figure 9-4 by the vertical distance *EF*. Notice that the average cost used to calculate these per-unit profits is the actual average cost experienced when the firm produces q^*. Now, total profits are found by multiplying this vertical distance by the number of units sold, q^*. These are therefore given by the area of the rectangle P^*EFA. In this case, these profits are positive because $P > SAC$. These could be zero if $P = SAC$, or even negative if $P < SAC$. Regardless of whether profits are positive or negative, we know that they are as large as possible because output level q^* obeys the marginal-revenue-equals-marginal-cost rule.[5]

The Firm's Short-Run Supply Curve

Firm's short-run supply curve The relationship between price and quantity supplied by a firm in the short run.

The positively sloped portion of the short-run marginal cost curve is the **firm's short-run supply curve** for this price-taking firm. That is, the curve shows how much the firm will produce for every possible market price. At a higher price of P^{**}, for example, the firm will produce q^{**} because it will find it in its interest to incur the higher marginal costs q^{**} entails. With a price of P^{***}, on the other hand, the firm opts to produce less (q^{***}) because only a lower output level will result in lower marginal costs to meet this lower price. By considering all possible prices that the firm might face, we can see from the marginal cost curve how much output the firm will supply at each price – if it is to maximize profits.

MICROQUIZ 9.4

Use the theory of short-run supply illustrated in Figure 9-4 to answer the following questions:

1. How will an increase in the fixed costs that Burger King must pay to heat its outlets affect the firm's short-run supply curve for Whoppers?
2. How will a €10 000 fine imposed on Burger King for littering by its customers affect the firm's short-run shutdown decision? Would your answer change if the fine were €1000 per day, to be ended once the littering stopped?

The Shutdown Decision

For very low prices, firms may not follow the $P = MC$ rule. The firm always has another option in the short run – it can choose to produce nothing. We therefore have to compare the profits obtainable if the firm opts to pursue this shutdown strategy to those obtainable if it follows the $P = MC$ rule. To do so, we must return to the distinction introduced in Chapter 8 between fixed and variable costs. In the short run, the firm must pay its fixed costs (for example, rent on its factory) whether or not it produces any output. If the firm shuts down, it suffers a loss of these fixed costs because it earns no revenues and incurs no variable costs. Can the firm do better than this dismal outcome? Because fixed costs are incurred in either case, the decision to produce must be based on a comparison between the total revenues a firm can receive for its output and the short-run variable costs (*SVC*) it incurs in producing this output. In algebraic terms, the firm will opt to produce something, providing

[5] Technically, the $P = MC$ rule is only a necessary condition for a maximum in profits. The value of q found by applying this rule would not yield maximum profits if the marginal cost curve had a negative slope at q^*. In that case, either increasing or decreasing q slightly would in fact increase profits. For all of our analysis, therefore, we will assume that the short-run marginal cost curve has a positive slope at the output level for which $P = SMC$.

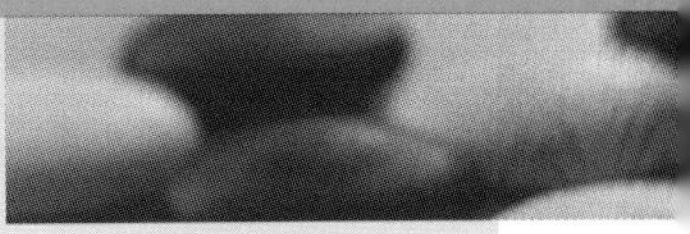

APPLICATION 9.4 *Why Is Drilling for Crude Oil Such a Boom or Bust Business?*

The production of crude oil by small operators provides a number of illustrations of the principles of short-run supply behavior by price-taking firms. Because prices for crude oil are set in international markets, these firms clearly are price takers, responding to the price incentives they face. Drillers face sharply increasing marginal costs as they drill to greater depths or in less-accessible areas. Hence, we should expect oil well activity to follow our model of how price-taking firms respond to price changes.

Some Historical Data

Table 1 shows US oil well drilling activity over the past three decades. The table also shows the average price of crude oil in the various years, adjusted for changing prices of drilling equipment. The tripling of real oil prices between 1970 and 1980 led to a tripling of drilling. In many cases, these additional wells were drilled in high-cost locations (for example, in deep water in the Gulf of Mexico or on the Arctic Slope in Alaska). Clearly, the late 1970s and early 1980s were boom times for oil drillers. As predicted, they responded to price signals being provided through the market.

Price Decline and Supply Behavior

Recessions in 1981 and 1990, combined with vast new supplies of crude oil (from the North Sea and Mexico, for example), put considerable pressure on oil prices. By 1990, real crude oil prices had declined by about 40 per cent from their levels of the early 1980s. US drillers were quick to respond to these changing circumstances. As Table 1 shows, less than half the number of wells were drilled in 1990 as in 1980. Real prices tended to stabilize during the 1990s, ending the decade much where they started. Drilling activity in the United States fell only modestly during the decade.

The Shutdown Decision

The decline in real oil prices during the 1980s also prompted oil well operators to shut down some marginal operations. Especially vulnerable were high-cost wells such as those that used pressurized steam or those that produced fewer than ten barrels per day. These shutdowns reached nearly 20 per cent of all wells before prices stabilized. The shutdown wells also provided a ready source of new supply should prices ever turn upward.

The 2004–2005 Price Increase

Crude oil prices did indeed rise dramatically starting in 2004. By mid-year 2005, the nominal price of crude oil had hit $60 per barrel (a real price of about $37 per barrel). Although drilling did pick up a bit late in 2004, producers responded rather cautiously to this new price, in part because they were not sure it would last. Another factor slowing the price response was the tendency to bring many formerly shutdown wells back on line. With the new higher price, operators found that they could now cover the high variable costs associated with these wells.

To Think About

1. Are US producers of crude oil accurately described as price takers? Isn't most crude oil in the US produced by giant firms like Exxon? (Perhaps some data on the subject would help here.)
2. How can firms continue to drill over 25 000 wells in the US each year? Hasn't all the oil in the US already been found long ago?

TABLE 1 World Oil Prices and Oil Well Drilling Activity in the United States

Year	World Price per Barrel	Real Price per Barrel*	Number of Wells Drilled
1970	$3.18	$7.93	21 177
1980	$21.59	$25.16	70 610
1990	$20.03	$16.30	31 555
2000	$23.00	$16.40	26 981

*NOMINAL PRICE DIVIDED BY PRODUCER PRICE INDEX FOR CAPITAL EQUIPMENT, 1982 = 1.00.
SOURCE: US DEPARTMENT OF ENERGY, WEBSITE: HTTP://WWW.EIA.DOE.GOV.

$$P \cdot q \geq SVC \qquad \{9.15\}$$

or, dividing by q,

$$P \geq SVC/q \qquad \{9.16\}$$

Shutdown price The price below which the firm will choose to produce no output in the short run. Equal to minimum average variable cost.

In words, price must exceed variable cost per unit (that is, average variable cost). In Figure 9-4, the minimum value for average variable cost is assumed to be P_1.[6] This is the **shutdown price** for this firm. For $P \geq P_1$, the firm will follow the $P = MC$ rule for profit maximization (even though profits may still be negative if price is below short-run average cost). In this case its supply curve will be its short-run marginal cost curve. For $P < P_1$, price does not cover the minimum average variable costs of production, and the firm will opt to produce nothing. This decision is illustrated by the heavy-collared segment $0P_1$ in Figure 9-4. The practical importance of shutdown decisions is illustrated in Application 9.4: *Why Is Drilling for Crude Oil Such a Boom or Bust Business?*

Hence, we have developed a rather complete picture of the short-run supply decisions of a price-taking firm. The twin assumptions of profit maximization and price-taking behavior result in a straightforward result. Notice that the information requirements for the firm are minimal. All it needs to know is the market price of the product it wishes to sell and information about the shape of its own marginal cost curve. In later chapters, we will encounter situations where firms need to know much more in order to make profit-maximizing decisions. But, for the moment, we have a very simple baseline from which to study the price-determination process.

[6]For values of q larger than q_1, following the $P = MC$ rule ensures price exceeds average variable cost because for all such values of output marginal cost exceeds average variable cost.

SUMMARY

In this chapter, we examined the assumption that firms seek to maximize profits in making their decisions. A number of conclusions follow from this assumption.

- In making output decisions, a firm should produce the output level for which marginal revenue equals marginal cost. Only at this level of production is the cost of extra output, at the margin, exactly balanced by the revenue it yields.
- Similar marginal rules apply to the hiring of inputs by profit-maximizing firms. These are examined in Chapter 15.
- For a firm facing a downward-sloping demand curve, marginal revenue will be less than price. In this case, the marginal revenue curve will lie below the market demand curve.
- When there are many firms producing the same output, it may make sense for any one of them to adopt price-taking behavior. That is, the firm assumes that its actions will not affect market price. So, marginal revenue is given by that market price.
- A price-taking firm will maximize profits by choosing that output level for which price (marginal revenue) is equal to marginal cost. For this reason, the firm's short-run supply curve is its short-run marginal cost curve (which is assumed to be positively sloped).
- If price falls below average variable cost, the profit-maximizing decision for a firm will be to produce no output. That is, it will shut down. The firm will still incur fixed costs in the short run, so its short-run profits will be negative.

REVIEW QUESTIONS

1 Why do economists assume that firms seek maximum economic profits? Because accounting rules determine what the euro value of profits actually is, why should firms be concerned with the economists' concept of cost? Which notion of profits do you believe is most important to entrepreneurs who are considering starting a business?

2 For its owners, a firm represents an asset that they own. Why would the pursuit of profit maximization by the firm make this asset as valuable as possible?

3 Explain whether each of the following actions would affect the firm's profit-maximizing decision. (Hint: How would each affect *MR* and *MC*?)

a An increase in the cost of a variable input such as labor.

b A decline in the output price for a price-taking firm.

c The imposition of a small fixed fee to be paid to the government for the right of doing business.

d The imposition of a 50 per cent tax on the firm's profits.

e The imposition of a per-unit tax on each unit the firm produces.

f Receipt of a no-strings-attached grant from the government.

g Receipt of a subsidy per unit of output from the government.

h Receipt of a subsidy per worker hired from the government.

4 Sally Greenhorn has just graduated from a prestigious university, but does not have the foggiest idea about her new job with a firm that sells shrink-wrapped dog biscuits. She has been given responsibility for a new line of turkey-flavored biscuits and must decide how many to produce. She opts for the following strategy: (1) Begin by hiring one worker and one dog biscuit machine; (2) If the revenues from this pilot project exceed its costs, add a second worker and machine; (3) If the additional revenues generated from the second worker/machine combination exceed what these cost, add a third; (4) Stop this process when adding a worker/machine combination brings less in revenues than it costs. Answer the following questions about SG's approach:

a Is SG using a marginal approach to her hiring of inputs?

b Does the approach adopted by SG also imply that she is following a $MR = MC$ rule for finding a profit-maximizing output?

c SG's distinguished professor of marketing examines her procedures and suggests she is mistaken in her approach. He insists that she should instead measure the profit on each new worker/machine combination employed and stop adding new output as soon as the last one added earns a lower profit than the previous one. How would you evaluate his distinguished advice?

5 What kind of demand curve does a price-taking firm face? For such a curve, what is the relationship between price and marginal revenue? Explain why an individual firm can be a price taker even though the entire market demand curve for its product may be downward-sloping.

6 Two features of the demand facing a firm will ensure that the firm must act as a price taker:

a That other firms be willing to provide all that is demanded at the current price, and

b That consumers of the firm's output regard it as identical to that of its competitors.

Explain why both of these conditions are required if the firm is to treat the price of its output as fixed. Describe what the demand facing the firm would be like if one of the conditions held but not the other.

7 A certain economics professor earns royalties from his textbook that are specified as 12 per cent of the book's total revenues. Assuming that the demand curve for this text is a downward-sloping straight line, how many copies of this book would the professor wish his or her publisher to sell? Is this the same number that the publisher itself would want to sell?

8 Show graphically the price that would yield exactly zero in economic profits to a firm in the

short run. With the price, why are profits maximized even though they are zero? Does this zero-profit solution imply that the firm's owners are starving?

9 Why do economists believe short-run marginal cost curves have positive slopes? Why does this belief lead to the notion that short-run supply curves have positive slopes? What kind of signal does a higher price send to a firm with increasing marginal costs? Would a reduction in output ever be the profit-maximizing response to an increase in price for a price-taking firm?

10 Wildcat John owns a few low-quality oil wells in Hawaii. He was heard complaining recently about the low price of crude oil: "With this \$50 per barrel price, I can't make any money – it costs me \$70 per barrel just to run my oil pumps. Still, I only paid \$1 an acre for my land many years ago, so I think I will just stop pumping for a time and wait for prices to get above \$70." What do you make of John's production decisions?

PROBLEMS

9.1 Beth's Lawn Mowing Service is a small business that acts as a price taker ($MR = P$). The prevailing market price of lawn mowing is €20 per acre. Although Beth can use the family mower for free (but see problem 9.2), she has other costs given by

$$\text{Total cost} = 0.1q^2 + 10q + 50$$

$$\text{Marginal cost} = 0.2q + 10$$

where q = the number of acres Beth chooses to mow in a week.

a How many acres should Beth choose to mow in order to maximize profit?

b Calculate Beth's maximum weekly profit.

c Plot these results on a graph and label Beth's supply curve.

9.2 Consider again the profit-maximizing decision of Beth's Lawn Mowing Service from problem 9.1. Suppose Beth's greedy father decides to charge for the use of the family lawn mower.

a If the lawn mower charge is set at €100 per week, how will this affect the acres of lawns Beth chooses to mow? What will her profits be?

b Suppose instead that Beth's father requires her to pay 50 per cent of weekly profits as a mower charge. How will this affect Beth's profit-maximizing decision?

c If Beth's greedy father imposes a charge of €2 per acre for use of the family mower, how will this affect Beth's marginal cost function? How will it affect her profit-maximizing decision? What will her profits be now? How much will Beth's greedy father get?

d Suppose finally that Beth's father collects his €2 per acre by collecting 10 per cent of the revenues from each acre Beth mows. How will this affect Beth's profit-maximizing decision? Explain why you get the same result here as for part c.

9.3 Widgets International faces a demand curve given by

$$Q = 10 - P$$

and has a constant marginal and average cost of €3 per widget produced. Complete the following table for the various production levels.

q	P	$TR (= P \cdot q)$	MR	MC	AC	TC	π
1							
2							
3							
4							
5							
6							
7							
8							
9							
10							

How many widgets will the firm produce in order to maximize profits? Explain briefly why this is so.

9.4 Suppose that a firm faces a demand curve that has a constant elasticity of −2. This demand curve is given by

$$q = 256/P^2$$

Suppose also that the firm has a marginal cost curve of the form

$$MC = 0.001q$$

a Plot these demand and marginal cost curves on a graph.

b Calculate the marginal revenue curve associated with the demand curve; plot this curve on a graph. (Hint: Use Equation 9.9 for this part of the problem.)

c At what output level does marginal revenue equal marginal cost?

9.5 Suppose a firm faces the following demand curve:

$$q = 60 - 2P$$

a Calculate the total revenue curve for the firm (that is, *TR* in terms of *q*).

b Using a tabular proof, show that the firm's *MR* curve is given by $MR = 30 - q$.

c Assume also that the firm has an *MC* curve given by $MC = 0.2q$. What output level should the firm produce to maximize profits?

d Plot the demand, *MC*, and *MR* curves and the point of profit maximization on a graph.

9.6 A local pizza shop has hired a consultant to help it compete with national chains in the area. Because most business is handled by these national chains, the local shop operates as a price taker. Using historical data on costs, the consultant finds that short-run total costs each day are given by, where *q* is daily pizza production. The consultant also reports that short-run marginal costs are given by

$$STC = 10 + q + 0.1q^2$$

a What is this price-taking firm's short-run supply curve?

b Does this firm have a shutdown price? That is, what is the lowest price at which the firm will produce any pizza?

c The pizza consultant calculates this shop's short-run average costs as

$$SAC = \frac{10}{q} + 1 + 0.1q$$

and claims that *SAC* reaches a minimum at $q = 10$. How would you verify this claim without using calculus?

d The consultant also claims that any price for pizza of less than €3 will cause this shop to lose money. Is the consultant correct? Explain.

e Currently the price of pizza is low (€2) because one major chain is having a sale. Because this price does not cover average costs, the consultant recommends that this shop cease operations until the sale is over. Would you agree with this recommendation? Explain.

9.7 The town where Beth's Lawn Mowing Service is located (see problems 9.1 and 9.2) is subject to sporadic droughts and monsoons. During periods of drought, the price for mowing lawns drops to €15 per acre, whereas, during monsoons, it rises to €25 per acre.

a How will Beth react to these changing prices?

b Suppose that weeks of drought and weeks of monsoons each occur half the time during a summer. What will Beth's average weekly profit be?

c Suppose Beth's kindly (but still greedy) father offers to eliminate the uncertainty in Beth's profits by agreeing to trade her the weekly profits based on a stable price of €20 per acre in exchange for the profits Beth actually makes. Should she take the deal?

d Plot your results on a graph and explain them intuitively.

9.8 In order to break the hold of Beth's greedy father over his struggling daughter (problems 9.1, 9.2, and 9.7), the government is thinking of instituting an income subsidy plan for the girl. Two plans are under consideration: (1) a flat grant of €200 per week to Beth; and (2) a grant of €4 per acre mowed.

a Which of these plans will Beth prefer?

b What is the cost of plan (2) to the government?

9.9 Suppose the production function for high-quality brandy is given by

$$q = \sqrt{K \cdot L}$$

where *q* is the output of brandy per week and *L* is labor hours per week. In the short run, *K* is fixed at 100, so the short-run production function is

$$q = 10\sqrt{L}$$

a If capital rents for €10 and wages are €5 per hour, show that short-run total costs are

$$STC = 1000 + 0.05q^2$$

b Given the short-run total cost curve in part a, short-run marginal costs are given by

$$SMC = 0.1q$$

With this short-run marginal cost curve, how much will the firm produce at a price of €20 per bottle of brandy? How many labor hours will be hired per week?

c Suppose that, during recessions, the price of brandy falls to €15 per bottle. With this price, how much would the firm choose to produce, and how many labor hours would be hired?

d Suppose that the firm believes that the fall in the price of brandy will last for only one week, after which it will wish to return to the level of production in part a. Assume also that, for each hour that the firm reduces its workforce below that described in part a, it incurs a cost of €1. If it proceeds as in part c, will it earn a profit or incur a loss? Explain.

9.10 Abby is the sole owner of a nail salon. In this problem, we explore whether sole ownership will affect profit-maximizing decisions.

a Suppose Abby has a utility function given by $U(\pi)$ – that is, she cares only about the monthly profits (π) the salon makes. This utility function exhibits diminishing marginal utility. Will Abby choose to maximize monthly profits?

b Suppose instead Abby's utility function is given by $U(\pi, x)$ where x is other things that Abby values. Plot on a graph Abby's indifference curves.

c Describe some possible factors that x might be. For each of these, describe what the relationship between π and x is. How would these relationships affect the budget constraint Abby faces?

d Based on your discussion in part c, under what conditions would it be reasonable to assume that Abby makes decisions in her salon in a profit-maximizing way? When would this assumption seem unreasonable?

e Would a prospective buyer be able to buy out Abby's business from her if she does not maximize profits?

PART FIVE
PERFECT COMPETITION

> *As every individual endeavors . . . to direct industry so that its produce may be of greatest value . . . he is led by an invisible hand to promote an end which was no part of his intention. By pursuing his own interest he frequently promotes that of society more effectively than when he really intends to promote it.*
> ADAM SMITH, *THE WEALTH OF NATIONS*, 1776

In this part, we look at price determination in markets with large numbers of demanders and suppliers. In such competitive markets, price-taking behavior is followed by all parties. Prices therefore convey important information about the relative scarcity of various goods and, under certain circumstances, help to achieve the sort of efficient overall allocation of resources that Adam Smith had in mind in his famous "invisible hand" analogy.

Chapter 10 develops the theory of perfectly competitive price determination in some detail. By focusing on the role of the entry and exit of firms in response to profitability in a market, the chapter shows that the supply–demand mechanism is considerably more flexible than is often assumed in simpler models. It also permits a more complete study of the relationship between goods' markets and the markets for the inputs that are employed in making these goods. The models developed in Chapter

10 are used in Chapter 11 to show how economists study the economic welfare of participants in real-world markets.

In Chapter 12, we examine how a complete set of competitive markets operates as a whole. That is, we develop an entire "general equilibrium" model of how a competitive economy operates. Such a model provides a more detailed picture of all of the effects that occur when something in the economy changes.

10

Perfect Competition in a Single Market

This chapter discusses how prices are determined in a single perfectly competitive market. The theory we develop here is an elaboration of Marshall's supply and demand analysis that is at the core of all of economics. We show how equilibrium prices are established and describe some of the factors that cause prices to change. In Chapter 11, we will then illustrate some of the many applications of this model.

Timing of a Supply Response

In the analysis of price determination, it is important to decide the length of time that is to be allowed for a **supply response** to changing demand conditions. The pattern of equilibrium prices will be different if we are talking about a very short period of time during which supply is essentially fixed and unchanging than if we are envisioning a very long-run process in which it is possible for entirely new firms to enter a market. For this reason, it has been traditional in economics to discuss pricing in three different time periods:

1. the very short run;
2. the short run, and
3. the long run.

Although it is not possible to give these terms an exact time length, the essential distinction among them concerns the nature of the supply response that is assumed to be possible. In the *very short run*, there can be no supply response – quantity supplied is absolutely fixed. In the *short run*, existing firms may change the quantity they are supplying but no new firms can enter the market. In the *long run*, firms can further change the quantity supplied and completely new firms may enter a market; this produces a very flexible supply response. This chapter discusses each of these different types of responses.

Pricing in the Very Short Run

Supply response The change in quantity of output supplied in response to a change in demand conditions.

Market period A short period of time during which quantity supplied is fixed.

Equilibrium price The price at which the quantity demanded by buyers of a good is equal to the quantity supplied by sellers of the good.

In the very short run or **market period**, there is no supply response. The goods are already "in" the marketplace and must be sold for whatever the market will bear. In this situation, price acts only to ration demand. The price will adjust to clear the market of the quantity that must be sold. Although the market price may act as a signal to producers in future periods, it does not perform such a function currently since current period output cannot be changed.

Figure 10-1 illustrates this situation.[1] Market demand is represented by the curve D. Supply is fixed at Q^*, and the price that clears the market is P_1. At P_1, people are willing to take all that is offered in the market. Sellers want to dispose of Q^* without regard to price (for example, the good in question may be perishable and will be worthless if not sold immediately). The price P_1 balances the desires of demanders with the desires of suppliers. For this reason, it is called an **equilibrium price**. In Figure 10-1, a price in excess of P_1 would not be an equilibrium price because people would demand less than Q^* (remember that firms are always willing to supply Q^* no matter what the price). Similarly, a price below P_1 would not be an equilibrium price because people would then demand more than Q^*. P_1 is the only equilibrium price possible when demand conditions are those represented by the curve D.

Shifts in Demand: Price as a Rationing Device

If the demand curve in Figure 10-1 shifted outward to D' (perhaps because incomes increased or because the price of some substitute increased), P_1 would no longer be

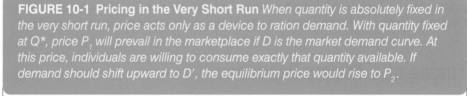

FIGURE 10-1 Pricing in the Very Short Run *When quantity is absolutely fixed in the very short run, price acts only as a device to ration demand. With quantity fixed at Q^*, price P_1 will prevail in the marketplace if D is the market demand curve. At this price, individuals are willing to consume exactly that quantity available. If demand should shift upward to D', the equilibrium price would rise to P_2.*

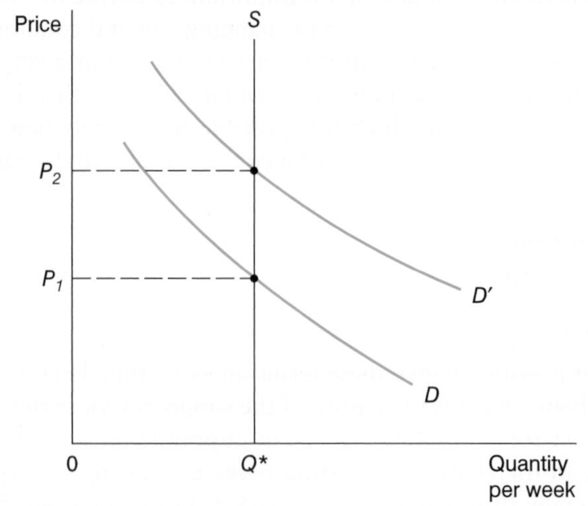

[1]As in previous chapters, we use Q to represent total quantity bought or sold in a market and q to represent the output of a single firm.

an equilibrium price. With the demand curve D', far more than Q^* is demanded at the price P_1. Some people who wish to make purchases at a price of P_1 would find that not enough of the good is now available to meet the increase in demand. In order to ration the available quantity among all demanders, the price would have to rise to P_2. At that new price, demand would again be reduced to Q^* (by a movement along D' in a north-westerly direction as the price rises). The price rise would restore equilibrium to the market. The curve labeled S (for "supply") in Figure 10-1 shows all the equilibrium prices for Q^* for any conceivable shift in demand. The price must always adjust to ration demand to exactly whatever supply is available. In Application 10.1: *Internet Auctions*, we look at how this price-setting mechanism works in practice.

Applicability of the Very-Short-Run Model

The model of the very-short-run is not particularly useful for most markets. Although the theory may adequately apply to some situations where goods are perishable, the far more common situation involves some degree of supply response to changing demand. It is usually presumed that a rise in price prompts producers to bring additional quantity into the market. We have already seen why this is true in Chapter 9 and will explore the response in detail in the next section.

Before beginning that analysis, note that increases in quantity supplied in response to higher prices need not come only from increased production. In a world in which some goods are durable (that is, last longer than a single market period), current owners of these goods may supply them in increasing amounts to the market as price rises. For example, even though the supply of Rembrandts is absolutely fixed, we would not draw the market supply curve for these paintings as a vertical line, such as that shown in Figure 10-1. As the price of Rembrandts rises, people (and museums) become increasingly willing to part with them. From a market point of view, the supply curve for Rembrandts has an upward slope even though no new production takes place. A similar analysis would follow for many types of durable goods, such as antiques, used cars, or company shares, all of which are not currently being produced. Here, we are more interested in how demand and production are related, however, so we do not look at these other cases in detail.

Short-Run Supply

In analysis of the short run, the number of firms in an industry is fixed. There is just not enough time for new firms to enter a market or for existing firms to exit completely. However, the firms currently operating in the market are able to adjust the quantity they are producing in response to changing prices. Because there are a large number of firms each producing the same good, each firm will act as a price taker. The model of short-run supply by a price-taking firm in Chapter 9 is therefore the appropriate one to use here. That is, each firm's short-run supply curve is simply the positively sloped section of its short-run marginal cost curve above the shutdown price. Using this model to record individual firms' supply decisions, we can add up all of these decisions into a single market supply curve.

MICROQUIZ 10.1

Suppose that a flower grower brings 100 boxes of roses to auction. There are many buyers at the auction; each may either offer to buy one box at the stated price by raising a bid paddle or decline to buy.

1. If the auctioneer starts at zero and calls off successively higher per-box prices, how will he or she know when an equilibrium is reached?
2. If the auctioneer starts off at an implausibly high price (€1000/box) and successively lowers that price, how will he or she know when an equilibrium is reached?

APPLICATION 10.1 *Internet Auctions*

Auctions on the Internet have rapidly become one of the most popular ways of selling all manner of goods. Websites offering auctions range from huge, all-inclusive listings such as those on eBay or Amazon to upmarket specialties (Sotheby's). Virtually every type of good can be found on some website. There are sites that specialize in collectibles, industrial equipment, office supplies, and the truly weird (check out Disturbingauctions.com). Occasionally, even human organs have appeared in Internet auctions, though, at least in the United Kingdom, selling such items is illegal and this may have been a hoax.

Is Supply Fixed in Internet Auctions?

There is a sense in which Internet auctions resemble the theoretical situation illustrated in Figure 10-1 – the goods listed are indeed in fixed supply and will be sold for whatever bidders are willing to pay. But this view of things may be too simple because it ignores dynamic elements that may be present in suppliers' decisions. Suppose, for example, that a supplier has ten copies of an out-of-print book to sell. Should he or she list all ten at once? Because buyers may search for what they want only infrequently, such a strategy may not be a good one. Selling all of the books at once may yield rather low prices for the final few sold because, at any one time, there are few demanders who value the books highly. But spreading the sales over several weeks may yield more favorable results. The book supplier will also watch auction prices of other sellers' offerings and will use price patterns in deciding precisely when to list the books to be sold. Hence, although the analysis of Figure 10-1 may be a good starting place for studying Internet auctions, any more complete understanding requires looking at complex sequences of decisions.

Special Features of Internet Auctions

A quick examination of auction sites on the Internet suggests that operators employ a variety of features in their auctions. Amazon, for example, has explicitly stated "reserve" prices that must be met before a bid will be considered. eBay does not explicitly report a reserve price, but many items do have reserve prices that can only be discovered through the bidding process. Some auctions provide you with a bidding history, whereas others only tell you the cumulative number of bids. A few auctions offer you the opportunity of buying a good outright at a relatively high price without going through the bidding process. For example, eBay has a "Buy It Now" price on many items. What purposes do these various features of Internet auctions serve? Presumably, an operator will only adopt a feature that promises to yield it better returns either in terms of attracting more buyers or (what may amount to the same thing) obtaining higher prices for sellers. But why do these features promise such higher returns? And why do auctioneers seem to differ in their opinions about what works? Attempts to answer these questions usually focus on the uncertainties inherent in the auction process and how bidders respond to them.[1]

Risks of Internet Auctions

Because buyers and sellers are total strangers in Internet auctions, a number of special provisions have been developed to mitigate the risks of fraud that the parties might encounter in such situations. The primary problem facing bidders in the auctions is in knowing that the goods being offered meet expected quality standards. An important way that many of the auctions help to reduce such uncertainty is through a grading process for sellers. Previous bidders provide rankings to the auction sites, and these are summarized for potential buyers. A good reputation probably results in a seller receiving higher bids. For sellers, the primary risk is that they will not be paid (or that a check will bounce). Various intermediaries (such as PayPal) have been developed to address this problem.

To Think About

1 A racetrack recently offered novelty key rings of a famous jockey for €3 each. One patron reportedly bought 100 of these, claiming that he could immediately resell them on the Internet for €10 each. What do you think?

2 Why does eBay keep its reserve prices secret? Doesn't this just frustrate bidders when they are told that their bids are unacceptable?

---

[1]For a discussion of these issues in auction design together with an analysis of various bidding strategies, see P. Bajari and A. Hortacsu, "Economic Insights from Internet Auctions", *Journal of Economic Literature* (June 2004): 457–486.

Construction of a Short-Run Supply Curve

The quantity of a good that is supplied to the market during a period is the sum of the quantities supplied by each of the existing firms. Because each firm faces the same market price in deciding how much to produce, the total supplied to the market also depends on this price. This relationship between market price and quantity supplied is called a **short-run market supply curve**.

Short-run market supply curve The relationship between market price and quantity supplied of a good in the short run.

Figure 10-2 illustrates the construction of the curve. For simplicity, we assume there are only two firms, A and B. The short-run supply (that is, marginal cost) curves for firms A and B are shown in Figure 10-2(a) and (b). The market supply curve shown in Figure 10-2(c) is the horizontal sum of these two curves. For example, at a price of P_1, firm A is willing to supply q_1^A, and firm B is willing to supply Q_1^B. At this price, the total supply in the market is given by Q_1, which is equal to $q_1^A + q_1^B$. The other points on the curve are constructed in an identical way. Because each firm's supply curve slopes upward, the market supply curve will also slope upward. This upward slope reflects the fact that short-run marginal costs increase as firms attempt to increase their outputs. They are willing to incur these higher marginal costs only at higher market prices.

The construction in Figure 10-2 uses only two firms; actual market supply curves represent the summation of many firms' supply curves. Each firm takes the market price as given and produces where price is equal to marginal cost. Because each firm operates on a positively sloped segment of its own marginal cost curve, the market supply curve will also have a positive slope. All of the information that is relevant to pricing from firms' points of view (such as their input costs, their current technical knowledge, or the nature of the diminishing returns they experience when trying to expand output) is summarized by this market supply curve. Should any of these factors change, the short-run supply curve would shift to a new position.

Short-Run Price Determination

We can now combine demand and supply curves to demonstrate how equilibrium prices are established in the short run. Figure 10-3 shows this process. In Figure 10-3(b), the market demand curve D and the short-run supply curve S intersect at a price of P_1 and

FIGURE 10-2 Short-Run Market Supply Curve *The supply (marginal cost) curves of two firms are shown in panel (a) and panel (b). The market supply curve in panel (c) is the horizontal sum of these curves. For example, at P_1, firm A supplies q_1^A, firm B supplies q_1^B, and total market supply is given by $Q_1 = q_1^A + q_1^B$.*

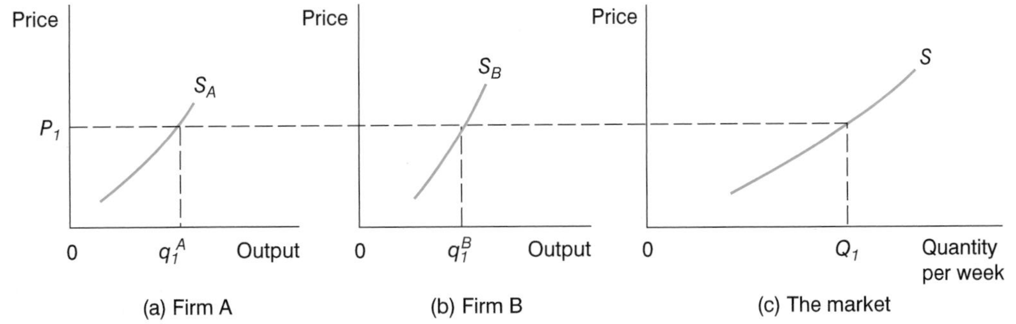

a quantity of Q_1. This price–quantity combination represents an equilibrium between the demands of individuals and the supply decisions of firms – the forces of supply and demand are precisely balanced. What firms supply at a price of P_1 is exactly what people want to buy at that price. This equilibrium tends to persist from one period to the next unless one of the factors underlying the supply and demand curves changes.

Functions of the Equilibrium Price

Here, the equilibrium price P_1 serves two important functions. First, this price acts as a signal to producers about how much should be produced. In order to maximize profits, firms produce that output level for which marginal costs are equal to P_1. In the aggregate, then, production is Q_1. A second function of the price is to ration demand. Given the market price of P_1, utility-maximizing consumers decide how much of their limited incomes to spend on that particular good. At a price of P_1, total quantity demanded is Q_1, which is precisely the amount that is produced. This is what economists mean by an equilibrium price. At P_1 each economic actor is content with what is transpiring. This is an "equilibrium" because no one has an incentive to change what he or she is doing. Any other price would not have this equilibrium property. A price in excess of P_1, for example, would cause quantity demanded to fall short of what is supplied. Some producers would not be able to sell their output and would therefore be forced to adopt other plans such as reducing production or selling at a cut-rate price. Similarly, at a price lower than P_1, quantity demanded would exceed the supply available and some demanders would be disappointed because they could not buy all they wanted. They might, for example, offer sellers higher prices so they can get the goods they want. Only at a price of P_1 would there be no such incentives to change behavior. This balancing of the forces of supply and demand at P_1 will tend to persist from one period to the next until something happens to change matters.

MICROQUIZ 10.2

How does the fact that there are many buyers and sellers in a competitive market enforce price-taking behavior? Specifically suppose that the equilibrium price of corn is €3 per bushel.

1 The owners of Yellow Ear Farm believe they deserve €3.25 per bushel because the farm has to use more irrigation in growing corn. Can this farm hold out for, and get, the price it wants?

2 United Soup Kitchens believes that it should be able to buy corn for €2.75 because it serves the poor. Can this charity find a place to buy at the price it is willing to pay?

FIGURE 10-3 Interactions of Many Individuals and Firms Determine Market Price in the Short Run *Market demand curves and market supply curves are each the horizontal sum of numerous components. These market curves are shown in panel (b). Once price is determined in the market, each firm and each individual treat this price as fixed in their decisions. If the typical person's demand curve shifts to d′, market demand will shift to D′ in the short run, and price will rise to P_2.*

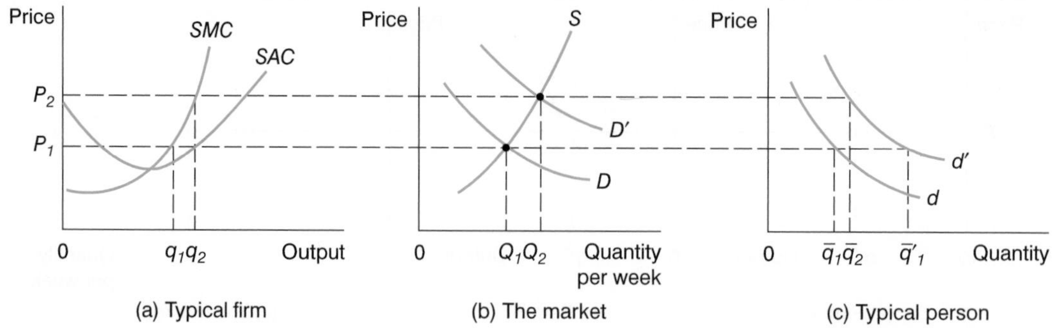

The implications of the equilibrium price (P_1) for a typical firm and for a typical person are shown in Figure 10-3(a) and (c), respectively. For the typical firm, the price P_1 causes an output level of q_1 to be produced. The firm earns a profit at this particular price because price exceeds short-run average total cost. The initial demand curve *d* for a typical person is shown in Figure 10-3(c). At a price of P_1, this person demands q_1. Adding up the quantities that each person demands at P_1 and the quantities that each firm supplies shows that the market is in equilibrium. The market supply and demand curves are a convenient way of doing that addition.

Effect of an Increase in Market Demand

To study a short-run supply response, let's assume that many people decide they want to buy more of the good in Figure 10-3. The typical person's demand curve shifts outward to d', and the entire market demand curve shifts. Figure 10-3(b) shows the new market demand curve, D'. The new equilibrium point is P_2, Q_2: At this point, supply–demand balance is re-established. Price has now increased from P_1 to P_2 in response to the shift in demand. The quantity traded in the market has also increased from Q_1 to Q_2.

The rise in price in the short run has served two functions. First, as shown in our analysis of the very short run, it has acted to ration demand. Whereas at P_1 a typical individual demanded $\bar{q}_1$, now at P_2 only $\bar{q}_2$ is demanded.

The rise in price has also acted as a signal to the typical firm to increase production. In Figure 10-3(a), the typical firm's profit-maximizing output level has increased from q_1 to q_2 in response to the price rise. That is the firm's short-run supply response: An increase in market price acts as an inducement to increase production. Firms are willing to increase production (and to incur higher marginal costs) because price has risen. If market price had not been permitted to rise (suppose, for example, government price controls were in effect), firms would not have increased their outputs. At P_1, there would have been an excess (unfilled) demand for the good in question. If market price is allowed to rise, a supply–demand equilibrium can be re-established so that what firms produce is again equal to what people demand at the prevailing market price. At the new price P_2, the typical firm has also increased its profits. This increased profitability in response to rising prices is important for our discussion of long-run pricing later in this chapter.

Shifts in Supply and Demand Curves

In previous chapters, we explored many of the reasons why either demand or supply curves might shift. Some of these reasons are summarized in Table 10-1. You may wish to review the material in Chapter 4, "Market Demand and Elasticity", and Chapter 8, "Costs", to see why these changes shift the various curves. These types of shifts in demand and supply occur frequently in real-world markets. When either a supply curve or a demand curve does shift, equilibrium price and quantity change. This section looks briefly at such change and how the outcome depends on the shapes of the curves.

Short-Run Supply Elasticity

Some terms used by economists to describe the shapes of demand and supply curves need to be understood before we can discuss the likely effects of these shifts. We already introduced the terminology for demand curves in Chapter 4. There, we developed the concept of the price elasticity of demand, which shows how the quantity demanded responds to changes in price. When demand is elastic, changes in price have a major impact on quantity demanded. In the case of inelastic demand, however, a price change does not have very much effect on the quantity that people choose to buy. Firms' short-run supply responses can be described along the same lines. If an increase in price causes firms to supply significantly more output, we say that the supply curve is "elastic" (at least in the range currently being observed). Alternatively, if the price increase has only a minor effect on the quantity firms choose to produce, supply is said to be inelastic. More formally

$$\text{Short-run supply elasticity} = \frac{\text{Percentage change in quantity supplied in short run}}{\text{Percentage change in price}} \quad \{10.1\}$$

For example, if the short-run supply elasticity is 2.0, each 1 per cent increase in price results in a 2 per cent increase in quantity supplied. Over this range, the short-run supply curve is rather elastic. If, on the other hand, a 1 per cent increase in price leads only to a 0.5 per cent increase in quantity supplied, the **short-run elasticity of supply** is 0.5, and we say that supply is inelastic. As we will see, whether short-run supply is elastic or inelastic can have a significant effect on how markets respond to economic events.

Short-run elasticity of supply The percentage change in quantity supplied in the short run in response to a 1 per cent change in price.

Shifts in Supply Curves and the Importance of the Shape of the Demand Curve

A shift inward in the short-run supply curve for a good might result, for example, from an increase in the prices of the inputs used by firms to produce the good. An increase in carpenters' wages raises homebuilders' costs and clearly affects their willingness to produce houses. The effect of such a shift on the equilibrium levels of *P* and *Q* depends on the shape of the demand curve for the product. Figure 10-4 illustrates two possible situations. The demand curve in Figure 10-4(a) is relatively price elastic; that is, a change in price substantially affects the quantity demanded. For this case, a shift in the supply curve from *S* to *S′* causes equilibrium prices to rise only moderately (from *P* to *P′*), whereas quantity is reduced sharply (from *Q* to *Q′*). Rather than being "passed on" in higher prices, the increase in the firms' input costs is met primarily by

TABLE 10-1 Reasons for a Shift in a Demand or Supply Curve

Demand	*Supply*
Shifts outward (→) because	Shifts outward (→) because
• Income increases	• Input prices fall
• Price of substitute rises	• Technology improves
• Price of complement falls	
• Preferences for good increase	
Shifts inward (←) because	Shifts inward (←) because
• Income falls	• Input prices rise
• Price of substitute falls	
• Price of complement rises	
• Preferences for good diminish	

a decrease in quantity produced (a movement down each firm's marginal cost curve) with only a slight increase in price.[2]

This situation is reversed when the market demand curve is inelastic. In Figure 10-4(b), a shift in the supply curve causes equilibrium price to rise substantially, but quantity is little changed because people do not reduce their demands very much if prices rise. Consequently, the shift upward in the supply curve is passed on to demanders almost completely in the form of higher prices. The result of this demonstration is almost counterintuitive. The impact, say, of a wage increase on house prices depends not so much on how suppliers react but on the nature of demand for houses. If we asked only how much builders' costs were increased by a wage increase, we might make a very inaccurate prediction of how prices would change. The effect of any given shift upward in a supply curve can only be determined with additional information about the nature of demand for the good being produced.

Shifts in Demand Curves and the Importance of the Shape of the Supply Curve

For similar reasons, a given shift in a market demand curve will have different implications for P and Q depending on the shape of the short-run supply curve. Two illustrations are shown in Figure 10-5. In Figure 10-5(a), the short-run supply curve for the good in question is relatively inelastic. As quantity expands, firms' marginal costs rise rapidly, giving the supply curve its steep slope. In this situation, a shift outward in the market demand curve (caused, for example, by an increase in consumer income) causes prices to increase substantially. Yet, the quantity supplied increases only slightly. The increase in demand (and in Q) has caused firms to move up their steeply sloped

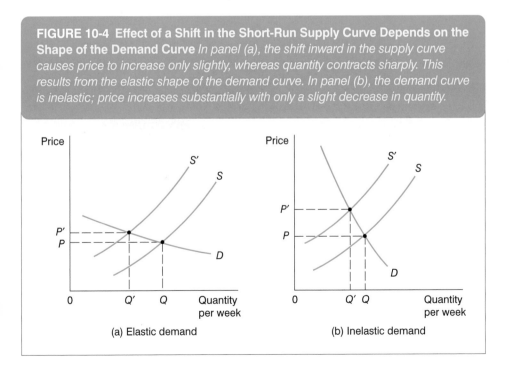

FIGURE 10-4 Effect of a Shift in the Short-Run Supply Curve Depends on the Shape of the Demand Curve *In panel (a), the shift inward in the supply curve causes price to increase only slightly, whereas quantity contracts sharply. This results from the elastic shape of the demand curve. In panel (b), the demand curve is inelastic; price increases substantially with only a slight decrease in quantity.*

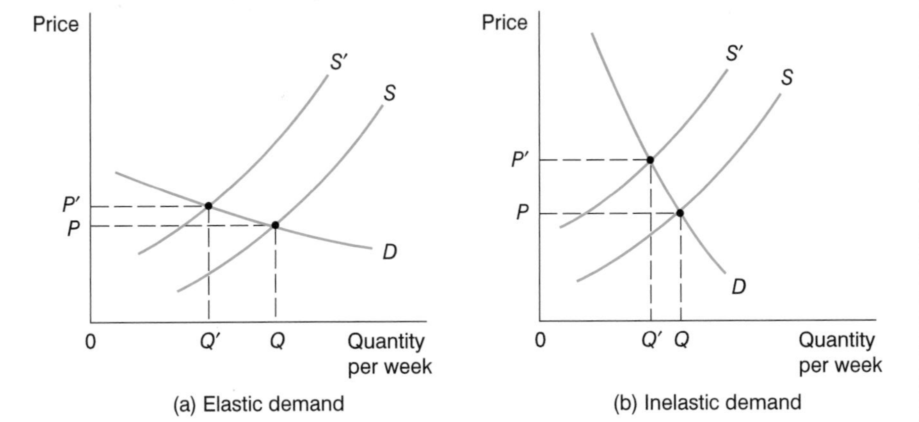

[2]Notice, for example, that on the supply curve S', the marginal cost of producing output level Q is considerably higher than the marginal cost of producing Q'.

marginal cost curves. The accompanying large increase in price serves to ration demand. There is little response in terms of quantity supplied.

Figure 10-5(b) shows a relatively elastic short-run supply curve. This kind of curve would occur for an industry in which marginal costs do not rise steeply in response to output increases. For this case, an increase in demand produces a substantial increase in Q. However, because of the nature of the supply curve, this increase is not met by great cost increases. Consequently, price rises only moderately.

These examples again demonstrate Marshall's observation that demand and supply together determine price and quantity. Recall from Chapter 1 Marshall's analogy: Just as it is impossible to say which blade of a scissors does the cutting, so too it is impossible to attribute price solely to demand or to supply characteristics. Rather, the effect that shifts in either a demand curve or a supply curve will have depends on the shapes of both of the curves. In predicting the effects of shifting supply or demand conditions on market price and quantity in the real world, this simultaneous relationship must be considered. Application 10.2: *Ethanol Subsidies in the United States and Brazil* illustrates how this short-run model might be used to examine some of the politics of government price-support schemes.

A Numerical Illustration

Changes in market equilibria can be illustrated with a simple numerical example. Suppose, as we did in Chapter 9, that the quantity of CDs demanded per week (Q) depends on their price (P) according to the simple relation

$$\text{Demand: } Q = 10 - P \tag{10.2}$$

Suppose also that the short-run supply curve for CDs is given by

$$\text{Supply: } Q = P - 2 \text{ or } P = Q + 2 \tag{10.3}$$

FIGURE 10-5 Effect of a Shift in the Demand Curve Depends on the Shape of the Short-Run Supply Curve *In panel (a), supply is inelastic; a shift in demand causes price to increase greatly with only a small increase in quantity. In panel (b), on the other hand, supply is elastic; price rises only slightly in response to a demand shift.*

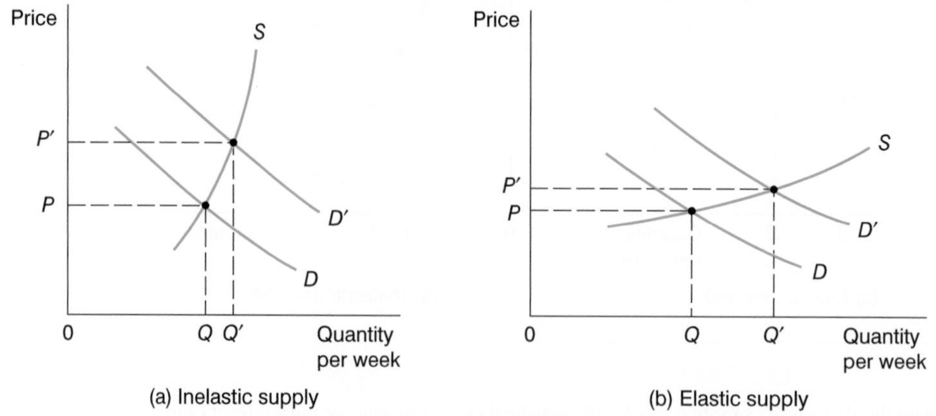

APPLICATION 10.2 *Ethanol Subsidies in the United States and Brazil*

Ethanol is another term for ethyl alcohol. In addition to its role as an intoxicant, the chemical also has potentially desirable properties as a fuel for cars because it burns cleanly and can be made from renewable resources such as sugar cane or corn. Ethanol can also be used as an additive to petrol, and some claim that this oxygenated product reduces air pollution. The EU's current non-binding target set in 2003 requires all Member States to have 5.75 per cent of transport run on bio fuels by 2010. Indeed, new proposals in 2007 aim to raise this figure to 10 per cent by 2020. In order to meet these challenging targets several governments have adopted subsidies for producers of bio fuel. In Italy, the government guarantees the purchase of bio fuel crops at €22 per 100 kilograms. This is nearly twice the €11-to-€12 rate per 100 kilograms of wheat guaranteed on the open market in 2006.

A Diagrammatic Treatment

One way to show the effect of a subsidy in a supply–demand graph is to treat it as a shift in the short-run supply curve.[1] In the United States, for example, producers of ethanol get what amounts to just over 14 cents-a-liter tax credit. As shown in Figure 1, this shifts the supply curve (which is the sum of ethanol producers' marginal cost curves) downward by 14 cents. This leads to an expansion of demand from its presubsidy level of Q_1 to Q_2. The total cost of the subsidy then depends not only on its per-liter amount but also on the extent of this increase in quantity demanded.

The Ethanol Subsidy and US Politics

Although the scientific basis for using ethanol as a fuel additive to reduce pollution has been challenged, the politics of the subsidy are unassailable. For example, a major beneficiary of the subsidy in the United States is the Archer Daniels Midland Company, a large corn processor. It is also a significant contributor to both major US political parties. The fact that ethanol subsidies are concentrated in Iowa is also politically significant, as that state hosts one of the earliest presidential primary races. Presidential hopefuls quickly see the wisdom of supporting subsidies. The 2005

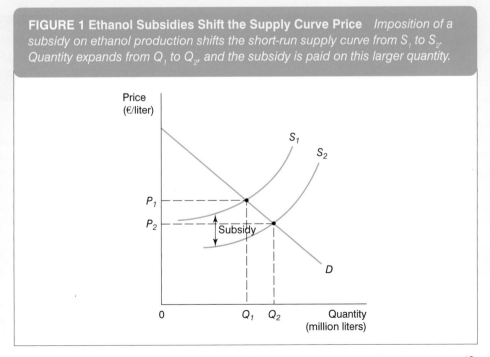

FIGURE 1 Ethanol Subsidies Shift the Supply Curve Price *Imposition of a subsidy on ethanol production shifts the short-run supply curve from S_1 to S_2. Quantity expands from Q_1 to Q_2, and the subsidy is paid on this larger quantity.*

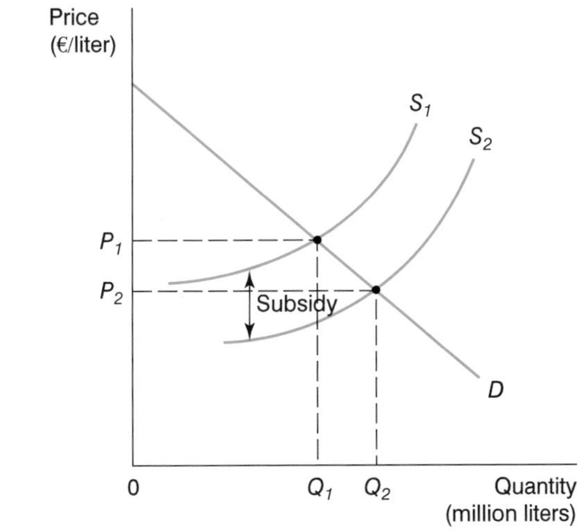

(*Continued*)

energy bill included production subsidies and other policies (such as requiring more cars be built with engines flexible enough to use ethanol) intended to more than double ethanol use (to eight billion barrels per year) by 2012.

Brazilian Politics

In Brazil, ethanol is made from sugar cane, one of the country's most important agricultural products. For many years, the government subsidized the production of ethanol and required that most cars' engines be adapted to run on it as a fuel. Economic liberalization during the 1990s led to a significant decline in the use of the fuel, however. In June of 1999, thousands of sugar-cane growers rallied in Brasilia, demanding that the government do more to support ethanol. But soaring sugar prices in 2000 made the government worry more about inflation. The required ethanol content of fuel was reduced by 20 per cent.

To Think About

1 Many of the purported benefits of ethanol use are environmental in nature. Assuming that these benefits actually exist, would an unsubsidized market provide the right level of ethanol use?

2 Who actually benefits from the ethanol subsidy: consumers, farm owners, or farm workers?

3 If bio fuels become more widely used, do you think there might be some losers as well as winners?

[1]A subsidy can also be shown as a "wedge" between the demand and supply curves – a procedure we use in Chapter 11 to study tax incidence.

Figure 10-6 plots these equations on a graph. As before, the demand curve (labeled *D* in the figure) intersects the vertical axis at P = €10. At higher prices, no CDs are demanded. The supply curve (labeled *S*) intersects the vertical axis at P = 2. This is the shutdown price for firms in the industry – at a price lower than €2, no CDs will be sold. As Figure 10-6 shows, these supply and demand curves intersect at a price of €6 per CD. At that price, people demand four CDs per week and firms are willing to supply four CDs per week. This equilibrium is also illustrated in Table 10-2, which shows the quantity of CDs demanded and supplied at each price. Only when P = €6

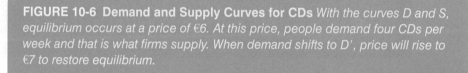

FIGURE 10-6 Demand and Supply Curves for CDs *With the curves D and S, equilibrium occurs at a price of €6. At this price, people demand four CDs per week and that is what firms supply. When demand shifts to D′, price will rise to €7 to restore equilibrium.*

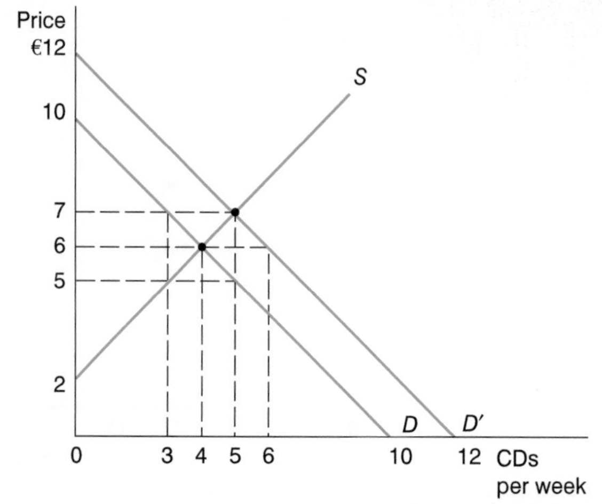

do these amounts agree. At a price of €5 per CD, for example, people want to buy five CDs per week but only three will be supplied; there is an excess demand of two CDs per week. Similarly, at a price of €7, there is an excess supply of two CDs per week.

If the demand curve for CDs were to shift outward, this equilibrium would change. For example, Figure 10-6 also shows the demand curve D', whose equation is given by

$$Q = 12 - P \quad \{10.4\}$$

With this new demand curve, equilibrium price rises to €7 and quantity also rises to five CDs per week. This new equilibrium is confirmed by the entries in Table 10-2, which show that this is the only price that clears the market given the new demand curve. For example, at the old price of €6, there is now an excess demand for CDs because the amount people want ($Q = 6$) exceeds what firms are willing to supply ($Q = 4$). The rise in price from €6 to €7 restores equilibrium both by prompting people to buy fewer CDs and by encouraging firms to produce more.

MICROQUIZ 10.3

Use the information on Case 1 in Table 10-2 to answer the following questions.

1 Suppose that the government confiscated two CDs per week as being "not suitable for young ears". What would be the equilibrium price of the remaining CDs?

2 Suppose that the government imposed a €4-per-CD tax, resulting in a €4 difference between what consumers pay and what firms receive for each CD. How many CDs would be sold? What price would buyers pay?

The Long Run

In perfectly competitive markets, supply responses are more flexible in the long run than in the short run for two reasons. First, firms' long-run cost curves reflect the greater input flexibility that firms have in the long run. Diminishing returns and the associated sharp increases in marginal costs are not such a significant issue in the long run. Second, the long run allows firms to enter

TABLE 10-2 Supply and Demand Equilibrium in the Market for CDs

	Supply	Demand	
Price	$Q = P - 2$ Quantity supplied (CDs per week)	Case 1 $Q = 10 - P$ Quantity demanded (CDs per week)	Case 2 $Q = 12 - P$ Quantity demanded (CDs per week)
€10	8	0	2
9	7	1	3
8	6	2	4
7	5	3	5
6	4	4	6
5	3	5	7
4	2	6	8
3	1	7	9
2	0	8	10
1	0	9	11
0	0	10	12

■ NEW EQUILIBRIUM. ■ INITIAL EQUILIBRIUM.

and exit a market in response to profit opportunities. These actions have important implications for pricing. We begin our analysis of these various effects with a description of the long-run equilibrium for a competitive industry. Then, as we did for the short run, we show how quantity supplied and prices change when conditions change.

Equilibrium Conditions

A perfectly competitive market is in long-run equilibrium when no firm has an incentive to change its behavior. Such an equilibrium has two components: Firms must be content with their output choices (that is, they must be maximizing profits), and they must be content to stay in (or out of) the market. We discuss each of these components separately.

Profit Maximization

As before, we assume that firms seek maximum profits. Because each firm is a price taker, profit maximization requires that the firm produce where price is equal to (long-run) marginal cost. This first equilibrium condition, $P = MC$, determines both the firm's output choice and its choice of a specific input combination that minimizes these costs in the long run.

Entry and Exit

A second feature of long-run equilibrium concerns the possibility of the entry of entirely new firms into a market or the exit of existing firms from that market. The perfectly competitive model assumes that such entry and exit entail no special costs. Consequently, new firms are lured into any market in which (economic) profits are positive because they can earn more there than they can in other markets. Similarly, firms leave a market when profits are negative. In this case, firms can earn more elsewhere than in a market where they are not covering all opportunity costs.

If profits are positive, the entry of new firms causes the short-run market supply curve to shift outward because more firms are now producing than were in the market previously. Such a shift causes market price (and market profits) to fall. The process continues until no firm contemplating entering the market would be able to earn an economic profit.[3] At that point, entry by new firms ceases and the number of firms has reached an equilibrium. When the firms in a market suffer short-run losses, some firms choose to leave, causing the supply curve to shift to the left. Market price then rises, eliminating losses for those firms remaining in the marketplace.

Long-Run Equilibrium

In this chapter, we assume that all the firms producing a particular good have the same cost curves; that is, we assume that no single firm controls any special resources or technologies.[4] Because all firms are identical, the equilibrium long-run position requires every firm to earn exactly zero economic profits. In graphic terms, long-run equilibrium price must settle at the low point of each firm's long-run average total cost curve.

[3]Remember, we are using the economic definition of profits here. Profits represent the return to the business owner in excess of that which is strictly necessary to keep him or her in the business. If an owner can earn just what he or she could earn elsewhere, there is no reason to enter a market.

[4]The important case of firms having different costs is discussed in Chapter 11. In that chapter, we see that very low-cost firms can earn positive, long-run profits. These represent a "rent" to whatever input provides the firms' unique low cost (e.g., especially fertile land or a low-cost source of raw materials).

Only at this point do the two equilibrium conditions hold: $P = MC$ (which is required for profit maximization) and $P = AC$ (which is the required zero-profit condition).

These two equilibrium conditions have rather different origins. Profit maximization is a goal of firms. The $P = MC$ rule reflects our assumptions about firms' behavior and is identical to the output-decision rule used in the short run. The zero-profit condition is not a goal for firms. Firms would obviously prefer to have large profits. The long-run operations of competitive markets, however, force all firms to accept a level of zero economic profits ($P = AC$) because of the willingness of firms to enter and exit. Although the firms in a perfectly competitive industry may earn either positive or negative profits in the short run, in the long run *only* zero profits prevail. That is, firms' owners earn only normal returns on their investments.

Long-Run Supply: The Constant Cost Case

The study of long-run supply depends crucially on how the entry of new firms affects the prices of inputs. The simplest assumption one might make is that entry has no effect on these prices. Under this assumption, no matter how many firms enter or leave a market, every firm retains exactly the same set of cost curves with which it started. There are many important cases for which this constant input cost assumption may be unrealistic; we analyze these cases later. For the moment, however, we wish to examine the equilibrium conditions for this **constant cost case**.

Constant cost case
A market in which entry or exit has no effect on the cost curves of firms.

Market Equilibrium

Figure 10-7 demonstrates long-run equilibrium for the constant cost case. For the market as a whole, in Figure 10-7(b), the demand curve is labeled D and the short-run

FIGURE 10-7 Long-Run Equilibrium for a Perfectly Competitive Market: Constant Cost Case *An increase in demand from D to D′ causes price to rise from P_1 to P_2 in the short run. This higher price creates profits, and new firms are drawn into the market. If the entry of these new firms has no effect on the cost curves of firms, new firms continue to enter until price is pushed back down to P_1. At this price, economic profits are zero. The long-run supply curve, LS, is therefore a horizontal line at P_1. Along LS, output is increased by increasing the number of firms that each produce q_1.*

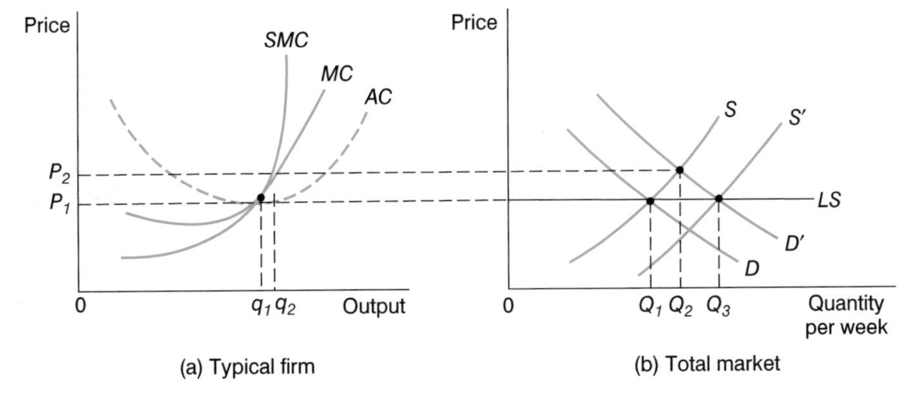

supply curve is labeled *S*. The short-run equilibrium price is therefore P_1. The typical firm in Figure 10-7(a) produces output level q_1, because at this level of output price is equal to short-run marginal cost (*SMC*). In addition, with a market price of P_1, output level q_1 is also a long-run equilibrium position for the firm. The firm is maximizing profits because price is equal to long-run marginal cost (*MC*). Figure 10-7(a) also shows a second long-run equilibrium property: Price is equal to long-run average total costs (*AC*). Consequently, economic profits are zero and there is no incentive for firms either to enter or to leave this market.

A Shift in Demand

Suppose now that the market demand curve shifts outward to D'. If *S* is the relevant short-run supply curve, then in the short run, price rises to P_2. The typical firm, in the short run, chooses to produce q_2 and (because $P_2 > AC$) earns profits on this level of output. In the long run, these profits attract new firms into the market. Because of the constant cost assumption, this entry of new firms has no effect on input prices. Perhaps this industry hires only a small fraction of the workers in an area and raises its capital in national markets. More inputs can therefore be hired without affecting any firms' cost curves. New firms continue to enter the market until price is forced down to the level at which there are again no economic profits being made. The entry of new firms therefore shifts the short-run supply curve to S', where the equilibrium price (P_1) is re-established. At this new long-run equilibrium, the price–quantity combination P_1, Q_3 prevails in the market. The typical firm again produces at output level q_1, although now there are more firms than there were in the initial situation.

Long-Run Supply Curve

By considering many potential shifts in demand, we can examine long-run pricing in this industry. Our discussion suggests that no matter how demand shifts, economic forces that cause price always to return to P_1 come into play. All long-run equilibria occur along a horizontal line at P_1. Connecting these equilibrium points shows the long-run supply response of this industry. This long-run supply curve is labeled *LS* in Figure 10-7. For a constant cost industry of identical firms, the long-run supply curve is a horizontal line at the low point of the firms' long-run average total cost curves. The fact that price cannot depart from P_1 in the long run is a direct consequence of the constancy of input prices as new firms enter. Application 10.3: *Film Rentals* looks at some cases where this is approximately true.

Shape of the Long-Run Supply Curve

Contrary to the short-run case, the long-run supply curve does not depend on the shape of firms' marginal cost curves. Rather, the zero-profit condition focuses attention on the low point of the long-run average cost curve as the factor most relevant to long-run price determination. In the constant cost case, the position of this low point does not change as new firms enter or leave a market. Consequently, only one price can prevail in the long run, regardless of how demand shifts, so long as input prices do not change. The long run supply curve is horizontal at this price.

Once the constant cost assumption is abandoned, this need not be the case. If the entry of new firms causes average costs to rise, the long-run supply curve has an upward slope. On the other hand, if entry causes average costs to decline, it is even possible for the long-run supply curve to be negatively sloped. We now discuss these possibilities.

APPLICATION 10.3 *Film Rentals*

Films have been available for home rental since the 1920s. Although the technology for showing films has changed dramatically over time (making it much cheaper and more widely available), the basic rental business has consistently exhibited the characteristics of a constant cost industry. Here, we look at a few recent implications of this fact.

The VCR Revolution

Once the VHS standard was adopted for videocassette recorders, ownership of the tape players grew phenomenally. By the end of the 1980s, more than 60 per cent of UK, and 70 per cent of US households owned this equipment, thereby creating the demand for film rentals on videotape. At first the rental industry was quite profitable, but there were no significant barriers to entry. Any would-be entrepreneur could rent space, put up a few shelves, and get in on the action. Because inputs used by the industry (low-wage workers and simple rental space) were readily available at market prices, the industry had a perfectly elastic long-run supply curve – it could easily meet exploding demand with no increase in price. Between 1982 and 1987, the number of tape rental outlets grew fourfold and the standard price for a rental movie fell to about $1.50 per night in the US. Even grocery stores and corner shops were stocking films for rental.

New Technology: The DVD

Introduction of DVD technology in the mid-1990s followed a similar path. Once a critical threshold of households owned DVD players, the rental market for movies on DVD emerged quickly. Existing video rental firms found that they could easily add a few DVD racks to their stores, and rental prices for DVDs soon came to approximate those for tapes (as might have been anticipated given the close substitutability between the two products). New outlets for DVD rentals, especially over the Internet, also enhanced the supply response. Again, the absence of barriers to entry together with the ready availability of inputs at constant prices (shelf space and workers) resulted in a close approximation to the constant cost model.

Sorting Out Future Technologies

This elastic supply response has also dictated a strict market test for innovations in the film rental business – such innovations must be cost-competitive with existing methods of distribution or they will not be adopted. The fate of "Divx" technology provides an instructive example. This approach (primarily organized in the US by the Circuit City chain of electronic stores) offered film rentals on non-returnable DVDs. The rental outlet monitored each showing through computer modems and imposed extra charges for additional viewing. Because consumers had to purchase special equipment, Divx gained few adherents. It was largely abandoned by 1999.

The market is changing fast with many newer technologies entering the rented market. The British Video Association reported in 2007 that the number of DVDs rented in Britain has fallen every year since 2001. In 2006 rentals, including online, were 116m, fewer than three per adult and a third of the market's heyday in 1989. The established high street rental businesses suffered an 18 per cent slump in their sales volumes in 2006, as the market became fiercely competitive with the likes of Sky Box Office, and Virgin Media's on demand service, and online postal services such as Amazon, Blockbuster.co.uk and LoveFilm. Even public libraries, which can offer a week-long rental for £1, have contributed to the change seeing their share of the market increase to 6.8 per cent in 2006.[1]

Such delivery offers consumers considerable advantages over rental by repeated trips to the rental shop. But the technology also poses questions about the viability of competitive distribution methods. Direct distribution of films to consumers might allow film studios to have more monopoly power in renting specific films than they now have with more competitive distribution schemes. Still, the studios would have to decide whether it would be better to exercise some monopoly in distribution, or continue with competitive distribution and exercise their monopoly solely in their pricing of the films themselves. As we will see in Chapter 13, this is a common problem for firms that seek to maintain monopoly power in selling

(Continued)

two or more related products. Profit-maximizing strategies for doing so may be quite complex depending on both the details of how the demands for the goods (here delivery of films and the films themselves) are related and on the nature of outside competition in the related markets. In general one might expect firms to make most of their profits from that market which they find to be least competitive.

To Think About

1 Looking at the Blockbuster chain of film rental outlets. Can Blockbuster raise its prices for rentals above the competitive level because it is so large? Has the firm's power to do so increased or decreased in recent years?

2 Although the home-movie rental industry has been an important source of income to film studios in recent years, they still prefer to open their films in theatres and embargo them for a time until DVDs are released. Why do the studios follow this practice? Can you think of other cases where products are released for sale in a piecemeal manner?

[1]Legal copies of new releases are also cheaper than ever, with the recent James Bond hit *Casino Royale* being offered at £7 by Asda supermarkets. Cut-prices have prompted rising sales and falling rentals. Having peaked in 1989 at 289m, rentals dwarfed sales of videos and DVDs for years. But in 2003 sales outstripped rentals for the first time and have done so ever since.

The Increasing Cost Case

The entry of new firms may cause the average cost of all firms to rise for several reasons. Entry of new firms may increase the demand for scarce inputs, driving up their prices. New firms may impose external costs on existing firms (and on themselves) in the form of air or water pollution, and new firms may place strains on public facilities (roads, courts, schools, and so forth), and these may show up as increased costs for all firms.

Increasing cost case A market in which the entry of firms increases firms' costs.

Figure 10-8 demonstrates market equilibrium for this **increasing cost case**. The initial equilibrium price is P_1. At this price, the typical firm in Figure 10-8(a) produces

FIGURE 10-8 Increasing Costs Result in a Positively Sloped Long-Run Supply Curve *Initially, the market is in equilibrium at P_1, Q_1. An increase in demand (to D') causes price to rise to P_2 in the short run, and the typical firm produces q_2 at a profit. This profit attracts new firms. The entry of these new firms causes costs to rise to the levels shown in (b). With this new set of curves, equilibrium is re-established in the market at P_3, Q_3. By considering many possible demand shifts and connecting all the resulting equilibrium points, the long-run supply curve LS is traced out.*

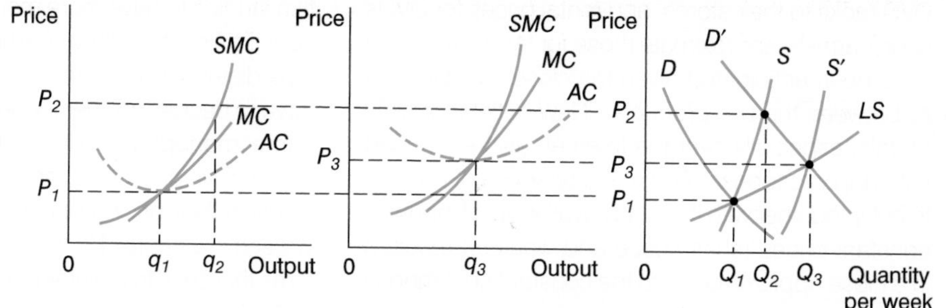

(a) Typical firm before entry (b) Typical firm after entry (c) The market

q_1 and total output, shown in Figure 10-8(c), is Q_1. Suppose that the demand curve for this product shifts outward to D' and that D' and the short-run supply curve (S) intersect at P_2. At this price, the typical firm produces q_2 and earns a substantial profit. This profit attracts new entrants into the market and shifts the short-run supply curve outward.

Suppose that the entry of new firms causes the costs of all firms to rise. The new firms may, for example, increase the demand for a particular type of skilled worker, driving up wages. A typical firm's new (higher) set of cost curves is shown in Figure 10-8(b). The new long-run equilibrium price for the industry is P_3 (here $P = MC = AC$), and at this price Q_3 is demanded. We now have two points (P_1, Q_1 and P_3, Q_3) on the long-run supply curve.[5] All other points on the curve can be found in an analogous way by considering every possible shift in the demand curve. These shifts would trace out the long-run supply curve *LS*. Here, *LS* has a positive slope because of the increasing costs associated with the entry of new firms. This positive slope is caused by whatever causes firms' costs to rise in response to entry.[6] Still, because the supply response is more flexible in the long run, the *LS* curve is somewhat flatter than its short-run counterpart.

Long-Run Supply Elasticity

As we have just shown, the long-run supply curve is constructed by considering all possible shifts in the demand curve for the product. In order to predict the effects that such increases in demand will have on market price, it is important to know something about the shape of the supply curve. A convenient measure for summarizing the shape of long-run supply curves is the **long-run elasticity of supply**. This concept records how proportional changes in price affect the quantity supplied, once all long-run adjustments have taken place. More formally:

Long-run elasticity of supply The percentage change in quantity supplied in the long run in response to a 1 per cent change in price.

$$\textit{Long-run supply elasticity} = \frac{\textit{Percentage change in quantity supplied in long run}}{\textit{Percentage change in price}} \quad \{10.5\}$$

An elasticity of 10, for example, would show that a 1 per cent increase in price would result in a 10 per cent increase in the long-run quantity supplied. We would say that long-run supply is very price elastic: The long-run supply curve would be nearly horizontal. A principal implication of such a high price elasticity is that long-run equilibrium prices would not increase very much in response to significant outward shifts in the market demand curve.

A small supply elasticity would have a quite different implication. If the elasticity were only 0.1, for example, a 1 per cent increase in price would increase quantity supplied by only 0.1 per cent. In other words, the long-run supply curve would be nearly vertical, and shifts outward in demand would result in rapidly rising prices without significant increases in quantity.

Estimating Long-Run Elasticities of Supply

Economists have devoted considerable effort to estimating long-run supply elasticities for competitive industries. Because economic growth leads to increased demands for

[5] Figure 10-8 also shows the short-run supply curve associated with the point P_3, Q_3. This supply curve has shifted to the right because more firms are producing now than were initially.

[6] In the next chapter, we encounter another reason for a positively sloped long-run supply curve – differences in costs among firms.

most products (especially natural resources and other primary products), the reason for this interest is obvious. If long-run supply elasticities are high, real resource prices will not increase rapidly over time. This seems to be the case for relatively abundant resources that can be obtained with only modest increases in costs, such as aluminum or coal. Over time, real prices for these goods have not risen very rapidly in response to increasing demand. Indeed, in some cases, real prices may even have fallen because of technical improvements in production.

On the other hand, cases in which long-run supply curves are inelastic can show sharply escalating real prices in response to increased demand. Again, the ultimate causes for such an outcome relate to conditions in the market for inputs. In cases such as rare minerals (platinum, for example, which is used in car exhaust systems), increased demand may require the exploitation of very costly deposits. Perhaps an even more important source of increasing input costs is the market for skilled labor. When expansion of a market, such as that for medical care or computer software, creates new demand for a specialized labor input, wages for these workers may rise sharply, and that gives the long-run supply curve its upward slope.

Table 10-3 summarizes a few studies of long-run supply elasticities. Although there are considerable uncertainties about some of these figures (and, in some cases, the markets may not obey all the assumptions of the perfectly competitive model), they still provide a good indication of the way in which conditions in input markets affect long-run supply elasticities. Notice, in particular, that the estimated elasticities for some natural resources are quite high – for these, the constant cost model may be approximately correct. For goods that encounter rising labor costs (medical care) or that require the use of increasingly high-cost locations (oil and farm crops), supply can be rather inelastic.

The Decreasing Cost Case

In some cases, entry may reduce costs. The entry of new firms may provide a larger pool of trained labor to draw from than was previously available, which would reduce

TABLE 10-3 Estimated Long-Run Supply Elasticities

Industry	*Elasticity estimate*
Agriculture	
Corn	+0.27
Soybeans	+0.13
Wheat	+0.03
Aluminium	Nearly infinite
Coal	+15.0
Medical care	+0.15 to +0.60
Natural gas (US)	+0.50
Crude oil (US)	+0.75

SOURCES: AGRICULTURE: J. S. CHOI AND P. G HELMBERGER, "HOW SENSITIVE ARE CROP YIELDS TO PRICE CHANGES AND FARM PROGRAMS?", *JOURNAL OF AGRICULTURE AND APPLIED ECONOMICS* (JULY 1993): 237–244. ALUMINUM: *CRITICAL MATERIALS COMMODITY ACTION ANALYSIS* (WASHINGTON, DC, US DEPARTMENT OF THE INTERIOR) 1975. COAL: MIT ENERGY LABORATORY REPORT, M. B. ZIMMERMAN, *THE SUPPLY OF COAL IN THE LONG RUN: THE CASE OF EASTERN DEEP COAL* (CAMBRIDGE, MA: SEPTEMBER 1975). MEDICAL CARE: L. PARINGER AND V. FON, "PRICE DISCRIMINATION IN MEDICINE: THE CASE OF MEDICARE", *QUARTERLY REVIEW OF ECONOMICS AND BUSINESS* (SPRING 1988): 49–68. ESTIMATES ARE BASED ON RESPONSIVENESS OF MEDICARE SERVICES TO FEES UNDER THE PROGRAM AND MAY OVERSTATE ELASTICITIES FOR THE ENTIRE MEDICAL CARE MARKET. NATURAL GAS: J. D. KHAZZOOM, "THE FPC STAFF'S MODEL OF NATURAL GAS SUPPLY IN THE UNITED STATES", *THE BELL JOURNAL OF ECONOMICS AND MANAGEMENT SCIENCE* (SPRING 1971). CRUDE OIL: D. N. EPPLE, *PETROLEUM DISCOVERIES AND GOVERNMENT POLICY* (CAMBRIDGE, MA: MARC BALLINGER PUBLISHING COMPANY, 1984), CHAPTER 3.

the costs of hiring new workers. The entry of new firms may also provide a "critical mass" of industrialization that permits the development of more efficient transportation, communications, and financial networks. Whatever the exact nature of the cost reductions, the final result is illustrated in Figure 10-9. The initial market equilibrium is shown by the price quantity combination P_1, Q_1 in Figure 10-9(c). At this price, the typical firm in Figure 10-9(a) produces q_1 and earns exactly zero in economic profits. Now suppose market demand shifts outward to D'. In the short run, price increases to P_2 and the typical firm produces q_2. At this price level, positive profits are earned. These profits cause new firms to enter the market. If these entries cause costs to decline, a new set of cost curves for the typical firm might resemble those in Figure 10-9(b). Now the new equilibrium price is P_3. At this price, Q_3 is demanded. By considering all possible shifts in demand, the long-run supply curve LS can be traced out. For this **decreasing cost case**, the long-run supply curve has a negative slope. In this case, increases in demand cause the market price of a product eventually to fall. Whether this explains recent large declines in the prices of telecommunications services is examined in Application 10.4: *How Do Network Externalities Affect Supply Curves?*

Decreasing cost case
A market in which the entry of firms decreases firms' costs.

MICROQUIZ 10.4

Table 10-3 reports that the estimated long-run elasticity of supply for natural gas in the United States is about 0.5. Hence, over the long-term we can expect each 10 per cent increase in natural gas production to be accompanied by a 20 per cent rise in relative price. Which interpretation (if either) of this fact is correct?

1 New firms should flock to this industry because it will be very profitable.

2 Existing firms will do very well in this market.

Infant Industries

The possibility of a negatively sloped long-run supply curve is believed to characterize some newly emerging, or "infant", industries. Initially, the costs of production of a new product may be very high. Few workers possess the skills needed to produce the good and procure other required inputs (such as communication networks or financing arrangements), which may be similarly underdeveloped. These difficulties are ameliorated as expanding production of the good yields a progressively larger pool of trained workers and a better-developed set of necessary services. Likewise, the improved availability of inputs causes the costs of all firms

FIGURE 10-9 Decreasing Costs Result in a Negatively Sloped Long-Run Supply Curve *Initially, the market is in equilibrium at P_1, Q_1. An increase in demand to D' causes price to rise to P_2 in the short run, and the typical firm produces q_2 at a profit. This profit attracts new firms. If the entry of these new firms causes costs to fall, a set of new cost curves might look like those in (b). With this new set of curves, market equilibrium is re-established at P_3, Q_3. By connecting such points of equilibrium, a negatively sloped long-run supply curve LS is traced out.*

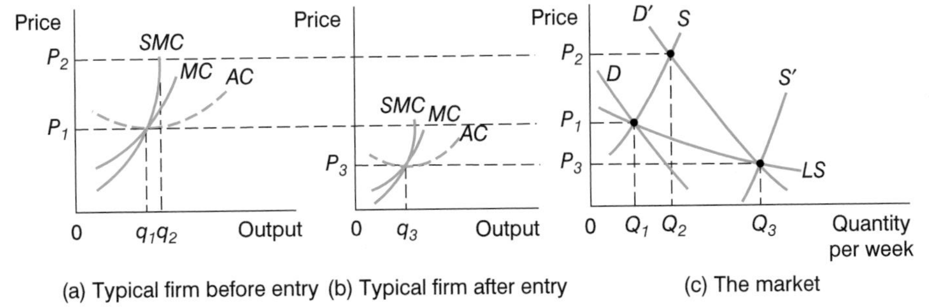

APPLICATION 10.4 *How Do Network Externalities Affect Supply Curves?*

Network externalities arise when adding additional users to a network causes costs to decline. Such externalities are common in many modern industries in telecommunication and Internet technology. Their presence sets the stage for declining prices as demand expands.

Metcalfe's Law

A basic property of communications networks is that they obey Metcalfe's Law, a principle named for Robert Metcalfe, a pioneer in the development of Ethernet technology. The law states that the usefulness of a given network varies directly with the square of the number of subscribers to that network.[1] This implies that the value of such a network expands much more rapidly than do the costs associated with establishing it. Such increasing returns combined with the impact of rapid change in communications technology itself have led to strong downtrends in the prices of many types of communications networks.

Some Examples

Examples of network externalities occur in the telecommunications, software, and Internet industries:

- **Telecommunications**: The benefits of having a phone or fax machine are greater the larger the number of people with whom one can communicate. Large telephone networks also facilitate other phone applications such as burglar alarm systems and mail-order operations.
- **Applications Software**: The greater the number of users of a given software package, the greater will be the benefits to users in terms of file sharing. For this reason, Microsoft Office has come to dominate the office software business. Microsoft also benefits from network externalities with their Windows operating systems because the large number of Windows installations makes it profitable for others to write applications software only for that system.
- **The Internet**: Network externalities in the Internet are similar to those in telecommunications. The ability of the Internet to carry any sort of digital file enables a much wider range of interactions than is possible with traditional phone networks, however. Especially problematic has been the ability of the Internet to foster piracy of intellectual property such as music or motion pictures.

Network Externalities and Supply Curves

Because prices for telecommunications and Internet services have fallen rapidly, it is tempting to argue that the presence of network externalities in these industries gives their long-run supply curves a negative slope. Falling prices just reflect movement along this supply curve as demand expands. Unfortunately, this analysis is unconvincing because the benefits of network externalities accrue largely to demanders,[2] not to suppliers, in terms of lower input costs. Yes, input prices for telecommunications have also been falling because of technical progress, but this effect is largely independent of network externalities. The prices of computers and digital watches have also been falling without reliance on significant network effects.

Economists remain undecided about the effect of network externalities on markets – especially about their impact on competition. The issue seems to be whether a firm can manage to appropriate some of the benefits of network externalities to itself (as seems to be the case with Microsoft Windows) or whether such externalities open the way for greater competition (as seems to be the case in telephone long-distance service). Developing models that differentiate between these two cases is an important area of economic research.

To Think About

1. Because additional users of a network generate gains to existing users, some economists have argued that new users should be subsidized. Will networks be "too small" without such subsidies?

2 Switching to a new network may pose substantial costs. For example, when a company adopts a new word-processing program, it will often incur large training costs. What economic factors would cause users to shift from an existing network to a new one?

[1]If there are n subscribers in a network, there are $n^2 - n$ possible connections among them (because a subscriber cannot connect to himself or herself). This expression may overstate the value of a network, however, because every potential connection is not equally valuable.

[2]For this reason, some authors refer to network externalities as "economies of scale on the demand side of the market".

within an infant industry to decline. For example, the development of the electronics industry in California's Silicon Valley or along routes 128 and 495 in Boston was undoubtedly aided by such cost-reducing economies stemming from the growing concentration of related firms in these areas.

Infant industries play an important role in discussions of international trade policy. Because new industries have high costs, it is argued, they may not be able to compete against lower-cost, foreign competition. Given adequate protection (in the form of a tariff or quota), the domestic industry would grow; costs would fall; and, eventually, firms would be able to meet foreign competition. This argument undoubtedly has held some validity in the past. For example, protection of the US textile industry in the early nineteenth century helped to make it become the world's largest. Today, however, the argument is often exploited by industries only wanting protection from foreign competitors. Detailed research is required to determine whether they really meet the conditions of an infant industry.

SUMMARY

The model of pricing in perfectly competitive markets is probably the most widely used economic model. Even when markets do not strictly obey all of the assumptions of perfect competition, it is still possible to use that model as a reasonable approximation of how such markets work. Some of the basic features of the perfectly competitive model that are highlighted in this chapter are:

- The short-run supply curve in a perfectly competitive market represents the horizontal sum of the short-run supply curves for many price-taking firms. The upward slope of the short-run supply curve reflects these firms' increasing short-run marginal costs.
- Equilibrium prices are determined in the short run by the interaction of the short-run supply curve with the market demand curve. At the equilibrium price, firms are willing to produce precisely the amount of output that people want to buy.
- Shifts in either the demand curve or the supply curve change the equilibrium price. The extent of such a change depends on the particular shapes of the two curves.
- Economic profits attract entrants into a perfectly competitive market in the long run. This entry continues until economic profits are reduced to zero. At that point, the market price equals long-run average cost and each firm is operating at the low point of its long-run average cost curve.
- Entry of new firms may have an effect on the prices of firms' inputs. In the constant cost case, however, input prices are not affected, so the long-run supply curve is horizontal. If entry raises input costs, the long-run supply curve is upward sloping. If entry reduces costs, the long-run supply curve is downward sloping.

REVIEW QUESTIONS

1 Each day 1000 fishing boats return to port with the fish that have been caught. These fish must be sold within a few hours or they will spoil. All of the fish are brought to a single marketplace, and each fisherman places a price on the fish he or she has for sale.

a How would a fisherman know that his or her price was too high?

b How would a fisherman know that his or her price was too low?

c As the day progresses, what would you expect to happen to the prices posted by the fisherman?

2 Many of the figures in this chapter show both an entire market and a single typical firm. How do these graphs reflect the assumption that each firm is selling the same good? How do these graphs reflect the assumption that firms are price takers for this good?

3 Why is the price for which quantity demanded equals quantity supplied called an "equilibrium price"? Suppose, instead, we viewed a demand curve as showing what price consumers are willing to pay and a supply curve as showing what price firms want to receive. Using this view of demand and supply, how would you define an "equilibrium quantity"?

4 For markets with inelastic demand and supply curves, most short-run movements will be in prices, not quantity. For markets with elastic demand and supply curves, most movements will be in quantity, not price. Do you agree? Illustrate your answer with a few simple graphs.

5 If long-run equilibrium in a perfectly competitive industry involves zero profits, why would anyone ever start a new business? What does an entrepreneur hope to achieve by starting a new firm? How might his or her initial success undermine this goal in the long term?

6 In long-run equilibrium in a perfectly competitive market, each firm operates at minimum average cost. Do firms also operate at minimum long-run average cost when such markets are out of equilibrium in the short run? Wouldn't firms make more in short-run profits if they opted always to produce that output level for which average costs were as small as possible?

7 Dr D. is a critic of standard microeconomic analysis. In one of his frequent tirades, he was heard to say: "Take the argument for upward-sloping, long-run supply curves. This is a circular argument if I ever heard one. Long-run supply curves are said to be upward sloping because input prices rise when firms hire more of them. And that occurs because the long-run supply curves for these inputs are upward sloping. Hence, the argument boils down to 'long-run supply curves are upward sloping because other supply curves are upward sloping'. What nonsense!" Does Dr D. have a point? How would you defend the analysis in this chapter?

8 Dr E. is an environmentalist and a critic of economics. On *The Tonight Program*, he attacks a book: "That text is typical – it includes all of this nonsense about long-run supply elasticities for natural resources like oil or coal. Any idiot knows that, because the earth has a finite size, all supply curves for natural resources are perfectly inelastic with respect to price. How can a rise in price for, say, oil lead to more oil when all of our oil was created eons ago? Focusing on these ridiculously high elasticity numbers just detracts from studying our real need – the need to conserve." How would you defend the analysis in this book against this tirade?

9 The long-run supply curve for gem diamonds is positively sloped because increases in diamond output increase the wages of diamond cutters. Explain why a decision by people to no longer buy diamond engagement rings would have disastrous consequences for diamond cutters but why such a trend would not really harm the owners of firms in the perfectly competitive gem diamond business.

10 "The existence of the decreasing cost case ultimately depends on the availability of inputs

that also have negatively sloped supply curves. If firms themselves took actions that reduced costs, they would appropriate these cost reductions for themselves, and they would not spread to other firms." Do you agree? Or may some cost reductions not be fully appropriable by the firm that causes them?

PROBLEMS

10.1 Suppose the daily demand curve for haddock at Peterhead is given by

$$Q_D = 1600 - 600P$$

where Q_D is demand in kilos per day and P is price per euro.

a If fishing boats land 1000 kilos one day, what will the price be?

b If the catch were to fall to 400 kilos, what would the price be?

c Suppose the demand for haddock shifts outward to

$$Q_D = 2200 - 600P$$

How would your answers to part a and part b change?

d Plot your results on a graph.

10.2 Suppose, as in problem 10.1, the demand for haddock is given by

$$Q_D = 1600 - 600P$$

but now assume that Peterhead fishermen can, at some cost, choose to sell their catch elsewhere. Specifically, assume that the amount they will sell in Peterhead is given by

$$Q_S = -1000 + 2000P \text{ for } Q_S \geq 0$$

where Q_S is the quantity supplied in kilos and P is the price per kilo.

a What is the lowest price at which haddock will be supplied to the Peterhead market?

b Given the demand curve for haddock, what will the equilibrium price be?

c Suppose now, as in problem 10.1, demand shifts to

$$Q_D = 2200 - 600P$$

What will be the new equilibrium price?

d Explain intuitively why price will rise by less in part c than it did in problem 10.1.

e Plot your results on a graph.

10.3 A perfectly competitive market has 1000 firms. In the very short run, each of the firms has a fixed supply of 100 units. The market demand is given by

$$Q = 160\,000 - 10\,000P$$

a Calculate the equilibrium price in the very short run.

b Calculate the demand schedule facing any one firm in the industry. Do this by calculating what the equilibrium price would be if one of the sellers decided to sell nothing or if one seller decided to sell 200 units. What do you conclude about the effect of any one firm on market price?

10.4 Assuming the same conditions as in problem 10.3, suppose now that in the short run each firm has a supply curve that shows the quantity the firm will supply (q_i) as a function of market price. The specific form of this supply curve is given by

$$q_i = -200 + 50P$$

Using this short-run supply response, supply new solutions to part a and part b in problem 10.3. Why do you get different solutions in this case?

10.5 Widgets, Inc., is a small firm producing widgets. The widget industry is perfectly competitive; Widgets, Inc., is a price taker. The short-run total cost curve for Widgets, Inc., has the form:

$$STC = 1/3\, q^3 + 10q^2 + 100q = 48$$

and the short-run marginal cost curve is given by

$$SMC = q^2 + 20q + 100$$

a Calculate the firm's short-run supply curve with q (the number of widgets produced per day) as a function of market price (P).

b How many widgets will the firm produce if the market price is $P = 121$? $P = 169$? $P = 256$? (Assume all of these prices exceed the firm's shutdown price.)

c How much profit will Widgets, Inc., make when $P = 121$? $P = 169$? $P = 256$?

10.6 Suppose there are 100 identical firms in the perfectly competitive note card industry. Each firm has a short-run total cost curve of the form:

$$STC = \frac{1}{300}q^3 + 0.2q^2 + 4q + 10$$

and marginal cost is given by

$$SMC = 0.01q^2 + 0.4q + 4$$

a Calculate the firm's short-run supply curve with q (the number of crates of note cards) as a function of market price (P).

b Calculate the industry supply curve for the 100 firms in this industry.

c Suppose market demand is given by $Q = -200P + 8000$. What will be the short-run equilibrium price-quantity combination?

d Suppose everyone starts writing more research papers and the new market demand is given by $Q = -200P + 10\,000$. What is the new short-run price–quantity equilibrium? How much profit does each firm make?

10.7 Suppose there are 1000 identical firms producing diamonds and that the short-run total cost curve for each firm is given by

$$STC = q^2 + wq$$

and short-run marginal cost is given by

$$SMC = 2q + w$$

where q is the firm's output level and w is the wage rate of diamond cutters.

a If $w = 10$, what will be the firm's (short-run) supply curve? What is the industry's supply curve? How many diamonds will be produced at a price of 20 each? How many more diamonds would be produced at a price of 21?

b Suppose that the wages of diamond cutters depend on the total quantity of diamonds produced and the form of this relationship is given by

$$w = 0.002Q$$

where Q represents total industry output, which is 1000 times the output of the typical firm. In this situation, show that the firm's marginal cost (and short-run supply) curve depends on Q. What is the industry supply curve? How much will be produced at a price of 20? How much more will be produced at a price of 21? What do you conclude about how the shape of the short-run supply curve is affected by this relationship between input prices and output?

10.8 Wheat is produced under perfectly competitive conditions. Individual wheat farmers have U-shaped, long-run, average-cost curves that reach a minimum average cost of €3 per bushel when 1000 bushels are produced.

a If the market demand curve for wheat is given by

$$Q_D = 2\,600\,000 - 200\,000P$$

where Q_D is the number of bushels demanded per year and P is the price per bushel, in long-run equilibrium what will be the price of wheat? How much total wheat will be demanded? How many wheat farms will there be?

b Suppose demand shifts outward to

$$Q_D = 3\,200\,000 - 200\,000P$$

If farmers cannot adjust their output in the short run (that is, suppose the *SMC* curve is vertical), what will market price be with this new demand curve? What will the profits of the typical farm be?

c Given the new demand curve described in part b, what will be the new long-run equilibrium? (That is, calculate market price, quantity of wheat produced, and the new equilibrium number of farms in this new situation.)

d Plot your results on a graph.

10.9 Petrol is sold through local filling stations under perfectly competitive conditions. All petrol station owners face the same long-run average cost curve given by

$$AC = 0.01q - 1 + 100/q$$

and the same long-run marginal cost curve given by

$$MC = 0.02q - 1$$

where q is the number of liters sold per day.

a Assuming the market is in long-run equilibrium, how much petrol will each individual owner sell per day? What are the long-run average cost and marginal cost at this output level?

b The market demand for petrol is given by

$$Q_D = 2\,500\,000 - 500\,000P$$

where Q_D is the number of liters demanded per day and P is the price per liter. Given your answer to part a, what will be the price of petrol in long-run equilibrium? How much petrol will be demanded, and how many petrol stations will there be?

c Suppose that because of the development of solar-powered cars, the market demand for petrol shifts inward to

$$Q_D = 2\,000\,000 - 1\,000\,000P$$

In long-run equilibrium, what will be the price of petrol? How much total petrol will be demanded, and how many petrol stations will there be?

d Plot your results on a graph.

10.10 A perfectly competitive painted men's tie industry has a large number of potential entrants. Each firm has an identical cost structure such that long-run average cost is minimized at an output of 20 units ($q_i = 20$). The minimum average cost is €10 per unit. Total market demand is given by

$$Q = 1500 - 50P$$

a What is the industry's long-run supply schedule?

b What is the long-run equilibrium price (P^*)? The total industry output (Q^*)? The output of each firm (q^*_i)? The number of firms? The profits of each firm?

c The short-run total cost curve associated with each firm's long-run equilibrium output is given by

$$STC = 0.5q^2 - 10q + 200$$

where $SMC = q - 10$. Calculate the short-run average and marginal cost curves. At what tie output level does short-run average cost reach a minimum?

d Calculate the short-run supply curve for each firm and the industry short-run supply curve.

e Suppose now painted ties become more fashionable and the market demand function shifts upward to $Q = 2000 - 50P$. Using this new demand curve, answer part b for the very short run when firms cannot change their outputs.

f In the short run, use the industry short-run supply curve to recalculate the answers to part b.

g What is the new long-run equilibrium for the industry?

11

Applying the Competitive Model

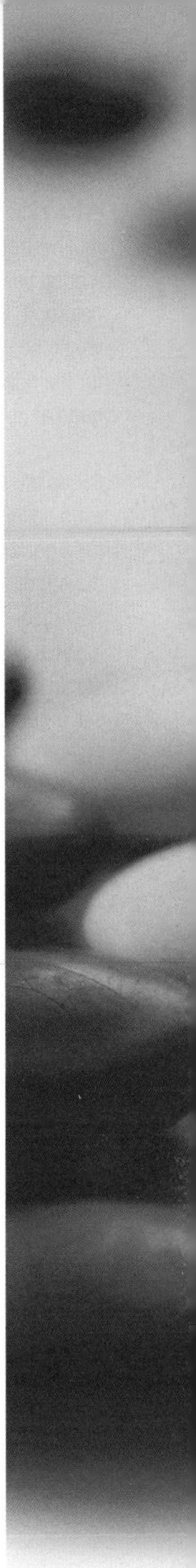

In Chapter 1, we met an educated parrot who became an economist by learning to say, "supply and demand!" This parrot knew that practically every applied economic model starts from the competitive case we studied in the previous chapter. Here, we will look at some of the most important of these applications.

Consumer and Producer Surplus

A simple supply–demand analysis can often be used to assess the well-being of market participants. For example, in Chapter 3 we introduced the notion of **consumer surplus** as a way of illustrating consumers' gains from market transactions. Figure 11-1 summarizes these ideas by showing the market for, say, fresh tomatoes. At the equilibrium price of P^*, individuals choose to consume Q^* tomatoes. Because the demand curve D shows what people are willing to pay for one more tomato at various levels of Q, the total value of tomato purchases to buyers (relative to a situation where no tomatoes are available) is given by the total area below the demand curve from $Q = 0$ to $Q = Q^*$ – that is, by area AEQ^*0. For this value, they pay an amount given by P^*EQ^*0, and hence receive a "surplus" (over what they pay) given by the grey shaded area AEP^*. Possible happenings in the tomato market that change the size of this area clearly affect the well-being of these market participants.

Figure 11-1 also can be used to illustrate the surplus value received by tomato producers relative to a situation where no tomatoes are produced. This measure is based on the intuitive notion that the supply curve S shows the minimum price that producers would accept for each unit produced. At the market equilibrium P^*, Q^*, producers receive total revenue of P^*EQ^*0. But under a scheme of selling one unit at a time at the lowest possible price, producers would have been willing to produce Q^* for a payment of BEQ^*0. At Q^*, therefore, they receive a **producer surplus**

Consumer surplus The extra value individuals receive from consuming a good over what they pay for it. What people would be willing to pay for the right to consume a good at its current price.

Producer surplus The extra value producers get for a good in excess of the opportunity costs they incur by producing it. What all producers would pay for the right to sell a good at its current market price.

given by the colored area P^*EB. To understand the precise nature of this surplus, we must again examine the short-run/long-run distinction in firms' supply decisions.

Short-Run Producer Surplus

The supply curve S in Figure 11-1 could be either a short-run or a long-run supply curve. However, in Chapter 10, we showed that the upward slope of S has rather different causes in these two cases. In the short run, the market supply curve is the horizontal summation of all firms' short-run marginal cost curves. The curve's positive slope reflects the diminishing returns to variable inputs that are encountered as output is increased. In this case, price exceeds marginal cost (as reflected by the supply curve) at all output levels, except Q^*. Production of each of these "intramarginal" units of output generates incremental profits for suppliers. Total short-run profits, then, are given by the sum of all of these profit increments (area P^*EB) plus profits when $Q = 0$. But, by definition, when $Q = 0$, profits are made up only of the loss of all fixed costs. Hence, short-run producer surplus (area P^*EB) reflects both actual profits in the short run and all fixed costs. This an appropriate measure of how much firms that decide to not shut down gain from participating in the market in the short run.[1] In this sense, it

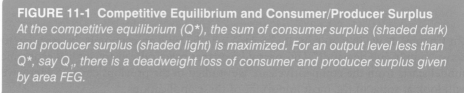

FIGURE 11-1 Competitive Equilibrium and Consumer/Producer Surplus
At the competitive equilibrium (Q^*), the sum of consumer surplus (shaded dark) and producer surplus (shaded light) is maximized. For an output level less than Q^*, say Q_1, there is a deadweight loss of consumer and producer surplus given by area FEG.

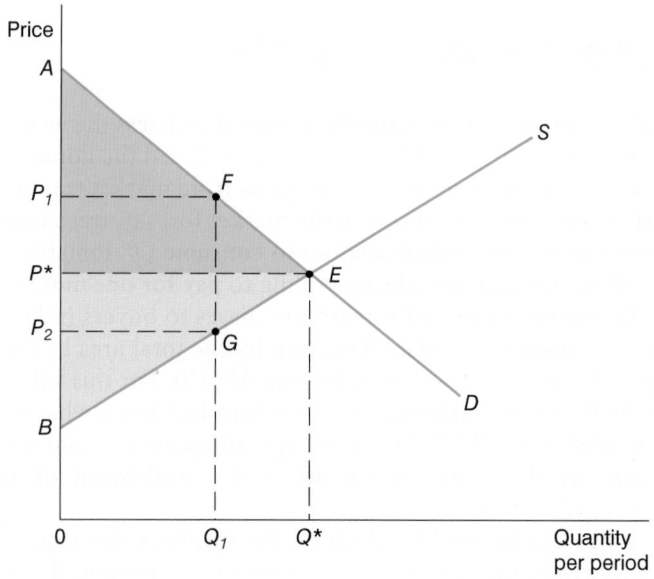

[1]Some algebra may clarify matters. Profits (π_m) at P^* are given by $\pi_m = P^*Q^* - TC$, whereas profits when shut down π_s are given by $\pi_s = -FC$. Hence, the gain from participating in the market is given by $\pi_m - \pi_s = \pi_m - (-FC) = \pi_m + FC$.

is the mirror image of consumer surplus, which measures how much consumers gain by being in the market rather than out of it.

Long-Run Producer Surplus

In the long run, positively sloped supply curves arise because firms experience increasing input costs. When the market is in equilibrium, each firm has zero profits and there are no fixed costs. Short-run producer surplus does not exist in this situation. Instead, long-run producer surplus now reflects the increasing payments being received by the firms' inputs as output expands. The area P^*EB in Figure 11-1 now measures all of these increased payments relative to a situation in which the industry produces no output, in which case these inputs would receive lower prices for their services.

Ricardian Rent

Long-run producer surplus can be most easily illustrated with a situation first described by David Ricardo in the early part of the nineteenth century.[2] Assume there are many parcels of land on which tomatoes might be grown. These range from very fertile land (low costs of production) to very poor, dry land (high costs). The long-run supply curve for tomatoes is constructed as follows. At low prices, only the best land is used to produce tomatoes and few are produced. As output increases, higher-cost plots of land are brought into production because higher prices make it profitable to grow tomatoes on this land. The long-run supply curve for tomatoes is positively sloped because of the increasing costs associated with using less-fertile land. Notice that this is a different reason than we discussed in Chapter 10. There, firms had identical cost curves and every firm's costs were affected by rising input prices. In the Ricardian example, firms' costs differ and costs of the marginal firm increase as more firms enter a market.

Ricardian rent Long-run profits earned by owners of low-cost firms. May be capitalized into the prices of these firms' inputs.

Market equilibrium in this situation is illustrated in Figure 11-2. At an equilibrium price of P^*, both the low-cost and the medium-cost farms earn (long-run) profits. The "marginal farm" earns exactly zero economic profits. Farms with even higher costs stay out of the market because they would incur losses at a price of P^*. Profits earned by the intramarginal farms can persist in the long run, however, because they reflect returns to a rare resource – low-cost land. Free entry cannot erode these profits even over the long term. The sum of these long-run profits constitutes total producer surplus as given by area P^*EB in Figure 11-2(d).

The long-run profits illustrated in Figure 11-2 are sometimes referred to as **Ricardian rent**. They represent the returns obtained by the owners of scarce resources (in this case, fertile tomato-growing land) in a marketplace. Often these rents are "capitalized" into the prices of these resources; in short, fertile land sells for higher prices than does poor land.

MICROQUIZ 11.1

The study of long-run producer surplus is one of the most important ways in which microeconomics ties together effects in various markets. Why are the following relationships true?

1. If the peanut harvesting industry is a price taker for *all* of the inputs it hires, there will be no long-run producer surplus in this industry.
2. If the only "scarce" resource in the potato harvesting industry is land for growing potatoes, total long-run producer surplus in this industry will be measured by total economic rents earned by potato-land owners. Do these rents "cause" high potato prices?

[2]See David Ricardo, *The Principles of Political Economy and Taxation* (1817; reprint, London: J.M. Dent and Son, 1965), Chapter 2 and Chapter 32.

Similarly, rich gold mines have higher prices than poor mines, favorably located retail space in shopping centers rents for more than out-of-the-way space, and airport landing slots at Heathrow airport near London are more valuable than slots at Luton airport which is not quite London despite the description of Luton, London that one often sees! (Hence the preference of low-cost carriers for such airports as the latter.)

Economic Efficiency

This description of producer and consumer surplus also provides a simple proof of why economists believe competitive markets produce "efficient" allocations of resources. Although a more detailed examination of that topic requires that we look at many markets (which we do in the next chapter), here we can return to Figure 11-1 as a simple illustration. Any output level for tomatoes other than Q^* in this figure is inefficient in that the sum total of consumer and producer surplus is not as large as possible. If Q_1 tomatoes were produced, for example, a total surplus of area *FEG* would be forgone. At Q_1 demanders are willing to pay P_1 for another tomato, which would cost only P_2 to

FIGURE 11-2 Ricardian Rent *Low-cost and medium-cost farms can earn long-run profits (shaded areas) if these costs reflect ownership of unique resources. Total Ricardian rent represents producer surplus—area P*EB in (d). Ricardian rents are usually capitalized into resource prices.*

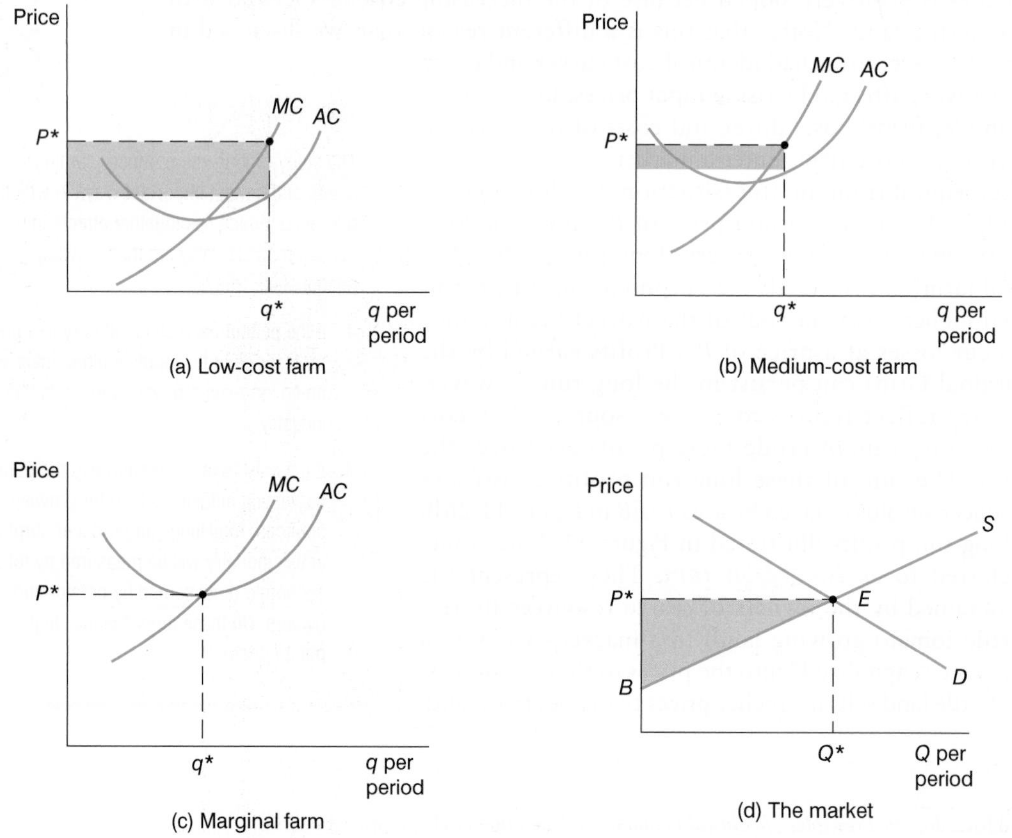

produce. That gap suggests that there exists a mutually beneficial transaction (such as producing one more tomato at a price of P^*) that could benefit both demanders (who would get the tomato for less than they were willing to pay) and suppliers (who would get more for the tomato than it would cost to produce). Only at Q^* are all such mutually beneficial transactions consummated and only then is the sum of consumer and producer surplus as large as possible.[3] Output level Q^* is said to be an **economically efficient allocation of resources** – a term we explore further in the next chapter. Application 11.1: *Does Buying Things on the Internet Improve Welfare?* shows how the extra welfare from expanding markets can be measured. Before turning to a number of other applications, a numerical example may help illustrate the efficiency concept.

Economically efficient allocation of resources An allocation of resources in which the sum of consumer and producer surplus is maximized. Reflects the best (utility-maximizing) use of scarce resources.

A Numerical Illustration

In Chapter 10, we looked at a hypothetical market for CDs in which demand was represented by

$$Q = 10 - P \qquad \{11.1\}$$

and supply by

$$Q = P - 2 \qquad \{11.2\}$$

We showed that equilibrium in this market occurs at $P^* = €6$ and $Q^* = 4$ CDs per week. Figure 11-3 repeats Figure 10–6 by providing an illustration of this equilibrium. At point E, consumers are spending €24 (= 6 × 4) per week for CDs. Total consumer surplus is given by the dark triangular area in the figure and amounts to €8 (= 1/2 of 4 × 4) per week. At E, producers also receive revenues of €24 per week and gain a producer surplus of €8 per week as reflected by the light triangle. Total consumer and producer surplus is therefore €16 per week.

The inefficiency of other potential CD output levels can also be illustrated with the help of Figure 11-3. If price remains at €6 but output is only three tapes per week, for example, consumers and producers each receive €7.50 per week of surplus in their transactions. Total consumer and producer surplus is €15 per week – a reduction of €1 from what it is at E. Total surplus would still be €15 per week with output of three CDs per week at any other price between €5 and €7. Once output is specified, the precise price at which transactions occur affects only the distribution of surplus between consumers and producers. The transaction price does not affect the total amount of surplus, which is always given by the area between the demand curve and the supply curve.

Output levels greater than four CDs per week are also inefficient. For example, production of five CDs per week at a transaction price of €6 would again generate consumer surplus of €7.50 (€8 for the four CDs transaction less a loss of €0.50 on the sale of the fifth CD, since the CD sells for more than people are willing to pay). Similarly, a producer surplus of €7.50 would occur, representing a loss of €0.50 in the production of the fifth CD. Total surplus at this point is now €15 per week, one euro less than at the market equilibrium. Again, the actual price assumed here doesn't matter – it is the fact that costs (reflected by the supply curve S) exceed individuals' willingness to pay (reflected by the demand curve D) for output levels greater than four CDs per week that results in the loss of total surplus value.

[3] Producing more than Q^* would also reduce total producer and consumer surplus since consumers' willingness to pay for extra output would fall short of the costs of producing that output.

APPLICATION 11.1 *Does Buying Things on the Internet Improve Welfare?*

Technical innovations together with significant network externalities have sharply reduced the transactions costs associated with conducting business over the Internet. These innovations offer the promise of transforming the way selling is done in many industries.

The Gains from Internet Trade

Figure 1 illustrates the nature of the gains from reduced transactions costs of Internet trading. The demand and supply curves in the figure represent consumers' and firms' behavior vis-à-vis any good that might be bought and sold over the Internet. Prior to the decline in Internet costs, per-unit transactions costs exceeded $P_2 - P_1$. Hence, no trading took place; buyers and sellers preferred traditional retail outlets. A fall in these costs increased Internet business. Assuming that the per-unit cost of making transactions fell to zero, the market would show a large increase in Internet trading, settling at the competitive equilibrium, P^*, Q^*. This new equilibrium promises substantial increases in both consumer and producer surplus.

The Growth of E-Commerce

Although Internet retailing is relatively new, its early growth has been remarkable. In America, in 2004, electronic retailing directly to consumers totaled about $45 billion, with business-to-business sales representing another $100 billion or more. The most important early inroads by Internet sales were in travel-related goods (airline and holiday reservations), online financial services, and in some narrow categories of consumer goods (for example, books sold by Amazon.com). These are goods for which Internet trading represented some of the largest reductions in transactions costs relative to traditional outlets. More recently, e-commerce has made inroads into many other areas as traditional retailers such as Tesco or Carrefour make

FIGURE 1 Reduced Transaction Costs Promote Internet Commerce *When transaction costs for Internet trading exceed $P_2 - P_1$, no transactions occur. As transaction costs decline, equilibrium approaches P^*, Q^*.*

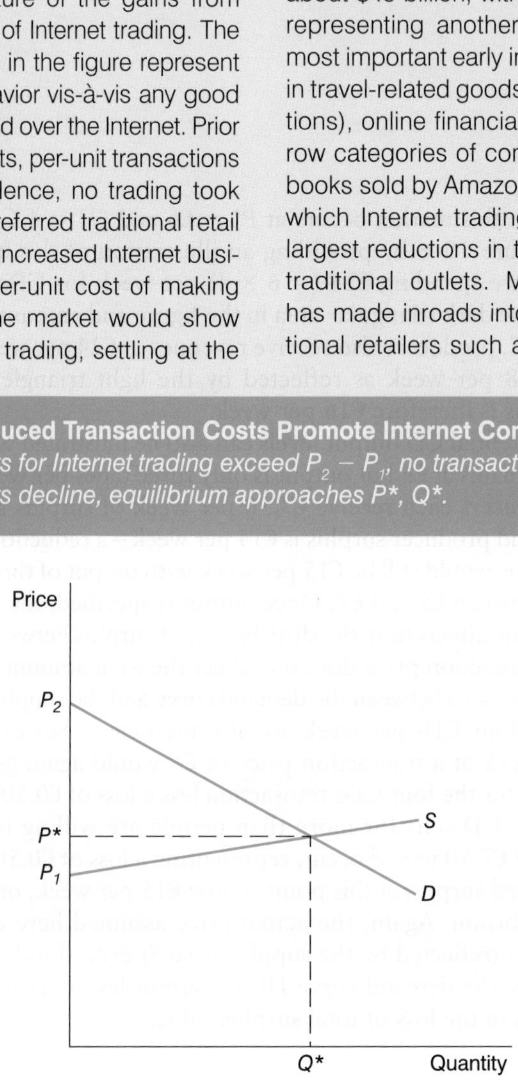

increasingly large fractions of their sales over the web.

The Value Added by Internet Retailers

One question raised by the growth of Internet selling is whether there will remain a separate role for retailers over the long term. If the Internet allows producers to reach customers directly, why would any role for retailing "middlemen" remain? The answer to this query lies in the nature of services that e-retailers can provide. In general, the primary good that such retailers provide is information. For example, Internet car sites (such as jamjar.com) not only provide comparative information about the features of various models, but can also point to the dealer that gives the best price. Internet travel services can search for the lowest fare or for the most convenient departure. Many retailing sites make use of customer profiles to suggest items they might like to buy. For example, Amazon.com uses a customer's past book purchases to suggest potential new ones. At LandsEnd.com you can even "try on" clothes. Hence, it appears that Internet retailing is evolving in ways that make the most use of the low cost of providing information to consumers.

To Think About

1 How will the growth of Internet retailing affect traditional "bricks and mortar" retailers such as Tesco, Carrefour or WalMart? What special services can these retailers offer that the Internet cannot? Are people willing to pay for such services?

2 One of the assumptions of perfect competition is perfect information. To what extent have search engines on the Internet made that assumption more realistic?

3 It has been said that the growth of the Internet means the "end of geography". Take education; why go to a university when all education can be provided online? What reasons can you think of as to why the Internet is *not* the end of geography?

FIGURE 11-3 Efficiency in CD Sales *Equilibrium in the CD market yields a price of €6 and a quantity of four CDs per week. Consumer surplus (shaded dark) and producer surplus (shaded light) are each €8. An output of three CDs per week would reduce the sum of consumer and producer surplus from €16 to €15.*

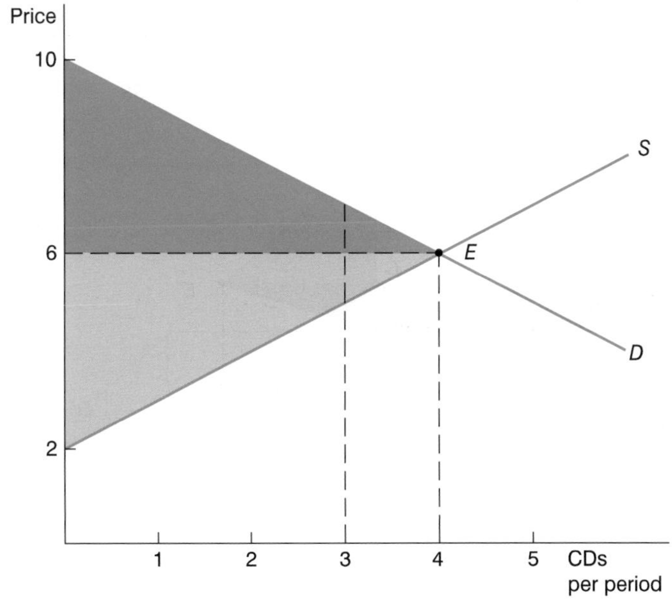

Price Controls and Shortages

Sometimes governments seek to control prices at below-equilibrium levels or intervene into a market to make it more "efficient". Although adoption of such policies is usually claimed to be based on noble motives (such as aiding the poor), frequently the controls or legislation distort the market in ways that were not anticipated and can deter long-run supply responses and create welfare losses for both consumers and producers. A simple analysis of this possibility is provided by Figure 11-4. Initially, the market is in long-run equilibrium at P_1, Q_1 (point *E*). An increase in demand from *D* to *D'* would cause the price to rise to P_2 in the short run and encourage entry by new firms. Assuming this market is characterized by increasing costs (as reflected in the long-run supply curve *LS*), price would fall somewhat as a result of this entry, ultimately settling at P_3. If these price changes were regarded as undesirable, the government could, in principle, prevent them by imposing a legally enforceable ceiling price of P_1. This would cause firms to continue to supply their previous output (Q_1); and, because at P_1 demanders now want to purchase Q_4, there will be a shortage, given by $Q_4 - Q_1$.

The welfare consequences of this price-control policy can be evaluated by comparing consumer- and producer-surplus measures prevailing under this policy to those that would have prevailed in the absence of controls. First, the buyers of Q_1 gain consumer surplus given by the blue area P_3CEP_1, because they can buy this good at a lower price than would exist in an uncontrolled market. This gain reflects a pure transfer to these buyers from the producer-surplus that would exist without

FIGURE 11-4 Price Controls and Shortages *A shift in demand from D to D' would raise price to P_2 in the short run. Entry over the long run would yield a final equilibrium of P_3 Q_3. Controlling the price at P_1 would prevent these actions and yield a shortage of $Q_4 - Q_1$. Relative to the uncontrolled situation, the price control yields a transfer from producers to consumers (shaded dark) and a deadweight loss of forgone transactions given by the two areas shaded light.*

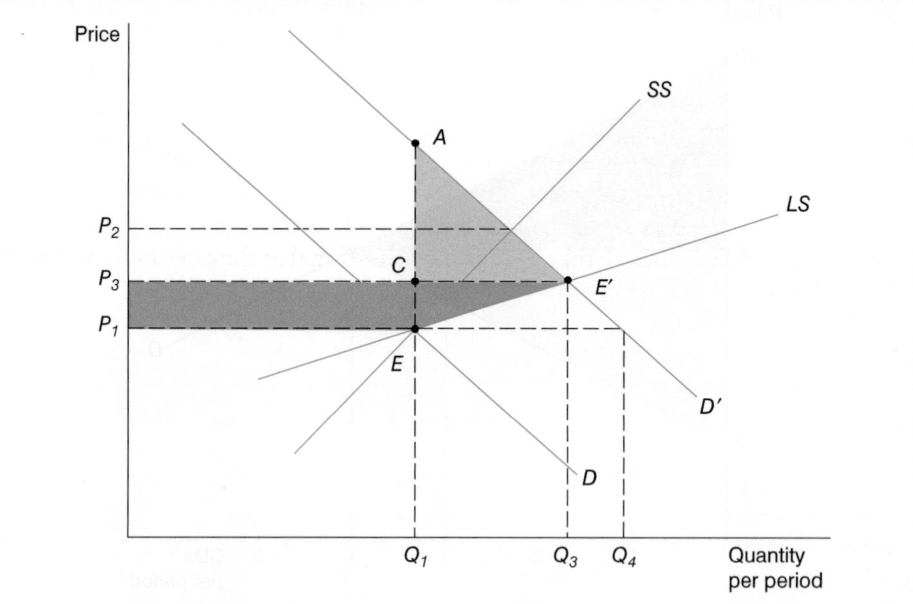

controls. What current consumers have gained from the lower price, producers have lost. Though as for any pure transfer, this does not represent a loss of overall welfare, it does clearly affect the relative well-being of the two types of market participants.

Second, the light shaded area $AE'C$ represents the value of additional consumer-surplus that would have been attained without controls. This represents what new consumers gain by being able to buy this good. Similarly, the dark shaded area $CE'E$ reflects additional producer surplus available in the uncontrolled situation. Together these two areas (that is, area $AE'E$) represent the total value of mutually beneficial transactions between willing buyers and sellers that are prevented by the government policy of controlling price. This is, therefore, a measure of the pure welfare costs of that policy (as distinct from its transfer effects).

Finally, the welfare analysis associated with Figure 11-4 also provides some insights about the politics of any price-control policy. Buyers who are able to get output Q_1 at a price of P_1 will be big supporters of the policy because they obtain substantial welfare benefits. Those benefits, however, come at the expense of producers of Q_1 who, because they earn less than they might, would likely oppose the policy. Both producers and consumers who wish to make transactions for amounts greater than Q_1 lose and they might also oppose the policy. They might, in fact, seek ways around the price controls by engaging in illegal transactions at prices higher than P_1.

In Application 11.2 *UK Government Intervention in the Housing Market* we look at how the UK government tried to influence the housing market. While not using direct price controls, a botched intervention design to help make the market more efficient for buyers of flats and houses had unforeseen consequences that impacted on both the market for buying homes and for renting them.

Tax Incidence

Another important application of the perfectly competitive model is to the study of the effects of taxes. Not only does the model permit an evaluation of how taxation alters the allocation of resources, but it also highlights the issue of who bears the actual burden of various taxes. By stressing the distinction between the legal obligation to pay a tax and the economic effects that may shift that burden elsewhere, **tax incidence theory** helps to clarify the ways in which taxes actually affect the well-being of market participants.

Tax incidence theory
The study of the final burden of a tax after considering all market reactions to it.

Figure 11-5 illustrates this approach by considering a "specific tax" of a fixed amount per unit of output that is imposed on all firms in a constant cost industry. Although legally the tax is required to be *paid* by the firm, this view of things is very misleading. To demonstrate this, we begin by showing that the tax can be analyzed as a shift downward in the demand curve facing this industry from D to D'. The vertical distance between the curves measures the amount of the per unit tax, t. For any price that consumers pay (say, P) firms get to keep only $P - t$. It is that after-tax demand curve D', then, that is relevant to firms' behavior. Consumers continue to pay a "gross" price as reflected by the demand curve D. The tax creates a "wedge" between what consumers pay and what firms actually get to keep.

The short-run effect of the tax is to shift the equilibrium from its initial position P_1, Q_1 to the point where the new demand curve D' intersects the short-run supply curve S. That intersection occurs at output level Q_2 at an after-tax price to the firm of P_2. Assuming this price exceeds average variable costs, the typical firm now produces output level q_2 at a loss.

APPLICATION 11.2 *UK Government Intervention in the Housing Market*

It seemed like a good idea; make every individual who wishes to sell their home in England compile a package of information which prospective buyers could look at. The package would include title deeds, copies of planning approvals, local searches, guarantees for any work done and an energy performance certificate. This would then make the quality of the housing more transparent and save buyers hundreds if not thousands of pounds in commissioning surveys of different properties – one home information pack (HIP) for all potential buyers to see at no cost to them. Rather the seller would bear the cost of roughly £400 to £500.

Due to be introduced on 1 June 2007, the scheme was shelved and at the time of writing had not come into force. However, in many respects the damage had been done. In an attempt to beat the charge of £500 many home owners brought their sale forward or to be more accurate placed their property on the market. For placing a home on the market is not the same thing as selling it. According to the National Association of Estate Agents the number of properties for sale went from 62 per agent in April 2007 to 72 in May 2007, a rise of 16.1 per cent.

With many sellers still expecting to receive offers for their properties based on the previous supply of properties to the market, asking prices were in many cases unrealistically set too high. As such, within a couple of months an oversupply of properties in the sales market developed.

Seeing that their properties were not selling many vendors decided that rather than lower their asking price, they would place their property on the rental market perhaps waiting on better times when they could get their favored price for their property. As such the knock-on effect was now into the rental market.

Voyce, who lives in Malvern Wells in Worcestershire, has let the flat, which was his former home, to corporate tenants since 2004, but is now struggling to attract interest. He has reduced the monthly rent from £1000 to £900 to make it more competitive. (*The Guardian* newspaper, 23 June 2007.)

Despite the above example, many properties remained vacant, unable to be rented out. That said, one needs to be careful. While there is a lot of anecdotal evidence that there was a rush to "beat HIPs", anecdotal evidence is not a replacement for scientific enquiry. In the first half of 2007 interest rates had been steadily rising and many commentators were predicting them to rise further. As such there could very well be more than one effect operating. Many people may have come to the conclusion that it was better to sell now while prices were still "good" rather than wait for the market to stall or even for house prices to fall (as they did in the UK in the early 1990s).

To Think About

1 Using a supply and demand diagram represent the initial state of the housing market, i.e. for selling residential property, in April 2007 and then on the same diagram show the effect of an increase in supply in May 2007 with sellers reluctant to lower their asking prices. Clearly indicate the oversupply of housing on your diagram.

2 Using a supply and demand diagram represent the initial state of the rental housing market before the increase in supply of properties for rent and then after.

3 Give the rise in UK interest rates what (eventually) should happen to the demand curves for housing in both markets?

Consumers will pay P_3 for output level Q_2. The graph reveals that $P_3 - P_2 = t$; in the short run, the tax is borne partially by consumers (who see the price they pay rise from P_1 to P_3) and partially by firms, which are now operating at a loss because they are receiving only P_2 (instead of P_1) for their output.

Long-Run Shifting of the Tax

In the long-run, firms do not continue to operate at a loss. Some firms leave the market bemoaning the role of oppressive taxation in bringing about their downfall. The industry short-run supply curve shifts leftward because fewer firms remain in the market. A new long-run equilibrium is established at Q_3 where the after-tax price received by those firms still in the industry enables them to earn exactly zero in economic profits. The firms remaining in the industry return to producing output level q_1. The price paid by buyers in the market is now P_4. In the long run, the entire amount of the tax has been shifted into increased prices. Even though the firm ostensibly *pays* the tax, the long run burden is borne completely by the consumers of this good.[4]

Long-Run Incidence with Increasing Costs

In the more realistic case of increasing costs, both producers and consumers pay a portion of this tax. Such a possibility is illustrated in Figure 11-6. Here, the long-run supply curve (*LS*) has a positive slope because the costs of various inputs are bid up as industry output expands. Imposition of the tax, *t*, shifts the after-tax demand curve inward to *D′*, and this brings about a fall in net price over the long-run from P_1 to P_2. Faced with the lower price, P_2, firms leave this industry, which has the

MICROQUIZ 11.2

Suppose a local government placed price controls on prescription drugs in expectation of a large increase in demand.

1. What aspect of drug firms' costs would determine the difference between the short-run and the long-run impact of this policy?
2. Explain how the losses of producer surplus from this policy would differ between the short run and the long run.

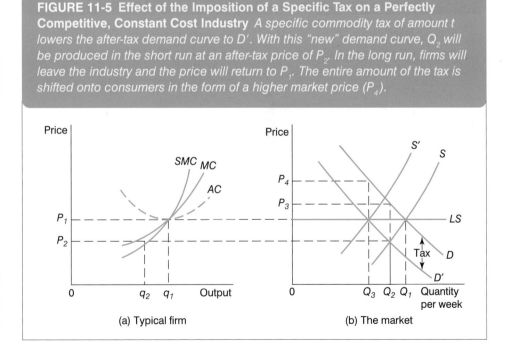

FIGURE 11-5 Effect of the Imposition of a Specific Tax on a Perfectly Competitive, Constant Cost Industry *A specific commodity tax of amount t lowers the after-tax demand curve to D′. With this "new" demand curve, Q_2 will be produced in the short run at an after-tax price of P_2. In the long run, firms will leave the industry and the price will return to P_1. The entire amount of the tax is shifted onto consumers in the form of a higher market price (P_4).*

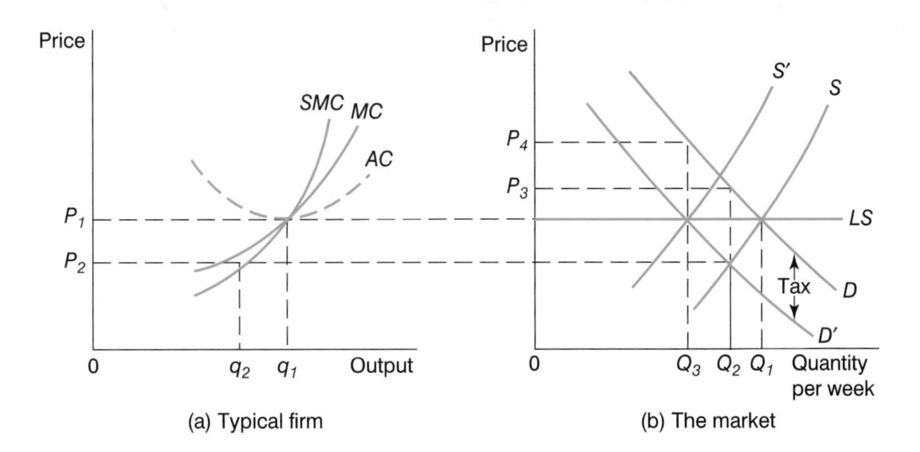

[4]Notice that owners of firms leaving the industry incur no long-run burden because they were initially earning zero economic profits, and, by assumption, can earn the same return elsewhere.

effect of reducing some inputs' prices. Long-run equilibrium is re-established at this lower net price, and consumers now pay a gross price of P_3, which exceeds what they paid previously. Total tax collections are given by the light shaded area $P_3ABE_2P_2$. These are partly paid by consumers (who pay P_3 instead of P_1) and partly by the owners of firms' inputs who are now paid based on a lower net price, P_2, instead of P_1.[5]

Incidence and Elasticity

A bit of geometric intuition suggests that the relative sizes of the price changes shown in Figure 11-6 depend on the elasticities of the demand and supply curves. Intuitively, the market participant with the more elastic response is able more easily to "get out of the way" of the tax, leaving the one with less-elastic response still in place to pay the most. We have already illustrated a special case of this principle in Figure 11-5. In that figure, the long-run elasticity of supply is infinite because of the constant-cost nature of the industry. Because the price received by firms (and by the inputs the firm employs) does not vary as output contracts as a result of the tax, the entire tax burden is shifted onto consumers. This outcome may be quite common in situations of some state or local taxes for which the good being taxed constitutes such a small portion of the national total that local supply is infinitely elastic. For example, a small town that tries

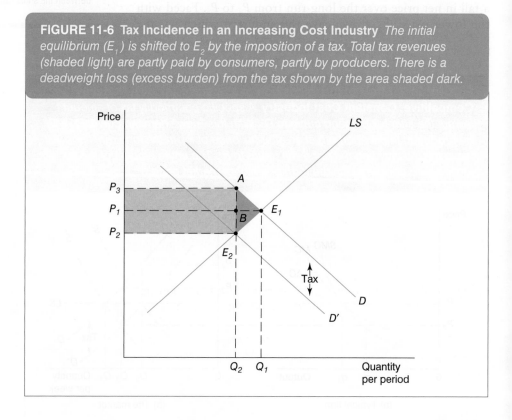

FIGURE 11-6 Tax Incidence in an Increasing Cost Industry *The initial equilibrium (E_1) is shifted to E_2 by the imposition of a tax. Total tax revenues (shaded light) are partly paid by consumers, partly by producers. There is a deadweight loss (excess burden) from the tax shown by the area shaded dark.*

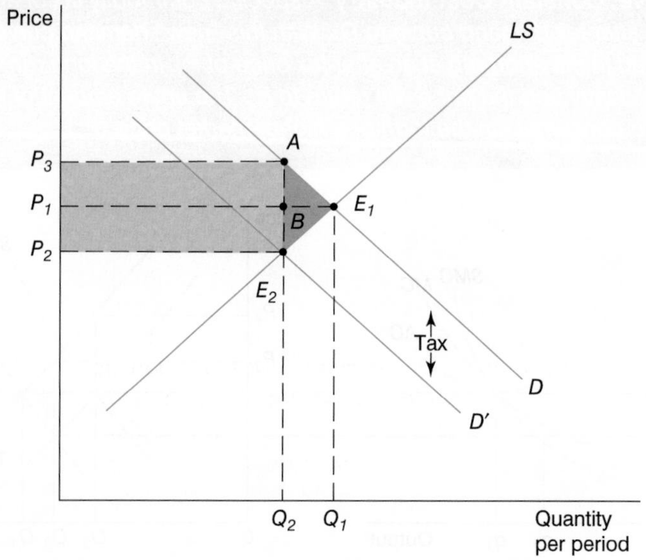

[5]Notice again that the firms' owners, *per se*, experience no losses here since they earned zero profits before the tax. Rather, the producer's share of the tax burden is borne by the owners of those inputs that have fallen in price.

to impose a large tax on its restaurants may find that the tax is quickly reflected in the price of restaurant meals. Some restaurant owners can avoid the tax by going elsewhere.

More generally, if demand is relatively inelastic whereas supply is elastic, demanders pay the bulk of a tax in the form of higher prices. Alternatively, if supply is relatively inelastic but demand is elastic, producers pay most of the tax. Indeed, in this case, we can push the analysis further by noting that the producer's share is paid primarily by those inputs that have inelastic supply curves because it is these inputs that experience the greatest drop in price when demand for their services declines. For example, the producer's share of a tax on gold or silver would be largely paid by mine owners because the supply of mining land to this industry may be very inelastic. The supply of mining machinery or mine workers may be more elastic, however, because these inputs may have good alternative sources of employment. Hence, they would pay little of the tax. Of course, taking account of all of these repercussions of a tax in various markets is sometimes very difficult and simple models of supply and demand may not be up to the task. Modern analyses of the tax incidence question use computer models of general equilibrium so that effects on many markets can be studied simultaneously. A brief look at these types of models is provided in the next chapter and in Application 11.3 *What's the Price of Eggs Got To Do With It?* we give a gentle introduction to the concept of general equilibrium.

Taxation and Efficiency

Because taxation reduces the output of the taxed commodity, there is a reallocation of production to other areas. This reallocation implies that some previously mutually beneficial transactions are forgone and that taxation reduces overall economic welfare. This loss can also be illustrated in Figure 11-6. The total loss in consumer surplus as a result of the tax is given by area $P_3AE_1P_1$. Of this area, P_3ABP_1 is transferred into tax revenues for the government and area AE_1B is simply lost. Similarly, the total loss of producer surplus is given by area $P_1E_1E_2P_2$ with area $P_1BE_2P_2$ being transferred into tax revenues and area BE_1E_2 being lost. By the standard of resource allocation efficiency, the effect of the transfer into tax revenues (which amounts in total to area $P_3AE_2P_2$) is ambiguous. Whether this reduces the welfare of consumers and producers as a whole depends on how wisely government funds are spent. If the government uses tax revenues to make investments that benefit everyone, the transfer may provide important social benefits to taxpayers. On the other hand, if the tax revenues end up in politicians' pockets or are used for frivolous things (such as palaces), the transfer represents a social loss as well as a personal cost to taxpayers. There is no ambiguity about the loss given by the red area AE_1E_2. This is a **deadweight loss** for which there are no compensating gains. Sometimes this loss is referred to as the "excess burden" of a tax; it represents the additional losses that consumers and producers incur as a result of a tax, over and above the actual tax revenues paid.

Deadweight loss
Losses of consumer and producer surplus that are not transferred to other parties.

MICROQUIZ 11.3

Suppose that a per-unit tax is imposed on the perfectly competitive golf-tee industry.

1. Why would you expect consumers to pay a larger share of this tax in the long run than in the short run?
2. How would you determine who pays the producer's share of this tax in the long run?

A Numerical Illustration

The effects of an excise tax can be illustrated by returning once again to our example of supply–demand equilibrium in the market for CDs. Suppose the government implements a

APPLICATION 11.3 *What's the Price of Eggs Got To Do With It?*

The price of a "traditional breakfast" for Americans has gone up in recent years; from 2006 to 2007 alone orange juice went up 25 per cent, eggs by 20 per cent, and milk by 5 per cent. Other countries are seeing similar trends developing.[1]

This may seem surprising when the International Grains Council estimated that world-wide grain production in 2007 would reach roughly 1670 million tonnes well up on the 2006 figure of 1569 million tons. All other things equal, this increased supply should mean lower prices. But not all other things were equal. While supply is increasing as farmers grow more grains, demand is increasing even faster.

Two main reasons can be identified for this surge in demand. Firstly, grains are used to make animal feed which then allows meat consumption. With the increasing prosperity of some countries like China meat consumption has been on the rise.

However, it is the growing demand for 'biofuels' in particular ethanol that is causing demand to surge. It has been estimated that ethanol distilleries in America for example consume 20 per cent of all of America's corn output and a growing number of governments throughout the world are encouraging their farmers to follow suit. Governments, seeing the price of oil at record levels (and being predicted to stay high for quite a long time), and also seeing the political instability in many parts of the world that supply oil, are trying to diversify for security considerations.

The implication of that is that farmers are growing less soya and wheat which pushes up these prices. In addition as all the different types of grain produced become more expensive to feed poultry and cattle, this pushes up the price of meat and eggs.

One reaction that might be expected to occur to excess demand (as well as for prices to increase) is for farmers to plant more grain crops and to try and increase the productivity of the land they farm. The best two candidate countries for bringing extra land into cultivation are Brazil and Ukraine. However, they are far from main markets and they have poor transport infrastructure for getting the crop to market. Genetically modified food could increase yields but they are expensive and politically controversial. Given, however, that the amount of ethanol production remains small relative to global oil needs, even an increase in supply of ethanol is unlikely to make much of an impact on world oil prices.

However, with the high price of oil and government subsides for biofuel production, any extra grain grown will in all probability simply be used to make more biofuel rather than more feedstock, ensuring meat and egg prices remain high.

To Think About

1. Let's assume for a minute that both Brazil and Ukraine have had and continue to have excellent transport links for delivering their crops to world markets. Do you think that the land currently lying fallow in Brazil and Ukraine would ever have been brought into cultivation in the past before the increased demand for biofuels took place? And what now with apparent long-run rising prices? Explain your reasoning using the concept of Ricardian rent.
2. Using 'simple' supply and demand diagrams show how the demand for grains – of whatever type – have grown over recent years. Are we talking here about movements along demand and supply curves or shifts of curves? And which one? Or both?
3. Chapter 12 looks at general equilibrium within markets which is the situation where all markets interact and each market for whatever good is not simply seen in isolation. If we break the grain market down into the market for wheat and soya and then the market for corn, show, on separate diagrams, how the demand and supply curves in the market for corn has changed over the years due to increased demand for biofuels and then on a separate diagram show how this changed market for corn has impacted on the supply and demand for wheat and soya.
4. In question 3 above, strictly speaking, we could have asked about how four markets have

interacted – the oil market; which then impacts on the market for ethanol; which then impacts on the corn market; which then impacts on the market for wheat and soya. From the information above is there likely to be any 'feed-back' from increased biofuel production on the price of oil?

5 Taking the market for ethanol and biofuels in general, how would you represent government subsidies to ethanol producers using a supply and demand framework?

[1]This application is based on an article from the *Economist* magazine, 21 June 2007.

€2 per CD tax that the retailer adds to the sales price for each tape sold. In this case, the supply function for tapes remains

$$\text{Supply: } Q = P - 2 \qquad \{11.3\}$$

where P is now the net price received by the seller. Demanders, on the other hand, must now pay $P + t$ for each CD, so their demand function becomes

$$\text{Demand: } Q = 10 - (P + t) \qquad \{11.4\}$$

or, since $t = 2$ here,

$$Q = 10 - (P + 2) = 8 - P \qquad \{11.5\}$$

Notice, as we have shown graphically, that the effect of the tax is to shift the net demand curve (that is, quantity demanded as a function of the net price received by firms) downward by the per-unit amount of the tax. Equating supply and demand in this case yields

$$\text{Supply} = P - 2 = \text{Demand} = 8 - P \qquad \{11.6\}$$

or $P^* = 5, Q^* = 3$. At this equilibrium, consumers pay €7 for each CD, and total tax collections are €6 per week (= €2 per CD times three CDs per week). As we showed previously, an output of three CDs per week generates a total consumer and producer surplus of €15 per week, of which €6 is now transferred into tax revenues. In this particular case, these revenues are half paid by firms (who see the net price fall from €6 to €5). The other half of tax revenues are paid by CD consumers who see the price they pay rise from €6 to €7. Of course, in other cases the split might not be so even – it would depend on the relative elasticities of supply and demand. Here the excess burden of the tax is €1 per week. This is a loss in consumer and producer surplus that is not collected in tax revenue. Looked at another way, the excess burden here represents about 17 per cent (= €1/€6) of total taxes collected. An efficient tax scheme would seek to keep such losses to a minimum.

MICROQUIZ 11.4

Graph this numerical illustration of taxation and use your graph to answer the following questions

1 What is the value of consumer and producer surplus after the tax is imposed? How do you know that the area of the "deadweight loss triangle" is €1 here?

2 Suppose that the tax were raised to €4. How much in extra tax revenue would be collected? How much bigger would the deadweight loss be?

3 How large a tax would foreclose all trading in CDs? What would tax collections be in this case? What would the deadweight loss be?

Transactions Costs

Although we have developed this discussion in terms of tax incidence theory, models incorporating a wedge between buyers' and sellers' prices have a number of other applications in economics. Perhaps the most important of these concern costs is associated with making market transactions. In some cases, these may be explicit. Most real estate transactions, for example, take place through a third-party broker, who charges a fee for the service of bringing buyer and seller together. Similar explicit transactions fees occur in the trading of stocks and bonds, boats and airplanes, and practically everything that is sold at auction. In all of these instances, buyers and sellers are willing to pay a fee to an agent or broker who facilitates the transaction. In other cases, transactions costs may be largely implicit. Individuals trying to purchase a used car, for example, spend considerable time and effort reading classified advertisements and examining vehicles. These activities amount to an implicit cost of making the transaction.

To the extent that transactions costs are on a per-unit basis (as they are in the real estate, securities, and auction examples), our previous taxation example applies exactly. From the point of view of the buyers – and sellers – it makes little difference whether t represents a per-unit tax or a per-unit transactions fee, since the analysis of the fee's effect on the market is the same. That is, the fee is shared between buyers and sellers, depending on the specific elasticities involved. Output in these markets is also lower than in the absence of such fees.[6]

A somewhat different analysis would hold, however, if transactions costs were a lump-sum amount per transaction. In that case, people would seek to reduce the number of transactions made, but existence of the charge would not affect the total amount bought over the long term. For example, driving to the supermarket is mainly a lump-sum transaction cost on shopping for groceries. Existence of such a charge may not significantly affect the price of food items or the amount of food consumed (unless it tempts people to grow their own). But the charge will cause individuals to shop less frequently, to buy larger quantities on each trip, and to hold larger inventories of food in their homes than would be the case if getting to the store were costless.

Trade Restrictions

Restrictions on the flow of goods in international commerce have effects similar to those we just examined for taxes. Impediments to free trade may reduce mutually beneficial transactions and cause significant transfers among the parties involved. Once again, the competitive model of supply and demand is frequently used to study these effects.

Gains from International Trade

Figure 11-7 illustrates the domestic demand and supply curves for a particular good, say, shoes. In the absence of international trade, the domestic equilibrium price of shoes would be P_D and quantity would be Q_D. Although this equilibrium would exhaust all mutually beneficial transactions between domestic shoe producers and domestic demanders, opening of international trade presents a number of additional options. If the world shoe price, P_W, is less than the prevailing domestic price, P_D, the opening of

[6]One shortcoming of this analysis is its failure to consider the possible benefits obtained from brokers. To the extent these services are valuable to the parties in the transaction, demand and supply curves shift outward to reflect this value. Hence, output may in some cases expand from the availability of agents that facilitate transactions (see Application 11.1).

trade will cause prices to fall to this world level.[7] This drop in price will cause quantity demanded to increase to Q_1, whereas quantity supplied by domestic producers will fall to Q_2. Imported shoes will amount to $Q_1 - Q_2$. In short, what domestic producers do not supply at the world price is instead provided by foreign sources.

The shift in the market equilibrium from E_0 to E_1 causes a large increase in consumer surplus given by area $P_D E_0 E_1 P_W$. Part of this gain reflects a transfer from domestic shoe producers (area $P_D E_0 A P_W$, which is shaded dark), and part represents an unambiguous welfare gain (the light shaded area $E_0 E_1 A$). The source of consumer gains here is obvious – buyers get shoes at a lower price than was previously available in the domestic market. As in our former analyses, losses of producer surplus are experienced by those inputs that give the domestic long-run supply curve its upward slope. If, for example, the domestic shoe industry experiences increasing costs because shoemaker wages are driven up as industry output expands, then the decline in output from Q_D to Q_2 as a result of trade will reverse this process, causing shoemaker wages to fall.

Tariffs

Shoemakers are unlikely to take these wage losses lying down. Instead, they will press the government for protection from the flood of imported footwear. Because the

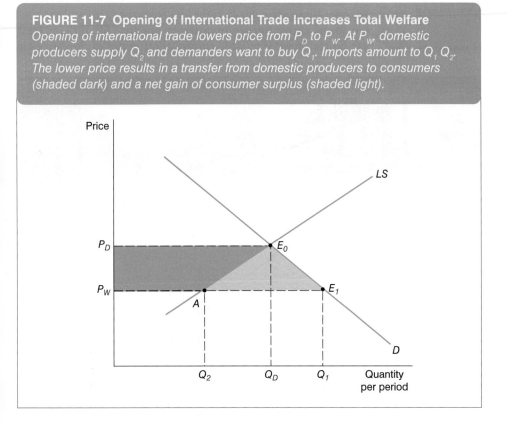

FIGURE 11-7 Opening of International Trade Increases Total Welfare

Opening of international trade lowers price from P_D to P_W. At P_W, domestic producers supply Q_2 and demanders want to buy Q_1. Imports amount to Q_1 Q_2. The lower price results in a transfer from domestic producers to consumers (shaded dark) and a net gain of consumer surplus (shaded light).

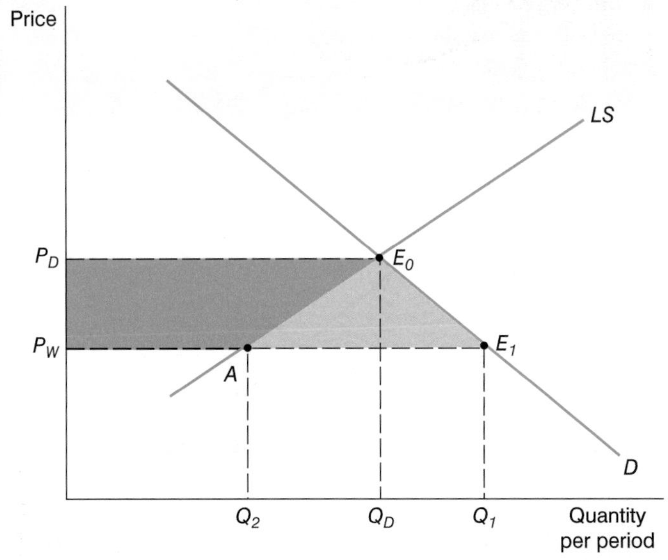

[7]Throughout our analysis, we assume that this country is a price taker in the world market and can purchase all of the imports it wishes without affecting the price, P_W. That is, the supply curve for the rest of the world is assumed to be infinitely elastic at P_W. This is not always the case especially in the case of countries like China and India whose purchases of commodities can help drive up the price.

Tariff A tax on an imported good. May be equivalent to a quota or a nonquantitative restriction on trade.

loss of producer surplus is experienced by relatively few individuals whereas consumer gains from trade are spread across many shoe buyers, shoemakers may have considerably greater incentives to organize opposition to imports than consumers would have to organize to keep trade open. The result may be adoption of protectionist measures.

Historically, the most important type of protection employed has been a **tariff**, that is, a tax on the imported good. Effects of such a tax are shown in Figure 11-8. Now comparisons begin from the free trade equilibrium E_1. Imposition of a per-unit tariff on shoes for domestic buyers of amount t raises the effective price to $P_W + t = P_R$. This price rise causes quantity demanded to fall from Q_1 to Q_3 whereas domestic production expands from Q_2 to Q_4. The total quantity of shoe imports falls from $Q_1 - Q_2$ to $Q_3 - Q_4$. Because each imported pair of shoes is now subject to a tariff, total tariff revenues are given by the area BE_2FC, that is, by $t(Q_3 - Q_4)$.

Imposition of the tariff on imported shoes creates a variety of welfare effects. Total consumer surplus is reduced by area $P_RE_2E_1P_W$. Part of this reduction, as we have seen, is transferred into tariff revenues and part is transferred into increased domestic producer's surplus (area P_RBAP_W, shown in light brown). The two dark brown triangles BCA and E_2E_1F represent losses of consumer surplus that are not transferred to anyone; these are a deadweight loss from the tariff and are similar to the excess burden imposed by any tax. All of these areas can be measured if reliable empirical estimates of the domestic

MICROQUIZ 11.5

Use Figure 11-8 to answer the following questions about the imposition of a tariff on a competitive industry.

1. Do domestic producers pay any of this tax? Do foreign producers pay any of this tax?
2. Who gains the increase in producer surplus that results from the tariff?
3. Are the sources of the deadweight losses represented by triangles ABC and E_2E_1F different? Explain.

FIGURE 11-8 Effects of a Tariff *Imposition of a tariff of amount t raises price to $P_R = P_W + t$. This results in collection of tariff revenue (medium brown), a transfer from consumers to producers (light brown), and two triangles measuring deadweight loss (dark brown). A quota has similar effects, though in this case no revenues are collected.*

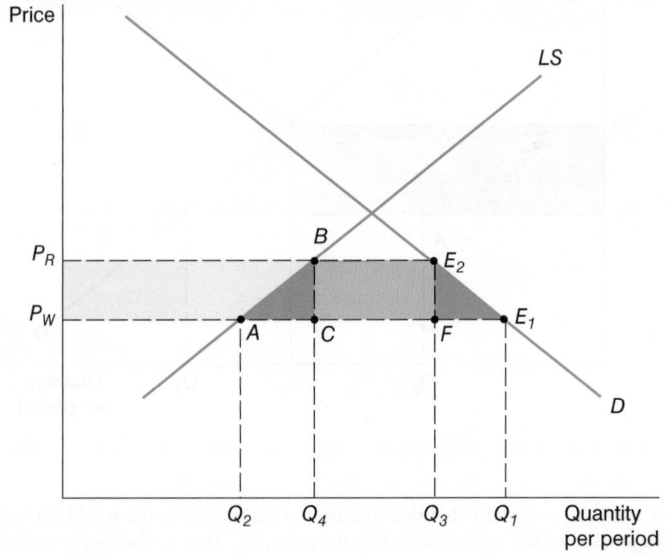

APPLICATION 11.4 *The Latest Episode in the Endless Saga of Steel Protectionism*

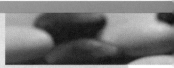

On March 6, 2002, President Bush announced that the United States would adopt a temporary tariff on steel imports. This tariff amounted to 30 per cent on many major steel products such as flat-rolled steel and steel bars. Other products were to be taxed at somewhat lower rates – ranging from 8 to 15 per cent. Two reasons were stated for the adoption of such large tariffs: (1) that some relief from foreign competition was needed to give the US industry time to adapt to new market realities; and (2) that many foreign governments subsidize their steel industries, so tariffs were needed to "level the playing field". Although the threat of adverse action by the World Trade Organization prompted the president to rescind these tariffs in late 2003, he promised to restore them should such concerns arise again in the future. Before discussing whether the arguments used for these temporary tariffs can withstand scrutiny, it may be useful to look at the history of protectionism in this industry.

Using Every Trick in the Protectionist Book

It would be hard to find an industry that has had the degree of special protection from imports that has characterized the US steel industry. Over the past 30 years, US steel producers have succeeded in getting the following protectionist measures enacted: (1) import quotas, (2) minimum price agreements with exporters, (3) "voluntary" export restraints by nations that export steel to the United States, and (4) temporary tariffs. In addition, steel firms have filed any number of lawsuits against exporting nations, alleging unfair trade practices, and the firms themselves have been the beneficiaries of various loan-guarantee and other subsidy programs. Often, such policies have been supported on the basis of the "importance" of the steel industry to the US economy – sometimes stressing the national defense uses of steel. However, because these arguments have been used many times before and are wearing a bit thin, they did not characterize the debate in 2002.

Assessing New Arguments for Steel Protection

The argument that the steel industry needed "breathing room" from foreign competition in order to adapt its technology to new market realities seems to be fallacious. Some segments of the industry are indeed plagued by old-style blast furnace technology. But adopting the tariffs simply raised prices and allowed firms that own this old technology to cover average costs. In the absence of such protection, the older plants would have been closed and US firms would have an incentive to adopt newer technologies that focus mainly on recycling scrap steel. The notion that foreign producers were selling steel in the United States at below cost is equally bogus. As a matter of economic logic, foreign firms would have no interest in serving a market where price did not cover average (or, perhaps, marginal) cost. On more practical grounds, US "antidumping" laws are notorious for their poor methodologies used to measure whether prices really do exceed costs. And purported "subsidies" by foreign governments (to the extent they exist at all) were probably much smaller than the subsidies many US firms received.

Effects of the Tariffs

Economists who study the steel industry concluded that the costs of the 2002 tariffs to the overall economy were large.[1] Estimated tariff revenues were about $900 million annually, and the gains in domestic producer surplus amounted to perhaps another $700 million. Balanced against this was an estimated loss of about $2.5 billion in consumer surplus. Overall then, there was an annual deadweight loss of about $900 million from the tariffs. One way of conceptualizing what this number means is to compare it to the jobs "saved" in the steel industry as a result of the tariff. A generous estimate of this effect might be about 5000 jobs.

(Continued)

Hence, the tariff package annually cost the economy about $180 000 per "job saved" in the steel industry. It seems likely that politicians will continue to be tempted to undertake such costly actions in the future.

To Think About

1 If the steel tariffs were mistaken, why do you think President Bush supported them? Why did he change his mind?

2 Steel firms argue that they have large "legacy costs" in terms of pensions promised to workers at their older plants. Tariffs would help them to pay those costs. Is this a good argument for tariff protection?

[1]All of the figures here are calculated from G. C. Hufbauer and B. Goodrich, *Time for a Grand Bargain in Steel?*, Washington DC, Institute for International Economics, 2002.

supply and demand curves for the imported good are available. Application 11.4: *The Latest Episode in the Endless Saga of Steel Protectionism* looks at a recent example.

Other Types of Trade Protection

In recent years, tariffs have come to play a reduced role in international trade. They have been gradually negotiated downward under the General Agreement on Tariffs and Trade (GATT). The decline in tariffs has not necessarily meant a decline in protectionism, however. In their place are a number of restrictive measures, including quotas, "voluntary" export restraints, and a series of non-quantitative restrictions such as those incorporated into seemingly beneficial health, safety, and environmental regulations. Many of these new types of restrictions can be illustrated by adapting the tariff diagram we have already developed in Figure 11-8.

A quota that limits imports to $Q_3 - Q_4$ would have effects that are very similar to those shown in the figure: Market price would rise to P_R; a substantial transfer from consumers to domestic producers would occur (area $P_R BAP_W$); and there would be deadweight losses represented by the dark brown triangular areas. With a quota, however, no revenues are collected by the government, so the loss of consumer surplus represented by area BE_2FC must go elsewhere. Often governments are in a position to determine who obtains these benefits by granting import licenses that allocate the quota amounts.

Non-quantitative restrictions such as health or other inspections also impose cost and time delays that are often treated as an "implicit" tariff on imports. An example of health restrictions occurred in 2003 when purported fear over mad cow disease led the United States to impose a ban on all imports of Canadian beef, even though the disease had showed up in only a single Canadian cow. Later in the same year, a similar discovery in the United States prompted many other countries (most importantly Japan) to impose a ban on US beef exports. In both cases, domestic producers of beef led the way in pushing the bans so as to "keep their herds safe". Examples of onerous inspection programs include a general unwillingness of the Japanese to accept results of pharmaceutical tests from other countries for imported drugs, French testing requirements for imported electronics, and restrictions on importing frozen chickens into the European Union. Figure 11-8 can often be adapted to illustrate the effects of such costly (and largely unwarranted) restrictions on trade.

APPLICATION 11.5 *The Sour Taste of US Sugar Policy*

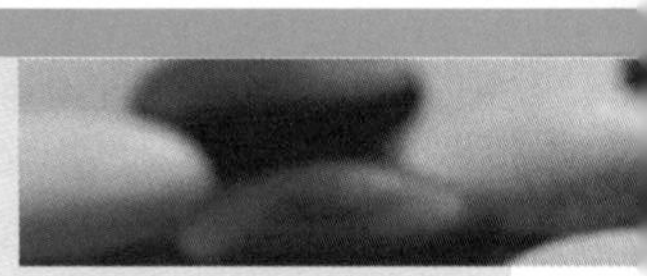

Perhaps no agricultural market has been so affected by the vagaries of politics than has the US market for raw sugar. Regulation of this market began during the economic depression of the 1930s. The Agricultural Adjustment Act of 1934 included price support provisions for domestically produced sugar, together with quantitative restrictions on the quantity of sugar that could be imported. Many of these provisions were reinstated into law under the Sugar Act of 1948, and that law (with occasional revisions) has been in effect ever since. A major component of the Sugar Act specifies "tariff-rate quotas" under which only certain limited quantities of raw sugar are allowed into the United States at world prices from 41 specified countries. Imports in excess of these quota amounts are subject to a prohibitive tariff of more than 15¢ per pound.

Direct Effects of the Quotas

The principal effect of these quotas on imported sugar is to raise the price of raw sugar in the United States. At the time of this writing, for example, the world price of sugar is about 9.5¢ per pound, whereas the domestic price of sugar in the US is about 22.3¢ per pound. As Figure 11-8 shows, this price differential is a direct result of the import quota. Because current consumption of sugar is approximately 17 billion pounds per year in the US, the extra cost paid by US consumers is about $2.2 billion per year. Some of this is transferred to domestic producers of sugar. An even larger portion is probably transferred to producers of high-fructose corn syrup – a perfect substitute for raw sugar in many liquid applications such as soft drinks. Finally, because consumers would have bought more sugar at the world price than they actually do under the quota regime, there are also deadweight losses from the quotas.

Indirect Effects of Sugar Policy

The indirect effects of US sugar policy may be even more significant than the direct ones. For example, one such effect is to expand domestic production of sugar cane significantly beyond what would occur under a free-trade regime.[1] Expansion of this industry in Florida has posed two sorts of problems. First, sugar cane workers are largely immigrants who earn very low wages in the dangerous job of cutting sugar cane. Second, intensive growing of sugar cane on the edge of the Everglades has created significant environmental degradation in this fragile ecosystem. Stresses produced by the sugar cane industry were largely responsible for the need to adopt a major program of reclamation for the Everglades.

Some authors have even claimed the US sugar policy may have played an important role in the Cuban revolution that brought Fidel Castro to power.[2] Quotas for imported Cuban sugar were reduced significantly under the Sugar Act of 1956. This meant that Cuban producers had to move away from a relatively stable American market for their output and face much greater risks on the world market. Although it may have taken some time for the consequences of this change to be fully felt in Cuba, there is no doubt that this was a major concern to politicians on all sides of the revolution. Of course, there were many other factors underlying the 1959 overthrow of the Batista regime in Cuba. But it is intriguing to speculate whether history might have been different if the US had adopted a more lenient policy toward imports of Cuban sugar (their principal crop) in the 1950s.

The longer-term consequences of US sugar policy toward Cuba also raise interesting questions. Because Cuba could not export sugar to the United States during the 1970s and 1980s, the country turned for sales mainly to the then Soviet Union and other Eastern Bloc countries. These countries tended to pay premium prices for Cuban sugar – a policy that meant that the Cuban industry remained relatively inefficient. With the demise of the Soviet Union, Cuba's share of world sugar production dropped significantly. Whether the country can return to the top ranks of sugar producers remains in doubt.

To Think About

1 Most studies find that the price elasticity of demand for sugar is about −0.30. How would you use this figure to get a rough estimate of the size of deadweight losses experienced by

(*Continued*)

US consumers because they are unable to buy sugar at world prices?

2 Explain the process through which the "price umbrella" created by sugar quotas can result in increased producer surplus for producers of high-fructose corn syrup.

[1]A significant portion of US sugar production is from sugar beets. These are grown in the upper Midwest, not in the semitropical climate necessary for sugar cane.

[2]See A. Dye and R. Sicotte, "The US Sugar Program and the Cuban Revolution", *Journal of Economic History* (September 2004): 673–706.

SUMMARY

In this chapter we showed how the competitive model of supply and demand can be used to investigate a wide range of actual economic activities and policies. Some of the general lessons from these applications include

- The concepts *consumer* and *producer surplus* provide useful ways of analyzing the effects of economic changes on the welfare of market participants. Changes in consumer surplus represent changes in the overall utility consumers receive from consuming a particular good. Changes in producer surplus represent changes in the returns inputs receive.
- In the short run, producer surplus represents the coverage of fixed costs plus whatever profits are received. In the long run, producer surplus represents the extra returns that inputs enjoy relative to a situation where no output of the good is produced.
- Ricardian rent is one type of producer surplus in which owners of resources that yield low costs receive long-run profits.
- In some cases, the long-run competitive equilibrium represents an economically efficient allocation of resources – it maximizes the sum of consumer and producer surplus.[8]
- Price controls involve both transfers between producers and consumers and losses of transactions that could benefit both consumers and producers.
- Tax incidence analysis concerns the determination of which market participants ultimately bear the burden of a tax. In general, this incidence falls mainly on participants who exhibit relatively inelastic responses to price changes. Taxes also involve deadweight losses in addition to the burden imposed by the actual tax revenues collected.
- Trade restrictions create both transfers between consumers and producers and deadweight losses of economic welfare. The effects of many types of trade restrictions can be modeled as being equivalent to a tariff.

[8]This conclusion is expanded upon in the next chapter.

REVIEW QUESTIONS

1 Early in Chapter 1, we defined *economics* as "the study of the allocation of scarce resources among alternative end uses". How does the observation that a competitive equilibrium exhausts all mutually beneficial transactions relate to this definition? What "scarce resources"

are being allocated by competitive markets? How are "alternative end uses" reflected by demand and supply curves?

2 A fledgling microeconomics student is having some trouble grasping the concept of short-run producer surplus. In exasperation, he blurts out, "This is absolute balderdash. I can understand that producer surplus is a good thing for firms because it measures the improvement in their welfare relative to a situation where they cannot participate in the market. But then I'm told that fixed costs are a component of short-run producer surplus. Aren't fixed costs a bad thing? They must be paid! How can they be one component of a good thing?" Can you set this student straight? (*Hint*: When is short-run producer surplus zero?)

3 "The size of producer surplus in the long run is ultimately determined by the elasticity of supply for the inputs to an industry." Use a series of graphs of both inputs' and goods' markets to explain this statement.

4 Suppose that all operators of fast-food restaurants must rent the land for their establishments from other landowners. All other aspects of the costs of fast-food establishments are identical. Why would rents differ among fast-food locations? Would these differences in rents necessarily cause differences in the prices of fast food? What do you make of the claim by Mr Z that "I simply can't make a go of my motorway service cafe – the landowner just wants too much rent"?

5 Would price controls involve welfare losses even in the constant cost case? What economic process would such controls short-circuit even in this case? Who would experience the welfare losses you describe?

6 "Firms don't pay taxes, only people pay taxes" is a favorite slogan of the *Wall Street Journal*. But our analysis in this chapter shows that in the long run (with an upward-sloping supply curve) at least some portion of a unit tax is paid out of producer surplus. Is the *Wall Street Journal* wrong?

7 Use a graphical analysis similar to Figure 11-6 to show that the allocation resulting from a per-unit subsidy also results in a deadweight loss. Explain in detail who loses what in this case.

8 It is relatively expensive to rent television sets in the United States so few people do so. But this is a market for which standard supply–demand analysis surely applies. How might you explain the low volume of sales in this market? (*Hint*: Why might transactions costs be high in the television rental case?)

9 Figure 11-8 shows that some part of the loss consumers suffer as a result of a tariff is transferred to domestic producers. Exactly how does this happen? Who actually gains from tariff protection?

10 Suppose that a nation institutes a costly inspection program on one of its imported goods. How would this affect equilibrium in the imported good's market? Explain how the various areas identified in Figure 11-8 should be interpreted in this circumstance.

PROBLEMS

11.1 Suppose that the demand for broccoli is given by

Demand: $Q = 1000 - 5P$

where Q is quantity per year measured in hundreds of kilos and P is price in euros per hundred kilo. The long-run supply curve for broccoli is given by

Supply: $Q = 4P - 80$

a Show that the equilibrium quantity here is $Q = 400$. At this output, what is the equilibrium price? How much in total is spent on broccoli? What is consumer surplus at this equilibrium? What is producer surplus at this equilibrium?

b How much in total consumer and producer surplus would be lost if $Q = 300$ instead of $Q = 400$?

c Show how the allocation of the loss of total consumer and producer surplus between suppliers and demanders described in part b depends on the price at which broccoli is sold. How would the loss be shared if $P = 140$? How about if $P = 95$?

d What would the total loss of consumer and producer surplus be if $Q = 450$ rather than $Q = 400$? Show that the size of this total loss also is independent of the price at which the broccoli is sold.

e Graph your results.

11.2 The handmade snuffbox industry is composed of 100 identical firms, each having short-run total costs given by

$$STC = 0.5q^2 + 10q + 5$$

and short-run marginal costs by

$$SMC = q + 10$$

where q is the output of snuffboxes per day.

a What is the short-run supply curve for each snuffbox maker? What is the short-run supply curve for the market as a whole?

b Suppose the demand for total snuffbox production is given by

$$Q = 1100 - 50P$$

What is the equilibrium in this marketplace? What is each firm's total short-run profit?

c Graph the market equilibrium and compute total producer surplus in this case.

d Show that the total producer surplus you calculated in part c is equal to total industry profits plus industry short-run fixed costs.

11.3 The perfectly competitive DVD copying industry is composed of many firms who can copy five DVDs per day at an average cost of €10 per DVD. Each firm must also pay a royalty to film studios, and the per-film royalty rate (r) is an increasing function of total industry output (Q) given by

$$r = 0.002Q$$

a Graph this royalty "supply" curve with r as a function of Q.

b Suppose the daily demand for copied DVDs is given by

$$\text{Demand: } Q = 1050 - 50P$$

Assuming the industry is in long-run equilibrium, what is the equilibrium price and quantity of copied DVDs? How many DVD firms are there? What is the per-film royalty rate? (*Hint*: Use $P = AC$. Now $AC = 10 + 0.002Q$.)

c Suppose that the demand for copied DVDs increases to

$$\text{Demand: } Q = 1600 - 50P$$

Now, what is the long-run equilibrium price and quantity for copied DVDs? How many DVD firms are there? What is the per-film royalty rate?

d Graph these long-run equilibria in the DVD market and calculate the increase in producer surplus between the situations described in part b and part c.

e Use the royalty supply curve graphed in part a to show that the increase in producer surplus is precisely equal to the increase in royalties paid as Q expands incrementally from its level in part b to its level in part c.

11.4 Consider again the market for broccoli described in problem 11.1.

a Suppose demand for broccoli shifted outward to

$$\text{Demand: } Q = 1270 - 5P$$

What would be the new equilibrium price and quantity in this market?

b What would the new levels of consumer and producer surplus in this market be?

c Suppose the government had prevented the price of broccoli from rising from its equilibrium level of problem 11.1. Describe how the consumer- and producer-surplus measures described in part b would be reallocated or lost entirely.

d Return now to the original demand curve in problem 11.1. Suppose that the government instituted a €45-per-hundred-kilo tax on broccoli.

i How would this tax affect equilibrium in the broccoli market?

ii How would this tax burden be shared between buyers and sellers of broccoli?

iii What is the excess burden of this tax?

11.5 Suppose that the demand for broccoli in problem 11.4 had instead been

Demand: Q = 2200 − 15P

a Recalculate the tax incidence outcomes from problem 11.4d using this new demand curve.

b Return now to the original demand curve in problem 11.1 but assume the supply for broccoli is given by

Supply: Q = 10P − 800.

Answer the tax incidence questions from problem 11.4d for this new supply-demand configuration.

c What can you conclude by comparing these three cases of tax incidence analysis (i.e., 11.4d, 11.5a, and 11.5b)?

11.6 Suppose that the government imposed a €3 tax on snuffboxes in the industry described in problem 11.2.

a How would this tax change the market equilibrium?

b How would the burden of this tax be shared between snuffbox buyers and sellers?

c Calculate the total loss of producer surplus as a result of the taxation of snuffboxes. Show that this loss equals the change in total short-run profits in the snuffbox industry. Why don't fixed costs enter into this computation of the change in short-run producer surplus?

11.7 Suppose that the government institutes a €5.50-per-film tax on the DVD copying industry described in problem 11.3.

a Assuming that the demand for copied films is that given in part c of problem 11.3, how does this tax affect the market equilibrium?

b How is the burden of this tax allocated between consumers and producers? What is the loss of consumer and producer surplus?

c Show that the loss of producer surplus as a result of this tax is borne completely by the film studios. Explain your results intuitively.

11.8 The domestic demand for MP3 players is given by

Demand: Q = 5000 − 100*P*

where price *P* is measured in euros and quantity *Q* is measured in thousands of MP3 players per year. The domestic supply curve for MP3 players is given by

Supply: Q = 150*P*

a What is the domestic equilibrium in the MP3 player market?

b Suppose MP3 players can be imported at a world price of €10 per MP3 player. If trade were unencumbered, what would the new market equilibrium be? How many MP3 players would be produced domestically? How many MP3 players would be imported?

c If domestic MP3 player producers succeeded in getting a €5 tariff implemented, how would this change the market equilibrium? How much would be collected in tariff revenues? How much consumer surplus would be transferred to domestic producers? What would the deadweight loss from the tariff be?

d Graph your results.

11.9 Using the supply and demand equations for MP3 players from problem 11.8, assess the impact of an import quota of 1.25 million MP3 players per year. Explain how this case differs from the case of the tariff studied in problem 11.8.

11.10 Suppose that the long-run supply curve for imported rice from the rest of the world has a positive slope, arising from generally increasing costs of production as such imports increase.

a How would you construct the total supply curve for rice, including both domestic and foreign producers, assuming that all producers and consumers are price takers?

b Using your supply curve from part a, illustrate the "free trade" equilibrium. Describe the welfare of various market participants relative to a situation of no imports.

c Show how you would illustrate a tariff on imported rice in your diagram. Again, discuss the welfare consequences of this tariff for all market participants. In particular, discuss the nature of the changes in foreign producer surplus that would be caused by the tariff.

d What are the most important differences between your analysis of a tariff in this situation and the analysis provided in Chapter 11 with perfectly elastic supply?

e In what ways does the price-taking assumption seem reasonable in this problem? Why might the assumption be unrealistic when thinking about the size of tariff the domestic government might choose?

12

General Equilibrium and Welfare

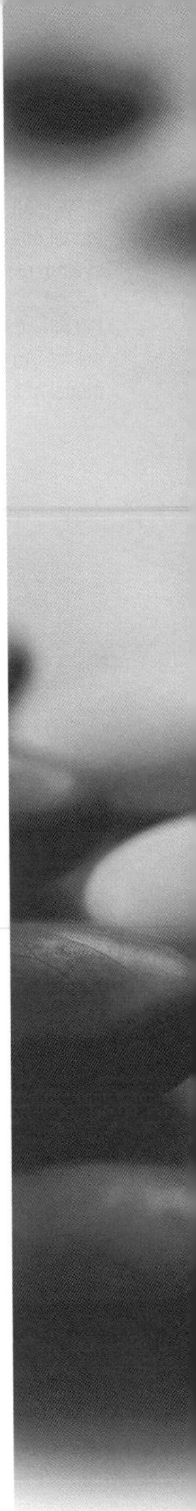

In Chapter 10 and Chapter 11, we looked only at a single competitive market in isolation. We were not concerned with how things that happened in that one market might affect other markets. For many economic issues, this narrowing of focus is helpful – we need only look at what really interests us. For other issues, however, any detailed understanding requires that we look at how many related markets work. For example, if we wished to examine the effects of all government taxes on the economy, we would need to look not only at a number of different product markets but also at markets for workers and for capital. Economists have developed both theoretical and empirical (computer) models for this purpose. These are called **general equilibrium models** because they seek to study market equilibrium in many markets at once. The models in Chapter 10 and Chapter 11, on the other hand, are called **partial equilibrium models** because they are concerned with studying equilibrium in only a single market. In this chapter, we take a very brief look at general equilibrium models. One purpose of this examination is to clarify further the concept of economic efficiency that we introduced in Chapter 11.

A Perfectly Competitive Price System

The most common type of general equilibrium model assumes that the entire economy works through a series of markets like those we studied in Chapter 10. Not only are all goods allocated through millions of competitive markets but also all inputs have prices that are established through the workings of supply and demand. In all of these many markets, a few basic assumptions are assumed to hold:

- All individuals and firms take prices as given – they are price takers.
- All individuals maximize utility.
- All firms maximize profits.

General equilibrium model An economic model of a complete system of markets.

Partial equilibrium model An economic model of a single market.

- All individuals and firms are fully informed; there are no transactions costs, and there is no uncertainty.

These assumptions should be familiar to you. They are ones we have been making throughout this book. One consequence of the assumptions (and a few others) is that it can be shown that when all markets work this way they establish equilibrium prices for all goods.[1] That is, at these prices, quantity supplied equals quantity demanded in every market.

Why Is General Equilibrium Necessary?

To see why we need a general model of this type, consider the market for tomatoes that we studied at the start of Chapter 11. Figure 12-1(a) shows equilibrium in this market by the intersection of the demand curve for tomatoes (*D*) with the supply curve for tomatoes (*S*). Initially, the price of tomatoes is given by P_1. Figure 12-1 also shows the markets for three other economic activities that are related to the tomato market: (b) the market for tomato pickers; (c) the market for cucumbers (a substitute for tomatoes in salads); and (d) the market for cucumber pickers. All of these markets are initially in equilibrium. The prices in these various markets will not change unless something happens to shift one of the curves.

Disturbing the Equilibrium

Suppose now that such a change does occur. Imagine a situation where the government announces that tomatoes have been found to cure the common cold so everyone decides to eat more of them. An initial consequence of this discovery is that the demand for tomatoes shifts outward to D'. In our analysis in Chapter 10, this shift would cause the price of tomatoes to rise and that would be, more or less, the end of the story. Now, however, we wish to follow the repercussions of what has happened in the tomato market into the other markets shown in Figure 12-1. A first possible reaction would be in the market for tomato pickers. Because tomato prices have risen, the demand for labor used to harvest tomatoes increases. The demand curve for labor in Figure 12-1(b) shifts to D'. This tends to raise the wages of tomato pickers, which, in turn, raises the costs of tomato growers. The supply curve for tomatoes (which, under perfect competition, reflects only growers' marginal costs) shifts to S'.

What happens to the market for cucumbers? Because people have an increased desire for tomatoes, they may reduce their demands for cucumbers because these tomato substitutes don't cure colds. The demand for cucumbers shifts inward to D', and cucumber prices fall. That reduces the demand for cucumber workers, and the wage associated with that occupation falls.

Re-establishing Equilibrium

We could continue this story indefinitely. We could ask how the lower price of cucumbers affects the tomato market. Or we could ask whether cucumber pickers, discouraged by their falling wages, might consider picking tomatoes, shifting the supply of labor curve

[1]Competitive markets can only establish relative, not absolute, prices. That is, these markets can only determine that one apple trades for two oranges, not whether apples and oranges cost €0.50 and €0.25 or €20 and €10. Absolute prices in an economy are determined by monetary factors, and we look briefly at these at the end of this chapter.

in Figure 12-1(b) outward. To follow this chain of events further or to examine even more markets related to tomatoes would add little to our story. Eventually we would expect all four markets in Figure 12-1 (and all the other markets we have not shown) to reach a new equilibrium, such as that illustrated by the lighter supply and demand curves in the figure. Once all the repercussions have been worked out, the final result would be a rise in tomato prices (to P_3), a rise in the wages of tomato pickers (to w_3), a fall in cucumber prices (to P_4), and a fall in the wages of cucumber pickers (to w_4). This is what we mean then by a smoothly working system of perfectly competitive markets. Following any disturbance, all the markets can eventually re-establish a new set of equilibrium prices at which quantity demanded is equal to quantity supplied in each market. In Application 12.1: *Modeling Excess Burden with a Computer* we show why using a model that allows for interconnections among markets provides a more realistic and complete picture of how taxes affect the economy than does the single-market approach we took in Chapter 11.

MICROQUIZ 12.1

Why are there two supply curves in Figure 12-1(a)? How does this illustrate "feedback" effects? Why would a partial equilibrium analysis of the effect of an increase in demand for tomatoes from *D* to *D′* give the wrong answer?

FIGURE 12-1 The Market Cost for Tomatoes and Several Related Markets *Initially, the market for tomatoes is in equilibrium (at P_1) as are the markets for tomato pickers, cucumbers, and cucumber pickers. An increase in demand for tomatoes disturbs these equilibria. Virtually all the supply and demand curves shift in the process of establishing a new general equilibrium.*

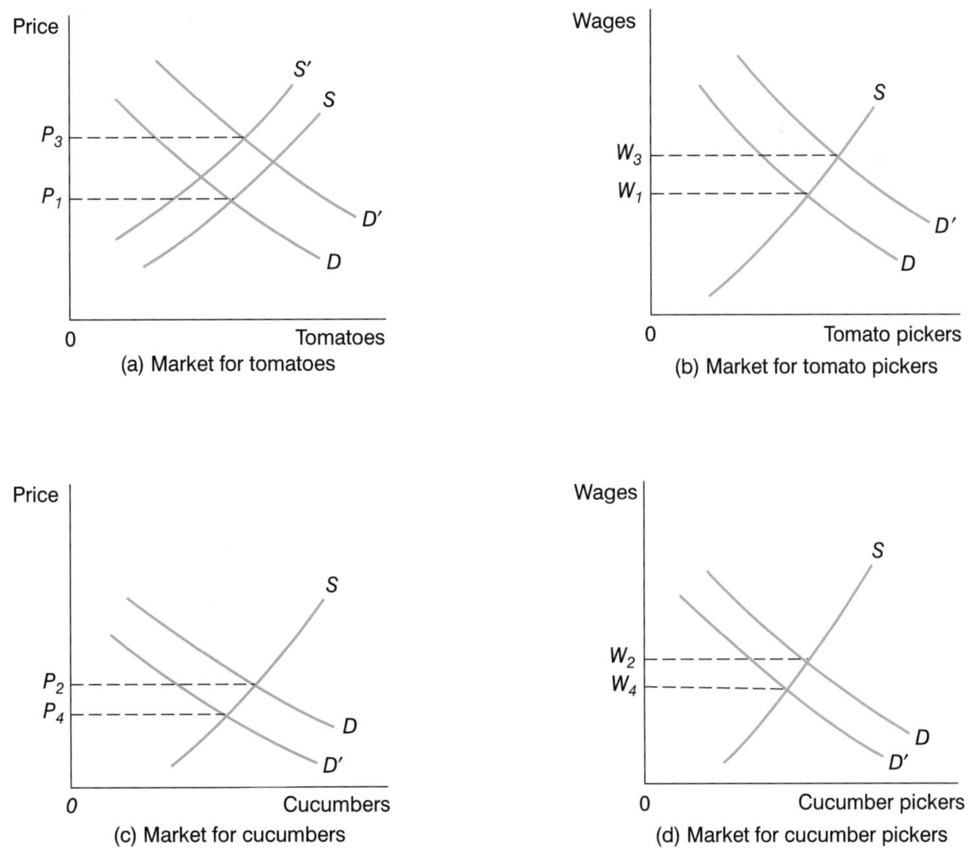

APPLICATION 12.1 *Modeling Excess Burden with a Computer*

In Chapter 11 we showed that many taxes create "excess burdens" in that they reduce total consumer well-being by more than the amounts collected in tax revenues. A primary shortcoming of our analysis of this issue was that we looked only at a single market – an approach that may significantly understate matters.

Excess Burden in General Equilibrium Models

More precise estimates of the effect of taxation can be obtained from large-scale general equilibrium models. One interesting comparison of excess burden estimates from such models to similar estimates from single-market models found that the simple models may underestimate excess burden by as much as 80 per cent.[1] For example, the authors look at a potential 5 per cent tax on energy consumption in the United States and find that the excess burden estimated from a simple model is about $0.5 billion per year, whereas it is $2.6 billion per year when studied in a complete model of the economy. The main reason for such large differences is that a single-market analysis fails to consider how an energy tax might affect workers' labor supply decisions.

Some Other Results

Other examples using general-equilibrium models to evaluate the excess burden of various tax systems are easy to find. For example, early studies of the entire tax system in the United Kingdom found that the distortions introduced by taxes resulted in a deadweight loss of 6 to 9 per cent of total GDP.[2] The tax system imposed particularly heavy costs on British manufacturing industries, perhaps contributing to the country's relatively poor economic performance prior to the Thatcher reforms.

Another set of examples is provided by papers that look at special tax breaks provided to homeowners in the United States. Probably the two most important such breaks are the deductibility of mortgage payments for homeowners and the failure to tax the in-kind services people receive from living in their own homes. This special treatment biases peoples' choices in favor of owning rather than renting and probably causes them to invest more in houses and less in other forms of saving. General equilibrium models generally support these predictions and conclude that special treatment of housing may impose significant efficiency costs on the US economy.[3]

The Progressive Nature of Tax

Finally, a number of authors have been interested in how the progressive income tax affects welfare in the United States, the United Kingdom (and elsewhere). The advantage of a progressive income tax is that it reduces inequality in after-tax incomes, thereby providing some implicit "insurance" to low-income people. The disadvantage of such tax schemes is that the high marginal tax rates required may adversely affect the work and savings behavior of high-income people. An interesting recent paper by Conesa and Krueger uses a computer general equilibrium model to determine whether the degree of progressivity in the US income tax is optimal,[4] or whether some different scheme would provide similar distributional benefits with less overall excess burden. They find that a flat tax (see Application 1A.2) with a large exemption might increase overall welfare by about 1.7 per cent relative to the current system.

To Think About

1. Why is the excess burden of a tax usually larger in a general-equilibrium model than in a model of a single market?
2. In general equilibrium models of taxation, tax incidence is studied by looking at the after-tax incomes of various groups of people. There is no notion that firms pay any taxes at all. What do you make of this?

[1]See L. H. Goulder and R. C. Williams III, "The Substantial Bias from Ignoring General Equilibrium Effects in Estimating Excess Burden and a Practical Solution", *Journal of Political Economy* (August 2003): 898–927.

[2]Many of the early uses of general equilibrium models to study tax systems are summarized in J. B. Shoven and J. Whalley, "Applied General Equilibrium Models of Taxation and International Trade", *Journal of Economic Literature* (September 1985): 1007–1051.

[3]See Y. Nakagami and A.M. Pereira, "Budgetary and Efficiency Effects of Housing Taxation in the United States", *Journal of Urban Economics* (September 1996): 68–86.

[4]J. C. Conesa and D. Kreuger, "On the Optimal Progressivity of the Income Tax Code", National Bureau of Economic Research Working Paper 11044 (January 2005).

A Simple General Equilibrium Model

One way to give the flavor of general equilibrium analysis is to look at a simple supply–demand model of two goods together. Ingeniously, we will call these two goods *X* and *Y*. The "supply" conditions for the goods are shown by the production possibility frontier *PP′* in Figure 12-2. This curve shows the various combinations of *X* and *Y* that this economy can produce if its resources are employed

FIGURE 12-2 Efficiency of Output Mix *In this economy, the production possibility frontier represents those combinations of X and Y that can be produced. Every point on the frontier is efficient in a technical sense. However, only the output combination at point E is a true utility maximum for the typical person. Only this point represents an economically efficient allocation of resources.*

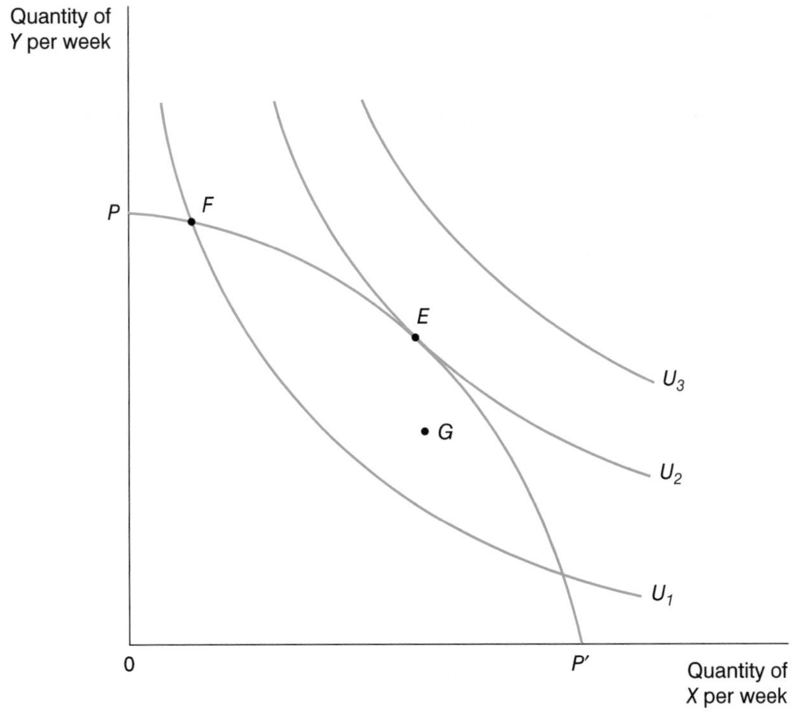

efficiently.[2] Figure 12-2 also shows a series of indifference curves representing the preferences of the consumers in this simple economy for the goods *X* and *Y*. These indifference curves represent the "demand" conditions in our model. Clearly, in this model, the best use of resources is achieved at point *E* where production is X^*, Y^*. This point provides the maximum utility that is available in this economy given the limitations imposed by scarce resources (as represented by the production possibility frontier). As in Chapter 11, we define this to be an **economically efficient allocation of resources**. Notice that this notion of efficiency really has two components. First, there is a "supply" component – X^*, Y^* is on the production possibility frontier. Any point inside the frontier would be inefficient because it would provide less utility than can potentially be achieved in this situation. The efficiency of X^*, Y^* also has a "demand" component because, from among all those points on *PP′*, this allocation of resources provides greatest utility. This reinforces the notion that the goal of economic activity is to improve the welfare of people. Here, people decide for themselves which allocation is the best.

Economically efficient allocation of resources An allocation of resources in which the sum of consumer and producer surplus is maximized. Reflects the best (utility-maximizing) use of scarce resources.

The efficient allocation shown at point *E* in Figure 12-2 is characterized by a tangency between the production possibility frontier and consumer's indifference curve. In Chapter 1 we saw that the slope of the production possibility frontier measures the relative opportunity cost of one good in terms of the other in production. The increasingly steep slope of the frontier shows that *X* becomes relatively more costly as its production is increased. On the other hand, in Chapter 2 we saw that the slope of an indifference curve shows how people are willing to trade one good for another in consumption (the marginal rate of substitution). That slope flattens as people consume more *X* because they seek balance in what they have. The tangency in Figure 12-2 therefore shows that one sign of efficiency is that the relative opportunity costs of goods in production should equal the rate at which people are willing to trade these goods for each other. In that way, an efficient allocation ties together technical information from the supply side of the market with information about preferences from the demand side. If these slopes were not equal (say at point *F*) the allocation of resources would be inefficient (utility would be U_1 instead of U_2). Although the description of an efficient allocation of resources in Figure 12-2 concerns only issues of technology and preferences, the tangency condition carries the suggestion that prices might have some connection to achieving this outcome because prices convey information about trade-offs. In the next section, we take that subject up in detail.

The Efficiency of Perfect Competition

In this simple model, the "economic problem" is how to achieve this efficient allocation of resources. One of the most important discoveries of modern welfare economics is to show that, under certain conditions, competitive markets can bring about this result. Because of the importance of this conclusion, it is sometimes called the **first theorem of welfare economics**. This "theorem" is simply a generalization of the efficiency result we described in Chapter 11 to many markets. Although a general proof of the theorem requires a lot of mathematics, we can give a glimpse of that proof by seeing how the efficient allocation shown in Figure 12-2 might be achieved through competitive markets.

First theorem of welfare economics A perfectly competitive price system will bring about an economically efficient allocation of resources.

[2] All of the points on *PP′* are sometimes referred to as being "technically efficient" in the sense that available inputs are fully employed and are being used in the right combinations by firms. Points inside *PP′* (such as *G*) are technically inefficient because it is possible to produce more of both goods. For an analysis of the relationship between input use and technical efficiency, see problem 12.9.

In Figure 12-3, we have redrawn the production possibility frontier and indifference curves from Figure 12-2. Now assume that goods *X* and *Y* are traded in perfectly competitive markets and that the initial prices of the goods are P_X^1 and P_Y^1, respectively. With these prices, profit-maximizing firms will choose to produce X_1, Y_1 because, from among all the combinations of *X* and *Y* on the production possibility frontier, this one provides maximum revenue and profits.[3]

On the other hand, given the budget constraint represented by line *CC*, individuals collectively will demand X'_1, Y'_1.[4] Consequently, at this price ratio,

FIGURE 12-3 How Perfectly Competitive Prices Bring about Efficiency *With an arbitrary initial price ratio, firms will produce X_1, Y_1; the economy's budget constraint will be given by line CC. With this budget constraint, individuals demand X'_1, Y_1, that is, there is an excess demand for good X ($X'_1 - X_1$) and an excess supply of good Y ($Y_1 - Y'_1$). The workings of the market will move these prices toward their equilibrium levels P^*_X, P^*_Y. At those prices, society's budget constraint will be given by the line C*C*, and supply and demand will be in equilibrium. The combination X*, Y* of goods will be chosen, and this allocation is efficient.*

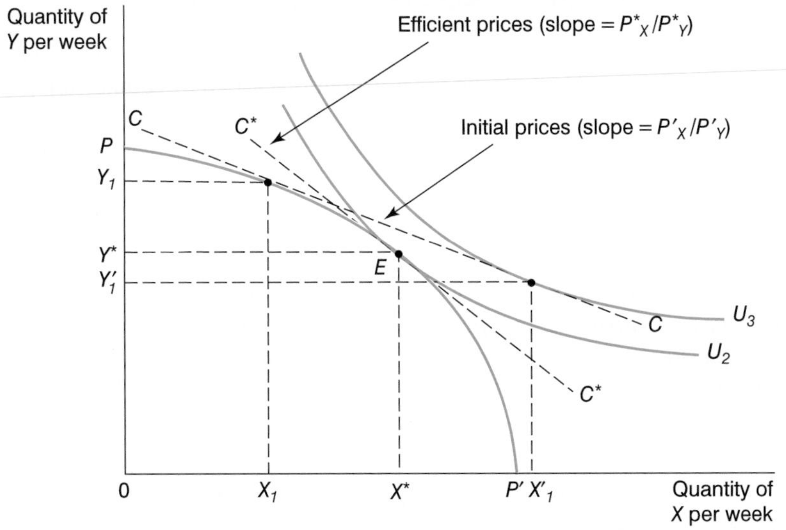

[3]The point provides maximum revenue because the prices of *X* and *Y* determine the slope of the line *CC*, which represents total revenue for the firm ($P^1_X + P^1_Y$), and this line is as far from the origin as possible given that production must take place on *PP′*. But the production possibility frontier assumes that input usage is fixed everywhere on and inside the frontier. Hence, maximization of revenue also amounts to maximization of profits.

[4]It is important to recognize why the budget constraint has this location. Because P^1_X and P^1_Y are given, the value of total production is

$$P^1_X \cdot X_1 + P^1_Y \cdot Y_1$$

This is the value of total output in the simple economy pictured in the figure. Because of the accounting identity "value of income = value of output", this is also the total income accruing to people in society. Society's budget constraint passes through X_1, Y_1 and has a slope of $-P^1_X/P^1_Y$. This is precisely the line labeled *CC* in the figure.

there is excess demand for good X (people want to buy more than is being produced), whereas there is an excess supply of good Y. The workings of the marketplace will cause P^1_X to rise and P^1_Y to fall. The price ratio P_X/P_Y will rise; the price line will move clockwise along the production possibility frontier. That is, firms will increase their production of good X and decrease their production of good Y. Similarly, people will respond to the changing prices by substituting Y for X in their consumption choices. The actions of both firms and individuals simultaneously eliminate the excess demand for X and the excess supply of Y as market prices change.

Equilibrium is reached at X^*, Y^*, with an equilibrium price ratio of P^*_X/P^*_X. With this price ratio, supply and demand are equilibrated for both good X and good Y. Firms, in maximizing their profits, given P^*_X and P^*_Y, will produce X^* and Y^*. Given the income that this level of production provides to people, they will purchase precisely X^* and Y^*. Not only have markets been equilibrated by the operation of the price system, but the resulting equilibrium is also economically efficient. As we showed previously, the equilibrium allocation X^*, Y^* provides the highest level of utility that can be obtained given the existing production possibility frontier. Figure 12-3 provides a simple two-good general equilibrium proof of the first theorem of welfare economics.

Prices, Efficiency, and Laissez-Faire Economics

We have shown that a perfectly competitive price system, by relying on the self-interest of people and of firms and by utilizing the information carried by equilibrium prices, can arrive at an economically efficient allocation of resources. This finding provides some "scientific" support for the laissez-faire position taken by many economists. For example, take Adam Smith's assertion that

> *The natural effort of every individual to better his own condition, when suffered to exert itself with freedom and security, is so powerful a principle that it is alone, and without any assistance, not only capable of carrying on the society to wealth and prosperity, but of surmounting a hundred impertinent obstructions with which the folly of human laws too often encumbers its operations . . . .*[5]

We have seen that this statement has considerable theoretical validity. As Smith noted, it is not the public spirit of the baker that provides bread for people to eat. Rather, bakers (and other producers) operate in their own self-interest in responding to market signals (Smith's invisible hand). In so doing, their actions are coordinated by the market into an efficient, overall pattern. The market system, at least in this simple model, imposes a very strict logic on how resources are used.

That efficiency theorem raises many important questions about the ability of markets to arrive at these perfectly competitive prices and about whether the theorem should act as a guide for government policy (for example, whether governments should avoid interfering in international markets as suggested by Application 12.2: *Gains from Free Trade and the NAFTA and CAFTA Debates*).

MICROQUIZ 12.2

Suppose that an economy produces only the two goods, left shoes (X) and right shoes (Y). Individuals only want to consume these in combinations for which $X = Y$.

1. Which point (or points) on the production possibility frontier would be economically efficient?
2. Why would a point on the production possibility frontier for which $X = 2Y$ be inefficient?

[5]Adam Smith, *The Wealth of Nations* (1776; repr., New York: Random House, 1937), 508. Citations are to the Modern Library edition.

APPLICATION 12.2 *Gains from Free Trade and the NAFTA and CAFTA Debates*

Free trade has been controversial for centuries. One of the most influential debates about trade took place following the Napoleonic Wars in Britain during the 1820s and 1830s. The primary focus of the debate concerned how eliminating high tariffs on imported grain would affect the welfare of various groups in society. Many of the same arguments made in the debate over these "Corn Laws" have reappeared nearly two centuries later in modern debates over free-trade policies.

General Equilibrium Theory of Free Trade

A general equilibrium model is needed to study the impact of free trade on various segments of society. One simple version of such a model is shown in Figure 1. The figure shows those combinations of grain (X) and manufactured goods (Y) that can be produced by, say, British factors of production. If the Corn Laws prevented all trade, point E would represent the domestic equilibrium. Britain would produce and consume quantities X_E and Y_E, and these would yield a utility level of U_2 to the typical British person. Removal of the tariffs would reduce the prevailing domestic price ratio to reflect world prices where grain is cheaper. At these world prices, Britain would reduce its production of grain from X_E to X_A and increase its production of manufactured goods from Y_E to Y_A. Trade with the rest of Europe would permit British consumption to move to point B. The country would import grain in amounts $X_B - X_A$ and export manufactured goods $Y_A - Y_B$. The utility of the typical British consumer would rise to U_3. Hence, adoption of free trade can involve substantial welfare gains.

But trade can also affect the prices of various inputs. Because British production has been reallocated from point E to point A, the demand for inputs used in the manufacturing industry will

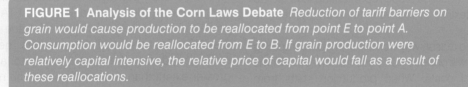

FIGURE 1 Analysis of the Corn Laws Debate *Reduction of tariff barriers on grain would cause production to be reallocated from point E to point A. Consumption would be reallocated from E to B. If grain production were relatively capital intensive, the relative price of capital would fall as a result of these reallocations.*

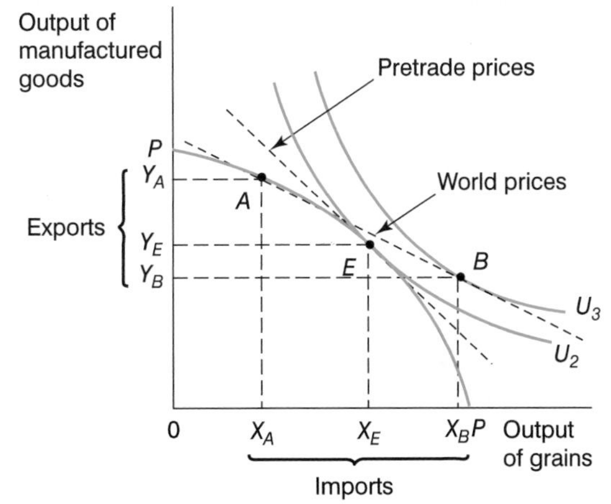

increase whereas the demand for inputs used to produce grain will fall. In the British case, this was good news for factory workers but bad news for landowners. Not surprisingly, the landowners strenuously fought repeal of the Corn Laws. Ultimately, however, the fact that both workers and typical British consumers gained from trade carried the day, and Britain became a leading proponent of free trade for the remainder of the nineteenth century.

Modern Resistance to Free Trade

Because opening of free trade has the capacity to affect the incomes of various inputs, that policy continues to be politically controversial to this day. In the United States and most Western countries, for example, export industries tend to demand skilled workers and significant amounts of high-tech capital equipment. Imports, on the other hand, tend to be produced by less-skilled workers. Hence, it might be expected that relaxation of trade barriers would result in rising wages for skilled workers but stagnating or falling wages for workers with fewer skills. This can be seen by the positions that unions take in trade debates – unions representing skilled workers (such as machinists, agricultural equipment workers, or workers in the chemical and petroleum industries) tend to support free trade, whereas those representing less-skilled workers (textiles or footwear, for example) tend to oppose it.

A related reason why workers in import-competing industries will oppose free trade initiatives concerns adjustment costs. When production shifts from import to export goods, workers must move out of industries that produce the imported goods. In general, it seems likely that they will eventually be reemployed in other industries, but they may have to learn new skills to get those jobs and the process of doing so may take some time. Many nations offer "trade-adjustment" policies that seek to mitigate the costs involved in such transitions by offering worker training or extra unemployment benefits. The US Trade Adjustment Assistance (TAA) program, for example, identifies workers for whom international trade was a cause of job loss. If these workers enter a training program (paid for through government vouchers) they may be able to collect unemployment benefits for up to 78 weeks – a full year longer than is provided for under the normal program of unemployment benefits. Workers who need remedial education can collect even more weeks of benefits. In combination with other assistance (such as subsidized health insurance benefits) TAA therefore provides a considerable cushion to workers affected by trade.[1] Whether such assistance can ever fully compensate for the costs individual workers incur from expansion of trade is an open question, however.

The NAFTA Debate

All of these issues were highlighted in the early 1990s debate over the North American Free Trade Agreement. That agreement significantly reduced trade barriers between the United States, Canada, and Mexico. Early computer modeling of the impact of the NAFTA did indeed suggest that the agreement might pose some short-term costs for low-wage workers.[2] But the models also showed that such costs were significantly outweighed by the gains to other workers and to consumers in all of the countries involved. Indeed, some of the more complicated general equilibrium models suggested that low-wage workers in the US might not be especially harmed by the agreement, because it might improve the operations of the labor markets in which they work.

The generally beneficial outcomes predicted by the general-equilibrium modeling of NAFTA largely seem to have materialized. Indeed, trade among the US, Canada, and Mexico has generally increased during the past decade to a much greater extent than was predicted by the models, especially in areas where goods had not traditionally been traded.[3] The relatively benign effect of this expansion of trade on input markets predicted in the models also seems to be supported by the actual data.

Other Free-Trade Agreements

The apparent success of NAFTA spawned suggestions for a number of additional trading pacts. Relatively modest agreements are now in effect between the United States and Australia, Chile, Singapore, Israel, and Jordan. In early 2005, Congress began debating the Central American Free Trade Agreement (CAFTA) that would eventually phase out all tariffs between the US and Central American countries (including the Dominican Republic). Major beneficiaries of the agreement in the United States are farmers and ranchers (who currently face numerous restrictions on exporting to Central America) and makers of yarn and fabrics (because the agreement will make garment factories in Central America more competitive with those in Asia). But, like its predecessor, CAFTA is controversial in many quarters and was weighted down with special provisions limiting imports of some goods (once again sugar gets special treatment – see Application 11.5). The agreement also imposed labor and environmental restrictions on some Central American countries, and some politicians tried to tie its passage to the adoption of restrictions on trade with China. Ultimately CAFTA passed Congress by a few votes in July 2005, but the fight over such a modest portion of US trade suggests that future free-trade agreements will be hard to achieve.

To Think About

1. Figure 1 shows that there are two sources of the utility gains from free trade: (1) a consumption gain because consumers can consume combinations of goods that lie outside a nation's production possibility frontier, and (2) a specialization effect because nations can specialize in producing goods with relatively high world prices. How would you show these effects in Figure 1? What would determine whether the effects were large or small?
2. Figure 1 shows that a nation will export goods that have a lower relative price domestically than they do in international markets (in this case, good *Y*). What factors will determine which goods have this characteristic? That is, what are the factors that determine a nation's "comparative advantage"?

[1]See K. Baicker and M. Rehavi, "Policy Watch: Trade Adjustment Assistance", *Journal of Economic Perspectives* (Spring, 2004): 239–255.

[2]See N. Lustig, B. Bosworth, and R. Lawrence, eds, *North American Free Trade* (Washington, DC: The Brookings Institution, 1992).

[3]T. J. Kehoe, "An Evaluation of the Performance of Applied General Equilibrium Models of the Impact of NAFTA", Research Department Staff Report 320, Federal Reserve Bank of Minneapolis (August 2003).

Why Markets Fail to Achieve Economic Efficiency

Showing that perfect competition is economically efficient depends crucially on all of the assumptions that underlie the competitive model. In this section, we examine some of the conditions that may prevent markets from generating an efficient allocation.

Imperfect Competition

Imperfect competition in a broad sense includes all those situations in which economic actors (that is, buyers or sellers) exert some market power in determining price. The essential aspect of all these situations is that marginal revenue is different from market price since the firm is no longer a price taker. Because of this, relative prices no longer accurately reflect marginal costs, and the price system no longer carries the information about costs necessary to ensure efficiency. The deadweight loss from monopoly that we will study in Chapter 13 is a good measure of this inefficiency.

Imperfect competition
A market situation in which buyers or sellers have some influence on the prices of goods or services.

Externalities

A price system can also fail to allocate resources efficiently when there are cost relationships among firms or between firms and people that are not adequately represented by market prices. Examples of these are numerous. Perhaps the most common is the case of a firm that pollutes the air with industrial smoke and other

Externality The effect of one party's economic activities on another party that is not taken into account by the price system.

debris. This is called an **externality**. The firm's activities impose costs on other people, and these costs are not taken directly into account through the normal operation of the price system. The basic problem with externalities is that firms' private costs no longer correctly reflect the social costs of production. In the absence of externalities, the costs a firm incurs accurately measure social costs. The prices of the resources the firm uses represent all the opportunity costs involved in production. When a firm creates externalities, however, there are additional costs – those that arise from the external damage. The fact that pollution from burning coal to produce steel causes diseases and general dirt and grime is as much a cost of production as are the wages paid to the firm's workers. However, the firm responds only to private input costs of steel production in deciding how much steel to produce. It disregards the social costs of its pollution. This results in a gap between market price and (social) marginal cost and therefore leads markets to misallocate resources. In Chapter 18, we look at this issue in some detail.

Public Goods

Public goods Goods that are both non-exclusive and non-rival.

A third potential failure of the price system to achieve efficiency stems from the existence of certain types of goods called **public goods**. These goods have two characteristics that make them difficult to produce efficiently through markets. First, the goods can provide benefits to one more person at zero marginal cost. In this sense the goods are "non-rival", in that the cost of producing them cannot necessarily be assigned to any specific user. Second, public goods are "non-exclusive" – no person can be excluded from benefiting from them. That is, people gain from the good being available, whether they actually pay for it or not.

To see why public goods pose problems for markets, consider the most important example, national defense. Once a national defense system is in place, one more person can enjoy its protection at zero marginal cost, so this good is non-rival. Similarly, all people in the country benefit from being protected whether they like it or not. It is not possible to exclude people from such benefits, regardless of what they do. Left to private markets, however, it is extremely unlikely that national defense would be produced at efficient levels. Each person would have an incentive to pay nothing voluntarily for national defense, in the hope that others would pay instead. Everyone would have an incentive to be a "free rider," relying on spending by others (which would never materialize). As a result, resources would then be under allocated to national defense in a purely market economy. To avoid such misallocations, communities will usually decide to have public goods (other examples are street lighting, traffic control systems, or mosquito control) produced by the government and will finance this production through some form of compulsory taxation. Economic issues posed by this process are also discussed in detail in Chapter 18.

Imperfect Information

Throughout our discussion of the connection between perfect competition and economic efficiency, we have been implicitly assuming that the economic actors involved are fully informed. The most important kind of information they are assumed to have is a knowledge of equilibrium market prices. If for some reason markets are unable to establish these prices or if demanders or suppliers do not know what these prices are, the types of "invisible hand" results we developed may not hold. Consider, for example, the problem that any consumer faces in trying to buy a new television. Not only does he or she have to make some kind of judgment about the quality of various brands (to determine what the available "goods" actually are) but this would-be buyer also faces the problem of finding out what various sellers are charging for a particular set. All of these kinds of problems have been assumed away so far by treating goods as being homogeneous and having a universally known market price. As we will see in Chapter 17, if such assumptions do not hold, the efficiency of perfectly competitive markets is more problematic.

Efficiency and Equity

So far in this chapter we have discussed the concept of economic efficiency and whether an efficient allocation of resources can be achieved through reliance on market forces. We have not mentioned questions of **equity** or fairness in the way goods are distributed among people. In this section, we briefly take up this question. We show not only that it is very difficult to define what an equitable distribution of resources is but also that there is no reason to expect that allocations that result from a competitive price system (or from practically any other method of allocating resources, for that matter) will be equitable.

Equity The fairness of the distribution of goods or utility.

Defining and Achieving Equity

A primary problem with developing an accepted definition of "fair" or "unfair" allocations of resources is that not everyone agrees as to what the concept means. Some people might call any allocation "fair" providing no one breaks any laws in arriving at it – these people would call only acquisition of goods by theft "unfair". Others may base their notions of fairness on a dislike for inequality. Only allocations in which people receive about the same levels of utility (assuming these levels could be measured and compared) would be regarded as fair. On a more practical level, some people think the current distribution of income and wealth in the United Kingdom is reasonably fair whereas others regard it as drastically unfair. Welfare economists have devised a number of more specific definitions, but these tend to give conflicting conclusions about which resource allocations are or are not equitable. There is simply no agreement on this issue.[6]

Equity and Competitive Markets

Even if everyone agreed on what a fair allocation of resources (and, ultimately, of people's utility) is, there would still be the question of how such a situation should be achieved. Can we rely on voluntary transactions among people to achieve fairness, or will something more be required? Some introspection may suggest why voluntary solutions will not succeed. If people start out with an unequal distribution of goods, voluntary trading cannot necessarily erase that inequality. Those who are initially favored will not voluntarily agree to make themselves worse off. Similar lessons apply to participation in competitive market transactions. Because these are voluntary, they may not be able to erase initial inequalities, even while promoting efficient outcomes.

Adopting coercive methods to achieve equity (such as taxes) may involve problems too. For example, in several places in this book, we have shown how taxes may affect people's behavior and result in efficiency losses that arise from this distortion. Using government's power to transfer income may therefore be a costly

[6]For a discussion of some recent thinking on this topic, see Amartya Sen's 1998 Nobel Prize Speech, reprinted in A. Sen, "The Possibility of Social Choice", *American Economic Review* (June 1999): 349–378.

activity; achieving equity may involve important losses of efficiency. Making decisions about equity–efficiency trade-offs is a major source of political controversy throughout the world.

The Edgeworth Box Diagram for Exchange

Edgeworth box diagram
A graphic device for illustrating all of the possible allocations of two goods (or two inputs) that are in fixed supply.

Issues about equity can best be illustrated with a graphic device called the **Edgeworth box diagram**. In this diagram, a box is used that has dimensions given by the total quantities of two goods available (we'll call these goods simply X and Y). The horizontal dimension of the box represents the total quantity of X available, whereas the vertical height of the box is the total quantity of Y. These dimensions are shown in Figure 12-4.

The point O_S is considered to be the origin for the first person (call her Smith). Quantities of X are measured along the horizontal axis rightward from O_S; quantities of Y, along the vertical axis upward from O_S. Any point in the box can be regarded as some allocation of X and Y to Smith. For example, at point E, Smith gets $X^E{}_S$ and $Y^E{}_S$. The useful property of the Edgeworth box is that the quantities received by the second person (say, Jones) are also recorded by point E. Jones simply gets that part of the total quantity that is left over. In fact, we can regard Jones's quantities as being measured from the origin O_J. Point E therefore also corresponds to the quantities $X^E{}_J$ and $Y^E{}_J$ for Jones. Notice that the quantities assigned to Smith and Jones in this manner exactly exhaust the total quantities of X and Y available.

MICROQUIZ 12.3

Draw simple supply and demand curve models for determining the prices of X and Y in Figure 12-4. Show the "disequilibrium" points X_1 and X_1' on your diagram for good X and points Y_1 and Y_1' on your diagram for good Y. Describe how *both* of these markets reach equilibrium simultaneously.

FIGURE 12-4 Edgeworth Box Diagram *The Edgeworth box diagram permits all possible allocations of two goods (X and Y) to be visualized. If we consider the corner O_S to be Smith's "origin" and O_J to be Jones's, then the allocation represented by point E would have Smith getting $X^E{}_S$ and $Y^E{}_S$, and Jones would receive what is left over ($X^E{}_J$, $Y^E{}_J$). One purpose of this diagram is to discover which of the possible locations within the box can be reached through voluntary exchange.*

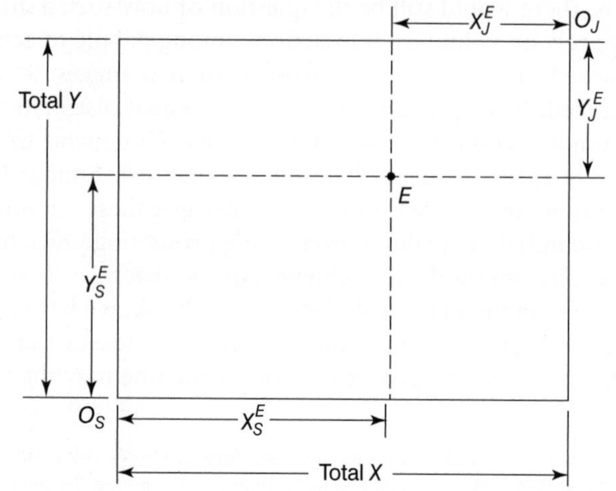

Mutually Beneficial Trades

Any point in the Edgeworth box represents an allocation of the available goods between Smith and Jones, and all possible allocations are contained somewhere in the box. To discover which of the allocations offer mutually beneficial trades, we must introduce these people's preferences. In Figure 12-5, Smith's indifference curve map is drawn with origin O_S. Movements in a north-easterly direction represent higher levels of utility to Smith. In the same figure, Jones's indifference curve map is drawn with the corner O_J as an origin. We have taken Jones's indifference curve map, rotated it 180 degrees, and fit it into the northeast corner of the Edgeworth box. Movements in a south-westerly direction represent increases in Jones's utility level.

Using these superimposed indifference curve maps, we can identify the allocations from which some mutually beneficial trades might be made. Any point for which the MRS for Smith is unequal to that for Jones represents such an opportunity. Consider an arbitrary initial allocation such as point E in Figure 12-5. This point lies on the point of intersection of Smith's indifference curve U^1_S and Jones's indifference curve U^3_J. Obviously, the marginal rates of substitution (the slopes of the indifference curves) are not equal at E. Any allocation in the oval-shaped area in Figure 12-5 represents a mutually beneficial trade for these two people – they can both move to a higher level of utility by adopting a trade that moves them into this area.

FIGURE 12-5 Edgeworth Box Diagram of Pareto Efficiency in Exchange
The points on the curve O_S, O_3 are efficient in the sense that at these allocations Smith cannot be made better off without making Jones worse off, and vice versa. An allocation such as E, on the other hand, is inefficient because both Smith and Jones can be made better off by choosing to move into the shaded area. Notice that along O_S, O_3 the MRS for Smith is equal to that for Jones. The line O_S, O_3 is called the contract curve.

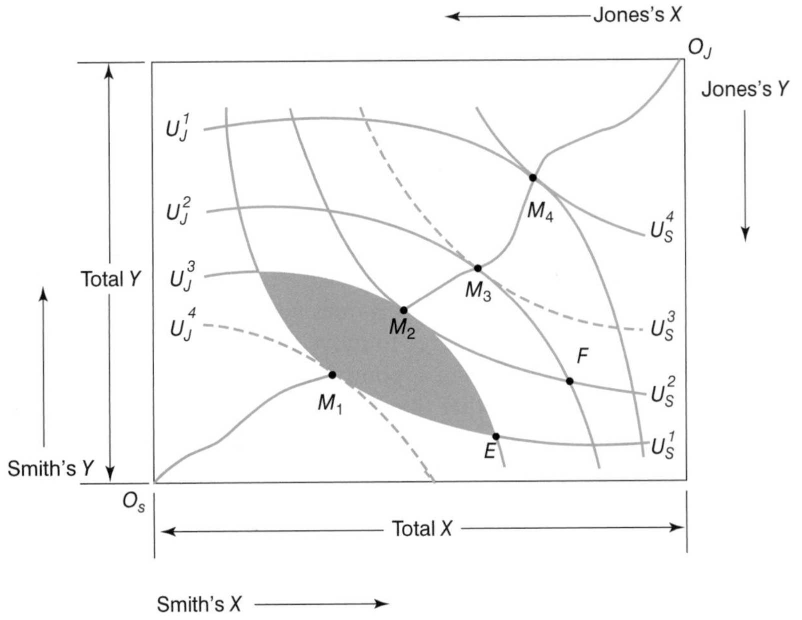

Efficiency in Exchange

When the marginal rates of substitution of Smith and Jones are equal, however, such mutually beneficial trades are not available. The points M_1, M_2, M_3, and M_4 in Figure 12-5 indicate tangencies of these individuals' indifference curves, and movement away from such points must make at least one of the people worse off. A move from M_2 to E, for example, reduces Smith's utility from U^2_S to U^1_S, even though Jones is made no worse off by the move. Alternatively, a move from M_2 to F makes Jones worse off but keeps the Smith utility level constant. In general, then, these points of tangency do not offer the promise of additional mutually beneficial trading. Such points are called **Pareto efficient allocations** after the Italian scientist Vilfredo Pareto (1878–1923), who pioneered in the development of the formal theory of exchange. Notice that the Pareto definition of efficiency does not require any interpersonal comparisons of utility; we never have to compare Jones's gains to Smith's losses or vice versa. Rather, individuals decide for themselves whether particular trades improve utility. For efficient allocations, there are no such additional trades to which both parties would agree.

Pareto efficient allocation An allocation of available resources in which no mutually beneficial trading opportunities are unexploited. That is, an allocation in which no one person can be made better off without someone else being made worse off.

Contract curve The set of efficient allocations of the existing goods in an exchange situation. Points off that curve are necessarily inefficient, since individuals can be made unambiguously better off by moving to the curve.

Initial endowments The initial holdings of goods from which trading begins.

Contract Curve

The set of all the efficient allocations in an Edgeworth box diagram is called the **contract curve**. In Figure 12-5, this set of points is represented by the line running from O_S to O_J and includes the tangencies M_1, M_2, M_3, and M_4 (and many other such tangencies). Points off the contract curve (such as E or F) are inefficient, and mutually beneficial trades are possible. But, as its name implies, moving onto the contract curve exhausts all such mutually beneficial trading opportunities. A move along the contract curve (say, from M_1 to M_2) does not represent a mutually beneficial trade because there will always be a winner (Smith) and a loser (Jones).

Efficiency and Equity

The Edgeworth box diagram not only permits a graphic description of Pareto efficiency, but also allows us to illustrate the problematic relationship between efficiency and equity. Suppose, for example, that everyone agreed that the only fair allocation is one of equal utilities. Perhaps everyone remembers his or her childhood experiences in dividing up a cake or chocolate bar where equal shares seemed to be the only reasonable solution. This desired allocation might be represented by point E in the Edgeworth exchange box in Figure 12-6. On the other hand, suppose Smith and Jones start out at point A – at which Smith is in a fairly favorable situation. As we described previously, any allocation between M_2 and M_3 is preferable to point A because both people would be better off by voluntarily making such a move. In this case, however, the point of equal utility (E) does not fall in this range. Smith would not voluntarily agree to move to point E since that would make her worse off than at point A. Smith would prefer to refrain from any trading rather than accept the "fair" allocation E. In the language of welfare economics, the **initial endowments** (that is, the starting place for trading) of Smith and Jones are so unbalanced that voluntary agreements will not result in the desired equal allocation of utilities. If point E is to be achieved, some coercion (such as taxation) must be used to get Smith to accept it. The idea that redistributive taxes might be used together with competitive markets to yield allocations of resources that are both efficient and

MICROQUIZ 12.4

What would the contract curve look like in the following situations?

1. Smith likes only good *X* and Jones likes only good *Y*.
2. Smith and Jones both view *X* and *Y* as perfect complements.
3. Smith and Jones are both always willing to substitute one unit of *X* for one unit of *Y* and remain equally well-off.

equitable has proven to be a tantalizing prospect for economists, as Application 12.3: *The Second Theorem of Welfare Economics* illustrates.

Money in General Equilibrium Models

Thus far in this chapter, we have shown how competitive markets can establish a set of relative prices at which all markets are in equilibrium simultaneously. At several places we stressed that competitive market forces determine only relative, not absolute, prices and that to examine how the absolute price level is determined we must introduce money into our models. Although a complete examination of this topic is more properly studied as part of macroeconomics, here we can briefly explore some questions of the role of money in a competitive economy that relate directly to microeconomics.

Nature and Function of Money

Money serves two primary functions in any economy: (1) it facilitates transactions by providing an accepted medium of exchange, and (2) it acts as a store of value so that economic actors can better allocate their spending decisions over time. Any commodity can serve as "money" provided it is generally accepted for exchange purposes and is durable from period to period. Today most economies tend to use government-created (fiat) money because the costs associated with its production (e.g., printing pieces of paper with portraits of past or present rulers or keeping records on magnetic tape) are very low. In earlier times, however, commodity money was common, with the particular good chosen ranging from the familiar (gold and silver) to the obscure

FIGURE 12-6 Voluntary Transactions May Not Result in Equitable Allocations *This Edgeworth box diagram for exchange is taken from Figure 12–5. Point E represents a "fair" sharing of the available goods (assuming that can be defined). If individuals' initial endowments are at point A, voluntary transactions cannot be relied on to reach point E since such an allocation makes Smith worse off than at A.*

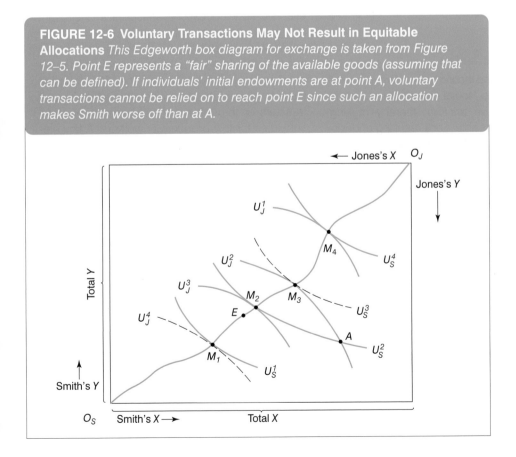

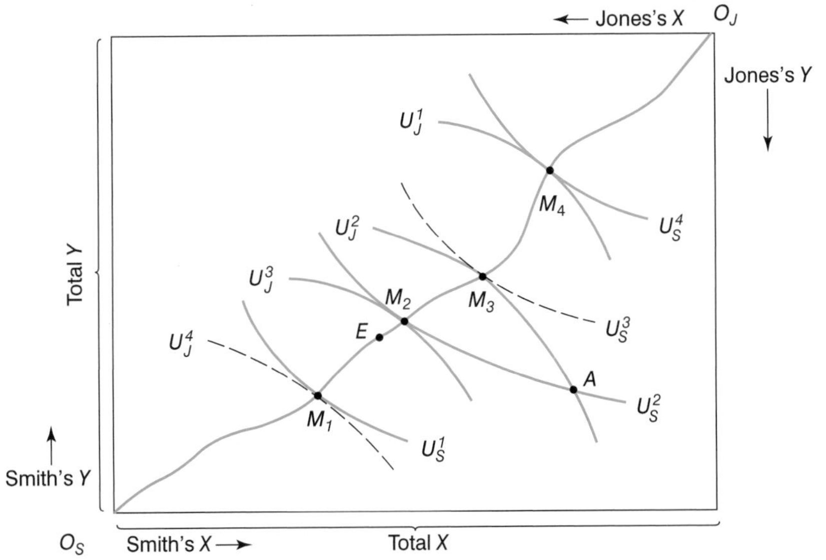

APPLICATION 12.3 *The Second Theorem of Welfare Economics*

Zealous students of microeconomics will be happy to know that there is, in fact, a "second" theorem of welfare economics that accompanies the more popular first "invisible hand" theorem. This second theorem focuses on equity and shows how competitive markets might be used to achieve that goal. Specifically, the theorem states that any desired allocation of utility among the members of society can be achieved through the operations of competitive markets, *providing* initial endowments are set appropriately. Suppose, for example, that equity dictated that the distribution of utility between Smith and Jones in Figure 12.5 must lie between M_2 and M_3 on the contract curve. The second theorem states that this can be achieved by adjusting initial endowments to point *F* and then allowing competitive trading between these two people. How this state of affairs might be achieved in the real world is the subject of this application.

Lump-Sum Redistribution

Sometimes the second theorem of welfare economics is paraphrased as "social policy should pursue efficiency (competitive pricing), thereby making the 'pie' as big as possible – any resulting undesirable inequalities can be patched up with lump-sum taxes and transfers". It is this vision that provides the impetus to the adherents of many "free-market" policies. But the view is probably too simplistic for at least two reasons. First, most real-world tax and transfer schemes depart significantly from the lump-sum ideal. That is, virtually all such schemes distort people's behavior and therefore cause welfare losses of their own. Second, this approach to achieving equity focuses on patching things up after competitive markets have reached equilibrium, but it is unclear whether any political system would in fact adopt such policies. Still, the lump-sum vision is an attractive one because efficiency gains from competitive markets offer opportunities for Pareto improvements, from which everyone can be made better off. The approach has been widely used in applied economics, especially in the field of law and economics, to evaluate various policy options.[1] For example, in the theory of contracts, a lawyer might argue that all contracts should be kept, regardless of unforeseen factors that may have occurred. Economists, on the other hand, have asked whether breaching some types of contracts might be efficient, creating added utility that could be shared by all parties.

Education and Initial Endowments

Another approach to finding desirable equity–efficiency trade-offs focuses specifically on using general-equilibrium models to study the relative merits of various ways of altering initial endowments. Because many people believe that education may be the best route to achieving a more equitable distribution of income, considerable attention has been devoted to looking at the potential effects of large educational subsidies. In one recent study, for example, the authors use a simple general-equilibrium model to study the equity–efficiency trade-offs that arise through the use of subsidies for higher education.[2] They then compare these to what might be obtained through taxes and transfers or through a general program of wage subsidies for low-productivity workers. A key element of their model is that people have differing abilities that affect both their chances for success in school, university, and their future wages. Greater subsidies for higher education help to equalize wages but also involve some deadweight losses because they lure people into higher education that is not a good match for their ability. Perhaps surprisingly, the authors conclude that education may not be an efficient way to alter initial endowments. They find that wage subsidies dominate both education and tax/transfer schemes in that any given level of government spending provides more final utility.

To Think About

1 Most general-equilibrium models of the trade-off between equity and efficiency look only at the distribution of utility among people in evaluating equity. Is this a limited view of "equity"?

Are there larger issues of "fairness" that should also be considered?

2 In general-equilibrium models, one can study the distribution of utility from two perspectives. The *ex ante* perspective looks at what people ultimately expect their utility to be before they engage in market transactions. That is, this perspective looks at opportunities. The *ex post* perspective looks at actual utility results after market transactions are completed. Which of these is the better way to look at the equity question?

[1]A good introductory discussion is in R. Posner, *Economic Analysis of Law*, 6th ed. (New York: Aspen Publishers, 2003), chaps. 1 and 2.

[2]E. A. Hanushek, C. K. Y. Leung, and K. Yilmaz, "Redistribution Through Education and Other Transfer Mechanisms", *Journal of Monetary Economics* (November 2003): 1719–1750.

and even bizarre (sharks' teeth or, on the island of Yap, large stone wheels). Societies probably choose the particular form that their money will take as a result of a wide variety of economic, historical, and political forces.

Money as the Accounting Standard

One of the most important functions money usually plays is to act as an accounting standard. All prices can be quoted in terms of this standard. In general, relative prices will be unaffected by which good (or possibly a basket of goods) is chosen as the accounting standard. For example, if one apple (good 1) exchanges for two plums (good 2):

$$\frac{P_1}{P_2} = \frac{2}{1} \tag{12.1}$$

and it makes little difference how those prices are quoted. If, for example, a society chooses clams as its monetary unit of account, an apple might exchange for four clams and a plum for two clams. If we denote clam prices of apples and plums by P_1' and P_2', respectively, we have

$$\frac{P'_1}{P'_2} = \frac{4}{2} = \frac{2}{1} = \frac{P_1}{P_2} \tag{12.2}$$

We could change from counting in clams to counting in sharks' teeth by knowing that ten sharks' teeth exchange for one clam. The price of our goods in sharks' teeth would be

$$P'_1 = 4 \cdot 10 = 40$$

and {12.3}

$$P'_2 = 2 \cdot 10 = 20$$

One apple (which costs 40 teeth) would still exchange for two plums that cost 20 teeth each.

Of course, using clams or sharks' teeth is not very common. Instead, societies usually adopt paper money as their accounting standard. An apple might exchange for half a piece of paper picturing Queen Elizabeth (i.e., £0.50) and a plum for one-fourth of such a piece of paper (£0.25). Thus, with this monetary standard, the relative price remains two for one. Choice of an accounting standard does not, however, necessarily dictate any particular absolute price level. An apple might exchange for four clams or four hundred, but, as long as a plum exchanges for half as many clams, relative prices will be unaffected by the absolute level that prevails. Absolute price levels are obviously important, however, especially to people who wish to use money as a store of value. A person with a large investment in clams obviously cares about how many apples he or she can buy with those clams. Although a complete theoretical treatment of the price level issue is beyond the scope of this book, we do offer some brief comments here.

Commodity Money

In an economy where money is produced in a way similar to any other good (gold is mined, clams are dug, or sharks are caught), the relative price of money is determined like any other relative price – by the forces of demand and supply. Economic forces that affect either the demand or supply of money will also affect these relative prices. For example, Spanish importation of gold from the New World during the fifteenth and sixteenth centuries greatly expanded gold supplies and caused the relative price of gold to fall. That is, the prices of all other goods rose relative to that of gold – there was general inflation in the prices of practically everything in terms of gold. Similar effects would arise from changes in any factor that affected the equilibrium price for the good chosen as money. Application 12.4: *Commodity Money* looks at some current debates about adopting a gold or other commodity standard.

Fiat Money and the Monetary Veil

For the case of fiat money produced by the government, the analysis can be extended a bit. In this situation, the government is the sole supplier of money and can generally choose how much it wishes to produce. What effects will this level of money production have on the real economy? In general, the situation would seem to be identical to that for commodity money. A change in the money supply will disturb the general equilibrium of all relative prices, and, although it seems likely that an expansion in supply will lower the relative price of money (that is, result in an inflation in the money prices of other goods), any more precise prediction would seem to depend on the results of a detailed general equilibrium model of supply and demand in many markets.

Beginning with David Hume, however, classical economists argued that fiat money differs from other economic goods and should be regarded as being outside the real economic system of demand, supply, and relative price determination. In this view, the economy can be dichotomized into a real sector in which relative prices are determined and a monetary sector where the absolute price level (that is, the value of fiat money) is set. Money, therefore, acts only as a "veil" for real economic activity; the quantity of money available has no effect on the real sector.[7] Whether this is true is an important unresolved issue in macroeconomics.

MICROQUIZ 12.5

Sometimes economists are not very careful when they draw supply and demand curves to state clearly whether the price on the vertical axis is a relative (real) price or a nominal price. How would a pure inflation (in which all prices rise together) affect

1. A supply and demand curve diagram that has relative price on the vertical axis?
2. A supply and demand curve diagram that has nominal price on the vertical axis?

[7] This leads directly to the quantity theory of the demand for money, first suggested by Hume:

$$D_M = \frac{1}{V} \cdot P \cdot Q$$

where D_M is the demand for money, V is the velocity of monetary circulation (the number of times a dollar is used each year), P is the overall price level, and Q is a measure of the quantity of transactions (often approximated by real GDP). If V is fixed and Q is determined by real forces of supply and demand, a doubling of the supply of money will result in a doubling of the equilibrium price level.

APPLICATION 12.4 *Commodity Money*

Throughout history both commodity and fiat money have been widely used. Today we are more accustomed to fiat money – money that is produced by the government at a cost much lower than its exchange value. The ability to control the supply of such money gives governments substantial power to control the general price level and many other macroeconomic variables. In contrast, the use of a particular commodity as money tends to arise by historical accident. Once a social consensus is reached that a certain good will serve as a medium of exchange, the amount of such money in circulation will be determined by the usual laws of supply and demand. Some economists believe this is a desirable feature of using commodity money because it severely limits what governments can do in terms of monetary policy. Regardless of where one comes down on this issue, examining some experiences with commodity money can provide insights about how the monetary and real sectors of any economy are related.

The Gold Standard

Gold has been used as money for thousands of years. In the nineteenth century, this use was formalized under the "gold standard". The process of establishing the standard started in 1821 with the British decision to make the pound freely tradable for gold at a fixed price. Germany and the United States quickly followed the British lead, and by the 1870s most of the world's major economies tied the values of their currencies to gold. This implicitly established an international system of fixed exchange rates. It also limited the power of governments to create fiat money because of the need to maintain a fixed price of their currencies in terms of gold.

Two features of economic life under the gold standard are worth noting. First, because economic output tended to expand more rapidly than the supply of gold during much of the nineteenth century, this was generally a period of falling prices. That is, the price of gold (and currencies tied to gold) increased relative to the price of other goods. Second, any periods of general inflation tended to be associated with new gold discoveries. This was especially true in the United States following gold discoveries in 1848 (in California) and in 1898 (in the Yukon).

Bimetallism

Gold and silver were both used as commodity money in the early history of the United States. The government set the official exchange ratio between the two metals, but that ratio did not always reflect true relative scarcities. Usually gold was defined to have an exchange value higher than its true market value, so gold was used for most monetary transactions. But that meant that money was tight because the gold supply was growing only slowly. William Jennings Bryan's famous "cross of gold" speech in 1896 was essentially a plea to raise the exchange value of silver so that the overall money supply could grow more rapidly. Much of the debate about bimetallism is also reflected in the Frank Baum story *The Wizard of Oz*. For example, the Wicked Witch of the East represents Eastern bankers who wished to maintain a gold-only standard.[1] More generally, experiences with bimetallism show how difficult it is to maintain fixed money prices for two different commodity moneys when the underlying values of the commodities are subject to the laws of supply and demand.

Cigarettes as Money

An interesting example of commodity money arising in strained circumstances is provided by R. A. Radford's famous account of his experiences in a POW camp during World War II.[2] Radford shows that prisoners soon settled on cigarettes as a commodity "money". It was mainly British or French cigarettes that were used as money, because American cigarettes were generally regarded as better for smoking. Arrival of Red Cross packages with fresh cigarette supplies generally led to an overall inflation in the cigarette prices of other goods.

(Continued)

To Think About

1 Suppose you could dictate which commodity would be used as a monetary standard, what criteria would you use in selecting the good to be used?

2 Radford's observation about American cigarettes is an example of Gresham's Law – that "bad" money drives out "good" money. Can you think of other historical examples of this phenomenon?

[1]For a complete discussion, see H. Rockoff, "*The Wizard of Oz* as a Monetary Allegory", *Journal of Political Economy* (August 1990): 739–760.

[2]R. A. Radford, "The Economic Organization of a POW Camp", *Economica* (November 1945): 189–201.

SUMMARY

We began this chapter with a description of a general equilibrium model of a perfectly competitive price system. In that model, relative prices are determined by the forces of supply and demand, and everyone takes these prices as given in their economic decisions. We then arrive at the following conclusions about such a method for allocating resources.

- Profit-maximizing firms will use resources efficiently and will therefore operate on the production possibility frontier.
- Profit-maximizing firms will also produce an economically efficient mix of outputs. The workings of supply and demand will ensure that the technical rate at which one good can be transformed into another in production (the rate of product transformation, RPT) is equal to the rate at which people are willing to trade one good for another (the MRS). Adam Smith's invisible hand brings considerable coordination into seemingly chaotic market transactions.
- Factors that interfere with the ability of prices to reflect marginal costs under perfect competition will prevent an economically efficient allocation of resources. Such factors include imperfect competition, externalities, and public goods. Imperfect information about market prices may also interfere with the efficiency of perfect competition.
- Under perfect competition, there are no forces to ensure that voluntary transactions will result in equitable final allocations. Achieving equity may require some coercion to transfer income or initial endowments. Such interventions may involve costs in terms of economic efficiency.
- A perfectly competitive price system establishes only relative prices. Introduction of money into the competitive model is needed to show how nominal prices are determined. In some cases the amount of money (and the absolute price level) will have no effect on the relative prices established in competitive markets.

REVIEW QUESTIONS

1 Why should an economist who is interested in only one market be concerned about general equilibrium relationships? Can't he or she just study shifts in supply or demand in this single market without worrying about what is happening elsewhere? Provide a specific example of general equilibrium feedback effects and of how omitting them might cause an analyst to make mistakes in his or her examination of a single market.

2 How does the approach to economic efficiency taken in Chapter 11 relate to the one taken here? How is the possible inefficiency in Figure 11-1 related to that in Figure 12-2?

3 Why are allocations on the production possibility frontier technically efficient? What is technically inefficient about allocations inside the frontier? Do inefficient allocations necessarily involve any unemployment of factors of production? In the model introduced in this chapter, would unemployment be technically inefficient?

4 Why does the slope of the production possibility frontier indicate relative opportunity costs? Why do economists expect the opportunity cost of *X* to increase as the output of *X* increases? Suppose opportunity costs were constant. What would the production possibility curve look like in this case and what would that imply about the marginal costs of *X* and *Y* production?

5 Suppose two countries had differing production possibility frontiers and were currently producing at points with differing slopes (that is, differing relative opportunity costs). If there were no transportation or other charges associated with international transactions, how might world output be increased by having these firms alter their production plans? Develop a simple numerical example of these gains for the case where both countries have linear production possibility frontiers (with different slopes). Interpret this result in terms of the concept of "comparative advantage" from the theory of international trade.

6 Use a simple two-goods model of resource allocation (such as that in Figure 12-2) to explain the difference between technical efficiency and economic (or allocative) efficiency. Would you agree with the statement that "economic efficiency requires technical efficiency, but many technically efficient allocations are not economically efficient"? Explain your reasoning with a graph.

7 In Chapter 10 we showed how a shift in demand or supply could be analyzed using a model of a single market. How would you illustrate an increase in the demand for good *X* in the general equilibrium model pictured in Figure 12-3? Why would such a shift in preferences cause the relative price of *X* to rise? What would happen to the market for good *Y* in this case? How would you conduct a similar analysis of an improvement in the technology for producing good *X*?

8 Relative prices convey information about both production possibilities and people's preferences. What exactly is that information and how does its availability help attain an efficient allocation of resources? In what ways does the presence of monopoly or externalities result in price information being "inaccurate"?

9 Suppose that the competitive equilibrium shown in Figure 12-3 were regarded as "unfair" because the relative price of *X* (an important necessity) is "too high". What would be the result of passing a law requiring that P_X/P_Y be lower?

10 In most of the theoretical examples in this book, prices have been quoted in dollars, euros, or cents. Is this choice of currency crucial? Would most examples be the same if prices had been stated in pounds, kroner, or yen? Or, would it have mattered if the dollars used were "1900 dollars" or "2000 dollars"? How would you change the endless hamburger–soft drink examples, say, to phrase them in some other currency? Would such changes result in any fundamental differences? Or, do most of the examples in this book seem to display the classical dichotomy between real and nominal magnitudes?

PROBLEMS

12.1 Suppose the production possibility frontier for cheeseburgers (*C*) and milkshakes (*M*) is given by

$$C + 2M = 600$$

a Plot this function on a graph.

b Assuming that people prefer to eat two cheeseburgers with every milkshake, how much of each product will be produced? Indicate this point on your graph.

c Given that this fast food economy is operating efficiently, what price ratio (P_C/P_M) must prevail?

12.2 Consider an economy with just one technique available for the production of each good, food and cloth:

Good	Food	Cloth
Labor per unit output	1	1
Land per unit output	2	1

a Supposing land is unlimited but labor equals 100, write and sketch the production possibility frontier.

b Supposing labor is unlimited but land equals 150, write and sketch the production possibility frontier.

c Supposing labor equals 100 and land equals 150, write and sketch the production possibility frontier. (*Hint*: What are the intercepts of the production possibility frontier? When is land fully employed? Labor? Both?)

d Explain why the production possibility frontier of part c is concave.

e Sketch the relative price of food as a function of its output in part c.

f If consumers insist on trading four units of food for five units of cloth, what is the relative price of food? Why?

g Explain why production is exactly the same at a price ratio of $P_F/P_C = 1.1$ as at $P_F/P_C = 1.9$.

h Suppose that capital is also required for producing food and cloth and that capital requirements per unit of food are 0.8 and per unit of cloth 0.9. There are 100 units of capital available. What is the production possibility curve in this case? Answer part e for this case.

12.3 Suppose the production possibility frontier for guns (*X*) and butter (*Y*) is given by

$$X^2 + 2Y^2 = 900$$

a Plot this frontier on a graph.

b If individuals always prefer consumption bundles in which $Y = 2X$, how much *X* and *Y* will be produced?

c At the point described in part b, what will be the slope of the production possibility frontier, and what price ratio will cause production to take place at that point? This slope should be approximated by considering small changes in *X* and *Y* around the optimal point.

d Show your solution on the figure from part a.

12.4 Robinson Crusoe obtains utility from the quantity of fish he consumes in one day (*F*), the quantity of coconuts he consumes that day (*C*), and the hours of leisure time he has during the day (*H*) according to the utility function:

$$\text{Utility} = F^{1/4} C^{1/4} H^{1/2}$$

Robinson's production of fish is given by

$$F = \sqrt{L_F}$$

(where L_F is the hours he spends fishing), and his production of coconuts is determined by

$$C = \sqrt{L_C}$$

(where L_C is the time he spends picking coconuts). Assuming that Robinson decides to work an eight-hour day (that is, $H = 16$), plot on a graph his production possibility curve for fish and coconuts. Show his optimal choices of those goods.

12.5 Suppose two individuals (Smith and Jones) each have ten hours of labor to devote to producing either ice cream (*X*) or chicken soup (*Y*). Smith's demand for *X* and *Y* is given by

$$X_S = \frac{0.3I_S}{P_X}$$

$$Y_S = \frac{0.7I_S}{P_Y}$$

whereas Jones's demands are given by

$$X_J = \frac{0.5I_J}{P_X}$$

$$Y_J = \frac{0.5I_J}{P_Y}$$

where I_S and I_J represent Smith's and Jones's incomes, respectively (which come only from working).

The individuals do not care whether they produce X or Y and the production function for each good is given by

$$X = 2L$$
$$Y = 3L$$

where L is the total labor devoted to production of each good. Using this information, answer the following:

a What must the price ratio, P_X/P_Y be?

b Given this price ratio, how much X and Y will Smith and Jones demand? (*Hint*: Set the wage equal to 1 here so that each person's income is 10.)

c How should labor be allocated between X and Y to satisfy the demand calculated in part b?

12.6 In the country of Ruritania there are two regions, A and B. Two goods (X and Y) are produced in both regions. Production functions for region A are given by

$$X_A = \sqrt{L_X}$$
$$Y_A = \sqrt{L_Y}$$

L_X and L_Y are the quantity of labor devoted to X and Y production, respectively. Total labor available in region A is 100 units. That is

$$L_X + L_Y = 100$$

Using a similar notation for region B, production functions are given by

$$X_B = \frac{1}{2}\sqrt{L_X}$$

$$Y_B = \frac{1}{2}\sqrt{L_Y}$$

There are also 100 units of labor available in region B:

$$L_X + L_Y = 100$$

a Calculate the production possibility curves for regions A and B.

b What condition must hold if production in Ruritania is to be allocated efficiently between regions A and B (assuming that labor cannot move from one region to the other)?

c Calculate the production possibility curve for Ruritania (again assuming that labor is immobile between regions). How much total Y can Ruritania produce if total X output is 12? (*Hint*: A graphic analysis may be of some help here.)

12.7 There are 200 kilos of food on an island that must be allocated between two marooned sailors. The utility function of the first sailor is given by

$$\text{Utility} = \sqrt{F_1}$$

where F_1 is the quantity of food consumed by the first sailor. For the second sailor, utility (as a function of food consumption) is given by

$$\text{Utility} = \frac{1}{2}\sqrt{F_2}$$

a If the food is allocated equally between the sailors, how much utility will each receive?

b How should food be allocated between the sailors to ensure equality of utility?

c Suppose that the second sailor requires a utility level of at least five to remain alive. How should food be allocated so as to maximize the sum of utilities subject to the restraint that the second sailor receives that minimum level of utility?

d What other criteria might you use to allocate the available food between the sailors?

12.8 Return to Problem 12.5 and now assume that Smith and Jones conduct their exchanges in paper money. The total supply of such money is €60 and each individual wishes to hold a stock of money equal to $\frac{1}{4}$ of the value of transactions made per period.

a What will the money wage rate be in this model? What will the nominal prices of X and Y be?

b Suppose the money supply increases to €90, how will your answers to part a change? Does this economy exhibit the classical dichotomy between its real and monetary sectors?

12.9 The Edgeworth box diagram can also be used to show how a production possibility frontier is constructed for an economy as a whole. Suppose there are only two goods that might be produced (X and Y), each using two inputs, capital (K) and labor (L). In order to construct the $X - Y$ production possibility frontier, we must look for efficient allocations of the total capital and labor available.

a Draw an Edgeworth box with dimensions given by the total quantities of capital and labor available (see Figure 12-4).

b Consider the lower-left corner of the box to be the origin for the isoquant map for good X. Draw a few of the X isoquants.

c Now consider the upper-right corner of the box to be the origin for the isoquant map for good Y. Draw a few Y isoquants (as in Figure 12-5) in the Edgeworth box.

d What are the efficient points in the box you have drawn? What condition must hold for a given allocation of K and L to be efficient?

e The production possibility frontier for X and Y consists of all the efficient allocations in the Edgeworth box. Explain why this is so. Also explain why inefficient points in the box would be *inside* the production possibility frontier.

f Use the connection between your box diagram and the production possibility frontier to discuss what the frontier would look like in the following cases.

i Production of good X uses only labor, production of good Y uses only labor.

ii Both X and Y are produced using K and L in the same fixed proportions as the inputs are available in the economy and both exhibit constant returns to scale.

iii Both X and Y have the same production function and both exhibit constant returns to scale.

iv Both X and Y are produced using the same production function and both exhibit increasing returns to scale.

12.10 Smith and Jones are stranded on a desert island. Each has in her possession some slices of ham (H) and cheese (C). Smith is a very choosy eater and will eat ham and cheese only in the fixed proportions of two slices of cheese to one slice of ham. Jones is more flexible in her dietary tastes and has a utility function given by $U_J = 4H + 3C$. Total endowments are 100 slices of ham and 200 slices of cheese.

a Draw the Edgeworth box diagram that represents the possibilities for exchange in this situation. What is the only exchange ratio that can prevail in any equilibrium?

b Suppose that Smith initially had $40H$ and $80C$. What would the equilibrium position be?

c Suppose that Smith initially had $60H$ and $80C$. What would the equilibrium position be?

d Suppose that Smith (much the stronger of the two) decides not to play by the rules of the game. Then what could the final equilibrium position be?

PART SIX
MARKET POWER

People of the same trade seldom meet together, even for merriment and diversion, but the conversation ends in a conspiracy against the public, or in some contrivance to raise prices.

ADAM SMITH, *THE WEALTH OF NATIONS*, 1776

In this part we explore the consequences of relaxing the price-taking assumption that we used throughout our study of perfect competition. That is, we look at situations where firms have the power to influence the prices they receive for what they produce.

The study of market power begins in Chapter 13, where we look at monopoly markets. Because these markets have only a single supplier, they are much easier to analyze than markets with several firms. The key point for a monopoly firm is that it can choose to set its price at any level it wishes, but in doing so it must take into account that setting higher prices will cause it to sell less. That is, the firm must be concerned with the fact that the marginal revenue from any sale will fall short of the market price at which a good sells (see Chapter 9). Because the monopoly opts for an output level for which price exceeds marginal cost, this output level will be inefficiently low.

Chapter 14 examines the question of market power in situations where there are two or more suppliers. Such markets are more difficult to study than either perfectly competitive markets or monopoly markets. They are unlike competitive markets because price-taking behavior by firms is unlikely – each firm will recognize that its actions do affect the price it ultimately receives. But the situation is also unlike a monopoly because any one firm cannot determine its profit-maximizing decisions in isolation – it must take into account whatever actions its rival(s) will undertake. In Chapter 14 we show how the concepts of strategic equilibrium developed in Chapter 6 can be used to study a number of increasingly complex types of market interaction.

13

Monopoly

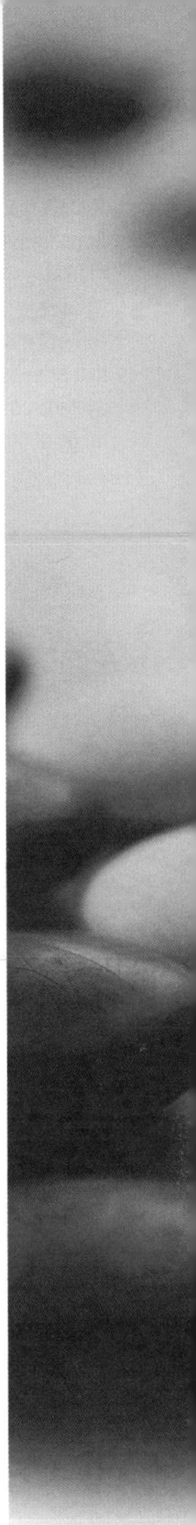

A market is described as a monopoly if it has only one supplier. This single firm faces the entire market demand curve. Using its knowledge of this demand curve, the monopoly makes a decision on how much to produce. Unlike the single competitive firm's output decision (which has no effect on market price), the monopoly output decision will completely determine the good's price.

Causes of Monopoly

The reason monopoly markets exist is that other firms find it unprofitable or impossible to enter the market. **Barriers to entry** are the source of all monopoly power. If other firms could enter the market, there would, by definition, no longer be a monopoly. There are two general types of barriers to entry: technical barriers and legal barriers.

Technical Barriers to Entry

A primary technical barrier to entry is that the production of the good in question exhibits decreasing average cost over a wide range of output levels. That is, relatively large-scale firms are more efficient than small ones. In this situation, one firm finds it profitable to drive others out of the industry by price cutting. Similarly, once a monopoly has been established, entry by other firms is difficult because any new firm must produce at low levels of output and therefore at high average costs. Because this barrier to entry arises naturally as a result of the technology of production, the monopoly created is sometimes called a **natural monopoly**.

The range of declining average costs for a natural monopoly need only be "large" relative to the market in question. Declining costs on some absolute scale are not necessary. For example, the manufacture of concrete does not exhibit declining average costs over a broad range of output when compared to a large national market. In any particular small town, however, declining average costs may permit a concrete monopoly to be established. The high costs of transporting concrete tend to create local monopolies for this good.

Barriers to entry Factors that prevent new firms from entering a market.

Natural monopoly A firm that exhibits diminishing average cost over a broad range of output levels.

Another technical basis of monopoly is special knowledge of a low-cost method of production. In this case, the problem for the monopoly firm fearing entry by other firms is to keep this technique uniquely to itself. When matters of technology are involved, this may be extremely difficult, unless the technology can be protected by a patent (discussed subsequently). Ownership of unique resources (such as mineral deposits or land locations) or the possession of unique managerial talents may also be a lasting basis for maintaining a monopoly.

Legal Barriers to Entry

Many pure monopolies are created as a matter of law rather than as a result of economic conditions. One important example of a government-granted monopoly position is the legal protection provided by a patent. Intel processing chips and most prescription drugs are just two notable examples of goods that would-be competitors may be prevented from copying by patent law. Because the basic technology for these products was assigned by the government to only one firm, a monopoly position was established. The rationale of the patent system, which in the United Kingdom is operated by the UK Intellectual Property Office, and in the United States was even originally established in the Constitution, is that it makes innovation more profitable and therefore encourages technical advancement. Whether or not the benefits of such innovative behavior exceed the cost of creating monopolies is an open question.

A second example of a legally created monopoly is the awarding of an exclusive franchise or license to serve a market. These are awarded in cases of public utility (gas and electric) services, communication services, the post office, some airline routes, some television and radio station markets, and a variety of other businesses. The (often dubious) argument usually put forward in favor of creating these monopolies is that having only one firm in the industry is more desirable than open competition.

In some instances, it is argued that restrictions on entry into certain industries are needed to ensure adequate quality standards (licensing of doctors, for example) or to prevent environmental harm (franchising businesses in the UK national parks). In many cases, there are sound reasons for such entry restrictions but, in some cases, as Application 13.1: *Should You Need a License to Shampoo a Dog*? shows, the reasons are obscure. The restrictions act mainly to limit the competition faced by existing firms and seem to make little economic sense.

Profit Maximization

As in any firm, a profit-maximizing monopoly will choose to produce that output level for which marginal revenue is equal to marginal cost. Because the monopoly, in contrast to a perfectly competitive firm, faces a downward-sloping demand curve for its product, marginal revenue is less than market price. To sell an additional unit, the monopoly must lower its price on all units to be sold in order to generate the extra demand necessary to find a taker for this marginal unit. In equating marginal revenue to marginal cost, the monopoly produces an output level for which price exceeds marginal cost. This feature of monopoly pricing is the primary reason for the negative effect of monopoly on resource allocation.

APPLICATION 13.1 *Should You Need a License to Shampoo a Dog?*

Governments license many occupations and impose stiff legal penalties on people who run a business without a license. For some of these occupations, licensing is clearly warranted – no one wants to be treated by a quack doctor, for example. However, in other cases, licensing restrictions may go too far. In the US for example, many states license such occupations as embalmers, dog-grooming specialists, appliance repairers, or golf-course designers. Here we look in more detail at three specific cases of how such licensing creates monopoly.

Dry Cleaning

One rationale for licensing is that existing firms find it in their interest to promote entry restrictions to reserve the market for themselves. A good illustration is provided by dry cleaners in California.[1] In order to enter the business, a would-be cleaner must pass examinations in a variety of specialties (fur cleaning, hat renovating, spot removal, and so forth). To do so, one must usually attend a dry-cleaning school. Those who try to evade the process and do laundry on the side face stiff fines and even jail sentences for "practicing dry cleaning without a license". Whether Californians have cleaner clothes than the rest of the United States as a result of all of this is unclear, though several studies have found that profits in the industry are higher in California than in other states.

German Chimney Sweeps

Germany's chimney sweeps provide an example of the perfect monopoly. In 1937 the chimney-sweep law was revised by Heinrich Himmler, then the acting interior minister. His rules tied chimney sweeps to their districts and decreed that they should be German, to enable him to use sweeps as local spies. Germany is divided into 7888 districts, each one assigned one sweep, who may employ one or more helpers. Although this is a private enterprise, the maintenance and inspection service provided is compulsory and prices are set by the local authority: sweeps cannot stray outside their district, nor can householders change their sweep. Here, chimney-sweeping and related gas and heating maintenance in Germany are treated as a matter of public safety. Annual or semi-annual visits are prescribed, keeping the sweeps busy all year round. The EU Commission is naturally unhappy with this lack of competition, but no amount of pressure seems to result in much change. Indeed, it appears that the number of deaths from carbon-monoxide poisoning in Germany is around one-tenth that in France or Belgium, and a poll by the Forsa agency suggests that 95 per cent of Germans are happy with their sweeps and the service they provide. The real question is whether a more competitive market would still ensure safety but at a lower cost, just as it does in the car servicing market.

London Taxis

Many cities, such as London, by various means, limit the number of taxis allowed on their streets. Ostensibly, the purpose of such strict licensing is to control unscrupulous cab drivers because they might overcharge passengers who are new to town. The famous "black cab" drivers take about two to three years to pass the onerous "*knowledge*" test of 320 routes. Many have argued that the cheap availability of satellite navigation systems have made this test virtually redundant. Indeed, its continued existence looks increasingly like a classic barrier to entry, especially as the strong taxi driver lobby, the London Taxi Drivers' Association (LTDA), fight tooth and nail to maintain it. Moreover, the lobby strongly support the regulations that only very specific cars can be used as taxis. A new taxi, for instance, costs about twice as much as a standard saloon, partly because it still has to be able to perform a U-turn in less than 7.62 m (25 ft), just as Victorian horse-drawn carriages could. This naturally results in deterring entry to any newcomers. This picture is not wholly inconsistent with evidence that tends to show that taxi fares are higher in strictly regulated markets. One study of Toronto, for example, found that prices are about 225 per cent higher than would prevail in an unregulated market.[2]

To Think About

1 Can you think of good reasons for regulating entry into the businesses described in this

(Continued)

application? Is licensing needed to ensure quality or to achieve other goals? How would you determine whether these goals are met?

2 Why do you think some countries or states have chosen to license certain occupations, whereas other places have not? Who are the gainers and losers under the current arrangement as compared to those in a competitive market? Why do you think that consumers do not protest more?

[1]See D. Kirp and E. Soffer, "Taking Californians to the Cleaners", *Regulation* (September/October 1985): 24–26. The puns in the article are highly recommended.

[2]D. W. Taylor, "The Economic Effects of the Direct Regulation of Taxicabs in Metropolitan Toronto", *Logistics and Transportation Review* (June 1989): 169–182.

A Graphic Treatment

The profit-maximizing output level for a monopoly is given by Q^* in Figure 13-1.[1] For that output, marginal revenue is equal to marginal costs, and profits are as large as possible given these demand and cost characteristics. If a firm produced slightly less than Q^*, profits would fall because the revenue lost from this cutback (*MR*) would exceed the decline in production costs (*MC*). A decision to produce

FIGURE 13-1 Profit Maximization and Price Determination in a Monopoly Market *A profit-maximizing monopolist produces that quantity for which marginal revenue is equal to marginal cost. In the diagram, this quantity is given by Q*, which yields a price of P* in the market. Monopoly profits can be read as the rectangle P*EAC.*

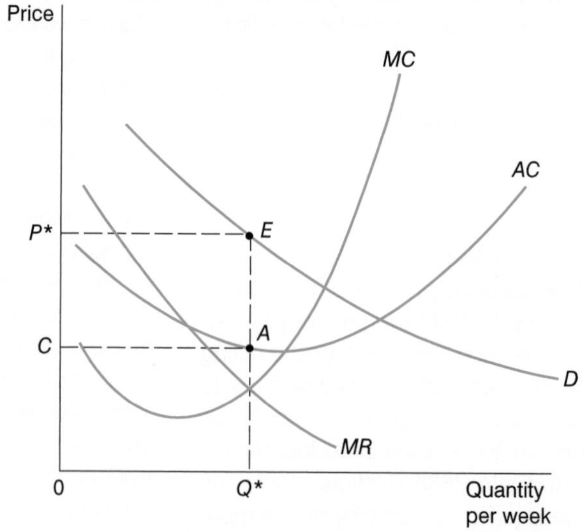

[1]In Figure 13-1 and in the other diagrammatic analyses in this chapter, no distinction is made between the behavior of a monopoly in the short run and in the long run. The analysis is the same in both cases, except that different sets of cost curves would be used depending on the possibilities for adjustment that would be feasible for the firm. In the short run, the monopoly follows the same shutdown rule as does a competitive firm. Notice also that we use "Q" for the monopoly output level because, by definition, this firm serves the entire market.

more than Q^* would also lower profits since the additional costs from increased production would exceed the extra revenues from selling the extra output. Consequently, profits are at a maximum at Q^*, and a profit-maximizing monopoly will choose this output level.

Given the monopoly's decision to produce Q^*, the demand curve D indicates that a market price of P^* will prevail. This is the price that demanders as a group are willing to pay for the output of the monopoly. In the market, an equilibrium price–quantity combination of P^*, Q^* will be observed.[2] This equilibrium will persist until something happens (such as a shift in demand or a change in costs) to cause the monopoly to alter its output decision.

Monopoly Supply Curve

In the theory of perfectly competitive markets we presented earlier, it was possible to speak of an industry supply curve. We constructed this curve by allowing the market demand curve to shift and observing the supply curve that was traced out by the series of equilibrium price–quantity combinations. This type of construction is not possible for monopoly markets. With a fixed market demand curve, the supply "curve" for a monopoly is only one point – namely, the point corresponding to the quantity at which $MR = MC$ (point E in Figure 13.1). If the demand curve were to shift, the marginal revenue curve would shift along with it and a new profit-maximizing output would be chosen. However, to connect the resulting series of equilibrium points would have little meaning and would not represent a supply curve. The set of points might have a very strange shape, depending on how the market demand curve's elasticity (and its associated MR curve) changed as the curve was shifted outward. In this sense, a monopoly market has no well-defined supply curve. Instead, each demand curve represents a unique profit-maximizing opportunity for the monopoly firm and each has to be studied independently.

Monopoly rents The profits that a monopolist earns in the long run.

Monopoly Profits

Economic profits earned by the monopolist can be read directly from Figure 13-1. These are shown by the rectangle P^*EAC and again represent the profit per unit (price minus average cost) times the number of units sold. These profits will be positive when, as in the figure, market price exceeds average total cost. Since no entry is possible into a monopoly market, these profits can exist even in the long run. For this reason, some authors call the profits that a monopolist earns in the long run **monopoly rents**. These profits can be regarded as a return to the factor that forms the basis of the monopoly (such as a patent, a favorable location, or the only alcohol license in town). Some other owner might be willing to pay that amount in rent for the right to operate the monopoly and obtain its profits. The huge prices paid for television stations or Premier League football television rights reflect the capitalized values of such rents.

MICROQUIZ 13.1

Monopoly behavior can also be modeled as a problem of choosing the profit-maximizing price.

1. Why can a monopoly choose either price or quantity for its output but not both?
2. How should the marginal revenue–marginal cost rule be stated when the monopolist is treated as a price setter?

[2]This combination must be on an elastic section of the demand curve. This is so because MC is positive, so for a profit maximum MR must also be positive. But, if marginal revenue is positive, demand must be elastic, as we showed in Chapter 9. One conclusion to be drawn is that markets that are found to operate along an inelastic portion of the demand curve probably are not characterized by strong monopoly power.

What's Wrong with Monopoly?

Firms that have a monopoly position in a market pose several problems for any economy. Here we look at two specific complaints: the profitability of monopoly and the effect of monopoly on resource allocation.

Monopoly Profits

Because perfectly competitive firms earn no economic profits in the long run, a firm with a monopoly position in a market can earn higher profits than if the market is competitive. This does not imply, however, that monopolies necessarily earn huge profits. Two equally strong monopolies may differ greatly in their profitability. It is the ability of monopolies to raise price above *marginal* cost that reflects their monopoly power. Since profitability reflects the difference between price and *average* cost, profits are not necessarily a definite consequence of monopoly power.

Figure 13-2 exhibits the cost and demand conditions for two firms with essentially the same degree of monopoly power (that is, the divergence between price and marginal cost is the same in both graphs). The monopoly in Figure 13-2(a) earns a high level of profits, whereas the one in Figure 13-2(b) actually earns zero in profits since price equals average cost. Hence, excess profitability is not inevitable, even for a strong monopoly. Indeed, if monopoly rents accrue mainly to the inputs a monopoly uses (for example, rent on a favourably located piece of land), the monopoly itself may appear to make no profits.

MICROQUIZ 13.2

Suppose there is an increase in the demand for Jedi lightsabers (a monopoly good).

1. Why might you expect both price and quantity to increase?
2. Could price and quantity move in opposite directions in some cases?

FIGURE 13-2 Monopoly Profits Depend on the Relationship between the Demand and Average Cost Curves *Both of the monopolies in this figure are equally "strong" in that they have similar divergences between market price and marginal cost. Because of the location of the demand and average cost curves, however, it turns out that the monopoly in graph (a) earns high profits, whereas that in graph (b) earns no profits. The size of profits is not a measure of the strength of a monopoly.*

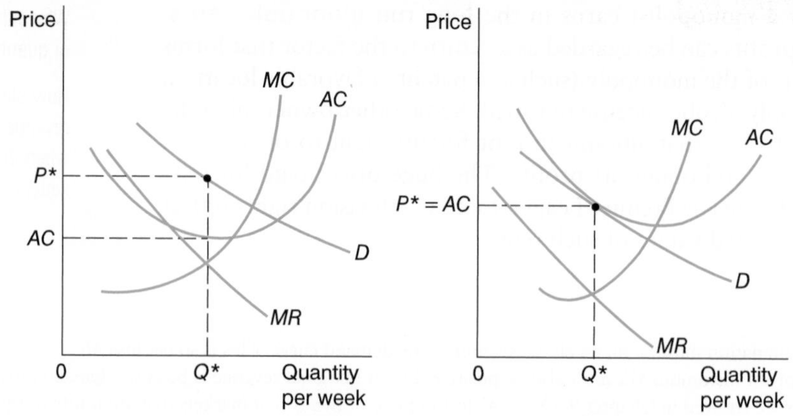

(a) Monopoly with large profits

(b) Zero-profit monopoly

More than the size of monopoly profits, people are likely to object to the distribution of these profits. If the profits go to relatively wealthy owners at the expense of less-well-to-do consumers, there may be valid objections to monopoly profits no matter what their size. Profits from a monopoly may not necessarily always go to the wealthy, however. For example, consider the decision of Navajo blanket makers to form a monopoly to sell their products to tourists at the Grand Canyon. In this situation, the monopoly profits make the income distribution more equal by transferring income from more wealthy tourists to low-income Navajos. Application 13.2: *Who Makes Money at Casinos?* describes how many groups have tried to make money from obtaining monopoly rights for gambling.

Monopoly and Resource Allocation

Economists (who tend to worry about such matters) raise a second objection to monopolies: Their existence distorts the allocation of resources. Monopolies intentionally restrict their production in order to maximize profits. The discrepancy between price and marginal cost shows that, at the monopoly's profit-maximizing output level, consumers are willing to pay more for an extra unit of output than it costs to produce that output. From a social point of view, output is too low and some mutually beneficial transactions are being missed.

Figure 13-3 illustrates this observation by comparing the output produced in a market characterized by perfect competition with the output produced in the same market

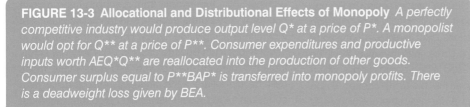

FIGURE 13-3 Allocational and Distributional Effects of Monopoly *A perfectly competitive industry would produce output level Q* at a price of P*. A monopolist would opt for Q** at a price of P**. Consumer expenditures and productive inputs worth AEQ*Q** are reallocated into the production of other goods. Consumer surplus equal to P**BAP* is transferred into monopoly profits. There is a deadweight loss given by BEA.*

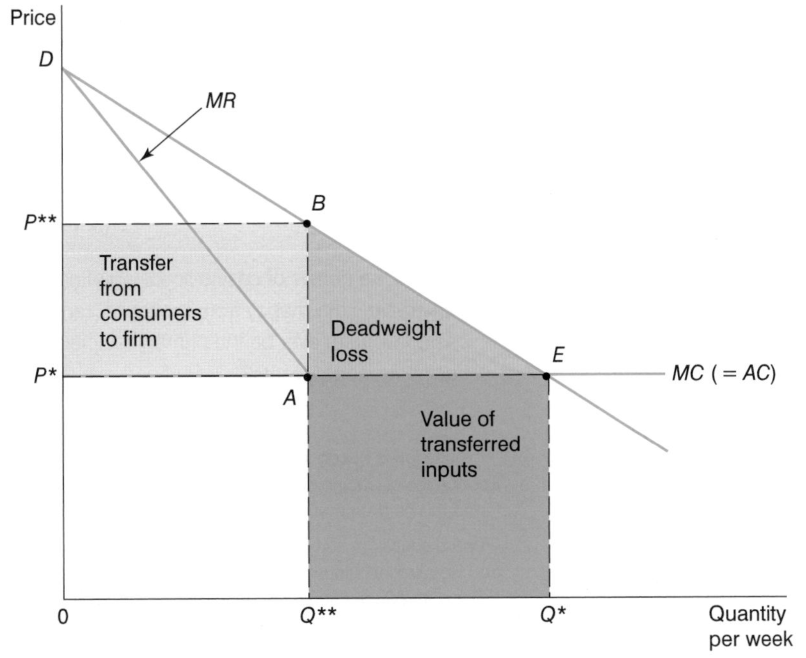

APPLICATION 13.2 *Who Makes Money at Casinos?*

Casino gambling is a big business in many countries. In the United States, casinos take in more than $50 billion each year in gross revenues. In some markets, casinos operate quite competitively. There are so many casinos in Las Vegas, for example, that it is unlikely that any one of them has much power to set prices monopolistically. However, many other areas have adopted entry restrictions on the numbers and sizes of casinos that are permitted. These restrictions provide the possibility for owners who can build casinos to capture substantial monopoly rents. Two illustrations are provided by riverboat casinos and by so-called Indian gaming.

Riverboat Gambling[1]

A number of states along the Mississippi River (Illinois, Iowa, Louisiana, and Mississippi) permit casino gambling only on riverboats. The number of riverboats is strictly regulated, as are many features of their operations. For example, some states have mandatory "cruising" requirements. Under such requirements, the riverboats must actually leave port and cruise along the river. Patrons must participate in the complete cruise, and once the cruise ends they must leave the boat. This might be contrasted to land-based casinos, where patrons can come and go as they like. The purported reason for this cruise requirement (as for many other seemingly odd regulations) is to limit compulsive gambling, but there is little evidence that the regulations have this effect.

One clear impact of the way that riverboat gambling is regulated is monopoly rents for a number of different parties. States are a prime beneficiary – they usually tax net profits from riverboats at more than 30 per cent – so obviously they have an incentive to adopt regulations that prevent the outbreak of competition. Some regulations themselves also create monopoly rents. For example, compulsory cruising rules benefit a variety of firms and workers engaged in river transportation who would not earn anything from stationary riverboats. Finally, the owners of the riverboats take in monopoly rents. Riverboat licenses are highly sought after and have sometimes been the fodder for major political scandals when bribes were involved in obtaining them.

Indian Gaming

The Indian Gaming Regulatory Act of 1988 clarified the relationship between states and the Native American tribes living within their borders, making it possible for these tribes to offer casino gambling under certain circumstances. Since the passage of the act, more than 120 tribes have adopted some form of legalized gambling. Revenue from this gambling amounts to about 20 per cent of all such spending in the United States. Indian gambling establishments range from slot machines in petrol stations or card tables in trailers to the luxurious Foxwoods Casino in Connecticut that employs more than 20 000 people and takes in nearly $1 billion in gambling revenues per year. Overall, revenues from legalized gambling have become an important source of income for many Indian tribes.

The distributional consequences of Indian gaming are generally beneficial. The tribes offering gambling include some of the poorest people in the United States. A number of studies have documented significant declines in those on welfare, with the introduction of gaming.[2] Still, the income from gambling can be quite unequally distributed, especially in the cases of smaller tribes (interestingly, the largest US tribe, the Navajos in Arizona, does not operate casinos). The very few actual Indian owners of the Foxwoods Casino make many millions of dollars each annually. Assorted lawyers, consultants, and local officials also probably share significantly in the booty.

To Think About

1. Much of the gambling in the United States is illegal. How does the presence of illegal gambling options affect the monopoly power of legalized gambling operations to set prices (that is, to set payouts to winners)? Who benefits from operations to stamp out illegal gambling?
2. How do the details of casino licensing affect which party makes the money from monopoly rents? Could casino workers ever be the primary recipients of casino monopoly rents?

[1]This section is based in part on W. R. Eadington, "The Economics of Casino Gambling", *Journal of Economic Perspectives* (Summer 1999): 173–192.

[2]For a discussion, see G. C. Anders, "Indian Gaming: Financial and Regulatory Issues", *Annals of the American Academy of Political and Social Science* (1998): 98–108.

when it contains only one firm. The figure assumes that the monopoly produces under conditions of constant marginal cost and that the competitive industry also exhibits constant costs with the same minimum long-run average cost as the monopolist[3] – an assumption we question in the next section. In this situation, a perfectly competitive industry would choose output level Q^*, where long-run supply and demand intersect. At this point, price is equal to average and marginal cost. A monopoly would choose output level Q^{**}, for which marginal revenue is equal to marginal cost. The restriction in output (Q^*–Q^{**}) is then some measure of the allocation harm done by monopoly. At Q^{**} people would be willing to pay P^{**} for additional output, which would only cost *MC*. However, the monopolist's market control and desire to maximize profits prevent the additional resources from being drawn into the industry to fill this demand.

As an admittedly inane example of this distortion, suppose a local burger bar has a monopoly in the production of chili hot dogs because its cook is the only one in town capable of concocting them. To maximize profits, the owner of the monopoly restricts chili-dog output to a point at which each dog sells for €2.00 but, at the margin, costs only €1.00 in terms of ingredients and the cook's time. Why is this inefficient? Because the well-being of both the cook and chili-dog consumers could be improved. If the cook agreed to sell chili-dogs at €1.50 to people who came around to the back door, overall welfare would be improved. Consumers would be better off (since they would save €0.50 per dog over what they would be willing to pay), and the cook would be better off (by effectively getting a higher wage). Of course, the owner would prevent these illicit sales because they would undercut the profits being made. But the fact that such unexploited mutually beneficial trading opportunities exist is clear evidence that resources (here, the cook's time) are not being used efficiently.

Monopolistic Distortions and Transfers of Welfare

Monopolies cause an artificial restriction in output together with an increase in price and thereby distort the allocation of resources. We can explore this distortion a bit further by looking at the changes involved. Figure 13-3 shows that, when the market is competitively organized, Q^* is produced at a price of P^*. As we showed before, the total value to consumers of this output level is given by the area under the demand curve (that is, by area DEQ^*0), for which they pay P^*EQ^*0. Total consumer surplus is given by the triangle DEP^*.

Allocational Effects

If this market is monopolized, only Q^{**} is produced and the price of this output is P^{**}. The restriction in output and consequent price rise has had several effects. The total value of this good that consumers receive has been reduced in Figure 13-3 by the area BEQ^*Q^{**}. This reduction is not a complete loss, however, because consumers previously had to pay AEQ^*Q^{**} for these goods and they may now spend this money elsewhere. Because the monopoly produces less, it needs to hire fewer inputs. These released inputs will be used to produce those other goods that consumers buy. The loss of consumer surplus given by the area *BEA* is, however, an unambiguous reduction in welfare as a result of the monopoly. Some authors refer to triangle *BEA* as the "deadweight loss" because it represents losses of

MICROQUIZ 13.3

What is lost from the "deadweight loss" that results from the monopolization of a market? Who loses this? Do the monopoly's profits make up for the deadweight loss?

[3]This assumption might be justified as reflecting the case of a competitive constant cost industry that has been completely captured by a monopolist.

mutually beneficial transactions between demanders and the suppliers of inputs (where opportunity costs are measured by *MC*). This loss is similar to the excess burden from a tax, which we illustrated in Chapter 11. It is the best single measure of the allocational harm caused by monopoly.

Distributional Effects

In addition to the allocational effect of monopolization of a market, there is a distributional effect, which can also be seen in Figure 13-3. At the monopoly's output level of Q^{**}, there exist monopoly profits given by the area $P^{**}BAP^{*}$. In the case of perfect competition, this area was a part of the consumer surplus triangle. If the market is a monopoly, that portion of consumer surplus is transferred into monopoly profits. The area $P^{**}BAP^{*}$ in Figure 13-3 does not necessarily represent a loss of social welfare. It does measure the redistributional effects of a monopoly, and these may or may not be undesirable.

Monopolists' Costs

Figure 13-3 assumes that monopolists and competitive firms have the same costs of production. Further thought suggests this may not in fact be the case. Monopoly profits, after all, provide a tantalizing target for firms, and they may spend real resources to achieve those profits. They may, for example, adopt extensive advertising campaigns or invest in ways to erect barriers to entry against other firms and hence obtain monopoly profits. Similarly, firms may seek special favors from the government in the form of tariff protection, restrictions on entry through licensing, or favorable treatment from a regulatory agency. Costs associated with these activities (such as lobbyists' salaries, legal fees, or advertising expenses) may make monopolists' costs exceed those in a competitive industry.

The possibility that costs may be different (and presumably higher) for a monopolist than for a firm in a competitive industry creates some complications for measuring monopolistic distortions to the allocation of resources. In this case, some potential monopoly profits are dissipated into monopoly-creating costs, and it is possible that some of those costs (advertising, for example) may even shift the demand curve facing the producer. Such effects seriously complicate Figure 13-3, and we do not analyze them in detail here.[4] Researchers who have tried to obtain empirical estimates of the monetary value of welfare losses from monopoly have found that these are quite sensitive to the assumptions made about monopolists' costs. Trivial figures of less than 0.5 per cent of GDP have been estimated under the assumption that monopolists are not cost increasing. Much more significant estimates (perhaps 5 per cent of GDP) have been derived under rather extreme assumptions about monopolists' higher costs. Despite the variation in these estimates, concern about potential losses from monopolization plays a large role in the actual regulation of business through antitrust laws. Application 13.3: *Making Money in Dallas* shows that a firm's ability to control prices can sometimes be temporary.

A Numerical Illustration of Deadweight Loss

As a numerical illustration of the types of calculations made by economists in studying the effects of monopoly, consider again the example of CD sales introduced in Chapter 9 and Chapter 11. Table 13-1 repeats some of the information about this market. Assume

[4]For a relatively simple treatment, see R. A. Posner, "The Social Costs of Monopoly and Regulation", *Journal of Political Economy* (August 1975): 807–827.

APPLICATION 13.3 *Making Money in Dallas*

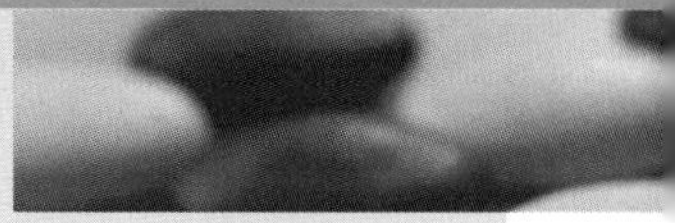

American Airlines is the largest carrier at the Dallas–Fort Worth Airport (DFW). Pricing of its flights from this hub has been subject to recurring controversies for many years as the airline has tried many schemes to get higher fares.

The Infamous Phone Call

In the opener to this part, we repeated Adam Smith's famous skepticism about innocent conversations between "people of the same trade". That skepticism appears to be amply justified by an infamous 1982 phone call between American Airlines CEO Robert Crandall and Braniff Airways CEO Howard Putnam about the pricing of flights to and from Dallas. Unfortunately for Mr Crandall, his conversation was taped by Mr Putnam. Portions of it later appeared in the *Wall Street Journal*.[1] One particularly colorful part of the conversation went:

Crandall: "I think it's dumb . . . to sit here and pound the *** out of each other . . . neither one of us making a *** dime."

Putnam: "Do you have a suggestion for me?"

Crandall: "Yes . . . Raise your *** fares 20 per cent. I'll raise mine the next morning!"

Such a "suggestion" represents a clear violation of Section I of the US Sherman Antitrust Act, which forbids all "conspiracies in restraint of trade". A subsequent investigation by the Justice Department, however, could find no evidence that American and Braniff ever carried out Crandall's plan.

Predatory Pricing in Dallas?

Sixteen years later, American Airlines' pricing policies in Dallas made the news again. This time the Justice Department charged American Airlines with illegally forcing smaller competitors out of Dallas by slashing ticket prices. According to the suit (filed in May 1999), after the small carriers left the market, American then boosted fares and reduced service. If true, this behavior might be illegal under Section II of the Sherman Act, which forbids "attempts to monopolize". To bolster its claim of such "predatory pricing" (see Chapter 14), the Justice Department looked at four specific routes, including the Dallas-to-Kansas City route on which American competed with Vanguard Airlines. The investigation showed that American dropped its $113 fare to $83 when Vanguard entered the market, only to raise it to $125 once the firm left the market. The question, of course, was whether such behavior was illegal or was simply what might have been expected in competitive markets. Ultimately the lawsuit was settled quietly

The Southwest Challenge

The major recent challenge to American Airlines at DFW airport has come from low-cost airlines, especially Southwest. Currently Southwest operates out of Love Field in Dallas, and a 1979 law allows it to make flights to and from only seven states. Anyone wishing to take Southwest to Dallas must change planes in one of these states. The general purposes of the law were to generate business for DFW and to protect American's position in Dallas. Because Southwest can operate at lower costs from Love Field, it argues that the law is anticonsumer and should be repealed.[2] By mid-2005 a major battle over the law was brewing in Congress, with heavy lobbying on both sides of the issue. Especially imaginative were some ads and bumper stickers originated by the pro-Southwest forces that all played off the theme "free Love". This is not the first time that Southwest has faced challenges in its strategy of using second-tier airports to challenge incumbent airlines' positions at major terminals. For example, the firm's entry into the Chicago market using Midway Airport was long opposed by major airlines using O'Hare. A similar recent controversy involves Southwest's decision to seek to operate out of Boeing Field in Seattle rather than using Seattle-Tacoma International Airport.

To Think About

1 Do airline executives really need to talk on the phone in order to figure out how to rig prices? How might the firms be able to coordinate pricing by using their computerized reservation

(Continued)

systems? (These systems have been the subject of antitrust scrutiny in recent years also.)

2 Southwest Airlines uses second-tier airports in many other cities, such as Midway in Chicago (instead of O'Hare) and Providence or Manchester near Boston (instead of Logan). Do such actions help to improve competition for airfares in these cities, more so than does a situation where all firms would have to use the same airport?

[1]The quotes appeared in the February 24, 1983 issue.

[2]Details on the campaign to open up Love Field can be found at http://www.setlovefree.com.

now that CDs have a marginal cost of €3. Under a situation of marginal cost pricing, CDs would also sell for €3 each and, as Table 13-1 shows, seven CDs per week would be bought. Consumer surplus can be computed as the amount people were willing to pay for each CD less what they actually pay (€3). For example, someone who was willing to pay €9 for the first CD sold paid only €3. He or she received a consumer surplus of €6. The sixth column of Table 13-1 makes a similar computation for each level of output from one to seven CDs. As the table shows, total consumer surplus is €21 per week when price is equal to marginal cost.

Suppose now that the CD market is monopolized by a single local merchant with a marginal cost of €3. This profit-maximizing firm will supply four CDs per week since at this level of output marginal revenue equals marginal cost. At this level of sales, price will be €6 per CD, profit per CD will be €3, and the firm will have total profits of €12. These profits represent a transfer of what was previously consumer surplus for the first four buyers of CDs. The seventh column of Table 13-1 computes consumer surplus figures for the monopolized situation. With a price of €6, for example, the buyer of the first CD now receives a consumer surplus of only €3 (€9 − €6); the other €3 he or she enjoyed under marginal cost pricing has been transferred into €3 of profits for the monopoly. As Table 13-1 shows, total consumer surplus under

TABLE 13-1 Effects of Monopolization on the Market for CDs

Demand Conditions					Consumer Surplus		
Price	*Quantity (CDs per Week)*	*Total Revenue*	*Marginal Revenue*	*Average and Marginal Cost*	*Under Perfect Competition*	*Under Monopoly*	*Monopoly Profits*
€9	1	€9	€9	€3	€6	€3	€3
8	2	16	7	3	5	2	3
7	3	21	5	3	4	1	3
6	4	24	3	3	3	0	3
5	5	25	1	3	2	—	—
4	6	24	−1	3	1	—	—
3	7	21	−3	3	0	—	—
2	8	16	−5	3	—	—	—
1	9	9	−7	3	—	—	—
0	10	0	−9	3	—	—	—
				Totals	*€21*	*€6*	*€12*

Competitive equilibrium: ($P = MC$). Monopoly equilibrium: ($MR = MC$).

the monopoly amounts to only €6 per week. When combined with the monopolist's profits of €12 per week, it is easy to see that there is now a deadweight loss of €3 per week (€21 − €18). Some part of what was previously consumer surplus has simply vanished with the monopolizing of the market.

Price Discrimination

So far in this chapter we have assumed that a monopoly sells all its output at one price. The firm was assumed to be unwilling or unable to adopt different prices for different buyers of its product. There are two consequences of such a policy. First, as we illustrated in the previous section, the monopoly must forsake some transactions that would in fact be mutually beneficial if they could be conducted at a lower price. The total value of such trades is given by area *BEA* in Figure 13-4 (which repeats Figure 13-3). Second, although the monopoly does succeed in transferring a portion of consumer surplus into monopoly profits, it still leaves some consumer surplus to those individuals who value the output more highly than the price that the monopolist charges (area *DBP*** in Figure 13-4). The existence of both of these areas of untapped opportunities suggests that a monopoly has the possibility of increasing its profits even more by practicing **price discrimination** – that is, by selling its output at different prices to different buyers. In this section, we examine some of these possibilities.

Price discrimination Selling identical units of output at different prices.

FIGURE 13-4 Targets for Price Discrimination *The monopolist's price-output choice (P**, Q**) provides targets for additional profits through successful price discrimination. It may obtain a portion of the consumer surplus given by area DBP** (light shaded) through discriminatory entry fees, whereas it can create additional mutually beneficial transactions (area BEA, dark shaded) through quantity discounts.*

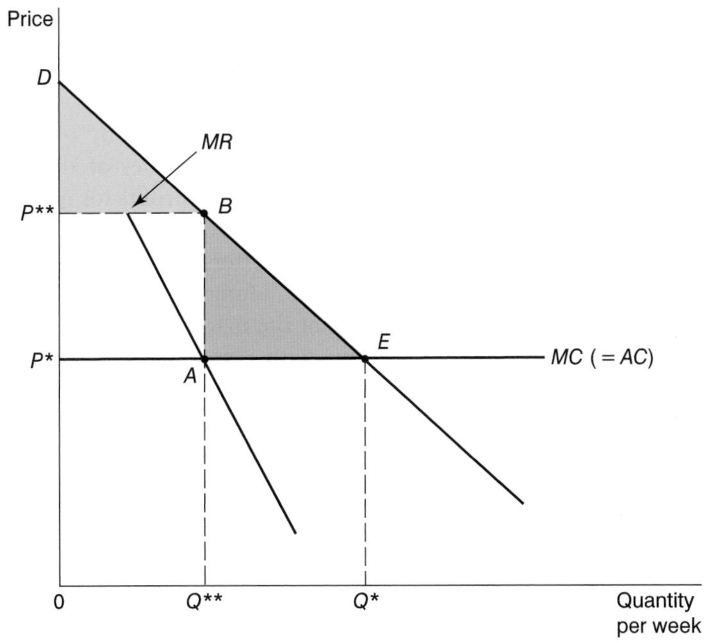

Perfect Price Discrimination

In theory, one way for a monopoly to practice price discrimination is to sell each unit of its output for the maximum amount that buyers are willing to pay for that particular unit. Under this scheme, a monopoly faced with the situation described in Figure 13-4 would sell the first unit of its output at a price slightly below $0D$, the second unit at a slightly lower price, and so forth. When the firm has the ability to sell one unit at a time in this way, there is no reason now to stop at output level Q^{**}. Because it can sell the next unit at a price only slightly below P^{**} (which still exceeds marginal and average cost by a considerable margin), it might as well do so. Indeed, the firm will continue to sell its output one unit at a time until it reaches output level Q^*. For output levels greater than Q^*, the price that buyers are willing to pay does not exceed average and marginal cost; hence, these sales would not be profitable.

Perfect price discrimination Selling each unit of output for the highest price obtainable. Extracts all of the consumer surplus available in a given market.

The result of this **perfect price discrimination** scheme is the firm's receiving total revenues of $0DEQ^*$,[5] incurring total costs of $0P^*EQ^*$, and, therefore, obtaining total monopoly profits given by area P^*DE. In this case, all of the consumer surplus available in the market has been transferred into monopoly profits. Consumers have had all the extra utility they might have received by consuming this good wrung out of them by the monopolist's price discrimination scheme.

Perhaps somewhat paradoxically, this perfect price discrimination scheme results in an equilibrium that is economically efficient. Because trading proceeds to the point at which price is equal to marginal cost, there are no further unexploited trading opportunities available in this marketplace. Of course, this solution requires that the monopoly knows a great deal about the buyers of its output in order to determine how much each is willing to pay. It also requires that no further trading occur in this good in order to prevent those who buy it at a low price from reselling to those who would have paid the most to the monopoly. The pricing scheme will not work for goods like toasters or concert tickets, which may easily be resold; but, for some services, such as medical office visits or personalized financial or legal planning, providers may have the required monopoly power and may know their buyers well enough to approximate such a scheme.

Quantity Discounts

One way to differentiate among buyers' willingness to pay is by offering quantity discounts. These have the advantage of retaining some sales at the monopolist's preferred price (P^{**} in Figure 13-4) but earning additional profits for quantities greater than Q^{**} sold at a lower price to consumers with lower marginal evaluations of the good. For example, the Pizza Hut restaurant chain offers customers a second pizza for much less than what it charges for the first one. Hungry consumers are tempted to make the additional purchase at a price that, at the margin, still yields profits for the restaurant. Similar quantity discounts occur with respect to supermarket coupons, video rental packages, and frequent-flier programs.

As for other price discrimination schemes, an important problem for the monopolist utilizing quantity discounts is to prevent further transactions between customers who pay a low price and those who pay a high price. In the case of Pizza Hut and

[5]Some authors refer to perfect price discrimination as "first-degree price discrimination". In this (relatively unhelpful) terminology, quantity discounts and two-part tariffs where each buyer faces the same pricing menu are referred to as "second-degree price discrimination" and market-separating strategies are referred to as "third-degree price discrimination".

APPLICATION 13.4 *Mrs Thatcher saw few Natural Monopolies*

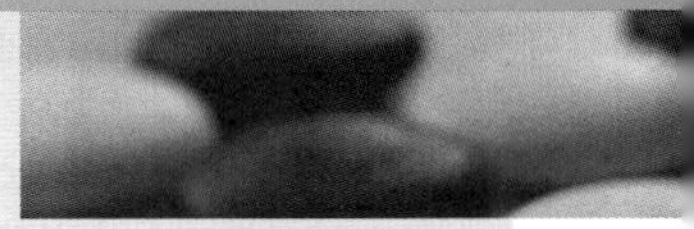

J.S. Mill is credited with first explaining in 1848 that natural monopolies are "those which are created by circumstances, and not by law". Since then, economists have rather taken it as gospel that certain industries display characteristics that mean that they should be seen as a distinguishing natural monopoly (created by nature), as compared to an artificial one (created by law). While the former was seen with favor, classical economists in particular, were strongly against the latter, considering it "unnatural".

Natural monopolies typically occur in two kinds of production: the first is characterized by the need of a very large infrastructure to start the operation, as in transport networks and some public utilities. The minimum efficient scale of production may only support one producer, nationally or locally. Two or more producers would all make a loss because there are very large "economies of scale" relative to the existing demand for the industry's product. Fixed costs are very high, but once the infrastructure is in place the marginal costs of production are smaller, and large economies of scale mean that LRAC are always falling. Competition is really impossible as no firm can enter the market in a modest way, no matter how attractive its service, or how appealing its prices. It is argued that natural gas supply, and electrical power distribution fall into this category because of the heavy initial investments in networks of electrical cables and gas pipes that are involved. Second, some industries such as telecommunications display strong network effects. Each customer gains every time a new consumer is wired up to the company's bank of clients; there are simply more people to ring. Therefore, one firm suffices.

So for decades governments around the world tolerated, and often encouraged natural monopolies in the belief that no consumer would favor a competitive situation where six firms took turns to regularly dig up the roads as they maintained "their" dedicated infrastructure. Any "market failure" could be dealt with, in the UK by nationalizing firms so they would serve the public good, or in the USA regulatory commissions could ensure the public were not ripped-off by over-zealous natural monopolies exploiting the status quo.

The Thatcher View

In the mid 1980s, the Thatcher government started to question this cozy arrangement. First, it was worried that nationalization in the UK had meant that supplier-side vested interest groups, managers, workers, even the government itself as a collector of industry surpluses, dominated most consumer demand interests. In the USA concern was also raised over "regulatory capture" as the industry and the regulator over time became very close friends, to the detriment of consumers. Second, the emergence of new digital technology meant that several firms could now use one network, and that customer usage, metering, billing, and supply could all be electronically calculated at a fraction of the cost of previous systems.

Armed with the technology and the political will, Margaret Thatcher transformed the industrial landscape as telecom, electricity, gas, buses and many other protected industries were opened up to competition. Much of the world followed suit. Industries could be privatized, but all that was needed was to liberalize the industry and allow open access to a range of suppliers, domestic or foreign.

The key is to understand that monopoly power comes from control of the distribution network. It is stopping competitors using "your" pipes, track, wires or distribution systems that give monopolists power. If the national network is operated by one company, as with National Grid plc, it can maintain and run the system, but allow anyone to use the highway to supply any customers; just as anyone can use the road network. This was not always realized in the early days as mistakes were made. British Gas was privatized from a public monopoly to a private monopoly in 1986. As such, its control of the gas pipe and distribution system frustrated competition until it was split into two companies, one producing gas, and one distributing gas through a

(Continued)

system that everyone would eventually get equal access to. By the electricity privatization of 1990 this mistake was identified, as distribution and production were separated from the start.

In the early stages of these industries the regulation of prices and service provision was necessary as the old incumbent industries still exercised great power. However, over time as competition has grown, regulation has adopted a very light-touch, or ceased altogether. After a slow start consumers have, in these old natural monopolistic industries, shown just the same behavior as they do elsewhere. They are concerned about quality, choice, service, safety, reliability, and price. If they are unhappy they do what 19 million UK electricity customers have done since 1990, they simply change companies, just as they might change their supermarket.

To Think About

1 Why was the success of transforming the natural monopolies of the gas, electricity, and telecom industries not possible with the water industry? What additional characteristics and problems does it display?

2 Even Mrs Thatcher did not tackle the natural monopoly of British Railways. Why do you think she avoided changing the industry, but John Major did not? How did John Major hope to transform the industry?

others, such resale is discouraged by custom; restaurant patrons seldom offer to buy a pizza for someone sitting at the next table (though a mutually beneficial transaction could probably be arranged). In the case of frequent-flier coupons, however, resales can be a major problem for airlines, and they take many precautions (not always successfully) to prevent low-cost tickets from competing with their more profitable ticket sales.

Two-Part Tariffs

Another way of increasing profits through price discrimination is to adopt a two-part pricing scheme under which consumers must pay an entry fee for the right to purchase the good being sold. The traditional example is popcorn pricing at cinemas. The entry fee for the film itself is the first part of this pricing scheme. Entry fees should be set in a way so as to extract as much of the available consumer surplus as possible from cinema goers. Presumably, this should involve a variety of quantity discount schemes coupled with special charges for very popular films. Popcorn itself should be priced in a way that maximizes admissions subject to the constraint that it cannot be sold below cost; that is, it should be priced at marginal cost, since this expands the pool of consumers paying entry fees.

Cinema owners price popcorn well above marginal cost because it is impossible to extract all available consumer surplus through entry price schemes. It is more profitable to raise popcorn prices above marginal cost and lose cinema attendance revenue extracted from some popcorn lovers with relatively little interest in films; the hope is to make up for this loss by extracting additional consumer surplus from film lovers who also buy popcorn.

Presenting a full analysis of optimal two-part pricing schemes is beyond our intentions here; but the prevalence of many kinds of pricing policies at restaurants, video stores, and resorts suggests that the topic is a fascinating one. Application 13.5: *Pricing at the Magic Kingdom* illustrates how Disney has tried many schemes to draw consumer surplus from the demanders of its unique offerings.

APPLICATION 13.5 *Pricing at the Magic Kingdom*

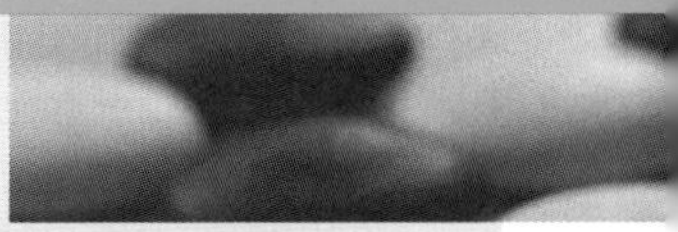

Disneyland and Disney World are unique entertainment attractions. Amusement park aficionados agree there are few substitutes for Disney's products. The company therefore occupies a clear monopolistic position with regard to its pricing, and it has not been shy about exploring a variety of approaches to price discrimination.

The Disneyland Passport

Prior to the 1980s, Disney used a complicated multipart pricing schedule for each of its rides.[1] Under that schedule, Disneyland patrons had to purchase a "passport", containing a ticket for admission to the park, together with coupons for admission to the rides themselves. (The contents of a fondly remembered passport are summarized in Table 1.) Disney enjoyed a great deal of pricing flexibility with the passport arrangement. It could vary the basic price of a passport; it could vary the composition of tickets contained in a passport; it could redefine which rides required which tickets, and it could alter the prices of extra tickets. Notice, for example, that the price of extra tickets for "E" rides was quite high (certainly well above marginal cost). This pricing policy was consistent with the low price elasticity of "E" ride fanatics.

Changes in Pricing Policy

Labor costs were substantially higher under the passport system (since many ticket collectors and salespersons were needed) than under the single-price admission policy followed at other amusement parks. Consequently, in the early 1980s, Disney moved away from individual tickets for rides and toward a single entry fee with zero marginal prices for all rides. This single fee still provided the company with numerous opportunities for price discrimination, such as the ability to charge reduced prices for multiday tickets and to charge lower rates for local residents.

Pricing at Disney World

The ever-growing number of attractions at Disney World in Orlando, Florida, has made it possible for Disney to return to pricing methods similar to those used prior to the 1980s, though on a larger scale. With four major theme parks (Magic Kingdom, EPCOT, Disney-MGM Studios, and Animal Kingdom), the company can develop tickets that offer any combination of these for varying lengths of time.

To Think About

1. The Disney website provides an education in pricing schemes.[2] Choose one of the options that Disney offers (such as Park Hopper, Magic Plus, or No Expiration) and explain what function this plays in the company's overall pricing scheme.

TABLE 1 Structure of a Typical Disneyland Passport

Item	*Example*	*Number of Tickets in Passport*	*Price of Extra Ticket*
Admission	—	1	$4.00
"A" ride	Shooting Gallery	2	0.25
"B" ride	Dumbo, train	3	0.50
"C" ride	Peter Pan's Flight	3	0.75
"D" ride	Autopia	2	1.00
"E" ride	Space Mountain	5	1.50

SOURCE: AUTHOR'S 1978 DISNEYLAND "PASSPORT".

(Continued)

2 Price discrimination schemes can work only if further trading among buyers is prevented. How do the Disney pricing schemes prevent such additional transactions?

[1]Disneyland inspired the first analytical treatment of two-part pricing – see W. Y. Oi, "A Disneyland Dilemma: Two-Part Tariffs for a Mickey Mouse Monopoly", *Quarterly Journal of Economics* (February 1971): 77–96.

[2]http://disneyworld.disney.go.com/wdw/index.

Market Separation

A final way in which a monopoly firm may be able to practice price discrimination for a single output is to separate its potential customers into two or more categories and to charge different amounts in these markets. If buyers cannot shift their purchasing from one market to another in response to price differences, this practice may increase profits over what is obtainable under a single-price policy.

Such a situation is shown graphically in Figure 13-5. The figure is drawn so that the market demand and marginal revenue curves in the two markets share the same vertical axis, which records the price charged for the good in each market. As before, the figure also assumes that marginal cost is constant over all levels of output. The profit-maximizing decision for the monopoly firm is to produce Q^*_1 in the first market and Q^*_2 in the second market; these output levels obey the $MR = MC$ rule for each market. The prices in the two markets are then P_1 and P_2, respectively. It is clear from the figure that the market with the less-elastic demand curve has the higher price.[6]

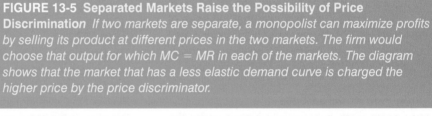

FIGURE 13-5 Separated Markets Raise the Possibility of Price Discrimination *If two markets are separate, a monopolist can maximize profits by selling its product at different prices in the two markets. The firm would choose that output for which MC = MR in each of the markets. The diagram shows that the market that has a less elastic demand curve is charged the higher price by the price discriminator.*

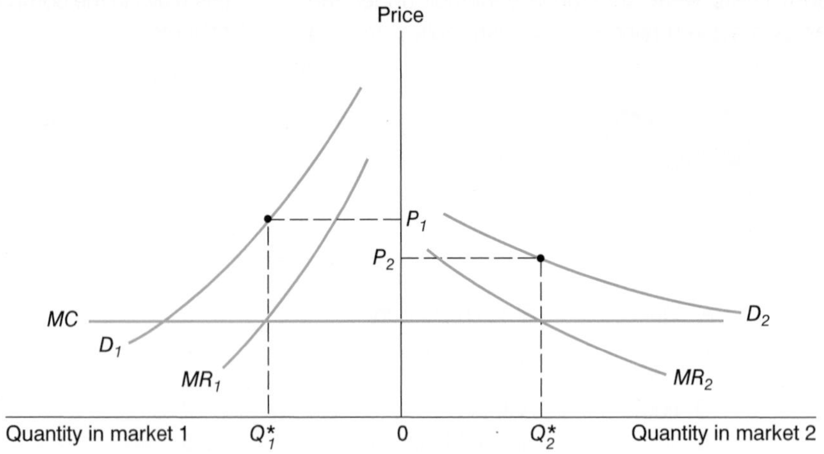

[6]*Proof*: Since $MR = P(1 + 1/e)$, $MR_1 = MR_2$ implies that $P_1(1 + 1/e_1) = P_2(1 + 1/e_2)$. If $e_1 > e_2$ (i.e., if the demand in market 1 is less elastic), then P_1 must exceed P_2 for this equality to hold.

The price-discriminating monopolist charges a higher price in that market in which quantity purchased is less responsive to price changes.

Whether a monopoly is successful in this type of price-discrimination depends critically on its ability to keep the markets separated. In some cases, that separation may be geographic. For example, book publishers tend to charge higher prices in the United States than abroad because foreign markets are more competitive and subject to illegal copying. In this case, the oceans enforce market separation; few people travel abroad simply to buy books. Such a discriminatory policy would not work if transportation costs were low, however. As chain stores that charge different prices in different parts of a town have discovered, people flock to where the bargains are.

Price-discrimination by time of sale may also be possible. For example, tickets to late-night or afternoon showings of films are usually cheaper than for evening shows. Discriminating against those who wish to attend peak-time shows succeeds because the good being purchased cannot be resold later. A firm that tried to sell toasters at two different prices during the day might discover itself to be in competition with savvy customers who bought when the price was low and undercut the firm by selling to other customers during high-price periods. If customers themselves can alter when they shop, a discriminatory policy may not work. A firm that offers lower post-Christmas prices may find its pre-Christmas business facing stiff competition from those sales. As always, the arrival of competition (even from a monopoly's other activities) makes it impossible to pursue pure monopoly pricing practices.

Pricing for Multiproduct Monopolies

If a firm has pricing power in markets for several related products, a number of additional price discrimination strategies become possible. All of these involve coordinating the prices of the goods in ways that convert more of available consumer surplus into profits than would be possible if the goods were priced independently. In some cases, firms can extend monopoly power directly by requiring that users of one product also buy a related, complementary product. For example, some producers of coffee machines require that replacement filters be bought through them and some makers of sophisticated lighting fixtures are the only sources of bulbs for them. Of course, a would-be buyer of such a product usually knows that the firm has a monopoly in replacement parts, so the firm must be careful not to scare off customers with exorbitant prices for those parts. It must also beware of potential entrants who may undersell it on the parts.

Other multiproduct schemes involve the creative pricing of bundles of goods. Car producers create various options packages, laptop computer makers configure their machines with specific components, and Chinese restaurants offer combination lunches. The key to the profitability of such bundling arrangements is to take advantage of differences among consumers in their relative preference for various items in the bundle. For example, some buyers of Chinese lunches may have a strong preference for starters and never eat a dessert, whereas others may skip the starters but never skip the dessert. But a properly priced "complete lunch" package may tempt starter fanciers to buy a dessert and vice versa. The restaurant can then obtain higher revenues (and profits) than if it only sold starters and desserts separately.

MICROQUIZ 13.4

Explain why the following versions of a profit-maximizing approach to market separation are not correct.

1. A firm with a monopoly in two markets and the same costs of serving them should charge a higher price in that market with a higher demand.
2. A firm with a monopoly in two markets with different marginal costs should always charge a higher price in the market with the higher marginal costs.

APPLICATION 13.6 *Bundling of Cable and Satellite Television Offerings*

The huge expansion in television offerings made possible by improvements in cable and satellite technology has created the possibility for many options for bundling programs to appeal to different categories of consumers.

Theory of Program Bundling

Figure 1 illustrates the theory of program bundling in a very simple case. The figure shows four consumers' willingness to pay for either sports or movie programming. Consumers *A* and *D* are true devotees, willing to pay $20 per month for sports (*A*) or movies (*D*) and nothing for the other option. Consumers *B* and *C* are more diverse in their interests, though their preferences are still rather different from each other. If the firm opts to sell each of the two packages separately, it should charge $15 for each. This will yield $60 to the firm. A bundling scheme, however, that charges $20 for each package if bought individually, but $23 if both are bought,[1] would yield $86. Bundling can offer a substantial increase in revenue to this provider.

Bundling by the DIRECTV Group, Inc.

These features of bundling are illustrated by the US firm, DIRECTV's price schedule for mid-2005 (see Table 1). Subscribers can add up to five options (which include the Sports Pack, HBO, and three other entertainment packages) to the basic package. The incremental cost to adding the first option ($12) is significantly higher than the per-option cost of adding subsequent options. This provision of the schedule allows DIRECTV to capture revenue from viewers who have very definitive viewing preferences (i.e., they like only sports). After purchasing the first option, incremental costs decline, thereby encouraging subscribers to add more options. But there are no added savings from purchasing "Total Choice Premium" (which includes all five options), perhaps because DIRECTV believes that some subscribers will simply opt for "the works" without any careful weighing of marginal benefits and costs.[2]

To Think About

1 Our hypothetical data and the actual data from DIRECTV suggest that bundling is profit maximiz-

FIGURE 1 *Four consumers have different preferences for movie and sports programming, making bundling profitable.*

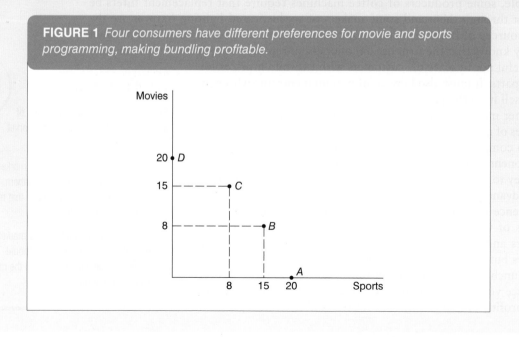

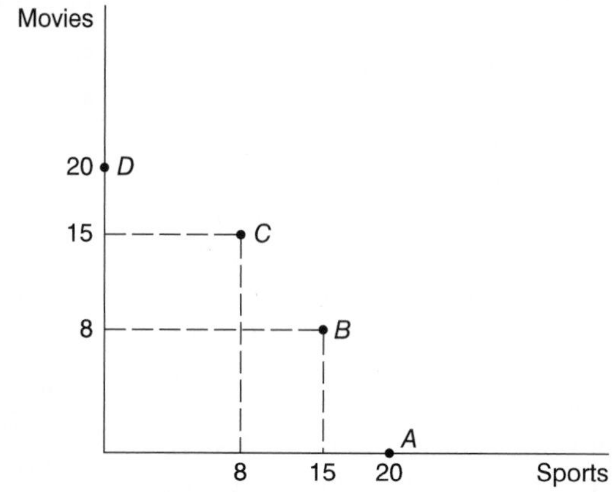

ing only when consumers have divergent preferences for the items being bundled. Why do you think that is a general result of bundling theory?

2 Why isn't bundling more extensive in retailing? For example, could supermarkets gain by offering shoppers prefilled shopping bags at modestly reduced prices?

[1]With this scheme, *A* and *D* would opt for single packages, and *B* and *C* would buy the combination.

[2]DIRECTV also offers options that can be added to its premium package, including all National Football League or English Premier League games, foreign language programming, and the Hot Network.

TABLE 1 Sample DIRECTV Program Bundles

Package	*Cost ($/mo.)*	*Incremental cost per option*
Total Choice Plus	45.99	—
TCP + 1 option	57.99	12.00
TCP + 3 options	78.99	10.50
TCP + 5 options	93.99	7.50
Total Choice Premium	93.99	—

SOURCE: HTTP://WWW.DIRECTV.COM

Application 13.6: *Bundling of Cable and Satellite Television Offerings* illustrates how such bundling provisions can be quite intricate in some cases.

Durable Goods

One interesting application of the theory of a multiproduct monopoly is the case of a monopoly that produces a durable good – that is, a good that can be used for several periods into the future. In this situation, the monopoly is essentially producing a good that will compete with its own future output. The firm must take some account of how trading in used goods will affect its ability to sell new ones. Consider, for example, Microsoft's decision to produce a new version of the Windows operating system, Vista. The firm knows that its primary competitor will come from computers equipped with older versions of Windows. It also knows that it will eventually want to replace this new version of Windows with an even newer version, so it is in effect designing its own future competition. Studying a firm's decisions in such situations can be quite complicated and this is a major current area for economic research.[7] Here we will look at two basic aspects of the problem: (1) How will the monopoly choose the durability of its goods; and (2) Does durability reduce monopoly power?

Durability On first thought, it would seem that a monopoly producer of a durable good should make a good that wears out as quickly as possible. In that way, it can minimize

[7]For a nice summary, see M. Waldman, "Durable Goods Theory for Real World Markets", *Journal of Economic Perspectives* (Winter 2003): 131–154.

the future competition from its own output. For example, in the 1960s many critics of the car industry claimed that firms practiced "planned obsolescence" to ensure that there would always be a market for their newer cars. Whether this example is representative of all durable goods monopolies, however, is open to question. The key point is that consumers care about the durability of the goods they buy. So a monopoly runs a risk of lost sales when it departs from choosing an optimal level of durability for its output. It turns out to be rather difficult to generalize about whether a monopoly would produce a less durable good than would firms in a competitive market – it all depends on the nature of the good and how consumers feel about durability.[8]

Durability and Monopoly Power It seems clear that durability must in some way reduce monopoly power. A firm that must compete with its own past output must have somewhat less power to set price than one that approaches pricing decisions in each period unhindered by any competition. Ronald Coase was the first economist to recognize this constraint that faces the monopoly producer of a durable good.[9] He argued that competition from used goods can potentially be so severe that the monopoly is forced into a strategy of pricing at marginal cost, thereby losing all of its monopoly power. To see why, suppose a monopoly produces the same durable good in two periods. It knows that units sold in the first period will be traded in the used market in the second period. Assuming there is perfect competition in the used-goods market, these goods will be priced at marginal cost in the second period. Hence, if it is to sell anything, the monopoly must also price its good at marginal cost in the second period. But, if consumers know that price will be set at marginal cost in period two, they would be foolish to pay more than that in period one – they can just wait for the price to come down. Hence the monopoly must choose $P = MC$ in period one as well.

Of course this "proof" is very simplistic and unrealistic. In the real world, firms can adopt all sorts of strategies to deal with the used-good "problem". They can develop newer versions of their goods and schedule their introductions for maximum impact. They may be able to differentiate among different types of buyers and charge more to those who want the newest version than to those who are willing to settle for last year's model. Or they may be able to lure consumers into buying new versions of their good by tying its purchase to the purchase of some other good (buyers of new PCs always get the most recent version of Windows, for example). Still, Coase's basic insight about the problems that used goods pose for monopolists has been very productive in getting economists to think about this issue in more detail.

Natural Monopolies

There are basically two solutions to minimizing the allocational harm caused by monopolies: (1) Make markets more competitive and (2) Regulate price in the monopoly market. In general, economists favor the first of these. Actions that loosen entry barriers (such as eliminating restrictive licensing requirements) can sharply reduce the power of a monopoly to control its prices. Similarly, antitrust laws can be used to reduce the power of monopoly firms to raise entry barriers on their own. Because direct price regulation can be problematic (as we shall see), pro-competitive solutions will generally work better. In the case of a natural

[8]There are cases where competitive firms and monopolies would choose the same level of durability. These were first discussed in P. L. Swan, "Durability of Consumption Goods", *American Economic Review* (December 1970): 884–894.

[9]R. Coase, "Durability and Monopoly", *Journal of Law and Economics* (April 1972): 143–149.

monopoly, however, that will not be the case. When average costs fall over the entire range of output, the cost-minimizing solution is to have only a single firm provide the good. Production by several firms would, by definition, be inefficient because it would involve extra costs. Hence, in a natural monopoly situation, direct price regulation may be the only option. How to achieve this regulation is an important subject in applied economics. The utility, communications, and transportation industries are all subject to price regulation in many countries. Although in many cases such regulation may be unwise because the industry is not really a natural monopoly, in other cases price regulation may be the only way to cause these industries to operate in socially desirable ways. Here we look at a few aspects of such price regulation.

Marginal Cost Pricing and the Natural Monopoly Dilemma

By analogy to the perfectly competitive case, many economists believe that it is important for the prices charged by natural monopolies to accurately reflect marginal costs of production. In this way, the deadweight loss from monopolies is minimized. The principal problem raised by a policy of enforced marginal cost pricing is that it may require natural monopolies to operate at a loss.

Natural monopolies, by definition, exhibit decreasing average costs over a broad range of output levels. The cost curves for such a firm might look like those shown in Figure 13-6. In the absence of regulation, the monopoly would produce output level Q_A and receive a price of P_A for its product. Profits in this situation are given by the rectangle P_AABC. A regulatory agency might set a price

MICROQUIZ 13.5

Does the regulatory pricing dilemma apply to a monopoly with a U-shaped average cost curve? Under what conditions would a regulated policy of marginal cost pricing create losses for the monopoly? Could the policy cause the monopoly to shut down?

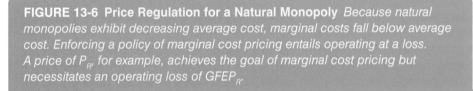

FIGURE 13-6 Price Regulation for a Natural Monopoly *Because natural monopolies exhibit decreasing average cost, marginal costs fall below average cost. Enforcing a policy of marginal cost pricing entails operating at a loss. A price of P_R, for example, achieves the goal of marginal cost pricing but necessitates an operating loss of $GFEP_R$.*

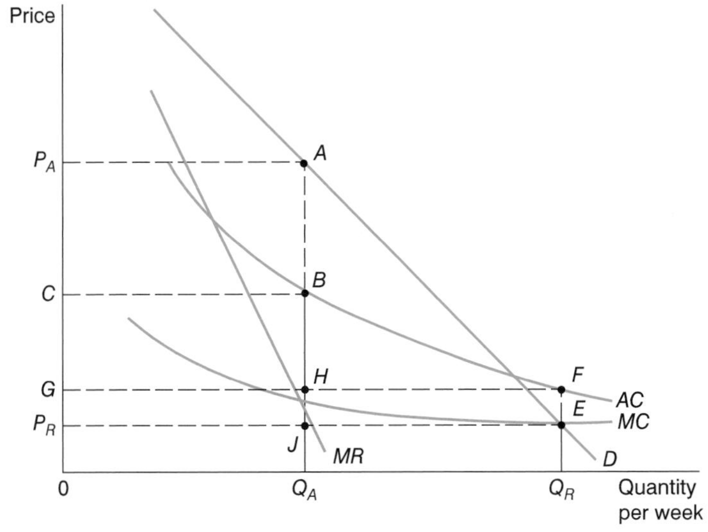

APPLICATION 13.7 *Does Anyone Understand Telephone Pricing?*

In 1974, the United States Department of Justice filed an antitrust suit against the American Telephone and Telegraph (AT&T) Company, charging unlawful monopolization of the markets for telephone equipment and long-distance service. Filing an antitrust suit against a regulated natural monopoly is rarely done, and legal wrangling over the suit lasted into the 1980s. A settlement was reached in late 1982, and, on 1 January 1984, AT&T formally divested itself of its seven local Bell Operating Companies (Ameritech, Atlantic Bell, Bell South, NYNEX, Pacific Telesis, Southwestern Bell, and US West). AT&T retained its long-distance operations. The goal of this huge restructuring was to improve the performance and competitiveness of the US telephone industry, but lingering effects of regulation have made these gains difficult to obtain.

Subsidization of Local Phone Service

Prior to the break-up, AT&T had been forced by regulators to provide local residential phone service at prices below average cost, making up these losses by charging above-average cost for long-distance calls (similar to the situation shown in Figure 13-6). Over the years immediately prior to the break-up, technical improvements (such as fiber-optics cables) sharply reduced the costs of long-distance service. But regulators chose to keep long-distance rates high and local rates low, increasing the subsidy to local subscribers. By the early 1980s, residential service was estimated to cost about $26 per month, but the typical charge was only $11 per month. Subsidies from long-distance and other sources made up the $15-per-month difference. After the break-up, state regulators were faced with the politically unappealing prospect of implementing huge increases in residential telephone rates. Not surprisingly, local regulators instead opted for a continuation of subsidies from AT&T (and, to a lesser extent, from other long-distance companies such as MCI or Sprint) to the local operators.

The Telecommunications Act of 1996

One promising route to lower costs for local phone service might be provided by increasing competition in these monopoly markets. Under the Telecommunications Act of 1996, the US government specified a number of steps that local providers should take to increase such competition.[1] Not surprisingly, the local firms have fought the implementation of many of these provisions in court, thereby making it very costly for any would-be competitor seeking to enter the local marketplace. Local, fixed-line phone service remains very much a monopoly enterprise. Regulators have continued to try to keep local prices low through more direct methods.

Technology Does Not Stand Still

Relentless improvement in telecommunications technology has not permitted phone markets to stand still. After 2000, overcapacity in fiber-optics cable, together with new phone transmission technology, has significantly reduced the prices and profitability of long-distance service. This led to the bankruptcy of some major providers (most notably, the WorldCom Corporation) and continuing troubles for AT&T itself. It also further reduced the ability of regulators to cross-subsidize local service. In addition, the rapid growth of cellular phone networks and the beginning of phone service over the Internet has called into question the continued viability of any sort of fixed-line local phone service. As is the case for any fast-moving market, local phone regulators are having a tough time keeping up with all of this. They have continued to try to practice cross-subsidization, primarily by charging business customers more for local service. But such differential pricing has led many firms to leave local phone networks. Regulators have also added a variety of tax-like charges to phone bills, but these also have proven to be controversial. It seems inevitable that prices of local phone service will increasingly come closer to approximating actual costs.

To Think About

1 Should local phone service be subsidized? Are there socially desirable benefits from ensuring that phone service is available to practically everyone? If so, who should pay the subsidy?

2 The original logic of the AT&T break-up was to treat the long-distance market as potentially competitive and the local exchange as a natural monopoly. Have changes in technology supported that view?

[1]For a discussion of some of these provisions, see R. G. Harris and C. J. Kraft, "Meddling Through: Regulating Local Telephone Competition in the United States", *Journal of Economic Perspectives* (Fall 1997): 93–112.

of P_R for this monopoly. At this price, Q_R is demanded, and the marginal cost of producing this output level is also P_R. Consequently, marginal cost pricing has been achieved. Unfortunately, because of the declining nature of the firm's cost curves, the price P_R (= marginal cost) falls below average costs. With this regulated price, the monopoly must operate at a loss given by area $GFEP_R$. Since no firm can operate indefinitely at a loss, this poses a dilemma for the regulatory agency: Either it must abandon its goal of marginal cost pricing, or the government must subsidize the monopoly forever.

Two-Tier Pricing Systems

One way out of the marginal cost pricing dilemma is a two-part pricing system. Under this system, the monopoly is permitted to charge some users a high price while maintaining a low price for "marginal" users. In this way, the demanders paying the high price in effect subsidize the losses of the low-price customers.

Such a pricing scheme can be illustrated with Figure 13-6. The regulatory agency might decide to permit the firm to charge one class of buyers the monopoly price P_A. At this price, Q_A is demanded. Other users (those who find this good less valuable to them) would be offered a marginal cost price of P_R and would demand $Q_R - Q_A$. With total output of Q_R, average costs are given by $0G$. With this two-tier price schedule, profits earned from those who pay the high price (given by the size of the rectangle P_AAHG) balance the losses incurred on sales to those who pay the low price (these losses are given by the area $HFEJ$). Here, the "marginal user" does indeed pay a price equal to marginal cost and the losses this entails are subsidized by profits from the "intramarginal user".

Although in practice it may not be so simple to establish pricing schemes that maintain marginal cost pricing and cover operating costs, many regulatory agencies do use multipart price schedules that intentionally discriminate against some users to the advantage of others. Application 13.7: *Does Anyone Understand Telephone Pricing?* illustrates how this was done for many years in the telephone industry and caused major problems in moving to a more competitive situation.

Rate of Return Regulation

Another approach to setting the price charged by a natural monopoly that is followed in many regulatory situations is to permit the monopoly to charge a price above average cost that will earn a "fair" rate of return on investment. Much effort is then spent on defining the "fair" rate and on developing how it might be measured. From an economic point of view, some of the most interesting questions about this procedure concern how rate of return regulation affects the firm's decisions. If, for example, the allowed rate of return exceeds what an owner might earn under competitive circumstances, the firm will have an incentive to use more capital input than needed to truly minimize costs. If regulators typically delay in making rate decisions, firms may be given incentives to minimize costs that would not otherwise exist since they cannot immediately recover their costs through higher rates. Although it is possible to develop formal models of all these possibilities, we will not do so here.

SUMMARY

A market in which there is a single seller is called a monopoly. In a monopoly situation, the firm faces the entire market demand curve. Contrary to the case of perfect competition, the monopolist's output decision completely determines market price. The major conclusions about pricing in monopoly markets are

- The profit-maximizing monopoly firm will choose an output level for which marginal revenue is equal to marginal cost. Because the firm faces a downward-sloping demand curve, market price will exceed both marginal revenue and marginal cost.
- The divergence between price and marginal cost is a sign that the monopoly causes resources to be allocated inefficiently. Buyers are willing to pay more for one more unit of output than it costs the firm to produce it, but the monopoly prevents this beneficial transaction from occurring. This is the deadweight loss of welfare from a monopoly.
- Because of barriers to entry, a monopoly may earn positive long-run economic profits. These profits may have undesirable distributional effects.
- A monopolist may be able to increase profits further by practicing price discrimination. Adoption of such schemes depends on the specific nature of demand in the market the monopoly serves.
- If a monopoly produces many different products or if its output is durable, the firm's pricing decisions are more complicated. In some cases, these greater complications will lead to greater monopoly power, whereas in others the potential for monopolistic distortions may be reduced.
- Governments may choose to regulate the prices charged by monopoly firms. In the case of a natural monopoly (for which average costs decline over a broad range of output), this poses a dilemma. The regulatory agency can opt for marginal cost pricing (in which case the monopoly will operate at a loss) or for average cost pricing (in which case an inefficient quantity will be produced).

REVIEW QUESTIONS

1 In everyday discussions, people tend to talk about monopoly firms "setting high prices", but in this chapter we have talked about choosing a profit-maximizing level of output. Are these two approaches saying the same thing? What kind of rule would a monopoly follow if it wished to choose a profit-maximizing price? Why not charge the highest price possible?

2 Why are barriers to entry crucial to the success of a monopoly firm? Explain why all monopoly profits will show up as returns to the factor or factors that provide the barrier to entry.

3 "At a monopoly firm's profit-maximizing output, price will exceed marginal cost simply because price exceeds marginal revenue for a downward-sloping demand curve." Explain why this is so and indicate what factors will affect the size of the price–marginal cost gap.

4 The following conversation was overheard during a microeconomics revision session:

Student A. "In order to maximize profits, a monopolist should obviously produce where the gap between price and *average* cost is the greatest."

Student B. "No, that will only maximize profit per unit. To maximize total profits, the firm should produce where the gap between price and *marginal* cost is the greatest since that will maximize monopoly power and hence profits."

Can you make any sense out of this drivel? Which concepts, if any, have these students not grasped sufficiently?

5 "Monopolies perpetuate inflation. When wages rise, a monopoly simply passes on the increased cost in its price. Competitive firms would not be able to do that." Do you agree? What are the differences between how a monopoly and a competitive firm respond to cost increases?

6 Figure 13-3 illustrates the "deadweight loss" from the monopolization of a market. What is this a loss of? In the chili-dog cook example, what is the world missing out on?

7 Suppose that the government instituted a per-unit tax on the output of a monopoly firm. How would you plot this situation on a graph? What would happen to the market equilibrium after implementation of such a tax? How would you analyze the tax incidence question – that is, how would you show which economic actor pays most of the tax?

8 Describe some of the transactions costs that must be present if a monopoly is to be able to practice price discrimination successfully. Are different types of costs more relevant to the practice of third-degree (market separation) price discrimination than to second-degree (price schedule) price discrimination?

9 Suppose that the Acme manufacturing company has a monopoly position in the market for the two principal types of roadrunner-catching equipment: roller skates and jet-assist backpacks. Describe in general terms how Acme should price both of these products when it knows that the demands for the two goods are related and that the costs of producing the two goods exhibit economies of scope (see Chapter 8).

10 What is a "natural monopoly"? Why does electric power distribution or local telephone service have the characteristics of a natural monopoly? Why might this be less true for electric power generation or long-distance telephone service?

PROBLEMS

13.1 A monopolist can produce at constant average and marginal costs of $AC = MC = 5$. The firm faces a market demand curve given by $Q = 53 - P$. The monopolist's marginal revenue curve is given by $MR = 53 - 2Q$.

a Calculate the profit-maximizing price-quantity combination for the monopolist. Also calculate the monopolist's profits and consumer surplus.

b What output level would be produced by this industry under perfect competition (where price = marginal cost)?

c Calculate the consumer surplus obtained by consumers in part b. Show that this exceeds the sum of the monopolist's profits and consumer surplus received in part a. What is the value of the "deadweight loss" from monopolization?

13.2 A monopolist faces a market demand curve given by

$$Q = 70 - P$$

The monopolist's marginal revenue function is given by

$$MR = 70 - 2Q$$

a If the monopolist can produce at constant average and marginal costs of $AC = MC = 6$, what output level will the monopolist choose in order to maximize profits? What is the price at this output level? What are the monopolist's profits?

b Assume instead that the monopolist has a cost structure where total costs are described by

$$TC = 0.25Q^2 - 5Q + 300$$

and marginal cost is given by

$$MC = 0.5Q - 5$$

With the monopolist facing the same market demand and marginal revenue, what price-quantity combination will be chosen now to maximize profits? What will profits be?

c Assume now that a third cost structure explains the monopolist's position, with total costs given by

$$TC = 0.333Q^3 - 26Q^2 + 695Q - 5800$$

and marginal costs given by

$$MC = Q^2 - 52Q + 695$$

Again, calculate the monopolist's price-quantity combination that maximizes profits. What will profits be? (*Hint*: Set $MC = MR$ as usual and use the quadratic formula or simple factoring to solve the equation for Q.)

d Plot on a graph the market demand curve, the MR curve, and the three marginal cost curves from part a, part b, and part c. Notice that the monopolist's profit-making ability is constrained by (1) the market demand curve it faces (along with its associated MR curve) and (2) the cost structure underlying its production.

13.3 A single firm monopolizes the entire market for Tony Blair facemasks and can produce at constant average and marginal costs of

$$AC = MC = 10$$

Originally, the firm faces a market demand curve given by

$$Q = 60 - P$$

and a marginal revenue function given by

$$MR = 60 - 2Q$$

a Calculate the profit-maximizing price-quantity combination for the firm. What are the firm's profits?

b Now assume that the market demand curve becomes steeper and is given by

$$Q = 45 - 0.5P$$

with the marginal revenue function given by

$$MR = 90 - 4Q$$

What is the firm's profit-maximizing price-quantity combination now? What are the firm's profits?

c Instead of the assumptions in part b, assume that the market demand curve becomes flatter and is given by

$$Q = 100 - 2P$$

with the marginal revenue function given by

$$MR = 50 - Q$$

What is the firm's profit-maximizing price-quantity combination now? What are the firm's profits?

d Plot on a graph the three different situations of part a, part b, and part c. Using your results, explain why there is no meaningful "supply curve" for this firm's mask monopoly.

13.4 Suppose that the market for hula hoops is monopolized by a single firm.

a Draw the initial equilibrium for such a market.

b Suppose now that the demand for hula hoops shifts outward slightly. Show that, in general (contrary to the competitive case), it will not be possible to predict the effect of this shift in demand on the market price of hula hoops.

c Consider three possible ways in which the price elasticity of demand might change as the demand curve shifts outward – it might increase, it might decrease, or it might stay the same. Consider also that marginal costs for the monopolist might be rising, falling, or constant in the range where $MR = MC$. Consequently, there are nine different combinations of types of demand shifts and marginal cost slope configurations. Analyze each of these to determine for which cases it is possible to make a definite prediction about the effect of the shift in demand on the price of hula hoops.

13.5 Suppose a company has a monopoly on a game called Monopoly and faces a demand curve given by

$$Q_T = 100 - P$$

and a marginal revenue function given by

$$MR = 100 - 2Q_T$$

where Q_T equals the combined total number of games produced per hour in the company's two factories ($Q_T = q_1 + q_2$). If factory 1 has a marginal cost function given by

$$MC_1 = q_1 - 5$$

and factory 2 has a marginal cost function given by

$$MC_2 = 0.5q_2 - 5$$

how much total output will the company choose to produce and how will it distribute this production between its two factories in order to maximize profits?

13.6 Suppose a textbook monopoly can produce any level of output it wishes at a constant marginal (and average) cost of €5 per book. Assume that the monopoly sells its books in two different markets that are separated by some distance. The demand curve in the first market is given by

$$Q_1 = 55 - P_1$$

and the curve in the second market is given by

$$Q_2 = 70 - 2P_2$$

a If the monopolist can maintain the separation between the two markets, what level of output should be produced in each market and what price will prevail in each market? What are total profits in this situation?

b How would your answer change if it only cost demanders €5 to mail books between the two markets? What would be the monopolist's new profit level in this situation? How would your answer change if mailing costs were 0? (*Hint*: Show that for a downward-sloping linear demand curve, profits are maximized when output is set at $Q^*/2$, where Q^* is the output level that would be demanded when $P = MC$. Use this result to solve the problem.)

13.7 Suppose a perfectly competitive industry can produce Roman candles at a constant marginal cost of €10 per unit. Once the industry is monopolized, marginal costs rise to €12 per unit because €2 per unit must be paid to politicians to ensure that only this firm receives a Roman candle license. Suppose the market demand for Roman candles is given by

$$Q_D = 1000 - 50P$$

and the marginal revenue function by

$$MR = 20 - Q/25$$

a Calculate the perfectly competitive and monopoly outputs and prices.

b Calculate the total loss of consumer surplus from monopolization of Roman candle production.

c Plot on a graph and discuss your results.

13.8 Consider the following possible schemes for taxing a monopoly:

i A proportional tax on profits.

ii A tax on each unit produced.

iii A proportional tax on the gap between price and marginal cost.

a Explain how each of these taxes would affect the monopolist's profit-maximizing output choice. Would the tax increase or decrease the deadweight loss from monopoly?

b Plot on a graph your results for these three cases.

13.9 Show that, with a linear demand curve, imposition of a per-unit tax on a monopoly will cause price to rise by less than the tax. Would this be true for a constant-elasticity demand curve?

13.10 Suppose a monopoly produces its output in a large number of identical plants, each characterized by a U-shaped, long-run average cost curve. How should the firm decide how much to produce and how many plants to utilize? Will each plant be operated at the low point of its average cost curve? Does this imply that production is efficient in this situation? How might a regulatory body enforce efficiency in this situation?

14

Imperfect Competition

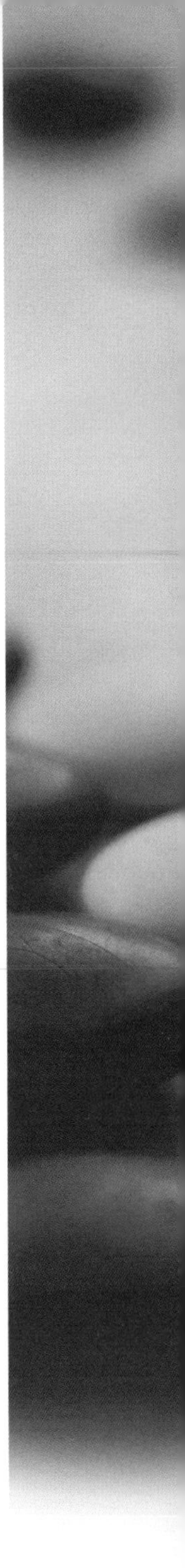

This chapter discusses markets that fall between the polar extremes of perfect competition and monopoly. Economists have proposed an array of models of imperfect competition. None has emerged as the "textbook" one, so we will study a variety of the basic models in current use. Several common principles will emerge from our study of these models of industries with few firms but more than one, called **oligopolies**. First, game theory is a valuable tool for studying oligopoly. Throughout this chapter, we will find ourselves applying the concepts of game theory developed in Chapter 6. Second, small changes in details concerning the variables that firms choose, the timing of their moves, or their information about market conditions or rival actions can have a dramatic effect on market outcomes. Last, we may simply have to accept the fact that predicting outcomes in imperfectly competitive industries is difficult based on theory alone; the best way to study real-world markets may involve a combination of theory and empirical evidence. Many of our boxed applications will include empirical evidence relevant to the issue under consideration.

Our analysis will proceed from the short-term decisions firms make (pricing and output decisions) to longer-term decisions (such as advertising, product design, and investment) and to the yet longer-term decisions (entry and exit).

Overview: Pricing of Homogeneous Goods

This section provides a brief overview of the rest of the chapter. To fix ideas, we will begin by looking at firms' pricing decisions in markets in which relatively few firms each produce the same good. As in previous chapters, we assume that the market is perfectly competitive on the demand side; that is, there are assumed to be many demanders, each of whom is a price taker. We also assume that there are no transactions or informational costs, so that the good in question obeys the law of one price. That is, we can talk accurately about the price of this good. Later in this chapter, we relax this assumption to consider cases where firms sell products that differ slightly from each other and may therefore have different prices.

Oligopoly A market with few firms, but more than one.

Competitive Outcome

It is difficult to predict exactly the possible outcomes for prices when there are few firms; prices depend on how aggressively firms compete, which in turn depends on which strategic variables firms choose, how much information firms have about rivals, and how often firms interact with each other in the market. The Bertrand model – which we will study in detail later in the chapter – in which identical firms choose prices simultaneously in their one meeting in the market, has a Nash equilibrium at point C in Figure 14-1. This figure assumes that marginal cost (and average cost) is constant for all output levels. Even though there may be only two firms in the market, in this equilibrium they behave as if they were perfectly competitive, setting price equal to marginal cost and earning zero profit. We will discuss whether the Bertrand model is a realistic depiction of actual firm behavior, but an analysis of the model shows that it is possible to think up rigorous game-theoretic models in which one extreme – the competitive outcome – can emerge in very concentrated markets with few firms.

Perfect Cartel Outcome

At the other extreme, firms as a group may act as a cartel, recognizing that they can affect price and coordinate their decisions. Indeed, they may be able to act as a perfect

FIGURE 14-1 Pricing under Imperfect Competition *Market equilibrium under imperfect competition can occur at many points on the demand curve. In this figure, which assumes that marginal costs are constant over all output ranges, the equilibrium of the Bertrand game occurs at point C, also corresponding to the perfectly competitive outcome. The perfect-cartel outcome occurs at point M, also corresponding to the monopoly outcome. Many solutions may occur between points M and C, depending on the specific assumptions made about how firms compete. For example, the equilibrium of the Cournot game might occur at a point such as A. The deadweight loss given by the shaded triangle is increasing as one moves from point C to M.*

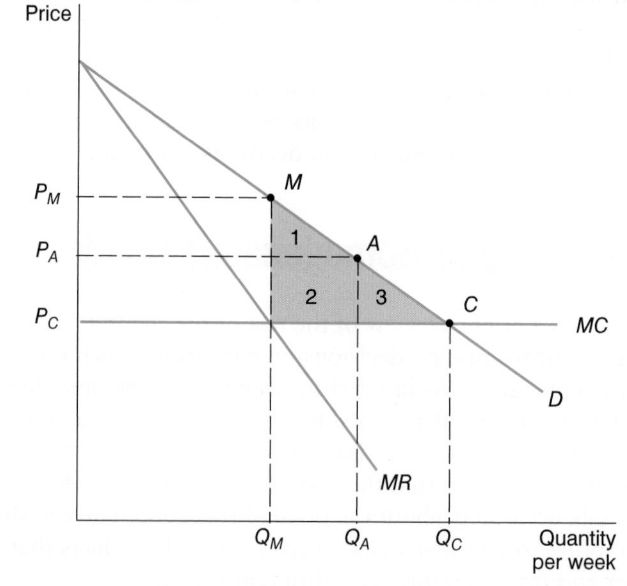

cartel, achieving the highest possible profits, namely, the profit a monopoly would earn in the market. Assuming, as before, that these marginal costs are equal and constant for all firms, the output choice is indicated by point *M* in Figure 14-1. Because this coordinated plan would have to specify an output level for each firm, the plan would also dictate how monopoly profits earned by the cartel are to be shared by its members.

One way to maintain a cartel is to bind firms with explicit pricing rules. Such explicit pricing rules are often prohibited by antitrust law. Firms do not need to resort to explicit pricing rules if they interact on the market repeatedly. They can collude tacitly. High collusive prices can be maintained with the tacit threat of a price war if any firm undercuts. We will analyze this game formally and discuss practical difficulties involved with trying to maintain collusion.

Other Possibilities

The Bertrand and cartel models determine the outer limits between which actual prices in an imperfectly competitive market are set (one such intermediate price is represented by point *A* in Figure 14-1). This band of outcomes may be very wide, and such is the wealth of models available that there may be a model for nearly every point within the band. For example, the Cournot model, in which firms set quantities rather than prices (as in the Bertrand model) leads to an outcome somewhere between C and *M* in Figure 14-1, such as point *A*. We will study the Cournot model in detail shortly. For another example, cartel models in which market characteristics make it difficult for firms to sustain a perfect cartel at point *M* may lead to a point such as *A* in the figure.

In the end, it may be difficult to predict which outcome between C and *M* will actually occur. The assumption that firms play a Nash equilibrium in simultaneous games and a sub game-perfect equilibrium in sequential games will help pin down firm behavior, but still the outcome will vary on the game that is being played, and there are many different, plausible ways to specify such a game. In the end, economists turn to data to determine the competitiveness of real-world industries, as discussed in Application 14.1: *Measuring Oligopoly Power*. It is important to know where the industry is on the line between points C and *M* because the well-being of society (as measured by the sum of consumer surplus and firms' profits) depends on where this point is. At point C, there is no deadweight loss and society is as well off as possible. At point *A*, the deadweight loss is given by the area of the shaded triangle 3. At point *M*, deadweight loss is even greater, given by the area of shaded regions 1, 2, and 3. The closer the imperfectly competitive outcome is to C and the farther it is from *M*, the better off society will be.

Cournot Model

The first model we will study is the **Cournot model**, named after the French economist who first proposed and analyzed it.[1] Since a formal development of the Cournot model can become quite mathematically complex, a simple numerical example can suffice.

Cournot model An oligopoly model in which firms simultaneously choose quantities of a homogeneous product.

Suppose there are two firms (*A* and *B*) that operate costless but healthy spa springs. Firms simultaneously choose the quantities q_A and q_B of water they will supply (in terms

[1]A. Cournot, *Researches into Mathematical Principles of the Theory of Wealth*, trans. N. T. Bacon (New York: Macmillan, 1897). Cournot was one of the first people to use mathematics in economics. Among other advances, he devised the concept of marginal revenue and used this concept both to discuss profit maximization by a monopoly and to develop a model in which two firms compete for the same market.

APPLICATION 14.1 *Measuring Oligopoly Power*

As Figure 14-1 shows, the variety of possible models of imperfect competition give a range of possibilities from the perfectly competitive outcome (point *C* in the figure) to the monopoly outcome achieved by a perfect cartel (point *M*). Because theory alone cannot determine where a real-world industry will fall between points *C* and *M*, economists have turned to data to help them answer the question.

Lerner Index

Asking where an industry falls between points *C* and *M* in Figure 14-1 is really just asking how competitive the industry is. The most widely used measure is called the Lerner index (*L*), which equals the percentage markup of price over marginal cost:

$$L = \frac{P - MC}{P}$$

(the index is expressed as a percentage to remove the units in which the product is measured). If the industry is perfectly competitive, the Lerner index equals zero since price equals marginal cost. For the monopoly/perfect cartel outcome, one can show that the Lerner index is related to the elasticity of market demand;[1] more precisely, the inverse of the absolute value of the elasticity,

$$L = \frac{1}{|e_{Q,P}|}$$

ranging from close to zero for very elastic demand curves to extremely high numbers for very inelastic demand curves.

Problems Measuring Marginal Cost

At first glance, it would seem a simple matter to calculate the Lerner index for an industry. One just needs to input information on price and marginal cost into the simple formula above. Unfortunately, this is not as easy as it sounds. Price data can be readily obtained just by looking at an advertisement or visiting a store. Unfortunately, data on marginal costs is not readily available. Firms often jealously guard cost information as being competitively sensitive, and a secret.

Economists have used three tacks to overcome this measurement problem. Up until recently, many utilities (telephone, electricity) were regulated by the government, with firms' prices set to a certain mark-up over cost. This form of regulation required the government to collect detailed cost information from the regulated firms, which became a data source for economists. A second tack is to look at an industry where the production process is simple enough that one can deduce marginal cost from using simple facts about the industry. One example is the early history of refined sugar, studied by Genesove and Mullin.[2] The main component of marginal cost is the cost of raw sugar: 108 pounds of raw sugar yields about 100 pounds of refined sugar. Combined with data on the wholesale price of raw sugar, around \$3.30 in 1900, and producers' statements reported in the trade press about the small additional costs of labor and energy to complete the refining process, around 25 cents, the authors came up with a plausible measure of marginal cost of $(108 \times \$3.30) + \$0.25 = \$3.81$ per hundred pounds. For most industries, where there are no direct measures of cost, a third tack is needed, involving estimating a sophisticated econometric model (based on the very same game-theory models studied in this chapter).

Industry Studies

Table 1 presents the estimated Lerner indexes from a number of studies. Note the broad range of possibilities. Rubber, coffee roasting, and sugar, for example, appear to be very competitive, with price being only around 5 per cent higher than marginal cost (that is, a Lerner index of around 0.05). Food processing, tobacco, and aluminum appear to be less competitive, with prices estimated to be more than double marginal cost (a Lerner index of more than 0.50). Competitiveness in Uruguayan banking appears to have improved considerably after removal of government entry restrictions.

General Lessons

What makes some of the industries in Table 1 more competitive than others? Unfortunately, there have not yet been enough studies done in a systematic way across industries to make such a comparison.

John Sutton has provided perhaps the most extensive synthesis across industries.[3] the clearest determinants of competitiveness appear to be the size of the market relative to fixed costs. Considering a large market such as that for cars in the United States, even if fixed costs (including the cost of setting up an assembly plant, the cost of advertising the new product line, and so forth) number in the billions of dollars, the market may be big enough to support a fair number of firms, leading to relatively stiff competition. In a smaller market such as Uruguay, there may be only space for one firm, with the resultant monopoly outcome. The nature of the fixed cost may matter as well. If fixed costs increase in proportion to market size, as, for example, with television advertising expenditures, larger markets may not support any more firms than small, and these large markets may exhibit high price-cost margins. Therefore, whether television and other forms of advertising are important for an industry (yes for cars, no for machine tools) might be an indicator of how competitive that industry is. Other factors that may reduce competitiveness include government restrictions on entry and barriers to international trade.

To Think About

1. Price data may have their own difficulties. Imagine trying to get price data on a new car model. How would you handle the fact that prices are usually set in customer-by-customer negotiations, usually below the manufacturer's retail price? How would you handle the fact that even for a given model there are numerous option packages available, which affect the car price?
2. Are there any surprises in Table 1? Where do you think such industries as home construction, beer, and computers would fit? How about higher education?

TABLE 1 Competitiveness of Various Industries

Industry	*Lerner index*
Aluminum	0.59
Cars	
Standard	0.10
Luxury	0.34
Banking (Uruguay)	
Before removing entry restrictions	0.88
After removing entry restrictions	0.44
Coffee roasting	0.06
Electrical machinery	0.20
Food processing	0.50
Petroleum	0.10
Refined sugar	0.05
Textiles	0.07
Tobacco	0.65

SOURCES: TAKEN FROM COMPILATIONS OF STUDIES BY T. F. BRESNAHAN, "EMPIRICAL STUDIES OF INDUSTRIES WITH MARKET POWER", IN *HANDBOOK OF INDUSTRIAL ORGANIZATION,* ED. R. SCHMALENSEE AND R. WILLIG (AMSTERDAM: NORTH-HOLLAND, 1989), TABLE 17.1 AND D. W. CARLTON AND J. M. PERLOFF, *MODERN INDUSTRIAL ORGANIZATION,* 4TH ED. (BOSTON: PEARSON, 2005), TABLE 8.7. ALUMINUM: V. SUSLOW, "ESTIMATING MONOPOLY BEHAVIOR WITH COMPETITIVE RECYCLING: AN APPLICATION TO ALCOA", *RAND JOURNAL OF ECONOMICS* (AUTUMN 1986): 389–403. AUTOS: T. F. BRESNAHAN, "DEPARTURES FROM MARGINAL-COST PRICING IN THE AMERICAN AUTOMOBILE INDUSTRY: ESTIMATES FOR 1977–1978", *JOURNAL OF ECONOMETRICS* (NOVEMBER 1981): 201–227. BANKING: P. SPILLER AND E. FAVARO, "THE EFFECTS OF ENTRY REGULATION ON OLIGOPOLISTIC INTERACTION: THE URUGUAYAN BANKING SECTOR", *RAND JOURNAL OF ECONOMICS* (SUMMER 1984): 244–254. COFFEE ROASTING: M. J. ROBERTS, "TESTING OLIGOPOLISTIC BEHAVIOR", *INTERNATIONAL JOURNAL OF INDUSTRIAL ORGANIZATION* (DECEMBER 1984): 367–383. ELECTRICAL MACHINERY, TEXTILES, TOBACCO: E. APPLEBAUM, "THE ESTIMATION OF THE DEGREE OF OLIGOPOLY POWER", *JOURNAL OF ECONOMETRICS* (AUGUST 1982): 287–299. FOOD PROCESSING: R. E. LOPEZ, "MEASURING OLIGOPOLY POWER AND PRODUCTION RESPONSES OF THE CANADIAN FOOD PROCESSING INDUSTRY", *JOURNAL OF AGRICULTURAL ECONOMICS* (JULY 1984): 219–230. GASOLINE: M. SLADE, "CONJECTURES, FIRM CHARACTERISTICS, AND MARKET STRUCTURE: AN EMPIRICAL ASSESSMENT", *INTERNATIONAL JOURNAL OF INDUSTRIAL ORGANIZATION* (DECEMBER 1986): 347–369. REFINED SUGAR: GENESOVE AND MULLIN, CITED IN FOOTNOTE 1.

(Continued)

[1]Using the fact from Equation 9.3 that $MR = MC$ for a profit-maximizing firm, the fact from Equation 9.9 that $MR = P + P/e_{q,P}$ and the fact that the elasticity of demand facing the firm $e_{q,P}$ equals market demand elasticity $e_{Q,P}$ for a monopoly, yields $P + P/e_{Q,P} = MC$. Rearranging terms,

$$P - MC = -P/e_{Q,P}, \text{ or } (P - MC)/P = -1/e_{Q,P} = 1/|e_{Q,P}|.$$

[2]D. Genesove and W. Mullin, "Testing Static Oligopoly Models: Conduct and Cost in the Sugar Industry, 1890–1914", *RAND Journal of Economics* (Summer 1998): 355–377.

[3]J. Sutton, *Sunk Costs and Market Structure* (Cambridge, Mass.: MIT Press, 1991).

of thousands of liters) in a single period of competition. We will assume spring water is a homogeneous product, so market price is a function of total quantity $Q = q_A + q_B$ produced. In particular, suppose market demand is given by the equation

$$Q = 120 - P \tag{14.1}$$

and market price by the inverse of Equation 14.1,

$$P = 120 - Q \tag{14.2}$$

We have just defined a game in which the players are the two firms, actions are quantities, and payoffs are profits (which can be computed from our specification of demand and costs). We will look for the Nash equilibrium of this game. Since quantities can be any number greater than or equal to zero, this is a game with continuous actions similar to the Tragedy of the Commons studied in Chapter 6. We will solve for the Nash equilibrium here in a similar way, so it may be helpful for the reader to review the definitions of Nash equilibrium and best-response function, and the analysis of the Tragedy of the Commons, all in Chapter 6, before proceeding.

Nash Equilibrium in the Cournot Model

For a pair of quantities, q_A and q_B, to be a Nash equilibrium, q_A must be a best response to q_B and vice versa. We therefore begin by computing the best-response function for firm *A*. Its best-response function tells us the value of q_A that maximizes *A*'s profit given for each possible choice q_B by firm *B*. In Chapter 9, we presented a rule for the profit-maximizing output choice that applies to any firm ranging from a perfectly competitive firm to a monopoly, namely that profits are maximized by the quantity where marginal revenue equals marginal cost. The same rule applies here.

Computing firm *A*'s marginal cost is easy here: production is costless, so *A*'s marginal cost is 0. Computing *A*'s marginal revenue is a bit more difficult. *A*'s total revenue equals its quantity q_A times market price $P = 120 - Q = 120 - q_A - q_B$:

$$q_A(120 - q_A - q_B) \tag{14.3}$$

Using the expression for total revenue in Equation 14.3, it can be shown,[2] or simply accepted as a fact, that marginal revenue equals

$$120 - 2q_A - q_B \tag{14.4}$$

[2]Distributing q_A among the terms in parentheses, Equation 14.3 can be rewritten as $120q_A - q^2_A - q_Aq_B$. Using calculus, one can differentiate this expression for total revenue with respect to q_A to find marginal revenue in Equation 14.4.

Equating marginal revenue in Equation 14.4 with the marginal cost of 0, and solving for q_A gives A's best-response function:

$$q_A = \frac{120 - q_B}{2} \qquad \{14.5\}$$

We can perform the same analysis for firm B and arrive at its best-response function, which expresses the profit-maximizing level of q_B as a function of q_A of the form

$$q_B = \frac{120 - q_A}{2} \qquad \{14.6\}$$

The best-response functions for both firms are shown in Figure 14-2.

Nash equilibrium requires each firm to play its best response to the other. The only point on Figure 14-2 where both are playing best responses is the intersection between their best-response functions. No other point would be stable (that is, would be a Nash equilibrium) because one firm or the other or both would have an incentive to deviate. It is easy to show (either using the graph or solving Equations 14.5 and 14.6 simultaneously) that the point of intersection is given by $q_A = 40$ and $q_B = 40$. In this Nash equilibrium, both firms produce 40, total output is 80, and the market price is €40 (= 120 − 80). Each firm earns revenue and profit equal to €1600, and total industry revenue and profit is €3200.

FIGURE 14-2 Cournot Best-Response Functions *Firm A's best-response function shows the profit-maximizing quantity it would choose for any quantity chosen by firm B. Firm B's best-response function shows the profit-maximizing quantity it would choose for any quantity chosen by firm A. Both firms must play best responses in the Nash equilibrium. The only point on both best-response functions is the point of intersection ($q_A = 40$, $q_B = 40$).*

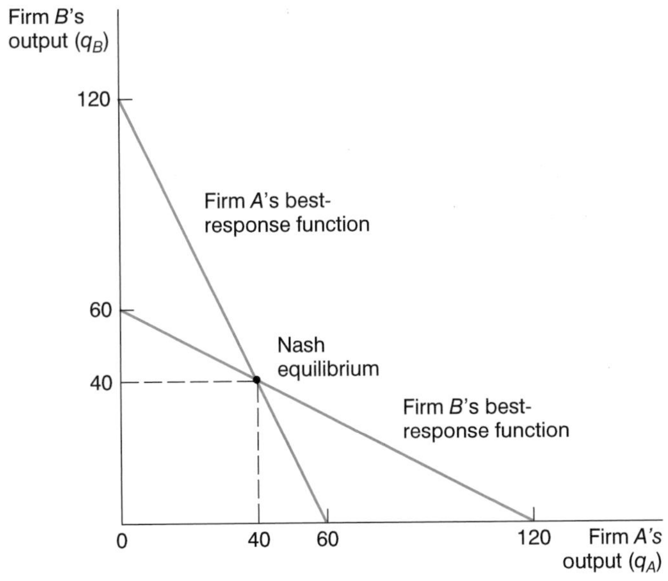

Comparisons and Antitrust Considerations

The Nash equilibrium of the Cournot model is somewhere between perfect competition and monopoly. With perfectly competitive firms, the price would be set at marginal cost, €0. Industry output would be 120, and industry revenue and profit would be €0. On the other hand, a monopoly's output would be 60, price would be €60, and revenue and profit would be €3600 (= €60 × 60).[3] Putting these results side by side, we see that equilibrium price and industry profit in the Cournot model is above the perfectly competitive level and below the monopoly level; industry output is below the perfectly competitive level and above the monopoly level. The firms manage not to compete away all the profits as in perfect competition. But the firms do not do as well as a monopoly would, either.

The industry does not attain the monopoly profit in the Cournot model because firms do not take into account the fact that an increase in their output lowers price and thus lowers the other firm's revenue. Firms "overproduce" in this sense. According to this model, firms would have an incentive to form a cartel with explicit rules limiting output. If such a cartel were illegal, the firms would have a motive to collude tacitly using self-enforcing strategies to reduce output and raise price toward the monopoly levels. With one period of competition, such collusion would be unstable; indeed, we showed that the only stable point is the Nash equilibrium of the Cournot model. Another way to increase profits would be for the firms to merge, essentially turning a Cournot model with two firms into a monopoly model with one firm.

Consumers benefit from the higher output and lower prices in the Cournot model compared to monopoly. Government authorities, through the antitrust laws, often prohibit conspiracies to form cartels and mergers that would increase concentration in the industry (certainly mergers from two to one firm would be examined critically by authorities). Assuming the government authorities act in the interest of consumers, the Cournot model provides some justification for these laws.

We noted at the outset that the methods used to solve the Cournot model are similar to those used to solve the Tragedy of the Commons from Chapter 6. In fact, except for the interpretation of the players' identities (shepherds versus spring-water producers) and actions (number of sheep versus thousands of liters of spring water), the two games are exactly the same. Indeed, the reader can verify that the equilibrium in both involves a choice of 40 units for each player.

MICROQUIZ 14.1

1 In Figure 14-2, how would an increase in *B*'s marginal cost from zero to a positive number shift its best-response function? Would it shift *A*'s? On a graph, indicate where the new Nash equilibrium would be.

2 On a graph, show how the best-response functions would shift and where the new Nash equilibrium would be if both firms' marginal costs increased by the same amount. What about a cost decrease? What about an increase in the demand intercept above 120?

Generalizations

The Cournot model can be relatively easily extended to cases involving more complex demand and cost assumptions or to situations involving three or more firms. As the number of firms grows large, it can be shown that the Nash equilibrium approaches the competitive case, with price approaching marginal cost. The ease with which the model can be extended, together with the fact that it produces what people think is a realistic outcome for most markets (that is, an outcome between perfect competition and monopoly), has made the Cournot model a workhorse for economists. Application 14.2: *Cournot in California* provides a good example of its use in economic and policy analysis.

[3]The monopoly's total revenue equals price, which we know from Equation 14.2 is $120 - Q$, times quantity Q – that is, $(120 - Q)Q$. Differentiating this expression for total revenue with respect to Q gives marginal revenue $120 - 2Q$. Equating marginal revenue with the marginal cost of 0 shows that the profit-maximizing monopoly output is 60.

APPLICATION 14.2 *Cournot in California*

Wholesale markets for electric power have been increasingly deregulated in many countries. In the United States, the process has evolved rather slowly because each state has a separate regulatory apparatus and moves toward deregulation have generated considerable political controversy. In California, the largest power market in the United States, deregulation of wholesale electricity sales was first authorized in 1996 and the actual trading of day-ahead electricity sales began in early 1998. Early attempts to model this process reached cautionary conclusions about the possibilities for market power in this trading. Subsequent events have tended to confirm these predictions.

Modeling Spot Markets in Electricity

Perhaps the most elaborate attempt at modeling the impact of electricity deregulation in California can be found in an important paper by Borenstein and Bushnell.[1] In this paper, the authors focus on the competition between the three major electricity-generating firms in the state (Pacific Gas and Electric, Southern California Edison, and San Diego Gas and Electric) together with a group of smaller in-state and out-of-state suppliers. They argue that the smaller suppliers can be treated as competitive suppliers but that the major in-state producers behave in the way assumed in the Cournot model. That is, each major supplier is assumed to choose its output levels (or, more precisely, its levels of electricity-generating capacity) in a way that treats output by other producers as fixed. The authors then study the resulting Cournot equilibrium under various assumptions about electricity demand and the behavior of out-of-state suppliers.

Results of the Modeling

Borenstein and Bushnell show that under certain circumstances there is substantial market power in California wholesale electricity markets. As we saw in Application 14.1, one way to measure that power is by the Lerner index, the gap between price and marginal cost expressed as a ratio of price. In periods of normal demand, the authors calculate values for this index in the range of 0.10 or less; the gap between price and marginal cost is less than 10 per cent of price. However, during peak hours of electric usage or during peak months (i.e., September), the index rises to well over 0.50; the gap between price and marginal cost is more than half of price. Hence, during such peak periods, equilibrium in these markets is far from the competitive ideal. Interestingly, the authors also show that market power can be significantly restrained by larger price elasticities of demand for electricity. But they point out that actual policies in California tend to keep price elasticities small by preventing increases in the wholesale price of electricity from being passed on to consumers.

Actual Price "Spikes" in California

Seldom has an economic model proven to be right so quickly. In the summer of 2000, California experienced a relatively modest shortfall in electric power availability because droughts in the Pacific Northwest reduced the supply of hydroelectric power. The result was a rapid spiking in the wholesale price of electricity in the late summer and fall. From a normal price of perhaps $50 per megawatt-hour in 1999, peak prices rose to over $500 per megawatt-hour and sometimes reached over $1000. These increases were, more or less, in line with what had been predicted by Borenstein and Bushnell. Because large California electric utilities had not been allowed to sign long-term power contracts, they had little choice but to buy at these prices. But the firms could not pass on these higher prices to their customers, so there were only modest reductions in demand. By 2001, several of California's largest utilities had filed for bankruptcy and had been forced to sell off major portions of their electricity distribution networks to the state.

To Think About

1. The model described in this application assumes that the major suppliers of electricity to California engaged in Cournot-type competition when electricity supplies were tight. Could the large price increases in 2000 also be explained with a competitive model?
2. One result of price spikes in the California electricity market was the filing of many lawsuits

(*Continued*)

against suppliers. Should firms engaged in Cournot-type competition be found guilty of a "conspiracy in restraint of trade"?

[1]S. Borenstein and J. Bushnell, "An Empirical Analysis of the Potential for Market Power in California's Electricity Industry", *Journal of Industrial Economics* (September 1999): 285–323.

Bertrand Model

Bertrand model An oligopoly model in which firms simultaneously choose prices for a homogeneous product.

We next turn to the **Bertrand model**, named after the economist who first proposed it.[4] Bertrand thought that Cournot's assumption that firms choose quantities was unrealistic, so he developed a model in which firms choose prices. In all other respects the model is the same as Cournot's. We will see that this seemingly small change in the strategic variable from quantities in the Cournot model to prices in the Bertrand model leads to a big change in the equilibrium outcome.

To state the model formally, suppose there are two firms in the market, A and B. They produce a homogeneous product at a constant marginal cost (and constant average cost), c. Note that this is a generalization of our assumption in the Cournot model that production was costless. Firms choose prices P_A and P_B simultaneously in a single period of competition. Firms' outputs are perfect substitutes, so all sales go to the firm with the lowest price, and sales are split evenly if $P_A = P_B$. We will generalize the demand curve beyond the particular linear one that we assumed in the Cournot model to be any downward-sloping demand curve.

We will look for the Nash equilibrium of the Bertrand model. It turns out that the marginal analysis (marginal revenue equals marginal cost) we used to derive the best-response functions in the Cournot model will not work here since the profit-functions are not smooth. Starting from equal prices, if one firm lowers its price by the smallest amount, its sales and profit would essentially double instantly. The model is simple enough that we will be able to leap to the right answer, and then we will spend some time verifying that our leap was in fact correct.

Nash Equilibrium in the Bertrand Model

The only Nash equilibrium in the Bertrand game is $P_A = P_B = c$. That is, the Nash equilibrium involves both firms charging marginal cost. In saying that this is the only Nash equilibrium, we are really making two statements that both need to be verified: one, that this outcome is a Nash equilibrium and, two, that there is no other Nash equilibrium.

To verify that this outcome is a Nash equilibrium, we need to show that both firms are playing a best response to each other or, in other words, that neither firm has an incentive to deviate to some other strategy. In equilibrium, firms charge a price equal to marginal cost, which in turn is equal to average cost. But a price equal to average cost means firms earn zero profit in equilibrium. Can a firm earn more than the zero it earns in equilibrium by deviating to some other price? No. If it deviates to a higher price, it will make no sales and therefore no profit, not strictly more than in equilibrium. If it deviates to a lower price, it will make sales but will earn a negative margin on each unit sold since price will be below marginal cost. So the firm will earn negative profit, less than in equilibrium. Because there is no possible profitable deviation for the firm, we have succeeded in verifying that both firms' charging marginal cost is a Nash equilibrium.

[4]J. Bertrand, "Théorie Mathematique de la Richess Sociale", *Journal de Savants* (1883): 499–508.

To verify that this outcome is the only Nash equilibrium, there are a number of cases to consider. It cannot be a Nash equilibrium for both firms to price above marginal cost. If the prices were unequal, the higher-pricing firm, which would get no demand and thus would earn no profit, would make positive sales and profit by lowering its price to undercut the other. If the above-marginal-cost prices were equal, either firm would have an incentive to deviate. By undercutting the price ever so slightly, price would hardly fall but sales would essentially double because the firm would no longer need to split sales with the other. A Nash equilibrium cannot involve a price less than marginal cost either because the low-price firm would earn negative profit and could gain by deviating to a higher price. For example, it could deviate by raising price to marginal cost, which, since it also equals average cost, would guarantee the firm zero, rather than negative, profit.

Bertrand Paradox

The Nash equilibrium of the Bertrand model is the same as the perfectly competitive outcome. Price is set to marginal cost, and firms earn zero profit. The result that the Nash equilibrium in the Bertrand model is the same as in perfect competition even though there are only two firms in the market is called the Bertrand Paradox. It is paradoxical that competition would be so tough with as few as two firms in the market. In one sense, the Bertrand Paradox is a general result in that we did not specify the marginal cost c or the demand curve, so the result holds for any c and any downward-sloping demand curve.

In another sense, the Bertrand Paradox is not very general; it can be undone by changing any of a number of the model's assumptions. For example, assuming firms choose quantity rather than price leads to the Cournot game, and we saw from our analysis of the Cournot game that firms do not end up charging marginal cost and earning zero profit. The Bertrand Paradox could also be avoided by making other assumptions, including the assumption that the marginal cost is higher for one firm than another, the assumption that products are slightly differentiated rather than being perfect substitutes, or the assumption that firms engage in repeated interaction rather than one round of competition. In the next section, we will see that the Bertrand Paradox can be avoided by assuming firms have capacity constraints rather than the ability to produce an unlimited amount at constant cost c.

Capacity Choice and Cournot Equilibrium

Capacity constraint
A limit to the quantity a firm can produce given the firm's capital and other available inputs.

The assumption that firms do not have **capacity constraints** is crucial for the stark result in the Bertrand model. Starting from equal prices, if a firm lowers its price slightly, its demand essentially doubles. The firm can satisfy this increased demand because it has no capacity constraints, giving firms a big incentive to undercut. If the undercutting firm could not serve all the demand at its lower price because of capacity constraints, that would leave some residual demand for the higher-priced firm, and would decrease the incentive to undercut.

In many settings, it is unrealistic to suppose that a firm can satisfy any number of customers, even if, say, the number of customers that usually showed up were to suddenly double. Consider a two-stage model in which firms build capacity in the first stage and choose prices in the second stage.[5] Firms cannot sell more in the

MICROQUIZ 14.2

In showing that no other outcome but marginal cost pricing for both firms is a Nash equilibrium in the Bertrand game, a case was left out. Show that it cannot be a Nash equilibrium for one firm to charge marginal cost when the other charges something above marginal cost.

[5]The model is due to D. Kreps and J. Scheinkman, "Quantity Precommitment and Bertrand Competition Yield Cournot Outcomes", *Bell Journal of Economics* (Autumn 1983): 326–337.

second stage than the capacity built in the first stage. If the cost of building capacity is sufficiently high, it turns out that the sub game-perfect equilibrium of this sequential game leads to the same outcome as the Nash equilibrium of the Cournot model.

To see this result, we will analyze the game using backward induction. Consider the second-stage pricing game supposing the firms have already built capacities $\bar{q}_A$ and $\bar{q}_B$ in the first stage. Let $\bar{P}$ be the price that would prevail when production is at capacity for both firms. A situation in which

$$P_A = P_B < \bar{P} \tag{14.7}$$

is not a Nash equilibrium. At this price, total quantity demanded exceeds total capacity, so firm *A* could increase its profits by raising price slightly and still selling $\bar{q}_A$. Similarly,

$$P_A = P_B > \bar{P} \tag{14.8}$$

is not a Nash equilibrium because now total sales fall short of capacity. At least one firm (say, firm *A*) is selling less than its capacity. By cutting price slightly, firm *A* can increase its profits by selling up to its capacity, $\bar{q}_A$. Hence, the Nash equilibrium of this second-stage game is for firms to choose the price at which quantity demanded exactly equals the total capacity built in the first stage[6]

$$P_A = P_B = \bar{P} \tag{14.9}$$

Anticipating that the price will be set such that firms sell all their capacity, the first-stage capacity-choice game is essentially the same as the Cournot game. The equilibrium quantities, price, and profits will thus be the same as in the Cournot game.

The principal lesson of the two-stage capacity/price game is that, even with Bertrand price competition, decisions made prior to this final (price-setting) stage of a game can have an important impact on market behavior. We will see this theme raised several times later in the chapter.

Comparing the Bertrand and Cournot Results

The contrast between the Bertrand and Cournot models is striking. The Bertrand model predicts competitive outcomes in a duopoly situation, whereas the Cournot model predicts prices above marginal cost and positive profits; that is, an outcome somewhere between competition and monopoly. These results suggest that actual behavior in duopoly markets may exhibit a wide variety of outcomes depending on the precise way in which competition occurs. The range of possibilities expands yet further if we add product differentiation or tacit collusion (issues we will study later in the chapter) to the model. Determining the competitiveness of a particular real-world industry is therefore a matter for careful empirical work, as discussed in Application 14.1.

Despite the differences between the Bertrand and Cournot models, the games offer some common insights. Indeed, the equilibrium outcomes from the two games resemble that from the Prisoners' Dilemma. The Nash equilibrium in all three games is not the best outcome for the players. Players could do better if they could cooperate on an outcome with lower outputs in Cournot, higher prices in Bertrand, or being Silent in

[6]For completeness, it should be noted that there is no pure-strategy Nash equilibrium of the second-stage game with unequal prices ($P_A \neq P_B$). The low-price firm would have an incentive to raise its price and/or the high-price firm would have an incentive to lower its price. For large capacities, there may be a complicated mixed-strategy Nash equilibrium, but this can be ruled out by supposing the cost of building capacity is sufficiently high.

the Prisoners' Dilemma. But cooperation is not stable because players have an individual incentive to deviate. In equilibrium of both the Cournot and Bertrand games, firms in a sense compete too hard for their own good (to the benefit of consumers, of course).

Product Differentiation

Up to this point, we have assumed that firms in an imperfectly competitive market all produce the same good. Consumers are indifferent about which firm's output they buy, and the law of one price holds. These assumptions may not be true in many real-world markets. Firms often devote considerable resources to make their products different from those of their competitors through such devices as quality and style variations, warranties and guarantees, special service features, and product advertising. These activities require firms to use additional resources, and firms choose to do so if profits are thereby increased. Product variation also results in a relaxation of the law of one price, since now the market consists of goods that vary from firm to firm and consumers may have preferences about which supplier to patronize.

Market Definition

That possibility introduces a certain fuzziness into what we mean by the "market for a good", since now there are many closely related, but not identical, products. For example, if toothpaste brands vary somewhat from supplier to supplier, should we consider all these products to be in the same market or should we differentiate among fluoridated products, gels, striped toothpaste, smokers' toothpaste, and so forth? Although this question is of great practical importance in industry studies, we do not pursue it here. Instead, we assume that the market is composed of a few slightly differentiated products that can be usefully grouped together because they are more substitutable for each other than for goods outside the group. More precisely, cross-price elasticities of demand are very large for the products in a group and low between products inside the group and products outside. Although this definition has its own ambiguities (arguments about the definition of a product group often dominate antitrust lawsuits, for example), it should suffice for our purposes.

Bertrand Model with Differentiated Products

For the moment, we will take as given the products in the product group under consideration and their characteristics. Below we will analyze the question of how differentiated a firm might want to make its product, including the nature of the product's design, its quality, and how much it is advertised.

One way to model differentiated products is to specify demand curves that are functions of the product's own price and also of the price of the other good. For example, if there are assumed to be two firms, A and B, each producing a single differentiated product, we might have a demand curve for firm A such as

$$q_A = \frac{1}{2} - P_A + P_B \qquad \{14.10\}$$

and for firm B such as

$$q_B = \frac{1}{2} - P_B + P_A \qquad \{14.11\}$$

A firm's demand is decreasing in its own price and increasing in the price of the other good. For example, the higher firm *B*'s price, the more of its consumers switch over and buy from *A*. Demand curves such as in Equation 14.10 and Equation 14.11 can be built up from models of individual consumer behavior, as in Application 14.3: *Competition on the Beach*.

MICROQUIZ 14.3

1 In Figure 14-3, how would an increase in *B*'s marginal cost shift its best-response function? Would it shift *A*'s? On a graph, indicate where the new Nash equilibrium might be.

2 On a graph, show how the best-response functions would shift and where the new Nash equilibrium would be if both firms' marginal costs increased by the same amount. What about a cost decrease? What about an increase in the demand intercept above $\frac{1}{2}$? What about a decrease in substitutability between the two goods?

Given the demand curves in Equation 14.10 and Equation 14.11 and some assumptions about costs, we could solve for the Nash equilibrium of a game in which firms choose price simultaneously, that is, a Bertrand game with differentiated, rather than homogeneous, products. With differentiated products, the profit functions are smooth, so one can use marginal analysis to compute the best-response functions, similar to the analysis of the Cournot model. Rather than working through the details of the computations, see Figure 14-3, which shows what the graphical solution for Nash equilibrium tends to look like in the typical Bertrand game with differentiated products. The best-response functions show the profit-maximizing price for a firm given a price charged by its competitor. The best-response functions tend to be upward-sloping: an increase in, for example, *B*'s price increases *A*'s demand, which

FIGURE 14-3 Bertrand Model with Differentiated Products *Given demand curves for differentiated products such as Equation 14.10 and Equation 14.11 and given assumptions about costs, one can derive best-response functions such as pictured here. A firm's best-response function gives the profit-maximizing price for a firm given a price charged by its competitor. Best-response functions are upward-sloping because A, for example, would respond to an increase in B's price, which would raise A's demand, by increasing price. The Nash equilibrium is the point of intersection between the two best-response functions, where A sets a price of P^*_A and B sets a price of P^*_B.*

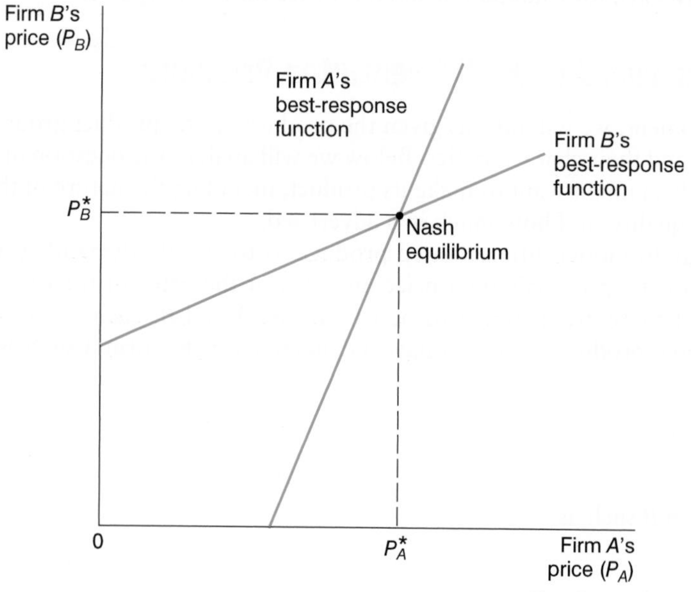

APPLICATION 14.3 *Competition on the Beach*

A simple way to model product differentiation is to assume that firms produce identical products but have different locations. Consumers do not like to travel and would pay a premium to buy from the closest firm.

Hotelling's Line

A widely used model of this type is Hotelling's line, shown in Figure 1.[1] Competition occurs along a linear "beach". The two ice cream stands (*A* and *B*) located on this beach will each draw the nearest customers (because ice cream will melt before a buyer gets back to his or her umbrella). Demand curves such as Equations 14.10 and 14.11 can be generated from this model, assuming that the ice cream stands are located at the ends of the beach and assuming the loss to consumers from melting ice cream is a particular value.

Competition between Politicians

While it is interesting to assume firms' locations are given (at the endpoints of the line or elsewhere) and to use the model to analyze price competition between them, the model can also be used to understand where firms will choose to operate. This can be done in a two-stage model in which firms first choose location then choose price. Assuming that price in the second stage is regulated (say the beach town mandates that ice cream be sold for €2 a cone), the Nash equilibrium of the first-stage location game is for both firms to locate right next to each other in the centre. Both firms get half of the demand that way. Neither has an incentive to deviate because it would get less than half the demand if it moved.

This model has been applied to political campaigns. Citizens locate along an ideological spectrum from the political left to right and prefer to vote for the candidate closest to their ideology. Two candidates choose their positions before the election. The fact that the candidates locate in the centre in the Nash equilibrium of this game helps explain the observation that candidates tend to "run to the centre" as an election progresses.

Television Scheduling

Models like the Hotelling line have been used to study other markets as well. For example, television networks can be thought of as locating their programs in the spectrum of viewer preferences defined along two dimensions – program content and broadcast timing. The Nash-equilibrium locations tend to be at the centre – that is, where there are concentrations of consumers with similar tastes – leading to much duplication of both program types and schedule timing. This has left room for specialized cable channels to pick off viewers with special preferences for programs or viewing times. In many cases (for example, the scheduling of sitcoms), these equilibria tend to be rather stable from season to season. Sometimes scheduling can be quite chaotic, however. For example, the scheduling of local news programs tends to fluctuate greatly, each station jockeying to gain only temporary advantage.[2]

FIGURE 1 Hotelling's Beach *Consumers are located uniformly along the line segment from 0 to 1. Firms A and B locate somewhere within the line segment. A variety of Nash equilibria are possible for this location game, depending on assumptions about the cost of travel for consumers.*

To Think About

1. How does a firm's location give it some pricing power among nearby consumers? Would such power exist if the costs of "traveling" were zero?
2. In 1972, the US Federal Trade Commission brought a complaint against Kellogg, General Foods, and General Mills, claiming that their proliferation of breakfast-cereal varieties left no room for the entry of competitors and allowed them to earn near monopoly profits. How might you think about the characteristics of cereal as belonging on a Hotelling line? Explain how the product-proliferation strategy might work.

[1]H. Hotelling, "Stability in Competition", *Economic Journal* (March 1929): 41–57.

[2]For an analysis of why no pure-strategy Nash equilibrium may exist in this situation, see M. Cancian, A. Bills, and T. Bergstrom, "Hotelling Location Problems with Directional Constraints: An Application to Television News Scheduling", *Journal of Industrial Economics* (March 1995): 121–123.

would lead *A* to respond by raising its price. This contrasts with the Cournot case, where the best-response functions were downward-sloping (see Figure 14-2). Whether the best-response functions are upward- or downward-sloping, the Nash equilibrium is given by their intersection.

Product Selection

The preceding analysis took the products' characteristics as given. But product characteristics – including color, size, functionality, quality of materials, etc. – are strategic choices for the firms just as are price and quantity. Application 14.3: *Competition on the Beach* suggests one formal way of thinking about a firm's choice of product characteristics. Consider a two-stage game in which firms choose product characteristics in the first stage and price (in the Bertrand model, the choice would be quantity in the Cournot model) in the second. In the application, a firm's choice of product characteristics is modeled as choosing a location on a Hotelling line (see Figure 1 in the application). Consumers are located along the line. The line can be thought of in the literal sense of differentiation in geographic location. Or it may represent differentiation in product space, for example different points on the color spectrum from red to violet.

There are two offsetting effects at work in the first-stage product-characteristics game. One effect is that firms prefer to locate near the greatest concentration of consumers because that is where demand is greatest. For example, if consumers' favorite colors are beige and metallic grey, carmakers will tend to produce beige and metallic-grey cars. This effect leads firms to locate near each other, that is, to produce very similar products. There is an offsetting strategic effect. Firms realize that if their products are close substitutes, they will compete aggressively in the second-stage price game. Locating further apart softens competition, leading to higher prices. This effect is shown in Figure 14-4. An increase in product differentiation between the two firms shifts their best-response functions out and leads to a Nash equilibrium with higher prices for both. Returning to the car example, if one firm happens to produce mostly saloons, the other might decide to specialize in another niche, say sport-utility vehicles. There may be little substitution between the two car classes, leaving a firm free to raise prices without fear of losing many customers to its competitor. How the two offsetting effects balance out is ambiguous. Depending on the specifics of the market, the sub game-perfect equilibrium of the two-stage game may involve the firmslocating close together in some cases and far apart in others.

If firms' products become too specialized, they risk the entry of another firm that might locate in the product space between them. We will take up the question of entry and entry deterrence in a later section.

Search Costs

Prices may differ across goods if products are differentiated. For example, one good may be constructed out of more durable materials than another, and the firm producing the higher-quality good may charge a higher price. Prices may differ even across homogeneous products if consumers are not fully informed about prices. One way to model imperfect price information is to assume that consumers know nothing about the prices any firms charge but can learn about the prices by paying a search cost. A search cost is the cost to the consumer in terms of time, effort, telephone or Internet charges, and/or fuel costs to contact a shop to learn the price it charges for the good. The introduction of search costs is a departure from the analysis in previous chapters, where it was implicitly assumed throughout that all consumers knew the prices for all goods.

There are many possible outcomes, depending on exactly how search costs are specified. An equilibrium that can arise if some consumers have low search costs and others have high search costs is for some firms to specialize in serving the

FIGURE 14-4 Increase in Product Differentiation Softens Price Competition *Two firms initially produce moderately differentiated products. The best-response functions for the game involving the simultaneous choice of prices are given by BR_A for A and BR_B for B. If the differentiation between the firms' products is increased, the best-response functions shift out to BR'_A and BR'_B. The Nash equilibrium (bold dot) shifts to one involving higher prices.*

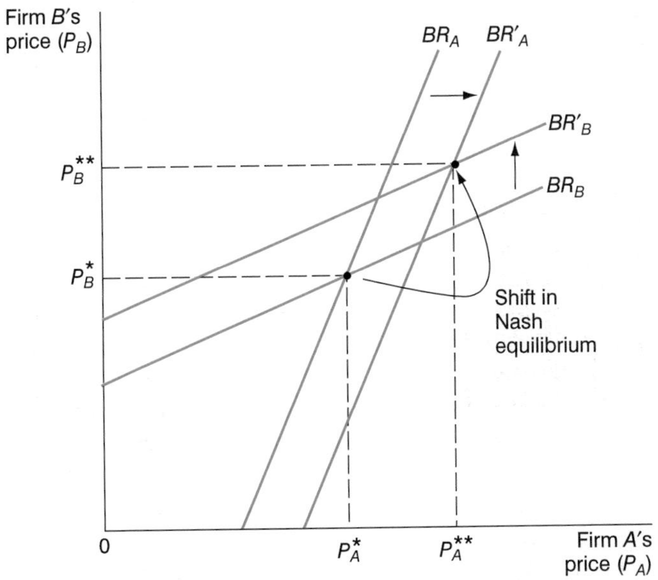

informed (low-search-cost) consumers at low prices and for other firms to specialize in serving the uninformed (high-search-cost) consumers at high prices.[7] The uninformed consumers are "ripped off" in the sense of paying a higher price than they would at another shop, but it is simply too costly for them to shop more to learn where the low prices are. Only by luck do some of them end up at a low-price retailer. How the conclusions of such a model might change with the growing use of the Internet for consumer search is explored in Application 14.4: *Searching the Internet*.

Advertising

Advertising can be classified into two types. A first type, informative advertising, provides "hard" information about prices, product attributes, and perhaps store locations and hours of operation. Classified ads in newspapers are a good example of this type of advertising. Economists tend to view informative advertising favorably, as a way to lower consumer search costs, increasing transparency and thus firms' competitiveness in the market. A second type of advertising, persuasive advertising, attempts to convince consumers to buy one product rather than another close – perhaps perfect – substitute. Persuasive advertising tends to involve "soft" information, perhaps involving images of attractive people enjoying the product, perhaps leading consumers to make positive associations with the images when they consume the product. Examples include television advertising of lager beers, some of which are chemically almost identical to cheaper, unadvertised beers. Some economists view persuasive advertising less favorably, as a way to soften price competition by increasing apparent rather than real product differentiation. This may provide one rationale for government bans on advertising. However, most studies show that such bans may harm consumers by leading to higher average prices.[8]

One glance at advertising in various media suggests that advertising is an important element of strategic competition between firms. The same strategic effects that arose in our discussion of investments in product differentiation also arise with advertising.

Tacit Collusion

We argued above that the Cournot and Bertrand games bear some resemblance to the Prisoners' Dilemma in that if the firms could cooperate to restrict output or raise prices, they could increase the profits of both, just as the players in the Prisoners' Dilemma would benefit from cooperating on being Silent. In Chapter 6 we concluded that if the Prisoners' Dilemma were repeated an indefinite number of times, the participants can devise ways to adopt more cooperative strategic choices. A similar possibility arises with the Cournot and Bertrand games. Repetition of these games offers a mechanism for the firms to earn higher profits by pursuing a monopoly pricing policy. The reader may want to review the discussion of indefinitely repeated games from Chapter 6 since the following analysis is closely related.

MICROQUIZ 14.4

Consider a two-stage model in which firms advertise in the first stage and then compete by choosing prices for differentiated products in the second stage.

1. What strategic effects would come into play if advertising increases the chance that consumers learn about both products rather than just knowing about one or the other?
2. What strategic effects would come into play if advertising persuades consumers that the product occupies a distinct niche?

[7] S. Salop and J. Stiglitz, "Bargains and Ripoffs: A Model of Monopolistically Competitive Price Dispersion", *Review of Economic Studies* (October 1977): 493–510.

[8] See, for example, L. Benham, "The Effects of Advertising on the Price of Eyeglasses", *Journal of Law and Economics* (October 1972): 337–352 and J. Milyo and J. Waldfogel, "The Effect of Price Advertising on Prices: Evidence in the Wake of 44 Liquormart", *American Economic Review* (December 1999): 1081–1096.

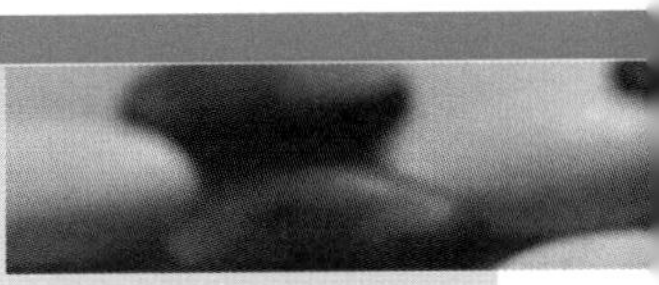

APPLICATION 14.4 *Searching the Internet*

The interplay between the Internet and consumer search costs is complex. On the one hand, the Internet dramatically lowers the cost of getting a price quote. Rather than driving to a store, the consumer can just make a few mouse clicks. In addition, the Internet makes it easier for firms to enter the market, since the cost of setting up a website may be lower than a "bricks and mortar" store. Entry should be expected to increase competitiveness in the market and result in lower prices. There is a twist to this story. Since starting up a store is as easy as setting up a website, fly-by-night firms using questionable sales tactics can proliferate because they only need to make a few sales to a few unsuspecting customers to be profitable. Firms can also use Internet technology against consumers to frustrate what should be efficient searches.

Price Dispersion for Books Online

It is hard to imagine a more homogeneous product than a particular book title. Yet studies of Internet bookstores indicate large price differences across retailers. One study found that the difference between the highest and lowest price for *New York Times* best-sellers was around $8, or 65 per cent of average price.[1] Large savings were available to consumers who were willing to shop at one of the alternatives to Amazon and Barnes & Noble, the two largest online bookstores, accounting for 80 per cent of online book sales during the period studied (1999–2000). The large price differences may stem from consumers' inability to use price-comparison sites efficiently to find smaller retailers willing to undercut the big bookstores' prices. Or consumers may stick with the large bookstores for fear of being "ripped off" by a retailer with an unknown reputation. As we will see in the discussion of "shady" strategies used by retailers of computer chips, such fears may be well founded.

Bait and Switch for Computer Chips

Ellison and Ellison discuss the example of the sale of computer processors and memory chips sold by retailers listed on various online price-comparison sites.[2] Price was the key advertised element on these sites: firms were listed in order from lowest to highest item price. But other product attributes were not listed there, including shipping costs, warranty and return policies, and product quality. Some retailers were found to have adopted the strategy of listing their low-quality items at very low prices but then trying to get the consumer to trade up to higher-quality substitutes when they clicked through to the retailer's website by indicating how lousy the low-quality item was, a sort of bait-and-switch strategy. For those consumers who truly wanted the lowest-quality items, this strategy led to considerable transparency. As a result, these consumers were extremely price sensitive, with estimated price elasticities on the order of −25 or more. Elasticities were less extreme for higher-quality items that required more searching on individual websites. Other retailers used the strategy of listing an item for $1 but then adding on a $40 shipping fee. Still other retailers used the strategy of tricking the algorithm used by the price-comparison sites into thinking they had zero prices, thus moving them high up on the list, even though they were actually among the higher-priced retailers.

The strategies for selling computer chips discussed above may be shady but are not illegal. Out-and-out fraud also plagues online shoppers. The most common frauds reported to the US Federal Trade Commission include Internet auction items that are never shipped, "free" Internet access services that lock the consumer into long-term contracts for high fees, and various scams to obtain consumers' credit card and bank account numbers.[3]

To Think About

1 How might a price-comparison website earn revenue? What motives would it have to make searches more or less transparent? How could the price-comparison website try to eliminate some of the retailers' obfuscation if it wanted to?

2 Compared to online retailers, "bricks and mortar" stores have the added expense of the physical space for consumers to see the items sold, but the "touch and feel factor" may be important for consumers' shopping experience. Describe the potential sales

(*Continued*)

problem of some online retailers in that an increase in the sales of one of a its products, results in a decrease in the sales of another item also produced by the same company. How might the manufacturer design contracts with online and "bricks and mortar" retailers to prevent this problem? What are the other relative cost/quality advantages of one form of retailing over the other?

[1]K. Clay, R. Krishnan, and E. Wolff, "Pricing Strategies on the Web: Evidence from the Online Book Industry", *Journal of Industrial Economics* (December 2001): 521–539.

[2]G. Ellison and S. F. Ellison, "Search, Obfuscation and Price Elasticities on the Internet", National Bureau of Economic Research working paper no. 10570 (June 2004).

[3]US Federal Trade Commission, "Dot Cons", October 2000, http://www.ftc.gov/bcp/conline/pubs/online/dotcons.htm, accessed on 18 October, 2005.

It should be emphasized that here we are adopting a non-cooperative approach to the collusion question by exploring models of "tacit" collusion. That is, we use game theory concepts to see whether firms can achieve monopoly profits through *self-enforcing* equilibrium strategies. A contrasting approach would be to assume that firms can form a cartel in which firms are bound to specific outputs and prices by *externally enforced* contracts. Governments have occasionally allowed cartel arrangements to be legally binding, in cases ranging from British shipping cartels in the 1800s to present-day professional sports leagues.[9] Ordinarily however, such cartels are illegal. In the United Kingdom, the Office of Fair Trading enforces action against cartels which is prohibited by the Competition Act 1998, and Article 81 of the EC Treaty. In addition, the Enterprise Act 2002 makes it a criminal offence for individuals to dishonestly take part in certain specified cartels, essentially those that involve price fixing, market sharing, limitation of production or supply or bid rigging. Similarly in the United States Section I of the Sherman Act of 1890 outlaws "conspiracies in restraint of trade", so would-be cartel members may expect a visit from law-enforcement officials. Similar laws exist in many other countries. Cartel arrangements may run into the same problems of potential instability as tacitly collusive arrangements, with cartel members secretly trying to chisel on the cartel arrangement when possible. Real-world markets often exhibit aspects of both tacit and explicit collusion, as Application 14.5: *The Great British Rip-Off*? shows.

To explore the ideas about the stability of collusion more fully (lessons which can be applied to the stability of cartels as well), we will focus on the case of the Bertrand game with homogeneous products (though the Cournot case would provide similar insights). Recall the Nash equilibrium of the game when it was repeated only once was marginal cost pricing for both firms, $P_A = P_B = c$. We will determine the conditions under which the two firms can earn the monopoly profit by tacitly colluding in a repeated game. We will use the sub game-perfect equilibrium concept to make sure collusion is not sustained by threats or promises that are not credible.

Finite Time Horizon

With any definite number of repetitions, the equilibrium is the same as when the game is not repeated. (We found this with the Prisoners' Dilemma in Chapter 6 as well.)

[9]On shipping cartels, see F. Scott Morton, "Entry and Predation: British Shipping Cartels, 1879–1929", *Journal of Economics and Management Strategy* (Winter 1997): 679–724. Note that, even if the cartel arrangements are not legally binding, they may be enforced with threats of violence, as with illegal drug cartels.

APPLICATION 14.5 *The Great British Rip-Off?*

Replica Football Shirts

In recent years as the English Premier Football League has grown popular on a world scale, so have sales of replica football shirts. This popular form of merchandising has become hugely lucrative to the larger clubs, and is worth millions of pounds in global income. Around 90 per cent of the sales of each new replica kit are in its first year, and 90 per cent of these sales are between the pre-season launch and Christmas.

However, doubt has always persisted amongst fans that they are being ripped-off by a cynical marketing exercise that sees club strips and logos change not only each session, but also sometimes during a season, and again for important European matches. In 2000, Manchester United actually launched five new kits after signing a £30 million sponsorship deal with Vodafone. It is now very big business with larger clubs having supermarket-sized merchandising shops within their grounds.[1]

During 2000 and 2001 suppliers of certain replica kit, including the top selling England and Manchester United shirts, were engaged in unlawful price-fixing. The Office of Fair Trading (OFT) found that ten companies had entered into agreements to set a minimum retail price in breach of the Chapter I Prohibition of the Competition Act 1998. To reflect the seriousness of the infringement, financial penalties totaling £18.6 million were imposed in August 2003. Among the businesses fined were JJB Sports (£8.373 m), Umbro (£6.641 m), Manchester United (£1.652 m), Allsports (£1.35 m), and even the FA (£198 000 reduced to £158 000 by leniency).

The OFT unearthed evidence of several agreements regarding the sale of certain England, Manchester United, Chelsea, Celtic, and Nottingham Forest replica kit manufactured under license by Umbro. These agreements were apparently policed through informal meetings and the monitoring of Umbro's retail customers, who, in some cases, were threatened with stock cancellations if they failed to stick to the agreed prices. Before the investigation into price-fixing began, it was difficult to buy an adult short-sleeved England shirt for less than £39.99. By Euro 2004, they were widely available for as little as £25.

The Chapter I prohibition of the Competition Act 2000, makes it illegal for companies to enter into agreements which have the object or effect of preventing, restricting or distorting competition. The OFT can also impose a penalty of 10 per cent of a firm's turnover for each year of infringement up to a maximum of three years.

It's not just the Big Boys

Collusive agreements are not just the prerogative of large national or global firms. In March 2004 nine roofing contractors were found by the OFT to have agreed to fix the prices of repair, maintenance, and improvement work for flat roofing in the West Midlands through collusive tendering in the period 2000–2002. They were fined nearly £300 000 in total.

These relatively small building firms were found to have been involved in a series of individual agreements or concerted practices in tendering for work on a number of schools, a community library, a shopping center, and a car park. The OFT concluded that the firms agreed to set tender prices so as to restrict or distort competition, meaning that local buyers were unable to obtain a fair competitive price when they sort out estimates and tenders for flat roof building work.

Such stitch-ups by businesses to fix prices by way of rigging tendering are among the most serious infringements of the Competition Act. Interestingly, financial penalties that are imposed can be subject to a "leniency policy" which can reduce any penalties for those who come forward with information in Competition Act cases.[2] Here, "spilling the beans" can be rewarded and Briggs Cladding & Roofing Limited were granted 100 per cent leniency, and Howard Evans (Roofing) Limited had its financial penalty reduced by 50 per cent.

To Think About

1 Why did those in the replica football shirt business opt for such an illegal scheme rather than

(Continued)

settling for some other form of tacit collusion? Consider what sort of control the football clubs might be able to exercise over the counterfeit market, and how price rigging might undermine their success.

2 Prosecutions in both the football replica shirt, and the roofing cases was considerably helped by one firm "spilling the beans" on the others, and getting a leniency opt-out. How fair is this approach? Are there any contradictions in it? Should it be extended and developed?

[1]When Newcastle United signed Alan Shearer, for example, the club made £250 000 on the *day* of this signing, just in terms of Shearer replica shirt sales. When Inter Milan, in contrast, signed Ronaldo the club had prepared no shirts carrying the Brazilian's favoured No. 9. Instead, counterfeit No. 9 shirts appeared to satisfy local demand, forcing the club to play their new star as a No. 10 in order to cash in later on official shirt sales.

[2]Total immunity from financial penalty is available to the *first* member of the cartel to come forward with relevant information. Significant reductions in penalty of up to 50 per cent are available in where a firm, although it's not the first to come forward with information, does so *before* the OFT has given written notice of its proposal to make a decision that the Chapter I prohibition has been infringed, or it would have qualified for total immunity had it not been the instigator or leader of the cartel or compelled others to join.

Using backward induction to solve for the sub game-perfect Nash equilibrium, no matter how the game was played up to the last period, the players will play the Nash equilibrium $P_A = P_B = c$ in the last period. Promises to play any other way are not credible. Because a similar argument also applies to any period prior to the last one, we can conclude that the only sub game-perfect equilibrium is one in which firms charge the competitive price in every period. The assumptions of the Bertrand model make tacit collusion impossible over any finite period.

Indefinite Time Horizon

If firms are viewed as having an indefinite time horizon, matters change significantly. In Chapter 6, we noted that the time horizon could be indefinite for two reasons. One is that there is uncertainty each period about whether the market opportunity will continue into the next period. This is the interpretation we pursued in Chapter 6. For completeness here, we will examine the alternative interpretation, that is, that the market continues with certainty each period but for an infinite number of periods. Let r now stand for the per-period interest rate (in Chapter 6 it stood for the probability the game continues into the next period rather than stopping for good). Firms care about the stream of profits over the game.

With an infinite number of periods, there is no "final" period for backward induction to unravel collusive strategies. Consider the trigger strategies in which each firm sets the monopoly price P_M in every period unless a firm has undercut this price previously. If any firm has undercut, players enter a price-war phase in which they set price to marginal cost c from then on. The threat of charging marginal cost for the rest of the game is credible, since this is equivalent to playing the Nash equilibrium of the one-period game over and over. To show that the proposed trigger strategies constitute a sub game-perfect equilibrium, it remains only to show that no firm has an incentive to undercut the collusive price P_M in a given period. Suppose firm A thinks about cheating in a given period. Knowing that firm B will choose $P_B = P_M$, A can set its price slightly below P_M and, in this period, obtain the entire market for itself. It will thereby earn (almost) the entire monopoly profit (π_M) in this period but will earn nothing in subsequent periods since undercutting will trigger a price war with marginal-cost prices. If instead of deviating, firm A continues with the collusive equilibrium, it earns its share of the monopoly profit ($\pi_M/2$) forever. Because the present value[10] of the stream of profits in the collusive equilibrium is

$$\frac{\pi_M}{2} \cdot \frac{1}{r} \tag{14.12}$$

cheating will be unprofitable if

$$\pi_M < \frac{\pi_M}{2} \cdot \frac{1}{r} \tag{14.13}$$

This condition holds for values of r less than $\frac{1}{2}$. We can therefore conclude that the trigger strategies constitute a sub game-perfect equilibrium for sufficiently low interest rates. To provide more intuition behind Equation 14.13, think about the interest rate as a measure of impatience. Impatient people like to buy things with their money immediately rather than waiting, so they need to be promised a large repayment, that is, a high interest rate, in order to get them to save. If the interest rate in 14.13 is high, meaning that firms are impatient, a firm would care more about the gain from undercutting, since this gain would be earned in the present period, than it would care about the loss of profits from the punishment, since this loss comes in the future, which the firm does not care about as much. Therefore, collusion would not be sustainable. Equation 14.13 says in effect that firms have to be patient enough to sustain collusion.

It should be emphasized that collusion sustained by the trigger strategies is tacit – firms never actually have to meet in the proverbial "smoke-filled room" to adopt strategies that yield monopoly profits – and is self-enforcing – firms do not need an external authority to enforce the outcome.

Generalizations and Limitations

It is straightforward to extend the analysis to allow for any number of firms, N. The profit from deviating would be the same as before, π_M. The present profit from continuing with the collusive equilibrium from Equation 14.12 becomes

$$\frac{\pi_M}{N} \cdot \frac{1}{r} \tag{14.14}$$

since in equilibrium with N firms, each firm only obtains $1/N$ of the monopoly profit. Thus the new condition for cheating to be unprofitable becomes

$$\pi_M < \frac{\pi_M}{N} \cdot \frac{1}{r} \tag{14.15}$$

This condition holds for r less than $1/N$. The higher N is, the lower $1/N$ is, and the less likely it is for the prevailing interest rate r to be less than $1/N$. Therefore, an increase in the number of firms makes it harder to sustain tacit collusion. What is bad for firms is good for consumers and society, since, if firms cannot tacitly collude, they will charge lower prices, raising consumer surplus and social welfare. This provides additional justification for antitrust authorities to prevent mergers where they think collusion might be a possibility.

The contrast between the competitive results of the Bertrand model and the monopoly results of the tacit-collusion model suggests that the viability of collusion in

[10]For a discussion of the present-value concept, see Chapter 16 and its appendix on compound interest.

game-theory models is very sensitive to the particular assumptions made. It was assumed that a firm can easily detect whether another has cheated. In practice, however, the deviator may cut price secretly, and other buyers may not learn about the deviation until much later. In the model, a lag in detection is similar to increasing the period length, which in turn is similar to increasing the interest rate (to see this, compare the interest repayment you would ask if you lent money for one month versus one year versus one decade). It is easy to see from the condition in Equation 14.13 that increasing the interest rate reduces the right-hand side and therefore makes collusion harder to sustain. Other firms may only learn about the price cut indirectly, perhaps because they see their own demands have fallen. To deter cheating in this case, firms may have to enter into price wars in demand downturns even if no firm has actually cheated.

If firms compete in quantities as in the Cournot model, or if firms produce differentiated rather than homogeneous products, the equation determining whether collusion can be sustained is slightly different from Equation 14.13. The profit from deviating on the left-hand side of 14.13 may not be as high because the deviator cannot capture the whole market with a tiny price cut. This effect would make collusion easier. The lost profits from punishment on the right-hand side of 14.13 may not be as severe because firms still earn positive profits in the Nash equilibrium they revert to following a deviation. This effect would make collusion harder. The two effects work in opposite directions, so whether collusion is easier or harder to sustain with quantity competition or with differentiated products compared to the basic Bertrand model is unclear.

Other categories of models have the two firms competing in several different markets. For example, two airlines might compete on a number of different city-pair routes. If collusion is harder to sustain on some routes than others, say, because there is less information on some routes about competitors' prices, the threat of a price war on all routes for undercutting on one may allow them to leverage the collusion that is easily sustained in some markets to the others. As might be imagined, results from the wide variety of models of tacit collusion are quite varied.[11] In all such models, the notions of Nash and sub game-perfect equilibria continue to play an important role in identifying whether tacit collusion can arise from strategic choices that appear to be viable.

Entry and Exit

The possibility of new firms entering an industry plays an important part in the theory of perfectly competitive price determination. Free entry ensures that any long-run profits are eliminated by new entrants and that firms produce at the low points of their long-run average cost curves. With relatively few firms, the first of these forces continues to operate. To the extent that entry is possible, long-run profits are constrained. If entry is completely costless, long-run economic profits are zero (as in the competitive case).

The treatment of entry and exit in earlier chapters left little room for strategic thinking. A potential entrant was concerned only with the relationship between prevailing market price and its own (average or marginal) costs. We assumed that making that comparison involved no special problems. Similarly, we assumed that firms will promptly leave a market they find to be unprofitable. Upon closer inspection, however, the entry and exit issue can become considerably more complex. The fundamental problem is that a firm wishing to enter or exit a market must make some conjecture about how its action will affect market price in subsequent periods. Making these conjectures obviously requires the firm to consider what its rivals will do. What appears

[11]See J. Tirole, *Theory of Industrial Organization* (Cambridge, MA: MIT Press, 1988), chap. 6.

to be a relatively straightforward decision, comparing price and average cost, may therefore involve a number of strategic ploys, especially when a firm's information about its rivals is imperfect.

Sunk Costs and Commitment

Many game-theory models of the entry process stress the importance of a firm's commitment to a specific market. If the nature of production requires that firms make specific capital investments in order to operate in a market and if these cannot easily be shifted to other uses, any firm that makes such investments has committed itself to being a market participant. As we saw in Chapter 8, expenditures on such investments are called *sunk costs*. Sunk costs might include expenditures on items such as unique types of equipment (for example, a newsprint-making machine) or on job-specific training for workers (developing the skills to use the newsprint machine). Sunk costs have many characteristics of fixed costs in that these costs are incurred even if no output is produced. Rather than being incurred periodically as are many fixed costs (heating the factory), these costs are incurred only once, as part of the entry process. More generally, any "sunk" decision is a decision that cannot be reversed later. When the firm makes such a decision, it has made a commitment in the market, which may have important consequences for its strategic behavior.

First-Mover Advantages

Although at first glance it might seem that incurring sunk costs by making the commitment to serve a market puts a firm at a disadvantage, in many models that is not the case. Rather, one firm can often stake out a claim to a market by making a commitment to serve it and in the process limit the kinds of actions its rivals find profitable. Many game-theory models, therefore, stress the advantage of moving first.

As a simple numerical example, consider again the Cournot model introduced earlier, wherein two springs can produce water costlessly and face market demand given by $Q = 120 - P$ (see Equation 14.1). We found that the Nash equilibrium quantities were 40 (thousand gallons) each, and firms each earned €1600. Suppose now, instead, that firm *A* has the option of moving first and committing to an output which *B* observes before *B* moves. We will use backward induction to solve for the sub game-perfect equilibrium of this sequential game. We thus solve for *B*'s equilibrium strategy first. Firm *B* will maximize profits given what *A* has done. We have solved for this best-response function already, in Equation 14.6, repeated here for reference:

$$q_B = \frac{120 - q_A}{2} \qquad \{14.16\}$$

Firm *A* can use this to compute the net demand for its own spring's water:

$$q_A = 120 - q_B - P = 120 - \left(\frac{120 - q_A}{2}\right) - P = 60 + \frac{q_A}{2} - P \qquad \{14.17\}$$

Solving for *P* gives

$$P = 60 - \frac{q_A}{2} \qquad \{14.18\}$$

Given this expression for A's inverse demand curve, it can be shown,[12] or taken as given, that A's marginal revenue curve is

$$60 - q_A \qquad \{14.19\}$$

Firm A maximizes its profit by choosing the quantity at which its marginal revenue in Equation 14.19 equals its marginal cost (recall 0 because production is costless), resulting in an output of $q_A = 60$. Given that firm A's output is 60, firm B chooses to produce

$$q_B = \frac{120 - q_A}{2} = \frac{120 - 60}{2} = 30 \qquad \{14.20\}$$

With total output of 90, spring water sells for €30, firm A's total profit is €1800 (= 60 × €30) – an improvement over the €1600 it earned in the Nash equilibrium of the Cournot model. Firm B's profit has correspondingly been reduced to €900 – a sign of the disadvantage faced by a later mover. Sometimes this solution is referred to as a **Stackelberg equilibrium**, after the German economist who first discovered the advantage of moving first in the sequential version of the Cournot model.

Stackelberg Equilibrium Subgame-perfect equilibrium of the sequential version of the Cournot game.

FIGURE 14-5 Stackelberg Equilibrium and Entry Deterrence *If firm A gets to move first, it effectively gets to choose a point on firm B's best-response function. Firm A will choose the point that maximizes its profit, the point labeled "Stackelberg equilibrium" involving $q_A = 60$. Increasing its output from the Cournot level to the Stackelberg level reduces B's profit. Firm A may wish to commit to an even higher output than in the Stackelberg equilibrium if this reduces B's anticipated profits below its fixed entry cost and thus deters B's entry.*

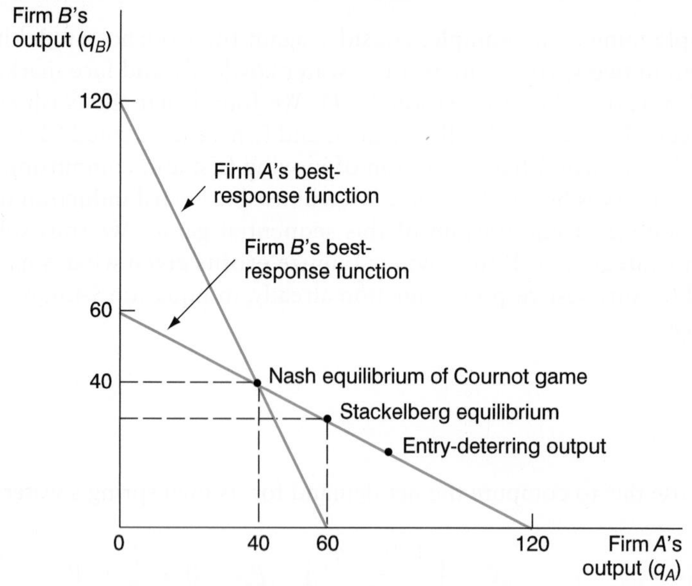

[12]Firm A's total revenue function is

$$P \cdot q_A = (60 - q_A/2) \cdot q_A = 60q_A - q_A^2/2$$

Differentiating this expression with respect to q_A gives the marginal revenue function $60 - q_A$.

Referring to Figure 14-5, which reproduces the best-response functions from Figure 14-2, if *A* gets to move first – knowing that *B* will choose a best response to its output and thus that the equilibrium point will be somewhere on *B*'s best-response function – *A* chooses the point that maximizes *A*'s profit. This point, the Stackelberg equilibrium, involves higher output for firm *A* than in the Nash equilibrium of the Cournot game. Firm *A*'s benefit from being the first mover is that by committing to a higher output, *A* induces *B* to reduce its output, and a lower output for *B* benefits *A* because price will be higher. The Stackelberg equilibrium is only feasible if *A*'s output decision is sunk, that is, irreversibly made, and observable to *B* before *B* moves. It is only because *A*'s decision is sunk that it is allowed to commit to an action that is not on its own best-response function. If *A* could not commit in this way, the outcome would return to the Nash equilibrium from the Cournot game, with both firms producing 40.

Entry Deterrence

In some cases, first-mover advantages may be large enough to deter all entry by rivals. Intuitively, it seems plausible that the first mover could opt for a very large capacity and thereby discourage all other firms from entering the market. The economic rationality of such a decision is not clear-cut, however. In the Cournot model, for example, the only sure way for one spring owner to deter all entry is to satisfy the total market demand at the firm's marginal and average costs; that is, firm *A* would have to offer $q_A = 120$, resulting in a price of zero, if it were to have a fully successful entry-deterrence strategy. Obviously, such a choice results in zero profits for the firm and would not be profit maximizing. Instead, it would be better for firm *A* to accept some entry.

With economies of scale in production, the possibility for profitable entry deterrence is increased. If the firm that is to move first can adopt a large enough scale of operation, it may be able to limit the scale of the potential entrant. The potential entrant will therefore experience such high average costs that there would be no way for it to earn a profit.

A Numerical Example

The simplest way to incorporate economies of scale into the Cournot model is to assume each spring owner must pay a fixed cost of operations. If that fixed cost is given by €785 (a carefully chosen number!), firm *B* would still find it attractive to enter if firm *A* moves first and opts to produce $q_A = 60$. In this case, firm *B* would earn profits of €115 (= €900 − €785) per period. However, if the first mover opts for $q_A = 64$, this would force firm *B* to choose $q_B = 28$ [= (120 − 64) ÷ 2]. At this combined output of 92, price would be €28 and firm *B* would make negative profits [profits = $TR - TC$ = $(28 \cdot 28) - 785 = -1$] and choose not to enter. Firm *A* would now have the market to itself, obtain a price of €56 (= 120 − 64), and earn profits of €2799 (= $(56 \cdot 64) - 785$). Economies of scale, combined with the ability to move first, provide firm *A* with a very profitable entry-deterring strategy. For this strategy to work, *A* must be able to make its sunk output decision before *B* makes its sunk entry decision.

MICROQUIZ 14.5

1. In the numerical example, suppose *B*'s entry costs were €700 rather than €785. How would this affect *A*'s entry-deterring strategy?
2. Suppose *B*'s entry costs were €910. How would this affect *A*'s entry-deterring strategy?

Limit Pricing

So far, our discussion of strategic considerations in entry decisions has focused on issues of sunk costs and output commitments. A somewhat different approach to the entry-deterrence question concerns the possibility that an incumbent monopoly could deter entry through its pricing policy alone. That is, are there situations where a monopoly might purposely choose a low ("limit") price with the goal of deterring entry into its market?

In most simple cases, the answer is no. The crucial issue is that prices are not usually "sunk". Prices are changed daily or even more frequently in some markets: for example, airlines change their fares on a minute-by-minute basis depending on seat availability. The price charged in one period may have no bearing on the price charged in later periods. If there is no link between the prices charged in different periods, there is no reason for an incumbent monopolist to limit its price before entry since setting a limit price $P_L < P_M$ (where P_M is the monopolist's profit-maximizing price) only reduces its current-period profits without any later strategic benefit.[13]

In richer models, there may be reasons why prices may be related across time. First, if prices are set in a national advertising campaign, it may be difficult to change prices quickly afterwards. For example, a camera manufacturer that advertises in a monthly magazine such as *Popular Photography* may find it difficult to change its price and advertise this price change within the month. Second, firms may face a learning curve, whereby costs fall with accumulated production as workers figure out how to produce more efficiently through experience. In the first study to quantify the learning curve, the cost of producing military aircraft during World War II was found to fall by 20 per cent for every doubling of output.[14] In the presence of a learning curve, a monopolist can reduce its costs by charging a low price and producing a lot initially, and thus be in a position to be an aggressive, low-cost competitor when potential entrants arrive, making entry for them less appealing. Third, there may be costs for consumers to switch between suppliers. Consumers having had a good experience with one product may be reluctant to switch to a product of uncertain quality. Consumers may have signed long-term agreements to stay with a certain supplier, as is the case with many mobile phone contracts. It may simply be a nuisance to contact the old and new suppliers to make the switch. In the presence of such switching costs, the monopolist may build a large customer base initially through low prices, making entry harder because the entrant may have to offer deep discounts to induce the incumbent's "captive" base of consumers to switch.

Incomplete Information

A fourth reason why initial prices may have a strategic effect is that a monopolist may know more about a particular market situation than does a potential entrant, and it may be able to take advantage of its superior knowledge to deter entry. As an example, consider the extensive form illustrated in Figure 14-6. Here, firm *A*, the incumbent monopolist, has an equal chance of having high or low production costs as a result of its past investments and luck. Firm *A* knows its own costs but *B* does not. The profitability of *B*'s entry into the market depends on *A*'s costs – with high costs, *B*'s entry is profitable ($\pi_B = 3$); whereas, if *A* has low costs, entry is unprofitable ($\pi_B = -1$). The situation is said to involve **incomplete information**, that is, at least one of the players is not certain what the payoffs in the game are. We will study games of incomplete information in more detail in Chapter 17. For now, note that the convention in games of incomplete information is to add a third player, "Nature", who chooses *A*'s costs at random.

Incomplete information Some players have information about the game that others do not.

[13]An influential model that can be viewed as an attempt to formalize the limit-pricing story is contestability. According to this model, a market is in equilibrium if incumbents at least break even at the current price and there is no possibility for another firm to make positive profits by entering at a slightly lower price. Incumbents are forced to charge limit prices to prevent entry, sometimes as low as average cost (thus earning zero profit). The implicit assumption that incumbents are forced to maintain the same price before and after entry may be difficult to justify

[14]T. P. Wright, "Factors Affecting the Cost of Airplanes", *Journal of Aeronautical Sciences* (February 1936): 122–128.

What is B to do? Without any further information, using the formula for expected values from Chapter 5, B's expected profit from entering equals the probability A's costs are high, $(\frac{1}{2})$ times B's profit from entering if A's costs are low (3), plus the probability A's costs are low, $(\frac{1}{2})$ times B's profit from entering if A's costs are low (-1), that is 1 $[= (\frac{1}{2})(3) + (\frac{1}{2})(-1)]$. Since this exceeds what B would earn if it didn't enter (0), B will enter if it does not have further information about A's costs.

The particularly intriguing aspects of this game concern whether A can influence B's assessment. If A's costs are low, it would like to tell B this and have B not enter, since A is better off if B does not enter. The difficulty is that even when A's costs are high, A would like to deter B's entry by lying and saying its costs are low. Firm B should not believe A's claim that its costs are low if there is nothing to back the claim up. Charging a low price initially might be a more credible signal. The price would have to be low enough to keep a high-cost A from pretending to be low-cost. That is, the loss to the high-cost A from charging the low price (rather than its monopoly price) would exceed the gain from deterring B's entry by misleading B into thinking that its costs were low. Such a signaling strategy would require the low-cost A to sacrifice some profits initially, but deterring B's entry may be worth it. This provides a possible rationale for setting a low price as an entry-deterrence strategy.

Predatory Pricing

Tools used to study limit pricing can also shed light on the possibility for **predatory pricing**. The difference between limit pricing and predatory pricing is in a sense semantic: limit pricing is a strategy to deter entry of rivals that have not yet entered, while predatory pricing is a strategy to induce exit of rivals that have already entered.

Predatory pricing An incumbent charging a low price in order to induce the exit of a rival.

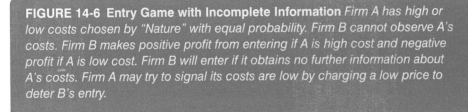

FIGURE 14-6 Entry Game with Incomplete Information *Firm A has high or low costs chosen by "Nature" with equal probability. Firm B cannot observe A's costs. Firm B makes positive profit from entering if A is high cost and negative profit if A is low cost. Firm B will enter if it obtains no further information about A's costs. Firm A may try to signal its costs are low by charging a low price to deter B's entry.*

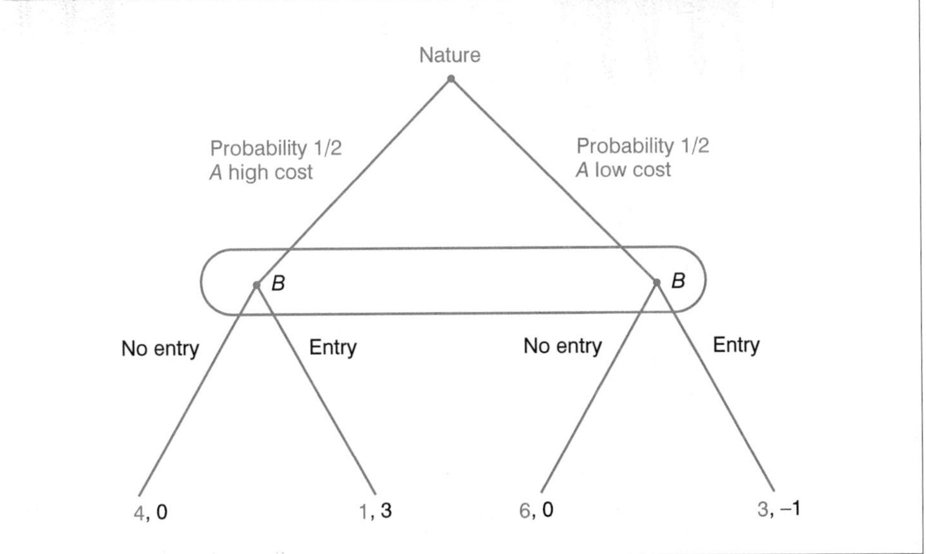

Ever since the formation of the Standard Oil monopoly in the late nineteenth century, part of the mythology of American business is that John D. Rockefeller was able to drive his competitors out of business by charging ruinously low (predatory) prices. Although both the economic logic and the empirical facts behind this version of the Standard Oil story have generally been discounted, the possibility of encouraging exit through predation continues to provide interesting opportunities for theoretical modeling.

The structure of some models of predatory behavior is similar to that used in limit pricing models. That is, the incumbent tries to signal its rival that market conditions are unfavorable, deterring entry of a potential competitor in the case of limit pricing and inducing the exit of a rival with predatory pricing. With predatory pricing, the incumbent may, for example, adopt a low-price policy in an attempt to signal to its rival that its costs are low or that market demand is weak. Once the rival is convinced of these market conditions, it may recalculate the expected profitability of continued operations and decide to exit the market.

Such models of predatory pricing may be less plausible than the related limit-pricing models. Predatory pricing requires the rival to have been participating in the market, during which time it could have learned about market conditions and be less subject to incomplete information than an entrant in a limit-pricing model. Another class of models that may be more plausible has firms investing continually to remain in the market. Firms that lack the resources to invest are forced to exit the market. In this setting, the incumbent has an incentive to use low prices to "beat up" its rival in order to exhaust any resources it may have available to invest. As with all predatory strategies, the incumbent sacrifices current profits for long-term gains anticipated when the rival exits. A subtle question is why the rival cannot borrow money from a bank or other financier as a commitment to stay in the market during the predatory episode, deterring predation by convincing the incumbent that predation will not induce the rival's exit. Economists have shown that if there is incomplete information on the financial market, that is, banks or other financiers do not have perfect information (say about a firm's prospects or effort in turning a profit), the firm may have difficulty borrowing an unlimited amount from a bank or other financier and predation may be a viable strategy. Incomplete information is a crucial element of most models of predatory pricing, whether the incomplete information is associated with the market in which the entrant sells the good or the market in which the entrant borrows money.

Other Models of Imperfect Competition

As should be clear from the analysis so far in this chapter, analyzing a full-blown game-theory model in which prices, output, product characteristics, entry, and exit are all strategic variables can become quite complicated. Economists have tried to simplify the analysis by coming up with short-hand models that focus on some strategic considerations and assume away others. We already studied the most famous short-hand model without thinking of it in these terms: perfect competition. It is not literally true, for example, that firms are price takers. If in an extreme case a firm were to increase its output a million fold, this output change would probably start to have an impact on market price. Such a million fold increase is out of the realm of possibility for small firms in perfectly competitive markets, so the assumption of price-taking behavior is probably not unreasonable. To aid the study of imperfect competition, economists have proposed some short-hand models that combine elements of perfect competition with elements of monopoly and oligopoly. Such models have proved useful in various applications, and so we study them now.

APPLICATION 14.6 *Find the Predatory Pricing*

Strong emotions sometimes seem to suggest that simple David and Goliath situations will often arise where a dominant strong player attempts to squeeze a smaller or weaker player out of the market, thus freeing up the environment for some good old fashioned consumer exploitation and dominance. However, this view has often been much harder to prove in practice, as competition authorities in Britain, the EU, and America have found predatory pricing to be far more elusive than the popular press would suggest. In fact some free-market economist claim the condition is incredibly rare.[1]

The Theory of Predatory Pricing

The economic theory behind predatory pricing is much less clear than the strong rhetoric often suggests. Economists have offered several rationalizations for predatory pricing, some discussed in the text. First, the predator may wish to signal to rivals that competition will be so tough, say because its costs are so low, that continuing in the market will be unprofitable for them. Such an argument requires rivals to lack knowledge about market conditions that they may reasonably be supposed to have.

Second, a would-be monopolist may wish to force smaller rivals to exit by exhausting their resources. Assuming the predatory firm is not much more efficient than rival firms, in order to cause them to earn negative profits, it must sell its output below average cost, perhaps below marginal cost. It must also be willing to absorb the extra sales that such lowered prices would bring. The predator must, therefore, operate with relatively large losses for some time in the hope that the smaller losses this may cause rivals will eventually prompt them to give up. It is unclear that the predator has longer staying power than its rivals in sticking to a low-price policy – especially since rivals know that price must eventually return to a normal, profitable level. It is also unclear that the predatory firm would prefer to force smaller rivals to exit rather than simply buying them in the marketplace.

Third, the firm may wish to establish a reputation for being a predator. By preying on existing rivals, the firm sacrifices current profits in return for the long-run benefit of scaring off future entrants. This theory requires entrants to believe there is at least a small chance that the predator does not sacrifice current profits when it preys. Again, such an argument requires rivals to lack knowledge about the market that they may reasonably be supposed to have.

The Volatile Newspaper Industry

The industry has often been portrayed as the Wild West, where robber barons play fast and loose in the cut throat world of competition. However all is often not as it seems. Two examples illustrate this.

In September 2002, Aberdeen Journals Ltd was fined £1.3 million by the OFT for abusing its dominant market position. A complaint from the Aberdeen & District Independent (a free weekly newspaper) alleged that Aberdeen Journals was acting unlawfully by the particularly low pricing of advertising space in its weekly free newspaper, the Aberdeen Herald & Post, and that the company deliberately incurred losses when selling advertising in an attempt to force out its only direct rival from that market. The OFT decided that Aberdeen Journals had infringed the Competition Act's Chapter II prohibition, which makes the abuse of a dominant position unlawful.

John Vickers, Director General of Fair Trading, said at the time "Aberdeen Journals deliberately incurred losses in a persistent campaign to remove its only direct rival from the market. This campaign continued despite the fact that the Competition Act 1998 prohibited predatory pricing from March 2000, and despite an OFT investigation already being in train. This was a serious infringement of the law, and the penalty should act as a deterrent to others."

After being shut down for nearly a year in the late 1970s, and emerging victorious after bruising battles with the print trade unions in the 1980s, *The Times*, under Rupert Murdoch's News International pursued a strategy that sought to dramatically increase circulation. Over nearly 12 years the paper followed a vicious price war, starting in 1993 when it cut the price of *The Times* from 45p to 30p. At times the price was

(Continued)

even down to 10p on Mondays. The *Independent* was plunged into a cash crisis which led to a succession of takeovers, and when in June 1994 *The Times* decreased is price again from 30p to 20p, it claimed it amounted to a £30 m a year subsidy. The OFT investigated, and in October 1994, Bryan Carsberg, Director General of Fair Trading, said that his inquiry into the price cuts had not established a case for formal action under the competition legislation. He stated, "The structure and characteristics of the market for national daily newspapers suggest that predation is unlikely to prove a feasible strategy for the owners or the *Daily Telegraph* or *The Times*". He added, "In view of the number of competing titles, it does not seem likely that a predator would be able to recoup any losses out of supranormal profits in the future. (. . .) *The Times* has been making losses for many years. (. . .) *The Times*' decision to reduce cover prices appears to be a reasonable commercial strategy designed to improve its competitive position in prevailing market circumstances."[2]

In the subsequent years the company was investigated a further three times over its low cost subscription offer and a host of other activities, and on each occasion was cleared. When the price war finished in September 2005, some estimates suggested that over the 12 years *The Times* has lost the best part of £175 m.

To Think About

1. If the facts do not always support the suspicion of predatory pricing why do you think that companies are often widely believed to have practiced it? What kinds of market-wide trends might be mistaken for predatory behavior?
2. When a firm dramatically reduces its prices, competitors often cry foul, and claim that a predatory pricing strategy is operating. What other strategies might a firm be following?

[1]See Thomas J. DiLorenzo, "The Myth of Predatory Pricing", Policy Analysis, No. 169 (1992), Cato Institute, available at: http://www.cato.org/pubs/pas/pa-169.html.

[2]Office of Fair Trading (OFT), Press Release, 21 October 1994.

Price Leadership

Price-leadership model A model with one dominant firm that behaves strategically and a group of small firms that behave as price takers.

The first short-hand model of imperfect competition we will study is the **price-leadership model**. This model resembles many real-world situations. In some markets, one firm or group of firms is looked upon as the leader in pricing, and all firms adjust their prices to what this leader does. Historical illustrations of this kind of behavior include the leadership of US Steel Corporation during the early post–World War II period and the pricing "umbrella" of IBM in the formative years of the computer industry.

Competitive fringe Group of firms that act as price takers in a market dominated by a price leader

A formal model of pricing in a market dominated by a leading firm is presented in Figure 14-7. The industry is assumed to be composed of a single price-setting leader and a **competitive fringe** of firms that take the leader's price as given in their decisions. The demand curve *D* represents the total market demand curve for the industry's product, and the supply curve *SC* represents the supply decisions of all the firms in the competitive fringe. Using these two curves, the demand curve (D') facing the industry leader is derived as follows. For a price of P_1 or above, the leader sells nothing since the competitive fringe would be willing to supply all that is demanded. For prices below P_2, the leader has the market to itself since the fringe is not willing to supply anything. Between P_2 and P_1, the curve D' is constructed by subtracting what the fringe will supply from total market demand. That is, the leader gets that portion of demand not taken by the fringe firms. D' is sometimes referred to as the price leader's residual demand curve.

Given the demand curve D', the leader can construct a marginal revenue curve for it (MR') and then refer to its own marginal cost curve (*MC*) to determine the profit-maximizing output level, Q_L. Market price is then P_L. Given that price, the competitive fringe produces Q_C, and total industry output is

$$Q_T\ (= Q_C + Q_L)$$

The price-leadership model takes a shortcut in assuming that the fringe firms are price takers rather than modeling their strategic behavior formally and applying game theory. The shortcut makes the analysis easier and is fitting if the fringe consists of a large number of small firms and if the dominant firm is quite a bit larger than any other firm. Another shortcut is that the model does not deal with how the price leader in an industry is chosen or what happens when a member of the fringe decides to challenge the leader for its position (and profits). Still, the model does show how elements of both the perfect competition and monopoly theories of price determination can be woven together to produce a model of pricing under imperfectly competitive conditions. Price leadership may be an important strategic element in a number of important markets, as Application 14.7: *Price Leadership in Financial Markets* illustrates.

Monopolistic Competition

Another model that weaves together elements of perfect competition and monopoly is **monopolistic competition**, illustrated in Figure 14-8. The monopoly aspect is that firms are assumed to have some control over the price they receive, perhaps because each produces a slightly differentiated product. Firms thus face downward-sloping demand curves, in contrast to the horizontal demand curve of perfect competition. The competitive aspect

Monopolistic competition Market in which each firm faces a downward-sloping demand curve and there are no barriers to entry.

FIGURE 14-7 Formal Model of Price-Leadership Behavior *The curve D′ shows the residual demand curve facing the price leader. It is derived by subtracting what is produced by the competitive fringe of firms (SC) from market demand (D). Given D′, the price leader's profit-maximizing output level is Q_L, and a price of P_L will prevail in the market.*

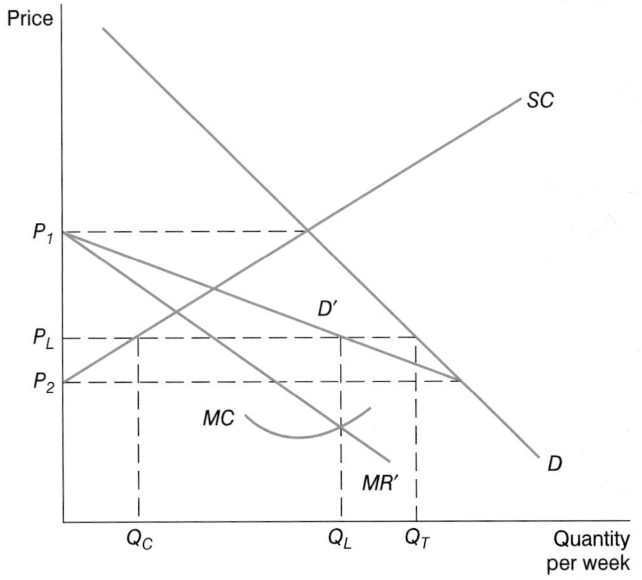

APPLICATION 14.7 *Price Leadership in Financial Markets*

Many financial markets are dominated by a few large firms. Because of the volatility of prices in these markets, smaller firms tend to look to these large firms in setting their own prices. In this application, we show how markets in both the United States and Germany tend to behave much like those illustrated in Figure 14-7.

Prime Rate at New York Commercial Banks

Major New York commercial banks quote a "prime rate", which purports to be the interest rate that they charge on loans to their most creditworthy customers. Although recent research suggests that the actual pricing of such loans is much more complex than this description implies, it is still true that the banks' prime rates provide a visible and influential indicator of what they charge.

Banks' costs of funds change on a day-to-day basis. The prime rate, however, tends to be rather sluggish, changing only occasionally by rather large amounts (say 0.25 per cent or more). It is when changes are needed that price leadership patterns are most clearly visible. One of the major banks (Citicorp or Morgan-Chase) will announce a new prime rate on a trial basis to see whether it will "stick". In a few days, either most other banks will have joined the new rate or the initiator will be forced to go back to the old rate. Because of the uncertainties involved in this procedure, the prime rate will tend to remain relatively stable for extended periods.

Figure 14-7 suggests that price leadership can be profitable for the leaders, and some evidence on the prime rate tends to confirm that possibility. Specifically, researchers have found an asymmetry in banks' changes in their prime rates: Rates tend to rise very soon after an increase in banks' costs but decline only slowly when costs fall. Banks' stock prices also tend to reflect this pattern.[1] A rise in the prime rate tends to hurt the stock prices of banks because such an increase is a signal that profits are being squeezed by costs. On the other hand, a fall in the prime rate tends to be good for bank stocks because it indicates a period of profitability on their loans.

Price Leadership in the Foreign Exchange Market

The market for world currencies is very large and very volatile. It is dominated by major financial institutions and is heavily influenced by the "intervention" of various nations' central banks in the market for their own currencies. Because such central bank intervention is usually not announced in advance, traders who are particularly well-informed may have an informational advantage in the market. One might expect, therefore, other firms to look to these firms as price leaders in particular currencies.

This presumption is supported by a 1997 study of trading in German marks (DM).[2] In this study, the author looked at every major transaction in trading DMs for US dollars over a 1-year period (1.5 million separate transactions). She found that one bank, the Deutsche Bank (the 13th-largest bank in the world), tended to play the role of leader in setting the DM/$ exchange rate for these transactions. This leadership role arose because of the bank's ability to foresee intervention by the German central bank (the Bundesbank) in exchange markets. Specifically, the author shows that changes in the exchange rate quoted by Deutsche Bank made between 25 minutes and 60 minutes before such intervention tended to be copied by many other large banks. These other banks presumably believed that Deutsche Bank had superior information about central bank intervention and were willing to follow that bank's pricing based on this belief. As the actual time of Bundesbank intervention approached, however, the information became more widely diffused, so no clear patterns emerged in price setting within 25 minutes of the intervention.

To Think About

1 Why do large commercial banks tend to converge to a single prime rate? Shouldn't there be

some variation in this rate among banks to reflect differences in their costs of funds and other operating characteristics?

2 Can you think of other situations where informational advantages about upcoming financial events may yield a price leadership position to a financial institution?

[1]For an analysis, see P. G. Nabar, S. Y. Park, and A. Saunders, "Prime Rate Changes: Is There an Advantage to Being First?", *Journal of Business* (January 1993): 69–92.

[2]B. Peiers, "Informed Traders, Intervention, and Price Leadership: A Deeper View of the Microstructure of the Foreign Exchange Market", *Journal of Finance* (September 1997): 1589–1614.

is that there is free entry. In the free-entry equilibrium, firm's profits are driven to zero, as follows. Initially, the demand curve facing the typical firm is given by d, and economic profits are being earned. New firms are attracted by these profits, and their entry shifts d inward (because now a larger number of substitute products are being sold on a given market). Indeed, entry can reduce profits to zero by shifting the demand curve to d'. The level of output that maximizes profits with this demand curve, q', is not, however, the same as that level at which average costs are minimized, q_{min}. Rather, the firm produces less than that output level and exhibits "excess capacity", given by $q_{min} - q'$.[15]

FIGURE 14-8 Monopolistic Competition *Initially the demand curve facing the firm is d. Marginal revenue is given by mr, and q* is the profit-maximizing output level. If entry is costless, new firms attracted by the possibility for profits may shift the firm's demand curve inward to d', where profits are zero. Output level q' is below the level q_{min}, where average costs reach a minimum. The firm exhibits excess capacity, given by $q_{min} - q'$.*

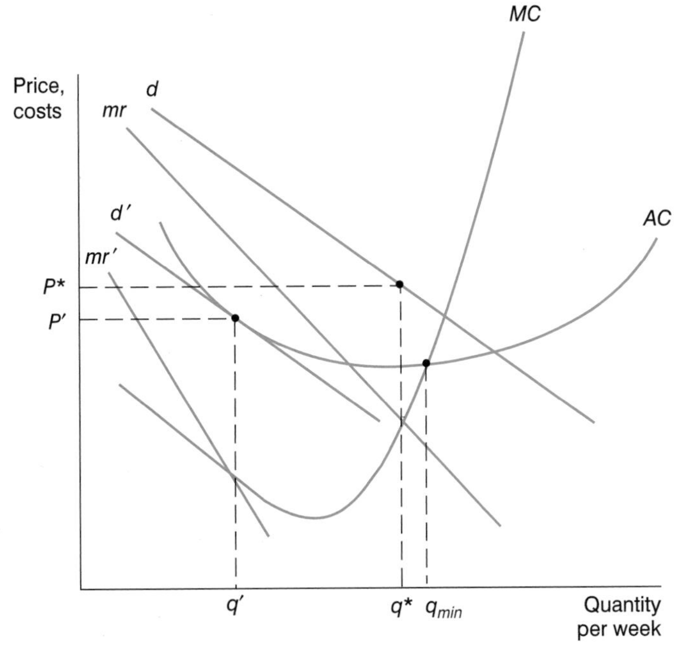

[15] This analysis was originally developed by E. H. Chamberlain, *The Theory of Monopolistic Competition* (Cambridge, MA: Harvard University Press, 1950).

Monopolistic competition brushes aside strategic considerations. The firm's demand curve is assumed to shift from d to d', without an explicit consideration of the process that leads to the demand shift. In a full-blown game-theory model, it is possible that free entry does not dissipate an incumbent's profits completely. Take the simple case in which firms produce very close substitutes and there is initially a monopoly in the market. Even though the monopolist might be earning lavish profits, other firms would hesitate to enter the market because entry would lead to a situation resembling the Bertrand Paradox (because products are close substitutes). The resulting profits may not be sufficient to cover even a modest fixed cost of entry. Brushing aside strategic considerations is probably only realistic if firms are small enough relative to the market that any given firm's strategic response would have little effect on other firms in the market. Monopolistic competition has thus been applied most successfully to the local competition in industries such as service stations, convenience stores, and restaurants, where there is some product differentiation (in terms of either product characteristics or store location) but entry occurs at a relatively small scale.

Barriers to Entry

The price-leadership and monopolistic-competition models aside, the rest of the models in this chapter are oligopoly models with only a few firms in the market. For example, there were only two firms in the market in our analysis of the Cournot and Bertrand models. For oligopoly models with few firms to have any applicability, market entry must be somewhat difficult. There might be some of the entry barriers already discussed in connection with monopoly in Chapter 13, which the reader should review again now.

Some new entry barriers arise specifically out of some features of imperfectly competitive markets. Product differentiation and advertising, for example, may raise entry barriers by promoting strong brand loyalty. The possibility of strategic pricing decisions may also deter entry for a number of reasons. Entry tends to make market competition more intense, reducing the profitability of subsequent entry. We saw this in the Cournot model, for example, where the equilibrium output increased from the monopoly to the perfectly competitive level as the number of firms increased. We also saw this in the repeated Bertrand model, where tacit collusion became harder to sustain as the number of firms increased. Incumbents may also manipulate their pricing decisions to convince firms wishing to enter that it would be unprofitable to do so.

Barriers to entry frequently are the central issue when government antitrust authorities decide merger cases. A merger immediately reduces the number of firms in the market (for example, a merger between two firms in a market with four leaves three of them). But the previous paragraph suggests that, according to various models studied so far, reducing the number of firms reduces competition and raises prices. Antitrust authorities, responsible for keeping consumer prices low, should be wary of allowing mergers if they believe the models. Concerns would be lessened if entry barriers were thought to be low enough that any short-term price increase would stimulate entry, and this entry would keep prices low in the long run. Merger cases sometimes hinge on measurements of the cost of entry and the length of time entry might be expected to take (that is, how long the "long run" is), with parties seeking approval for their merger of course arguing that entry will likely be quick and easy.

MICROQUIZ 14.6

1. List the two key features of the model of monopolistic competition.
2. Does the fact that firms have "excess capacity" in the model mean that the government should restrict entry in such a market, or would there be a potential loss from doing so?

SUMMARY

In this chapter, we studied models of imperfectly competitive industries, which lie between the extremes of monopoly and perfect competition. Such markets are characterized by relatively few firms that have some effect on market price – they are not price takers – but no single firm exercises complete market control. In these circumstances, there is no generally accepted model of market behavior. We presented a variety of models that economists use to study such industries, often called oligopolies. Some of the main points about the models in this chapter are the following.

- Because there are few firms, the strategic interaction among them becomes an important consideration. The concepts introduced in game theory, in particular Nash and subgame-perfect equilibrium, are useful to develop a formal understanding of this strategic interaction.
- Equilibrium outcomes with few firms may vary greatly from one resembling perfect competition (in the Bertrand model) to one resembling the monopoly outcome (in the model with tacit collusion), and outcomes in between (in the Cournot model).
- Best-response-function diagrams provide a useful tool to analyze oligopoly models such as Cournot and Bertrand with differentiated products.
- Small details about the market – including the strategic variable chosen (prices versus quantities), the nature of product differentiation, the presence of capacity constraints, information about market conditions, and repeated interaction – may have a big impact on the equilibrium.
- Firms may attempt to regain monopoly profits dissipated through imperfect competition by forming a cartel or through tacit collusion. Whether the cartel/collusion is sustainable depends on the trade-off between the short-term gain from cheating and the long-term loss if cheating leads to breakdown of the cartel/collusion. The cartel/collusion is more stable the fewer the number of firms and the more patient they are.
- Two-stage models can be used to understand a broad range of strategic choices beyond standard pricing and output decisions, including advertising, product selection, capacity choice, entry-deterring strategies, and so forth.
- Pricing strategies that deter entry (limit pricing) or induce exit (predatory pricing) are difficult to rationalize without subtle arguments involving asymmetric information about market conditions or about financing opportunities.
- Short-hand models such as monopolistic competition and price-leadership models can be quite useful for situations in which full-blown game-theoretic models might prove too complicated.

REVIEW QUESTIONS

1 Why is the intersection between firms' best-response functions in Figure 14-2 for the Cournot model or 14–3 for the Bertrand model with differentiated products a graphical illustration of the Nash equilibrium concept?

2 Commercial fishing is an industry that is often given as an example of quantity competition, as in the Cournot model. Can you think of others? Can you give examples of industries in which firms compete in prices? In which of these cases are capacity constraints important, so that the two-stage model of capacity investment and price competition might apply?

3 The Bertrand Paradox relies on the assumption that the demand for any one firm's product is very responsive to pricing by the other firm. Why is this

assumption crucial for the competitive results in the Bertrand model? How would those results be affected if consumers were reluctant to shift purchases from one firm to another because of consumer switching costs? What other assumptions are crucial for the Bertrand Paradox?

4 Find examples of informative and of persuasive advertising in your newspaper. Find examples in commercials during your favorite television show. Do the particular ads you picked out persuade you to buy a broad product (orange juice) or a particular brand (Tropicana)?

5 "No cartel in history has ever succeeded for very long. There is just too much opportunity to cheat." What does it mean for a cartel member to "cheat"? What would a member of, say, the OPEC cartel actually do if it were to cheat? Why would this undermine the cartel?

6 Consider a two-stage game in which firms first make a strategic choice such as product design, location on a Hotelling line, capacity, advertising, etc., and, second, compete in prices or quantities. Why is subgame-perfect equilibrium a useful equilibrium concept? What sort of "crazy" Nash equilibria might be ruled out?

7 Consider the market for high-definition televisions, which can be expected to grow in popularity over time as consumers become familiar with it and more programs are developed for it. If there is a first-mover advantage in building capacity, what determines which firm will move first? If firms race to pre-empt each other to be the first mover, is there some profit-maximizing condition that would determine how long before the anticipated peak in demand firms would start building capacity?

8 Explain the difference between entry deterrence through first-mover investments and entry deterrence through pricing. What assumptions are required for each of these entry-deterrence strategies to be successful? Describe a hypothetical situation under which each strategy might work for an incumbent monopolist.

9 Suppose a firm is considering investing in research that would lead to a cost-saving innovation. Assuming the firm can retain this innovation solely for its own use, will the additional profits from the lower (marginal) cost be greater if the firm is a monopolist or competes against another, say, in a Cournot or Bertrand model?

10 In Figure 14-8, the demand curve facing a firm in a monopolistically competitive industry is shown as being tangent to its average cost curve at q'. Explain why this is a long-run equilibrium position for this firm. That is, why does marginal revenue equal marginal cost, and why are long-run profits zero?

PROBLEMS

14.1 The pricing game between two firms, which can each set either a low or a high price, is given by the following normal form.

		B	
		Low Price	High Price
A	Low Price	2, 2	4, 1
	High Price	1, 4	3, 3

a Find the Nash equilibrium or equilibria of the game.

b How would you label the actions to make this a quantity game like Cournot?

14.2 Refer to Figure 14-1. Suppose demand is

$$Q = 10\,000 - 1000P$$

and marginal cost is constant at $MC = 6$. From the given demand curve, one can compute the following marginal revenue curve

$$MR = 10 - \frac{Q}{500}$$

a Graph the demand, marginal cost, and marginal revenue curves.

b Calculate the price and quantity associated with point C, the perfectly competitive outcome. Compute industry profit, consumer surplus, and social welfare.

c Calculate the price and quantity associated with point M, the monopoly/perfect cartel outcome. Compute industry profit, consumer surplus, social welfare, and deadweight loss.

d Calculate the price and quantity associated with point A, a hypothetical imperfectly competitive outcome, assuming that it lies at a price halfway between C and M. Compute industry profit, consumer surplus, social welfare, and deadweight loss.

14.3 Return to the example used in the text for the Cournot model, where demand was equal to

$$Q = 120 - P$$

Suppose that instead of costless production, marginal and average costs are constant at

$$MC = AC = 30$$

Compute the Nash equilibrium quantities, prices, and profits.

14.4 Consider the model of Bertrand competition with differentiated products from the text. Let the demand curves for firms A and B be given by Equation 14.10 and Equation 14.11, and let the firms' marginal costs be constant, given by c_A and c_B. It can be shown that the best-response function for firm A is

$$p_A = \frac{1 + 2p_B + c_A}{4}$$

and for firm B is

$$p_B = \frac{1 + 2p_A + c_B}{4}$$

a Graph the two best-response functions. Find the Nash equilibrium assuming $c_A = c_B = 0$ algebraically and indicate it on the graph.

b Indicate on the graph how an increase in c_B would shift the best-response functions and change the equilibrium.

c Indicate on the graph where analogue to the Stackelberg equilibrium might be, with firm A choosing price first and then firm B. Is it better to be the first or the second mover when firms choose prices?

14.5 Suppose firms A and B operate under conditions of constant marginal and average cost but that $MC_A = 10$ and $MC_B = 8$. The demand for the firms' output is given by

$$Q = 500 - 20P$$

a If the firms practice Bertrand competition, what will the Nash-equilibrium market price be? (It may help to assume that prices can only be in increments of a penny, so that prices of 9.98, 9.99, and 10 are possible, but not 9.995.)

b What will the profits be for each firm?

c Which aspects of the Bertrand Paradox show up in this example, if any?

14.6 Consider the example of the Stackelberg model discussed in the text. Firms choose quantities, with firm A moving first, and then firm B. As in the text, market demand is given by

$$Q = 120 - P$$

and production is costless.

a Recall that firm B's best-response function is

$$q_B = \frac{120 - q_A}{2}$$

Substitute this best-response function into the equation for A's profit, (Equation 14.3), to express A's profit as a function of q_A, labeled π_A. Next, substitute this best-response function into the analogous equation for B's profit to compute B's profit as a function of q_A, labeled π_B. Finally, write the expression for A's profit if B produces zero as a function of q_A, labeled π_M (where the M subscript stands for the fact that A is a monopoly if B produces zero).

b Use the formulae from part a to fill in the following table.

q_A	π_A	π_B	π_M
0			
20			
40			
60			
80			
100			
120			

c Does your table from part b confirm the result from the text that firm *A* would choose $q_A = 60$ in the Stackelberg game? How much would *A* have to produce to deter *B*'s entry if *B* had a fixed cost of entry equal to a bit more than 400? If *B* had a fixed cost of entry a bit more than 100? Would it be worthwhile for *A* to deter *B*'s entry in these cases?

14.7 Using Equation 14.15 from the text, graph the relationship between the number of firms in the market, N, and the interest rate, r, needed to sustain collusion in an indefinitely repeated game. What is the greatest number of firms for which collusion would be sustainable at current interest rates (take the period length to be one year, so that the annual interest rate is the relevant rate)?

14.8 Consider a two-period model with two firms, *A* and *B*. In the first period, they simultaneously choose one of two actions, Enter or Don't enter. Entry requires the expenditure of a fixed entry cost of 10. In the second period, whichever firms enter play a pricing game as follows. If no firm enters, the pricing game is trivial and profits are zero. If only one firm enters, it earns the monopoly profit of 30. If both firms enter, they engage in competition as in the Bertrand model with homogeneous products.

a Using backward induction, fold the game back to the first period in which firms make their choice of Enter or Don't enter. Write down the normal form (a 2 by 2 matrix) for this game.

b Solve for the mixed-strategy Nash equilibrium of this game (see Chapter 6 for a discussion of mixed strategies).

c Compare the results from the mixed-strategy Nash equilibrium to the Bertrand Paradox.

14.9 The text mentioned a model of predatory pricing in which an incumbent tries to "beat up" a rival, exhausting the resources the rival needs to continue operating in the market, causing it to exit. Consider a specific example of this sort of model given by the extensive form in Figure 14-9. As the figure shows, there are three possible outcomes. If the entrant *E* does not enter, leaving the incumbent *I* to operate alone, the incumbent

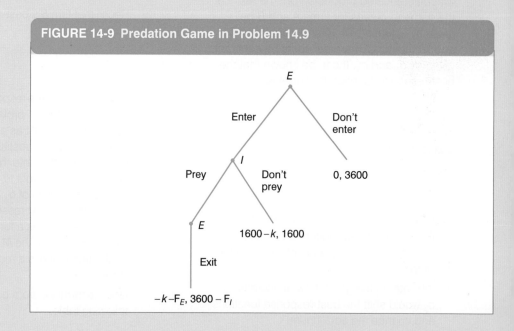

FIGURE 14-9 Predation Game in Problem 14.9

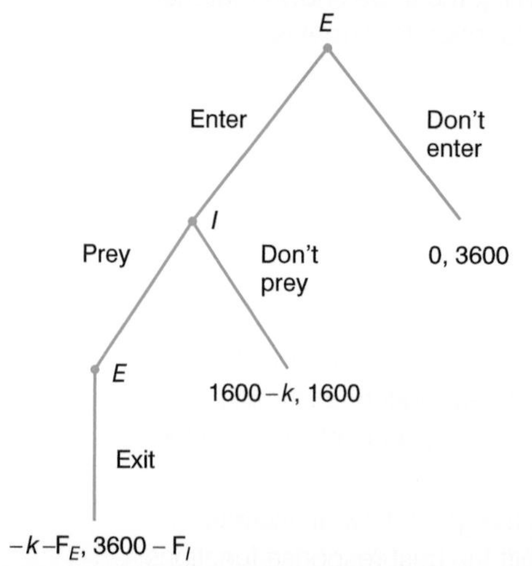

earns 3600. If the entrant spends fixed entry cost $K < 1600$ and is not preyed upon, each firm earns 1600 (not including the entry cost). If the entrant comes in and the incumbent preys upon the entrant, it can exhaust the entrant's resources and force it to exit the industry. The period of predation costs the entrant F_E and the incumbent F_I (where F stands for "fighting"). Compute the subgame-perfect equilibrium for $F_I > 2000$ and for $F_I < 2000$. Is predation ever observed in equilibrium? Would a law prohibiting predation affect the equilibrium?

14.10 Suppose that the total market demand for crude oil is given by

$$Q_D = 70\,000 - 2000P$$

where Q_D is the quantity of oil in thousands of barrels per year and P is the dollar price per barrel. Suppose also that there are 1000 identical small producers of crude oil, each with marginal costs given by

$$MC = q + 5$$

where q is the output of the typical firm.

a Assuming that each small oil producer acts as a price taker, calculate the typical firm's supply curve ($q = \ldots$), the market supply curve ($Q_S = \ldots$), and the market equilibrium price and quantity (where $Q_D = Q_S$).

b Suppose a practically infinite source of crude oil is discovered in London by a would-be price leader and that this oil can be produced at a constant average and marginal cost of $AC = MC = \$15$ per barrel. Assume also that the supply behavior of the competitive fringe described in part a is unchanged by this discovery. Calculate the demand curve facing the price leader.

c Assuming that the price leader's marginal revenue curve is given by

$$MR = 25 - \frac{Q}{1500}$$

how much should the price leader produce in order to maximize profits? What price and quantity will now prevail in the market?

PART SEVEN
FURTHER TOPICS

The economic approach provides a valuable unified framework for understanding all human behavior.

GARY BECKER, *THE ECONOMIC APPROACH TO HUMAN BEHAVIOR,* 1976

You don't have to believe Gary Becker's grand conclusion to agree with the general idea that economic thinking has proved valuable in understanding many aspects of our modern world. In this part, we look at some applications of that approach that expand beyond the focus of previous chapters exclusively on markets for goods.

Part Seven begins with the study of input markets in Chapter 15. Our presentation follows the general sort of supply/demand modeling we have used throughout the book, but in this case the roles of the economic actors involved are reversed. That is, firms operate on the demand side of input markets whereas individuals are the suppliers.

Chapter 16 looks at the role of time in microeconomics. When transactions occur over time, one must necessarily consider interest rates because these are the "prices" that tie time periods together. In Chapter 16, we show how market forces establish interest rates and how interest rates affect economic behavior.

In Chapter 17, we will look further at questions about the role of information in economic activity. We will be especially concerned with situations in which different economic actors have different information – that is, situations in which information is said to be "asymmetric".

Earlier, in Chapter 12, we showed that Adam Smith's famous "Invisible Hand Theorem" does not necessarily hold true in situations where third parties are affected by economic transactions. In Chapter 18, the final chapter in this book, we take up this subject in detail. Two types of externalities will be of central concern to us: environmental externalities and "public good" externalities. In some cases there are effective, market-based solutions to these problems. In other cases, however, solutions must be found in the political process, if at all.

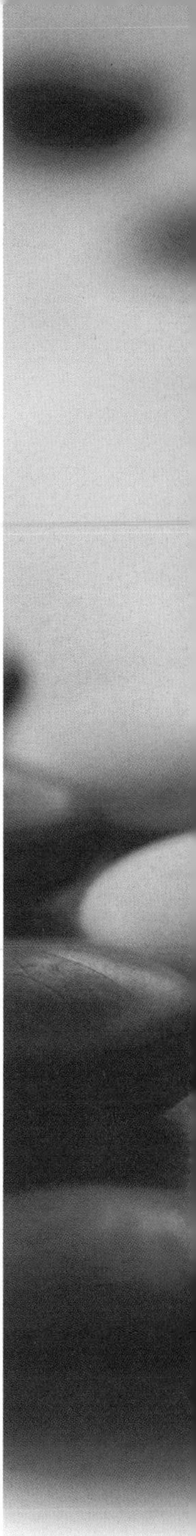

15

Pricing in Input Markets

Input prices are also determined by the forces of demand and supply. In this case, however, market roles are reversed. Now firms are on the demand side of the market, hiring inputs to meet their production needs. These inputs are supplied by individuals through the jobs they take and the capital resources that their savings provide. In this chapter, we will explore some models of how prices are determined in this process. We begin with a fairly extensive discussion of demand, then very briefly summarize the nature of supply decisions. The remainder of the chapter is devoted to examining how demand and supply interact to determine prices. The appendix to this chapter explores questions of labor supply in somewhat more detail. Chapter 16 covers those issues in input pricing that relate specifically to time and interest rates.

Marginal Productivity Theory of Input Demand

In Chapter 11, we looked briefly at Ricardo's theory of economic rent. This theory was an important start to the development of marginal economics. Ricardo's notion that price is determined by the costs of the "marginal" producer in many ways represents the seed from which modern microeconomics grew. One application of his approach was the development of the "marginal productivity" theory of the demand for factors of production. This section investigates that theory in detail.

Profit-Maximizing Behavior and the Hiring of Inputs

The basic concept of the marginal productivity theory of factor demand was stated in Chapter 9 when we discussed profit-maximization. There we showed that one implication of the profit-maximization hypothesis is that the firm will make marginal input choices. More precisely, we showed that a profit-maximizing firm will hire additional units of any input up to the point at which the additional revenue from hiring one more unit of the input is exactly equal to the cost of hiring that unit. If we use ME_K and ME_L to denote the marginal expense associated with hiring one more unit of capital and labor, respectively, and let MR_K and MR_L be the extra revenue that hiring these units of capital and labor allows the firm to bring in, then profit-maximization requires that

$$ME_K = MR_K$$
$$ME_L = MR_L \quad \{15.1\}$$

Price-Taking Behavior

If the firm is a price taker in the capital and labor markets, it is easy to simplify the marginal expense idea. In this case, the firm can always hire an extra hour of capital input at the prevailing rental rate (v) and an extra hour of labor at the wage rate (w). Therefore, the profit-maximizing requirement reduces to

$$v = ME_K = MR_K$$
$$w = ME_L = MR_L \quad \{15.2\}$$

These equations simply say that a profit-maximizing firm that is a price taker for the inputs it buys should hire extra amounts of these inputs up to the point at which their unit cost is equal to the revenue generated by the last one hired. If the firm's hiring decisions affect input prices, it will have to take that into account. We will look at such a situation later in this chapter.

Marginal Revenue Product

To analyze the additional revenue yielded by hiring one more unit of an input is a two-step process. First we must ask how much output the additional input can produce. As we discussed in Chapter 7, this magnitude is given by the input's marginal physical productivity. For example, if a firm hires one more worker for an hour to make shoes, the worker's marginal physical productivity (MP_L) is simply the number of additional pairs of shoes per hour that the firm can make.

Once the additional output has been produced, it must be sold. Assessing the value of that sale is the second step in analyzing the revenue yielded by hiring one more unit of an input. We have looked at this issue quite extensively in previous chapters – the extra revenue obtained from selling an additional unit of output is, by definition, marginal revenue (MR). So, if an extra worker can produce two pairs of shoes per hour and the firm can take in €4 per pair from selling these shoes, then hiring the worker for an hour has increased the firm's revenues by €8. This is the figure the firm will compare to the worker's hourly wage to decide whether he or she should be hired. So now our profit-maximizing rules become

$$v = ME_K = MR_K = MP_K \times MR$$
$$w = ME_L = MR_L = MP_L \times MR \quad \{15.3\}$$

Marginal revenue product The extra revenue obtained from selling the output produced by hiring an extra worker or machine.

The terms on the right side of Equation 15.3 are called the **marginal revenue product** of capital and labor, respectively. They show how much extra revenue is brought in by hiring one more unit of the input. These are precisely what we need to study the demand for inputs and how the demand might change if wages or rental rates change.

A Special Case – Marginal Value Product

The profit-maximizing rules for input choices can be made even clearer if we assume that the firm we are examining sells its output in a competitive market. In that case, the firm will also be a price taker in the goods market, so the marginal revenue it takes in from selling one more unit of output is the market price (*P*) at which the output sells. Using the result that, for a price taker in the goods market, marginal revenue is equal to price, Equation 15.3 becomes

$$v = MP_K \times P$$

$$w = MP_L \times P \qquad \{15.4\}$$

as the conditions for a profit maximum.[1] We call the terms on the right-hand side of Equation 15.4 the **marginal value product (MVP)** of capital and labor, respectively, since they do indeed put a value on these inputs' marginal physical productivities. Our final condition for maximum profits in this simple situation is

Marginal value product (MVP) A special case of marginal revenue product in which the firm is a price taker for its output.

$$v = MVP_K$$

$$w = MVP_L \qquad \{15.5\}$$

To see why these are required for profit-maximization, consider again our shoe worker example. Suppose the worker can make two pairs of shoes per hour and that shoes sell for €4. The worker's marginal value product is €8 per hour. If the hourly wage is less than this (say, €5 per hour), the firm can increase profits by €3 by employing the worker for one more hour; profits were not at a maximum, so the extra labor should be hired. Similarly, if the wage is €10 per hour, profits would rise by €2 if one less hour of labor were used. Only if the wage and labor's marginal value product are equal will profits truly be as large as possible.

MICROQUIZ 15.1

Suppose that a firm has a monopoly in the goods it sells but must hire its two inputs in competitive markets.

1. Will this monopoly hire workers up to the point at which $w = MVP_L$ and $v = MVP_K$?
2. Will this monopoly be minimizing the total costs of the output level that it chooses to produce?

Responses to Changes in Input Prices

Suppose the price of any input (say, labor) were to fall. It seems reasonable that firms might demand more of this input in response to such a change. In this section, we provide a detailed analysis of why the model of a profit-maximizing firm supports this conclusion.

[1]Equation 15.4 implies cost-minimization for this firm. Dividing the two equations gives

$$MP_L/MP_K = w/v$$

but in Chapter 7 we showed that *RTS* (of *L* for *K*) = MP_L/MP_K. A firm that pursues a marginal productivity approach to input demand will equate

$$RTS \text{ (of } L \text{ for } K) = w/v$$

and this is required for (long-run) cost-minimization.

APPLICATION 15.1 *The Demand for Labor under Monopoly*

The following application is slightly more demanding. In particular see the sections on some simple rules of calculus in the Mathematical Note to Application 15.1 on page 486. For those students who would rather not approach calculus at this stage of their academic careers you may proceed to the next section without loss of continuity.

Under the assumption of perfect competition in the product market and in the input market for labor a firm maximizes profits as follows

$$\max_n \Pi = pq(n) - wn \qquad \{1\}$$

In words, profit equals the price of the product, p, multiplied by the output of the firm, q, (which in turn, in the short-run, depends on the quantity of labor hired) *less* the wage rate paid in the firm multiplied by the quantity of labor hired. If we now take the derivative of equation 15.1 with respect to n we obtain

$$\frac{d\Pi}{dn} = pq'(n) - w = 0 \qquad \{2\}$$

Given that $q'(n)$ equals the marginal physical product of labor, if we take w to the right hand side of equation 15.2 and then divide through by p we obtain

$$q'(n) = \frac{w}{p} \qquad \{3\}$$

In words, the firm maximizes profits where the marginal product of labor is equal to the real wage paid by the firm.[1]

Using calculus we now derive the monopolists labor demand curve. It should be emphasized that we still assume that the labor market is perfectly competitive with the wage being established at the level of the overall market demand for the particular types of labor that may be demanded by the monopolist.[2] We start by recognizing that price is now a decreasing function of output which we did *not* under the assumption of perfect competition. That is,

$$p = p(q) \qquad \{4\}$$

A firm's revenue can be written generally as:

$$R(q) = p(q)q \qquad \{5\}$$

That is, revenue equals price (which is a function of output) multiplied by the output of the firm. The firm's short-run production function is

$$q = q(n) \qquad \{6\}$$

which assumes a fixed level of capital in the short-run. The firm selects n to maximize profits given by

$$\max_n \Pi = p(q(n))q(n) - wn \qquad \{7\}$$

In words, if we break {7} down into four parts, the above says that

- i profit, Π, in the short-run, is equal to
- ii price, p, (which in turn is a function of output, q, which in turn depends on the amount of labor hired, n)
- iii multiplied by output, q, (which depends on the amount of labor hired) which has been sold in the market
- iv *less* the wage bill (which is equal to the wage rate, w, multiplied by the amount of labor hours worked, n.)

The first order condition is

$$\frac{d\Pi}{dn} = \frac{dp}{dq}\frac{dq}{dn}q(n) + p(q(n))\frac{dq}{dn} - w = 0 \qquad \{8\}$$

If you do not fully understand how we derive {8} then see the Mathematical Note to Application 15.1 toward the end of this chapter (page 486).

Notice also that:

$$\frac{dp}{dq} = MR = \text{Marginal Revenue and}$$

$$\frac{dq}{dn} = MPP_L = \text{Marginal Physical Product of Labor}$$

If we now take w to the right hand side of equation {8} and multiply the left hand side by

$$\frac{p}{p}$$

we arrive at

$$p\left[\frac{dp}{dq}\frac{dq}{dn}\frac{q}{p} + \frac{dq}{dn}\right] = w \qquad \{9\}$$

or

$$p\left[\frac{dp}{dq}\frac{q}{p} + 1\right]\frac{dq}{dn} = w \qquad \{10\}$$

We now recognize that

$$\left(\frac{dq}{q}\right) \div \left(\frac{dp}{p}\right) = \eta \qquad \{11\}$$

where η = the elasticity of output with respect to price but

$$\left(\frac{dq}{q}\right) \div \left(\frac{dp}{p}\right) = \left(\frac{dq}{q}\right) \times \left(\frac{p}{dp}\right) = \left(\frac{dq}{dp}\right) \times \left(\frac{p}{q}\right) \qquad \{12\}$$

In equation {10} above we have the inverse of this and so we may write

$$p\left[\frac{1}{\eta} + 1\right]\frac{dq}{dn} = w \qquad \{13\}$$

Given, however, that we know *a priori* that as output rises price will fall, the elasticity will be negative and so we write equation {13} as

$$p\left[1 - \frac{1}{\eta}\right]\frac{dq}{dn} = w \qquad \{14\}$$

or

$$\left[1 - \frac{1}{\eta}\right]\frac{dq}{dn} = \frac{w}{p} \qquad \{15\}$$

or

$$(1 - 1/\eta) \times MPP_L = \textit{real wage} \qquad \{16\}$$

Under perfect competition in the product market and input market, the nominal wage is equal to the marginal physical product of labor multiplied by the product price which equals the marginal revenue product of labor. The marginal revenue product of labor then "traces out" the labor demand curve on the downward part of the slope.

$$\textit{nominal wage} = MPP_L \times p \qquad \{17\}$$

or

$$\textit{real wage} = MPP_L \qquad \{18\}$$

As can be seen this differs from the situation under monopoly by the factor

$$(1 - 1/\eta)$$

To Think About

1 As η, the elasticity of output with respect to price, gets larger and larger what will happen to $1/\eta$? As a consequence of this what will happen to the real wage and the marginal product of labor?

2 Given your answers to 1) is demand for labor greater or less under monopoly conditions compared to perfect competition?

[1]Strictly speaking we should now show that the second derivative is less than zero for us to make the claim of the firm maximizing profits. Given our assumption of diminishing returns to labor holding capital fixed in the short-run we will take it as read that this is the case.

[2]Do not confuse the fact that a monopolist has by definition a monopoly on the supply of a particular product to the *product market* with demand for labor on the *input* side of the market. A monopolist producer of product "*A*" may recruit cleaners but other (different) industries producing products "*B*", "*C*", "*D*", etc. also require cleaners. Each of these different industries will demand cleaners. The combined demand among all these industries intersecting with the overall supply curve of cleaners will determine the going wage rate for cleaners. The same argument applies to the monopolist's demand for, say, IT technicians. Other (different) industries will also need IT technicians.

Single Variable Input Case

Let's look first at the case where a firm has fixed capital input and can only vary its labor input in the short run. In this case, labor input will exhibit diminishing marginal physical productivity, so labor's *MVP* ($= P \times MP_L$) will decline as increasing numbers of labor hours are hired. The downward-sloping MVP_L curve in Figure 15-1 illustrates this possibility. With a wage rage of w_1, a profit-maximizing firm will hire L_1 labor hours.

If the wage rate were to fall to w_2, more labor (L_2) would be demanded. At such a lower wage, more labor can be hired because the firm can "afford" to have a lower marginal physical productivity from the labor it employs. If it continued to hire only L_1, the firm would not be maximizing profits since, at the margin, labor would now be capable of producing more in additional revenue than hiring additional labor would cost. When only one input can be varied, the assumption of a diminishing marginal productivity of labor ensures that a fall in the price of labor will cause more labor to be hired.[2] The marginal value product curve shows this response.

A Numerical Example

As a numerical example of these input choices, let's look again at the hiring decision for Hamburger Heaven first discussed in Chapter 7. Table 15-1 repeats the productivity information for the case in which Hamburger Heaven uses four grills ($K = 4$). As the table shows, the marginal productivity of labor declines as more workers are assigned to use grills each hour – the 1st worker hired turns out 20 (heavenly) hamburgers per hour, whereas the 10th hired produces only 3.2 hamburgers per hour. To calculate these workers' marginal value products, we simply multiply these physical productivity figures by the price of hamburgers, €1.00. These results appear in the final column of Table 15-1. With a market wage of €5.00 per hour, Hamburger

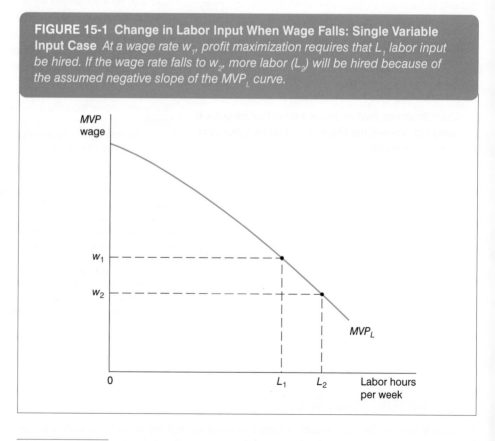

FIGURE 15-1 Change in Labor Input When Wage Falls: Single Variable Input Case *At a wage rate w_1, profit maximization requires that L_1 labor input be hired. If the wage rate falls to w_2, more labor (L_2) will be hired because of the assumed negative slope of the MVP_L curve.*

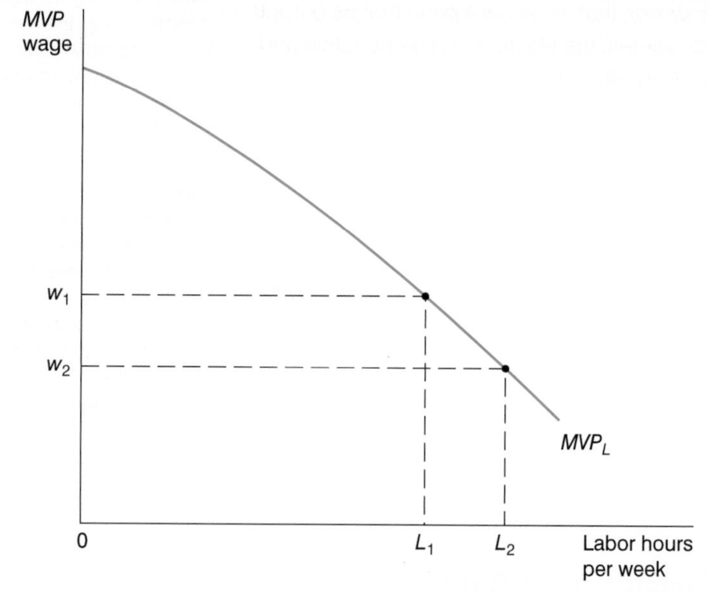

[2]Because the marginal productivity of labor is positive, hiring more labor also implies that output will increase when w declines.

Heaven should hire four workers. The marginal value product of each of these workers exceeds €5.00, so the firm earns some incremental profit on each of them. The fifth worker's *MVP* is only €4.70, however, so it does not make sense to add that worker.

At a wage other than €5.00 per hour, Hamburger Heaven would hire a different number of workers. At €6.00 per hour, for example, only three workers would be hired. With wages of €4.00 per hour, on the other hand, six workers would be employed. The *MVP* calculation provides complete information about Hamburger Heaven's short-run hiring decisions. Of course, a change in the wages of burger flippers might also cause the firm to reconsider how many grills it uses – a subject we now investigate.

Two Variable Input Case

For the case where the firm can vary two (or more) inputs, the story is more complex. The assumption of a diminishing marginal physical product of labor can be misleading here. If w falls, there will be a change not only in labor input but also in capital input as a new cost-minimizing combination of inputs is chosen (see our analysis in Chapter 8). When capital input changes, the entire MP_L function shifts (workers now have a different amount of capital to work with), and our earlier analysis of how wages affect hiring cannot be made. The remainder of this section presents a series of observations that establish that even with many inputs, a fall in w will lead to an increase in the quantity of labor demanded.

Substitution Effect

In some ways analyzing the two-input case is similar to our analysis of the individual's response to a change in the price of a good in Chapter 3. When w falls, we can decompose the total effect on the quantity of L hired into two components: a substitution effect and an output effect.

To study the **substitution effect**, we hold q constant at q_1. With a fall in w, there will be a tendency to substitute labor for capital in the production of q_1. This effect is illustrated in Figure 15-2(a). Because the condition for minimizing the cost of producing q_1 requires that $RTS = w/v$, a fall in w will necessitate a movement from input combination A to combination B. It is clear from the diagram that this substitution effect

Substitution effect In the theory of production, the substitution of one input for another while holding output constant in response to a change in the input's price.

TABLE 15-1 Hamburger Heaven's Profit-Maximizing Hiring Decision

Labor input per hour	*Hamburgers produced per hour*	*Marginal product (hamburgers)*	*Marginal value product (€1.00 per hamburger)*
1	20.0	20.0	€20.00
2	28.3	8.3	8.30
3	34.6	6.3	6.30
4	40.0	5.4	5.40
5	44.7	4.7	4.70
6	49.0	4.3	4.30
7	52.9	3.9	3.90
8	56.6	3.7	3.70
9	60.0	3.4	3.40
10	63.2	3.2	3.20

must cause labor input to rise in response to the fall in w because of the convex shape of the q_1 isoquant. The firm now decides to produce q_1 in a more labor-intensive way.

Output Effect

Output effect The effect of an input price change on the amount of the input that the firm hires that results from a change in the firm's output level.

It is, however, not correct to hold q output constant when w falls. When the firm changes its level of production – the **output effect** – the analogy to a person's utility-maximization problem breaks down. The reason for this is that consumers have budget constraints, but firms do not. Firms produce as much as profit-maximization requires; their need for inputs is derived from these production decisions. In order to investigate what happens to the quantity of output produced, we must therefore investigate the firm's profit-maximizing output decision. A fall in w, because it changes relative factor costs, will shift the firm's expansion path. Consequently, all the firm's cost curves will be shifted, and probably some output level other than q_1 will be chosen.

Figure 15-2(b) illustrates the most common case. As a result of the fall in w, the marginal cost curve for the firm has shifted downward to MC'. The profit-maximizing level of output rises from q_1 to q_2.[3] The profit-maximizing condition ($P = MC$) is now satisfied at a higher level of output. Returning to Figure 15-2(a), this increase in output will cause even more labor input to be demanded. The combined result of both the substitution and the output effects is to move the input choice to point C on the firm's isoquant for output level q_2. Both effects work to increase L in response to a decrease in w.[4]

FIGURE 15-2 Substitution and Output Effects of a Decrease in Price of Labor *When the price of labor falls, the substitution effect causes more labor to be purchased even if output is held constant. This is shown as a movement from point A to point B in panel (a). The change in w will also shift the firm's marginal cost curve. A normal situation might be for the MC curve to shift downward in response to a decrease in w, as shown in panel (b). With this new curve (MC') a higher level of output (q_2) will be chosen. The hiring of labor will increase (to L_2) from this output effect.*

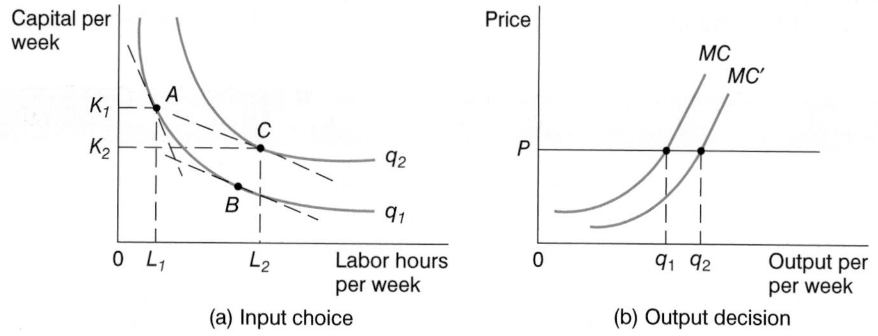

[3]Price (P) is assumed to be constant. If all firms in an industry were confronted with a decline in w, all would change their output levels; the industry supply curve would shift outward, and consequently P would fall. As long as the market demand curve for the firm's output is negatively sloped, however, the analysis in this chapter would not be seriously affected by this observation since the lower P will lead to more output being demanded.

[4]No definite statement can be made about how the quantity of capital (or any other input) changes in response to a decline in w. The substitution and output effects work in opposite directions (as can be seen in Figure 15-2), and the precise outcome depends on the relative sizes of these effects.

Summary of Firm's Demand for Labor

We conclude therefore that a profit-maximizing firm will increase its hiring of labor for two reasons. First, the firm will substitute the now-cheaper labor for other inputs that are now relatively more expensive. This is the substitution effect. Second, the wage decline will reduce the firm's marginal costs, thereby causing it to increase output and to increase the hiring of all inputs including labor. This is the output effect.

This conclusion holds for any input. Naturally, it can be reversed to show that an increase in the price of an input will cause the firm to hire less of that input. We have shown that the firm's demand curve for an input will be unambiguously downward sloping: the lower its price, the more of the input will be demanded.[5]

Responsiveness of Input Demand to Price Changes

The notions of substitution and output effects help to explain how responsive to price changes the demand for an input might be. Suppose the wage rate rose. We already know that less labor will be demanded. Now we wish to investigate whether this decrease in quantity demanded will be large or small.

Ease of Substitution

First, consider the substitution effect. The decrease in the hiring of labor from a rise in w will depend on how easy it is for firms to substitute other factors of production for labor. Some firms may find it relatively simple to substitute machines for workers, and for these firms the quantity of labor demanded will decrease substantially. Other firms may produce with a fixed proportions technology. For them substitution will be impossible. The size of the substitution effect may also depend on the length of time allowed for adjustment. In the short run, a firm may have a stock of machinery that requires a fixed complement of workers. Consequently, the short-run substitution possibilities are slight. Over the long-run, however, this firm may be able to adapt its machinery to use less labor per machine; the possibilities of substitution may now be substantial. For example, a rise in the wages of coal miners will have little short-run substitution effect since existing coal-mining equipment requires a certain number of workers to operate it. In the long-run, however, there is clear evidence that mining can be made more capital intensive by designing more complex machinery. In the long-run, capital has been substituted for labor on a large scale.

Costs and the Output Effect

An increase in the wage rate will also raise firms' costs. In a competitive market, this will cause the price of the good being produced to rise, and people will reduce their purchases of that good. Consequently, firms will lower their levels of production;

MICROQUIZ 15.2

In America there was (and still is in places) a "tradition" that a customer has their car filled up with petrol by a forecourt attendant. Suppose that an American State passes a law that requires that every petrol pump has exactly one attendant, and suppose that petrol pumps are always in use filling motorists' cars.

1. Will a rise in attendants' wages cause fewer to be hired? Explain.
2. Suppose attendants' wages represent one-third of the total cost of petrol to motorists and that the price elasticity of demand for petrol is -0.50. What is the elasticity of demand for petrol pump attendants?

[5]Actually, a proof of this assertion is not as simple as is implied here. The complicating factor arises when the input in question is "inferior", and it is no longer true that the marginal cost curve shifts downward when the price of such a factor declines. Nevertheless, as long as the good that is being produced has a downward-sloping demand curve, the firm's demand for the input will also be negatively sloped.

APPLICATION 15.2 *Controversy over the Minimum Wage*

Increasing the minimum wage rates is always a contentious political issue, in part because some economists believe that such an increase may be counterproductive. Nevertheless, 18 out of the 25 Member States of the European Union had legal minimum wage levels as shown in Table 1 below.

As can be seen from Table 1 the countries of the EU 25 can be divided into three groupings based on the euro figure of the minimum wage: the top group

TABLE 1 Statutory Minimum Wages Throughout Geographical Europe in January 2006[1]

	*Euro**	*PPS**	*National Currency*	*Percentage of Employees Receiving the minimum wage in 2004*
Belgium	1 234	1 184	1 234	—
Czech Republic	261	431	7 570	2.0
Estonia	192	305	3000	5.7
Greece**	668	785	668	—
Spain	631	722	631	0.8
France	1 218	1 128	1 218	15.6
Ireland	1 293	1 050	1 293	3.1
Latvia	129	240	90	—
Lithuania	159	292	550	12.1
Luxembourg	1 503	1 417	1503	18.0
Hungary	247	401	62 500	8.0
Malta	580	776	249	1.5
Netherlands	1 273	1 210	1 273	2.1
Poland	234	379	899	4.5
Portugal	437	510	437	5.5
Slovenia	512	676	123 000	2.0
Slovakia	183	314	6 900	1.9
United Kingdom	1 269	1 202	862	1.4
Bulgaria	82	191	160	—
Romania	90	189	330	12.0
Turkey	331	517	531	—
USA	753	779	893	1.4

SOURCE: EUROSTAT NEWS RELEASE 92/2006 – 13 JULY 2006 "MINIMUM WAGES IN THE EU25". EUROSTAT © EUROPEAN COMMUNITIES, (2006).

* Figures refer to statutory minimum wage levels as of 1 january 2006. The average exchange rate for December 2005 was used to convert the national currency figure to euros. The concept of Purchasing Power Standard allows (here) comparison of minimum wages in different countries once the prices of goods and services have been taken into account. So if a minimum wage in one country is twice as large as the minimum wage in another country but the prices of goods and services is also twice as large then the minimum wages are really at the same level *in terms of what they are able to purchase*.

** The figures for Greece refer to minimum wages for non-manual workers. A different rate applies to manual workers.

in terms of the highest euro payments takes in Luxembourg, Ireland, Netherlands, United Kingdom, Belgium, and France. The middle group of countries comprises Greece, Spain, Malta, Slovenia and Portugal. The low end comprises the countries of Latvia, Lithuania, Slovakia, Estonia, Poland, Hungary, and the Czech Republic. Given the graphical analysis which follows, one should not attach any normative inference to the use of the words low and high minimum wages. It *may* well be that "low" minimum wages are the most appropriate measure (combined with others) given the state of the labor market in different EU25 countries.

A Graphic Analysis

Figure 1 illustrates the possible effects of a minimum wage. Figure 1(a) shows the supply and demand curves for labor. Given these curves, an equilibrium wage rate, w_1, is established in the market. At this wage, a typical firm hires l_1 (shown on the firm's isoquant map in Figure 1[b]). Suppose now that a minimum wage of w_2 is imposed by law. This new wage will cause the typical firm to reduce its demand for labor from l_1 to l_2. At the same time, more labor (L_3) will be supplied at the specified minimum wage than was supplied at the lower wage rate. The imposition of the minimum wage will result in an excess of the supply of labor over the demand for labor of $L_3 - L_2$.

Minimum Wages and Teenage Unemployment

There is some empirical evidence that changes in the minimum wage law have had serious effects in increasing teenage unemployment. Teenagers are the labor-market participants most likely to be affected by minimum wage laws, because their skills usually represent the lower end of the spectrum. Minority group members, for whom unemployment rates often exceed 30 per cent, may be especially vulnerable.

Disputes over the Evidence

In an influential 1994 study, David Card and Alan Krueger challenged the belief that minimum wages reduce employment opportunities.[2] In this study, the authors compared employment levels at fast-food restaurants in New Jersey and Pennsylvania following increases in the New Jersey minimum wage. They concluded that there was no negative effect from the wage increase. That finding has not been universally accepted, however. An analysis of somewhat different data from similar fast-food franchises (Burger King, Wendy's, and KFC) in these states reached the opposite conclusion. More generally, the methods used in the Card-Krueger study have been subject to considerable dispute.[3] Still, although theoretical models provide the clear prediction that higher minimum

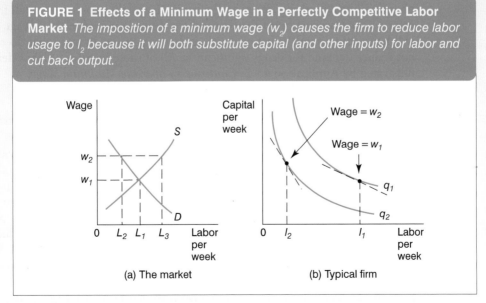

FIGURE 1 Effects of a Minimum Wage in a Perfectly Competitive Labor Market *The imposition of a minimum wage (w_2) causes the firm to reduce labor usage to l_2 because it will both substitute capital (and other inputs) for labor and cut back output.*

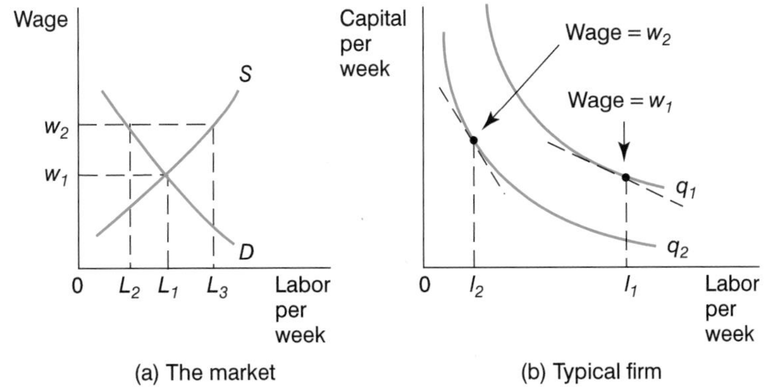

(Continued)

wages should reduce employment, measuring this effect empirically has proven rather difficult.[4]

To Think About

1. What factors will determine whether an increase in the minimum wage increases or decreases total wages received by workers affected by it?
2. Would an increase in minimum wage necessarily reduce employment in every industry?

[1]The minimum wage levels quoted above refer to full-time salaried workers in each country. Other categories of workers based on, say, age, disability etc., may also exist. The figure quoted is a gross amount, i.e. before taxes and social security contributions are taken off and in most cases are paid monthly. The legislation of some countries, however, is to quote the minimum wage as so much per hour, or day or week. These figures have been suitably converted to a monthly rate. In Spain and Greece where the minimum wage is paid 14 times per year a suitable adjustment has been made.

[2]David Card and Alan Krueger, "Minimum Wages and Employment: A Case Study of the Fast-Food Industry in New Jersey and Pennsylvania", *American Economic Review* (September 1994): 722–793.

[3]The controversy over the Card-Krueger results is summarized in the July 1995 issue of *Industrial and Labor Relations Review*.

[4]For an interesting, though unnecessarily opinionated, summary, see A. B. Krueger, "Teaching the Minimum Wage in Econ 101 in Light of the New Economics of the Minimum Wage", *Journal of Economic Education* (Summer 2001): 243–258.

because less output is being produced, the output effect will cause less labor to be demanded. In this way, the output effect reinforces the substitution effect. The size of this output effect will depend on (1) how large the increase in marginal costs brought about by the wage rate increase is, and (2) how much the quantity demanded will be reduced by a rising price. The size of the first of these components depends on how "important" labor is to total production costs, whereas the size of the second depends on how price-elastic the demand for the product is.

In industries for which labor costs are a major portion of total costs and for which demand is very elastic, output effects will be large. For example, an increase in wages for restaurant workers is likely to induce a large negative output effect in the demand for such workers, since labor costs are a significant portion of restaurant operating costs and the demand for meals eaten out is relatively price-elastic. An increase in wages will cause a big price rise, and this will cause people to reduce sharply the number of meals they eat out. On the other hand, output effects in the demand for pharmaceutical workers are probably small. Direct labor costs are a small fraction of drug production costs, and the demand for drugs is price-inelastic. Wage increases will have only a small effect on costs, and any increases in price that do result will not reduce demand for drugs significantly. All of these features of labor demand are illustrated by Application 15.2: *Controversy over the Minimum Wage*.

Input Supply

Firms get their inputs from three primary sources. Labor is provided by individuals who choose among available employment opportunities. Capital equipment is produced primarily by other firms and may be bought outright or rented for a period. Finally, natural resources are extracted from the ground and may be used directly (Exxon produces petrol from the crude oil it extracts) or sold to other firms (DuPont buys a petroleum feedstock from Exxon). Studying the supply decisions for firms that produce capital equipment and natural resources doesn't require us to develop any new tools. We already know how to model this supply, since nothing in our prior discussion required that firms produce their output only for consumers. Hence, we can safely assume that firms that produce inputs to be sold to other firms have upward-sloping supply curves.[6]

[6]That is, unless these firms are monopolies, in which case our analysis in Chapter 13 would apply.

Studying labor supply, however, raises different issues. This input (which constitutes the majority of most firms' costs) is supplied by individuals, so our previous models of firms are not much help in analyzing labor supply. Indeed, individuals are also partly involved in the supply of capital. In this case individuals provide the funds (usually channeled through banks or securities) that firms use to finance capital purchases. Again, models of firms' supply behavior do not help us to understand this process. In the appendix to this chapter, we look in detail at models of labor supply. Here we summarize our findings as they relate to drawing labor supply curves. Input supply questions that are related to interest rates (such as the supply of loans for firms or the decision to supply a natural resource) will be taken up in Chapter 16.

Labor Supply and Wages

For individuals, the wages they can earn represent the opportunity cost of not working at a paying job. Of course, no one works 24 hours a day, so individuals incur these opportunity costs regularly. They may refuse jobs with long hours, opt for early retirement, or choose to work in their homes. Presumably, all such decisions will be made to maximize utility. That is, individuals will balance the monetary rewards from working against the psychic benefits of other, non-paid activities.

A change in the wage rate, because it changes opportunity costs, will alter individuals' decisions. Although, as we show in the appendix to this chapter, the story is relatively complicated, in general we might expect that a rise in the wage would encourage market work. With higher wages, people might voluntarily agree to work overtime or to moonlight, they might retire later, or they might do less at home. In graphical terms, the supply curve for labor is positively sloped – higher wages cause more labor to be supplied.

Two additional observations should be kept in mind about labor supply. First, "wages" should be interpreted broadly to include all forms of compensation. Fringe benefits (such as health insurance), paid vacations, and firm-paid child care are important supplements to cash earnings. When we speak of the market wage w, we include all such returns to workers and these also represent costs to firms.

A second important lesson of labor supply theory is that supply decisions are based on individual preferences. If people prefer some jobs to others, perhaps because some offer a more pleasant work environment, labor supply curves will differ. Similarly, if attitudes toward work change, labor supply curves will shift (as seems to have been the case for married women during the 1960s and 1970s). Hence, a wide variety of "non-economic" factors may shift labor supply curves.

Equilibrium Input Price Determination

Bringing the various strands of our analysis together provides a straightforward view of how input prices are determined. This process is illustrated by the familiar demand (*D*) and supply (*S*) curves in Figure 15-3. For this figure we have chosen to depict equilibrium wage determination in the general labor market, but the graph would serve equally well for workers with specific skills or for any other input market. Given this demand–supply configuration, the equilibrium wage is w^*, and L^* units of labor are employed. As for any market, this equilibrium will tend to persist from period to period until demand or supply curves shift. As described earlier, in Application 15.2, government wage regulation may affect this equilibrium outcome.

Shifts in Demand and Supply

Although you should by now be familiar with analyses in which demand or supply curves shift, the details of input markets are sufficiently different from those for goods markets, so that some review may be in order. Marginal productivity theory provides the guide for understanding shifts in demand. Any factor that shifts a firm's underlying production function (such as the development of labor-saving technologies) will shift its input demand curve. In addition, because the demand for inputs is ultimately derived from the demand for the goods those inputs produce and the prices paid for those goods, happenings in product markets also can shift input demand curves. An increased demand for four-wheel-drive vehicles raises the price of the vehicles and increases the demand for workers who make them. On the other hand, a decline in the price of clothing brought on, say, by an increase in imports would reduce the demand for apparel workers. This situation can be reflected in Figure 15-3 by the shift in the demand curve to D'. The impact of such a shift would be to reduce equilibrium wages of apparel workers from w^* to w' and equilibrium employment from L^* to L'. If the adjustment in wages does not occur quickly (perhaps because wages are fixed by custom or long-term contract) some unemployment may be experienced in moving to this new equilibrium.

MICROQUIZ 15.3

In the United States, Social Security taxes of about 6 per cent are levied on workers, with a matching 6 per cent paid by firms. What will determine who *actually pays* these taxes?

Input supply curves are shifted by a variety of factors. For inputs that are produced by other firms (power tools, railroad locomotives, and so forth), the standard supply analysis applies – supply curves are shifted by anything that affects the input producers' costs. For labor input, changes in individuals'

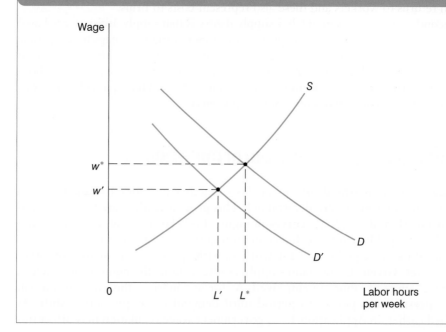

FIGURE 15-3 Equilibrium in an Input Market *An equilibrium wage (w^*) in the labor market is determined by demand (D) and supply (S). A shift in demand to D' would lower the wage to w' and the quantity of labor demanded to L'. If the wage does not adjust immediately, there may be some unemployment.*

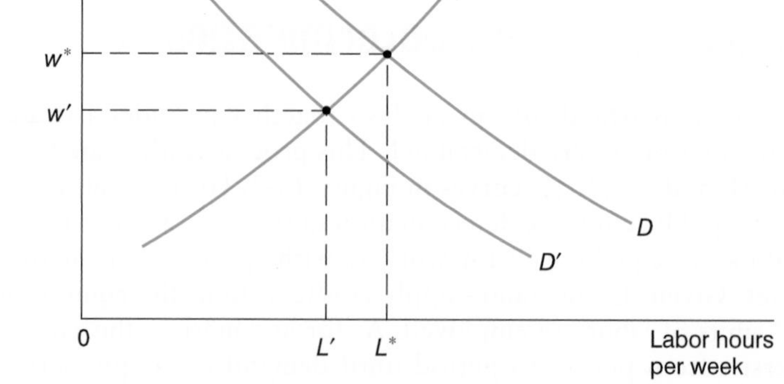

preferences (both for "work" in general and for the characteristics of specific jobs) will shift supply.

All these various reasons for shifting demand or supply curves for inputs are summarized in Table 15-2. It is important to keep these various factors in mind when you try to understand how the economy as a whole operates. Because people get their incomes from input markets, any investigation of well-being requires an understanding of these factors. Application 15.3: *What Characterizes Low-Paying Jobs in the European Union?* examines some recent trends.

Monopsony

In some situations, a firm may not be a price taker for the inputs it buys. It may be necessary for the firm to offer a wage above that currently prevailing to attract more employees, or the firm may be able to get a better price on some equipment by restricting its purchases. To explore these situations, it is most convenient to examine the polar case of **monopsony** (a single buyer) in an input market.

Monopsony Condition in which one firm is the only hirer in a particular input market.

Marginal Expense

If there is only one buyer of an input, that firm faces the entire market supply curve for the input. In order to increase its hiring of labor, say, by one or more units, the firm must move to a higher point on this supply curve. This will involve paying not only a higher wage to the last worker hired but also additional wages to those workers already employed. The extra cost of hiring the added worker therefore exceeds his or her wage rate, and the price-taking assumption we made earlier no longer holds. Instead, for a monopsonist facing an upward-sloping supply curve for an input, the **marginal expense** will exceed the market price of the input. For labor input, for example, the marginal expense (ME_L) of hiring one more worker exceeds the market wage (w).

Marginal expense The cost of hiring one more unit of an input. Will exceed the price of the input if the firm faces an upward-sloping supply curve for the input.

Notice the similarity between the concept of the marginal expense of an input and the marginal revenue for a monopolist. Both concepts are intended to be used

TABLE 15-2 Factors That Shift Input Demand and Supply Curves

Demand	*Labor Supply*	*Capital Supply*
Demand Shifts Outward		Supply Shifts Outward
Rise in output price	Decreased preference for leisure	Fall in input costs of equipment makers
Increase in marginal productivity	Increased desirability of job	Technical progress in making equipment
Demand Shifts Inward		Supply Shifts Inward
Fall in output price	Increased preference for leisure	Rise in input costs of equipment makers
Decrease in marginal productivity	Decreased desirability of job	

APPLICATION 15.3 *What Characterizes Low-Paying Jobs in the European Union?*

Wages earned by workers have exhibited a large degree of inequality throughout history. In *The Republic*, for example, Plato laments the fact that some workers make more than 10 times what others make. In recent years, wage inequality seems to have increased throughout the world. Below we present data for the European Union taken from work carried out by Eurostat and "DARES" – the Directorate of the French Ministry for Employment and Solidarity. These two bodies looked at the concept of a low wage using data from a 1996 survey called the European Community Household Panel using data from countries where it was available and deals with employees working at least 15 hours per week.

For each of the countries listed in Table 1 the low-wage threshold has been set at 60 per cent of the national median monthly wage.[1] As can be seen, the number of low wage employees varies a great deal within the EU from 6 per cent to 7 per cent in Denmark and Portugal to 21 per cent in the United Kingdom.

Now one needs to be careful here since an individual can have a low wage for one of two reasons; the wage rate – the amount paid per hour is very low or the wage rate per hour may be reasonably high but the total number of hours worked per week or month is very low. Clearly some individuals may have the misfortune to fall into both categories.

The Netherlands and the United Kingdom have a far larger proportion of their workforce working less than 30 hours compared to southern EU states. On the other hand Greece has the highest percentages of low wage rates while Belgium and Denmark have the lowest.

It turns out that low wages are more common in the service sector of the economy and among those who are on fixed-term contracts. Public sector workers are less affected than the private sector. Finally of all those who have low wage jobs, 77 per cent of them are women. This despite the fact that at the time in 1996 they made up roughly 38 per cent of all employees.

Another point to consider is that while wage rates are linked to the skill and educational level of the individual, the decision to work part-time can be voluntary or involuntary. In the survey mentioned here,

TABLE 1 Proportion of Low Wages, Part-Time Work, Low-Remuneration Rates and D5/D1 Ratio in the EU

	B	*DK*	*D*	*EL*	*E*	*F*	*IRL*	*I*	*L*	*NL*	*A*	*P*	*UK*	*EU-13*
Low wages (%)	9	7	17	17	13	13	18	10	16	16	16	6	21	15
Part-time work (%)	11	9	12	5	6	9	11	8	9	18	11	3	17	11
Low-remuneration rates (%)	4	4	11	16	12	9	13	10	14	6	8	6	9	9
D5/D1 ratio	1.6	1.5	2.4	2.6	1.9	2.0	2.2	1.8	2.0	2.0	2.1	1.5	2.5	2.2

SOURCE: STATISTICS IN FOCUS, *LOW-WAGE EMPLOYEES IN EU COUNTRIES,* ERIC MARLIER (EUROSTAT) AND SOPHIE PONTHIEUX (DARES) POPULATION AND SOCIAL CONDITIONS, THEME 3 – 11/2000. EUROSTAT © EUROPEAN COMMUNITIES, (2000).
KEY TO COUNTRIES: B, BELGIUM; DK, DENMARK; D, GERMANY; EL BELGIUM, E, SPAIN; F, FRANCE; IRL, IRELAND; I, ITALY; L, LUXEMBOURG; NL, NETHERLANDS; A, AUSTRIA; P, PORTUGAL; UK, UNITED KINGDOM. DATA FOR FINLAND AND SWEDEN NOT AVAILABLE. EU CALCULATIONS INCLUDE ONLY INDIVIDUALS AGED 16 TO 64 INCLUSIVE

20 per cent of women who worked part-time in 1996 stated that they did so through choice; almost 50 per cent said it was due to family commitments (domestic work, looking after children, sick relatives etc.). In 19 per cent of cases they did so as they could not find full-time jobs.

The ratio D5/D1 given in Table 1 is the ratio of the median wage to the upper end of the first wage decile.[2] The bigger this number the farther away are the low earners from those on median earnings and is hence an indication of how large is the wage dispersion.

To Think About

1 If someone is on a low wage by the definition given above does this automatically mean that they will have a low standard of living? Or vice-versa, does having a high wage guarantee a high standard of living? Explain your reasoning.

2 At what stage of someone's career is an individual more likely to have a low wage? Why do you think women are more represented in the category of having low wages?

3 If a country has a low D5/D1 ratio does this imply that the majority of people have a very good standard of living. [*Hint*: Look at the D5/D1 ratio for Portugal and Denmark.]

[1]Recall that the median of the numbers 1, 3, 6, 7, 10, 12, 15, 20, 45 is 10, i.e. the middle number but the mean value is roughly 13.2.

[2]If you arrange all the wages that people receive in a country (or in the above case a sample) from lowest to highest then divided the sample now into tenths. The bottom tenth will contain 10 per cent of the sample with the lowest wages.

when firms possess market power and their choices have an effect on prices. In such situations, firms are no longer price takers. Instead, firms will recognize that their actions affect prices and will use this information in making profit-maximizing decisions.

A Numerical Illustration

This distinction is easiest to see with a numerical example. Suppose that Disneyland Paris is the only hirer of people in the part of France where the entertainment resort is located who are both acrobats and jugglers and who are able to speak four foreign languages. Suppose also that the number of people willing to take this job (L) is a simple positive function of the hourly wage (w) given by

$$L = \frac{1}{2}w \qquad \{15.6\}$$

This relationship between the wage and the number of people who offer their services as special entertainers is shown in the first two columns of Table 15-3. Total labor costs ($w \cdot L$) are shown in the third column, and the marginal expense of hiring each entertainer is shown in the fourth column. The extra expense associated with adding another entertainer always exceeds the wage rate paid to that person. The reason is clear. Not only does a newly hired entertainer receive the higher wage, but all previously hired entertainers also get a higher wage. A monopsonist will take these extra expenses into account in its hiring decisions.

A graph can be used to help to clarify this relationship. Figure 15-4 shows the supply curve (S) for acrobats and jugglers. If Disneyland Paris wishes to hire three entertainers, it must pay €6 per hour, and total outlays will be €18 per hour. This situation is reflected by point A on the supply curve. If Disneyland Paris tries to hire a fourth entertainer with the specific skills it requires, it must offer €8 per hour to everyone – it must move to point *B* on the supply curve. Total outlays are now €32 per hour, so the marginal expense of hiring the fourth worker is €14 per hour. By comparing the sizes of the total outlay rectangles, we can see why the marginal expense is higher than the wage paid to the fourth worker. That worker's hourly wage is shown by the darker rectangle – it is €8 per hour. The other three workers, who were previously earning €6 per hour, now earn €8. This extra outlay is shown in lighter shade. Total labor expenses for four entertainers exceed those for three by the area of both rectangles. In this case, marginal expense exceeds the wage because Disneyland Paris is the sole hirer of people in this unusual occupation.

Monopsonist's Input Choice

As for any profit-maximizing firm, a monopsonist will hire an input up to the point at which the additional revenue and additional cost of hiring one more unit are equal. For the case of labor, this requires

$$ME_L = MVP_L \quad \{15.7\}$$

In the special case of a price taker that faces an infinitely elastic labor supply ($ME_L = w$), Equations 15.5 and 15.7 are identical. However, if the firm faces a positively sloped labor supply curve, Equation 15.7 dictates a different level of input choice, as we now show.

A Graphical Demonstration

The monopsonist's choice of labor input is illustrated in Figure 15-5. The firm's demand curve for labor (*D*) is drawn initially on the assumption that the firm is a price taker. The ME_L curve associated with the labor supply curve (*S*) is constructed in much the same way that the marginal revenue curve associated with a demand curve can be constructed. Because *S* is positively sloped, the ME_L curve always lies above *S*. The profit-maximizing level of labor input for the monopsonist is given by L_1. At this level of input use, marginal expense is equal to marginal value product (*MVP*). At L_1 the wage rate in the market is given by w_1. The quantity of labor demanded falls short of that which would be hired in a perfectly competitive market (L^*). The firm has restricted input demand to take advantage of its monopsonistic position in the labor market.

The formal similarities between this analysis and the monopoly analysis we presented in Chapter 13 should be clear. In particular, the actual "demand curve" for a

TABLE 15-3 Labor Costs of Hiring Special Entertainers in Disneyland Paris

Hourly wage	Workers supplied per hour	Total labor cost per hour	Marginal expense
€2	1	€2	€2
4	2	8	6
6	3	18	10
8	4	32	14
10	5	50	18
12	6	72	22
14	7	98	26

monopsonist consists of a single point. In Figure 15-5 this point is given by L_1, w_1. The monopsonist has chosen this point as the most desirable of all those points on the supply curve *S*. The firm would not choose another point unless some external change (such as a shift in the demand for the firm's output or a change in technology) affects labor's marginal value product.

Monopsonists and Resource Allocation

In addition to restricting its input demand, the monopsonist pays an input less than its marginal value product. This result is also illustrated in Figure 15-5. At the monopsonist's preferred choice of labor input (L_1), a wage of w_1 prevails in the market. For this level of input demand, the firm is willing to pay an amount equal to MVP_1: This is the amount of extra revenue that hiring another worker would provide to the firm. At L_1 the monopsonist pays workers less than they are "worth" to the firm. This is a clear indication that this firm uses too little labor. Total output could be increased by drawing labor from elsewhere in the economy into this industry. It should be clear from the figure that the extent of this misallocation of resources will be greater the more inelastic the supply of labor is to the monopsonist. The less responsive to low wages the supply of labor is, the more the monopsonist can take advantage of this situation.

MICROQUIZ 15.4

Is there a deadweight loss from the monopsony pictured in Figure 15-5? How would this loss be shown graphically? Who would suffer this loss?

Causes of Monopsony

To practice monopsonistic behavior a firm must possess considerable power in the market for a particular input. If the market is

FIGURE 15-4 Marginal Expense of Hiring Special Entertainers *Since Disneyland Paris is (in this example) the only hirer of acrobats and jugglers who can speak four foreign languages, it must raise the hourly wage offered from €6 to €8 if it wishes to hire a fourth warden. The marginal expense of hiring that warden is €14—his or her wage (€8, shown in dark) plus the extra €2 per hour that must be paid to the other three wardens (shown in light).*

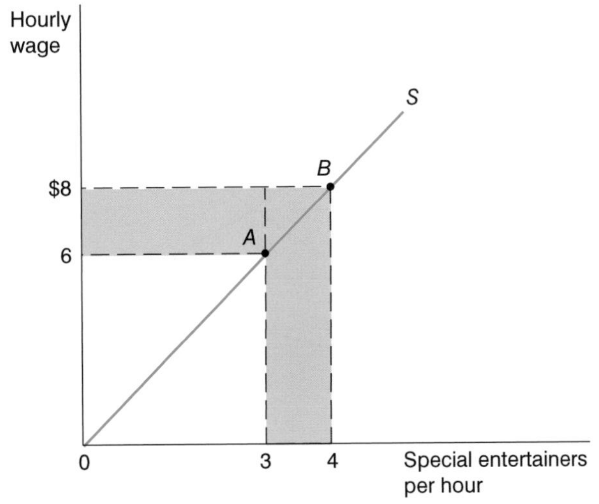

reasonably competitive, this cannot occur because other firms will recognize the profit potential reflected in the gap between *MVP*s and input costs. They will therefore bid for these inputs, driving their prices up to equality with marginal value products. Under such conditions the supply of labor to any one firm will be nearly infinitely elastic (because of the alternative employment possibilities available), and monopsonistic behavior will be impossible. Our analysis suggests monopsonistic outcomes will be observed in real-world situations in which, for some reason, effective competition for inputs is lacking. For example, some firms may occupy a monopsonistic position by being the only source of employment in a small town. Because moving costs for workers are high, alternative employment opportunities for local workers are unattractive, and the firm may be able to exert a strong effect on wages paid. Similarly, it may sometimes be the case that only one firm hires a particularly specialized type of input. If the alternative earnings prospects for that input are unattractive, its supply to the firm will be inelastic, presenting the firm with the opportunity for monopsonistic behavior. For example, marine engineers with many years of experience in designing nuclear submarines must work for the one or two companies that produce these vessels. Because other jobs would not make use of these workers' specialized training, alternative employment is not particularly attractive. Since the government occupies a monopoly position in the production of a number of goods requiring specialized inputs (space travel, armed forces, and national political offices, to name a few), it would be expected to be in a position to exercise monopsony power. In other cases a group of firms may combine to form a cartel in their hiring decisions (and, perhaps, in their output decisions too). Application 15.4: *Labor Demand in the United Kingdom* looks a little deeper at how demand for labor is forever changing and its relationship with hours worked.

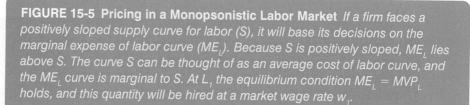

FIGURE 15-5 Pricing in a Monopsonistic Labor Market *If a firm faces a positively sloped supply curve for labor (S), it will base its decisions on the marginal expense of labor curve (ME_L). Because S is positively sloped, ME_L lies above S. The curve S can be thought of as an average cost of labor curve, and the ME_L curve is marginal to S. At L_1 the equilibrium condition $ME_L = MVP_L$ holds, and this quantity will be hired at a market wage rate w_1.*

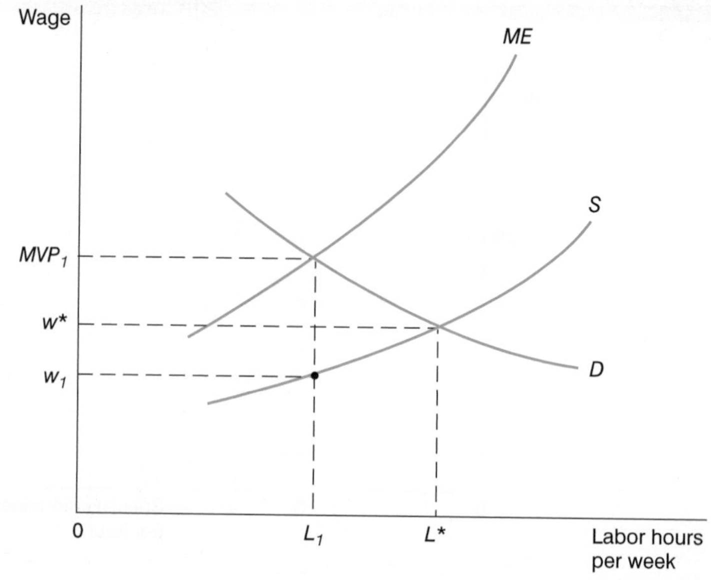

APPLICATION 15.4 *Labor Demand in the United Kingdom*

Labor demand is not static. That is, demand for labor is continuously changing over time. From Table 1 we can see a "snap shot" of the situation in Great Britain and two regions of that country over a 20-year period starting with 1983, followed by 1993, and then finally in 2003. The percentage figures working in specific industries illustrate a common observation in mature industrialized economies. Namely, the gradual decline of manufacturing as a source of large-scale employment and the rise of the service sector.

While the patterns of demand change are quite similar for both regions of Great Britain, the higher percentage figure for those working in manufacturing and other industries in general, reflects the higher industrialization that the North East of England witnessed since the industrial revolution and hence the different patterns of localized labor demand.

In the text we have concentrated on the marginal product of labor in helping us determine the demand for labor. In a more general sense other factors of both a micro and macro nature will play a role in helping shape the demand for labor at the firm level and at a national level. One such factor, product demand changes combined with total hours worked,

TABLE 1 Proportions of Employee Jobs by Broad Industry Sector for Great Britain and Selected Regions for the Years 1983, 1993 and 2003

	Great Britain			*London*			*North East of England*		
	1983	*1993*	*2003*	*1983*	*1993*	*2003*	*1983*	*1993*	*2003*
All									
Manufacturing	23	17	13	15	8	6	24	20	16
Services	67	76	81	79	88	90	64	72	77
Other Industries	10	7	6	6	4	4	16	8	7
Employee Jobs (thousands = 100%)	21 967	22 452	25 554	3703	3359	3972	1125	1128	1212
Men									
Manufacturing	29	24	19	19	11	8	31	28	26
Services	56	65	71	73	84	86	49	57	62
Other Industries	15	11	10	8	6	7	20	15	12
Employee Jobs (thousands = 100%)	12 241	11 249	12 886	2097	1722	2100	627	562	600
Women									
Manufacturing	16	10	7	10	6	4	15	12	6
Services	81	87	91	87	92	95	82	86	92
Other Industries	3	3	2	2	2	1	3	2	2
Employee Jobs (thousands = 100%)	9 727	11 203	12 669	1606	1638	1873	498	566	612

SOURCE: EMPLOYER SURVEYS. DISPLAYED IN "THE DEMAND FOR LABOUR IN THE UK", (2004) BY RICHARD D. WILLIAMS. THE OFFICE FOR NATIONAL STATISTICS. CROWN COPYRIGHT.

(*Continued*)

helps us to see that in reality our model of labor demand outlined in the text is a simplification which although powerful in giving us insights into how the firm rationalizes its demand for labor is nevertheless a first approximation.

Figure 1 shows the output of the United Kingdom along with total employment and total hours worked over the period 1993 to 2003. Firms, when faced with, say, a positive change in the demand for their product can actually decide to either increase the amount of labor (and/or by implication other factors of production as well) or increase the amount of hours that each factor of production works. If the firm decides on the latter course then this will be conditional on how much "slack" or unused capacity exists within the firm.

Notice that changes in output "leads" both total hours worked and total employment. Why should this be the case? A manager or owner of a firm when he or she observes an increase, or indeed a decrease, in the demand for the firm's product or service will not know immediately if this is the start of a prolonged trend. Perhaps it is just a temporary "blip" and very soon it will be back to "normal".

If at every sudden change of product demand a manager fires or hires workers (or again purchases new machinery) the manager may very well find that the change in product demand is temporary but he or she will be left in the position of having just hired extra staff which due to labor legislation he cannot simply fire immediately. Costs for the firm will have increased but there is no long-lasting increase in product demand. Only when the owner/manager is convinced that the shift in demand is "permanent" will new hiring/redundancy decisions be made.

During that period of uncertainty, it is probably much safer and perhaps easier to simply offer overtime to existing employees or to cut back on hours worked of existing employees rather than hire new employees. As such, when there is a change in demand for the firms product we should observe that total hours worked leads total employment which, roughly speaking it does. Notice in Figure 1, for example, that from Q3 in 1994 output starts to fall. It is total hours worked which first responds, falling roughly in Q4 of 1994. However, the total numbers in employment actually keep rising until Q4 of 1995.

To Think About

1 Due to an unexpected increase in product demand a manager decides to increase the

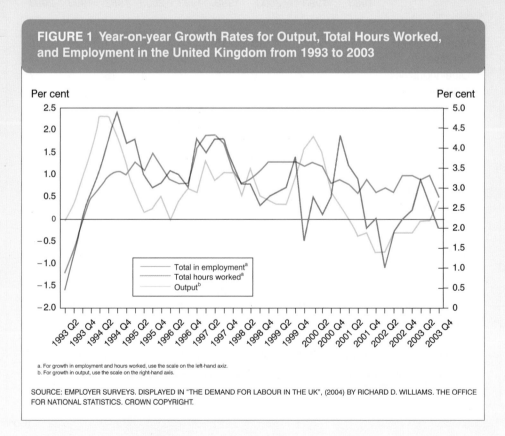

FIGURE 1 Year-on-year Growth Rates for Output, Total Hours Worked, and Employment in the United Kingdom from 1993 to 2003

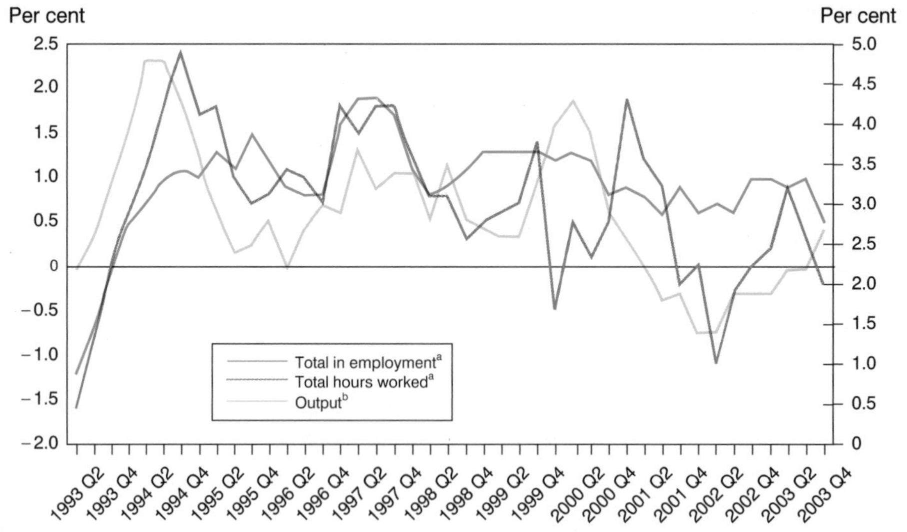

a. For growth in employment and hours worked, use the scale on the left-hand axiz.
b. For growth in output, use the scale on the right-hand axis.

SOURCE: EMPLOYER SURVEYS. DISPLAYED IN "THE DEMAND FOR LABOUR IN THE UK", (2004) BY RICHARD D. WILLIAMS. THE OFFICE FOR NATIONAL STATISTICS. CROWN COPYRIGHT.

amount of hours worked by her workforce rather than hire new employees. The total amount of capital, however, is not increased. Assuming spare capital capacity, what will the effect be on the marginal product of labor and capital?

2 Even if legislation allowed an owner of a firm to instantly dismiss employees in the event of a drop in demand for the firm's product, why might the owner *not* wish to do this? [*Hint*: Are there any costs associated with hiring and training employees?]

Bilateral Monopoly

In some cases there may be monopoly power on both sides of an input market. That is, suppliers of the input may have a monopoly, and the buyer of the input may be a monopsony. In this situation of **bilateral monopoly** the price of the input is indeterminate and will ultimately depend on the bargaining abilities of the parties involved.

Bilateral monopoly
A market in which both suppliers and demanders have monopoly power. Pricing is indeterminate in such markets.

Figure 15-6 illustrates this general result. Although the "supply" and "demand" curves in this diagram intersect at P^*, Q^*, this market equilibrium will not occur, because neither the supplier nor the demander of the input is a price taker. Instead, the monopoly supplier of the input will use the marginal revenue curve (*MR*) associated with the demand curve *D* to calculate a preferred price–quantity combination of P_1, Q_1. The monopsonistic buyer of this input, on the other hand, will use the marginal expense curve (*ME*) to calculate a preferred equilibrium of P_2, Q_2. Although both the monopolist and monopsonist here seek to restrict the quantity hired, the two opposing players in this market differ significantly on what they think the input should be paid. This will lead to some sort of bargaining between the two parties,

FIGURE 15-6 Bilateral Monopoly *When both demanders and suppliers have monopoly power, price will be indeterminate. Suppliers will want P_1, Q_1, but demanders will want P_2, Q_2.*

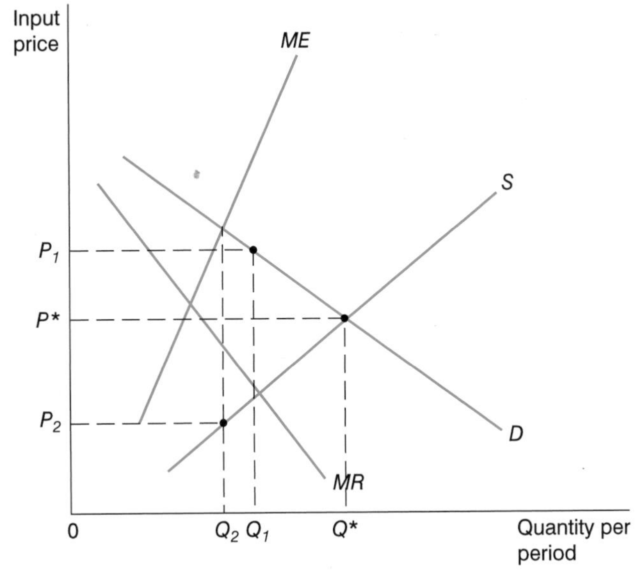

APPLICATION 15.5 *The Beautiful Game and the Payment of Wages to Footballers – Does it make the people happy?*[1]

"It is simply insane for any player to 'earn' £6m–£8m a year when the annual budget of even a club competing in the UEFA Champions League may be less than half that. What logic, right or economic necessity would qualify a man in his mid-20s to demand to earn in a month a sum that his own father – and the majority of fans – could not hope to earn in a decade?"

Joseph S. Blatter, President of FIFA, 11 October 2005.[2]

I was only in the game for the love of football – and I wanted to bring back happiness to the people of Liverpool.

(Bill Shankly, Liverpool FC's greatest manager after retiring at the age of 60 in 1974)

What determines the wage of a footballer or of a football "superstar"? In Britain – at one time – back in 1901 it was very simple: there was a maximum wage which originally was set at £4 per week. By 1922 it had risen to £8 per week (£6 in the summer). This should be compared to average weekly earnings of male employees in engineering in 1924 of £2.65 per week. The maximum rose to £20 per week by 1958 (£17 in the summer) when, for comparison, the average male manual employee was earning £12.83 per week. In 1961, however, the maximum wage was abolished.

Up to that time the main beneficiaries of this maximum wage had been the paying spectator where in 1960 "the average admission price was only 23 per cent higher in real terms than in 1926, despite the very much larger rise in real disposable incomes that had taken place in the meantime" (page 91 of Dobson and Goddard).

In 1963 a High Court ruling in the case of the football player George Eastman ruled against his employer Newcastle United. Players now became "free agents" if a contract was not offered at the expiry of an existing one. One direct consequence was a sharp rise in wages. "Famously, the weekly wage of Fulham and England captain Johnny Haynes increased almost immediately to £100: a rise of more than 400 per cent relative to the old maximum" (page 92 of Dobson and Goddard). In recent years wages have been awarded by clubs which make the £100 per week for Johnny Haynes (even allowing for inflation) look like small change.

If, instead of looking at the overall club total we look at individual salaries, then the Guardian newspaper reports[3] that the average Premiership footballer earns a basic salary of £676 000 per year (£13K per week) but that figure can rise by anything from 60 per cent to 100 per cent when bonuses are included also.

Players can also expect their wages to vary depending on the position they play – with strikers earning the highest wages at an average of £806 000 in the Premiership. Top flight midfielders can expect to earn an average of £754 000, with

TABLE 1 Average Wages and Salaries of Club per Week (£000)

	Premier League	Division One	Division Two	Division Three	All
1994	5 312	2 541	1 096	743	2 397
1995	6 568	2 485	1 256	788	2 735
1996	8 494	3 263	1 324	941	3 289
1997	10 905	3 768	1 734	1 051	4 080
1998	15 222	5 605	2 179	1 201	5 653
1999	19 545	5 343	2 861	1 302	6 729

SOURCE: DELOITTE AND TOUCHE (1999, 2000) QUOTED IN DOBSON AND GODDARD (2001, PAGE 97) *defenders on £653 000 and goalkeepers being paid £533 000.*

(Guardian Newspaper, 2 October 2006)

How is this phenomenal amount spent on wages to be justified? Rosen (1981) accounts for this phenomenon through two key aspects of consumer tastes and production technology. First, *Imperfect Substitution* between sellers of certain services. As Rosen comments

Hearing a succession of mediocre singers does not add up to a single outstanding performance. If a surgeon is 10 per cent more successful in saving lives than his fellows, most people would be willing to pay more than a 10 per cent premium for his services. A company involved in a $30 million law suit is rash to scrimp on the legal talent it engages.

(ibid., page 846)

This imperfect substitution helps to explain the (very) skewed earnings distribution that can be observed in football and other "labor markets".

A second feature of the labor market for footballers is the concentration of output on a few individuals. (By output we mean the playing of high-quality games, or rock star performances, top ace golfers etc.) Rosen explains this by liking the services of such "mega-stars" to *public goods*. (See Chapter 18 for a full explanation.) Public goods have the characteristics of having a zero marginal cost of production and the inability to exclude individuals from consuming the product or service. National defense and street lighting are standard textbook examples.

The joint consumption of an outstanding performance by David Beckham or Wayne Rooney are the fans in the stadium or those paying for a chance to watch on TV in their homes or in a public house where the games are screened.

Thus a performer or an author must put out more or less the same effort whether 10 or a 1000 people show up in the audience or buy the book.

(ibid., page 847)

Unlike pure public goods, however, customers can be excluded – fans can be excluded from stadia if they do not pay, pay-to-view customers must do exactly that, pay or not view; and if you don't buy a pint in a bar that has satellite TV you will not be welcome back!

The combination of imperfect substitution and joint consumption of technology makes for the possibility of talented individuals to command both large markets and very large incomes.

It should not be thought, however, that this imperfect substitution and joint consumption will lead to endless increases in wages indefinitely. Eventually internal and external diseconomies of scale will set in. What do we mean by this? As the number of football games played increases, the player (regardless of talent) will become more and more tired so affecting performance (as with rock stars, celebrity golfers, big-named authors etc.). As such, marginal costs start to rise. These are the internal diseconomies of scale.

External diseconomies of scale are associated with the medium through which the service (output) is transmitted to the customer. Live music played to a small select audience is superior to music played in an open-air park which in turn is superior to CD recorded music which in turn is superior to that of radio music of the songs. Each level increases the size of the market but at the cost of lowering quality. In doing so the willingness to pay for such output is reduced. So too with professional footballers.

To Think About

1 While the above application gives the theoretical points as regards top players' wages, there are nevertheless implications for the game itself which may or may not be favorable. In 1995 the European Court ruled that football players should be free to move throughout Europe at the expiry of their contracts without the permission of their club (the so-called Bosman ruling). They were, through their agents, free to negotiate with new prospective clubs. Given this "free movement of labor" what implications do you think this ruling has had on the game of football?

(*Hints*: There are quite a few implications. However, to start you off you may not know but Glasgow Celtic was the first British team to win the European Cup in 1967. Famously all the players who played that day in Lisbon, Portugal were

(*Continued*)

born within a 30-mile radius of Glasgow. Are big name clubs likely to nurture local talent in the same way or simply "buy off the shelf"? Also does the Bosman ruling increase or decrease monopsony power of football clubs? What was likely to be the impact on top footballers' wages? If more money is paid directly to top players what implication does that have for money available to develop the game of football?)

[1]Much of the information for this case study is taken from two excellent sources. First, the reader is recommended to read the *Economics of Football* by Stephen Dobson and John Goddard (2001). The book, while technical in places, nevertheless entwines the historical and current settings of the game along with theoretical underpinnings in more detail than can be presented here. In addition the paper by S. Rosen ("The Economics of Superstars", *American Economic Review*, Vol. 71, No.5 (1981): 85–858) is drawn on here to present the theoretical view as to why some superstars are paid what they are paid. The journal article by Rosen is a bit heavier but the reader is encouraged to read through it to deepen his or her knowledge of the theory behind the wages of "talented" individuals. Certainly any reader who wished to specialize in a study of the wages of superstars (from whatever background – sport, pop music, actors etc.) would need to tackle this article at some stage.

[2]See http://www.fifa.com/en/organisation/president/index/0,4095,110409,00.html?articleid=110409 Accessed 29 September 2006.

[3]See http://football.guardian.co.uk/News_Story/0,,1751542,00.html Accessed 2 October 2006.

with suppliers holding out for P_1 and demanders offering only P_2. Protracted labor disputes in major industries and "holdouts" by sports and entertainment celebrities are evidence of this type of market structure. Application 15.5: *The Beautiful Game and the Payment of Wages to Footballers – Does it make the people happy*? looks at various types of imperfect competition in the market for football players.

SUMMARY

In this chapter we illustrated some models of markets for inputs. The conclusions of this examination include the following:

- Firms will hire any input up to the point at which the marginal expense of hiring one more unit is equal to the marginal revenue yielded by selling what that input produces.
- If the firm is a price-taker in both the market for its inputs and the market for its output, profit-maximization requires that it employ that level of inputs for which the market price of each input (for example, the wage) is equal to the marginal value product of that input (for example, $P \times MP_L$).
- If the price of an input rises, the firm will hire less of it for two reasons. First, the higher price will cause the firm to substitute other inputs for the one whose price has risen. Second, the higher price will raise the firm's costs and reduce the amount it is able to sell. This output effect will also cause fewer units of the input to be hired.
- Input supply curves are positively sloped. Capital equipment supply is much like the supply of any good. Labor supply involves individual choices (see the appendix to this chapter).
- Equilibria in input markets resemble those in goods' markets, though reasons for shifts in supply and demand curves are somewhat different.
- If a firm is the sole hirer of an input (a monopsony), its hiring decisions will affect market prices of inputs. The marginal expense associated with hiring an additional unit of an input will exceed that input's price. Firms will take this into account in their hiring decisions – they will restrict hiring below what it would be under competitive conditions.

REVIEW QUESTIONS

1 In the supply–demand model of input pricing, who are the demanders? What type of assumptions would you use to explain their behavior? In this model, who are the suppliers? What types of assumptions would you use to explain their behavior?

2 Profit-maximization implies that firms will make input choices in a marginal way. Explain why the following marginal rules found in this chapter are specific applications of this general idea

a $MR_L = ME_L$

b $MP_L \times MR = ME_L = w$

c $MVP_L = ME_L = w$

d $MVP_L = w$

e $MVP_L = ME_L > w$

If firms follow these various rules, will they also be producing a profit-maximizing level of output? That is, will they produce that quantity for which $MR = MC$? Will they also be minimizing costs if they use these rules? Explain your answers both intuitively and with algebra.

3 Explain why if a price-taking firm has only one variable input the *MVP* curve is also its demand curve for that input, but if the firm has two or more variable inputs, its demand curve for one of them reflects a whole family of *MVP* curves.

4 A fall in the price of an input induces a profit–maximizing firm to experience both substitution and output effects that cause it to hire more of that input. Explain how the profit-maximizing assumption is used in explaining the direction of each of these effects. Did you have to use the assumption that the input is not inferior in your analysis? Do you think a similar statement can be made about inferior inputs?

5 Suppose the price of an input used by firms with fixed-proportions production functions were to fall. Why would such a change not cause any substitution effects for these firms' input demand? Would there, however, be output effects? What would determine the size of these effects?

6 If the pricing of any input can be explained by a simple supply–demand model, what labels should be put on the axes? What types of influences might cause the demand curve or the supply curve to shift?

7 In Chapter 11 we described the notions of consumer and producer surplus as they relate to a competitive equilibrium. How should similar areas be interpreted in a supply–demand graph of the competitive equilibrium in a factor market?

8 In Chapter 13, we showed the relationship between marginal revenues and market price for a monopoly to be given by

$$MR = P\left(1 + \frac{1}{c}\right)$$

where *e* is the price elasticity of demand for the product. For a monopsony, a similar relationship holds for the marginal expense associated with hiring more labor:

$$ME = w\left(1 + \frac{1}{e}\right)$$

where *e* is the elasticity of supply of labor to the firm. Use this equation to show

a that for a firm that is a price taker in the labor market, $ME = w$;

b that $ME > w$ for a firm facing a labor supply curve that is not infinitely elastic at the prevailing wage; and

c that the gap between *ME* and *w* is larger the smaller *e* is.

Explain all of these results intuitively.

9 How would you measure the strength of a monopsonist in an input market? Would a monopsony necessarily be very profitable? What would you need to add to Figure 15–5 in order to show a monopsonist's profit graphically?

10 "In a situation of bilateral monopoly, the two parties are more likely to agree on quantity than on price." Explain why this is the case.

PROBLEMS

15.1 A landowner has three farms (*A*, *B*, and *C*) of differing fertility. The levels of output for the three farms with one, two, and three laborers employed are as follows

Number of laborers	Level of Output Farm *A*	Farm *B*	Farm *C*
1	10	8	5
2	17	11	7
3	21	13	8

For example, if one laborer were hired for each farm, the total output would be $10 + 8 + 5 = 23$. This would represent a poor allocation of labor, since if the farm *C* laborer were assigned to farm *A* the total output would be $17 + 8 = 25$.

a If market conditions caused the landowner to hire five laborers, what would be the most productive allocation of that labor? How much would be produced? What is the marginal product of the last worker?

b If we assume that farm output is sold in a perfectly competitive market with one unit of output priced at €1, and we assume that labor market equilibrium occurs when five workers are hired, what wage is paid? How much profit does the landowner receive?

15.2 Assume that the quantity of envelopes licked per hour by Sticky Gums, Inc., is

$$q = 10\,000\sqrt{L}$$

where *L* is the number of laborers hired per hour by the firm. Assume further that the envelope-licking business is perfectly competitive with a market price of €0.01 per envelope. The marginal product of a worker is given by

$$MP_L = 5000/\sqrt{L}$$

a How much labor would be hired at a competitive wage of €10? €5? €2? Use your results to sketch a demand curve for labor.

b Assume that Sticky Gums hires its labor at an hourly wage of €10. What quantity of envelopes will be licked when the price of a licked envelope is €0.10? €0.05? €0.02? Use your results to sketch a supply curve for licked envelopes.

15.3 Suppose there are a fixed number of 1000 identical firms in the perfectly competitive concrete pipe industry. Each firm produces the same fraction of total market output and each firm's production function for pipe is given by

$$q = \sqrt{KL}$$

and for this production function

$$RTS\ (L \text{ for } K) = K/L$$

Suppose also that the market demand for concrete pipe is given by

$$Q = 400\,000 - 100\,000P$$

where *Q* is total concrete pipe.

a If $w = v = €1$, in what ratio will the typical firm use *K* and *L*? What will be the long-run average and marginal cost of pipe?

b In the long-run equilibrium, what will be the market equilibrium price and quantity for concrete pipe? How much will each firm produce? How much labor will be hired by each firm and in the market as a whole?

c Suppose the market wage, *w*, rose to €2 while *v* remained constant at €1. How will this change the capital–labor ratio for the typical firm, and how will it affect its marginal costs?

d Under the conditions of part *c*, what will the long-run market equilibrium be? How much labor will now be hired by the concrete pipe industry?

e How much of the change in total labor demand from part *b* to part *d* represents the substitution effect resulting from the change in wage and how much represents the output effect?

15.4 Suppose the demand for labor is given by

$$L = -50w + 450$$

and the supply is given by

$$L = 100w$$

where L represents the number of people employed and w is the real wage rate per hour.

a What will be the equilibrium levels for w and L in this market?

b Suppose the government wishes to raise the equilibrium wage to €4 per hour by offering a subsidy to employers for each person hired. How much will this subsidy have to be? What will the new equilibrium level of employment be? How much total subsidy will be paid?

c Suppose instead the government declared a minimum wage of €4 per hour. How much labor would be demanded at this price? How much unemployment would there be?

d Graph your results.

15.5 Assume that the market for rental cars for business purposes is perfectly competitive, with the demand for this capital input given by

$$K = 1500 - 25v$$

and the supply given by

$$K = 75v - 500$$

where K represents the number of cars rented by firms and v is the rental rate per day.

a What will be the equilibrium levels for v and K in this market?

b Suppose that following an oil embargo petrol prices rise so dramatically that now business firms must take account of petrol prices in their car rental decisions. Their demand for rental cars is now given by

$$K = 1700 - 25v - 300g$$

where g is the per-liter price of petrol. What will be the equilibrium levels for v and K if g = €2? If g = €3?

c Graph your results.

d Since the oil embargo brought about decreased demand for rental cars, what might be the implication for other capital input markets as a result? For example, employees may still need transportation, so how might the demand for mass transit be affected? Since business people also rent cars to attend meetings, what might happen in the market for telephone equipment as employees drive less and use the telephone more? Can you think of any other factor input markets that might be affected?

15.6 Suppose that the supply curve for the labor to a firm is given by

$$L = 100w$$

and the marginal expense of labor curve is given by

$$ME_L = L/50$$

where w is the market wage. Suppose also that the firm's demand for labor (marginal revenue product) curve is given by

$$L = 1000 - 100MRP_L$$

a If the firm acts as a monopsonist, how many workers will it hire in order to maximize profits? What wage will it pay? How will this wage compare to the MRP_L at this employment level?

b Assume now that the firm must hire its workers in a perfectly competitive labor market, but it still acts as a monopoly when selling its output. How many workers will the firm hire now? What wage will it pay?

c Graph your results.

15.7 Carl the clothier owns a large garment factory on a remote island. Carl's factory is the only source of employment for most of the islanders, and thus Carl acts as a monopsonist. The supply curve for garment workers is given by

$$L = 80w$$

and the marginal-expense-of-labor curve is given by

$$ME_L = L/40$$

where L is the number of workers hired and w is their hourly wage. Assume also that Carl's labor demand (marginal value product) curve is given by

$$L = 400 - 40MVP_L$$

a How many workers will Carl hire in order to maximize his profits, and what wage will he pay?

b Assume now that the government implements a minimum-wage law covering all garment workers. How many workers will Carl now hire, and how much unemployment will there be if the minimum wage is set at €3 per hour? €3.33 per hour? €4.00 per hour?

c Graph your results.

d How does the imposition of a minimum wage under monopsony differ in results from a minimum wage imposed under perfect competition (assuming the minimum wage is above the market-determined wage)?

15.8 The Ajax Coal Company is the only employer in its area. It can hire any number of female workers or male workers it wishes. The supply curve for women is given by

$$L_f = 100w_f$$

$$ME_f = L_f/50$$

and for men by

$$L_m = 9w_m^2$$

$$ME_m = \frac{1}{2}\sqrt{L_m}$$

where w_f and w_m are, respectively, the hourly wage rate paid to female and male workers. Assume that Ajax sells its coal in a perfectly competitive market at €5 per tonne and that each worker hired (both men and women) can mine two tonnes per hour. If the firm wishes to maximize profits, how many female and male workers should be hired and what will the wage rates for these two groups be? How much will Ajax earn in profits per hour on its mining machinery? How will that result compare to one in which Ajax was constrained (say, by market forces) to pay all workers the same wage based on the value of their marginal products?

Note: The following problems involve mainly the material from the Appendix to Chapter 15.

15.9 Mrs Smith has a guaranteed income of €10 per day from an inheritance. Her preferences require her always to spend half her potential income on leisure (*H*) and consumption (*C*).

a What is Mrs Smith's budget constraint in this situation?

b How many hours will Mrs Smith devote to work and to leisure in order to maximize her utility, given that her market wage is €1.25? €2.50? €5.00? €10.00?

c Graph the four different budget constraints and sketch in Mrs Smith's utility-maximizing choices. (*Hint*: When graphing budget constraints, remember that when $H = 24$, $C = 10$, not 0.)

d Graph Mrs Smith's supply-of-labor curve.

15.10 How will Mrs Smith's supply-of-labor curve (calculated in part d of problem 15.9) shift if her inheritance increases to €20 per day? Graph both supply curves to illustrate this shift.

Appendix to Chapter 15

Labor Supply

In this appendix, we use the utility-maximization model to study individual labor-supply decisions. The ultimate goal of this discussion is to provide additional details about the labor supply curves that we used to study how wages are determined in Chapter 15.

Allocation of Time

Part Two studied how an individual chooses to allocate a fixed amount of income among a variety of available goods. People must make similar choices in deciding how they will spend their time. The number of hours in a day (or in a year) is absolutely fixed, and time must be used as it passes by. Given this fixed amount of time, any person must decide how many hours to work; how many hours to spend consuming a wide variety of goods, ranging from cars and television sets to operas; how many hours to devote to self-maintenance; and how many hours to sleep. Table 15A-1 shows that there is considerable variation in time use between men and women and among various countries around the world. By studying the division of time people choose to make among their activities, economists are able to understand labor-supply decisions. Viewing work as only one of a number of choices open to people in the way

TABLE 15A-1 Time Allocation (Percentage of Time during Typical Week)

	Men			*Women*		
	US	*Japan*	*Russia*	*US*	*Japan*	*Russia*
Market work	28.3%	33.6%	35.1%	15.4%	15.3%	25.4%
Housework	8.2	2.1	7.1	18.2	18.5	16.1
Personal care and sleep	40.6	43.1	40.4	42.6	42.9	41.6
Leisure and other	22.9	21.2	17.4	23.8	23.3	16.9

SOURCE: ADAPTED FROM F. T. JUSTER AND F. P. STAFFORD, "THE ALLOCATION OF TIME: EMPIRICAL FINDINGS, BEHAVIORAL MODELS AND PROBLEMS AND MEASUREMENT", *JOURNAL OF ECONOMIC LITERATURE* (JUNE 1991), TABLE 1.

they spend their time enables us to understand how these decisions may be adjusted in response to changing opportunities.

A Simple Model of Time Use

Leisure Time spent in any activity other than market work.

We assume that there are only two uses to which any person may devote his or her time: either engaging in market work at a wage rate of w per hour or not working. We refer to non-work time as **leisure**, but to economists this word does not mean idleness. Time that is not spent in market work can be used in many productive ways: for work in the home, for self-improvement, or for consumption (it takes time to use a television set or a bowling ball).[1] All of these activities contribute to a person's well-being, and time will be allocated to them in a utility-maximizing way.

More specifically, assume that utility depends on consumption of market goods (C) and on the amount of leisure time (H) used. Figure 15A-1 shows an indifference curve map for this utility function. The diagram has the familiar shape introduced in Chapter 2. It shows those combinations of C and H that yield an individual various levels of utility.

Now we must describe the budget constraint that faces this person. If the period we are studying is one day, the individual will work $(24 - H)$ hours. That is, he or she will work all of the hours not devoted to leisure. For this work, she or he will earn w per hour and will use this to buy consumption goods.

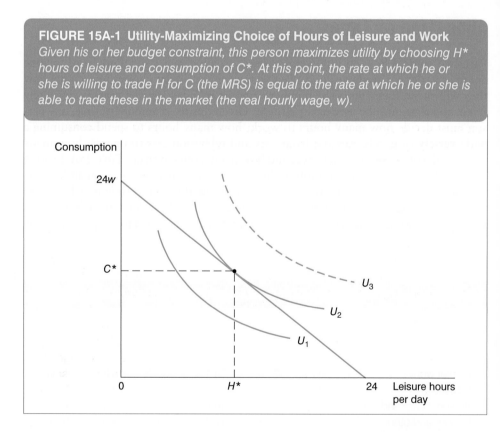

FIGURE 15A-1 Utility-Maximizing Choice of Hours of Leisure and Work
Given his or her budget constraint, this person maximizes utility by choosing H hours of leisure and consumption of C*. At this point, the rate at which he or she is willing to trade H for C (the MRS) is equal to the rate at which he or she is able to trade these in the market (the real hourly wage, w).*

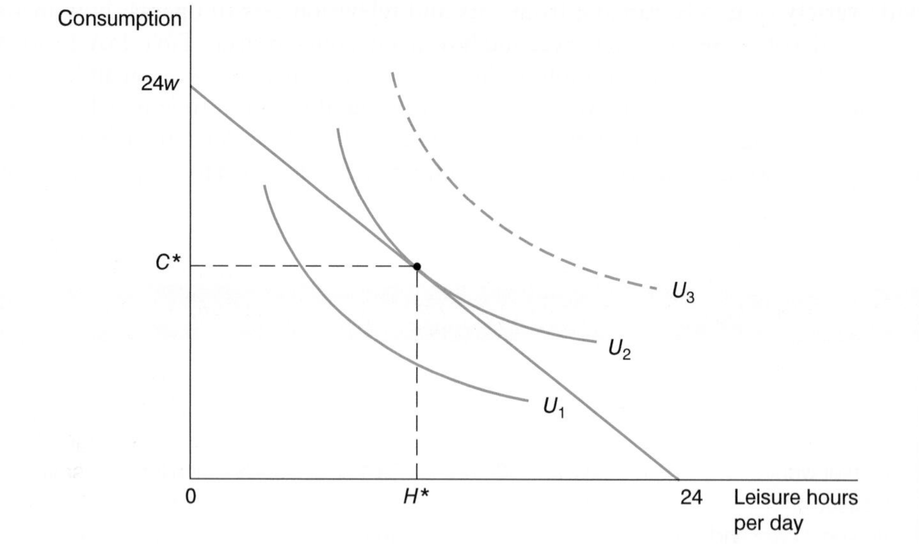

[1]For the classic treatment of the allocation of time, See G. S. Becker, "A Theory of the Allocation of Time". *The Economic Journal* (September 1965): 493–517.

APPLICATION 15A.1 *Changing Labor Force Participation of Younger Women and Older Men*

The two most important trends in labor market behavior in the United States and many other industrialized countries during the past 50 years are: (1) the increasing number of women who hold paying jobs and (2) the decline in labor force participation for older men.

Increasing Female Labor Force Participation

For women in the age category 25–34, the increase in labor force participation has been spectacular. Between 1960 and 2004, the fraction of women age 25 to 34 in the labor force more than doubled. Many reasons have been put forward to explain this major social phenomenon. Economists have primarily tended to focus on expanding job opportunities and rising real wage rates as the primary explanation. Because many women in this age bracket have good alternative uses for their time (such as working in the home rather than in the market), substitution effects from higher wages would be expected to be larger than income effects for this segment of the population. Sociologists, on the other hand, tend to attribute increasing work by women to changing cultural and political factors. This is, they attribute the change to a shift in women's labor supply curves rather than to movements along a relatively fixed supply curve motivated by wage changes. Regardless of whether changes in wages motivated changing cultural norms or changing norms affected wages, the study of women's labor supply behavior is one of the most interesting topics in labor economics because it illustrates considerable variability in responses to changing conditions.

Declining Labor Force Participation for Older Men

Recent trends in labor force participation for older men have been precisely opposite that for younger women. Between 1960 and 1985, the labor force participation rate for men age 65 and over fell to less than half its initial level before rebounding slightly over the next two decades. This pattern is all the more puzzling given the significant improvements in the health status of older men that occurred over this period. Because many older men credit poor health as the reason they are not employed, such improvements should have resulted in more, rather than less, labor force activity for this group.

Research on reasons for the decline in labor force participation by older men has focused primarily on issues related to retirement. Of course, compulsory retirement at age 65 is now illegal in most occupations. But financial incentives in many company pension plans tend to favor such a retirement date. The US Social Security program also has provisions that discourage some older workers from taking jobs. Most important, workers who retire before Social Security's "normal retirement age" (scheduled to slowly rise to 67 under current laws) incur an implicit tax of 50 per cent on any earnings they may have. Prior to 1990 this "earnings test" applied to all workers under age 70. Its elimination may in part explain the upturn in labor force participation rates for this group in recent years.

To Think About

1 How does taxation affect the labor supply of women? Would you expect higher taxes to lead to more or fewer hours worked? For married couples, how does income taxation affect their joint labor supply decisions?

2 Workers, of course, know that they will be eligible for Social Security when they retire. How does this knowledge affect both their work behavior and their savings decisions during their pre-retirement years?

The Opportunity Cost of Leisure

Each extra hour of leisure this person takes reduces his or her income (and consumption) by w dollars. The hourly wage therefore reflects the opportunity cost of leisure. People have to "pay" this cost for each hour they do not work. The wage rate used to make these calculations should be a real wage in that it should represent how workers can turn their earnings into actual consumer goods. A nominal wage of €1 per hour provides the same purchasing power when the typical item costs €0.25 as does a wage of €100 per hour when that item sells for €25. In either case, the person must work 15 minutes to buy the item. Alternately, in both cases, the opportunity cost of taking one more hour of leisure is to do without four consumption items.

Utility Maximization

To show the utility-maximizing choices of consumption and leisure, we must first graph the budget constraint. This is done in Figure 15A-1. If this person doesn't work at all, he or she can enjoy 24 hours of leisure. This is shown as the horizontal intercept of the budget constraint. If, on the other hand, this person works 24 hours per day, he or she will be able to buy $(24 \cdot w)$ in consumption goods. This establishes the vertical intercept in the figure. The slope of the budget constraint is $-w$. This reflects opportunity costs – each added hour of leisure must be "purchased" by doing without w worth of consumption items. For example, if w = €10, this person will earn €240 if he or she works 24 hours per day. Each hour not worked has an opportunity cost of €10.

Given this budget constraint, this person will maximize utility by choosing to take H^* hours of leisure and to work the remaining time. With the income earned from this work, he or she will be able to buy C^* units of consumption goods. At the utility-maximizing point, the slope of the budget $(-w)$ is equal to the slope of indifference curve U_2. In other words, the person's real wage is equal to the marginal rate of substitution of leisure hours for consumption.

If this were not true, utility would not be as large as possible. For example, suppose a person's *MRS* were equal to 5, indicating a willingness to give up 5 units of consumption to get an additional hour of leisure. Suppose also that the real wage is €10. By working one more hour, he or she is able to earn enough to buy 10 units (that is, €10 worth) of consumption. This is clearly an inefficient situation. By working one hour more, this person can buy 10 extra units of consumption; but he or she required only 5 units of consumption to be as well-off as before. By working the extra hour, this person earns 5 (= 10 − 5) more units of consumption than required. Consequently he or she could not have been maximizing utility in the first place. A similar proof can be constructed for any case in which the *MRS* differs from the market wage, which proves that the two trade-off rates must be equal for a true utility maximum.

Substitution effect of a change in *w* Movement along an indifference curve in response to a change in the real wage. A rise in *w* causes an individual to work more.

MICROQUIZ 15A.1

How would you graph the utility maximizing choices for individuals with the following preferences?

1. Ms Steady always works exactly seven hours each day no matter what wage is offered to her.
2. Mr Mellow currently doesn't work, but might if the right wage were offered.

Income and Substitution Effects of a Change in the Real Wage Rate

A change in the real wage rate can be analyzed the same way we studied a price change in Chapter 3. When w rises, the price of leisure becomes higher – people must give up more in lost wages for each hour of leisure consumed. The **substitution effect** of an increase in w on the hours of leisure is therefore to reduce them. As leisure becomes more expensive, there is reason to consume less of it. However, the **income effect** of a rise in the wage tends to increase leisure. Because leisure is a normal good, the higher income resulting from a higher w increases the demand for it. Hence income and substitution effects work in the opposite direction. It is impossible to predict whether an increase in w will increase or decrease the demand for leisure time. Because leisure and work are mutually exclusive ways to use time, this also shows that it is impossible to predict what will happen to the number of hours worked when wages change.

Income effect of a change in w Movement to a higher indifference curve in response to a rise in the real wage rate. If leisure is a normal good, a rise in w causes an individual to work less.

A Graphical Analysis

Figure 15A-2 illustrates two different reactions to an increase in w. In both graphs, the initial wage rate is w_0, and the optimal choices of consumption and leisure are given by C_0 and H_0. When the wage rate increases to w_1, the utility-maximizing combination moves to C_1, H_1. This movement can be divided into two effects. The substitution effect is represented by the movement along the indifference curve U_0 from H_0 to S. This effect works to reduce the number of hours of leisure in both parts of Figure 15A-2. People substitute consumption for leisure since the relative price of leisure has increased.

The movement from S to C_1, H_1 represents the income effect of a higher real wage. Because leisure time is a normal good, increases in income cause more leisure to be demanded. Consequently, the income and substitution effects induced by the increase in w work in opposite directions. In Figure 15A-2(a) the demand for leisure is reduced by the rise in w; that is, the substitution effect outweighs the income effect. On the other hand, in Figure 15A-2(b) the income effect is stronger and the demand for leisure increases in response to an increase in w. This person actually chooses to work fewer hours when w increases. In the analysis of demand, we would have considered this result unusual – when the price of leisure rises, this person demands more of it. For the case of normal consumption goods, income and substitution effects work in the same direction, and both cause quantity to decline when price increases. In the case of leisure, however, income and substitution effects work in opposite directions. An increase in w makes a person better-off because he or she is a *supplier* of labor. In the case of a consumption good, an individual is made worse off by a rise in price because he or she is a *consumer* of that good. Consequently, it is not possible to predict exactly how a person will respond to a wage increase – he or she may work more or fewer hours depending on his or her preferences.

Market Supply Curve for Labor

If we are willing to assume that in most cases substitution effects of wage changes outweigh income effects, individual labor supply curves will have positive slopes. We can construct a market-supply-of-labor curve from these individual supply curves by "adding" them up. At each possible wage rate, we add together the quantity of labor offered by each person in order to arrive at a market total. One particularly interesting aspect of this procedure is that, as the wage rate rises, more people may be induced to enter the labor force. That is, rising wages may induce some people who were not previously employed to take

MICROQUIZ 15A.2

Suppose the government of a European country is choosing between two types of income tax: (1) a proportional tax on wages and (2) a lump-sum tax of a fixed-euro amount. How would each of these taxes be expected to affect the labor supply of a typical person?

jobs. Figure 15A-3 illustrates this possibility for a simple case of two individuals. For a real wage below w_1, neither person chooses to work in the market. Consequently, the market supply curve of labor (Figure 15A-3[c]) shows that no labor is supplied at real wages below w_1. A wage in excess of w_1 causes person 1 to enter the labor market. However, as long as wages fall short of w_2, person 2 will not work. Only at a

FIGURE 15A-2 Income and Substitution Effects of a Change in the Real Wage Rate *Because the individual is a supplier of labor, the income and substitution effects of an increase in the real wage rate affect the hours of leisure demanded (or hours of work) in opposite directions. In panel (a), the substitution effect (movement to point S) outweighs the income effect and a higher wage causes hours of leisure to decline to H_1. Hours of work, therefore, increase. In panel (b), the income effect is stronger than the substitution effect and H increases to H_1. Hours of work in this case fall.*

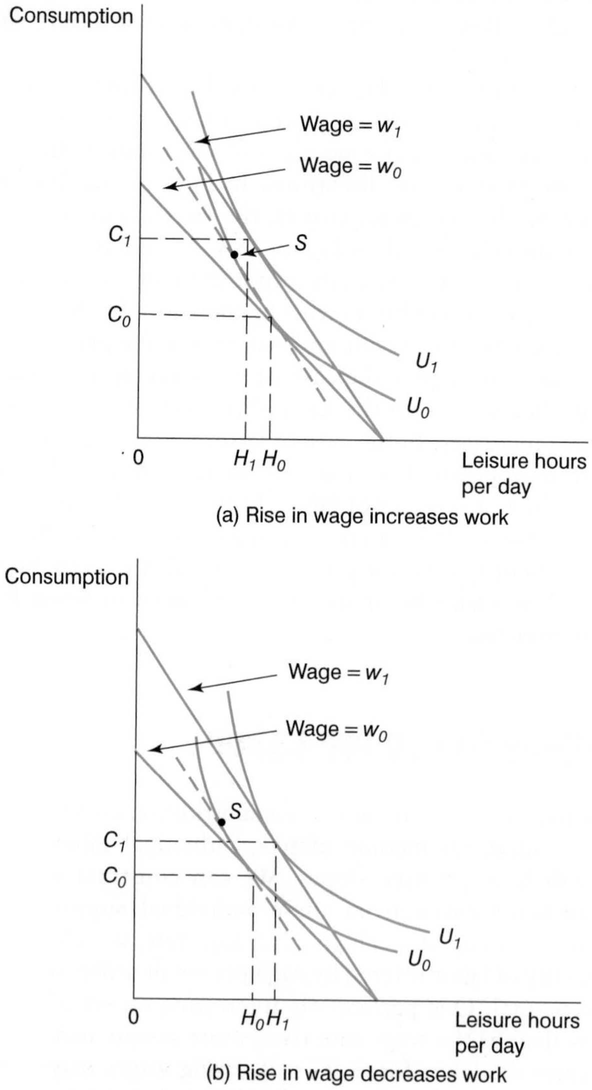

APPLICATION 15A.2 *Mr Demand seeks lady of quality in the form of Ms Supply but in India and China she is playing hard to get . . .*

Day after day, day after day,
We stuck, nor breath nor motion;
As idle as a painted ship
Upon a painted ocean.
Water, water, everywhere,
And all the boards did shrink;
Water, water, everywhere,
Nor any drop to drink.
(The Rime of the Ancient Mariner
by Samuel Coleridge, 1797)

This is an abridged version of an article that appeared in the *Financial Times* on 19 July 2006 by Jo Johnson and Richard McGregor. Read the article carefully and then answer the questions that follow.

When Ishmael Chawla advertises for software developers in New Delhi, he braces himself for rejection. "More than half our candidates don't show up for a scheduled interview", says Mr Chawla, 33, who manages the Indian operations of LiveCareer, a San Francisco-based provider of online career counseling. "Even then we probably have one qualified person for every 20 we interview – and by qualified, I essentially mean 'trainable'."

In China, the skills shortage is so severe in some sectors that even local Chinese companies are forced to look offshore for suitable staff. The country, unlike many in the developing world, had long been able to meet its own needs for commercial pilots, for instance. Not now.

Huang Mei, an official at United Eagle Airlines, a new private airline in western China, says the carrier could not have got off the ground on schedule without foreign pilots. "Although we need to pay them an annual salary of Rmb800 000 (Euros 80 000), the overall cost is reasonable compared to paying for the training of someone from scratch", says Ms Huang.

India and China, which represent 40 per cent of the world's supply of labor, have an abundance of unskilled workers and a daunting backlog of unemployed. Over the next five years, according to United Nations predictions, they will respectively contribute an additional 71 m and 44 m to the global labor pool, the lion's share of demographic growth. During this time the US workforce will expand by 10 m, Europes will not increase and Japans will decline by 3 m.

Yet shortages of skilled labor are biting across an ever greater swath of both economies, with significant implications for global business. The idea that both countries are fathomless wells of good-value talent is colliding with a very different reality. Companies that have offshored production there in anticipation of savings are feeling the pinch of labor markets that have tightened much more rapidly than expected.

China produces 600 000 university-trained engineers every year, for example, a figure often cited to illustrate the country's inexorable rise as a technology power. But a McKinsey survey of nine occupations found that fewer than one in ten were employable by multinationals.

Chinese students are the product of an education system built around rote learning. As a result, the pool of engineers suitable to work for multinationals is about 160 000, less than one-third of the graduates or about the same number produced each year by the UK, according to McKinsey.

While 3 m students graduate from Indian universities each year, only about 25 per cent of engineering graduates and 10–15 per cent of general college graduates are considered suitable for direct employment in the offshore information technology and business process outsourcing industries, according to a recent study by India's National Association of Software and Service Companies.

"While some young men, on the brink of starvation, desperately look for work, employers elsewhere look – with almost similar desperation – for appropriate persons to fill tens of thousands of vacancies", says Kiran Karnik, Nasscom president.

Even Infosys, an Indian information technology group that receives 1.4 m job applications every

(Continued)

year, this week revealed it would be boosting pay rates for entry-level employees by 12.5 per cent from April next year to Rs270 000 (Dollars 5750, Pounds 3125, Euros 4570).

The sheer pace of economic expansion and change is also a reason for the squeeze on talent. The education and training systems have simply not been able to keep up. "If there wasn't a shortage, it would be strange", says Gordon Orr, of McKinsey in Shanghai. "But it's a real constraint in building successful companies."

Such risks also apply to the hiring of local managers in China. Many are over promoted and overpaid, because of the lack of available talent. If they are not up to the job, "it takes about 18 months for them to be found out, but things are so tight that they move to another position in the market at a premium", says Steve Mullinjer, of headhunter Heidrick & Struggles in Shanghai.

To Think About

1 Using labor demand and labor supply curves, how would you represent the situation in the labor market for skilled and unskilled labor at a particular point in time? (*Hint*: Use different demand curves and different supply curves for the *separate* markets for skilled labor and that for unskilled labor.)

2 "Even Infosys, an Indian information technology group that receives 1.4 m job applications every year, this week revealed it would be boosting pay rates for entry-level employees by 12.5 per cent from April next year to Rs270 000 (Dollars 5750, Pounds 3125, Euros 4570)". Represent this change in the starting wage by the use of labor supply and demand analysis. (*Hint*: Here we are talking about shifts in a particular curve.)

3 What evidence is there in the article that firms are not prepared to train up personnel themselves? Is there any evidence in the article that firms are rational in this approach?

4 In your opinion, who is to blame and what can be done about the shortage of skilled labor in China and India? Is it the respective governments or the companies that hire skilled labor? (This is an open-ended question where several points of view are relevant.)

5 Jumping ahead to Chapter 17 where we cover adverse selection, we define adverse selection (in brief here) as a situation where information is not shared equally between the buyer and a seller in a market transaction. One side of the transaction has either good or bad news which if revealed to the other party would affect the price paid (if at all) for the good or service being sold. Referring to the case of labor offering itself for hire in the article what evidence is there that adverse selection has operated in the labor markets described?

FIGURE 15A-3 Construction of the Market Supply Curve for Labor *As the real wage rises, the supply of labor may increase for two reasons. First, higher real wages may cause each person to work more hours. Second, higher wages may induce more people (for example, person 2) to enter the labor market.*

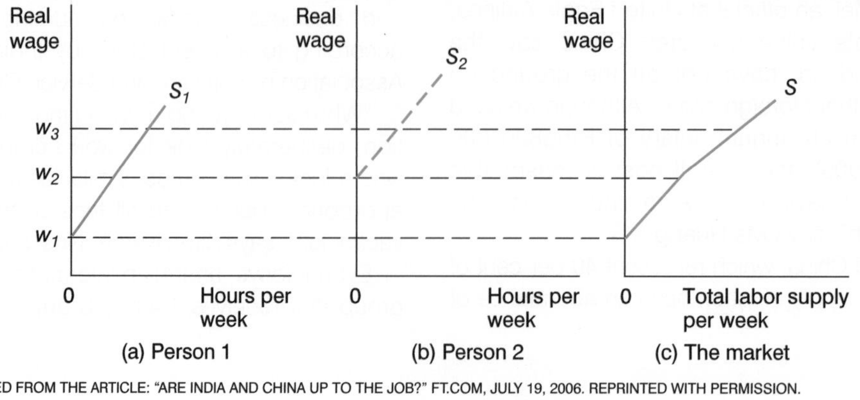

SOURCE: ABRIDGED FROM THE ARTICLE: "ARE INDIA AND CHINA UP TO THE JOB?" FT.COM, JULY 19, 2006. REPRINTED WITH PERMISSION.

wage rate above w_2 will both people choose to take a job. As Figure 15A-3(c) shows, the possibility of the entry of these new workers makes the market supply of labor somewhat more responsive to wage rate increases than would be the case if we assumed that the number of workers was fixed. Changing wage rates may not only induce current workers to alter their hours of work, but, perhaps more important, they may change the composition of the workforce.

SUMMARY

In this appendix, we have examined the utility-maximizing model of labor supply. This model is another application of the economic theory of choice that we described earlier in this textbook. Although the results are quite similar to those we derived before, the focus here on labor supply provides a number of new insights, including:

- Labor supply decisions by individuals can be studied as one aspect of their allocation of time. The market wage represents an opportunity cost for individuals if they choose not to engage in market work.
- A rise in the market wage induces income and substitution effects into individuals' labor supply decisions. These effects operate in opposite directions. A higher wage causes a substitution effect favoring more market work but an income effect favoring more leisure.
- Construction of the labor supply curve also requires the consideration of labor force participation decisions by individuals.

Mathematical Note to Application 15.1

The Power Rule

If we have the following function

$$y = kx^n \quad \{A15.1\}$$

Where k is a constant number and n is an index number, then the derivative of {A15.1} is

$$\frac{dy}{dx} = nkx^{n-1} \quad \{A15.2\}$$

Example:

$$y = 7x^{-5} \quad \{A15.3\}$$

So the derivative is

$$\frac{dy}{dx} = -5 \times 7(x)^{-5-1} = -35x^{-6} \quad \{A15.4\}$$

We "bring down" the index number −5 and multiply it against the number 7. We then subtract 1 from −5 to give us −6 (recalling that a minus number minus another minus number gives us a "bigger" minus number).

The Product Rule

If we have the following *functions* (i.e. more than one function) being multiplied against each other

$$y = f(x) \times g(x) \quad \{A15.5\}$$

then the derivative is as follows

$$\frac{dy}{dx} = f'(x) \times g(x) + f(x) \times g'(x) \quad \{A15.6\}$$

Notice we use the Power Rule to take the derivative of the first function in {A15.6} but "leave alone" the second function. We then repeat the process but reverse it, i.e. "leave the first function alone" and take the derivative of the second function using the Power Rule. We then complete the process by adding our two calculations together.

Example: If we wish to find the derivative, i.e. the rate of change of the following function,

$$y = (x^2 + 5x) \times (4x^4 - 3x^2 + 7x + 5) \quad \{A15.7\}$$

we end up with

$$\frac{dy}{dx} = (2x + 5) \times (4x^4 - 3x^2 +$$

$$7x + 5) + (x^2 + 5) \times (16x^3 - 6x^2 + 7) \qquad \{A15.8\}$$

The Chain Rule

In order to understand the Chain Rule you need to understand that as well as being able to multiply two functions together as in the Product Rule, we can also have a function contained within a function. So if we have

$$y = f(g(x)) \qquad \{A15.9\}$$

Then the first derivative is given by

$$\frac{dy}{dx} = f'(\bullet) \times g'(x) \qquad \{A15.10\}$$

Where $f'(\bullet)$ is implying through the use of • that we do nothing to the *inside* function but only differentiate the *outside* function. We then finish by using the Power Rule and multiplying against $f'(\bullet)$.

Example:

$$y = 3x(5x^3 - 2x^2 + 6)^3 \qquad \{A15.11\}$$

The first derivative of this is given by

$$\frac{dy}{dx} = 3 \times 3x(5x^3 - 2x^2 + 6)^{3-1} \times (3 \times 5(x)^{3-1} - 2 \times 2(x)^{2-1})$$

$$= 9x(5x^3 - 2x^2 + 6)^2 \times (15x^2 - 4x) \qquad \{A15.12\}$$

Making Sense of Equation {7}

Now that you have grasped the Power, Product, and Chain Rules you are now in a position to make sense of Equation {7} in the main text in order to differentiate $p(q(n)).q(n)$. The key to understanding {7} is to realize that the expression needs a combination of both the Product and Chain Rules.

We can represent {7} as $p(\bullet) . q(\bullet)$ where $p(\bullet) = p(q(n))$ and $q(\bullet) = q(n)$. Recall the product rule tells us to differentiate the first argument and leave the second as it is – "untouched". So we have

$$p'(\bullet) . q(\bullet) \qquad \{A15.13\}$$

We then do the same thing except reverse the order of operation. This gives us

$$p(\bullet) . q'(\bullet) \qquad \{A15.14\}$$

Now add the two together

$$p'(\bullet) . q(\bullet) + p(\bullet) . q'(\bullet) \qquad \{A15.15\}$$

But while that is the end of the matter for $q(\bullet)$ or $q'(\bullet)$ not so for $p(\bullet) = p(q(n))$. We have a function, $q(n)$, contained within a function, $p(\bullet)$. Since we are differentiating with respect to n, differentiating $p(\bullet)$ gives us

$$\frac{dp}{dq}$$

since price is a function of output and then differentiating the inside function, $q(n)$ gives us

$$\frac{dq}{dn}$$

We then by the Chain Rule multiply these two together to give

$$\frac{dp}{dq}\frac{dq}{dn}$$

Finally, we do not forget $-wn$ at the end of equation {7} which we differentiate using the Power Rule to leave us with $-w$. Putting the whole thing together gives us equation {8}.

16

Capital and Time

In this chapter, we look at capital markets. In some respects, this material is not very different from the discussion of general input markets in the previous chapter. Firms acquire capital equipment for the same reason that they hire any input – to maximize profits. Hence, the general rule of hiring an input up to the point at which its marginal revenue product is equal to its market rental rate continues to apply. The main new dimension added in the study of capital markets is the need to explicitly consider questions of time. Because machinery may produce valuable output for many years into the future, we need to take account of the fact that values that occur in different time periods can be compared only after taking account of the potential interest payments that might have been earned. A primary purpose of this chapter then is to show clearly how interest rates affect the rental rates on capital equipment and thereby determine how much capital is hired.

Time Periods and the Flow of Economic Transactions

Before starting our investigation, it may be best to get some conceptual issues out of the way. As everyone knows, time is continuous – it just keeps passing by, much like a river. Often, however, it is useful to divide time up into discrete intervals such as days, months, or years. This is true also for economic activity. Although economic activity (such as producing and selling cars) proceeds more or less continuously, it is often convenient to divide up this activity into discrete intervals and speak of markets as reaching an equilibrium on a per-day, per-month, or per-year basis. This is how we have proceeded in this book by, for example, noting on most graphs that they refer to "quantity per period". Hence, these magnitudes are a "flow" per period. Just as one might measure the flow of a river on the basis of gallons per hour, so too economic transactions are usually measured as a per-period flow. For example, gross domestic product (GDP) is measured as total output per year, and total peanut output is measured in kilograms per year.

There are two important ways in which transactions can occur across periods. First, some goods may be "durable" in that they last more than one period. Most relevant to this chapter, firms buy machinery and hope to be able to use it for many periods into the future. In deciding whether to make such a purchase, firms must think about the future. Economic models that take account of these decisions are usually fairly straightforward generalizations of the models we have already studied. Still, many new and interesting issues do arise when such future expectations are taken into account.

A second way that transactions can occur across periods is through borrowing and lending. An individual can borrow to increase his or her spending in one period but knows that the loan must be repaid (by spending less) in the next period. Similarly, a firm may borrow in one period to buy equipment that then generates future returns with which to repay the loan. In the next section, we see how this demand and supply for loans determines the interest rate to be paid. Then we show how this interest rate becomes the primary "price" that ties together all transactions that take place over time – especially firms' investment decisions. The appendix to this chapter examines some of the mathematical concepts that relate to interest rates.

Individual Savings – The Supply Of Loans

When individuals save out of their current incomes, these savings have two important economic effects. First, they free up some resources that might otherwise have been devoted to produce goods for their own consumption. These resources can be used to produce the kinds of investment goods (buildings and equipment) that firms need. Second, savings also provide the funds that firms can use to finance the purchase of these investment goods. Usually, individuals "lend" their funds, not directly to firms but indirectly through financial intermediaries such as banks or the stock market. In the study of how interest rates are determined, however, we think of individuals' savings decisions as directly providing the supply of loans to firms.

Two-Period Model of Saving

Individual savings decisions can be illustrated with a simple utility-maximization model. Suppose that we are concerned only with two periods – this year and next year. Consumption this year is denoted by C_0 and consumption next year is denoted by C_1, and these are the only items that provide utility to this individual. He or she has a current income of Y euros that can either be spent now on C_0 or saved to buy C_1 next year. Any income saved this year earns interest (at a real interest rate of r[1]) before it is used to buy C_1. The individual's problem then is to maximize utility given this budget constraint.

A Graphical Analysis

Figure 16-1 shows this utility-maximization process. The indifference curves show the utility obtainable from various combinations of C_0 and C_1. To understand the (intertemporal) budget constraint in this problem, consider first the case where

[1]That is, the interest rate is adjusted for any possible change in purchasing power between the two periods. Hence, this real interest rate provides information to the consumer about how *real* consumption this year can be traded for *real* consumption next year. In Application 16.4, we look at the real interest rate concept in more detail.

$C_1 = 0$. Then $C_0 = Y$, and no income is saved for use in period 2. On the other hand, if all income is saved, $C_0 = 0$ and $C_1 = (1 + r)Y$. In year 2, this person can consume all of his or her income plus the interest earned on that income. For example, if $r = 0.05$ (that is, 5 per cent), C_1 will be $1.05Y$. Waiting for the interest to be earned has made it possible for this person to have relatively more consumption in period 2 than in period 1.

Given the two intercepts in Figure 16-1, the entire budget constraint can be constructed as the black straight line joining them. Utility maximization is achieved at C_0^*, C_1^* at which point the marginal rate of substitution (*MRS*) is equal to $(1 + r)$. That is, utility maximization requires equating the rate at which this person is willing to trade C_0 for C_1 to the rate at which he or she is able to trade these goods for each other in the market through saving. The interest rate is clearly an important part of this story because it measures the opportunity cost that the individual incurs when he or she chooses to consume now rather than in the future.

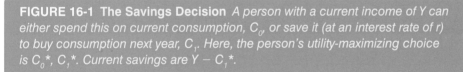

MICROQUIZ 16.1

One way to study the results of Figure 16-1 and Figure 16-2 is by thinking about the "relative price" of C_1 in terms of C_0.

1 Explain why the relative price of C_1 is given by $1/(1 + r)$. If $r = 0.10$, what is the relative price of C_1? Explain the meaning of this "price".

2 Explain why an increase in *r* reduces the relative price of C_1. Why is the individual's reaction to such a price decline ambiguous here, whereas that was not the case in Chapter 3?

Substitution and Income Effects of a Change in *r*

A change in the real interest rate, *r*, changes the "price" of future versus current consumption. The substitution and income effects of this price change are illustrated in Figure 16-2 for an increase in *r*. In this case, the rise in *r* to *r′* causes this individual to move along the U_2 indifference curve to point *S* – this is the substitution

FIGURE 16-1 The Savings Decision *A person with a current income of Y can either spend this on current consumption, C_0, or save it (at an interest rate of r) to buy consumption next year, C_1. Here, the person's utility-maximizing choice is C_0^*, C_1^*. Current savings are $Y - C_1^*$.*

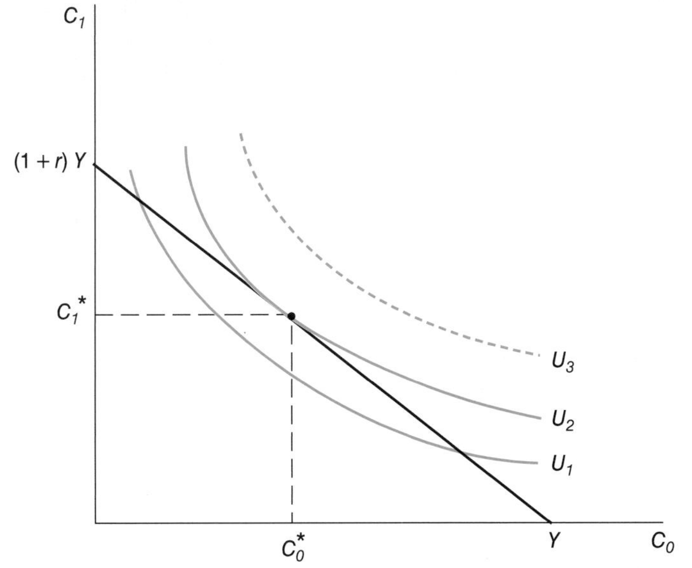

effect. With a higher r, the opportunity cost of C_0 rises and this person substitutes C_1 for C_0 – that is, he or she saves more. But the rise in r also shifts this person's budget constraint outward because he or she is made better off by this rise. This income effect causes the preferred consumption point to move from S to C_0^{**}, C_1^{**}. Assuming that both C_0 and C_1 are normal goods, they should both be increased by this move. The final effect of an increase in r on C_0 (and hence on savings) is indeterminate – the substitution effect increases savings (C_0 falls) whereas the income effect decreases savings (C_0 rises). The net effect depends on the relative sizes of these two effects.[2] In general, economists believe that the substitution effect is probably the stronger of the two effects so that a rise in r encourages savings. This is the final result pictured in Figure 16-2. But there is considerable disagreement about the actual size of this effect, as Application 16.1: *Do We Need Tax Breaks for Savers?* illustrates.

Firms' Demand for Capital and Loans

In Chapter 15, we saw that profit-maximizing firms rent additional capital equipment up to the point at which the marginal revenue product of the equipment is equal to the rental rate on the equipment, v. To understand the connections between this demand and the demand for loans, we need to understand the nature of the determinants of this

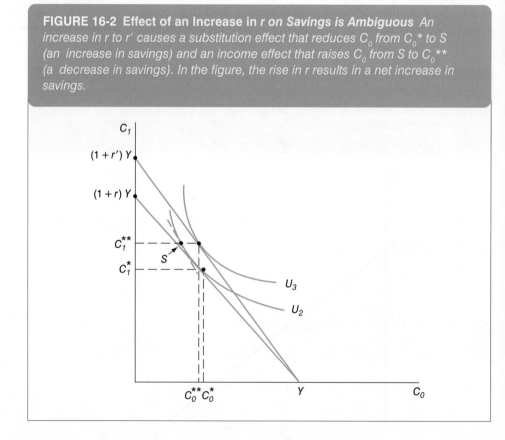

FIGURE 16-2 Effect of an Increase in *r* on Savings is Ambiguous *An increase in r to r′ causes a substitution effect that reduces C_0 from C_0* to S (an increase in savings) and an income effect that raises C_0 from S to C_0** (a decrease in savings). In the figure, the rise in r results in a net increase in savings.*

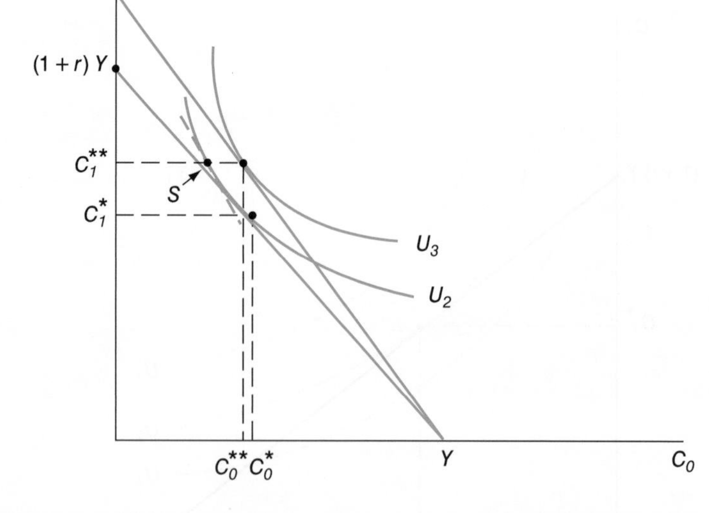

[2]This ambiguity is identical to that encountered in looking at the effect on labor supply of an increase in the real wage – see the appendix to Chapter 15 for a discussion.

APPLICATION 16.1 *Do We Need Tax Breaks for Savers?*

Personal savings rates in the United States are very low by international standards. In 2005, total personal savings amounted to only about 1.3 per cent of disposable income. That figure represented both a steep decline from earlier savings levels in the United States and a markedly lower rate than exists in many other countries[1] (where rates above 10 per cent are common). These low savings rates have prompted a variety of concerns. Some observers worry about whether individuals will have adequate savings for their own retirement or for various emergencies. Others worry that inadequate savings will fail to provide sufficient capital accumulation for future generations. As a result, many tax-favored plans for savings have been introduced in recent years.

Recent Savings Incentive Plans

Many recent savings incentive plans have a similar structure. All of them allow a tax deduction for contributions to the plans[2]. Savings in the plans are then not subject to the federal income tax until benefits are paid out at retirement. The three principal types of such plans are

- Individual Retirement Accounts (IRAs), which are set up by individuals acting on their own. Only low-income individuals receive an income tax deduction for IRA contributions, but everyone can avoid taxation of returns from assets in the plans until they retire.
- 401(k) plans are set up by employers who sometimes make matching contributions to their workers' plans. Both contributions and asset returns are tax-exempt until retirement.
- Keogh plans are similar to IRAs and 401(k) plans, but the plans are intended for self-employed individuals. They generally have higher contribution limits than the other plans do.

Theoretical Effects on Savings

The effect of these various tax benefits on total personal savings is ambiguous. Although special tax treatment does raise the after-tax interest rate for savers, our discussion of Figure 16-2 showed that the effect of such a change on savings is uncertain – income and substitution effects of increases in the effective interest rate work in opposite directions. In addition, the fact that the special tax treatment does not apply to all savings but only to contributions to specific plans gives individuals an incentive to shift their assets into the tax-favored plans without actually changing the total amount of their savings. Hence, the rapid growth of the plans should not be taken as an indication of the plans' ability to stimulate savings.

Research on Savers and Spenders

Because savings incentive plans involve significant losses in tax revenues, much research has been undertaken to determine whether the plans are achieving their goal of increasing savings. Most studies use data on individual savings behavior to detect such influences. Unfortunately, this research has been plagued by one serious problem: it appears that different people have very different attitudes toward saving. Some people are serious savers who will accumulate assets in many forms. Other people are only spenders who never put anything aside. Individuals who participate in one of the special saving plans have shown that they fit into the "saver" category. But to compare their savings behavior to the behavior of those individuals without the plans runs the danger of concluding that the plans themselves increase savings. A more correct interpretation is that plan participation acts only to identify savers who are predisposed to save more. Researchers have been unable to resolve this sample selection problem and the true impact of the special savings plans remains largely unknown.

To Think About

1. The taxation of interest income always distorts individuals' choices between present and future consumption. Would a move from income taxation to a scheme that only taxes consumption change this situation?

(Continued)

2 Most of the special savings plans in the US tax code have income limitations on who can participate in them and how much they can contribute in any year. Why do such restrictions exist? Are they a good idea?

[1]To some extent the low savings rate in the United States may reflect faulty measurement. See W. G. Gale and J. Sabelhaus, "Perspectives on the Household Savings Rate", *Brookings Papers on Economic Activity*, no. 1 (1999): 181–224.

[2]Roth IRAs, which became available in 1998, do not allow current deductibility, but all retirement benefits are non-taxable when received.

rental rate. We begin by assuming that firms rent all of the capital that they use from other firms. Cases in which firms directly own their own equipment are then easy to explain.

Rental Rates and Interest Rates

Many types of capital equipment are in fact rented in the real world. Hertz rents millions of cars each year to other firms; banks and insurance companies actually own many commercial planes that they rent to airlines; and construction firms rent specialized equipment (for example, heavy-lifting cranes) when they need it. In these cases, the per-period rate that firms have to pay to rent this equipment (v) is determined by the average costs that the rental firms (for example, Hertz) incur. Two such costs are especially important: depreciation costs and borrowing costs. Depreciation costs reflect the physical wear and tear on equipment that occurs during each period that it is used. Borrowing costs may be either explicit or implicit for the firm providing the equipment. If they have financed the purchase of their equipment with a loan, interest payments on that loan are an explicit cost.[3] If, on the other hand, they have bought equipment with internal funds, interest payments are an implicit or opportunity cost. By having the funds tied up in the equipment, the firm is forgoing what it could have earned by putting them in the bank. Hence, interest costs are always relevant to the firm that supplies the rented equipment, no matter how they have actually financed the equipment purchase.

In general, it might be expected that both depreciation and borrowing costs are proportional to the market price of the equipment being rented. If P represents that price, d is the per-period rate of depreciation, and r is the interest rate, we have the following expression for the per-period rental rate (v):

$$\text{Rental rate} = v = \text{Depreciation} + \text{Borrowing costs} = dP + rP = (d + r)P \qquad \{16.1\}$$

For example, suppose Citicorp owns a Boeing 777 that it leases to United Airlines. Suppose also that the current value of the plane is \$50 million, that the plane is expected to deteriorate at a rate of 10 per cent each year, and that the real interest rate is 5 per cent. Then Citicorp's total costs of owning the plane are \$7.5 million (\$5 million in depreciation and \$2.5 million in interest costs). If it is to break even in its plane rental business, that is the rate it must charge United each year for the plane.

Equation 16.1 clearly shows why firms' demand for equipment is negatively related to the interest rate. When the interest rate is high, rental rates on equipment are high and firms try to substitute toward cheaper inputs. When interest rates are low, rental rates are low and firms opt to rent more equipment. Such changes in equipment rentals also bring about accompanying changes in the demand for loans with which to finance the equipment. When interest rates are high, the demand for loans contracts because there is

[3]Financing through offering stock would involve similar costs, though we do not examine that case.

little need to finance equipment purchases. With low interest rates, loan volume picks up as a consequence of the rental firms' needs to add to their available equipment.

Ownership of Capital Equipment

Of course, most capital equipment is owned by the firms that use it; only a relatively small portion is rented. But that distinction does not affect the validity of Equation 16.1. Firms that own equipment are really in two businesses – they produce goods and they lease capital equipment to themselves. In their role as equipment leasers, firms are affected by the same economic considerations as are firms whose primary business is leasing. The implicit rental rates that they pay are the same regardless of who owns the equipment.[4] Application 16.2: *Do Taxes Affect Investment?* shows how Equation 16.1 can be used to study the ways in which government tax policy can be used to influence firms' decisions to purchase capital equipment.

Determination of the Real Interest Rate

Now that we have described the two sides of the market for loans, we are ready to describe how the real interest rate is determined. Figure 16-3 shows that the supply of loans is an upward-sloping function of the real interest rate, *r*. This slope reflects

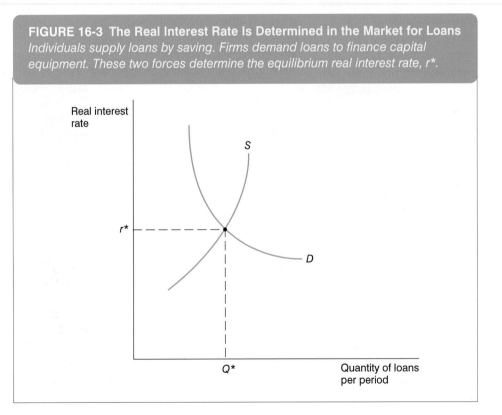

FIGURE 16-3 The Real Interest Rate Is Determined in the Market for Loans
Individuals supply loans by saving. Firms demand loans to finance capital equipment. These two forces determine the equilibrium real interest rate, r.*

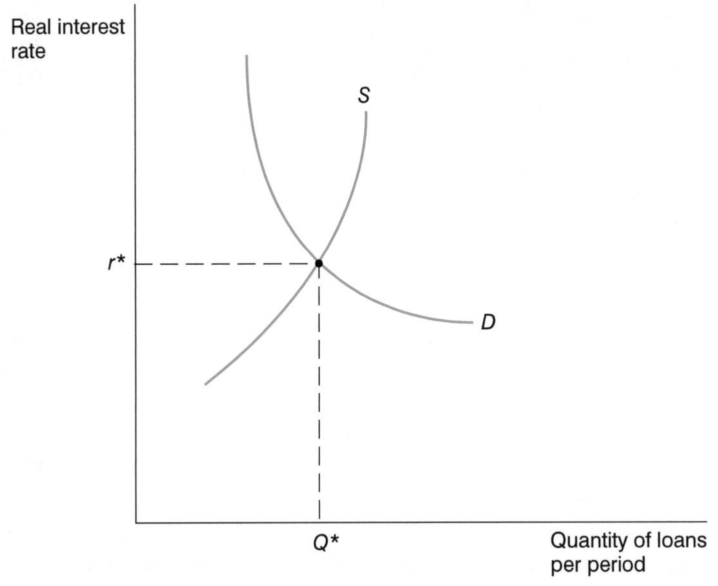

[4]The mathematical relationship between the present-value calculations that owners must make in deciding whether to purchase new equipment and the rental rate they implicitly pay on the equipment is examined in the appendix to this chapter.

APPLICATION 16.2 *Do Taxes Affect Investment?*

Although a tax on pure economic profits would not affect firms' input choices, the actual US corporate income tax departs in several ways from such a pure tax. Most important, opportunity costs of equity capital are not deductible under US tax law and allowable depreciation charges for tax purposes often fall short of true economic depreciation. Equation 16.1 should therefore be modified to take into account how the corporate income tax actually affects the rental rate for capital input. This can be done by writing

$$v = (r + d)P(1 + t) \qquad \{i\}$$

where t is the effective tax rate per unit of capital. In the usual case, t is positive. But in some cases, the government may subsidize certain types of capital input, so t then would be negative. Because taxes change the rental rate that firms must pay for their capital, they can obviously affect input choices.

Elements of Tax Policy

Federal tax policy toward investment has undergone many changes in recent years. Three specific elements of tax policy have been frequently adjusted:

- The corporate tax rate has been reduced on several occasions.
- "Accelerated" depreciation schedules have been adopted to bring depreciation allowances more into line with actual economic depreciation that machines experience.
- Investment tax credits for certain types of capital purchases have been enacted and then abolished.

Brief History of Tax Policy

Major reductions in rates of capital taxation were implemented in 1962 during the administration of President Kennedy. At that time, depreciation schedules, especially for producers' equipment, were made much more generous. A temporary 7 per cent tax credit on all new investment was also enacted. According to some estimates, these changes may have increased total purchases of capital equipment by as much as 20 per cent.[1]

Similar changes were instituted early in the administration of President Reagan (1981). Especially important was the adoption of more generous depreciation schedules for buildings and longer-lived equipment. In some cases, these allowances may have resulted in a subsidy for these investments. But the initial Reagan policies were significantly modified in 1982, so the most generous of the policies had little time to influence investment behavior, which remained sluggish through much of the 1980s.

Policy changes instituted during the administration of President Clinton primarily involved investment tax credits. Such credits were adopted for research and development expenditures and for smaller firms' new investments. Tax incentives under the second Bush administration have been rather narrowly focused (such as credits on investments in ethanol production).

Effects of Tax Policies

Although it seems clear in principle that changes in tax policies can affect rental rates on capital, the evidence about whether tax changes have had important effects on firms' input choices is quite ambiguous. One reason that the impacts may be rather small is that tax benefits for investment may also raise the price of capital equipment, thereby largely offsetting their direct effect on lowering rental rates (see Equation i). There is some empirical evidence supporting this possibility.[2] Another possibility is that the highly selective (and political) nature of investment incentives may only have caused firms to change what they buy, but not their overall level of investment.

To Think About

1. Why would the US government wish to adopt tax policies that encourage investment?
2. Much of the discussion of tax policy toward capital focuses on depreciation allowances. Why should the precise rules for allocating a machine's cost over the years affect the machine's rental rate? (*Hint*: Depreciation rules affect the tax rate on a machine (t) not

the actual rate of physical deterioration of the machine (d).)

[1]R. E. Hall and D. W. Jorgenson, "Tax Policy and Investment Behavior", *American Economic Review* (June 1967): 391–414. Hall and Jorgenson show precisely how various elements of tax policy affect the rental rate on capital.

[2]See A. Goolsbee, "Investment Tax Incentives, Prices, and the Supply of Capital Goods", *Quarterly Journal of Economics* (February 1999): 121–149.

our assumption that individuals increase their savings (and loans to firms) as the interest rate rises. The demand for loans is negatively sloped because of the inhibiting effect that higher interest rates have on firms' equipment rental rates. Equilibrium then occurs at r^*, Q^*, where the quantity of loans demanded is equal to the quantity supplied. This equilibrium real interest rate provides the price that links economic periods together.

Because charging of interest on loans has been controversial throughout history (see Application 16.3: *Usury*), it may be useful to explore the nature of the equilibrium pictured in Figure 16-3 more fully. There are two reasons why we might expect the equilibrium real interest rate (r^*) shown in the figure to be positive. From the perspective of the individuals providing loans, they will expect some return for doing so. Borrowers, after all, are asking savers to defer some of their possible consumption into the future. Our observations of a natural degree of "impatience" in people would suggest that they seek some sort of compensation for doing so. From the point of view of borrowers, firms will be willing to pay something to lenders because they find that buying capital equipment is profitable. Take the simple case where machines do not depreciate. Then Equation 16.1 shows that firms will employ additional capital equipment up to the point at which $r = v/P$ – that is, up to the point at which the interest rate they must pay is equal to the rate of return they earn by buying the machine (at the price P) and thereby save the cost of renting the machine from someone else (v). Hence, in a market economy, interest rates are jointly determined by the willingness of people to lend and the productivity of capital investments made by borrowers.

Changes in the Real Interest Rate

This simple theory of how the real interest rate is determined also provides insights about why that interest rate might change. On one hand, any factor that increases firms' demand for capital equipment also increases the demand for loans. Such factors include technical progress that makes equipment more productive, declines in the actual market prices of such equipment, or more optimistic views by firms about the strength of demand for their products in the future. All such effects shift the demand for loans outward, increasing the real interest rate. On the other hand, any factor that affects individual savings affects the supply of loans. For example, availability of government-provided pension benefits in the future may reduce individuals' current savings, thereby raising real interest rates. Similarly, reductions in taxes on savings may increase the supply of loans and reduce the real interest rate. Application 16.4: *Inflation-Indexed Bonds* looks at one way in which changes in real interest rates might actually be measured.

MICROQUIZ 16.2

A "pure" inflation (in which all prices change by the same amount) should not have any real effect on firms' decisions. Use Equation 16.1 together with the theory of input demand from Chapter 15 to explain why this is so for firms' decisions about how much capital to use.

APPLICATION 16.3 *Usury*

Although the equilibrium pictured in Figure 16-3 seems reasonable, probably no price has been as controversial over many centuries as has the interest rate on loans. Most major religions have, at one time or another, condemned interest payments as being exploitive. Many philosophers, especially those who take a Marxist perspective, have come to similar conclusions. To this day, many nations sharply restrict interest rates, and most US states have "usury laws" that limit what consumers can be charged for credit. In this application, we look briefly at the controversy over interest, with the primary goal of differentiating between positive and normative (see Chapter 1) views of the issue.

Religious and Literary Views

Opposition to the payment of interest on loans dates back at least to the Greek philosophers. Alfred Marshall reports that Aristotle viewed money as "barren" and deriving interest from it as "unnatural".[1] In the Old Testament of the Bible, Moses states that "If you lend money to any of my people with you who is poor, you shall not be to him as a creditor, and you shall not exact interest from him". Later biblical references clarify the nature of this prohibition somewhat by implying that interest is barred only in transactions in which "brothers" lend to "brothers" (usually taken to mean Jews lending to Jews). Interest on loans to "foreigners" is permissible. Other religions that have taken a negative view of interest payments include the Hindu religion in India and most sects of the Muslim religion (to be examined shortly).[2]

World literature has sometimes reflected these religious views. For example, Dante reserved a special place in hell for usurers. In probably the most famous case, Shakespeare's play *The Merchant of Venice* focused on the moneylender Shylock and on his lending contract that demanded a "pound of flesh" if the merchant Antonio was unable to repay his loan. Other literary references can be found in such diverse works as the writings of St Thomas Aquinas and Mahatma Gandhi.

Normative Basis for Usury Restrictions

Most usury restrictions are derived from two related notions: (1) that borrowers are usually in need and requiring interest payments worsens their situation and (2) that lenders incur no real costs when they provide loans. These beliefs then lead to the conclusion that interest should not be charged. Notice that this is a normative statement about how the economy *should* operate (a normative conclusion about which people may differ). The equilibrium shown in Figure 16-3 makes a positive prediction about how interest rates arise in the real world. Reconciling this prediction with individuals' normative views can sometimes be quite difficult.

Muslim Mortgages

The difficulties are clearly illustrated in the problems faced by some American Muslims who wish to take out mortgages to buy homes. The Koran generally forbids paying or receiving interest, so Muslims who both wish to obey their religious heritage and to purchase good houses face the prospect of having to save for many years before getting a house. Recently US financial institutions have developed a variety of special types of mortgages that Islamic scholars have deemed consistent with the Koran. The general idea of these loans (sometimes called *Murabaha* loans) is to have the financial institution buy a house and lease it back to the resident. The resident then pays the going rental rate for the house plus an extra amount that allows him or her slowly to buy the house. Because the financial institution has an equity investment in the house and therefore incurs risk on the resident's behalf, earning a "profit" is viewed as being consistent with Islamic law.

To Think About

1 In the New Testament Jesus expels "money-changers" from his local temple. According to some research, these people were involved in lending. Other research indicates they may have been foreign exchange traders. Do you

think Jesus should have behaved differently with respect to these two professions?

2 Most states require that lenders publish the "true annual interest charge" on any loans they make. How should this law be interpreted in the case of Muslim mortgages?

[1]A. Marshall, *Principles of Economics*, 8th ed. (London: Macmillan & Co., 1950), 585.

[2]A good summary of religious views is provided in E. L. Glaeser and J. Scheinkman, "Neither Borrower nor a Lender be: An Economic Analysis of Interest Restrictions and Usury Laws", *Journal of Law and Economics* (April 1998): 1–36.

Present Discounted Value

Probably the most important lesson from studying the economics of decision-making over time is that interest rates must be taken into account. Transactions that take place at different times cannot be compared directly because of interest that was or might have been earned (or paid) between the two dates. For example, a promise to pay a euro today is not the same as a promise to pay a euro in one year. The euro today is more valuable because it can be invested at interest for the year. In order to bring comparability to transactions that occur over time, actual euro amounts must always be adjusted for the effects of potential interest payments.

Single-Period Discounting

With only two periods, this process is very simple. Because any euro invested today grows by a factor of $(1 + r)$ next year, the present value of a euro that is not received until next year is $1/(1 + r)$ euros. For example, if $r = 0.05$, an investment of €1 today will grow to €1.05 next year. Hence, the promise of €1 next year is worth about €0.95 today.[5] That is, investing €0.95 today will yield €1 in one year. The discount factor $1/(1 + r)$ must always be applied to calculate the **present value** of funds to be paid one year in the future. The first row of Table 16-1 illustrates this discount factor for various interest rates – clearly, the higher the interest rate, the smaller the discount factor.

Present value
Discounting the value of future transactions back to the present day to take account of the effect of potential interest payments.

TABLE 16-1 Present Discounted Value of €1 for Various Time Periods and Interest Rates

	Interest rate			
Years until payment is received	*1 per cent*	*3 per cent*	*5 per cent*	*10 per cent*
1	€0.99010	€0.97087	€0.95238	€0.90909
2	0.98030	0.94260	0.90703	0.82645
3	0.97059	0.91516	0.86386	0.75131
5	0.95147	0.86281	0.78351	0.62093
10	0.90531	0.74405	0.61391	0.38555
25	0.78003	0.47755	0.29531	0.09230
50	0.60790	0.22810	0.08720	0.00852
100	0.36969	0.05203	0.00760	0.00007

[5]To be precise, $1/(1.05) = 0.95238$.

APPLICATION 16.4 *Inflation-Indexed Bonds*

Most government bonds take no explicit account of economy-wide inflation. They make nominal interest payments and allow the market for the bonds to take inflationary expectations into account. In recent years, however, a number of nations have begun to offer "inflation-indexed" bonds that adjust payments for changes in the overall price level. Therefore, in principle these bonds pay a real interest rate. The government of Israel is the most significant issuer of inflation-indexed bonds. In that country, over 80 per cent of all government bonds are indexed. Australia, Turkey, and Brazil are also significant issuers of such bonds. The US Treasury began issuing inflation-indexed bonds in 1997, although these bonds make up a small portion of total government debt.

Real and Nominal Interest Rates

Exploring the relationship between real and nominal interest rates requires a bit of math. Suppose you are promised a (nominal) interest rate of i for making a one-period loan of €1 but that you expect the price level to increase by p^e next year. Then the real value of your repayment will be

$$\text{Real value of payment} = \frac{1+i}{1+p^e} \qquad \{i\}$$

But, as we have already seen, this real payment is also given by $(1 + r)$, where r is the real interest rate. So

$$1 + r = \frac{1+i}{1+p^e} \text{ or } (1 + r)(1 + p^e) = 1 + i \qquad \{ii\}$$

Expanding the left side of Equation (ii) yields

$$1 + r + p^e + rp^e = 1 + i \text{ or } i = r + p + p^e + rp^e \qquad \{iii\}$$

If both r and p^e are small, this leads to the approximation

$$i = r + p^e \qquad \{iv\}$$

That is, nominal and real interest rates differ by the expected rate of inflation, p^e. Looked at in another way, Equation iv also gives a way of estimating general inflationary expectations. For example, on 22 August 2005, the nominal yield on a ten-year US Treasury bond was 4.21 per cent. The yield on a ten-year indexed bond was 1.81 per cent, so it appears that, on this date, individuals were expecting inflation rates to average about 2.4 per cent per year over the next ten years.

The Design of Inflation-Indexed Bonds[1]

One should be cautious in using this method for assessing expectations about inflation, however, because it depends crucially on the assumption that inflation-indexed bonds actually pay a real interest rate. In the United States, inflation adjustment is accomplished by adjusting both the annual interest payment and the final redemption value of the bond each year to changes in the Consumer Price Index (CPI). That approach at first seems unobjectionable. Indeed, it seems generous given the general belief that the CPI may overstate actual inflation (see Application 3.2). However, the US Internal Revenue Service has decided that both the higher interest payments caused by inflation adjustment and the annual increase in the redemption value of the bond represent currently taxable income. Hence, the actual, after-tax real interest rate promised by inflation-indexed bonds may be much lower than reported.

A second complexity involved in using Equation iv to compute expected inflation is that nominal and inflation-indexed bonds are subject to differing risk factors. For nominal bonds, of course, the greatest risk is inflation. So nominal bonds might be expected to pay higher interest rates simply to compensate investors not only for expected inflation but also for the variability associated with that expectation. For inflation-indexed bonds, most risks relate to fears about changes in government policy toward them. The bonds would seem to be especially vulnerable to possible changes in the way the CPI is computed.

To Think About

1 Equations i–iv look only at interest rates and inflation over a single period. How do you think that the relationship embodied in Equation iv

would be changed if one were interested in multiple-year compounding?

2 Why are inflationary payments for indexed bonds taxed? Do these represent real income to the bondholders? If this is done to be consistent with the way nominal interest rates are taxed in the United States, is this approach to taxation a mistake?

[1] This section is based on R. W. Kopcke and R. C. Kimball, "Inflation-Indexed Bonds: The Dog That Didn't Bark", *New England Economic Review* (January–February 1999): 3–24.

Multiperiod Discounting

Generalizing the discounting concept to any number of periods is easy. As we show in the appendix to this chapter, the present value of €1 that is not to be paid until n years in the future is given by

$$\text{Present value of €1 in } n \text{ years} = €1/(1 + r)^n \qquad \{16.2\}$$

This discounting factor allows the user to take into account the compound interest that is forgone by waiting for n years to obtain funds, rather than obtaining them immediately. The entries in Table 16-1 show how this discount term depends both on the interest rate (r) and on the number of years until payment is received (n). For high values of r and/or high values of n, this factor can be very small. For example, the promise of €1 in ten years with an interest rate of 10 per cent is worth only €0.39 today. If payment is delayed for 100 years (again with a 10 per cent interest rate), its present value is worth less than one hundredth of a cent! Such calculations make clear that the present value of payments long into the future may be very low, so we should not be surprised that such distant payments play a rather small part in most economic decisions.

Present Value and Economic Decisions

When looking at economic decisions over time, the concepts of utility maximization by individuals and profit maximization by firms continue to be relevant. But they must be restated to allow for the discounting that should be done in all multiperiod situations. For firms, this reformulation is easy to understand. Instead of assuming that firms "maximize profits", we now assume that they "maximize the present value of all future profits". Virtually all of the results of the theory of profit maximization continue to hold under this revised formulation.[6] For example, profit maximization requires that firms whose revenues and costs may not occur at the same time choose that output level for which the *present value* of marginal revenue equals the *present value* of marginal cost. Similarly, such firms should hire inputs up to the point at which the *present value* of the marginal revenue product is equal to the *present value* of the input's cost. Sometimes economists state the profit-maximization assumption a little differently when speaking about decisions over time – they assume that firms make decisions that seek to "maximize the present value of the firm".

MICROQUIZ 16.3

A European lottery is currently offering a payoff of €20 million, which it will pay to the lucky winner in 20 annual €1 million installments. Is this really a €20 million prize? How would you decide its actual value?

[6] For some illustrations, see review question 16.8. In the theory of corporate finance, some issues do arise in choosing which interest rate to use to compute the present value of future profits, but we do not pursue those issues here.

APPLICATION 16.5 *Discounting Cash Flows and Derivative Securities*

The concept of present value can be applied to any pattern of cash inflows or outflows. This provides a general way to think about transactions that are really quite complex. Here, we look at two examples.

Mortgage-Backed Securities

Mortgages on houses are the most prevalent type of loan individuals make. These loans commit homeowners to pay a fixed monthly charge, typically for 30 years. Most mortgages also permit early repayments with no penalties. Because mortgages are so long-lived, an active secondary market in them has been developed that permits the initial lender to sell the mortgage to someone else. Often, many mortgages are bundled together in order to achieve economies of scale in buying and selling. Recent innovations in financial markets have carried this process one step further by creating new securities that represent only one portion of the cash flow from a pool of mortgages. These new securities are called "collateralized mortgage obligations" (CMOs). For example, one CMO might promise only the monthly interest payments from a given pool of mortgages. Another might promise all of the actual mortgage repayments from the same pool.

Calculation of the present value of a CMO is in principle a straightforward application of Equation 16A.25 in the appendix to this chapter. Each expected cash flow must be appropriately discounted to the present day. Unfortunately, the fact that people can change their mortgage payoff practices rather sharply as conditions change makes the actual calculation subject to considerable uncertainty in practice.

The Fannie Mae Mismatch

An illustration of this problem occurred in the fall of 2002 as declining interest rates caused many people to pay off long-term mortgages. This posed special problems for Fannie Mae – the largest dealer in mortgage-backed securities in the United States. The expected timing of the firm's receipts from mortgages became much shorter than the timing of payments they owed to their bondholders. This timing mismatch posed risks for the company because its net worth (the present value of assets minus the present value of liabilities) could have dropped sharply if interest rates fell further (do you see why?). Although interest rates stabilized during the next few years, Fannie Mae has continued to have problems in accounting for its complex streams of mortgage payments.

Derivatives and Hedging Risks

CMOs are one example of a "derivative security" – a security whose value "derives" from some other asset. Because such securities are very complex, firms need to be especially careful that they have not exposed themselves to too much risk in taking derivative positions. One way that they seek to do that is to aggregate all of the expected cash flows from the many derivatives that they own into a single stream of expected payments and receipts. Then they can use a version of Equation 16A.25 to see how the present values of their overall position might be affected by various happenings.

The Long-Term Capital Management Fiasco

This type of risk assessment was practiced extensively by the Long-Term Capital Management hedge fund – a fund run in part by two recent Nobel prize winners in economics. Although the fund thought that it had most scenarios accounted for, the summer of 1998 proved to be devastating, primarily because cash flows did not follow expected historical relationships. Ultimately, the US Federal Reserve had to orchestrate a multibillion-dollar bailout for the fund despite the sophistication with which it approached risk assessment. The value of the procedure proved to be only as good as the data the firm had.[1]

To Think About

1. Although any cash flow, no matter how complex, can be converted to a single value by discounting using Equation 16A.25, there still is the matter

of which interest rate to use in the computation. How would you choose an interest rate?

2 For a simple derivative security (such as a repayment CMO), how would you evaluate the relationship between the cash flows promised and other economic data (such as general interest rates or the growth rate of the economy)?

[1]The Long-Term Capital story is told in the fascinating video *The Trillion-Dollar Gamble* (Boston, MA: WGBH Videos, 1999).

But this amounts to just another version of profit maximization, because a firm is only worth the future profits that it generates.

Present-value concepts are also important to individuals. Although we do not explore these connections here, problem 16.8 and problem 16.9 provide you with some practice in avoiding common deceptive sales practices that are based on a failure of consumers to understand how interest rates work. Application 16.5: *Discounting Cash Flows and Derivative Securities* shows a few more complicated illustrations of present-value calculations that can confuse even the most astute investor.

Pricing of Exhaustible Resources

One important way in which considerations of time and interest rates enter into economics is in the pricing of natural resources – especially those that are not renewable. Ever since Robert Malthus started worrying about population growth in nineteenth-century England, there have been recurrent concerns that we are "running out" of such resources and that market pressures may be accelerating that process. In this section, we try to shed some light on this important issue by focusing on the ways in which resource scarcity might be expected to affect the current pricing of those resources.

Scarcity Costs

What makes the production of non-renewable resources different from the production of other types of economic goods is that the current production from a finite stock of the resource reduces the amount that is available in the future. This contrasts with the usual case in which firms' production decisions during one year have no effect on the next year's production. Firms involved in the production of an exhaustible resource must therefore take an additional cost into account: the opportunity cost of not being able to make some sales in the future. These extra costs are defined as the **scarcity costs**. Of course, recognition of these costs does not mean that a firm thinking about producing from a finite resource stock always opts to produce nothing, constantly hoarding its resource holdings for sale at some future date. But the firm must be careful to incorporate all opportunity costs into its decisions.

Scarcity costs The opportunity costs of future production forgone because current production depletes exhaustible resources.

The implications of scarcity costs are illustrated in Figure 16-4. In the absence of scarcity costs, the industry supply curve for the resource would be given by S. This curve reflects the marginal costs of actually producing the resource (that is, the costs of drilling, mining, and/or refining). Scarcity costs shift firms' marginal cost curves upward because of the extra opportunity cost of forgone future sales that they represent. The new market supply curve is therefore S' and the gap between S and S' represents scarcity costs. Current output falls from Q^* to Q' and market price rises from P^* to P' once these costs are taken into account. These changes effectively encourage "conservation" of the resource – firms withhold some extra resources from the market, intending to sell them sometime in the future.

The Size of Scarcity Costs

The actual value of scarcity costs depends on firms' views about what prices for the resource will be in the future. Knowledge of these prices is required if resource owners are to be able to calculate correctly the present value of revenues that will be forgone by producing the resource now out of their currently available stock.[7] As a simple example, suppose that the owner of a copper mine believes that copper will sell for €1 per kilo in ten years. Hence, selling a kilo today means forgoing a €1 sale in ten years because the supply of copper in the mine is fixed. With a real interest rate of, say, 5 per cent, Table 16-1 shows that the present value of this opportunity cost is about €0.61. Assuming that the owner of the mine is indifferent about whether the copper is sold today or in ten years, the current market price should be about €0.61 because that is the only price that reflects an equilibrium between present and future sales. If the actual marginal cost of copper production is, say, €0.35 per kilo, then scarcity costs would be €0.26 per kilo. Price would exceed the actual

MICROQUIZ 16.4

Suppose that kryptonite is discovered on Earth and that one firm owns the entire world supply.

1 Should the monopoly firm take scarcity costs into account?

2 Will the monopoly produce less kryptonite than would a competitive industry?

FIGURE 16-4 Scarcity Costs Associated with Exhaustible Resources *Firms that produce exhaustible resources take into account both current marginal production costs and the opportunity costs of forgone future production. The market supply curve for such firms (S′) is above their marginal cost curves to the extent of those scarcity costs.*

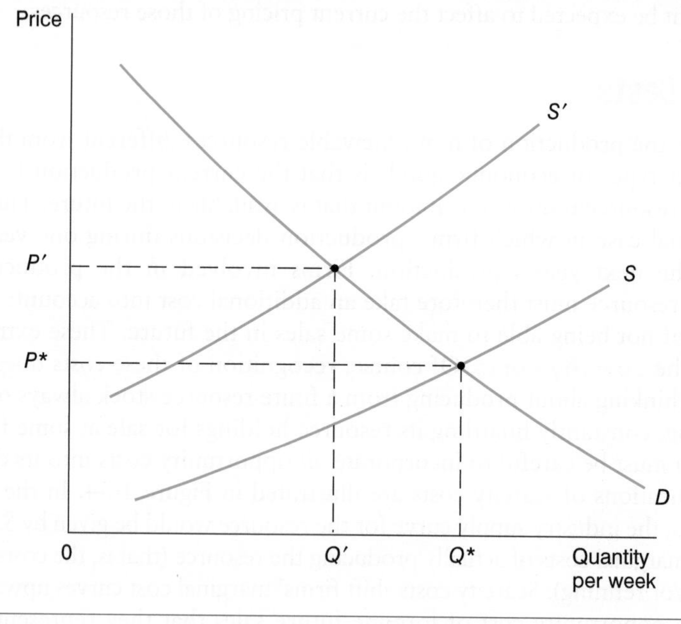

[7]If the firm does not actually own the resource (suppose it is mining on public land, for example), it may not take scarcity costs into account because it may believe that it will not have access to the resource in the future. In Chapter 18, we explicitly consider the externalities created when resources are "owned" in common.

APPLICATION 16.6 *Are Any Resources Scarce?*

The question "Are any resources scarce?" is, of course, intentionally provocative. After all, Earth is of finite size, so (barring mining on other planets) the total quantity of natural resources is ultimately fixed. Any production today necessarily reduces the amount that can be produced tomorrow. By this test, all natural resources are scarce. The economic consequences of this scarcity, however, are not obvious.

Resource Price Trends

During the past century, the primary trend for natural resource prices has been downward in real terms. As Table 1 shows, annual rates of decline between 1 and 2 per cent characterize the price histories for such diverse resources as petroleum, coal, and aluminum. Similarly, farmland prices seem to have declined in real terms, though at a slower rate than natural resources. It is difficult to infer actual scarcity values from these figures because declining relative costs of extraction and development may have masked rising scarcity costs. Since 1970, the decline in real resource prices appears to have slowed and this may indeed indicate an increasing relevance of scarcity costs. Nevertheless, the prospect of rising real resource prices driven by scarcity is not yet a forgone conclusion.

TABLE 1 Real Prices for Natural Resources *(1990 = 100)*

Resource	*1870*	*1910*	*1950*	*1970*	*1990*
Petroleum	700	250	150	80	100
Coal	550	350	200	110	100
Copper	1000	500	250	160	100
Iron ore	1000	750	200	120	100
Aluminum	—	800	180	110	100
Farmland	200	375	80	105	100

SOURCE: ADAPTED FROM W. D. NORDHAUS, "LETHAL MODEL 2: LIMITS TO GROWTH REVISITED", *BROOKINGS PAPERS ON ECONOMIC ACTIVITY*, NO. 2 (1992):24–26.

Implications of Scarcity

Even if real prices of natural resources were to follow a rising path indicating their scarcity, market reactions to the trend could be quite complex. The ultimate effect on overall output (GDP) would depend on such factors as the ability of firms to substitute inputs that have stable prices for those that were rising in price, the tendency of rising resource prices to induce various types of resource-saving technical innovations, and the willingness of consumers to reduce their consumption of resource-intensive goods. Modeling all of these various reactions is a formidable undertaking. One fairly careful estimate suggests that resource scarcity might reduce real economic growth rates by about 0.3 per cent by the year 2050, with more than half of the decline being attributed to the increasing scarcity of energy resources.[1] Whether this relatively modest estimate will prove accurate is, of course, anyone's guess.

To Think About

1 How should changing costs of resource extraction be factored into an explanation of market prices? In what way might such changes mask changing scarcity values? What is the maximum effect that changing relative extraction costs might be expected to have?

2 Why do economists and environmentalists have such different views on resource scarcity? Don't environmentalists understand that the price system works to mitigate the effects of scarcity? Or is it economists who mistakenly assume that markets will work efficiently when the environment is threatened?

[1] W. D. Nordhaus, "Lethal Model 2: Limits to Growth Revisited", *Brooking Papers on Economic Activity*, No. 2 (1992):1–43.

marginal cost of production by €0.26 per kilo. In this case, the fact that price exceeds marginal cost is not a sign of inefficiency as it has been in several other situations we've looked at. Instead, the price here reflects efficiency in resource use in that consumers are paying all of the costs associated with the current production of the resource.

Time Pattern of Resource Prices

An important implication of this discussion is that, in the absence of any change in real production costs or in firms' expectations about future prices, the relative price of resources should be expected to rise over time at the real rate of interest. In our previous example, because the real rate of interest was assumed to be 5 per cent, real copper prices would be expected to rise at 5 per cent per year. Only by following that time path would prices always be equal to the present value of €1 in ten years.

This result can be shown intuitively from another perspective. Any firm that owns a quantity of a finite natural resource evaluates that holding in the way it evaluates any other investment. Since the real interest rate represents the rate of return on such alternative investments, only if resource prices rise at this rate do they provide a competitive return to the owner. If prices were rising more slowly than the real rate of interest, natural resources would be an inferior investment and firms should put their funds elsewhere. A rate of increase in prices faster than the real interest rate is also unsustainable because investors would quickly bid up the current price of resources to attempt to capture those desirable returns. This important result about resource pricing can be used to study a variety of important economic issues, as Application 16.6: *Are Any Resources Scarce?* shows.

SUMMARY

In this chapter, we have examined economic issues associated with decisions that are made over time in capital markets. The discussion focused primarily on the role of the real interest rate (r) in providing a "price" that connects one period to the next. Some of the important results of this examination included:

- Real interest rates affect individuals' savings decisions. Although income and substitution effects of a change in the real interest rate work in opposite directions, it is generally believed that the (intertemporal) substitution effect is stronger. Hence, an increase in r causes savings (and loans) to increase.
- The real interest rate represents a cost of capital to firms regardless of whether they rent or own their equipment. An increase in r raises the rental rate on capital equipment and reduces its usage. This also reduces the demand for loans.
- Real interest rates are determined by the supply and demand for loans. Loans are supplied by individuals through their savings decisions. Loans are demanded by firms to finance their purchases of capital equipment.
- Expenditures or receipts in different periods cannot be compared directly because of the opportunity cost of interest payments. Such flows must be discounted so that they can be compared on a common, present-value basis. Investment decisions are an especially important situation where discounting is required.
- Production of finite resources involves additional costs reflecting scarcity. These costs arise because current production involves an opportunity cost in terms of forgone future sales.

REVIEW QUESTIONS

1 Some economic variables are "stocks" in that they represent the total value of something at a point in time, rather than a per-period "flow". Explain the connection between the following flow and stock variables:

Flow	*Stock*
Individual savings	Individual wealth
Firm investment	Firm capital
Education	Human capital
Gold production	Gold

2 Explain why the intertemporal budget constraint pictured in Figure 16-1 can be interpreted as requiring that individuals choose C_0 and C_1 so that the present value of this consumption is equal to their current income.

3 Suppose that an individual obtains the same utility from a given level of consumption regardless of whether it is consumed now or next period. Suppose also that the marginal utility of consumption is diminishing. Why would you expect this person to be "impatient", that is, always choosing C_0 to be greater than C_1? (*Hint*: What is the relative "price" of C_1 in terms of C_0?)

4 Sometimes retirement planners suggest that people set a "target" for retirement income. For example, the advice might be, "Be sure to have accumulated €1 000 000 by the time you are 60". Assuming that the target remains unchanged, how would an increase in the real interest rate affect a person's level of savings to reach this target? Is it appropriate to hold the target constant when the real interest rate changes?

5 P. T. Blowhard is the CEO of Ditch Industries. He was heard to make the following statement about his choice of inputs for digging ditches: "We borrowed €100 000 to buy this DitchWitch, and we're still paying €8000 per year in interest on that loan even though the machine is now essentially worthless to any other firm. We could save money by borrowing €70 000 to buy a new DitchKing machine that would do the same job with only €5600 in interest." What do you make of this argument? Assuming the machines are perfect substitutes, costs would be minimized by using the one with the lower rental rate. Which one has the lower rental rate?

6 CEO Blowhard continues his economic wisdom by discussing his rationale for calculating the present value of the rents he might save by purchasing a building to house his firm: "We could save €25 000 per year in rent by purchasing our own building. Over a 25-year horizon, Nicholson and Snyder's Table 16A-3 (see Appendix to Chapter 16) tells me that the present value of these savings is about €350 000 using a real interest rate of 5 per cent. But that is clearly an understatement since our rents are bound to rise because of general inflation. Hence, I'm sure it would be worthwhile for us to purchase a building costing up to at least €500 000." Has the CEO got it right now? How should he take into account the expected inflationary increases in rent in the future?

7 Figure 16-3 shows how the real interest rate is determined by the supply and demand for loans. Explain why this process also determines the rate of return that any capital owner should expect to earn on investments in physical capital. That is, how do you reconcile a "loanable funds" theory of interest rates with a "return on capital" theory of interest rates? If you are adventuresome, you might also seek to reconcile these theories with whatever theory of interest rates you learned in macroeconomics.

8 Suppose that a monopoly farmer of Wonder Grain must pay all of its costs of production in this year but that it must wait until next year to sell its output. Why would the farm's profit-maximizing output be the level for which $MR = MC(1 + r)$? Explain why this profit-maximizing condition takes *all* costs into account. Would this farmer produce more or less output if he or she could defer paying costs until next period? Explain why the firm should also hire any input, such as labor, up to the point at which $MRP_L = w(1 + r)$.

9 Why do scarcity costs occur only in the case of finite resources? Do producers of renewable resources such as fish or trees also incur

scarcity costs? Explain the differences between these cases.

10 Our theory of the pricing of exhaustible resources concludes that the prices of such resources should increase (relative to prices of other goods) at a rate equal to the real rate of interest. What does this conclusion assume about the costs involved in actually producing natural resources?

a That they are constant.

b That they increase at the overall rate of inflation.

c That they also increase relative to prices of other goods at the real rate of interest.

Explain your answer and discuss how resource prices would be expected to move if your assumption were not true.

PROBLEMS

16.1 The budget constraint facing an individual planning his or her consumption over two periods is an intertemporal one in which the present value of consumption expenditures must equal the present value of incomes in the two periods

$$C_0 + C_1/(1 + r) = Y_0 + Y_1/(1 + r)$$

where Y and C represent income and consumption respectively and the subscripts represent the two time periods.

a Explain the meaning of this constraint.

b If $Y_0 > C_0$, this individual is saving in period 0. Why does this imply that $Y_1 < C_1$?

c If this individual is saving in period 0, why is $Y_0 - C_0$ less than $C_1 - Y_1$?

16.2 Flexible Felix views present and future consumption as perfect substitutes. He does, however, discount future consumption by a bit to reflect the uncertainties of his life. His utility function is therefore given by

$$U(C_0, C_1) = C_0 + C_1/(1 + \delta)$$

where δ (which is a small positive number) is the "discount rate" he applies to C_1.

a Graph Felix's indifference curve map.

b Show that if r (the real interest rate) exceeds δ, then $C_0 = 0$.

c Show that if $r < \delta$, then $C_1 = 0$

d What do you conclude about the relationship between a person's saving behavior and his or her "impatience"?

16.3 Two roommates, Prudence and Glitter, graduate from university and get identical jobs that pay them €50 000 this year and €55 000 next year. The roommates have different utility functions so that the marginal rates of substitution are given by

$$MRS \text{ for Prudence} = C_1/3C_0$$

$$MRS \text{ for Glitter} = 3C_1/C_0$$

Assume that the real interest rate is 10 per cent.

a What is the present value of each student's income?

b Focusing first on Prudence, what is her condition for utility maximization?

c How should Prudence choose C_0 and C_1 so as to satisfy the condition for utility maximization and so that the present value of her consumption equals the present value of her income? How much will Prudence borrow or save in period 0?

d Answer part c for Glitter.

16.4 The Robotics Corporation produces cuddly toys using only computer-driven robots. The quantity of toys (T) produced per year is given by

$$T = 10\sqrt{R}$$

where R is the number of robots used during each year of production.

a If the market price of robots is €2000, the real interest rate is 0.05, and the depreciation rate on robots is 0.10, what is the firm's implicit rental rate for robot use?

b What is the firm's total cost function for production of T?

c If cuddly toys sell for €60, how many will this firm choose to produce? (*Hint*: If Total Cost $= kT^2$, then calculus shows that Marginal Cost $= 2kT$.)

d How many robots will the firm employ for the year?

16.5 Acme Landfill Company is considering the purchase of ten better garbage collection lorries. Each lorry costs €50 000 and will last seven years. The firm estimates that the purchase will increase its annual revenues by €100 000 per year for as long as the lorries last. If the real interest rate is 10 per cent, should the firm buy the ten lorries? Would your answer change if the real interest rate fell to 8 per cent?

16.6 Scottish whisky increases in value as it ages, at least up to a point. For any period of time, t, the value of a barrel is given by

$$V = 100t - 6t^2$$

This function implies that the proportional rate of growth of the value of the scotch is $(100 - 12t)/V$.

a Graph this whisky value function.

b At what value of t is the barrel of whisky most valuable?

c If the real interest rate is 5 per cent, when should this distiller bottle the whisky for immediate sale?

d How would the distiller's decision change if the real interest rate were 10 per cent? (*Hint*: You will have to use the quadratic equation to solve part d here.)

16.7 In order to calculate scarcity costs for any finite resource, a price at some future date must be assumed. Suppose, for example, that the real price of platinum will be €4000 per gram in 25 years.

a If the real interest rate is 5 per cent and no change is expected in the real costs of producing platinum over the next 25 years, what should the equilibrium price be today?

b If the current cost of producing platinum is €100 per gram, what are current scarcity costs?

c What will scarcity costs be in 25 years?

d Assuming that resource markets are in equilibrium and that real production costs for platinum continue to remain constant, what is the real equilibrium price of the metal in 50 years?

Note: Problems 16.8–16.10 make extensive use of the material on compound interest that is in the appendix to this chapter..

16.8 A persistent life insurance salesman makes the following pitch: "At your age (40) a €100 000 whole life policy is a much better buy than a term policy. The whole life policy requires you to pay €2000 per year for the next four years but nothing after that. A term policy will cost you €400 per year for as long as you own it. Let's assume you live 35 more years – that means you'll end up paying €8000 for the whole life policy and €14 000 for the term policy. The choice is obvious!"

a Is the choice so obvious? How does the best buy depend on the interest rate?

b If the interest rate is 10 per cent, which policy is the best buy?

16.9 A car salesman once made the following pitch to one of your authors: "If you buy this €10 000 car with cash you will lose at least €1500 over the next three years in forgone interest (assumed to be 5 per cent per year). If you take one of our low-cost auto loans you only have to pay €315 per month for the next three years. That amounts to €11 340 – €10 000 for the car and €1340 in interest. With our car loan you will actually save €160 in interest." What do you make of this argument?

16.10 Although perpetual bonds are illegal, sometimes it is easiest to assume that interest payments last forever to show some simple results based on Equation 16A.24. Use that equation to show that

a Assuming no inflation, the value of a bond that pays €10 per year is €200 with a real rate of interest of 5 per cent.

b If inflation is 3 per cent per year and interest payments rise at that rate, the current value of the perpetual bond is still €200.

c If inflation is 3 per cent per year and the bond's payments are fixed at €10, that the current value of the perpetual bond is €125 can be shown in two ways

i By assuming that the nominal rate of interest is 8 per cent and using that rate for discounting.

ii By adjusting the €10 payment for inflation in each period and using a real discount rate of 5 per cent. (*Hint*: This latter proof is easiest if you use the approximation $[1 + r][1 + i] \approx 1 + r + i$ for small values of r [the real interest rate] and i [the inflation rate].)

Appendix to Chapter 16

Compound Interest

People encounter compound interest concepts almost every day. Calculating returns on bank accounts, deciding on the true cost of an automobile loan, and buying a home with a mortgage all involve the use of interest rate computations. This appendix shows how some of those computations are made. The methods introduced are useful not only in economics classes but in many personal economic decisions too.

Interest

Interest is payment for the time value of money. A borrower gets to use funds for his or her own purposes for a time and in return pays the lender some compensation. Interest rates are usually stated as some percentage of the amount borrowed (the principal). For example, an annual interest rate of 5 per cent would require someone who borrowed €100 to pay €5 per year in interest.

Interest Payment for the current use of funds.

Throughout this appendix, we assume that the market has established an annual interest rate, i, and that this interest rate will persist from one year to the next. It is a relatively simple matter to deal with interest rates that change from one period to another, but we do not consider them here. We are also not particularly interested in whether i is a "nominal" interest rate (such as a rate quoted by a bank) or a "real" interest rate that has been adjusted for any inflation that may occur over time.[1] The mathematics of compound interest is the same for both nominal and real interest rates.

Compound Interest

If you hold funds in a bank for more than one period, you receive **compound interest** – that is, you receive interest not only on your original principal but also on the interest that you earned in prior periods and left in the bank. Compounding is relatively complicated and results in rather dramatic growth over long periods.

Compound interest Interest paid on prior interest earned.

[1]For a discussion of the relationship between nominal and real interest rates, see Application 16.4.

Interest for One Year

If you invest €1 at the interest rate of i, at the end of one year you will have

$$€1 + €1 \cdot i = €1 \cdot (1 + i) \qquad \{16A.1\}$$

For example, if i is 5 per cent, at the end of one year, you will have

$$€1 + €1 \cdot (0.05) = €1 \cdot (1.05) = €1.05 \qquad \{16A.2\}$$

Interest for Two Years

If at the end of the first year, you leave your money in the bank, you will now earn interest on both the original €1 and on your first year's interest. At the end of two years you will therefore have

$$€1 \cdot (1 + i) + €1 \cdot (1 + i) \cdot i = €1 \cdot (1 + i)(1 + i) = €1 \cdot (1 + i)^2 \qquad \{16A.3\}$$

To understand this equation, it is helpful to expand the term $(1 + i)^2$. Remember from algebra that

$$(1 + i)^2 = 1 + 2i + i^2 \qquad \{16A.4\}$$

At the end of two years, €1 will grow to

$$€1 \cdot (1 + i)^2 = €1 \cdot (1 + 2i + i^2) = €1 + €1 \cdot (2i) + €1 \cdot i^2 \qquad \{16A.5\}$$

At the end of two years, you will have the sum of three amounts

1. Your original €1
2. Two years' simple interest on your original €1, that is, $€1 \cdot 2i$
3. Interest on your first year's interest, that is, $[(€1 \cdot i) \cdot i] = €1 \cdot i^2$

If the interest rate is 5 per cent, at the end of two years you will have

$$€1 \cdot (1.05)^2 = €1 \cdot (1.1025) = €1.1025 \qquad \{16A.6\}$$

This represents the sum of your original €1, two years' interest on the €1 (that is, €0.10), and interest on the first year's interest (5 per cent of €0.05, which is €0.0025). The fact that you will have more than €1.10 is a reflection of compounding (that is, earning interest on past interest). As we look at longer and longer periods of time, the effects of this compounding become much more pronounced.

Interest for Three Years

If you now leave these funds, which after two years amount to $€1 \cdot (1 + i)^2$, in the bank for another year, at the end of this third year you will have

$$€1 \cdot (1 + i)^2 + €1 \cdot (1 + i)^2 \cdot i = €1 \cdot (1 + i)^2(1 + i) = €1 \cdot (1 + i)^3 \qquad \{16A.7\}$$

For an interest rate of 5 per cent, this amounts to

$$€1 \cdot (1 + 0.05)^3 = €1 \cdot 1.157625 = €1.157625 \qquad \{16A.8\}$$

The fact that you get more than your original €1 and three years' simple interest (€0.15) again reflects the effects of compounding.

A General Formula

By now the pattern should be clear. If you leave your €1 in the bank for any number of years, n, you will have, at the end of that period

$$\text{Value of €1 compounded for } n \text{ years} = €1 \cdot (1 + i)^n \tag{16A.9}$$

With a 5 per cent interest rate and a period of ten years, you would have

$$€1 \cdot (1.05)^{10} = €1 \cdot 1.62889\ldots = €1.62889 \tag{16A.10}$$

Without compounding you would have had €1.50 – your original €1 plus ten years' interest at €0.05 per year. The extra €0.12889 comes about through compounding.

To illustrate the effects of compounding further, Table 16A-1 shows the value of €1 compounded for various time periods and interest rates.[2] Notice how compounding becomes very important for long periods. For instance, the table shows that, at a 5 per cent interest rate, €1 grows to be €131.50 over 100 years. This represents the original €1, simple interest of €5 (€0.05 per year for 100 years), and a massive €125.50 in interest earned on prior interest. At higher interest rates, the effect of compounding is even more pronounced because there is even more prior interest on which to earn interest. At a 1 per cent interest rate, only about 26 per cent of the funds accumulated over 100 years represents the effects of compounding. At a 10 per cent interest rate, more than 99.9 per cent of the huge amount accumulated represents the effects of compounding.

MICROQUIZ 16A.1

The term $(1 + i)^3$ can be expanded to be $1 + 3i + 3i^2 + i^3$. Carefully explain why each of these terms is required in order to reflect the complete effects of compounding. You may have to do some factoring to make your explanation clear.

TABLE 16A-1 Effects of Compound Interest for Various Interest Rates and Time Periods with an Initial Investment of €1

	Interest Rate			
Years	*1%*	*3%*	*5%*	*10%*
1	€1.01	€1.03	€1.05	€1.10
2	1.0201	1.0609	1.1025	1.2100
3	1.0303	1.0927	1.1576	1.3310
5	1.051	1.159	1.2763	1.6105
10	1.1046	1.344	1.6289	2.5937
25	1.282	2.094	3.3863	10.8347
50	1.645	4.384	11.4674	117.3909
100	2.705	19.219	131.5013	13 780.6123

[2]All calculations in this appendix were done on a Hewlett-Packard financial calculator – a device that is highly recommended. Advanced versions of Texas Instruments calculators also have nice financial options.

Compounding with Any Euro Amount

The use of €1 in all of the computations we have made so far was for convenience only. Any other amount of money grows in exactly the same way. Investing €1000 is just the same as investing a thousand one-euro bills – at an interest rate of 5 per cent this amount would grow to €1050 at the end of 1 year [€1000 · (1.05)]; it would grow to €1629 at the end of 10 years [€1000 · (1.629)]; and to €131 501 at the end of 100 years [€1000 · 131.501].

Algebraically, D euros invested for n years at an interest rate of i will grow to

$$\text{Value of } €D \text{ invested for } n \text{ years} = €D \cdot (1 + i)^n \qquad \{16A.11\}$$

Application 16A.1: *Compound Interest Gone Berserk* illustrates some particularly extreme examples of using this formula.

Present Discounted Value

Because interest is paid on invested euros, a euro you get today is more valuable than one you won't receive until next year. You could put a euro you receive today in a bank and have more than a euro in one year. If you wait a year for the euro, you will do without this interest that you could have earned.

Present value
Discounting the value of future transactions back to the present day to take account of the effect of potential interest payments.

Economists use the concept of present discounted value – or, more simply, **present value** – to reflect this opportunity cost notion. The present discounted value of the euro you will not get for one year is simply the amount you would have to put in a bank now to have €1 at the end of one year. If the interest rate is 5 per cent, for example, the present value of €1 to be obtained in one year is about €0.95 – if you invest €0.95 today, you will have €1 in one year, so €0.95 accurately reflects the present value of €1 in one year.

An Algebraic Definition

More formally, if the interest rate is i, the present discounted value of €1 in one year is €1/(1 + i) since

$$\frac{€1}{1 + i} \cdot (1 + i) = €1 \qquad \{16A.12\}$$

If i = 5 per cent, the present discounted value (*PDV*) of €1 in one year is

$$PDV = \frac{€1}{1.05} = €0.9524 \qquad \{16A.13\}$$

and

$$€0.9524 \cdot 1.05 = €1 \qquad \{16A.14\}$$

A similar computation would result for any other interest rate. For example, the *PDV* of €1 payable in one year is €0.971 if the interest rate is 3 per cent, but €0.909 when the interest rate is 10 per cent. With a higher interest rate, the *PDV*

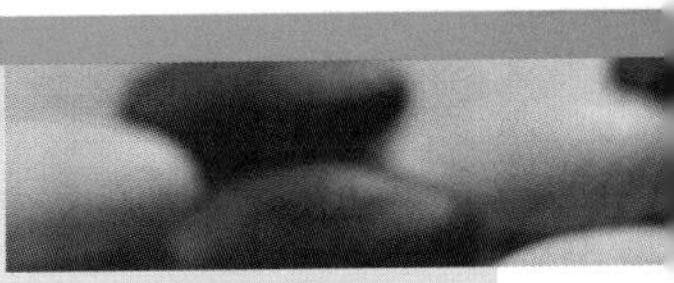

APPLICATION 16A.1 *Compound Interest Gone Berserk*

The effect of compounding can be gigantic if a sufficiently long period is used. Here are three of your authors' favorite examples.

Manhattan Island

Legend has it that in 1623 Dutch settlers "purchased" Manhattan Island from Native Americans living there for trinkets worth about \$24. The usual version of the story claims that the sellers were robbed in this transaction. But suppose they had invested the money? Real returns on stocks have averaged about 7 per cent, so let's calculate how the \$24 invested in stocks would have grown during the 383 years since the sale.

$$\text{Value of \$24 in 2006} = 24 \cdot (1.07)^{383}$$
$$= 24 \cdot (179\,467\,930\,000)$$
$$= 4\,307\,230\,320\,000$$

That is, the funds would have grown to be more than \$4 trillion – a value that is probably greater than the land on Manhattan Island is worth today.

Horse Manure in Philadelphia

In the 1840s the horse population of Philadelphia was growing at 10 per cent per year. The city fathers, fearing excessive crowding, decided to restrict the number of horses in the city. It's a good thing! If the horse population of 50 000 in 1845 had continued to grow at 10 per cent per year, there would have been quite a few of them in 2005.

$$\text{Number of horses in 2005} = 50\,000 \cdot (1.10)^{160}$$
$$= 50\,000 \cdot (4\,195\,943) = 209\,797\,172\,000$$

More than 200 billion horses would have posed some problems for the city. Assuming each horse produces 0.25 cubic feet of manure per day, there would be about 2000 feet of manure per year covering each square foot of Philadelphia today. Luckily the City of Brotherly Love (author Nicholson's hometown) was spared this fate through timely government action. (For those "interested" in horse manure see Application 18.7.)

Rabbits in Australia

Rabbits were first introduced into Australia in 1860. They found a country relatively free of natural predators and multiplied rapidly. If we assume that two rabbits started this process and that the population was growing at 100 per cent per year, in only 20 years there were

$$\text{Number of rabbits in 1880} = 2 \cdot (1 + 1)^{20}$$
$$= 2^{21}$$
$$= 2\,097\,152$$

If the growth continued for the next 125 years, by 2005 there would have been 2^{146} rabbits, amounting to many trillions of rabbits per square foot of Australia. Clearly they built the "rabbit-proof fence" for a purpose.

To Think About

1. The preposterous numbers in these examples suggest there is something wrong with the calculations. Can you put your finger on precisely why each is pure nonsense?
2. Compounding with high interest rates can produce astounding results. Often people look at very high interest rates (50 per cent or more) in some developing countries and calculate how rich they will be in only a few years. What are they forgetting?

is lower because the opportunity costs involved in waiting to get the euro are greater.

Waiting two years to get paid involves even greater opportunity costs than waiting one year since now you forgo two years' interest. At an interest rate of 5 per cent, €0.907 will grow to be €1 in two years – that is, €1 = €0.907 · $(1.05)^2$. Consequently, the present value of €1 payable in two years is only €0.907. More generally, for any interest rate, i, the present value of €1 payable in two years is

$$PDV \text{ of } €1 \text{ payable in two years} = €1/(1 + i)^2 \quad \{16A.15\}$$

and, for the case of a 5 per cent interest rate,

$$PDV \text{ of } €1 \text{ payable in two years} = €1/(1.05)^2$$
$$= €1/1.1025$$
$$= €0.907 \quad \{16A.16\}$$

General *PDV* Formulas

The pattern again should be obvious. With an interest rate of i, the present value of €1 payable after any number of years, n, is simply

$$PDV \text{ of } €1 \text{ payable in } n \text{ years} = €1/(1 + i)^n \quad \{16A.17\}$$

Calculating present values is the reverse of computing compound interest. In the compound interest case (Equation 16A.9), the calculation requires multiplying by the interest factor $(1 + i)^n$, whereas in the present discounted value case (Equation 16A.17) the calculation proceeds by dividing by that factor. Similarly, the present value of any number of euros (€D) payable in n years is given by

$$PDV \text{ of } €D \text{ payable in } n \text{ years} = €D/(1 + i)^n \quad \{16A.18\}$$

Again, by comparing Equation 16A.11 and Equation 16A.18, you can see the different ways that the interest factor $(1 + i)^n$ enters into the calculations.

In Table 16A-2, your authors have again put their calculators to work to compute the present discounted value of €1 payable at various times and for various interest rates. The entries in this table are the reciprocals of the entries in Table 16A-1 because compounding and taking present values are different ways of looking at the same process. In Table 16A-2, the *PDV* of €1 payable in some particular year is smaller the

TABLE 16A-2 Present Discounted Value of €1 for Various Time Periods and Interest Rates

Years until payment is received	Interest rate 1%	3%	5%	10%
1	€0.99010	€0.97087	€0.95238	€0.90909
2	0.98030	0.94260	0.90703	0.82645
3	0.97059	0.91516	0.86386	0.75131
5	0.95147	0.86281	0.78351	0.62093
10	0.90531	0.74405	0.61391	0.38555
25	0.78003	0.47755	0.29531	0.09230
50	0.60790	0.22810	0.08720	0.00852
100	0.36969	0.05203	0.00760	0.00007

NOTE: THESE AMOUNTS ARE THE RECIPROCALS OF THOSE IN TABLE 16A-1.

higher the interest rate. Similarly, for a given interest rate, the *PDV* of €1 is smaller the longer it is until the €1 will be paid. With a 10 per cent interest rate, for example, a euro that will not be paid for 50 years is worth less than 1 cent (€0.00852) today. Application 16A.2: *Zero-Coupon Bonds* shows how such *PDV* calculations apply to a popular type of financial asset.

Discounting Payment Streams

Euros payable at different points of time have different present values. One must be careful in calculating the true worth of streams of payments that occur at various times into the future – simply adding them up is not appropriate. Consider a situation that has irritated your authors for some time. Many lotteries promise grand prizes of €1 million (or, sometimes, much more) that they pay to the winners over 25 years. But €40 000 per year for 25 years is not "worth" €1 million. Indeed, at a 10 per cent interest rate, the present value of such a stream is only €363 200 – much less than half the amount falsely advertised by the lottery. This section describes how such a calculation can be made. There is really nothing new to learn about discounting streams of payments – performing the calculations always involves making careful use of the general discounting formula. However, repeated use of that formula may be very time consuming (if a stream of income is paid, say, at 100 different times in the future), and our main purpose here is to present a few shortcuts.

An Algebraic Presentation

Consider a stream of payments that promises €1 per year starting next year and continuing for three years. By applying Equation 16A.18, it is easy to see that the present value of this stream is

$$PDV = \frac{€1}{1+i} + \frac{€1}{(1+i)^2} + \frac{€1}{(1+i)^3} \qquad \{16A.19\}$$

If the interest rate is 5 per cent, this value would be

$$\frac{€1}{1.05} + \frac{€1}{(1.05)^2} + \frac{€1}{(1.05)^3} = €0.9523 + €0.9070 + €0.8639$$
$$= €2.7232 \qquad \{16A.20\}$$

Consequently, just as for the lottery, €1 a year for three years is not worth €3 but quite a bit less because of the need to take forgone interest into account in making present value calculations. If the promised stream of payments extends for longer than three years, additional terms should be added to Equation 16A.19. The present value of €1 per year for five years is

$$PDV = \frac{€1}{1+i} + \frac{€1}{(1+i)^2} + \frac{€1}{(1+i)^3} + \frac{€1}{(1+i)^4} + \frac{€1}{(1+i)^5} \qquad \{16A.21\}$$

which amounts to about €4.33 at a 5 per cent interest rate. Again, €1 per year for five years is not worth €5.

MICROQUIZ 16A.2

If the interest rate is 5 per cent, would you rather have €1000 in five years or €3000 in 25 years? Would your answer change if the interest rate were 10 per cent?

APPLICATION 16A.2 *Zero-Coupon Bonds*

US Treasury notes pay their interest semiannually. In the past, each bond had a series of coupons for these interest payments. An owner would clip off a payment coupon and turn it in to the Treasury for payment. This is the origin of the term "coupon-clipper" for elderly Scrooge-type characters living off their bond holdings. Today, of course, coupons are a thing of the past. Bond owners are recorded on computer files, and checks are routinely sent out to them when interest payments are due. Still, the idea that bonds are nothing more than a big coupon book of interest payments to be made at specific dates has spawned a variety of innovations.

Invention of Zero-Coupon Bonds

One of the most important such innovations occurred in the late 1970s when large financial institutions started buying large numbers of US Treasury bonds and "stripping" off the interest (and principal) payments into separate financial assets. For example, consider a recent ten-year Treasury note that promises 20 semiannual interest payments of $20 on each $1000 bond together with a return of the $1000 principal in ten years. A large financial institution can buy $100 million of such bonds and sell off $2 million worth of interest payments for each of the 20 semiannual interest payment dates into the future. The firm can also sell $100 million of principal payments due in ten years. Hence it has created 21 new financial assets based on its underlying bond holdings. Because the payments promised by these assets are supported by actual bond holdings of the financial institution, they are a low-risk investment for people who will need their funds at specific dates in the future.

Applying the *PDV* Formula

Because the interest and principal payments will not be received until some date in the future, we must use present value calculations to determine what they are worth today. For example, a promised interest payment of $20 in, say, six years with an interest rate of 5 per cent would be worth $\$20/(1+i)^6 = \$20/(1.05)^6 = \$14.92$ today. A buyer that paid $14.92 for the promise of $20 in six years would achieve a return of 5 per cent on his or her funds and would avoid the hassle of having to deal with periodic interest payments.

Yields

The calculations for zero-coupon bonds appearing daily in the financial press work a bit differently than this hypothetical example. Specifically, the prices for a given date's interest payments are determined in the market and an implicit yield on this price is calculated using the present value formula. For example, today's *Wall Street Journal* reports that a $100 interest payment "strip" payable in ten years currently sells for $65. We can compute the yield on this investment by solving the following equation for *i*:[1]

$$65 = \frac{100}{(1+i)^{10}} \text{ or } (1+i)^{10} = \frac{100}{65}$$

$$= 1.5385 \text{ so } (1+i) = (1.5385)^{0.1} = 1.0440$$

So the implicit yield on this strip is 4.4 per cent. A person who buys the strip today and holds it until it matures will be assured of making 4.4 per cent on his or her money.

To Think About

1. Does an investor who buys a zero-coupon bond have to hold onto the asset until it comes due? Suppose that a person who bought the ten-year strip described above decided to sell it after four years. What would determine the yield he or she actually received on the investment? What would determine the yield this seller could get if he or she wanted to invest the proceeds for a new ten-year period?
2. US Treasury "bills" operate much like strips. Bills with a maturity value of, say, $1000 are sold on a discount basis and the buyer receives an implicit yield by holding to maturity. For example, a 65-day Treasury bill with a maturity value of $1000 currently sells $994. What is the annual yield on this investment? (*Hint*: You must first compute the daily yield on this investment. Then you must compound this daily yield over 365 days to get an effective annual yield.)

[1] The actual computation is more complicated than this because interest is assumed to be compounded daily and the calculation must take account of the precise number of days involved.

The *PDV* equation can be generalized to any number of years (n) by just adding the correct number of terms

$$PDV = \frac{€1}{1+i} + \frac{€1}{(1+i)^2} + \cdots + \frac{€1}{(1+i)^n} \qquad \{16A.22\}$$

Table 16A-3 uses this formula to compute the value of €1 per year for various numbers of years and interest rates. Several features of the numbers in this table are important to keep in mind when discussing present values. As noted previously, none of the streams is worth in present value terms the actual number of euros paid. The figures are always less than the number of years for which €1 will be paid. Even for low interest rates, the difference is substantial. With a 3 per cent interest rate, €1 per year for 100 years is worth only €31 in present value. At higher interest rates, the effect of discounting is even more pronounced. A euro each year for 100 years is worth (slightly) less than €10 in present value terms with an interest rate of 10 per cent.

Perpetual Payments

The value of a stream of payments that goes on "forever" at €1 per year is reported as the final entry in each column of Table 16A-3. To understand how this is calculated, we can pose the question in a slightly different way. How much (€X) would you have to invest at an interest rate of i to yield €1 a year forever? That is, we wish to find €X that satisfies the equation

$$€1 = i \cdot €X \qquad \{16A.23\}$$

But this just means that

$$€X = €1/i \qquad \{16A.24\}$$

which is the way the entries in the table were computed. For example, the present value of €1 per year forever with an interest rate of 5 per cent is €20 (= €1/0.05). With an interest rate of 10 per cent, the figure would be €10 (= €1/0.10). Such a permanent payment stream is called a **perpetuity**. Although these are technically illegal

Perpetuity A promise of a certain number of euros each year, forever.

TABLE 16A-3 Present Value of €1 per Year for Various Time Periods and Interest Rates

	Interest Rate			
Years of payment	*1%*	*3%*	*5%*	*10%*
1	€0.99	€0.97	€0.95	€0.91
2	1.97	1.91	1.86	1.74
3	2.94	2.83	2.72	2.49
5	4.85	4.58	4.33	3.79
10	9.47	8.53	7.72	6.14
25	22.02	17.41	14.09	9.08
50	39.20	25.73	18.26	9.91
100	63.02	31.60	19.85	9.99
Forever	100.00	33.33	20.00	10.00

in the United States (however, many people set up "permanent" endowments for cemetery plots, scholarships, and prize funds), other countries do permit such limitless contracts to be written. In the United Kingdom, for example, perpetuities originally written in the 1600s are still bought and sold. Equation 16A.24 shows that, even though such perpetuities in effect promise an infinite number of euros (since the payments never cease), in present-value terms they have quite modest values. Indeed, for relatively high interest rates, there isn't much difference between getting €1 a year for 25 or 50 years and getting it forever. At an interest rate of 10 per cent, for example, the present value of a perpetuity (which promises an infinite number of euros) is only €0.92 greater than a promise of a euro a year for only 25 years. The infinite number of euros to be received after year 25 are only worth €0.92 today.[3]

Varying Payment Streams

The present value of a payment stream that consists of the same number of euros each year can be calculated by multiplying the value of €1 per year by that amount. In the lottery illustration with which we began this section, for example, we calculated the present value of €40 000 per year for 25 years. This is 40 000 times the entry for €1 per year for 25 years at 10 per cent from Table 16A-3 (40 000 · €9.08 = €363 200). The present value of any other constant stream of euro payments can be calculated in a similar fashion.

When payments vary from year to year, the computation can become more cumbersome. Each payment must be discounted separately using the correct discount factor from Equation 16A.18. We can show this computation in its most general form by letting D_i represent the amount to be paid in any year i. Then the present value of this stream would be

$$PDV = \frac{D_1}{1+i} + \frac{D_2}{(1+i)^2} + \frac{D_3}{(1+i)^3} + \cdots + \frac{D_n}{(1+i)^n} \qquad \{16A.25\}$$

Here, each D could be either positive or negative depending on whether funds are to be received or paid out. In some cases, the computations may be very complicated, as

[3]Using the formula for perpetuities provides a simple way of computing streams that run for only a limited number of years. Suppose we wished to evaluate a stream of €1 per year for 25 years at a 10 per cent interest rate. If we used Equation 16A.22, we would need to evaluate 25 terms. Instead, we could note that a 25-year stream is an infinite stream less all payments for year 26 and beyond. The present value of a perpetual stream is

$$\frac{€1}{i} = \frac{€1}{0.10} = €\,10$$

whereas the present value of a perpetual stream that starts in year 25 is

$$\frac{€10}{(1+i)^{25}} = \frac{€10}{(1+0.10)^{25}} = \frac{€10}{10.83} = €\,0.92$$

The value of a 25-year stream is

$$€10 - €0.92 = €9.08$$

which is the figure given in Table 16A-3.

More generally, a stream of €1 per year for n years at the interest rate i has a present value of

$$PDV = \frac{€1}{i} - \frac{€1/i}{(1+i)^n} = \frac{€1}{i}\left(1 - \frac{1}{(1+i)^n}\right)$$

we saw in Application 16.4. Still, Equation 16A.25 provides a uniform way to approach all present value problems.

Calculating Yields

Equation 16A.25 can also be used to compute the **yield** promised by any payment stream. That is, we can use the equation to compute the implied interest rate that discounts any payment stream to the present price that a buyer must pay for the rights to the stream. If we let P be the price of the payment stream and if we know the periodic payments to be made ($D_1 \ldots D_n$), then Equation 16A.25 becomes

Yield The effective (internal) rate of return promised by a payment stream that can be purchased at a certain price.

$$P = PDV = \frac{D_1}{1+i} + \frac{D_2}{(1+i)^2} + \cdots + \frac{D_n}{(1+i)^n} \qquad \{16A.26\}$$

where now i is an unknown to be computed. Solving this equation can be clarified if we let $\delta = 1/(1 + i)$. Then Equation 16A.26 can be written as

$$P = \delta D_1 + \delta^2 D_2 + \cdots + \delta^n D_n \qquad \{16A.27\}$$

which is an n-degree polynomial in the unknown δ. This polynomial equation can usually be solved for δ and hence for the yield (or "internal rate of return") on the flow of payments.

Reading Bond Tables

One of the most common applications of this type of calculation is the computation of yields on bonds. Most ordinary bonds promise to pay a stream of annual interest payments for a given number of years and to make a final repayment of principal when the bond matures. For example, the bond tables in the *Wall Street Journal* list a "6.25 per cent bond maturing in May 2030", which currently sells for \$1260. This bond is simply a promise to pay 6.25 per cent of its initial face amount (\$1000) each year and then to repay the \$1000 principal when interest payments end in 25 years. The yield on this bond is found by solving the following equation for δ [and, also for $i = (1 - \delta)/\delta$]:[4]

$$1260 = 62.5\delta + 62.5\delta^2 + \ldots + 62.5\delta^{25} + 1000\delta^{25} \qquad \{16A.28\}$$

The result of this calculation is given as 4.46 per cent – that is the yield on this particular bond. Notice that in this case the yield is less than the interest rate quoted on the bond, in part because the bond's current price is greater than \$1000.

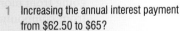

MICROQUIZ 16A.3

For the bond described in the text, how would the yield be affected by

1. Increasing the annual interest payment from \$62.50 to \$65?
2. Increasing the repayment amount from \$1000 to \$1100?
3. Shortening the maturity date from 2030 to 2025?

Frequency of Compounding

So far we have talked only about interest payments that are compounded once a year. That is, interest is paid at the end of each year and does not itself start to earn interest until the next year begins. In the past, that was how banks worked. Every January, depositors were expected to bring in their bank books so

[4]The actual calculation is a bit more complicated than described here because adjustments have to be made for the actual dates at which interest and principal payments are to be made. Typically, interest payments are made semiannually.

that the past year's interest could be added. People who withdrew money from the bank prior to January 1 often lost all the interest they had earned so far in the year.

Since the 1960s, however, banks and all other financial institutions have started to use more frequent, usually daily, compounding. This has provided some extra interest payments to investors, because more frequent compounding means that prior interest earned begins itself to earn interest more quickly. In this section, we use the tools we have developed so far to explore this issue.

Semiannual Compounding

As before, assume the annual interest rate is given by i (or in some of our examples 5 per cent). But now suppose the bank agrees to pay interest two times a year – on January 1 and on July 1. If you deposit €1 on January 1, by July 1 it will have grown to be $€1 \cdot (1 + i/2)$ since you will have earned half a year's interest. With an interest rate of 5 per cent, you will have €1.025 on July 1. For the second half of the year, you will earn interest on €1.025, not just on €1. At the end of the year, you will have $€1.025 \cdot 1.025 = €1.05063$, which is slightly larger than the €1.05 you would have with annual compounding. More generally, with an interest rate of i, semiannual compounding would yield

$$€1(1 + i/2)(1 + i/2) = €1(1 + i/2)^2 \tag{16A.29}$$

at the end of one year. That this is superior to annual compounding can be shown with simple algebra

$$€1 \cdot (1 + i/2)^2 = €1(1 + i + i^2/4) = €1 \cdot (1 + i) + €1 \cdot i^2/4 \tag{16A.30}$$

which is clearly greater than $€1 \cdot (1 + i)$. The final term in Equation 16A.30 reflects the interest earned in the first half of the year, $€1 \cdot (i/2)$, times the interest rate in the second half of the year $(i/2)$. This is the bonus earned by semiannual compounding.

A General Treatment

We could extend this algebraic discussion to more frequent compounding – quarterly, monthly, or daily – but little new information would be added. More frequent compounding would continue to increase the effective yield that the 5 per cent annual interest rate actually provides. Table 16A-4 shows how the frequency of compounding has this effect over time periods of various durations. The gains of using monthly rather than annual compounding are relatively large, especially over long periods of time when small differences in effective yields can make a big difference. Gains in going from monthly to daily compounding are fairly small, however. The extra yield from compounding even more frequently (every second?) is even smaller. Application 16A.3: *Continuous Compounding* shows that, for some purposes, using such frequent compounding can make calculations much easier.

The Present Discounted Value Approach to Investment Decisions

The present discounted value concept provides an alternative way of approaching the theory of capital demand that we discussed in Chapter 16. When a firm buys a machine, it is in effect buying a stream of net revenues in future periods. In order

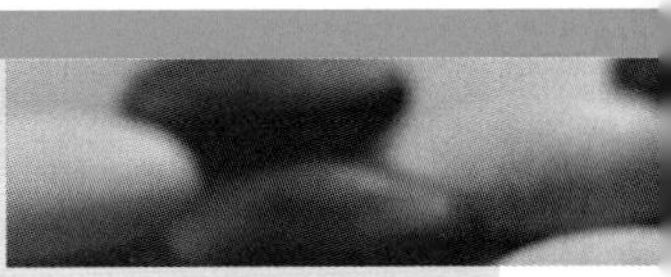

APPLICATION 16A.3 *Continuous Compounding*

Perhaps surprisingly, the mathematics involved with "continuous" compounding (that is compounding that occurs every instant of time) is really quite simple. A familiarity with continuous compounding can allow you to make very good approximations to interest calculations that would otherwise be very cumbersome.

The Amazing e

One of the most important constants[1] in mathematics is the number "e", which takes a value of approximately 2.718281828. The mathematician Euler discovered the constant in 1727, thereby explaining why this letter was chosen. The constant seems to turn up everywhere in mathematics. For us, the most important property of e is that it is used in continuous compounding. Consider an annual interest rate of *i* that will be compounded *n* times in one year. The result of this compounding will be

$$\left(1+\frac{i}{n}\right)^{n} i$$

If *n* approaches infinity, the value of this expression is precisely e^i. For example, if $i = 0.05$, $e^i = e^{0.05} = 1.05127$. So an annual interest rate of 5 per cent that is continuously compounded has an effective annual yield of 5.13 per cent. If compounding extends for *t* years, €1 becomes $€1 \cdot (e^i)^t = €1 \cdot e^{it}$.

The Rule of 70

A simple application of continuous compounding is to provide a rule of thumb for calculating doubling time for any given interest rate. To find the time anything doubles we wish to solve the equation $e^{it} = 2$ for *t*. Taking natural logarithms yields

$$t^* = \frac{\ln 2}{i} = \frac{0.6913}{i}$$

If we approximate 0.6913 as 0.7, this is the "rule of 70". To find any doubling time, just divide the interest rate into 0.70. For example, anything growing at 5 per cent per year will double in about 14 (= 0.7/0.05) years.

Growth Rates of Products and Ratios

When economic magnitudes follow exponential growth rates, calculations combining two or more series can be especially simple. For example, suppose we have two series, *x* and *y* growing at rates of r_1 and r_2 respectively. Then the product $x \cdot y$ is growing like

$$z = x \cdot y = e^{r_1 t} \cdot e^{r_2 t} = e^{1r_1 + r_2 2t} \qquad \{i\}$$

That is, the product of the two variables is growing at a rate which equals the *sum* of the individual growth rates. If, for example, real GDP is growing at 3 per cent per year and inflation is 2 per cent per year, nominal GDP is growing at 5 per cent per year. A similar result works for growth rates in the ratio of two variables. That is, the ratio of two variables grows at a rate which equals the *difference* in their growth rates. For example, if real GDP is growing at 3 per cent per year and population growth is 1 per cent per year, per capita GDP is growing at 2 per cent per year.

Discounting

With continuous compounding, the appropriate discount factor is e^{-it}, which plays the same role that $1/(1 + i)^t$ does in discrete discounting. Any continuous stream of payments can be discounted to the present day by using this factor. As a simple example, the value of payments of €1 per year for 25 years discounted at an interest rate of 5 per cent is given by

$$\begin{aligned} PDV &= \int_0^{25} €1 \cdot e^{-0.05t}\,dt = €1 \cdot \frac{e^{-0.05t}}{-0.05}\Big|_0^{25} \\ &= €1\left(\frac{e^{-1..25}}{-0.05} - \frac{1}{-0.05}\right) \\ &= €20(1 - e^{-1.25}) = €14.27 \end{aligned} \qquad \{ii\}$$

To Think About

1 The US consumer price index was 152 in 1995 and 195 in 2005. How would you use continuous compounding formulas to calculate the annual rate of change during this ten-year period?

2 How would you change Equation (ii) to calculate the value of a euro per year forever?

[1]One indication of the significance of e is that Google in its initial public offering in 2004 sold precisely €2 718 281 828 worth of stock. That is, it sold "e billion" worth of shares. The firm's 2005 stock offering was based on π.

to decide whether to purchase the machine, the firm must assign some value to this stream. Because the revenues will accrue to the firm in many future periods, the logic of the preceding pages suggests that the firm should compute the present discounted value of this stream. Only by doing so will the firm have taken adequate account of the opportunity costs associated with alternative assets it might have bought.

Consider a firm in the process of deciding whether to buy a particular machine. The machine is expected to last n years and will give its owner a stream of real returns (that is, marginal value products) in each of the n years. Let the return in year i be represented by R_i. If r is the real interest rate on alternative investments, and if this rate is expected to prevail for the next n years, the present discounted value (*PDV*) of the machine to its owner is given by

$$PDV = \frac{R_1}{1+r} = \frac{R_2}{(1+r)^2} + \cdots + \frac{R_n}{(1+r)^n} \qquad \{16A.31\}$$

This represents the total value of the stream of payments that is provided by the machine, once adequate account is taken of the fact that these payments occur in different years. If the *PDV* of this stream of payments exceeds the price (*P*) of the machine, the firm should make the purchase. Even when opportunity costs are taken into account, the machine promises to return more than it will cost to buy and firms would rush out to buy machines. On the other hand, if *P* exceeds the machine's *PDV*, the firm would be better off investing its funds in some alternative that promises a rate of return of r. When account is taken of forgone returns, the machine does not pay for itself. No profit-maximizing firm would buy such a machine.

In a competitive market, the only equilibrium that can persist is one where the price of a machine is exactly equal to the present discounted value of the net revenues it provides. Only in this situation will there be neither an excess demand for machines nor an excess supply of machines. Hence, market equilibrium requires that

$$P = PDV = \frac{R_1}{1+r} = \frac{R_2}{(1+r)^2} + \cdots + \frac{R_n}{(1+r)^n} \qquad \{16A.32\}$$

TABLE 16A-4 Value of €1 at a 5 per cent Annual Interest Rate Compounded with Different Frequencies and Terms

	Frequency			
Years on deposit	Annual	Semiannual	Monthly	Daily
1	€1.0500	€1.0506	€1.0512	€1.0513
2	1.1025	1.1038	1.1049	1.1052
3	1.1576	1.1596	1.1615	1.1618
5	1.2763	1.2801	1.2834	1.2840
10	1.6289	1.6386	1.6471	1.6487
25	3.3863	3.4371	3.4816	3.4900
50	11.4674	11.8137	12.1218	12.1803
100	131.5013	139.5639	146.9380	148.3607

Present Discounted Value and the Rental Rate

For simplicity, assume now that machines do not depreciate and that the marginal value product is the same in every year. This uniform return will then also equal the rental rate for machines (v), since that is what another firm would be willing to pay for the machine's use during each period. With these simplifying assumptions, we may write the present discounted value from machine ownership as

$$PDV = \frac{v}{1+r} = \frac{v}{(1+r)^2} + \cdots + \frac{v}{(1+r)^n} + \cdots \quad \{16A.33\}$$

where the dots (. . .) indicate that payments go on forever. But because in equilibrium $P = PDV$, our earlier discussion of perpetuities gives

$$P = \frac{v}{r} \quad \{16A.34\}$$

or

$$v = rP \quad \{16A.35\}$$

which is the same as Equation 16.1 when $d = 0$. For this case, the present discounted value criterion gives results identical to those outlined earlier using the rental rate approach. In equilibrium, a machine must promise owners the prevailing rate of return.

MICROQUIZ 16A.4

Equation 16A.33 assumes that machines do not depreciate. How should the equation be changed if the machine deteriorates at the rate of d per year? If the machine still lasts forever (even though it will be very deteriorated), will its rental rate be given by the formula in Chapter 16 – that is, $v = (r + d)P$?

SUMMARY

This appendix surveys mathematical calculations involving compound interest concepts. Euros payable at different points in time are not equally valuable (because those payable in the distant future require the sacrifice of some potential interest), and it is important to be careful in making comparisons among alternative payment schedules. Discussing this issue we show the following:

- In making compound interest calculations, it is necessary to take account of interest that is paid on prior interest earned. The interest factor $(1 + i)^n$ – where n is the number of years over which interest is compounded – reflects this compounding.
- Euros payable in the future are worth less than euros payable currently. To compare euros that are payable at different dates requires using present discounted value computations to allow for the opportunity costs associated with forgone interest.
- Evaluating payment streams requires that each individual payment be discounted by the appropriate interest factor. It is incorrect simply to add together euros payable at different times.
- More frequent compounding leads to higher effective returns because prior interest paid begins to earn interest more quickly. There is an upper limit to the increased yield provided, however.
- The present discounted value formula provides an alternative approach to investment decisions that reaches the same result already derived in Chapter 16.

17

Asymmetric Information

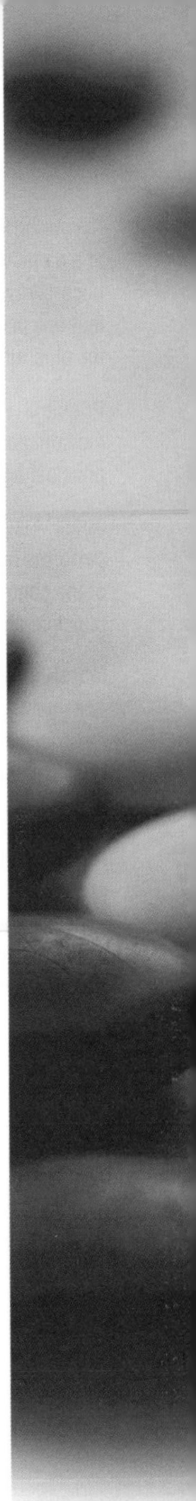

In previous chapters, we have seen how markets can allocate goods efficiently and examined some of the factors (such as monopoly) that can prevent such a result. In this chapter, we will see that another factor, participants' lack of full information about the market, can also lead markets to be inefficient. Using game theory, we will analyze a series of models in which one player has better information about the uncertain economic environment than others. This extra information is variously referred to as hidden, private, or **asymmetric information**. Game theory will enable us to better understand the range of clever strategies that might be used to cope with asymmetric information. We will see again and again that, even if market participants can resort to such clever strategies, the market will still not be as efficient as it would be if all participants had full information.

The tools developed in this chapter will allow us to analyze an array of important and interesting economic situations. How does a boss ensure that an employee is working hard when the boss cannot observe every move the employee makes? How does the firm ensure it hires talented employees when such talent is difficult to measure? Can the employer use a person's education as a signal of talent? How should a coffee shop set prices and cup sizes to extract the most money from coffee drinkers, whose demands might be unknown to the shop? Will used-car markets consist of mostly lemons if buyers cannot judge quality? Will high-risk consumers, the most expensive to insure, be the only ones to buy health insurance? When should a player bluff in poker?

Games of asymmetric information are the focus of much recent research in economics. Given the complexity of the subject, we will only provide a brief overview in this chapter, but it should be sufficient to give you a taste of the exciting developments in this area. We begin with perhaps the simplest setting in which to study asymmetric information, contracts between just two parties where one or the other has better information. Even in this simple setting, called the principal-agent model, a large number of interesting applications can be studied. Then we will move on to more complicated settings.

Principal-Agent Model

Asymmetric information In a game with uncertainty, information that one player has but the other does not.

Principal Player offering the contract in a principal-agent model.

Agent Player who performs under the terms of the contract in a principal-agent model.

Moral-hazard problem The agent's actions affect the principal but the principal does not directly observe the actions.

Adverse-selection problem A version of the principal-agent model in which the agent's type is private information.

We will begin our study of games of asymmetric information by focusing on a simple but influential game, called the principal-agent model. The game involves a contract signed between two players in an environment involving uncertainty. The player making the contract offer is called the **principal**. The player who decides whether to accept the contract or not and then performs under the terms of the contract is called the **agent**. The agent is typically the party with the private information.

The principal-agent model encompasses a wide variety of applications as shown in Table 17-1. Note that the same party might be a principal in one setting and an agent in another. For example, a company's CEO is the principal in dealings with the company's employees but is the agent of the firm's owners, the shareholders. We will study a number of the applications from Table 17-1 in detail throughout the remainder of the chapter, beginning with two that will help introduce some of the chapter's main ideas in Application 17.1: *Principals and Agents in Franchising and Medicine*.

The analysis turns out to be somewhat different depending on whether the agent has private information about an action under his or her control or about an innate characteristic outside his or her control (the agent's "type"). See Table 17-1 for some examples of each case. The case of hidden actions is referred to as the **moral-hazard problem** and the case of hidden types is referred to as the **adverse-selection problem**. We will study each in turn, beginning with moral hazard.

Moral Hazard: Manager's Private Information About Effort

We will base our discussion of the moral-hazard problem on the first case from Table 17-1, in which shareholders hire a manager to run the firm for them. The moral-hazard problem is that the manager can increase the firm's profit by working harder, but the shareholders cannot observe the manager's effort, and so the manager's effort cannot be specified directly in a contract. Instead, the shareholders will have to induce the manager to work hard through the design of the manager's incentive contract, which will link the manager's pay to firm performance.

TABLE 17-1 Applications of the Principal-Agent Model

		Agent's private information	
Principal	*Agent*	*Hidden action*	*Hidden type*
Shareholders	Manager	Effort, executive decisions	Managerial skill
Manager	Employee	Effort	Job skill
Patient	Doctor	Effort, unnecessary procedures	Medical knowledge, severity of condition
Student	Tutor	Preparation, patience	Subject knowledge
Monopoly	Customers	Quality of fabrication	Valuation for good
Health insurer	Insurance purchaser	Risky activity	Pre-existing condition
Parent	Child	Delinquency	Moral fibre

APPLICATION 17.1 *Principals and Agents in Franchising and Medicine*

Problems in principal-agent relationships arise in economic situations as diverse as fast-food operations and the provision of medical care. A closer examination shows that these two situations have much in common.

Franchising

Many large businesses operate their local retail outlets through franchise contracts. The McDonald's Corporation, for example, does not actually own every place that displays the golden arches. Instead, local restaurants are usually owned by small groups of investors who have bought a franchise from the parent company. The widespread use of franchise contracts by McDonald's and other retailers suggests that they are very useful in solving the principal-agent problems that arise in the industry.[1]

One problem that has to be solved is to get retail outlets to operate at the lowest cost possible. Fast food restaurants operate on thin margins; a small cost increase may turn a very profitable outlet into an unprofitable one. Keeping costs low and operations running smoothly requires constant attention by the manager. It seems impossible for central headquarters to monitor the daily operation of thousands of far-flung restaurants. Franchise contracts offer a solution. The franchisee gets to keep a large share of the profits generated by the local restaurant, thereby providing significant incentives to manage it efficiently without direct monitoring.

In solving one problem, franchise contracts raise another. McDonald's success depends on consistency across restaurants. A customer knows exactly what a McDonald's hamburger will taste like from whether they are in America or Europe. A franchisee who only keeps a share of local profits may be inclined to cut costs by cutting quality since the loss of consistency across franchises matters less to the local restaurant than the parent company. Franchise contracts contain additional provisions to help maintain consistent quality. McDonald's franchisees, for example, must meet certain food-quality and service standards, and they must purchase their supplies (hamburgers, frozen fries, buns, napkins, and so forth) from firms that also meet standards set by the parent company. In return, the franchisee gets some management assistance and enjoys the reputation of the McDonald's trademark (together with its national advertising).

Doctors and Patients

A similar set of problems occurs between doctors and their patients in many countries. When people are sick, they often have very little idea of what is wrong or what the most promising treatment is. They place themselves under a doctor's care in the belief that the doctor has better information on which to base decisions about the proper course of action. The doctor then acts as an agent for the patient. But there are several reasons why a doctor might not choose exactly what a fully informed patient would choose. The doctor generally pays none of the patient's bills; to the doctor, the price of anything prescribed is essentially zero. Indeed, since the doctor may in many instances also be the provider of care, he or she may even benefit financially from the services prescribed. A number of studies have gathered evidence on such doctor-induced demand, and most have reported relatively small but significant effects. In China public hospitals now charge commercial rates for new drugs and most treatments. Given that the salaries of health care workers is usually linked to the amount of income they generate for their hospitals this can act as a powerful incentive to overprescribe drugs or carry out unnecessary treatments.

Doctors as Double Agents

In America most medical care consumers have insurance. As such, because insurance companies must rely on doctors to deliver care, this raises a second principal-agent situation in which the companies need some way to ensure that doctors will not overprescribe care. With traditional fee-for-service insurance, providing such incentives to doctors is very difficult because the company cannot monitor every doctor decision. This is one reason that many health care plans in America have adopted "prepaid" features such as those found in health maintenance organizations (HMOs). Under these plans, insured patients pay an annual fee covering all of their medical needs. That annual fee then becomes a budget constraint for doctors, who now may more carefully consider the costs of the care they deliver.

In the United Kingdom the principal-agent problem exists but from a different perspective. There it is the government of the country (and behind the government the ultimate principals – the tax payers) rather than insurance companies which are affected by the inability of the government to monitor every clinical decision taken by doctors. In the United Kingdom most patients are treated by the National Health Service which is a state organization. The doctors within the NHS acting as agents of the government presumably prescribe drugs and treatment as they see fit based on the condition of the patient although the effect of hard sell advertising from pharmaceutical firms should not be underestimated. However, there has been an explosion of prescriptions for drugs. Over a five year period from 2002 to 2007 the number of prescriptions handed out by GPs (doctors at local health clinics) rose by 27 per cent taking the annual drugs bill to about £10 billion in 2007. The (expensive) irony is that it is estimated £200 million of the drugs prescribed annually are never actually taken by the patient. Most governments in Europe as such have in effect caps over which their national drugs bill cannot rise. In the UK discussions have been underway between the pharmaceutical firms and the government over how to control costs of drugs. One suggestion has been to link the price of drugs to how effective they are. Either way, as can be seen, the principal-agent problem is no mere theoretical discussion but has acute consequences for patients and taxpayers alike.

To Think About

1 Many US states have enacted laws that protect franchisees from their larger parent firms. For example, some states do not allow the establishment of new franchises from the same parent if that would be "unfair" to existing firms. How would such restrictions affect the efficiency of franchise contracts?

[1]For a summary of empirical evidence, see R.S. Thompson, "Company Ownership vs. Franchising: Issues and Evidence", *Journal of Economic Studies*, 19, no. 4 (1992): 31–42.

The setting can be modeled as a sequential game in which the shareholders move first, offering a contract to the manager, and the manager moves second, deciding whether to accept the contract, and if the contract is accepted, choosing how much effort to expend. We will use the subgame-perfect equilibrium concept, which in this context ensures that

1 the manager accepts the contract if it provides him or her with at least as high a payoff as the best alternative if the contract were rejected; and
2 the manager chooses effort to maximize his or her utility, taking into account contractual pay and effort costs.

In other words, the manager works in his or her self-interest, not in the interest of the shareholders directly. The manager only works in the shareholders' interest indirectly if incentives are provided in the contract.

The last point is central to our analysis of the moral-hazard problem. When an organization involves more than one individual (here a firm involving shareholders and a manager), it cannot simply be assumed that they act in concert. Such an assumption would be inconsistent with everything we have assumed about the behavior of microeconomic agents. Throughout the text we have assumed that agents act in their own best interest, whether consumers maximizing utility, firms maximizing profit, or players playing best responses in games. Our analysis of the principal-agent problem can be thought of as the natural extension of maximizing behavior to organizations involving more than one party.

Full Information About Effort

Suppose first that shareholders can observe the manager's effort perfectly. Figure 17-1 provides an illustration of this full-information case. In the top panel, the firm's gross profit is shown to be increasing in the manager's effort. To be clear about the terms used here, "gross profit" will mean revenue minus the cost of all the inputs not including payments to the manager; "profit" without any modifier will mean what it usually does, namely revenue minus the cost of all inputs, including payments to the manager. By distinguishing between gross profit and profit we will be able to focus our attention on payments to the manager that flow from the incentive contract offered to the manager. In the figure, the units of effort have been chosen so that the gross-profit curve is the 45-degree line, with one unit of effort leading to a €1 increase in gross profit (this is not a crucial point – the gross profit line could have any slope or indeed could be a concave curve). The cost of effort to the employee is increasing and convex. Effort is

FIGURE 17-1 Effort Choice Under Full Information *If the shareholders could specify the manager's effort in a contract, they would choose the level e* producing the highest joint surplus. In the upper panel, e* corresponds to the greatest distance between the firm's gross profit line and the manager's effort cost curve. In the lower panel, e* is given by the intersection between the firm's marginal gross profit curve (MP) and the manager's marginal effort cost line (MC).*

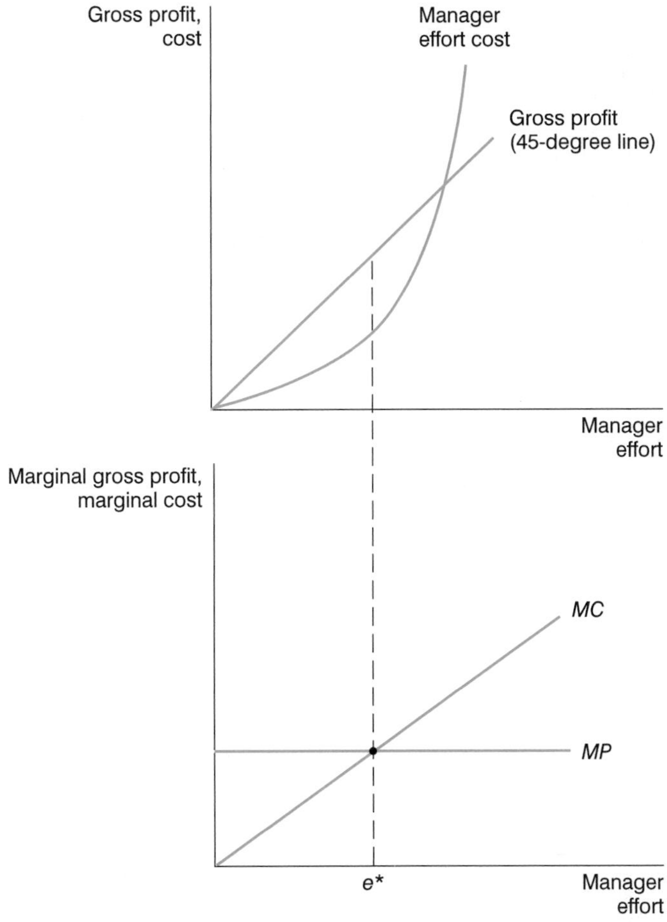

costly for the manager and becomes increasingly costly at high levels of effort. The lower panel translates the gross profit and cost curves into their marginal counterparts by taking the slopes of the curves. Here, the efficient outcome (the outcome maximizing the joint surplus of shareholders and manager) is found by equating marginal gross profit for the firm with the marginal cost of effort for the employee, that is, the intersection between the two curves in the bottom panel of Figure 17-1. Effort level e^* would be the level required by the shareholders if effort were observable and a contract could be written with the manager along the lines of "in order to receive any pay, you need to exert e^* units of effort".

Incentive Schemes When Effort Is Unobservable

Suppose now that effort is not observable and so cannot be specified in a contract. Regardless of what interpretation is given to the term "effort", it is realistic to assume effort is unobservable. Whether effort is interpreted as concentrating intensely on the job, undertaking productive yet distasteful activities (such as firing employees or issuing negative performance reviews), or doing without expensive perks (such as fancy offices or corporate jets), it is difficult to imagine how shareholders could monitor any of these things well.[1]

While the shareholders may not be able to observe the manager's effort, they can observe the firm's balance sheet, and in particular its gross profit, and may be able to provide incentives to exert effort by conditioning the manager's pay on gross profit. The lines in Figure 17-2 represent incentive contracts. The steeper the slope of the

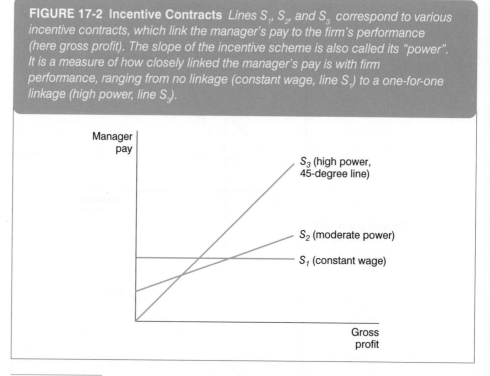

FIGURE 17-2 Incentive Contracts *Lines S_1, S_2, and S_3 correspond to various incentive contracts, which link the manager's pay to the firm's performance (here gross profit). The slope of the incentive scheme is also called its "power". It is a measure of how closely linked the manager's pay is with firm performance, ranging from no linkage (constant wage, line S_1) to a one-for-one linkage (high power, line S_3).*

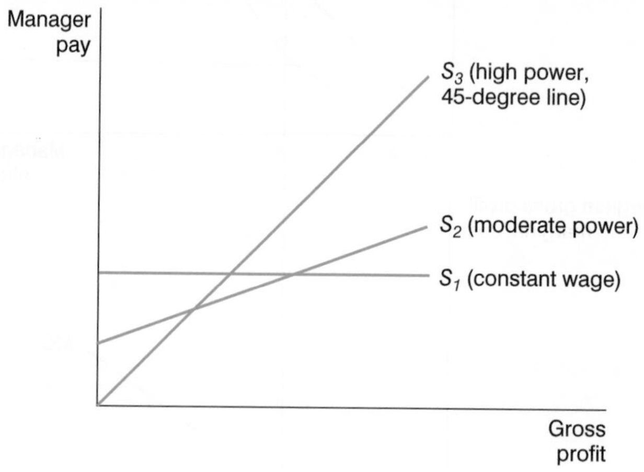

[1]Some economists believe that, far from being lazy, managers have the opposite problem: they enjoy the prestige of running the biggest firm possible. Managers may try to "build an empire", authorizing investment projects without regard to their profitability. It would be difficult for shareholders to second-guess which investments were profitable, given the expertise to make such decisions may have been the reason for hiring the manager to begin with.

incentive contract, also called the "power" of the incentive contract, the more closely the manager's pay is tied to gross profit. Line S_1 corresponds to a constant wage that does not depend at all on how well the firm does. This incentive contract has the lowest-possible power. With lines S_2 and S_3, the manager's pay increases with the firm's gross profits. Line S_2 has a moderate slope and thus is a moderate-powered incentive contract. The manager's pay increases with gross profit, but not very quickly. Line S_3 is a high-powered incentive contract. The manager's pay increases one-for-one with gross profit.

Figure 17-3 graphs the marginal pay implied by the incentive contracts from Figure 17-2. Graphically, the marginal pay is the slope of the incentive contract. The marginal pay corresponding to the flat wage, line S_1, lies along the horizontal axis of Figure 17-3. Higher-powered incentive schemes correspond to higher marginal pay curves. The figure superimposes the manager's marginal cost of effort from the lower panel of Figure 17-1. The manager's equilibrium effort is given by the intersection between the marginal cost of effort and the marginal pay curves. The flat wage results in no effort (e_1). In other words, if the manager's pay does not depend on the firm's performance, he or she will have no incentive to exert effort. The medium-powered incentive contract results in moderate effort (e_2), and the high-powered incentive contract results in the highest effort of the three (e_3).

In sum, while the shareholders cannot observe effort directly, they can induce effort indirectly by having the manager's pay depend on what can be observed, namely gross profit. The manager's effort incentives are determined by the slope of the incentive contract.

We can say more about the equilibrium effort induced by incentive contract S_3 from Figure 17-2. Because S_3 is the 45-degree line (equivalently, it has a slope equal to 1), it provides efficient incentives for the manager to exert effort. The marginal pay line, which the manager uses along with his or her marginal cost curve to compute equilibrium effort, is the same as the marginal gross profit curve from the bottom panel of Figure 17-1. Thus, the manager chooses the same effort as in the full-information case, e^*. This is a general result: the manager can be induced to

FIGURE 17-3 Manager Equilibrium Effort Choice *The manager's effort choice is given by the intersection of marginal pay and marginal effort cost. The marginal pay associated with constant wage scheme S_1 leads to no effort; effort is increasing in the power of the incentive scheme.*

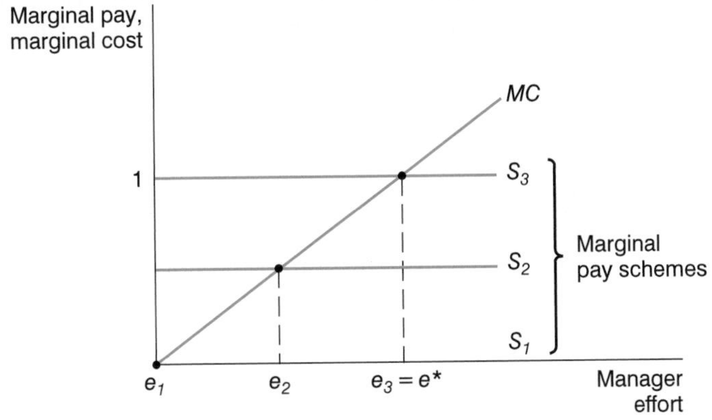

exert the efficient level of effort, even if there is asymmetric information about effort, by having the manager's incentive contract increase one-for-one with firm performance.

Incentive contract S_3 turns out to be equivalent to having the shareholders sell the firm to the manager. The manager captures all the increase in gross profit from an increase in his or her effort. Of course the shareholders would not give the firm's profit stream away for free; they would require a fixed payment from the manager up front to buy their shares, and the manager would be willing to pay for the right to get all the firm's gross profit. While having the manager buy out the firm may seem outlandish, there was a wave of such buyouts in the 1980s, culminating in the \$25 billion buyout of RJR Nabisco.[2]

There are other practical ways of increasing the power of the manager's incentive scheme besides selling the firm to the manager. The manager can be offered a bonus tied to the performance of the firm. The manager can receive shares of the firm's stock, the value of which automatically fluctuates with the fortunes of the firm. Stock options, analyzed in Application 17.2: *The Good and Bad Effects of Stock Options*, are becoming an increasingly popular form of incentive pay for managers.

Problems with High-Powered Incentives

High-powered incentives would seem to solve the moral-hazard problem. Unfortunately, there are factors outside of our simple model that lead to problems with high-powered incentive schemes.

The problem that has received the greatest attention in the economics literature is risk aversion on the part of managers. Suppose that there is uncertainty regarding the firm's gross profit. While the manager's effort will increase the chance of high profits, there are other random factors outside of the manager's control that also may matter. Agricultural output will depend on the weather. Clothing sales may depend on fads in fashion. If gross profit depends on random factors in addition to the manager's effort, then tying the manager's pay to gross profit will introduce uncertainty into the manager's pay. The higher the power of the incentive scheme, the more uncertainty is introduced. Of course a constant wage has no uncertainty. On the other hand, a high-powered incentive scheme such as S_3 in Figure 17-2 will cause managerial pay to fluctuate one-for-one with these random economic factors. As discussed in Chapter 5, risk-averse individuals dislike uncertainty; they need to be paid to accept even fair gambles. Introducing uncertainty in the manager's pay by tying it to uncertain gross profit exposes the manager to risk. Exposing the manager to risk is costly for the shareholders. The manager would trade a lower salary for less risk. The shareholders would profit from trading salary for risk because shareholders typically hold diversified portfolios of small amounts of many different firms' stock. The benefits of diversification were discussed in Chapter 5. Diversified shareholders are likely to be much less risk averse than the manager and thus able to bear risk at very little cost. In the end, shareholders may prefer to lower the power of the incentive contract and thereby reduce the manager's risk exposure.

Managerial risk aversion would not prevent the shareholders and manager from attaining the efficient outcome if effort were

MICROQUIZ 17.1

Figure 17-1 shows why e^* is the effort level that is best from the joint perspective of the firm and the manager. Explain why the firm would not want to induce higher effort than e^* in the full-information equilibrium even though gross profit is increasing in e.

[2]See Application 9.1 for more detail on the 1980s management buyout craze. In the application, it is suggested that tax avoidance, rather than enhanced incentives, was the primary rationale for management buyouts during this period.

APPLICATION 17.2 The Good and Bad Effects of Stock Options

Stock options grant to the holder the ability to buy shares at a fixed price. If the market price of these shares rises, option holders will benefit because they can buy the stock at less than the market price (and perhaps resell it, making a quick profit). Options are usually granted by firms to their executives as one way of providing incentives to manage the firm in a way that will increase the price of its shares.

The Explosion in Stock Options

Use of stock options as a form of executive compensation has grown rapidly in recent years. In 1980, most firms did not offer options to their executives and, in those that did, the value of options constituted a fairly small percent of total compensation. By 2000, top executives of the largest companies received more than half their total compensation in the form of stock options, sometimes amounting to options worth hundreds of millions of dollars. There are many reasons for the increased popularity of stock options as a form of compensation. Rising stock prices throughout the decade of the 1990s undoubtedly made this form of compensation more attractive to executives. From the perspective of firms, the accounting treatment of options (which are often assigned a zero cost to the firm granting them) made them a low-cost way to pay their executives. A special provision in American tax laws enacted in 1993 specified that firms could not deduct executive pay of more than $1 million per year unless that pay was tied to company performance – a further spur to the use of options.

Incentive Effects of Options

Stock options clearly do succeed in tying an executive's compensation to the performance of a company's stock. By one estimate, stock options provide more than 50 times the pay-to-performance ratio provided by conventional pay packages.[1] Dollar for dollar, options also provide more pay-to-performance incentives than would a simple grant of shares to the executive. For example, it would cost the firm $1 million to grant 10 000 shares of $100 stock to an executive. The executive would gain $100 000 from a 10 per cent increase in firm value. If the executive were instead given 100 000 options to buy the stock at $100, the executive would gain ten times more ($1 million) from a 10 per cent increase in firm value.

But the exact incentive effects of stock options are complex, depending on precisely how the options are granted and the ways in which the stock price for the firm performs. For example, options are less valuable when the firm pays large dividends to its shareholders, so the executive may have an incentive to hold back on dividend increases. For another example, options are more valuable when the price of a company's stock is more volatile. This is because the option holder's gain from stock price increases is unbounded above but is bounded below by zero for falls in the stock price (the option is simply "out of the money"). Options may therefore induce executives to make more risky investments than they ordinarily would.

Unanticipated Incentive Effects – Accounting Fraud

Executives with significant holdings of stock options can make huge amounts of money if the values of their shares rise. In recent years, it has been common to see executives making hundreds of millions of dollars on such stock price movements. One unintended effect of giving CEOs such a large stake in seeing a higher stock price has been to encourage them to seek to manipulate information that can affect the price of their shares. Executives of the WorldCom Corporation, for example, hid nearly $4 billion in corporate expenses in 2001 so that their company would look more profitable. The firm's CEO benefited handsomely when he bailed out of the firm's stock. Accounting fiascos such as those at Enron and Tyco also seem to have been motivated in part by the desire to keep stock prices up so options holders could benefit. Whether stock-option contracts can be

(continued)

adjusted to reduce the incentives for such actions remains an open question.

To Think About

1 Michael Eisner, CEO of the Walt Disney Corporation, once received over $500 million in stock options. Do you think he managed the company better than if he had been awarded only $50 million's worth?

2 If the price of a company's stock declines, stock options may become worthless. What would be the effect of a policy that promised to adjust the purchase price specified in the option contract downward when this happens?

[1] B. J. Hall and J. B. Liebman, "Are CEOs Really Paid Like Bureaucrats?", *Quarterly Journal of Economics* (August 1998): 653–691.

observable. The manager's pay could be conditioned directly on effort, which would be in the manager's control and about which he or she would have no uncertainty. Asymmetric information about effort forces the incentive contract to be conditioned on the firm's uncertain gross profit rather than effort, which then exposes the manager to risk.

To summarize the main point of this subsection, there is a trade-off between effort incentives and risk. High-powered incentive schemes induce a lot of effort, but expose risk-averse managers to a lot of risk and may require a high fixed payment to the manager to accept the risk. At the other extreme, a constant wage induces no effort but does not expose the manager to any risk. The optimum in the presence of a risk-averse manager may involve some compromise between the two extremes.

There are other problems with high-powered incentives besides risk aversion. First, the manager may not be able to afford to buy out the firm. Second, if the manager gets most of the benefit from increasing gross profit, the shareholders may not take all the steps they can to increase gross profit. For example, the manager of a McDonald's franchise may be reluctant to sign a contract that has most of his or her pay tied to the franchise's gross profit if there is the possibility that McDonald's could open up a second franchise nearby and "steal" some business from the first. The coach of a football team may be reluctant to have his salary tied to the team's winning percentage if he fears the owners may try to save salary expenses by trading away some of the better players. Third, even if the shareholders cannot take actions to affect gross profit, they may have a better idea about the firm's prospects than an incoming manager. Shareholders might try to recruit the manager by inflating gross profit prospects, making a high-powered incentive contract seem lucrative for the manager. The skeptical manager might instead insist on a constant wage that would be the same whether or not shareholders were honest about prospects for the firm's gross profit.

Substitutes for High-Powered Incentives

If it is too difficult for shareholders to offer the manager high-powered incentives for the reasons mentioned above, they may have to resort to other strategies to get the manager to work hard. One possibility is monitoring. As discussed above, measuring something as nebulous as effort might be prohibitively difficult. Even if it were possible to measure effort, many of the shareholders may hold so few shares of the firm's stock that it might not be worth their while to supervise the manager individually. Shareholders could consider hiring someone to supervise the manager. But what would guarantee this supervisor would work hard? The same moral-hazard problems may confront the supervisor as the manager. In addition, there might be an incentive for the manager to bribe the supervisor to issue a good report about his or her efforts.

The possibility of firing the manager may provide crude incentives. Even if the shareholders themselves do not fire the manager, the manager may be fired as a result of a takeover. The way a takeover might work is that a corporate raider might see that a firm's stock price is low due to an underperforming manager. The raider would buy a controlling share of the firm's stock, fire the manager, bring in a new management team, and profit from the resulting increased stock price. The initial manager may wish to keep the firm performing well so that the stock price remains too high to be a takeover target.

Another possibility is that the manager works hard to look good for future employers. A successful lower-level manager may be a prime candidate for promotion to a higher level. A CEO who succeeds in running a small firm may be a prime candidate to run a larger firm. It can be argued that such situations may lead agents to overwork. Agents may try to convince potential employers that they are more talented than they really are by substituting hard work for any shortcomings in talent. Potential employers may not be fooled, but in the "rat race" that is the job market, agents may have to overwork just to avoid being mistaken for being less talented than they actually are.

Manager's Participation Decision

We have discussed part of the manager's decision problem: the amount of effort she exerts in equilibrium given the terms of the contract. Recall that the effort choice was determined by the slope of the incentive contract. We need to study the decision of the manager to sign the contract to begin with. The decision to sign the contract, called the participation decision, is determined by the level of pay, which, holding the slope of the incentive contract constant, depends on the incentive contract's intercept. Figure 17-4 draws several incentive schemes with the same slope, so they would

FIGURE 17-4 Manager's Participation Decision *Fixing the slope of the incentive scheme, the intercept of the scheme determines the manager's participation decision. Depending on the best alternative available to the manager if he or she does not sign the contract, the intercept could be at 0 as with line S_2, could involve a positive fixed transfer as in S_3, or could involve negative fixed transfer (that is, a payment from the manager to the firm for the right to participate) as in S_1. The shareholders will choose the lowest intercept subject to having the manager participate.*

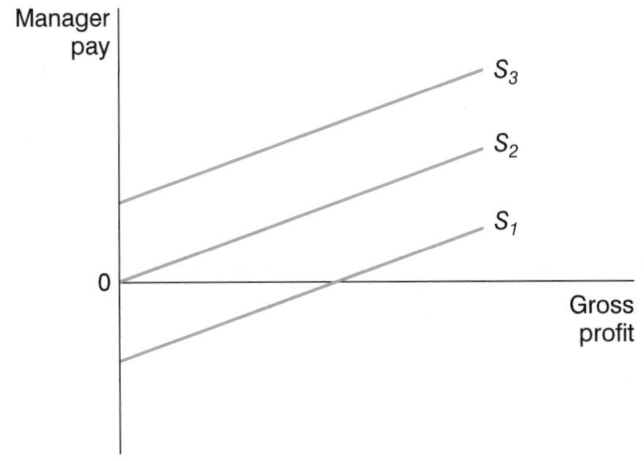

induce the same level of effort, but with different intercepts. Line S_2 has an intercept at 0. This is a pure profit-sharing arrangement. If no gross profit is earned, the manager gets no pay. Above that, the manager gets a share of the gross profit. As drawn, with a slope of about $\frac{1}{2}$, the manager gets about half of the firm's gross profit. Line S_3 has a positive intercept, equal to the fixed part of the manager's pay earned even if the firm does not make any gross profit. This contract could be implemented by providing the manager with a fixed salary together with incentive pay in the form of bonuses based on gross profit, or stock or stock options. There is even the possibility of requiring a payment from the manager to participate, as with S_1. The manager has to "buy in" to participate. Such contracts are sometimes seen in franchising. A potential manager of, say, a McDonald's franchise, is often required to put up some money to set up the local franchise, in return for a share of the franchise profits. This would correspond to a negative intercept as in S_1.

Which scheme – S_1, S_2, or S_3, among others – would the shareholders choose to offer the manager? The best one for the shareholders is the one with the lowest intercept that would still be accepted by the manager. This incentive contract makes the manager indifferent between accepting the contract and not. If the contract left some positive surplus to the manager so that the manager strictly preferred to accept the contract, it would be possible for the shareholders to lower the fixed part of the manager's pay (or increase the manager's payment to them), thereby increasing shareholder profit, and still have the manager be willing to sign the contract.

Comparison to the Standard Model: Summing Up

To sum up, it is natural to ask how the results in the presence of the moral-hazard problem accord with the results from the standard model of a perfectly competitive market with no private information. First, the presence of moral hazard raises the possibility of slack and inefficiency completely absent in the standard model. The manager does not exert as much effort as he or she would if effort were observable. Even if shareholders do the best they can in the presence of asymmetric information to provide incentives for effort, they must balance the benefits of incentives against the cost of exposing the manager to too much risk.

Second, while the manager can be regarded as an input like any other (capital, labor, materials, and so forth) in the standard model, in the presence of the moral-hazard problem the manager becomes a unique sort of input. It is not enough to pay a fixed unit price for this input as a firm would the rental rate for capital or the wage rate for labor. How productive the manager is depends on how the manager's compensation is structured.

Adverse Selection: Consumer's Private Information About Valuation

Next we turn to the other main issue in the principal-agent model, the adverse-selection problem. Whereas with the moral-hazard problem, the agent had private information about an action he or she chose, with the adverse-selection problem, the agent has private information about his or her type, that is, a characteristic that is innate – not chosen – by the agent.

To make the analysis concrete, we will consider the application in which the principal is a monopoly firm and the agent is a customer. Consumers differ in how much they value the good, but these valuations are not observable to the monopolist. The monopolist offers the customer a menu of different-sized bundles at different prices. This setup is identical to the model of second-degree price discrimination studied in Chapter 13. With second-degree price discrimination, the monopolist is not restricted to a constant price per unit but rather offers a menu of bundles at different prices, perhaps involving price discounts for large purchases, and has the consumers select bundles from the menu themselves. We will build on the earlier analysis by being slightly more detailed here and highlighting the important features of the adverse-selection problem.

Examples of this sort of second-degree include a coffee shop's offering a $\frac{1}{3}$ of a liter cup at €1.50 and a $\frac{2}{3}$ of a liter cup at €2.50. Bundles can be distinguished by quality instead of quantity as well. Airlines' first class has plusher seats, more leg room, and better meals than economy class, comforts which may cost three or four times the economy fare. How does the monopolist decide on such a menu of quantity/price bundles or quality/price bundles, which constitutes, in effect, the contract offered to the customer? We will investigate this question carefully in the next several subsections.

One Consumer Type

In this section we examine the monopolist's problem of selling a bundle to consumers who all obtain the same surplus from the good – that is, they are all the same type. To simplify the analysis, we will consider a single representative consumer. Whatever the size of the bundle the monopolist chooses to offer, it may as well ask the highest price for the bundle that the consumer would be willing to pay. The most the consumer would pay for the bundle rather than doing without it is called **gross consumer surplus**. Gross consumer surplus is related to (ordinary) consumer surplus, defined in Chapter 3. Both are measures of consumers' valuation for a good. Whereas consumer surplus subtracts the amount the consumer pays for the bundle from the amount the consumer would be willing to pay, gross consumer surplus does not. Consider Figure 17-5, which reproduces the figure originally used to define

Gross consumer surplus The most consumers would pay for a bundle rather than doing without it.

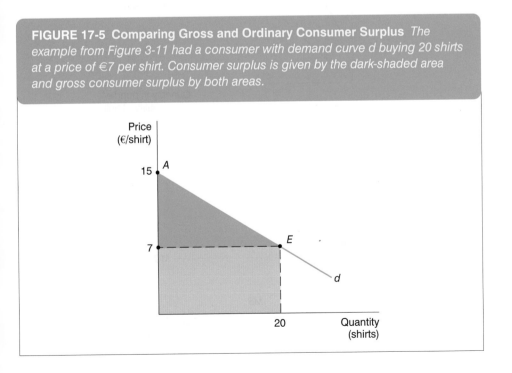

FIGURE 17-5 Comparing Gross and Ordinary Consumer Surplus *The example from Figure 3-11 had a consumer with demand curve d buying 20 shirts at a price of €7 per shirt. Consumer surplus is given by the dark-shaded area and gross consumer surplus by both areas.*

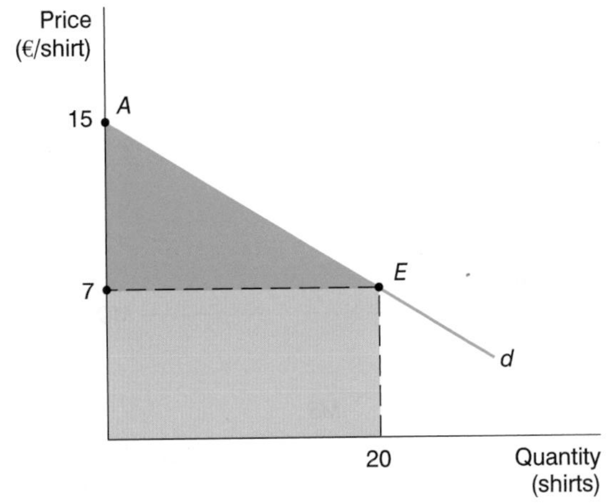

consumer surplus (Figure 3–11). Gross consumer surplus equals the whole area under the demand curve, the light- and dark-shaded regions. Consumer surplus subtracts the amount paid for the good (the light-shaded area), leaving just the dark-shaded area. Since we are interested in computing how much the consumer is willing to pay for the bundle, the measure that does not subtract off consumer payments, gross consumer surplus, is the relevant concept here.

The monopolist chooses the quantity in the bundle, q^*, to maximize profit. The monopolist's profit equals the difference between the revenue received from selling the bundle at the highest price it can charge and the cost of producing the bundle. In the top panel of Figure 17-6, the monopolist's profit is the vertical distance between the gross consumer surplus and total cost curves. The profit-maximizing bundle q^* maximizes this distance. Equivalently, in the lower panel of Figure 17-6, q^* is given by the intersection of marginal surplus *MS* (the slope of the gross consumer surplus

FIGURE 17-6 Profit-Maximizing Bundle with One Consumer Type *Facing a single, representative consumer, the monopolist chooses a bundle q* maximizing the consumer's and monopolist's combined surplus, found in the upper panel as the greatest vertical distance between gross consumer surplus and the total cost curves or equivalently in the lower panel by the intersection of the marginal surplus and marginal cost curves. The monopolist charges a bundle price equal to the shaded area (A and B) and earns profit equal to the area of A.*

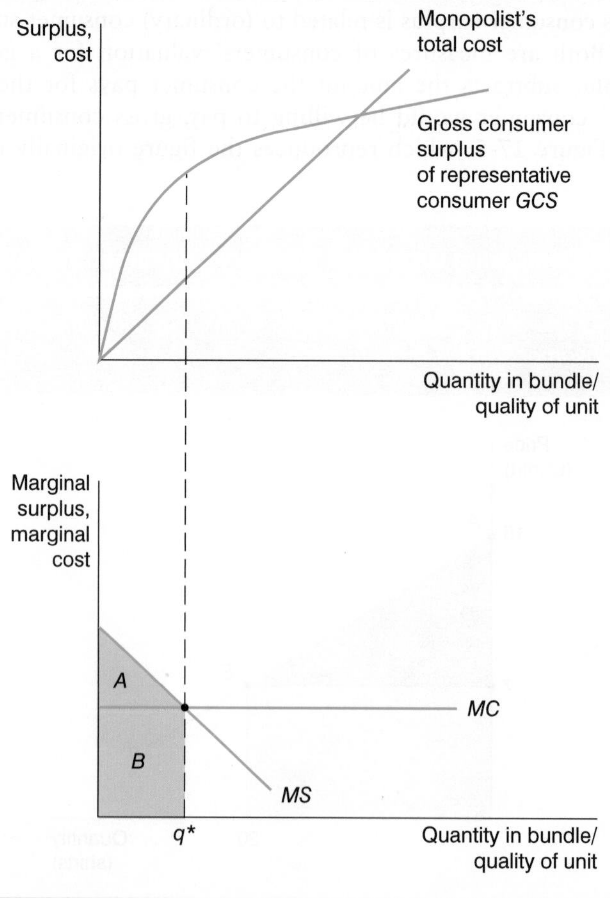

curve) and the monopolist's marginal cost *MC*. Just as in Figure 17-5, where gross consumer surplus equals the area under the demand curve down to the horizontal axis, in Figure 17-6 gross consumer surplus from the bundle equals the area under the marginal surplus curve up to q^*, that is, the shaded area *A* and *B* on the graph. The monopolist receives this amount as revenue from the bundle. The monopolist's profit equals the shaded area minus the shaded rectangle *B*, which represents the total cost of producing this bundle, leaving triangle *A* for profit.

Two Consumer Types, Full Information

If the monopolist has full information about types and can act on this information (that is, can require a consumer to buy only the bundle directed at his or her particular type and not some other bundle and can prevent consumers from selling repackaged bundles among themselves), the analysis of two consumer types adds nothing new to the analysis of one consumer type. Figure 17-7 provides a graph for the two-type case that is related to the bottom panel of Figure 17-6. There is still one representative consumer, but with certain probability the consumer may have a high value for the product (the "high-value type") and with complementary probability may have a low value (the "low-value type"). The marginal consumer surplus for the high-value type lies above the low-value types.

The profit-maximizing bundle for the low-value type involves q_L units, given by the intersection between the low type's marginal consumer surplus and the monopolist's marginal cost. The bundle price equals the area of the light-shaded regions (*A* and *B*). The monopolist's profit equals the area of region *A*. Similarly, the profit-maximizing bundle for the high-value type involves q_H units given by the intersection between the high type's marginal consumer surplus and the monopolist's marginal cost. The bundle price equals the area of the entire shaded region *A*, *B*, *C*, and *D*, and the monopolist's profit equals the areas of *A* and *C*.

MICROQUIZ 17.2

Refer to Figure 17-5.

1 Compute consumer surplus.

2 Compute gross consumer surplus.

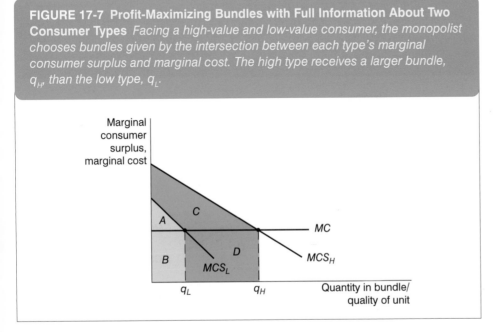

FIGURE 17-7 Profit-Maximizing Bundles with Full Information About Two Consumer Types *Facing a high-value and low-value consumer, the monopolist chooses bundles given by the intersection between each type's marginal consumer surplus and marginal cost. The high type receives a larger bundle, q_H, than the low type, q_L.*

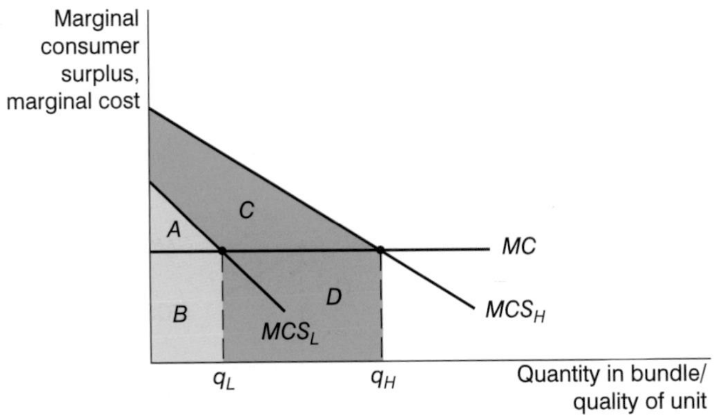

Two Consumer Types, Asymmetric Information

The menu of bundles that maximized profit in the full information case will not work if the monopolist cannot observe the consumer's types. The q_H-unit bundle meant for the high-value type is priced to extract all of his or her consumer surplus. The high type would obtain positive surplus from instead purchasing the q_L-unit bundle meant for the low-value type. Figure 17-8 shows why. The high type's gross consumer surplus from the q_L-unit bundle equals the area under the marginal consumer surplus curve up to the quantity q_L, that is, the area of the shaded regions *A*, *B*, and *C′*. After subtracting off the bundle's price (the light-shaded areas *A* and *B*), the high-value type is left with positive surplus equal to the area of the dark-shaded region *C′*. This is better than purchasing the q_H-unit bundle and getting no surplus.

Incentive-compatible Describes contract that gets the agent to make the intended choice.

The q_H-unit bundle sold at a price that extracts all of the high type's consumer surplus is not **incentive-compatible**. Left the choice between the two bundles, the high type would have an incentive to choose the bundle meant for the other type. The q_H-unit bundle could be made incentive-compatible for the high type by reducing its price so that the high type would be left with at least as much surplus as if he or she bought the q_L-unit bundle. In particular, the price for the q_H-unit bundle would have to be reduced by the area of region *C′* (and so equal the combined area of regions *A*, *B*, *C′*, and *D*).

The monopolist can do even better than this. The monopolist can reduce the quantity associated with the bundle meant for the low-value type. On the one hand, reducing quantity reduces the profit from the sale of the bundle to low-value consumers. But a bigger effect is that the bundle meant for the low-value type becomes much less attractive to the high-value type. The high-value type places a high value on quantity, and a reduction in quantity "scares him or her off" from choosing the low-value bundle. As a result, the monopolist does not need to leave the high type with as much surplus, and can raise the price charged for the q_H-unit bundle.

The profit-maximizing bundles are shown in Figure 17-9. Reducing the quantity in the low type's bundle from q_L to q'_L does reduce the profit from sales to low-value

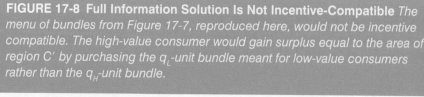

FIGURE 17-8 Full Information Solution Is Not Incentive-Compatible *The menu of bundles from Figure 17-7, reproduced here, would not be incentive compatible. The high-value consumer would gain surplus equal to the area of region C′ by purchasing the q_L-unit bundle meant for low-value consumers rather than the q_H-unit bundle.*

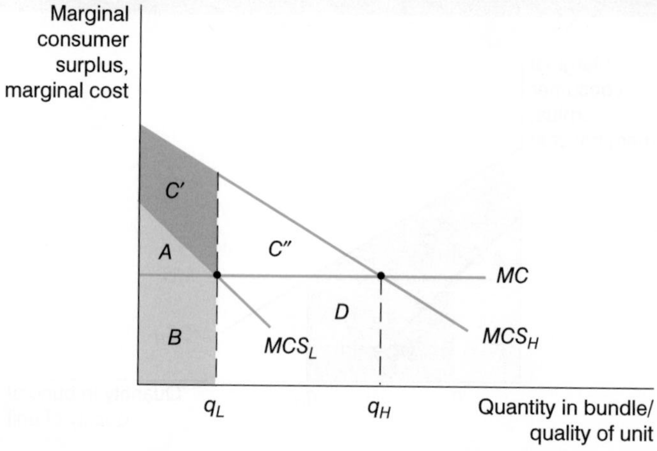

consumers, by an amount equal to the black-hatched triangle. But this reduction in quantity makes the low type's bundle much less attractive to the high type. After all, the high type obtains high marginal consumer surplus from additional units and so loses a lot if quantity is reduced. The price at which the q_H-unit bundle is sold can be increased by the area of the gray-hatched region and still be incentive-compatible, that is, still ensure that the high type buys the q_H-unit bundle rather than the bundle meant for the low type.

By distorting the low type's quantity, the monopolist sacrifices efficiency. The low type would be willing to pay more than what it costs to increase the size of his or her bundle. The monopolist's gain is that it can squeeze more revenue out of the high type. As shown in Figure 17-9, the revenue squeezed from the high type (the gray-hatched region) can be much larger than the loss from selling an inefficiently small bundle to the low type (the black-hatched triangle).

How much the monopolist distorts the low type's quantity downward depends on how many consumers are of each type. If there are a lot of low-value consumers, the monopolist would not be willing to distort the quantity in their bundle very much, since the loss from this distortion would be substantial and there would not be many high-value consumers from whom to squeeze additional revenue. The more high-value consumers, the more the monopolist is willing to distort the quantity in the low type's bundle downward. Indeed, if there are enough high-value consumers, the monopolist may decide not to serve the low-value consumers at all and just offer one bundle that would be purchased by the high types. This would allow the monopolist to squeeze all of the surplus from the high types, because they would have no other option left.

Examples

Consider the example of a coffee shop. Suppose it offers two cup sizes: small, directed at the typical coffee drinker, and large, directed at the true coffee hound. As a thought experiment, suppose the shop can identify which consumers are typical and which

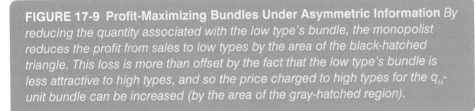

FIGURE 17-9 Profit-Maximizing Bundles Under Asymmetric Information *By reducing the quantity associated with the low type's bundle, the monopolist reduces the profit from sales to low types by the area of the black-hatched triangle. This loss is more than offset by the fact that the low type's bundle is less attractive to high types, and so the price charged to high types for the q_H-unit bundle can be increased (by the area of the gray-hatched region).*

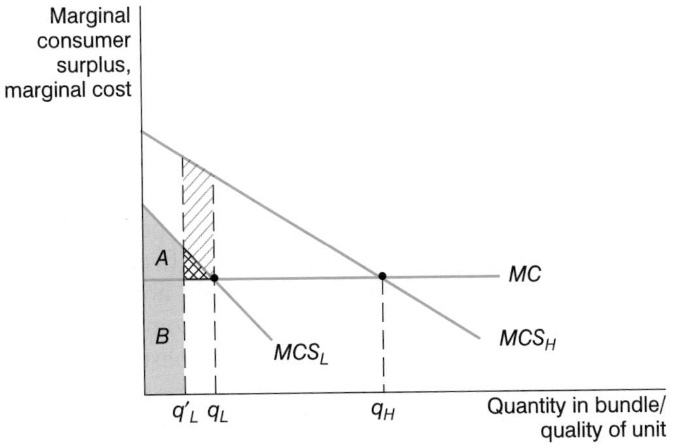

are coffee hounds and can force each type to buy the cup meant for it (so, for example, anyone identified as a coffee hound would be forbidden to buy one or more small cups of coffee). The profit-maximizing menu in this thought experiment might involve selling a $\frac{1}{3}$ of a liter cup for €1.50 to typical coffee drinkers and a $\frac{2}{3}$ of a liter cup for €5.00 to coffee hounds, extracting all the surplus from both. Now leave this thought experiment aside and suppose, more realistically, that there is asymmetric information about types. The shop would not know which consumers are coffee hounds and so could not prevent them from buying the small cup. Coffee hounds indeed would buy the small cup, unless the price of the large cup were reduced, say to €2.00. The coffee shop could do even better by reducing the size of the small cup, say to $\frac{1}{4}$ of a liter, and selling it for a lower price, say €1.25. This would make the small cup less attractive to coffee hounds and allow the shop to increase the price for the large cup, say to €2.50. Notice that the coffee shop is not squeezing all of the profit out of the typical coffee drinker that it could. The typical coffee drinker may be willing to pay the extra 25 cents for the difference between a $\frac{1}{4}$ and $\frac{1}{3}$ of a liter cup of coffee, and the marginal cost of this difference may be just a few pennies. But if a $\frac{1}{3}$ of a liter cup were available, coffee hounds may not be willing to pay as much as €2.50 for the $\frac{2}{3}$ of a liter cup. The size of the small cup is reduced, not to harm the typical coffee drinker, but to squeeze more revenue out of the coffee hounds. If enough customers are coffee hounds, the shop may decide only to offer the large cup at the price of €5.00 that extracted all of the coffee hound's surplus in the thought experiment. The shop would effectively have full information about the consumer's type because only coffee hounds would show up to buy at such a high price.

The same logic holds for airplane fares reinterpreting q to be the quality level of a single flight rather than the quantity in a bundle. Consumers only demand one flight at any one time, but the quality of that flight may vary depending on the size of the seat, the quality of the meal, and other amenities together represented by q. The airline might offer two or three different classes of travel on one flight, say economy, business, and first class. The typical economy-class passenger may be willing to pay more than the marginal cost of expanding the seat size and serving a better meal: it may only cost, say, €50 (in terms of a larger airplane, more fuel, and better food ingredients) to gain enough leg room and to serve a decent enough meal to make the economy-class flight reasonably comfortable. But the airline may still keep economy seats small and limit meals. If economy-class is too comfortable, there may be little reason for business- and first-class passengers to pay the exorbitant prices for those seats. Some discomfort in economy-class "scares" business-class and first-class passengers from buying economy tickets.

Discussion

The adverse-selection problem prevents the principal from being able to squeeze all surplus from all agents. The high types have to be left with some surplus, or else they will choose the contract option meant for the low types. We ignored the possibility that low types might buy the bundle meant for the high types. This is typically not a problem. In the monopoly-consumer application, low types have low marginal surplus, they are not willing to pay a lot for large bundles. (Even if low-value consumers were willing to buy the high types' bundle, this would not be a "problem" for the monopolist because the monopolist makes more profit from the sale of the high types' bundle than the low types'.) Consequently, the monopolist does not need to distort the quantity associated with the high types' bundle to preserve incentive compatibility for the low types. The high types are sold the efficient quantity at which marginal consumer surplus equals marginal cost. The only quantity that needs to be distorted to preserve incentive compatibility is the quantity in the low types' bundle.

We have discussed one important issue with adverse selection in the principal-agent model: the contract has to be structured so that it is incentive compatible for the high types. The only remaining issue is the agent's participation decision. In the monopoly-consumer application, consumers must choose to buy a bundle rather than go without. The high types earn positive surplus, so there is no question that they participate. The price for the low types' bundle must be low enough that they purchase as well: the price must be no greater than their gross consumer surplus from the bundle (the area of light-shaded regions *A* and *B* in Figure 17-9). There is one case in which the low types' participation decision does not matter. This is when, as discussed above, the monopolist does not bother to serve the low types and only offers a bundle to the high types.

It is worth emphasizing how adverse selection affects the efficiency of markets. Compared to the standard model in which firms have full information, market outcomes are typically less efficient in the presence of the adverse-selection problem. Output is lower. The monopolist sacrifices efficiency in order to extract more surplus from some consumer types.

Warranty and Insurance Contracts

Moral-hazard and adverse-selection problems present themselves in a unique way when the firm sells not a simple good such as coffee but a more complicated contract such as a warranty or insurance to the consumer. Whereas a cup of coffee costs the same to make regardless of to whom it is sold, the cost of fulfilling a contract may depend on the consumer's action (moral hazard) or the consumer's type (adverse selection).

Consider a warranty promising to replace a lawn mower with a new one if the first one breaks down. Whether the mower breaks down depends on its quality (indeed, the warranty was presumably offered in the first place to address consumer concerns about the risk of low quality). But whether the mower breaks down also depends on consumer behavior. Does the customer operate it carefully, not smashing into fences and running over stumps? With an unconditional warranty, the consumer will have little incentive to prevent the mower's breaking down by being careful. This will result in a higher number of mowers breaking down and being returned, and a higher replacement cost for the firm, than if the customer was more careful. Because the customer's care is likely to be unobservable, there is little left for the firm to do except perhaps raise the price of the warranted good to reflect the higher cost or limit the terms of the warranty.

Lawn mower warranties may also lead to an adverse-selection problem. More careless users and also more intensive users will be attracted to mowers carrying full warranties, because the firm will bear the high cost of likely replacement instead of the consumer. An increase in the percentage of these "high-cost" consumers will force the firm to raise price in equilibrium, which may lead careful customers to drop the good and substitute instead toward a less-expensive good with more limited or no warranties. These effects may continue to spiral until only the most intense or careless users buy the good with the full warranty.

The same effects arise with insurance. Insurance shifts losses from the customer to the insurance company. This reduces the customer's incentive to take care to avoid the loss, the moral-hazard problem again. The consumer is less inclined to drive carefully, buy fire extinguishers and alarms, lock the doors against thieves, eat well to avoid heart disease, and so forth. This inefficient care leads insurance to be more expensive than it would otherwise be. Often the only recourse the insurance company has to solve the problem is to provide less than full insurance (requiring some coinsurance or excess) so as to provide at least some small incentive for the customer to take care.

As Application 17.3: *Adverse Selection in Insurance* discusses, the adverse-selection problem presents itself in an interesting way in insurance markets. The riskiest

APPLICATION 17.3 *Adverse Selection in Insurance*

The earliest application of the idea of adverse selection, and indeed the genesis of the term itself, was in the study of insurance markets. As we saw in Chapter 5, actuarially fair insurance can increase the utility of risk-averse individuals, implying that individuals who face very different probabilities of loss should pay different insurance premiums. The difficulty faced by insurers in this situation is in estimating an individual's probability of loss so that insurance can be correctly priced. When insurers possess less information than do insurance buyers, adverse selection may undermine the entire insurance market.

A Theoretical Model

This possibility is illustrated in Figure 1, which assumes that two individuals initially face identical consumption prospects represented by point *A*. If person 1 has a relatively low risk of incurring state 2, costs of insurance will be low and this individual's budget constraint is given by *AE*. If insurance is fairly priced, this risk-averse individual would choose to fully insure by moving to point *E* on the certainty line. For person 2, losses are more likely. Fair insurance costs are represented by *AF*. This person, too, might choose to be fully insured by moving to point *F*. If the insurance company cannot tell how risky a particular customer is, however, this twin solution is unstable. Person 2 will recognize that he or she can gain utility by purchasing a policy intended for person 1. The additional losses this implies means that the insurer will lose money on policy *AE* and will have to increase its price, thereby reducing person 1's utility. Whether there is a final solution to this type of adverse selection is a complex question. It is possible that person 1 may choose to face the world uninsured rather than buy an unfairly priced policy.[1]

Safe-Driver Policies

Adverse selection arises in all sorts of insurance, ranging from life insurance to health insurance to flood insurance to automobile insurance. Consider the case of automobile insurance. Traditionally, insurers have used accident data to devise group rating factors that assign higher premium costs to groups such as young males and urban dwellers, who tend to be more likely to have accidents.

FIGURE 1 Adverse Selection in Insurance Markets *Two individuals face identical consumption prospects at A. Low-risk individuals can buy insurance at a rate reflected by AE; high-risk individuals must pay the rate reflected by AF. If insurers cannot distinguish among individuals, high-risk people will choos AE-type policies and cause them to be unprofitable. Low-risk individuals will be made worse off by the absence of such policies.*

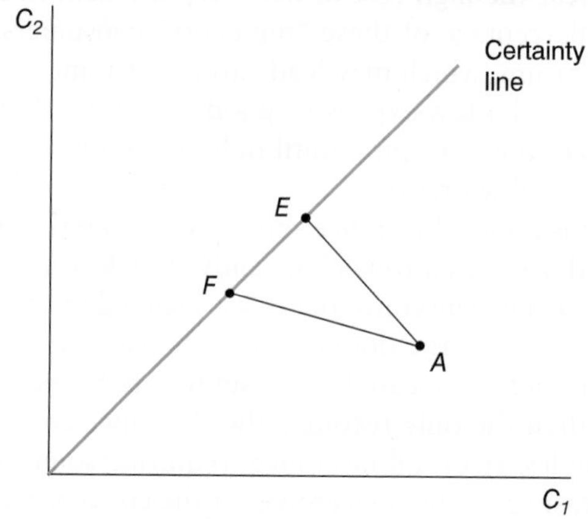

Recently, however, this rate-setting procedure has come under attack as unfairly lumping both safe and unsafe drivers together. A 1989 ballot initiative in California, for example, sharply limited the use of rating factors by requiring them to be primarily individual-based rather than group-based. Because data on individuals is hard to obtain and not very good at predicting accidents, the main result has been to force rates together for all groups. The main beneficiary of the law seems to have been young male drivers in Los Angeles. Figure 1 suggests that individuals in safer groups (females and rural California residents) may have been the losers.

To Think About

1. How are low-risk individuals made worse off by adverse selection?
2. Can you think of other types of situations where risk ratings might differ among individuals? How would you decide which risk differences should be reflected in differences in rates and which should not?

[1]For one of the original discussions of this issue, see M. Rothschild and J. Stiglitz, "Equilibrium in Competitive Insurance Markets: An Essay on the Economics of Imperfect Information", *Quarterly Journal of Economics* (November 1976): 629–650.

consumers obtain the most benefit from insurance, and so gravitate toward the fullest insurance policies, yet these are the consumers who are the most expensive to serve. This may lead insurance companies to try to find observable indicators of risk, so that the riskier consumers can be charged higher prices or be refused insurance. If companies cannot sort consumers based on observable characteristics, they can resort to menus with options involving more complete insurance, targeted at the higher-risk classes, requiring significantly higher premiums. If the insurance company cannot resort to these strategies, it may be forced to raise prices, driving less risky consumers (better drivers, owners of houses in safer areas, people with no known family history of disease) toward less complete insurance or, in the extreme, leading them to go without insurance.

As we have seen previously, with warranty and insurance markets the presence of private information (in the form of either the moral-hazard or adverse-selection problem) leads to inefficiency. It is efficient for risk-neutral companies to provide full coverage to risk-averse consumers. But as we saw, the equilibrium in the presence of private information involves reduced warranty or insurance coverage, either because the firm imposes excesses or co-payments or because price has to be raised, driving certain classes of consumers to forgo coverage entirely.

In Application 17.6: *Can Wages above Market Clearing Levels Counteract Adverse Selection?* we briefly explore why, in some circumstances, paying wages above the market clearing rate can counteract adverse selection amongst potential employees and *increase* profits.

Asymmetric Information in Competitive Markets

The principal-agent model studied so far is a very simple setting since it involved just a single principal and a single agent. (Sometimes the agent was a representative of a larger population, but this did not complicate the analysis since the agents did not directly compete.) In this section, we will see how the results change in a market setting, with competing agents, or competing principals, or both.

Moral Hazard with Several Agents

Adding agents to the basic principal-agent model can make the moral-hazard problem better or worse, depending on the details of the setting. Suppose first that a single principal needs to hire a team of several agents to perform a task. The moral-hazard problem may be more severe in this setting. Each of the agents may slack off, relying on the efforts of the others. In large teams, it may be difficult to identify who is working hard and who is not, possibly leading all of them to slack. It is hard to provide a large number of agents with high-powered incentives because even if the firm is sold to the team of them, each would only obtain a small fraction of the firm's gross profit.

On the other hand, if there are many agents in the market, but each works for a separate firm/principal, moral hazard may be less of a problem than it would be with one agent. By comparing the performance of their own firms with that of others', uncertainty about agents' efforts can be reduced. If a firm's gross profit is low, but so are the gross profits of similar firms, it can be inferred that the poor performance was due to random market forces rather than the agent's slacking off. On the other hand, if all firms but one perform well, it becomes increasingly clear that the one agent had slacked off. Such comparisons are most useful when firms operate in similar lines of business that are exposed to similar market forces.

Auctions and Adverse Selection

With the adverse-selection problem, how the results change when players are added also depends on the specifics of the situation. Consider the monopoly-consumer model, but suppose the monopoly has a limited number of units to sell to several competing consumers (if the monopoly produced an unlimited amount at a constant marginal cost, consumers would not end up competing even if there were many of them, so nothing would change from our previous analysis of the adverse-selection problem). The result would be an auction setting. Auctions have received a great deal of attention in the economics literature since William Vickery's foundational work for which he won the Nobel Prize in economics.[3] Auctions continue to grow in significance as a market mechanism, used for selling goods ranging from airwave spectrum, to Treasury bills, to repossessed houses, to collectibles on the Internet auction site eBay.

Competition among consumers in an auction can help the monopolist solve the adverse-selection problem. High-value consumers are pushed to bid high to avoid losing the good to another bidder. The exact outcome of the auction depends on the nature of the economic environment (which consumers know what information when) and the auction format.

There are a host of different auction formats. Auctions can involve sealed bids or open outcries. Sealed-bid auctions can be first price (the highest bidder wins the object and has to pay his or her bid) or second price (the highest bidder still wins but only has to pay the next-highest bid). Open-outcry auctions can be ascending, as in the so-called English auction when buyers yell out successively higher bids until no one is willing to top the last, or descending, as in the so-called Dutch auction when the auctioneer starts with a very high price and lowers it continuously until one of the participants stops the auction by accepting the price at that point. The monopolist can decide whether or not to set a "reserve clause", which requires bids to be over a certain threshold or else the object will not be sold. Even more exotic auction formats are possible. In an "all-pay" auction, for example, bidders pay their bids even if they lose.

A powerful and somewhat surprising result due to Vickery is that in simple settings (risk-neutral bidders who each know their valuation for the good perfectly, no collusion, and so forth), many of the different auction formats listed previously (and more besides) provide the monopolist with the same expected revenue in equilibrium.

[3] W. Vickery, "Counterspeculation, Auctions, and Competitive Sealed Tenders", *Journal of Finance* (March 1961), 8–37.

To see why this result is surprising, consider two formats in more detail, a first-price, sealed-bid auction and a second-price, sealed-bid auction. Suppose that a single object is to be auctioned. In the first-price, sealed-bid auction, all bidders simultaneously submit secret bids. The auctioneer unseals the bids and awards the object to the highest bidder, who pays his or her bid. In equilibrium, bidders bid strictly less than their gross consumer surplus for the object (we will call this their valuations for short). Bidders would receive zero surplus from bidding their valuations (losing bidders get no surplus; the winning bidder would have to pay his or her entire surplus back to the monopolist and again get no surplus). By bidding less than his or her valuation, there is a chance that others' valuations, and thus bids, are low enough so that the bidder wins the object and makes a positive surplus.

In a second-price, sealed-bid auction, the highest bidder pays the next-highest bid rather than his or her own. In this auction format, a bidder's dominant strategy is to bid his or her valuation. This is an interesting result in its own right and worth analyzing in some detail. Let b_1 be player 1's bid and b_2 be player 2's. Table 17-2 presents the normal form for the game. It is partial in that it only shows player 1's payoffs and only shows two strategies for player 1, bidding his or her valuation ($b_1 = 50$) and bidding less ($b_1 = 30$). Looking at the first column of the matrix, if $b_2 < 30$, player 1 wins the object, pays b_2, and obtains payoff $50 - b_2$ whether he or she bids 30 or 50. The payoffs from the two strategies tie. Looking at the last column, if $b_2 > 50$, player 1 loses the object and gets payoff 0 whether he or she bids 30 or 50. Again, the payoffs from the two strategies tie. Looking at the middle column, however, if b_2 is between 30 and 50, then bidding 50 is better than 30 for player 1 because he or she loses the object and earns a payoff of 0 by bidding 30 but wins the object and earns payoff $50 - b_2 > 0$ by bidding 50. As the underlined payoffs indicate, bidding 50 is always at least as good for player 1 as bidding 30 and is strictly better against some of player 2's strategies. Similar arguments can be used to show that bidding 50 dominates any of player 1's alternatives, implying that bidding 50 is a dominant strategy for player 1.

With an understanding of equilibrium bidding in second-price auctions, we can compare first- and second-price, sealed-bid auctions. Each format has plusses and minuses regarding the revenue the monopolist earns from it. On one hand, bidders shade their bids below their valuations in the first-price auction but not in the second-price auction, a "plus" for second-price auctions. On the other hand, the winning bidder pays the highest bid in the first-price auction but only the second-highest bid in the second-price auction, a "plus" for first-price auctions. The surprising result is

MICROQUIZ 17.3

The analysis in Table 17-2 shows that player 1 prefers to bid 50 (his or her valuation) rather than 30 (a lower bid than his or her valuation). Use a similar analysis to show that player 1 would prefer to bid 50 than 70 (a higher bid than his or her valuation).

TABLE 17-2 Bidding Valuation 50 is Player 1's Dominant Strategy in a Second-Price Auction

		Player 2		
		$b_2 < 30$	$30 < b_2 < 50$	$b_2 > 50$
Player 1	$b_1 = 30$	$\underline{50 - b_2}$	0	$\underline{0}$
	$b_1 = 50$	$\underline{50 - b_2}$	$\underline{50 - b_2}$	$\underline{0}$

that these plusses and minuses balance perfectly so that they both provide the monopolist with the same expected revenue.

In more complicated settings, the long list of different auction formats do not necessarily yield the same revenue. One complication that is frequently considered is to suppose that the good has the same value to all the bidders but they do not know exactly what that value is. Each bidder only has an imprecise estimate of what that value might be. For example, bidders for oil fields may have each conducted their own surveys of the likelihood that there is oil below the surface. All bidders' surveys taken together may give a clear picture of the likelihood of oil, but each one separately may only give a rough idea. For another example, the value of a piece of art depends in part on its resale value (unless the bidder plans on keeping it in the family forever), which in turn depends on others' valuations; each bidder knows his or her own valuation but perhaps not others'. Such a setting is called a **common-values setting**.

Common-values setting An object has the same value to all bidders, but each only has an imprecise estimate of that value.

Winner's curse Winning reveals that all other bidders thought the good was worth less than the highest bidder did.

The most interesting new issue that arises in a common-values setting is the **winner's curse**. The winning bidder realizes that every other bidder probably thought the good was worth less than he or she did, meaning that he or she probably overestimated the value of the good. The winner's curse sometimes leads inexperienced bidders to regret having won the auction. Sophisticated bidders take account of the winner's curse by shading down their bids below their imprecise estimates of the value of the good, so that they never regret having won the auction in equilibrium.

Analysis of the common-values setting becomes complicated, and the different auction formats listed here no longer yield equivalent revenue. Roughly speaking, auctions that incorporate other bidders' information in the price paid tend to provide the monopolist with more revenue. For example, a second-price auction tends to be better than a first-price auction because the price paid in a second-price auction depends on what other bidders think the object is worth. If other bidders thought the object was not worth much, the second-highest bid will be low and the price paid by the winning bidder will be low, helping to solve the winner's curse problem.

Adverse Selection in the Market for Lemons

Whereas in the auction setting we supposed there was a single seller who was matched with several potential buyers, we could imagine markets in which many buyers and many sellers are matched. A particularly intriguing problem may arise in such markets if each seller has private information about the quality of the good he or she is selling. As George Akerlof showed in the article for which he won the Nobel Prize in economics, in equilibrium sometimes only the lowest-quality goods, the "lemons", get sold.[4]

To gain more insight about this result, consider the used-car market. Suppose used cars are of two types (good cars and lemons) and only the owner of a car knows which type his or her car is. Since buyers cannot differentiate between good cars and lemons, all used cars of a particular type will sell for the same price – somewhere between the true worth of the two types. The owner of a car will choose to keep his or her car if it is a good one (since a good car is worth more than the prevailing market price) but will sell the car if it is a lemon (since a lemon is worth less than the market price). Consequently, only lemons will be brought to the used-car market, and the quality of cars traded will be less than expected.

The lemons problem leads the market for used cars to be much less efficient than it would be in the standard competitive model in which quality is known (indeed, in

[4]G. A. Akerlof, "The Market for 'Lemons': Quality Uncertainty and the Market Mechanism", *Quarterly Journal of Economics* (August 1970): 488–500.

the standard model, there is no issue about knowing the quality of different goods, since typically they all are assumed to be of the same quality). Whole segments of the market disappear – along with the gains from trade in these segments – because higher-quality items are no longer traded. In the extreme, the market can simply break down with nothing (or perhaps just a few of the worst items) being sold.

The lemons problem can be mitigated by trustworthy used-car dealers, by development of car-buying expertise by the general public, by sellers providing proof that their cars are trouble-free, or by sellers offering money-back guarantees. But anyone who has ever shopped for a used car knows the problem of potential lemons is a very real one. Application 17.4: *Looking for Lemons* discusses the evidence for the lemons problem in markets ranging from lorries to football players.

Signaling

Our analysis of the adverse-selection problem so far has mainly focused on the case in which the uninformed party makes the first move, offering a contract to the party with private information. For example, the monopolist made the first move by offering a menu of different bundles to consumers, who had private information about their valuations (their types); consumers moved next by choosing which bundle to purchase.

The reverse is also possible. The player with private information can take the first action and thereby signal something about his or her type. Examples abound. A student may seek additional education as a signal that he or she is unusually talented to prospective employers. (Although see Application 17.5 *Is Education a Signal*? where we touch on the theory of countersignaling.) A person may drive a fancy car as a signal of wealth to prospective spouses or buy large diamond rings as a signal of his or her affection. A professional-looking website may signal to customers that the business is not a fly-by-night operation. An incumbent firm may price low to convince future entrants that it is a "tough" competitor. A high bet may signal that a poker player has a good hand (though the player may be bluffing).[5]

In formal terms, such settings are known as signaling games. In a signaling game, Nature moves first, choosing the first player's type at random from a number of possibilities. The first player's type is private information, unknown to the second player, who only knows the probabilities that Nature might choose one type or the other. The first player makes a move called a signal since it is observed by the second player. Based on the information provided by the signal, the second player updates his or her beliefs about the first player's type. Then the second player chooses his or her move and the game ends.

MICROQUIZ 17.4

Consider the market for used cars.

1. What information about the car might an owner know better than a prospective buyer, and so be a source of private information?
2. Whose interest is it in to "solve" the lemons problem, the seller, the buyer, or both? What measures can each side take to solve the problem?

Spence's Education Model

We will analyze signaling games in terms of a single application, Spence's education model,[6] named after Michael Spence, who received the Nobel Prize in economics for developing it (a prize

[5] The lemons problem can be thought of as a version of a signaling model. By offering a car for sale, the seller is signaling something about the quality of the car, namely, that the car is not so high quality that the seller is willing to keep it rather than selling it at the going market price. Of course, this is a signal that the seller would rather not send.

[6] A. M. Spence, "Job Market Signaling", *Quarterly Journal of Economics* (August 1973): 355–377.

APPLICATION 17.4 *Looking for Lemons*

Economists have spent some time trying to find markets in which the quality deterioration predicted by the lemons model is apparent. Here, we look at three such investigations.

Pickup Trucks

Although used pickup trucks might be expected to exhibit quality deterioration because of asymmetric information between buyers and sellers, that does not appear to be the case. A 1982 study of pickup purchases during the 1970s found that about 60 per cent of such trucks were bought used.[1] After controlling for the mileage that trucks had traveled, the author found no difference in the repair records for trucks purchased new versus those purchased used. The author offered two explanations for the relatively good quality of used pickups. First, pickup buyers may have some expertise in truck repair or can gain that expertise by looking at several pickups before buying. Second, it seems possible that, in some cases, sellers provide repair records in order to get good prices for their trucks.

Professional Footballers

Professional football players often, for various reasons, wish to be placed on the transfer market. Because a player's present team may know much more about his physical condition and general skills than does a would-be hirer, the market for "used players" may provide another case where asymmetric information leads to quality deterioration. Of course, teams undoubtedly recognize the adverse incentives inherent in the trading of free agents. So, detailed physical examinations and other kinds of tryouts have become commonplace in recent years. No team wants to be saddled with a multimillion-pound "dud" if that can be avoided.

Thoroughbreds

Many racehorse "yearlings" are sold at auction. One of the largest of these is the Keeneland auction that is held in September near Lexington, Kentucky in America. An article examining the sale prices from this auction in 1994 found evidence that lemons may appear among the thoroughbreds.[2] The authors divided sellers at the auction into two groups – those stables that both breed and race horses and those that are only in the breeding business. They reasoned that breeder-only stables would bring all of their yearlings to the auction but that those stables that also raced would have an incentive to keep the best horses for themselves. Although a would-be buyer has relatively little information about the racing quality of any yearling, he or she does know the nature of the stable from which it comes and therefore is in a position to suspect that the racers' offerings will contain relatively more lemons.

Evidence on auction prices tended to confirm these expectations. The authors found that, after holding constant such factors as the quality of the yearlings' parents, yearlings from stables that are heavily involved in racing tended to have lower prices than did those from breeder-only stables. Specifically, the authors estimated that each race that a stable entered in 1993 tended to reduce the price of its 1994 yearlings by nearly one percentage point. Apparently, buyers at the Keeneland auction were cautious about buying yearlings from breeders who may have incentives to take the best horses out of their offerings.

To Think About

1 Each of these examples suggests that buyers may take steps to address problems raised by asymmetric information. Do sellers have similar incentives to provide information to buyers?

2 The late 1990s saw a huge number of initial offerings of common stock by Internet start-up companies. How might the lemons model be applied to these initial offerings? Did subsequent events bear out the model?

---

[1] E. W. Bond, "A Direct Test of the 'Lemons' Model: The Market for Used Pickup Trucks", *American Economic Review* (September 1982): 836–840.

[2] B. Chezum and D. Wimmer, "Roses or Lemons: Adverse Selection in the Market for Thoroughbred Yearlings", *Review of Economics and Statistics* (August 1997): 521–526.

shared with George Akerlof, encountered earlier in the lemons problem, and Joseph Stiglitz, another foundational contributor to the economics of asymmetric information). Workers have an equal chance of being one of two types, high skill or low skill. A low-skill worker generates no producer surplus for the firm, and a high-skill worker generates gross profit π (where gross profit means profit not including the worker's wage, which will be computed and subtracted off later). Skill is private information for workers and cannot be observed by employers. Before the hiring decision, workers can obtain education. We will make the extreme assumption that education does nothing to enhance a worker's productivity directly. Rather, it may provide a signal of skill to future employers because high-skill workers find it easier to obtain more education. Let c be the cost of obtaining an education, where $c = c_L$ for a low-skill worker, $c = c_H$ for a high-skill worker, and $c_L > c_H$. The assumption that it is easier for high-skill workers to obtain education is crucial in the signaling model. If education were as costly or more costly for the high-skill workers to obtain, education could not provide a signal of skill.

The game tree for the Spence signaling game is shown in Figure 17-10. Nature moves first, choosing the worker's skill, low or high, with probability $\frac{1}{2}$ each. The worker observes his or her skill and then makes the decision to get an education or not (this could be thought of as additional education beyond high school or an advanced degree beyond university, such as an MBA). The firm observes the education decision but not the worker's type. Assume the firm is representative of a large number of firms

FIGURE 17-10 Spence Signalling Game in Extensive Form *Nature chooses worker skill at random. The worker then makes an education decision. The ovals around selected decision points for the firm indicate that the firm observes the worker's education decision but not skill. The payoffs, calculated in the text, provide the worker with a competitive wage based on the representative firm's beliefs about the worker's skill.*

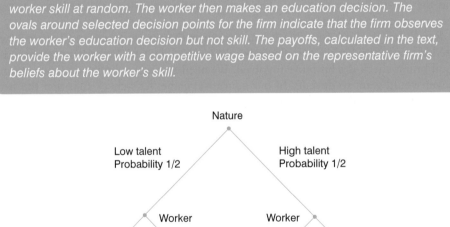

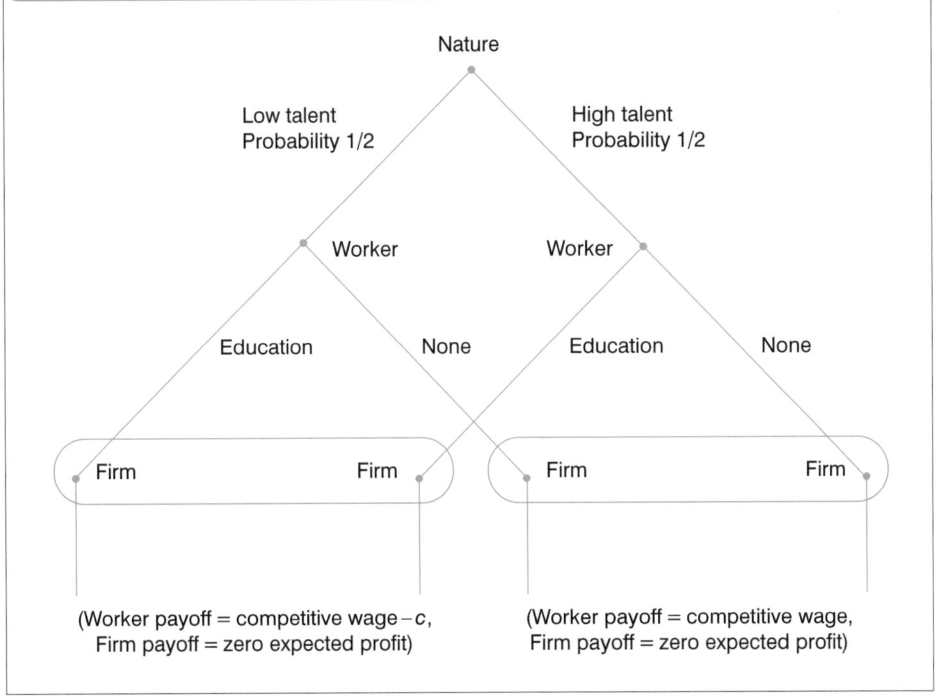

that compete for the worker. The worker's wage is set competitively; that is, all the expected gross profit is incorporated into the wage, so the firm earns zero expected profit after subtracting off the wage.

Signaling games often have multiple equilibria, and that is true in this game. In searching for these equilibria, it often helps to look for two different kinds, separating equilibria and pooling equilibria. In a **separating equilibrium**, each different type of worker chooses a different action, so the action is a perfect signal of the worker's skill. In a **pooling equilibrium**, all types choose the same action, so the equilibrium action is an uninformative signal. The uninformed player knows nothing beyond the initial probabilities Nature used to draw the first player's type.

Separating equilibrium Each type chooses a different action in a signaling game.

Pooling equilibrium All types choose the same action in a signaling game.

Separating Equilibrium

Let's begin by looking for a separating equilibrium. There is only one sensible possibility for a separating equilibrium: the high-skill type chooses to get an education and the low-skill type does not. (The other possibility is that the low-skill type obtains an education and the high-skill type does not, but this outcome does not make sense.) How would the competitive wage be set in this equilibrium? If the firm sees the worker get an education, it knows the worker must be high skill and would generate gross profit of π. Competition among firms for the worker would drive the wage up to π and the firm would earn zero profit net of the wage. If the firm sees that the worker did not get an education, it knows the worker must be low skill and would generate no gross profit. The firm would pay the worker a wage of zero. To summarize the strategies in this separating equilibrium, the high-skill type gets an education and the low-skill type does not. The firm pays wage π to an educated worker and zero to an uneducated worker.

Recall that to check for a Nash equilibrium in the simple games in Chapter 6, we needed to check whether any player would want to deviate. In signaling games, the equilibrium check is a bit more involved. We need to check whether *any type* of any player would want to deviate. In our education game, let's check first that the firm would not want to deviate from the proposed separating equilibrium. There is no reason for the firm to offer higher wages, since it is able to hire the worker at the present wages. If the firm offers a lower wage, it will lose the worker to some other firm on the competitive market and will earn zero profit, which is not strictly more than it earns in equilibrium (also zero profit). Next we need to check whether either type of worker would want to deviate. In equilibrium, the high-skill worker earns the wage π minus the cost of education c_H. If the high-skill worker deviates by choosing no education, the firm would believe the worker is low skill and pay a zero wage, and the worker would earn nothing (though he or she would save the cost of getting an education). For the high-skill worker not to want to deviate,

$$\pi - c_H > 0 \qquad \{17.1\}$$

In equilibrium, the low-skill worker's payoff is zero. If the low-skill worker deviates by pretending to be high skill and obtaining an education, he or she would earn the high-skill wage π minus the cost of education c_L. For the low-skill worker not to want to deviate in this way

$$\pi - c_L < 0 \qquad \{17.2\}$$

Putting conditions 17.1 and 17.2 together, a separating equilibrium requires $c_H < \pi < c_L$. In other words, for the separating equilibrium to work, the gap between the high- and low-skill workers' cost of obtaining an education must be large enough that the return to education, π, falls somewhere in between the two types' costs of obtaining an education.

In the separating equilibrium, each worker is paid according to his or her productivity. There is some deadweight loss in that the high type has to pay the cost of getting an education, which is socially wasteful since it does not add to productivity. An education is still a worthwhile investment for the high type because it results in a better wage.

Pooling Equilibria

Next we will look for a pooling equilibrium, in particular, a pooling equilibrium in which both types of worker obtain an education. The idea is that the low-skill worker chooses the same action as the high-skill worker to prevent being distinguished from the high-skill types and paid a lower wage. In equilibrium, the firm learns nothing about the worker's skill from seeing the fact that the worker is educated. The firm's best guess is that the worker is high or low skill with equal probability $\frac{1}{2}$, the same probabilities that Nature used to choose the worker type initially. The firm's expected gross profit from the worker equals the probability of high skill, $\frac{1}{2}$, times the gross profit from a high-skill worker, p, plus the probability of low skill, $\frac{1}{2}$, times the gross profit from a low-skill worker, 0: $(\frac{1}{2})(\pi) + (\frac{1}{2})(0) = \pi/2$. Thus the competitive wage is $\pi/2$.

We need to check whether any type of any player would want to deviate from the proposed pooling equilibrium. As with the separating equilibrium, here the competitive wage is set so that the firm earns zero expected profit and would not gain from deviating. The question remains whether either type of worker would want to deviate by choosing not to get an education. Since education is costliest for the low-skill worker, it is this type's deviation we have to worry about. In equilibrium, the low-skill worker earns the wage $\pi/2$ minus the cost of education c_L. What it earns by deviating to "no education" depends on the competitive wage paid to uneducated workers, which in turn depends on what the firm believes about an uneducated worker's skill. The rules of probability provide little guidance as to what this belief should be because seeing an uneducated worker is a totally unexpected event for the firm; the firm never encounters such a worker in equilibrium. Game theorists have devoted considerable attention to this thorny question of what might be sensible beliefs after something unexpected happens, and there is unfortunately no settled answer. In the present application, it is plausible to assume that the firm has pessimistic beliefs about an uneducated worker's skill, that is, the firm believes that if the worker chooses not to get an education, he or she is certainly a low-skill worker.[7] If so, by deviating to "no education", a low-skill worker would save the cost of education but would get a wage of zero for a total payoff of zero. The low-skill worker would choose not to deviate if $\pi/2 - c_L > 0$. For the proposed pooling equilibrium to work, the low-skill worker's cost of pooling with the high-skill type by obtaining an education cannot be too high relative to the expected wage.

We could also look for a pooling equilibrium in which both types choose not to get an education. Whether or not such an equilibrium exists again depends on the firm's beliefs following an unexpected event, this time, the unexpected event of seeing an educated worker. As long as the firm is not too confident that an educated worker is

[7]Alternatively, it is also plausible to assume that the firm learns nothing about the worker's type if it observes an uneducated worker. Given this belief, there is no reason for workers to obtain an education, and the pooling equilibrium, in which both types obtain an education, would not exist.

APPLICATION 17.5 *Is Education a Signal?*

Spence's model assumes that education does nothing to improve workers' productivity. School is just a testing ground in which students can demonstrate their ability to prospective employers. This assumption is extreme: it is hard to imagine that in going to high school, college, or university students learn nothing that would be useful for a later job. An interesting question is whether education has any signaling value at all and if so, how much of the value of education can be ascribed to signaling and how much to increased productivity.

High School Drop Out

In an area with limited access to university (say an area far from urban life and a smaller or nonexistent state system), some talented students will end up not going to university and only getting high school qualifications. If the signaling model is correct, in particular the logic of the pooling equilibrium, the presence of high-ability students in the pool of high school leavers would increase the value of a high school qualifications to lower-ability students who might otherwise have dropped out. Employers would not be able to distinguish low- from high-ability students among high school leavers and would only know that the average skill was higher given the presence of the high-ability students, raising the wage for the whole pool of high school leavers. The increased value of high school qualifications would lead to a lower dropout rate for the lower-ability students. On the other hand, if employers can perfectly observe ability and do not rely on education as a signal, having talented students in the pool of high school leavers would not provide a benefit to low-ability students and would not affect their dropout rate.

Kelly Bedard proposed this test of the signaling model and carried it out using a sample of US students who attended colleges in the early 1970s in America.[1] The presence of a college in a locality increased college attendance, and, as predicted by the signaling model, increased the high school dropout rate. In particular, a 10 per cent increase in college access increased the high school dropout rate by about 3 per cent.

Self-Employment

Another ingenious test of the signaling model relied on the difference between self-employed and other workers.[2] While education may serve as a signal of ability for workers who seek to be hired by a firm, self-employed workers know their own abilities. For them, education can only increase productivity. A study of Hong Kong workers found that the self-employed had lower returns to education than other workers. This result is consistent with the signaling model since it suggests that education had an additional value, presumably a signaling value, for workers who are hired by firms.

Three Classes of Individuals

An interesting development as regards signaling theory was proposed in a recent paper.[3] In this paper three classes of individuals are assumed – low-, medium- and high-ability individuals. The theory of "countersignaling" is a theory proposing that some high-ability individuals will pretend to be less bright than they really are. Why should they do this? While an employer may be able to distinguish between high- and low-ability individuals, how does he or she distinguish between high- and medium-ability individuals given they are very close in ability and at job interviews, for example, medium-ability people may "shine on the day"? Or to turn it around how do high-ability individuals distinguish themselves from medium-ability candidates when going for a job interview?

Medium-ability individuals will boast of their achievements (at school or university) by talking, perhaps at length, of their grades to set themselves apart from low quality candidates. The high-quality candidates, however, will not even bother to mention their grades knowing the grades will automatically set themselves apart from low-quality candidates and at the same time medium-quality candidates. It is almost as if the medium-quality candidates lack confidence in themselves and need to "speak aloud" to convince not only the potential employer but even themselves. As the authors of the paper put it,

The nouveau riche flaunt their wealth, but the old rich scorn such gauche displays. Minor officials

prove their status with petty displays of authority, while the truly powerful show their strength through gestures of magnanimity. People of average education show off the studied regularity of their script, but the well educated often scribble illegibly. Mediocre students answer a teacher's easy questions, but the best students are embarrassed to prove their knowledge of trivial points. Acquaintances show their good intentions by politely ignoring one's flaws, while close friends show intimacy by teasingly highlighting them. People of moderate ability seek formal credentials to impress employers and society, but the talented often downplay their credentials even if they have bothered to obtain them. A person of average reputation defensively refutes accusations against his character, while a highly respected person finds it demeaning to dignify accusations with a response. (page 631)

To Think About

1 Even if the employer must resort to using education as a signal rather than observing ability directly, wouldn't he or she quickly be able to learn the worker's ability by observing performance on the job? Shouldn't the wage adjust to reflect what the employer learns? What barriers might there be to learning and adjusting wages?

2 Would you advocate that your university *not* release your grades or class rank to prospective schools or employers? Does your answer depend on your performance in university so far? What would be the effect on student effort of such a policy?

3 A medium-ability candidate for a job interview reading about the theory of countersignaling may pretend to be a high-ability candidate by not boasting or emphasizing his or her achievements at school or university. But does the fact that the medium-quality individual has understood the need to do this not in the end show he or she may indeed be of high-ability?

[1]K. Bedard, "Human Capital versus Signaling Models: University Access and High School Dropouts", *Journal of Political Economy* (August 2001): 749–775.

[2]J. S. Heywood and X. Wei, "Education and Signaling: Evidence from a Highly Competitive Labor Market", *Education Economics* (April 2004): 1–16.

[3]N. Feltovich, R. Harbaugh and T. To, "Too cool for school? Signaling and countersignaling", *RAND Journal of Economics*, (Volume 33, No. 4, Winter 2002): 630 -649.

high skill, there will exist a pooling equilibrium in which both types of worker do not get an education.

The Spence model is a nice setting in which to study signaling games because it involves issues familiar to students. The question is whether there is any truth to the model. How much of the return to education is due to its signaling value and how much due to the fact that it increases productivity? Application 17.5: *Is Education a Signal*? discusses researchers' attempts to measure whether there is a signaling component to education.

Predatory Pricing and Other Signaling Games

The Spence model is but one application of signaling games. Another important application, alluded to in Chapter 14 on imperfect competition, is predatory pricing, where an incumbent firm prices low for a sufficient time to induce the exit of a rival. As noted in Chapter 14, it is difficult to rationalize predatory pricing as an equilibrium strategy unless there is some private information in the game.

One possibility is that the incumbent has private information about its cost. The lower the incumbent's cost, the lower the prices it would charge, whether it is a monopolist or competes against an entrant. The lower the incumbent's prices, the less an

MICROQUIZ 17.5

Suppose it is more expensive for the high-skill worker to get an education: $c_L < c_H$.

1 Will there be a separating equilibrium?

2 Can there be pooling equilibria?

APPLICATION 17.6 Can Wages above Market Clearing Levels Counteract Adverse Selection?

In the text we looked at how managers are motivated and how the shareholders could account for the unseen behavior of their managers acting on their behalf. However, "What about the workers?" as the old saying goes. How does an employer know that the individual they are going to employ has high productivity? Linked to this is the question, why don't many employers use the fact that at times there are unemployed individuals to lower the wages they pay by taking on unemployed who may be so desperate to get a job that they will undercut the wage paid to current employees?

The theory of efficiency wages potentially has an answer. The argument runs as follows: even if we assume no government legislation in the field of hiring and firing and that employers have a "free-hand" to do as they like, employers may still not take on unemployed at lower wage rates and sack existing workers as anyone prepared to work for lower wages is signaling their true productivity level to a potential employer. This is assuming that effort (and hence productivity) and the minimum wage at which people are prepared to work (known as the reservation wage) are positively related.

The efficiency wage is defined as the wage per unit of effort and the relationship between the wage and productivity is shown in Figure 1 below where the curved line traces out this relationship and is given by *E(w)*.

The gradient of the dashed line coming from the origin shows the value of the wage per unit of effort, i.e. w/E. $E(w)^e$ shows the wage and level of effort where the efficiency wage is minimized. At any other wage level the efficiency wage is higher implying that from the firm's perspective the money paid in the form of wages is not generating effort (or productivity) at the same efficient levels as $E(w)^e$.

At this point many textbooks would quote the example of Hendry Ford (the car manufacturer) and the "five-dollar day" (see the To Think About section below for an explanation). Here, however, we introduce the reader to perhaps the first industrialist who used efficiency wages to boost productivity by both attracting and developing high-productivity workers within his enterprises. The individual is called Robert Owen (1771–1858), a Welshman who is best known for his social experiments at his cotton mills in New Lanark, Scotland in the early part of the 19th century.[1]

Owen himself is described in the textbooks as a utopian socialist although with historical hindsight many of his ideas and practices at his mills were more akin to modern human resource practices. As he himself wrote:

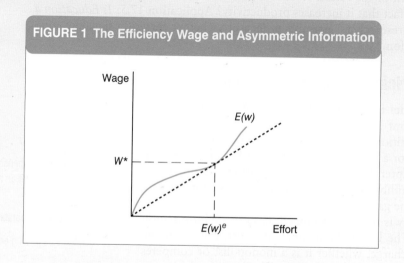

FIGURE 1 The Efficiency Wage and Asymmetric Information

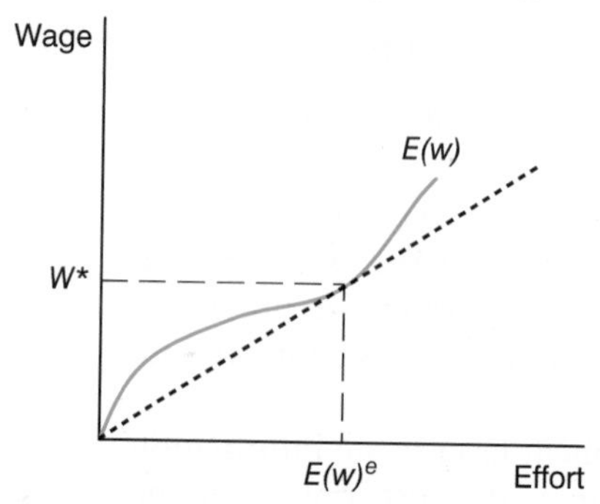

The working classes may be injuriously degraded and oppressed in three ways: 1st When they are neglected in infancy; 2nd When they are overworked by their employer, and are thus rendered incompetent from ignorance to make a good use of high wages when they can procure them. 3rd When they are paid low wages for their labor.
(On the employment of children in manufactories, 1818.)

Unlike his fellow industrialists he did allow small children to work in the mills; education was provided along with (for the time) decent housing for the workers and especially the children of the workers. No corporal punishment was allowed both inside the mills and in the classrooms. Recreation also played an important part in the lives of the workers with weekly dances for all and music and dancing lessons for children at the school provided by Owen.

When the children were educated, their parents worked the shortest hours in Britain and enjoyed the benefits of free medical care, a savings bank and cheap goods from the non-profit-making company shop.

All of the above allowed Owen to make "£60 000 a year" which was quite a tidy sum for the early part of the 19th century.[2]

The above, and more, was not a panacea but it must be seen in the light of conditions prevailing at other mills during the industrial revolution. As such it may be more accurate to see Owen's industrial relations practices as offering a *social* efficiency wage to his workforce. The net result, however, was similar to Hendry Ford's in encouraging workers to be loyal and productive. The main distinction is that he believed that it was possible to mould the person and so the productivity of the current workforce by the way they were treated and not simply attract more productive types although attract them he did.

To Think About

1 Go to your university or college library and find the article by Daniel Raff and Lawrence Summers, "Did Henry Ford Pay Efficiency Wages?"[3] Read the article (which is by no means too technical and as such is quite readable). Do you agree with Henry Ford that his decision to dramatically raise wages above the then prevailing market rates was one of the "finest cost cutting moves we ever made"? (Quoted in Raff and Summers, page S59.)

2 To what extent do you think that the theory of efficiency wages can help explain why an individual remains unemployed despite him being willing to work for lower wages than currently hired workers?

[1]For those who wish to delve into this area of economic and social history more fully then you will come across the name David Dale. This gentleman was the precursor to Owen at the mills in New Lanark, with Owen marrying Dale's daughter and taking over from Dale on his retirement, and he deserves some credit also for the working conditions at these mills.

[2]*The Scotsman* newspaper, 7 September 2001, accessed online 5 October 2006.

[3]Daniel M. G. Raff, and Lawrence H. Summers, "Did Henry Ford Pay Efficiency Wages?" (October 1989). NBER Working Paper No. W2101. Available at SSRN: http://ssrn.com/abstract=344867.

entrant would earn in competition with the incumbent. The incumbent's cost may be so low that the entrant would be unprofitable in competition with it. If the entrant knew the incumbent's costs were this low, it would not enter the market or would exit if it had entered. Such a low-cost incumbent may gain from signaling its costs are low to separate itself from a higher-cost one against which entry might be profitable. The low-cost incumbent could try to signal its type by pricing low during an initial period, low enough that a high-cost type would rather have the entrant in the market rather than charge such a low price during the initial period. There may also be equilibria of the predation game, in which the high-cost type of incumbent pools with the low-cost

MICROQUIZ 17.6

Following the example of Figure 17-10, draw the extensive form for the predatory-pricing signaling game outlined in the text, that is, the game in which an incumbent's price may serve as a signal of its costs (high or low) to another firm that is deciding whether to enter the market.

type by pricing low during the initial period, if by doing so it would prevent entry by preventing the entrant from learning its type.

As mentioned previously, there are a wide variety of other applications of signaling games. Poker can be analyzed as a signaling game. An interesting feature of poker is that extreme types on both ends, players with very good hands as well as players with very bad hands, gain from pooling with other types. A player with a very good hand would like opponents to believe his or her hand is not so good so that they continue betting; a player with a bad hand would like to bluff that his or her hand is good so that others fold.

Inefficiency in Signaling Games

The presence of private information typically leads to inefficiency in signaling games. In the Spence education model, depending on the equilibrium, one or the other type of worker, or even sometimes both, obtained an education even though education had no social benefit in terms of raising productivity. In the standard model in which firms had full information about worker productivity, there would be no need for workers to seek wasteful education. This is a typical finding in signaling games. Players with private information depart from the efficient action choice to provide an informative signal to other players.[8]

[8]The need to signal private information can increase efficiency in rare cases. Paradoxically, if the market is already inefficient, say because of monopoly or externalities, adding another source of inefficiency in the form of private information can improve matters. For example, in the predation model with a monopoly incumbent firm, lowering its price to signal low cost leads to higher consumer surplus and perhaps higher social welfare, at least in the initial period.

SUMMARY

In this chapter, we extended our analysis of game theory to situations in which one player has private information, either about its type (adverse selection) or an action it can choose (moral hazard). Some of the main points in this chapter are the following.

- Compared to the standard competitive model in which there is full information, private information typically leads markets to operate inefficiently. Depending on the model, private information can lead to slack, undersupply, or distortion of other economic decisions. In the extreme, private information can lead the entire market to break down.
- Inefficiency does not stem from a failure of firms to maximize profit or consumers to maximize utility. Players are still assumed to maximize their payoffs, but maximizing payoffs in the presence of asymmetric information leads to inefficiency.
- The principal-agent model is a simple starting point to study games of private information. The principal must design the contract it offers to the agent carefully, recognizing that the contract must give the agent the incentives to make the right choices and must be attractive enough to get the agent to accept the contract in the first place.
- With the moral-hazard problem, the agent will only work hard if given an incentive contract tying pay to performance. But tying pay to performance has the drawback of exposing the agent to risk for which the agent has to be compensated.

- With the adverse-selection problem, the principal may distort the low type's contract option in order to make it less attractive to the high type. This allows the principal to increase the price charged for the high type's contract option.
- Having consumers compete in an auction helps the monopolist solve the adverse-selection problem. In simple settings, many different auction formats produce equivalent revenues, but this no longer holds in more complicated settings.
- In a "lemons market", sellers have private information about their own good's quality. The market may unravel as no seller with a quality good would be willing to sell at the prevailing price.
- In a signaling game, the player with private information about its type makes the first move. Signaling games often have multiple equilibria, including separating equilibria, in which the first mover's action perfectly identifies its type, and pooling equilibria, in which all types choose the same action.

REVIEW QUESTIONS

1 Consider the moral-hazard problem that arises when a risk-averse manager, whose effort is unobservable, runs a firm on behalf of shareholders. Explain how the trade-off between incentives and risk prevents the firm from obtaining the fully efficient outcome. How can the moral-hazard problem be eliminated if effort is observable? How can the moral-hazard problem be eliminated if effort is unobservable but the manager is risk neutral?

2 Many contracts between professional athletes and the teams on which they play involve incentive provisions. Can you provide some examples? Do you think moral hazard is a serious problem for professional athletes? Why or why not? Discuss the problem of using incentive contracts for unproven rookies, whose playing time may depend on the discretion of the coach. How might incentive contracts worsen the problem with performance-enhancing drugs such as steroids?

3 For each of the following types of insurance, explain how the moral-hazard problem might arise. Explain how the adverse-selection problem might arise.

   a Life insurance
   b Health insurance
   c Homeowners' insurance
   d Automobile insurance
   e Unemployment insurance

   How might an insurance company adjust the insurance contract to mitigate the moral-hazard and adverse-selection problems?

4 A computer manufacturer offers an optional extended warranty on the laptops it sells. What signal does the fact that the manufacturer offers this warranty send to potential consumers about laptop quality? Does this reduce consumers' incentives to purchase the extended warranty? Suppose consumers are of two types, heavy users who travel with laptops, exposing them to the risk of accidental damage, and light users. Explain how market forces may lead the price of the extended warranty to reflect the heavy users' risk of damage rather than the average consumers'.

5 Consider the problem of a monopolist setting a menu of price/quantity bundles when there are two types of consumer and types are unobservable. The source of inefficiency in this setting is that the monopolist distorts the quantity in the low demanders' bundle. Why does the monopolist do this? Explain with reference to Figure 17-9. Why isn't the quantity in the high demanders' bundle also distorted?

6 The famous comedian Groucho Marx once quipped that "I would never join a club that would have me as a member". Modified to apply to market settings, the quote might be rewritten, "I would never buy from a seller who was willing to sell to me". Under what sort of market conditions would this quote apply? Connect this quote to Akerlof's lemons model. Among other things, use this quote to help identify the source of inefficiency in the lemons model.

7 Why is it a good idea to bid your (known) valuation in a second-price, sealed-bid auction? Why is it a bad idea to bid your (known) valuation in a first-price, sealed-bid auction? Explain, with reference to the "winner's curse", why it is an even worse idea to bid what you think your valuation is when you are not exactly sure of its value.

8 Consider a signaling model in which the first player may be one of two types. What determines the other player's beliefs about the first player's type before observing the first-player's signal? After observing the first player's signal, what beliefs must the second player have about the first player's type in a separating equilibrium? What beliefs must the second player have in a pooling equilibrium?

9 In the Spence model of education signaling we studied, what was inefficient about the equilibria? Why did the presence of asymmetric information (the fact that firms do not know the workers' productivities, but the workers themselves do) lead to this inefficiency? We saw that there were at least three possible equilibria that arose under certain conditions: a pooling equilibrium in which both types (high and low productivity) obtained an education, a pooling equilibrium in which neither type did, and a separating equilibrium in which only the high-productivity worker obtained an education. Are any of these equilibria more efficient than the others? Do workers enjoy having private information, or does your answer depend on the worker's type?

10 Suppose you invented a test that can easily measure worker productivity in Spence's signaling model. Who would be interested in paying for the test? Would workers pay to take it? Would firms pay to be able to administer it? One way for the firm to "test" workers is to have an initial probationary period during which it observes workers' productivity and fires them or adjusts their wages according to how the workers perform. What effect would this strategy have on the return to education? Can you think of real-world markets in which firms use such strategies?

PROBLEMS

17.1 Draw the following incentive contracts on the same graph, with gross profit (revenue minus costs for all inputs, not including payments to the manager) for the firm on the horizontal axis and manager pay on the vertical axis as in Figure 17-2. Draw a second graph with the marginal pay implied by each contract.

a The manager is paid €50 000 plus a 40 per cent share of gross profit.

b The manager buys out the firm (so the manager gets all the gross profits) for €100 000.

c The manager is paid a constant €75 000.

d The manager is paid €60 000 plus a bonus if the firm's gross profit is more than €90 000.

17.2 Clare manages a piano store. Her utility function is given by

$$\text{Utility} = w - 100$$

where w is the total of all monetary payments to her and 100 represents the cost to her of the effort of running the store. Clare's next best alternative to managing the store provides her with zero utility. The store's gross profit depends on random factors. There is a 50 per cent chance it earns €1000 (where by earnings we mean gross profits, not including payments to the manager) and a 50 per cent chance it earns only €400.

a If shareholders offered to share half of the store's gross profit, what would her expected utility be? Would she accept such a contract? What if she were only given a quarter share? What would be the lowest share she would accept to manage the firm?

b What is the most Clare would pay to buy out the store if shareholders decided to sell it to her?

c Suppose instead that shareholders decided to offer her a €100 bonus if the store earns €1000. What fixed salary would Clare need to be paid in addition to get her to accept the contract?

17.3 Return to problem 17.2. Suppose that Clare can still choose to exert effort, as in the previous problem, but that she can also choose not to exert effort. If she does not exert effort, she has no effort cost, so her utility is just the wage, w; the shop's return is €400 for certain.

a If shareholders offered to share half of the store's gross profit, what effort would Clare choose? Would she accept such a contract? What if she were only given a quarter share? What would be the lowest share that would get her to exert effort?

b Suppose instead that shareholders decided to offer her a €100 bonus if the store earns €1000. Show that this would not get her to work hard. What is the minimum bonus that she would need to be paid? What fixed salary would she need to be paid in addition to get her to accept the contract?

17.4 A ready-to-eat cereal manufacturer faces two types of consumers, adults and children, having the following schedule of gross surpluses for each additional unit of cereal consumed.

Gram of cereal	Marginal surplus this gram provides adults in cents	Marginal surplus this gram provides children in cents
First	20	40
Second	16	32
Third	12	24
Fourth	8	16
Fifth	4	8
Sixth	0	0
Seventh	0	0

Cereal costs €0.15 per gram to produce. The manufacturer has full information about types because adults hate sweet children's cereal and children hate the fiber-filled adult cereal. What is the optimal bundle to offer adults and to children in this full-information setting?

17.5 L. L. Bean, among other stores, has a policy of replacing shoes that wear out with new ones. Suppose there are two types of shoe buyers. Half of them have desk jobs and only have a 20 per cent chance of wearing out their shoes. The other half have active jobs (construction, nursing) and have a 60 per cent chance of wearing out their shoes. A pair of shoes costs €25 to produce.

a If the store cannot distinguish between the two types, what is the lowest price it can charge for shoes and still break even on average? (This is the price that would prevail in a competitive market.)

b What would happen to the equilibrium if the desk workers' valuation for shoes was less than the market price in part a? What is a possible source of inefficiency in this new equilibrium?

c Compute the competitive equilibrium if shoe manufacturers can charge an extra price for shoes with a replacement guarantee, assuming that only the active workers purchase the guarantee.

17.6 Suppose 100 cars will be offered on the used-car market, 50 of them good cars, each worth €10 000 to a buyer, and 50 of them lemons, each worth €2000.

a Compute a buyer's maximum willingness to pay for a car if he or she cannot observe the car's type.

b Suppose that there are enough buyers that competition among them leads cars to be sold at their maximum willingness to pay. What would the market equilibrium be if sellers value good cars at €8000? At €6000?

17.7 Tess and Meg are the only two bidders in an auction for a van Gogh painting. Each can be one of two types with equal probability: a low-value consumer with valuation €1 million or a high-value consumer with valuation €2 million. Each knows her own type but only knows the probabilities of the other's type.

a Suppose they compete in a sealed-bid, second-price auction. What are the equilibrium bidding strategies? Compute the seller's expected revenue.

b Repeat part a supposing there are three identical bidders. What if there are N bidders?

c Explain how your answer from parts a and b can be used to compute the seller's expected revenue from a first-price, sealed-bid auction.

17.8 An incumbent firm may be a low-cost type, with constant marginal cost of production 10, or a high-cost type, with marginal cost of production 20, with probabilities t and $1 - t$, respectively. The incumbent's type is private information. The incumbent produces as a monopolist in the first period. An entrant who has marginal cost 15 may enter the market between periods. Entry requires at least a small fixed investment. If the entrant comes in the market, it learns what the incumbent's marginal cost is, and firms engage in Bertrand competition in homogeneous products in the second period (see Chapter 14 for a discussion of Bertrand competition). Consumer demand is the same in each period. Suppose there is no discounting between periods, so the incumbent's objective is to maximize the sum of first- plus second-period profit.

a What is the Nash equilibrium of the second-stage game if the entrant enters? Solve the game for each type of incumbent.

b Argue that the entrant would not enter if it believes the incumbent is certainly low cost but would enter if it believes the incumbent is certainly high cost.

c Assume that the low-cost type's monopoly price is greater than 20. Use your answer from part b to argue that 20 is the highest possible price that the low-cost type of incumbent can charge in a separating equilibrium.

17.9 A firm earns gross profit (profit not including the wage) of 100 from a low-ability worker and 200 from a high-ability worker. A quarter of the workers are low-ability and the rest are high-ability.

a If competitive firms have no signals available, what is the equilibrium wage they would pay?

b Under what conditions on the cost of getting an education for each type, c_L and c_H, is there a separating equilibrium?

c Suppose $c_L = 50$ and $c_H = 0$. Outline a pooling equilibrium in which both types get an education. Be sure to specify the firm's out-of-equilibrium beliefs if it were to meet an uneducated worker. Similarly, outline a pooling equilibrium in which neither type gets an education.

18

Externalities and Public Goods

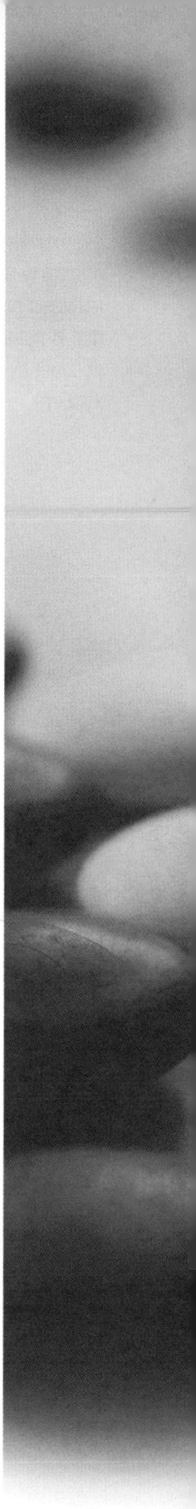

Although markets can yield economically efficient allocations, in many important cases they may fail to do so. In this chapter, we look at two specific examples. We begin by describing the general problem of "externalities" – that is, situations where the production or consumption of certain kinds of goods affects third parties not actually involved in the transaction. We also look at various ways that problems raised by externalities in private markets might be addressed. The concluding sections of the chapter then focus on a specific type of externality – the benefits that individuals receive from public goods. Our particular interest there is on asking how well various methods of public decision-making (for example, voting) allocate resources to this kind of good.

Defining Externalities

An **externality** is an effect of one economic actor's activities on another actor's well-being that is not taken into account by the normal operations of the price system. This definition stresses the direct, non-market effect of one actor on another, such as soot falling out of the air or toxic chemicals appearing in drinking water. The definition does not include effects that take place through the market. If I buy a shirt that is on sale before you get there, I may keep you from getting it and thereby affect your well-being. That is not an externality in our sense because the effect took place in a market setting.[1] Its occurrence does not affect the ability of markets to allocate resources efficiently since whether you or I get the shirt is only a distributional question. Real externalities can occur between any two economic actors. Here, we first illustrate negative (harmful) and positive (beneficial) externalities between firms. We then consider externalities between people and firms and conclude with a few externalities between people.

[1]Sometimes such effects are called "pecuniary" externalities to distinguish them from the "technological" externalities we will be discussing.

Externalities between Firms

Externality The effect of one party's economic activities on another party that is not taken into account by the price system.

Consider two firms – one producing eyeglasses, another producing charcoal (this is an actual example from nineteenth-century English law). The production of charcoal is said to have an external effect on the production of eyeglasses if the output of eyeglasses depends not only on the amount of inputs chosen by the eyeglass firm but also on the level at which the production of charcoal is carried on. Suppose these two firms are located near each other, and the eyeglass firm is downwind from the charcoal firm. In this case, the output of eyeglasses may depend not only on the level of inputs the eyeglass firm uses itself but also on the amount of charcoal in the air, which affects its precision grinding wheels. The level of pollutants, in turn, is determined by the output of the charcoal firm. Increases in charcoal output would cause fewer high-quality eyeglasses to be produced even though the eyeglass firm has no control over this negative effect.[2]

The relationship between two firms may also be beneficial. Most examples of positive externalities are rather bucolic in nature. Perhaps the most famous, proposed by James Meade, involves two firms, one producing honey by raising bees and the other producing apples.[3] Because the bees feed on apple blossoms, an increase in apple production will improve productivity in the honey industry. The beneficial effects of having well-fed bees is a positive externality to the beekeeper. Similarly, bees pollinate apple crops and the beekeeper provides an external benefit to the orchard owner. Later in this chapter, we examine this situation in greater detail because, surprisingly enough, the beekeeper–apple grower relationship has played an important role in economic research on the significance of externalities.

Externalities between Firms and People

Firms may impact directly on people's well-being. A cement firm that spews dust into the air imposes costs on people living near the plant in the form of ill health and increased dirt and grime. Similar effects arise from firms' pollution of water (for example, mining firms that dump their waste into a river, reducing the river's recreational value to people who wish to fish there), misuse of land (opencast mining that is an eyesore and may interfere with water supplies), and production of noise (airports that are located near major cities). In all of these cases, at least on first inspection, it seems that firms will not take any of these external costs into account when deciding how much to produce.

Of course, people may also have external effects on firms. Drivers' car pollution harms the productivity of citrus growers, cleaning up litter and graffiti is a major expense for shopping centers, and the noise of Saturday night rock concerts on university campuses probably affects hotel and guest house rentals. In these cases, there may be no simple way for the affected parties to force the people who generate the externalities to take the full costs of their actions into account.

Externalities between People

Finally, the activity of one person may affect the well-being of someone else. Playing a radio too loud, smoking cigars, or driving during peak hours are all consumption

[2]We will find it necessary to redefine the assumption of "no control" considerably as the analysis of this chapter proceeds.

[3]James Meade, "External Economies and Diseconomies in a Competitive Situation", *Economic Journal* (March 1952): 54–67.

activities that may negatively affect the utility of others. Planting an attractive garden or shoveling the snow off one's sidewalk may, on the other hand, provide beneficial externalities. Often, however, these activities will not be reflected in market transactions among the people involved.

Reciprocal Nature of Externalities

Although these examples of externalities picture one actor as the cause of the problem and some other actor as the helpless victim (or beneficiary), that is not a very useful way of looking at the problem. By definition, externalities require (at least) two parties, and in a sense each should be regarded as the "cause". If the producer of eyeglasses had not located its factory near the charcoal furnace, it would not have suffered any negative effects on its grinding wheels; if individuals didn't live below airport flight paths, noise would only be a minor problem; and if you were out of earshot, it wouldn't matter that someone else had the radio's volume turned up. Recognizing these reciprocal relationships is not intended to exonerate polluters, only to clarify the nature of the problem. In all of these cases, two economic actors are seeking to use the same resource, and (as we illustrate in Application 18.1: *Passive Smoking*) there are no unambiguous economic principles for deciding whose claim is stronger. (In addition, in Application 18.7: *Where There's Muck There's Brass*, we look at situations where the actions of economic agents can result in situations where the effect has both a positive and a negative externality at the *same* time.)

Externalities and Allocational Efficiency

It has traditionally been argued that the presence of externalities such as those we have just described can cause a market to operate inefficiently. We discussed the reasons for this briefly in Chapter 12 and repeat these reasons here using the example of eyeglass and charcoal producers. Production of eyeglasses produces no externalities but is negatively affected by the level of charcoal output. We now show that resources may be allocated inefficiently in this situation. Remember that for an allocation of resources to be efficient price must be equal to true social marginal cost in each market. If the market for eyeglasses is perfectly competitive (as we assume both markets to be), their price will indeed be equal to this good's private marginal cost. Since there are no externalities in eyeglass production, there is no need to make a distinction between private and social marginal cost in this case.

For charcoal production, the story is more complex. The producer of charcoal will still produce that output for which price is equal to private marginal cost. This is a direct result of the profit-maximization assumption. However, because of the negative effect that production of charcoal has on eyeglass production, it will not be the case that private and social marginal costs of charcoal production are equal. Rather, the **social cost** of charcoal production is equal to the private cost *plus* the cost that charcoal production imposes on eyeglass firms in terms of reduced or inferior output. The charcoal-producing firm does not recognize this effect and produces too much charcoal. Society would be made better off by reallocating resources away from charcoal production and toward the production of other goods.

Social costs Costs of production that include both input costs and costs of the externalities that production may cause.

A Graphical Demonstration

Figure 18-1 illustrates the misallocation of resources that results from the externality in charcoal production. Assuming that the charcoal producer is a price taker, the

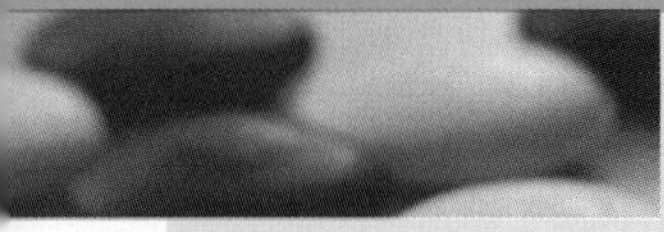

APPLICATION 18.1 *Passive Smoking*

Many of the economic issues that arise in cases of externalities are illustrated by controversies over second-hand smoke or passive smoking. The term second-hand smoke (more formally, environmental tobacco smoke, or ETS) refers to the effects of smokers' consumption of cigarettes and other tobacco products on third-party bystanders. This is a separate issue from the harmful effects of smoking on smokers themselves – an activity that generally does not involve externalities, strictly defined.

Health Effects of Passive Smoking

Few doubt that passive smoking is annoying; it is also, however, a serious health hazard. The Environmental Protection Agency in the United States estimates that approximately 2200 people die annually in the country as a result of the increased incidence of lung cancer among those exposed to ETS. The agency suggests that the figure could be much higher if possible effects of ETS on heart disease were also taken into account. The *British Medical Journal* published an article in 1997 in which 37 passive smoking studies were analyzed.[1] The study found a 24 per cent increase in lung cancer among people living with smokers. In addition, an editorial in the *British Medical Journal* of 18 October 1997 outlines the extensive studies in many different countries that confirm the link between passive smoking and various illnesses.

Reciprocal Nature of the ETS Externality

As for all externalities, the ETS externality involves reciprocal effects. Smokers harm bystanders with their smoke, but attempts to limit the "rights" of smokers impose inconveniences that need not arise if the bystanders were not present. Although inconvenience effects of restrictions on smokers are seldom mentioned, they are not necessarily trivial. For example, one study of the potential impact of workplace restrictions in America on smoking calculates a loss in smokers' consumer surplus of approximately \$20 billion per year.[2] Of course, such estimates may be as far off the mark. But the fact that any specification of rights will significantly affect the welfare of the parties involved makes the issue a controversial one in deciding how a particular resource (air) should be used.

Private Actions

For many years, decisions regarding second-hand smoke were handled through private transactions. People decided when and where to smoke in their homes or in homes they were visiting. Railroads designated smoking cars; airlines and restaurants had smoking sections; and workers would negotiate among themselves over whether smoking on the job would be permitted. Such private restrictions on smoking have been tightened in recent years, mainly in response to market pressures. For example, all airlines have banned smoking from all flights, and many restaurants have gone smoke free. Most hotel chains now offer non-smoking rooms, and some have begun segregating smokers and non-smokers by floors. Smoking has also been banned from most public venues such as cinemas or sports arenas.

Public Actions

In addition, a number of countries such as the Republic of Ireland and the United Kingdom have prohibited smoking in (indoor) public places completely. Huddles of smokers standing outside pubs in both the Republic of Ireland and the United Kingdom in the middle of winter will be familiar sights to any visitor to these countries. Some economists have asked whether such additional restrictions (beyond those adopted privately) are really efficient. They ask for clear evidence that private choices by smokers and non-smokers have not been adequate for ameliorating most of the adverse effects of smoking externalities. Given the declining number of smokers and the increasing aggressiveness with which non-smokers pursue their rights, however, it seems likely that smoking regulations will become increasingly restrictive throughout many other countries.

To Think About

1 Some people argue that smokers create additional "externalities" in their behavior by driving up health-care and insurance costs for non-smokers. Are such effects "externalities"? How,

if at all, do they distort the allocation of resources? How would an efficient market handle smoking risks in, say, health-insurance premiums?

2 Non-smokers can often avoid ETS through their own behavior (for example, by refusing to patronize establishments that permit smoking). How, if at all, should the costs that non-smokers incur by taking such actions be taken into account in defining an optimal policy toward ETS?

[1]A. K. Hackshaw, M. Law, and N. J. Wald, "The accumulated evidence on lung cancer and environmental tobacco smoke", *British Medical Journal,* no. 315 (1997): 980–988.

[2]W. K. Viscusi, "Second-hand Smoke: Facts and Fantasy", *Regulation*, no. 3 (1995): 42–49.

demand curve for its output is a horizontal line at the prevailing market price (say, P^*). Profits are maximized at q^*, where price is equal to the private marginal cost of producing charcoal (*MC*). Because of the externality that charcoal production imposes on eyeglass makers, however, the social marginal cost of this production (*MCS*) exceeds *MC* as shown in Figure 18-1. The vertical gap between the *MCS* and the *MC* curves measures the harm that producing an extra unit of charcoal imposes on eyeglass makers. At q^*, the social marginal cost of producing charcoal

MICROQUIZ 18.1

At several places in previous chapters we have illustrated "deadweight loss" triangles. Explain why the triangle *ABE* in Figure 18-1 represents exactly the same kind of deadweight loss as in the monopoly case.

FIGURE 18-1 An Externality in Charcoal Production Causes an Inefficient Allocation of Resources *Because production of charcoal imposes external costs on eyeglass makers, social marginal costs (MCS) exceed private marginal costs (MC). In a competitive market, the firm would produce q* at a price of P*. At q*, however, MCS > P* and resource allocation could be improved by reducing output to q'. With bargaining among the parties, however, output level q' may be arrived at voluntarily.*

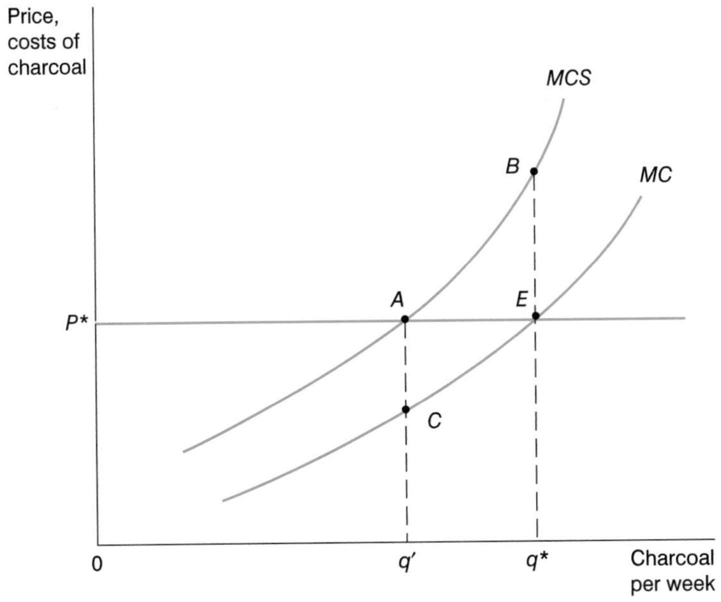

exceeds the price people are willing to pay for this output (P^*). Resources are misallocated, and production should be reduced to q' where social marginal cost and price are equal. In making this reduction, the reduction in total social costs (area ABq^*q') exceeds the reduction in total spending on charcoal (given by area AEq^*q'). This comparison shows that the allocation of resources is improved by a reduction in charcoal output because social costs are reduced to a greater extent than are consumers' expenditures on charcoal. Consumers can reallocate their spending toward something else that involves lower social costs than charcoal does.

Property Rights, Bargaining, and the Coase Theorem

Property rights The legal specification of who owns a good and the trades the owner is allowed to make with it.

Common property Property that may be used by anyone without cost.

Private property Property that is owned by specific people who may prevent others from using it.

The conclusion that externalities always distort the allocation of resources should not be accepted uncritically. To explore the issue further, we need to introduce the concept of property rights to show how these rights might be traded voluntarily between the two firms. Simply put, **property rights** are the legal specification of who owns a good and of the types of trades that the current owner is allowed to make. Some goods may be defined as **common property** that is owned by society at large and may be used by anyone; others may be defined as **private property** that is owned by specific people. Private property may either be *exchangeable* or *non-exchangeable*, depending on whether the good in question may or may not be traded to someone else. In this book, we have been primarily concerned with exchangeable private property and we consider these types of property rights here.

Costless Bargaining and Competitive Markets

For the purposes of the charcoal–eyeglass externality, it is interesting to consider the nature of the property right that might be attached to the air shared by the charcoal and eyeglass firms. Suppose property rights were defined so as to give sole rights to use of the air to one of the firms, but that the firms were free to bargain over exactly how the air might be used. At first, you might think that if rights to the air were given to the charcoal producer, pollution would result; whereas, if rights were given to the eyeglass firm, the air would remain pure and grinding machines would work properly. This might not be the case, because your snap conclusion disregards the bargains that might be reached by the two parties. Indeed, some economists have argued that if there are no transactions (bargaining) costs, the two parties left on their own will arrive at the efficient output (q'), and this result will be true regardless of who "owns" the rights to use the air.

Ownership by the Polluting Firm

Suppose the charcoal firm owns the right to use the air as it wishes. It must then add the costs (if any) related to this ownership into its total costs. What are the costs associated with air ownership? Again, the opportunity cost notion provides the answer. For the charcoal firm, the costs of using the air as a dumping place for its dust are what someone else is willing to pay for this resource in its best alternative use. In our example, only the eyeglass maker has some alternative uses for the air (to keep it clean), and the amount that this firm would be willing to pay for clean air is precisely equal to the external damage done by charcoal pollution. If the charcoal firm calculates its costs correctly, its marginal cost curve (including the implicit cost of air use rights) becomes *MCS* in Figure 18-1. The firm will therefore produce q' and sell the remaining air use rights to the eyeglass maker for a fee of some amount between *AEC* (the lost profits from producing q' rather than q^* tonnes of charcoal) and *ABEC* (the maximum amount the eyeglass maker would pay to avoid having charcoal output increased from q' to q^*).

Ownership by the Injured Firm

A similar result would occur if eyeglass makers owned the rights to use the air as they pleased. In this case, the charcoal producer would be willing to pay up to its total profits for the right to pollute the air (assuming, as we have all along, that there is no less damaging way to make charcoal). The eyeglass maker will accept these payments as long as they exceed the costs imposed on it by the charcoal firm's pollution. The ultimate result of bargaining will be for the charcoal firm to offer a payment for the right to "use" the air to dispose of the amount of soot and ash associated with output level q'. The eyeglass maker will not sell the rights to undertake any further pollution into "its" air because, beyond q', what the charcoal firm would be willing to pay ($P^* - MC$) falls short of the cost of this additional pollution ($MCS - MC$). Again, as when the charcoal firm had the property rights for air usage, an efficient allocation can be reached by relying on voluntary bargaining between the two firms. In both situations, some production of charcoal takes place, and there will therefore be some air pollution. Having no charcoal output (and no pollution) would be inefficient in the same sense that producing q^* is inefficient – scarce resources would not be efficiently allocated. In this case, there is some "optimal level" of charcoal output, eyeglass output, and of air pollution that may be achieved through bargains between the firms involved.

Coase theorem If bargaining is costless, the social cost of an externality will be taken into account by the parties, and the allocation of resources will be the same no matter how property rights are assigned.

The Coase Theorem

We have shown that the two firms left on their own can arrive at the efficient output level (q'). Assuming that making such transactions is costless, both parties will recognize the advantages of striking a deal. Each will be led by the "invisible hand" to the same output level that would be achieved through an ideal merger. That solution will be reached no matter how the property rights associated with air use are assigned. The pollution-producing firm has exactly the same incentives to choose an efficient output level as does the injured firm. The ability of the two firms to bargain freely causes the true social costs of the externality to be recognized by each in its decisions. This result is sometimes referred to as the **Coase theorem** after the economist Ronald Coase, who first proposed it in this form.[4] Application 18.2: *Property Rights and Nature* looks at some examples of how a proper definition of property rights can often improve the allocation of resources in the presence of externalities.

MICROQUIZ 18.2

The Coase theorem requires both that property rights be fully specified and that there be no transactions costs.

1. Would efficiency be achieved if transactions costs were zero but property rights did not exist?
2. Would efficiency be achieved if transactions costs were high but property rights were fully defined? Would your answer to this question depend on which party was assigned the property rights?

Distributional Effects

There are distributional effects that do depend on who is assigned the property rights to use the air. If the charcoal firm is given the air rights, it will get the fee paid by the eyeglass

[4] See Ronald Coase, "The Problem of Social Cost", *Journal of Law and Economics* (October 1960): 1–44.

APPLICATION 18.2 *Property Rights and Nature*

The notion that the specification and enforcement of private property rights may aid in coping with externalities has provided a number of surprising insights. Some of the most picturesque of these involve natural surroundings.

Bees and Apples

Bees pollinate apple trees, and apple blossoms provide nectar with which bees produce honey. Despite the seeming complexity of these externalities, it appears that markets function quite well in this situation. In many locales, contractual bargaining between beekeepers and orchard owners is well developed. Standard contracts provide for the renting of bees for the pollination of many crops. Research has shown that the rents paid in these contracts accurately reflect the value of honey that is yielded from the rentals. Apple growers, for example, must pay higher rents than clover growers because apple blossoms yield considerably less honey.[1] Because bargaining among those affected by these externalities is relatively costless, this seems to be a situation where the Coase theorem applies directly.

Shellfish

Over-fishing results from an externality – no single fisher takes into account the fact that his or her catch will reduce the amounts that others can catch. In the open seas, there is no easy solution to this sort of externality – costs of enforcing property rights are just too high. But in coastal situations, where property can be effectively policed, the harmful effects of over-fishing can be ameliorated. When these rights are defined and enforced, private owners will recognize how their harvesting practices affect their own fish stocks.

This possibility has been especially well documented for coastal shellfish, such as oysters and lobsters. In cases where property rights to specific fishing grounds are well defined, average catches are much higher over the long run. For example, one comparison of oyster yields in two states in America – Virginia and Maryland – during the 1960s found that catches were nearly 60 per cent higher in Virginia. The authors attributed this finding to the fact that Virginia state law made it much easier to enforce private coastal fishing rights than did Maryland law.[2] Similar results have been found by comparing harvest yields between family-owned and communal lobster beds on the Maine coast.

Elephants

The potential conservationist value of property rights enforcement has also been discovered by African nations who are seeking to preserve their elephant herds. In the past, ivory hunters have been ruthless in their killing of elephants. Strong, international sanctions have been largely ineffective in preventing the carnage. During the 1980s, for example, elephant populations declined by more than 50 per cent in East African countries, such as Kenya.

Several southern African nations, most notably Botswana, have taken a different approach to elephant preservation. These countries have allowed villages to capitalize on their local elephant herds by giving them the right to sell a limited number of elephant hunting permits and by encouraging them to develop tourism in protected elephant areas. Essentially, the elephants have been converted into the private property of villages, which now have an incentive to maximize the value of this asset. Elephant herds have more than doubled in Botswana.

To Think About

1. In the bees–apples case, considerable bargaining may be required to reach a satisfactory contract, and, in some instances, the bees may wander out of their contracted areas. What factors would determine whether it will be cost effective to develop private property contracts in such situations?
2. Isn't the notion of "privatizing wildlife" (as Botswana has done for elephants) crass commercialism? Wouldn't a better solution be to develop a conservationist ethic under which everyone agreed to nurture the planet's wild heritage?

---

[1] The classic examination of this question is S. N. S. Cheung, "The Fable of the Bees: An Economic Investigation", *Journal of Law and Economics* (April 1973): 11–33.

[2] R. J. Agnello and L. P. Donnelly, "Property Rights and Efficiency in the Oyster Industry", *Journal of Law and Economics* (October 1975): 521–533.

maker, which will make the charcoal producer at least as well off as it was producing q^*. If the eyeglass firm gets the rights, it will receive a fee for air use that at least covers the damage the air pollution does. Because, according to the Coase result, the final allocation of resources will be unaffected by the way in which property rights are assigned,[5] any assessment of the desirability of the various possibilities might be made on equity grounds. For example, if the owners of the charcoal firm were very wealthy and those who make eyeglasses were poor, we might argue that ownership of the air use rights should be given to eyeglass makers on the basis of distributional equity. If the situation were reversed, one could argue for giving the charcoal firm the rights. The price system may often be capable of solving problems in the allocation of resources caused by externalities, but, as always, it will not necessarily achieve equitable solutions. Such issues of equity in the assignment of property rights arise in every allocational decision, not only in the study of externalities, however.

The Role of Transactions Costs

The result of the Coase theorem depends crucially on the assumption of zero transactions costs. If the costs of striking bargains were high, the workings of this voluntary exchange system might not be capable of achieving an efficient result. In the next section, we examine situations where transactions costs are high and show that competitive markets will need some help if they are to achieve efficient results.

Externalities with High Transactions Costs

When transactions costs are high, externalities may cause real losses in economic welfare. The fundamental problem is that, with high transactions costs, economic actors face no pressure to recognize the third-party effects they may be causing. All solutions to externality problems in these cases must therefore find some way to get the actors to "internalize" the third-party effects they cause. In this section, we look at three such methods, each of which has both advantages and disadvantages.

Legal Redress

The operation of the law may sometimes provide a way for taking externalities into account. If those who are injured by an externality have the right to sue for damages in a court of law, the possibility of such suits may lead to internalization. For example, if the charcoal producer shown in Figure 18-1 can be sued for the harm that it does to eyeglass makers, payment of damages will increase the costs associated with charcoal production. Hence, the charcoal marginal cost curve will shift upward to *MCS* and an efficient allocation of resources will be achieved.

This discussion suggests that different types of law might be applied in cases of externalities, depending on whether transactions costs are high or low. When transactions costs are low, careful specification of rights under property law can be used to achieve efficient results because the Coase theorem applies. When transactions costs are high, the law of "torts" (harms) should be used because lawsuits can get those who create externalities to recognize the damage that they do. Hence,

[5]Assuming that the wealth effects of how property rights are assigned do not affect demand and cost relationships in the charcoal market.

the possibility of legal redress provides an important complement to the Coase theorem.[6]

Of course, using the legal system requires real resources. Lawyers, judges, and expert witnesses do not come cheap. These costs may multiply rapidly as the number of injured parties increases. Hence, any full assessment of the desirability of using the law to obtain market-like solutions to the externality problem must take the costs of using the law into account. Still, it seems clear that in many cases of externalities, such as automobile accidents or other types of personal injuries, use of the legal system may prove to be expeditious. Application 18.3: *Product Liability* looks at some advantages and disadvantages of using legal approaches to issues of product safety.

Taxation

A second way to achieve internalization is through taxation. This remedy was first suggested by the welfare economist A. C. Pigou in the 1920s,[7] and it remains the standard economists' solution for many types of externalities.

The taxation solution is illustrated in Figure 18-2. Again, MC and MCS represent the private and social marginal costs of charcoal production, and the market price of charcoal is given by P^*. An excise tax of amount t would reduce the net price received by the firm to $P^* - t$, and at that price the firm would choose to produce q'. The tax causes the firm to reduce its output to the socially optimal amount. At q', the firm incurs private marginal costs of $P^* - t$ and imposes external costs on eyeglass makers of t per unit. The per-unit tax is therefore exactly equal to the extra costs that charcoal producers impose on eyeglass producers.[8] The problem then for government regulators is to decide on the proper level for such a **Pigovian tax**.

Pigovian tax A tax or subsidy on an externality that brings about an equality of private and social marginal costs.

Regulation of Externalities

A third set of ways to control externalities in situations of high transactions costs is through regulation. In order to look at some of the issues that arise in regulation, let's consider the case of policy toward environmental pollution. The horizontal axis in Figure 18-3 shows percentage reductions in environmental pollution from some source below what would occur in the absence of any regulation. The curve MB in the figure shows the additional social benefits obtained by reducing such pollution by one more unit. These benefits consist of possibly improved health, the availability of additional recreational or aesthetic benefits, and improved production opportunities for other firms. As for most economic activities, this provision of benefits is assumed to exhibit diminishing returns – the curve MB slopes downward to reflect the fact that the marginal benefits from additional reductions in pollution decline as stricter controls are implemented.

[6] These insights were first noted in G. Calabresi and A. D. Melamed, "Property Rules, Liability Rules, and Inalienability", *Harvard Law Review* (March 1972): 1089–1128. Notice that the lawsuits described here are intended only to recover "compensatory damages" that compensate for the harm that externalities do. See Application 18.3 for a discussion of "positive" damages.

[7] A. C. Pigou, *The Economics of Welfare*, 4th ed. (London: Macmillan, 1946); Pigou also stressed the desirability of providing subsidies to firms that produce beneficial externalities.

[8] If the charcoal firm here represents an entire industry, then the tax would, as in Chapter 11, raise the market price of charcoal. If the industry exhibited constant costs, in the long run, price would rise by the exact amount of the tax, and demand would be reduced to the socially optimal level by that price rise. In this case, the tax would be fully paid by charcoal consumers in the long run. If charcoal production exhibited increasing costs, some portion of the Pigovian tax would be paid by suppliers of inputs to the charcoal industry.

APPLICATION 18.3 *Product Liability*

Concerns about product safety have multiplied significantly in recent years. Here we look at some of the law and economics behind this trend.

A Coase Theorem

Situations in which products cause injuries are not necessarily externalities under our definition because the product supplier and the consumer have a market relationship between one another. With perfect information and low transactions costs, the Coase theorem suggests that it may be possible to achieve an efficient allocation even when products are dangerous. A simple illustration is provided in Figure 1 for the case of, say, chainsaws. Use of chainsaws provides utility to people (try cutting up a fallen tree without one) but also cause injuries. Under a legal specification of *caveat emptor* (let the buyer beware), consumers would be responsible for all injuries caused. The demand curve for saws would be given by D. The supply curve for chainsaws would reflect only production costs and would be given by S. Market equilibrium occurs at P^*, Q^*.

Suppose instead that suppliers are liable for all injuries that chainsaws cause. Costs of these injuries (c) would shift the supply curve upward to S'. Demanders would now know that they would be compensated for the injuries they sustain from chainsaw operation, so they would be willing to pay c more for any output level – demand would shift upward by c. The new market equilibrium would be given by $P^* + c$, Q^*. That is, quantity produced would remain the same, but the price would now explicitly reflect injury costs. Regardless of the legal regime that is in place, the efficient quantity of chainsaws will be produced.

Imperfect Information

Outcomes under the two legal regimes will differ if the parties to chainsaw transactions are not perfectly informed. In this case, attaining an efficient solution will require that the liability be placed on the best-informed party. For example, suppose that most chainsaw injuries occur because, unknown to consumers, firms produce mechanically defective saws. Placing the legal liability on the firms will ensure that they take injury costs into account. On the other hand, if most injuries occur because people do dumb things with their chainsaws, efficiency

FIGURE 1 Coase Theorem for Product Liability *If demanders bear liability for injuries, market equilibrium will be at P*, Q*. If suppliers bear liability, equilibrium will be at P* + c, Q*. The same quantity is produced under both legal regimes.*

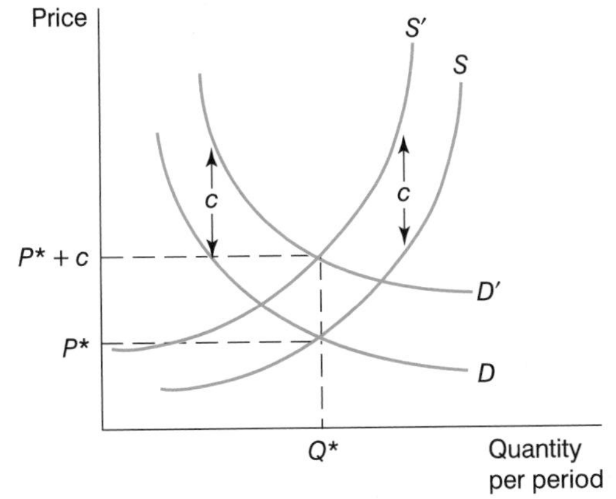

(Continued)

can be obtained by opting for *caveat emptor* in order to give users an incentive to be careful.

Punitive Damages

Efficiency is achieved in Figure 1 under the various legal regimes because the parties are made to internalize the costs of injuries into their decisions. In legal jargon, payment of these costs is called "compensatory damages" because such payments accurately compensate for injuries incurred. In the US legal system (though not in some other countries' systems), parties injured by a product can also sue for "punitive damages". These damages are intended to "send a message" rather than compensate for actual physical harm. In general, economists doubt the wisdom of such damages because they may over-deter valuable production and cause firms to adopt excessive safety features that would not meet a cost-benefit test.

To Think About

1 Sketch the analysis which shows that the safety of chainsaws will be optimal regardless of whether firms or consumers bear liability for injuries.

2 A lawsuit against the Merck drug company awarded $3 million in compensatory damages and $220 million in punitive damages in a case involving the pain medication Vioxx. What is the likely effect of such a legal result?

The curve *MC* in Figure 18-3 represents the marginal costs incurred in reducing environmental emissions. The positive slope of this curve reflects our usual assumptions of increasing marginal costs. Controlling the first 50 or 60 per cent of pollutants is a relatively low-cost activity, but controlling the last few percentage points is rather costly. As reductions in emissions approach 100 per cent, marginal costs rise very rapidly.

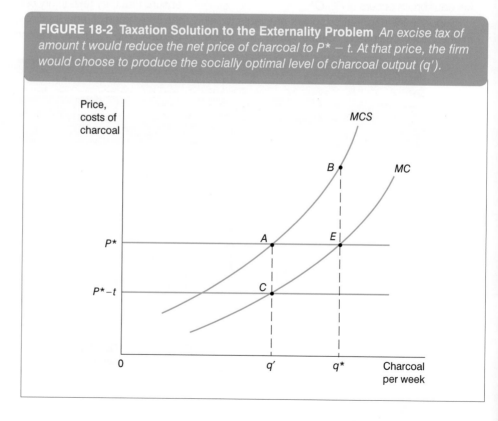

FIGURE 18-2 Taxation Solution to the Externality Problem *An excise tax of amount t would reduce the net price of charcoal to P* – t. At that price, the firm would choose to produce the socially optimal level of charcoal output (q′).*

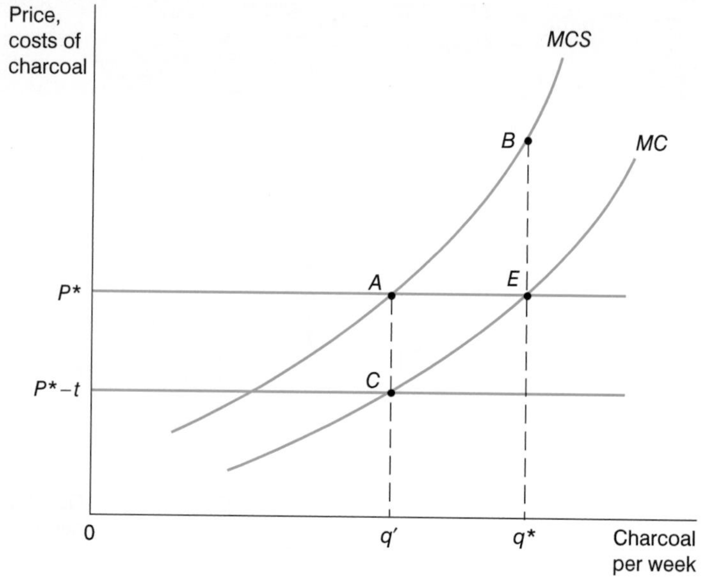

Optimal Regulation

Given this configuration, it is clear that R^* is the optimal level of pollution reduction. For reductions less than R^* (say, R_L), the marginal benefits associated with further tightening of environmental controls exceed the marginal cost of achieving lower pollution levels, so emissions should be reduced further. Reductions in excess of R^* are also inefficient – environmental control can be pushed too far. At R_H, the marginal cost of emissions control exceeds the marginal benefits obtained, so less-strict regulation may be desirable. To non-economists, the notion that there is an optimal level of pollution (that R^* is less than 100 per cent) may sound strange, but this result reflects the general principles of efficient resource allocation we have been studying throughout this book.

Fees, Permits, and Direct Controls

There are three general ways that emissions reductions of R^* might be attained through regulatory policy. First, the government may adopt a Pigovian-type "effluent fee" of f^* for each per cent that pollution is not reduced. Faced with such a charge, the polluting firm will choose the optimal emissions reduction level, R^*. For reductions less than R^*, the fee exceeds the marginal cost of pollution abatement, so a profit-maximizing firm will opt for abatement. Reductions in emissions of more than R^* would be unprofitable, however, so the firm will opt to pay the fee on $(100 - R^*)$ of its pollutants. One important feature of the fee approach is that the firm itself is free to choose whatever combination of output reduction and adoption of pollution control technology achieves R^* at minimal cost.

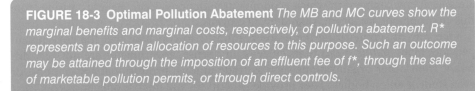

FIGURE 18-3 Optimal Pollution Abatement *The MB and MC curves show the marginal benefits and marginal costs, respectively, of pollution abatement. R* represents an optimal allocation of resources to this purpose. Such an outcome may be attained through the imposition of an effluent fee of f*, through the sale of marketable pollution permits, or through direct controls.*

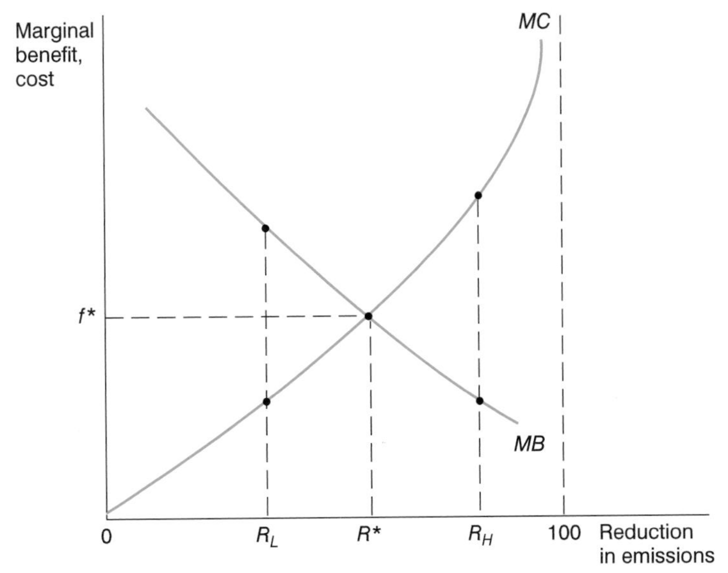

A similar allocational result would be attained if governmental regulators issued permits that allow firms to "produce" $(100 - R^*)$ per cent of their unregulated emissions levels. Figure 18-3 implies that, if such permits were freely tradable, they would sell for a price of f^*. In this case, a competitive market for pollution permits ensures that the optimal level of emissions reductions will be attained at minimal social cost.

A third regulatory strategy would be simply to implement reductions of R^* through direct controls. In this case, which tends to be the one most often followed in the United States, firms would be told the level of emissions they would be allowed. Such a direct approach can, in principle, duplicate the allocations provided by lawsuits, Pigovian taxation, or marketable permits. If, as is often the case, direct control is also accompanied by specification of the precise mechanism by which R^* is to be achieved (for example, through the installation of a special kind of pollution-control equipment) the cost-minimization incentives incorporated in the other approaches may be lost. Application 18.4: *Regulating Power Plant Emissions* looks at a situation where a variety of regulatory strategies has been used.

Public Goods

The activities of governments can have important externalities. For many of the goods that governments provide, the benefits are shared by all citizens. For example, one of the primary functions of all governments is the provision of a common defense. All citizens benefit from this whether or not they pay taxes for it. More generally, the government establishes such things as property rights and laws of contract that create a legal environment in which economic transactions occur. Benefits arising from this environment are, again, shared by all citizens.

One way of summarizing these observations is to conclude that the government provides many *public goods* to its citizens. In a sense, governments are not very different from other organizations such as trade unions, professional associations, or even student union bodies. They provide benefits to, and impose obligations on, their members. Governments differ primarily because they may be able to achieve economies of scale by virtue of their all-inclusive character and because they have the ability to finance their activities through compulsory taxation.

MICROQUIZ 18.3

Suppose that the government does not have detailed information about the costs of the firms that produce pollution.

1. Why are the three methods described here for attaining R^* superior to a regulatory strategy that requires firms to install a specific technology that would allow them to attain R^*?
2. How do the three strategies minimize the information that the government needs?

Attributes of Public Goods

The preceding discussion of public goods is circular – governments are defined as producers of public goods, and public goods are defined as the stuff governments produce. Many economists (starting with Paul Samuelson) have tried to attach a more specific, technical definition to the term *public good*.[9] The purpose of such a definition is to differentiate those goods that are public by nature from those that are suitable for private markets. The most common definitions of public goods stress two attributes that seem to characterize many of the goods governments produce: nonexclusivity and nonrivalry.

[9]See Paul A. Samuelson, "The Pure Theory of Public Expenditure", *Review of Economics and Statistics* (November 1954): 387–389. Usually the implication is that governments should not produce private goods because competitive markets will do a better job.

APPLICATION 18.4 *Regulating Power Plant Emissions*

The majority of electric power plants throughout the world burn fossil fuels. This burning results in the emission of a variety of unhealthy by-products. Most important, burning combines the sulfur in coal or oil with oxygen to produce sulfuric acid. This pollutant has been associated with the creation of the "acid rain" that harms the lakes and forests of the eastern United States, Canada, Europe, Russia, and China. Burning of fossil fuels also produces other potentially harmful by-products such as mercury, nitric acid, and carbon dioxide.

Regulation of Production Technology

Most power-plant regulation has followed a "command-and-control" (CAC) approach. Under this approach, air-quality standards are defined by law, and plants are required to install specific equipment that enables them to meet the standards. To achieve the defined goal, most large power plants must install "scrubbers" that clean the exhaust fumes in their stacks. A variety of studies have found that these regulations are not especially cost-effective. A primary reason for the extra costs is the inflexibility of the regulations – plants are not free to adapt the required technology to prevailing meteorological or geographical realities. Studies of cost-effectiveness conclude that, in the United States, costs may have exceeded a least-cost ideal by a factor of two or more.

Emission Charges

An alternative, more efficient approach favoured by many economists would follow Pigou's proposal by imposing a tax on power plants for their harmful emissions. With such a charge, utility owners would be free to choose any technology that promised emissions reductions at a marginal cost that is equal to or less than this charge. Computer simulations of the effect suggest that it would be considerably more cost-effective. Both Japan and France have made significant use of the emissions-charge approach.

Emissions Trading

In Europe, the European Union Emissions Trading Scheme (ETS) was set up in 2005 to cover five industries and take in about 13,000 factories and power stations. For those firms with an energy use above 20 MW/hour, participation is obligatory. For every tonne of CO_2 that a firm emits above its limit it can be finned 40 euros. Since then carbon-trading has expanded with talk for example of Britain and the American state of California linking up in a carbon-trading scheme.

The ETS, however, is an example of how a good theoretical idea, which has potential to ameliorate externalities, can have its "teething" problems when implemented (at least initially). First, the permits, which allow so much carbon to be produced, were handed out to firms rather than auctioned as had been advocated by economists. Less developed countries, who also issue their own permits and which could be used by firms under the Kyoto Agreement were selling their permits for about half the price of the European ones. A classic arbitrage situation arose (buy cheap, sell dear) whereby the polluting firms sold the permits they had received, purchased the cheaper ones from developing countries and kept the difference in price between the two types of permits as profit.

Second, initial estimates of carbon emissions from the industries covered were (it turned out) way off the mark. This has caused the price of the permits to vary, at times, quite dramatically, so making it harder to establish a stable market for the permits and for the industries concerned to plan ahead by weighing the costs of installing cleaner new technologies or simply buying permits that allow more emissions.

Finally, given that cleaner technologies normally require a payback period of at least five years, polluting firms were reluctant to invest in such technology given the ETS was initially set up to run for only three years to 2008. Why invest in new technology to clean up your carbon emissions if the price of carbon emitting permits makes it less costly to buy the permits instead? But if there is uncertainty on the exact details of what will be done by policy makers after 2008 in terms of new permits issued (and hence the price of permits) then perhaps, so the logic goes, better to "wait and see" and put off any investment decisions until the situation is clearer.

(Continued)

A market-based solution is still a very attractive option for cutting CO_2 emissions. However, the lesson here seems to be that implementation requires forethought.

To Think About

1 Would a tax on fossil fuels have the same effects on firms' input and output choices as a tax on emissions themselves? Which taxation scheme would provide the most cost-efficient pollution reduction incentives?

2 Emissions trading credits have sometimes been purchased by environmental groups in order to obtain pollution reductions greater than allowed under the trading regimes. Does this purchasing subvert the efficiency goals of the program?

Nonexclusivity

One property that distinguishes many public goods is whether people may be excluded from the benefits the goods provide. For most private goods, exclusion is indeed possible. I can easily be excluded from consuming a hamburger if I don't pay for it. In some cases, exclusion is either very costly or impossible. National defense is the standard example. Once an army or navy is set up, everyone in a country benefits from its protection whether they pay for it or not. Similar comments apply on a local level to such goods as flood control or inoculation programs against disease. In these cases, once the programs are implemented, all of the residents of a community benefit from them and no one can be excluded from those benefits, regardless of whether he or she pays for them. These **nonexclusive goods** pose problems for markets because people are tempted to "let the other guy do it" and benefit from this person's spending.

Nonexclusive goods Goods that provide benefits that no one can be excluded from enjoying.

Nonrivalry

A second property that characterizes many public goods is nonrivalry. **Nonrival goods** are goods for which benefits can be provided to additional users at zero marginal social cost. For most goods, consumption of additional amounts involves some marginal costs of production. Consumption of one more hot dog, for example, requires that various resources be devoted to its production. For some goods, however, this is not the case. Consider one more automobile crossing a bridge during an off-peak period. Because the bridge is already there anyway, one more vehicle crossing it requires no additional resources and does not reduce consumption of anything else. One more viewer tuning into a television channel involves no additional cost, even though this action would result in additional consumption taking place. Consumption by additional users of such a good is nonrival in that this additional consumption involves zero marginal social costs of production; such consumption does not reduce other people's ability to consume. Again, goods with the nonrival property pose problems for markets because the efficient price (= marginal cost) is zero.

Nonrival goods Goods that additional consumers may use at zero marginal costs.

Categories of Public Goods

The concepts of nonexclusivity and nonrivalry are in some ways related. Many goods that are nonexclusive are also nonrival. National defense and mosquito control are two examples of goods for which exclusion is not possible and for which additional consumption takes place at zero marginal cost. Many other instances might be suggested.

These concepts are not identical. Some goods may possess one property but not the other. It is, for example, impossible (or at least very costly) to exclude some fishing boats from ocean fisheries, yet one more boat imposes social costs in the form of a reduced catch for all concerned. Similarly, use of a bridge during off-peak hours may be nonrival, but it is possible to exclude potential users by erecting toll booths. Table 18-1 presents a cross-classification of goods by their possibilities for exclusion and their rivalry. Several examples of goods that fit into each of the categories are provided. Many of the examples in boxes other than the upper left corner in the table are often produced by the government. Nonrival goods are sometimes privately produced – there are private bridges, swimming pools, and motorways that consumers must pay to use even though this use involves zero marginal cost. Nonpayers can be excluded from consuming these goods, so a private firm may be able to cover its costs.[10] Still, even in this case, the resulting allocation of resources will be inefficient because price will exceed marginal cost.

For simplicity we define **public goods** as having both of the properties listed in Table 18-1. That is, such goods provide nonexclusive benefits and can be provided to one more user at zero marginal cost. Public goods are both nonexclusive and nonrival.

Public goods Goods that are both nonexclusive and nonrival.

Public Goods and Market Failure

The definition of public goods suggests why private markets may not produce them in adequate amounts. For exclusive private goods, the purchaser of that good can appropriate the entire benefits of the good. If Smith eats a pork chop, for example, that means the chop yields no benefits to Jones. The resources used to produce the pork chop can be seen as contributing only to Smith's welfare, and he or she is willing to pay whatever this is worth.

For a public good, this will not be the case. In buying a public good, any one person will not be able to appropriate all the benefits the good offers. Because others cannot be excluded from benefiting from the good and because others can use the good at no cost, society's potential benefits from the public good will exceed the benefits that accrue to any single buyer. However, the purchaser will not take the potential benefits of this purchase to others into account in his or her expenditure decisions. Consequently, private markets will tend to under-allocate resources to public goods. Before starting our general treatment of the topic, it may be useful to look at one type of public good, ideas, that can be produced privately with a little help, as Application 18.5: *Ideas and Public Goods* shows.

TABLE 18-1 Types of Public and Private Goods

		Exclusive: Yes	Exclusive: No
Rival	Yes	Hot dogs, cars, houses	Fishing grounds, public grazing land, clean air
Rival	No	Bridges, swimming pools, scrambled satellite television signal	National defense, flood control, justice, ideas

[10]Nonrival goods that permit imposition of an exclusion mechanism are sometimes referred to as *club goods* since provision of such goods might be organized along the lines of private clubs. Such clubs might then charge a "membership" fee and permit unlimited use by members. The optimal size of a club is determined by the economies of scale present in the production process for the club good. For an analysis, see R. Cornes and T. Sandler, *The Theory of Externalities, Public Goods, and Club Goods* (Cambridge, England: Cambridge University Press, 1986).

APPLICATION 18.5 *Ideas as Public Goods*

Ideas for new products or artistic creations have both of the properties that define public goods. Ideas are nonexclusive because no one can be prevented from using them. They are also nonrival because additional people may use ideas at zero marginal cost. Because of these properties, it seems likely that valuable ideas will be under-produced in a market economy. People will be reluctant to invest time in thinking up new inventions or in developing works of art and literature when they know that others can easily copy their work. This fact is recognized all over the world where individuals or firms may register an invention or a new innovation with a national patent office which then gives them the exclusive use for a temporary period to the patented idea. The disadvantage is that the owner of this property is given what may result in a temporary monopoly in its use. Finding a proper trade-off between these effects has proven to be elusive both in the United States and internationally.[1]

Within Europe ideas can be patented at the European level through the European Patent Office (EPO). Established in 1977 it covers 32 European countries as of March 2007. Once a European patent is granted, there is no need to seek a patent in other countries that are signed up to the EPO. The other two main patent offices are the United States Patent and Trademark Office (USPTO) and the Japan Patent Office (JPO). Known as the Trilateral Offices they work closely together but with interesting differences. With the exception of the USPTO the other two main patent offices use the "first-to-file" system – the person or firm first to file a patent application is granted the patent regardless of who or what firm actually made the initial invention. With the USPTO it is the reverse – as long as you can show you invented "it" first then it is not important if you fail to be the first to patent your invention. As an example of where intellectual property is infringed upon we turn now to music and motion pictures.

Music and Motion Pictures

Music and motion pictures are protected by copyright laws. These laws are intended to provide an economic incentive to individuals who create such works, by enabling them to capture the fruits of their efforts. Copyright law originated in the early eighteenth century and for most of its existence applied mainly to printed works. The advent of recording technologies, especially those that use digital files, has vastly expanded the problems that arise in seeking to enforce the law. Because digital files can be copied at essentially zero marginal cost, creators can easily lose control of their intellectual property. Illegal copying and distribution of music has probably progressed the most rapidly due in part to success of the MP3 format. By some estimates, less than one-third of music files that are transferred among listeners result in royalty payments to artists. DVD files of motion pictures have been following a similar route. Often copies of new motion pictures are available before the films ever appear in cinemas. Major recording and film firms continue to search for both legal and technological fixes to these problems.

To Think About

1. Some economists have suggested that the allocational inefficiencies caused by patent and copyright monopolies might be ameliorated if we instead adopted a system of government-sponsored rewards to inventors and artists. What would be the economic advantage of such a scheme? What would be the major drawbacks?
2. What do you think are the pros and cons of the "first-to-file" and "first-to-invent" systems of patent registration?

[1] For a complete discussion of the issues raised in this application see W. M. Landes and R. A. Posner, *The Economic Structure of Intellectual Property Law* (Cambridge, Mass.: Harvard University Press, 2003). See also the European Patent website (http://www.epo.org/index.html) for more details of the differences between different world-wide patent offices in how they operate and the up and coming patent offices especially in China, South Korea, India, and other emerging economies.

A Graphical Demonstration

One way to show why markets under-allocate resources to public goods is by looking at the demand curve associated with such goods. In the case of a private good, we found the market demand curve (see Chapter 4) by summing people's demands horizontally. At any price, the quantities demanded by each person are summed up to calculate the total quantity demanded in the market. The market demand curve shows the marginal evaluation that people place on an additional unit of output. For a public good (which is provided in about the same quantity to everyone), we must add individual demand curves vertically. To find out how society values some level of public good production, we must ask how each person values this level of output and then add up these valuations.

This idea is represented in Figure 18-4 for a situation with only two people. The total demand curve for the public good is the vertical sum of each person's demand curve. Each point on the curve represents what person 1 and person 2 together are willing to pay for the particular level of public good production. Producing one more unit of the public good would benefit both people because the good is nonexclusive; so, to evaluate this benefit, we must add up what each person would be willing to pay. This is shown in Figure 18-4 by adding what person 1 is willing to pay to what person 2 is willing to pay. In private markets, on the other hand, the production of

FIGURE 18-4 Derivation of the Demand for a Public Good *Because a public good is nonexclusive, the price that people are willing to pay for one more unit (their marginal valuations) is equal to the sum of what each individual would pay. Here person 1's willingness to pay is added vertically to person 2's to get the total demand for the public good.*

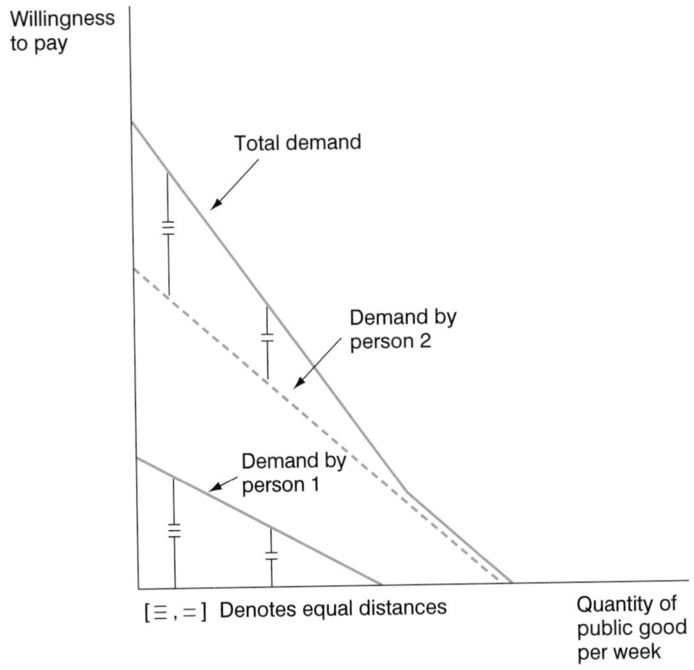

one more unit benefits only the person who ultimately consumes it. Because each person's demand curve in Figure 18-4 is below the total demand for the public good, no single buyer is willing to pay what the good is worth to society as a whole. Therefore, in many cases, private markets may undervalue the benefits of public goods because they take no account of the externalities the goods create. Hence, resources will be under allocated to them.

Solutions to the Public Goods Problem

Because private markets will not allocate resources efficiently to the production of public goods, some other mechanism must be found. Unfortunately, as anyone who tries to organize a picnic (or get his or her children to clean their rooms) quickly discovers, getting people to provide public goods voluntarily is a difficult task. Because people know that they will benefit from the good regardless of whether or not they contribute to its production, everyone will have an incentive to be a **free rider**. That is, they will refrain from contributing to production in the hope that someone else will. In general, this will result in the underproduction of the public good in question.

Free rider A consumer of a nonexclusive good who does not pay for it in the hope that other consumers will.

Nash Equilibrium and Underproduction

One approach that illustrates this underproduction relies on the concept of Nash equilibrium, first introduced in Chapter 6. Consider the situation of two roommates illustrated in Table 18-2. Each roommate may either clean the room or not. A clean room provides more utility than a dirty room to both of the players in this game. But each player would also prefer to have a clean room cleaned by his or her roommate to one in which the cleaning is shared. On the other hand, each roommate prefers a dirty room to one that he or she has had to clean alone. In this game (which resembles the Prisoner's Dilemma game in Chapter 16), the only Nash equilibrium is for neither player to clean the room. Any choice by one player to clean would induce the other to shirk. But this dirty equilibrium is inferior to a situation where both players clean the room – a Pareto improvement that would require some degree of coercion to enforce (or a moral responsibility which can sometimes take time for individuals to develop).

MICROQUIZ 18.4

1. Explain why a public good must have the nonexclusivity feature if free riding is to occur.
2. Would a public good that had the nonrivalry property but not the nonexclusivity property be subject to free riding? Why might such a good be produced at inefficient levels anyway?

TABLE 18-2 Utilities from Room Cleaning: The Nash Equilibrium Underproduces Public Goods

		B's Strategies	
		Clean	Do not clean
A's Strategies	Clean	A:2 B:2	A:0 B:3
	Do not clean	A:3 B:0	A:1 B:1

Compulsory Taxation

Although the room-cleaning example is a trivial one in comparison to issues of public goods production that involve national defense or providing for public health, the nature of the problem is the same for any public good. The free-rider problem is inescapable. Hence, some compulsory mechanism must be found to ensure efficient production. Most often, this solution relies on some form of tax-like measure. That is, members of a group who are expected to benefit from a public good must in some way be forced to pay for it in the optimal amounts. The fact that there can be an efficient equilibrium with compulsory taxation was first illustrated by the Swedish economist Erik Lindahl in 1919. Lindahl's argument can be shown graphically for a society with only two individuals (again, the ever-popular Smith and Jones). In Figure 18-5, the curve labeled *SS* shows Smith's demand for a particular public good. Rather than using the price of the public good on the vertical axis, we instead record the share of a public good's cost that Smith must pay (which varies from 0 per cent to 100 per cent). The negative slope of *SS* indicates that, at a higher tax "price" for the public good, Smith will demand a smaller quantity of it.

Jones's demand for the public good is derived in much the same way. Now, however, we record the proportion paid by Jones on the right-hand vertical axis on Figure 18-5 and reverse the scale so that moving up the axis results in a lower tax price paid. Given this convention, Jones's demand for the public good (*JJ*) has a positive slope.

FIGURE 18-5 Lindahl Equilibrium in the Demand for a Public Good *The curve SS shows that Smith's demand for a public good increases as the tax share that Smith must pay falls. Jones's demand curve for the public good (JJ) is constructed in a similar way. The point C represents a Lindahl equilibrium at which 0E of the public good is supplied, with Smith paying 60 per cent of the cost. Any other quantity of the public good is not an equilibrium since either too much or too little funding would be available.*

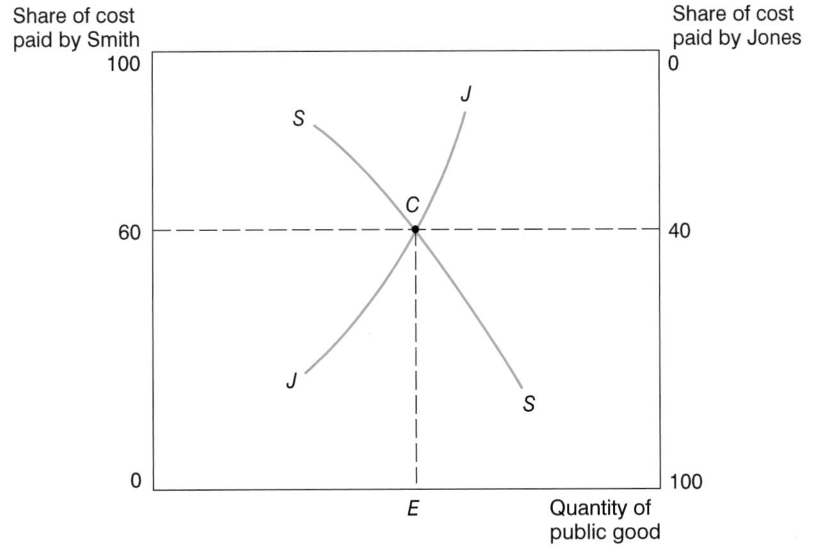

The Lindahl Equilibrium

The two demand curves in Figure 18-5 intersect at C, with an output level of 0*E* for the public good. At this output level, Smith is willing to pay, say, 60 per cent of the good's cost, whereas Jones pays 40 per cent. That point C is an equilibrium is suggested by the following argument. For output levels less than 0*E*, the two people combined are willing to pay more than 100 per cent of the public good's cost. They will vote to increase its level of production (but see the warnings about this statement in the next section). For output levels greater than 0*E*, the people are not willing to pay the total cost of the public good being produced and may vote for reductions in the amount being provided. Only for output level 0*E* is there a **Lindahl equilibrium** where the tax shares precisely pay for the level of public good production undertaken by the government.

Lindahl equilibrium
Balance between people's demand for public goods and the tax shares that each must pay for them.

Not only does this allocation of tax responsibilities result in an equilibrium in people's demands for public goods, but it is also possible to show that this equilibrium is efficient. The tax shares introduced in Lindahl's solution to the public goods problem play the role of "pseudo prices" that mimic the functioning of a competitive price system in achieving efficiency. Unfortunately, for reasons we now examine, this solution is not a particularly practical one.

Revealing the Demand for Public Goods

Although the Lindahl equilibrium is efficient, computation of the optimal tax shares requires knowledge of individuals' demands for public goods. A major problem is how to get people to reveal those demands. In usual market transactions, people reveal their demands by either choosing to buy or not to buy a given product. If I really like Steven Spielberg films, I reveal that by renting them (buying a DVD). By declining to rent (purchase) Oliver Stone films, I reveal that they are not worth the price (though for many other people that is not the case). Getting people to reveal their demands for public goods is much more difficult, however, because of the free-rider problem. If each person knows that his or her tax share will be based on his or her personal demand for public goods, there is a clear incentive to try to hide this true demand. Of course, the government may try any number of clever schemes to try to induce people to show their true preferences; but, often, this proves to be a very frustrating task. Application 18.6: *Fund-Raising on Public Broadcasting* describes one such situation that is probably very familiar to many of you. In the end, any government will probably have to depart from the Lindahl ideal and resort to more pragmatic ways of determining how much will be spent on public goods.

Local Public Goods

Some economists believe that the problem of revealing the demand for public goods may be more tractable on a local than on a national level.[11] Because people are relatively free to move from one locality to another, they may indicate their preferences for local public goods by choosing to live in communities that offer them utility-maximizing public-goods taxation packages. "Voting with one's feet" provides a mechanism for revealing demand for public goods in much the same way that "currency voting" reveals

[11]See C. M. Tiebout, "A Pure Theory of Local Expenditures", *Journal of Political Economy* (October 1956): 416–424.

APPLICATION 18.6 *Fund-Raising on Public Broadcasting*

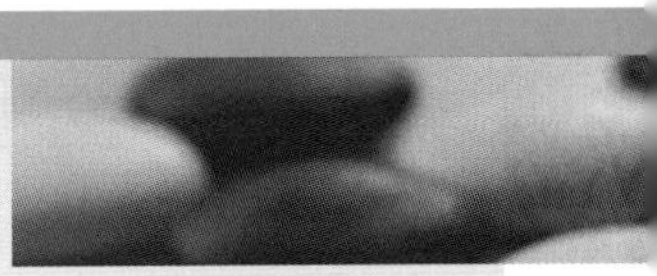

The creation of public radio and television broadcasting corporations in the United States in the 1960s was viewed as a revolution in media design. Rather than being financed solely by taxes (as is the case in many other countries), public radio and television in the United States were intended to be supported in large part by their listeners and viewers through voluntary contributions.

Is Public Broadcasting a Public Good?

Over-the-air television and radio broadcasting would seem to meet the definition of a public good. Broadcasting is nonexclusive in that no listener or viewer can be excluded for using what is "on the air". And the good is nonrival because costs are not increased if an additional user tunes in. However, thriving commercial markets in both television and radio should raise some caution in jumping to the conclusion that such broadcasting is necessarily underproduced in private markets.

It is the complementary relationship between advertising and broadcasting that mitigates the problems raised by the public-good nature of broadcasting. Viewed as a mechanism for delivering advertising messages, broadcasting is both exclusive (those who do not pay cannot advertise) and rival (when one advertiser buys a time slot, no one else can use it). Hence, a general underprovision of broadcasting seems unlikely. Instead, the rationale for public broadcasting must rest on the notion that certain types of programming (e.g., children's, cultural, or public affairs) will be unattractive to advertisers and will therefore be underprovided in private markets.[1] It is this type of programming that was intended to be supported through government grants and voluntary public contributions.

The Consequences of Free Riders

Unfortunately, the free rider problem common to most public goods has tended to undermine this voluntary support. By most estimates, fewer than 10 per cent of the viewers of public television make voluntary contributions. Approximately the same percentage applies to public radio as well.[2] Although the broadcasters have tried to encourage contributions through extensive fund-raising campaigns and more subtle pressures to make non-contributors feel guilty, these have met with, at best, partial success. Hence, public broadcasting has had to turn increasingly to advertising – a funding source that was originally considered to be contrary to its philosophy. Today, most public television shows are preceded by a series of short advertising messages and the viewer is reminded of these at the end of the show. Public radio has been under somewhat less pressure to advertise, but in this case too the time devoted to advertising has been lengthening in recent years.

Technology and Public Television

The situation of public television has been aggravated in recent years by the spread of cable television. Because cable access substantially increases the number of viewing options, the notion that there are untapped areas of viewer preferences that public broadcasting might serve has become increasingly dubious. Public television shows have become indistinguishable from those offered by such commercial cable networks as A&E, The Learning Channel, History Channel, and House and Garden Television. Indeed, these new networks have been increasingly competing with public television for the same shows, drawing several popular offerings into the commercial venue. Voluntary support for public television has been declining (at least in some areas) and the long-run viability of this "public good" remains in doubt.

To Think About

1 Is there a conflict between what advertisers will support and what viewers wish to see on television? Does the support mechanism for public broadcast mitigate these conflicts?

2 In many countries, public broadcasting is supported through direct taxation. Does this solve the problem of free riders? How would you determine whether such direct government support improves welfare?

---

[1]Judging whether the market would have provided such programming is difficult because public broadcasting can also crowd out private options. For a discussion, see S. T. Berry and J. Waldfogel, "Public Radio in the United States: Does It Correct Market Failure or Cannibalize Commercial Stations?", *Journal of Public Economics* (February 1999): 189–211.

[2]For a discussion of direct evidence on free riding in public radio, see E. J. Brunner, "Free Riders or Easy Riders? An Examination of Voluntary Provision of Public Radio", *Public Choice* (December 1998): 587–604.

demand for private goods. People who want high-quality schools or a high level of police protection can "pay" for them by choosing to live in highly taxed communities. Those who prefer not to receive such benefits can choose to live elsewhere. These observations suggest that some decentralization of government functions may be desirable.

Voting for Public Goods

Voting is used to decide questions about the production and financing of public goods in many institutions. In some instances, people vote directly on policy questions. That is the case in New England town meetings (a region within the United States) and many other American statewide referenda and for many of the public policies adopted in Switzerland. Direct voting also characterizes the social decision procedure used for many smaller groups and clubs such as farmers' cooperatives, university faculties, or the local Rotary Club. In other cases, societies have found it more convenient to utilize a representative form of government in which people directly vote only for political representatives, who are then charged with making decisions on policy questions.

To study how decisions about public goods are made, we begin with an analysis of direct voting. Direct voting is important, not only because such a procedure may apply to some cases but also because elected representatives often engage in direct voting (such as the European Parliament), and the theory we illustrate applies to those instances also. Later in the chapter, we take up special problems of representative government.

Majority Rule

Because so many elections or votes are conducted by majority rule, we often tend to regard that procedure as a natural and, perhaps, optimal one for making social choices. But a quick examination suggests that there is nothing particularly sacred about a rule requiring that a policy obtain 50 per cent of the vote to be adopted. In the European Union, for example, the countries that comprise the European Union have 345 votes distributed between them with the Council of Europe. The votes of each country are roughly proportional to their respective populations. For those decisions that do not require unanimity, then at least two-thirds of member countries must vote for the proposal and roughly 74 per cent of all possible votes must be cast in favor of the proposal. (Given the fluidity of European Union politics no doubt the above will change in due course. However, the point remains as regards the so-called "natural" cross-over boundary of 50 per cent).

Our discussion of the Lindahl equilibrium concept suggests that there does indeed exist a distribution of tax shares that would obtain unanimous support in voting for public goods. But arriving at such unanimous agreements poses difficult information problems and may be subject to strategic ploys and free rider behavior by the voters involved. To examine in detail the forces that lead societies to move away from unanimity and to choose some other determining fraction would take us too far afield here. We instead assume throughout our discussion of voting that decisions are made by majority rule. You may be able to think of some situations that might call for a decisive proportion other than 50 per cent.

The Paradox of Voting

In the 1780s, the French social theorist M. de Condorcet observed an important peculiarity of majority-rule voting systems – they may not arrive at a clear decision but instead may cycle among alternative options. Condorcet's paradox is illustrated for a simple case in Table 18-3. Suppose there are three voters (Smith, Jones, and Fudd) choosing among three policy options. These policy options represent three levels of spending on a particular public good (*A* = low, *B* = medium, and *C* = high). Preferences of Smith, Jones, and Fudd among the three policy options are indicated by the order listed in the table. For example, Smith prefers option *A* to option *B* and option *B* to option *C*, but Jones prefers option *B* to option *C* and option *C* to option *A*. The preferences described in Table 18-3 give rise to Condorcet's paradox.

Consider a vote between options *A* and *B*. Option *A* would win, because it is favored by Smith and Fudd and opposed only by Jones. In a vote between options *A* and *C*, option *C* would win, again by two votes to one. But in a vote of option *C* versus option *B*, the previously defeated option *B* would win, and consequently social choices would cycle. In subsequent elections, any choice that was initially decided upon could later be defeated by an alternative, and no decision would ever be reached. In this situation, the option finally chosen will depend on such seemingly unimportant issues as when the balloting stops or how items are ordered on an agenda rather than being derived in some rational way from the preferences of voters.

Single-Peaked Preferences and the Median Voter Theorem

Condorcet's voting paradox arises because of the degree of irreconcilability in the preferences of voters. We might ask whether restrictions on the types of preferences allowed might yield situations where stable voting outcomes are more likely. A fundamental result about this probability was discovered by Duncan Black in 1948.[12] Black showed that stable voting outcomes can always occur in cases where the issue being voted upon is one-dimensional (such as how much to spend on public goods) and where voters' preferences are "single-peaked".

To understand what *single-peaked* means, consider again Condorcet's paradox. In Figure 18-6, we illustrate the preferences that gave rise to the paradox by assigning hypothetical utility levels to options *A*, *B*, and *C* that are consistent with the preferences recorded in Table 18-3. For Smith and Jones, preferences are single-peaked – as levels of public goods' expenditures rise, there is only one local utility-maximizing choice (*A* for Smith, *B* for Jones). Fudd's preferences, on the other hand, have two local peaks (*A* and *C*). It is these preferences that produced the

TABLE 18-3 Preferences That Produce the Paradox of Voting

Voter	Order of preferences		
Smith	*A*	*B*	*C*
Jones	*B*	*C*	*A*
Fudd	*C*	*A*	*B*

A = Low-spending policy. B = Medium-spending policy. C = High-spending policy.

[12]Duncan Black, "On the Rationale of Group Decision Making", *Journal of Political Economy* (February 1948): 23–24.

cyclical voting pattern. If, instead, Fudd had preferences represented by the dashed line in Figure 18-6 (where *C* is now the only local peak), there would be no paradox. In that case, option *B* would be chosen, since that option would defeat both *A* and *C* by votes of two to one. Here, *B* is the preferred choice of the *median voter* (Jones), whose preferences are "between" the preferences of Smith and the opposing preferences of Fudd.

Black's result is quite general and applies to any number of voters. If choices are one-dimensional and preferences are single-peaked, majority rule will result in selection of that project that is most favored by the **median voter**. Therefore, that voter's preference will determine what social choices are made.

Median voter A voter whose preferences for a public good represent the middle point of all voters' preferences for the good.

Voting and Efficient Resource Allocation

Voting does in fact determine the allocation of resources to the production of public goods in many cases. The important economic question is whether that allocation is efficient or whether it results in misallocations that might be as bad as leaving the production of public goods to private markets. Unfortunately, economists have found relatively little correspondence between the efficient allocations called for by the Lindahl approach to public goods demand and the actual allocations that will be adopted under a median-voter approach. For example, virtually every Western country has seen an increase in the share of GDP devoted to the production of public goods since World War II. Undoubtedly, this reflects, at least in part, the attitudes of the median voters in these countries; but there is no agreement among economists about whether this trend reflects a move toward greater efficiency as previously unmet demands for public goods are satisfied or some failure in voting mechanisms that causes public goods to be overproduced.

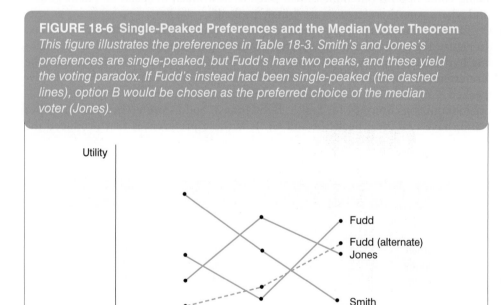

FIGURE 18-6 Single-Peaked Preferences and the Median Voter Theorem
This figure illustrates the preferences in Table 18-3. Smith's and Jones's preferences are single-peaked, but Fudd's have two peaks, and these yield the voting paradox. If Fudd's instead had been single-peaked (the dashed lines), option B would be chosen as the preferred choice of the median voter (Jones).

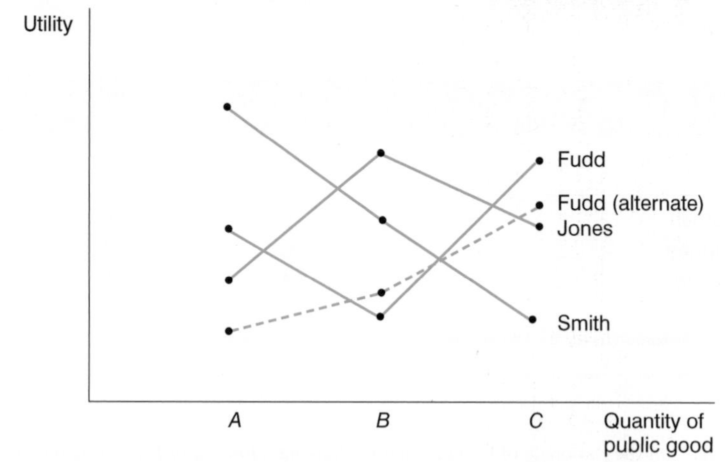

APPLICATION 18.7 *Where There's Muck There's Brass*

Externalities can be seen as either positive or negative. Here we present an example of an externality that is both positive and negative at the same time . . . depending on your perspective! When horse transportation was the main way of getting around and of transporting goods an unavoidable negative externality for those who got around on foot and had to cross streets was the horse excrement that resulted from this mode of transportation. Getting your feet stuck on this material or having to endure the smell at the height of the summer was not pleasant at all.

On the other hand, for farmers or the keen gardener such manure or dung could aid the growth of crops and plants no end. In the absence of cheap, mass-produced fertilizers one could think of manure as an "organic fertilizer". The reader will, no doubt, rest easy in their bed tonight to know that a 450 kg horse (about 1000 lbs) produces about 8.16 metric tonnes (9 imperial tons) of manure each year. This is high in nitrogen, phosphorous, and potassium, all needed for growing crops. For the farmer then, manure was a positive externality from

FIGURE 1 Where There's Muck There's Brass . . .[1]

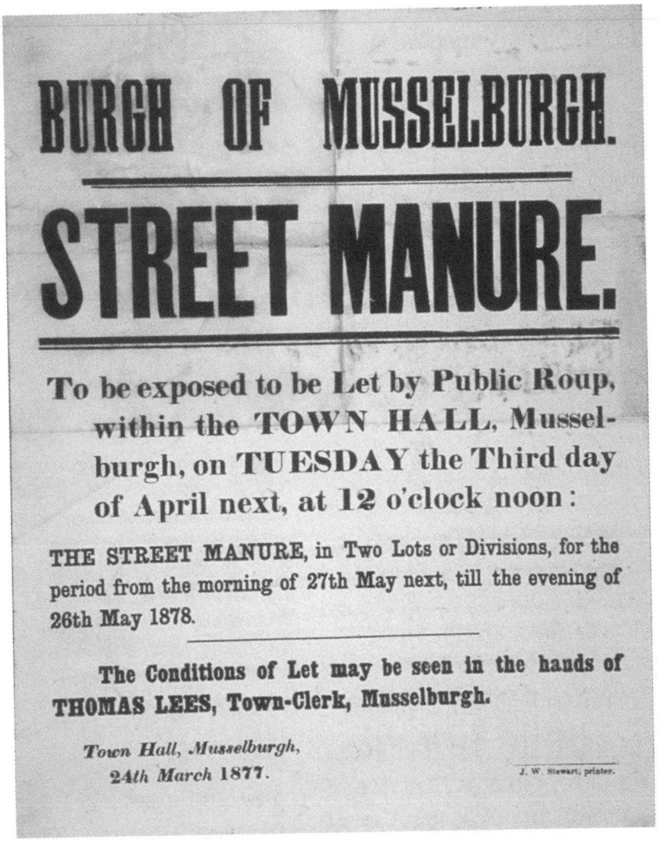
BURGH OF MUSSELBURGH.

STREET MANURE.

To be exposed to be Let by Public Roup, within the TOWN HALL, Musselburgh, on TUESDAY the Third day of April next, at 12 o'clock noon:

THE STREET MANURE, in Two Lots or Divisions, for the period from the morning of 27th May next, till the evening of 26th May 1878.

The Conditions of Let may be seen in the hands of THOMAS LEES, Town-Clerk, Musselburgh.

Town Hall, Musselburgh,
24th March 1877.

J. W. Stewart, printer.

SOURCE: © EAST LOTHIAN MUSEUMS SERVICE. LICENSOR WWW.SCRAN.AC.UK.

the economic activity of transportation and not a negative one.

As can be seen from Figure 1 such a positive externality had (and still does) have a market value. Here in the little Scottish town of Musselburgh in May 1878 a public auction was to take place by public roup. Roup here does not mean a disease in chicken (as it can) but auction by public outcry.

However, it is not just with horse manure that negative externalities to one can become positive externalities to another. A very interesting (almost entertaining) article by Ralph Turvey explores economic growth and refuse in London in the 19th and 20th centuries. The reader is encouraged to read the full article.[2]

Even dog shit (yes you read correctly), known as "pure" from its purifying and cleansing properties, had its uses. It was sold by the bucketful to Bermondsey (a district of London) tanners who used it in the manufacture of morocco and kid leather.

What is interesting from Mr Turvey's article is how technological development affected the development of household waste and hence negative externalities.

> *One such factor was the growing use of disposable packaging. In 1860, the first paper bag machine was invented. In the 1895 edition of Mrs Beeton's Book of Household Management, it was noted that the widespread use of tinned provisions had sprung up within the last quarter of a century. In 1885, Lever introduced the branded, heavily advertised and wrapped Sunlight Soap, soap having hitherto been sold by the grocer cutting and weighing a piece off a large bar. Then, in 1889, the principle of the folding box or carton was introduced from the United States by Parmenter, who got his first order for 100 000 cartons for Murray's Caramels. He subsequently made cartons for eggs, butter and Robertson's Table Jelly. Huntley and Palmers of Reading introduced wrapping biscuits in paper packets until 1905.*
>
> (Page 11 of Mr Harvey's article)

The ash from coal fires was also used in the manufacture of bricks. As Turvey remarks, "London refuse was thus used for growth as well as resulting from it. While the cities of the ancient world were built in successive layers on the ashes of previous generations, nineteenth and early twentieth century London was built with the ashes of current generations." However, with the advent of gas heating and cooking this went into decline.

To Think About

1 It is mentioned in the application that technological progress contributed to refuse increase in the 19th century. How might economic growth contribute *or* lessen household waste? [*Hint*: Think of the sale of second-hand clothes for example.]

2 The public auction in Musselburgh for the right to collect street manure was conducted by public outcry. Bidders would presumably know how much they could get from local farmers for each kilo of dung they collected. They might even have been able to work out how much it would cost the council, and also themselves, to clear the streets of Musselburgh of dung. The council presumably knew this information as well. What does this imply about the range of possible bids that would be shouted out? Is the open-outcry auction the best method for maximizing revenue in this case?

---

[1] "Where there's muck there's brass" is a 20th century expression that originated in Yorkshire, England where the word brass is still used as a slang term for money. The meaning is that where there are dirty jobs to be done, then there is money to be made. Further, lest the good people of Musselburgh be offended at their town being highlighted with the subject of manure it should be noted the town is more famous, or perhaps should be more famous, as having the oldest existing golf course in the world.

> *Golf has been played in Scotland at least from the 15th century. Documents show that golf has been played in East Lothian* (the district where Musselburgh is located – Authors) *since the 17th century with evidence that it was present the century before. The Earl of Moray accused Mary Queen of Scots (1542–1587) of playing golf at Seton House in Musselburgh in 1567 (a few days after the murder of her husband, Lord Darnley). The oldest existing course in the county is Musselburgh Links – The Old Course (dating from at least 1672). The Honourable Company of Edinburgh Golfers (now at Muirfield) has records going back to 1744, which makes it the earliest known golf club in the world (ten years before The Society Club of St. Andrews Golfers was established).*

See http://www.scotlandsgolfholidays.co.uk/history.aspx. Accessed 16 September 2007.

[2] Ralph Turvey, "Economic Growth and Domestic Refuse in London," from *LSE on Social Science: A Century Anthology* (1996), LSE Books.

One of the primary problems with voting for public goods as a method of allocating resources is simply that votes by themselves do not provide enough information for achieving efficient resource allocation. Because resources have real costs, any proper allocational mechanism must in some way reveal the willingness of people to pay those costs. But voting does not offer voters any way to indicate the intensity with which they desire specific public goods. Nor are the options presented to voters usually very explicit about potential trade-offs involved in choosing one good over another. Economists and political scientists have proven to be quite innovative in dreaming up more informative voting schemes that give people some say on how strongly they feel about public spending options. But none of these, so far, has been especially effective in getting people to reveal their demands for public goods. The market mechanism has proven to be a remarkably effective way of gathering this sort of information with regard to allocating resources to the production of private goods, but it has been much more difficult to find a similarly effective method for allocations to public goods.

Representative Government and Bureaucracies

In large, complex societies, the problem of allocating resources to public-goods production is made even more complex by the necessity of operating many governmental functions through representative legislative bodies or through administrative bureaucracies. Both elected representatives and people who work in government departments can be viewed as agents for voters who are the ultimate demanders of public goods. But, as in any principal/agent relationship, there may be important differences in motives between voters and the people they have chosen to represent them. As was the case in the situations we studied in Chapter 17, agents may be able to take advantage of the informational asymmetries between themselves and the principals they represent (here, the voters) in ways that increase their own utility but distort the allocation of resources away from the voters' true demands for public goods. Hence, just as private markets may fail to provide efficient allocations in the presence of public goods, so too may governments fail in the provision of such goods. For example, many economic actors may find it in their interests to use the government to obtain monopoly gains for themselves that would not otherwise be obtainable without government help. They may, for example, enlist the government's aid in limiting competition in their markets or they may seek spending that benefits them alone. Through such **rent-seeking behavior** they may be able to get governmental agents to distort the allocations of resources away from what the voters would actually prefer if their preferences could be measured directly. To study all of the ways in which this might happen would, however, take us far beyond the intended subject matter of this book.

Rent-seeking behavior
Firms or individuals influencing government policy to increase their own welfare.

SUMMARY

We began this chapter with a demonstration of the misallocation of resources that may be created by an externality. We then proceeded to look at a number of consequences of this observation.

- When transactions costs are low and property rights are fully specified, no governmental intervention may be required to cope with an externality. Private negotiations between the parties may result in an efficient allocation regardless of how the property rights are assigned (the Coase theorem).

- Some externalities, such as those associated with environmental pollution, involve high transactions costs. In this case, legal redress or governmental intervention may be required to achieve an efficient allocation (although intervention does not guarantee such a result).
- The traditional method for correcting the allocational harm of an externality, first proposed by A. C. Pigou, is to impose an optimal tax on the firm creating the externality.
- Environmental regulation can proceed through the use of fees, pollution permits, or direct control. In the simplest case, these can have identical outcomes. In actuality, however, the incentives incorporated under each may yield quite different results.
- Pure public goods have the property of nonexclusivity and nonrivalry – once the good is produced, no one can be excluded from receiving the benefits it provides, but additional people may benefit from the good at zero cost. These properties pose a problem for private markets because people will not freely choose to purchase public goods in economically efficient amounts. Resources may be under-allocated to public goods.
- In theory, compulsory taxation can be used to provide public goods in efficient quantities by charging taxpayers what the goods are worth to each of them. However, measuring this demand may be very difficult because each person has an incentive to act as a free rider by understating his or her demands.
- Direct voting may produce paradoxical results. However, in some cases, majority rule will result in the adoption of policies favored by the median voter.

REVIEW QUESTIONS

1 If one firm raises the costs of another firm by bidding against it for its inputs, that is not an externality by our definition. But, if a firm raises the costs of another firm by polluting the environment, that is an externality. Explain the distinction between these two situations. Why does the second lead to an inefficient allocation of resources but the first does not?

2 Our general definition of economic efficiency focuses on mutually beneficial transactions. Explain why the presence of externalities may result in some mutually beneficial transactions being forgone. Illustrate these using Figure 18-1.

3 The proof of the Coase theorem requires that firms recognize both the explicit and implicit costs of their decision. Explain a situation where a firm's failure to curtail pollution may cause it to incur implicit costs. Why is the assumption of zero bargaining costs crucial if the firm is to take account of these costs?

4 Explain why the level of emissions control R^* in Figure 18-3 is economically efficient. Why would the levels of abatement given by R_L and R_H result in inefficiency? What kinds of inefficient trades would be occurring at these levels of abatement?

5 Figure 18-3 shows that an emissions fee can be chosen that attains the same level of pollution reduction as does direct control. Explain why firms would make the same choices under either control method. Would this equivalence necessarily hold if government regulators did not know the true marginal costs of emissions control?

6 For each of the following goods, explain whether it possesses the nonexclusive property, the nonrival property, or both. If the good does not have the characteristics of a public good but is, nevertheless, produced by the government, can you explain why?

a Television receivers

b Over-the-air television transmissions

c Cable television transmissions

d Elementary education

e University education

f Electric power

g Delivery of first-class mail

h Low-income housing within the South East of England

7 The Lindahl solution to the public-goods problem promises economic efficiency on a voluntary basis. Why would each person voluntarily agree to the tax assessments determined under the Lindahl solution? What choice is he or she being asked to make?

8 Why is the "paradox of voting" a paradox? What, if anything, is undesirable about a voting scheme that cycles? How will issues be decided in such cases?

9 "Under perfect competition, voting with euros achieves economic efficiency, but democratic voting (one person–one vote) offers no such promise." Do you agree? Why does the specification of one vote per person interfere with the ability to achieve economic efficiency? Is it an issue with regard to efficiency that under perfect competition some people have more euros (and so more votes) than other people?

10 Why would individuals or firms engage in rent-seeking behavior? How much will they spend on such behavior? Are there externalities associated with rent seeking?

PROBLEMS

18.1 A firm in a perfectly competitive industry has patented a new process for making widgets. The new process lowers the firm's average costs, meaning this firm alone (although still a price taker) can earn real economic profits in the long run.

a If the market price is €20 per widget and the firm's marginal cost curve is given by $MC = 0.4q$, where q is the daily widget production for the firm, how many widgets will the firm produce?

b Suppose a government study has found that the firm's new process is polluting the air and the study estimates the social marginal cost of widget production by this firm to be $MCS = 0.5q$. If the market price is still €20, what is the socially optimal level of production for the firm? What should the amount of a government-imposed excise tax be in order to bring about this optimal level of production?

18.2 On the island of Pago-Pago, there are two lakes and 20 fishermen. Each fisherman gets to fish on either lake and gets to keep the average catch on that lake. On Lake X, the total number of fish caught is given by

$$F^X = 10L_X - \frac{1}{2}L_X^2$$

where L_X is the number of fishers on the lake. The amount an additional fisher will catch is $MP_X = 10 - L_X$. For Lake Y, the relationship is

$$F^Y = 5L_Y$$

a Under this organization of society, what will the total number of fish caught be? Explain the nature of the externality in this equilibrium.

b The chief of Pago-Pago, having once read an economics book, believes that she can raise the total number of fish caught by restricting the number of fishers allowed on Lake X. What is the correct number of fishers on Lake X to allow in order to maximize the total catch of fish? What is the number of fish caught in this situation?

c Being basically opposed to coercion, the chief decides to require a fishing license for Lake X. If the licensing procedure is to bring about the optimal allocation of labor, what should the cost of a license be (in terms of fish)?

18.3 Suppose that the oil industry in Utopia is perfectly competitive and that all firms draw oil from a single (and practically inexhaustible) pool. Each competitor believes that he or she can sell all the oil he or she can produce at a stable world price of \$10 per barrel and that the cost of operating a well for one year is \$1000. Total output per year (Q) of the oil field is a function of the number of wells (N) operating in the field. In particular,

$$Q = 500N - N^2$$

and the amount of oil produced by each well (q) is given by

$$q = \frac{Q}{N} = 500 - N$$

The output from the Nth well is given by

$$MP_N = 500 - 2N$$

a Describe the equilibrium output and the equilibrium number of wells in this perfectly competitive case. Is there a divergence between private and social marginal cost in the industry?

b Suppose that the government nationalizes the oil field. How many oil wells should it operate? What will total output be? What will the output per well be?

c As an alternative to nationalization, the Utopian government is considering an annual license fee per well to discourage over-drilling. How large should this license fee be to prompt the industry to drill the optimal number of wells?

18.4 Mr Wile E. Coyote purchases a variety of equipment with which to catch roadrunners. Invariably he finds that the equipment fails to work as promised. For example, the roadrunner rocket pack he purchased misfired and pushed him backwards over a steep cliff, the roadrunner flamethrower only singed his whiskers, and the spring-mounted net ended up capturing him instead of the roadrunner.

a Show how the Coase theorem would apply to transactions between predators and companies manufacturing roadrunner-catching equipment. In the full information case, would the equipment have efficient operating characteristics regardless of how legal liability is defined?

b Many predators, including Mr Coyote, are rather careless in how they use their equipment. If this carelessness is not affected by assignment of legal liability and if it is fully understood by producers, would its presence change your answer to part a?

c Suppose predators became even more careless when they knew manufacturers would have legal liability for any injuries. How would this affect your answer to part a?

d Assume that a single firm (the famous Acme Manufacturing Company) has a monopoly in the supply of roadrunner-catching equipment. How, if at all, would this change your answer to part a?

(Note: This question was motivated by the great comic essay by Ian Frazier, *Coyote v. Acme*, New York: Farrar, Straus, and Giroux, 1996.)

18.5 As an illustration of the apple–bee externality, suppose that a beekeeper is located next to a 20-acre apple orchard. Each hive of bees is capable of pollinating $\frac{1}{4}$ acre of apple trees, thereby raising the value of apple output by €25.

a Suppose the market value of the honey from one hive is €50 and that the beekeeper's marginal costs are given by

$$MC = 30 + 0.5Q$$

where Q is the number of hives employed. In the absence of any bargaining, how many hives will the beekeeper have and what portion of the apple orchard will be pollinated?

b What is the maximum amount per hive the orchard owner would pay as a subsidy to the beekeeper to prompt him or her to install extra hives? Will the owner have to pay this much to prompt the beekeeper to use enough hives to pollinate the entire orchard?

18.6 A government study has concluded that the marginal benefits from controlling cow-induced methane production are given by

$$MB = 100 - R$$

where R represents the percentage reduction from unregulated levels. The marginal cost to farmers of methane reduction (through better cow feed) is given by

$$MC = 20 + R$$

a What is the socially optimal level of methane reduction?

b If the government were to adopt a methane fee that farmers must pay for each per cent of methane they do not reduce, how should this fee be set to achieve the optimal level of R?

c Suppose there are two farmers in this market with differing costs of methane reduction. The first has marginal costs given by

$$MC_1 = 20 + \frac{2}{3}R_1$$

whereas the second has marginal costs given by

$$MC_2 = 20 + 2R_2$$

Total methane reduction is the average from these two farms. If the government mandates that each farm reduce methane by the optimal amount calculated in part a, what will the overall reduction be and what will this reduction cost (assuming there are no fixed costs to reducing methane)?

d Suppose, instead, that the government adopts the methane fee described in part b. What will be the total reduction in methane and what will this reduction cost?

e Explain why part c and part d yield different results.

18.7 Suppose there are only two people in society. The demand curve for person A for rat infestation control is given by

$$q_A = 100 - P$$

For person B, the demand curve for rat infestation control is given by

$$q_B = 200 - P$$

a Suppose rat infestation control is a nonexclusive good – that is, once it is produced everyone benefits from it. What would be the optimal level of this activity if it could be produced at a constant marginal cost of €50 per unit?

b If rat infestation control were left to the private market, how much might be produced? Does your answer depend on what each person assumes the other will do?

c If the government were to produce the optimal amount of rat infestation control, how much would this cost? How should the tax bill for this amount be allocated between the individuals if they are to share it in proportion to benefits received from rat infestation control?

18.8 Suppose there are three people in society who vote on whether the government should undertake specific projects. Let the net benefits of a particular project be €150, €140, and €50 for persons A, B, and C, respectively.

a If the project costs €300 and these costs are to be shared equally, would a majority vote to undertake the project? What would be the net benefits to each person under such a scheme? Would total net benefits be positive?

b Suppose the project cost €375 and again costs were to be shared equally. Now would a majority vote for the project and total net benefits be positive?

c Suppose (presumably contrary to fact) votes can be bought and sold in a free market. Describe what kinds of results you might expect in part a and part b.

18.9 The town of Pleasantville is thinking of building a swimming pool. Building and operating the pool will cost the town €5000 per day. There are three groups of potential pool users in Pleasantville: (1) 1000 families who are each willing to pay €3 per day for the pool; (2) 1000 families who are each willing to pay €2 per day for the pool; and (3) 1000 families who are each willing to pay €1 per day for the pool. Suppose also that the intended pool is large enough so that whatever number of families come on any day will not affect what people are willing to pay for the pool.

a Which property of public goods does this pool have? Which does it not have?

b Would building the pool be an efficient use of resources?

c Consider four possible prices for family admission to the pool: (1) €3; (2) €2; (3) €1; and (4) €0. Which of these prices would result in covering the cost of the pool? Which of the prices would achieve an efficient allocation of resources?

d Is there any pricing scheme for admission to this pool that would both cover the pool's cost and achieve an efficient allocation of resources?

e Suppose that this pool has a capacity of only 2000 families per day. If more than 2000 families are admitted, the willingness to pay of any family (with children or not) falls to €0.50 per day. Now what is the efficient pricing scheme for the pool?

18.10 The demand for Starburst fruit chews is given by

$$Q = 200 - 100P$$

and these confections can be produced at a constant marginal cost of €0.50.

a How much will Sweettooth, Inc., be willing to pay in bribes to obtain a monopoly concession from the government for Starburst fruit chews production?

b Do the bribes represent a welfare cost from rent seeking?

c What is the welfare cost of this rent-seeking activity?

SOLUTIONS TO ODD-NUMBERED PROBLEMS

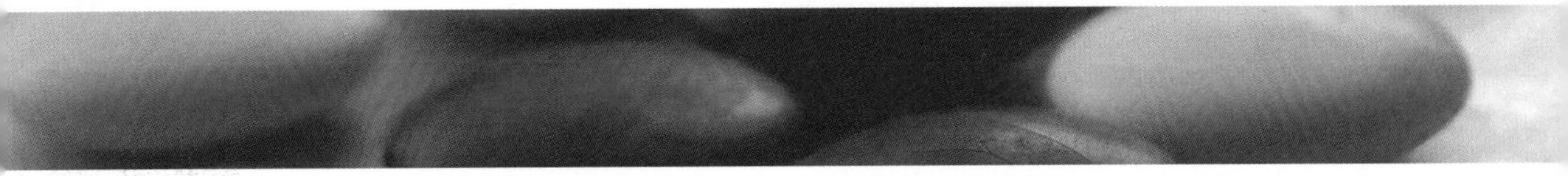

This section contains solutions to all of the odd-numbered problems in the text. Solutions to all of the text problems are contained in the *Instructor's Manual*.

Chapter 1

1.1 a

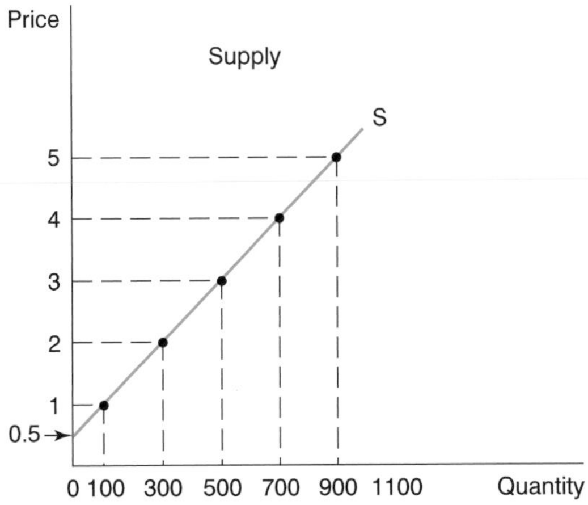

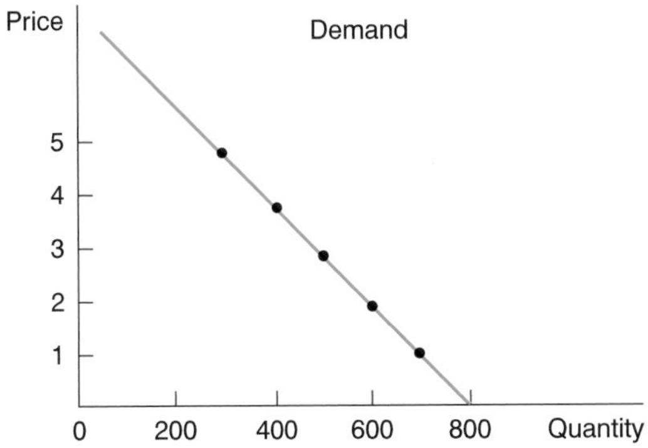

b The supply points seem to be on a straight line. Use

$$\frac{\Delta Q}{\Delta P} = 200.$$ So, $Q = a + 200P$. At $P = 1$, $Q = 100$ this implies $a = -100$. So the final supply equation is $Q_S = -100 + 200P$. Applying the same logic to the demand data yields $Q_D = 800 - 100P$.

c If $P = 0$, $Q_S = -100$ (= 0 because can't have negative supply), $Q_D = 800$, $ED = 800$.

d If $P = 6$, $Q_S = 1100$, $Q_D = 200$, $ES = 900$.

1.3 a

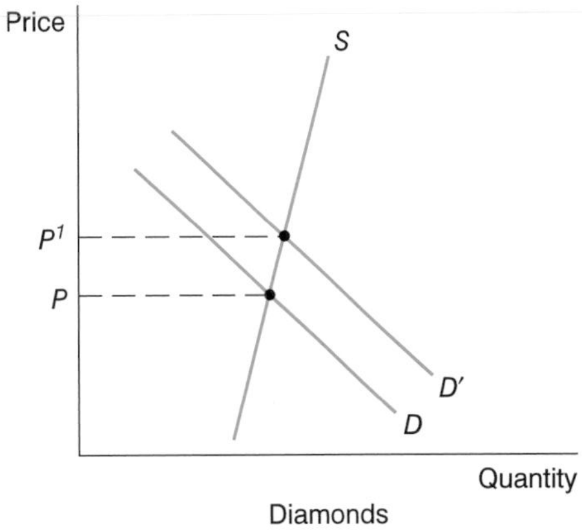

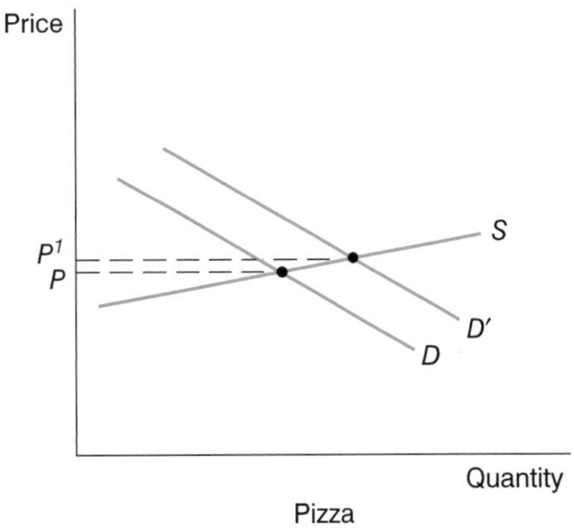

b For diamond suppliers the shift in demand causes costs to rise significantly. For pizza suppliers the rise is only modest even though the increase in demand is of roughly the same magnitude.

c $PD = a + bQD$. Where the subscript D represents diamonds, a and b are coefficients and P and Q have their normal meaning. This implies $QD = PD/b - a/b$ and $PP = c + dQP$. Where the subscript P represents pizzas, c and d are coefficients and P and Q have their normal meaning. This implies $QP - PP/d - c/d$. Given the shape of the supply curves that were derived in part a of the question, we need the supply curve of diamonds to be steeply sloped. That is, the coefficient on price for diamonds ($1/b$) should be small (shallow slope) and the coefficient on price for pizzas ($1/d$) should be large (steep slope).

1.5

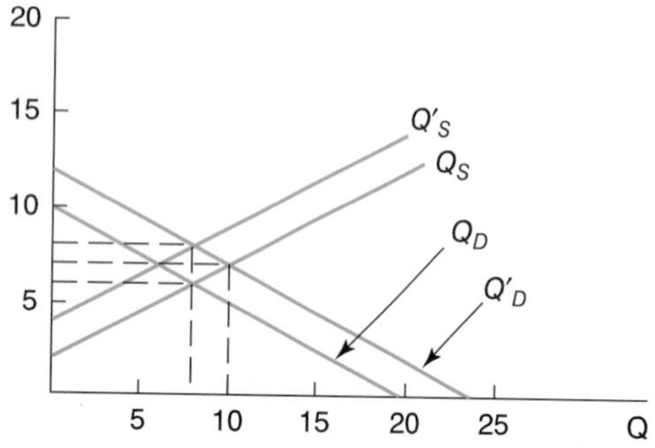

The algebraic solution proceeds as follows:

a $Q_D = -2P + 20$.
$Q_S = 2P - 4$.
Set $Q_D = Q_S$: $-2P + 20 = 2P - 4$
$24 = 4P$
$P = 6$.
Substituting for P gives: $Q_D = Q_S = 8$.

b Now $Q_D' = -2P + 24$.
Set $Q_D = Q_S$: $-2P + 24 = 2P - 4$
$28 = 4P$
$P = 7$.
Substituting gives: $Q_D = Q_S = 10$.

c $P = 8$, $Q = 8$ (see graph).

1.7 a

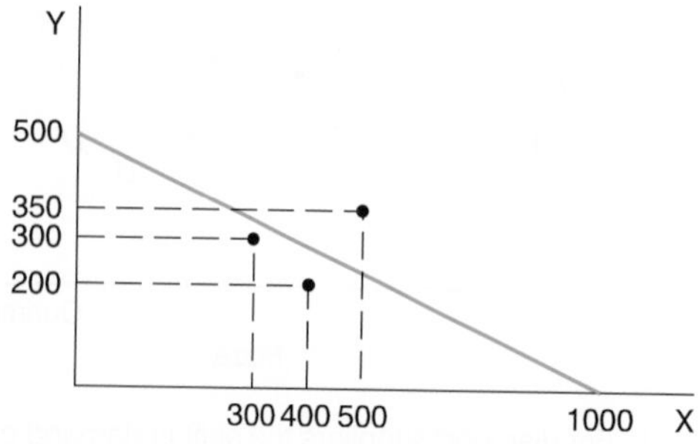

b Both these points lie below the frontier.

c This point lies beyond the frontier.

d Opportunity cost of $1Y$ is $2X$ no matter how much is produced.

1.9 a $X^2 + 4Y^2 = 100$.
If $X = Y$, then $5X^2 = 100$, and $X = \sqrt{20}$ and $Y = \sqrt{20}$.

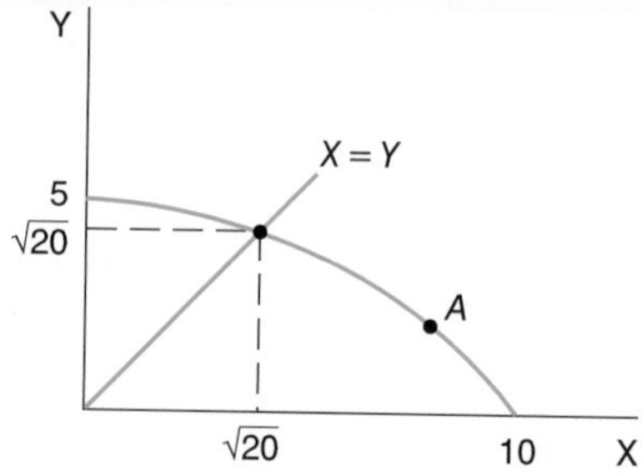

b If only X is produced, $X = 10$. So can trade any combination for which $X + Y = 10$.

c Because consumers wish X and Y in equal amounts, should have $X = Y = 5$.

d Costs of forgone trade would be a loss of X of $5 - \sqrt{20} \approx 0.53$. Loss in Y would be the same.

Chapter 2

2.1 a $\dfrac{€8.00}{€.40/\text{apple}} = 20$ apples can be bought.

b $\dfrac{€8.00}{€.10/\text{banana}} = 80$ bananas can be bought.

c 10 apples cost:
10 apples · €.40/apple = €4.00, so there is €8.00 – €4.00 = €4.00 left to spend on bananas, which means
$\dfrac{€4.00}{€.10/\text{banana}} = 40$ bananas can be bought.

d One less apple frees €.40 to be spent on bananas, so $\dfrac{€.40}{€.10/\text{banana}} = 4$ more bananas can be bought.

e €8.00 = €.40 · number of apples + €10 · number of bananas = $.40A + .10B$.

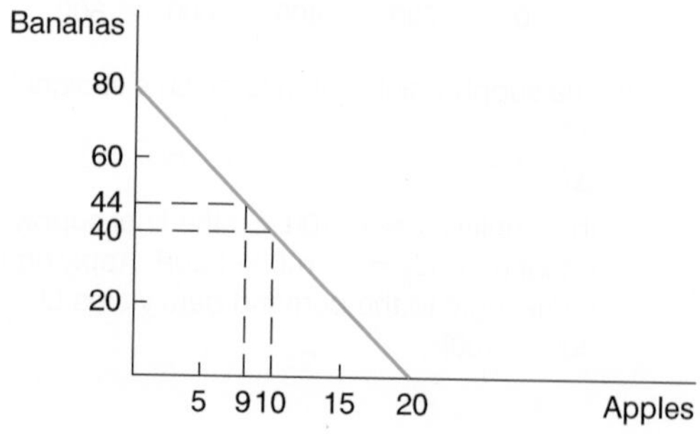

2.3 a If $U = \sqrt{C \cdot D}$ indifference curves are hyperbolas

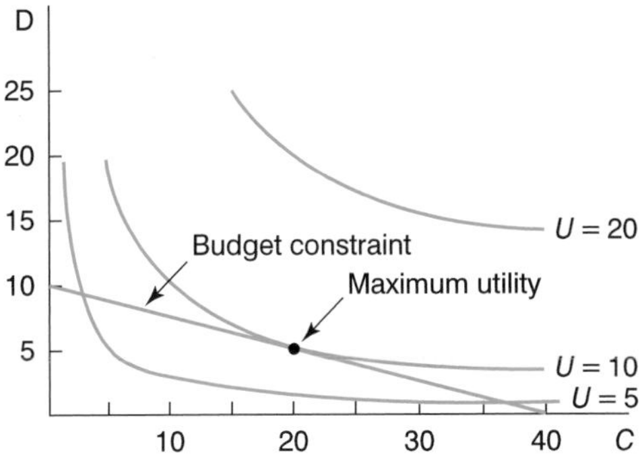

b Budget constraint is $200 = 5C + 20D$ shown on graph

c With 200 can buy 10D. With $D = 10$, $C = 0$, and $U = 0$

d See graph. If, say, spend 100 on C and 100 on D can only buy $C = 20$, $D = 5$. Well below $U = 20$.

e With $C = 20$, $D = 5$, $U = 10$

f To show solution in e is highest, try

$C = 40, D = 0, U = 0$

$C = 24, D = 4, U = \sqrt{96} < 10$

$C = 16, D = 6, U = \sqrt{96} < 10$

$C = 0, D = 10, U = 0$

so $C = 20$, $D = 5$, looks like maximum.

2.5

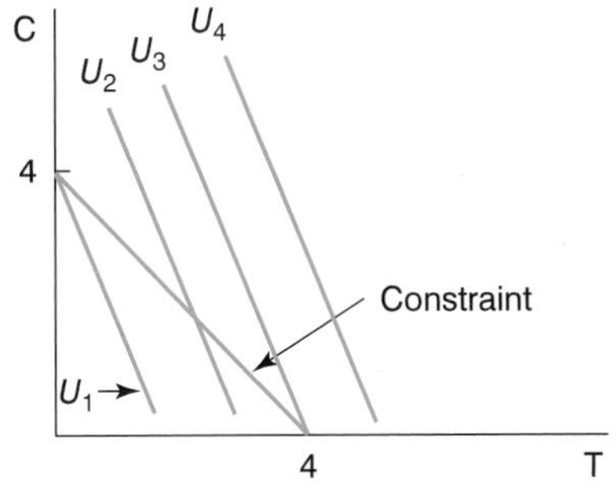

Her indifference curves are straight lines: Slope of these lines is $-4/3$. Therefore, $MRS = 4/3$ – this person is willing to give up 4/3 units of C to get one more T. She would buy where her budget constraint intersects her indifference curve (maximizing U), which is at $T = 4$, $C = 0$. If she had more income, she would not buy more coffee (she would maximize utility by buying more tea). If the price of coffee fell to €2, she would buy all coffee maximizing her utility at $U = 3C + 4T = 3(6) + 4(0) = 18$.

2.7

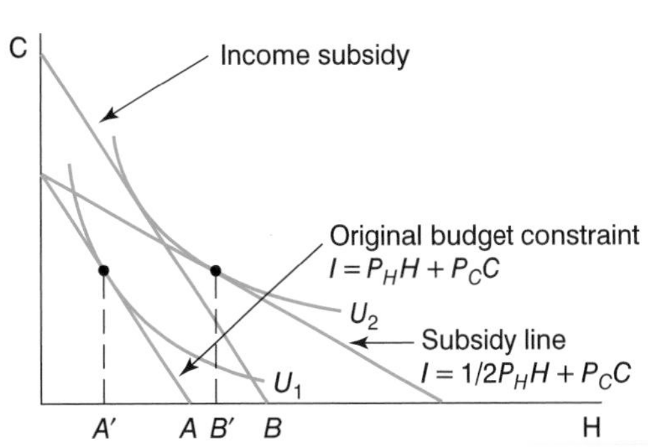

Income subsidy is cheaper since $AB < A'B'$

d The income grant is smaller because it does not distort market prices. The subsidy is more costly because it encourages people to buy more of the subsidized even though it is not really cheaper.

2.9

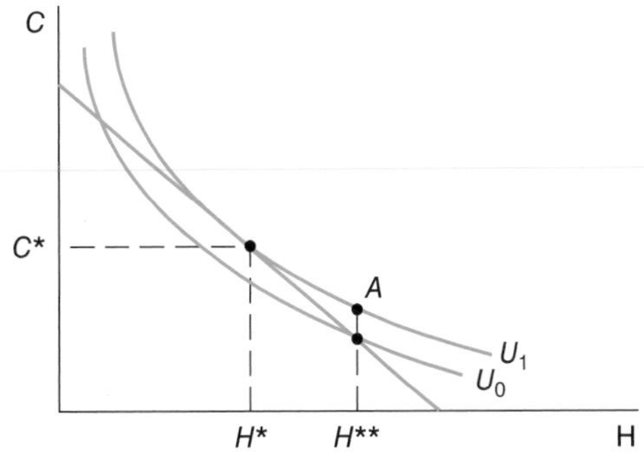

The figure shows that an unconstrained choice will yield utility level U_1 with choices of C^*, H^*. If the government requires purchase of H^{**}, utility would fall to U_0. Low-income consumers are most likely to be constrained by $H \geq H^{**}$. To return to U_1, budget constraint must allow this person to reach point A.

Chapter 3

3.1 a $I = €200$; $S = J$.

$P_S S + P_J J = 20S + 20S = 200$; $40S = 200$

$S = 5, J = 5$

b $P_S S + P_J J = I$; $20S + 30S = 200$; $50S = 200$.

$S = 4, J = 4$

c

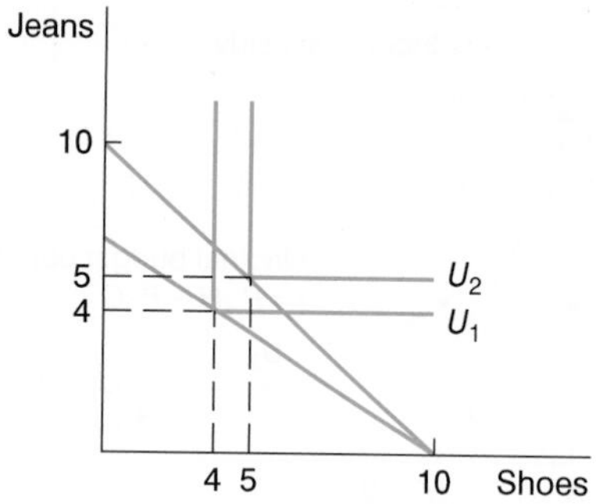

Elizabeth's indifference curves are L-shaped since she only gains utility when shoes and jeans are purchased in a one-to-one proportion. Ten shoes and five pairs of jeans yield the same utility as five shoes and five pairs of jeans.

d The change from U_2 to U_1 is entirely attributable to the income effect. There is no substitution effect due to Elizabeth's insistence on a fixed proportion of jeans and shoes.

e $S = J$ throughout because of her preferences.

$20S + P_J S = 200$

$$S = J = \frac{200}{20 + P_J}$$

The following choices will be made:

P_J	$S = J$
30	4
20	5
10	$6^{2/3}$
5	8

f

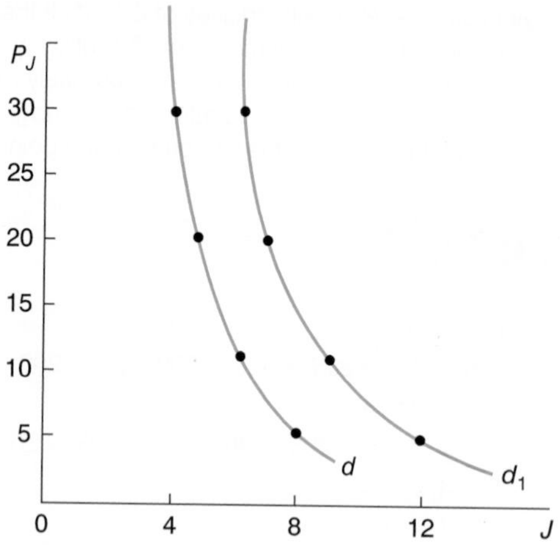

g Now $S = J = \dfrac{300}{20 + P_J}$

P_J	$S = J$
30	6
20	7.5
10	10
5	12

More J is demanded at each price (see graph in part f).

h Now: $S = J = \dfrac{200}{30 + P_J}$

This will shift both demand curves inward.

3.3 a Demand functions are

$P_F F = I/3$ or $F = I/3P_F$

$P_S S = 2I/3$ or $S = 2I/3P_S$.

If I, P_F and P_S all change by the same a proportion, quantities of F and S demanded will not change.

If $I = 20\,000$

$$F = \frac{20\,000}{3P_F}$$

$$S = \frac{40\,000}{3P_F}$$

If $Z = 50\,000$

$$F = \frac{50\,000}{3P_F}$$

$$S = \frac{100\,000}{3P_F}$$

b

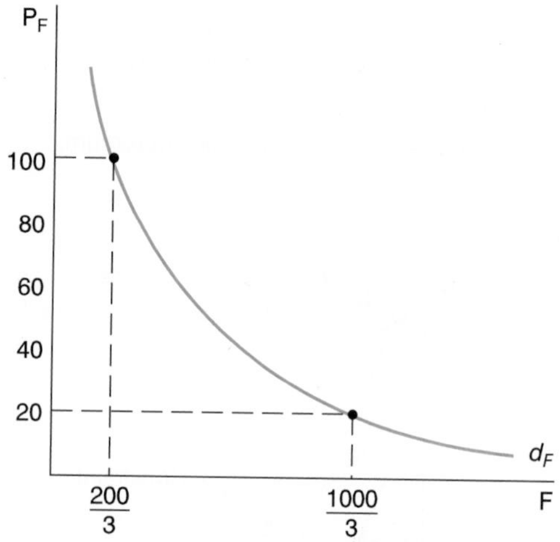

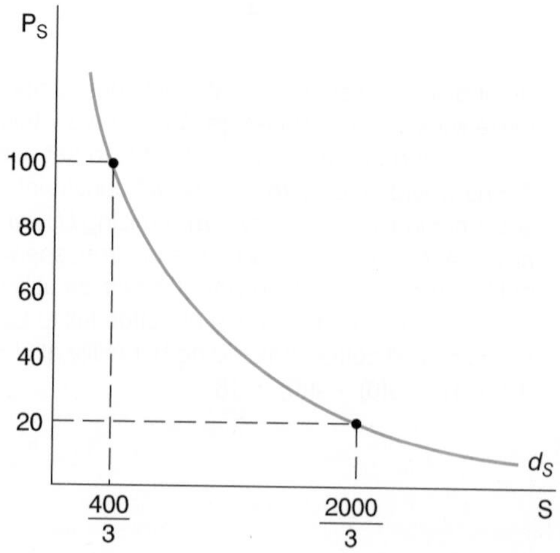

c Increase in income would shift both d_F and d_S outward.

d Part a shows that P_F does not enter into the shelter demand function. Since food always constitutes one-third of income, a change in P_F with no change in I does not change spending on either food or shelter. Since P_S has not changed, S does not change.

3.5 a With fixed proportions the individual does not substitute away from the taxed commodity even though its price has risen. There is no need to adjust for such substitution when setting tax rates.

b

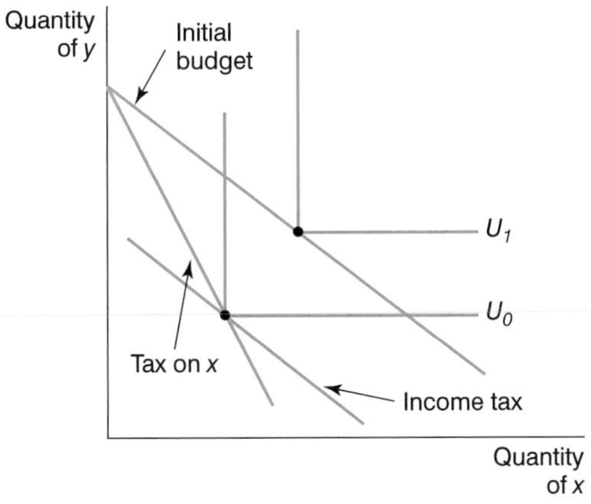

c Welfare type programs will be more efficient in raising utility for a given expenditure if they focus on subsidizing goods that are not very responsive to price.

3.7 a This person's initial endowment provides utility of U_0.

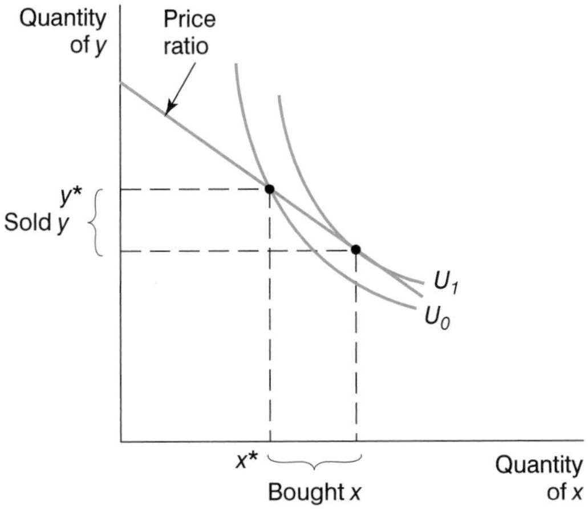

b The budget constraint passes through the initial endowment with a slope given by the ratio of market prices (see figure).

c Both preferences and market prices will determine where the utility-maximizing point occurs on this person's budget constraint.

d How this person moves along the budget constraint depends on what the MRS is at the initial endowment. If the MRS is less than the price ratio, he or she will sell X and buy more Y. If the MRS is greater than the price ratio at the initial endowment, this person will buy more X by selling Y (as shown in figure).

e A rise in the price of X will rotate the budget constraint clockwise around the initial endowment. If this person is initially a seller of good X this will raise utility. If this person is initially a buyer of good X, utility will decline.

3.9 a This is simply a matter of definition – starting from a specific utility-maximizing point, the regular demand curve examines the consequence of changing price, holding income and other prices constant. The compensated demand curve examines the consequence of changing price, holding utility and other prices constant.

b The compensated demand curve does not incorporate income effects. Therefore, the impact of a given price change is smaller than would be the case with a regular demand curve (assuming the good is a normal good).

c Because the construction of a compensated demand curve can be based on any utility level and because utility levels vary along the regular demand curve, any point on the regular demand curve can be a basis for constructing a unique compensated demand curve.

d There are no substitution effects in Irving's demand for Chianti. His compensated demand curve is perfectly inelastic at the prevailing level of Chianti consumption. A change in Chianti consumption would change utility and represent a different compensated demand curve. Irving's regular demand curve for Chianti is not perfectly inelastic because it also involves income effects when the price of this wine changes.

Chapter 4

4.1 $Q = 500 - 50P$.

a If $P = 2, Q = 400$.
$P = 3, Q = 350$.
$P = 4, Q = 300$.
$P = 0, Q = 500$.

b

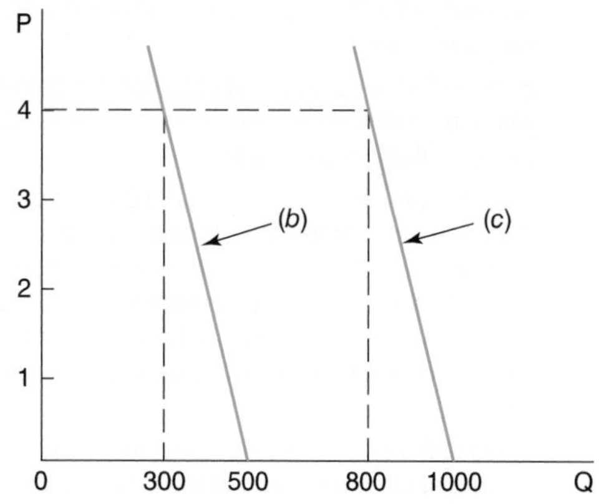

c $Q = 1000 - 50P$.
If $P = 2$, $Q = 900$.
$P = 3$, $Q = 850$.
$P = 4$, $Q = 800$.
$P = 0$, $Q = 1000$.

4.3 a Demand function (Q)

	(i)	*(ii)*	*(iii)*
$P = 1$	100	100	100
$P = 1.1$	90.9	95.3	86.7

b Demand function (i) has $e = -1$.
Demand function (ii) has $e = -0.5$.
Demand function (iii) has $e = -1.5$.

Note: Values are not exact because of the relatively large price change. Elasticities would more closely predict changes in Q for smaller changes.

c Demand function (Q)

	(i)	*(ii)*	*(iii)*
$P = 4$	25	50	12.5
$P = 4.4$	22.7	47.7	10.8

These results mirror those in part a and show the constant elasticity of the demand functions.

4.5 a

	Tom	*Dick*	*Harry*	*Total*
$P = 50$	0	0	0	0
$= 35$	30	20	0	50
$= 25$	50	60	25	135
$= 10$	80	120	100	300
$= 00$	100	160	150	410

b "Total" column in part a.

c

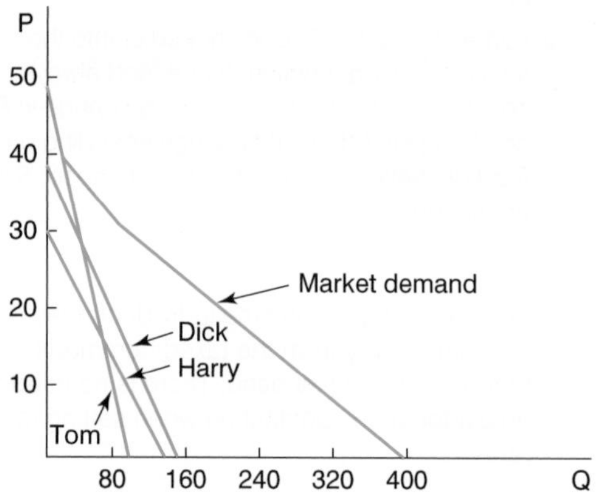

d Above graph.

4.7 a P falls by 10 per cent, so purchases will increase by $10(1.3) = 13$ per cent.

b I rises by 5 per cent, so purchases will increase by $5(1.7) = 8.5$ per cent.

c P' falls by 20 per cent, so purchases fall by $20(0.8) = 16$ per cent.

d Summing all the changes gives $+13 + 8.5 - 16 = +5.5$ per cent increase in purchases.

4.9 a Compensated demand is totally inelastic: $e_S = 0$.

b Since there are only two goods to buy, $e_{F,I} = 1$.

c $S_F = 1/3$.

d $e_{F,P} = -1/3$. If P_F rises by, say, 3 per cent, one will have to reduce spending on both food and shelter by 1 per cent to compensate for the price rise. Hence $e_{F,P} = -1$ per cent/+3 per cent $= -1/3$.

e $e_{F,P} = e_S - s_F e_{F,I} - 1/3 = 0 - 1/3(1)$

f $F = I/3\,P_F$.

g Here $e_{F,P} = -1$, $s_{F'} = 1/3$, $e_{F,I} = 1$.
$e_S = e_{F,P} + s_F e_{F,I} = -1 + 1/3(1) = -2/3$.
Now there is some substitution effect in food purchases.

h Denote shelter by H. With fixed proportions, $e_S = 0$, $e_{H,I} = 1$, $s_H = 2/3$ $e_{H,P} = 0 - 2/3(1) = -2/3$.
If $H = 2I/3P_{H'}$ $e_{H,P} = -1$, $s_H = 2/3$, $e_{H,I} = 1$
$e_S = -1 + 2/3(1) = -1/3$.

Chapter 5

5.1 a $E(1) = 0.50(100) + 0.50(-100) = 0$
$E(2) = 0.75(100) + 0.25(-300) = 0$
$E(3) = 0.90(100) + 0.10(-900) = 0$

b Assume current income is €1000.

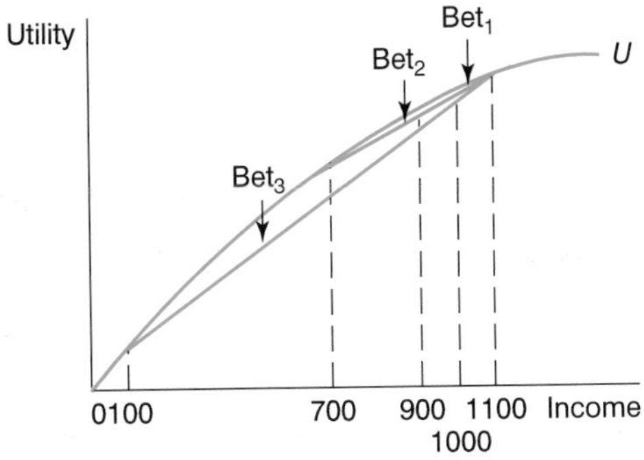

c Bet 1 will be preferred since it has smaller variability.

5.3 a Strategy one:

Outcome	*Probability*
12 eggs	0.5
0 eggs	0.5

Expected value $= 0.5 \cdot 12 + 0.5 \cdot 0 = 6$

Strategy two:

Outcome	*Probability*
12 eggs	0.25
6 eggs	0.5
0 eggs	0.25

Expected value $= (0.25 \cdot 12) + (0.5 \cdot 6) + (0.25 \cdot 0)$
$= 3 + 3 = 6.$

b

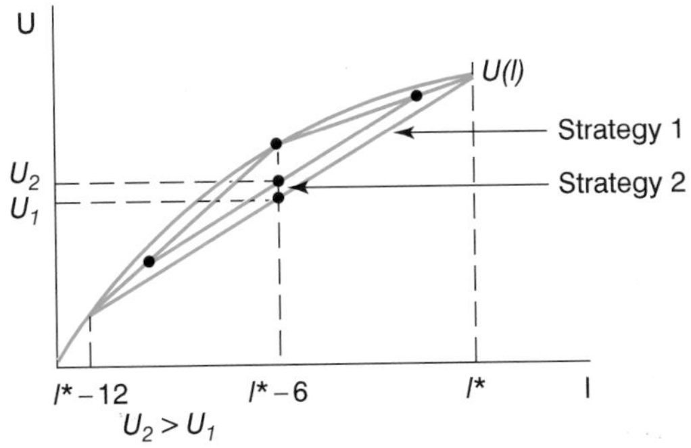

c Gains from diversification are offset by costs of extra trips, so there may be an optimal number of such trips.

5.5 a $E(U) = 0.75 \log(10\,000) + 0.25 \log(9000) = 3.9886$

b $E(U)$ with insurance $= \log(9750) = 3.9890$
$\therefore U_w > U_{w.o}$.

c Will pay up to point where $U_w = U_{w.o}$. So want $3.9886 = \log(10\,000 - P)$ where P is the premium cost.
$10^{3.9886} = 10\,000 - P = 9.741$

$P_{max} = €259.$

d Fair insurance: $E(L) = 0.30 \cdot 1000 = €300$ Since €300 > €259, she will not buy this insurance even though this is fair insurance. This is an example of moral hazard.

5.7 a $U = ln$ (€18 000) = 9.798

b $U = ln$ (€18 300) = 9.815

c If Molly invests €100 in the trip, she will have a wealth of €17 900 if Crazy Eddie does not have the set and €18 200 if he does. $E(U) = 0.5 ln(17\,900) + 0.5\, ln(18\,200) = 9.801$. Since this exceeds the utility from part a, it is worth the trip.

5.9 a Now Equations (1) in Application 5.4 are $k(20) - L = 0$ $k(30) - L = 2$. The solution is $k = 0.2$, $L = 4$. Net cost for this purchase is \$1. That is now the value of the option, which is lower than in the application because the higher strike price allows for less profit.

b Now the net cost is $0.3(27) - 6 = 2.10$. This is the value of the option. An increase from the original cost because the replicating portfolio is now more expensive. Notice that this case is a bit artificial because the rise in Microsoft price does not affect expected future prices.

c Now the replicating portfolio is found by $k(18) - L = 0$, $k(32) - L = 5$. Solution is $k = 0.36$, $L = 6.48$. Cost of this portfolio is 2.52. This is an increase from the value in the application because of increased volatility.

d Interest payments can be treated as creating a difference between the amount borrowed and the amount repaid. If, for example, the interest rate were 5 per cent per period (paid at the end of the period), the amount repaid in the replicating portfolio would be $1.05L$. For the example in the application, the replicating k would remain 0.3, but the loan amount would fall to $6/1.05 = 5.71$. Hence the cost of the portfolio would rise to $7.50 - 5.71 = 1.79$, which would be the cost of the option now.

Chapter 6

6.1 **a** *A* plays Up; *B* plays Left.

b *A*'s dominant strategy is Up. *B* does not have a dominant strategy.

6.3 **a**

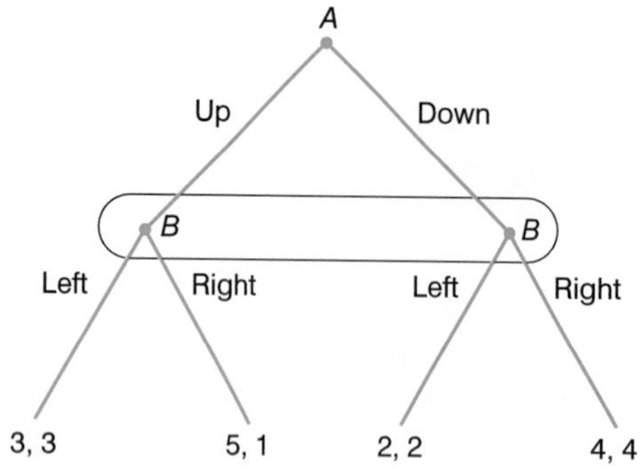

b

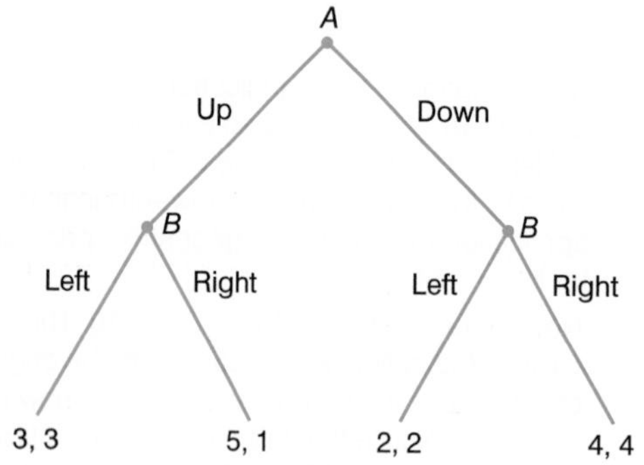

c

		Left|Up Left|Down	Left|Up Right|Down	Right|Up Left|Down	Right|Up Right|Down
A	Up	3, 3	3, 3	5, 1	5, 1
	Down	2, 2	4, 4	2, 2	4, 4

There are two Nash equilibria: first, *A* plays Up, and *B* plays "Left | Up, Left | Down"; second, *A* plays Down, and *B* plays "Left | Up, Right | Down." The second is a subgame-perfect equilibrium.

6.5 **a**

		B: Shirk	*B*: Work
A	Shirk	0, 0	4, −2
	Work	−2, 4	1, 1

b Both shirk.

c Shirking is a dominant strategy for both. Game resembles the Prisoners' Dilemma

6.7 **a** Using the underlining method shows that Confessing is a dominant strategy for both and that both Confessing is a Nash equilibrium.

b Expected payoff in equilibrium is

$$1 + (r)(1) + (r^2)(1) + (r^3)(1) + \ldots$$
$$= (1)(1 + r + r^2 + r^3 + \ldots)$$
$$= 1/(1 - r).$$

If a player deviates to Confess in the first period, his or her payoff is 3 in the first period and 0 from then on. For the trigger strategies to be an equilibrium, $1/(1 - r) \geq 3$, implying $r \geq 2/3$.

c The expected equilibrium payoff is the same as in part b, $1/(1 - r)$. If a player deviates from tit-for-tat, he or she earns 3 in the first period, 0 in the second, and then the players return to the original equilibrium for an expected payoff of

$$3 + (r)(0) + (r^2)(1) + (r^3)(1) + \ldots$$
$$= 2 + 1 + (r)(1 - 1) + (1)(r^2 + r^3 + \ldots)$$
$$= 2 - r + (1)(1 + r + r^2 + r^3 + \ldots)$$
$$= 2 - r + 1/(1 - r).$$

For this payoff from deviating to be less than the equilibrium payoff, $2 - r \leq 0$, implying $r \geq 2$. This is impossible since *r* is a probability. So players cannot sustain cooperation on Silent using tit-for-tat.

6.9 **a** There are four pure-strategy Nash equilibria, one in which none of the three locate in the shopping center and three different ones in which two locate in the shopping center and the third does not (so three different ones, one for each different left-out store *A*, *B*, and *C*).

b Playing cooperatively, they might reach one of the three outcomes in which two of the stores locate in the shopping center and the third does not. The sum of the payoffs is the highest in these outcomes, 4. The stores locating in the shopping center may pay the left-out one for not locating there, perhaps each paying 2/3 so that total surplus is split evenly.

Chapter 7

7.1 **a** $K = 6$, $q = 6K + 4L = 6(6) + 4L = 36 + 4L$.
If $q = 60$, $4L = 60 - 36 = 24$, $L = 6$.
If $q = 100$, $4L = 100 - 36 = 64$, $L = 16$.

b $K = 8$, $q = 6K + 4L = 6(8) + 4L = 48 + 4L$.
If $q = 60$, $4L = 60 - 48 = 12$, $L = 3$.
If $q = 100$, $4L = 100 - 48 = 52$, $L = 13$.

c $RTS = 2/3$. If L increases by 1 unit, q can remain constant by decreasing K by 2/3 units.

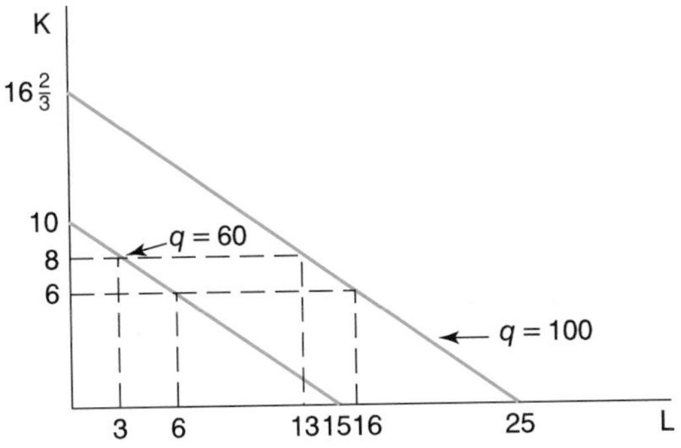

7.3 a

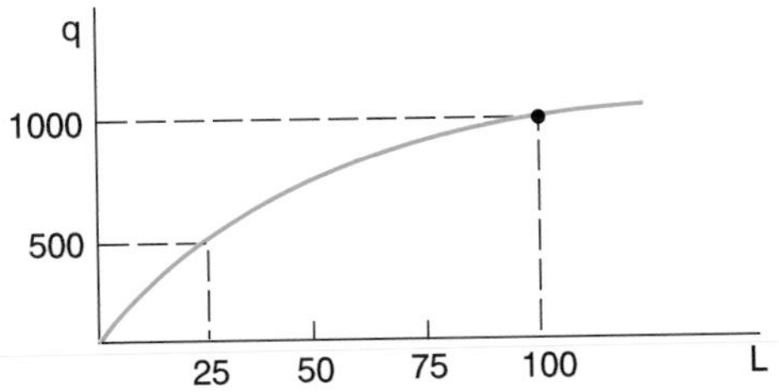

b $AP_L = \frac{q}{L} = \frac{100}{\sqrt{L}}$

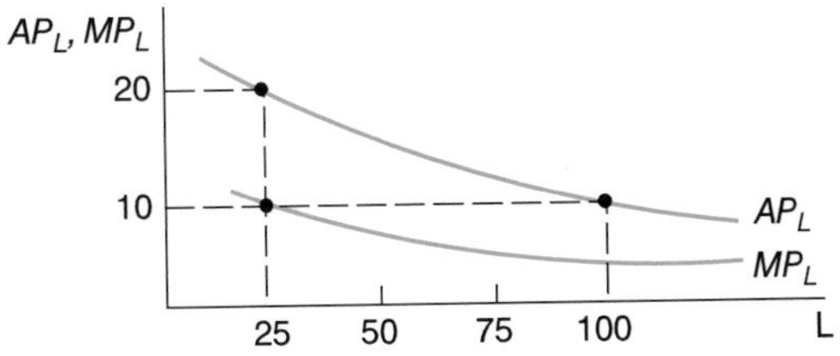

c Graph above. Since the AP_L is everywhere decreasing, then each additional worker must be contributing less than the average of the existing workers, bringing the average down. Therefore, the marginal productivity must be lower than the average.

Here $MP_L = \frac{1}{2}AP_L$.

7.5 a

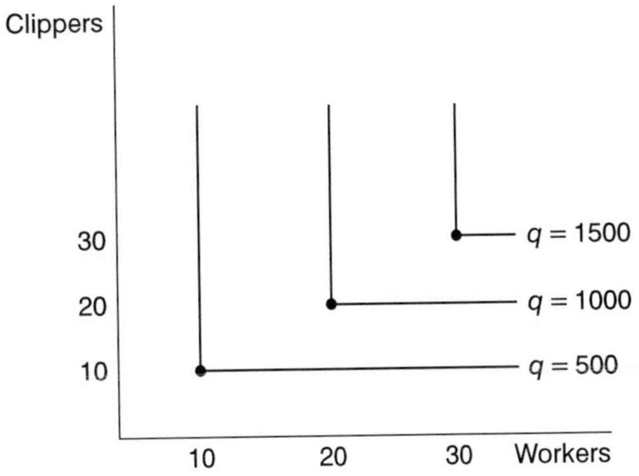

Will operate at the vertex of the isoquants.

b Hire 20 workers, $q = 1000$.

c Depends on whether grapes can be sold for a price exceeding average cost.

d

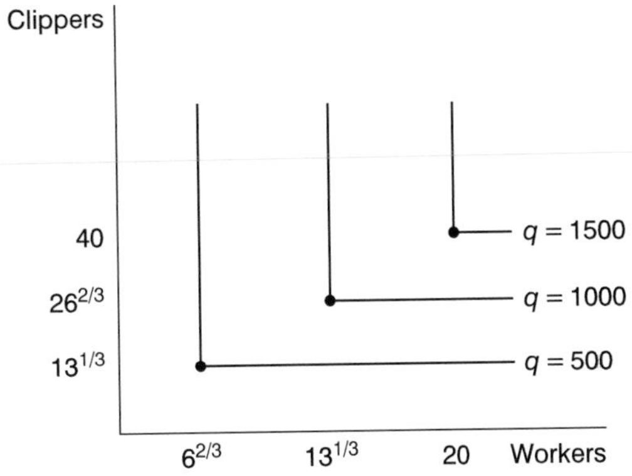

Choice would depend on clipper costs and wages for ambidextrous workers.

7.7 a In 7.4, $a = b = 1/2$.

b If we use $2K$, $2L$, have $q = (2K)^a(2L)^b = 2^{a+b}K^aL^b$ and if $a + b = 1$, this is twice K^aL^b.

c, d From b, it follows that output will less than double or more than double if $a + b < 1$ or $a + b > 1$.

e Function can exhibit any returns to scale desired depending on the values of a and b.

7.9 a $q = 100 = 1000$, so $= 10$, or, $K \cdot L = 100$.

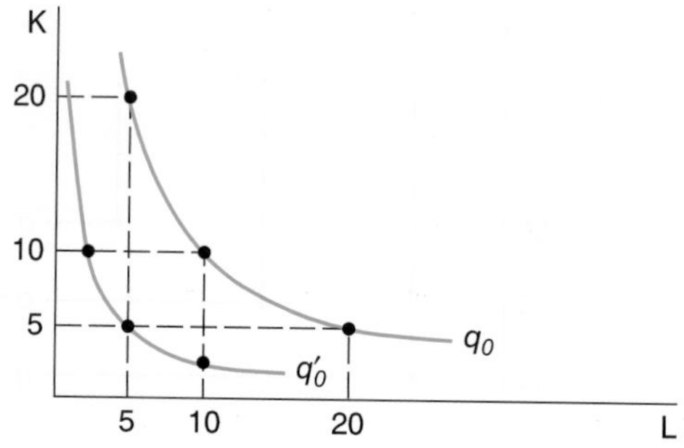

b $K = 10, L = 10$

$AP_L = q/L = 1000/10 = 100$ boxes per hour per worker.

c If $q = 200\sqrt{KL} = 1000$, $\sqrt{KL} = 5$, or $KL = 25$. Isoquant shifts to q'_0. Now, if $K = 10$, $L = 2.5$. $AP_L = q/L = 1000/2.5 = 400$ boxes per hour per worker.

d $q = (1.05)^t\, 100\sqrt{KL} = 1{,}000$, so $\sqrt{KL} = 10/(1.05)^t$ or $KL = 100/(1.05)^{2t}$. Hence, the amounts of capital and labor required to produce 1000 units of output fall over time. If $K = 10$, $L = 10$, $AP_L = 1000(1.05)^t/10 = 100(1.05)^t$. Therefore the average product of labor grows over time at 5 per cent per year.

Chapter 8

8.1 a

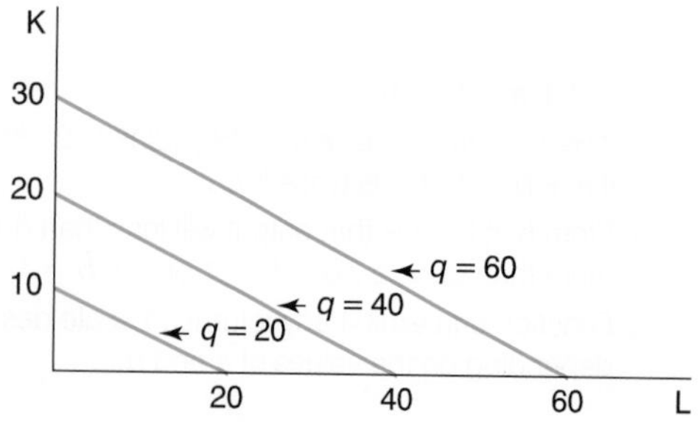

$RTS = 1/2$ since, if L is increased by one, K can be reduced by 1/2 while holding q constant.

b Since $RTS = 1/2 < w/v = 1$, the manufacturer will use only K. For $q = 20$, $K = 10$; $q = 40$, $K = 20$; $q = 60$, $K = 30$. The manufacturer's expansion path is simply the K-axis.

c If v = €3, $RTS = 1/2 > w/v = 1/3$, the manufacturer will use only L. For $q = 20$, $L = 20$; $q = 40$, $L = 40$; $q = 60$, $L = 60$. Now the manufacturer's expansion path is the L-axis.

8.3 a This is a cubic cost curve. It resembles Figure 8-3(d).

b $AC = TC/q = q^2 - 40q + 430$

This is a parabola. It reaches a minimum at the axis of symmetry:

$q = -(-40)/2 = 20$

At $q = 20$, $AC = 400 - 800 + 430 = 30$.

c At $q = 20$, $MC = 3(400) - 1600 + 430 = 30$.

d

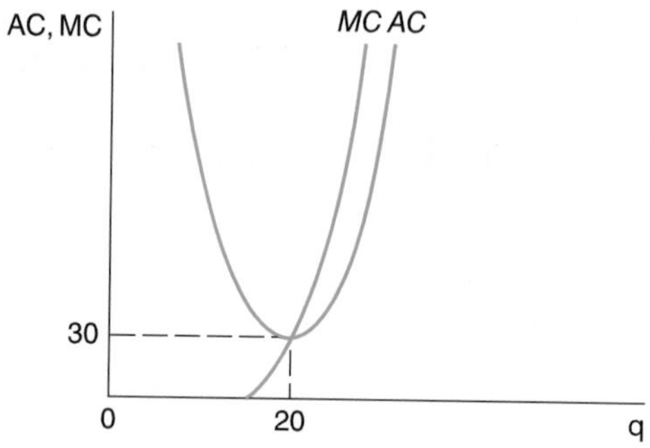

8.5 a $q = 2\sqrt{K \cdot L}$. $K = 100$, $q = 2\sqrt{100 \cdot L}$.

$$q = 20\sqrt{L}.\ \sqrt{L} = \frac{q}{20}.\ L = \frac{q^2}{400}$$

$$STC = vK + wL = 1(100) + 4\frac{(q^2)}{400}$$

$$= 100 + \frac{(q^2)}{100}.$$

$$SAC = \frac{STC}{q} = \frac{100}{q} + \frac{q}{100}$$

b $SMC = \dfrac{q}{50}$.

If $q = 25$, $STC = 100 + \dfrac{(25)^2}{100} = 106.25$.

$$SAC = \frac{100}{25} + \frac{25}{100} = 4.25.$$

$$SMC = \frac{25}{50} = 5.$$

If $q = 50$, $STC = 100 + \dfrac{(50)^2}{100} = 125$.

$$SAC = \frac{100}{50} + \frac{50}{100} = 2.50.$$

$$SMC = \frac{50}{50} = 1.$$

If $q = 100$, $STC = 100 + \dfrac{(100)^2}{100} = 200$.

$$SAC = \frac{100}{100} + \frac{100}{100} = 2.$$

$SMC = \frac{100}{50} = 2.$

If $q = 200$, $STC = 100 + \frac{(200)^2}{100} = 500.$

$SAC = \frac{100}{200} + \frac{200}{100} = 2.50.$

$SMC = \frac{200}{50} = 4.$

c

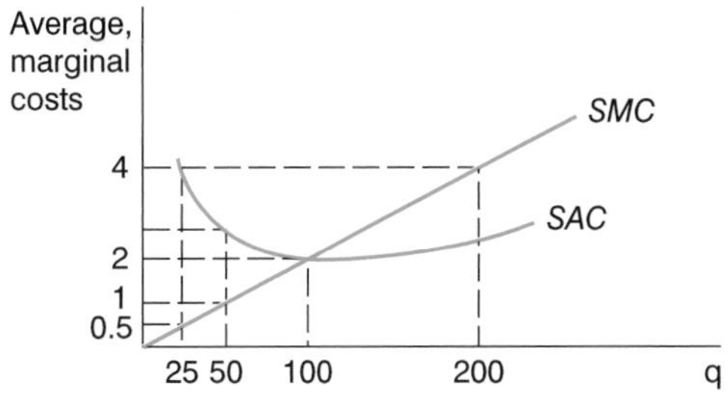

d As long as the marginal cost of producing one more unit is below the average cost curve, average costs will be falling. Similarly, if the marginal cost of producing one more unit is higher than the average cost, then average costs will be rising. Therefore, the *SMC* curve must intersect the *SAC* curve at its lowest point.

8.7 Minimizing costs requires equal marginal productivities of labor in each plant. If labor were more productive in one plant than another, costs could be lowered by moving workers.

a $MP_{L_1} = MP_{L_2}$. $5/2\sqrt{L_1} = 5/\sqrt{L_2}$.

$2\sqrt{L_1} = \sqrt{L_2}$. $L_2 = 4L_1$.

$q_1 = 5\sqrt{L_1}$; $q_2 = 10\sqrt{L_2} = 10\sqrt{4L_1} = 20\sqrt{L_1}$.

Hence $q_2 = 4q_1$

b $4q_1 = q_2$, so $q_1 = 1/5q \cdot q_2 = 4/5q$ where q is total output.

$STC \text{ (Plant 1)} = 25 + wL_1 = 25 + \frac{q_1^2}{25}$

$STC \text{ (Plant 2)} = 100 + wL_2 = 100 + \frac{q_2^2}{100}$

$STC = STC \text{ (Plant 1)} + STC \text{ (Plant 2)}$

$= 25 + \frac{q_1^2}{25} + 100 + \frac{q_2^2}{100}$

$= 125 + \frac{(1/5q)^2}{25} + \frac{(4/5q)^2}{100}$

$= 125 + \frac{1/25q^2}{25} + \frac{16/25q^2}{100}$

$= 125 + \frac{20/25q^2}{100}$

$MC = \frac{2q}{125}$. $AC = \frac{125}{q} + \frac{q}{125}$.

$MC\ (100) = \frac{200}{125} = €1.60.$

$MC\ (125) = €2.00$ $MC(200) = €3.20.$

c Because of constant returns to scale, in the long run one can change *K*. It is really not important where production occurs. Production could be split evenly or produced all in one plant.

$TC = K + L = 2q$. $AC = 2 = MC$.

d If there were decreasing returns to scale, then each firm should have equal share of production. *AC* and *MC*, no longer constant, are increasing functions of *q* preventing either plant from being too large.

8.9 a Now $K = L$, so $q = 20L$.

$TC = vK + wL = 5K + 5L = 10L$,

so $TC = 0.5q$

$AC = TC/q = 0.5$

$MC = \Delta TC/\Delta q = 0.5$.

These costs are half what they were before.

b All costs will fall at the rate of *r* per year.

Chapter 9

9.1 a Set $P = MC$, $20 = 0.2q + 10$. $q = 50$.

b Maximum profits $= TR - TC$

$= (50 \cdot 20) - [0.1(50)^2 + 10(50) + 50]$

$= 1000 - 800 = 200.$

c

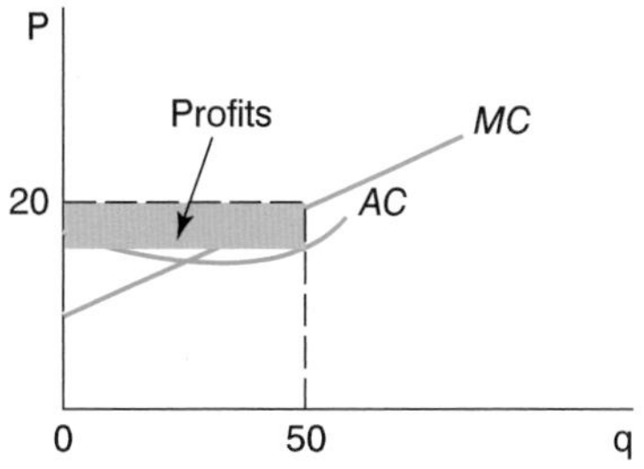

9.3

q	P	TR (= Pq)	MR	MC	AC	TC	π (= TR − TC)
1	9	9	9	3	3	3	6
2	8	16	7	3	3	6	10
3	7	21	5	3	3	9	12
4	6	24	3	3	3	12	12
5	5	25	1	3	3	15	10
6	4	24	−1	3	3	18	6
7	3	21	−3	3	3	21	0
8	2	16	−5	3	3	24	−8
9	1	9	−7	3	3	27	−18
10	0	0	−9	3	3	30	−30

Maximum profits occur at $q = 4$. At $q = 4$, the additional revenue of producing one more unit (3) is exactly equal to the cost of that added unit, and therefore it is profitable. For $q > 4$, profits fall and become negative for $q \geq 8$.

9.5 a Since $q = 60 - 2P$, solving for P yields $2P = 60 - q$ or $P = 30 - q/2$.

Hence, $TR = P \cdot q = q(30 - q/2)$, so $TR = 30q - q^2/2$

b That $MR = 30 - q$ can be shown through calculus. A tabular proof is illustrated in the following table.

P	$q = 60 - 2P$	Pq	MR	$MR = 30 - q$
20	20	400		
19.5	21	409.5	9.5	9
19	22	418	8.5	8
18.5	23	425.5	7.5	7
18	24	432	6.5	6
17.5	25	437.5	5.5	5
17	26	442	4.5	4
16.5	27	445.5	3.5	3
16	28	448	2.5	2
15.5	29	449.5	1.5	1
15	30	450	0.5	0

Hence MR is approximately that given by the equation $MR = 30 - q$.

c To maximize profits set $MC = MR$, $0.2q = 30 - q$, so $q = 150 - 5q$, $6q = 150$. Hence, $q = 25$, $P = 17.5$, $MR = MC = 5$.

d The graph shows the linear D, MR, and MC curves.

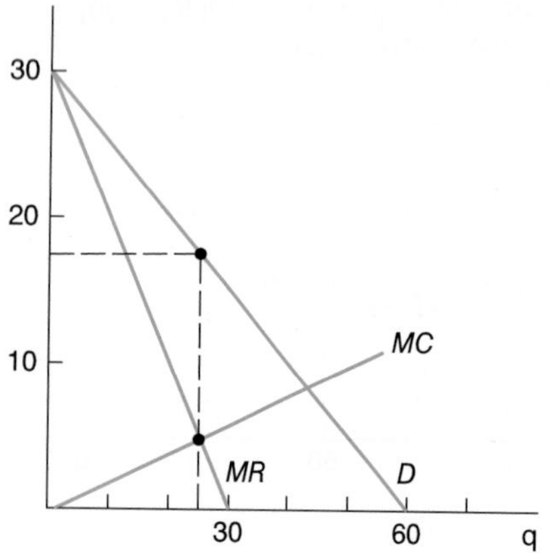

9.7 a Beth's supply function is $q = 5P - 50$.

If $P = 15$, $q = 25$.

If $P = 25$, $q = 75$.

b When $P = 15$, $\pi = 15 \cdot 25 - 362.5 = 375 - 362.5 = 12.5$.

When $P = 25$, $\pi = 25 \cdot 75 - 1362.5 = 1875 - 1362.5 = 512.5$.

Average $\pi = (512.5 + 12.5) \div 2 = 262.5$.

c If $P = 20$, $q = 50$, $\pi = 1000 - 800 = 200$. The father's deal makes Beth worse off.

d

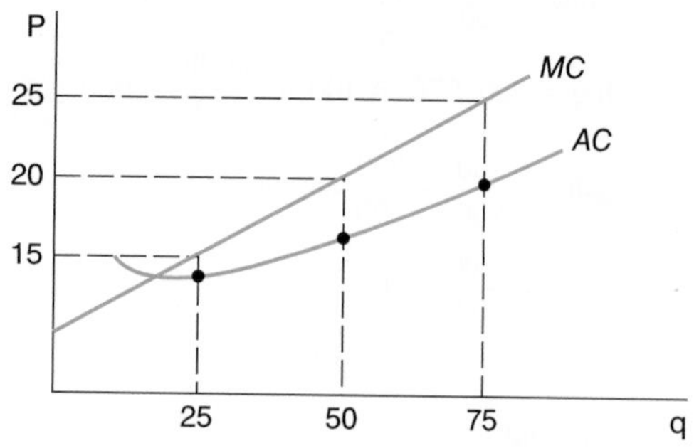

Since high profits are associated with high P, q combination, it's more profitable to let price fluctuate.

9.9 a $STC = vK + wL$

$= 10 \cdot 100 + wL$

$= 1000 + 5L$,

but $q = 10\sqrt{L}$, so $L = \frac{q^2}{100}$.

Hence, $STC = 1000 + q^2/20$.

b Use $P = MC$.

$20 = 0.1q$, so $q = 200$.

$L = q^2/100$, so $L = 400$.

c If $P = 15$, $P = MC$ implies $15 = 0.1q$ or $q = 150$, $L = 225$.

d Cost will be 175 to reduce L from 400 to 225. With $q = 150$, Profits $= TR - TC = 15(150) - (1000 + 0.05q^2) = 2250 - (1000 + 1125) = 125$. After paying severance cost of 175, the firm will incur a loss of 50. Note that if the firm continues to hire 400 workers it will have no severance costs and profits of $TR - TC = 15(200) - [1000 + 0.05(200)^2] = 3000 - (1000 + 2000) = 0$, which is better than in part d. An output level of 180 ($L = 324$) would yield an overall profit for the firm.

Chapter 10

10.1 a Set supply equal to demand to find equilibrium price:

$Q_S = 1000 = Q_D = 1600 - 600P$.

$1000 = 1600 - 600P$.

$600 = 600P$

$P = 1$/kilo

b $Q_S = 400 = 1600 - 600P$.

$600P = 1200$.

$P = 2$/kilo

c $Q_S = 1000 = 2200 = 600P$.

$1200 = 600P$.

$P = 2$/kilo

$Q_S = 400 = 2200 - 600P.$
$600P = 1800.$
$P = 3/\text{kilo}$

d

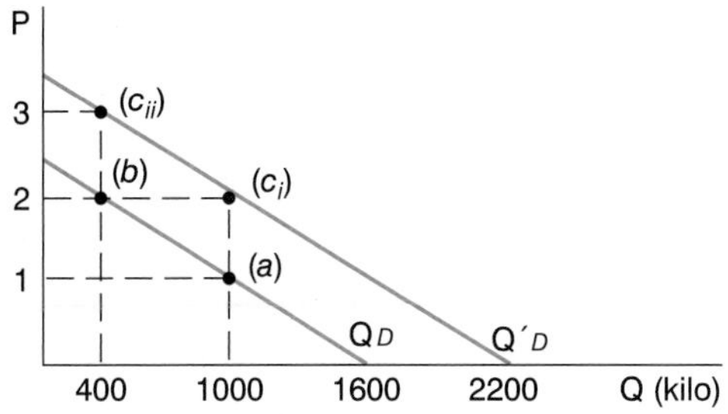

10.3 a Supply = 100 000. In equilibrium 100 000 = Q_S = Q_D = 160 000 − 10 000P, or P = 6.

b For any one firm, quantity supplied by other firms is fixed at 99 900. Demand curve is

Q'_D = 160 000 − 10 000P − 99 900 = 60 100 − 10 000P.

If quantity supplied is 0, $Q'_S = 0 = Q'_D$ = 60 100 − 10 000P, or P = 6.01.

If quantity supplied is 200, $Q'_S = 200 = Q'_D$ = 60 100 − 10 000P, or P = 5.99.

Elasticity = Slope of demand · P/Q for market.

$$e_{Q,P} = -10\,000.\frac{6}{100\,000} = -0.6.$$

For a single firm, demands is much more elastic

$$e_{Q,P} = -10\,000.\frac{6}{100} = -600.$$

A change in quantity supplied does not affect price very much.

10.5 a Short run: $MR = P$, so $P = MC$.

$P = q^2 + 20q + 100.$

$P = (q + 10)^2.$

$\sqrt{P} = q + 10.\ q = \sqrt{P} - 10.$

b $P = 121, q = \sqrt{121} - 10 = 1.$

$P = 169, q = \sqrt{169} - 10 = 3$

$P = 256, q = \sqrt{256} - 10 = 6.$

c $\pi = TR - TC.\ P = 121.$

$\pi = 1 \cdot (121) - [0.33(1)^3 + 10(1)^2 + 100(1) + 48].$
$= 121 - 158.33 = -37.33.$

$P = 169.$

$\pi = 3(169) - [.33(3)^3 + 10(3)^2 + 100(3) + 48].$
$= 507 - 447 = 60.$

$P = 256.$

$\pi = 6(256) - [.33(6)^3 + 10(6)^2 + 100(6) + 48].$
$= 1536 - 1080 = 456.$

10.7 $STC = q^2 + wq = q^2 + 0.002Qq$

a If $w = 10$, $STC = q^2 + 10q$. $SMC = 2q + 10 = P$.

Hence, $q = P/2 - 5$.

Industry Supply:

$$Q = \sum_{1}^{1000} q = 500P - 5000$$

At $P = 20$, $Q = 5000$; at $P = 21$, $Q = 5500$.

b Here $MC = 2q + 0.002Q$. Set $= P$.

$q = P/2 - 0.001Q.$

$$\text{Total } Q = \sum_{1}^{1000} q = 500P - Q.$$

Therefore, $Q = 250P$.

$P = 20, Q = 5000.$

$P = 21, Q = 5250.$

Supply is more steeply sloped in this case of interactions – increasingly production bids up the wages of diamond cutters.

10.9 a In long-run equilibrium, $AC = P$ and $MC = P$, so $AC = MC$.

$$0.01q - 1 + \frac{100}{q} = 0.02q - 1$$

$$\frac{100}{q} = 0.01q.$$

$$\frac{10\,000}{q} = q, \text{ so } q^2 = 10\,000$$

$q = 100$ liters

$$AC = 0.01(100) - 1 + \frac{100}{100} = 1 - 1 + 1 = 1.$$

$MC = 0.02(100) - 1 = 2 - 1 = 1.$

b In the long run, $P = MC$; P = €1.

Q_D = 2 500 000 − 500 000(1) = 2 000 000 liters.

The market supplies 2 000 000 liters, so

$$\frac{2\,000\,000 \text{ liters}}{100 \text{ liters/station}} = 20\,000 \text{ petrol stations.}$$

c In the long run, P = €1 still since the AC curve has not changed. Q_D
= 2 000 000 − 1 000 000(1)
= 1 000 000 liters.

$$\frac{1\,000\,000 \text{ liters}}{100 \text{ liters/station}} = 10\,000 \text{ petrol stations.}$$

d The graph for answer c would be:

Petrol Industry

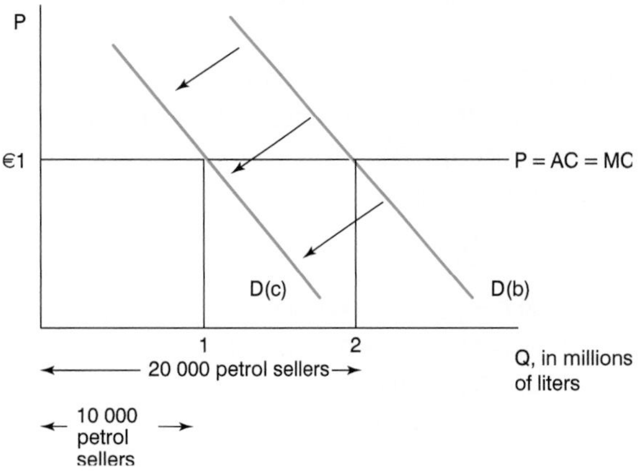

20 000 petrol sellers

However, a different interpretation might be:

Firm

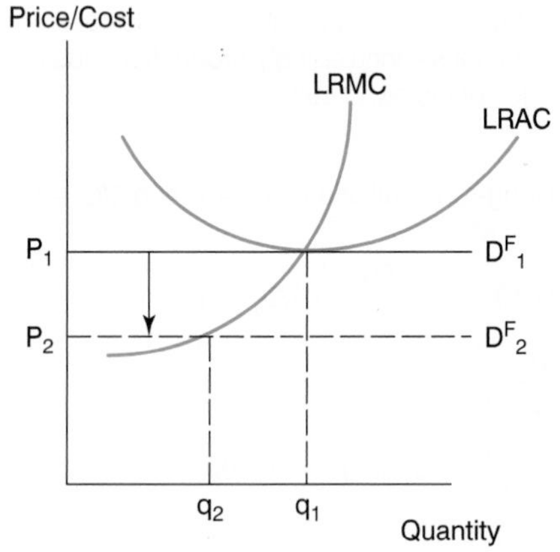

Industry

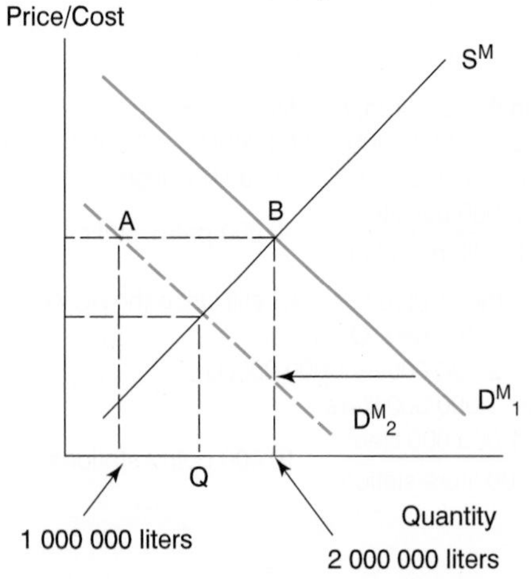

Strictly speaking the answer to 10c depends on the assumption that the price of petrol stays the same at one euro. In that situation 1 000 000 liters are demanded and sold. Strictly speaking at one euro (shown as P1) and with a new market demand curve given by D^M_2 there will excess supply of petrol given by AB.

But this is only a short-run assumption until the market has time to adjust. Individual petrol stations will find that they minimise their losses where P_2 = LRMC (they are minimising losses since the price which is set at the industry level and not the firm level is below what they need to cover LRAC). At a market price of P_2, Q millions of liters would be demanded and sold.

Some petrol stations, however, will "weather the storm" and make cost savings (reduce wages where they can, renegotiate rental rates for forecourts etc.); some petrol stations will not and will go out of business. As these petrol stations go out of business the industry supply curve will shift left and eventually meet a falling LRAC curve of those petrol stations which have managed to make cost savings (shifts in curves not shown). The eventual price will lie somewhere between P_1 and P_2.

Chapter 11

11.1 **a** With $Q = 400$, demand curve yields $400 = 1000 - 5P$, or $P = 120$. For supply, $400 = 4P - 80$, or $P = 120$. Hence, P is an equilibrium price. Total spending on broccoli is $400 \cdot 120 = 48\,000$.

On the demand curve when $Q = 0$, $P = 200$. Hence, area of the consumer surplus triangle is $0.5(200 - 120)(400) = 16\,000$.

On the supply curve, $P = 20$ when $Q = 0$. Producer surplus is then $0.5(120 - 20)(400) = 20\,000$.

b With $Q = 300$, the total loss of surplus would be given by the area of the triangle between the demand and supply curves, which is $0.5(140 - 95)(100) = 2250$.

c With $P = 140$, consumer surplus is $0.5(200 - 140)(300) = 9000$. Producer surplus is $0.5(95 - 20)(300) + 45(300) = 24\,750$.

Consumers lose 7000, producers gain 4750, net loss is 2250.

With $P = 95$, consumer surplus is $0.5(200 - 140)(300) + 45(300) = 22\,500$.

Producer surplus is $0.5(95 - 20)(300) = 11\,250$.

Consumers gain 6500, producers lose 8750; again net loss is 2250.

d With $Q = 450$, demand price would be 110, supply price is 132.50. Total loss of surplus is $0.5(132.5 - 110)(5) = 562.50$.

Net loss is shared depending on where price falls between 110 and 132.5.

e

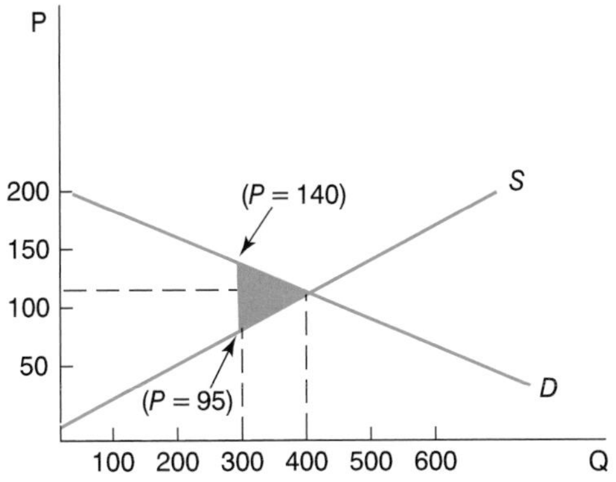

0.5(2 − 1)(1000 − 500) = 500 + 250 = 750, which is precisely the increase in producer surplus in part d.

11.3 a

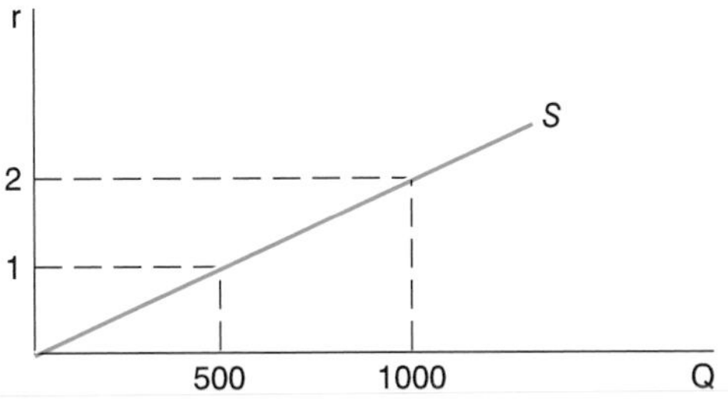

b Since $P = AC = 10 + r = 10 + 0.002Q$, substitute this into demand: $Q = 1050 - 50P = 1050 - 500 - 0.1Q$, or $1.1Q = 550$, $Q = 500$. Since each firm produces 5 DVDs, there will be 100 firms. Royalty is $r = 0.002(500) = 1$, so $P = 11$.

c With $Q = 1600 - 50P$, same substitution gives $Q = 1600 - 500 - 0.1Q$ or $1.1Q = 1100$, $Q = 1000$. So now there are 200 firms and $r = 0.002(1000) = 2$, so $P = 12$.

d

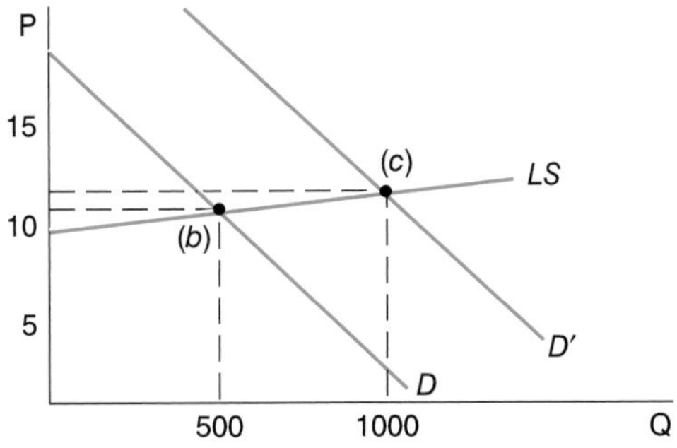

Producer surplus when $P = 11$ is $0.5(11 - 10)(500) = 250$. When $P = 12$, it is $0.5(12 - 10)(1000) = 1000$.

e Royalties when $Q = 500$ are 500. Increment when Q rises from 500 to 1000 is $(2 - 1)(500) + 0.5(2 - 1)(1000 - 500) = 500 + 250 = 750$, which is precisely the increase in producer surplus in part d.

11.5 a *Supply:* $Q = 4P - 80$
Demand: $Q = 2200 - 15P$
Equilibrium without tax: $19P = 2280$
$P^* = 120$ $Q^* = 400$
Equilibrium with tax: $4P - 80 = 2200 - 15(P + 45) = 1525 - 15P$
$P^* = 84.5$, $P^* + 45 = 129.5$, $Q^* = 258$
Here consumers pay less of the tax, producers pay more of the tax than in problem 11.4d because demand is more price-responsive in this case.

b *Supply:* $Q = 10P - 800$
Demand: $1000 - 5P$
Equilibrium without tax: $P^* = 120$, $Q^* = 400$
Equilibrium with tax: $10P - 800 = 1000 - 5(P + 45) = 775 - 5P$
$P^* = 105$, $P^* + 45 = 150$, $Q^* = 250$
Now consumers pay more of the tax, firms pay less because supply is more price-responsive.

c Tax incidence is determined by relative price responsiveness (that is by the relative elasticities of supply and demand).

11.7 a With the tax demand is now

$$Q = 1050 - 50(P + 5.5).$$

Since $P = 10 + 0.002Q$, this means

$$Q = 1050 - 500 - 0.1Q - 275$$

or

$$1.1Q = 825,\ Q = 750,\ P = 11.5.$$

Price to consumers is 17.

b Total tax collections are
5.5(750) = 4125.
Consumers pay (17 − 12)(750) = 3750
Producers pay (12 − 11.5)(750) = 375.
Consumer surplus is now 0.5(32 − 17)(750) = 5625 whereas previously it was 0.5(32 − 12)(1000) = 10 000, so the loss is 4375: 3750 of tax revenue and 625 from foregone transactions.
Producer surplus was 1000; now it is 0.5(11.5 − 10)(750) = 562.5 a loss of 437.5.

c All of the lost producer surplus is a loss of royalties. Now $r = 0.002(750) = 1.5$ whereas previously $r = 2$. Loss is $(2 - 1.5)(750) + 0.5(2 - 1.5)(250) = 375 + 62.5 = 437.5$.

11.9 This will be the same equilibrium as in problem 11.8: $P^* = 15$, $Q^* = 3500$. Now there will be no tariff revenues collected. Quota "rents" will accrue to whoever has the right to import the MP3 players.

Chapter 12

12.1 a The production possibility frontier for M and C is shown as:

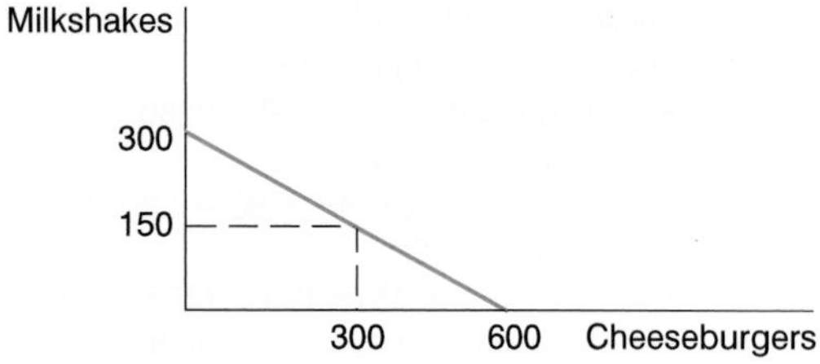

b If people want $M = \frac{1}{2}C$ and technology requires $C + 2M = 600$, then $C + 2(\frac{1}{2}C) = 600.2C = 600$, or $C = 300$. $M = 150$.

c Negative slope $= RPT = \frac{1}{2}$. If efficiency holds, $RPT = MRS = P_C/P_M$, so $P_C/P_M = 1/2$

12.3 a The frontier is a quarter ellipse:

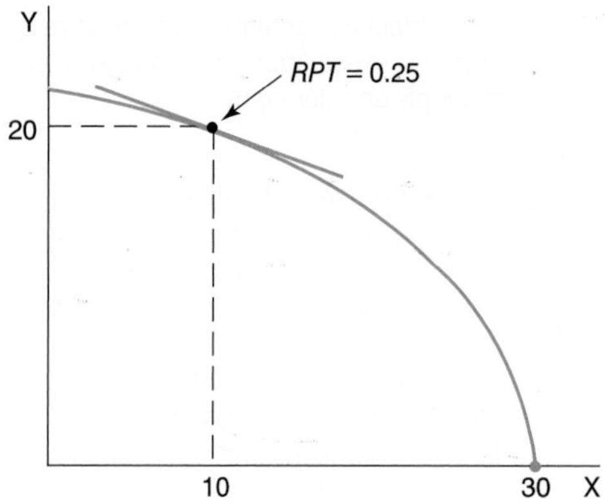

b If $Y = 2X$, $X^2 + 2(2X)^2 = 900$.
$9X^2 = 900$; $X = 10$, $Y = 20$. This point is shown on the frontier in part a.

c If $X = 9$ on the production possibility frontier,
$Y = \sqrt{\frac{819}{2}} = 20.24$.

If $X = 11$ on the frontier,
$Y = \sqrt{\frac{779}{2}} = 19.75$.

Hence, the RPT is $-\frac{\Delta Y}{\Delta X} = \frac{0.50}{2} = 0.25$.

12.5 a $P_X P_Y = 3/2$, since $RPT = -\frac{\Delta Y}{\Delta X} = -\frac{(-3)}{2}$ from the production technology which depends on labor only.

b If wage = 1, Smith spends 3 on X, 7 on Y, Jones spends 5 on X, 5 on Y.
Total spent on X is 8, total on Y is 12.
Total spending equals total income (20).
Since $w = 1$, average cost of X is $\frac{1}{2}$, of Y is $\frac{1}{3}$. So, $P_x = \frac{1}{2}$, $P_Y = \frac{1}{3}$.
With these prices, Smith demands $6X$, $21Y$ and Jones demands $10X$, $15Y$.

c Production is $X = 16$, $Y = 36$. 20 hours of labor are allocated: 8 to X production, 12 to Y production.

12.7 200 total kilos of food, $U_1 = \sqrt{F_1}$, $U_2 = 1/2\sqrt{F_2}$.

a With 100 kilos each $U_1 = 10$, $U_2 = 5$.

b Equal utilities require $\sqrt{F_1} = 1/2\sqrt{F_2}$,
$F_1 = 1/4F_2$.
$F_1 = 40$, $F_2 = 160$

c With $U_2 \geq 5$, best choice is $U_2 = 5$, since extra food yields more utility to person 1. Hence, $F_2 = 100$, $F_1 = 100$.

d Perhaps one might opt for maximizing the sum of utilities. This yields the very unequal result of $F_1 = 160$, $F_2 = 40$, $U_1 = 4\sqrt{10}$, $U_2 = \sqrt{10}$. But $U_1 + U_2 = 5\sqrt{10} = 15.8$, which exceeds value in the other parts.

12.9 a–d Construction closely follows that used for the Edgeworth Exchange diagram.

e The inefficient points in the Edgeworth Box are allocations where it is possible to increase output of both goods. Points inside the production possibility frontier have this same feature.

f i The axes of the Edgeworth Box are the efficient allocations.

ii Efficient allocations lie along the main diagonal of the Box. The production possibility frontier is a straight line.

iii In this case too the production possibility frontier is a straight line. Only with differing input intensities would the frontier have a concave shape.

iv The frontier would be convex.

Chapter 13

13.1 a $P = 53 - Q$.
For maximum profits, set $MR = MC$.
$MR = 53 - 2Q = MC = 5$.

$Q = 24$, $P = 29$.
$\pi = TR - TC = 24 \cdot 29 - 24 \cdot 5$
$= 696 - 120 = 576$.

Consumer surplus $= \frac{1}{2}(53 - 29)\cdot 24 = 288.$

b $MC = P = 5$, $P = 5$, $Q = 48$.

c Consumer surplus $= \frac{1}{2}(48)^2 = 1152$.

$1152 >$ Profits + consumer surplus $= 576 + 288 = 864$.

Deadweight loss $= 1152 - 864 = 288$.
Also $1/2\Delta Q \cdot \Delta P = 1/2(24)(24)$.

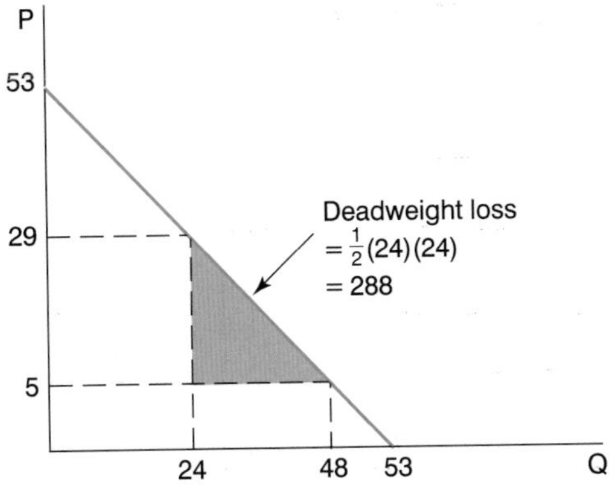

13.3 **a** $AC = MC = 10$, $Q = 60 - P$, $MR = 60 - 2Q$.
For profit maximization, $MC = MR$.
$10 = 60 - 2Q$, $2Q = 50$, $Q = 25$, $P = 35$.
$\pi = TR - TC = (25)(35) - (25)(10) = 625$.

b $AC = MC = 10$, $Q = 45 - 0.5P$. $MR = 90 - 4Q$.
For profit maximization, $MC = MR$, $10 = 90 - 4Q$, $80 = 4Q$, $Q = 20$, $P = 50$.
$\pi = (20)(50) - (20)(10) = 800$.

c $AC = MC = 10$, $Q = 100 - 2P$, $MR = 50 - Q$.
For profit maximization, $MC = MR$, $10 = 50 - Q$, $Q = 40$, $P = 30$.
$\pi = (40)(30) - (40)(10) = 800$.

d

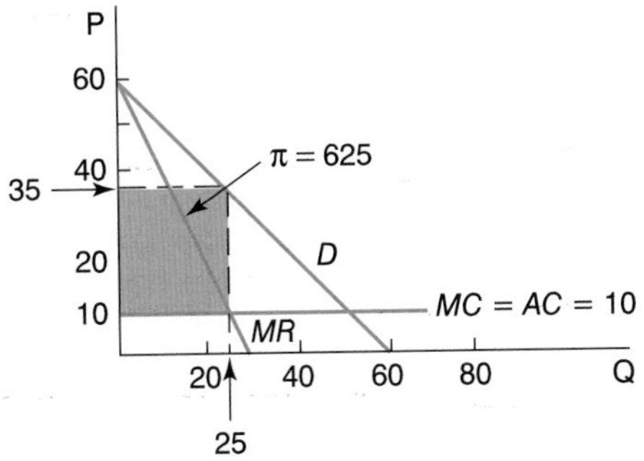

Part a

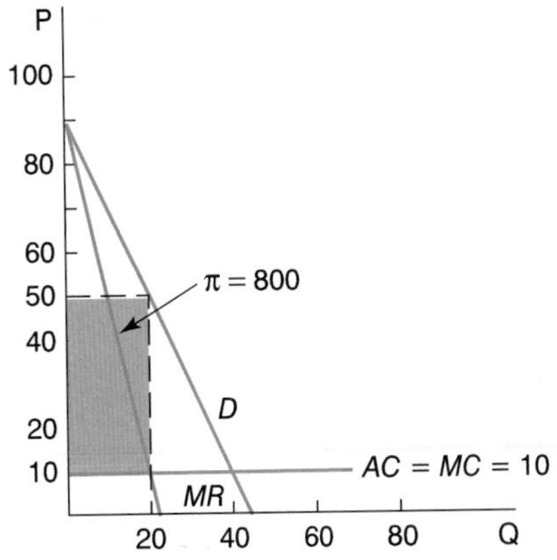

Part b

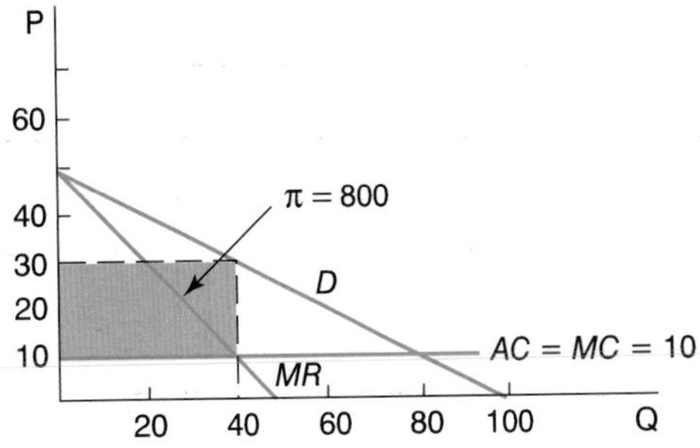

Part c

The supply curve for a monopoly is the single point on the demand curve that corresponds to profit maximization. Any attempt to connect equilibrium points (price/quantity points) on the market demand curves has little meaning and brings about a strange shape. One reason for this is that as the demand curve shifts, its elasticity (and its *MR* curve) often changes, bringing about widely varying price and quantity combinations.

13.5 A multiplant monopolist will still produce where $MR = MC$ and will equalize MC among factories.
$MR = 100 - 2(q_1 + q_2)$ and $MC_1 = MC_2$
$q_1 - 5 = 0.5q_2 - 5$. $q_1 = 0.5q_2$
$MR = 100 - 2(0.5q_2 + q_2)$.
$MR = MC_2$, $100 - 2(1.5q_2) = 0.5q_2 - 5$.
$3.5q_2 = 105$.
$q_2 = 30$ and $q_1 = 15$, so $Q_T = 45$.

13.7 $Q_D = 1000 - 50P$; $MR = 20 - Q/25$ $MC = 10$ under *PC*; $MC = 12$ under monopoly

a *Perfect competition*:
$P = MC = 10$.
$Q_D = 1000 - 50(10) = 500 = Q_S$.
Monopoly:
$MC = MR$
$12 = 20 - Q/25$
$300 = 500 - Q$
$Q = 200$;
$200 = 1000 - 50P$;
$50P = 800$; $P = 16$

b Loss of consumer surplus due to monopolization can easily be obtained from the graph (shaded portion). Area of shaded portion = $(16 - 10)(200) + 1/2\,(16 - 10)(500 - 200) = 1200 + 900 = 2100$.

This area is much larger than loss of consumer surplus if monopolist's $MC = 10$.

c

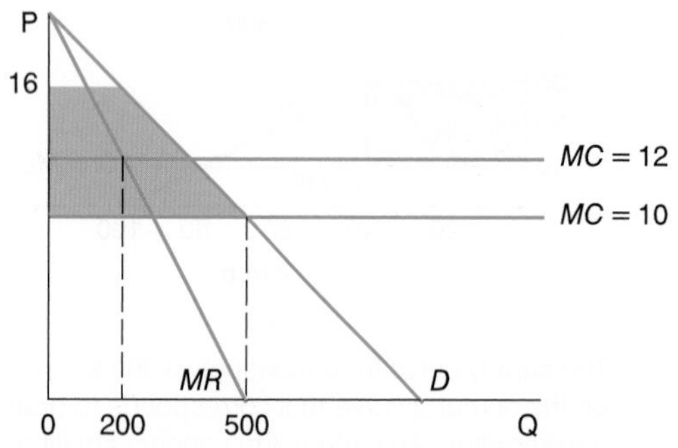

13.9 With a constant marginal cost, the graph shows that the rise in price will be less than the rise in marginal revenue as shown in the attached graph. The reason for this is that the *MR* curve is steeper than the demand curve so that a given fall in quantity causes a smaller vertical move along the demand curve. With an increasing marginal cost curve, the increase in price would be even smaller because *MR* increases by only a portion of the tax.

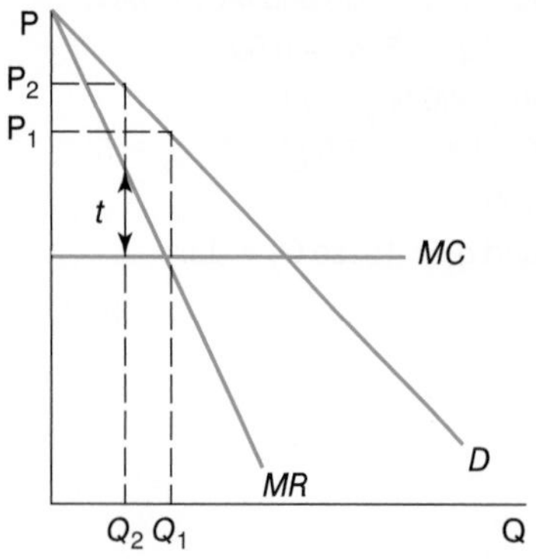

With a constant elasticity demand curve, the case is reversed, at least with constant *MC*.

Since $MR = P\left(1 + \frac{1}{e}\right)$ or $P^* = \frac{MC}{1 + \frac{1}{e}}$.

With constant MC, a unit tax will raise price to:

$$P^{**} = \frac{MC + t}{1 + \frac{1}{e}} = P^* + \frac{t}{1 + \frac{1}{e}} < P^* + t$$

because $e < -1$. An upward sloping *MC* curve will complicate matters, however, because the first term in this expression will fall with the implementation of the tax.

Chapter 14

14.1 a The Nash equilibrium is for both to price low.

b You could relabel "Low Price" as "High Output" and "High Price" as "Low Output".

14.3 Equation (14.4) states the marginal revenue for Cournot firm *A* with the given demand curve is
$120 - 2q_A - q_B$.
Equating this marginal revenue with marginal cost 30 yields
$120 - 2q_A - q_B = 30$
implying
$90 - 2q_A - q_B = 0$.
Similarly, for firm *B*,
$90 - 2q_B - q_A = 0$.
Solving the two preceding equations simultaneously gives
$q^*_A = q^*_B = 30$.
Industry output = 30 + 30 = 60.
To find *P*, solve $60 = 120 - P$, implying $P = 60$.
Firm profit = (60 − 30) (30) = 900.
Industry profit = 2 × 900 = 1800.

14.5 a There are many Nash equilibria. Firm *A* charges any price along the one-cent-increment grid from €8.02 to €10.01 (inclusive). Firm *B* undercuts *A* by one cent. All of these involve weakly dominated actions for firm *A* except the highest price one, in which it charges €10.01 and *B* charges €10. Firm *B* gets all the demand. Assume throughout the remainder of the answer that this is the Nash equilibrium that is played. Leaving the complications associated with the large number of equilibria aside, it is sufficient that students realize that prices will be around €10 and the low-cost firm will make all the sales.

b *A* earns zero profit. *B* earns

$$10 - 6 = 4$$

per unit and sells

$$Q = 500 - 20 \times 10 = 300$$

units for a profit of

$$4 \times 300 = 1200.$$

c Price equals marginal cost as in the Bertrand Paradox, though the price is equal to the high-cost firm's marginal cost. One of the firms earns zero profit as in the Bertrand Paradox, but unlike in the Bertrand Paradox one of the firms earns positive profit.

14.7 Dividing both sides of equation (14.15) by π_A, collusion is sustainable for *N* as high as $1/r$. The graph of $N = 1/r$ is below.

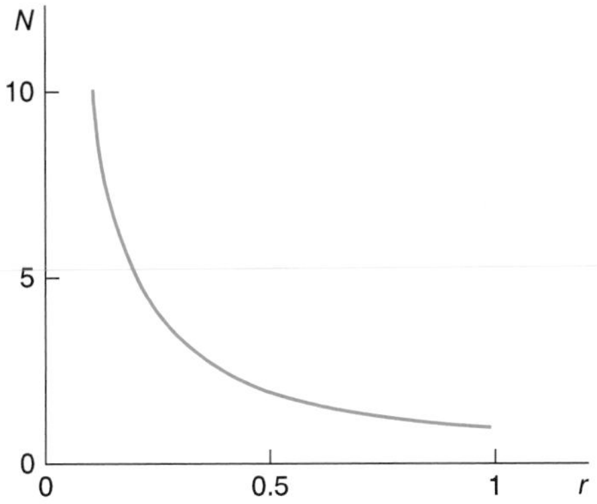

Using the prime rate as of this writing, 6.75 per cent, or $r = 0.0675$, we have

$1/0.0675 \approx 14.8.$

Collusion would be sustainable with 14 or fewer firms.

14.9 First suppose $F_I > 2000$. Then *I* will not prey. *E* earns $1600 - K > 0$ if it enters, and so will enter.

Next suppose $F_I < 2000$. Then *I* would prey if *E* entered. *E* would earn $-K - F_E < 0$ if it entered, and so would choose not to.

Predation would not be observed in either case. The only case in which *I* would be inclined to prey (if $F_I < 2000$), *E* does not enter and so there is no firm to prey upon.

Chapter 15

15.1 **a** With five workers, put each successively where its MP_L is greatest. First worker goes to A, second goes to B, third goes to *A*, fourth goes to *C*, fifth goes to *A*. Output = 21 + 8 + 5 = 34. *MP* of last worker is 4.

b $P \cdot MP_L = €1.00 \cdot 4 = €4.00 = w$. With five workers, the wage bill is $wL = €20$. Profits are $\pi = TR - TC = PQ - wL = €34 - €20 = €14$.

15.3 **a** $w = v = €1$, so *K* and *L* will be used in a one-to-one ratio.

$TC = w\ ?L + vK = L + K = 2L$, so

$$AC = \frac{2L}{q} = \frac{2L}{\sqrt{KL}} = \frac{2L}{\sqrt{LL}} = 2 \text{ and } MC = 2.$$

b Since $P = 2$, quantity demanded is $Q = 400\,000 - 100\,000(2) = 200\,000$ pipe.

$$q = \frac{200\,000 \text{ pipe}}{1000 \text{ firms}} = 200\text{pipe/firm}.$$

$q = 200 = \sqrt{L \cdot K} = L?$ so 200 workers are hired per firm, 200 000 by the industry.

c When $w = €2$ and $v = €1$, cost minimization requires $K/L = 2$.

$TC = wL + vK$, so $= 2L + K = 4L = 2\sqrt{2} \cdot q$ so $AC = MC = 2\sqrt{2}$.

d $P = 2\sqrt{2}$, $Q = 400\,000 - 100\,000(2\sqrt{2}) = 117\,157$.

$$L = \frac{200\,000}{\sqrt{2}} = 141\,000 \text{ workers hired by the industry.}$$

e If $Q = 200\,000$ at the new wage,

$$L = \frac{200\,000}{\sqrt{2}} = 141\,000 \text{ workers would have been hired by the industry.}$$

So if *Q* were unchanged, 59 000 fewer workers would have been hired = substitution effect. The remaining 58 000 fewer workers (141 000 − 83 000) are the result of the lower output; that is, the output effect.

15.5 **a** Demand: $K = 1500 - 25v$

Supply: $K = 75v - 500$

Equilibrium is found by setting quantity supplied equal to quantity demanded.

$$75v - 500 = 1500 - 25v$$
$$100v = 2000$$
$$v = 20, K = 1000.$$

b Now demand is $K = 1700 - 25v - 300g$.

If $g = 2$, $K = 1700 - 25v - 600 = 1100 - 25v$.

The new equilibrium is

$$75v - 500 = 1100 - 25v.$$
$$100v = 1600$$
$$v = 16, K = 700.$$

If $g = 3$, demand is $K = 1700 - 25v - 900 = 800 - 25v$, and the equilibrium is $75v - 500 = 800 - 25v$.

$100v = 1300$

$v = 13, K = 475.$

c The graph shows these changing equilibria as demand shifts in along a stationary supply curve.

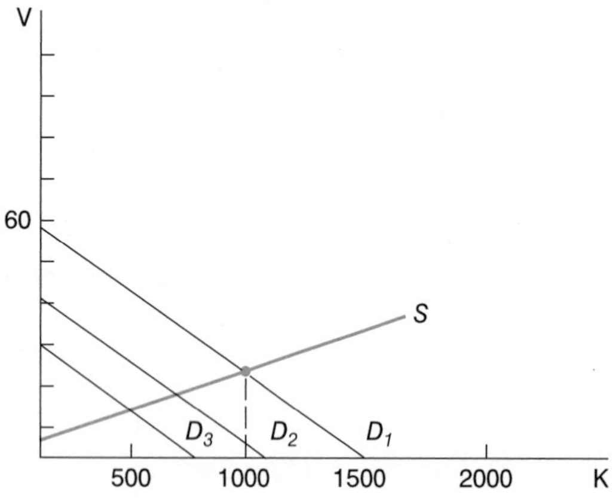

d The changing equilibrium would probably affect many markets and a general equilibrium model would be needed to examine all the possibilities.

15.7 Supply: $L = 80w$. $ME_L = \frac{L}{40}$.

Demand: $L = 400 - 40\,MVP_L$

a For monopsonist $ME_L = MVP_L$.

$L = 400 - 40MVP_L$.

$40MVP_L = 400 - L$

$MVP_L = 10 - \frac{L}{40}$

Using the profit maximizing condition,

$\frac{L}{40} = 10 - \frac{L}{40} \cdot \frac{2L}{40} = 10$

$L = 200.$

Get w from supply curve:

$w = \frac{L}{80} = \frac{200}{80} = €2.50$

b For Carl, the marginal expense of labor now equals the minimum wage, and, in equilibrium, the marginal expense of labor will equal the marginal revenue product of labor.

$w_m = ME_L = MVP_L$.

$w_m = €3.00.$

Carl's Demand	*Supply*
$L = 400 - 40MVP_L$	$L = 80w$
$L = 400 - 40(3)$	$L = 80(3)$
$L = 280.$	$L = 240.$

Demand > supply. Carl will hire 240 workers, with no unemployment. To study effects of minimum, try €3.33 and €4.00.

$w_m = €3.33$

$L = 400 - 40(3.33) = 267.$ $\quad L = 80(3.33) = 267.$

Demand = supply, Carl will hire 267 workers, with no unemployment.

$w_m = €4.00$

$L = 400 - 40(4.00) = 240.$ $\quad L = 80(4.00) = 320.$

Supply > demand, Carl will hire 240 workers, unemployment = 80.

c

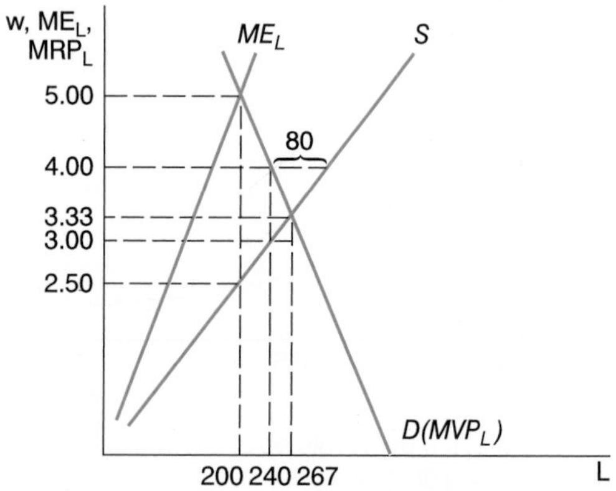

d Under perfect competition, a minimum wage means higher wages but fewer workers employed. Under monopsony, a minimum wage may result in higher wages and more workers employed as shown by some of the cases studied in part b.

15.9 **a** Budget constraint: $C = w(24 - H) + 10$.

b Due to Mrs Smith's preferences, she insists on spending half of potential income ($w \cdot 24 + 10$) on consumption and half on leisure. This means value of consumption = value of leisure (i.e., $w \cdot H$) for all wage rates.

$C = wH$

Substituting for C:

$w(24 - H) + 10 = wH$

$24 - H + 10/w = H$

$2H = 24 + 10/w$

$H = 12 + 5/w$

For w = €1.25; $H = 16$; $C = 1.25(24 - 16) + 10 = 20$.

For w = €2.50; $H = 14$; $C = 2.50(24 - 14) + 10 = 35$.

For w = €5.00; $H = 13$; $C = 5.00(24 - 13) + 10 = 65$.

For w = €10.00; $H = 12.5$; $C = 10.00(24 - 12.5) + 10 = 125$.

c The graph shows Mrs Smith's changing choices as the wage rises. Hours of leisure H fall toward 12 as w rises.

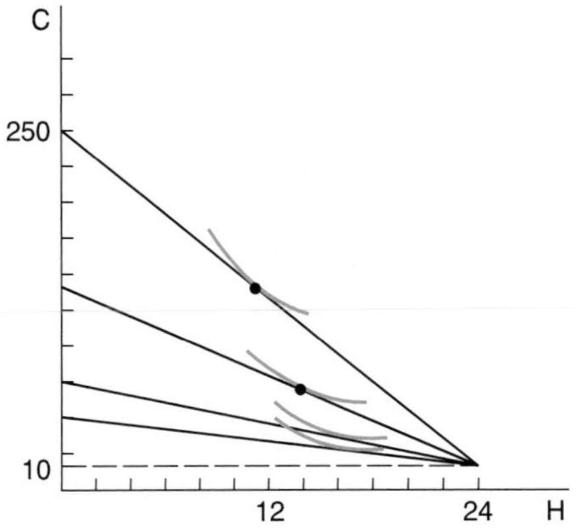

d Mrs Smith's labor supply curve can be constructed directly from the data in part b. It is upward sloping, being asymptotic to 12 hours as w rises.

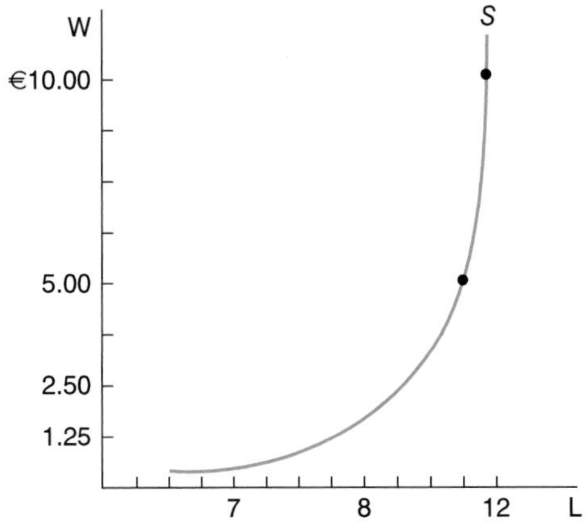

Chapter 16

16.1 a The budget constraint shows that spending must equal income in present-value terms, but income and consumption are not constrained to be equal in either period.

b If this individual saves in period zero, consumption will of necessity exceed income in period 1.

c Because period 0 savings ($= Y_0 - C_0$) earn interest, more can be spent in terms of dissaving ($= C_1 - Y_1$) in period 1.

16.3 a Present value of income is $50\,000 + 55\,000/(1 + r) = 50\,000 + 55\,000/1.1 = 100\,000$

b Prudence has $MRS = 1 + r$, or $C_1/3\,C_0 = 1.1$.

c Budget constraint in present value terms is $100\,000 = C_0 + C_1/1.1$.

Using the utility maximizing condition from part b gives

$100\,000 = C_0 + 3.3\,C_0/1.1$.

Hence $C_0 = 25\,000$. Savings in period 0 are 25 000. With these savings $C_1 = 55\,000 + 25\,000\,(1.1) = 82\,500$.

d For Glitter, $MRS = 3\,C_1/C_0 = 1.1$. Substitution into budget constraint (Prudence and Glitter have the same budget constraint) yields $100\,000 = C_0 + 1.1\,C_0/3.3 = 4\,C_0/3$.

Hence, for her, $C_0 = 75\,000$. Savings in period 0 are − 25 000. Glitter borrows 25 000 and repays 25 000 (1.1) = 27 500. Hence $C_1 = 27\,500$.

16.5 Assuming revenues are received at the end of each year gives a present value of €486 841 when $r = 0.1$. This falls short of the current purchase price of €500 000 for the ten trucks. When $r = 0.08$, the present value of future revenue is €520 637, which means that the investment would be profitable.

16.7 a Price should be $4000/(1.05)^{25} = 4000 / 3.3864 = 1181$.

b Scarcity costs = 1181 − 100 = 1081

c Assuming real production costs stay at €100, scarcity costs in 25 years are €3900.

d In 50 years price is $1181(1.05)^{50} = 4000(1.05)^{25} = 13\,545$.

16.9 The fallacy here is that the calculation assumes that you have borrowed €10 000 for all 3 years. Since the repayment plan includes some repayment of the €10 000 too, the effective amount borrowed is only about half that amount. The actual effective interest rate on the loan, assuming that the €315 payments are made at the start of each month, is about 8.7 per cent, well above the 5 per cent opportunity cost.

Chapter 17

17.1

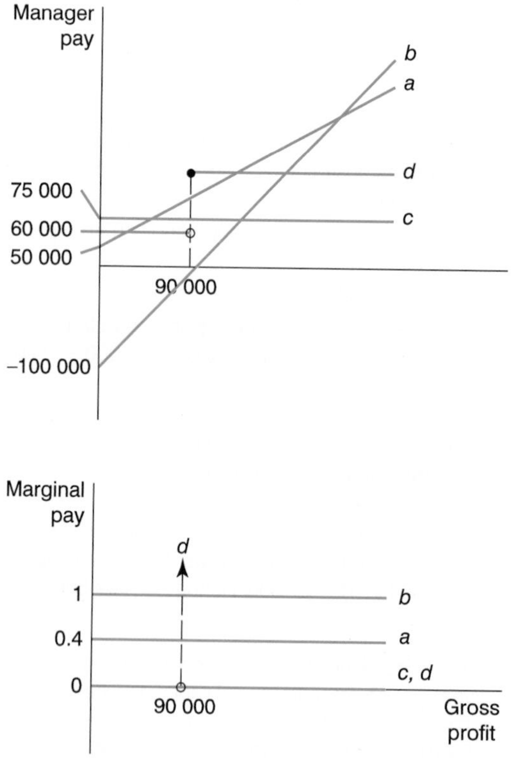

17.3 **a** From part a of problem 17.2, if she receives half of a firm's return, Clare's expected utility from exerting effort is 250. If she does not exert effort, her utility is

$$400/2 = 200 < 250.$$

So she will exert effort. We saw in problem 17.2 that she would accept the contract. With a quarter share of gross profit, by part a of problem 17.2 her expected utility from working is 75. Her expected utility from not working is

$$400/4 = 100 > 75.$$

Clare would accept the contract and not exert effort.

For Clare to exert effort, her gross-profit share must solve

$$(0.5)(1000\,s) + (0.5)(400\,s) - 100 \geq 400\,s, \text{ or } s \geq 1/3.$$

b If she works hard, her expected utility with the bonus is

$$(0.5)(100) - 100 = -50.$$

If she does not work hard, her utility is 0. So she would not work hard. (Adding a fixed part to the wage would not change the answer.)

The bonus b that would induce her to work hard solves

$$(0.5)\,b - 100 \geq 0,$$

or $b \geq 200$.

She would not need an additional fixed wage since the bonus also would give her at least as much expected utility as her outside option.

17.5 **a** The expected cost of a replacement pair is $(0.5)[(0.2)(25) + (0.8)(0)] + (0.5)[(0.6)(25) + (0.4)(0)] = €10$.

The first term is the product of the probability of a desk worker times the expected replacement cost for a desk worker; the second is the product of the probability of an active user times the expected replacement cost for an active user.

Added to the €25 cost of the original pair, the expected cost is $10 + 25 = €35$.

b Desk workers would drop out of the market. All consumers would be active users. Total expected cost would rise to 25 (for the original pair) + (0.6)(25) (expected replacement cost) = €40.

The inefficiency is that desk workers may value shoes at more than the $25 + (0.2)(25) = €30$ cost of serving them, but are not served in equilibrium.

c Shoes sell for €25. Replacement guarantees sell for $(0.6)(25) = €15$.

17.7 **a** The equilibrium is for each to bid her valuation. The price paid will be €1 million unless both have high values, in which case the price will be €2 million. Expected revenue thus is

$$(3/4)(1 \text{ million}) + (1/4)(2 \text{ million}) = €1.25 \text{ million}.$$

b With three bidders, the price paid will be €2 million if at least two have high valuations and €1 million otherwise. The probability of at least two having high valuations is 1/2. You can see this by listing the $2^3 = 8$ equally likely permutations of valuations (*LHL*, *HHL*, and so forth) and noting that half of them involve two or more high valuations *H*. Expected revenue equals

$$(1/2)(2 \text{ million}) + (1/2)(1 \text{ million}) = €1.5 \text{ million}.$$

With *N* bidders, expected revenue increases in *N*. Computing the probability of at least two high valuations is a difficult mathematical exercise that students are not expected to be able to solve. For the record, expected revenue can be shown to be

$$\left[1-(N+1)\left(\frac{1}{2}\right)^N\right](2\text{ million})+$$

$$(N+1)\left(\frac{1}{2}\right)^N(1\text{ million}).$$

c Expected revenue is the same for a first-price as from a second-price auction by the revenue-equivalence theorem.

17.9 a (1/4)(100) + (3/4)(200) = 175.

b $$200 - c_L \geq 100$$

and

$$200 - c_H < 100$$

or together,

$$c_L \leq 100 < c_H.$$

c There is a pooling equilibrium in which both get an education. This is an equilibrium as long as the firm's beliefs are that an uneducated worker is unproductive. By obtaining an education in this equilibrium, low-productivity workers obtain surplus

$$175 - c_L = 175 - 50 = 125.$$

If a low-productivity worker does not get an education, his or her surplus is 100 < 125. So the low-productivity worker would indeed prefer to get an education. Of course a high-productivity worker would as well since he or she has a lower cost of obtaining an education.

There is also a pooling equilibrium in which neither type gets an education. This is an equilibrium if the firm believes an educated worker is equally likely to be high- or low-ability. There would be no return to education, and so both types would not get an education in equilibrium.

Chapter 18

18.1 a $MC = 0.4q$. P = €20. Set $P = MC$. $20 = 0.4q$, $q = 50$.

b $MCS = 0.5q$. Set $P = MCS$. $20 = 0.5q$. $q = 40$.

At optimal production level of $q = 40$, the marginal cost of production is $MC = 0.4q = 0.4(40) = 16$, so the excise tax $t = 20 - 16$ = €4.

18.3 $AC = MC$ = 1000/well.

a Produce where revenue/well = 1000 = 10q = 5000 − 10N. N = 400. There is an externality here because drilling another well reduces output in *all* wells.

b Produce where $MVP = MC$ of well.
Total value = $5000N - 10N^2$.
$MVP = 5000 - 20N = 1000$. $N = 200$.

c Let Tax = X. Want revenue/well − X = 1000 when $N = 200$.
At $N = 200$, average revenue per well = 3000.
Charge X = 2000.

18.5 a For profit maximization, set $P = MC$, $50 = 30 + 0.5Q$. Hence $Q = 40$ hives. There will be enough bees to pollinate only 10 acres.

b Orchard owner would pay up to €25 per hive. A €20 subsidy would result in total receipts per hive of 70, and profit maximization would dictate $70 = 30 + 0.5Q$ or $Q = 80$ – enough hives to pollinate the entire 20 acres.

18.7 a Marginal valuation for person $A = P = 100 - q_A$; for B, Marginal valuation $= P = 200 - q_B$. Because of the public good nature of rat infestation control, these should be added "vertically".

Marginal value $= 300 - 2q$ (since $q_A = q_B$). Set this equal to marginal cost of 50, which gives $q = 125$.

b Private market problem could result in having no production. Each person would let the other do it.

c Total cost = 50 · 125 = €6250. Area under demand curve for A = €5000, for B = €17 188. One solution would be to share costs in proportion to these values.

18.9 a This pool is excludable, unlike many public goods. It is nonrival, however, because there is a zero marginal cost for one more user.

b Families as a whole are willing to pay €6000 per day for the pool, which would cost only €5000 per day. Building the pool would improve the allocation of resources.

c None of these prices would cover the cost of the pool. A price of either €1 or €0 would be efficient but would require the pool to operate at a loss.

d An efficient pricing scheme would require those who value the pool most to pay more. There is no single price policy that both covers the pool's cost and yields an efficient allocation.

e The economic value of the pool is maximized when it is used by 2000 families. To avoid operating at a loss, however, it still will be necessary for those who value the pool at €3 to pay that amount.

BRIEF ANSWERS TO MICROQUIZZES

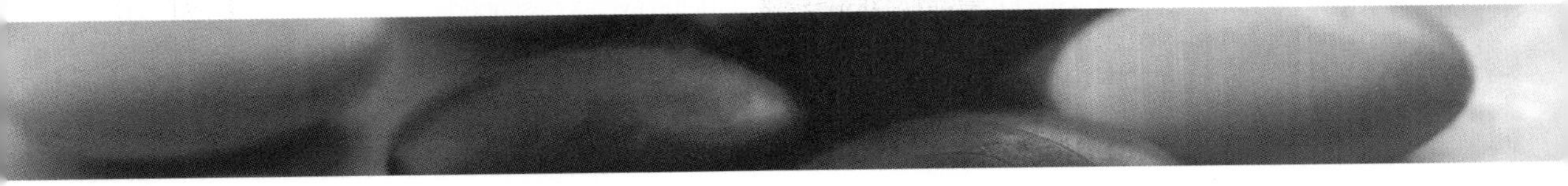

MICROQUIZ 1.1 The curve is a "frontier" because it shows *the most* of one good that can be produced if the output of the other good is held fixed (assuming that resource availability is also held constant). With a *concave* shape, the opportunity cost of producing, say, X increases as X output increases. If the frontier were *convex*, the opportunity cost of producing more X would fall as X output expanded. That might happen, for example, if X production exhibited major economies of scale.

MICROQUIZ 1.2 Supply and demand curves show economic actors' voluntary reactions to alternative prices. At the intersection of these curves, therefore, both parties to the transaction are satisfied. Any other P, Q combination would not lie at the intersection, so at least one party would not be at a position voluntarily chosen.

MICROQUIZ 1.3 Consumer income, the prices of goods related to computers, or people's preferences for computing could all shift the demand. Supply would be shifted by anything that affects the costs of making computers. The price of computers *does not* shift either curve because the curves themselves reflect demanders' and suppliers' reactions to all possible prices.

MICROQUIZ 1A.1 The intercept is in the same units as the dependent variable – 100 000 kilos per week. The slope is the change in the dependent variable for a unit change in the independent variable – 5000 kilos per week for each one euro per kilo increase in the price. If flounder were measured in kilos and price in cents, the equation would be: $Q = 100\,000 + 50P$.

MICROQUIZ 1A.2 If $Y = -5X/6 + 10$, $Y = 0$ when $X = 12$. Comparison of the graphs shows that the same change in X-intercept can come about through parallel shifts by suitably changing the Y-intercept.

MICROQUIZ 1A.3 Here, each extra worker hour increases the grape harvest by 20 pounds per hour. The average productivity is given by $Q/L = 100/L + 20$. The value of this expression is 30 for $L = 10$, 25 for $L = 20$, and 22 for $L = 50$.

MICROQUIZ 1A.4 All three sets of contour lines are the same. This shows that certain transformations of the function $Y = X \cdot Z$ have no effect on the appearance of the contour lines.

MICROQUIZ 1A.5 The shift outward in Figure 1A-6 comes about because the intercept in the equation $X + Y = 3$ changes to 5. This is a change in one of the factors held constant under *ceteris paribus*. Figure 1A-6 resembles a market in which there has been an increase in demand, perhaps from an increase in consumers' incomes.

MICROQUIZ 1A.6 With approach 1 it is likely that many other factors that affect broccoli demand change over time. Hence the points will not lie along a single demand curve. The averaging process suggested in approach 2 may improve matters, but it is still unlikely that the unmeasured factors that affect broccoli demand will cancel out across cities through this process.

MICROQUIZ 2.1 Completeness implies that all of the points in the positive quadrant of the graph can be ranked. If, say, point X_1, Y_1 is preferred to X^*, Y^*, then any other point in the "?" areas for which $X \geq X_1$ and $Y \geq Y_1$ will also be preferred to X^*, Y^*.

MICROQUIZ 2.2 Positively sloped indifference curves would imply that an increase in the amount of X consumed would have to be met by an *increase* in the amount of Y consumed to keep the individual equally well-off. But this would imply that an increase in either X or Y alone would diminish utility – a contradiction to the definition of economic "goods". The MRS cannot be computed at E or F because the indifference curve is not known at those points. All that is known is that E lies above U_I, F below it.

MICROQUIZ 2.3 The budget constraint in this case would be a straight line with intercepts of 5 on the Frisbee axis and 10 on the beach ball axis. A doubling of income would double both of these intercepts. When Frisbees cost €25, the Frisbee intercept becomes 4 and the beach ball intercept remains at 10.

MICROQUIZ 2.4 With these prices, an individual can forgo one film DVD and buy an additional 1.7 music CDs or give up 1.7 CDs to get a DVD. If the MRS is 2 CDs for 1 DVD, he or she is willing to give up more CDs than required to get a DVD. Hence, he or she should buy fewer CDs and more DVDs in order to maximize utility.

MICROQUIZ 2.5

1 In Figure 2-8(c), utility maximization requires that if *MRS* $> P_X/P_Y$ even when $Y = 0$, then $Y = 0$ is the best choice. In Figure 2-9(c), the *MRS* is 1 since these are identical goods, so if $P_X/P_Y > 1$ should choose $X = 0$. Your authors never eat butter beans because $P_{butters}/P_Y >$ *MRS* even when limas = 0. Because butter beans sell at a positive price, however, someone must like these dreadful vegetables.

2 The equilibrium in Figure 2-9(d) will exist at the vertex of the indifference curves for any price ratio. No matter what the separate prices are of left and right shoes, this person will always consume them in pairs (unless he or she cannot afford a single pair).

MICROQUIZ 3.1 In the first case, housing and other goods will both increase directly in proportion to income. In the second, the goods will increase in proportion to income until housing reaches an "adequate" level; then, no more will be bought, and all extra income will be used to purchase other goods.

MICROQUIZ 3.2

1 Brands of petrol are perfect substitutes so any significant variation in price would cause most demanders to switch to the lower cost brand.

2 Supermarket retailers sell many of the same products sold by local retailers, at a lower price. Because the goods themselves are perfect substitutes, demanders will patronize the lower price retailer.

MICROQUIZ 3.3 A decrease in the price of tea will have a substitution effect that reduces coffee purchases but an income effect that increases coffee purchases (assuming coffee is a normal good). A decrease in the price of cream will increase coffee purchases because the goods are complementary. It will also increase coffee purchases because of a positive income effect (again, assuming that coffee is a normal good). The income effects are in the same direction in both of these cases, but the substitution effects are in different directions.

MICROQUIZ 3.4 Reporter 1 confuses a movement along the demand curve for apples (the freeze raises price causing such a move) and a shift of a curve. The curve does not shift, so there are no "lower prices" as a result. Reporter 2 also makes the confusion by implying that demand falls and remains low. The freeze-induced movement along the demand curve can be reversed by a more normal crop. Notice how all of this could be clarified by showing a graph of the events described.

MICROQUIZ 3.5 Consumer surplus is measured on a demand curve for which the axes are price (in euros say, per unit) and quantity (units). Therefore, areas are measured in €/unit · units = € – consumer surplus is a monetary measure that can be compared to other monetary figures. If price rose by 10 per cent the decline in consumer surplus would be greater than 10 per cent.

MICROQUIZ 4.1 Case 1 would shift the demand for nutmeg *outward* so that at each price quantity demanded would increase by 2 million kilos per year. That is, the curve would be shifted to the right by an amount of 2 million kilos measured horizontally. Case 2 would shift the demand for nutmeg *upward* by €1 at each quantity. That is, the curve would shift upward in a vertical direction by €1.

MICROQUIZ 4.2

1 In the left hand panel, a fall in price would cause total spending to fall – demand is inelastic. In the right hand panel such a decline would cause total spending to rise – demand is elastic.

2 The per cent change in total spending for a 1 per cent change in market price is given by $1 + e_{QP}$ as can be shown by

$$\frac{\Delta PQ/PQ}{\Delta P/P} = \frac{(\Delta P \cdot Q + \Delta Q \cdot P)/PQ}{\Delta P/P} = 1 + \frac{\Delta Q/Q}{\Delta P/P}.$$

Hence, this information would also yield a precise estimate of the price elasticity of demand.

MICROQUIZ 4.3 If every good had an income elasticity of demand greater than 1, then a 1 per cent increase in income would cause total spending to rise by more than 1 per cent – an impossibility given the budget constraint. If every income elasticity of demand were less than 1, then a 1 per cent increase in income would increase total spending by less than 1 per cent – leaving some income unspent (which would not maximize utility in a one-period model). If 95 per cent of income were spent on housing, a high income elasticity of demand would result in housing expenditures quickly exhausting income when income rises. For example, suppose a consumer had an income of €100, spending €95 on housing. If the income elasticity of demand for housing were 2, then a 10 per cent increase in income (to €110) would cause a 20 per cent increase in spending on housing (to €114). Hence, housing spending would now exceed income, an impossibility.

MICROQUIZ 4.4 A fall in the price of beer will cause consumers to substitute beer for pizza. But it will also increase overall purchasing power, which will tend to increase pizza purchases. The substitution and income effects work in opposite directions. Because a 10 per cent increase in all prices and income must leave demand unchanged, the sum of these three elasticities must be zero.

MICROQUIZ 5.1

1 0.

2 €200.

3 €100.

MICROQUIZ 5.2 If the utility of wealth function were linear, the person would be risk neutral. He or she would prefer risk if the function were convex (rather than concave as shown in Figure 5-1).

MICROQUIZ 5.3

1 The expected value of the bet is zero in either case, but the variability of outcomes is much higher with the single flip.

2 The expected time to be served is the same under either approach, but the variability is higher with lines for each teller (the feeling that one has chosen the wrong line is universal).

3 Your authors feel that any scoring in sports involves some randomness. Hence, sports in which many goals are scored will be more likely to reveal the best team than sports where only a few goals are scored (true, soccer fans will probably disagree).

MICROQUIZ 5.4

1 The proposed transaction is to buy the film at €100 million. The expected value of this transaction depends on the expected film revenue and on the probability Lucas will make the movie. Both of these features add variability to the transaction's value. Presumably the duration of the option is infinite.

2 The value of the option is expected film revenue minus €100 million discounted to the present day and by the probability the film will be made.

MICROQUIZ 5.5

1 There is no risk because C is the same no matter which state of the world occurs.

2 The actuarially fair slope is $-0.6/0.4 = -1.5$ – this person should be able to trade 1 unit of C_1 for 1.5 units of C_2 because State 1 is more likely to occur.

3 The slope of the indifference curve is determined by the expected MRS, which is also given by the ratios of the expected marginal utility of C_1 to the expected marginal utility of C_2.

4 If the probabilities of State 1 and State 2 are 0.6 and 0.4 respectively, then the expected MRS is $0.6MU(C_1)/0.4MU(C_2)$. Setting this equal to the actuarially fair price ratio (0.6/0.4) implies that $MU(C_1) = MU(C_2)$. If the marginal utility function is the same for both states of the world, this implies $C_1 = C_2$ – that the person is on the Certainty Line.

MICROQUIZ 6.1

1 $(1/2)(1) + (1/2)(-1) = 0$.

2 $(1/2)(-1) + (1/2)(1) = 0$.

3 Parts 1 and 2 showed that A's expected payoff from playing either heads or tails is 0. Therefore, A's expected payoff from the indicated mixed strategy is $(1/2)(0) + (1/2)(0) = 0$.

4 $(1/3)(0) + (2/3)(0) = 0$.

MICROQUIZ 6.2

1 No.

2 No. If a player has a dominant strategy, he or she would obtain a higher expected surplus from playing it than any other strategy and so would play the dominant strategy with probability one.

MICROQUIZ 6.3

1 The payoff vector (2,1) is associated with two different Nash equilibria. In the first one, B always plays ballet no matter what A does. In the second, B always follows A. These are two very different strategies.

2 There are three different ways B could end up playing Ballet. He could play the strategy of always choosing Ballet. He could play the strategy of following A, and A could have played Ballet. Or he could play the strategy of doing the opposite of A, and A could have chosen Boxing. To be clear about which strategy B is actually playing, one needs to specify a complete contingent plan following any action by A.

MICROQUIZ 6.4

1 $r = 0$.

2 Relenting would make sustaining cooperation more difficult. Only the threat of punishment deters deviation from cooperation. Relenting reduces the severity of the punishment, and less severe punishments have less deterrence value.

MICROQUIZ 6.5

1 The three equations, found by equating marginal benefits with marginal costs (zero) are $120 - 2s_A - s_B - s_C = 0$, $120 - s_A - 2s_B - s_C = 0$, and $120 - s_A - s_B - 2s_C = 0$. Solving them simultaneously, $s^*_A = s^*_B = s^*_C = 30$.

MICROQUIZ 7.1 In Case 1, the marginal product of labor is 50 apples per hour. The average productivity of labor declines as L increases because the fixed term, "10", is divided by progressively larger amounts of labor. In Case 2, the marginal product of labor is five books dusted per minute. The average productivity of labor increases as L increases because the "−10" term is divided by progressively larger amounts of labor input.

MICROQUIZ 7.2 The RTS here is: $\frac{1}{2}$ hour of labor time can be substituted for an increase in shovel size. The one-hole isoquant is two points: (a) 1 hour, small shovel; (b) $\frac{1}{2}$ hour, large shovel. A worker using a small shovel can dig $\frac{1}{2}$ the hole in $\frac{1}{2}$ an hour. If he or she then switches to the large shovel, the hole can be completed in $\frac{1}{4}$ an hour. Hence, this production technique would use $\frac{3}{4}$ an hour of labor time.

MICROQUIZ 7.3

1 Clearly a doubling of K and L would double output here. So the function exhibits constant returns to scale.
2 The function assumes that K and L are perfect substitutes. The RTS for this function is a constant – it does not diminish as L increases.
3 The function implies that q can be produced without using any labor input – a situation that is unlikely.

MICROQUIZ 7.4

1 At least in part technical progress, though some substitution also.
2 At least in part technical progress, though some substitution also.
3 Almost exclusively substitution of capital for labor.
4 Almost entirely technical progress.

MICROQUIZ 8.1 Rent payments are for housing services. Someone who lives in his or her own house similarly pays for such services in the form of forgone earnings on the funds invested. So, the key question is which form of housing consumption provides the services at lower costs (including opportunity costs). Paying off the mortgage converts explicit interest costs into implicit ones (the forgone earnings one could obtain by investing funds tied up in the house). If opportunity costs are the same as mortgage costs, burning the mortgage has no significance.

MICROQUIZ 8.2

1. With fixed proportions, it will take 10 labor hours and 20 hours of capital services to produce 100 units of output. Total cost will be $10 \cdot 10 + 20 \cdot 4 = 180$. If capital rental rates rise to 10, the firm will continue to use the same fixed proportions but its total costs will increase to 300.
2. With this production function, the RTS (L for K) is 2. That is, an extra unit of labor can substitute for two units of capital. With $w = 10$ and $v = 4$, cost minimization requires that the firm use only capital: if it hires 20 units to produce 100 units of output, total costs are 80 (they would be 100 if only labor were used). If v increases to 10, labor becomes the less expensive input. The firm will use $L = 10$ and incur total costs of 100.

MICROQUIZ 8.3

1 Average will be $(80 \cdot 5 + 60 \cdot 2)/7 = 520/7 = 74.3$.
2 Need $(520 + 3x)/10 = 80$, $3x = 280$, $x = 93.3$.
3 When the marginal score falls below the average, the average falls. When the marginal score exceeds the average, the average rises.

MICROQUIZ 8.4

1 *SAC* exceeds *AC* for every output level except q^*, because at all other output levels the firm is using a level of capital input that is not cost minimizing.
2 *SMC* exceeds *MC* for $q > q^*$, because there are more significant diminishing returns to variable inputs in the short run (when some inputs are fixed) than in the long run.
3 An increase in K above K^* would shift the *SAC* and *SMC* rightward along the *AC* curve.

MICROQUIZ 8.5 The larger the fraction of total costs that are attributable to labor, the greater will be the effect of the increase in wages on total costs. If the firm is able to substitute capital for labor, the extent of this cost increase may be ameliorated.

MICROQUIZ 9.1

1 Profit per unit is greatest when the gap between average revenue and average cost is greatest. That may not be where marginal revenue and marginal costs are equal. Even if application of the $MR = MC$ rule reduces profit per unit, it will increase *total* profits.
2 Since price is equal to "average revenue", the proposed rule would indeed maximize profit per unit. When average revenue is fixed, minimizing average cost would achieve this goal. For the reasons listed in 1, however, this would not maximize *total* profits.

MICROQUIZ 9.2

1 The demand for any one crossing is elastic. When all crossings are taken together, however, the demand is inelastic.
2 The same argument applies here. The demand for meals in any one town may be elastic, but, if the tax increase is statewide, consumers cannot so easily escape it.

MICROQUIZ 9.3

1 Equation 9.9 implies that $MR/P = 1 + 1/e$. Hence, the less elastic is the demand (assuming $e < -1$), the smaller will be the ratio MR/P.
2 Equation 9.9 implies that the *percentage* change in P will be the same as the *percentage* change in MR if e does not change. If e changes, the two percentages may differ.

MICROQUIZ 9.4

1 An increase in fixed costs will affect neither the *SMC* curve nor the shutdown point.

2 The fine could be treated as a fixed cost and therefore would have no effect on supply decisions. A daily fine would still be treated as a fixed cost in Whopper supply decisions. But it might provide an incentive to the firm to adopt new, less littering packaging materials.

MICROQUIZ 10.1

1 When only 100 paddles are in the air.

2 When paddles in the air increase to 100. (Are these two prices the same?)

MICROQUIZ 10.2

1 The farmer cannot get the €3.25, even though his or her costs may require that, because any buyer can get all the corn desired at €3.

2 No seller will sell to the soup kitchen at €2.75 if he or she can make €3 elsewhere (unless the seller derives utility from helping the poor).

MICROQUIZ 10.3

1 The price would rise to €7. Demand would be 3 and supply would be $5 - 2 = 3$.

2 Trial and error using Table 10-2 suggests that a price to buyers of €8 and to sellers of €4 would create the necessary tax "wedge". In this case, the quantity demanded and supplied would be 2.

MICROQUIZ 10.4

1 Assuming the industry as perfectly competitive, economic profits will be zero despite the price rise, since costs will rise too (rising costs are the explanation of the noninfinite elasticity of supply).

2 Existing firms will also continue to earn zero profits because their costs too will rise.

MICROQUIZ 11.1

1 If expansion of the industry does not lead to increases in the prices of any inputs, the long-run supply curve will be perfectly elastic.

2 As the demand for potato land increases, its price will rise. This will be the sole reason for rising potato prices. Producer surplus will be the extra rents earned by potato landowners. The rents do not "cause" the price increase – rather, they are a result of it.

MICROQUIZ 11.2

1 The short-run impact would depend on the extent of the increase in demand and on the supply response that was prevented by the price control. The size of the latter effect would depend on the short-run elasticity of supply, which in turn is determined by diminishing returns in the short run. The long-run impact would depend on the long-run elasticity of supply, which depends on the possibility of rising input costs (e.g., for research inputs).

2 In the short run, firms would lose producer surplus in the form of short-run profits. In the long run, the losses would accrue to the inputs that, in the absence of the price control, would have increased in price.

MICROQUIZ 11.3

1 Because short-run supply is less elastic than long-run supply.

2 One would need to examine the reasons for the upward slope in the long-run supply curve. Owners of inputs that cause the upward slope would pay the producer's share of the tax.

MICROQUIZ 11.4

1 Consumer surplus is $\frac{1}{2}(10 - 7)(3) = 4.5$. Producer surplus is $\frac{1}{2}(5 - 2)(3) = 4.5$. Taxes are 6. Hence, total surplus plus taxes amount to 15. Prior to the tax, consumer surplus was 8 and producer surplus was 8. With the tax, there is a deadweight loss of 1. That can also be computed as $\frac{1}{2}(t)(\Delta Q) = \frac{1}{2}(2)(1) = 1$.

2 With a tax of 4, $P - 2 = 10 - (P + 4)$, or $P = 4$; $P + t = 8$; and $Q = 2$. Deadweight loss is $\frac{1}{2}(t)(\Delta Q) = \frac{1}{2}(4)(2) = 4$. Consumer surplus $= \frac{1}{2}(10 - 8)(2) = 2$, producer surplus $= \frac{1}{2}(4 - 2)(2) = 2$, and tax collections are 8. Adding the three gives 12, a loss of 4 from total surplus when there are no taxes.

3 With a tax of, say, 8, $Q = 0$. All producer and consumer surplus would be lost. There would be no tax collected.

MICROQUIZ 11.5

1 Relative to a situation of free trade, domestic producers pay none of this tax. Assuming that the foreign supply curve is infinitely elastic, foreign producers pay none of the tax either. The tariff is paid solely by domestic consumers.

2 The increase in producer surplus from the tariff goes to those inputs that give rise to the positively sloped long-run supply curve.

3 Both areas are losses of consumer surplus that are not captured by firms nor by the government.

MICROQUIZ 12.1 The primary reason for the second supply curve is to allow for repercussions in labor markets that serve the tomato industry. The rise in tomato pickers' wages shifts the supply curve. A model that looked at the effect of the shift in demand without considering these labor market effects would underpredict the impact of the increase in demand on tomato prices.

MICROQUIZ 12.2

1 Only the point for which $X = Y$ on the frontier would be economically efficient.

2 A point for which $X = 2Y$ on the frontier is inefficient because utility can be improved by producing more Y and less X until a point where $X = Y$ is reached.

MICROQUIZ 12.3 The initial price of X would be below equilibrium. The initial price for Y would be above equilibrium. Raising P_X and lowering P_Y would restore equilibrium in both markets simultaneously.

MICROQUIZ 12.4

1 The only efficient point is where Smith gets all the X and Jones gets all the Y.

2 In this case, only the points on the diagonal of the box would be efficient.

3 In this case, all of the points in the box would be efficient.

MICROQUIZ 12.5

a A pure inflation would have no effect on relative prices, hence, with a correctly drawn supply-demand diagram, neither the demand curve nor the supply curve should shift.

b If the supply–demand curve (incorrectly) shows nominal price on the vertical axis, a pure inflation would shift both demand and supply curves up by precisely the same amounts. Equilibrium quantity would remain unchanged.

MICROQUIZ 13.1

1 The monopoly is constrained by the demand curve for its product. That curve provides a menu of price-quantity combinations – once one variable is chosen, the other is defined as well.

2 The profit maximization rule for price setting must still focus on the MR/MC idea. The price should be chosen so that the extra revenue from lowering the price slightly (this amount must be positive because the monopoly will operate only where demand is elastic) is just equal to the extra costs involved in producing the extra output that is sold.

MICROQUIZ 13.2

1 The increase in demand will shift the marginal revenue curve outward. If MC is positively sloped, quantity will increase. Since MR has also increased, P will increase unless the elasticity of demand changes greatly (see part 2).

2 Although quantity will always rise when MR shifts outward along a positively sloped MC curve, price itself could fall if demand became much more elastic. Since $MR = P(1 + 1/e)$, a large enough increase in $(1 + 1/e)$ could allow P to fall even though MR increases.

MICROQUIZ 13.3 The deadweight loss of consumer surplus is fundamentally a loss of utility to consumers – they receive less utility than they would if the market were competitive. Monopoly profits are a transfer from consumer surplus to the monopoly. They are not part of the deadweight loss.

MICROQUIZ 13.4

1 The notion of "higher demand" is meaningless. It is elasticity of demand that matters.

2 The monopoly should set $MR = MC$ in both markets. If the elasticities in the markets differ, this need not imply that the market with higher MC will have a higher price.

MICROQUIZ 13.5 With U-shaped average costs, there is no regulatory dilemma – the regulator can set $P = MC =$ minimum AC and achieve efficiency with zero economic profits. If P is set below AC, losses will result. Clearly, P could also be set below the shutdown price.

MICROQUIZ 14.1

1 B's best-response function would shift in toward the origin. A's would not shift. The new Nash equilibrium would be at the point of intersection between B's new best-response function and A's unchanged one. The new Nash equilibrium would involve higher output for A and lower for B.

2 If costs for both increased, both best-response functions would shift in toward the origin. The Nash equilibrium would involve lower output for both. If costs decreased, the opposite would happen. An increase in the demand intercept would cause both best-response functions to shift out from the original and the Nash equilibrium quantities to increase.

MICROQUIZ 14.2 It cannot be a Nash equilibrium because the firm that charges marginal cost earns zero profit in the outcome but could earn positive profit by deviating to a price slightly higher than marginal cost and less than the other firm's price.

MICROQUIZ 14.3

1 B's best-response function would shift up. A's would not shift. The new Nash equilibrium would involve higher prices for both.

2 Both firms' best-response functions would shift away from the origin. The new Nash equilibrium would involve higher prices for both. A cost decrease would have the opposite effect. An increase in the demand intercept would shift the best-response functions away from the origin and result in higher Nash equilibrium prices. A decrease in substitutability is tricky to formalize. Thought about the right way, it would probably result in best-response functions shifting out and increasing Nash equilibrium prices.

MICROQUIZ 14.4

1 An increase in this sort of advertising would make the products closer substitutes and intensify second-stage price competition between them. Recognizing this effect, firms may cut back on advertising to keep competition softer and prices higher.

2 This sort of advertising would have the opposite effect as in part 1.

MICROQUIZ 14.5

1 *A* would have to produce more to deter *B*'s entry (complicated calculations show that *A* would be required to produce about 67 to deter *B*'s entry).

2 *A* can deter *B*'s entry simply producing the Stackelberg output of 60. This also happens to be the monopoly output. The implication is that *A*'s simply operating as a monopolist ignoring *B* is sufficient to deter *B*'s entry.

MICROQUIZ 14.6

1 Downward-sloping demand and free entry (so zero profits).

2 The potential loss would be a loss of product diversity. The fact that demand curves facing individual firms are assumed to be downward-sloping in the monopolistic-competition model is often justified by the assumption that firms' products are at least slightly differentiated. If a firm exits, consumers lose the variety of the good it offers and thus lose some consumer surplus.

MICROQUIZ 15.1

1 The monopoly will hire labor up to the point at which $w = MR \cdot MP_L$ and capital up to the point at which $v = MR \cdot MP_K$. Because $MR < P$, $w < MVP_L$, $v < MVP_K$.

2 Even for the monopoly, $w/v = MP_L/MP_K$ (the *MR* term cancels out), so the firm is minimizing cost.

MICROQUIZ 15.2

1 There will be no substitution effects from the wage increase. But the wage increase may cause a rise in petrol prices and therefore a fall in the demand for petrol and for attendants to pump it.

2 Because of the fixed-proportions nature of production, again there is no need to worry about substitution effects. A 10 per cent rise in wages will raise petrol prices by 3.33 per cent. That will result in a decline in purchases of 1.67 per cent and a similar decline in hiring of attendants. Hence, the elasticity of demand is $-0.167(= -1.67/10)$.

MICROQUIZ 15.3 As for any tax, the actual incidence of the 12 per cent total tax depends on the elasticities of supply and demand.

MICROQUIZ 15.4 Yes, there is a deadweight loss triangle in Figure 15-5 that is similar to the deadweight loss from monopoly. Part of the loss is suffered by suppliers who receive lower wages than they would under competition; part is suffered by demanders who cannot convert all of the surplus they would enjoy under competition into monopsony profits.

MICROQUIZ 15A.1

1 The indifference curves have income and substitution effects of increases in *w* always precisely balanced at 7 hours of work.

2 The indifference curve map intersects the leisure axis with a slope steeper than the prevailing wage rate.

MICROQUIZ 15A.2 The proportional tax on wages effectively reduces the wage rate, inducing income and substitution effects in labor supply – the substitution effect would favor less work, the income effect more work. A lump-sum tax would have no substitution effect, only an income effect favoring more work.

MICROQUIZ 16.1

1 C_1 is effectively "cheaper" than C_0 because interest can be earned before C_1 is purchased. If $r = 0.10$, the relative price of C_1 is $1/1.1 = 0.909$. Refraining from buying 0.909 units of C_0 permits this person to buy one unit of C_1.

2 An increase in *r* reduces $1/(1 + r)$. For example, if $r = 0.15$, the relative price of C_1 is 0.870, a reduction from 0.909. This price decline has both income and substitution effects that favor consuming more C_1. The ambiguity is in the effect on C_0: a higher relative price of C_0 creates substitution effects causing C_0 to fall but income effects causing C_0 to rise (because the higher interest rate increases the person's purchasing power in this case).

MICROQUIZ 16.2 A pure inflation would not affect the real interest rate nor the depreciation rate in Equation 16.1. It would raise the price of machinery, *P*, and the price of the firm's output, P^*, both by the same amount. Hence, in the equation $MVP_K = P^* \, MP_K = v = P(r + d)$, the effects of inflation would appear on both sides and would cancel out, leaving the firm's capital use decision unchanged.

MICROQUIZ 16.3 Clearly, the present value of the payments is not €20 million. To calculate the present value, one would need to assume a specific nominal interest rate (nominal because the lottery payments are nominal). At 5 per cent, for example, €1 million per year for 20 years has a present value of €12.5 million, significantly less than €20 million. At a 10 per cent interest rate, the present value is only €8.5 million.

MICROQUIZ 16.4

1 The finite nature of the resource poses the same sort of opportunity cost for the monopoly as for a competitive firm.

2 If the future price is assumed to be the same for the monopoly and the competitive firm, the result that the resource price must rise at the rate of interest implies that the monopoly price will be identical to the competitive price in all time periods. The firm cannot exercise its monopoly power.

MICROQUIZ 16A.1 If €1 is invested for 3 years, the terms in the expansion have the following meanings:

a 1 – the original euro is returned.

b $3i$ – interest is earned on the original euro in each year.

c $3i^2$ – interest earned on Year 1's interest in Year 2 (i^2) plus interest on Year 1's interest in Year 3 (i^2) plus interest on Year 2's interest in Year 3 (i^2), which equals $3i^2$ in all.

d i^3 – interest earned in Year 3 on the interest earned in Year 2 on Year 1's interest.

MICROQUIZ 16A.2 With a 5 per cent interest rate, the present value of €1000 in 5 years is €784 (see Table 16A-2). The value of €3000 in 25 years is 3(295) = €885, so it is worth the wait. If the interest rate is 10 per cent, the €1000 has a present value of €621, and the €3000 has a present value of €277: With the higher interest rate, the wait is clearly not worthwhile.

MICROQUIZ 16A.3

1 Increasing the annual payment to \$65 would raise the yield to 4.66 per cent.

2 Increasing the maturity value to \$1100 would raise the yield to 4.64 per cent.

3 Reducing the maturity to 23 years would lower the yield to 4.38 per cent (because the \$1000 face value of the bond is returned sooner).

MICROQUIZ 16A.4 Depreciation can be handled by assuming that the machine's rental rate deteriorates at the rate d per period. Hence, in Period n, the numerator to Equation 16A.33 should be $v/(1 + d)^n$. The equation therefore becomes $\sum_1^n v/(1 + r)^i (1 + d)^i$. Because $(1 + r)(1 + d) \approx (1 + r + d)$, this can be approximated by $\sum_1^n v/(1 + r + d)^i$, and taking n to infinity yields $P = v/(r + d)$, which is Equation 16.1.

MICROQUIZ 17.1 The manager has to be paid enough to get him or her to work at the firm rather than somewhere else. The more effort the firm tries to induce from the manager, the more the manager has to be paid to compensate. So while gross profit may be increasing in e above e*, profit (gross profit minus manager pay) is not.

MICROQUIZ 17.2

1 Consumer surplus = area of shaded triangle = (15 − 7)(10)(1/2) = 40.

2 Gross consumer surplus = area of shaded triangle and rectangle = 40 + (20)(7) = 40 + 140 = 180.

MICROQUIZ 17.3 There are three ranges for player 2's bid: first, 2 could bid below 50; second, between 50 and 70; and third, above 70. First, if 2 bids below 50, player 1 would win the object whether he or she bid 50 or 70 and would pay the other player's bid regardless. Second, if 2 bids between 50 and 70, 1 would win the object and earn a negative surplus (equal to the difference between his or her valuation 50 and player 2's bid) if it bid 70; if it bid 50 it would lose the object and earn zero surplus. Third, if 2 bids above 70, 1 loses the object and pays nothing whether its bid is 50 or 70.

MICROQUIZ 17.4

1 The seller may know how diligently the car was maintained, whether the car had sustained an accident, whether the car is prone to breakdown, how the car handles in different driving conditions, and so forth.

2 Sellers of higher-quality cars and buyers would benefit from solving the lemons problem. The lemons problem results in mutually advantageous trades not being executed. Some solutions were offered in the text: seller reputation, buyer knowledge about quality indicators, certification by an independent repair shop (hired by either the buyer or the seller), money-back guarantees offered by the seller, seller-provided repair histories, and so forth.

MICROQUIZ 17.5

1 No. If there were, high types would have to prefer to separate than pool. The higher wage must compensate them for any higher education cost. But then a low type would benefit from mimicking the high-type's education level. It would get the same wage as a high type but would have to pay a lower education cost.

2 Yes. For example, there is a pooling equilibrium in which no one gets an education. This equilibrium could be supported by out-of-equilibrium beliefs that an educated worker has an equal chance of being a high or low type (so education does not change the firm's initial beliefs).

MICROQUIZ 17.6 A possible extensive form is below.

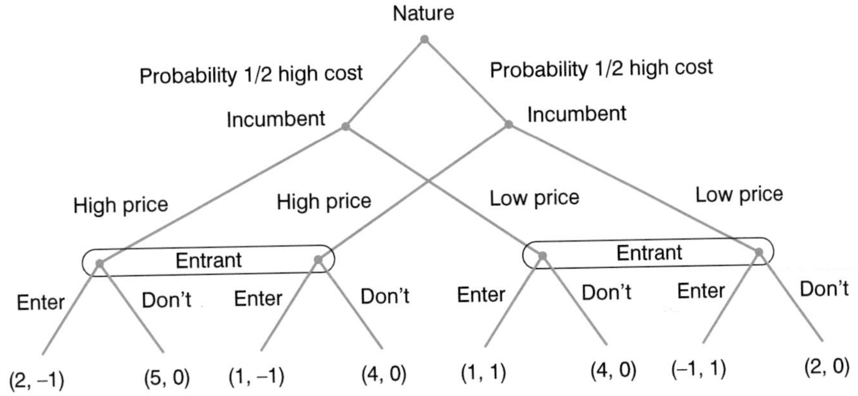

MICROQUIZ 18.1 These deadweight losses are losses of utility that would have gone to consumers under an alternative market equilibrium, just as in the monopoly case.

MICROQUIZ 18.2

1 In the absence of enforceable property rights, Coase-type exchanges would not occur because neither party could be sure that the other would stick to the agreement.

2 With high transactions costs, property rights' assignments matter. The rights should be assigned to the party most likely to internalize the externality. This observation is crucial to the study of law and economics.

MICROQUIZ 18.3

1 Under all three strategies, firms are left on their own to choose cost-minimizing control strategies. The requirement of specific technologies for all firms would not be likely to result in cost minimization.

2 The government does not need to know anything about the specific cost functions of firms under any of the three market-based strategies.

MICROQUIZ 18.4

1 Free riding arises because individuals obtain benefits from the public good without paying for them. That requires nonexclusion. If exclusion were possible (even if the good were nonrival), production could take place in "clubs".

2 To achieve efficiency with nonrival goods requires that the price for each use be zero. With such a price there would be no way to pay the production costs of the good unless the good could be organized as a club with an entry fee.

GLOSSARY

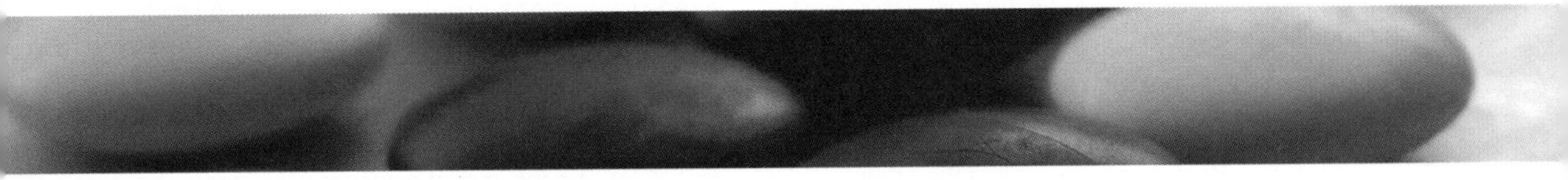

A

accounting cost The concept that inputs cost what was paid for them. (p. 236)

adverse-selection problem A version of the principal-agent model in which the agent's type is private information. (p. 528)

agent Player who performs under the terms of the contract in a principal-agent model. (p. 528)

asymmetric information In a game with uncertainty, information that one player has but the other does not. (p. 527)

average cost Total cost divided by output; a common measure of cost per unit. (p. 243)

average effect The ratio of *Y* to *X* at a particular value of *X*. (Also the slope of the ray from the origin to the function.) (p. 33)

B

backward induction Solving for equilibrium by working backwards from the end of the game to the beginning. (p. 188)

barriers to entry Factors that prevent new firms from entering a market. (p. 373)

Bertrand model An oligopoly model in which firms simultaneously choose prices for a homogeneous product. (p. 412)

best response A strategy that produces the highest payoff among all possible strategies for a player given what the other player is doing. (p. 167)

best-response function Function giving the payoff-maximizing choice for one player for each of a continuum of actions of the other player. (p. 178)

bilateral monopoly A market in which both suppliers and demanders have monopoly power. Pricing is indeterminate in such markets. (p. 469)

budget constraint The limit that income places on the combinations of goods that an individual can buy. (p. 61)

C

capacity constraint A limit to the quantity a firm can produce given the firm's capital and other available inputs. (p. 413)

***ceteris paribus* assumption** In economic analysis, holding all other factors constant so that only the factor being studied is allowed to change. (p. 48)

Coase theorem If bargaining is costless, the social cost of an externality will be taken into account by the parties, and the allocation of resources will be the same no matter how property rights are assigned. (p. 571)

common property Property that may be used by anyone without cost. (p. 570)

common-values setting Object has the same value to all bidders but each only has an imprecise estimate of that value. (p. 550)

competitive fringe Group of firms that act as price takers in a market dominated by a price leader. (p. 434)

complements Two goods such that when the price of one increases, the quantity demanded of the other falls. (p. 96)

complete preferences The assumption that an individual is able to state which of any two options is preferred. (p. 51)

composite good Combining expenditures on several different goods whose relative prices do not change into a single good for convenience in analysis. (p. 70)

compound interest Interest paid on prior interest earned. (p. 511)

constant cost case A market in which entry or exit has no effect on the cost curves of firms. (p. 305)

consumer surplus The extra value individuals receive from consuming a good over what they pay for it. What people would be willing to pay for the right to consume a good at its current price. (pp. 103, 319)

contour lines Lines in two dimensions that show the sets of values of the independent variables that yield the same value for the dependent variable. (p. 38)

contract curve The set of efficient allocations of the existing goods in an exchange situation. Points off that curve are necessarily inefficient, since individuals can be made unambiguously better off by moving to the curve. (p. 360)

Cournot model An oligopoly model in which firms simultaneously choose quantities of a homogeneous product. (p. 405)

cross-price elasticity of demand The percentage change in the quantity demanded of a good in response to a 1 per cent change in the price of another good. (p. 127)

D

deadweight loss Losses of consumer and producer surplus that are not transferred to other parties. (p. 331)

decreasing cost case A market in which the entry of firms decreases firms' costs. (p. 311)

demand function A representation of how quantity demanded depends on prices, income, and preferences. (p. 77)

dependent variable In algebra, a variable whose value is determined by another variable or set of variables. (p. 25)

diminishing returns Hypothesis that the cost associated with producing one more unit of a good rises as more of that good is produced. (p. 13)

diversification The spreading of risk among several options rather than choosing only one. (p. 148)

dominant strategy Best response to all of the other player's strategies. (p. 173)

E

economic cost The amount required to keep an input in its present use; the amount that it would be worth in its next best alternative use. (p. 236)

economic profits (π) The difference between a firm's total revenues and its total economic costs. (p. 238)

economically efficient allocation of resources An allocation of resources in which the sum of consumer and producer surplus is maximized. Reflects the best (utility-maximizing) use of scarce resources. (pp. 323, 350)

economics The study of the allocation of scarce resources among alternative uses. (p. 4)

economies of scope Reductions in the costs of one product of a multiproduct firm when the output of another product is increased. (p. 254)

Edgeworth box diagram A graphic device for illustrating all of the possible allocations of two goods (or two inputs) that are in fixed supply. (p. 358)

elasticity The measure of the percentage change in one variable brought about by a 1 per cent change in some other variable. (p. 116)

equilibrium price The price at which the quantity demanded by buyers of a good is equal to the quantity supplied by sellers of the good. (pp. 14, 292)

equity The fairness of the distribution of goods or utility. (p. 357)

expansion path The set of cost-minimizing input combinations a firm will choose to produce various levels of output (when the prices of inputs are held constant). (p. 242)

expected value The average outcome from an uncertain gamble. (p. 139)

extensive form Representation of a game as a tree. (p. 170)

externality The effect of one party's economic activities on another party that is not taken into account by the price system. (pp. 356, 565)

F

fair games Games that cost their expected value. (p. 140)

fair insurance Insurance for which the premium is equal to the expected value of the loss. (p. 144)

firm Any organization that turns inputs into outputs. (p. 205)

firm's short-run supply curve The relationship between price and quantity supplied by a firm in the short run. (p. 282)

first theorem of welfare economics A perfectly competitive price system will bring about an economically efficient allocation of resources. (p. 350)

fixed costs Costs associated with inputs that are fixed in the short run. (p. 248)

fixed-proportions production function A production function in which the inputs must be used in a fixed ratio to one another. (p. 221)

focal point Logical outcome on which to coordinate, based on information outside of the game. (p. 181)

free rider A consumer of a nonexclusive good who does not pay for it in the hope that other consumers will. (p. 584)

functional notation A way of denoting the fact that the value taken on by one variable (Y) depends on the value taken on by some other variable (X) or set of variables. (p. 25)

G

general equilibrium model An economic model of a complete system of markets. (p. 345)

Giffen's paradox A situation in which an increase in a good's price leads people to consume more of the good. (p. 87)

gross consumer surplus Most consumers would pay for a bundle rather than doing without it. (p. 539)

H

homogeneous demand function Quantity demanded does not change when prices and income increase in the same proportion. (p. 78)

I

imperfect competition A market situation in which buyers or sellers have some influence on the prices of goods or services. (p. 355)

incentive-compatible Describes contract that gets the agent to make the intended choice. (p. 542)

income effect (in demand theory) The part of the change in quantity demanded that is caused by a change in real income. A movement to a new indifference curve. (p. 81)

income effect of a change in *w* Movement to a higher indifference curve in response to a rise in the real wage rate. If leisure is a normal good, a rise in w causes an individual to work less. (p. 481)

income elasticity of demand The percentage change in the quantity demanded of a good in response to a 1 per cent change in income. (p. 127)

incomplete information Some players have information about the game that others do not. (pp. 197, 430)

increase or decrease in demand The change in demand for a good caused by changes in the price of another good, in income, or in preferences. Graphically represented by a shift of the entire demand curve. (p. 101)

increase or decrease in quantity demanded The increase or decrease in quantity demanded caused by a change in the good's price. Graphically represented by the movement along a demand curve. (p. 101)

increasing cost case A market in which the entry of firms increases firms' costs. (p. 308)

independent variable In an algebraic equation, a variable that is unaffected by the action of another variable and may be assigned any value. (p. 25)

indifference curve A curve that shows all the combinations of goods or services that provide the same level of utility. (p. 52)
indifference curve map A contour map that shows the utility an individual obtains from all possible consumption options. (p. 55)
individual demand curve A graphic representation of the relationship between the price of a good and the quantity of it demanded by a person, holding all other factors constant. (p. 97)
inferior good A good that is bought in smaller quantities as income increases. (p. 79)
initial endowments The initial holdings of goods from which trading begins. (p. 360)
intercept The value of *Y* when *X* equals zero. (p. 27)
interest Payment for the current use of funds. (p. 511)
isoquant A curve that shows the various combinations of inputs that will produce the same amount of output. (p. 213)
isoquant map A contour map of a firm's production function. (p. 213)

L

leisure Time spent in any activity other than market work. (p. 478)
Lindahl equilibrium Balance between people's demand for public goods and the tax shares that each must pay for them. (p. 586)
linear function An equation that is represented by a straight-line graph. (p. 27)
long run The period of time in which a firm may consider all of its inputs to be variable in making its decisions. (p. 246)
long-run elasticity of supply The percentage change in quantity supplied in the long run in response to a 1 per cent change in price. (p. 309)

M

marginal cost The additional cost of producing one more unit of output. (p. 244)
marginal effect The change in *Y* brought about by a one unit change in *X* at a particular value of *X*. (Also the slope of the function.) (p. 33)
marginal expense The cost of hiring one more unit of an input. Will exceed the price of the input if the firm faces an upward-sloping supply curve for the input. (p. 461)
marginal product The additional output that can be produced by adding one more unit of a particular input while holding all other inputs constant. (p. 206)
marginal rate of substitution (MRS) The rate at which an individual is willing to reduce consumption of one good when he or she gets one more unit of another good. The negative of the slope of an indifference curve. (p. 53)
marginal rate of technical substitution (RTS) The amount by which one input can be reduced when one more unit of another input is added while holding output constant. The negative of the slope of an isoquant. (p. 214)
marginal revenue The extra revenue a firm receives when it sells one more unit of output. (p. 271)
marginal revenue curve A curve showing the relation between the quantity a firm sells and the revenue yielded by the last unit sold. Derived from the demand curve. (p. 276)
marginal revenue product The extra revenue obtained from selling the output produced by hiring an extra worker or machine. (p. 448)
marginal value product (MVP) A special case of marginal revenue product in which the firm is a price taker for its output. (p. 449)
market demand The total quantity of a good or service demanded by all potential buyers. (p. 111)
market demand curve The relationship between the total quantity demanded of a good or service and its price, holding all other factors constant. (p. 111)
market line A line showing the relationship between risk and annual returns that an investor can achieve by mixing financial assets. (p. 155)
market period A short period of time during which quantity supplied is fixed. (p. 292)
median voter A voter whose preferences for a public good represent the middle point of all voters' preferences for the good. (p. 590)
microeconomics The study of the economic choices individuals and firms make and of how those choices create markets. (p. 4)
mixed strategy Randomly selecting from several possible actions. (p. 173)
models Simple theoretical descriptions that capture the essentials of how the economy works. (p. 4)
monopolistic competition Market in which each firm faces a downward-sloping demand curve and there are no barriers to entry. (p. 435)
monopoly rents The profits that a monopolist earns in the long run. (p. 377)
monopsony Condition in which one firm is the only hirer in a particular input market. (p. 461)
moral-hazard problem The agent's actions benefit the principal but the principal does not directly observe the actions. (p. 528)

N

Nash equilibrium A set of strategies, one for each player, that are each best responses against one another. (p. 167)
natural monopoly A firm that exhibits diminishing average cost over a broad range of output levels. (p. 373)
nonexclusive goods Goods that provide benefits that no one can be excluded from enjoying. (p. 580)
nonrival goods Goods that additional consumers may use at zero marginal costs. (p. 580)
normal form Representation of a game using a payoff matrix. (p. 169)
normal good A good that is bought in greater quantities as income increases. (p. 78)

O

oligopoly A market with few firms, but more than one. (p. 403)
opportunity cost The cost of a good as measured by the alternative uses that are forgone by producing the good. (pp. 5, 235)

option A contract offering the right, but not the obligation, to complete an economic transaction over a specified period. (p. 150)

output effect The effect of an input price change on the amount of the input that the firm hires that results from a change in the firm's output level. (p. 454)

P

Pareto efficient allocation An allocation of available resources in which no mutually beneficial trading opportunities are unexploited. That is, an allocation in which no one person can be made better off without someone else being made worse off. (p. 360)

partial equilibrium model An economic model of a single market. (p. 345)

perfect price discrimination Selling each unit of output for the highest price obtainable. Extracts all of the consumer surplus available in a given market. (p. 386)

perpetuity A promise of a certain number of euros each year, forever. (p. 519)

Pigovian tax A tax or subsidy on an externality that brings about an equality of private and social marginal costs. (p. 574)

pooling equilibrium All types choose the same action in a signaling game. (p. 554)

positive–normative distinction Distinction between theories that seek to explain the world as it is and theories that postulate the way the world should be. (p. 19)

predatory pricing An incumbent charging a low price in order to induce the exit of a rival. (p. 431)

present value Discounting the value of future transactions back to the present day to take account of the effect of potential interest payments. (pp. 499, 514)

price discrimination Selling identical units of output at different prices. (p. 385)

price elasticity of demand The percentage change in the quantity demanded of a good in response to a 1 per cent change in its price. (p. 116)

price-leadership model A model with one dominant firm that behaves strategically and a group of small firms that behave as price takers. (p. 434)

price taker A firm or individual whose decisions regarding buying or selling have no effect on the prevailing market price of a good. (p. 272)

principal Player offering the contract in a principal-agent model. (p. 528)

private property Property that is owned by specific people who may prevent others from using it. (p. 570)

probability The relative frequency with which an event occurs. (p. 139)

producer surplus The extra value producers get for a good in excess of the opportunity costs they incur by producing it. What all producers would pay for the right to sell a good at its current market price. (p. 319)

production function The mathematical relationship between inputs and outputs. (p. 205)

production possibility frontier A graph showing all possible combinations of goods that can be produced with a fixed amount of resources. (p. 4)

proper subgame Part of the game tree including an initial decision not connected to another in an oval and everything branching out below it. (p. 186)

property rights The legal specification of who owns a good and the trades the owner is allowed to make with it. (p. 570)

public goods Goods that are both nonexclusive and nonrival. (pp. 356, 581)

pure strategy A single action played with certainty. (p. 173)

R

rental rate (v) The cost of hiring one machine for one hour. (p. 236)

rent-seeking behavior Firms or individuals influencing government policy to increase their own welfare. (p. 593)

returns to scale The rate at which output increases in response to proportional increases in all inputs. (p. 215)

Ricardian rent Long-run profits earned by owners of low-cost firms. May be capitalized into the prices of these firms' inputs. (p. 321)

risk aversion The tendency of people to refuse to accept fair games. (p. 140)

S

scarcity costs The opportunity costs of future production forgone because current production depletes exhaustible resources. (p. 503)

separating equilibrium Each type chooses a different action in a signaling game. (p. 554)

short run The period of time in which a firm must consider some inputs to be fixed in making its decisions. (p. 246)

short-run elasticity of supply The percentage change in quantity supplied in the short run in response to a 1 per cent change in price. (p. 298)

short-run market supply curve The relationship between market price and quantity supplied of a good in the short run. (p. 295)

shutdown price The price below which the firm will choose to produce no output in the short run. Equal to minimum average variable cost. (p. 284)

simultaneous equations A set of equations with more than one variable that must be solved together for a particular solution. (p. 39)

slope The direction of a line on a graph; shows the change in Y that results from a unit change in X. (p. 27)

social costs Costs of production that include both input costs and costs of the externalities that production may cause. (p. 567)

Stackelberg Equilibrium Subgame-perfect equilibrium of the sequential version of the Cournot game. (p. 428)

stage game Simple game that is played repeatedly. (p. 191)

statistical inference Use of actual data and statistical techniques to determine quantitative economic relationships. (p. 43)

subgame-perfect equilibrium Strategies that form a Nash equilibrium on every proper subgame. (p. 186)

substitutes Two goods such that if the price of one increases, the quantity demanded of the other rises. (p. 96)

substitution effect (in demand theory) The part of the change in quantity demanded that is caused by substitution of one good for another. A movement along an indifference curve. (p. 81, 453)

substitution effect (in production theory) The substitution of one input for another while holding output constant in response to a change in the input's price. (p. 453)

substitution effect of a change in *w* Movement along an indifference curve in response to a change in the real wage. A rise in *w* causes an individual to work more. (p. 480)

sunk cost Expenditure that once made cannot be recovered. (p. 236)

supply-demand model A model describing how a good's price is determined by the behavior of the individuals who buy the good and of the firms that sell it. (p. 11)

supply response The change in quantity of output supplied in response to a change in demand conditions. (p. 291)

T

tariff A tax on an imported good. May be equivalent to a quota or a nonquantitative restriction on trade. (p. 336)

tax incidence theory The study of the final burden of a tax after considering all market reactions to it. (p. 327)

technical progress A shift in the production function that allows a given output level to be produced using fewer inputs. (p. 223)

testing assumptions Verifying economic models by examining the validity of the assumptions on which they are based. (p. 16)

testing predictions Verifying economic models by asking if they can accurately predict real-world events. (p. 16)

theory of choice The interaction of preferences and constraints that causes people to make the choices they do. (p. 47)

transitivity of preferences The property that if *A* is preferred to *B*, and *B* is preferred to *C*, then *A* must be preferred to *C*. (p. 51)

trigger strategy Strategy in a repeated game where the player stops cooperating in order to punish another player's break with cooperation. (p. 191)

U

utility The pleasure or satisfaction that people get from their economic activity. (p. 47)

V

variable costs Costs associated with inputs that can be varied in the short run. (p. 248)

variables The basic elements of algebra, usually called *X*, *Y*, and so on, that may be given any numerical value in an equation. (p. 25)

W

wage rate (*w*) The cost of hiring one worker for one hour. (p. 236)

winner's curse Winning reveals that all other bidders thought the good was worth less than the highest bidder did. (p. 550)

Y

yield The effective (internal) rate of return promised by a payment stream that can be purchased at a certain price. (p. 521)

INDEX